Title 49 —Transportation
Subtitle B —Other Regulations Relating to Transportation
Chapter III —Federal Motor Carrier Safety Administration, Department of Transportation
Subchapter A —General Regulations

Part 303 Civil Rights
  § 303.1 Purpose.
  § 303.3 Application of this part.

PART 303—CIVIL RIGHTS

Authority: Public Law 105–159, 113 Stat. 1748, Title I, sections 107(a) and 106 (Dec. 9, 1999) (49 U.S.C. 113); 42 U.S.C. 2000d, *et seq.;* and 49 CFR 1.87.

Source: 70 FR 7414, Feb. 14, 2005, unless otherwise noted.

§ 303.1 Purpose.

The purpose of this part is to provide guidelines and procedures for implementing the Federal Motor Carrier Safety Administration's (FMCSA) Title VI program under Title VI of the Civil Rights Act of 1964 and related civil rights laws and regulations. For FMCSA-only programs or activities, Federal financial assistance recipients or grantees will continue to apply and use the Departmental Title VI provisions at 49 CFR part 21. For joint and multi-agency programs/projects, FMCSA Federal assistance recipients or grantees must use the Title VI requirements at 49 CFR part 21, unless agreement is reached by the Federal funding agencies for the recipients to use the Title VI procedures of another agency.

§ 303.3 Application of this part.

The provisions of this part are applicable to all elements of the FMCSA and to any program or activity for which Federal financial assistance is authorized under a law administered by the FMCSA. This part provides Title VI guidelines for State Departments of Transportation and local State agencies, including their sub-recipients, to implement Title VI. It also applies to money paid, property transferred, or other Federal financial assistance extended under any program of the FMCSA after the date of this part.

Title 49 —Transportation
Subtitle B —Other Regulations Relating to Transportation
Chapter III —Federal Motor Carrier Safety Administration, Department of Transportation
Subchapter A —General Regulations

PART 325—COMPLIANCE WITH INTERSTATE MOTOR CARRIER NOISE EMISSION STANDARDS

Authority: 42 U.S.C. 4917; 49 U.S.C. 301; and 49 CFR 1.87.

Source: 40 FR 42437, Sept. 12, 1975, unless otherwise noted.

Editorial Note: Nomenclature changes to part 325 appear at 66 FR 49869, Oct. 1, 2001.

Subpart A—General Provisions

§ 325.1 Scope of the rules in this part.

(a) The rules in this part prescribe procedures for inspection, surveillance, and measurement of motor vehicles and motor vehicle equipment operated by motor carriers to determine whether those vehicles and that equipment conform to the Interstate Motor Carrier Noise Emission Standards of the Environmental Protection Agency, 40 CFR part 202.

(b) Except as provided in paragraph (c) of this section, the rules in this part apply to motor carriers engaged in interstate commerce. The rules apply at any time or under any condition of highway grade, load, acceleration or deceleration.

(c) The rules in this part do not apply to—

   (1) A motor vehicle that has a Gross Vehicle Weight Rating (GVWR) of 10,000 pounds (4,536 kg.) or less;

   (2) A combination of motor vehicles that has a Gross Combination Weight Rating (GCWR) of 10,000 pounds (4,536 kg.) or less;

   (3) The sound generated by a warning device, such as a horn or siren, installed in a motor vehicle, unless such device is intentionally sounded in order to preclude an otherwise valid noise emission measurement;

   (4) An emergency motor vehicle, such as a fire engine, an ambulance, a police van, or a rescue van, when it is responding to an emergency call;

   (5) A snow plow in operation; or

   (6) The sound generated by auxiliary equipment which is normally operated only when the motor vehicle on which it is installed is stopped or is operating at a speed of 5 miles per hour (8 kph) or less, unless such device is intentionally operated at speeds greater than 5 mph (8 kph) in order to preclude an otherwise valid noise measurement. Examples of that type of auxiliary equipment include, but are not limited to, cranes, asphalt spreaders, ditch diggers, liquid or slurry pumps, auxiliary air compressors, welders, and trash compactors.

[40 FR 42437, Sept. 12, 1975, as amended at 78 FR 58477, Sept. 24, 2013]

§ 325.3 [Reserved]

§ 325.5 Definitions.

(a) *Statutory definitions.* All terms defined in the Noise Control Act of 1972 (Pub. L. 92–574, 86 Stat. 1234) are used as they are defined in that Act.

(b) *Definitions in standards.* All terms defined in § 202.10 of the Interstate Motor Carrier Noise Emission Standards, 40 CFR 202.10, are used as they are defined in that section.

(c) *Additional definitions.*

(1) *Hard test site* means any test site having the ground surface covered with concrete, asphalt, packed dirt, gravel, or similar reflective material for more than $1/2$ the distance between the microphone target point and the microphone location point.

(2) *Soft test site* means any test site having the ground surface covered with grass, other ground cover, or similar absorptive material for $1/2$ or more of the distance between the microphone target point and the microphone location point.

(3) *Ground cover* means any of various low, dense-growing plants, such as ivy, myrtle, low weeds, or brush.

(4) *Traffic railing* means any longitudinal highway traffic barrier system installed along the side or median of a highway. For the purpose of this part, a traffic railing must have at least 35 percent of its vertical height, from the ground surface to the top of the railing, open to free space in order to qualify as an acceptable object within a noise measurement test site. Further, for the purposes of this part, posts or other discrete supports shall be ignored when ascertaining open free space.

(5) *Relatively flat* when used to describe a noise measurement site means a site which does not contain significant concave curvatures or slope reversals that may result in the focusing of sound waves toward the microphone location point.

§ 325.7 Allowable noise levels.

Motor vehicle noise emissions, when measured according to the rules of this part, shall not exceed the values specified in Table 1.

Table 1—Maximum Permissible Sound Level Readings (Decibel (A))[1][2]

	Highway operation test				Stationary tests	
	Soft site		Hard Site		Soft site	Hard site
	35 mi/h or less	Above 35 mi/h	35 mi/h or less	Above 35 mi/h		
If the distance between the microphone location point and the microphone target point is—						
31 ft (9.5m) or more but less than 35 ft (10.7m)	87	91	89	93	89	91
35 ft (10.7m) or more but less than 39 ft (11.9m)	86	90	88	92	88	90

	Highway operation test				Stationary tests	
	Soft site		Hard Site		Soft site	Hard site
	35 mi/h or less	Above 35 mi/h	35 mi/h or less	Above 35 mi/h		
39 ft (11.9m) or more but less than 43 ft (13.1m)	85	89	87	91	87	89
43 ft (13.1m) or more but less than 48 ft (14.6m)	84	88	86	90	86	88
48 ft (14.6m) or more but less than 58 ft (17.1m)	83	87	85	89	85	87
58 ft (17.1m) or more but less than 70 ft (21.3m)	82	86	84	88	84	86
70 ft (21.3m) or more but less than 83 ft (25.3m)	81	85	83	87	83	85

[1] The speeds shown refer to measurements taken at sites having speed limits as indicated. These speed limits do not necessarily have to be posted.

[2] This table is based on motor carrier noise emission requirements specified in 40 CFR 202.20 and 40 CFR 202.21.

[40 FR 42437, Sept. 12, 1975, as amended at 54 FR 50385, Dec. 6, 1989]

§ 325.9 Measurement tolerances.

(a) Measurement tolerances will be allowed to take into account the effects of the following factors:

(1) The consensus standard practice of reporting filed sound level measurements to the nearest whole decibel.

(2) Variations resulting from commercial instrument tolerances.

(3) Variations resulting from the topography of the noise measurement site.

(4) Variations resulting from atmospheric conditions such as wind, ambient temperature, and atmospheric pressure.

(5) Variations resulting from reflected sound from small objects allowed within the test site.

(6) The interpretation of the effects of the above cited factors by enforcement personnel.

(b) Measurement tolerances shall not exceed 2 decibels for a given measurement.

Subpart B—Administrative Provisions

§ 325.11 Issuance, amendment, and revocation of the rules in this part.

The procedures specified in part 389 of this chapter for the issuance, amendment, or revocation of the Federal Motor Carrier Safety Regulations apply to rulemaking proceedings for the issuance, amendment, or revocation of the rules in this part.

§ 325.13 Inspection and examination of motor vehicles.

(a) *Authority.* Any special agent of the Federal Motor Carrier Safety Administration (designated in appendix B to part 390 of this chapter) is authorized to inspect, examine, and test a motor vehicle operated by a motor carrier in accordance with the procedures specified in this part for the purpose of ascertaining whether the motor vehicle and equipment installed on the motor vehicle conforms to the Interstate Motor Carrier Noise Emission Standards of the Environmental Protection Agency, 40 CFR part 202.

(b) A motor carrier, its officers, drivers, agents, and employees must, at any time, submit a motor vehicle used in its operations for inspection, examination, and testing for the purpose of ascertaining whether the motor vehicle and equipment installed on it conforms to the Interstate Motor Carrier Noise Emission Standards of the Environmental Protection Agency, 40 CFR part 202.

(c) *Prescribed inspection report.* Form MCS–141, Noise Level Compliance Check shall be used to record findings from motor vehicles selected for noise emission inspection by authorized employees.

(d) *Motor carrier's disposition of form MCS–141.*

(1) The driver of any motor vehicle receiving a Form MCS–141 shall deliver such MCS–141 to the motor carrier operating the vehicle upon his/her arrival at the next terminal or facility of the motor carrier, if such arrival occurs within twenty-four (24) hours. If the driver does not arrive at a terminal or facility of the motor carrier operating the vehicle within twenty-four (24) hours he/she shall immediately mail the Form MCS–141 to the motor carrier. For operating convenience, motor carriers may designate any shop, terminal, facility, or person to which it may instruct its drivers to deliver or forward Form MCS–141. It shall be the sole responsibility of the motor carrier that Form MCS–141 is returned to the Federal Motor Carrier Safety Administration, in accordance with the terms prescribed thereon and in paragraphs (d) (2) and (3) of this section. A driver, if himself/herself a motor carrier, shall return Form MCS–141 to the Federal Motor Carrier Safety Administration, in accordance with the terms prescribed thereon and in paragraphs (d) (2) and (3) of this section.

(2) Motor carriers shall carefully examine Forms MCS–141. Appropriate corrective action shall be taken on vehicles found to be not in compliance with the requirements of this part.

(3) Motor carriers must complete the "Motor Carrier Certification of Action Taken" on Form MCS–141 in accordance with the terms prescribed thereon. Motor carriers must return Forms MCS–141 to the Division Office at the address indicated on Form MCS–141 within fifteen (15) days following the date of the vehicle inspection.

[40 FR 42437, Sept. 12, 1975, as amended at 41 FR 10226, Mar. 10, 1976; 54 FR 50385, Dec. 6, 1989; 60 FR 38743, July 28, 1995; 66 FR 49869, Oct. 1, 2001; 78 FR 58477, Sept. 24, 2013; 88 FR 80179, Nov. 17, 2023]

Subpart C—Instrumentation

§ 325.21 Scope of the rules in this subpart.

The rules in this subpart specify criteria for sound level measurement systems which are used to make the sound level measurements specified in subpart D and subpart E of this part.

§ 325.23 Type of measurement systems which may be used.

The sound level measurement system must meet or exceed the requirements of American National Standard Specification for Sound Level Meters (ANSI S1.4–1971), approved April 27, 1971, issued by the American National Standards Institute,[1] throughout the applicable frequency range for either:

(a)   A Type 1 sound level meter;

(b)   A Type 2 sound level meter; or

(c)   A Type S sound level meter which has—

    (1)   A weighing frequency response;

    (2)   Fast dynamic characteristics of its indicating instrument; and

    (3)   A relative response level tolerance consistent with those of either a Type 1 or Type 2 sound level meter, as specified in section 3.2 of ANSI S1.4–1971.

§ 325.25 Calibration of measurement systems.

(a)

    (1)   The sound level measurement system must be calibrated and appropriately adjusted at one or more frequencies in the range from 250 to 1,000 Hz at the beginning of each series of measurements and at intervals of 5–15 minutes thereafter, until it has been determined that the sound level measurement system has not significantly drifted from its calibrated level. Once this fact has been established, calibrations may be made at intervals once every hour. A significant drift shall be considered to have occurred if a 0.3 dB or more excursion is noted from the system's predetermined reference calibration level. In the case of systems using displays with whole decibel increments, the operator may visually judge when the 0.3 dB drift has been met or exceeded.

    (2)   The sound level measurement system must be checked periodically by its manufacturer, a representative of its manufacturer, or a person of equivalent special competence to verify that its accuracy meets the manufacturer's design criteria.

(b)   An acoustical calibrator of the microphone coupler type designed for the sound level measurement system in use shall be used to calibrate the sound level measurement system in accordance with paragraph (a) of this section. The calibration must meet or exceed the accuracy requirements specified in section 5.4.1 of the American National Standard Institute Standard *Methods for Measurements of Sound Pressure Levels* (ANSI S1.13–1971) for field method measurements.

[40 FR 42437, Sept. 12, 1975, as amended at 41 FR 10227, Mar. 10, 1976]

§ 325.27 Use of a windscreen.

A properly installed windscreen, of the type recommended by the manufacturer of the Sound Level Measurement System, shall be used during the time that noise emission measurements are being taken.

[1] Copies of the specification may be secured from the American National Standards Institute, 1430 Broadway, New York, New York, 10018.

Subpart D—Measurement of Noise Emissions; Highway Operations

§ 325.31 Scope of the rules in this subpart.

The rules in this subpart specify conditions and procedures for measurement of the sound level generated by a motor vehicle engaged in a highway operation for the purpose of ascertaining whether the motor vehicle conforms to the Standards for Highway Operations set forth in 40 CFR 202.20.

§ 325.33 Site characteristics; highway operations.

(a) Measurement shall be made at a test site which is adjacent to, and includes a portion of, a traveled lane of a public highway. A microphone target point shall be established on the centerline of the traveled lane of the highway, and a microphone location point shall be established on the ground surface not less than 31 feet (9.5 m) or more than 83 feet (25.3 m) from the microphone target point and on a line that is perpendicular to the centerline of the traveled lane of the highway and that passes through the microphone target point. In the case of a standard test site, the microphone location point is 50 feet (15.2 m) from the microphone target point. Within the test site is a triangular measurement area. A plan view diagram of a standard test site, having an open site within a 50-foot (15.2 m) radius of both the microphone target point and the microphone location point, is shown in Figure 1. Measurements may be made at a test site having smaller or greater dimensions in accordance with the rules in subpart F of this part.

Figure 1
STANDARD TEST SITE;
HIGHWAY OPERATIONS

(b) The test site must be an open site, essentially free of large sound-reflecting objects. However, the following objects may be within the test site, including the triangular measurement area:

(1) Small cylindrical objects such as fire hydrants or telephone or utility poles.

(2) Rural mailboxes.

(3) Traffic railings of any type of construction except solid concrete barriers (see § 325.5(c)(4)).

(4) One or more curbs having a vertical height of 1 foot (.3 m) or less.

(c) The following objects may be within the test site if they are outside of the triangular measurement area of the site:

    (1) Any vertical surface (such as billboard), regardless of size, having a lower edge more than 15 feet (4.6 m) higher than the surface of the traveled lane of the highway.

    (2) Any uniformly smooth sloping surface slanting away from the highway (such as a rise in grade alongside the highway) with a slope that is less than 45 degrees above the horizontal.

    (3) Any surface slanting away from the highway that is 45 degrees or more and not more than 90 degrees above the horizontal, if all points on the surface are more than 15 feet (4.6 m) above the surface of the traveled lane of the highway.

(d) The surface of the ground within the measurement area must be relatively flat (see § 325.5(c)(5)). The site shall be a "soft" test site. However, if the site is determined to be "hard," the correction factor specified in § 325.75(a) of this part shall be applied to the measurement.

(e) The traveled lane of the highway within the test site must be dry, paved with relatively smooth concrete or asphalt, and substantially free of—

    (1) Holes or other defects which would cause a motor vehicle to emit irregular tire, body, or chassis impact noise; and

    (2) Loose material, such as gravel or sand.

(f) The traveled lane of the highway on which the microphone target point is situated must not pass through a tunnel or underpass located within 200 feet (61 m) of that point.

[40 FR 42437, Sept. 12, 1975, as amended at 54 FR 50385, Dec. 6, 1989]

§ 325.35 Ambient conditions; highway operations.

(a)

    (1) *Sound.* The ambient A-weighted sound level at the microphone location point shall be measured, in the absence of motor vehicle noise emanating from within the clear zone, with fast meter response using a sound level measurement system that conforms to the rules of § 325.23.

    (2) The measured ambient level must be 10 dB(A) or more below that level specified in § 325.7, Table 1, which corresponds to the maximum permissible sound level reading which is applicable at the test site at the time of testing.

(b) *Wind.* The wind velocity at the test shall be measured at the beginning of each series of noise measurements and at intervals of 5–15 minutes thereafter until it has been established that the wind velocity is essentially constant. Once this fact has been established, wind velocity measurements may be made at intervals of once every hour. Noise measurements may only be made if the measured wind velocity is 12 mph (19.3 kph) or less. Gust wind measurements of up to 20 mph (33.2 kph) are allowed.

(c) *Precipitation.* Measurements are prohibited under any condition of precipitation, however, measurements may be made with snow on the ground. The ground surface within the measurement area must be free of standing water.

[40 FR 42437, Sept. 12, 1975, as amended at 41 FR 10227, Mar. 10, 1976; 41 FR 28267, July 9, 1976]

§ 325.37 Location and operation of sound level measurement system; highway operations.

(a) The microphone of a sound level measurement system that conforms to the rules in § 325.23 of this part shall be located at a height of not less than 2 feet (.6 m) nor more than 6 feet (1.8 M) above the plane of the roadway surface and not less than $3^1/_2$ feet (1.1 m) above the surface on which the microphone stands. The preferred microphone height on flat terrain is 4 feet (1.2 m).

(b)

   (1) When the sound level measurement system is hand-held or is otherwise monitored by a person located near its microphone, the holder must orient himself/herself relative to the highway in a manner consistent with the recommendation of the manufacturer of the sound level measurement system.

   (2) In no case shall the holder or observer be closer than 2 feet (.6 m) from the system's microphone, nor shall he/she locate himself/herself between the microphone and the vehicle being measured.

(c) The microphone of the sound level measurement system shall be oriented toward the traveled lane of the highway at the microphone target point at an angle that is consistent with the recommendation of the system's manufacturer. If the manufacturer of the system does not recommend an angle of orientation for its microphone, the microphone shall be oriented toward the highway at an angle of not less than 70 degrees and not more than perpendicular to the horizontal plane of the traveled lane of the highway at the microphone target point.

(d) The sound level measurement system shall be set to the A-weighting network and "fast" meter response mode.

[40 FR 42437, Sept. 12, 1975, as amended at 41 FR 10227, Mar. 10, 1976]

§ 325.39 Measurement procedure; highway operations.

(a) In accordance with the rules in this subpart, a measurement shall be made of the sound level generated by a motor vehicle operating through the measurement area on the traveled lane of the highway within the test site, regardless of the highway grade, load, acceleration or deceleration.

(b) The sound level generated by the motor vehicle is the highest reading observed on the sound level measurement system as the vehicle passes through the measurement area, corrected, when appropriate, in accordance with the rules in subpart F of this part. (Table 1 in § 325.7 lists the range of maximum permissible sound level readings for various test conditions.) The sound level of the vehicle being measured must be observed to rise at least 6 dB(A) before the maximum sound level occurs and to fall at least 6 dB(A) after the maximum sound level occurs in order to be considered a valid sound level reading.

[40 FR 42437, Sept. 12, 1975, as amended at 41 FR 10227, Mar. 10, 1976]

Subpart E—Measurement of Noise Emissions; Stationary Test

§ 325.51 Scope of the rules in this subpart.

(a) The rules in this subpart specify conditions and procedures for measuring the sound level generated by a vehicle when the vehicle's engine is rapidly accelerated from idle to governed speed at wide open throttle with the vehicle stationary, its transmission in neutral, and its clutch engaged, for the purpose of ascertaining whether the motor vehicle conforms to the Standard for Operation Under Stationary Test, 40 CFR 202.21.

(b) The rules in this subpart apply only to a motor vehicle that is equipped with an engine speed governor.

(c) Tests conducted in accordance with the rules of this subpart may be made on either side of the vehicle.

§ 325.53 Site characteristics; stationary test.

(a)

    (1) The motor vehicle to be tested shall be parked on the test site. A microphone target point shall be established on the ground surface of the site on the centerline of the lane in which the motor vehicle is parked at a point that is within 3 feet (.9 m) of the longitudinal position of the vehicle's exhaust system outlet(s). A microphone location point shall be established on the ground surface not less than 31 feet (9.5 m) and not more than 83 feet (25.3 m) from the microphone target point. Within the test site is a triangular measurement area. A plan view diagram of a standard test site, having an open site within a 50-foot (15.2 m) radius of both the microphone target point and the microphone location point, is shown in Figure 2.

Figure 2
STANDARD TEST SITE;
STATIONARY TEST

    (2) Measurements may be made at a test site having smaller or greater dimensions in accordance with the rules in subpart F of this part.

(b) The test site must be an open site, essentially free of large sound-reflecting objects. However, the following objects may be within the test site, including the triangular measurement area:

    (1) Small cylindrical objects such as fire hydrants or telephone or utility poles.

    (2) Rural mailboxes.

    (3) Traffic railings of any type of construction except solid concrete barriers (see § 325.5(c)(4)).

(4) One or more curbs having a height of 1 foot (.3 m) or less.

(c) The following objects may be within the test site if they are outside of the triangular measurement area of the site:

(1) Any vertical surface, regardless of size (such as a billboard), having a lower edge more than 15 feet (4.6 m) above the ground.

(2) Any uniformly smooth surface slanting away from the vehicle with a slope that is less than 45 degrees above the horizontal.

(3) Any surface slanting away from the vehicle that is 45 degrees or more and not more than 90 degrees above the horizontal, if all points on the surface are more than 15 feet (4.6 m) above the surface of the ground in the test site.

(d) The surface of the ground within the measurement area must be relatively flat. (See § 325.5(c)(5)). The site shall be a "hard" site. However, if the site is determined to be "soft," the correction factor specified in § 325.75(b) of this part shall be applied to the measurement.

[40 FR 42437, Sept. 12, 1975, as amended at 41 FR 10227, Mar. 10, 1976; 54 FR 50385, Dec. 6, 1989]

§ 325.55 Ambient conditions; stationary test.

(a)

(1) *Sound.* The ambient A-weighted sound level at the microphone location point shall be measured, in the absence of motor vehicle noise emanating from within the clear zone, with fast meter response using a sound level measurement system that conforms to the rules of § 325.23.

(2) The measured ambient level must be 10 dB(A) or more below that level specified in § 325.7, Table 1, which corresponds to the maximum permissible sound level reading which is applicable at the test site at the time of testing.

(b) *Wind.* The wind velocity at the test site shall be measured at the beginning of each series of noise measurements and at intervals of 5–15 minutes thereafter until it has been established that the wind velocity is essentially constant. Once this fact has been established, wind velocity measurements may be made at intervals of once every hour. Noise measurements may only be made if the measured wind velocity is 12 mph (19.3 kph) or less. Gust wind measurements of up to 20 mph (33.2 kph) are allowed.

(c) *Precipitation.* Measurements are prohibited under any conditions of precipitation, however, measurements may be made with snow on the ground. The ground within the measurement area must be free of standing water.

[40 FR 42437, Sept. 12, 1975, as amended at 41 FR 28267, July 9, 1976]

§ 325.57 Location and operation of sound level measurement systems; stationary test.

(a) The microphone of a sound level measurement system that conforms to the rules in § 325.23 shall be located at a height of not less than 2 feet (.6 m) nor more than 6 feet (1.8 m) above the plane of the roadway surface and not less than $3^1/_2$ feet (1.1 m) above the surface on which the microphone stands. The preferred microphone height on flat terrain is 4 feet (1.2 m).

(b) When the sound level measurement system is hand-held or otherwise monitored by a person located near its microphone, the holder must orient himself/herself relative to the highway in a manner consistent with the recommendation of the manufacturer of the sound level measurement system. In no case shall the holder or observer be closer than 2 feet (.6 m) from the system's microphone, nor shall he/she locate himself/herself between the microphone and the vehicle being measured.

(c) The microphone of the sound level measurement system shall be oriented toward the vehicle at an angle that is consistent with the recommendation of the system's manufacturer. If the manufacturer of the system does not recommend an angle of orientation for its microphone, the microphone shall be oriented at an angle of not less than 70 degrees and not more than perpendicular to the horizontal plane of the test site at the microphone target point.

(d) The sound level measurement system shall be set to the A-weighting network and "fast" meter response mode.

[40 FR 42437, Sept. 12, 1975, as amended at 41 FR 10227, Mar. 10, 1976]

§ 325.59 Measurement procedure; stationary test.

In accordance with the rules in this subpart, a measurement shall be made of the sound level generated by a stationary motor vehicle as follows:

(a) Park the motor vehicle on the test site as specified in § 325.53 of this subpart. If the motor vehicle is a combination (articulated) vehicle, park the combination so that the longitudinal centerlines of the towing vehicle and the towed vehicle or vehicles are in substantial alinement.

(b) Turn off all auxiliary equipment which is installed on the motor vehicle and which is designed to operate under normal conditions only when the vehicle is operating at a speed of 5 mph (8 kph) or less. Examples of such equipment include cranes, asphalt spreaders, liquid or slurry pumps, auxiliary air compressors, welders, and trash compactors.

(c) If the motor vehicle's engine radiator fan drive is equipped with a clutch or similar device that automatically either reduces the rotational speed of the fan or completely disengages the fan from its power source in response to reduced engine cooling loads, park the vehicle before testing with its engine running at high idle or any other speed the operator may choose, for sufficient time but not more than 10 minutes, to permit the engine radiator fan to automatically disengage when the vehicle's noise emissions are measured under stationary test.

(d) With the motor vehicle's transmission in neutral and its clutch engaged, rapidly accelerate the vehicle's engine from idle to its maximum governed speed with wide open throttle. Return the engine's speed to idle.

(e) Observe the maximum reading on the sound level measurement system during the time the procedures specified in paragraph (d) of this section are followed. Record that reading, if the reading has not been influenced by extraneous noise sources such as motor vehicles operating on adjacent roadways.

(f) Repeat the procedures specified in paragraphs (d) and (e) of this section until the first two maximum sound level readings that are within 2 dB(A) of each other are recorded. Numerically average those two maximum sound level readings. When appropriate, correct the average figure in accordance with the rules in subpart F of this part.

(g) The average figure, corrected as appropriate, contained in accordance with paragraph (f) of this section, is the sound level generated by the motor vehicle for the purpose of determining whether it conforms to the Standard for Operation Under Stationary Test, 40 CFR 202.21. (Table 1 in § 325.7 lists the range of maximum permissible sound level readings for various test conditions.)

[40 FR 42437, Sept. 12, 1975, as amended at 41 FR 10226, Mar. 10, 1976]

Subpart F—Correction Factors

§ 325.71 Scope of the rules in this subpart.

(a) The rules in this subpart specify correction factors which are added to, or subtracted from, the reading of the sound level generated by a motor vehicle, as displayed on a sound level measurement system, during the measurement of the motor vehicle's sound level emissions at a test site which is not a standard site.

(b) The purpose of adding or subtracting a correction factor is to equate the sound level reading actually generated by the motor vehicle to the sound level reading it would have generated if the measurement had been made at a standard test site.

§ 325.73 Microphone distance correction factors.[1]

If the distance between the microphone location point and the microphone target point is other than 50 feet (15.2 m), the maximum observed sound level reading generated by the motor vehicle in accordance with § 325.39 of this part or the numerical average of the recorded maximum observed sound level readings generated by the motor vehicle in accordance with § 325.59 of this part shall be corrected as specified in the following table:

Table 2—Distance Correction Factors

If the distance between the microphone location point and the microphone target point is	The value dB(A) to be applied to the observed sound level reading is—
31 feet (9.5 m) or more but less than 35 feet (10.7 m)	−4
35 feet (10.7 m) or more but less than 39 feet (11.9 m)	−3
39 feet (11.9 m) or more but less than 43 feet (13.1 m)	−2
43 feet (13.1 m) or more but less than 48 feet (14.6 m)	−1
48 feet (14.6 m) or more but less than 58 feet (17.7 m)	0
58 feet (17.7 m) or more but less than 70 feet (21.3 m)	+ 1
70 feet (21.3 m) or more but less than 83 feet (25.3 m)	+ 2

[40 FR 42437, Sept. 12, 1975, as amended at 54 FR 50385, Dec. 6, 1989]

[1] Table 1, in § 325.7 is a tabulation of the maximum allowable sound level readings taking into account both the distance correction factors contained in § 325.73 and the ground surface correction factors contained in § 325.75.

§ 325.75 Ground surface correction factors.[1]

(a) *Highway operations.* When measurements are made in accordance with the rules in subpart D of this part upon a test site which is "hard," a correction factor of 2 dB(A) shall be subtracted from the maximum observed sound level reading generated by the motor vehicle to determine whether the motor vehicle conforms to the Standards for Highway Operations, 40 CFR 202.20.

(b) *Stationary test*. When measurements are made in accordance with the rules in subpart E of this part upon a test site which is "soft," a correction factor of 2 dB(A) shall be added to the numerical average of the recorded maximum observed sound level readings generated by the motor vehicle to determine whether the motor vehicle conforms to the Standard for Operation Under Stationary Test, 40 CFR 202.21.

[1] Table 1, in § 325.7 is a tabulation of the maximum allowable sound level readings taking into account both the distance correction factors contained in § 325.73 and the ground surface correction factors contained in § 325.75.

§ 325.77 Computation of open site requirements—nonstandard sites.

(a) If the distance between the microphone location point and the microphone target point is other than 50 feet (15.2 m), the test site must be an open site within a radius from both points which is equal to the distance between the microphone location point and the microphone target point.

(b) Plan view diagrams of nonstandard test sites are shown in Figures 3 and 4. Figure 3 illustrates a test site which is larger than a standard test site and is based upon a 60-foot (18.3 m) distance between the microphone location point and the microphone target point. (See § 325.79(b)(1) for an example of the application of the correction factor to a sound level reading obtained at such a site.) Figure 4 illustrates a test site which is smaller than a standard test site and is based upon a 35-foot (10.7 m) distance between the microphone location point and the microphone target point. (See § 325.79(b)(2) for an example of the application of the correction factor to a sound level reading obtained at such a site.)

Figure 3
NON-STANDARD TEST SITE;
(60 FT (18.3M) DISTANCE BETWEEN
MICROPHONE LOCATION AND TARGET POINTS)

Figure 4
NON-STANDARD TEST SITE;
(35 FT.(10.7M) DISTANCE BETWEEN
MICROPHONE LOCATION AND TARGET POINTS)

§ 325.79 Application of correction factors.

(a) If two correction factors apply to a measurement they are applied cumulatively.

(b) The following examples illustrate the application of correction factors to sound level measurement readings:

(1) *Example 1—Highway operations.* Assume that a motor vehicle generates a maximum observed sound level reading of 86 dB(A) during a measurement in accordance with the rules in subpart D of this part. Assume also that the distance between the microphone location point and the microphone target point is 60 feet (18.3 m) and that the measurement area of the test site is acoustically "hard." The corrected sound level generated by the motor vehicle would be 85 dB(A), calculated as follows:

86 dB(A) Uncorrected reading

+ 1 dB(A) Distance correction factor

−2 dB(A) Ground surface correction factor

_____

85 dB(A) Corrected reading

(2) *Example 2—Stationary test.* Assume that a motor vehicle generates maximum sound level readings which average 88 dB(A) during a measurement in accordance with the rules in subpart E of this part. Assume also that the distance between the microphone location point and the microphone target point is 35 feet (10.7 m), and that the measurement area of the test site is acoustically "soft." The corrected sound level generated by the motor vehicle would be 87 dB(A), calculated as follows:

88 dB(A) Uncorrected average of readings

−3 dB(A) Distance correction factor

+ 2 dB(A) Ground surface correction factor

———————

87 dB(A) Corrected reading

Subpart G—Exhaust Systems and Tires

§ 325.91 Exhaust systems.

A motor vehicle does not conform to the visual exhaust system inspection requirements, 40 CFR 202.22, of the Interstate Motor Carrier Noise Emission Standards, if inspection of the exhaust system of the motor vehicle discloses that the system—

(a) Has a defect which adversely affects sound reduction, such as exhaust gas leaks or alteration or deterioration of muffler elements, (small traces of soot on flexible exhaust pipe sections shall not constitute a violation of this subpart);

(b) Is not equipped with either a muffler or other noise dissipative device; or

(c) Is equipped with a cut-out, by-pass, or similar device, unless such device is designed as an exhaust gas driven cargo unloading system.

[40 FR 42437, Sept. 12, 1975, as amended at 75 FR 57193, Sept. 20, 2010]

§ 325.93 Tires.

(a) Except as provided in paragraph (b) of this section, a motor vehicle does not conform to the visual tire inspection requirements, 40 CFR 202.23, of the Interstate Motor Carrier Noise Emissions Standards, if inspection of any tire on which the vehicle is operating discloses that the tire has a tread pattern composed primarily of cavities in the tread (excluding sipes and local chunking) which are not vented by grooves to the tire shoulder or circumferentially to each other around the tire.

(b) Paragraph (a) of this section does not apply to a motor vehicle operated on a tire having a tread pattern of the type specified in that paragraph, if the motor carrier who operates the motor vehicle demonstrates to the satisfaction of the Administrator or his/her designee that either—

(1) The tire did not have that type of tread pattern when it was originally manufactured or newly remanufactured; or

(2) The motor vehicle generates a maximum sound level reading of 90 dB(A) or less when measured at a standard test site for highway operations at a distance of 15.3 meters (50 feet) and under the following conditions:

(i) The measurement must be made at a time and place and under conditions specified by the Administrator or his/her designee.

(ii) The motor vehicle must be operated on the same tires that were installed on it when the inspection specified in paragraph (a) of this section occurred.

(iii) The motor vehicle must be operated on a highway having a posted speed limit of more than 56.3 kph (35 mph).

(iv) The sound level measurement must be made while the motor vehicle is operating at the posted speed limit.

[40 FR 42437, Sept. 12, 1975, as amended at 60 FR 38743, July 28, 1995; 66 FR 49869, Oct. 1, 2001]

SUBCHAPTER B—FEDERAL MOTOR CARRIER SAFETY REGULATIONS

PART 350—COMMERCIAL MOTOR CARRIER SAFETY ASSISTANCE PROGRAM

AUTHORITY: 49 U.S.C. 13902, 31101–31104, 31108, 31136, 31140–31141, 31161, 31310–31311, 31502; and 49 CFR 1.73.

SOURCE: 65 FR 15102, Mar. 21, 2000, unless otherwise noted.

Subpart A—General

§ 350.101 What is the Motor Carrier Safety Assistance Program (MCSAP)?

The MCSAP is a Federal grant program that provides financial assistance to States to reduce the number and severity of accidents and hazardous materials incidents involving commercial motor vehicles (CMV). The goal of the MCSAP is to reduce CMV-involved accidents, fatalities, and injuries through consistent, uniform, and effective CMV safety programs. Investing grant monies in appropriate safety programs will increase the likelihood that safety defects, driver deficiencies, and unsafe motor carrier practices will be detected and corrected before they become contributing factors to accidents. The MCSAP also sets forth the conditions for participation by States and local jurisdictions and promotes the adoption and uniform enforcement of safety rules, regulations, and standards compatible with the Federal Motor Carrier Safety Regulations (FMCSRs) and Federal Hazardous Material Regulations (HMRs) for both interstate and intrastate motor carriers and drivers.

§ 350.103 What is the purpose of this part?

The purpose of this part is to ensure the Federal Motor Carrier Safety Administration (FMCSA), States, and other political jurisdictions work in partnership to establish programs to improve motor carrier, CMV, and driver safety to support a safe and efficient transportation system.

§ 350.105 What definitions are used in this part?

10-year average accident rate means for each State, the aggregate number of large truck-involved fatal crashes (as reported in the Fatality Analysis Reporting System (FARS)) for a 10-year period divided by the aggregate vehicle miles traveled (VMT) (as defined by the Federal Motor Carrier Safety Administration (FMCSA)) for the same 10-year period.

Accident rate means for each State, the total number of fatal crashes involving large trucks (as measured by the FARS for each State) divided by the total VMT as defined by the FMCSA for each State for all vehicles.

Agency means Federal Motor Carrier Safety Administration.

Administrative Takedown Funds means funds deducted by the FMCSA each fiscal year from the amount made available for the MCSAP for expenses incurred in the administration of the MCSAP, including expenses to train State and local government employees.

Administrator means Federal Motor Carrier Safety Administrator.

Basic Program Funds means the total MCSAP funds less the High Priority Activity, Border Activity, Administrative Takedown, and Incentive Funds.

Border Activity Funds means funds provided to States, local governments, and other persons carrying out programs, activities, and projects relating to CMV safety and regulatory enforcement supporting the North American Free Trade Agreement (NAFTA) at the U.S. border. Up to 5 percent of total MCSAP funds are available for these activities.

Commercial motor vehicle (CMV) means a motor vehicle that has any of the following characteristics:

(1) A gross vehicle weight (GVW), gross vehicle weight rating (GVWR), gross combination weight (GCW), or gross combination weight rating (GCWR) of 4,537 kilograms (10,001 pounds) or more.

(2) Regardless of weight, is designed or used to transport 16 or more passengers, including driver.

(3) Regardless of weight, is used in the transportation of hazardous materials and is required to be placarded pursuant to 49 CFR part 172, subpart F.

Commercial vehicle safety plan (CVSP) means the document outlining the State's CMV safety objectives, strategies, activities and performance measures.

Compatible or *Compatibility* means State laws and regulations applicable to interstate commerce and to intrastate movement of hazardous materials are identical to the FMCSRs and the HMRs or have the same effect as the FMCSRs. State laws applicable to intrastate commerce are either identical to, or have the same effect as, the FMCSRs or fall within the established limited variances under § 350.341.

High Priority Activity Funds means funds provided for carrying out high-priority activities and projects that improve CMV safety and compliance with CMV safety regulations (including activities and projects that are national in scope), increase public awareness and education, demonstrate new technologies, and reduce the number and rate of accidents involving CMVs.

Incentive Funds means funds awarded to States achieving reductions in CMV involved fatal accidents, CMV fatal accident rate, or meeting specified CMV safety program performance criteria.

Large truck means a truck over 10,000 pounds gross vehicle weight rating including single unit trucks and truck tractors (FARS definition).

Motor carrier means a for-hire motor carrier or private motor carrier. The term includes a motor carrier's agents, officers, or representatives responsible for hiring, supervising, training, assigning, or dispatching a driver or concerned with the installation, inspection, and maintenance of motor vehicle equipment or accessories or both.

New Entrant Funds means funds provided to State and local governments to conduct safety audits on New Entrant motor carriers under the New Entrant Safety Assurance Program.

North American Standard Inspection means the methodology used by State CMV safety inspectors to conduct safety inspections of CMVs. This consists of various levels of inspection of the vehicle or driver or both. The inspection criteria are developed by the FMCSA in conjunction with the Commercial Vehicle Safety Alliance (CVSA), an association of States, Canadian Provinces, and Mexico whose members agree to adopt these standards for inspecting CMVs in their jurisdiction.

Operating authority means the registration required by 49 U.S.C. 13902, 49 CFR part 365, 49 CFR part 368, and 49 CFR 392.9a.

[65 FR 15102, Mar. 21, 2000, as amended at 71 FR 50866, Aug. 28, 2006; 72 FR 36769, July 5, 2007]

§350.107 What jurisdictions are eligible for MCSAP funding?

All of the States, the District of Columbia, the Commonwealth of Puerto Rico, the Commonwealth of the Northern Mariana Islands, American Samoa, Guam, and the Virgin Islands are eligible to receive MCSAP grants directly from the FMCSA. For purposes of this subpart, all references to "State" or "States" include these jurisdictions.

§350.109 What are the national program elements?

The national program elements include the following five activities:

(a) Driver/vehicle inspections.
(b) Traffic enforcement.
(c) Compliance reviews.
(d) Public education and awareness.
(e) Data collection.

§350.111 What constitutes traffic enforcement for the purpose of the MCSAP?

Traffic enforcement means enforcement activities of State or local officials, including the stopping of vehicles operating on highways, streets, or roads for moving violations of State or local motor vehicle or traffic laws (e.g., speeding, following too closely, reckless driving, improper lane changes).

[72 FR 36769, July 5, 2007]

Subpart B—Requirements for Participation

§350.201 What conditions must a State meet to qualify for Basic Program Funds?

Each State must meet the following 26 conditions:

(a) Assume responsibility for improving motor carrier safety and adopting and enforcing State safety laws and regulations that are compatible with the FMCSRs (49 CFR parts 390–397) and the HMRs (49 CFR parts 107 (subparts F and G only), 171–173, 177, 178 and 180), except as may be determined by the Administrator to be inapplicable to a State enforcement program.

(b) Implement performance-based activities, including deployment of technology to enhance the efficiency and effectiveness of CMV safety programs.

(c) Designate, in its State Certification, the lead State agency responsible for implementing the CVSP.

(d) Ensure that only agencies having the legal authority, resources, and qualified personnel necessary to enforce the FMCSRs and HMRs or compatible State laws or regulations are assigned to perform functions in accordance with the approved CVSP.

(e) Allocate adequate funds for the administration of the CVSP including the enforcement of the FMCSRs, HMRs, or compatible State laws or regulations.

(f) Maintain the aggregate expenditure of funds by the State and its political subdivisions, exclusive of Federal funds, for CMV safety programs eligible for funding under this part, at a level at least equal to the average level of expenditure for the 3 full fiscal years beginning after October 1 of the year 5 years prior to the beginning of each Government fiscal year.

(g) Provide legal authority for a right of entry and inspection adequate to carry out the CVSP.

(h) Prepare and submit to the FMCSA, upon request, all reports required in connection with the CVSP or other conditions of the grant.

(i) Adopt and use the reporting standards and forms required by the FMCSA to record work activities performed under the CVSP.

(j) Require registrants of CMVs to declare, at the time of registration, their knowledge of applicable FMCSRs, HMRs, or compatible State laws or regulations.

(k) Grant maximum reciprocity for inspections conducted under the North American Standard Inspection through the use of a nationally accepted system that allows ready identification of previously inspected CMVs.

(l) Conduct CMV size and weight enforcement activities funded under this program only to the extent those activities do not diminish the effectiveness of other CMV safety enforcement programs.

(m) Coordinate the CVSP, data collection and information systems, with State highway safety programs under title 23 United States Code (U.S.C.).

(n) Ensure participation in SAFETYNET and other information systems by all appropriate jurisdictions receiving funding under this section.

(o) Ensure information is exchanged with other States in a timely manner.

(p) Emphasize and improve enforcement of State and local traffic laws and regulations related to CMV safety.

(q) Promote activities in support of the national program elements listed in § 350.109, including the following three activities:

(1) Activities aimed at removing impaired CMV drivers from the highways through adequate enforcement of restrictions on the use of alcohol and controlled substances and by ensuring ready roadside access to alcohol detection and measuring equipment.

(2) Activities aimed at providing an appropriate level of training to MCSAP personnel to recognize drivers impaired by alcohol or controlled substances.

(3) Interdiction activities affecting the transportation of controlled substances by CMV drivers and training on appropriate strategies for carrying out those interdiction activities.

(r) Enforce requirements relating to the licensing of CMV drivers, including checking the status of commercial drivers' licenses (CDL).

(s) Establish a program to ensure that accurate, complete, and timely motor carrier safety data are collected and reported, and ensure the State's participation in a national motor carrier safety data correction system prescribed by FMCSA.

(t)(1) Enforce registration (i.e., operating authority) requirements under 49 U.S.C. 13902, 49 CFR part 365, 49 CFR part 368, and 49 CFR 392.9a by prohibiting the operation of (i.e., placing out of service) any vehicle discovered to be operating without the required operating authority or beyond the scope of the motor carrier's operating authority.

(2) Enforce financial responsibility requirements under 49 U.S.C. 13906, 31138, 31139, and 49 CFR part 387.

(u) Adopt and maintain consistent, effective, and reasonable sanctions for violations of CMV, driver, and hazardous materials regulations.

(v) Ensure that MCSAP agencies have policies that stipulate roadside inspections will be conducted at locations that are adequate to protect the safety of drivers and enforcement personnel.

(w) Include in the training manual for the licensing examination to drive a CMV and the training manual for the licensing examination to drive a non-CMV information on best practices for driving safely in the vicinity of non-CMVs and CMVs.

(x) Conduct comprehensive and highly visible traffic enforcement and CMV safety inspection programs in high-risk locations and corridors.

(y) Except in the case of an imminent or obvious safety hazard, ensure that an inspection of a vehicle transporting passengers for a motor carrier of passengers is conducted at a station, terminal, border maintenance facility, destination, or other location where a motor carrier may make a planned stop.

(z) Enforce requirements relating to FMCSA remedial directives issued in accordance with 49 CFR part 385, subpart J, including providing inspection services for verification of electronic on-board recorder installation and operation as provided in §385.811(b).

[65 FR 15102, Mar. 21, 2000, as amended at 67 FR 55165, Aug. 28, 2002; 67 FR 61820, Oct. 2, 2002; 71 FR 50866, Aug. 28, 2006; 72 FR 36769, July 5, 2007; 75 FR 17240, Apr. 5, 2010]

§350.203 [Reserved]

§350.205 How and when does a State apply for MCSAP funding?

(a) The lead agency, designated by the Governor, must submit the State's CVSP to the Motor Carrier State Director, FMCSA, on or before August 1 of each year.

(b) This deadline may, for good cause, be extended by the State Director for a period not to exceed 30 calendar days.

(c) For a State to receive funding, the CVSP must be complete and include all required documents.

§350.207 What response does a State receive to its CVSP submission?

(a) The FMCSA will notify the State, in writing, within 30 days of receipt of the CVSP whether:

(1) The plan is approved.

(2) Approval of the plan is withheld because the CVSP does not meet the requirements of this part, or is not adequate to ensure effective enforcement of the FMCSRs and HMRs or compatible State laws and regulations.

(b) If approval is withheld, the State will have 30 days from the date of the notice to modify and resubmit the plan.

(c) Disapproval of a resubmitted plan is final.

(d) Any State aggrieved by an adverse decision under this section may seek judicial review under 5 U.S.C. chapter 7.

§350.209 How does a State demonstrate that it satisfies the conditions for Basic Program funding?

(a) The Governor, the State's Attorney General, or other State official specifically designated by the Governor, must execute a State Certification as described in §350.211.

(b) The State must submit the State Certification along with its CVSP, and supplement it with a copy of any State law, regulation, or form pertaining to CMV safety adopted since the State's last certification that bears on the items contained in §350.201 of this subpart.

§350.211 What is the format of the certification required by §350.209?

The State's certification must be consistent with the following content:

I (name), (title), on behalf of the State (or Commonwealth) of (State), as requested by the Administrator as a condition of approval of a grant under the authority of 49 U.S.C. 31102, as amended, do hereby certify as follows:

1. The State has adopted commercial motor carrier and highway hazardous materials safety rules and regulations that are compatible with the FMCSRs and the HMRs.

2. The State has designated (name of State CMV safety agency) as the lead agency to administer the CVSP for the grant sought and (names of agencies) to perform defined functions under the plan. These agencies have the legal authority, resources, and qualified personnel necessary to enforce the State's commercial motor carrier, driver, and highway hazardous materials safety laws or regulations.

3. The State will obligate the funds or resources necessary to provide a matching share to the Federal assistance provided in the grant to administer the plan submitted and to enforce the State's commercial motor carrier safety, driver, and hazardous materials laws or regulations in a manner consistent with the approved plan.

4. The laws of the State provide the State's enforcement officials right of entry and inspection sufficient to carry out the purposes of the CVSP, as approved, and provide that the State will grant maximum reciprocity for inspections conducted pursuant to the North American Standard Inspection procedure, through the use of a nationally accepted system allowing ready identification of previously inspected CMVs.

5. The State requires that all reports relating to the program be submitted to the appropriate State agency or agencies, and the

State will make these reports available, in a timely manner, to the FMCSA on request.

6. The State has uniform reporting requirements and uses FMCSA designated forms for record keeping, inspection, and other enforcement activities.

7. The State has in effect a requirement that registrants of CMVs declare their knowledge of the applicable Federal or State CMV safety laws or regulations.

8. The State must maintain the average aggregate expenditure of the State and its political subdivisions, exclusive of Federal assistance and State matching funds, for CMV safety programs eligible for funding under the Basic program at a level at least equal to the average level of expenditure for the 3 full fiscal years beginning after October 1 of the year 5 years prior to the beginning of each Government fiscal year. These expenditures must cover at least the following four program areas, as applicable:

a. Motor carrier safety programs in accordance with 49 CFR 350.109.

b. Size and weight enforcement programs in accordance with 49 CFR 350.309(c)(1).

c. Drug interdiction enforcement programs in accordance with 49 CFR 350.309(c)(2).

d. Traffic safety programs in accordance with 49 CFR 350.309(d).

9. The State will ensure that CMV size and weight enforcement activities funded with MCSAP funds will not diminish the effectiveness of other CMV safety enforcement programs.

10. The State will ensure that violation fines imposed and collected by the State are consistent, effective, and equitable.

11. The State will establish a program to provide FMCSA with accurate, complete, and timely reporting of motor carrier safety information that includes documenting the effects of the State's CMV safety programs; participate in a national motor carrier safety data correction program (DataQs); participate in SAFETYNET; and ensure information is exchanged in a timely manner with other States.

12. The State will ensure that the CVSP, data collection, and information systems are coordinated with the State highway safety program under title 23, U.S. Code. The name of the Governor's highway safety representative (or other authorized State official through whom coordination was accomplished) is _____. (Name)

13. The State has undertaken efforts to emphasize and improve enforcement of State and local traffic laws as they pertain to CMV safety.

14. The State will ensure that MCSAP agencies have departmental policies stipulating that roadside inspections will be conducted at locations that are adequate to protect the safety of drivers and enforcement personnel.

15. The State will ensure that requirements relating to the licensing of CMV drivers are enforced, including checking the status of CDLs.

16. The State will ensure that MCSAP-funded personnel, including sub-grantees, meet the minimum Federal standards set forth in 49 CFR part 385, subpart C for training and experience of employees performing safety audits, compliance reviews, or driver/vehicle roadside inspection.

17. The State will enforce operating authority requirements under 49 CFR 392.9a by prohibiting the operation of any vehicle discovered to be operating without the required operating authority or beyond the scope of the motor carrier's operating authority.

18. The State will enforce the financial responsibility requirements under 49 CFR part 387 as applicable to CMVs subject to the provisions of 49 CFR 392.9a.

19. The State will include, in the training manual for the licensing examination to drive a non-CMV and the training manual for the licensing examination to drive a CMV, information on best practices for safe driving in the vicinity of noncommercial and commercial motor vehicles.

20. The State will conduct comprehensive and highly visible traffic enforcement and CMV safety inspection programs in high-risk locations and corridors.

21. The State will ensure that, except in the case of an imminent or obvious safety hazard, an inspection of a vehicle transporting passengers for a motor carrier of passengers is conducted at a station, terminal, border crossing, maintenance facility, destination, or other location where motor carriers may make planned stops.

Date _____

Signature _____

[65 FR 15102, Mar. 21, 2000, as amended at 67 FR 12779, Mar. 19, 2002; 67 FR 61820, Oct. 2, 2002; 72 FR 36770, July 5, 2007]

§ 350.213 What must a State CVSP include?

The State's CVSP must reflect a performance-based program, and contain the following eighteen items:

(a) A general overview section that must include the following two items:

(1) A statement of the State agency goal or mission.

(2) A program summary of the effectiveness of the prior years' activities in reducing CMV accidents, injuries and fatalities, and improving driver and motor carrier safety performance. Data periods used must be consistent from year to year. This may be calendar year or fiscal year or any 12-month period of time for which the State's data

is current. The summary must show trends supported by safety and program performance data collected over several years. It must identify safety or performance problems in the State and those problems must be addressed in the new or modified CVSP.

(b) A brief narrative describing how the State program addresses the national program elements listed in §350.109. The plan must address these elements even if there are no planned activities in a program area. The rationale for the resource allocation decision must be explained. The narrative section must include a description of how the State supports the activities identified in §350.201(q) and (t).

(1) Activities aimed at removing impaired CMV drivers from the highways through adequate enforcement of restrictions on the use of alcohol and controlled substances and by ensuring ready roadside access to alcohol detection and measuring equipment.

(2) Activities aimed at providing an appropriate level of training to MCSAP personnel to recognize drivers impaired by alcohol or controlled substances.

(3) Interdiction activities affecting the transportation of controlled substances by CMV drivers and training on appropriate strategies for carrying out those interdiction activities.

(4) Activities to enforce registration requirements under 49 U.S.C. 13902 and 49 CFR part 365 and financial responsibility requirements under 49 U.S.C. 13906, 31138 and 31139 and 49 CFR part 387.

(c) A definitive problem statement for each objective, supported by data or other information. The CVSP must identify the source of the data, and who is responsible for its collection, maintenance, and analysis.

(d) Performance objectives, stated in quantifiable terms, to be achieved through the State plan. Objectives must include a measurable reduction in highway accidents or hazardous materials incidents involving CMVs. The objective may also include documented improvements in other program areas (e.g., legislative or regulatory authority, enforcement results, or resource allocations).

(e) Strategies to be employed to achieve performance objectives. Strategies may include education, enforcement, legislation, use of technology and improvements to safety infrastructure.

(f) Specific activities intended to achieve the stated strategies and objectives. Planned activities must be eligible under this program as defined in §§350.309 and 350.311.

(g) Specific quantifiable performance measures, as appropriate. These performance measures will be used to assist the State in monitoring the progress of its program and preparing an annual evaluation.

(h) A description of the State's method for ongoing monitoring of the progress of its plan. This should include who will conduct the monitoring, the frequency with which it will be carried out, and how and to whom reports will be made.

(i) An objective evaluation that discusses the progress towards individual objectives listed under the "Performance Objectives" section of the previous year's CVSP and identifies any safety or performance problems discovered. States will identify those problems as new objectives or make modifications to the existing objectives in the next CVSP.

(j) A budget which supports the CVSP, describing the expenditures for allocable costs such as personnel and related costs, equipment purchases, printing, information systems costs, and other eligible costs consistent with §§350.311 and 350.309.

(k) A budget summary form including planned expenditures for that fiscal year and projected number of activities in each national program element, except data collection.

(l) The results of the annual review to determine the compatibility of State laws and regulations with the FMCSRs and HMRs.

(m) A copy of any new law or regulation affecting CMV safety enforcement that was enacted by the State since the last CVSP was submitted.

(n) Executed State Certification as outlined in §350.211.

(o) Executed MCSAP–1 form.

(p) List of MCSAP contacts.

(q) Annual Certification of Compatibility, §350.331.

(r) State Training Plan.

[65 FR 15102, Mar. 21, 2000, as amended at 67 FR 61820, Oct. 2, 2002; 67 FR 63019, Oct. 9, 2002]

§ 350.215 What are the consequences for a State that fails to perform according to an approved CVSP or otherwise fails to meet the conditions of this part?

(a) If a State is not performing according to an approved plan or not adequately meeting conditions set forth in § 350.201, the Administrator may issue a written notice of proposed determination of nonconformity to the Governor of the State or the official designated in the plan. The notice will set forth the reasons for the proposed determination.

(b) The State will have 30 days from the date of the notice to reply. The reply must address the deficiencies or incompatibility cited in the notice and provide documentation as necessary.

(c) After considering the State's reply, the Administrator will make a final decision.

(d) In the event the State fails timely to reply to a notice of proposed determination of nonconformity, the notice becomes the Administrator's final determination of nonconformity.

(e) Any adverse decision will result in immediate cessation of Federal funding under this part.

(f) Any State aggrieved by an adverse decision under this section may seek judicial review under 5 U.S.C. chapter 7.

Subpart C—Funding

§ 350.301 What level of effort must a State maintain to qualify for MCSAP funding?

(a) The State must maintain the average aggregate expenditure of the State and its political subdivisions, exclusive of Federal funds and State matching funds, for CMV safety programs eligible for funding under this part at a level at least equal to the average level of expenditure for the 3 full fiscal years beginning after October 1 of the year 5 years prior to the beginning of each Government fiscal year.

(b) Determination of a State's level of effort must not include the following three things:

(1) Federal funds received for support of motor carrier and hazardous materials safety enforcement.

(2) State matching funds.

(3) State funds used for federally sponsored demonstration or pilot CMV safety programs.

(c) The State must include costs associated with activities performed during the base period by State or local agencies currently receiving or projected to receive funds under this part. It must include only those activities which meet the current requirements for funding eligibility under the grant program.

[65 FR 15102, Mar. 21, 2000, as amended at 72 FR 36770, July 5, 2007]

§ 350.303 What are the State and Federal shares of expenses incurred under an approved CVSP?

(a) The FMCSA will reimburse up to 80 percent of the eligible costs incurred in the administration of an approved CVSP.

(b) In-kind contributions are acceptable in meeting the State's matching share if they represent eligible costs as established by 49 CFR part 18 or agency policy.

§ 350.305 Are U.S. Territories subject to the matching funds requirement?

The Administrator waives the requirement for matching funds for the Virgin Islands, American Samoa, Guam, and the Commonwealth of the Northern Mariana Islands.

§ 350.307 How long are MCSAP funds available to a State?

The funds obligated to a State will remain available for the rest of the fiscal year in which they were obligated and the next full fiscal year. The State must account for any prior year's unexpended funds in the annual CVSP. Funds must be expended in the order in which they are obligated.

§ 350.309 What activities are eligible for reimbursement under the MCSAP?

The primary activities eligible for reimbursement are:

(a) The five national program elements listed in § 350.109 of this part.

(b) Sanitary food transportation inspections performed under 49 U.S.C. 5708.

(c) The following two activities, when accompanied by an appropriate North American Standard Inspection and inspection report:

(1) Enforcement of CMV size and weight limitations at locations other than fixed weight facilities; at specific locations such as steep grades or mountainous terrains where the weight of a CMV can significantly affect the safe operation of the vehicle; or at ports where intermodal shipping containers enter and leave the United States.

(2) Detection of the unlawful presence of a controlled substance in a CMV or on the person of any occupant (including the operator) of the vehicle.

(d) Documented enforcement of State traffic laws and regulations designed to promote the safe operation of CMVs, including documented enforcement of such laws and regulations relating to non-CMVs when necessary to promote the safe operation of CMVs, if the number of motor carrier safety activities (including roadside safety inspections) conducted in the State is maintained at a level at least equal to the average level of such activities conducted in the State in fiscal years 2003, 2004, and 2005. The State may not use more than 5 percent of its MCSAP Basic Program funds for enforcement activities relating to non-CMVs unless the Administrator determines that a higher percentage will result in significant increases in CMV safety.

[65 FR 15102, Mar. 21, 2000, as amended at 72 FR 36770, July 5, 2007]

§350.311 What specific items are eligible for reimbursement under the MCSAP?

All reimbursable items must be necessary, reasonable, allocable to the approved CVSP, and allowable under this part and 49 CFR part 18. The eligibility of specific items is subject to review by the FMCSA. The following six types of expenses are eligible for reimbursement:

(a) Personnel expenses, including recruitment and screening, training, salaries and fringe benefits, and supervision.

(b) Equipment and travel expenses, including per diem, directly related to the enforcement of safety regulations, including vehicles, uniforms, communications equipment, special inspection equipment, vehicle maintenance, fuel, and oil.

(c) Indirect expenses for facilities, except fixed scales, used to conduct inspections or house enforcement personnel, support staff, and equipment to the extent they are measurable and recurring (*e.g.*, rent and overhead).

(d) Expenses related to data acquisition, storage, and analysis that are specifically identifiable as program-related to develop a data base to coordinate resources and improve efficiency.

(e) Clerical and administrative expenses, to the extent necessary and directly attributable to the MCSAP.

(f) Expenses related to the improvement of real property (e.g., installation of lights for the inspection of vehicles at night). Acquisition of real property, land, or buildings are not eligible costs.

§350.313 How are MCSAP funds allocated?

(a) After deducting administrative expenses authorized in 49 U.S.C. 31104(e), the MCSAP funds are allocated as follows:

(1) An amount of the MCSAP funds appropriated for each fiscal year up to the maximum allowed by law may be distributed for High Priority Activities and Projects at the discretion of the Administrator.

(2) An amount of the MCSAP funds appropriated for each fiscal year up to the maximum allowed by law may be distributed for safety audits of New Entrant motor carriers under the New Entrant Safety Assurance Program at the discretion of the Administrator.

(3) The remaining funds will be allocated among qualifying States in two ways:

(i) As Basic Program Funds in accordance with §350.323 of this part,

(ii) As Incentive Funds in accordance with §350.327 of this part.

(b) The funding provided in paragraphs (a)(1) and (a)(2) of this section may be awarded through contract, cooperative agreement, or grant. The FMCSA will notify States if it intends to solicit State grant proposals for any portion of this funding.

(c) The funding provided under paragraph (a)(1) of this section may be made available to State agencies, local governments, and organizations representing government agencies or officials that use and train qualified officers and employees in coordination with State motor vehicle safety agencies. At least 90 percent of the amount set aside in a fiscal year shall be awarded in grants to State agencies and local government agencies.

(d) The funding provided under paragraph (a)(2) of this section may be made available to State and local governments. If the Administrator determines that a State or local government is not able to use government employees to conduct New Entrant motor carrier audits, the Administrator may use the funds under paragraph (a)(2) to conduct audits for such State or local governments.

[65 FR 15102, Mar. 21, 2000, as amended at 72 FR 36770, July 5, 2007]

§ 350.315 How may Basic Program Funds be used?

Basic Program Funds may be used for any eligible activity or item consistent with §§ 350.309 and 350.311.

§ 350.317 What are Incentive Funds and how may they be used?

Incentive Funds are monies, in addition to Basic Program Funds, provided to States that achieve reduction in CMV-involved fatal accidents, CMV fatal accident rate, or that meet specified CMV safety performance criteria. Incentive Funds may be used for any eligible activity or item consistent with §§ 350.309 and 350.311.

§ 350.319 What are permissible uses of High Priority Activity Funds?

(a) The FMCSA may generally use these funds to support, enrich, or evaluate State CMV safety programs and to accomplish the five objectives listed below:

(1) Implement, promote, and maintain national programs to improve CMV safety.

(2) Increase compliance with CMV safety regulations.

(3) Increase public awareness about CMV safety.

(4) Provide education on CMV safety and related issues.

(5) Demonstrate new safety related technologies.

(b) These funds will be allocated, at the discretion of the FMCSA, to States, local governments, and other organizations that use and train qualified officers and employees in coordination with State safety agencies.

(c) The FMCSA will notify the States when such funds are available.

(d) The Administrator may set aside an amount of MCSAP funding up to the maximum allowed by law for these projects and activities in each fiscal year.

(e) FMCSA will reimburse up to 80 percent of the eligible costs in the administration of an approved project plan, except that approved public information and education activities may be reimbursed up to 100 percent of the eligible costs.

[65 FR 15102, Mar. 21, 2000, as amended at 72 FR 36771, July 5, 2007]

§ 350.321 What are permissible uses of New Entrant Funds?

(a) These funds may be used to conduct safety audits on New Entrant motor carriers under the New Entrant Safety Assurance Program.

(b) New Entrant funds will be allocated, at the discretion of FMCSA, to State and local governments.

(c) FMCSA will notify States when such funds are available.

(d) The Administrator may designate up to the maximum amount allowed by law of MCSAP funding for these projects in each fiscal year. FMCSA will reimburse up to 100 percent of the eligible costs in the administration of an approved project plan.

[72 FR 36771, July 5, 2007]

§ 350.323 What criteria are used in the Basic Program Funds allocation?

(a) The funds are distributed proportionally to the States using the following four, equally weighted (25 percent), factors.

(1) 1997 Road miles (all highways) as defined by the FMCSA.

(2) All vehicle miles traveled (VMT) as defined by the FMCSA.

(3) Population—annual census estimates as issued by the U.S. Census Bureau.

(4) Special fuel consumption (net after reciprocity adjustment) as defined by the FMCSA.

(b) Distribution of Basic Program Funds is subject to a maximum and minimum allocation as illustrated in the Table to this section, as follows:

TABLE TO §350.323(b)—BASIC PROGRAM FUND ALLOCATION LIMITATIONS

Recipient	Maximum allocation	Minimum allocation
States and Puerto Rico ...	4.944% of the Basic Program Funds	$350,000 or 0.44% of Basic Program Funds, whichever is greater.
U.S. Territories	$350,000 (fixed amount)	

§350.325 [Reserved]

§350.327 How may States qualify for Incentive Funds?

(a) A State may qualify for Incentive Funds if it can demonstrate that its CMV safety program has shown improvement in any or all of the following five categories:

(1) Reduction of large truck-involved fatal accidents.

(2) Reduction of large truck-involved fatal accident rate or maintenance of a large truck-involved fatal accident rate that is among the lowest 10 percent of such rates of MCSAP recipients.

(3) Upload of CMV accident reports in accordance with current FMCSA policy guidelines.

(4) Verification of CDLs during all roadside inspections.

(5) Upload of CMV inspection data in accordance with current FMCSA policy guidelines.

(b) Incentive Funds will be distributed based upon the five following safety and program performance factors:

(1) Five shares will be awarded to States that reduce the number of large truck-involved fatal accidents for the most recent calendar year for which data are available when compared to the 10-year average number of large truck-involved fatal accidents ending with the preceding year. The 10-year average will be computed from the number of large truck-involved fatal crashes, as reported by the FARS, administered by the National Highway Traffic Safety Administration (NHTSA).

(2) Four shares will be awarded to States that reduce the fatal-accident rate for the most recent calendar year for which data are available when compared to each State's average fatal accident rate for the preceding 10-year period. States with the lowest 10 percent of accident rates in the most recent calendar year for which data are available will be awarded three shares if the rate for the State is the same as its average accident rate for the preceding 10-year period.

(3) Two shares will be awarded to States that upload CMV accident data within FMCSA policy guidelines.

(4) Two shares will be awarded to States that certify their MCSAP inspection agencies have departmental policies that stipulate CDLs are verified, as part of the inspection process, through Commercial Driver's License Information System (CDLIS), National Law Enforcement Tracking System (NLETS), or the State licensing authority.

(5) Two shares will be awarded to States that upload CMV inspection reports within current FMCSA policy guidelines.

(c) The total of all States' shares awarded will be divided into the dollar amount of Incentive Funds available, thereby establishing the value of one share. Each State's incentive allocation will then be determined by multiplying the State's percentage participation in the formula allocation of Basic Program Funds, by the number of shares it received that year, multiplied by the dollar value of one share.

(d) States may use Incentive Funds for any eligible CMV safety purpose.

(e) Incentive Funds are subject to the same State matching requirements as Basic Program Funds.

(f) A State must annually certify compliance with the applicable incentive criteria to receive Incentive Funds. A State must submit the required certification as part of its CVSP or as a separate document.

§ 350.329 How may a State or local agency qualify for High Priority or Border Activity Funds?

(a) States must meet the requirements of § 350.201, as applicable.

(b) Local agencies must meet the following nine conditions:

(1) Prepare a proposal in accordance with § 350.213, as applicable.

(2) Coordinate the proposal with the State lead MCSAP agency to ensure the proposal is consistent with State and national CMV safety program priorities.

(3) Certify that your local jurisdiction has the legal authority, resources, and trained and qualified personnel necessary to perform the functions specified in the proposal.

(4) Designate a person who will be responsible for implementation, reporting, and administering the approved proposal and will be the primary contact for the project.

(5) Agree to fund up to 20 percent of the proposed request.

(6) Agree to prepare and submit all reports required in connection with the proposal or other conditions of the grant.

(7) Agree to use the forms and reporting criteria required by the State lead MCSAP agency and/or the FMCSA to record work activities to be performed under the proposal.

(8) Certify that the local agency will impose sanctions for violations of CMV and driver laws and regulations that are consistent with those of the State.

(9) Certify participation in national data bases appropriate to the project.

§ 350.331 How does a State ensure its laws and regulations are compatible with the FMCSRs and HMRs?

(a) A State must review any new law or regulation affecting CMV safety as soon as possible, but in any event immediately after enactment or issuance, for compatibility with the FMCSRs and HMRs.

(b) If the review determines that the new law or regulation is incompatible with the FMCSRs and/or HMRs, the State must immediately notify the Motor Carrier State Director.

(c) A State must conduct an annual review of its laws and regulations for compatibility and report the results of that review in the annual CVSP in accordance with § 350.213(l) along with a certification of compliance, no later than August 1 of each year. The report must include the following two items:

(1) A copy of the State law, regulation, or policy relating to CMV safety that was adopted since the State's last report.

(2) A certification, executed by the State's Governor, Attorney General, or other State official specifically designated by the Governor, stating that the annual review was performed and that State CMV safety laws remain compatible with the FMCSRs and HMRs. If State CMV laws are no longer compatible, the certifying official shall explain.

(d) As soon as practical after the effective date of any newly enacted regulation or amendment to the FMCSRs or HMRs, but no later than three years after that date, the State must amend its laws or regulations to make them compatible with the FMCSRs and/or HMRs, as amended.

§ 350.333 What are the guidelines for the compatibility review?

(a) The State law or regulation must apply to all segments of the motor carrier industry (i.e., for-hire and private motor carriers of property and passengers).

(b) Laws and regulations reviewed for the CDL compliance report are excluded from the compatibility review.

(c) Definitions of words or terms must be consistent with those in the FMCSRs and HMRs.

(d) A State must identify any law or regulation that is not the same as the corresponding Federal regulation and evaluate it in accordance with the table to this section as follows:

TABLE TO §350.333—GUIDELINES FOR THE STATE LAW AND REGULATION COMPATIBILITY REVIEW

Law or regulation has same effect as corresponding Federal regulation	Applies to interstate or intrastate commerce	Less stringent or more stringent	Action authorized
(1) Yes			Compatible—Interstate and intrastate commerce enforcement authorized.
(2) No	Intrastate		Refer to §350.341
(3) No	Interstate	Less stringent	Enforcement prohibited.
(4) No	Interstate	More stringent	Enforcement authorized if the State can demonstrate the law or regulation has a safety benefit or does not create an undue burden upon interstate commerce (See 49 CFR Part 355).

§350.335 What are the consequences if my State has laws or regulations incompatible with the Federal regulations?

(a) A State that currently has compatible CMV safety laws and regulations pertaining to interstate commerce (i.e., rules identical to the FMCSRs and HMRs) and intrastate commerce (i.e., rules identical to or within the tolerance guidelines for the FMCSRs and identical to the HMRs) but enacts a law or regulation which results in an incompatible rule will not be eligible for Basic Program Funds nor Incentive Funds.

(b) A State that fails to adopt any new regulation or amendment to the FMCSRs or HMRs within three years of its effective date will be deemed to have incompatible regulations and will not be eligible for Basic Program nor Incentive Funds.

(c) Those States with incompatible laws or regulations pertaining to intrastate commerce and receiving 50 percent of their basic formula allocation on April 20, 2000 will continue at that level of funding until those incompatibilities are removed, provided no further incompatibilities are created.

(d) Upon a finding by the FMCSA, based upon its own initiative or upon a petition of any person, including any State, that your State law, regulation or enforcement practice pertaining to CMV safety, in either interstate or intrastate commerce, is incompatible with the FMCSRs or HMRs, the FMCSA may initiate a proceeding under §350.215 for withdrawal of eligibility for all Basic Program and Incentive Funds.

(e) Any decision regarding the compatibility of your State law or regulation with the HMRs that requires an interpretation will be referred to the Research and Special Programs Administration of the DOT for such interpretation before proceeding under §350.215.

§350.337 How may State laws and regulations governing motor carriers, CMV drivers, and CMVs in interstate commerce differ from the FMCSRs and still be considered compatible?

States are not required to adopt 49 CFR parts 398 and 399, subparts A through E and H of part 107, and §§171.15 and 171.16, as applicable to either interstate or intrastate commerce.

§350.339 What are tolerance guidelines?

Tolerance guidelines set forth the limited deviations from the FMCSRs allowed in your State's laws and regulations. These variances apply only to motor carriers, CMV drivers and CMVs engaged in intrastate commerce and not subject to Federal jurisdiction.

§350.341 What specific variances from the FMCSRs are allowed for State laws and regulations governing motor carriers, CMV drivers, and CMVs engaged in intrastate commerce and not subject to Federal jurisdiction?

(a) A State may exempt a CMV from all or part of its laws or regulations applicable to intrastate commerce, provided that neither the GVW, GVWR, GCW, nor GCWR of the vehicle equals or exceeds 11,801 kg (26,001 lbs.). However, a State may not exempt a CMV

31

from such laws or regulations if the vehicle:

(1) Transports hazardous materials requiring a placard.

(2) Is designed or used to transport 16 or more people, including the driver.

(b) State laws and regulations applicable to intrastate commerce may not grant exemptions based upon the type of transportation being performed (*e.g.*, for-hire, private, etc.).

(c) A State may retain those exemptions from its motor carrier safety laws and regulations that were in effect before April, 1988, are still in effect, and apply to specific industries operating in intrastate commerce.

(d) State laws and regulations applicable to intrastate commerce must not include exemptions based upon the distance a motor carrier or driver operates from the work reporting location. This prohibition does not apply to those exemptions already contained in the FMCSRs nor to the extension of the mileage radius exemption contained in 49 CFR 395.1(e) from 100 to 150 miles.

(e) Hours of service—State hours-of-service limitations applied to intrastate transportation may vary to the extent of allowing the following:

(1) A 12-hour driving limit, provided driving a CMV after having been on duty more than 16 hours is prohibited.

(2) Driving prohibitions for drivers who have been on duty 70 hours in 7 consecutive days or 80 hours in 8 consecutive days.

(f) Age of CMV driver—All CMV drivers must be at least 18 years of age.

(g) Grandfather clauses—States may provide grandfather clauses in their rules and regulations if such exemptions are uniform or in substantial harmony with the FMCSRs and provide an orderly transition to full regulatory adoption at a later date.

(h) Driver qualifications:

(1) Intrastate drivers who do not meet the physical qualification standards in 49 CFR 391.41 may continue to be qualified to operate a CMV in intrastate commerce if the following three conditions are met:

(i) The driver was qualified under existing State law or regulation at the time the State adopted physical quali-

fication standards compatible with the Federal standards in 49 CFR 391.41.

(ii) The otherwise non-qualifying medical or physical condition has not substantially worsened.

(iii) No other non-qualifying medical or physical condition has developed.

(2) The State may adopt or continue programs granting variances to intrastate drivers with medical or physical conditions that would otherwise be non-qualifying under the State's equivalent of 49 CFR 391.41 if the variances are based upon sound medical judgment combined with appropriate performance standards ensuring no adverse affect on safety.

§ 350.343 **How may a State obtain a new exemption for State laws and regulations for a specific industry involved in intrastate commerce?**

The FMCSA strongly discourages exemptions for specific industries, but will consider such requests if the State submits documentation containing information supporting evaluation of the following 10 factors:

(a) Type and scope of the industry exemption requested, including percentage of industry affected, number of vehicles, mileage traveled, number of companies involved.

(b) Type and scope of the requirement to which the exemption would apply.

(c) Safety performance of that specific industry (*e.g.*, accident frequency, rates and comparative figures).

(d) Inspection information (*e.g.*, number of violations per inspection, driver and vehicle out-of-service information).

(e) Other CMV safety regulations enforced by other State agencies not participating in the MCSAP.

(f) Commodity transported (*e.g.*, livestock, grain).

(g) Similar variations granted and the circumstances under which they were granted.

(h) Justification for the exemption.

(i) Identifiable effects on safety.

(j) State's economic environment and its ability to compete in foreign and domestic markets.

§350.345 How does a State apply for additional variances from the FMCSRs?

Any State may apply to the Administrator for a variance from the FMCSRs for intrastate commerce. The variance will be granted only if the State satisfactorily demonstrates that the State law, regulation or enforcement practice:

(a) Achieves substantially the same purpose as the similar Federal regulation.

(b) Does not apply to interstate commerce.

(c) Is not likely to have an adverse impact on safety.

PART 355—COMPATIBILITY OF STATE LAWS AND REGULATIONS AFFECTING INTERSTATE MOTOR CARRIER OPERATIONS

Subpart A—General Applicability and Definitions

AUTHORITY: 49 U.S.C. 504 and 31101 et seq.; 49 CFR 1.73.

SOURCE: 57 FR 40962, Sept. 8, 1992, unless otherwise noted.

EDITORIAL NOTE: Nomenclature changes to part 355 appear at 66 FR 49870, Oct. 1, 2001.

Subpart A—General Applicability and Definitions

§355.1 Purpose.

(a) To promote adoption and enforcement of State laws and regulations pertaining to commercial motor vehicle safety that are compatible with appropriate parts of the Federal Motor Carrier Safety Regulations.

(b) To provide guidelines for a continuous regulatory review of State laws and regulations.

(c) To establish deadlines for States to achieve compatibility with appropriate parts of the Federal Motor Carrier Safety Regulations with respect to interstate commerce.

§355.3 Applicability.

These provisions apply to any State that adopts or enforces laws or regulations pertaining to commercial motor vehicle safety in interstate commerce.

§355.5 Definitions.

Unless specifically defined in this section, terms used in this part are subject to the definitions in 49 CFR 390.5.

Compatible or *Compatibility* means that State laws and regulations applicable to interstate commerce and to intrastate movement of hazardous materials are identical to the FMCSRs and the HMRs or have the same effect as the FMCSRs; and that State laws applicable to intrastate commerce are either identical to, or have the same effect as, the FMCSRs or fall within the established limited variances under §§350.341, 350.343, and 350.345 of this subchapter.

Federal Hazardous Materials Regulations (FMHRs) means those safety regulations which are contained in parts 107, 171–173, 177, 178 and 180, except part 107 and §§171.15 and 171.16.

Federal Motor Carrier Safety Regulations (FMCSRs) means those safety regulations which are contained in parts 390, 391, 392, 393, 395, 396, and 397 of this subchapter.

State means a State of the United States, the District of Columbia, the Commonwealth of Puerto Rico, the Commonwealth of the Northern Mariana Islands, American Samoa, Guam and the Virgin Islands.

[57 FR 40962, Sept. 8, 1992, as amended at 65 FR 15109, Mar. 21, 2000]

Subpart B—Requirements

§355.21 Regulatory review.

(a) *General.* Each State shall annually analyze its laws and regulations, including those of its political subdivisions, which pertain to commercial motor vehicle safety to determine whether its laws and regulations are compatible with the Federal Motor Carrier Safety Regulations. Guidelines for the regulatory review are provided in the appendix to this part.

(b) *Responsibility.* The State agency designated as lead agency for the administration of grants made pursuant to part 350 of this subchapter is responsible for reviewing and analyzing State laws and regulations for compliance with this part. In the absence of an officially designated Motor Carrier Safety Assistance Program (MCSAP) lead agency or in its discretion, the State shall designate another agency responsible to review and determine compliance with these regulations.

(c) *State review.* (1) The State shall determine which of its laws and regulations pertaining to commercial motor vehicle safety are the same as the Federal Motor Carrier Safety or Federal Hazardous Materials Regulations. With respect to any State law or regulation which is not the same as the FMCSRs (FHMRs must be identical), the State shall identify such law or regulation and determine whether:

(i) It has the same effect as a corresponding section of the Federal Motor Carrier Safety Regulations;

(ii) It applies to interstate commerce;

(iii) It is more stringent than the FMCSRs in that it is more restrictive or places a greater burden on any entity subject to its provisions.

(2) If the inconsistent State law or regulation applies to interstate commerce and is more stringent than the FMCSRs, the State shall determine:

(i) The safety benefits associated with such State law or regulation; and

(ii) The effect of the enforcement of such State law or regulation on interstate commerce.

(3) If the inconsistent State law or regulation does not apply to interstate commerce or is less stringent than the FMCSRs, the guidelines for participation in the Motor Carrier Safety Assistance Program in §§ 350.341, 350.343, and 350.345 of this subchapter shall apply.

[57 FR 40962, Sept. 8, 1992, as amended at 65 FR 15109, Mar. 21, 2000]

§ 355.23 Submission of results.

Each State shall submit the results of its regulatory review annually with its certification of compliance under § 350.209 of this subchapter. It shall submit the results of the regulatory review with the certification no later than August 1 of each year with the Commercial Vehicle Safety Plan (CVSP). The State shall include copies of pertinent laws and regulations.

[65 FR 15109, Mar. 21, 2000]

§ 355.25 Adopting and enforcing compatible laws and regulations.

(a) *General.* No State shall have in effect or enforce any State law or regulation pertaining to commercial motor vehicle safety in interstate commerce which the Administrator finds to be incompatible with the provisions of the Federal Motor Carrier Safety Regulations.

(b) *New state requirements.* No State shall implement any changes to a law or regulation which makes that or any other law or regulation incompatible with a provision of the Federal Motor Carrier Safety Regulations.

(c) *Enforcement.* To enforce compliance with this section, the Administrator will initiate a rulemaking proceeding under part 389 of this subchapter to declare the incompatible State law or regulation pertaining to commercial motor vehicle safety unenforceable in interstate commerce.

(d) *Waiver of determination.* Any person (including any State) may petition for a waiver of a determination made under paragraph (c) of this section. Such petition will also be considered in a rulemaking proceeding under part 389. Waivers shall be granted only upon a satisfactory showing that continued enforcement of the incompatible State law or regulation is not contrary to the public interest and is consistent with the safe operation of commercial motor vehicles.

(e) *Consolidation of proceedings.* The Administrator may consolidate any action to enforce this section with other proceedings required under this section if the Administrator determines that such consolidation will not adversely affect any party to any such proceeding.

APPENDIX A TO PART 355—GUIDELINES
FOR THE REGULATORY REVIEW

Each State shall review its laws and regulations to achieve compatibility with the Federal Motor Carrier Safety Regulations (FMCSRs). Each State shall consider all related requirements on enforcement of the State's motor carrier safety regulations. The documentation shall be simple and brief.

SCOPE

The State review required by § 355.21 may be limited to those laws and regulations previously determined to be incompatible in the report of the Commercial Motor Vehicle Safety Regulatory Review Panel issued in August 1990, or by subsequent determination by the Administrator under this part, *and* any State laws or regulations enacted or issued after August 1990.

APPLICABILITY

The requirements must apply to all segments of the motor carrier industry common, contract, and private carriers of property and for-hire carriers of passengers.

DEFINITIONS

Definitions of terms must be consistent with those in the FMCSRs.

DRIVER QUALIFICATIONS

Require a driver to be properly licensed to drive a commercial motor vehicle; require a driver to be in good physical health, at least 21 years of age, able to operate a vehicle safely, and maintain a good driving record; prohibit drug and alcohol abuse; require a motor carrier to maintain a driver qualification file for each driver; and require a motor carrier to ensure that a driver is medically qualified.

NOTE: The requirements for testing apply only to drivers of commercial motor vehicles as defined in 49 CFR part 383.

DRIVING OF MOTOR VEHICLES

Prohibit possession, use, or driving under the influence of alcohol or other controlled substances (while on duty); and establish 0.04 percent as the level of alcohol in the blood at which a driver is considered under the influence of alcohol.

PARTS AND ACCESSORIES NECESSARY FOR SAFE
OPERATION

Require operational lights and reflectors; require systematically arranged and installed wiring; and require brakes working at the required performance level, and other key components included in 49 CFR part 393.

HOURS OF SERVICE OF DRIVERS

Prohibit a motor carrier from allowing or requiring any driver to drive: More than 10 hours following 8 consecutive hours off duty; after being on duty 15 hours, after being on duty more than 60 hours in any 7 consecutive days; or after being on duty more than 70 hours in any 8 consecutive days.

Require a driver to prepare a record-of-duty status for each 24-hour period. The driver and motor carrier must retain the records.

INSPECTION AND MAINTENANCE

Prohibit a commercial motor vehicle from being operated when it is likely to cause an accident or a breakdown; require the driver to conduct a walk-around inspection of the vehicle before driving it to ensure that it can be safely operated; require the driver to prepare a driver vehicle inspection report; and require commercial motor vehicles to be inspected at least annually.

HAZARDOUS MATERIALS

Require a motor carrier or a person operating a commercial motor vehicle transporting hazardous materials to follow the safety and hazardous materials requirements.

STATE DETERMINATIONS

1. Each State must determine whether its requirements affecting interstate motor carriers are "less stringent" than the Federal requirements. "Less stringent" requirements represent either gaps in the State requirements in relation to the Federal requirements as summarized under item number one in this appendix or State requirements which are less restrictive than the Federal requirements.

a. An example of a gap is when a State does not have the authority to regulate the safety of for-hire carriers of passengers or has the authority but chooses to exempt the carrier.

b. An example of a less restrictive State requirement is when a State allows a person under 21 years of age to operate a commercial motor vehicle in interstate commerce.

2. Each State must determine whether its requirements affecting interstate motor carriers are "more stringent" than the Federal requirements: "More stringent" requirements are more restrictive or inclusive in relation to the Federal requirements as summarized under item number one in this appendix. For example, a requirement that a driver must have 2 days off after working 5 consecutive days. The State would demonstrate that its more stringent requirements:

a. Have a "safety benefit;" for example, result in fewer accidents or reduce the risk of accidents;

b. do not create "an undue burden on interstate commerce," e.g., do not delay, interfere with, or increase that cost or the administrative burden for a motor carrier transporting property or passengers in interstate commerce; and

c. Are otherwise compatible with Federal safety requirements.

3. A State must adopt and enforce in a consistent manner the requirements referenced in the above guidelines in order for the FMCSA to accept the State's determination that it has compatible safety requirements affecting interstate motor carrier operations. Generally, the States would have up to 3 years from the effective date of the new Federal requirement to adopt and enforce compatible requirements. The FMCSA would specify the deadline when promulgating future Federal safety requirements. The requirements are considered of equal importance.

[57 FR 40962, Sept. 8, 1992, as amended by 58 FR 33776, June 21, 1993; 62 FR 37151, July 11, 1997; 65 FR 15110, Mar. 21, 2000]

PART 356—MOTOR CARRIER ROUTING REGULATIONS

AUTHORITY: 5 U.S.C. 553; 49 U.S.C. 13301 and 13902; and 49 CFR 1.73.

SOURCE: 62 FR 32041, June 12, 1997, unless otherwise noted.

EDITORIAL NOTE: Nomenclature changes to part 356 appear at 66 FR 49870, Oct. 1, 2001.

§ 356.1 Authority to serve a particular area—construction.

(a) *Service at municipality.* A motor carrier of property, motor passenger carrier of express, and freight forwarder authorized to serve a municipality may serve all points within that municipality's commercial zone not beyond the territorial limits, if any, fixed in such authority.

(b) *Service at unincorporated community.* A motor carrier of property, motor passenger carrier of express, and freight forwarder, authorized to serve an unincorporated community having a post office of the same name, may serve all points in the United States not beyond the territorial limits, if any, fixed in such authority, as follows:

(1) All points within 3 miles of the post office in such unincorporated community if it has a population of less than 2,500; within 4 miles if it has a population of 2,500 but less than 25,000; and within 6 miles if it has a population of 25,000 or more;

(2) At all points in any municipality any part of which is within the limits described in paragraph (b)(1) of this section; and

(3) At all points in any municipality wholly surrounded, or so surrounded except for a water boundary, by any municipality included under the terms of paragraph (b)(2) of this section.

§ 356.3 [Reserved]

§ 356.5 Traversal authority.

(a) *Scope.* An irregular route motor carrier may operate between authorized service points over any reasonably direct or logical route unless expressly prohibited.

(b) *Requirements.* Before commencing operations, the carrier must, regarding each State traversed:

(1) Notify the State regulatory body in writing, attaching a copy of its operating rights;

(2) Designate a process agent; and

(3) Comply with 49 CFR 387.315.

§ 356.7 Tacking.

Unless expressly prohibited, a motor common carrier of property holding separate authorities which have common service points may join, or *tack,* those authorities at the common point, or *gateway,* for the purpose of performing through service as follows:

(a) Regular route authorities may be tacked with one another;

(b) Regular route authority may be tacked with irregular route authority;

(c) Irregular route authorities may be tacked with one another if the authorities were granted pursuant to application filed on or before November 23, 1973, and the distance between the points at which service is provided, when measured through the gateway point, is 300 miles or less; and

(d) Irregular route authorities may be tacked with one another if the authorities involved contain a specific provision granting the right to tack.

§356.9 Elimination of routing restrictions—regular route carriers.

(a) *Regular route authorities—construction.* All certificates that, either singly or in combination, authorize the transportation by a motor common carrier of property over:

(1) A single regular route or;

(2) Over two or more regular routes that can lawfully be tacked at a common service point, shall be construed as authorizing transportation between authorized service points over any available route.

(b) *Service at authorized points.* A common carrier departing from its authorized service routes under paragraph (a) of this section shall continue to serve points authorized to be served on or in connection with its authorized service routes.

(c) *Intermediate point service.* A common carrier conducting operations under paragraph (a) of this section may serve points on, and within one airline mile of, an alternative route it elects to use if all the following conditions are met:

(1) The carrier is authorized to serve all intermediate points (without regard to nominal restrictions) on the underlying service route;

(2) The alternative route involves the use of a superhighway (i.e., a limited access highway with split-level crossings);

(3) The alternative superhighway route, including highways connecting the superhighway portion of the route with the carrier's authorized service route,

(i) Extends in the same general direction as the carrier's authorized service route and

(ii) Is wholly within 25 airline miles of the carrier's authorized service route; and

(4) Service is provided in the same manner as, and subject to any restrictions that apply to, service over the authorized service route.

§356.11 Elimination of gateways—regular and irregular route carriers.

A motor common carrier of property holding separate grants of authority (including regular route authority), one or more of which authorizes transportation over irregular routes, where the authorities have a common service point at which they can lawfully be tacked to perform through service, may perform such through service over any available route.

§356.13 Redesignated highways.

Where a highway over which a regular route motor common carrier of property is authorized to operate is assigned a new designation, such as a new number, letter, or name, the carrier shall advise the FMCSA by letter, and shall provide information concerning the new and the old designation, the points between which the highway is redesignated, and each place where the highway is referred to in the carrier's authority. The new designation of the highway will be shown in the carrier's certificate when the FMCSA has occasion to reissue it.

PART 360—FEES FOR MOTOR CARRIER REGISTRATION AND INSURANCE

Sec.
360.1 Fees for records search, review, copying, certification, and related services.
360.3 Filing fees.
360.5 Updating user fees.

AUTHORITY: 31 U.S.C. 9701; 49 U.S.C. 13908(c) and 14504(c)(2); and 49 CFR 1.73.

SOURCE: 64 FR 7137, Feb. 12, 1999, unless otherwise noted.

EDITORIAL NOTE: Nomenclature changes to part 360 appear at 66 FR 49870, Oct. 1, 2001.

§360.1 Fees for records search, review, copying, certification, and related services.

Certifications and copies of public records and documents on file with the Federal Motor Carrier Safety Administration will be furnished on the following basis, pursuant to the Freedom of Information Act regulations at 49 CFR Part 7:

(a) Certificate of the Director, Office of Data Analysis and Information Systems, as to the authenticity of documents, $9.00;

(b) Service involved in checking records to be certified to determine authenticity, including clerical work, etc., incidental thereto, at the rate of $16.00 per hour;

(c) Copies of the public documents, at the rate of $.80 per letter size or legal size exposure. A minimum charge of $5.00 will be made for this service; and

(d) Search and copying services requiring ADP processing, as follows:

(1) A fee of $42.00 per hour for professional staff time will be charged when it is required to fulfill a request for ADP data.

(2) The fee for computer searches will be set at the current rate for computer service. Information on those charges can be obtained from the Office of Data Analysis and Information Systems (MC-PSDRIS).

(3) Printing shall be charged at the rate of $.10 per page of computer generated output with a minimum charge of $.25. A charge of $30 per reel of magnetic tape will be made if the tape is to be permanently retained by the requestor.

§ 360.3 Filing fees.

(a) *Manner of payment.* (1) Except for the insurance fees described in the next sentence, all filing fees will be payable at the time and place the application, petition, or other document is tendered for filing. The service fee for insurance, surety or self-insurer accepted certificate of insurance, surety bond or other instrument submitted in lieu of a broker surety bond must be charged to an insurance service account established by the Federal Motor Carrier Safety Administration in accordance with paragraph (a)(2) of this section.

(2) *Billing account procedure.* A written request must be submitted to the Office of Enforcement and Compliance, Insurance Compliance Division (MC-PSDECI) to establish an insurance service fee account.

(i) Each account will have a specific billing date within each month and a billing cycle. The billing date is the date that the bill is prepared and printed. The billing cycle is the period be-

tween the billing date in one month and the billing date in the next month. A bill for each account which has activity or an unpaid balance during the billing cycle will be sent on the billing date each month. Payment will be due 20 days from the billing date. Payments received before the next billing date are applied to the account. Interest will accrue in accordance with 4 CFR 102.13.

(ii) The Debt Collection Act of 1982, including disclosure to the consumer reporting agencies and the use of collection agencies, as set forth in 4 CFR 102.5 and 102.6 will be utilized to encourage payment where appropriate.

(iii) An account holder who files a petition in bankruptcy or who is the subject of a bankruptcy proceeding must provide the following information to theOffice of Enforcement and Compliance, Insurance Division (MC-PSDECI):

(A) The filing date of the bankruptcy petition;

(B) The court in which the bankruptcy petition was filed;

(C) The type of bankruptcy proceeding;

(D) The name, address, and telephone number of its representative in the bankruptcy proceeding; and

(E) The name, address, and telephone number of the bankruptcy trustee, if one has been appointed.

(3) Fees will be payable to the Federal Motor Carrier Safety Administration by a check payable in United States currency drawn upon funds deposited in a United States or foreign bank or other financial institution, money order payable in United States' currency, or credit card (VISA or MASTERCARD).

(b) Any filing that is not accompanied by the appropriate filing fee is deficient except for filings that satisfy the deferred payment procedures in paragraph (a) of this section.

(c) *Fees not refundable.* Fees will be assessed for every filing in the type of proceeding listed in the schedule of fees contained in paragraph (f) of this section, subject to the exceptions contained in paragraphs (d) and (e) of this section. After the application, petition, or other document has been accepted for filing by the Federal Motor Carrier Safety Administration, the filing fee will not be refunded, regardless of whether the application, petition, or other document is granted or approved, denied, rejected before docketing, dismissed, or withdrawn.

(d) *Related or consolidated proceedings.* (1) Separate fees need not be paid for related applications filed by the same applicant which would be the subject of one proceeding. (This does not mean requests for multiple types of operating authority filed on forms in the OP–1 series under the regulations at 49 CFR part 365. A separate filing fee is required for each type of authority sought in each transportation mode, e.g., common, contract, and broker authority for motor property carriers.)

(2) Separate fees will be assessed for the filing of temporary operating authority applications as provided in paragraph (f)(6) of this section, regardless of whether such applications are related to an application for corresponding permanent operating authority.

(3) The Federal Motor Carrier Safety Administration may reject concurrently filed applications, petitions, or other documents asserted to be related and refund the filing fee if, in its judgment, they embrace two or more severable matters which should be the subject of separate proceedings.

(e) *Waiver or reduction of filing fees.* It is the general policy of the Federal Motor Carrier Safety Administration not to waive or reduce filing fees except as described as follows:

(1) Filing fees are waived for an application or other proceeding which is filed by a Federal government agency, or a State or local government entity. For purposes of this section the phrases "Federal government agency" or "government entity" do not include a quasi-governmental corporation or government subsidized transportation company.

(2) In extraordinary situations the Federal Motor Carrier Safety Administration will accept requests for waivers or fee reductions in accordance with the following procedure:

(i) *When to request.* At the time that a filing is submitted to the Federal Motor Carrier Safety Administration the applicant may request a waiver or reduction of the fee prescribed in this part. Such request should be addressed to the Director, Office of Data Analysis and Information Systems.

(ii) *Basis.* The applicant must show the waiver or reduction of the fee is in the best interest of the public, or that payment of the fee would impose an undue hardship upon the requestor.

(iii) *Federal Motor Carrier Safety Administration action.* The Director, Office of Data Analysis and Information Systems, will notify the applicant of the decision to grant or deny the request for waiver or reduction.

(f) Schedule of filing fees.

Type of Proceeding		Fee
Part I: Licensing:		
(1)	An application for motor carrier operating authority, a certificate of registration for certain foreign carriers, property broker authority, or freight forwarder authority.	$300
(2)	A petition to interpret or clarify an operating authority	3,000
(3)	A request seeking the modification of operating authority only to the extent of making a ministerial correction, when the original error was caused by applicant, a change in the name or owner of a plant site, or the change of a highway name or number.	50
(4)	A petition to renew authority to transport explosives	250
(5)	An application for authority to deviate from authorized regular-route authority.	150
(6)	An application for motor carrier temporary authority issued in an emergency situation.	100
(7)	Request for name change of a motor carrier, property broker, or freight forwarder.	14
(8)	An application involving the merger, transfer, or lease of the operating rights of motor passenger and property carriers, property brokers, and household goods freight forwarders under 49 U.S.C. 10321 and 10926.	300
(9)–(49)	[Reserved]	
Part II: Insurance:		
(50)	(i) An application for original qualification as self-insurer for bodily injury and property damage insurance (BI&PD).	4,200
	(ii) An application for original qualification as self-insurer for cargo insurance.	420

39

Type of Proceeding		Fee
(51)	A service fee for insurer, surety, or self-insurer accepted certificate of insurance, surety bond, and other instrument submitted in lieu of a broker surety bond.	$10 per accepted certificate, surety bond or other instrument submitted in lieu of a broker surety bond.
(52)	A petition for reinstatement of revoked operating authority	80
(53)–(79)	[Reserved].	
Part III: Services:		
(80)	Request for service or pleading list for proceedings	13 per list
(81)	Faxed copies of operating authority to applicants or their representatives who did not receive a served copy.	5

(g) *Returned check policy.* (1) If a check submitted to the FMCSA for a filing or service fee is dishonored by a bank or financial institution on which it is drawn, the FMCSA will notify the person who submitted the check that:

(i) All work will be suspended on the filing or proceeding, until the check is made good;

(ii) A returned check charge of $6.00 and any bank charges incurred by the FMCSA as a result of the dishonored check must be submitted with the filing fee which is outstanding; and

(iii) If payment is not made within the time specified by the FMCSA, the proceeding will be dismissed or the filing may be rejected.

(2) If a person repeatedly submits dishonored checks to the FMCSA for filing fees, the FMCSA may notify the person that all future filing fees must be submitted in the form of a certified or cashier's check, money order, or credit card.

[64 FR 7137, Feb. 12, 1999, as amended at 67 FR 61820, Oct. 2, 2002]

§ 360.5 Updating user fees.

(a) *Update.* Each fee established in this part may be updated in accordance with this section as deemed necessary by the FMCSA.

(b) *Publication and effective dates.* Updated fees shall be published in the FEDERAL REGISTER and shall become effective 30 days after publication.

(c) *Payment of fees.* Any person submitting a filing for which a fee is established shall pay the fee in effect at the time of the filing.

(d) *Method of updating fees.* Each fee shall be updated by updating the cost components comprising the fee. Cost components shall be updated as follows:

(1) Direct labor costs shall be updated by multiplying base level direct labor costs by percentage changes in average wages and salaries of FMCSA employees. Base level direct labor costs are direct labor costs determined by the cost study in *Regulations Governing Fees For Service*, 1 I.C.C. 2d 60 (1984), or subsequent cost studies. The base period for measuring changes shall be April 1984 or the year of the last cost study.

(2) Operations overhead shall be developed each year on the basis of current relationships existing on a weighted basis, for indirect labor applicable to the first supervisory work centers directly associated with user fee activity. Actual updating of operations overhead will be accomplished by applying the current percentage factor to updated direct labor, including current governmental overhead costs.

(3)(i) Office general and administrative costs shall be developed each year on the basis of current levels costs, i.e., dividing actual office general and administrative costs for the current fiscal year by total office costs for the office directly associated with user fee activity. Actual updating of office general and administrative costs will be accomplished by applying the current percentage factor to updated direct labor, including current governmental overhead and current operations overhead costs.

(ii) FMCSA general and administrative costs shall be developed each year on the basis of current level costs; i.e., dividing actual FMCSA general and administrative costs for the current fiscal year by total agency expenses for the current fiscal year. Actual updating of FMCSA general and administrative costs will be accomplished by applying the current percentage factor to updated direct labor, including current governmental overhead, operations overhead and office general and administrative costs.

(4) Publication costs shall be adjusted on the basis of known changes in the costs applicable to publication of material in the FEDERAL REGISTER or FMCSA Register.

(This rounding procedures excludes copying, printing and search fees.)

(e) *Rounding of updated fees.* Updated fees shall be rounded in the following manner:

(1) Fees between $1 and $30 will be rounded to the nearest $1;

(2) Fees between $30 and $100 will be rounded to the nearest $10;

(3) Fees between $100 and $999 will be rounded to the nearest $50; and

(4) Fees above $1,000 will be rounded to the nearest $100.

PART 365—RULES GOVERNING APPLICATIONS FOR OPERATING AUTHORITY

Subpart A—How To Apply for Operating Authority

Subpart B—How To Oppose Requests for Authority

Subpart C—General Rules Governing the Application Process

Subpart D—Transfer of Operating Rights Under 49 U.S.C. 10926

Subpart E—Special Rules for Certain Mexico-Domiciled Carriers

AUTHORITY: 5 U.S.C. 553 and 559; 49 U.S.C. 13101, 13301, 13901–13906, 14708, 31138, and 31144; 49 CFR 1.73.

SOURCE: 59 FR 63728, Dec. 9, 1994, unless otherwise noted. Redesignated at 61 FR 54707, Oct. 21, 1996.

EDITORIAL NOTE: Nomenclature changes to part 365 appear at 66 FR 49870, Oct. 1, 2001.

Subpart A—How To Apply for Operating Authority

§ 365.101 Applications governed by these rules.

These rules govern the handling of applications for operating authority of the following type:

(a) Applications for certificates and permits to operate as a motor common or contract carrier of property or passengers.

(b) Applications for permits to operate as a freight forwarder.

(c) [Reserved]

(d) Applications for licenses to operate as a broker of motor vehicle transportation.

(e) Applications for certificates under 49 U.S.C. 13902(b)(3) to operate as a motor carrier of passengers in intrastate commerce over regular routes if such intrastate transportation is to be provided on a route over which the carrier provides interstate transportation of passengers.

(f) [Reserved]

(g) Applications for temporary motor carrier authority.

(h) Applications for Mexico-domiciled motor carriers to operate in foreign commerce as common, contract or private motor carriers of property (including exempt items) between Mexico and all points in the United States. Under NAFTA Annex I, page I-U-20, a Mexico-domiciled motor carrier may not provide point-to-point transportation services, including express delivery services, within the United States for goods other than international cargo.

(i) Applications for non-North America-domiciled motor carriers to operate in foreign commerce as for-hire motor carriers of property and passengers within the United States.

[59 FR 63728, Dec. 9, 1994, as amended at 60 FR 63981, Dec. 13, 1995; 62 FR 49940, Sept. 24, 1997; 67 FR 12714, Mar. 19, 2002; 67 FR 61820, Oct. 2, 2002; 73 FR 76488, Dec. 16, 2008; 74 FR 2901, Jan. 16, 2009]

§ 365.103 Modified procedure.

The FMCSA will handle licensing application proceedings using the modified procedure, if possible. The applicant and protestants send statements made under oath (verified statements) to each other and to the FMCSA. There are no personal appearances or formal hearings.

§ 365.105 Starting the application process: Form OP–1.

(a) Each applicant must file the appropriate form in the OP–1 series. Form OP–1 must be filed when requesting authority to operate as a motor property carrier, a broker of general freight, or a broker of household goods; Form OP–1(P) must be filed when requesting authority to operate as a motor passenger carrier; Form OP–1(FF) must be filed when requesting authority to operate as a freight forwarder; Form OP–1(MX) must be filed by a Mexico-domiciled motor property,

including household goods, carrier, or a motor passenger carrier requesting authority to operate within the United States; and effective December 16, 2009. Form OP–1(NNA) must be filed by a non-North America-domiciled motor property, including household goods, carrier or a motor passenger carrier requesting authority to operate within the United States. A separate filing fee in the amount set forth at 49 CFR 360.3(f)(1) is required for each type of authority sought.

(b) Obtain forms at a FMCSA Division Office in each State or at one of the FMCSA Service Centers. Addresses and phone numbers for the Division Offices and Service Centers can be found at: *http://www.fmcsa.dot.gov/aboutus/ fieldoffices.* The forms and information about filing procedures can be downloaded at: *http:// www.fmcsa.dot.gov/factsfigs/formspubs;* and from the do-it-yourself website at: *http://www.diy.dot.gov.*

[66 FR 49870, Oct. 1, 2001, as amended at 67 FR 12714, Mar. 19, 2002; 67 FR 61820, Oct. 2, 2002; 73 FR 76488, Dec. 16, 2008]

§ 365.107 Types of applications.

(a) Fitness applications. Motor property applications and certain types of motor passenger applications require only the finding that the applicant is fit, willing and able to perform the involved operations and to comply with all applicable statutory and regulatory provisions. These applications can be opposed only on the grounds that applicant is not fit [*e.g.*, is not in compliance with applicable financial responsibility and safety fitness requirements]. These applications are:

(1) Motor common and contract carrier of property (except household goods) , Mexican motor property carriers that perform private carriage and transport exempt items, and motor contract carrier of passengers transportation.

(2) Motor carrier brokerage of general commodities (except household goods).

(3) Certain types of motor passenger applications as described in Form OP–1 (P).

(b) Motor passenger "public interest" applications as described in Form OP–1 (P).

(c) Intrastate motor passenger applications under 49 U.S.C. 13902(b)(3) as described in Form OP–1, Schedule B.

(d) Motor common carrier of household goods applications, including Mexican carrier applicants. These applications require a finding that:

(1) The applicant is fit, willing, and able to provide the involved transportation and to comply with all applicable statutory and regulatory provisions; and

(2) The service proposed will serve a useful public purpose, responsive to a public demand or need.

(e) Motor contract carrier of household goods, household goods property broker, and freight forwarder applications. These applications require a finding that:

(1) The applicant is fit, willing, and able to provide the involved transportation and to comply with all applicable statutory and regulatory provisions; and

(2) The transportation to be provided will be consistent with the public interest and the national transportation policy of 49 U.S.C. 13101.

(f) Temporary authority (TA) for motor and water carriers. These applications require a finding that there is or soon will be an immediate transportation need that cannot be met by existing carrier service.

(g) In view of the expedited time frames established in this part for processing requests for permanent authority, applications for TA will be entertained *only* in exceptional circumstances (*i.e.*, natural disasters or national emergencies) when evidence of immediate service need can be specifically documented in a narrative supplement appended to Form OP–1 for motor property carriers, Form OP–1MX for Mexican property carriers and, Form OP–1(P) for motor passenger carriers.

[59 FR 63728, Dec. 9, 1994, as amended at 60 FR 63981, Dec. 13, 1995; 62 FR 49940, Sept. 24, 1997; 67 FR 61820, Oct. 2, 2002]

§ 365.109 FMCSA review of the application.

(a) FMCSA staff will review the application for correctness, completeness, and adequacy of the evidence (the *prima facie* case).

(1) Minor errors will be corrected without notification to the applicant.

(2) Materially incomplete applications will be rejected. Applications that are in substantial compliance with these rules may be accepted.

(3) All motor carrier applications will be reviewed for consistency with the FMCSA's operational safety fitness policy. Applicants with "Unsatisfactory" safety fitness ratings from DOT will have their applications rejected.

(4) FMCSA staff will review completed applications that conform with the FMCSA's safety fitness policy and that are accompanied by evidence of adequate financial responsibility.

(5) Financial responsibility is indicated by filing within 20 days from the date an application notice is published in the FMCSA Register:

(i) *Form BMC–91 or 91X or BMC 82 surety bond*—Bodily injury and property damage (motor property and passenger carriers; household goods freight forwarders that provide pickup or delivery service directly or by using a local delivery service under their control).

(ii) *Form BMC–84*—Surety bond or Form BMC–85—trust fund agreement (property brokers of general commodities and household goods).

(iii) *Form BMC 34 or BMC 83 surety bond*—Cargo liability (household goods motor carriers and household goods freight forwarders).

(6) Applicants also must submit Form BOC–3—designation of legal process agents—within 20 days from the date an application notice is published in the *FMCSA Register*.

(7) Applicants seeking to conduct operations for which tariffs are required may not commence such operations until tariffs are in effect.

(8) All applications must be completed in English.

(b) A summary of the application will be published as a preliminary grant of authority in the *FMCSA Register* to give notice to the public in case anyone wishes to oppose the application.

[59 FR 63728, Dec. 9, 1994, as amended at 60 FR 63981, Dec. 13, 1995; 67 FR 61820, Oct. 2, 2002; 75 FR 35328, June 22, 2010]

§ 365.111 Appeals to rejections of the application.

(a) An applicant has the right to appeal rejection of the application. The appeal must be filed at the FMCSA within 10 days of the date of the letter of rejection.

(b) If the appeal is successful and the filing is found to be proper, the application shall be deemed to have been properly filed as of the decision date of the appeal.

§ 365.113 Changing the request for authority or filing supplementary evidence after the application is filed.

(a) Once the application is filed, the applicant may supplement evidence only with approval of the FMCSA.

(b) Amendments to the application generally are not permitted, but in appropriate instances may be entertained at the discretion of the FMCSA.

§ 365.115 After publication in the FMCSA Register.

(a) Interested persons have 10 days from the date of *FMCSA Register* publication to file protests. See Subpart B of this part.

(b) If no one opposes the application, the grant published in the *FMCSA Register* will become effective by issuance of a certificate, permit, or license.

§ 365.117 Obtaining a copy of the application.

After publication, interested persons may request a copy of the application by contacting the FMCSA-designated contract agent (as identified in the *FMCSA Register*).

§ 365.119 Opposed applications.

If the application is opposed, opposing parties are required to send a copy of their protest to the applicant.

§ 365.121 Filing a reply statement.

(a) If the application is opposed, applicant may file a reply statement. This statement is due within 20 days after *FMCSA Register* publication.

(b) The reply statement may not contain new evidence. It shall only rebut or further explain matters previously raised.

(c) The reply statement need not be notarized or verified. Applicant understands that the oath in the application form applies to all evidence submitted in the application. Separate legal arguments by counsel need not be notarized or verified.

§ 365.123 Applicant withdrawal.

If the applicant wishes to withdraw an application, it shall request dismissal in writing.

Subpart B—How To Oppose Requests for Authority

§ 365.201 Definitions.

A person wishing to oppose a request for permanent authority files a *protest*. A person filing a valid protest becomes a *protestant*.

§ 365.203 Time for filing.

A protest shall be filed (received at the FMCSA) within 10 days after notice of the application appears in the *FMCSA Register*. A copy of the protest shall be sent to applicant's representative at the same time. Failure timely to file a protest waives further participation in the proceeding.

§ 365.205 Contents of the protest.

(a) All information upon which the protestant plans to rely is put into the protest.

(b) A protest must be verified, as follows:

I, _____, verify under penalty of perjury under laws of the United States of America, that the information above is true and correct. Further, I certify that I am qualified and authorized to file this protest. (*See* 18 U.S.C. 1001 and 18 U.S.C. 1621 for penalties.)

(Signature and Date)

(c) A protest not in substantial compliance with applicable statutory standards or these rules may be rejected.

(d) Protests must respond directly to the statutory standards for FMCSA review of the application. As these standards vary for particular types of applications, potential protestants should refer to the general criteria addressed at § 365.107 and may consult the FMCSA at (202) 366–9805 for further assistance in developing their evidence.

[59 FR 63728, Dec. 9, 1994. Redesignated at 61 FR 54707, Oct. 21, 1996, as amended at 62 FR 49940, Sept. 24, 1997]

§365.207   Withdrawal.

A protestant wishing to withdraw from a proceeding shall inform the FMCSA and applicant in writing.

Subpart C—General Rules Governing the Application Process

§365.301   Applicable rules.

Generally, all application proceedings are governed by the FMCSA's Rules of Practice at part 386 of this chapter except as designated below.

§365.303   Contacting another party.

When a person wishes to contact a party or serve a pleading or letter on that party, it shall do so through its representative. The phone and FAX numbers and address of applicant's representative shall be listed in the *FMCSA Register*.

§365.305   Serving copies of pleadings.

(a) An applicant must serve all pleadings and letters on the FMCSA and all known participants in the proceeding, except that a reply to a motion need only be served on the moving party.

(b) A protestant need serve only the FMCSA and applicant with pleadings or letters.

§365.307   Replies to motions.

Replies to motions filed under this part are due within 5 days of the date the motion is filed at the FMCSA.

§365.309   FAX filings.

FAX filings of applications and supporting evidence are not permitted. To assist parties in meeting the expedited time frames established for protesting an application, however, the FMCSA will accept FAX filings of protests and any reply or rebuttal evidence. FAX filings of these pleadings must be followed by the original document, plus one copy for FMCSA recordkeeping purposes.

Subpart D—Transfer of Operating Rights Under 49 U.S.C. 10926

Source: 53 FR 4852, Feb. 18, 1988, unless otherwise noted. Redesignated at 61 FR 54707, Oct. 21, 1996.

§365.401   Scope of rules.

These rules define the procedures that enable motor passenger and property carriers,, property brokers, and household goods freight forwarders to obtain approval from the FMCSA to merge, transfer, or lease their operating rights in financial transactions not subject to 49 U.S.C. 11343. Transactions covered by these rules are governed by 49 U.S.C. 10321 and 10926. The filing fee is set forth at 49 CFR 360.3(f)(8).

[53 FR 4852, Feb. 18, 1988, as amended at 67 FR 61820, Oct. 2, 2002]

§365.403   Definitions.

For the purposes of this part, the following definitions apply:

(a) *Transfer.* Transfers include all transactions (*i.e.*, the sale or lease of interstate operating rights,[1] or the merger of two or more carriers or a carrier into a noncarrier) subject to 49 U.S.C. 10926, as well as the sale of property brokers' licenses under 49 U.S.C. 10321.

(b) *Operating rights.* Operating rights include:

(1) Certificates and permits issued to motor carriers;

(2) Permits issued to freight forwarders;

(3) Licenses issued to property brokers; and

(4) Certificates of Registration issued to motor carriers. The term also includes authority held by virtue of the gateway elimination regulations published in the FEDERAL REGISTER as letter-notices.

---

[1] The execution of a chattel mortgage, deed of trust, or other similar document does not constitute a transfer or require the FMCSA's approval. However, a foreclosure for the purpose of transferring an operating right to satisfy a judgment or claim against the record holder may not be effected without approval of the FMCSA.

(c) *Certificate of registration.* The evidence of a motor carrier's right to engage in interstate or foreign commerce within a single State is established by a corresponding State certificate.

(d) *Person.* An individual, partnership, corporation, company, association, or other form of business, or a trustee, receiver, assignee, or personal representative of any of these.

(e) *Record holder.* The person shown on the records of the FMCSA as the legal owner of the operating rights.

(f) *Control.* A relationship between persons that includes actual control, legal control, and the power to exercise control, through or by common directors, officers, stockholders, a voting trust, a holding or investment company, or any other means.

(g) *Category 1 transfers.* Transactions in which the person to whom the operating rights would be transferred is not an FMCSA carrier and is not affiliated with any FMCSA carrier.

(h) *Category 2 transfers.* Transactions in which the person to whom the operating rights would be transferred is an FMCSA carrier and/or is affiliated with an FMCSA carrier.

[53 FR 4852, Feb. 18, 1988, as amended at 67 FR 61821, Oct. 2, 2002]

§ 365.405 Applications.

(a) *Procedural requirements.* (1) At least 10 days before consummation, an original and two copies of a properly completed Form OP-FC-1 and any attachments (*see* paragraph (b)(1)(viii) of this section) must be filed with the Federal Motor Carrier Safety Administration, IT Operations Division (MC–RIO), 1200 New Jersey Ave., SE., Washington, DC 20590–0001.

(2) At any time after the expiration of the 10-day waiting period, applicants may consummate the transaction, subject to the subsequent approval of the application by the FMCSA, as described below. The transferee may commence operations under the rights acquired from the transferor upon its compliance with the FMCSA's regulations governing insurance, and process agents. *See* 49 CFR parts 387, subpart C, and 366, respectively. In the alternative, applicants may wait until the FMCSA has issued a decision on their application before transferring the op-

erating rights. If the transferee wants the transferor's operating authority to be reissued in its name, it should furnish the FMCSA with a statement executed by both transferor and transferee indicating that the transaction has been consummated. Authority will not be reissued until after the FMCSA has approved the transaction.

(b) *Information required.* (1) In category 1 and category 2 transfers, applicants must furnish the following information:

(i) Full name, address, and signatures of the transferee and transferor.

(ii) A copy of the transferor's operating authority involved in the transfer proceeding.

(iii) A short summary of the essential terms of the transaction.

(iv) If relevant, the status of proceedings for the transfer of State certificate(s) corresponding to the Certificates of Registration being transferred.

(v) A statement as to whether the transfer will or will not significantly affect the quality of the human environment.

(vi) Certification by transferor and transferee of their current respective safety ratings by the United States Department of Transportation (*i.e.*, satisfactory, conditional, unsatisfactory, or unrated).

(vii) Certification by the transferee that it has sufficient insurance coverage under 49 U.S.C. 13906 for the service it intends to provide.

(viii) Information to demonstrate that the proposed transaction is consistent with the national transportation policy and satisfies the criteria for approval set forth at § 365.409 of this part. (Such information may be appended to the application form and, if provided, would be embraced by the oath and verification contained on that form.)

(ix) If motor carrier operating rights are being transferred, certification by the transferee that it is not domiciled in Mexico nor owned or controlled by persons of that country.

(2) Category 2 applicants must also submit the following additional information:

(i) Name(s) of the carrier(s), if any, with which the transferee is affiliated.

(ii) Aggregate revenues of the transferor, transferee, and their carrier affiliates from interstate transportation sources for a 1-year period ending not earlier than 6 months before the date of the agreement of the parties concerning the transaction. If revenues exceed $2 million, the transfer may be subject to 49 U.S.C. 14303 rather than these rules.

[53 FR 4852, Feb. 18, 1988, as amended at 54 FR 35343, Aug. 25, 1989; 62 FR 49940, Sept. 24, 1997; 67 FR 61821, Oct. 2, 2002; 68 FR 56198, Sept. 30, 2003; 72 FR 55699, Oct. 1, 2007]

§ 365.407 Notice.

The FMCSA will give notice of approved transfer applications through publication in the *FMCSA Register.*

§ 365.409 FMCSA action and criteria for approval.

A transfer will be approved under this section if:

(a) The transaction is not subject to 49 U.S.C. 14303; and

(b) The transaction is consistent with the public interest; however,

(c) If the transferor or transferee has an "Unsatisfactory" safety fitness rating from DOT, the transfer may be denied. If an application is denied, the FMCSA will set forth the basis for its action in a decision or letter notice. If parties with "Unsatisfactory" safety fitness ratings consummate a transaction pursuant to the 10-day rule at § 365.405 of this part prior to the notification of FMCSA action, they do so at their own risk and subject to any conditions we may impose subsequently. Transactions that have been consummated but later are denied by the FMCSA are null and void and must be rescinded. Similarly, if applications contain false or misleading information, they are void *ab initio.*

[53 FR 4852, Feb. 18, 1988, as amended at 56 FR 46735, Sept. 16, 1991; 62 FR 49940, Sept. 24, 1997]

§ 365.411 Responsive pleadings.

(a) Protests must be filed within 20 days after the date of publication of an approved transfer application in the *FMCSA Register.* Protests received prior to the notice will be rejected. Applicants may respond within 20 days after the due date of protests. Petitions for reconsideration of decisions denying applications must be filed within 20 days after the date of service of such decisions.

(b) Protests and petitions for reconsideration must be filed with the Federal Motor Carrier Safety Administration, IT Operations Division (MC–RIO), 1200 New Jersey Ave., SE., Washington, DC 20590–0001, and be served on appropriate parties.

[53 FR 4852, Feb. 18, 1988, as amended at 67 FR 61821, Oct. 2, 2002; 68 FR 56198, Sept. 30, 2003; 72 FR 55699, Oct. 1, 2007]

§ 365.413 Procedures for changing the name or business form of a motor carrier, freight forwarder, or property broker.

(a) *Scope.* These procedures apply in the following circumstances:

(1) A change in the form of a business, such as the incorporation of a partnership or sole proprietorship;

(2) A change in the legal name of a corporation or partnership or change in the trade name or assumed name of any entity;

(3) A transfer of operating rights from a deceased or incapacitated spouse to the other spouse;

(4) A reincorporation and merger for the purpose of effecting a name change;

(5) An amalgamation or consolidation of a carrier and a noncarrier into a new carrier having a different name from either of the predecessor entities; and

(6) A change in the State of incorporation accomplished by dissolving the corporation in one State and reincorporating in another State.

(b) *Procedures.* To accomplish these changes, a letter must be sent to the Federal Motor Carrier Safety Administration, IT Operations Division (MC–RIO), 1200 New Jersey Ave., SE., Washington, DC 20590–0001. The envelope should be marked "NAME CHANGE". The applicant must provide:

(1) The docket number(s) and name of the carrier requesting the change;

(2) A copy of the articles of incorporation and the State certificate reflecting the incorporation;

(3) The name(s) of the owner(s) of the stock and the distribution of the shares;

(4) The names of the officers and directors of the corporation; and

(5) A statement that there is no change in the ownership, management, or control of the business. When this procedure is being used to transfer operating rights from a deceased or incapacitated spouse to the other spouse, documentation that the other spouse has the legal right to effect such change must be included with the request. The fee for filing a name change request is in § 360.3(f) of this chapter.

[53 FR 4852, Feb. 18, 1988, as amended at 54 FR 47364, Nov. 14, 1989; 62 FR 49940, Sept. 24, 1997; 68 FR 56198, Sept. 30, 2003; 72 FR 55699, Oct. 1, 2007]

Subpart E—Special Rules for Certain Mexico-domiciled Carriers

SOURCE: 67 FR 12714, Mar. 19, 2002, unless otherwise noted.

§ 365.501　Scope of rules.

(a) The rules in this subpart govern the application by a Mexico-domiciled motor carrier to provide transportation of property or passengers in interstate commerce between Mexico and points in the United States beyond the municipalities and commercial zones along the United States-Mexico international border.

(b) A Mexico-domiciled carrier may not provide point-to-point transportation services, including express delivery services, within the United States for goods other than international cargo.

§ 365.503　Application.

(a) Each applicant applying under this subpart must submit an application that consists of:

(1) Form OP-1 (MX)—Application to Register Mexican Carriers for Motor Carrier Authority To Operate Beyond U.S. Municipalities and Commercial Zones on the U.S.-Mexico Border;

(2) Form MCS-150—Motor Carrier Identification Report; and

(3) A notification of the means used to designate process agents, either by submission in the application package of Form BOC-3—Designation of Agents-Motor Carriers, Brokers and Freight Forwarders or a letter stating that the applicant will use a process agent service that will submit the Form BOC-3 electronically.

(b) The Federal Motor Carrier Safety Administration (FMCSA) will only process your application if it meets the following conditions:

(1) The application must be completed in English;

(2) The information supplied must be accurate, complete, and include all required supporting documents and applicable certifications in accordance with the instructions to Form OP-1 (MX), Form MCS-150, and Form BOC-3;

(3) The application must include the filing fee payable to the FMCSA in the amount set forth at 49 CFR 360.3(f)(1); and

(4) The application must be signed by the applicant.

(c) You must submit the application to the address provided in Form OP-1(MX).

(d) You may obtain the application forms from any FMCSA Division Office or download it from the FMCSA website at: *http://www.fmcsa.dot.gov/factsfigs/formspubs.htm.*

§ 365.505　Re-registration and fee waiver for certain applicants.

(a) If you filed an application using Form OP-1(MX) before May 3, 2002, you are required to file a new Form OP-1(MX). You do not need to submit a new fee when you file a new application under this subpart.

(b) If you hold a Certificate of Registration issued before April 18, 2002, authorizing operations beyond the municipalities along the United States-Mexico border and beyond the commercial zones of such municipalities, you are required to file an OP-1(MX) if you want to continue those operations. You do not need to submit a fee when you file an application under this subpart.

(1) You must file the application by November 4, 2003.

(2) The FMCSA may suspend or revoke the Certificate of Registration of any applicable holder that fails to comply with the procedures set forth in this section.

(3) Certificates of Registration issued before April 18, 2002, will remain valid

until the FMCSA acts on the OP–1(MX) application.

[67 FR 12714, Mar. 19, 2002, as amended at 68 FR 56198, Sept. 30, 2003]

§ 365.507 FMCSA action on the application.

(a) The FMCSA will review and act on each application submitted under this subpart in accordance with the procedures set out in this part.

(b) The FMCSA will validate the accuracy of information and certifications provided in the application by checking data maintained in databases of the governments of Mexico and the United States.

(c) *Pre-authorization safety audit.* Every Mexico-domiciled carrier that applies under this part must satisfactorily complete an FMCSA-administered safety audit before FMCSA will grant provisional operating authority to operate in the United States. The safety audit is a review by the FMCSA of the carrier's written procedures and records to validate the accuracy of information and certifications provided in the application and determine whether the carrier has established or exercises the basic safety management controls necessary to ensure safe operations. The FMCSA will evaluate the results of the safety audit using the criteria in Appendix A to this subpart.

(d) If a carrier successfully completes the pre-authorization safety audit and the FMCSA approves its application submitted under this subpart, FMCSA will publish a summary of the application as a preliminary grant of authority in the FMCSA Register to give notice to the public in case anyone wishes to oppose the application, as required in § 365.109(b) of this part.

(e) If the FMCSA grants provisional operating authority to the applicant, it will assign a distinctive USDOT Number that identifies the motor carrier as authorized to operate beyond the municipalities in the United States on the U.S.-Mexico international border and beyond the commercial zones of such municipalities. In order to operate in the United States, a Mexico-domiciled motor carrier with provisional operating authority must:

(1) Have its surety or insurance provider file proof of financial responsibility in the form of certificates of insurance, surety bonds, and endorsements, as required by § 387.301 of this subchapter;

(2) File a hard copy of, or have its process agent(s) electronically submit, Form BOC–3—Designation of Agents-Motor Carriers, Brokers and Freight Forwarders, as required by part 366 of this subchapter; and

(3) Comply with all provisions of the safety monitoring system in subpart B of part 385 of this subchapter, including successfully passing CVSA Level I inspections at least every 90 days and having decals affixed to each commercial motor vehicle operated in the United States as required by § 385.103(c) of this subchapter.

(f) The FMCSA may grant permanent operating authority to a Mexico-domiciled carrier no earlier than 18 months after the date that provisional operating authority is granted and only after successful completion to the satisfaction of the FMCSA of the safety monitoring system for Mexico-domiciled carriers set out in subpart B of part 385 of this subchapter. Successful completion includes obtaining a satisfactory safety rating as the result of a compliance review.

§ 365.509 Requirement to notify FMCSA of change in applicant information.

(a) A motor carrier subject to this subpart must notify the FMCSA of any changes or corrections to the information in parts I, IA or II submitted on the Form OP–1(MX) or the Form BOC–3—Designation of Agents—Motor Carriers, Brokers and Freight Forwarders during the application process or after having been granted provisional operating authority. The carrier must notify the FMCSA in writing within 45 days of the change or correction.

(b) If a carrier fails to comply with paragraph (a) of this section, the FMCSA may suspend or revoke its operating authority until it meets those requirements.

§ 365.511 Requirement for CVSA inspection of vehicles during first three consecutive years of permanent operating authority.

A Mexico-domiciled motor carrier granted permanent operating authority must have its vehicles inspected by Commercial Vehicle Safety Alliance (CVSA)-certified inspectors every three months and display a current inspection decal attesting to the successful completion of such an inspection for at least three consecutive years after receiving permanent operating authority from the FMCSA.

APPENDIX A TO SUBPART E OF PART 365—EXPLANATION OF PRE-AUTHOR-IZATION SAFETY AUDIT EVALUATION CRITERIA FOR MEXICO-DOMICILED MOTOR CARRIERS

I. GENERAL

(a) Section 350 of the Fiscal Year 2002 DOT Appropriations Act (Pub. L. 107–87) directed the FMCSA to perform a safety audit of each Mexico-domiciled motor carrier before the FMCSA grants the carrier provisional operating authority to operate beyond United States municipalities and commercial zones on the United States-Mexico international border.

(b) The FMCSA will decide whether it will conduct the safety audit at the Mexico-domiciled motor carrier's principal place of business in Mexico or at a location specified by the FMCSA in the United States, in accordance with the statutory requirements that 50 percent of all safety audits must be conducted onsite and on-site inspections cover at least 50 percent of estimated truck traffic in any year. All records and documents must be made available for examination within 48 hours after a request is made. Saturdays, Sundays, and Federal holidays are excluded from the computation of the 48-hour period.

(c) The safety audit will include:

(1) Verification of available performance data and safety management programs;

(2) Verification of a controlled substances and alcohol testing program consistent with part 40 of this title;

(3) Verification of the carrier's system of compliance with hours-of-service rules in part 395 of this subchapter, including record-keeping and retention;

(4) Verification of proof of financial responsibility;

(5) Review of available data concerning the carrier's safety history, and other information necessary to determine the carrier's preparedness to comply with the Federal Motor Carrier Safety Regulations, parts 382 through 399 of this subchapter, and the Federal Hazardous Material Regulations, parts 171 through 180 of this title;

(6) Inspection of available commercial motor vehicles to be used under provisional operating authority, if any of these vehicles have not received a decal required by § 385.103(d) of this subchapter;

(7) Evaluation of the carrier's safety inspection, maintenance, and repair facilities or management systems, including verification of records of periodic vehicle inspections;

(8) Verification of drivers' qualifications, including confirmation of the validity of the Licencia de Federal de Conductor of each driver the carrier intends to assign to operate under its provisional operating authority; and

(9) An interview of carrier officials to review safety management controls and evaluate any written safety oversight policies and practices.

(d) To successfully complete the safety audit, a Mexico-domiciled motor carrier must demonstrate to the FMCSA that it has the required elements in paragraphs (c)(2), (3), (4), (7), and (8) above and other basic safety management controls in place which function adequately to ensure minimum acceptable compliance with the applicable safety requirements. The FMCSA developed a "safety audit evaluation criteria," which uses data from the safety audit and roadside inspections to determine that each applicant for provisional operating authority has basic safety management controls in place.

(e) The safety audit evaluation process developed by the FMCSA is used to:

(1) Evaluate basic safety management controls and determine if each Mexico-domiciled carrier and each driver is able to operate safely in the United States beyond municipalities and commercial zones on the United States-Mexico international border; and

(2) Identify motor carriers and drivers who are having safety problems and need improvement in their compliance with the FMCSRs and the HMRs, before FMCSA grants the carriers provisional operating authority to operate beyond United States municipalities and commercial zones on the United States-Mexico international border.

II. SOURCE OF THE DATA FOR THE SAFETY AUDIT EVALUATION CRITERIA

(a) The FMCSA's evaluation criteria are built upon the operational tool known as the safety audit. The FMCSA developed this tool to assist auditors and investigators in assessing the adequacy of a Mexico-domiciled carrier's basic safety management controls.

(b) The safety audit is a review of a Mexico-domiciled motor carrier's operation and is used to:

(1) Determine if a carrier has the basic safety management controls required by 49 U.S.C. 31144;

(2) Meet the requirements of Section 350 of the DOT Appropriations Act; and

(3) In the event that a carrier is found not to be in compliance with applicable FMCSRs and HMRs, the safety audit can be used to educate the carrier on how to comply with U.S. safety rules.

(c) Documents such as those contained in driver qualification files, records of duty status, vehicle maintenance records, and other records are reviewed for compliance with the FMCSRs and HMRs. Violations are cited on the safety audit. Performance-based information, when available, is utilized to evaluate the carrier's compliance with the vehicle regulations. Recordable accident information is also collected.

III. OVERALL DETERMINATION OF THE CARRIER'S BASIC SAFETY MANAGEMENT CONTROLS

(a) The carrier will not be granted provisional operating authority if the FMCSA fails to:

(1) Verify a controlled substances and alcohol testing program consistent with part 40 of this title;

(2) Verify a system of compliance with hours-of-service rules of this subchapter, including recordkeeping and retention;

(3) Verify proof of financial responsibility;

(4) Verify records of periodic vehicle inspections; and

(5) Verify drivers' qualifications of each driver the carrier intends to assign to operate under such authority, as required by parts 383 and 391 of this subchapter, including confirming the validity of each driver's Licencia de Federal de Conductor.

(b) If the FMCSA confirms each item under II (a)(1) through (5) above, the carrier will be granted provisional operating authority, except if FMCSA finds the carrier has inadequate basic safety management controls in at least three separate factors described in part III below. If FMCSA makes such a determination, the carrier's application for provisional operating authority will be denied.

IV. EVALUATION OF REGULATORY COMPLIANCE

(a) During the safety audit, the FMCSA gathers information by reviewing a motor carrier's compliance with "acute" and "critical" regulations of the FMCSRs and HMRs.

(b) Acute regulations are those where noncompliance is so severe as to require immediate corrective actions by a motor carrier regardless of the overall basic safety management controls of the motor carrier.

(c) Critical regulations are those where noncompliance relates to management and/or operational controls. These are indicative of breakdowns in a carrier's management controls.

(d) The list of the acute and critical regulations, which are used in determining if a carrier has basic safety management controls in place, is included in Appendix B, VII. List of Acute and Critical Regulations to part 385 of this subchapter.

(e) Noncompliance with acute and critical regulations are indicators of inadequate safety management controls and usually higher than average accident rates.

(f) Parts of the FMCSRs and the HMRs having similar characteristics are combined together into six regulatory areas called "factors." The regulatory factors, evaluated on the adequacy of the carrier's safety management controls, are:

(1) Factor 1—General: Parts 387 and 390;

(2) Factor 2—Driver: Parts 382, 383 and 391;

(3) Factor 3—Operational: Parts 392 and 395;

(4) Factor 4—Vehicle: Part 393, 396 and inspection data for the last 12 months;

(5) Factor 5—Hazardous Materials: Parts 171, 177, 180 and 397; and

(6) Factor 6—Accident: Recordable Accident Rate per Million Miles.

(g) For each instance of noncompliance with an acute regulation, 1.5 points will be assessed.

(h) For each instance of noncompliance with a critical regulation, 1 point will be assessed.

(i) *Vehicle Factor.* (1) When at least three vehicle inspections are recorded in the Motor Carrier Management Information System (MCMIS) during the twelve months before the safety audit or performed at the time of the review, the Vehicle Factor (part 396) will be evaluated on the basis of the Out-of-Service (OOS) rates and noncompliance with acute and critical regulations. The results of the review of the OOS rate will affect the Vehicle Factor as follows:

(i) If the motor carrier has had at least three roadside inspections in the twelve months before the safety audit, and the vehicle OOS rate is 34 percent or higher, one point will be assessed against the carrier. That point will be added to any other points assessed for discovered noncompliance with acute and critical regulations of part 396 to determine the carrier's level of safety management control for that factor.

(ii) If the motor carrier's vehicle OOS rate is less than 34 percent, or if there are less than three inspections, the determination of the carrier's level of safety management controls will only be based on discovered noncompliance with the acute and critical regulations of part 396.

(2) Over two million inspections occur on the roadside each year in the United States. This vehicle inspection information is retained in the MCMIS and is integral to evaluating motor carriers' ability to successfully maintain their vehicles, thus preventing them from being placed OOS during roadside inspections. Each safety audit will continue to have the requirements of part 396, Inspection, Repair, and Maintenance, reviewed as indicated by the above explanation.

(j) *Accident Factor.* (1) In addition to the five regulatory factors, a sixth factor is included in the process to address the accident history of the motor carrier. This factor is the recordable accident rate, which the carrier has experienced during the past 12 months. Recordable accident, as defined in 49 CFR 390.5, means an accident involving a commercial motor vehicle operating on a public road in interstate or intrastate commerce which results in a fatality; a bodily injury to a person who, as a result of the injury, immediately receives medical treatment away from the scene of the accident; or one or more motor vehicles incurring disabling damage as a result of the accident requiring the motor vehicle to be transported away from the scene by a tow truck or other motor vehicle.

(2) Experience has shown that urban carriers, those motor carriers operating entirely within a radius of less than 100 air miles (normally urban areas), have a higher exposure to accident situations because of their environment and normally have higher accident rates.

(3) The recordable accident rate will be used in determining the carrier's basic safety management controls in Factor 6, Accident. It will be used only when a carrier incurs two or more recordable accidents within the 12 months before the safety audit. An urban carrier (a carrier operating entirely within a radius of 100 air miles) with a recordable rate per million miles greater than 1.7 will be deemed to have inadequate basic safety management controls for the accident factor. All other carriers with a recordable accident rate per million miles greater than 1.5 will be deemed to have inadequate basic safety management controls for the accident factor. The rates are the result of roughly doubling the United States national average accident rate in Fiscal Years 1994, 1995, and 1996.

(4) The FMCSA will continue to consider preventability when a new entrant contests the evaluation of the accident factor by presenting compelling evidence that the recordable rate is not a fair means of evaluating its accident factor. Preventability will be determined according to the following standard: "If a driver, who exercises normal judgment and foresight, could have foreseen the possibility of the accident that in fact occurred, and avoided it by taking steps within his/her control which would not have risked causing another kind of mishap, the accident was preventable."

(k) *Factor Ratings.* (1) The following table shows the five regulatory factors, parts of the FMCSRs and HMRs associated with each factor, and the accident factor. Each carrier's level of basic safety management controls with each factor is determined as follows:

(i) Factor 1—General: Parts 390 and 387;
(ii) Factor 2—Driver: Parts 382, 383, and 391;
(iii) Factor 3—Operational: Parts 392 and 395;

(iv) Factor 4—Vehicle: Parts 393, 396 and the Out of Service Rate;
(v) Factor 5—Hazardous Materials: Part 171, 177, 180 and 397; and
(vi) Factor 6—Accident: Recordable Accident Rate per Million Miles;

(2) For paragraphs III (k)(1)(i) through (v) (Factors 1 through 5), if the combined violations of acute and or critical regulations for each factor is equal to three or more points, the carrier is determined not to have basic safety management controls for that individual factor.

(3) For paragraphs III (k)(1)(vi), if the recordable accident rate is greater than 1.7 recordable accidents per million miles for an urban carrier (1.5 for all other carriers), the carrier is determined to have inadequate basic safety management controls.

(l) Notwithstanding FMCSA verification of the items listed in part II (a)(1) through (5) above, if the safety audit determines the carrier has inadequate basic safety management controls in at least three separate factors described in part III, the carrier's application for provisional operating authority will be denied. For example, FMCSA evaluates a carrier finding:

(1) One instance of noncompliance with a critical regulation in part 387 scoring one point for Factor 1;
(2) Two instances of noncompliance with acute regulations in part 382 scoring three points for Factor 2;
(3) Three instances of noncompliance with critical regulations in part 396 scoring three points for Factor 4; and
(4) Three instances of noncompliance with acute regulations in parts 171 and 397 scoring four and one-half (4.5) points for Factor 5.

Under this example, the carrier will not receive provisional operating authority because it scored three or more points for Factors 2, 4, and 5 and FMCSA determined the carrier had inadequate basic safety management controls in at least three separate factors.

PART 366—DESIGNATION OF PROCESS AGENT

AUTHORITY: 49 U.S.C. 13303, 13304, and 14704; and 49 CFR 1.73.

SOURCE: 55 FR 11197, Mar. 27, 1990, unless otherwise noted. Redesignated at 61 FR 54707, Oct. 21, 1996.

EDITORIAL NOTE: Nomenclature changes to part 366 appear at 66 FR 49870, Oct. 1, 2001.

§ 366.1 Applicability.

These rules, relating to the filing of designations of persons upon whom court process may be served, govern motor carriers and brokers and, as of the moment of succession, their fiduciaries (as defined at 49 CFR 387.319(a)).

[55 FR 11197, Mar. 27, 1990. Redesignated at 61 FR 54707, Oct. 21, 1996; 62 FR 49940, Sept. 24, 1997]

§ 366.2 Form of designation.

Designations shall be made on Form BOC–3, *Designation of Agent for Service of Process.* Only one completed current form may be on file. It must include all States for which agent designations are required. One copy must be retained by the carrier or broker at its principal place of business.

§ 366.3 Eligible persons.

All persons (as defined at 49 U.S.C. 13102(16)) designated must reside or maintain an office in the State for which they are designated. If a State official is designated, evidence of his willingness to accept service of process must be furnished.

[55 FR 11197, Mar. 27, 1990. Redesignated at 61 FR 54707, Oct. 21, 1996; 62 FR 49940, Sept. 24, 1997]

§ 366.4 Required States.

(a) *Motor carriers.* Every motor carrier (of property or passengers) shall make a designation for each State in which it is authorized to operate and for each State traversed during such operations. Every motor carrier (including private carriers) operating in the United States in the course of transportation between points in a foreign country shall file a designation for each State traversed.

(b) *Brokers.* Every broker shall make a designation for each State in which its offices are located or in which contracts will be written.

[55 FR 11197, Mar. 27, 1990, as amended at 55 FR 47338, Nov. 13, 1990]

§ 366.5 Blanket designations.

Where an association or corporation has filed with the FMCSA a list of process agents for each State, motor carriers may make the required designations by using the following statement:

Those persons named in the list of process agents on file with the Federal Motor Carrier Safety Administration by _____

(Name of association or corporation) and any subsequently filed revisions thereof, for the States in which this carrier is or may be authorized to operate, including States traversed during such operations, except those States for which individual designations are named.

§ 366.6 Cancellation or change.

A designation may be canceled or changed only by a new designation except that, where a carrier or broker ceases to be subject to § 366.4 in whole or in part for 1 year, designation is no longer required and may be canceled without making another designation.

[55 FR 11197, Mar. 27, 1990. Redesignated at 61 FR 54707, Oct. 21, 1996; 62 FR 49940, Sept. 24, 1997]

PART 367—STANDARDS FOR REGISTRATION WITH STATES

Subpart A—[Reserved]

Subpart B—Fees Under the Unified Carrier Registration Plan and Agreement

Sec.
367.20 Fees under the Unified Carrier Registration Plan and Agreement for each registration year until any subsequent adjustment in the fees becomes effective.
367.30 Fees under the Unified Carrier Registration Plan and Agreement for registration years beginning in 2010.

AUTHORITY: 49 U.S.C. 13301, 14504a; and 49 CFR 1.73.

SOURCE: 58 FR 28933, May 18, 1993, unless otherwise noted. Redesignated at 61 FR 54707, Oct. 21, 1996.

EDITORIAL NOTE: Nomenclature changes to part 367 appear at 66 FR 49870, Oct. 1, 2001.

Subpart A—[Reserved]

Subpart B—Fees Under the Unified Carrier Registration Plan and Agreement

§ 367.20 Fees under the Unified Carrier Registration Plan and Agreement for each registration year until any subsequent adjustment in the fees becomes effective.

FEES UNDER THE UNIFIED CARRIER REGISTRATION PLAN AND AGREEMENT FOR EACH REGISTRATION YEAR

Bracket	Number of commercial motor vehicles owned or operated by exempt or non-exempt motor carrier, motor private carrier, or freight forwarder	Fee per company for exempt or non-exempt motor carrier, motor private carrier, or freight forwarder	Fee per company for broker or leasing company
B1	0–2	$39	$39
B2	3–5	116	
B3	6–20	231	
B4	21–100	806	
B5	101–1,000	3,840	
B6	1,001 and above	37,500	

[72 FR 48590, Aug. 24, 2007, as amended at 73 FR 10158, Feb. 26, 2008]

§ 367.30 Fees under the Unified Carrier Registration Plan and Agreement for registration years beginning in 2010.

FEES UNDER THE UNIFIED CARRIER REGISTRATION PLAN AND AGREEMENT FOR EACH REGISTRATION YEAR

Bracket	Number of commercial motor vehicles owned or operated by exempt or non-exempt motor carrier, motor private carrier, or freight forwarder	Fee per entity for exempt or non-exempt motor carrier, motor private carrier, or freight forwarder	Fee per entity for broker or leasing company
B1	0–2	$76	$76
B2	3–5	227	
B3	6–20	452	
B4	21–100	1,576	
B5	101–1,000	7,511	
B6	1,001 and above	73,346	

[75 FR 22012, Apr. 27, 2010]

PART 368—APPLICATION FOR A CERTIFICATE OF REGISTRATION TO OPERATE IN MUNICIPALITIES IN THE UNITED STATES ON THE UNITED STATES-MEXICO INTERNATIONAL BORDER OR WITHIN THE COMMERCIAL ZONES OF SUCH MUNICIPALITIES.

Sec.
368.1 Certificate of registration.
368.2 Definitions.
368.3 Applying for a certificate of registration.
368.4 Requirement to notify FMCSA of change in applicant information.
368.5 Re-registration of certain carriers holding certificates of registration.
368.6 FMCSA action on an application.
368.7 Requirement to carry certificate of registration in the vehicle.
368.8 Appeals.

AUTHORITY: 49 U.S.C. 13301 and 13902; Pub. L. 106–159, 113 Stat. 1748; and 49 CFR 1.73.

SOURCE: 67 FR 12660, Mar. 19, 2002, unless otherwise noted.

§ 368.1 Certificate of registration.

(a) A Mexico-domiciled motor carrier must apply to the FMCSA and receive a Certificate of Registration to provide interstate transportation in municipalities in the United States on the United States-Mexico international border or within the commercial zones of such municipalities as defined in 49 U.S.C. 13902(c)(4)(A).

(b) A certificate of registration permits only interstate transportation of property in municipalities in the United States on the United States-Mexico international border or within the commercial zones of such municipalities. A holder of a Certificate of Registration who operates a vehicle beyond this area is subject to applicable penalties and out-of-service orders.

§ 368.2 Definitions.

Interstate transportation means transportation described at 49 U.S.C. 13501, and transportation in the United States otherwise exempt from the Secretary's jurisdiction under 49 U.S.C. 13506(b)(1).

Mexico-domiciled motor carrier means a motor carrier of property whose principal place of business is located in Mexico.

§ 368.3 Applying for a certificate of registration.

(a) If you wish to obtain a certificate of registration under this part, you must submit an application that includes the following:

(1) Form OP-2—Application for Mexican Certificate of Registration for Foreign Motor Carriers and Foreign Motor Private Carriers Under 49 U.S.C. 13902;

(2) Form MCS-150—Motor Carrier Identification Report; and

(3) A notification of the means used to designate process agents, either by submission in the application package of Form BOC-3—Designation of Agents—Motor Carriers, Brokers and Freight Forwarders or a letter stating that the applicant will use a process agent service that will submit the Form BOC-3 electronically.

(b) The FMCSA will only process your application for a Certificate of Registration if it meets the following conditions:

(1) The application must be completed in English;

(2) The information supplied must be accurate and complete in accordance with the instructions to the Form OP-2, Form MCS-150 and Form BOC-3;

(3) The application must include all the required supporting documents and applicable certifications set forth in the instructions to the Form OP-2, Form MCS-150 and Form BOC-3;

(4) The application must include the filing fee payable to the FMCSA in the amount set forth in 49 CFR 360.3(f)(1); and

(5) The application must be signed by the applicant.

(c) If you fail to furnish the complete application as described under paragraph (b) of this section your application may be rejected.

(d) If you submit false information under this section, you will be subject to applicable Federal penalties.

(e) You must submit the application to the address provided in the instructions to the Form OP-2.

(f) You may obtain the application described in paragraph (a) of this section from any FMCSA Division Office or download it from the FMCSA web site at: *http://www.fmcsa.dot.gov/factsfigs/formspubs.htm.*

§ 368.4 Requirement to notify FMCSA of change in applicant information.

(a) You must notify the FMCSA of any changes or corrections to the information in Parts I, IA or II submitted on the Form OP-2 or the Form BOC-3—Designation of Agents—Motor Carriers, Brokers and Freight Forwarders during the application process or while you have a Certificate of Registration. You must notify the FMCSA in writing within 45 days of the change or correction.

(b) If you fail to comply with paragraph (a) of this section, the FMCSA may suspend or revoke the Certificate of Registration until you meet those requirements.

§ 368.5 Re-registration of certain carriers holding certificates of registration.

(a) Each holder of a certificate of registration that permits operations only in municipalities in the United States along the United States-Mexico international border or in commercial zones of such municipalities issued before April 18, 2002, who wishes to continue solely in those operations must submit an application according to procedures established under § 368.3 of this part, except the filing fee in paragraph (b)(4) of that section is waived. You must file your application by October 20, 2003.

(b) The FMCSA may suspend or revoke the certificate of registration of any registrant that fails to comply with the procedures set forth in this section.

(c) Certificates of registration issued before April 18, 2002, remain valid until the FMCSA acts on the OP-2 application filed according to paragraph (a) of this section.

§ 368.6 FMCSA action on the application.

(a) The Federal Motor Carrier Safety Administration will review the application for correctness, completeness, and adequacy of information. Non-material errors will be corrected without notice to the applicant. Incomplete applications may be rejected.

(b) If the applicant does not require or is not eligible for a Certificate of Registration, the FMCSA will deny the application and notify the applicant.

(c) The FMCSA will validate the accuracy of information and certifications provided in the application against data maintained in databases of the governments of Mexico and the United States.

(d) If the FMCSA determines that the application and certifications demonstrate that the application is consistent with the FMCSA's safety fitness policy, it will issue a provisional Certificate of Registration, including a distinctive USDOT Number that identifies the motor carrier as permitted to provide interstate transportation of property solely in municipalities in the United States on the U.S.-Mexico international border or within the commercial zones of such municipalities.

(e) The FMCSA may issue a permanent Certificate of Registration to the holder of a provisional Certificate of Registration no earlier than 18 months after the date of issuance of the Certificate and only after completion to the satisfaction of the FMCSA of the safety monitoring system for Mexico-domiciled carriers set out in subpart B of part 385 of this subchapter.

(f) Notice of the authority sought will not be published in either the FEDERAL REGISTER or the FMCSA Register.

Protests or comments will not be allowed. There will be no oral hearings.

§ 368.7 Requirement to carry certificate of registration in the vehicle.

A holder of a Certificate of Registration must maintain a copy of the Certificate of Registration in any vehicle providing transportation service within the scope of the Certificate, and make it available upon request to any State or Federal authorized inspector or enforcement officer.

§ 368.8 Appeals.

An applicant has the right to appeal denial of the application. The appeal must be in writing and specify in detail why the agency's decision to deny the application was wrong. The appeal must be filed with the Director, Office of Data Analysis and Information Systems within 20 days of the date of the letter denying the application. The decision of the Director will be the final agency order.

PART 369—REPORTS OF MOTOR CARRIERS

AUTHORITY: 5 U.S.C. 553 and 559; 16 U.S.C. 1456; 49 U.S.C. 14123; 49 CFR 1.73.

§ 369.1 Annual reports of motor carriers of property, motor carriers of household goods, and dual property carriers.

(a) *Annual Report Form M.* All class I and class II common and contract carriers of property, including household goods and dual property motor carriers, must file Motor Carrier Annual Report Form M (Form M). Carriers must file the annual report on or before March 31 of the year following the year to which it relates. For classification criteria, see § 369.2.

(b) *Quarterly Report Form QFR.* All class I common motor carriers of property and class I household goods motor carriers must file Motor Carrier Quarterly Report Form QFR (Form QFR). The quarterly accounting periods end on March 31, June 30, September 30, and December 31. The quarterly reports must be filed within 30 calendar days after the end of the reporting quarter.

(c) *Where to file reports.* Carriers must file the quarterly and annual reports with the Federal Motor Carrier Safety Administration at the address in § 369.6. You can obtain blank copies of the report forms from the Federal Motor Carrier Safety Administration.

[64 FR 13921, Mar. 23, 1999. Redesignated at 71 FR 45742, Aug. 10, 2006, and amended at 71 FR 45743, Aug. 10, 2006]

§ 369.2 Classification of carriers—motor carriers of property, household goods carriers, and dual property carriers.

(a) Common and contract motor carriers of property are grouped into the following three classes:

Class I. Carriers having annual carrier operating revenues (including interstate and intrastate) of $10 million or more after applying the revenue deflator formula in Note A.

Class II. Carriers having annual carrier operating revenues (including interstate and intrastate) of at least $3 million but less than $10 million after applying the revenue deflator formula in Note A.

Class III. Carriers having annual carrier operating revenues (including interstate and intrastate) of less than $3 million after applying the revenue deflator formula in Note A.

(b)(1) The class to which any carrier belongs shall be determined by annual carrier operating revenues (excluding revenues from private carriage, compensated intercorporate hauling, and leasing vehicles with drivers to private carriers) after applying the revenue deflator formula in Note A. Upward and downward classification will be effective as of January 1 of the year immediately following the third consecutive year of revenue qualification.

(2) Any carrier which begins new operations by obtaining operating authority not previously held or extends its existing authority by obtaining additional operating rights shall be classified in accordance with a reasonable estimate of its annual carrier operating revenues after applying the revenue deflator formula shown in Note A.

(3) When a business combination occurs such as a merger, reorganization, or consolidation, the surviving carrier shall be reclassified effective as of January 1 of the next calendar year on the basis of the combined revenues for the year when the combination occurred after applying the revenue deflator formula shown in Note A.

(4) Carriers must notify the Federal Motor Carrier Safety Administration (FMCSA) of any change in classification or any change in annual operating revenues that would cause a change in classification. The carrier may request a waiver or an exception from these regulations in unusual or extenuating circumstances, where the classification process will unduly burden the carrier, such as partial liquidation or curtailment or elimination of contracted services. The request must be in writing, specifying the conditions justifying the waiver or exception. FMCSA will notify the carriers of any change in classification.

(5) Carriers not required to file an Annual Report Form M may be required to file the Worksheet for Calculating Carrier Classification. All carriers will be notified of any classification changes.

NOTE A: Each carrier's operating revenues will be deflated annually using the Producers Price Index (PPI) of Finished Goods before comparing those revenues with the dollar revenue limits prescribed in paragraph (a) of this section. The PPI is published monthly by the Bureau of Labor Statistics. The formula to be applied is as follows:

$$\text{Current year's annual operating revenues} \times \frac{\text{1994 average PPI}}{\text{Current year's average PPI}} = \text{Adjusted annual operating revenues}$$

[52 FR 10383, Apr. 1, 1987, as amended at 59 FR 5111, Feb. 3, 1994; 59 FR 49848, Sept. 30, 1994. Redesignated at 63 FR 52193, Sept. 30, 1998, and amended at 64 FR 13921, 13922, Mar. 23, 1999; 68 FR 4719, Jan. 30, 2003. Resesignated at 71 FR 45742, Aug. 10, 2006, and amended at 71 FR 45743, Aug. 10, 2006]

§ 369.3 Classification of carriers—motor carriers of passengers.

(a) Common and contract carriers of passengers are grouped into the following two classes:

Class I—Carriers having average annual gross transportation operating revenues (including interstate and intrastate) of $5 million or more from passenger motor carrier operations after applying the revenue deflator formula as shown in the Note.

Class II—Carriers having average annual gross transportation operating revenues (including interstate or intrastate) of less than $5 million from passenger motor carrier operations after applying the revenue deflator formula as shown in the Note.

(b)(1) The class to which any carrier belongs shall be determined by annual carrier operating revenues after applying the revenue deflator formula as shown in the Note. Upward and downward reclassification will be effective as of January 1 of the year immediately following the third consecutive year of revenue qualification.

(2) Any carrier which begins new operations (obtains operating authority not previously held) or extends its existing authority (obtains additional operating rights) shall be classified in accordance with a reasonable estimate of its annual carrier operating revenues after applying the revenue deflator formula shown in the Note.

(3) When a business combination occurs, such as a merger, reorganization, or consolidation, the surviving carrier shall be reclassified effective as of January 1 of the next calendar year on the basis of the combined revenues for the year when the combination occurred after applying the revenue deflator formula shown in the Note.

(4) Carriers shall notify the FMCSA of any change in classification or when their annual operating revenues exceed the Class II limit by writing to the Federal Motor Carrier Safety Administration at the address in § 369.6. In unusual circumstances where the classification regulations and reporting requirements will unduly burden the carrier, the carrier may request from the FMCSA a waiver from these regulations. This request shall be in writing specifying the conditions justifying the waiver. The FMCSA then shall notify carriers of any change in classification or reporting requirements.

(c) For classification purposes, the FMCSA shall publish in the FEDERAL REGISTER annually an index number which shall be used for adjusting gross annual operating revenues. The index number (deflator) is based on the Producer Price Index of Finished Goods and is used to eliminate the effects of inflation from the classification process.

NOTE: Each carrier's operating revenues will be deflated annually using the Producers Price Index (PPI) of Finished Goods before comparing them with the dollar revenue limits prescribed in paragraph (a) of this section. The PPI is published monthly by the Bureau of Labor Statistics. The formula to be applied is as follows:

$$\text{Current year's annual operating revenues} \times \frac{\text{1986 average PPI}}{\text{Current year's average PPI}} = \text{Adjusted annual operating revenues}$$

[53 FR 4029, Feb. 11, 1988. Redesignated at 63 FR 52193, Sept. 30, 1998, and amended at 68 FR 4719, Jan. 30, 2003. Redesignated at 71 FR 45742, Aug. 10, 2006, and amended at 71 FR 45743, Aug. 10, 2006]

§369.4 Annual and quarterly reports of Class I carriers of passengers.

(a) All Class I motor carriers of passengers shall complete and file Motor Carrier Quarterly and Annual Report Form MP–1 for Motor Carriers of Passengers (Form MP–1). Other than Class I carriers are not required to file Form MP–1.

(b) Motor Carrier Quarterly and Annual Report Form MP–1 shall be used to file both quarterly and annual selected motor carrier data. The annual accounting period shall be based either (1) on the 31st day of December in each year, or (2) an accounting year of thirteen 4-week periods ending at the close of the last 7 days of each calendar year. A carrier electing to adopt an accounting year of thirteen 4-week periods shall file with the FMCSA a statement showing the day on which its accounting year will close. A subsequent change in the accounting period may not be made except by authority of the FMCSA. The quarterly accounting period shall end on March 31, June 30, September 30, and December 31. The quarterly report shall be filed within 30 days after the end of the reporting quarter. The annual report shall be filed on or before March 31 of the year following the year to which it relates.

(c) The quarterly and annual report shall be filed in duplicate to the Federal Motor Carrier Safety Administration at the address in §369.6. Copies of Form MP–1 may be obtained from the FMCSA.

[52 FR 20400, June 1, 1987. Redesignated at 63 FR 52193, Sept. 30, 1998, as amended at 68 FR 4719, Jan. 30, 2003. Redesignated at 71 FR 45742, Aug. 10, 2006, and amended at 71 FR 45743, Aug. 10, 2006]

§369.5 Records.

Books, records and carrier operating documents shall be retained as prescribed in 49 CFR part 379, Preservation of Records.

[52 FR 10383, Apr. 1, 1987. Redesignated at 63 FR 52193, Sept. 30, 1998. Redesignated at 71 FR 45742, Aug. 10, 2006, and amended at 71 FR 45743, Aug. 10, 2006]

§369.6 Address.

The following address must be used by motor carriers when submitting a report, requesting an exemption from filing a report, or requesting an exemption from public release of a report: Federal Motor Carrier Safety Administration, Office of Information Technology (MC–RI), 1200 New Jersey Ave., SE., Washington, DC 20590–0001. This address may also be used for general correspondence regarding the data collection program described in this section.

[64 FR 13923, Mar. 23, 1999, as amended at 68 FR 4719, Jan. 30, 2003. Redesignated at 71 FR 45742, Aug. 10, 2006, and amended at 71 FR 45743, Aug. 10, 2006; 72 FR 55699, Oct. 1, 2007]

§369.8 Requests for exemptions from filing.

(a) *In General.* This section governs requests for exemptions from filing of reports required under §369.1.

(b) *Criteria.* The Federal Motor Carrier Safety Administration (FMCSA) may grant a request upon a proper showing that the exemption is necessary to preserve confidential business information that is not otherwise publicly available. Information is considered to be confidential when:

(1) Disclosure of the information in the carrier's report would be likely to cause substantial harm to the carrier's competitive position; or

(2) Disclosure of information in the report would be likely to impair protectable government interests.

(c) *Contents of a request.* The contents of a request for an exemption from filing must contain, at a minimum, the contents that are required for a request for an exemption from public release contained in §369.9(c). A carrier's request may include any other grounds as to why the request should be granted.

(d) *When requests are due.* The timing of a request for an exemption from filing is the same as the timing for a request for an exemption from public release contained in §369.9(d). The table below summarizes report and request due dates.

Report	Report due by	Request due by
Annual Form M	March 31	March 31
First Quarter Form QFR	April 30	March 31
Second Quarter Form QFR	July 31	March 31
Third Quarter Form QFR	October 31	March 31
Fourth Quarter Form QFR	January 31	March 31

(e) *Decision to grant or deny a request.* (1) A request will be denied if it fails to provide all of the supporting information required in paragraph (c) of this section or if the supporting information is insufficient to establish that information in the carrier's report meets the criteria in paragraph (b) of this section.

(2) FMCSA will grant or deny each request within a reasonable period of time. FMCSA will notify the carrier of its decision. The decision by FMCSA shall be administratively final.

(f) *Pendency.* While a request is pending, the carrier is required to submit any reports required under § 369.1.

(g) *Period of exemptions.* If a request for an exemption under this section is granted, the carrier will be exempt from the reporting requirements of § 369.1 for a period of three reporting years.

(h) *Modification of a decision to grant a request.* If a request is granted it remains in effect in accordance with its terms, unless modified by a later finding that the decision was clearly erroneous. If FMCSA believes such a finding should be made, FMCSA will notify the requesting carrier in writing of the reasons for the modification. The carrier may seek reconsideration of the modification.

[64 FR 13922, Mar. 23, 1999. Redesignated at 71 FR 45742, Aug. 10, 2006, and amended at 71 FR 45743, Aug. 10, 2006]

§ 369.9 Requests for exemptions from public release.

(a) *In General.* This section governs requests for exemptions from public release of reports filed under § 369.1.

(b) *Criteria.* The Federal Motor Carrier Safety Administration (FMCSA) will grant a request upon a proper showing that the carrier is not a publicly held corporation or that the carrier is not subject to financial reporting requirements of the Securities and Exchange Commission, and that the exemption is necessary to avoid competitive harm and to avoid the disclosure of information that qualifies as trade secret or privileged or confidential information under 5 U.S.C. 552(b)(4). Information is considered to be confidential when:

(1) Disclosure of the information in the carrier's report would be likely to cause substantial harm to the carrier's competitive position; or

(2) Disclosure of information in the report would be likely to impair protectable government interests.

(c) *Contents of a request.* A request for an exemption from public release must contain information supporting the claim. While the supporting information may contain opinions, the request must consist of objective data to the extent possible. General or nonspecific assertions or analysis will be insufficient to support a request if FMCSA is unable to find that the criteria are met. The supporting information must show:

(1) That the information claimed to be confidential is a trade secret, or commercial or financial information that is privileged or confidential.

(2) Measures taken by the carrier to ensure that the information has not been disclosed or otherwise made available to any person, company, or organization other then the carrier.

(3) Insofar as is known by the carrier, the extent to which the information has been disclosed, or otherwise become available, to persons other than the carrier, and why such disclosure or availability does not compromise the confidential nature of the information.

(4) If the carrier asserts that disclosure would be likely to result in substantial competitive harm, what the harmful effects of disclosure would be, why the effects should be viewed as substantial, and the causal relationship between the effects and disclosure.

(5) If the carrier asserts that disclosure would be likely to impair protectable government interests, what the effects of disclosure are likely to be and why disclosure is likely to impair such interests.

(d) *When requests are due.* (1) Requests for an exemption under this section may be made at any time during the year. However, a request will be deemed applicable to only those reports due on or after the date the request is received. Requests received after a report's due date will only be considered for the following year's report.

(2) A request will be deemed received on the date the request is physically received or, if it is sent by mail, on the date it is postmarked.

(3) FMCSA will only allow a late request if there are extenuating circumstances and the carrier gives adequate notice within a reasonable time of the extenuating circumstances.

(4) A carrier submitting a request relating to the annual report can also request that it cover the quarterly reports for the upcoming year. In this case FMCSA will decide both requests at the same time. Requests covering the quarterly reports must be received by the due date of the annual report which relates to the prior year. The table in paragraph (e) of this section summarizes report, request, and decision due dates.

(e) *Decision to grant or deny a request.* (1) After each due date of each annual report specified in §369.1, FMCSA will publish a notice in the FEDERAL REGISTER requesting comments on any requests received under this section that are valid and pending.

(2) A request will be granted only if it provides all of the supporting information required in paragraph (c) of this section and if the supporting information is sufficient to establish that information in the carrier's report meets the criteria in paragraph (b) of this section.

(3) If the carrier fails to comply with the timing requirements of paragraph (d) of this section, the claim for confidentiality will be waived unless FMCSA is notified of extenuating circumstances before the information is disclosed to the public and FMCSA finds that the extenuating circumstances warrant consideration of the claim.

(4) FMCSA will grant or deny each request no later than 90 days after the request's due date as defined in paragraph (d) of this section. The decision by FMCSA shall be administratively final. The table below summarizes report, request, and decision due dates.

Report	Report due	Request due	Decision due
Annual Form M	March 31	March 31	June 30
First Quarter Form QFR	April 30	March 31	June 30
Second Quarter Form QFR	July 31	March 31	June 30
Third Quarter Form QFR	October 31	March 31	June 30
Fourth Quarter Form QFR	January 31	March 31	June 30

(5) If a request is granted, FMCSA will notify carrier of that decision and of any appropriate limitations.

(6) If a request for confidentiality is denied, FMCSA will notify the carrier of that decision and that the information will be made available to the public not less than ten working days after the carrier has received notice of the denial. The notice will specify the reasons for denying the request.

(f) *Pendency.* A request is deemed pending from the date it is received by FMCSA until it is granted or denied by FMCSA. FMCSA will not release publicly, unless otherwise required by law, any report for which a valid request for an exemption from public release is pending.

(g) *Period of exemptions.* If a request for an exemption under this section is granted, FMCSA will not publicly release the reports covered by the granted exemption, unless otherwise required by law, for a period of three years from the report's due date.

(h) *Modification of a decision to grant a request.* If a request is granted it remains in effect in accordance with its terms, unless modified by a later finding that the decision was clearly erroneous. If FMCSA believes such a finding should be made, FMCSA will notify the requesting carrier in writing of the reasons for the modification and that the carrier's report will be made available to the public in not less than ten working days from the date of receipt of notice under this paragraph. The carrier may seek reconsideration of the modification.

[64 FR 13922, Mar. 23, 1999. Redesignated at 71 FR 45742, Aug. 10, 2006, and amended at 71 FR 45743, Aug. 10, 2006]

§ 369.10 Public release of motor carrier of property data.

(a) *In general.* Unless otherwise provided in this section, the data contained in a report filed under § 369.1 shall be made publicly available, but no sooner than the due date for the report.

(b) *Exceptions relating to exemptions from public release.* (1) If a request for an exemption from public release is pending under § 369.9, FMCSA will not publicly release the reports covered by the request until at least the time that a decision to grant or deny the request is made.

(2) If a carrier is granted an exemption from public release under § 369.9, FMCSA will not publicly release the reports covered by the granted exemption for a period of three years from the report's due date.

(c) *Other exceptions.* Notwithstanding any other provision of this part, information may be released:

(1) If the data are included in aggregate industry statistics that do not identify the individual carrier;

(2) To other components of the Department of Transportation for their internal use only;

(3) If required by law;

(4) With the consent of the carrier filing the report; or

(5) To contractors, if necessary for the performance of a contract with FMCSA.

[64 FR 13923, Mar. 23, 1999, as amended at 68 FR 4719, Jan. 30, 2003. Redesignated at 71 FR 45742, Aug. 10, 2006, and amended at 71 FR 45743, Aug. 10, 2006]

§ 369.11 Quarterly reports of passenger revenues, expenses, and statistics.

Commencing with reports for the quarter ended March 31, 1968, and for subsequent quarters thereafter, until further order, all class I common and contract motor carriers of passengers, as defined in § 369.3(a), shall compile and file quarterly reports in accordance with Motor Carrier Quarterly and Annual Report, Form MP-1. Such quarterly reports shall be filed in duplicate in the FMCSA Office of Information Management at the address in § 369.6, within 30 days after the close of the period to which it relates.

[43 FR 46975, Oct. 12, 1978. Redesignated at 63 FR 52193, Sept. 30, 1998, as amended at 68 FR 4719, Jan. 30, 2003. Redesignated at 71 FR 45742, Aug. 10, 2006, and amended at 71 FR 45743, Aug. 10, 2006]

PART 370—PRINCIPLES AND PRACTICES FOR THE INVESTIGATION AND VOLUNTARY DISPOSITION OF LOSS AND DAMAGE CLAIMS AND PROCESSING SALVAGE

Sec.
370.1 Applicability of regulations.
370.3 Filing of claims.
370.5 Acknowledgment of claims.
370.7 Investigation of claims.
370.9 Disposition of claims.
370.11 Processing of salvage.

AUTHORITY: 49 U.S.C. 13301 and 14706; and 49 CFR 1.73.

SOURCE: 62 FR 32042, June 12, 1997, unless otherwise noted.

EDITORIAL NOTE: Nomenclature changes to part 370 appear at 66 FR 49870, Oct. 1, 2001.

§ 370.1 Applicability of regulations.

The regulations set forth in this part shall govern the processing of claims for loss, damage, injury, or delay to property transported or accepted for transportation, in interstate or foreign commerce, by each motor carrier, water carrier, and freight forwarder (hereinafter called carrier), subject to 49 U.S.C. subtitle IV, part B.

§ 370.3 Filing of claims.

(a) *Compliance with regulations.* A claim for loss or damage to baggage or for loss, damage, injury, or delay to cargo, shall not be voluntarily paid by a carrier unless filed, as provided in paragraph (b) of this section, with the receiving or delivering carrier, or carrier issuing the bill of lading, receipt, ticket, or baggage check, or carrier on whose line the alleged loss, damage, injury, or delay occurred, within the specified time limits applicable thereto and as otherwise may be required by law, the terms of the bill of lading or other contract of carriage, and all tariff provisions applicable thereto.

(b) *Minimum filing requirements.* A written or electronic communication (when agreed to by the carrier and shipper or receiver involved) from a claimant, filed with a proper carrier within the time limits specified in the bill of lading or contract of carriage or transportation and:

(1) Containing facts sufficient to identify the baggage or shipment (or shipments) of property,

(2) Asserting liability for alleged loss, damage, injury, or delay, and

(3) Making claim for the payment of a specified or determinable amount of money, shall be considered as sufficient compliance with the provisions for filing claims embraced in the bill of lading or other contract of carriage; *Provided, however,* That where claims are electronically handled, procedures are established to ensure reasonable carrier access to supporting documents.

(c) *Documents not constituting claims.* Bad order reports, appraisal reports of damage, notations of shortage or damage, or both, on freight bills, delivery receipts, or other documents, or inspection reports issued by carriers or their inspection agencies, whether the extent of loss or damage is indicated in dollars and cents or otherwise, shall, standing alone, not be considered by carriers as sufficient to comply with the minimum claim filing requirements specified in paragraph (b) of this section.

(d) *Claims filed for uncertain amounts.* Whenever a claim is presented against a proper carrier for an uncertain amount, such as "$100 more or less," the carrier against whom such claim is filed shall determine the condition of the baggage or shipment involved at the time of delivery by it, if it was delivered, and shall ascertain as nearly as possible the extent, if any, of the loss or damage for which it may be responsible. It shall not, however, voluntarily pay a claim under such circumstances unless and until a formal claim in writing for a specified or determinable amount of money shall have been filed in accordance with the provisions of paragraph (b) of this section.

(e) *Other claims.* If investigation of a claim develops that one or more other carriers has been presented with a similar claim on the same shipment, the carrier investigating such claim shall communicate with each such other carrier and, prior to any agreement entered into between or among them as to the proper disposition of such claim or claims, shall notify all claimants of the receipt of conflicting or overlapping claims and shall require further substantiation, on the part of each claimant of his/her title to the property involved or his/her right with respect to such claim.

§370.5 Acknowledgment of claims.

(a) Each carrier shall, upon receipt in writing or by electronic transmission of a proper claim in the manner and form described in the regulations in the past, acknowledge the receipt of such claim in writing or electronically to the claimant within 30 days after the date of its receipt by the carrier unless the carrier shall have paid or declined such claim in writing or electronically within 30 days of the receipt thereof. The carrier shall indicate in its acknowledgment to the claimant what, if any, additional documentary evidence or other pertinent information may be required by it further to process the claim as its preliminary examination of the claim, as filed, may have revealed.

(b) The carrier shall at the time each claim is received create a separate file and assign thereto a successive claim file number and note that number on all documents filed in support of the claim and all records and correspondence with respect to the claim, including the acknowledgment of receipt. At the time such claim is received the carrier shall cause the date of receipt to be recorded on the face of the claim document, and the date of receipt shall also appear in the carrier's acknowledgment of receipt to the claimant. The carrier shall also cause the claim file number to be noted on the shipping order, if in its possession, and the delivery receipt, if any, covering such shipment, unless the carrier has established an orderly and consistent internal procedure for assuring:

(1) That all information contained in shipping orders, delivery receipts, tally sheets, and all other pertinent records made with respect to the transportation of the shipment on which claim is made, is available for examination upon receipt of a claim;

(2) That all such records and documents (or true and complete reproductions thereof) are in fact examined in the course of the investigation of the claim (and an appropriate record is made that such examination has in fact taken place); and

(3) That such procedures prevent the duplicate or otherwise unlawful payment of claims.

§ 370.7 Investigation of claims.

(a) *Prompt investigation required.* Each claim filed against a carrier in the manner prescribed in this part shall be promptly and thoroughly investigated if investigation has not already been made prior to receipt of the claim.

(b) *Supporting documents.* When a necessary part of an investigation, each claim shall be supported by the original bill of lading, evidence of the freight charges, if any, and either the original invoice, a photographic copy of the original invoice, or an exact copy thereof or any extract made therefrom, certified by the claimant to be true and correct with respect to the property and value involved in the claim; or certification of prices or values, with trade or other discounts, allowance, or deductions, of any nature whatsoever and the terms thereof, or depreciation reflected thereon; *Provided, however,* That where property involved in a claim has not been invoiced to the consignee shown on the bill of lading or where an invoice does not show price or value, or where the property involved has been sold, or where the property has been transferred at bookkeeping values only, the carrier shall, before voluntarily paying a claim, require the claimant to establish the destination value in the quantity, shipped, transported, or involved; *Provided, further,* That when supporting documents are determined to be a necessary part of an investigation, the supporting documents are retained by the carriers for possible FMCSA inspection.

(c) *Verification of loss.* When an asserted claim for loss of an entire package or an entire shipment cannot be otherwise authenticated upon investigation, the carrier shall obtain from the consignee of the shipment involved a certified statement in writing that the property for which the claim is filed has not been received from any other source.

§ 370.9 Disposition of claims.

(a) Each carrier subject to 49 U.S.C. subtitle IV, part B which receives a written or electronically transmitted claim for loss or damage to baggage or for loss, damage, injury, or delay to property transported shall pay, decline, or make a firm compromise settlement offer in writing or electronically to the claimant within 120 days after receipt of the claim by the carrier; *Provided, however,* That, if the claim cannot be processed and disposed of within 120 days after the receipt thereof, the carrier shall at that time and at the expiration of each succeeding 60-day period while the claim remains pending, advise the claimant in writing or electronically of the status of the claim and the reason for the delay in making final disposition thereof and it shall retain a copy of such advice to the claimant in its claim file thereon.

(b) When settling a claim for loss or damage, a common carrier by motor vehicle of household goods as defined in § 375.1(b)(1) of this chapter shall use the replacement costs of the lost or damaged item as a base to apply a depreciation factor to arrive at the current actual value of the lost or damaged item: *Provided,* That where an item cannot be replaced or no suitable replacement is obtainable, the proper measure of damages shall be the original costs, augmented by a factor derived from a consumer price index, and adjusted downward by a factor depreciation over average useful life.

§370.11 Processing of salvage.

(a) Whenever baggage or material, goods, or other property transported by a carrier subject to the provisions in this part is damaged or alleged to be damaged and is, as a consequence thereof, not delivered or is rejected or refused upon tender thereof to the owner, consignee, or person entitled to receive such property, the carrier, after giving due notice, whenever practicable to do so, to the owner and other parties that may have an interest therein, and unless advised to the contrary after giving such notice, shall undertake to sell or dispose of such property directly or by the employment of a competent salvage agent. The carrier shall only dispose of the property in a manner that will fairly and equally protect the best interests of all persons having an interest therein. The carrier shall make an itemized record sufficient to identify the property involved so as to be able to correlate it to the shipment or transportation involved, and claim, if any, filed thereon. The carrier also shall assign to each lot of such property a successive lot number and note that lot number on its record of shipment and claim, if any claim is filed thereon.

(b) Whenever disposition of salvage material or goods shall be made directly to an agent or employee of a carrier or through a salvage agent or company in which the carrier or one or more of its directors, officers, or managers has any interest, financial or otherwise, that carrier's salvage records shall fully reflect the particulars of each such transaction or relationship, or both, as the case may be.

(c) Upon receipt of a claim on a shipment on which salvage has been processed in the manner prescribed in this section, the carrier shall record in its claim file thereon the lot number assigned, the amount of money recovered, if any, from the disposition of such property, and the date of transmittal of such money to the person or persons lawfully entitled to receive the same.

PART 371—BROKERS OF PROPERTY

Subpart A—General Requirements

Subpart B—Special Rules for Household Goods Brokers

AUTHORITY: 49 U.S.C. 13301, 13501, and 14122; subtitle B, title IV of Pub. L. 109–59; and 49 CFR 1.73.

SOURCE: 45 FR 68942, Oct. 17, 1980, unless otherwise noted. Redesignated at 61 FR 54707, Oct. 21, 1996.

Subpart A—General Requirements

§371.1 Applicability.

This part applies, to the extent provided therein, to all brokers of transportation by motor vehicle as defined in §371.2.

[32 FR 20034, Dec. 20, 1967, as amended at 62 FR 15421, Apr. 1, 1997]

§ 371.2 Definitions.

(a) *Broker* means a person who, for compensation, arranges, or offers to arrange, the transportation of property by an authorized motor carrier. Motor carriers, or persons who are employees or bona fide agents of carriers, are not brokers within the meaning of this section when they arrange or offer to arrange the transportation of shipments which they are authorized to transport and which they have accepted and legally bound themselves to transport.

(b) *Bona fide agents* are persons who are part of the normal organization of a motor carrier and perform duties under the carrier's directions pursuant to a preexisting agreement which provides for a continuing relationship, precluding the exercise of discretion on the part of the agent in allocating traffic between the carrier and others.

(c) *Brokerage* or *brokerage service* is the arranging of transportation or the physical movement of a motor vehicle or of property. It can be performed on behalf of a motor carrier, consignor, or consignee.

(d) *Non-brokerage service* is all other service performed by a broker on behalf of a motor carrier, consignor, or consignee.

§ 371.3 Records to be kept by brokers.

(a) A broker shall keep a record of each transaction. For purposes of this section, brokers may keep master lists of consignors and the address and registration number of the carrier, rather than repeating this information for each transaction. The record shall show:

(1) The name and address of the consignor;

(2) The name, address, and registration number of the originating motor carrier;

(3) The bill of lading or freight bill number;

(4) The amount of compensation received by the broker for the brokerage service performed and the name of the payer;

(5) A description of any non-brokerage service performed in connection with each shipment or other activity, the amount of compensation received for the service, and the name of the payer; and

(6) The amount of any freight charges collected by the broker and the date of payment to the carrier.

(b) Brokers shall keep the records required by this section for a period of three years.

(c) Each party to a brokered transaction has the right to review the record of the transaction required to be kept by these rules.

[45 FR 68942, Oct. 17, 1980. Redesignated at 61 FR 54707, Oct. 21, 1996, as amended at 62 FR 15421, Apr. 1, 1997]

§ 371.7 Misrepresentation.

(a) A broker shall not perform or offer to perform any brokerage service (including advertising), in any name other than that in which its registration is issued.

(b) A broker shall not, directly or indirectly, represent its operations to be that of a carrier. Any advertising shall show the broker status of the operation.

[45 FR 68942, Oct. 17, 1980. Redesignated at 61 FR 54707, Oct. 21, 1996, as amended at 62 FR 15421, Apr. 1, 1997]

§ 371.9 Rebating and compensation.

(a) A broker shall not charge or receive compensation from a motor carrier for brokerage service where:

(1) The broker owns or has a material beneficial interest in the shipment or

(2) The broker is able to exercise control over the shipment because the broker owns the shipper, the shipper owns the broker, or there is common ownership of the two.

(b) A broker shall not give or offer to give anything of value to any shipper, consignor or consignee (or their officers or employees) except inexpensive advertising items given for promotional purposes.

§ 371.10 Duties and obligations of brokers.

Where the broker acts on behalf of a person bound by law or the FMCSA regulation as to the transmittal of bills or payments, the broker must also abide by the law or regulations which apply to that person.

[45 FR 68943, Oct. 17, 1980, as amended at 62 FR 15421, Apr. 1, 1997]

§371.13 Accounting.

Each broker who engages in any other business shall maintain accounts so that the revenues and expenses relating to the brokerage portion of its business are segregated from its other activities. Expenses that are common shall be allocated on an equitable basis; however, the broker must be prepared to explain the basis for the allocation.

[45 FR 68943, Oct. 17, 1980]

Subpart B—Special Rules for Household Goods Brokers

SOURCE: 75 FR 72996, Nov. 29, 2010, unless otherwise noted.

§371.101 If I operate as a household goods broker in interstate or foreign commerce, must I comply with subpart B of this part?

Yes, you must comply with all regulations in this subpart when you operate as a household goods broker offering services to individual shippers in interstate or foreign commerce. The regulations in this subpart do not apply to a household goods broker when providing services to commercial or government shippers in interstate or foreign commerce.

§371.103 What are the definitions of terms used in this subpart?

FMCSA means the Federal Motor Carrier Safety Administration within the U.S. Department of Transportation.

Household goods has the same meaning as the term is defined in §375.103 of this subchapter.

Household goods broker means a person, other than a motor carrier or an employee or bona fide agent of a motor carrier, that as a principal or agent sells, offers for sale, negotiates for, or holds itself out by solicitation, advertisement, or otherwise as selling, providing, or arranging for, transportation of household goods by motor carrier for compensation.

Individual shipper has the same meaning as the term is defined in §375.103 of this subchapter.

§371.105 Must I use a motor carrier that has a valid U.S. DOT number and valid operating authority issued by FMCSA to transport household goods in interstate or foreign commerce?

You may only act as a household goods broker for a motor carrier that has a valid, active U.S. DOT number and valid operating authority issued by FMCSA to transport household goods in interstate or foreign commerce.

§371.107 What information must I display in my advertisements and Internet Web homepage?

(a) You must prominently display in your advertisements and Internet Web homepage(s) the physical location(s) (street or highway address, city, and State) where you conduct business.

(b) You must prominently display your U.S. DOT registration number(s) and MC license number issued by the FMCSA in your advertisements and Internet Web homepage(s).

(c) You must prominently display in your advertisements and Internet Web site(s) your status as a household goods broker and the statement that you will not transport an individual shipper's household goods, but that you will arrange for the transportation of the household goods by an FMCSA-authorized household goods motor carrier, whose charges will be determined by its published tariff.

(d) If you provide estimates on any carrier's behalf pursuant to §371.113(b), you must prominently display in your Internet Web site(s) that the estimate must be based on the carrier's tariff and that the carrier is required to make its tariff available for public inspection upon a reasonable request.

(e) You may only include in your advertisements or Internet Web site(s) the names or logos of FMCSA-authorized household goods motor carriers with whom you have a written agreement as specified in §371.115 of this part.

§371.109 Must I inform individual shippers which motor carriers I use?

(a) You must provide to each potential individual shipper who contacts you a list of all authorized household goods motor carriers you use, including

67

their U.S. DOT registration number(s) and MC license numbers. You may provide the list electronically or on paper.

(b) You must provide to each potential individual shipper who contacts you a statement indicating that you are not a motor carrier authorized by the Federal Government to transport the individual shipper's household goods, and you are only arranging for an authorized household goods motor carrier to perform the transportation services and, if applicable, additional services. You may provide the statement electronically or on paper.

§ 371.111 Must I provide individual shippers with Federal consumer protection information?

(a) You must provide potential individual shippers with Federal consumer protection information by one of the following three methods:

(1) Provide a hyperlink on your Internet Web site to the FMCSA Web site containing the information in FMCSA's publications "Ready to Move?—Tips for a Successful Interstate Move" and "Your Rights and Responsibilities When You Move."

(2) Distribute to each shipper and potential shipper at the time you provide an estimate, copies of FMCSA's publications "Ready to Move?—Tips for a Successful Interstate Move" and "Your Rights and Responsibilities When You Move."

(3) Distribute to each shipper and potential shipper at the time you provide an estimate, copies of "Ready to Move?—Tips for a Successful Interstate Move" and "Your Rights and Responsibilities When You Move" as modified and produced by the authorized, lawful motor carrier to which you intend to provide the shipment under your written agreement required by § 371.115.

(b) If an individual shipper elects to waive physical receipt of the Federal consumer protection information by one of the methods described in paragraphs (a)(2) and (a)(3) of this section, and elects to access the same information via the hyperlink on the Internet as provided in paragraph (a)(1) of this section, you must include a clear and concise statement on the written estimate described in § 371.113 that the individual shipper expressly agreed to ac-

cess the Federal consumer protection information on the Internet.

(c) You must obtain a signed, dated, electronic or paper receipt showing the individual shipper has received both booklets that includes, if applicable, verification of the shipper's agreement to access the Federal consumer protection information on the Internet.

(d) You must maintain the signed receipt required by paragraph (c) of this section for three years from the date the individual shipper signs the receipt.

§ 371.113 May I provide individual shippers with a written estimate?

(a) You may provide each individual shipper with an estimate of transportation and accessorial charges. If you provide an estimate, it must be in writing and must be based on a physical survey of the household goods conducted by the authorized motor carrier on whose behalf the estimate is provided if the goods are located within a 50-mile radius of the motor carrier's or its agent's location, whichever is closer. The estimate must be prepared in accordance with a signed, written agreement, as specified in § 371.115 of this subpart.

(b) You must base your estimate upon the published tariffs of the authorized motor carrier who will transport the shipper's household goods.

(c)(1) A shipper may elect to waive the physical survey required in paragraph (a) of this section by written agreement signed by the shipper before the shipment is loaded.

(2) The household goods broker must explain the physical survey waiver agreement to the individual shipper in plain English. The physical survey waiver agreement must be printed on the written estimate and must be printed at no less than 7-point font size and with the font typeface Universe.

(3) A copy of the waiver agreement must be retained as an addendum to the bill of lading and is subject to the same record inspection and preservation requirements as are applicable to bills of lading.

(d) You must keep the records required by this section for three years following the date you provide the

68

written estimate for an individual shipper who accepts the estimate and has you procure the transportation.

§371.115 Must I maintain agreements with motor carriers before providing written estimates on behalf of these carriers?

(a) In order to provide estimates of charges for the transportation of household goods, you must do so in accordance with the written agreement required by §375.409 of this subchapter. Your written agreement with the motor carrier(s) must include the following items:

(1) Your broker name as shown on your FMCSA registration, your physical address, and your U.S. DOT registration number and MC license number;

(2) The authorized motor carrier's name as shown on its FMCSA registration, its physical address, and its U.S. DOT registration number and MC license number;

(3) A concise, easy to understand statement that your written estimate to the individual shipper:

(i) Will be exclusively on behalf of the authorized household goods motor carrier;

(ii) Will be based on the authorized household goods motor carrier's published tariff; and

(iii) Will serve as the authorized household goods motor carrier's estimate for purposes of complying with the requirements of part 375 of this chapter, including the requirement that the authorized household goods motor carrier relinquishes possession of the shipment upon payment of no more than 110 percent of a non-binding estimate at the time of delivery;

(4) Your owner's, corporate officer's, or corporate director's signature lawfully representing your household goods broker operation and the date;

(5) The signature of the authorized household goods motor carrier's owner, corporate officer, or corporate director lawfully representing the household goods motor carrier's operation and the date; and

(b) The signed written agreement required by this section is public information and you must produce it for review upon reasonable request by a member of the public.

(c) You must keep copies of the agreements required by this section for as long as you provide estimates on behalf of the authorized household goods motor carrier and for three years thereafter.

§371.117 Must I provide individual shippers with my policies concerning cancellation, deposits, and refunds?

(a) You must disclose prominently on your Internet Web site and in your agreements with prospective shippers your cancellation policy, deposit policy, and policy for refunding deposited funds in the event the shipper cancels an order for service before the date an authorized household goods motor carrier has been scheduled to pick up the shipper's property.

(b) You must maintain records showing each individual shipper's request to cancel a shipment and the disposition of each request for a period of three years after the date of a shipper's cancellation request. If you refunded a deposit, your records must include:

(1) Proof that the individual shipper cashed or deposited the check or money order, if the financial institution provides documentary evidence; or

(2) Proof that you delivered the refund check or money order to the individual shipper.

§371.121 What penalties may FMCSA impose for violations of this part?

The penalty provisions of 49 U.S.C. chapter 149, *Civil and Criminal Penalties* apply to this subpart. These penalties do not overlap. Notwithstanding these civil penalties, nothing in this section deprives an individual shipper of any remedy or right of action under existing law.

PART 372—EXEMPTIONS, COMMERCIAL ZONES, AND TERMINAL AREAS

Subpart A—Exemptions

Sec.

sold or arranged by anyone for compensation.

AUTHORITY: 49 U.S.C. 13504 and 13506; and 49 CFR 1.73.

EDITORIAL NOTE: Nomenclature changes to part 372 appear at 66 FR 49870, Oct. 1, 2001.

Subpart A—Exemptions

SOURCE: 32 FR 20036, Dec. 20, 1967, unless otherwise noted. Redesignated at 61 FR 54708, Oct. 21, 1996.

§ **372.101 Casual, occasional, or reciprocal transportation of passengers for compensation when such transportation is sold or arranged by anyone for compensation.**

The partial exemption from regulation under the provisions of 49 U.S.C. subtitle IV, part B of the casual, occasional, and reciprocal transportation of passengers by motor vehicle in interstate or foreign commerce for compensation as provided in 49 U.S.C. 13506(b) be, and it is hereby, removed to the extent necessary to make applicable all provisions of 49 U.S.C. subtitle IV, part B to such transportation when sold or offered for sale, or provided or procured or furnished or arranged for, by any person who sells, offers for sale, provides, furnishes, contracts, or arranges for such transportation for compensation or as a regular occupation or business.

[32 FR 20036, Dec. 20, 1967. Redesignated at 61 FR 54708, Oct. 21, 1996, as amended at 62 FR 15421, Apr. 1, 1997]

§ **372.103 Motor vehicles employed solely in transporting school children and teachers to or from school.**

The exemption set forth in 49 U.S.C. 13506(a)(1) shall not be construed as being inapplicable to motor vehicles being used at the time of operation in the transportation of schoolchildren and teachers to or from school, even though such motor vehicles are employed at other times in transportation beyond the scope of the exemption.

[36 FR 9022, May 18, 1971, as amended at 62 FR 15421, Apr. 1, 1997]

§ **372.107 Definitions.**

As used in the regulations in this part, the following terms shall have the meaning shown:

(a) *Cooperative association.* The term "cooperative association" means an association which conforms to the following definition in the Agricultural Marketing Act, approved June 15, 1929, as amended (12 U.S.C. 1141j):

As used in this Act, the term *cooperative association* means any association in which farmers act together in processing, preparing for market, handling, and/or marketing the farm products of persons so engaged, and also means any association in which farmers act together in purchasing, testing, grading, processing, distributing, and/or furnishing farm supplies and/or farm business services. Provided, however, That such associations are operated for the mutual benefit of the members thereof as such producers or purchasers and conform to one or both of the following requirements:

First. That no member of the association is allowed more than one vote because of the amount of stock or membership capital he may own therein; and

Second. That the association does not pay dividends on stock or membership capital in excess of 8 per centum per annum.

And in any case to the following:

Third. That the association shall not deal in farm products, farm supplies and farm business services with or for nonmembers in an amount greater in value than the total amount of such business transacted by it with or for members. All business transacted by any cooperative association for or on behalf of the United States or any agency or instrumentality thereof shall be disregarded in determining the volume of member and nonmember business transacted by such association.

Associations which do not conform to such definition are not eligible to operate under the partial exemption of 49 U.S.C. 13506(a)(5).

(b) *Federation of cooperative associations.* The term "federation of cooperative associations" means a federation composed of either two or more cooperative associations, or one or more farmers, which federation possesses no greater powers or purposes than a cooperative association as defined in paragraph (a) of this section. Federations of cooperative associations which do not conform to such definition are not eligible to operate under the partial exemption of 49 U.S.C. 13506(a)(5).

(c) *Member.* The term "member" means any farmer or cooperative association which has consented to be, has been accepted as, and is a member in good standing in accordance with the constitution, bylaws, or rules of the cooperative association or federation of cooperative associations.

(d) *Farmer.* The term "farmer" means any individual, partnership, corporation, or other business entity to the extent engaged in farming operations either as a producer of agricultural commodities or as a farm owner.

(e) *Interstate transportation.* The term "interstate transportation" means transportation by motor vehicle in interstate or foreign commerce subject to the FMCSA's jurisdiction as set forth in 49 U.S.C. 13501.

(f) *Member transportation.* The term "member transportation" means transportation performed by a cooperative association or federation of cooperative associations for itself or for its members, but does not include transportation performed in furtherance of the nonfarm business of such members.

(g) *Nonmember transportation.* The term "nonmember transportation" means transportation performed by a cooperative association or federation of cooperative associations other than member transportation as defined in paragraph (f) of this section.

(h) *Fiscal year.* The term "fiscal year" means the annual accounting period adopted by the cooperative association or federation of cooperative associations for Federal income tax reporting purposes.

[43 FR 2397, Jan. 17, 1978, as amended at 45 FR 45524, July 3, 1980; 47 FR 13353, Mar. 30, 1982; 47 FR 15142, Apr. 8, 1982]

§372.109 Computation of tonnage allowable in nonfarm-non-member transportation.

Interstate transportation performed by a cooperative association or federation of cooperative associations for nonmembers who are not farmers, cooperative associations, or federations of associations or the United States Government for compensation, (except transportation otherwise exempt under subtitle IV, part B, chapter 135 of title 49 of the United States Code) shall be limited to that which is incidental to its primary transportation operation and necessary for its effective performance. It shall in no event exceed 25 percent of its total interstate transportation services in any fiscal year, measured in terms of tonnage. A cooperative association or federation of cooperative associations may transport its own property, its members' property, property of other farmers and the property of other cooperatives or federations in accordance with existing law, except where the provisions of §372.111 may be applicable to the limit on member/nonmember transportation.

(a) The phrase "incidental to its primary transportation operation and necessary for its effective performance" means that the interstate transportation of the cooperative association or federation of cooperation association for nonmembers as described above is performed with the same trucks or tractors employed in a prior or subsequent trip in the primary transportation operation of the cooperative association or federation, that it is not economically feasible to operate the trucks or tractors empty on return trips (outbound trips in cases where the primary transportation operation is inbound to the association or federation), and that the additional income obtained from such transportation is necessary to make the primary transportation operation financially practicable. Transportation for nonmembers as described above performed by a cooperative or federation through the use of trucks or tractors trip-leased for one-way movements with the cooperative association or federation acting as leasee, is not incidental and necessary;

(b) The base tonnage to which the 25-percent limitation is applied is all tonnage of all kinds transported by the cooperative association or federation of cooperative associations in interstate or foreign commerce, whether for itself, its members or nonmembers, for or on behalf of the United States or any agency or instrumentality thereof, and that performed within the exemption provided by 49 U.S.C. 13506(a)(5).

[43 FR 2397, Jan. 17, 1978, as amended at 43 FR 21894, May 22, 1978; 45 FR 45524, July 3, 1980; 62 FR 49940, Sept. 24, 1997]

§ 372.111 Nonmember transportation limitation and record keeping.

(a) *Overall limitation of nonmember transportation.* No cooperative association or federation of cooperative associations may engage in nonmember interstate transportation for compensation in any fiscal year which, measured in terms of tonnage, exceeds its total interstate member transportation in such fiscal year.

(b) *Records of interstate transportation when nonmember transportation is performed.* Any cooperative association or federation of cooperative associations performing interstate transportation for nonmembers shall prepare and retain for a period of at least two years written records of all interstate transportation performed for members and nonmembers. These records shall contain:

(1) The date of the shipment,

(2) The names and addresses of the consignor and consignee,

(3) The origin and destination of the shipment,

(4) A description of the articles in the shipment,

(5) The weight or volume of the shipment,

(6) A description of the equipment used either by unit number or license number and, in the event this equipment is nonowned, the name and address of its owners and drivers,

(7) The total charges collected,

(8) A copy of all leases executed by the cooperative association or federation of cooperative associations to obtain equipment to perform transportation under 49 U.S.C. 13506(a)(5),

(9) Whether the transportation performed is:

(i) Member transportation,

(ii) Nonmember transportation for nonmembers who are farmers, cooperative associations, or federations thereof,

(iii) Other nonmember transportation, and if of class (iii), how the transportation was incidental and necessary as defined in § 372.109(a).

[43 FR 2397, Jan. 17, 1978, as amended at 45 FR 45524, July 3, 1980; 62 FR 38036, July 16, 1997; 62 FR 49940, Sept. 24, 1997]

§ 372.113 [Reserved]

§ 372.115 Commodities that are not exempt under 49 U.S.C. 13506(a)(6).

49 U.S.C. 13506(a)(6) provides an exemption from regulation for motor vehicles used in carrying ordinary livestock, fish, and unmanufactured agricultural commodities. Certain specific commodities have been statutorily determined to be non-exempt. Administrative Ruling No. 133, which is reproduced below, is a list of those commodities that are non-exempt by statute.

ADMINISTRATIVE RULING NO. 133

LIST OF COMMODITIES THAT ARE NOT EXEMPT BY STATUTE UNDER 49 U.S.C. 13506(A)(6)

Animal fats
Butter

Canned fruits and vegetables
Carnauba wax as imported in slabs or chunks
Cattle, slaughtered
Charcoal
Cheese
Coal
Cocoa beans
Coffee, beans, roasted, or instant
Copra meal
Cotton yarn
Cottonseed cake or meal
Diatomaceous earth
Dinners, frozen
Feeds:

  Alfalfa meal
  Alfalfa pellets
  Beet pulp
  Bran shorts
  Copra meal
  Corn gluten
  Distilled corn grain residues, with or without solubles added
  Fish meal
  Hominy feed
  Middlings
  Pelletized ground refuse screenings
  Wheat bran
  Wheat shorts

Fertilizer, commercial
Fish:

  Canned or salted as a treatment for preserving
  Cooked or partially cooked fish or shrimp, frozen or unfrozen
  Hermetically sealed in containers as a treatment for preserving
  Oil from fishes
  Preserved, or treated for preserving, such as smoked, salted, pickled, spiced, corned or kippered

Flagstone
Flaxseed meal
Flour
Forest products:

  Resin products, such as turpentine

Fruits and Berries:

  Bananas, fresh, dried, dehydrated, or frozen
  Canned
  Frozen
  Hulls of oranges after juice extractions
  Juice, fruit, plain or concentrated
  Pies, frozen
  Preserved, such as jam
  Purees, strawberry and other, frozen

Grains:

  Oils extracted from grain
  Popcorn, popped
  Rice, precooked
  Wheat germ

Gravel
Hair, hog or other animal, product of slaughter of animal

Hay, sweetened with 3 percent molasses by weight
Hemp fiber
Hides, green and salted
Insecticides
Limestone, agricultural
Livestock:

  Monkeys
  Race horses
  Show horses
  Zoo animals

Lumber, rough sawed or planed
Maple syrup
Meal:

  Alfalfa
  Copra
  Cottonseed
  Fish
  Flaxseed
  Linseed
  Peanut
  Soybean

Meat and meat products, fresh, frozen or canned
Milk and Cream:

  Chocolate
  Condensed
  Sterilized in hermetically sealed cans

Molasses
Nuts (including peanuts):

  Peanut meal
  Roasted or boiled

Oil, mint
Oil, extracted from vegetables, grain, seed, fish or other commodity
Pelts
Pies, frozen
Pigeons, racing
Pulp, beet
Pulp, sugar cane
Rock (except natural crushed, vesicular rock to be used for decorative purposes)
Rubber, crude, in bales
Rubber, latex, natural, liquid, from which water has been extracted and to which ammonia has been added
Sand
Seeds:

  Oil extracted from seeds

Skins, animal
Soil, potting
Soil, top
Soup, frozen
Sugar
Sugar cane pulp
Sugar raw
Syrup, cane
Syrup, maple
Tea
Tobacco:

  Cigars and cigarettes

Homogenized

Smoking

Top Soil

Trees:

Sawed into lumber

Vegetables:

Candied sweet potatoes, frozen

Canned

Cooked

French fried potatoes

Oil, extracted from vegetables

Soup, frozen

Soybean meal

Wool imported from a foreign country

Wool tops and noils

Wool waste (carded, spun, woven, or knitted)

Wool yarn

Note 1: Under 49 U.S.C. 13506(a)(6)(D), any listed fish or shellfish product that is not intended for human consumption is *exempt.*

Note 2: Under 49 U.S.C. 13506(a)(6)(E), any listed livestock feed, poultry feed, agricultural seeds, or plants that are transported to a site of agricultural production or to a business enterprise engaged in the sale to agricultural producers of goods used in agricultural production is *exempt*

[53 FR 17707, May 18, 1988, as amended at 62 FR 15421, Apr. 1, 1997]

§ 372.117 **Motor transportation of passengers incidental to transportation by aircraft.**

(a) *Passengers having an immediately prior or subsequent movement by air.* The transportation of passengers by motor vehicle is transportation incidental to transportation by aircraft provided (1) that it is confined to the transportation of passengers who have had or will have an immediately prior or immediately subsequent movement by air and (2) that the zone within which motor transportation is incidental to transportation by aircraft, except as it may be individually determined as provided in section (c) herein, shall not exceed in size the area encompassed by a 25-mile radius of the boundary of the airport at which the passengers arrive or depart and by the boundaries of the commercial zones (as defined by the Secretary) of any municipalities any part of whose commercial zones falls within the 25-mile radius of the pertinent airport.

(b) *Substituted motor-for-air transportation due to emergency conditions.* Transportation of passengers by motor vehicle is transportation incidental to

transportation by aircraft if it constitutes substituted motor-for-air service performed at the expense of the air carrier in emergency situations arising from the inability of the air carrier to perform air transportation due to adverse weather conditions, equipment failure, or other causes beyond the control of the air carrier.

(c) *Individual determination of exempt zones.* Upon its own motion or upon petition filed by any interested person, the Secretary may in an appropriate proceeding, determine whether the area within which the transportation by motor vehicle of passengers having an immediately prior or subsequent movement by air must be performed, in order to come within the provisions of paragraph (a) of this section, should be individually determined with respect to any particular airport or city served by an airport, and whether there should be established therefor appropriate boundaries differing in extent from this defined in paragraph (a)(2) of this section.

(d) *Exempt zones and operations*—(1) *Dulles and Baltimore-Washington International Airports.* The transportation by motor vehicle, in interstate or foreign commerce, of passengers, having an immediately prior or subsequent movement by air, between Dulles International Airport, near Chantilly, Va., and Baltimore-Washington International Airport, near Baltimore, Md., is partially exempt from regulation under 49 U.S.C. 13506(a)(8)(A).

(2) *Savannah, Ga., Airport.* The transportation by motor vehicle, in interstate or foreign commerce, of passengers, having an immediately prior or subsequent movement by air, between Savannah, Ga., Airport and all points on Hilton Head Island, SC, is partially exempt from regulation under 49 U.S.C. 13506(a)(8)(A).

(3) *Chicago O'Hare International Airport (Chicago, Ill.).* The transportation by motor vehicle, in interstate or foreign commerce, of passengers, having an immediately prior or subsequent movement by air, between O'Hare International Airport, at Chicago, Ill., on the one hand, and, on the other, points in Indiana on and north of U.S. Highway 30 and on and west of Indiana Highway 49, is partially exempt from

regulation under 49 U.S.C. 13506(a)(8)(A).

[32 FR 20036, Dec. 20, 1967, as amended at 37 FR 5252, Mar. 11, 1972; 42 FR 10003, Feb. 18, 1977; 42 FR 15705; Mar. 23, 1977; 62 FR 15421, Apr. 1, 1997]

Subpart B—Commercial Zones

SOURCE: 41 FR 56653, Dec. 29, 1976, unless otherwise noted. Redesignated at 61 FR 54708, Oct. 21, 1996.

§372.201 Albany, NY.

The zone adjacent to, and commercially a part of Albany, N.Y., within which transportation by motor vehicle, in interstate or foreign commerce, not under common control, management, or arrangement for a continuous carriage or shipment to or from a point beyond such zone, is partially exempt from regulations under 49 U.S.C. 13506(b)(1) includes and is comprised of all points as follows:

(a) The municipality of Albany, N.Y., itself.

(b) All points within a line drawn eight miles beyond the municipal limits of Albany.

(c) All points in that area more than eight miles beyond the municipal limits of Albany bounded by a line as follows: Beginning at that point on the western boundary of Cohoes, N.Y., where it crosses the line described in paragraph (b) of this section, thence along the western and northern boundary of Cohoes to the Mohawk River thence along such river to the northern boundary of the Town of Waterford thence along the northern and eastern boundaries of the Town of Waterford to the northern boundary of the City of Troy (all of which city is included under the next provision).

(d) All of any municipality any part of which is within the limits of the combined areas defined in paragraphs (b) and (c) of this section, and

(e) All of any municipality wholly surrounded, or so surrounded except for a water boundary, by the municipality of Albany or any other municipality included under the terms of paragraph (d) of this section.

[41 FR 56653, Dec. 29, 1976, as amended at 62 FR 15422, Apr. 1, 1997]

§372.203 Beaumont, TX.

The zone adjacent to, and commercially a part of Beaumont, Tex., within which transportation by motor vehicle in interstate or foreign commerce, not under common control, management, or arrangement for a continuous carriage or shipment to or from a point beyond such zone, is partially exempt from regulation under 49 U.S.C. 13506(b)(1) includes and is comprised of all points as follows:

(a) The municipality of Beaumont, Tex., itself;

(b) All points within a line drawn 8 miles beyond the municipal limits of Beaumont;

(c) All points in Jefferson County and Orange County, Tex.;

(d) All of any municipality any part of which is within the limits of the combined areas defined in paragraphs (b) and (c) of this section, and

(e) All of any municipality wholly surrounded, or so surrounded except for a water boundary, by the municipality of Beaumont or by any other municipality included under the terms of paragraph (d) of this section.

[41 FR 56653, Dec. 29, 1976, as amended at 62 FR 15422, Apr. 1, 1997]

§372.205 Charleston, S.C.

The zone adjacent to, and commercially a part of Charleston, S.C., within which transportation by motor vehicle in interstate or foreign commerce, not under common control, management, or arrangement for a continuous carriage or shipment to or from a point beyond such zone, is partially exempt from regulation under 49 U.S.C. 13506(b)(1) includes and is comprised of all points as follows:

(a) The municipality of Charleston, S.C., itself;

(b) All points within a line drawn 6 miles beyond the municipal limits of Charleston;

(c) Those points in Charleston County, S.C., which are not within the areas described in paragraph (b) of this section; and those points in Berkley County, S.C., which are not within the areas described in paragraph (b) of this section, and which are west of South Carolina Highway 41; and all points in Dorchester County, SC.

(d) All of any municipality any part of which is within the limits of the combined areas defined in paragraphs (b) and (c) of this section, and

(e) All of any municipality wholly surrounded, or so surrounded except for a water boundary, by the municipality of Charleston or by any other municipality included under the terms of paragraph (d) of this section.

[41 FR 56653, Dec. 29, 1976, as amended at 46 FR 28658, May 28, 1981; 62 FR 15422, Apr. 1, 1997]

§ 372.207 Charleston, WV.

The zone adjacent to, and commercially a part of Charleston, W. Va., within which transportation by motor vehicle in interstate or foreign commerce, not under common control, management, or arrangement for a continuous carriage or shipment to or from a point beyond such zone, is partially exempt from regulation under 49 U.S.C. 13506(b)(1) includes and is comprised of all points as follows:

(a) The municipality of Charleston, W. Va., itself;

(b) All points within a line drawn 6 miles beyond the municipal limits of Charleston;

(c) Those points in Kanawha County, W. Va., which are not within the area described in paragraph (b) of this section; and those points in Putnam County, W. Va., south of West Virginia Highway 34;

(d) All of any municipality any part of which is within the limits of the combined areas defined in paragraphs (b) and (c) of this section, and

(e) All of any municipality wholly surrounded, or so surrounded except for a water boundary, by the municipality of Charleston or by any other municipality included under the terms of paragraph (d) of this section.

[41 FR 56653, Dec. 29, 1976, as amended at 62 FR 15422, Apr. 1, 1997]

§ 372.209 Lake Charles, LA.

The zone adjacent to, and commercially a part of Lake Charles, La., within which transportation by motor vehicle in interstate or foreign commerce, not under common control, management, or arrangement for a continuous carriage or shipment to or from a point beyond such zone, is partially exempt from regulation under 49 U.S.C. 13506(b)(1) includes and is comprised of all points as follows:

(a) The municipality of Lake Charles, La., itself;

(b) All points within a line drawn 6 miles beyond the municipal limits of Lake Charles;

(c) Those points in Calcasieu Parish, La., which are not within the area described in paragraph (b) of this section; and which are east of Louisiana Highway 27 (western section);

(d) All of any municipality any part of which is within the limits of the combined areas defined in paragraphs (b) and (c) of this section, and

(e) All of any municipality wholly surrounded, or so surrounded except for a water boundary, by the municipality of Lake Charles or by any other municipality included under the terms of paragraph (d) of this section.

[41 FR 56653, Dec. 29, 1976, as amended at 62 FR 15422, Apr. 1, 1997]

§ 372.211 Pittsburgh, PA.

The zone adjacent to, and commercially a part of Pittsburgh within which transportation by motor vehicle in interstate or foreign commerce, not under common control, management, or arrangement for a continuous carriage or shipment to or from a point beyond such zone, is partially exempt from regulation under 49 U.S.C. 13506(b)(1) includes and is comprised of all points as follows:

(a) The municipality of Pittsburgh, Pa., itself;

(b) All points within a line drawn 15 miles beyond the municipal limits of Pittsburgh;

(c) Those points in Allegheny County, Pa., which are not within the area described in paragraph (b) of this section;

(d) All of any municipality any part of which is within the limits of the combined areas defined in paragraphs (b) and (c) of this section, and

(e) All of any municipality wholly surrounded, or so surrounded except for a water boundary, by the municipality of Pittsburgh by any other municipality included under the terms of paragraph (d) of this section.

[41 FR 56654, Dec. 29, 1976, as amended at 62 FR 15422, Apr. 1, 1997]

§372.213 Pueblo, CO.

The zone adjacent to, and commercially a part of Pueblo, Colo., within which transportation by motor vehicle in interstate or foreign commerce, not under common control, management, or arrangement for a continuous carriage or shipment to or from a point beyond such zone, is partially exempt from regulations under 49 U.S.C. 13506(b)(1) includes and is comprised of all points as follows:

(a) The municipality of Pueblo, Colo., itself;

(b) All points within a line drawn 6 miles beyond the municipal limits of Pueblo;

(c) Those points in Pueblo County, Colo., which are not within the area described in paragraph (b) of this section;

(d) All of any municipality any part of which is within the limits of the combined areas defined in paragraphs (b) and (c) of this section, and

(e) All of any municipality wholly surrounded, or so surrounded except for a water boundary, by the municipality included under the terms of paragraph (d) of this section.

[41 FR 56654, Dec. 29, 1976, as amended at 62 FR 15422, Apr. 1, 1997]

§372.215 Ravenswood, WV.

The zone adjacent to, and commercially a part of Ravenswood, W. Va., within which transportation by motor vehicle in interstate or foreign commerce, not under common control, management, or arrangement for a continuous carriage or shipment to or from a point beyond such zone, is partially exempt from regulation under 49 U.S.C. 13506(b)(1) includes and is comprised of all points as follows:

(a) The municipality of Ravenswood, W. Va., itself;

(b) All points within a line drawn 4 miles beyond the municipal limits of Ravenswood;

(c) Those points in Jackson County, W. Va., which are not within the area described in paragraph (b) of this sec-

tion, and which are north of U.S. Highway 33;

(d) All of any municipality any part of which is within the limits of the combined areas defined in paragraphs (b) and (c) of this section, and

(e) All of any municipality wholly surrounded, or so surrounded except for a water boundary, by the municipality of Ravenswood or by any other municipality included under the terms of paragraph (d) of this section.

[41 FR 56654, Dec. 29, 1976, as amended at 62 FR 15422, Apr. 1, 1997]

§372.217 Seattle, WA.

The zone adjacent to, and commercially a part of Seattle, Wash., within which transportation by motor vehicle in interstate or foreign commerce, not under common control, management, or arrangement for a continuous carriage or shipment to or from a point beyond such zone, is partially exempt from regulation under 49 U.S.C. 13506(b)(1) includes and is comprised of all points as follows:

(a) The municipality of Seattle, Wash., itself;

(b) All points within a line drawn 15 miles beyond the municipal limits of Seattle;

(c) Those points in King County, Wash., which are not within the area described in paragraph (b) of this section, and which are west of a line beginning at the intersection of the line described in paragraph (b) of this section and Washington Highway 18, thence northerly along Washington Highway 18 to junction of Interstate Highway 90, thence westerly along Interstate Highway 90 to junction Washington Highway 203, thence northerly along Washington Highway 203 to the King County line; and those points in Snohomish County, Wash., which are not within the area described in paragraph (b) of this section and which are west of Washington Highway 9; and those points in Kitsap County, Wash., which are not within the area described in paragraph (b) of this section lying within the area bounded by a line beginning at the intersection of the line described in paragraph (b) of this section and Washington Highway 3 to the boundary of Olympic View Industrial

Park/Bremerton-Kitsap County Airport, thence westerly, southerly, easterly, and northerly along the boundary of Olympic View Industrial Park/Bremerton-Kitsap County Airport to its juncture with Washington Highway 3 to its intersection with the line described in paragraph (b) of this section.

(d) All of any municipality any part of which is within the limits of the combined areas defined in paragraphs (b) and (c) of this section, and

(e) All of any municipality wholly surrounded, or so surrounded except for a water boundary, by the municipality of Seattle or by any other municipality included under the terms of paragraph (d) of this section.

[41 FR 56654, Dec. 29, 1976, as amended at 46 FR 25314, May 6, 1981; 62 FR 15422, Apr. 1, 1997]

§ 372.219 Washington, DC

The zone adjacent to, and commercially a part of Washington, D.C., within which transportation by motor vehicle in interstate or foreign commerce, not under common control, management, or arrangement for a continuous carriage or shipment to or from a point beyond such zone, is partially exempt from regulation under 49 U.S.C. 13506(b)(1) includes and is comprised of all points as follows:

(a) The municipality of Washington, D.C., itself;

(b) All points within a line drawn 15 miles beyond the municipal limits of Washington, DC

(c) All points in Fairfax and Loudoun Counties, VA, and all points in Prince William County, VA, including the City of Manassas, VA, and the City of Manassas Park, VA.

(d) All of any municipality any part of which is within the limits of the combined areas defined in paragraphs (b) and (c) of this section, and

(e) All of any municipality wholly surrounded, or so surrounded except for a water boundary, by the municipality of Washington, D.C., or by any other municipality included under the terms of paragraph (d) of this section.

[41 FR 56654, Dec. 29, 1976, as amended at 46 FR 56424, Nov. 17, 1981; 62 FR 15422, Apr. 1, 1997]

§ 372.221 Twin Cities.

For the purpose of determining commercial zones, utilizing the general population-mileage formula as set forth in § 372.241, each of the following combinations of cities shall be considered as a single municipality:

(a) Having a population equal to the sum of their combined populations, and

(b) Having boundaries comprised of their combined corporate limits, with the common portion thereof disregarded:

(1) Bluefield, Va.-W. Va.

(2) Bristol, Va.-Tenn.

(3) Davenport, Iowa, and Rock Island and Moline, Ill.

(4) Delmar, Del-Md.

(5) Harrison, Ohio-West Harrison, Ind.

(6) Junction City, Ark.-La.

(7) Kansas City, Mo.-Kansas City, Kans.

(8) Minneapolis-St. Paul, Minn.

(9) St. Louis, Mo.-East St. Louis, Ill.

(10) Texarkana, Ark.-Tex.

(11) Texhoma, Tex.-Okla.

(12) Union City, Ind.-Ohio.

[41 FR 56654, Dec. 29, 1976, as amended at 62 FR 15422, Apr. 1, 1997]

§ 372.223 Consolidated governments.

The zone adjacent to, and commercially a part of a consolidated government within which transportation by motor vehicle, in interstate or foreign commerce, not under common control, management, or arrangement for a continuous carriage or shipment to or from a point beyond the zone, is partially exempt from regulation under 49 U.S.C. 13506(b)(1) includes and is comprised of all points as follows:

(a) All points within the boundaries of the consolidated government.

(b) All points beyond the boundaries of the consolidated government which were at any time within the commercial zone of the formerly independent core municipality.

(c) When the present population of the formerly independent core municipality is identifiable, all points beyond the boundaries of the consolidated government which are within the territory determined by the most recent population-mileage formula measured from the limits of the formerly independent core municipality.

(d) All of any municipality wholly surrounded, or so surrounded except for a water boundary, by the consolidated government or by any other municipality included under the terms of paragraphs (a), (b), or (c) of this section.

[41 FR 56654, Dec. 29, 1976, as amended at 62 FR 15422, Apr. 1, 1997]

§372.225 Lexington-Fayette Urban County, KY.

The zone adjacent to and commercially a part of Lexington-Fayette Urban County, Ky., within which transportation by motor vehicle, in interstate or foreign commerce, not under a common control, management, or arrangement for a continuous carriage or shipment to or from a point beyond the zone, is partially exempt from regulation under 49 U.S.C. 13506(b)(1) includes and is comprised of all points as follows:

(a) Lexington-Fayette Urban County, Ky., itself.

(b) All other municipalities and unincorporated areas within 5 miles of the intersection of U.S. Highway 27 (Nicholasville Road) with the corporate boundary line between Jessamine County, Ky., and Lexington-Fayette Urban County, Ky.

[39 FR 18769, May 30, 1974. Redesignated at 41 FR 56655, Dec. 29, 1976. Further redesignated at 55 FR 42198, Oct. 18, 1990, as amended at 62 FR 15422, Apr. 1, 1997]

§372.227 Syracuse, NY.

The zone adjacent to, and commercially a part of Syracuse, N.Y., within which transportation by motor vehicle, in interstate or foreign commerce, not under common control, management, or arrangement for shipment to or from points beyond such zone, is partially exempt from regulation under 49 U.S.C. 13506(b)(1) includes and is comprised of all points as follows:

(a) The municipality of Syracuse, N.Y., itself;

(b) All points within a line drawn 10 miles beyond the municipal limits of Syracuse;

(c) Those points in the towns of Van Buren and Lysander, Onondaga County, N.Y., which are not within the area de-

scribed in paragraph (b) of this section, but which are within an area bounded by a line beginning at the intersection of new New York Highway 48 with the line described in (b) of this sectio, thence northwesterly along new New York Highway 48 to junction New York Highway 370, thence westerly along New York Highway 370 to junction Emerick Road, thence northerly along Emerick Road to junction Dunham Road, thence northerly along Dunham road to junction New York Highway 192, thence easterly along New York Highway 192 to junction new New York Highway 48, thence northerly along new New York Highway 48 to junction New York Highway 213, thence easterly along New York Highway 213 to junction New York Highway 213A, thence easterly along New York Highway 213A to junction New York Highway 37, thence southerly along New York Highway 37 to its intersection with the line in (b) above;

(d) All of any municipality any part of which is within the limits of the combined area defined in (b) and (c) of this section, and

(e) All of any municipality wholly surrounded, or so surrounded except for a water boundary, by the municipality of Syracuse or any other municipality included under the terms of (d) of this section.

[42 FR 44816, Sept. 7, 1977. Redesignated at 55 FR 42198, Oct. 18, 1990, as amended at 62 FR 15422, Apr. 1, 1997]

§372.229 Spokane, WA.

The zone adjacent to, and commercially a part of Spokane, WA, within which transportation by motor vehicle, in interstate or foreign commerce, not under control, management, or arrangement for shipment to or from points beyond such zone, is partially exempt from regulation under 49 U.S.C. 13506(b)(1) includes and is comprised of all points as follows:

(a) The municipality of Spokane, WA, itself,

(b) All points within a line drawn 8 miles beyond the municipal limits of Spokane;

(c) All points within that area more than 8 miles beyond the municipal limits of Spokane bounded by a line as follows: From the intersection of the line described in (b) of this section and U.S. Highway 2, thence westerly along U.S. Highway 2 to junction Brooks Road, thence southerly along Brooks Road to junction Hallett Road, thence easterly along Hallett Road to its intersection with the line described in (b) of this section;

(d) All of any municipality any part of which is within the limits of the combined areas in (b) and (c) of this section; and

(e) All of any municipality wholly surrounded, or so surrounded except for a water boundary, by the municipality of Spokane or any other municipality included under the terms of (d) of this section.

[45 FR 62085, Sept. 18, 1980. Redesignated and amended at 55 FR 42198, Oct. 18, 1990; 62 FR 15422, Apr. 1, 1997]

§ 372.231 Tacoma, WA.

The zone adjacent to, and commercially a part of Tacoma, WA, within which transportation by motor vehicle, in interstate or foreign commerce, not under common control, management, or arrangement for shipment to or from points beyond such zone, is partially exempt from regulation under 49 U.S.C. 13506(b)(1), includes and is comprised of all points as follows:

(a) The municipality of Tacoma, WA, itself;

(b) All points within a line drawn 8 miles beyond the municipal limits of Tacoma;

(c) Those points in Pierce County, WA, which are not within the area described in paragraph (b) of this section, but which are on Washington Highway 162 beginning at its intersection with the line described in paragraph (b) of this section, extending to and including Orting, WA, and all points within the Orting commercial zone.

(d) All of any municipality any part of which is within the limits of the combined area defined in (b) and (c) of this section, and

(e) All of any municipality wholly surrounded, or so surrounded except for a water boundary, by the municipality of Tacoma or any other municipality

included under the terms of (d) of this section.

[45 FR 66460, Oct. 7, 1980. Redesignated at 55 FR 42198, Oct. 18, 1990, as amended at 62 FR 15422, Apr. 1, 1997]

§ 372.233 Chicago, IL.

The zone adjacent to, and commercially a part of Chicago, IL, within which transportation by motor vehicle, in interstate or foreign commerce, not under common control, management, or arrangement for a shipment to or from such zone, is partially exempt from regulation under 49 U.S.C. 13506(b)(1), includes and is comprised of all points as follows:

(a) The municipality of Chicago, IL, itself;

(b) All points within a line drawn 20 miles beyond the municipal limits of Chicago;

(c) All points in Lake County, IL.

(d) All of any municipality any part of which is within the limits of the combined area defined in paragraphs (b) and (c) of this section, and

(e) All of any municipality wholly surrounded, or so surrounded except for a water boundary, by the municipality included under the terms of paragraph (d) of this section.

[46 FR 11286, Feb. 6, 1981. Redesignated at 55 FR 42198, Oct. 18, 1990, as amended at 62 FR 15422, Apr. 1, 1997]

§ 372.235 New York, NY.

The zone adjacent to, and commercially a part of, New York, NY, within which transportation by motor vehicle, in interstate or foreign commerce, not under common control, management, or arrangement for shipment to or from points beyond such zone is partially exempt from regulation under 49 U.S.C. 13506(b)(1), includes and is comprised of all points as follows:

(a) The municipality of New York, NY, itself;

(b) All points within a line drawn 20 miles beyond the municipal limits of New York, NY;

(c) All points in Morris County, NJ;

(d) All of any municipality any part of which is within the limits of the combined areas defined in paragraphs (b) and (c); and

(e) All of any municipality wholly surrounded, or so surrounded except by a water boundary, by the municipality of New York or by any other municipality included under the terms of paragraph (d) of this section.

[50 FR 34478, Aug. 26, 1985. Redesignated at 55 FR 42198, Oct. 18, 1990, as amended at 62 FR 15422, Apr. 1, 1997]

§372.237 Cameron, Hidalgo, Starr, and Willacy Counties, TX.

(a) Transportation within a zone comprised of Cameron, Hidalgo, Starr, and Willacy Counties, TX, by motor carriers of property, in interstate or foreign commerce, not under common control, management, or arrangement for shipment to or from points beyond such zone, is partially exempt from regulation under 49 U.S.C. 13506(b)(1).

(b) To the extent that commercial zones of municipalities within the four counties (as determined under §372.241) extend beyond the boundaries of this four-county zone, the areas of such commercial zones shall be considered to be part of the zone and partially exempt from regulation under 49 U.S.C. 13506(b)(1).

[51 FR 1815, Jan. 15, 1986. Redesignated at 55 FR 42198, Oct. 18, 1990, as amended at 62 FR 15422, Apr. 1, 1997]

§372.239 Definitions.

For the purposes of this part, the following terms are defined:

(a) *Municipality* means any city, town, village, or borough which has been created by special legislative act or which has been, otherwise, individually incorporated or chartered pursuant to general State laws, or which is recognized as such, under the Constitution or by the laws of the State in which located, and which has a local government. It does not include a town of the township or New England type.

(b) *Contiguous municipalities* means municipalities, as defined in paragraph (a) of this section, which have at some point a common municipal or corporate boundary.

(c) *Unincorporated area* means any area not within the corporate or municipal boundaries of any municipality as defined in paragraph (a) of this section.

[32 FR 20048, Dec. 20, 1967]

§372.241 Commercial zones determined generally, with exceptions.

The commercial zone of each municipality in the United States, with the exceptions indicated in the note at the end of this section, within which the transportation of passengers or property, in interstate or foreign commerce, when not under a common control, management, or arrangement for a continuous carriage or shipment to or from a point without such zone, is exempt from all provisions of 49 U.S.C. subtitle IV, part B shall be deemed to consist of:

(a) The municipality itself, hereinafter called the base municipality;

(b) All municipalities which are contiguous to the base municipality;

(c) All other municipalities and all unincorporated areas within the United States which are adjacent to the base municipality as follows:

(1) When the base municipality has a population less than 2,500 all unincorporated areas within 3 miles of its corporate limits and all of any other municipality any part of which is within 3 miles of the corporate limits of the base municipality,

(2) When the base municipality has a population of 2,500 but less than 25,000 all unincorporated areas within 4 miles of its corporate limits and all of any other municipality any part of which is within 4 miles of the corporate limits of the base municipality.

(3) When the base municipality has a population of 25,000 but less than 100,000 all unincorporated areas within 6 miles of its corporate limits and all of any other municipality any part of which is within 6 miles of the corporate limits of the base municipality, and

(4) When the base municipality has a population of 100,000 but less than 200,000 all unincorporated areas within 8 miles of its corporate limits and all of any other municipality any part of which is within 8 miles of the corporate limits of the base municipality.

(5) When the base municipality has a population of 200,000 but less than 500,000 all unincorporated areas within 10 miles of its corporate limits and all of any other municipality any part of which is within 10 miles of the corporate limits of the base municipality.

(6) When the base municipality has a population of 500,000 but less than 1 million, all unincorporated areas within 15 miles of its corporate limits and all of any other municipality any part of which is within 15 miles of the corporate limits of the base municipality.

(7) When the base municipality has a population of 1 million or more, all unincorporated areas within 20 miles of its corporate limits and all of any other municipality any part of which is within 20 miles of the corporate limits of the base municipality, and

(d) All municipalities wholly surrounded, or so surrounded except for a water boundary, by the base municipality, by any municipality contiguous thereto, or by any municipality adjacent thereto which is included in the commercial zone of such base municipality under the provisions of paragraph (c) of this section.

NOTE: Except: Municipalities the commercial zones of which have been or are hereafter individually or specially determined.

[32 FR 20048, Dec. 20, 1967, as amended at 34 FR 9870, June 26, 1969; 34 FR 15482, Oct. 4, 1969; 41 FR 56655, Dec. 29, 1976; 62 FR 15422, Apr. 1, 1997]

§ 372.243 Controlling distances and population data.

In the application of § 372.241:

(a) Air-line distances or mileages about corporate limits of municipalities shall be used.

(b) The population of any municipality shall be deemed to be the highest figure shown for that municipality in any decennial census since (and including) the 1940 decennial census.

(c) Contraction of municipal boundaries will not alter the size of commercial zones.

[32 FR 20040, Dec. 20, 1967, as amended at 37 FR 15701, Aug. 4, 1972; 50 FR 10233, Mar. 14, 1985; 62 FR 15422, Apr. 1, 1997]

Subpart C—Terminal Areas

SOURCE: 32 FR 20049, Dec. 20, 1967, unless otherwise noted. Redesignated at 61 FR 54708, Oct. 21, 1996.

§ 372.300 Distances and population data.

In the application of this subpart, distances and population data shall be determined in the same manner as provided in 49 CFR 372.243. See also definitions in 49 CFR 372.239.

[62 FR 15422, Apr. 1, 1997]

§ 372.301 Terminal areas of motor carriers and freight forwarders at municipalities served.

The terminal area within the meaning of 49 U.S.C. 13503 of any motor carrier of property or freight forwarder subject to 49 U.S.C. subtitle IV, part B at any municipality authorized to be served by such motor carrier of property or motor carrier of passengers in the transportation of express or freight forwarder, within which transportation by motor carrier in the performance of transfer, collection, or delivery services may be performed by, or for, such motor carrier of property or freight forwarder without compliance with the provisions of 49 U.S.C. subtitle IV, part B consists of and includes all points or places which are:

(a) Within the commercial zone, as defined by the Secretary, of that municipality, and

(b) Not beyond the limits of the operating authority of such motor carrier of property or freight forwarder.

[62 FR 15422, Apr. 1, 1997]

§ 372.303 Terminal areas of motor carriers and freight forwarders at unincorporated communities served.

The terminal areas within the meaning of 49 U.S.C. 13503 of any motor carrier of property or freight forwarder subject to 49 U.S.C. subtitle IV, part B, at any unincorporated community having a post office of the same name which is authorized to be served by such motor carrier of property or motor carrier of passengers in the transportation of express or freight forwarder, within which transportation by motor vehicle in the performance of transfer, collection, or delivery services may be performed by, or for, such motor carrier of property or freight forwarder without compliance with the provisions of 49 U.S.C. subtitle IV, part B, consists of:

(a) All points in the United States which are located within the limits of the operating authority of the motor carrier of property or freight forwarder involved, and within 3 miles of the post office at such authorized unincorporated point if it has a population less than 2,500, within 4 miles if it has a population of 2,500 but less than 25,000, or within 6 miles if it has a population of 25,000 or more;

(b) All of any municipality any part of which is included under paragraph (a) of this section; and

(c) Any municipality wholly surrounded by any municipality included under paragaph (b) of this section, or so wholly surrounded except for a water boundary.

[32 FR 20049, Dec. 20, 1967, as amended at 41 FR 56655, Dec. 29, 1976; 51 FR 44297, Dec. 9, 1986; 62 FR 15423, Apr. 1, 1997]

PART 373—RECEIPTS AND BILLS

Subpart A—Motor Carrier Receipts and Bills

AUTHORITY: 49 U.S.C. 13301, 13531 and 14706; and 49 CFR 1.73.

Subpart A—Motor Carrier Receipts and Bills

SOURCE: 55 FR 11198, Mar. 27, 1990, unless otherwise noted. Redesignated at 61 FR 54708, Oct. 21, 1996.

§373.101 Motor carrier bills of lading.

Every motor common carrier shall issue a receipt or bill of lading for property tendered for transportation in interstate or foreign commerce containing the following information:

(a) Names of consignor and consignee.

(b) Origin and destination points.

(c) Number of packages.

(d) Description of freight.

(e) Weight, volume, or measurement of freight (if applicable to the rating of the freight).

The carrier shall keep a record of this information as prescribed in 49 CFR part 379.

[55 FR 11198, Mar. 27, 1990, as amended at 56 FR 30874, July 8, 1991; 62 FR 15423, Apr. 1, 1997]

§373.103 Expense bills.

(a) *Property.* Every motor common carrier shall issue a freight or expense bill for each shipment transported containing the following information:

(1) Names of consignor and consignee (except on a reconsigned shipment, not the name of the original consignor).

(2) Date of shipment.

(3) Origin and destination points (except on a reconsigned shipment, not the original shipping point unless the final consignee pays the charges from that point).

(4) Number of packages.

(5) Description of freight.

(6) Weight, volume, or measurement of freight (if applicable to the rating of the freight).

(7) Exact rate(s) assessed.

(8) Total charges due, including the nature and amount of any charges for special service and the points at which such service was rendered.

(9) Route of movement and name of each carrier participating in the transportation.

(10) Transfer point(s) through which shipment moved.

(11) Address where remittance must be made or address of bill issuer's principal place of business.

The shipper or receiver owing the charges shall be given the original freight or expense bill and the carrier shall keep a copy as prescribed at 49 CFR part 379. If the bill is electronically transmitted (when agreed to by the carrier and payor), a receipted copy shall be given to the payor upon payment.

(b) *Charter service.* Every motor passenger common carrier providing charter service shall issue an expense bill containing the following information:

(1) Serial number, consisting of one of a series of consecutive numbers assigned in advance and imprinted on the bill.

(2) Name of carrier.

(3) Names of payor and organization, if any, for which transportation is performed.

(4) Date(s) transportation was performed.

(5) Origin, destination, and general routing of trip.

(6) Identification and seating capacity of each vehicle used.

(7) Number of persons transported.

(8) Mileage upon which charges are based, including any deadhead mileage, separately noted.

(9) Applicable rates per mile, hour, day, or other unit.

(10) Itemized charges for transportation, including special services and fees.

(11) Total charges assessed and collected.

The carrier shall keep a copy of all expense bills issued for the period prescribed at 49 CFR part 379. If any expense bill is spoiled, voided, or unused for any reason, a copy or written record of its disposition shall be retained for a like period.

[55 FR 11198, Mar. 27, 1990, as amended at 59 FR 2303, Jan. 14, 1994; 61 FR 19860, May 3, 1996; 62 FR 15423, Apr. 1, 1997]

§ 373.105 Low value packages.

The carrier and shipper may elect to waive the above provisions and use a more streamlined recordkeeping or documentation system for distribution of "low value" packages. This includes the option of shipping such packages under the provisions of 49 U.S.C. 14706(c). The shipper is responsible ultimately for determining which packages should be designated as low value. A useful guideline for this determination is an invoice value less than or equal to the costs of preparing a loss or damage claim.

[55 FR 11198, Mar. 27, 1990. Redesignated at 61 FR 54708, Oct. 21, 1996, as amended at 62 FR 15423, Apr. 1, 1997]

Subpart B—Freight Forwarders; Bills of Lading

§ 373.201 Receipts and bills of lading for freight forwarders.

Each freight forwarder must issue the shipper a receipt or through bill of lading, covering transportation from origin to ultimate destination, on each shipment for which it arranges transportation in interstate commerce. Where a motor carrier receives freight at the origin and issues a receipt therefor on its form with a notation showing the freight forwarder's name, then the freight forwarder, upon receiving the shipment at the "on line" or consolidating station, must issue a receipt or through bill of lading on its form as of the date the carrier receives the shipment.

[74 FR 15393, Apr. 6, 2009]

PART 374—PASSENGER CARRIER REGULATIONS

374.405 Baggage excess value declaration procedures.

Subpart E—Incidental Charter Rights

374.501 Applicability.
374.503 Authority.
374.505 Exceptions.

AUTHORITY: 49 U.S.C. 13301 and 14101; and 49 CFR 1.73.

EDITORIAL NOTE: Nomenclature changes to part 374 appear at 66 FR 49871, Oct. 1, 2001.

Subpart A—Discrimination in Operations of Interstate Motor Common Carriers of Passengers

SOURCE: 36 FR 1338, Jan. 28, 1971, unless otherwise noted. Redesignated at 61 FR 54709, Oct. 21, 1996.

§374.101 Discrimination prohibited.

No motor common carrier of passengers subject to 49 U.S.C. subtitle IV, part B shall operate a motor vehicle in interstate or foreign commerce on which the seating of passengers is based upon race, color, creed, or national origin.

[36 FR 1338, Jan. 28, 1971. Redesignated at 61 FR 54709, Oct. 21, 1996, as amended at 62 FR 15423, Apr. 1, 1997]

§374.103 Notice to be printed on tickets.

Every motor common carrier of passengers subject to 49 U.S.C. subtitle IV, part B shall cause to be printed on every ticket sold by it for transportation on any vehicle operated in interstate or foreign commerce a plainly legible notice as follows: "Seating aboard vehicles operated in interstate or foreign commerce is without regard to race, color, creed, or national origin."

NOTE: The following interpretation of the provisions of §374.103 (formerly §1055.2) appears at 27 FR 230, Jan. 9, 1962:
The words, "Seating aboard vehicles operated in interstate or foreign commerce is without regard to race, color, creed, or national origin", should appear on the face of every ticket coming within the purview of the section. If the ticket is in parts or consists of additional elements, such as coupons, identification stubs, or checks, it shall be sufficient for the purposes of §374.103 that the notice appear only once on the ticket and be placed on the face of that portion of the ticket which is held by the passenger.

[36 FR 1338, Jan. 28, 1971. Redesignated at 61 FR 54709, Oct. 21, 1996, as amended at 62 FR 15423, Apr. 1, 1997]

§374.105 Discrimination in terminal facilities.

No motor common carrier of passengers subject to 49 U.S.C. subtitle IV, part B shall in the operation of vehicles in interstate or foreign commerce provide, maintain arrangements for, utilize, make available, adhere to any understanding for the availability of, or follow any practice which includes the availability of, any terminal facilities which are so operated, arranged, or maintained as to involve any separation of any portion thereof, or in the use thereof on the basis of race, color, creed, or national origin.

[36 FR 1338, Jan. 28, 1971. Redesignated at 61 FR 54709, Oct. 21, 1996, as amended at 62 FR 15423, Apr. 1, 1997]

§374.107 Notice to be posted at terminal facilities.

No motor common carrier of passengers subject to 49 U.S.C. subtitle IV, part B shall in the operation of vehicles in interstate or foreign commerce utilize any terminal facility in which there is not conspicuously displayed and maintained so as to be readily visible to the public a plainly legible sign or placard containing the full text of these regulations. Such sign or placard shall be captioned: "Public Notice: Regulations Applicable to Vehicles and Terminal Facilities of Interstate Motor Common Carriers of Passengers, by order of the Secretary, U.S. Department of Transportation."

[36 FR 1338, Jan. 28, 1971. Redesignated at 61 FR 54709, Oct. 21, 1996, as amended at 62 FR 15423, Apr. 1, 1997]

§374.109 Carriers not relieved of existing obligations.

Nothing in this regulation shall be construed to relieve any interstate motor common carrier of passengers subject to 49 U.S.C. subtitle IV, part B of any of its obligations under 49 U.S.C.

subtitle IV, part B or its certificate(s) of public convenience and necessity.

[36 FR 1338, Jan. 28, 1971. Redesignated at 61 FR 54709, Oct. 21, 1996, as amended at 62 FR 15423, Apr. 1, 1997]

§ 374.111 Reports of interference with regulations.

Every motor common carrier of passengers subject to 49 U.S.C. subtitle IV, part B operating vehicles in interstate or foreign commerce shall report to the Secretary, within fifteen (15) days of its occurrence, any interference by any person, municipality, county, parish, State, or body politic with its observance of the requirements of these regulations in this part. Such report shall include a statement of the action that such carrier may have taken to eliminate any such interference.

[36 FR 1338, Jan. 28, 1971. Redesignated at 61 FR 54709, Oct. 21, 1996, as amended at 62 FR 15423, Apr. 1, 1997]

§ 374.113 Definitions.

For the purpose of these regulations the following terms and phrases are defined:

(a) *Terminal facilities.* As used in these regulations the term "terminal facilities" means all facilities, including waiting room, rest room, eating, drinking, and ticket sales facilities which a motor common carrier makes available to passengers of a motor vehicle operated in interstate or foreign commerce as a regular part of their transportation.

(b) *Separation.* As used in § 374.105, the term "separation" includes, among other things, the display of any sign indicating that any portion of the terminal facilities are separated, allocated, restricted, provided, available, used, or otherwise distinguished on the basis of race, color, creed, or national origin.

[36 FR 1338, Jan. 28, 1971. Redesignated at 61 FR 54709, Oct. 21, 1996, as amended at 62 FR 15423, Apr. 1, 1997]

Subpart B—Limitation of Smoking on Interstate Passenger Carrier Vehicles

§ 374.201 Prohibition against smoking on interstate passenger-carrying motor vehicles.

(a) All motor common carriers of passengers subject to 49 U.S.C. subtitle IV, part B, shall prohibit smoking (including the carrying of lit cigars, cigarettes, and pipes) on vehicles transporting passengers in scheduled or special service in interstate commerce.

(b) Each carrier shall take such action as is necessary to ensure that smoking by passengers, drivers, and other employees is not permitted in violation of this section. This shall include making appropriate announcements to passengers, the posting of the international no-smoking symbol, and the posting of signs in all vehicles transporting passengers in letters in sharp color contrast to the background, and of such size, shape, and color as to be readily legible. Such signs and symbols shall be kept and maintained in such a manner as to remain legible and shall indicate that smoking is prohibited by Federal regulation.

(c) The provisions of paragraph (a) of this section shall not apply to charter operations as defined in § 374.503 of this part.

[56 FR 1745, Jan. 17, 1991. Redesignated at 61 FR 54709, Oct. 21, 1996, as amended at 62 FR 15423, Apr. 1, 1997]

Subpart C—Adequacy of Intercity Motor Common Carrier Passenger Service

SOURCE: 55 FR 11199, Mar. 27, 1990, unless otherwise noted. Redesignated at 61 FR 54709, Oct. 21, 1996.

§ 374.301 Applicability.

These rules govern only motor passenger common carriers conducting regular-route operations.

§ 374.303 Definitions.

(a) *Carrier* means a motor passenger common carrier.

(b) *Bus* means a passenger-carrying vehicle, regardless of design or seating capacity, used in a carrier's authorized operations.

(c) *Facility* means any structure provided by or for a carrier at or near which buses pick up or discharge passengers.

(d) *Terminal* means a facility operated or used by a carrier chiefly to furnish passengers transportation services and accommodations.

(e) *Station* means a facility, other than a terminal, operated by or for a carrier to accommodate passengers.

(f) *Service* means passenger transportation by bus over regular routes.

(g) *Commuter service*, means passenger transportation wholly between points not more than 100 airline miles apart and not involving through-bus, connecting, or interline services to or from points beyond 100 airline miles. The usual characteristics of commuter service include reduced fare, multiple-ride, and commutation tickets, and peak morning and evening operations.

(h) *Baggage* means property a passenger takes with him for his personal use or convenience.

(i) *Restroom* means a room in a bus or terminal equipped with a toilet, washbowl, soap or a reasonable alternative, mirror, wastebasket, and toilet paper.

[55 FR 11199, Mar. 27, 1990, as amended at 68 FR 56198, Sept. 30, 2003; 74 FR 2901, Jan. 16, 2009]

§374.305 Ticketing and information.

(a) *Information service*. (1) During business hours at each terminal or station, information shall be provided as to schedules, tickets, fares, baggage, and other carrier services.

(2) Carrier agents and personnel who sell or offer to sell tickets, or who provide information concerning tickets and carrier services, shall be competent and adequately informed.

(b) *Telephone information service*. Every facility where tickets are sold shall provide telephonic information to the traveling public, including current bus schedules and fare information, when open for ticket sales.

(c) *Schedules*. Printed, regular-route schedules shall be provided to the traveling public at all facilities where tickets for such services are sold. Each schedule shall show the points along the carrier's route(s) where facilities

are located or where the bus trips originate or terminate, and each schedule shall indicate the arrival or departure time for each such point.

(d) *Ticket refunds*. Each carrier shall refund unused tickets upon request, consistent with its governing tariff, at each place where tickets are sold, within 30 days after the request.

(e) *Announcements*. No scheduled bus (except in commuter service) shall depart from a terminal or station until a public announcement of the departure and boarding point has been given. The announcement shall be given at least 5 minutes before the initial departure and before departures from points where the bus is scheduled to stop for more than 5 minutes.

§374.307 Baggage service.

(a) *Checking procedures*. (1) Carriers shall issue receipts, which may be in the form of preprinted tickets, for all checked services baggage.

(2)(i) If baggage checking service is not provided at the side of the bus, all baggage checked at a baggage checking counter at least 30 minutes but not more than 1 hour before departure shall be transported on the same schedule as the ticketed passenger.

(ii) If baggage checking service is provided at the side of the bus, passengers checking baggage at the baggage checking counter less than 30 minutes before the scheduled departure shall be notified that their baggage may not travel on the same schedule. Such baggage must then be placed on the next available bus to its destination. All baggage checked at the side of the bus during boarding, or at alternative locations provided for such purpose, shall be transported on the same schedule as the ticketed passenger.

(b) *Baggage security*. All checked baggage shall be placed in a secure or attended area prohibited to the public. Baggage being readied for loading shall not be left unattended.

(c) *Baggage liability*. (1) No carrier may totally exempt its liability for articles offered as checked baggage, unless those articles have been exempted by the Secretary. (Other liability is subject to subpart D of this part). A notice listing exempted articles shall be prominently posted at every location where baggage is accepted for checking.

(2) Carriers may refuse to accept as checked baggage and, if unknowingly accepted, may disclaim liability for loss or damage to the following articles:

(i) Articles whose transportation as checked baggage is prohibited by law or regulation;

(ii) Fragile or perishable articles, articles whose dimensions exceed the size limitations in the carrier's tariff, receptacles with articles attached or protruding, guns, and materials that have a disagreeable odor;

(iii) Money; and

(iv) Those other articles that the Secretary exempts upon petition by the carrier.

(3) Carriers need not offer excess value coverage on articles of extraordinary value (including, but not limited to, negotiable instruments, papers, manuscripts, irreplaceable publications, documents, jewelry, and watches).

(d) *Express shipments.* Passengers and their baggage always take precedence over express shipments.

(e) *Baggage at destination.* All checked baggage shall be made available to the passenger within a reasonable time, not to exceed 30 minutes, after arrival at the passenger's destination. If not, the carrier shall deliver the baggage to the passenger's local address at the carrier's expense.

(f) *Lost or delayed baggage.* (1) Checked baggage that cannot be located within 1 hour after the arrival of the bus upon which it was supposed to be transported shall be designated as lost. The carrier shall notify the passenger at that time and furnish him with an appropriate tracing form.

(2) Every carrier shall make available at each ticket window and baggage counter a single form suitable both for tracing and for filing claims for lost or misplaced baggage. The form shall be prepared in duplicate and signed by the passenger and carrier representative. The carrier or its agent shall receive the signed original, with any necessary documentation and additional information, and the claim check, for which a receipt shall be given. The passenger shall retain the duplicate copy.

(3) The carrier shall make immediate and diligent efforts to recover lost baggage.

(4) A passenger may fill out a tracing form for lost unchecked baggage. The carrier shall forward recovered unchecked baggage to the terminal or station nearest the address shown on the tracing form and shall notify the passenger that the baggage will be held on a will-call basis.

(g) *Settlement of claims.* Notwithstanding 49 CFR 370.9, if lost checked baggage cannot be located within 15 days, the carrier shall immediately process the matter as a claim. The date on which the carrier or its agent received the tracing form shall be considered the first day of a 60-day period in which a claim must be resolved by a firm offer of settlement or by a written explanation of denial of the claim.

[55 FR 11199, Mar. 27, 1990. Redesignated at 61 FR 54709, Oct. 21, 1996, as amended at 62 FR 15423, Apr. 1, 1997]

§ 374.309   Terminal facilities.

(a) *Passenger security.* All terminals and stations must provide adequate security for passengers and their attendants and be regularly patrolled.

(b) *Outside facilities.* At terminals and stations that are closed when buses are scheduled to arrive or depart, there shall be available, to the extent possible, a public telephone, outside lighting, posted schedule information, overhead shelter, information on local accommodations, and telephone numbers for local taxi service and police.

(c) *Maintenance.* Terminals shall be clean.

§ 374.311   Service responsibility.

(a) *Schedules.* Carriers shall establish schedules that can be reasonably met, including connections at junction points, to serve adequately all points.

(b) *Continuity of service.* No carrier shall change an existing regular-route schedule without first displaying conspicuously a notice in each facility and on each bus affected. Such notice shall be displayed for a reasonable time before it becomes effective and shall contain the carrier's name, a description of the proposed schedule change, the effective date thereof, the reasons for the change, the availability of alternate service, and the name and address of the carrier representative passengers may contact.

(c) *Trip interruptions.* A carrier shall mitigate, to the extent possible, any passenger inconvenience it causes by disrupting travel plans.

(d) *Seating and reservations.* A carrier shall provide sufficient buses to meet passengers' normal travel demands, including ordinary weekend and usual seasonal or holiday demand. Passengers (except commuters) shall be guaranteed, to the extent possible, passage and seating.

(e) *Inspection of rest stops.* Each carrier shall inspect periodically all rest stops it uses to ensure that they are clean.

[55 FR 11199, Mar. 27, 1990. Redesignated at 61 FR 54709, Oct. 21, 1996, as amended at 62 FR 15423, Apr. 1, 1997; 74 FR 2901, Jan. 16, 2009]

§374.313 Equipment.

(a) *Temperature control.* A carrier shall maintain a reasonable temperature on each bus (except in commuter service).

(b) *Restrooms.* Each bus (except in commuter service) seating more than 14 passengers (not including the driver) shall have a clean, regularly maintained restroom, free of offensive odor. A bus may be operated without a restroom if it makes reasonable rest stops.

(c) *Bus servicing.* Each bus shall be kept clean, with all required items in good working order.

§374.315 Transportation of passengers with disabilities.

Service provided by a carrier to passengers with disabilities is governed by the provisions of 42 U.S.C. 12101 *et seq.*, and regulations promulgated thereunder by the Secretary of Transportation (49 CFR parts 27, 37, and 38) and the Attorney General (28 CFR part 36), incorporating the guidelines established by the Architectural and Transportation Barriers Compliance Board (36 CFR part 1191).

[57 FR 35764, Aug. 11, 1992]

§374.317 Identification—bus and driver.

Each bus and driver providing service shall be identified in a manner visible to passengers. The driver may be identified by name or company number.

§374.319 Relief from provisions.

(a) *Petitions.* Where compliance with any rule would impose an undue burden on a carrier, it may petition the Federal Motor Carrier Safety Administration either to treat it as though it were conducting a commuter service or to waive the rule. The request for relief must be justified by appropriate verified statements.

(b) *Notice to the public.* The carrier shall display conspicuously, for at least 30 days, in each facility and on each bus affected, a notice of the filing of any petition. The notice shall contain the carrier's name and address, a concise description of and reasons for the relief sought, and a statement that any interested person may file written comments with the Federal Motor Carrier Safety Administration (with one copy mailed to the carrier) on or before a specific date that is at least 30 days later than the date the notice is posted.

[55 FR 11199, Mar. 27, 1990. Redesignated at 61 FR 54709, Oct. 21, 1996, as amended at 62 FR 15423, Apr. 1, 1997]

Subpart D—Notice of and Procedures for Baggage Excess Value Declaration

SOURCE: 40 FR 1249, Jan. 7, 1975, unless otherwise noted. Redesignated at 61 FR 54709, Oct. 21, 1996.

§374.401 Minimum permissible limitations for baggage liability.

(a) Motor common carriers of passengers and baggage subject to 49 U.S.C. 13501 may not publish tariff provisions limiting their liability for loss or damage to baggage checked by a passenger transported in regular route or special operations unless:

(1) The amount for which liability is limited is $250 or greater per adult fare, and

(2) The provisions permit the passenger, for an additional charge, to declare a value in excess of the limited amount, and allow the passenger to recover the increased amount (but not higher than the actual value) in event of loss or damage. The carriers may publish a maximum value for which they will be liable, but that maximum value may not be less than $1,000. Appropriate identification must be attached securely by the passenger to each item of baggage checked, indicating in a clear and legible manner the name and address to which the baggage should be forwarded if lost and subsequently recovered. Identification tags shall be made immediately available by the carriers to passengers upon request.

(3) Carriers need not offer excess value coverage on articles listed in § 374.307(c)(3).

(49 U.S.C. 10321, 5 U.S.C. 553)

[46 FR 22899, Apr. 22, 1981, as amended at 47 FR 21840, May 20, 1982; 62 FR 15423, Apr. 1, 1997]

§ 374.403 Notice of passenger's ability to declare excess value on baggage.

(a) All motor common carriers of passengers and baggage subject to 49 U.S.C. subtitle IV, part B, which provide in their tariffs for the declaration of baggage in excess of a free baggage allowance limitation, shall provide clear and adequate notice to the public of the opportunity to declare such excess value on baggage.

(b) The notice referred to in paragraph (a) of this section shall be in large and clear print, and shall state as follows:

NOTICE—BAGGAGE LIABILITY

This motor carrier is not liable for loss or damage to properly identified baggage in an amount exceeding $____. If a passenger desires additional coverage for the value of his baggage he may, upon checking his baggage, declare that his baggage has a value in excess of the above limitation and pay a charge as follows:

IDENTIFY YOUR BAGGAGE

Under FMCSA regulations, all baggage must be properly identified. Luggage tags should indicate clearly the name and address to which lost baggage should be forwarded.

Free luggage tags are available at all ticket windows and baggage counters.

The statement of charges for excess value declaration shall be clear, and any other pertinent provisions may be added at the bottom in clear and readable print.

(c) The notice referred to in paragraphs (a) and (b) of this section shall be (1) placed in a position near the ticket seller, sufficiently conspicuous to apprise the public of its provisions, (2) placed on a form to be attached to each ticket issued (and the ticket seller shall, where possible, provide oral notice to each ticket purchaser to read the form attached to the ticket), (3) placed in a position at or near any location where baggage may be checked, sufficiently conspicuous to apprise each passenger checking baggage of its provisions, and (4) placed in a position at each boarding point or waiting area used by the carrier at facilities maintained by the carrier or its agents, sufficiently conspicuous to apprise each boarding passenger of the provisions of the said notice.

[40 FR 1249, Jan. 7, 1975, as amended at 62 FR 15423, Apr. 1, 1997]

§ 374.405 Baggage excess value declaration procedures.

All motor common carriers of passengers and baggage subject to 49 U.S.C. subtitle IV, part B, which provide in their tariffs for the declaration of baggage value in excess of a free baggage allowance limitation, shall provide for the declaration of excess value on baggage at any time or place where provision is made for baggage checking, including (a) at a baggage checking counter until 15 minutes before scheduled boarding time, and (b) at the side of the bus or at a baggage checking counter in reasonable proximity to the boarding area during boarding at a terminal or any authorized service point.

[40 FR 1249, Jan. 7, 1975, as amended at 62 FR 15423, Apr. 1, 1997]

Subpart E—Incidental Charter Rights

AUTHORITY: 5 U.S.C. 553 and 559 and 49 U.S.C. 10321, 10922, and 10932.

SOURCE: 54 FR 46619, Nov. 6, 1989, unless otherwise noted. Redesignated at 61 FR 54709, Oct. 21, 1996.

§ 374.501 Applicability.

The regulations in this part apply to incidental charter rights authorized under 49 U.S.C. 13506 [49 U.S.C. 10932(c)]. These regulations do not apply to interpreting authority contained in a certificate to transport passengers in special and/or charter operations.

[54 FR 46619, Nov. 6, 1989. Redesignated at 61 FR 54709, Oct. 21, 1996, as amended at 62 FR 15423, Apr. 1, 1997]

§ 374.503 Authority.

Motor carriers transporting passengers, in interstate or foreign commerce, over regular routes authorized in a certificate issued as a result of an application filed before January 2, 1967, may transport special or chartered parties, in interstate or foreign commerce, between any points and places in the United States (including Alaska and Hawaii). The term "special or chartered party" means a group of passengers who, with a common purpose and under a single contract, and at a fixed charge for the vehicle in accordance with the carrier's tariff, have acquired the exclusive use of a passenger-carrying motor vehicle to travel together as a group to a specified destination or for a particular itinerary.

§ 374.505 Exceptions.

(a) Incidental charter rights do not authorize the transportation of passengers to whom the carrier has sold individual tickets or with whom the carrier has made separate and individual transportation arrangements.

(b) Service provided under incidental charter rights may not be operated between the same points or over the same route so frequently as to constitute a regular-route service.

(c) Passenger transportation within the Washington Metropolitan Area Transit District (as defined in the Washington Metropolitan Area Transportation Regulation Compact, Pub. L. No. 86–794, 74 Stat. 1031 (1960), as amended by Pub. L. No. 87–767, 76 Stat. (1962) is not authorized by these regulations, but is subject to the jurisdiction and regulations of the Washington Metropolitan Area Transportation Commission.

(d) A private or public recipient of governmental assistance (within the meaning of 49 U.S.C. 13902(b)(8)) may provide service under incidental charter rights only for special or chartered parties originating in the area in which the private or public recipient provides regularly scheduled mass transportation services under the specific qualifying certificate that confers its incidental charter rights.

[54 FR 46619, Nov. 6, 1989. Redesignated at 61 FR 54709, Oct. 21, 1996, as amended at 62 FR 15423, Apr. 1, 1997]

PART 375—TRANSPORTATION OF HOUSEHOLD GOODS IN INTERSTATE COMMERCE; CONSUMER PROTECTION REGULATIONS

Subpart A—General Requirements

AUTHORITY: 5 U.S.C. 553; 49 U.S.C. 13102, 13301, 13704, 13707, 14104, 14706, 14708; subtitle B, title IV of Pub. L. 109–59; and 49 CFR 1.73.

SOURCE: 68 FR 35091, June 11, 2003 unless otherwise noted.

Subpart A—General Requirements

§ 375.101 Who must follow the regulations in this part?

You, a household goods motor carrier engaged in the interstate transportation of household goods, must follow the regulations in this part when offering your services to individual shippers. You are subject to this part only when you transport household goods for individual shippers by motor vehicle in interstate commerce. Interstate commerce is defined in § 390.5 of this subchapter.

[72 FR 36771, July 5, 2007]

§ 375.103 What are the definitions of terms used in this part?

Terms used in this part are defined as follows. You may find other terms used in these regulations defined in 49 U.S.C. 13102. The definitions contained in this statute control. If terms are used in this part and the terms are neither defined here nor in 49 U.S.C. 13102, the terms will have the ordinary practical meaning of such terms.

Advertisement means any communication to the public in connection with an offer or sale of any interstate household goods transportation service. This includes written or electronic database listings of your name, address, and telephone number in an on-line database. This excludes listings of your name, address, and telephone number in a telephone directory or similar publication. However, Yellow Pages advertising is included in the definition.

Cashier's check means a check that has all four of the following characteristics:

(1) Drawn on a bank as defined in 12 CFR 229.2.

(2) Signed by an officer or employee of the bank on behalf of the bank as drawer.

(3) A direct obligation of the bank.

(4) Provided to a customer of the bank or acquired from the bank for remittance purposes.

Certified scale means any scale inspected and certified by an authorized scale inspection and licensing authority, and designed for weighing motor vehicles, including trailers or semitrailers not attached to a tractor, or designed as a platform or warehouse type scale.

Commercial shipper means any person who is named as the consignor or consignee in a bill of lading contract who is not the owner of the goods being transported but who assumes the responsibility for payment of the transportation and other tariff charges for the account of the beneficial owner of the goods. The beneficial owner of the goods is normally an employee of the consignor and/or consignee. A freight forwarder tendering a shipment to a carrier in furtherance of freight forwarder operations is also a commercial shipper. The Federal government is a government bill of lading shipper, not a commercial shipper.

Force majeure means a defense protecting the parties in the event that a part of the contract cannot be performed due to causes which are outside the control of the parties and could not be avoided by exercise of due care.

Government bill of lading shipper means any person whose property is transported under the terms and conditions of a government bill of lading issued by any department or agency of the Federal government to the carrier responsible for the transportation of the shipment.

Household goods, as used in connection with transportation, means the personal effects or property used, or to be used, in a dwelling, when part of the equipment or supplies of the dwelling. Transportation of the household goods must be arranged and paid for by the individual shipper or by another individual on behalf of the shipper. Household goods includes property moving from a factory or store if purchased with the intent to use in a dwelling and transported at the request of the householder, who also pays the transportation charges.

Household goods motor carrier means—

(1) In general, a motor carrier that, in the ordinary course of its business of providing transportation of household goods, offers some or all of the following additional services:

(i) Binding and nonbinding estimates;

(ii) Inventorying;

(iii) Protective packing and unpacking of individual items at personal residences;

(iv) Loading and unloading at personal residences.

(2) The term includes any person considered to be a household goods motor carrier under regulations, determinations, and decisions of the Federal Motor Carrier Safety Administration in effect on the date of enactment of the Household Goods Mover Oversight Enforcement and Reform Act of 2005 (August 10, 2005).

(3) The term does not include any motor carrier providing transportation of household goods in containers or trailers that are entirely loaded and unloaded by an individual other than an employee or agent of the motor carrier.

Individual shipper means any person who—

(1) Is the shipper, consignor, or consignee of a household goods shipment;

(2) Is identified as the shipper, consignor, or consignee on the face of the bill of lading;

93

(3) Owns the goods being transported; and

(4) Pays his or her own tariff transportation charges

May means an option. You may do something, but it is not a requirement.

Must means a legal obligation. You must do something.

Order for service means a document authorizing you to transport an individual shipper's household goods.

Reasonable dispatch means the performance of transportation on the dates, or during the period, agreed upon by you and the individual shipper and shown on the Order For Service/Bill of Lading. For example, if you deliberately withhold any shipment from delivery after an individual shipper offers to pay the binding estimate or 110 percent of a non-binding estimate, you have not transported the goods with reasonable dispatch. The term "reasonable dispatch" excludes transportation provided under your tariff provisions requiring guaranteed service dates. You will have the defenses of force majeure, *i.e.*, superior or irresistible force, as construed by the courts.

Should means a recommendation. We recommend you do something, but it is not a requirement.

Surface Transportation Board means an agency within the Department of Transportation. The Surface Transportation Board regulates household goods carrier tariffs among other responsibilities.

Tariff means an issuance (in whole or in part) containing rates, rules, regulations, classifications or other provisions related to a motor carrier's transportation services. The Surface Transportation Board requires a tariff contain specific items under § 1312.3(a) of this title. These specific items include an accurate description of the services offered to the public and the specific applicable rates (or the basis for calculating the specific applicable rates) and service terms. A tariff must be arranged in a way that allows for the determination of the exact rate(s) and service terms applicable to any given shipment.

We, us, and *our* means the Federal Motor Carrier Safety Administration (FMCSA).

You and *your* means a household goods motor carrier engaged in the interstate transportation of household goods and its household goods agents.

[68 FR 35091, June 11, 2003, as amended at 72 FR 36771, July 5, 2007]

§ 375.105 What are the information collection requirements of this part?

(a) The information collection requirements of this part have been reviewed by the Office of Management and Budget pursuant to the Paperwork Reduction Act of 1995 (44 U.S.C. 3501 *et seq.*) and have been assigned OMB control number 2126–0025.

(b) The information collection requirements are found in the following sections: Section 375.205, Section 375.207, Section 375.209, Section 375.211, Section 375.213, Section 375.215, Section 375.217, Section 375.303, Section 375.401, Section 375.403, Section 375.405, Section 375.409, Section 375.501, Section 375.503, Section 375.505, Section 375.507, Section 375.515, Section 375.519, Section 375.521, Section 375.605, Section 375.607, Section 375.609, Section 375.803, Section 375.805, and Section 375.807.

[69 FR 10575, Mar. 5, 2004]

Subpart B—Before Offering Services to My Customers

LIABILITY CONSIDERATIONS

§ 375.201 What is my normal liability for loss and damage when I accept goods from an individual shipper?

(a) In general, you are legally liable for loss or damage if it happens during performance of any transportation of household goods and all related services identified on your lawful bill of lading.

(b) Full Value Protection Obligation—In general, your liability is for the household goods that are lost, damaged, destroyed, or otherwise not delivered to the final destination in an amount equal to the replacement value of the household goods. The maximum amount is the declared value of the shipment. The declared value is subject to rules issued by the Surface Transportation Board (STB) and applicable tariffs.

(c) If the shipper waives, in writing, your liability for the full value of the household goods, then you are liable for loss of, or damage to, any household goods to the extent provided in the STB released rates order. Contact the STB for a current copy of the Released Rates of Motor Carrier Shipments of Household Goods. The rate may be increased annually by the motor carrier based on the U.S. Department of Commerce's Cost of Living Adjustment.

(d) As required by §375.303(g), you may have additional liability if you sell liability insurance and fail to issue a copy of the insurance policy or other appropriate evidence of insurance.

(e) You must, in a clear and concise manner, disclose to the individual shipper the limits of your liability.

[68 FR 35091, June 11, 2003, as amended at 72 FR 36771, July 5, 2007]

§375.203 What actions of an individual shipper may limit or reduce my normal liability?

(a) If an individual shipper includes perishable, dangerous, or hazardous articles in the shipment without your knowledge, you need not assume liability for those articles or for the loss or damage caused by their inclusion in the shipment. If the shipper requests that you accept such articles for transportation, you may elect to limit your liability for any loss or damage by appropriately published tariff provisions.

(b) If an individual shipper agrees to ship household goods released at a value greater than 60 cents per pound ($1.32 per kilogram) per article, your liability for loss and damage may be limited to $100 per pound ($220 per kilogram) per article if the individual shipper fails to notify you in writing of articles valued at more than $100 per pound ($220 per kilogram).

(c) If an individual shipper notifies you in writing that an article valued at greater than $100 per pound ($220 per kilogram) will be included in the shipment, the shipper will be entitled to full recovery up to the declared value of the article or articles, not to exceed the declared value of the entire shipment.

GENERAL RESPONSIBILITIES

§375.205 May I have agents?

(a) You may have agents provided you comply with paragraphs (b) and (c) of this section. A household goods agent is defined as either one of the following two types of agents:

(1) A *prime agent* provides a transportation service for you or on your behalf, including the selling of, or arranging for, a transportation service. You permit or require the agent to provide services under the terms of an agreement or arrangement with you. A prime agent does not provide services on an emergency or temporary basis. A prime agent does not include a household goods broker or freight forwarder.

(2) An *emergency or temporary agent* provides origin or destination services on your behalf, excluding the selling of, or arranging for, a transportation service. You permit or require the agent to provide such services under the terms of an agreement or arrangement with you. The agent performs such services only on an emergency or temporary basis.

(b) If you have agents, you must have written agreements between you and your prime agents. You and your retained prime agent must sign the agreements.

(c) Copies of all your prime agent agreements must be in your files for a period of at least 24 months following the date of termination of each agreement.

§375.207 What items must be in my advertisements?

(a) You and your agents must publish and use only truthful, straightforward, and honest advertisements.

(b) You must include, and you must require each of your agents to include, in all advertisements for all services (including any accessorial services incidental to or part of interstate household goods transportation), the following two elements:

(1) Your name or trade name, as it appears on our document assigning you a U.S. DOT number, or the name or trade name of the motor carrier under whose operating authority the advertised service will originate.

(2) Your U.S. DOT number, assigned by us authorizing you to operate as a for-hire motor carrier transporting household goods.

(c) Your FMCSA-assigned U.S. DOT number must be displayed only in the following form in every advertisement: U.S. DOT No. (*assigned number*).

§ 375.209 How must I handle complaints and inquiries?

(a) You must establish and maintain a procedure for responding to complaints and inquiries from your individual shippers.

(b) Your procedure must include all four of the following items:

(1) A communications system allowing individual shippers to communicate with your principal place of business by telephone.

(2) A telephone number.

(3) A clear and concise statement about who must pay for complaint and inquiry telephone calls.

(4) A written or electronic record system for recording all inquiries and complaints received from an individual shipper by any means of communication.

(c) You must produce a clear and concise written description of your procedure for distribution to individual shippers.

§ 375.211 Must I have an arbitration program?

(a) You must have an arbitration program for individual shippers to resolve disputes about property loss and damage and disputes about whether carrier charges in addition to those collected at delivery must be paid. You must establish and maintain an arbitration program with the following 11 minimum elements:

(1) You must design your arbitration program to prevent you from having any special advantage in any case where the claimant resides or does business at a place distant from your principal or other place of business.

(2) Before execution of the order for service, you must provide notice to the individual shipper of the availability of neutral arbitration, including all three of the following items:

(i) A summary of the arbitration procedure.

(ii) Any applicable costs.

(iii) A disclosure of the legal effects of election to use arbitration.

(3) Upon the individual shipper's request, you must provide information and forms you consider necessary for initiating an action to resolve a dispute under arbitration.

(4) You must require each person you authorize to arbitrate to be independent of the parties to the dispute and capable of resolving such disputes, and you must ensure the arbitrator is authorized and able to obtain from you or the individual shipper any material or relevant information to carry out a fair and expeditious decisionmaking process.

(5) You must not charge the individual shipper more than one-half of the total cost for instituting the arbitration proceeding against you. In the arbitrator's decision, the arbitrator may determine which party must pay the cost or a portion of the cost of the arbitration proceeding, including the cost of instituting the proceeding.

(6) You must refrain from requiring the individual shipper to agree to use arbitration before a dispute arises.

(7) Arbitration must be binding for claims of $10,000 or less, if the individual shipper requests arbitration.

(8) Arbitration must be binding for claims of more than $10,000, if the individual shipper requests arbitration and the carrier agrees to it.

(9) If all parties agree, the arbitrator may provide for an oral presentation of a dispute by a party or representative of a party.

(10) The arbitrator must render a decision within 60 days of receipt of written notification of the dispute, and a decision by an arbitrator may include any remedies appropriate under the circumstances.

(11) The arbitrator may extend the 60-day period for a reasonable period if you or the individual shipper fail to provide, in a timely manner, any information the arbitrator reasonably requires to resolve the dispute.

(b) You must produce and distribute a concise, easy-to-read, accurate summary of your arbitration program, including the items in this section.

[68 FR 35091, June 11, 2003, as amended at 69 FR 10575, Mar. 5, 2004; 72 FR 36772, July 5, 2007]

§375.213 What information must I provide to a prospective individual shipper?

(a) When you provide the written estimate to a prospective individual shipper, you must also provide the individual shipper with a copy of Department of Transportation publication FMCSA–ESA–03–005 (or its successor publication) entitled "Ready to Move?—Tips for a Successful Interstate Move." You may provide the individual shipper with a paper copy or you may provide a hyperlink on your Internet Web site to the FMCSA Web site containing the information in FMCSA's publication "Ready to Move?—Tips for a Successful Interstate Move."

(b) Before you execute an order for service for a shipment of household goods, you must furnish to your prospective individual shipper all five of the following documents:

(1) The contents of appendix A of this part, entitled "Your Rights and Responsibilities When You Move" (Department of Transportation publication FMCSA–ESA–03–006, or its successor publication). You may provide the individual shipper with a paper copy or you may provide a hyperlink on your Internet Web site to the FMCSA Web site containing the information in FMCSA's publication "Your Rights and Responsibilities When You Move."

(2) A concise, easy-to-read, accurate estimate of your charges.

(3) A notice of the availability of the applicable sections of your tariff for the estimate of charges, including an explanation that individual shippers may examine these tariff sections or have copies sent to them upon request.

(4) A concise, easy-to-read, accurate summary of your arbitration program.

(5) A concise, easy-to-read, accurate summary of your customer complaint and inquiry handling procedures. Included in this description must be both of the following two items:

(i) The main telephone number the individual shipper may use to communicate with you.

(ii) A clear and concise statement concerning who must pay for telephone calls.

(c) To comply with paragraph (b)(1) of this section, you must ensure that the text and general order of the document you produce and distribute to prospective individual shippers are consistent with the text and general order of appendix A to this part. The following three items also apply:

(1) If we, the Federal Motor Carrier Safety Administration, choose to modify the text or general order of appendix A, we will provide the public appropriate notice in the FEDERAL REGISTER and an opportunity for comment as required by part 389 of this chapter before making you change anything.

(2) If you publish the document, you may choose the dimensions of the publication as long as the type font size is 10 points or larger and the size of the booklet is at least as large as 36 square inches (232 square centimeters).

(3) If you publish the document, you may choose the color and design of the front and back covers of the publication. The following words must appear prominently on the front cover in 12-point or larger bold or full-faced type: "Your Rights and Responsibilities When You Move. Furnished by Your Mover, as Required by Federal Law." You may substitute your name or trade name in place of "Your Mover" if you wish (for example, *Furnished by XYZ Van Lines, as Required by Federal Law*).

(d) Paragraphs (c)(2) and (c)(3) of this section do not apply to exact copies of appendix A published in the FEDERAL REGISTER, the Code of Federal Regulations, or on FMCSA's Web site.

(e) If an individual shipper elects to waive physical receipt of the Federal consumer protection information by one of the methods described in paragraphs (a) and (b)(1) of this section, and elects to access the same information via the hyperlink on the Internet as provided in paragraphs (a) and (b)(1) of this section:

(1) You must include a clear and concise statement on the written estimate described in §375.401 that the individual

shipper expressly agreed to access the Federal consumer protection information on the Internet.

(2) You must obtain a signed, dated, electronic or paper receipt showing the individual shipper has received both booklets that includes, if applicable, verification of the shipper's agreement to access the Federal consumer protection information on the Internet.

(3) You must maintain the signed receipt required by paragraph (e)(2) of this section for three years from the date the individual shipper signs the receipt.

[72 FR 36772, July 5, 2007, as amended at 75 FR 72998, Nov. 29, 2010]

COLLECTING TRANSPORTATION CHARGES

§ 375.215 How must I collect charges?

You must issue an honest, truthful freight or expense bill in accordance with subpart A of part 373 of this chapter. All rates and charges for the transportation and related services must be in accordance with your appropriately published tariff provisions in effect, including the method of payment.

§ 375.217 How must I collect charges upon delivery?

(a) You must specify the form of payment when you prepare the estimate. You and your agents must honor the form of payment at delivery, except when a shipper agrees to a change in writing.

(b) You must specify the same form of payment provided in paragraph (a) of this section when you prepare the order for service and the bill of lading.

(c) Charge or credit card payments:

(1) If you agree to accept payment by charge or credit card, you must arrange with the individual shipper for the delivery only at a time when you can obtain authorization for the shipper's credit card transaction.

(2) Paragraph (c)(1) of this section does not apply to you when you have equipped your motor vehicle(s) to process card transactions.

(d) You may maintain a tariff setting forth nondiscriminatory rules governing collect-on-delivery service and the collection of collect-on-delivery funds.

(e) If an individual shipper pays you at least 110 percent of the approximate costs of a non-binding estimate on a collect-on-delivery shipment, you must relinquish possession of the shipment at the time of delivery.

[68 FR 35091, June 11, 2003, as amended at 69 FR 10575, Mar. 5, 2004]

§ 375.219 May I extend credit to shippers?

You may extend credit to shippers, but, if you do, it must be in accordance with § 375.807.

§ 375.221 May I use a charge or credit card plan for payments?

(a) You may provide in your tariff for the acceptance of charge or credit cards for the payment of freight charges. Accepting charge or credit card payments is different than extending credit to shippers in §§ 375.219 and 375.807. Once you provide an estimate you are bound by the provisions in your tariff regarding payment as of the estimate date, until completion of any transaction that results from that estimate, unless otherwise agreed with a shipper under § 375.217(a).

(b) You may accept charge or credit cards whenever shipments are transported under agreements and tariffs requiring payment by cash, certified check, money order, or a cashier's check.

(c) If you allow an individual shipper to pay for a freight or expense bill by charge or credit card, you are deeming such payment to be the same as payment by cash, certified check, money order, or a cashier's check.

(d) The charge or credit card plans you participate in must be identified in your tariff rules as items permitting the acceptance of the charge or credit cards.

(e) If an individual shipper causes a charge or credit card issuer to reverse a charge transaction, you may consider the individual shipper's action tantamount to forcing you to provide an involuntary extension of your credit. In such instances, the rules in § 375.807 apply.

Subpart C—Service Options Provided

§375.301 What service options may I provide?

(a) You may design your household goods service to provide individual shippers with a wide range of specialized service and pricing features. Many carriers provide at least the following five service options:

(1) Space reservation.

(2) Expedited service.

(3) Exclusive use of a vehicle.

(4) Guaranteed service on or between agreed dates.

(5) Liability insurance.

(b) If you sell liability insurance, you must follow the requirements in §375.303.

§375.303 If I sell liability insurance coverage, what must I do?

(a) You, your employee, or an agent may sell, offer to sell, or procure liability insurance coverage for loss or damage to shipments of any individual shipper only when the individual shipper releases the shipment for transportation at a value not exceeding 60 cents per pound ($1.32 per kilogram) per article.

(b) You may offer, sell, or procure any type of insurance policy on behalf of the individual shipper covering loss or damage in excess of the specified carrier liability.

(c) If you sell, offer to sell, or procure liability insurance coverage for loss or damage to shipments:

(1) You must issue to the individual shipper a policy or other appropriate evidence of the insurance that the individual shipper purchased.

(2) You must provide a copy of the policy or other appropriate evidence to the individual shipper at the time you sell or procure the insurance.

(3) You must issue policies written in plain English.

(4) You must clearly specify the nature and extent of coverage under the policy.

(5) Your failure to issue a policy, or other appropriate evidence of insurance purchased, to an individual shipper will subject you to full liability for any claims to recover loss or damage attributed to you.

(6) You must provide in your tariff for the provision of selling, offering to sell, or procuring liability insurance coverage. The tariff must also provide for the base transportation charge, including your assumption of full liability for the value of the shipment. This would be in the event you fail to issue a policy or other appropriate evidence of insurance to the individual shipper at the time of purchase.

[69 FR 10575, Mar. 5, 2004]

Subpart D—Estimating Charges

§375.401 Must I estimate charges?

(a) You must conduct a physical survey of the household goods to be transported and provide the prospective individual shipper with a written estimate, based on the physical survey, of the charges for the transportation and all related services. There are *two exceptions* to the requirement to conduct a physical survey:

(1) If the household goods are located beyond a 50-mile radius of the location of the household goods motor carrier's agent preparing the estimate, the requirement to base the estimate on a physical survey does not apply.

(2) An individual shipper may elect to waive the physical survey. The waiver agreement is subject to the following requirements:

(i) It must be in writing;

(ii) It must be signed by the shipper before the shipment is loaded; and

(iii) The household goods motor carrier must retain a copy of the waiver agreement as an addendum to the bill of lading with the understanding that the waiver agreement will be subject to the same record retention requirements that apply to bills of lading, as provided in §375.505(d).

(b) Before you execute an order for service for a shipment of household goods for an individual shipper, you must provide a written estimate of the total charges and *indicate whether it is a binding or a non-binding estimate*, as follows:

(1) *A binding estimate* is an agreement made in advance with your individual shipper. It guarantees the total cost of the move based upon the quantities and services shown on your estimate,

99

which shall be based on the physical survey of the household goods, if required. You may impose a charge for providing a written binding estimate. The binding estimate must indicate that you and the shipper are bound by the charges.

(2) *A non-binding estimate* is what you believe the total cost will be for the move, based upon both the estimated weight or volume of the shipment and the accessorial services requested and the physical survey of the household goods, if required. A non-binding estimate is not binding on you. You will base the final charges upon the actual weight of the individual shipper's shipment and the tariff provisions in effect. You may not impose a charge for providing a non-binding estimate.

(c) You must specify the form of payment you and your agent will honor at delivery. Payment forms may include, but are not limited to, cash, a certified check, a money order, a cashier s check, a specific charge card such as American Express™, a specific credit card such as Visa™, or your credit as allowed by § 375.807.

(d) For non-binding estimates, you must provide your reasonably accurate estimate of the approximate costs the individual shipper should expect to pay for the transportation and services of such shipments. If you provide an inaccurately low estimate, you may be limiting the amount you will collect at the time of delivery as provided in § 375.407.

(e) If you provide a shipper with an estimate based on volume that will later be converted to a weight-based rate, you must provide the shipper an explanation in writing of the formula used to calculate the conversion to weight. You must specify the final charges will be based on actual weight and services subject to the 110 percent rule at delivery.

(f) You must determine charges for any accessorial services such as elevators, long carries, etc., before preparing the order for service and the bill of lading for binding or non-binding estimates. If you fail to ask the shipper about such charges and fail to determine such charges before preparing the order for service and the bill of lading, you must deliver the goods and bill the

shipper after 30 days for the additional charges.

(g) You and the individual shipper must sign the estimate of charges. You must provide a dated copy of the estimate of charges to the individual shipper at the time you sign the estimate.

(h) Before loading a household goods shipment, and upon mutual agreement of both you and the individual shipper, you may amend an estimate of charges. You may not amend the estimate after loading the shipment.

[68 FR 35091, June 11, 2003, as amended at 72 FR 36772, July 5, 2007]

§ 375.403 How must I provide a binding estimate?

(a) You may provide a guaranteed binding estimate of the total shipment charges to the individual shipper, so long as it is provided for in your tariff. The individual shipper must pay the amount for the services included in your estimate. You must comply with the following 11 requirements:

(1) You must base the binding estimate on the physical survey unless one of the exceptions provided in § 375.401(a)(1) and (2) applies.

(2) You must provide the binding estimate in writing to the individual shipper or other person responsible for payment of the freight charges.

(3) You must retain a copy of each binding estimate as an attachment to be made an integral part of the bill of lading contract.

(4) You must clearly indicate upon each binding estimate's face that the estimate is binding upon you and the individual shipper. Each binding estimate must also clearly indicate on its face that the charges shown apply only to those services specifically identified in the estimate.

(5) You must clearly describe binding-estimate shipments and all services you are providing.

(6) If it appears an individual shipper has tendered additional household goods or requires additional services not identified in the binding estimate, you are not required to honor the estimate. If an agreement cannot be reached as to the price or service requirements for the additional goods or services, you are not required to service the shipment. However, if you do

service the shipment, before loading the shipment you must do one of the following three things:

(i) Reaffirm your binding estimate.

(ii) Negotiate a revised written binding estimate listing the additional household goods or services.

(iii) Agree with the individual shipper, in writing, that both of you will consider the original binding estimate as a non-binding estimate subject to §375.405.

(7) Once you load a shipment, failure to execute a new binding estimate or a non-binding estimate signifies you have reaffirmed the original binding estimate. You may not collect more than the amount of the original binding estimate, except as provided in paragraphs (a)(8) and (9) of this section.

(8) If you believe additional services are necessary to properly service a shipment after the bill of lading has been issued, you must inform the individual shipper what the additional services are before performing those services. You must allow the shipper at least one hour to determine whether he or she wants the additional services performed. If the individual shipper agrees to pay for the additional services, you must execute a written attachment to be made an integral part of the bill of lading contract and have the individual shipper sign the written attachment. This may be done through fax transmissions; e-mail; overnight courier; or certified mail, return receipt requested. You must bill the individual shipper for the additional services after 30 days from delivery. If the individual shipper does not agree to pay the additional services, the carrier should perform only those additional services as are required to complete the delivery, and bill the individual shipper for the additional services after 30 days from delivery, except that you may collect at delivery charges for impracticable operations that do not exceed 15 percent of all other charges due at delivery.

(9) If the individual shipper requests additional services after the bill of lading has been issued, you must inform the individual shipper of the additional charges involved. You may require full payment at destination for these additional services and for 100 percent of the original binding estimate. If applicable, you also may require payment at delivery of charges for impracticable operations (as defined in your carrier tariff) not to exceed 15 percent of all other charges due at delivery. You must bill and collect from the individual shipper any applicable charges not collected at delivery in accordance with subpart H of this part.

(10) Failure to relinquish possession of a shipment upon the individual shipper's offer to pay the binding estimate amount (or, in the case of a partial delivery, a prorated percentage of the binding estimate as set forth in paragraph (a)(11) of this section) plus charges for any additional services requested by the shipper after the bill of lading has been issued and charges, if applicable, for impracticable operations (subject to a maximum amount as set forth in paragraph 9 of this section), constitutes a failure to transport a shipment with "reasonable dispatch" and subjects you to cargo delay claims pursuant to part 370 of this chapter.

(11) If you make only a partial delivery of the shipment, you may not demand upon delivery full payment of the binding estimate. You may demand only a prorated percentage of the binding estimate. The prorated percentage must be the percentage of the weight of that portion of the shipment delivered relative to the total weight of the shipment. For example, if you deliver only 2,500 pounds of a shipment weighing 5,000 pounds, you may demand payment at destination for only 50 percent of the binding estimate.

(b) In accordance with §375.401(a), you may impose a charge for providing a written binding estimate. If you do not provide a binding estimate to an individual shipper, you must provide a non-binding estimate in accordance with §375.405.

(c) You must retain a copy of the binding estimate for each move you perform for at least one year from the date you made the estimate and keep it as an attachment to be made an integral part of the bill of lading contract.

[68 FR 35091, June 11, 2003, as amended at 69 FR 10575, Mar. 5, 2004; 69 FR 17317, May 5, 2004; 72 FR 36773, July 5, 2007]

§ 375.405 How must I provide a nonbinding estimate?

(a) If you do not provide a binding estimate to an individual shipper in accordance with § 375.403, you must provide a non-binding written estimate to the individual shipper.

(b) If you provide a non-binding estimate to an individual shipper, you must provide your reasonably accurate estimate of the approximate costs the individual shipper should expect to pay for the transportation and services of the shipment. You must comply with the following ten requirements:

(1) You must provide reasonably accurate non-binding estimates based upon both the estimated weight or volume of the shipment and services required and the physical survey of the household goods, if required. If you provide a shipper with an estimate based on volume that will later be converted to a weight-based rate, you must provide the shipper an explanation in writing of the formula used to calculate the conversion to weight.

(2) You must explain to the individual shipper that final charges calculated for shipments moved on nonbinding estimates will be those appearing in your tariffs applicable to the transportation. You must explain that these final charges may exceed the approximate costs appearing in your estimate.

(3) You must furnish non-binding estimates without charge and in writing to the individual shipper or other person responsible for payment of the freight charges.

(4) You must retain a copy of each non-binding estimate as an attachment to be made an integral part of the bill of lading contract.

(5) You must clearly indicate on the face of a non-binding estimate that the estimate is not binding upon you and the charges shown are the approximate charges to be assessed for the service identified in the estimate. The estimate must clearly state that the shipper will not be required to pay more than 110 percent of the non-binding estimate at the time of delivery.

(6) You must clearly describe on the face of a non-binding estimate the entire shipment and all services you are providing.

(7) If it appears an individual shipper has tendered additional household goods or requires additional services not identified in the non-binding estimate, you are not required to honor the estimate. If an agreement cannot be reached as to the price or service requirements for the additional goods or services, you are not required to service the shipment. However, if you do service the shipment, before loading the shipment, you must do one of the following two things:

(i) Reaffirm your non-binding estimate.

(ii) Negotiate a revised written non-binding estimate listing the additional household goods or services.

(8) Once you load a shipment, failure to execute a new non-binding estimate signifies you have reaffirmed the original non-binding estimate. You may not collect more than 110 percent of the amount of the original non-binding estimate at destination, except as provided in paragraphs (b)(9) and (10) of this section.

(9) If you believe additional services are necessary to properly service a shipment after the bill of lading has been issued, you must inform the individual shipper what the additional services are before performing those services. You must allow the shipper at least one hour to determine whether he or she wants the additional services performed. If the individual shipper agrees to pay for the additional services, you must execute a written attachment to be made an integral part of the bill of lading contract and have the individual shipper sign the written attachment. This may be done through fax transmissions; e-mail; overnight courier; or certified mail, return receipt requested. You must bill the individual shipper for the additional services after 30 days from delivery. If the individual shipper does not agree to pay the additional services, the carrier should perform only those additional services as are required to complete the delivery, and bill the individual shipper for the additional services after 30 days from delivery, except that you may collect at delivery charges for impracticable operations that do not exceed 15 percent of all other charges due at delivery.

(10) If the individual shipper requests additional services after the bill of lading has been issued, you must inform the individual shipper of the additional charges involved. You may require full payment at destination for these additional services and (unless you make only a partial delivery, in which case you must collect a prorated percentage of the original non-binding estimate as set forth in §375.407(c) of this part) for up to 110 percent of the original non-binding estimate. If applicable, you also may require payment at delivery of charges for impracticable operations (as defined in your carrier tariff) not to exceed 15 percent of all other charges due at delivery. You must bill and collect from the individual shipper any applicable charges not collected at delivery in accordance with subpart H of this part.

(c) If you furnish a non-binding estimate, you must enter the estimated charges upon the order for service and upon the bill of lading.

(d) You must retain a copy of the non-binding estimate for each move you perform for at least one year from the date you made the estimate and keep it as an attachment to be made an integral part of the bill of lading contract.

[68 FR 35091, June 11, 2003, as amended at 69 FR 10576, Mar. 5, 2004; 72 FR 36773, July 5, 2007]

§375.407 Under what circumstances must I relinquish possession of a collect-on-delivery shipment transported under a non-binding estimate?

(a) If an individual shipper pays you up to 110 percent of the non-binding estimate on a collect-on-delivery shipment (or, in the case of a partial delivery, a prorated percentage of the non-binding estimate as set forth in paragraph (c) of this section), you must relinquish possession of the shipment at the time of delivery. If there are either charges for any additional services requested by the shipper after the bill of lading has been issued and/or charges, if applicable, for impracticable operations (subject to a maximum amount as set forth in paragraph (d) of this section), and the shipper also pays you for such charges, you must relinquish pos-

session of the shipment at the time of delivery. You must accept the form of payment agreed to at the time of estimate, unless the shipper agrees in writing to a change in the form of payment.

(b) Failure to relinquish possession of a shipment after the individual shipper offers to pay you up to 110 percent of the approximate costs of a non-binding estimate plus any additional charges described in paragraph (a) of this section constitutes a failure to transport a shipment with "reasonable dispatch" and subjects you to cargo delay claims pursuant to part 370 of this chapter.

(c) If you make only a partial delivery of the shipment, you may not demand full payment of the non-binding estimate. You may demand at delivery only a prorated percentage of the non-binding estimate (or a prorated percentage of an amount up to 110 percent of the non-binding estimate). The prorated percentage must be the percentage of the weight of that portion of the shipment delivered relative to the total weight of the shipment. For example, if you deliver only 2,500 pounds of a shipment weighing 5,000 pounds, you may demand payment of 50 percent of not more than 110 percent of the non-binding estimate.

(d) You may not demand payment of charges for impracticable operations, as defined in your tariff, of more than 15 percent of all other charges due at delivery. You must bill and collect from the individual shipper charges for impracticable operations not collected at delivery in accordance with subpart H of this part.

[72 FR 36774, July 5, 2007]

§375.409 May household goods brokers provide estimates?

(a) Subject to the limitations in §371.113(a) of this subchapter, household goods brokers may provide estimates to individual shippers provided there is a written agreement between the broker and you, the motor carrier, adopting the broker's estimate as your own estimate. If you, the motor carrier, make such an agreement with a household goods broker, you must ensure compliance with all requirements of this part pertaining to estimates, including the requirement that you must relinquish possession of the shipment if the shipper pays you no more than 110 percent of a non-binding estimate at the time of delivery.

(b) Your written agreement with the household goods broker(s) must include the items required in § 371.115(a) of this subchapter.

[75 FR 72998, Nov. 29, 2010]

Subpart E—Pick Up of Shipments of Household Goods

BEFORE LOADING

§ 375.501 Must I write up an order for service?

(a) Before you receive a shipment of household goods you will move for an individual shipper, you must prepare an order for service. The order for service must contain the information described in the following 15 items:

(1) Your name and address and the FMCSA U.S. DOT number assigned to the mover who is responsible for performing the service.

(2) The individual shipper's name, address, and, if available, telephone number(s).

(3) The name, address, and telephone number of the delivering mover's office or agent located at or nearest to the destination of the shipment.

(4) A telephone number where the individual shipper/consignee may contact you or your designated agent.

(5) One of the following three entries must be on the order for service:

(i) The agreed pickup date and agreed delivery date of the move.

(ii) The agreed period(s) of the entire move.

(iii) If you are transporting the shipment on a guaranteed service basis, the guaranteed dates or periods for pickup, transportation, and delivery. You must enter any penalty or per diem requirements upon the agreement under this item.

(6) The names and addresses of any other motor carriers, when known, who will participate in interline transportation of the shipment.

(7) The form of payment you and your agents will honor at delivery. The payment information must be the same that was entered on the estimate.

(8) The terms and conditions for payment of the total charges, including notice of any minimum charges.

(9) The maximum amount you will demand at the time of delivery to obtain possession of the shipment, when you transport on a collect-on-delivery basis.

(10) A statement of the declared value of the shipment, which is the maximum amount of your liability to the individual shipper under your Full Value Protection for the replacement value of any household goods that are lost, damaged, destroyed, or otherwise not delivered to the final destination. If the individual shipper waives, in writing, your Full Value Protection liability, you must include a copy of the waiver; the Surface Transportation Board's required released rates valuation statement; and the charges, if any, for optional valuation coverage (other than Full Value Protection). The released rates may be increased annually by the motor carrier based on the U.S. Department of Commerce's Cost of Living Adjustment.

(11) A complete description of any special or accessorial services ordered and minimum weight or volume charges applicable to the shipment, subject to the following two conditions:

(i) If you provide service for individual shippers on rates based upon the transportation of a minimum weight or volume, you must indicate on the order for service the minimum weight- or volume-based rates, and the minimum charges applicable to the shipment.

(ii) If you do not indicate the minimum rates and charges, your tariff must provide you will compute the final charges relating to such a shipment based upon the actual weight or volume of the shipment.

(12) Any identification or registration number you assign to the shipment.

(13) *For non-binding estimates*, your reasonably accurate estimate of the amount of the charges, the method of payment of total charges, and the maximum amount (no more than 110 percent of the non-binding estimate) you will demand at the time of delivery to relinquish possession of the shipment.

(14) *For binding estimates,* the amount of charges you will demand based upon the binding estimate and the terms of payment under this estimate.

(15) Whether the individual shipper requests notification of the charges before delivery. The individual shipper must provide you with the fax number(s) or address(es) where you will transmit the notifications by fax transmission; e-mail; overnight courier; or certified mail, return receipt requested.

(b) You, your agent, or your driver must inform the individual shipper if you reasonably expect a special or accessorial service is necessary to safely transport a shipment. You must refuse to accept the shipment when you reasonably expect a special or accessorial service is necessary to safely transport a shipment and the individual shipper refuses to purchase the special or accessorial service. You must make a written note if the shipper refuses any special or accessorial services that you reasonably expect to be necessary.

(c) You and the individual shipper must sign the order for service. You must provide a dated copy of the order for service to the individual shipper at the time you sign the order.

(d)(1) You may provide the individual shipper with blank or incomplete estimates, orders for service, bills of lading, or any other blank or incomplete documents pertaining to the move.

(2) You may require the individual shipper to sign an incomplete document at origin provided it contains all relevant shipping information except the actual shipment weight and any other information necessary to determine the final charges for all services performed.

(e) You must provide the individual shipper the opportunity to rescind the order for service without any penalty for a three-day period after the shipper signs the order for service, if the shipper scheduled the shipment to be loaded more than three days after signing the order.

(f) Before loading the shipment, and upon mutual agreement of both you and the individual shipper, you may amend an order for service.

(g) You must retain a copy of the order for service for each move you

perform for at least one year from the date you made the order for service and keep it as an attachment to be made an integral part of the bill of lading contract.

(h) You have the option of placing the valuation statement on either the order for service or the bill of lading, provided the order for service or bill of lading states the appropriate valuation selected by the shipper.

[68 FR 35091, June 11, 2003, as amended at 69 FR 10576, Mar. 5, 2004; 72 FR 36774, July 5, 2007]

§375.503 Must I write up an inventory?

(a) You must prepare a written, itemized inventory for each shipment of household goods you transport for an individual shipper. The inventory must identify every carton and every uncartoned item that is included in the shipment. When you prepare the inventory, an identification number that corresponds to the inventory must be placed on each article that is included in the shipment.

(b) You must prepare the inventory before or at the time of loading in the vehicle for transportation in a manner that provides the individual shipper with the opportunity to observe and verify the accuracy of the inventory if he or she so requests.

(c) You must furnish a complete copy of the inventory to the individual shipper before or at the time of loading the shipment. A copy of the inventory, signed by both you and the individual shipper, must be provided to the shipper, together with a copy of the bill of lading, before or at the time you load the shipment.

(d) Upon delivery, you must provide the individual shipper with the opportunity to observe and verify that the same articles are being delivered and the condition of those articles. You must also provide the individual shipper the opportunity to note in writing any missing articles and the condition of any damaged or destroyed articles. In addition, you must also provide the shipper with a copy of all such notations.

(e) You must retain inventories for each move you perform for at least one

105

year from the date you made the inventory and keep it as an attachment to be made an integral part of the bill of lading contract.

[68 FR 35091, June 11, 2003, as amended at 69 FR 10576, Mar. 5, 2004]

§ 375.505   Must I write up a bill of lading?

(a) You must issue a bill of lading. The bill of lading must contain the terms and conditions of the contract. A bill of lading may be combined with an order for service to include all the items required by § 375.501 of this subpart. You must furnish a partially complete copy of the bill of lading to the individual shipper before the vehicle leaves the residence at origin. The partially complete bill of lading must contain all relevant shipment information, except the actual shipment weight and any other information necessary to determine the final charges for all services performed.

(b) On a bill of lading, you must include the following 14 items:

(1) Your name and address, or the name and address of the motor carrier issuing the bill of lading.

(2) The names and addresses of any other motor carriers, when known, who will participate in transportation of the shipment.

(3) The name, address, and telephone number of your office (or the office of your agent) where the individual shipper can contact you in relation to the transportation of the shipment.

(4) The form of payment you and your agents will honor at delivery. The payment information must be the same that was entered on the estimate and order for service.

(5) When you transport on a collect-on-delivery basis, the name, address, and if furnished, the telephone number, facsimile number, or e-mail address of a person to notify about the charges. The notification may also be made by overnight courier or certified mail, return receipt requested.

(6) *For non-guaranteed service,* the agreed date or period of time for pickup of the shipment and the agreed date or period of time for the delivery of the shipment. The agreed dates or periods for pickup and delivery entered upon the bill of lading must conform to the agreed dates or periods of time for pickup and delivery entered upon the order for service or a proper amendment to the order for service.

(7) *For guaranteed service,* subject to tariff provisions, the dates for pickup and delivery, and any penalty or per diem entitlements due the individual shipper under the agreement.

(8) The actual date of pickup.

(9) The company or carrier identification number of the vehicle(s) upon which you load the individual shipper's shipment.

(10) The terms and conditions for payment of the total charges, including notice of any minimum charges.

(11) The maximum amount you will demand at the time of delivery to obtain possession of the shipment, when you transport under a collect-on-delivery basis.

(12) A statement of the declared value of the shipment, which is the maximum amount of your liability to the individual shipper under your Full Value Protection for the replacement value of any household goods that are lost, damaged, destroyed, or otherwise not delivered to the final destination. If the individual shipper waives, in writing, your Full Value Protection liability for the declared value of the household goods, you must include a copy of the waiver; the Surface Transportation Board's required released rates valuation statement; and the charges, if any, for optional valuation coverage (other than Full Value Protection). The released rates may be increased annually by the motor carrier based on the U.S. Department of Commerce's Cost of Living Adjustment.

(13) Evidence of any insurance coverage sold to or procured for the individual shipper from an independent insurer, including the amount of the premium for such insurance.

(14) Each attachment to the bill of lading. Each attachment is an integral part of the bill of lading contract. If not provided elsewhere to the shipper, the following three items must be added as an attachment to the bill of lading.

(i) The binding or non-binding estimate.

(ii) The order for service.

(iii) The inventory.

(c) A copy of the bill of lading must accompany a shipment at all times while in your (or your agent's) possession. Before the vehicle leaves the residence of origin, the bill of lading must be in the possession of the driver responsible for the shipment.

(d) You must retain bills of lading for each move you perform for at least one year from the date you created the bill of lading.

(e) You have the option of placing the valuation statement on either the order for service or the bill of lading, provided the order for service or bill of lading states the appropriate valuation selected by the shipper.

[68 FR 35091, June 11, 2003, as amended at 69 FR 10576, Mar. 5, 2004; 72 FR 36774, July 5, 2007]

WEIGHING THE SHIPMENT

§375.507 Must I determine the weight of a shipment?

(a) When you transport household goods on a non-binding estimate dependent upon the shipment weight, you must determine the weight of each shipment transported before the assessment of any charges.

(b) You must weigh the shipment upon a certified scale.

(c) You must provide a written explanation of volume to weight conversions, when you provide an estimate by volume and convert the volume to weight.

§375.509 How must I determine the weight of a shipment?

(a) You must weigh the shipment by using one of the following two methods:

(1) *First method—origin weigh.* You determine the difference between the tare weight of the vehicle before loading at the origin of the shipment and the gross weight of the same vehicle after loading the shipment.

(2) *Second method—back weigh.* You determine the difference between the gross weight of the vehicle with the shipment loaded and the tare weight of the same vehicle after you unload the shipment.

(b) The following three conditions must exist for both the tare and gross weighings:

(1) The vehicle must have installed or loaded all pads, dollies, hand trucks, ramps, and other equipment required in the transportation of the shipment.

(2) The driver and other persons must be off the vehicle at the time of either weighing.

(3) The fuel tanks on the vehicle must be full at the time of each weighing, or, in the alternative, when you use the *first method—origin weigh,* in paragraph (a)(1) of this section, where the tare weighing is the first weighing performed, you must refrain from adding fuel between the two weighings.

(c) You may detach the trailer of a tractor-trailer vehicle combination from the tractor and have the trailer weighed separately at each weighing provided the length of the scale platform is adequate to accommodate and support the entire trailer at one time.

(d) You must use the net weight of shipments transported in containers. You must calculate the difference between the tare weight of the container (including all pads, blocking and bracing used in the transportation of the shipment) and the gross weight of the container with the shipment loaded in the container.

§375.511 May I use an alternative method for shipments weighing 3,000 pounds or less?

For shipments weighing 3,000 pounds or less (1,362 kilograms or less), you may weigh the shipment upon a platform or warehouse certified scale before loading for transportation or after unloading.

§375.513 Must I give the individual shipper an opportunity to observe the weighing?

You must give the individual shipper or any other person responsible for the payment of the freight charges the right to observe all weighings of the shipment. You must advise the individual shipper, or any other person entitled to observe the weighings, where and when each weighing will occur. You must give the person who will observe the weighings a reasonable opportunity to be present to observe the weighings.

107

§ 375.515 May an individual shipper waive his/her right to observe each weighing?

(a) If an individual shipper elects not to observe a weighing, the shipper is presumed to have waived that right.

(b) If an individual shipper elects not to observe a reweighing, the shipper must waive that right in writing. The individual shipper may send the waiver notification via fax transmission; e-mail; overnight courier; or certified mail, return receipt requested.

(c) Waiver of the right to observe a weighing or re-weighing does not affect any other rights of the individual shipper under this part or otherwise.

[68 FR 35091, June 11, 2003, as amended at 69 FR 10576, Mar. 5, 2004]

§ 375.517 May an individual shipper demand re-weighing?

After you inform the individual shipper of the billing weight and total charges and before actually beginning to unload a shipment weighed at origin (*first method* under § 375.509(a)(1)), the individual shipper may demand a re-weigh. You must base your freight bill charges upon the re-weigh weight.

§ 375.519 Must I obtain weight tickets?

(a) You must obtain weight tickets whenever we require you to weigh the shipment in accordance with this subpart. You must obtain a separate weight ticket for each weighing. The weigh master must sign each weight ticket. Each weight ticket must contain the following six items:

(1) The complete name and location of the scale.

(2) The date of each weighing.

(3) The identification of the weight entries as being the tare, gross, or net weights.

(4) The company or carrier identification of the vehicle.

(5) The last name of the individual shipper as it appears on the bill of lading.

(6) The carrier's shipment registration or bill of lading number.

(b) When both weighings are performed on the same scale, one weight ticket may be used to record both weighings.

(c) As part of the file on the shipment, you must retain the original weight ticket or tickets relating to the determination of the weight of a shipment.

(d) All freight bills you present to an individual shipper must include true copies of all weight tickets obtained in the determination of the shipment weight in order to collect any shipment charges dependent upon the weight transported.

§ 375.521 What must I do if an individual shipper wants to know the actual weight or charges for a shipment before I tender delivery?

(a) If an individual shipper of a shipment being transported on a collect-on-delivery basis specifically requests notification of the actual weight or volume and charges on the shipment, you must comply with this request. This requirement is conditioned upon the individual shipper's supplying you with an address or telephone number where the individual shipper will receive the communication. You must make your notification by telephone; in person; fax transmissions; e-mail; overnight courier; or certified mail, return receipt requested.

(b) The individual shipper must receive your notification at least one full 24-hour day before any tender of the shipment for delivery, excluding Saturdays, Sundays and Federal holidays.

(c) You may disregard the 24-hour notification requirement on shipments in any one of the following three circumstances:

(1) The shipment will be back weighed (*i.e.*, weighed at destination).

(2) Pickup and delivery encompass two consecutive weekdays, if the individual shipper agrees.

(3) The shipment is moving under a non-binding estimate and the maximum payment required at time of delivery is 110 percent of the estimated charges, but only if the individual shipper agrees to waive the 24-hour notification requirement.

[68 FR 35091, June 11, 2003, as amended at 69 FR 10576, Mar. 5, 2004]

Subpart F—Transportation of Shipments

§375.601 Must I transport the shipment in a timely manner?

Yes. Transportation in a timely manner is also known as "reasonable dispatch service." You must provide reasonable dispatch service to all individual shippers, except for transportation on the basis of guaranteed pickup and delivery dates.

§375.603 When must I tender a shipment for delivery?

You must tender a shipment for delivery for an individual shipper on the agreed delivery date or within the period specified on the bill of lading. Upon the request or concurrence of the individual shipper, you may waive this requirement.

§375.605 How must I notify an individual shipper of any service delays?

(a) When you are unable to perform either the pickup or delivery of a shipment on the dates or during the periods specified in the order for service and as soon as the delay becomes apparent to you, you must notify the individual shipper of the delay, at your expense, in one of the following six ways:

(1) By telephone.

(2) In person.

(3) Fax transmissions.

(4) E-mail.

(5) Overnight courier.

(6) Certified mail, return receipt requested.

(b) You must advise the individual shipper of the dates or periods you expect to be able to pick up and/or deliver the shipment. You must consider the needs of the individual shipper in your advisement. You also must do the following four things:

(1) You must prepare a written record of the date, time, and manner of notification.

(2) You must prepare a written record of your amended date or period for pick-up or delivery.

(3) You must retain these records as a part of your file on the shipment. The retention period is one year from the date of notification.

(4) You must furnish a copy of the notice to the individual shipper by first class mail or in person if the individual shipper requests a copy of the notice.

[68 FR 35091, June 11, 2003, as amended at 69 FR 10576, Mar. 5, 2004]

§375.607 What must I do if I am able to tender a shipment for final delivery more than 24 hours before a specified date?

(a) You may ask the individual shipper to accept an early delivery date. If the individual shipper does not concur with your request or the individual shipper does not request an early delivery date, you may, at your discretion, place a shipment in storage under your own account and at your own expense in a warehouse located near the destination of the shipment. If you place the shipment in storage, you must comply with paragraph (b) of this section. You may comply with paragraph (c) of this section, at your discretion.

(b) You must immediately notify the individual shipper of the name and address of the warehouse where you place the shipment. You must make and keep a record of your notification as a part of your shipment records. You have responsibility for the shipment under the terms and conditions of the bill of lading. You are responsible for the charges for redelivery, handling, and storage until you make final delivery.

(c) You may limit your responsibility under paragraph (b) of this section up to the agreed delivery date or the first day of the period of time of delivery as specified in the bill of lading.

§375.609 What must I do for shippers who store household goods in transit?

(a) If you are holding goods for storage-in-transit (SIT) and the period of time is about to expire, you must comply with this section.

(b) You must notify the individual shipper, in writing of the following four items:

(1) The date of conversion to permanent storage.

(2) The existence of a nine-month period after the date of conversion to permanent storage when the individual shipper may file claims against you for

loss or damage occurring to the goods in transit or during the storage-in-transit period.

(3) The fact your liability is ending.

(4) The fact the individual shipper's property will be subject to the rules, regulations, and charges of the warehouseman.

(c) You must make this notification at least 10 days before the expiration date of either one of the following two periods:

(1) The specified period of time when the goods are to be held in storage.

(2) The maximum period of time provided in your tariff for storage-in-transit.

(d) You must notify the individual shipper by facsimile transmission; e-mail; overnight courier; or certified mail, return receipt requested.

(e) If you are holding household goods in storage-in-transit for a period of time less than 10 days, you must give notification to the individual shipper of the information specified in paragraph (b) of this section one day before the expiration date of the specified time when the goods are to be held in such storage.

(f) You must maintain a record of notifications as part of the records of the shipment.

(g) Your failure or refusal to notify the individual shipper will automatically effect a continuance of your carrier liability according to the applicable tariff provisions with respect to storage-in-transit, until the end of the day following the date when you actually gave notice.

[68 FR 35091, June 11, 2003, as amended at 69 FR 10577, Mar. 5, 2004]

Subpart G—Delivery of Shipments

§ 375.701 May I provide for a release of liability on my delivery receipt?

(a) Your delivery receipt or shipping document must not contain any language purporting to release or discharge you or your agents from liability.

(b) The delivery receipt may include a statement the property was received in apparent good condition except as noted on the shipping documents.

§ 375.703 What is the maximum collect-on-delivery amount I may demand at the time of delivery?

(a) On a binding estimate, the maximum amount is the exact estimate of the charges, plus charges for any additional services requested by the shipper after the bill of lading has been issued and charges, if applicable, for impracticable operations as defined in your carrier tariff. The maximum amount of charges for impracticable operations you may collect on delivery is an amount equal to 15 percent of all other charges due at delivery.

(b) On a non-binding estimate, the maximum amount is 110 percent of the non-binding estimate of the charges, plus charges for any additional services requested by the shipper after the bill of lading has been issued and charges, if applicable, for impracticable operations as defined in your carrier tariff. The maximum amount of charges for impracticable operations you may collect on delivery is an amount equal to 15 percent of all other charges due at delivery.

[72 FR 36774, July 5, 2007]

§ 375.705 If a shipment is transported on more than one vehicle, what charges may I collect at delivery?

(a) At your discretion, you may do one of the following three things:

(1) You may defer the collection of all charges until you deliver the entire shipment.

(2) If you have determined the charges for the entire shipment, you may collect charges for the portion of the shipment tendered for delivery. You must determine the percentage of the charges for the entire shipment represented by the portion of the shipment tendered for delivery.

(3) If you cannot reasonably calculate the charges for the entire shipment, you must determine the charges for the portion of the shipment being delivered. You must collect this amount. The total charges you assess for the transportation of the separate portions of the shipment must not be more than the charges due for the entire shipment.

(b) In the event of the loss or destruction of any part of a shipment transported on more than one vehicle, you must collect the charges as provided in §375.707.

§375.707 If a shipment is partially lost or destroyed, what charges may I collect at delivery?

(a) (1) If a shipment is partially lost or destroyed, you may collect at delivery:

(i) A prorated percentage of the binding estimate or a prorated percentage of up to 110 percent of the non-binding estimate. The prorated percentage is equal to the percentage of the weight of that portion of the shipment delivered relative to the total weight of the shipment. For example, if you deliver only 2,500 pounds of a shipment weighing 5,000 pounds, you may demand at destination, as applicable, only 50 percent of a binding estimate or 50 percent of not more than 110 percent of a non-binding estimate;

(ii) Charges for any additional services requested by the shipper after the bill of lading has been issued; and

(iii) Charges for impracticable operations, if applicable, except that such charges must not exceed 15 percent of all other charges due at delivery.

(iv) Any specific valuation charge due.

(2) You must bill and collect from the individual shipper any remaining charges not collected at delivery in accordance with subpart H of this part.

(b) You must determine, at your own expense, the proportion of the shipment, based on actual or constructive weight, not lost or destroyed in transit.

(c) You may disregard paragraph (a)(1) of this section if loss or destruction was due to an act or omission of the individual shipper.

(d) The individual shipper's rights are in addition to, and not in lieu of, any other rights the individual shipper may have with respect to a shipment of household goods you or your agent(s) partially lost or destroyed in transit. This applies whether or not the individual shipper exercises any rights to obtain a refund of the portion of your published freight charges corresponding to the portion of the lost or destroyed shipment (including any charges for accessorial or terminal services) at the time you dispose of claims for loss, damage, or injury to articles in the shipment under part 370 of this chapter.

[72 FR 36775, July 5, 2007]

§375.709 If a shipment is totally lost or destroyed, what charges may I collect at delivery?

(a) You are forbidden from collecting, or requiring an individual shipper to pay, any freight charges (including any charges for accessorial or terminal services) when a household goods shipment is *totally lost or destroyed* in transit. The following two conditions also apply:

(1) You must collect any specific valuation charge due.

(2) You may disregard paragraph (a) of this section if loss or destruction was due to an act or omission of the individual shipper.

(b) The individual shipper's rights are in addition to, and not in lieu of, any other rights the individual shipper may have with respect to a shipment of household goods you or your agent(s) totally lost or destroyed in transit. This applies whether or not the individual shipper exercises its rights provided in paragraph (a) of this section.

Subpart H—Collection of Charges

§375.801 What types of charges apply to subpart H?

This subpart applies to all shipments of household goods that:

(a) Entail a balance due freight or expense bill, or

(b) Are transported on an extension of credit basis.

[69 FR 10577, Mar. 5, 2004]

§375.803 How must I present my freight or expense bill?

You must present your freight or expense bill in accordance with §375.807 of this subpart.

[69 FR 10577, Mar. 5, 2004]

§375.805 If I am forced to relinquish a collect-on-delivery shipment before the payment of ALL charges, how do I collect the balance?

On "collect-on-delivery" shipments, you must present your freight bill for all transportation charges within 15 days as required by §375.807.

§ 375.807 What actions may I take to collect the charges upon my freight bill?

(a) You must present a freight bill within 15 days (excluding Saturdays, Sundays, and Federal holidays) of the date of delivery of a shipment at its destination.

(b) The credit period must be seven days (including Saturdays, Sundays, and Federal holidays).

(c) You must provide in your tariffs the following four things:

(1) You must automatically extend the credit period to a total of 30 calendar days for any shipper who has not paid your freight bill within the 7-day period. However, for charges for impracticable operations that are not collected at delivery, you may not extend the credit period beyond 30 days after you present your freight bill.

(2) You will assess a service charge to each individual shipper equal to one percent of the amount of the freight bill, subject to a $20 minimum charge, for the extension of the credit period. You will assess the service charge for each 30-day extension the charges go unpaid.

(3) You must deny credit to any shipper who fails to pay a duly-presented freight bill within the 30-day period. You may grant credit to the individual shipper when the individual shipper satisfies he/she will promptly pay all future freight bills duly presented.

(4) You must ensure all payments of freight bills are strictly in accordance with the rules and regulations of this part for the settlement of your rates and charges.

[68 FR 35091, June 11, 2003, as amended at 72 FR 36775, July 5, 2007]

Subpart I—Penalties

§ 375.901 What penalties do we impose for violations of this part?

The penalty provisions of 49 U.S.C. Chapter 149, Civil and Criminal Penalties apply to this part. These penalties do not overlap. Notwithstanding these civil penalties, nothing in this section shall deprive any holder of a receipt or a bill of lading any remedy or right of action under existing law.

APPENDIX A TO PART 375—YOUR RIGHTS AND RESPONSIBILITIES WHEN YOU MOVE

OMB No. 2126–0025

FURNISHED BY YOUR MOVER, AS REQUIRED BY FEDERAL LAW

AUTHORITY: 49 U.S.C. 13301, 13704, 13707, and 14104; 49 CFR 1.73.

What Is Included in This Pamphlet?

In this pamphlet, you will find a discussion of each of these topics:
Why Was I Given This Pamphlet?
What Are the Most Important Points I Should Remember From This Pamphlet?
What If I Have More Questions?

SUBPART A—GENERAL REQUIREMENTS

Who must follow the regulations?
What definitions are used in this Pamphlet?

SUBPART B—BEFORE REQUESTING SERVICES FROM ANY MOVER

What is my mover's normal liability for loss or damage when my mover accepts goods from me?
What actions by me limit or reduce my mover's normal liability?
What are dangerous or hazardous materials that may limit or reduce my mover's normal liability?
May my mover have agents?
What items must be in my mover's advertisements?
How must my mover handle complaints and inquiries?
Do I have the right to inspect my mover's tariffs (schedules of charges) applicable to my move?
Must my mover have an arbitration program?
Must my mover inform me about my rights and responsibilities under Federal Law?
What other information must my mover provide to me?
How must my mover collect charges?
May my mover collect charges upon delivery?
May my mover extend credit to me?
May my mover accept charge or credit cards for my payments?

SUBPART C—SERVICE OPTIONS PROVIDED

What service options may my mover provide?
If my mover sells liability insurance coverage, what must my mover do?

SUBPART D—ESTIMATING CHARGES

Must my mover estimate the transportation and accessorial charges for my move?
How must my mover estimate charges under the regulations?

What payment arrangements must my mover have in place to secure delivery of my household goods shipment?

SUBPART E—PICKUP OF MY SHIPMENT OF HOUSEHOLD GOODS

Must my mover write up an order for service?

Must my mover write up an inventory of the shipment?

Must my mover write up a bill of lading?

Should I reach an agreement with my mover about pickup and delivery times?

Must my mover determine the weight of my shipment?

How must my mover determine the weight of my shipment?

What must my mover do if I want to know the actual weight or charges for my shipment before delivery?

SUBPART F—TRANSPORTATION OF MY SHIPMENT

Must my mover transport the shipment in a timely manner?

What must my mover do if it is able to deliver my shipment more than 24 hours before I am able to accept delivery?

What must my mover do for me when I store household goods in transit?

SUBPART G—DELIVERY OF MY SHIPMENT

May my mover ask me to sign a delivery receipt releasing it from liability?

What is the maximum collect-on-delivery amount my mover may demand I pay at the time of delivery?

If my shipment is transported on more than one vehicle, what charges may my mover collect at delivery?

If my shipment is partially or totally lost or destroyed, what charges may my mover collect at delivery?

How must my mover calculate the charges applicable to the shipment as delivered?

SUBPART H—COLLECTION OF CHARGES

Does this subpart apply to most shipments?

How must my mover present its freight or expense bill to me?

If I forced my mover to relinquish a collect-on-delivery shipment before the payment of ALL charges, how must my mover collect the balance?

What actions may my mover take to collect from me the charges in its freight bill?

Do I have a right to file a claim to recover money for property my mover lost or damaged?

SUBPART I—RESOLVING DISPUTES WITH MY MOVER

What may I do to resolve disputes with my mover?

WHY WAS I GIVEN THIS PAMPHLET?

The Federal Motor Carrier Safety Administration's (FMCSA) regulations protect consumers on interstate moves and define the rights and responsibilities of consumers and household goods carriers.

The household goods carrier (mover) gave you this booklet to provide information about your rights and responsibilities as an individual shipper of household goods. Your primary responsibility is to select a reputable household goods carrier, ensure that you understand the terms and conditions of the contract, and understand and pursue the remedies that are available to you in case problems arise. You should talk to your mover if you have further questions. The mover will also furnish you with additional written information describing its procedure for handling your questions and complaints. The additional written information will include a telephone number you can call to obtain additional information about your move.

WHAT ARE THE MOST IMPORTANT POINTS I SHOULD REMEMBER FROM THIS PAMPHLET?

1. Movers must give written estimates.

2. Movers may give binding estimates.

3. Non-binding estimates are not always accurate; actual charges may exceed the estimate.

4. If your mover provides you (or someone representing you) with any partially complete document for your signature, you should verify the document is as complete as possible before signing it. Make sure the document contains all relevant shipping information, except the actual shipment weight and any other information necessary to determine the final charges for all services performed.

5. You may request from your mover the availability of guaranteed pickup and delivery dates.

6. Be sure you understand the mover's responsibility for loss or damage, and request an explanation of the difference between valuation and actual insurance.

7. You have the right to be present each time your shipment is weighed.

8. You may request a reweigh of your shipment.

9. If you agree to move under a non-binding estimate, you should confirm with your mover—in writing—the method of payment at delivery as cash, certified check, cashier's check, money order, or credit card.

10. Movers must offer a dispute settlement program as an alternative means of settling loss or damage claims. Ask your mover for details.

11. You should ask the person you speak to whether he or she works for the actual mover or a household goods broker. A household goods broker must not represent itself

113

as a mover. The broker is responsible only for arranging the transportation. It does not own the trucks used to transport the shipment and is required to find an authorized mover to provide the transportation. You should know that a household goods broker generally has no authority to provide you with an estimate for the move, unless the broker has a written agreement with the household goods carrier. If a household goods broker provides you with an estimate without a written agreement with the carrier, the estimate may not be binding and you may instead be required to pay the actual charges assessed by the mover. A household goods broker is not responsible for loss or damage.

12. You may request complaint information about movers from the Federal Motor Carrier Safety Administration under the Freedom of Information Act. You may be assessed a fee to obtain this information. See 49 CFR part 7 for the schedule of fees.

13. You should seek estimates from at least three different movers. You should not disclose any information to the different movers about their competitors, as it may affect the accuracy of their estimates.

WHAT IF I HAVE MORE QUESTIONS?

If this pamphlet does not answer all of your questions about your move, do not hesitate to ask for additional information from your mover's representative who handled the arrangements for your move, the driver who transports your shipment, or the mover's main office.

SUBPART A—GENERAL REQUIREMENTS

The primary responsibility for your protection lies with you in selecting a reputable household goods carrier, ensuring you understand the terms and conditions of your contract with your mover, and understanding and pursuing the remedies that are available to you in case problems arise.

WHO MUST FOLLOW THE REGULATIONS?

The regulations inform motor carriers engaged in the interstate transportation of household goods (household goods motor carriers or movers) what standards they must follow when offering services to you. You, an individual shipper, are not directly subject to the regulations. However, your mover may be required by the regulations to demand that you pay on time. The regulations apply only to a mover that both transports your household goods by motor vehicle in interstate commerce—that is, when you are moving from one State to another—and provides certain types of additional services. The regulations do not apply when your interstate move takes place within a single commercial zone. A commercial zone is roughly equivalent to the local metropolitan area of a city or town. For example, a move between Brooklyn, NY, and Hackensack, NJ, would be considered within the New York City commercial zone and would not be subject to these regulations. Commercial zones are defined in 49 CFR part 372.

WHAT DEFINITIONS ARE USED IN THIS PAMPHLET?

Accessorial (Additional) Services—These are services such as packing, appliance servicing, unpacking, or piano stair carries that you request be performed (or that are necessary because of landlord requirements or other special circumstances). Charges for these services may be in addition to the line-haul charges.

Advanced Charges—These are charges for services performed by someone other than the mover. A professional, craftsman, or other third party may perform these services at your request. The mover pays for these services and adds the charges to your bill of lading charges.

Advertisement—This is any communication to the public in connection with an offer or sale of any interstate household goods transportation service. This will include written or electronic database listings of your mover's name, address, and telephone number in an online database. This excludes listings of your mover's name, address, and telephone number in a telephone directory or similar publication. However, Yellow Pages advertising is included within the definition.

Agent—A local moving company authorized to act on behalf of a larger, national company.

Appliance Service by Third Party—The preparation of major electrical appliances to make them safe for shipment. Charges for these services may be in addition to the line-haul charges.

Bill of Lading—The receipt for your goods and the contract for their transportation.

Carrier—The mover transporting your household goods.

Collect on Delivery (COD)—This means payment is required at the time of delivery at the destination residence (or warehouse).

Certified Scale—Any scale designed for weighing motor vehicles, including trailers or semi-trailers not attached to a tractor, and certified by an authorized scale inspection and licensing authority. A certified scale may also be a platform or warehouse type scale that is properly inspected and certified.

Estimate, Binding—This is a written agreement made in advance with your mover. It guarantees the total cost of the move based upon the quantities and services shown on the estimate.

Estimate, Non-Binding—This is what your mover believes the cost will be, based upon the estimated weight of the shipment and the accessorial services requested. A non-binding estimate is not binding on the mover. The final charges will be based upon the actual weight of your shipment, the services provided, and the tariff provisions in effect.

Expedited Service—This is an agreement with the mover to perform transportation by a set date in exchange for charges based upon a higher minimum weight.

Flight Charge—A charge for carrying items up or down flights of stairs. Charges for these services may be in addition to the line-haul charges.

Guaranteed Pickup and Delivery Service—An additional level of service featuring guaranteed dates of service. Your mover will provide reimbursement to you for delays. This premium service is often subject to minimum weight requirements.

High-Value Article—These are items included in a shipment valued at more than $100 per pound ($220 per kilogram).

Household Goods, as used in connection with transportation, means the personal effects or property used, or to be used, in a dwelling, when part of the equipment or supplies of the dwelling. Transportation of the household goods must be arranged and paid for by you or by another individual on your behalf. This may include items moving from a factory or store when you purchase them to use in your dwelling. You must request that these items be transported, and you (or another individual on your behalf) must pay the transportation charges to the mover.

Household Goods Motor Carrier means a motor carrier that, in the ordinary course of its business of providing transportation of household goods, offers some or all of the following additional services: (1) Binding and non-binding estimates, (2) Inventory, (3) Protective packing and unpacking of individual items at personal residences, and (4) Loading and unloading at personal residences. The term does not include a motor carrier when the motor carrier provides transportation of household goods in containers or trailers that are entirely loaded and unloaded by an individual other than an employee or agent of the motor carrier.

Individual Shipper—Any person who—

1. Is the shipper, consignor, or consignee of a household goods shipment;

2. Is identified as the shipper, consignor, or consignee on the face of the bill of lading;

3. Owns the goods being transported; and

4. Pays his or her own tariff transportation charges.

Impracticable Operations generally refer to services required when operating conditions make it physically impossible for the motor carrier to perform pickup or delivery with its normally assigned road-haul equipment, so that the carrier must use smaller equipment and/or additional labor to complete pickup or delivery of the shipment. A mover may require *payment of additional charges for impracticable operations* even if you do not request these services. The specific services considered to be impracticable operations by your mover are defined in your mover's tariff.

Inventory—The detailed descriptive list of your household goods showing the number and condition of each item.

Line-Haul Charges—The charges for the vehicle transportation portion of your move. These charges, if separately stated, apply in addition to the accessorial service charges.

Long Carry—A charge for carrying articles excessive distances between the mover's vehicle and your residence. Charges for these services may be in addition to the line-haul charges.

May—An option. You or your mover may do something, but it is not a requirement.

Mover—A household goods motor carrier and its household goods agents.

Must—A legal obligation. You or your mover must do something.

Order for Service—The document authorizing the mover to transport your household goods.

Order (Bill of Lading) Number—The number used to identify and track your shipment.

Peak Season Rates—Higher line-haul charges applicable during the summer months.

Pickup and Delivery Charges—Separate transportation charges applicable to transporting your shipment between the storage-in-transit warehouse and your residence.

Reasonable Dispatch—The performance of transportation on the dates, or during the period of time, agreed upon by you and your mover and shown on the Order for Service/Bill of Lading. For example, if your mover deliberately withholds any shipment from delivery after you offer to pay the binding estimate or up to 110 percent of a non-binding estimate, plus any charges for additional services you requested that were not included in the estimate and/or permissible charges for impracticable operations, your mover has not transported the goods with reasonable dispatch. The term "reasonable dispatch" excludes transportation provided under your mover's tariff provisions requiring guaranteed service dates. Your mover will have the defense of force majeure, i.e., that the contract cannot be performed owing to causes that are outside the control of the parties and could not be avoided by exercise of due care.

Should—A recommendation. We recommend you or your mover do something, but it is not a requirement.

Shuttle Service—The use of a smaller vehicle to provide service to residences not accessible to the mover's normal line-haul vehicles.

Storage-In-Transit (SIT)—The temporary warehouse storage of your shipment pending further transportation, with or without notification to you. If you (or someone representing you) cannot accept delivery on the agreed-upon date or within the agreed-upon time period (for example, because your home is not quite ready to occupy), your mover may place your shipment into SIT without notifying you. In those circumstances, you will be responsible for the added charges for SIT service, as well as the warehouse handling and final delivery charges. However, your mover also may place your shipment into SIT if your mover was able to make delivery before the agreed-upon date (or before the first day of the agreed-upon delivery period) but you did not concur with early delivery. In those circumstances, your mover must notify you immediately of the SIT, and your mover is fully responsible for redelivery charges, handling charges, and storage charges.

Surface Transportation Board—An agency within the U.S. Department of Transportation that regulates household goods carrier tariffs, among other responsibilities. The Surface Transportation Board's address is 395 E Street, SW., Washington, DC 20423–0001. Tele. 202–245–0245.

Tariff—An issuance (in whole or in part) containing rates, rules, regulations, classifications, or other provisions. The Surface Transportation Board requires that a tariff contain three specific items. First, an accurate description of the services the mover offers to the public. Second, the specific applicable rates (or the basis for calculating the specific applicable rates) and service terms for services offered to the public. Third, the mover's tariff must be arranged in a way that allows you to determine the exact rate(s) and service terms applicable to your shipment.

Valuation—The degree of worth of the shipment. The valuation charge compensates the mover for assuming a greater degree of liability than is provided for in its base transportation charges.

Warehouse Handling—A charge may be applicable each time SIT service is provided. Charges for these services may be in addition to the line-haul charges. This charge compensates the mover for the physical placement and removal of items within the warehouse.

We, Us, and *Our*—The Federal Motor Carrier Safety Administration (FMCSA).

You and *Your*—You are an individual shipper of household goods. You are a consignor or consignee of a household goods shipment and your mover identifies you as such in the bill of lading contract. You own the goods being transported and pay the transportation charges to the mover.

Where may other terms used in this pamphlet be defined? You may find other terms used in this pamphlet defined in 49 U.S.C. 13102. The statute controls the definitions in this pamphlet. If terms are used in this pamphlet and the terms are defined neither here nor in 49 U.S.C. 13102, the terms will have the ordinary practical meaning of such terms.

Subpart B—Before Requesting Services From Any Mover

What Is My Mover's Normal Liability for Loss or Damage When My Mover Accepts Goods From Me?

In general, your mover is legally liable for loss or damage that occurs during performance of any transportation of household goods and of all related services identified on your mover's lawful bill of lading.

Your mover is liable for loss of, or damage to, any household goods to the extent provided in the current Surface Transportation Board's Released Rates Order. You may obtain a copy of the current Released Rates Order by contacting the Surface Transportation Board at the address provided under the definition of the Surface Transportation Board. The rate may be increased annually by your mover based on the U.S. Department of Commerce's Cost of Living Adjustment. Your mover may have additional liability if your mover sells liability insurance to you.

All moving companies are required to assume liability for the value of the goods transported. However, there are different levels of liability, and you should be aware of the amount of protection provided and the charges for each option.

Basically, most movers offer two different levels of liability under the terms of their tariffs and the Surface Transportation Board's Released Rates Orders. These orders govern the moving industry. The levels of liability are as follows:

(1) FULL VALUE PROTECTION (FVP). This is the most comprehensive option available for the protection of your goods. Unless you waive full-value protection in writing and agree to Release Value Protection as described below, your shipment will be transported under your mover's *full (replacement) value* level of liability. If any article is lost, destroyed, or damaged while in your mover's custody, your mover will, at its option, either: repair the article to the extent necessary to restore it to the same condition as when it was received by your mover, or pay you for the cost of such repairs; replace the article with an article of like kind; or pay you for the cost of a replacement article at the current market replacement value, regardless of the age of the lost or damaged article. Your mover will charge you for this level of protection, or you may select the Alternative Level of Liability described below.

The cost for FVP is based on the value that you place on your shipment. For example, the valuation charge for a shipment valued at $25,000 would be about $250.00. However, the exact cost for full-value protection may vary by mover and may be further subject to various deductible levels of liability that could reduce your cost. Ask your mover for the details and cost of its specific plan.

Under the FVP level of liability, movers are permitted to limit their liability for loss of, or damage to, articles of extraordinary value, unless you specifically list on the shipping documents such articles for which you want liability coverage. An article of extraordinary value is any item whose value exceeds $100 per pound (for example, jewelry, silverware, china, furs, antiques, oriental rugs and computer software). Ask your mover for a complete explanation of this limitation before your move. It is your responsibility to study this provision carefully and to make the necessary declaration.

(2) RELEASED VALUE of 60 Cents Per Pound Per Article. This is the most economical protection option available; however, this no-cost option provides only minimal protection. Under this option, the mover assumes liability for no more than 60 cents per pound per article. Loss or damage claims are settled based on the weight of the article multiplied by 60 cents per pound. For example, if a 10-pound stereo component valued at $1,000 were lost or destroyed, the mover would be liable for no more than $6.00 (10 pounds × 60 cents per pound). Obviously, you should think carefully before agreeing to such an arrangement. There is no extra charge for this minimal protection, but you must sign a specific statement on the bill of lading agreeing to it. If you do not select this Alternative Level of Liability, your shipment will be transported at the Full (Replacement) Value level of liability and you will be assessed the applicable valuation charge.

These two levels of liability are not insurance agreements governed by State insurance laws but instead are contractual tariff levels of liability authorized under Released Rates Orders of the Surface Transportation Board of the U.S. Department of Transportation.

In addition to these options, some movers may also offer to sell, or procure for you, separate liability insurance from a third-party insurance company when you release your shipment for transportation at the minimum released value (60 cents per pound [$1.32 per kilogram] per article). This is not valuation coverage governed by Federal law but optional insurance regulated under State law. If you purchase this separate coverage and your mover is responsible for loss or damage, the mover is liable only for an amount not exceeding 60 cents per pound ($1.32 per kilogram) per article, and the balance of the loss is recoverable from the insurance company up to the amount of insurance purchased. The mover's representative can advise you of the availability of such liability insurance, and the cost.

If you purchase liability insurance from or through your mover, the mover is required to issue a policy or other written record of the purchase and to provide you with a copy of the policy or other document at the time of purchase. If the mover fails to comply with this requirement, the mover becomes fully liable for any claim for loss or damage attributed to its negligence.

WHAT ACTIONS BY ME LIMIT OR REDUCE MY MOVER'S NORMAL LIABILITY?

Your actions may limit or reduce your mover's normal liability under the following three circumstances:

(1) You include perishable, dangerous, or hazardous materials in your household goods without your mover's knowledge.

(2) You choose the alternative level of liability (60 cents per pound per article) but ship household goods valued at more than 60 cents per pound ($1.32 per kilogram) per article.

(3) You fail to notify your mover in writing of articles valued at more than $100 per pound ($220 per kilogram). (If you *do* notify your mover, you will be entitled to full recovery up to the declared value of the article or articles, not to exceed the declared value of the entire shipment.)

WHAT ARE DANGEROUS OR HAZARDOUS MATERIALS THAT MAY LIMIT OR REDUCE MY MOVER'S NORMAL LIABILITY?

Federal law forbids you to ship hazardous materials in your household goods boxes or luggage without informing your mover. A violation can result in 5 years' imprisonment and penalties of $250,000 or more (49 U.S.C. 5124). You could also lose or damage your household goods by fire, explosion, or contamination.

If you offer hazardous materials to your mover, you are considered a hazardous materials shipper and must comply with the hazardous materials requirements in 49 CFR parts 171, 172, and 173, including but not limited to package labeling and marking, shipping papers, and emergency response information. Your mover must comply with 49 CFR parts 171, 172, 173, and 177 as a hazardous materials carrier.

Hazardous materials include explosives, compressed gases, flammable liquids and solids, oxidizers, poisons, corrosives, and radioactive materials. Examples: Nail polish remover, paints, paint thinners, lighter fluid, gasoline, fireworks, oxygen bottles, propane cylinders, automotive repair and maintenance chemicals, and radio-pharmaceuticals.

There are special exceptions for small quantities (up to 70 ounces total) of medicinal and toilet articles carried in your household goods and certain smoking materials carried on your person. For further information, contact your mover.

117

MAY MY MOVER HAVE AGENTS?

Yes, your mover may have agents. If your mover has agents, your mover must have written agreements with its prime agents. Your mover and its retained prime agent must sign their agreements. Copies of your mover's prime agent agreements must be in your mover's files for a period of at least 24 months following the date of termination of each agreement.

WHAT ITEMS MUST BE IN MY MOVER'S ADVERTISEMENTS?

Your mover must publish and use only truthful, straightforward, and honest advertisements. Your mover must include certain information in all advertisements for all services (including any accessorial services incidental to or part of interstate transportation). Your mover must require each of its agents to include the same information in its advertisements. The information must include the following two pieces of information about your mover:

(1) Name or trade name of the mover under whose U.S. DOT number the advertised service will originate.

(2) U.S. DOT number assigned by FMCSA authorizing your mover to operate. Your mover must display the information as: U.S. DOT No. (assigned number).

You should compare the name or trade name of the mover and its U.S. DOT number to the name and U.S. DOT number on the sides of the truck(s) that arrive at your residence. The names and numbers should be identical. If the names and numbers are not identical, you should ask your mover immediately why they are not. You should not allow the mover to load your household goods on its truck(s) until you obtain a satisfactory response from the mover's local agent. The discrepancies may warn of problems you will have later in your business dealings with this mover.

HOW MUST MY MOVER HANDLE COMPLAINTS AND INQUIRIES?

All movers are expected to respond promptly to complaints or inquiries from you, the customer. Should you have a complaint or question about your move, you should first attempt to obtain a satisfactory response from the mover's local agent, the sales representative who handled the arrangements for your move, or the driver assigned to your shipment.

If for any reason you are unable to obtain a satisfactory response from one of these persons, you should then contact the mover's principal office. When you make such a call, be sure to have available your copies of all documents relating to your move. *Particularly important is the number assigned to your shipment by your mover.*

Interstate movers are also required to offer neutral arbitration as a means of resolving consumer disputes involving loss of or damage to your household goods shipment and disputes regarding charges that your mover billed in addition to those collected at delivery. Your mover is required to provide you with information regarding its arbitration program. You have the right to pursue court action under 49 U.S.C. 14706 to seek judicial redress directly rather than participate in your mover's arbitration program.

All interstate moving companies are required to maintain a complaint and inquiry procedure to assist their customers. At the time you make the arrangements for your move, you should ask the mover's representative for a description of the mover's procedure, the telephone number to be used to contact the mover, and whether the mover will pay for such telephone calls. Your mover's procedure must include the following four things:

(1) A communications system allowing you to communicate with your mover's principal place of business by telephone.

(2) A telephone number.

(3) A clear and concise statement about who must pay for complaint and inquiry telephone calls.

(4) A written or electronic record system for recording all inquiries and complaints received from you by any means of communication.

Your mover must give you a clear and concise written description of its procedure. You may want to be certain that the system is in place.

DO I HAVE THE RIGHT TO INSPECT MY MOVER'S TARIFFS (SCHEDULES OF CHARGES) APPLICABLE TO MY MOVE?

Federal law requires your mover to advise you of your right to inspect your mover's tariffs (its schedules of rates or charges) governing your shipment. Movers' tariffs are made a part of the contract of carriage (bill of lading) between you and the mover. You may inspect the tariff at the mover's facility, or, upon request, the mover will furnish you a free copy of any tariff provision containing the mover's rates, rules, or charges governing your shipment.

Tariffs may include provisions limiting the mover's liability. This is generally described in a section on declaring value on the bill of lading. A second tariff provision may set the periods for filing claims. This is generally described in Section 6 on the reverse side of a bill of lading. A third tariff provision may reserve your mover's right to assess additional charges for additional services performed. For non-binding estimates, another tariff provision may base charges upon the exact weight of the goods transported. Your mover's tariff may contain other provisions that apply to your move. Ask your mover what they might be, and request a copy.

MUST MY MOVER HAVE AN ARBITRATION PROGRAM?

Your mover must have an arbitration program for your use in resolving disputes concerning loss of or damage to your household goods and disputes regarding charges that were billed to you in addition to those collected at delivery of your shipment. You have the right not to participate in the arbitration program. You may pursue court action under 49 U.S.C. 14706 to seek judicial remedies directly. Your mover must establish and maintain an arbitration program with the following 11 minimum elements:

(1) The arbitration program offered to you must prevent your mover from having any special advantage because you live or work in a place distant from the mover's principal or other place of business.

(2) Before your household goods are tendered for transport, your mover must provide notice to you of the availability of neutral arbitration, including the following three things:

(a) A summary of the arbitration procedure.

(b) Any applicable costs.

(c) A disclosure of the legal effects of electing to use arbitration.

(3) Upon your request, your mover must provide information and forms it considers necessary for initiating an action to resolve a dispute under arbitration.

(4) Each person authorized to arbitrate must be independent of the parties to the dispute and capable of resolving such disputes fairly and expeditiously. Your mover must ensure the arbitrator is authorized and able to obtain from you or your mover any material or relevant information to carry out a fair and expeditious decision-making process.

(5) You must not be required to pay more than one-half of the arbitration's cost. The arbitrator may determine the percentage of payment of the costs for each party in the arbitration decision, but must not make you pay more than half.

(6) Your mover must not require you to agree to use arbitration before a dispute arises.

(7) You and your mover will be bound by arbitration for claims of $10,000 or less if you request arbitration.

(8) You and your mover will be bound by arbitration for claims of more than $10,000 only if you request arbitration and your mover agrees to it.

(9) If you and your mover both agree, the arbitrator may provide for an oral presentation of a dispute by a party or representative of a party.

(10) The arbitrator must render a decision within 60 days of receipt of written notifica-

tion of the dispute, and a decision by an arbitrator may include any remedies appropriate under the circumstances.

(11) The 60-day period may be extended for a reasonable period if either you or your mover fails to provide information in a timely manner. Your mover must produce and distribute a concise, easy-to-read, accurate summary of its arbitration program.

MUST MY MOVER INFORM ME ABOUT MY RIGHTS AND RESPONSIBILITIES UNDER FEDERAL LAW?

Yes, your mover must inform you about your rights and responsibilities under Federal law. Your mover must produce and distribute this document. It should follow the general order and contain the text of appendix A to 49 CFR part 375.

WHAT OTHER INFORMATION MUST MY MOVER PROVIDE ME?

At the time your mover provides a written estimate, it must provide you with a copy of the U.S. Department of Transportation publication FMCSA–ESA–03–005 entitled "Ready to Move?" (or its successor publication). Before your mover executes an order for service for a shipment of household goods, your mover must furnish you with the following four documents:

1. The contents of Appendix A, "Your Rights and Responsibilities When You Move"—this booklet.

2. A concise, easy-to-read, and accurate summary of your mover's arbitration program.

3. A notice of availability of the applicable sections of your mover's tariff for the estimate of charges, including an explanation that you may examine the tariff sections or have copies sent to you upon request.

4. A concise, easy-to-read, accurate summary of your mover's customer complaint and inquiry handling procedures. Included in this summary must be the following two items:

(a) The main telephone number you may use to communicate with your mover.

(b) A clear and concise statement concerning who must pay for telephone calls.

Your mover may, at its discretion, provide additional information to you.

HOW MUST MY MOVER COLLECT CHARGES?

Your mover must issue you an honest, truthful freight or expense bill for each shipment transported. Your mover's freight or expense bill must contain the following 17 items:

(1) Name of the consignor.

(2) Name of the consignees.

(3) Date of the shipment.

(4) Origin point.

(5) Destination points.

(6) Number of packages.

(7) Description of the freight.

(8) Weight of the freight (if your shipment is moved under a non-binding estimate).

(9) Exact rate(s) assessed.

(10) Disclosure of the actual rates, charges, and allowances for the transportation service, when your mover electronically presents or transmits freight or expense bills to you. These rates must be in accordance with the mover's applicable tariff.

(11) An indication of whether adjustments may apply to the bill.

(12) Total charges due and acceptable methods of payment.

(13) The nature and amount of any special service charges.

(14) The points where special services were rendered.

(15) Route of movement and name of each mover participating in the transportation.

(16) Transfer points where shipments moved.

(17) Address where you must pay or address of bill issuer's principal place of business.

Your mover must present its freight or expense bill to you within 15 days of the date of delivery of a shipment at its destination. The computation of time excludes Saturdays, Sundays, and Federal holidays. If your mover lacks sufficient information to compute its charges, your mover must present its freight bill for payment within 15 days of the date when sufficient information does become available.

MAY MY MOVER COLLECT CHARGES UPON DELIVERY?

Yes. Your mover must specify the form of payment acceptable at delivery when the mover prepares an estimate and order for service. The mover and its agents must honor the form of payment at delivery, except when you mutually agree to a change in writing. The mover must also specify the same form of payment when it prepares your bill of lading, unless you agree to a change. See also "May my mover accept charge or credit cards for my payments?"

You must be prepared to pay 10 percent more than the estimated amount, if your goods are moving under a non-binding estimate. Every collect-on-delivery shipper must have available 110 percent of the estimate at the time of delivery. In addition, your mover may also collect at the time of delivery the charges for any additional services you requested after the contract with your mover was executed (charges therefore not included in the estimate) and any charges for impracticable operations needed to accomplish delivery, as defined by the carrier's tariff. Charges collected at the time of delivery for impracticable operations may not exceed 15 percent of all other charges due at the time of delivery. You must pay all remaining charges for impracticable operations within

30 days after you receive the mover's freight bill.

MAY MY MOVER EXTEND CREDIT TO ME?

Extending credit to you is not the same as accepting your charge or credit card(s) as payment. Your mover may extend credit to you in the amount of the tariff charges. If your mover extends credit to you, your mover becomes like a bank offering you a line of credit, whose size and interest rate are determined by your ability to pay its tariff charges within the credit period. Your mover must ensure you will pay its tariff charges within the credit period. Your mover may relinquish possession of freight before you pay its tariff charges, at its discretion.

The credit period must begin on the day following presentation of your mover's freight bill to you. Under Federal regulation, the standard credit period is 7 days, excluding Saturdays, Sundays, and Federal holidays. Your mover must also extend the credit period to a total of 30 calendar days if the freight bill is not paid within the 7-day period. A service charge equal to one percent of the amount of the freight bill, subject to a $20 minimum, will be assessed for this extension and for each additional 30-day period the charges go unpaid.

Your failure to pay within the credit period will require your mover to determine whether you will comply with the Federal household goods transportation credit regulations in good faith in the future before extending credit again.

MAY MY MOVER ACCEPT CHARGE OR CREDIT CARDS FOR MY PAYMENTS?

Your mover may allow you to use a charge or credit card for payment of the freight charges. Your mover may accept charge or credit cards whenever you ship with it under an agreement and tariff requiring payment by cash or cash equivalents. Cash equivalents are a certified check, money order, or cashier's check (a check that a financial institution—bank, credit union, savings and loan—draws upon itself and that is signed by an officer of the financial institution).

If your mover allows you to pay for a freight or expense bill by charge or credit card, your mover deems such a payment to be equivalent to payment by cash, certified check, or cashier's check. It must note in writing on the order for service and the bill of lading whether you may pay for the transportation and related services using a charge or credit card. You should ask your mover at the time the estimate is written whether it will accept charge or credit cards at delivery.

The mover must specify what charge or credit cards it will accept, such as American Express™, Discover™, MasterCard™, or

Visa™. If your mover agrees to accept payment by charge or credit card, you must arrange with your mover for the delivery only at a time when your mover can obtain authorization for your credit card transaction. If you cause a charge or credit card issuer to reverse a transaction, your mover may consider your action tantamount to forcing your mover to provide an involuntary extension of its credit.

SUBPART C—SERVICE OPTIONS PROVIDED

WHAT SERVICE OPTIONS MAY MY MOVER PROVIDE?

Your mover may provide any service options it chooses. It is customary for movers to offer several price and service options.

The total cost of your move may increase if you want additional or special services. Before you agree to have your shipment moved under a bill of lading providing special service, you should have a clear understanding with your mover of what the additional cost will be. You should always consider whether other movers might provide the services you need without requiring you to pay the additional charges.

One service option is a *space reservation*. If you agree to have your shipment transported under a space reservation agreement, you will pay for a minimum number of cubic feet of space in the moving van regardless of how much space in the van your shipment actually occupies.

A second option is *expedited service*. This aids you if you must have your shipments transported on or between specific dates when the mover could not ordinarily agree to do so in its normal operations.

A third customary service option is exclusive use of a vehicle. If for any reason you desire or require that your shipment be moved by itself on the mover's truck or trailer, most movers will provide such service.

Another service option is *guaranteed service on or between agreed dates*. You enter into an agreement with the mover where the mover provides for your shipment to be picked up, transported to destination, and delivered on specific guaranteed dates. If the mover fails to provide the service as agreed, you are entitled to be compensated at a predetermined amount or a daily rate (per diem) regardless of the expense you might actually have incurred as a result of the mover's failure to perform.

Before requesting or agreeing to any of these price and service options, be sure to ask the mover's representatives about the final costs you will pay.

Transport of Shipments on Two or More Vehicles

Although all movers try to move each shipment on one truck, it becomes nec-essary, at times, to divide a shipment among two or more trucks. This may occur if your mover has underestimated the cubic feet (meters) of space required for your shipment and it will not all fit on the first truck. Your mover will pick up the remainder, or "leave behind," on a second truck at a later time, and this part of your shipment may arrive at the destination later than the first truck. When this occurs, your transportation charges will be determined as if the entire shipment had moved on one truck.

If it is important for you to avoid this inconvenience of a "leave behind," be sure your estimate includes an accurate calculation of the cubic feet (meters) required for your shipment. Ask your estimator to use a "Table of Measurements" form in making this calculation. Consider asking for a binding estimate. A binding estimate is more likely to be conservative with regard to cubic feet (meters) than a non-binding estimate. If the mover offers space reservation service, consider purchasing this service for the necessary amount of space plus some margin for error. In any case, you would be prudent to "prioritize" your goods in advance of the move so the driver will load the more essential items on the first truck if some are left behind.

IF MY MOVER SELLS LIABILITY INSURANCE COVERAGE, WHAT MUST MY MOVER DO?

If your mover provides the service of selling additional liability insurance, your mover must follow certain regulations.

Your mover, its employees, or its agents may sell, offer to sell, or procure additional liability insurance coverage for you for loss of or damage to your shipment if you release the shipment for transportation at a value not exceeding 60 cents per pound ($1.32 per kilogram) per article.

Your mover may offer, sell, or procure any type of insurance policy covering loss or damage in excess of its specified liability.

Your mover must issue you a policy or other appropriate evidence of the insurance you purchased. Your mover must provide a copy of the policy or other appropriate evidence to you at the time your mover sells or procures the insurance. Your mover must issue policies written in plain English.

Your mover must clearly specify the nature and extent of coverage under the policy. Your mover's failure to issue you a policy, or other appropriate evidence of insurance you purchased, will subject your mover to full liability for any claims to recover loss or damage attributed to it.

Your mover's tariff must provide for liability insurance coverage. The tariff must also provide for the base transportation charge, including its assumption of full liability for the value of the shipment. This would offer you a degree of protection in the event your mover fails to issue you a policy or other appropriate evidence of insurance at the time of purchase.

SUBPART D—ESTIMATING CHARGES

MUST MY MOVER ESTIMATE THE TRANSPORTATION AND ACCESSORIAL CHARGES FOR MY MOVE?

We require your mover to prepare a written estimate on every shipment transported for you. You are entitled to a copy of the written estimate when your mover prepares it. Your mover must provide you a written estimate of all charges, including transportation, accessorial, and advance charges. Your mover's "rate quote" is not an estimate. You and your mover must sign the estimate of charges. Your mover must provide you with a dated copy of the estimate of charges at the time you sign the estimate.

If the location you are moving from is within a 50-mile radius of your mover's (or its agent's) place of business, the estimate that your mover provides you must be based on a physical survey of your goods. You have the right to waive the requirement for a physical survey if you choose, but your waiver must be in the form of a written agreement signed by you before your shipment is loaded.

You should be aware that if you receive an estimate from a household goods broker, the mover may not be required to accept the estimate. Be sure to obtain a written estimate from a mover who tells you orally that it will accept the broker's estimate.

Your mover must specify the form of payment the mover and its delivering agent will honor at delivery. Payment forms may include but are not limited to cash, certified check, money order, cashier's check, a specific charge card such as American Express™, a specific credit card such as Visa™, and your mover's own credit.

Before loading your household goods, and upon mutual agreement between you and your mover, your mover may amend an estimate of charges. Your mover may not amend the estimate after loading the shipment.

A *binding estimate* is a written agreement made in advance with your mover, indicating you and the mover are bound by the charges. It guarantees the total cost of the move based upon the quantities and services shown on your mover's estimate.

A *non-binding estimate* is what your mover believes the total cost will be for the move, based upon the estimated weight of the shipment and the accessorial services requested. A non-binding estimate is not binding on your mover. Your mover will base the final charges upon the actual weight of your shipment, the services provided, and its tariff provisions in effect. You must be prepared to pay 10 percent more than the estimated amount at delivery.

You must also be prepared to pay at delivery the charges for any additional services you requested after the contract was executed (charges therefore not included in the estimate) and any charges for impracticable operations. Impracticable operations are defined in your mover's tariff. You should ask to see the mover's tariff to determine what services constitute impracticable operations. Charges for impracticable operations due at delivery must not exceed 15 percent of all other charges due at delivery.

HOW MUST MY MOVER ESTIMATE CHARGES UNDER THE REGULATIONS?

Binding Estimates

Your mover may charge you for providing a binding estimate. The binding estimate must clearly describe the shipment and all services provided.

When you receive a binding estimate, you cannot be required to pay any more than the estimated amount at delivery. If you have requested the mover provide more services than those included in the estimate, your mover will collect the charges for those services when your shipment is delivered. However, charges for impracticable operations due at delivery must not exceed 15 percent of all other charges due at delivery.

A binding estimate must be in writing, and a copy must be made available to you before you move.

If you agree to a binding estimate, you are responsible for paying the charges due by cash, certified check, money order, or cashier's check. The charges are due your mover at the time of delivery unless your mover agrees, before you move, to extend credit or to accept payment by a specific charge card such as American Express™ or a specific credit card such as Visa™. If you are unable to pay at the time the shipment is delivered, the mover may place your shipment in storage at your expense until you pay the charges.

Other requirements of binding estimates include the following eight elements:

(1) Your mover must retain a copy of each binding estimate as an attachment to the bill of lading.

(2) Your mover must clearly indicate upon each binding estimate's face that the estimate is binding upon you and your mover. Each binding estimate must also clearly indicate on its face that the charges shown are the charges to be assessed for only those services specifically identified in the estimate.

(3) Your mover must clearly describe binding estimate shipments and all services to be provided.

(4) If, before loading your shipment, your mover believes you are tendering additional household goods or are requiring additional

services not identified in the binding estimate, and you and your mover cannot reach an agreement, your mover may refuse to service the shipment. If your mover agrees to service the shipment, your mover must do one of the following three things:

(a) Reaffirm the binding estimate.

(b) Negotiate a revised written binding estimate listing the additional household goods or services.

(c) Add an attachment to the contract, in writing, stating you both will consider the original binding estimate as a non-binding estimate. Before you agree to this option, read the information about non-binding estimates in the next section of this pamphlet. Accepting a non-binding estimate may seriously affect how much you may pay for the entire move.

(5) Once your mover loads your shipment, your mover's failure to execute a new binding estimate or to agree with you to treat the original estimate as a non-binding estimate signifies it has reaffirmed the original binding estimate. Your mover may not collect more than the amount of the original binding estimate, except as provided in the next two paragraphs.

(6) If you request additional services after the bill of lading is executed, your mover will collect the charges for these additional services when your shipment is delivered.

(7) If your mover must perform impracticable operations, as defined in its tariff, to accomplish the delivery of your shipment, your mover will collect the charges for these services when your shipment is delivered. However, charges for impracticable operations collected at delivery must not exceed 15 percent of all other charges due at delivery. Any remaining impracticable operations charges must be paid within 30 days after you receive the mover's freight bill.

(8) Failure of your mover to relinquish possession of a shipment upon your offer to pay the binding estimate amount plus the cost of any additional services you requested after the bill of lading was executed and any charges for impracticable operations (not to exceed 15 percent of all other charges due at delivery) constitutes your mover's failure to transport a shipment with "reasonable dispatch" and subjects your mover to cargo delay claims pursuant to 49 CFR part 370.

Non-Binding Estimates

Your mover is not permitted to charge you for giving a non-binding estimate.

A non-binding estimate is not a bid or contract. Your mover provides it to you to give you a general idea of the cost of the move, but it does not bind your mover to the estimated cost. You should expect the final cost to be more than the estimate. The actual cost will be in accordance with your mover's tariffs. Federal law requires your mover to collect the charges shown in its tariffs, re-

gardless of what your mover writes in its non-binding estimates. That is why it is important to ask for copies of the applicable portions of the mover's tariffs before deciding on a mover. The charges contained in movers' tariffs are essentially the same for shipments of equal weight moving equal distances. Even if you obtain different non-binding estimates from different movers, you must pay only the amount specified in your mover's tariff. Therefore, a non-binding estimate may differ substantially from the amount that you ultimately will pay.

You must be prepared to pay 10 percent more than the estimated amount at the time of delivery. Every collect-on-delivery shipper must have available 110 percent of the estimate at the time of delivery. If you order additional services from your mover after the mover issues the bill of lading, the mover will collect the charges for those additional services when your shipment is delivered.

Non-binding estimates must be in writing and clearly describe the shipment and all services provided. Any time a mover provides such an estimate, the amount of the charges estimated must be on the order for service and bill of lading related to your shipment. When you are given a non-binding estimate, do not sign or accept the order for service or bill of lading unless the mover enters the amount estimated on each form it prepares.

Other requirements of non-binding estimates include the following 10 elements:

(1) Your mover must provide reasonably accurate non-binding estimates based upon the estimated weight of the shipment and services required.

(2) Your mover must explain to you that all charges on shipments moved under non-binding estimates will be those appearing in your mover's tariffs applicable to the transportation. If your mover provides a non-binding estimate of approximate costs, your mover is not bound by such an estimate.

(3) Your mover must furnish non-binding estimates without charge and in writing to you.

(4) Your mover must retain a copy of each non-binding estimate as an attachment to the bill of lading.

(5) Your mover must clearly indicate on the face of a non-binding estimate that the estimate is not binding upon your mover and the charges shown are the approximate charges to be assessed for the services identified in the estimate.

(6) Your mover must clearly describe on the face of a non-binding estimate the entire shipment and all services to be provided.

(7) If, before loading your shipment, your mover believes you are tendering additional household goods or requiring additional services not identified in the non-binding estimate, and you and your mover cannot reach an agreement, your mover may refuse to

service the shipment. If your mover agrees to service the shipment, your mover must do one of the following two things:

(a) Reaffirm the non-binding estimate.

(b) Negotiate a revised written non-binding estimate listing the additional household goods or services.

(8) Once your mover loads your shipment, your mover's failure to execute a new estimate signifies it has reaffirmed the original non-binding estimate. Your mover may not collect more than 110 percent of the amount of this estimate at destination for the services and quantities shown on the estimate.

(9) If you request additional services after the bill of lading is executed, your mover will collect the charges for these additional services when your shipment is delivered.

(10) If your mover must perform impracticable operations, as defined in its tariff, to accomplish the delivery of your shipment, your mover will collect the charges for these services when your shipment is delivered. However, charges for impracticable operations collected at delivery must not exceed 15 percent of all other charges due at delivery. Any remaining impracticable operations charges must be paid within 30 days after you receive the mover's freight bill.

If your mover furnishes a non-binding estimate, your mover must enter the estimated charges upon the order for service and the bill of lading. Your mover must retain a record of all estimates of charges for each move performed for at least one year from the date your mover made the estimate.

WHAT PAYMENT ARRANGEMENTS MUST MY MOVER HAVE IN PLACE TO SECURE DELIVERY OF MY HOUSEHOLD GOODS SHIPMENT?

If your total bill is 110 percent or less of the non-binding estimate, the mover can require payment in full upon delivery. If the bill exceeds 110 percent of the non-binding estimate, your mover must relinquish possession of the shipment at the time of delivery upon payment of 110 percent of the estimated amount, and defer billing for the remaining charges for at least 30 days.

There are two exceptions to this requirement. Your mover may demand at the time of delivery payment of the charges for any additional services you requested after the bill of lading was executed (charges therefore not included in the estimate). Your mover may also require you to pay charges for impracticable operations at the time of delivery, provided these do not exceed 15 percent of all other charges due at delivery. Impracticable operations charges that exceed 15 percent of all other charges due at delivery are due within 30 days after you receive the mover's freight bill. Your mover should have specified its acceptable form of payment on the estimate, order for service, and bill of lading.

Your mover's failure to relinquish possession of a shipment after you offer to pay 110 percent of the estimated charges, plus the charges for any additional services you requested after the bill of lading was executed (charges therefore not included in the estimate) and any charges for impracticable operations (not to exceed 15 percent of all other charges due at delivery), constitutes its failure to transport the shipment with "reasonable dispatch" and subjects your mover to your cargo delay claims under 49 CFR part 370.

SUBPART E—PICKUP OF MY SHIPMENT OF HOUSEHOLD GOODS

MUST MY MOVER WRITE UP AN ORDER FOR SERVICE?

We require your mover to prepare an order for service on every shipment transported for you. You are entitled to a copy of the order for service when your mover prepares it.

The order for service is not a contract. Should you cancel or delay your move or decide not to use the mover, you should promptly cancel the order.

If you or your mover change any agreed-upon dates for pickup or delivery of your shipment, or agree to any change in the non-binding estimate, your mover may prepare a written change to the order for service. The written change must be attached to the order for service.

The order for service must contain the following 15 elements:

(1) Your mover's name and address and the U.S. DOT number assigned to your mover.

(2) Your name, address and, if available, telephone number(s).

(3) The name, address, and telephone number of the delivering mover's office or agent at or nearest to the destination of your shipment.

(4) A telephone number where you may contact your mover or its designated agent.

(5) One of the following three dates and times:

(i) The agreed-upon pickup date and agreed delivery date of your move.

(ii) The agreed-upon period(s) of the entire move.

(iii) If your mover is transporting the shipment on a guaranteed service basis, the guaranteed dates or periods of time for pickup, transportation, and delivery. Your mover must enter any penalty or per diem requirements upon the agreement under this item.

(6) The names and addresses of any other motor carriers, when known, that will participate in interline transportation of the shipment.

(7) The form of payment your mover will honor at delivery. The payment information must be the same as was entered on the estimate.

(8) The terms and conditions for payment of the total charges, including notice of any minimum charges.

(9) The maximum amount your mover will demand, based on the mover's estimate, for you to obtain possession of the shipment at the time of delivery, when the household goods are transported on a collect-on-delivery basis.

(10) If not provided in the Bill of Lading, the Surface Transportation Board's required released rates valuation statement, and the charges, if any, for optional valuation coverage. The STB's required released rates may be increased annually by your mover based on the U.S. Department of Commerce's Cost of Living Adjustment.

(11) A complete description of any special or accessorial services ordered and minimum weight or volume charges applicable to the shipment.

(12) Any identification or registration number your mover assigns to the shipment.

(13) For non-binding estimated charges, your mover's reasonably accurate estimate of the amount of the charges, the method of payment of total charges, and the maximum amount (110 percent of the non-binding estimate) your mover will demand at the time of delivery for you to obtain possession of the shipment.

(14) For binding estimated charges, the amount of charges your mover will demand based upon the binding estimate and the terms of payment under the estimate.

(15) An indication of whether you request notification of the charges before delivery. You must provide your mover with the telephone number(s) or address(es) where your mover will transmit such communications.

You and your mover must sign the order for service. Your mover must provide a dated copy of the order for service to you at the time your mover signs the order. Your mover must provide you the opportunity to rescind the order for service without any penalty for a 3-day period after you sign the order for service, if you scheduled the shipment to be loaded more than 3 days after you sign the order.

Your mover should provide you with documents that are as complete as possible, and with all charges clearly identified. However, as a practical matter, your mover usually cannot give you a complete bill of lading before transporting your goods. This is both because the shipment cannot be weighed until it is in transit and because other charges for service, such as unpacking, storage-in-transit, and various destination charges, cannot be determined until the shipment reaches its destination.

Therefore, your mover can require you to sign a partially complete bill of lading if it contains all relevant information except the actual shipment weight and any other information necessary to determine the final charges for all services provided. Signing the bill of lading allows you to choose the valuation option, request special services, and/or acknowledge the terms and conditions of released valuation.

Your mover also may provide you, strictly for informational purposes, with blank or incomplete documents pertaining to the move. Before loading your shipment, and upon mutual agreement between you and your mover, your mover may amend an order for service. Your mover must retain records of an order for service it transported for at least one year from the date your mover wrote the order.

Your mover must inform you, before or at the time of loading, if the mover reasonably expects a special or accessorial service is necessary to transport a shipment safely. Your mover must refuse to accept the shipment when your mover reasonably expects a special or accessorial service is necessary to transport a shipment safely but you refuse to purchase the special or accessorial service. Your mover must make a written note if you refuse any special or accessorial services that your mover reasonably expects to be necessary.

Must My Mover Write Up an Inventory of the Shipment?

Yes. Your mover must prepare an inventory of your shipment before or at the time of loading. If your mover's driver fails to prepare an inventory, you should write a detailed inventory of your shipment listing any damage or unusual wear to any items. The purpose is to make a record of the existence and condition of each item.

After completing the inventory, you should sign each page and ask the mover's driver to sign each page. Before you sign it, it is important you make sure that the inventory lists every item in the shipment and that the entries regarding the condition of each item are correct. You have the right to note any disagreement. If an item is missing or damaged when your mover delivers the shipment, your subsequent ability to dispute the items lost or damaged may depend upon your notations.

You should retain a copy of the inventory. Your mover may keep the original if the driver prepared it. If your mover's driver completed an inventory, the mover must attach the complete inventory to the bill of lading as an integral part of the bill of lading.

Must My Mover Write Up a Bill of Lading?

The bill of lading is the *contract* between you and the mover. The mover is required by law to prepare a bill of lading for every shipment it transports. *The information on a bill of lading is required to be the same information shown on the order for service.* The driver who loads your shipment must give you a copy of the bill of lading before or at the time of loading your furniture and other household goods.

It is your responsibility to read the bill of lading before you accept it. It is your responsibility to understand the bill of lading before you sign it. If you do not agree with something on the bill of lading, do not sign it until you are satisfied it is correct.

The bill of lading requires the mover to provide the service you have requested. You must pay the charges set forth in the bill of lading. *The bill of lading is an important document. Do not lose or misplace your copy.* Have it available until your shipment is delivered, all charges are paid, and all claims, if any, are settled.

A bill of lading must include the following 14 elements:

(1) Your mover's name and address, or the name and address of the motor carrier issuing the bill of lading.

(2) The names and addresses of any other motor carriers, when known, who will participate in the transportation of the shipment.

(3) The name, address, and telephone number of the office of the motor carrier you must contact in relation to the transportation of the shipment.

(4) The form of payment your mover will honor at delivery. The payment information must be the same that was entered on the estimate and order for service.

(5) When your mover transports your shipment under a collect-on-delivery basis, your name, address, and telephone number where the mover will notify you about the charges.

(6) *For non-guaranteed service,* the agreed-upon date or period of time for pickup of the shipment and the agreed-upon date or period of time for the delivery of the shipment. The agreed-upon dates or periods for pickup and delivery entered upon the bill of lading must conform to the agreed-upon dates or periods of time for pickup and delivery entered upon the order for service or a proper amendment to the order for service.

(7) For *guaranteed service,* the dates for pickup and delivery and any penalty or per diem entitlements due you under the agreement.

(8) The actual date of pickup.

(9) The identification number(s) of the vehicle(s) in which your mover loads your shipment.

(10) The terms and conditions for payment of the total charges including notice of any minimum charges.

(11) The maximum amount your mover, based on the estimate, will demand from you at the time of delivery for you to obtain possession of your shipment, when your mover transports under a collect-on-delivery basis.

(12) If not provided for in the Order for Service, the Surface Transportation Board's required released rates valuation statement, and the charges, if any, for optional valuation coverage. The Board's required released rates may be increased annually by your mover based on the U.S. Department of Commerce's Cost of Living Adjustment.

(13) Evidence of any insurance coverage sold to or procured for you from an independent insurer, including the amount of the premium for such insurance.

(14) Each attachment to the bill of lading. Each attachment is an integral part of the bill of lading contract. If not provided to you elsewhere by the mover, the following three items must be added as attachments:

(i) The binding or non-binding estimate.

(ii) The order for service.

(iii) The inventory.

A copy of the bill of lading must accompany your shipment at all times while it is in the possession of your mover or its agent(s). When your mover loads the shipment on a vehicle for transportation, the bill of lading must be in the possession of the driver responsible for the shipment. Your mover must retain bills of lading for shipments it transported for at least one year from the date your mover created the bill of lading.

SHOULD I REACH AN AGREEMENT WITH MY MOVER ABOUT PICKUP AND DELIVERY TIMES?

You and your mover should reach an agreement for pickup and delivery times. It is your responsibility to determine on what date, or between what dates, you need to have the shipment picked up and on what date, or between what dates, you require delivery. It is your mover's responsibility to tell you if it can provide service on or between those dates, or, if not, on what other dates it can provide the service.

In the process of reaching an agreement with your mover, you may find it necessary to alter your moving and travel plans if no mover can provide service on the specific dates you desire.

Do not agree to have your shipment picked up or delivered "as soon as possible." The dates or periods you and your mover agree upon should be definite.

Once an agreement is reached, your mover must enter those dates upon the order for service and the bill of lading.

Once your goods are loaded, your mover is contractually bound to provide the service described in the bill of lading. Your mover's only defense for not providing the service on the dates called for is the defense of force majeure. This is a legal term. It means that when circumstances change, were not foreseen, and are beyond the control of your mover, preventing your mover from performing the service agreed to in the bill of lading, your mover is not responsible for damages resulting from its nonperformance.

This may occur when you do not inform your mover of the exact delivery requirements. For example, because of restrictions trucks must follow at your new location, the mover may not be able to take its truck down the street of your residence and may need to shuttle the shipment using another type of vehicle.

MUST MY MOVER DETERMINE THE WEIGHT OF MY SHIPMENT?

Generally, yes. If your mover transports your household goods on a non-binding estimate, your mover must determine the actual weight of the shipment in order to calculate its lawful tariff charge. If your mover provided a binding estimate and has loaded your shipment without claiming you have added additional items or services, the weight of the shipment will not affect the charges you will pay.

Your mover must determine the weight of your shipment before requesting you to pay for any charges dependent upon your shipment's weight.

Most movers have a minimum weight charge for transporting a shipment. Generally, the minimum is the charge for transporting a shipment of at least 3,000 pounds (1,362 kilograms).

If your shipment appears to weigh less than the mover's minimum weight, your mover must advise you on the order for service of the minimum cost before transporting your shipment. Should your mover fail to advise you of the minimum charges and your shipment is less than the minimum weight, your mover must base your final charges upon the actual weight, not upon the minimum weight.

HOW MUST MY MOVER DETERMINE THE WEIGHT OF MY SHIPMENT?

Your mover must weigh your shipment upon a certified scale.

The weight of your shipment must be obtained by using one of two methods:

Origin Weighing—Your mover may weigh your shipment in the city or area where it loads your shipment. If it elects this option, the driver must weigh the truck before coming to your residence. This is called the *tare weight*. At the time of this first weighing, the truck may already be partially loaded with another shipment(s). This will not affect the weight of your shipment. The truck should also contain the pads, dollies, hand trucks, ramps, and other equipment normally used in the transportation of household goods shipments.

After loading, the driver will weigh the truck again to obtain the loaded weight, called the *gross weight*. The net weight of your shipment is then obtained by sub-

tracting the *tare weight* before loading from the *gross weight*.

Gross Weight less the Tare Weight Before Loading = Net Weight.

Destination Weighing (Also called *Back Weighing*)—The mover is also permitted to determine the weight of your shipment at the destination after it delivers your load. Weighing your shipment at destination instead of at origin will not affect the accuracy of the shipment weight. *The most important difference is that your mover will not determine the exact charges on your shipment before it is unloaded.*

Destination weighing is done in reverse of origin weighing. After arriving in the city or area where you are moving, the driver will weigh the truck. Your shipment will still be on the truck. Your mover will determine the *gross weight* before coming to your new residence to unload. After unloading your shipment, the driver will again weigh the truck to obtain the *tare weight*. The net weight of your shipment will then be obtained by subtracting the *tare weight* after delivery from the *gross weight*.

Gross Weight less the Tare Weight After Delivery = Net Weight.

At the time of both weighings, your mover's truck must have installed or loaded all pads, dollies, hand trucks, ramps, and other equipment required in the transportation of your shipment. The driver and other persons must be off the vehicle at the time of both weighings. The fuel tanks on the vehicle must be full at the time of each weighing; or, if the fuel tanks are not full, your mover must not add fuel between the two weighings when the tare weighing is the first weighing performed.

Your mover may detach the trailer of a tractor-trailer vehicle combination from the tractor and have the trailer weighed separately at each weighing, provided the length of the scale platform is adequate to accommodate and support the entire trailer.

Your mover may use an alternative method to weigh your shipment if it weighs 3,000 pounds (1,362 kilograms) or less. The only alternative method allowed is weighing the shipment upon a platform or warehouse certified scale before loading your shipment for transportation or after unloading.

Your mover must use the net weight of shipments transported in large containers, such as ocean or railroad containers. Your mover will calculate the difference between the tare weight of the container (including all pads, blocking and bracing used in the transportation of your shipment) and the gross weight of the container with your shipment loaded in the container.

You have the right, and your mover must inform you of your right, to observe all weighings of your shipment. Your mover must tell you where and when each weighing

127

will occur. Your mover must give you a reasonable opportunity to be present to observe the weighings.

You may waive your right to observe any weighing or reweighing. This does not affect any of your other rights under Federal law.

Your mover may request that you waive your right to have a shipment weighed upon a certified scale. Your mover may want to weigh the shipment upon a trailer's onboard, non-certified scale. You should demand your right to have a certified scale used. The use of a non-certified scale may cause you to pay a higher final bill for your move, if the non-certified scale does not accurately weigh your shipment. Remember that certified scales are inspected and approved for accuracy by a government inspection or licensing agency. Non-certified scales are not inspected and approved for accuracy by a government inspection or licensing agency.

Your mover must obtain a separate weight ticket for each weighing. The weigh master must sign each weight ticket. Each weight ticket must contain the following six items:

(1) The complete name and location of the scale.

(2) The date of each weighing.

(3) Identification of the weight entries as being the tare, gross, or net weights.

(4) The company or mover identification of the vehicle.

(5) Your last name as it appears on the Bill of Lading.

(6) Your mover's shipment registration or Bill of Lading number.

Your mover must retain the original weight ticket or tickets relating to the determination of the weight of your shipment as part of its file on your shipment. When both weighings are performed on the same scale, one weight ticket may be used to record both weighings.

Your mover must present all freight bills with true copies of all weight tickets. If your mover does not present its freight bill with all weight tickets, your mover is in violation of Federal law.

Before the driver actually begins unloading your shipment weighed at origin and after your mover informs you of the billing weight and total charges, you have the right to demand a reweigh of your shipment. If you believe the weight is not accurate, you have the right to request your mover reweigh your shipment before unloading.

You have the right, and your mover must inform you of your right, to observe all reweighings of your shipment. Your mover must tell you where and when each reweighing will occur. Your mover must give you a reasonable opportunity to be present to observe the reweighing. You may waive your right to observe any reweighing; however, you must waive that right in writing. You may send the written waiver via fax or

e-mail, as well as by overnight courier or certified mail, return receipt requested. This does not affect any of your other rights under Federal law.

Your mover is prohibited from charging you for the reweighing. If the weight of your shipment at the time of the reweigh is different from the weight determined at origin, your mover must recompute the charges based upon the reweigh weight.

Before requesting a reweigh, you may find it to your advantage to estimate the weight of your shipment using the following three-step method:

1. Count the number of items in your shipment. Usually there will be either 30 or 40 items listed on each page of the inventory. For example, if there are 30 items per page and your inventory consists of four complete pages and a fifth page with 15 items listed, the total number of items will be 135. *If an automobile is listed on the inventory, do not include this item in the count of the total items.*

2. Subtract the weight of any automobile included in your shipment from the total weight of the shipment. If the automobile was not weighed separately, its weight can be found on its title or license receipt.

3. Divide the number of items in your shipment into the weight. If the average weight resulting from this exercise ranges between 35 and 45 pounds (16 and 20 kilograms) per article, it is unlikely a reweigh will prove beneficial to you. In fact, it could result in your paying higher charges.

Experience has shown that the average shipment of household goods will weigh about 40 pounds (18 kilograms) per item. If a shipment contains a large number of heavy items, such as cartons of books, boxes of tools or heavier than average furniture, the average weight per item may be 45 pounds or more (20 kilograms or more).

WHAT MUST MY MOVER DO IF I WANT TO KNOW THE ACTUAL WEIGHT OR CHARGES FOR MY SHIPMENT BEFORE DELIVERY?

If you request notification of the actual weight and charges of your shipment, your mover must comply with your request if it is moving your goods on a collect-on-delivery basis. This requirement is conditioned upon your supplying your mover with an address or telephone number where you will receive the communication. Your mover must make its notification by telephone; fax transmissions; e-mail; overnight courier; certified mail, return receipt requested; or in person.

You must receive the mover's notification at least one full 24-hour day before its scheduled delivery, excluding Saturdays, Sundays, and Federal holidays.

Your mover may disregard this 24-hour notification requirement on shipments subject to one of the following three things:

(1) Back weigh (when your mover weighs your shipment at its destination).

(2) Pickup and delivery encompassing two consecutive weekdays, if you agree.

(3) Maximum payment amounts at time of delivery of 110 percent of the estimated charges, if you agree.

SUBPART F—TRANSPORTATION OF MY SHIPMENT

MUST MY MOVER TRANSPORT THE SHIPMENT IN A TIMELY MANNER?

Yes, your mover must transport your household goods in a timely manner. This is also known as "reasonable dispatch service." Your mover must provide reasonable dispatch service to you, except for transportation on the basis of guaranteed delivery dates.

When your mover is unable to perform either the pickup or delivery of your shipment on the dates or during the periods of time specified in the order for service, your mover must notify you of the delay, at the mover's expense. As soon as the delay becomes apparent to your mover, it must give you notification it will be unable to provide the service specified in the terms of the order for service. Your mover may notify you of the delay in any of the following ways: By telephone; fax transmissions; e-mail; overnight courier; certified mail, return receipt requested; or in person.

When your mover notifies you of a delay, it also must advise you of the dates or periods of time it may be able to pick up and/or deliver the shipment. Your mover must consider your needs in its advisement. Your mover must prepare a written record of the date, time, and manner of its notification.

Your mover must prepare a written record of its amended date or period for delivery. Your mover must retain these records as a part of its file on your shipment. The retention period is one year from the date of notification. Your mover must furnish a copy of the notification to you either by first class mail or in person, if you request a copy of the notice.

Your mover must tender your shipment for delivery on the agreed-upon delivery date or within the period specified on the bill of lading. Upon your request or concurrence, your mover may deliver your shipment on another day.

The establishment of a delayed pickup or delivery date does not relieve your mover from liability for damages resulting from your mover's failure to provide service as agreed. However, when your mover notifies you of alternate delivery dates, it is your responsibility to be available to accept delivery on the dates specified. If you are not available and are not willing to accept delivery, your mover has the right to place your shipment in storage at your expense or hold the shipment on its truck and assess additional charges.

If after the pickup of your shipment, *you* request your mover to change the delivery date, most movers will agree to do so provided your request will not result in unreasonable delay to its equipment or interfere with another customer's move. However, your mover is under no obligation to consent to amended delivery dates. Your mover has the right to place your shipment in storage at your expense if you are unwilling or unable to accept delivery on the date agreed to in the bill of lading.

If your mover fails to pick up and deliver your shipment on the date entered on the bill of lading and you have expenses you otherwise would not have had, you may be able to recover those expenses from your mover. This is what is called an inconvenience or delay claim. Should your mover refuse to honor such a claim and you continue to believe you are entitled to be paid damages, you may take your mover to court under 49 U.S.C. 14706. *The Federal Motor Carrier Safety Administration (FMCSA) has no authority to order your mover to pay such claims.*

While we hope your mover delivers your shipment in a timely manner, you should consider the possibility your shipment may be delayed, and find out what payment you can expect if a mover delays service through its own fault, before you agree with the mover to transport your shipment.

WHAT MUST MY MOVER DO IF IT IS ABLE TO DELIVER MY SHIPMENT MORE THAN 24 HOURS BEFORE I AM ABLE TO ACCEPT DELIVERY?

At your mover's discretion, it may place your shipment in storage. This will be under its own account and at its own expense in a warehouse located in proximity to the destination of your shipment. Your mover may do this if you fail to request or concur with an early delivery date, and your mover is able to deliver your shipment more than 24 hours before your specified date or the first day of your specified period.

If your mover exercises this option, your mover must immediately notify you of the name and address of the warehouse where your mover places your shipment. Your mover must make and keep a record of its notification as a part of its shipment records. Your mover has full responsibility for the shipment under the terms and conditions of the bill of lading. Your mover is responsible for the charges for redelivery, handling, and storage until it makes final delivery. Your mover may limit its responsibility to the agreed-upon delivery date or the first day of the period of delivery as specified in the bill of lading.

WHAT MUST MY MOVER DO FOR ME WHEN I
STORE HOUSEHOLD GOODS IN TRANSIT?

If you request your mover to hold your
household goods in storage-in-transit and
the storage period is about to expire, your
mover must notify you, in writing, about the
four following items:

(1) The date when storage-in-transit will
convert to permanent storage.

(2) The existence of a 9-month period after
the date of conversion to permanent storage,
during which you may file claims against
your mover for loss or damage occurring to
your goods while in transit or during the
storage-in-transit period.

(3) The date your mover's liability will
end.

(4) Your property will be subject to the
rules, regulations, and charges of the warehouseman.

Your mover must make this notification at
least 10 days before the expiration date of
one of the following two periods of time:

(1) The specified period of time when your
mover is to hold your goods in storage.

(2) The maximum period of time provided
in its tariff for storage-in-transit.

Your mover must notify you by facsimile
transmission; overnight courier; e-mail; or
certified mail, return receipt requested.

If your mover holds your household goods
in storage-in-transit for less than 10 days,
your mover must notify you, one day before
the storage-in-transit period expires, of the
same information specified above.

Your mover must maintain a record of all
notifications to you as part of the records of
your shipment. Under the applicable tariff
provisions regarding storage-in-transit, your
mover's failure or refusal to notify you will
automatically extend your mover's liability
until the end of the day following the date
when your mover actually gives you notice.

SUBPART G—DELIVERY OF MY SHIPMENT

MAY MY MOVER ASK ME TO SIGN A DELIVERY
RECEIPT PURPORTING TO RELEASE IT FROM
LIABILITY?

At the time of delivery, your mover will
expect you to sign a receipt for your shipment. Normally, you will sign each page of
your mover's copy of the inventory.

Your mover's delivery receipt or shipping
document must not contain any language
purporting to release or discharge it or its
agents from liability.

Your mover may include a statement
about your receipt of your property in apparent good condition, except as noted on the
shipping documents.

Do not sign the delivery receipt if it contains any language purporting to release or
discharge your mover or its agents from liability. Strike out such language before
signing, or refuse delivery if the driver or

mover refuses to provide a proper delivery
receipt.

WHAT IS THE MAXIMUM COLLECT-ON-DELIVERY
AMOUNT MY MOVER MAY DEMAND I PAY AT
THE TIME OF DELIVERY?

On a binding estimate, the maximum
amount is the exact estimate of the charges,
plus the charges for any additional services
you requested after the bill of lading was executed (charges therefore not included in the
estimate) and any charges for impracticable
operations (not to exceed 15 percent of all
other charges due at delivery). Your mover
must specify on the estimate, order for service, and bill of lading the form of payment
acceptable to it (for example, a certified
check).

On a non-binding estimate, the maximum
amount is 110 percent of the approximate
costs, plus the charges for any additional
services you requested after the bill of lading
was executed (charges therefore not included
in the estimate) and any charges for impracticable operations (not to exceed 15 percent
of all other charges due at delivery). Your
mover must specify on the estimate, order
for service, and bill of lading the form of
payment acceptable to it (for example, cash).

IF MY SHIPMENT IS TRANSPORTED ON MORE
THAN ONE VEHICLE, WHAT CHARGES MAY
MY MOVER COLLECT AT DELIVERY?

Although all movers try to move each
shipment on one truck, it becomes necessary
at times to divide a shipment among two or
more trucks. This frequently occurs when an
automobile is included in the shipment and
transported on a specially designed vehicle.
When this occurs, your transportation
charges are the same as if the entire shipment moved on one truck.

If your shipment is divided for transportation on two or more trucks, the mover
may require payment for each portion as it
is delivered.

Your mover may delay the collection of all
the charges until the entire shipment is delivered, at its discretion, not yours. When
you order your move, you should ask the
mover about its policies in this regard.

IF MY SHIPMENT IS PARTIALLY LOST OR DE-
STROYED, WHAT CHARGES MAY MY MOVER
COLLECT AT DELIVERY?

Movers customarily make every effort to
avoid losing, damaging, or destroying any of
your items while your shipment is in their
possession for transportation. However, despite the precautions taken, articles are
sometimes lost or destroyed during the
move.

In addition to any money you may recover
from your mover to compensate for lost or
destroyed articles, you also may recover the
transportation charges represented by the

portion of the shipment lost or destroyed. Your mover may apply this paragraph only to the transportation of household goods. Your mover may disregard this paragraph if loss or destruction was due to an act or omission by you. Your mover must require you to pay any specific valuation charge due.

For example, if you pack a hazardous material (i.e., gasoline, aerosol cans, motor oil, etc.) and your shipment is partially lost or destroyed by fire in storage or in the mover's trailer, your mover may require you to pay for the full cost of transportation.

If your shipment is partially lost or destroyed, your mover is permitted to collect at delivery only a prorated percentage based on the freight charges for the goods actually delivered, plus the charges for any additional services you requested after the bill of lading was executed and any charges for impracticable operations. Charges for impracticable operations collected at delivery must not exceed 15 percent of the total charges your mover collects at delivery.

Your mover is forbidden from collecting, or requiring you to pay, any freight charges (including any charges for accessorial or terminal services) when your household goods shipment is *totally lost or destroyed* in transit, unless the loss or destruction was due to an act or omission by you.

HOW MUST MY MOVER CALCULATE THE CHARGES APPLICABLE TO THE SHIPMENT AS DELIVERED?

Your mover must multiply the percentage equal to the weight of the portion of the shipment delivered to the total weight of the shipment times the total charges applicable to the shipment tendered by you to obtain the total charges it must collect from you.

If your mover's computed charges exceed the charges otherwise applicable to the shipment as delivered, the lesser of those charges must apply. This will apply only to the transportation of your household goods.

Your mover must require you to pay any specific valuation charge due.

Your mover may not refund the freight charges if the loss or destruction was due to an act or omission by you. For example, you fail to disclose to your mover that your shipment contains perishable live plants. Your mover may disregard its loss or destruction of your plants because you failed to inform your mover you were transporting live plants.

Your mover must determine, at its own expense, the proportion of the shipment, based on actual or constructive weight, not lost or destroyed in transit.

Your rights are in addition to, and not in lieu of, any other rights you may have with respect to your shipment of household goods your mover lost or destroyed, or partially lost or destroyed, in transit. This applies whether or not you have exercised your rights provided above.

SUBPART H—COLLECTION OF CHARGES

DOES THIS SUBPART APPLY TO MOST SHIPMENTS?

It applies to all shipments of household goods that involve a balance due freight or expense bill or are shipped on credit.

HOW MUST MY MOVER PRESENT ITS FREIGHT OR EXPENSE BILL TO ME?

At the time of payment of transportation charges, your mover must give you a freight bill identifying the service provided and the charge for each service. It is customary for most movers to use a copy of the bill of lading as a freight bill; however, some movers use an entirely separate document for this purpose.

Except in those instances where a shipment is moving on a binding estimate, the freight bill must specifically identify each service performed, the rate or charge per service performed, and the total charges for each service. *If this information is not on the freight bill, do not accept or pay the freight bill.*

Movers' tariffs customarily specify that freight charges must be paid in cash, by certified check, or by cashier's check. When this requirement exists, the mover will not accept personal checks. At the time you order your move, you should ask your mover about the form of payment your mover requires.

Some movers permit payment of freight charges by use of a charge or credit card. However, do not assume your nationally recognized charge, credit, or debit card will be acceptable for payment. Ask your mover at the time you request an estimate. Your mover must specify the form of payment it will accept at delivery.

If you do not pay the transportation charges at the time of delivery, your mover has the right, under the bill of lading, to refuse to deliver your goods. The mover may place them in storage, at your expense, until the charges are paid. However, the mover must deliver your goods upon payment of 100 percent of a binding estimate, plus the charges for any additional services you requested after the bill of lading was executed (charges therefore not included in the estimate) and any charges for impracticable operations (not to exceed 15 percent of all other charges due at delivery).

If, before payment of the transportation charges, you discover an error in the charges, you should attempt to correct the error with the driver or the mover's local agent, or by contacting the mover's main office. If an error is discovered after payment, you should write the mover (the address will be on the freight bill) explaining the error, and request a refund.

Movers customarily check all shipment files and freight bills after a move has been completed to make sure the charges were accurate. If an overcharge is found, you should be notified and a refund should be made. If an undercharge occurred, you may be billed for the additional charges due.

On "to be prepaid" shipments, your mover must present its freight bill for all transportation charges within 15 days of the date your mover received the shipment. This period excludes Saturdays, Sundays, and Federal holidays.

On "collect" shipments, your mover must present its freight bill for all transportation charges on the date of delivery, or, at its discretion, within 15 days, calculated from the date the shipment was delivered at your destination. This period excludes Saturdays, Sundays, and Federal holidays. (Bills for additional charges based on the weight of the shipment will be presented 30 days after delivery; charges for impracticable operations not paid at delivery are due within 30 days of the invoice.) Your mover's freight bills and accompanying written notices must state the following five items:

(1) Penalties for late payment.
(2) Credit time limits.
(3) Service or finance charges.
(4) Collection expense charges.
(5) Discount terms.

If your mover extends credit to you, freight bills or a separate written notice accompanying a freight bill or a group of freight bills presented at one time must state, "You may be subject to tariff penalties for failure to timely pay freight charges," or a similar statement. Your mover must state on its freight bills or other notices when it expects payment and any applicable service charges, collection expense charges, and discount terms.

When your mover lacks sufficient information to compute its tariff charges at the time of billing, your mover must present its freight bill for payment within 15 days following the day when sufficient information becomes available. This period excludes Saturdays, Sundays, and Federal holidays.

Your mover must not extend additional credit to you if you fail to furnish sufficient information to your mover. Your mover must have sufficient information to render a freight bill within a reasonable time after shipment.

When your mover presents freight bills by mail, it must deem the time of mailing to be the time of presentation of the bills. The term "freight bills," as used in this paragraph, includes both paper documents and billing by use of electronic media such as computer tapes, disks, or the Internet (e-mail).

When you mail acceptable checks or drafts in payment of freight charges, your mover must deem the act of mailing the payment within the credit period to be the proper collection of the tariff charges within the credit period for the purposes of Federal law. In case of a dispute as to the date of mailing, your mover must accept the postmark as the date of mailing.

IF I FORCED MY MOVER TO RELINQUISH A COLLECT-ON-DELIVERY SHIPMENT BEFORE THE PAYMENT OF ALL CHARGES, HOW MUST MY MOVER COLLECT THE BALANCE?

On "collect-on-delivery" shipments, your mover must present its freight bill for transportation charges within 15 days, calculated from the date the shipment was delivered at your destination. This period excludes Saturdays, Sundays, and Federal holidays. (Bills for additional charges based on the weight of the shipment will be presented 30 days after delivery; charges for impracticable operations not paid at delivery are due within 30 days of the invoice.)

WHAT ACTIONS MAY MY MOVER TAKE TO COLLECT FROM ME THE CHARGES IN ITS FREIGHT BILL?

Your mover must present a freight bill within 15 days (excluding Saturdays, Sundays, and Federal holidays) of the date of delivery of a shipment at your destination. (Bills for additional charges based on the weight of the shipment will be presented 30 days after delivery; charges for impracticable operations not paid at delivery are due within 30 days of the invoice.)

Your mover must provide in its tariffs the following three things:

(1) A provision indicating its credit period is a total of 30 calendar days.

(2) A provision indicating you will be assessed a service charge by your mover equal to one percent of the amount of the freight bill, subject to a $20 minimum charge, for the extension of the credit period. The mover will assess the service charge for each 30-day extension that the charges go unpaid.

(3) A provision that your mover must deny credit to you if you fail to pay a duly presented freight bill within the 30-day period. Your mover may grant credit to you, at its discretion, when you satisfy your mover's condition that you will pay all future freight bills duly presented. Your mover must ensure all your payments of freight bills are strictly in accordance with Federal rules and regulations for the settlement of its rates and charges.

DO I HAVE A RIGHT TO FILE A CLAIM TO RECOVER MONEY FOR PROPERTY MY MOVER LOST OR DAMAGED?

Should your move result in the loss of or damage to any of your property, you have the right to file a claim with your mover to recover money for such loss or damage.

You should file a claim as soon as possible. If you fail to file a claim within 9 months, your mover may not be required to accept your claim. If you institute a court action and win, you may be entitled to attorney's fees if you submitted your claim to the carrier within 120 days after delivery or the scheduled date of delivery (whichever is later), and (1) the mover did not advise you during the claim settlement process of the availability of arbitration as a means for resolving the dispute; (2) a decision was not rendered through arbitration within the time required by law; or (3) you are instituting a court action to enforce an arbitration decision with which the mover has not complied.

While the Federal Government maintains regulations governing the processing of loss and damage claims (49 CFR part 370), it cannot resolve those claims. If you cannot settle a claim with the mover, you may file a civil action to recover your claim in court under 49 U.S.C. 14706. You may obtain the name and address of the mover's agent for service of legal process in your State by contacting the Federal Motor Carrier Safety Administration. You may also obtain the name of a process agent via the Internet. Go to *http://www.fmcsa.dot.gov* then click on Licensing and Insurance (L&I) section.

In addition, your mover must participate in an arbitration program. As described earlier in this pamphlet, an arbitration program gives you the opportunity to settle, through a neutral arbitrator, certain types of unresolved loss or damage claims and disputes regarding charges that were billed to you by your mover after your shipment was delivered. You may find submitting your claim to arbitration under such a program to be a less expensive and more convenient way to seek recovery of your claim. Your mover is required to provide you with information about its arbitration program before you move. If your mover fails to do so, ask the mover for details of its program.

SUBPART I—RESOLVING DISPUTES WITH MY MOVER

WHAT MAY I DO TO RESOLVE DISPUTES WITH MY MOVER?

The Federal Motor Carrier Safety Administration Does Not Help You Settle Your Dispute With Your Mover

Generally, you must resolve your own loss and damage disputes with your mover. You enter a contractual arrangement with your mover. You are bound by each of the following three things:

(1) The terms and conditions you negotiated before your move.

(2) The terms and conditions you accepted when you signed the bill of lading.

(3) The terms and conditions you accepted when you signed for delivery of your goods.

You have the right to take your mover to court. We require your mover to offer you arbitration to settle your disputes with it.

[72 FR 36775, July 5, 2007]

PART 376—LEASE AND INTERCHANGE OF VEHICLES

Subpart A—General Applicability and Definitions

Sec.
376.1 Applicability.
376.2 Definitions.

Subpart B—Leasing Regulations

376.11 General leasing requirements.
376.12 Written lease requirements.

Subpart C—Exemptions for the Leasing Regulations

376.21 General exemptions.
376.22 Exemption for private carrier leasing and leasing between authorized carriers.
376.26 Exemption for leases between authorized carriers and their agents.

Subpart D—Interchange Regulations

376.31 Interchange of equipment.

Subpart E—Private Carriers and Shippers

376.42 Lease of equipment by regulated carriers.

AUTHORITY: 49 U.S.C. 13301 and 14102; and 49 CFR 1.73.

SOURCE: 44 FR 4681, Jan. 23, 1979, unless otherwise noted. Redesignated at 61 FR 54707, Oct. 21, 1996.

EDITORIAL NOTE: Nomenclature changes to part 376 appear at 66 FR 49871, Oct. 1, 2001.

Subpart A—General Applicability and Definitions

§376.1 Applicability.

The regulations in this part apply to the following actions by motor carriers registered with the Secretary to transport property:

(a) The leasing of equipment with which to perform transportation regulated by the Secretary.

(b) The leasing of equipment to motor private carrier or shippers.

(c) The interchange of equipment between motor common carriers in the performance of transportation regulated by the Secretary.

[44 FR 4681, Jan. 23, 1979. Redesignated at 61 FR 54707, Oct. 21, 1996, as amended at 62 FR 15423, Apr. 1, 1997]

§ 376.2 Definitions.

(a) *Authorized carrier.* A person or persons authorized to engage in the transportation of property as a motor carrier under the provisions of 49 U.S.C. 13901 and 13902.

(b) *Equipment.* A motor vehicle, straight truck, tractor, semitrailer, full trailer, any combination of these and any other type of equipment used by authorized carriers in the transportation of property for hire.

(c) *Interchange.* The receipt of equipment by one motor common carrier of property from another such carrier, at a point which both carriers are authorized to serve, with which to continue a through movement.

(d) *Owner.* A person (1) to whom title to equipment has been issued, or (2) who, without title, has the right to exclusive use of equipment, or (3) who has lawful possession of equipment registered and licensed in any State in the name of that person.

(e) *Lease.* A contract or arrangement in which the owner grants the use of equipment, with or without driver, for a specified period to an authorized carrier for use in the regulated transportation of property, in exchange for compensation.

(f) *Lessor.* In a lease, the party granting the use of equipment, with or without driver, to another.

(g) *Lessee.* In a lease, the party acquiring the use of equipment with or without driver, from another.

(h) *Sublease.* A written contract in which the lessee grants the use of leased equipment, with or without driver, to another.

(i) *Addendum.* A supplement to an existing lease which is not effective until signed by the lessor and lessee.

(j) *Private carrier.* A person, other than a motor carrier, transporting property by motor vehicle in interstate or foreign commerce when (1) the person is the owner, lessee, or bailee of the property being transported; and (2) the property is being transported for sale, lease, rent, or bailment, or to further a commercial enterprise.

(k) *Shipper.* A person who sends or receives property which is transported in interstate or foreign commerce.

(l) *Escrow fund.* Money deposited by the lessor with either a third party or the lessee to guarantee performance, to repay advances, to cover repair expenses, to handle claims, to handle license and State permit costs, and for any other purposes mutually agreed upon by the lessor and lessee.

(m) *Detention.* The holding by a consignor or consignee of a trailer, with or without power unit and driver, beyond the free time allocated for the shipment, under circumstances not attributable to the performance of the carrier.

[44 FR 4681, Jan. 23, 1979, as amended at 49 FR 47850, Dec. 7, 1984; 62 FR 15424, Apr. 1, 1997]

Subpart B—Leasing Regulations

§ 376.11 General leasing requirements.

Other than through the interchange of equipment as set forth in § 376.31, and under the exemptions set forth in subpart C of these regulations, the authorized carrier may perform authorized transportation in equipment it does not own only under the following conditions:

(a) *Lease.* There shall be a written lease granting the use of the equipment and meeting the requirements contained in § 376.12.

(b) *Receipts for equipment.* Receipts, specifically identifying the equipment to be leased and stating the date and time of day possession is transferred, shall be given as follows:

(1) When possession of the equipment is taken by the authorized carrier, it shall give the owner of the equipment a receipt. The receipt identified in this section may be transmitted by mail, telegraph, or other similar means of communication.

(2) When possession of the equipment by the authorized carrier ends, a receipt shall be given in accordance with the terms of the lease agreement if the lease agreement requires a receipt.

(3) Authorized representatives of the carrier and the owner may take possession of leased equipment and give and

receive the receipts required under this subsection.

(c) *Identification of equipment.* The authorized carrier acquiring the use of equipment under this section shall identify the equipment as being in its service as follows:

(1) During the period of the lease, the carrier shall identify the equipment in accordance with the FMCSA's requirements in 49 CFR part 390 of this chapter (Identification of Vehicles).

(2) Unless a copy of the lease is carried on the equipment, the authorized carrier shall keep a statement with the equipment during the period of the lease certifying that the equipment is being operated by it. The statement shall also specify the name of the owner, the date and length of the lease, any restrictions in the lease relative to the commodities to be transported, and the address at which the original lease is kept by the authorized carrier. This statement shall be prepared by the authorized carrier or its authorized representative.

(d) *Records of equipment.* The authorized carrier using equipment leased under this section shall keep records of the equipment as follows:

(1) The authorized carrier shall prepare and keep documents covering each trip for which the equipment is used in its service. These documents shall contain the name and address of the owner of the equipment, the point of origin, the time and date of departure, and the point of final destination. Also, the authorized carrier shall carry papers with the leased equipment during its operation containing this information and identifying the lading and clearly indicating that the transportation is under its responsibility. These papers shall be preserved by the authorized carrier as part of its transportation records. Leases which contain the information required by the provisions in this paragraph may be used and retained instead of such documents or papers. As to lease agreements negotiated under a master lease, this provision is complied with by having a copy of a master lease in the unit of equipment in question and where the balance f documentation called for by this paragraph is included in the freight documents prepared for the specific movement.

(2) [Reserved]

[44 FR 4681, Jan. 23, 1979, as amended at 49 FR 47269, Dec. 3, 1984; 49 FR 47850, Dec. 7, 1984; 50 FR 24649, June 12, 1985; 51 FR 37406, Oct. 22, 1986; 62 FR 15424, Apr. 1, 1997]

§376.12 Written lease requirements.

Except as provided in the exemptions set forth in subpart C of this part, the written lease required under §376.11(a) shall contain the following provisions. The required lease provisions shall be adhered to and performed by the authorized carrier.

(a) *Parties.* The lease shall be made between the authorized carrier and the owner of the equipment. The lease shall be signed by these parties or by their authorized representatives.

(b) *Duration to be specific.* The lease shall specify the time and date or the circumstances on which the lease begins and ends. These times or circumstances shall coincide with the times for the giving of receipts required by §376.11(b).

(c) *Exclusive possession and responsibilities.* (1) The lease shall provide that the authorized carrier lessee shall have exclusive possession, control, and use of the equipment for the duration of the lease. The lease shall further provide that the authorized carrier lessee shall assume complete responsibility for the operation of the equipment for the duration of the lease.

(2) Provision may be made in the lease for considering the authorized carrier lessee as the owner of the equipment for the purpose of subleasing it under these regulations to other authorized carriers during the lease.

(3) When an authorized carrier of household goods leases equipment for the transportation of household goods, as defined by the Secretary, the parties may provide in the lease that the provisions required by paragraph (c)(1) of this section apply only during the time the equipment is operated by or for the authorized carrier lessee.

(4) Nothing in the provisions required by paragraph (c)(1) of this section is intended to affect whether the lessor or driver provided by the lessor is an independent contractor or an employee of the authorized carrier lessee. An independent contractor relationship may

135

exist when a carrier lessee complies with 49 U.S.C. 14102 and attendant administrative requirements.

(d) *Compensation to be specified.* The amount to be paid by the authorized carrier for equipment and driver's services shall be clearly stated on the face of the lease or in an addendum which is attached to the lease. Such lease or addendum shall be delivered to the lessor prior to the commencement of any trip in the service of the authorized carrier. An authorized representative of the lessor may accept these documents. The amount to be paid may be expressed as a percentage of gross revenue, a flat rate per mile, a variable rate depending on the direction traveled or the type of commodity transported, or by any other method of compensation mutually agreed upon by the parties to the lease. The compensation stated on the lease or in the attached addendum may apply to equipment and driver's services either separately or as a combined amount.

(e) *Items specified in lease.* The lease shall clearly specify which party is responsible for removing identification devices from the equipment upon the termination of the lease and when and how these devices, other than those painted directly on the equipment, will be returned to the carrier. The lease shall clearly specify the manner in which a receipt will be given to the authorized carrier by the equipment owner when the latter retakes possession of the equipment upon termination of the lease agreement, if a receipt is required at all by the lease. The lease shall clearly specify the responsibility of each party with respect to the cost of fuel, fuel taxes, empty mileage, permits of all types, tolls, ferries, detention and accessorial services, base plates and licenses, and any unused portions of such items. The lease shall clearly specify who is responsible for loading and unloading the property onto and from the motor vehicle, and the compensation, if any, to be paid for this service. Except when the violation results from the acts or omissions of the lessor, the authorized carrier lessee shall assume the risks and costs of fines for overweight and oversize trailers when the trailers are pre-loaded, sealed, or the load is containerized, or when the trailer or lading is otherwise outside of the lessor's control, and for improperly permitted overdimension and overweight loads and shall reimburse the lessor for any fines paid by the lessor. If the authorized carrier is authorized to receive a refund or a credit for base plates purchased by the lessor from, and issued in the name of, the authorized carrier, or if the base plates are authorized to be sold by the authorized carrier to another lessor the authorized carrier shall refund to the initial lessor on whose behalf the base plate was first obtained a prorated share of the amount received.

(f) *Payment period.* The lease shall specify that payment to the lessor shall be made within 15 days after submission of the necessary delivery documents and other paperwork concerning a trip in the service of the authorized carrier. The paperwork required before the lessor can receive payment is limited to log books required by the Department of Transportation and those documents necessary for the authorized carrier to secure payment from the shipper. In addition, the lease may provide that, upon termination of the lease agreement, as a condition precedent to payment, the lessor shall remove all identification devices of the authorized carrier and, except in the case of identification painted directly on equipment, return them to the carrier. If the identification device has been lost or stolen, a letter certifying its removal will satisfy this requirement. Until this requirement is complied with, the carrier may withhold final payment. The authorized carrier may require the submission of additional documents by the lessor but not as a prerequisite to payment. Payment to the lessor shall not be made contingent upon submission of a bill of lading to which no exceptions have been taken. The authorized carrier shall not set time limits for the submission by the lessor of required delivery documents and other paperwork.

(g) *Copies of freight bill or other form of freight documentation.* When a lessor's revenue is based on a percentage of the gross revenue for a shipment, the lease must specify that the authorized carrier will give the lessor, before or at the time of settlement, a copy of the rated freight bill or a computer-generated document containing the same information, or, in the case of contract carriers, any other form of documentation actually used for a shipment containing the same information that would appear on a rated freight bill. When a computer-generated document is provided, the lease will permit lessor to view, during normal business hours, a copy of any actual document underlying the computer-generated document. Regardless of the method of compensation, the lease must permit lessor to examine copies of the carrier's tariff or, in the case of contract carriers, other documents from which rates and charges are computed, provided that where rates and charges are computed from a contract of a contract carrier, only those portions of the contract containing the same information that would appear on a rated freight bill need be disclosed. The authorized carrier may delete the names of shippers and consignees shown on the freight bill or other form of documentation.

(h) *Charge-back items.* The lease shall clearly specify all items that may be initially paid for by the authorized carrier, but ultimately deducted from the lessor's compensation at the time of payment or settlement, together with a recitation as to how the amount of each item is to be computed. The lessor shall be afforded copies of those documents which are necessary to determine the validity of the charge.

(i) *Products, equipment, or services from authorized carrier.* The lease shall specify that the lessor is not required to purchase or rent any products, equipment, or services from the authorized carrier as a condition of entering into the lease arrangement. The lease shall specify the terms of any agreement in which the lessor is a party to an equipment purchase or rental contract which gives the authorized carrier the right to make deductions from the lessor's compensation for purchase or rental payments.

(j) *Insurance.* (1) The lease shall clearly specify the legal obligation of the authorized carrier to maintain insurance coverage for the protection of the public pursuant to FMCSA regulations under 49 U.S.C. 13906. The lease shall

further specify who is responsible for providing any other insurance coverage for the operation of the leased equipment, such as bobtail insurance. If the authorized carrier will make a charge back to the lessor for any of this insurance, the lease shall specify the amount which will be charged-back to the lessor.

(2) If the lessor purchases any insurance coverage for the operation of the leased equipment from or through the authorized carrier, the lease shall specify that the authorized carrier will provide the lessor with a copy of each policy upon the request of the lessor. Also, where the lessor purchases such insurance in this manner, the lease shall specify that the authorized carrier will provide the lessor with a certificate of insurance for each such policy. Each certificate of insurance shall include the name of the insurer, the policy number, the effective dates of the policy, the amounts and types of coverage, the cost to the lessor for each type of coverage, and the deductible amount for each type of coverage for which the lessor may be liable.

(3) The lease shall clearly specify the conditions under which deductions for cargo or property damage may be made from the lessor's settlements. The lease shall further specify that the authorized carrier must provide the lessor with a written explanation and itemization of any deductions for cargo or property damage made from any compensation of money owed to the lessor. The written explanation and itemization must be delivered to the lessor before any deductions are made.

(k) *Escrow funds.* If escrow funds are required, the lease shall specify:

(1) The amount of any escrow fund or performance bond required to be paid by the lessor to the authorized carrier or to a third party.

(2) The specific items to which the escrow fund can be applied.

(3) That while the escrow fund is under the control of the authorized carrier, the authorized carrier shall provide an accounting to the lessor of any transactions involving such fund. The carrier shall perform this accounting in one of the following ways:

(i) By clearly indicating in individual settlement sheets the amount and description of any deduction or addition made to the escrow fund; or

(ii) By providing a separate accounting to the lessor of any transactions involving the escrow fund. This separate accounting shall be done on a monthly basis.

(4) The right of the lessor to demand to have an accounting for transactions involving the escrow fund at any time.

(5) That while the escrow fund is under the control of the carrier, the carrier shall pay interest on the escrow fund on at least a quarterly basis. For purposes of calculating the balance of the escrow fund on which interest must be paid, the carrier may deduct a sum equal to the average advance made to the individual lessor during the period of time for which interest is paid. The interest rate shall be established on the date the interest period begins and shall be at least equal to the average yield or equivalent coupon issue yield on 91-day, 13-week Treasury bills as established in the weekly auction by the Department of Treasury.

(6) The conditions the lessor must fulfill in order to have the escrow fund returned. At the time of the return of the escrow fund, the authorized carrier may deduct monies for those obligations incurred by the lessor which have been previously specified in the lease, and shall provide a final accounting to the lessor of all such final deductions made to the escrow fund. The lease shall further specify that in no event shall the escrow fund be returned later than 45 days from the date of termination.

(l) *Copies of the lease.* An original and two copies of each lease shall be signed by the parties. The authorized carrier shall keep the original and shall place a copy of the lease on the equipment during the period of the lease unless a statement as provided for in § 376.11(c)(2) is carried on the equipment instead. The owner of the equipment shall keep the other copy of the lease.

(m) This paragraph applies to owners who are not agents but whose equipment is used by an agent of an authorized carrier in providing transportation on behalf of that authorized carrier. In this situation, the authorized carrier is obligated to ensure that these owners receive all the rights and benefits due an owner under the leasing regulations, especially those set forth in paragraphs (d)–(k) of this section. This is true regardless of whether the lease for the equipment is directly between the authorized carrier and its agent rather than directly between the authorized carrier and each of these owners. The lease between an authorized carrier and its agent shall specify this obligation.

[44 FR 4681, Jan. 23, 1979, as amended at 45 FR 13092, Feb. 28, 1980; 47 FR 28398, June 30, 1982; 47 FR 51140, Nov. 12, 1982; 47 FR 54083, Dec. 1, 1982; 49 FR 47851, Dec. 7, 1984; 51 FR 37406, 37407, Oct. 22, 1986; 52 FR 2412, Jan. 22, 1987; 57 FR 32905, July 24, 1992; 62 FR 15424, Apr. 1, 1997]

Subpart C—Exemptions for the Leasing Regulations

§ 376.21 General exemptions.

Except for § 376.11(c) which requires the identification of equipment, the leasing regulations in this part shall not apply to:

(a) Equipment used in substituted motor-for-rail transportation of railroad freight moving between points that are railroad stations and on railroad billing.

(b) Equipment used in transportation performed exclusively within any commercial zone as defined by the Secretary.

(c) Equipment leased without drivers from a person who is principally engaged in such a business.

(d) Any type of trailer not drawn by a power unit leased from the same lessor.

[44 FR 4681, Jan. 23, 1979. Redesignated at 61 FR 54707, Oct. 21, 1996, as amended at 62 FR 15424, Apr. 1, 1997]

§ 376.22 Exemption for private carrier leasing and leasing between authorized carriers.

Regardless of the leasing regulations set forth in this part, an authorized carrier may lease equipment to or from another authorized carrier, or a private carrier may lease equipment to an authorized carrier under the following conditions:

(a) The identification of equipment requirements in §376.11(c) must be complied with;

(b) The lessor must own the equipment or hold it under a lease;

(c) There must be a written agreement between the authorized carriers or between the private carrier and authorized carrier, as the case may be, concerning the equipment as follows:

(1) It must be signed by the parties or their authorized representatives.

(2) It must provide that control and responsibility for the operation of the equipment shall be that of the lessee from the time possession is taken by the lessee and the receipt required under §376.11(b) is given to the lessor until:

(i) Possession of the equipment is returned to the lessor and the receipt required under §376.11(b) is received by the authorized carrier; or

(ii) In the event that the agreement is between authorized carriers, possession of the equipment is returned to the lessor or given to another authorized carrier in an interchange of equipment.

(3) A copy of the agreement must be carried in the equipment while it is in the possession of the lessee.

(4) Nothing in this section shall prohibit the use, by authorized carriers, private carriers, and all other entities conducting lease operations pursuant to this section, of a master lease if a copy of that master lease is carried in the equipment while it is in the possession of the lessee, and if the master lease complies with the provisions of this section and receipts are exchanged in accordance with §376.11(b), and if records of the equipment are prepared and maintained in accordance with §376.11(d).

(d) Authorized and private carriers under common ownership and control may lease equipment to each other under this section without complying with the requirements of paragraph (a) of this section pertaining to identification of equipment, and the requirements of paragraphs (c)(2) and (c)(4) of this section pertaining to equipment receipts. The leasing of equipment be-

tween such carriers will be subject to all other requirements of this section.

[49 FR 9570, Mar. 14, 1984, as amended at 49 FR 47269, Dec. 3, 1984; 49 FR 47851, Dec. 7, 1984; 62 FR 15424, Apr. 1, 1997; 63 FR 40838, July 31, 1998]

§376.26 Exemption for leases between authorized carriers and their agents.

The leasing regulations set forth in §376.12(e) through (l) do not apply to leases between authorized carriers and their agents.

[47 FR 28398, June 30, 1982, as amended at 62 FR 15424, Apr. 1, 1997]

Subpart D—Interchange Regulations

§376.31 Interchange of equipment.

Authorized common carriers may interchange equipment under the following conditions:

(a) *Interchange agreement.* There shall be a written contract, lease, or other arrangement providing for the interchange and specifically describing the equipment to be interchanged. This written agreement shall set forth the specific points of interchange, how the equipment is to be used, and the compensation for such use. The interchange agreement shall be signed by the parties or by their authorized representatives.

(b) *Operating authority.* The carriers participating in the interchange shall be registered with the Secretary to provide the transportation of the commodities at the point where the physical exchange occurs.

(c) *Through bills of lading.* The traffic transported in interchange service must move on through bills of lading issued by the originating carrier. The rates charged and the revenues collected must be accounted for in the same manner as if there had been no interchange. Charges for the use of the interchanged equipment shall be kept separate from divisions of the joint rates or the proportions of such rates accruing to the carriers by the application of local or proportional rates.

(d) *Identification of equipment.* The authorized common carrier receiving the equipment shall identify equipment operated by it in interchange service as follows:

(1) The authorized common carrier shall identify power units in accordance with the FMCSA's requirements in 49 CFR part 390 of this chapter (Identification of Vehicles). Before giving up possession of the equipment, the carrier shall remove all identification showing it as the operating carrier.

(2) Unless a copy of the interchange agreement is carried on the equipment, the authorized common carrier shall carry a statement with each vehicle during interchange service certifying that it is operating the equipment. The statement shall also identify the equipment by company or State registration number and shall show the specific point of interchange, the date and time it assumes responsibility for the equipment, and the use to be made of the equipment. This statement shall be signed by the parties to the interchange agreement or their authorized representatives. The requirements of this paragraph shall not apply where the equipment to be operated in interchange service consists only of trailers or semitrailers.

(3) Authorized carriers under common ownership and control may interchange equipment with each other without complying with the requirements of paragraph (d)(1) of this section pertaining to removal of identification from equipment.

(e) *Connecting carriers considered as owner*—An authorized carrier receiving equipment in connection with a through movement shall be considered to be the owner of the equipment for the purpose of leasing the equipment to other authorized carriers in furtherance of the movement to destination or the return of the equipment after the movement is completed.

[44 FR 4681, Jan. 23, 1979. Redesignated at 61 FR 54707, Oct. 21, 1996, as amended at 62 FR 15424, Apr. 1, 1997; 63 FR 40838, July 31, 1998]

Subpart E—Private Carriers and Shippers

§ 376.42 Lease of equipment by regulated carriers.

Authorized carriers may lease equipment and drivers from private carriers,

for periods of less than 30 days, in the manner set forth in § 376.22.

[49 FR 9570, Mar. 14, 1984, as amended at 51 FR 37034, Oct. 17, 1986; 62 FR 15424, Apr. 1, 1997]

PART 377—PAYMENT OF TRANSPORTATION CHARGES

Subpart A—Handling of C.O.D. Shipments

Sec.
377.101 Applicability.
377.103 Tariff requirements.
377.105 Collection and remittance.

Subpart B—Extension of Credit to Shippers by Motor Common Carriers, Water Common Carriers, and Household Goods Freight Forwarders

377.201 Scope.
377.203 Extension of credit to shippers.
377.205 Presentation of freight bills.
377.207 Effect of mailing freight bills or payments.
377.209 Additional charges.
377.211 Computation of time.
377.213–377.215 [Reserved]
377.217 Interline settlement of revenues.

AUTHORITY: 49 U.S.C. 13101, 13301, 13701, 13702, 13706, 13707, and 14101; and 49 CFR 1.73.

EDITORIAL NOTE: Nomenclature changes to part 377 appear at 66 FR 49871, Oct. 1, 2001.

Subpart A—Handling of C.O.D. Shipments

SOURCE: 32 FR 20050, Dec. 20, 1967, unless otherwise noted. Redesignated at 61 FR 54708, Oct. 21, 1996.

§ 377.101 Applicability.

The rules and regulations in this part apply to the transportation by motor vehicle of c.o.d. shipments by all common carriers of property subject to 49 U.S.C. 13702, except such transportation which is auxiliary to or supplemental of transportation by railroad and performed on railroad bills of lading, and except such transportation which is performed for freight forwarders and on freight forwarder bills of lading.

[32 FR 20050, Dec. 20, 1967. Redesignated at 61 FR 54708, Oct. 21, 1996, as amended at 62 FR 15424, Apr. 1, 1997]

§377.103 Tariff requirements.

No common carrier of property subject to the provisions of 49 U.S.C. 13702, except as otherwise provided in §377.101, shall render any c.o.d. service unless such carrier has published, posted and filed tariffs which contain the rates, charges and rules governing such service, which rules shall conform to the regulations in this part.

[32 FR 20050, Dec. 20, 1967. Redesignated at 61 FR 54708, Oct. 21, 1996, as amended at 62 FR 15424, Apr. 1, 1997]

§377.105 Collection and remittance.

Every common carrier of property subject to 49 U.S.C. 13702, except as otherwise provided in §377.101, which chooses to provide c.o.d. service may publish and maintain, or cause to be published and maintained for its account, a tariff or tariffs which set forth nondiscriminatory rules governing c.o.d. service and the collection and remittance of c.o.d. funds. Alternatively, any carrier that provides c.o.d. service, but does not wish to publish and maintain, or cause to be published and maintained, its own nondiscriminatory tariff, may adopt a rule requiring remittance of each c.o.d. collection directly to the consignor or other person designated by the consignor as payee within fifteen (15) days after delivery of the c.o.d. shipment to the consignee.

[52 FR 45966, Dec. 3, 1987, as amended at 62 FR 15424, Apr. 1, 1997]

Subpart B—Extension of Credit to Shippers by Motor Common Carriers, Water Common Carriers, and Household Goods Freight Forwarders

SOURCE: 50 FR 2290, Jan. 16, 1985, unless otherwise noted. Redesignated at 61 FR 54709, Oct. 21, 1996.

§377.201 Scope.

(a) *General.* These regulations apply to the extension of credit in the transportation of property under Federal Motor Carrier Safety Administration regulation by motor carriers and household goods freight forwarders, except as otherwise provided.

(b) *Exceptions.* These regulations do not apply to—

(1) Contract carriage operations.

(2) Transportation for—

(i) The United States or any department, bureau, or agency thereof,

(ii) Any State, or political subdivision thereof,

(iii) The District of Columbia.

(3) Property transportation incidental to passenger operations.

[50 FR 2290, Jan. 16, 1985, as amended at 51 FR 44297, Dec. 9, 1986; 62 FR 15424, Apr. 1, 1997]

§377.203 Extension of credit to shippers.

(a) *Authorization to extend credit.* (1) A carrier that meets the requirements in paragraph (a)(2) of this section may—

(i) Relinquish possession of freight in advance of the payment of the tariff charges, and

(ii) Extend credit in the amount of such charges to those who undertake to pay them (such persons are called *shippers* in this part).

(2) For such authorization, the carrier shall take reasonable actions to assure payment of the tariff charges within the credit periods specified—

(i) In this part, or

(ii) In tariff provisions published pursuant to the regulations in paragraph (d) of this section.

(b) *When the credit period begins.* The credit period shall begin on the day following presentation of the freight bill.

(c) *Length of credit period.* Unless a different credit period has been established by tariff publication pursuant to paragraph (d) of this section, the credit period is 15 days. It includes Saturdays, Sundays, and legal holidays.

(d) *Carriers may establish different credit periods in tariff rules.* Carriers may publish tariff rules establishing credit periods different from those in paragraph (c) of this section. Such credit periods shall not be longer than 30 calendar days.

(e) *Service charges.* (1) Service charges shall not apply when credit is extended and payments are made within the standard credit period. The term *standard credit period,* as used in the preceding sentence, means—

(i) The credit period prescribed in paragraph (c) of this section, or

141

(ii) A substitute credit period published in a tariff rule pursuant to the authorization in paragraph (d) of this section.

(2) Carriers may, by tariff rule, extend credit for an additional time period, subject if they wish to a service charge for that additional time. The combined length of the carrier's standard credit period (as defined in paragraph (e)(1) of this section) and its additional credit period shall not exceed the 30-day maximum credit period prescribed in paragraph (d) of this section. When such a tariff rule is in effect, shippers may elect to postpone payment until the end of the extended credit period if, in consideration therefor, they include any published service charges when making their payment.

(3) Carriers may, by tariff rule, establish service charges for payments made after the expiration of an authorized credit period. Such a rule shall—

(i) Institute such charges on the day following the last day of an authorized credit period, and

(ii) Notify shippers—

(A) That its only purpose is to prevent a shipper who does not pay on time from having free use of funds due to the carrier,

(B) That it does not sanction payment delays, and

(C) That failure to pay within the authorized credit period will, despite this provision for such charges, continue to require the carrier, before again extending credit, to determine in good faith whether the shipper will comply with the credit regulations in the future.

(4) Tariff rules that establish charges pursuant to paragraph (e) (2) or (3) of this section may establish minimum charges.

(f) *Discounts.* Carriers may, by tariff rule, authorize discounts for early freight bill payments when credit is extended.

(g)(1) *Collection expense charges.* Carriers may, by tariff rule, assess reasonable and certain liquidated damages for all costs incurred in the collection of overdue freight charges. Carriers may use one of two methods in their tariffs:

(i) The first method is to assess liquidated damages as a separate additional charge to the unpaid freight bill.

In doing so, the tariff rule shall disclose the exact amount of the charges by stating either a dollar or specified percentage amount (or a combination of both) of the unpaid freight bill. The tariff shall further specify the time period (which shall at least allow for the authorized credit period) within which the shipper must pay to avoid such liquidated damages.

(ii) The second method is to require payment of the full, nondiscounted rate instead of the discounted rate otherwise applicable. The difference between the discount and the full rate constitutes a carrier's liquidated damages for its collection effort. Under this method the tariff shall identify the discount rates that are subject to the condition precedent and which require the shipper to make payment by a date certain. The date certain may not be set to occur by the carrier until at least after the expiration of the carrier's authorized credit period.

(2) The damages, the timing of their applicability, and the conditions, if any, as provided by the tariff-rule methods allowed under paragraphs (g)(1) (i) and (ii) of this section also:

(i) Shall be clearly described in the tariff rule;

(ii) Shall be applied without unlawful prejudice and/or unjust discrimination between similarly situated shippers and/or consignees;

(iii) Shall be applied only to the nonpayment of original, separate and independent freight bills and shall not apply to aggregate *balance-due* claims sought for collection on past shipments by a bankruptcy trustee, or any other person or agent;

(iv) Shall not apply to instances of clear clerical or ministerial error such as non-receipt of a carrier's freight bill, or shipper's payment check lost in the mail, or carrier mailing of the freight bill to the wrong address;

(v) Shall not apply in any way to a charge for a transportation service if the carrier's bill of lading independently provides that the shipper is liable for fees incurred by the carrier in the collection of freight charges on that same transportation service;

(vi) shall be applied only after the authorized credit period, and when the carrier has issued a revised freight bill

142

or notice of imposition of collection expense charges for late payment within 90 days after expiration of the authorized credit period.

(3) As an alternative to the tariff-rule methods allowed under paragraphs (g)(1) (i) and (ii) of this section, a carrier may, wholly outside of its tariff, assess collection charges though contract terms in a bill of lading. By using the carrier and its bill of lading, the shipper accepts the bill of lading terms.

(h) *Discrimination prohibited.* Tariff rules published pursuant to paragraphs (d), (e), and (f) of this section shall not result in unreasonable discrimination among shippers.

[50 FR 2290, Jan 16, 1985, as amended at 53 FR 6991, Mar. 4, 1988; 54 FR 30748, July 24, 1989]

§377.205 Presentation of freight bills.

(a) *"To be prepaid" shipments.* (1) On "to be prepaid" shipments, the carrier shall present its freight bill for all transportation charges within the time period prescribed in paragraph (a)(2) of this section, except—

(i) As noted in paragraph (d) of this section, or

(ii) As otherwise excepted in this part.

(2) The time period for a carrier to present its freight bill for all transportation charges shall be 7 days, measured from the date the carrier received the shipment. This time period does not include Saturdays, Sundays, or legal holidays.

(b) *"Collect" shipments.* (1) On "collect" shipments, the carrier shall present its freight bill for all transportation charges within the time period prescribed in paragraph (b)(2) and of this section, except—

(i) As noted in paragraph (d) of this section, or

(ii) As otherwise excepted in this part.

(2) The time period for a carrier to present its freight bill for all transportation charges shall be 7 days, measured from the date the shipment was delivered at its destination. This time period does not include Saturdays, Sundays, or legal holidays.

(c) *Bills or accompanying written notices shall state penalties for late payment, credit time limits and service charge and/or collection expense charge and discount terms.* When credit is extended, freight bills or a separate written notice accompanying a freight bill or a group of freight bills presented at one time shall state that "failure timely to pay freight charges may be subject to tariff penalties" (or a statement of similar import). The bills or other notice shall also state the time by which payment must be made and any applicable service charge and/or collection expense charge and discount terms.

(d) *When the carrier lacks sufficient information to compute tariff charges.* (1) When information sufficient to enable the carrier to compute the tariff charges is not then available to the carrier at its billing point, the carrier shall present its freight bill for payment within 7 days following the day upon which sufficient information becomes available at the billing point. This time period does not include Saturdays, Sundays, or legal holidays.

(2) A carrier shall not extend further credit to any shipper which fails to furnish sufficient information to allow the carrier to render a freight bill within a reasonable time after the shipment is tendered to the origin carrier.

(3) As used in this paragraph, the term "shipper" includes, but is not limited to, freight forwarders, and shippers' associations and shippers' agents.

[50 FR 2290, Jan 16, 1985, as amended at 54 FR 30748, July 24, 1989; 62 FR 15424, Apr. 1, 1997]

§377.207 Effect of mailing freight bills or payments.

(a) *Presentation of freight bills by mail.* When carriers present freight bills by mail, the time of mailing shall be deemed to be the time of presentation of the bills. The term *freight bills*, as used in this paragraph, includes both paper documents and billing by use of electronic media such as computer tapes or disks, when the mails are used to transmit them.

(b) *Payment by mail.* When shippers mail acceptable checks, drafts, or money orders in payment of freight charges, the act of mailing them within the credit period shall be deemed to be the collection of the tariff charges within the credit period for the purposes of the regulations in this part.

(c) *Disputes as to date of mailing.* In case of dispute as to the date of mailing, the postmark shall be accepted as such date.

§ 377.209 Additional charges.

When a carrier—

(a) Has collected the amount of tariff charges represented in a freight bill presented by it as the total amount of such charges, and

(b) Thereafter presents to the shipper another freight bill for additional charges—

the carrier may extend credit in the amount of such additional charges for a period of 30 calendar days from the date of the presentation of the freight bill for the additional charges.

§ 377.211 Computation of time.

Time periods involving calendar days shall be calculated pursuant to 49 CFR 386.32(a).

[50 FR 2290, Jan 16, 1985. Redesignated at 61 FR 54709, Oct. 21, 1996, as amended at 62 FR 15424, Apr. 1, 1997]

§§ 377.213–377.215 [Reserved]

§ 377.217 Interline settlement of revenues.

Nothing in this part shall be interpreted as affecting the interline settlement of revenues from traffic which is transported over through routes composed of lines of common carriers subject to the Secretary's jurisdiction under 49 U.S.C. subtitle IV, part B.

[50 FR 2290, Jan 16, 1985. Redesignated at 61 FR 54709, Oct. 21, 1996, as amended at 62 FR 15424, Apr. 1, 1997]

PART 378—PROCEDURES GOVERNING THE PROCESSING, INVESTIGATION, AND DISPOSITION OF OVERCHARGE, DUPLICATE PAYMENT, OR OVERCOLLECTION CLAIMS

AUTHORITY: 49 U.S.C. 13321, 14101, 14704 and 14705; and 49 CFR 1.73.

SOURCE: 43 FR 41040, Sept. 14, 1978, unless otherwise noted. Redesignated at 61 FR 54707, Oct. 21, 1996.

§ 378.1 Applicability.

The regulations set forth in this part govern the processing of claims for overcharge, duplicate payment, or overcollection for the transportation of property in interstate or foreign commerce by motor common carriers and household goods freight forwarders subject to 49 U.S.C. subtitle IV, part B.

[43 FR 41040, Sept. 14, 1978, as amended at 51 FR 44297, Dec. 9, 1986; 62 FR 15424, Apr. 1, 1997]

§ 378.2 Definitions.

(a) *Carrier* means a motor common carrier or household goods freight forwarder subject to 49 U.S.C. subtitle IV, part B.

(b) *Overcharge* means an overcharge as defined in 49 U.S.C. 14704(b). It also includes duplicate payments as defined in paragraph (c) of this section and overcollections as defined in paragraph (d) of this section when a dispute exists between the parties concerning such charges.

(c) *Duplicate payment* means two or more payments for transporting the same shipment. Where one or more payment is not in the exact amount of the applicable tariff rates and charges, refunds shall be made on the basis of the excess amount over the applicable tariff rates and charges.

(d) *Overcollection* means the receipt by a household goods carrier of a payment in excess of the transportation and/or accessorial charges applicable to a particular shipment of household goods, as defined in part 375 of this chapter, under tariffs lawfully on file with the United States Department of Transportation's Surface Transportation Board.

(e) *Unidentified payment* means a payment which a carrier has received but which the carrier is unable to match with its open accounts receivable or otherwise identify as being due for the performance of transportation services.

(f) *Claimant* means any shipper or receiver, or its authorized agent, filing a request with a carrier for the refund of an overcharge, duplicate payment, or overcollection.

[43 FR 41040, Sept. 14, 1978, as amended at 44 FR 66832, Nov. 21, 1979; 51 FR 34989, Oct. 1, 1986; 51 FR 44297, Dec. 9, 1986; 62 FR 15424, Apr. 1, 1997]

§378.3 **Filing and processing claims.**

(a) A claim for overcharge, duplicate payment, or overcollection shall not be paid unless filed in writing or electronically communicated (when agreed to by the carrier and shipper or receiver involved) with the carrier that collected the transportation charges. The collecting carrier shall be the carrier to process all such claims. When a claim is filed with another carrier that participated in the transportation, that carrier shall transmit the claim to the collecting carrier within 15 days after receipt of the claim. If the collecting carrier is unable to dispose of the claim for any reason, the claim may be filed with or transferred to any participating carrier for final disposition.

(b) A single claim may include more than one shipment provided the claim on each shipment involves:

(1) The same tariff issue or authority or circumstances,

(2) Single line service by the same carrier, or

(3) Service by the same interline carriers.

[43 FR 41040, Sept 14, 1978, as amended at 47 FR 12804, Mar. 25, 1982]

§378.4 **Documentation of claims.**

(a) Claims for overcharge, duplicate payment, or overcollection shall be accompanied by sufficient information to allow the carriers to conduct an investigation and pay or decline the claim within the time limitations set forth in §378.8. Claims shall include the name of the claimant, its file number, if any, and the amount of the refund sought to be recovered, if known.

(b) Except when the original freight bill is not a paper document but is electronically transmitted, claims for overcharge shall be accompanied by the original freight bill. Additional information may include, but is not limited to, the following:

(1) The rate, classification, or commodity description or weight claimed to have been applicable.

(2) Complete tariff authority for the rate, classification, or commodity description claimed.

(3) Freight bill payment information.

(4) Other documents or data which is believed by claimant to substantiate the basis for its claim.

(c) Claims for duplicate payment and overcollection shall be accompanied by the original freight bill(s) for which charges were paid (except when the original freight bill is not a paper document but is electronically transmitted) and by freight bill payment information.

(d) Regardless of the provisions of paragraphs (a), (b), and (c) of this section, the failure to provide sufficient information and documentation to allow a carrier to conduct an investigation and pay or decline the claim within the allowable time limitation shall not constitute grounds for disallowance of the claim. Rather, the carrier shall comply with §378.5(c) to obtain the additional information required.

(e) A carrier shall accept copies instead of the orginal documents required to be submitted in this section where the carrier is furnished with an agreement entered into by the claimant which indemnifies the carrier for subsequent duplicate claims which might be filed and supported by the original documents.

[43 FR 41040, Sept. 14, 1978, as amended at 44 FR 4679, Jan. 23, 1979; 47 FR 12804, Mar. 25, 1982; 62 FR 15424, Apr. 1, 1997]

§378.5 **Investigation of claims.**

(a) Upon receipt of a claim, whether written or otherwise, the processing carrier shall promptly initiate an investigation and establish a file, as required by §378.6.

(b) If a carrier discovers an overcharge, duplicate payment, or overcollection which has not been the subject of a claim, it shall promptly initiate an investigation and comply with the provisions in §378.9.

(c) In the event the carrier processing the claim requires information or documents in addition to that submitted with the claim, the carrier shall promptly notify the claimant and request the information required. This includes notifying the claimant that a written or electronically transmitted claim must be filed before the carrier becomes subject to the time limits for settling such a claim under § 378.8.

[43 FR 41040, Sept. 14, 1978, as amended at 47 FR 12804, Mar. 25, 1982; 62 FR 15424, 15425, Apr. 1, 1997]

§ 378.6 Claim records.

At the time a claim is received the carrier shall create a separate file and assign it a successive claim file number and note that number on all documents filed in support of the claim and all records and correspondence with respect to the claim, including the written or electronic acknowledgment of receipt required under § 378.7. If pertinent to the disposition of the claim, the carrier shall also note that number on the shipping order and delivery receipt, if any, covering the shipment involved.

[47 FR 12804, Mar. 25, 1982, as amended at 62 FR 15425, Apr. 1, 1997]

§ 378.7 Acknowledgment of claims.

Upon receipt of a written or electronically transmitted claim, the carrier shall acknowledge its receipt in writing or electronically to the claimant within 30 days after the date of receipt except when the carrier shall have paid or declined in writing or electronically within that period. The carrier shall include the date of receipt in its written or electronic claim which shall be placed in the file for that claim.

[47 FR 12804, Mar. 25, 1982]

§ 378.8 Disposition of claims.

The processing carrier shall pay, decline to pay, or settle each written or electronically communicated claim within 60 days after its receipt by that carrier, except where the claimant and the carrier agree in writing or electronically to a specific extension based upon extenuating circumstances. If the carrier declines to pay a claim or makes settlement in an amount different from that sought, the carrier shall notify the claimant in writing or

electronically, of the reason(s) for its action, citing tariff authority or other pertinent information developed as a result of its investigation.

[47 FR 12804, Mar. 25, 1982]

§ 378.9 Disposition of unidentified payments, overcharges, duplicate payments, and overcollections not supported by claims.

(a)(1) Carriers shall establish procedures for identifying and properly applying all unidentified payments. If a carrier does not have sufficient information with which properly to apply such a payment, the carrier shall notify the payor of the unidentified payment within 60 days of receipt of the payment and request information which will enable it to identify the payment. If the carrier does not receive the information requested within 90 days from the date of the notice, the carrier may treat the unidentified payment as a payment in fact of freight charges owing to it. Following the 90-day period, the regular claims procedure under this part shall be applicable.

(2) Notice shall be in writing and clearly indicate that it is a final notice and not a bill. Notice shall include: The check number, amount, and date; the payor's name; and any additional basic information the carrier is able to provide. The final notice also must inform payor that: (i) Applicable regulations allow the carrier to conditionally retain the payment as revenue in the absence of a timely response by the payor; and (ii) following the 90-day period the regular claims procedure shall be applicable.

(3) Upon a carrier's receipt of information from the payor, the carrier shall, within 14 days: (i) Make a complete refund of such funds to the payor; or (ii) notify the payor that the information supplied is not sufficient to identify the unapplied payment and request additional information; or (iii) notify the payor of the carrier's determination that such payment was applicable to particular freight charges lawfully due the carrier. Where no refund is made by the carrier, the carrier shall advise the payor of its right to file a

formal claim for refund with the carrier in accordance with the regular claims procedure under this part.

(b) When a carrier which participates in a transportation movement, but did not collect the transporation charges, finds that an overpayment has been made, that carrier shall immediately notify the collecting carrier. When the collecting carrier (when single or joint line haul) discovers or is notified by such a participating carrier that an overcharge, duplicate payment, or overcollection exists for any tranportation charge which has not been the subject of a claim, the carrier shall create a file as if a claim had been submitted and shall record in the file the date it discovered or was notified of the overpayment. The carrier that collected the charges shall then refund the amount of the overpayment to the person who paid the transportation charges or to the person that made duplicate payment within 30 days from the date of such discovery or notification.

[43 FR 41040, Sept. 14, 1978, as amended at 44 FR 66832, Nov. 21, 1979]

PART 379—PRESERVATION OF RECORDS

AUTHORITY: 49 U.S.C. 13301, 14122 and 14123; and 49 CFR 1.73.

SOURCE: 62 FR 32044, June 12, 1997, unless otherwise noted.

EDITORIAL NOTE: Nomenclature changes to part 379 appear at 66 FR 49871, Oct. 1, 2001.

§379.1 Applicability.

(a) The preservation of record rules contained in this part shall apply to the following:

(1) Motor carriers and brokers;

(2) Water carriers; and

(3) Household goods freight forwarders.

(b) This part applies also to the preservation of accounts, records and memoranda of traffic associations, weighing and inspection bureaus, and other joint activities maintained by or on behalf of companies listed in paragraph (a) of this section.

§379.3 Records required to be retained.

Companies subject to this part shall retain records for the minimum retention periods provided in appendix A to this part. After the required retention periods, the records may be destroyed at the discretion of each company's management. It shall be the obligation of the subject company to maintain records that adequately support financial and operational data required by the Secretary. The company may request a ruling from the Secretary on the retention of any record. The provisions of this part shall not be construed as excusing compliance with the lawful requirements of any other governmental body prescribing longer retention periods for any category of records.

§379.5 Protection and storage of records.

(a) The company shall protect records subject to this part from fires, floods, and other hazards, and safeguard the records from unnecessary exposure to deterioration from excessive humidity, dryness, or lack of ventilation.

(b) The company shall notify the Secretary if prescribed records are substantially destroyed or damaged before the term of the prescribed retention periods.

§379.7 Preservation of records.

(a) All records may be preserved by any technology that is immune to alteration, modification, or erasure of the underlying data and will enable production of an accurate and unaltered paper copy.

(b) Records not originally preserved on hard copy shall be accompanied by a statement executed by a person having personal knowledge of the facts indicating the type of data included within

147

the records. One comprehensive statement may be executed in lieu of individual statements for multiple records if the type of data included in the multiple records is common to all such records. The records shall be indexed and retained in such a manner as will render them readily accessible. The company shall have facilities available to locate, identify and produce legible paper copies of the records.

(c) Any significant characteristic, feature or other attribute that a particular medium will not preserve shall be clearly indicated at the beginning of the applicable records as appropriate.

(d) The printed side of forms, such as instructions, need not be preserved for each record as long as the printed matter is common to all such forms and an identified specimen of the form is maintained on the medium for reference.

§ 379.9　Companies going out of business.

The records referred to in the regulations in this part may be destroyed after business is discontinued and the company is completely liquidated. The records may not be destroyed until dissolution is final and all pending transactions and claims are completed. When a company is merged with another company under jurisdiction of the Secretary, the successor company shall preserve records of the merged company in accordance with the regulations in this part.

§ 379.11　Waiver of requirements of the regulations in this part.

A waiver from any provision of the regulations in this part may be made by the Secretary upon his/her own initiative or upon submission of a written request by the company. Each request for waiver shall demonstrate that unusual circumstances warrant a departure from prescribed retention periods, procedures, or techniques, or that compliance with such prescribed requirements would impose an unreasonable burden on the company.

§ 379.13　Disposition and retention of records.

The schedule in appendix A to this part shows periods that designated records shall be preserved. The descriptions specified under the various general headings are for convenient reference and identification, and are intended to apply to the items named regardless of what the records are called in individual companies and regardless of the record media. The retention periods represent the prescribed number of years from the date of the document and not calendar years. Records not listed in appendix A to this part shall be retained as determined by the management of each company.

APPENDIX A TO PART 379—SCHEDULE OF RECORDS AND PERIODS OF RETENTION

Item and category of records	Retention period
A. Corporate and General	
1. Incorporation and reorganization:	
(a) Charter or certificate of incorporation and amendments	Note A.
(b) Legal documents related to mergers, consolidations, reorganization, receiverships and similar actions which affect the identity or organization of the company.	Note A.
2. Minutes of Directors, Executive Committees, Stockholders and other corporate meetings.	Note A.
3. Titles, franchises and authorities:	
(a) Certificates of public convenience and necessity issued by regulating bodies.	Until expiration or cancellation.
(b) Operating authorizations and exemptions to operate	Until expiration or cancellation.
(c) Copies of formal orders of regulatory bodies served upon the company.	Note A.
(d) Deeds, charters, and other title papers	Until disposition of property.
(e) Patents and patent records	Note A.
4. Annual reports or statements to stockholders	3 years.
5. Contracts and agreements:	
(a) Service contracts, such as for operational management, accounting, financial or legal services, and agreements with agents.	Until expiration or termination plus 3 years.

Item and category of records	Retention period
(b) Contracts and other agreements relating to the construction, acquisition or sale of real property and equipment except as otherwise provided in (a) above.	Until expiration or termination plus 3 years.
(c) Contracts for the purchase or sale of material and supplies except as provided in (a) above.	Until expiration.
(d) Shipping contracts for transportation or caretakers of freight	Until expiration.
(e) Contracts with employees and employee bargaining groups	Until expiration.
(f) Contracts, leases and agreements, not specifically provided for in this section.	Until expiration or termination plus 1 year.
6. Accountant's auditor's, and inspector's reports:	
(a) Certifications and reports of examinations and audits conducted by public accountants.	3 years.
(b) Reports of examinations and audits conducted by internal auditors, time inspectors, and others.	3 years.
7. Other	Note A.
B. Treasury	
1. Capital stock records:	
(a) Capital stock ledger	Note A.
(b) Capital stock certificates, records of or stubs of	Note A.
(c) Stock transfer register	Note A.
2. Long-term debt records:	
(a) Bond indentures, underwritings, mortgages, and other long-term credit agreements.	Until redemption plus 3 years.
(b) Registered bonds and debenture ledgers	Until redemption plus 3 years.
(c) Stubs or similar records of bonds or other long-term debt issued	Note A.
3. Authorizations from regulatory bodies for issuance of securities including applications, reports, and supporting papers.	Note A.
4. Records of securities owned, in treasury, or held by custodians, detailed ledgers and journals, or their equivalent.	Until the securities are sold, redeemed or otherwise disposed of.
5. Other	Note A.
C. Financial and Accounting	
1. Ledgers:	
(a) General and subsidiary ledgers with indexes	Until discontinuance of use plus 3 years.
(b) Balance sheets and trial balance sheets of general and subsidiary ledgers.	3 years.
2. Journals:	
(a) General journals	Until discontinuance of use plus 3 years.
(b) Subsidiary journals and any supporting data, except as otherwise provided for, necessary to explain journal entries.	3 years.
3. Cash books:	
(a) General cash books	Until discontinuance of use plus 3 years.
(b) Subsidiary cash books	3 years.
4. Vouchers:	
(a) Voucher registers, indexes, or equivalent	3 years.
(b) Paid and canceled vouchers, expenditure authorizations, detailed distribution sheets and other supporting data including original bills and invoices, if not provided for elsewhere.	3 years.
(c) Paid drafts, paid checks, and receipts for cash paid out	3 years.
5. Accounts receivable:	
(a) Record or register of accounts receivable, indexes thereto, and summaries of distribution.	3 years after settlement.
(b) Bills issued for collection and supporting data	3 years after settlement.
(c) Authorization for writing off receivables	1 year.
(d) Reports and statements showing age and status of receivables	1 year.
6. Records of accounting codes and instructions	3 years after discontinuance.
7. Other	Note A.
D. Property and Equipment	

Note.—All accounts, records, and memoranda necessary for making a complete analysis of the cost or value of property shall be retained for the periods shown. If any of the records elsewhere provided for in this schedule are of this character, they shall be retained for the periods shown below, regardless of any lesser retention period assigned.

1. Property records:	
(a) Records which maintain complete information on cost or other value of all real and personal property or equipment.	3 years after disposition of property.
(b) Records of additions and betterments made to property and equipment.	3 years after disposition of property.
(c) Records pertaining to retirements and replacements of property and equipment.	3 years after disposition of property.
(d) Records pertaining to depreciation	3 years after disposition of property.
(e) Records of equipment number changes	3 years after disposition of property.
(f) Records of motor and engine changes	3 years after disposition of property.
(g) Records of equipment lightweighed and stenciled	Only current or latest records.
2. Engineering records of property changes actually made	3 years after disposition of property.

Item and category of records	Retention period
3. Other	Note A.
E. Personnel and Payroll	
1. Personnel and payroll records	1 year.
F. Insurance and Claims	
1. Insurance records:	
(a) Schedules of insurance against fire, storms, and other hazards and records of premium payments.	Until expiration plus 1 year.
(b) Records of losses and recoveries from insurance companies and supporting papers.	1 year after settlement.
(c) Insurance policies	Until expiration of coverage plus 1 year.
2. Claims records:	
(a) Claim registers, card or book indexes, and other records which record personal injury, fire and other claims against the company, together with all supporting data.	1 year after settlement.
(b) Claims registers, card or book indexes, and other records which record overcharges, damages, and other claims filed by the company against others, together with all supporting data.	1 year after settlement.
(c) Records giving the details of authorities issued to agents, carriers, and others for participation in freight claims.	3 years.
(d) Reports, statements and other data pertaining to personal injuries or damage to property when not necessary to support claims or vouchers.	3 years.
(e) Reports, statements, tracers, and other data pertaining to unclaimed, over, short, damaged, and refused freight, when not necessary to support claims or vouchers.	1 year.
(f) Authorities for disposal of unclaimed, damaged, and refused freight	3 years.
3. Other	Note A.
G. Taxes	
1. Taxes.	Note A.
H. Purchases and Stores	
1. Purchases and stores.	Note A.
I. Shipping and Agency Documents	
1. Bills of lading and releases:	
(a) Consignors' shipping orders, consignors' shipping tickets, and copies of bills of lading, freight bills from other carriers and other similar documents furnished the carrier for movement of freight.	1 year.
(b) Shippers' order-to-notify bills of lading taken up and canceled	1 year.
2. Freight waybills:	
(a) Local waybills	1 year.
(b) Interline waybills received from and made to other carriers	1 year.
(c) Company freight waybills	1 year.
(d) Express waybills	1 year.
3. Freight bills and settlements:	
(a) Paid copy of freight bill retained to support receipt of freight charges:	
(1) Bus express freight bills provided no claim has been filed	1 year.
(2) All other freight bills	1 year.
(b) Paid copy of freight bill retained to support payment of freight charges to other carriers:	
(1) Bus express freight bills provided no claim has been filed	1 year.
(2) All other freight bills	1 year.
(c) Records of unsettled freight bills and supporting papers	1 year after disposition.
(d) Records and reports of correction notices	1 year.
4. Other freight records:	
(a) Records of freight received, forwarded, and delivered	1 year.
(b) Notice to consignees of arrival of freight; tender of delivery	1 year.
5. Agency records (to include conductors, pursers, stewards, and others):	
(a) Cash books	1 year.
(b) Remittance records, bank deposit slips and supporting papers	1 year.
(c) Balance sheets and supporting papers	1 year.
(d) Statements of corrections in agents' accounts	1 year.
(e) Other records and reports pertaining to ticket sales, baggage handled, miscellaneous collections, refunds, adjustments, etc..	1 year.
J. Transportation	
1. Records pertaining to transportation of household goods:	
(a) Estimate of charges	1 year.
(b) Order for service	1 year.
(c) Vehicle-load manifest	1 year.
(d) Descriptive inventory	1 year.
2. Records and reports pertaining to operation of marine and floating equipment:	
(a) Ship log	3 years.
(b) Ship articles	3 years.
(c) Passenger and room list	3 years.

Item and category of records	Retention period
(d) Floatmen's barge, lighter, and escrow captain's reports, demurrage records, towing reports and checks sheets.	2 years.
3. Dispatchers' sheets, registers, and other records pertaining to movement of transportation equipment.	3 years.
4. Import and export records including bonded freight and steamship engagements.	2 years.
5. Records, reports, orders and tickets pertaining to weighting of freight	3 years.
6. Records of loading and unloading of transportation equipment	2 years.
7. Records pertaining to the diversion or reconsignment of freight, including requests, tracers, and correspondence.	2 years.
8. Other	Note A.
K. Supporting Data for Reports and Statistics	
1. Supporting data for reports filed with the Federal Motor Carrier Safety Administration, the Surface Transportation Board, the Department of Transportation's Bureau of Transportation Statistics and regulatory bodies:	
(a) Supporting data for annual financial, operating and statistical reports.	3 years.
(b) Supporting data for periodical reports of operating revenues, expenses, and income.	3 years.
(c) Supporting data for reports detailing use of proceeds from issuance or sale of company securities.	3 years.
(d) Supporting data for valuation inventory reports and records. This includes related notes, maps and sketches, underlying engineering, land, and accounting reports, pricing schedules, summary or collection sheets, yearly reports of changes and other miscellaneous data, all relating to the valuation of the company's property by the Federal Highway Administration, the Surface Transportation Board, the Department of Transportation's Bureau of Transportation Statistics or other regulatory body.	3 years after disposition of the property.
2. Supporting data for periodical reports of accidents, inspections, tests, hours of service, repairs, etc..	3 years.
3. Supporting data for periodical statistical of operating results or performance by tonnage, mileage, passengers carried, piggyback traffic, commodities, costs, analyses of increases and decreases, or otherwise.	3 years.
M. Miscellaneous	
1. Index of records	Until revised as record structure changes.
2. Statement listing records prematurely destroyed or lost	For the remainder of the period as prescribed for records destroyed.

NOTE A—Records referenced to this note shall be maintained as determined by the designated records supervisory official. Companies should be mindful of the record retention requirements of the Internal Revenue Service, Securities and Exchange Commission, State and local jurisdictions, and other regulatory agencies. Companies shall exercise reasonable care in choosing retention periods, and the choice of retention periods shall reflect past experiences, company needs, pending litigation, and regulatory requirements.

PART 380—SPECIAL TRAINING REQUIREMENTS

Subpart A—Longer Combination Vehicle (LCV) Driver-Training and Driver-Instructor Requirements—General

Subpart B—LCV Driver-Training Program

Subpart C—LCV Driver-Instructor Requirements

Subpart D—Driver-Training Certification

Subpart E—Entry-Level Driver Training Requirements

380.513 Required information on the training certificate.

APPENDIX TO PART 380—LCV DRIVER TRAINING PROGRAMS, REQUIRED KNOWLEDGE AND SKILLS

AUTHORITY: 49 U.S.C. 31133, 31136, 31307, and 31502; sec. 4007(a) and (b) of Pub. L. 102–240 (105 Stat. 2151–2152); and 49 CFR 1.73.

SOURCE: 69 FR 16732, Mar. 30, 2004, unless otherwise noted.

Subpart A—Longer Combination Vehicle (LCV) Driver-Training and Driver-Instructor Requirements—General

§ 380.101 Purpose and scope.

(a) *Purpose.* The purpose of this part is to establish minimum requirements for operators of longer combination vehicles (LCVs) and LCV driver-instructors.

(b) *Scope.* This part establishes:

(1) Minimum training requirements for operators of LCVs;

(2) Minimum qualification requirements for LCV driver-instructors; and

(3) Procedures for determining compliance with this part by operators, instructors, training institutions, and employers.

§ 380.103 Applicability.

The rules in this part apply to all operators of LCVs in interstate commerce, employers of such persons, and LCV driver-instructors.

§ 380.105 Definitions.

(a) The definitions in part 383 of this subchapter apply to this part, except where otherwise specifically noted.

(b) As used in this part:

Classroom instructor means a qualified LCV driver-instructor who provides knowledge instruction that does not involve the actual operation of a longer combination vehicle or its components. Instruction may take place in a parking lot, garage, or any other facility suitable for instruction.

Longer combination vehicle (LCV) means any combination of a truck-tractor and two or more trailers or semi-trailers, which operate on the National System of Interstate and Defense Highways with a gross vehicle weight (GVW) greater than 36,288 kilograms (80,000 pounds).

LCV Double means an LCV consisting of a truck-tractor in combination with two trailers and/or semi-trailers.

LCV Triple means an LCV consisting of a truck-tractor in combination with three trailers and/or semi-trailers.

Qualified LCV driver-instructor means an instructor meeting the requirements contained in subpart C of this part. There are two types of qualified LCV driver-instructors: (1) classroom instructor and (2) skills instructor.

Skills instructor means a qualified LCV driver-instructor who provides behind-the-wheel instruction involving the actual operation of a longer combination vehicle or its components outside a classroom.

Training institution means any technical or vocational school accredited by an accrediting institution recognized by the U.S. Department of Education. A motor carrier's training program for its drivers or an entity that exclusively offers services to a single motor carrier is not a training institution.

§ 380.107 General requirements.

(a) Except as provided in § 380.111, a driver who wishes to operate an LCV shall first take and successfully complete an LCV driver-training program that provides the knowledge and skills necessary to operate an LCV. The specific types of knowledge and skills that a training program shall include are outlined in the appendix to this part.

(b) Before a person receives training:

(1) That person shall present evidence to the LCV driver-instructor showing that he/she meets the general requirements set forth in subpart B of this part for the specific type of LCV training to be taken.

(2) The LCV driver-instructor shall verify that each trainee applicant meets the general requirements for the specific type of LCV training to be taken.

(c) Upon successful completion of the training requirement, the driver-student shall be issued an LCV Driver Training Certificate by a certifying official of the training entity in accordance with the requirements specified in subpart D of this part.

§380.109 Driver testing.

(a) *Testing methods.* The driver-student must pass knowledge and skills tests in accordance with the following requirements, to determine whether a driver-student has successfully completed an LCV driver-training program as specified in subpart B of this part. The written knowledge test may be administered by any qualified driver-instructor. The skills tests, based on actual operation of an LCV, must be administered by a qualified LCV skills instructor.

(1) All tests shall be constructed to determine if the driver-student possesses the required knowledge and skills set forth in the appendix to this part for the specific type of LCV training program being taught.

(2) Instructors shall develop their own tests for the specific type of LCV-training program being taught, but those tests must be at least as stringent as the requirements set forth in paragraph (b) of this section.

(3) LCV driver-instructors shall establish specific methods for scoring the knowledge and skills tests.

(4) Passing scores must meet the requirements of paragraph (b) of this section.

(5) Knowledge and skills tests shall be based upon the information taught in the LCV training programs as set forth in the appendix to this part.

(6) Each knowledge test shall address the training provided during both theoretical and behind-the-wheel instruction, and include at least one question from each of the units listed in the table to the appendix to this part, for the specific type of LCV training program being taught.

(7) Each skills test shall include all the maneuvers and operations practiced during the Proficiency Development unit of instruction (behind-the-wheel instruction), as described in the appendix to this part, for the specific type of LCV training program being taught.

(b) *Proficiency determinations.* The driver-student must meet the following conditions to be certified as an LCV driver:

(1) Answer correctly at least 80 percent of the questions on each knowledge test; and

(2) Demonstrate that he/she can successfully perform all of the skills addressed in paragraph (a)(7) of this section.

(c) *Automatic test failure.* Failure to obey traffic laws or involvement in a preventable crash during the skills portion of the test will result in automatic failure. Automatic test failure determinations are made at the sole discretion of the qualified LCV driver-instructor.

(d) *Guidance for testing methods and proficiency determinations.* Motor carriers should refer to the Examiner's Manual for Commercial Driver's License Tests for help in developing testing methods and making proficiency determinations. You may obtain a copy of this document by contacting the American Association of Motor Vehicle Administrators (AAMVA), 4300 Wilson Boulevard, Suite 400, Arlington, Virginia 22203.

§380.111 Substitute for driver training.

(a) *Grandfather clause.* The LCV driver-training requirements specified in subpart B of this part do not apply to an individual who meets the conditions set forth in paragraphs (b), (c), and (d) of this section. A motor carrier must ensure that an individual claiming eligibility to operate an LCV on the basis of this section meets these conditions before allowing him/her to operate an LCV.

(b) An individual must certify that, during the 2-year period immediately preceding the date of application for a Certificate of Grandfathering, he/she had:

(1) A valid Class A CDL with a "double/triple trailers" endorsement;

(2) No more than one driver's license;

(3) No suspension, revocation, or cancellation of his/her CDL;

(4) No convictions for a major offense while operating a CMV as defined in §383.51(b) of this subchapter;

(5) No convictions for a railroad-highway grade crossing offense while operating a CMV as defined in §383.51(d) of this subchapter;

(6) No convictions for violating an out-of-service order as defined in §383.51(e) of this subchapter;

153

(7) No more than one conviction for a serious traffic violation, as defined in § 383.5 of this subchapter, while operating a CMV; and

(8) No convictions for a violation of State or local law relating to motor vehicle traffic control arising in connection with any traffic crash while operating a CMV.

(c) An individual must certify and provide evidence that he/she:

(1) Is regularly employed in a job requiring the operation of a CMV that re-quires a CDL with a double/triple trailers endorsement; and

(2) Has operated, during the 2 years immediately preceding the date of application for a Certificate of Grandfathering, vehicles representative of the type of LCV that he/she seeks to continue operating.

(d) A motor carrier must issue a Certificate of Grandfathering to a person who meets the requirements of this section and must maintain a copy of the certificate in the individual's Driver Qualification file.

Longer Combination Vehicle (LCV) Driver-Training Certificate of Grandfathering

I certify that _____ has presented evidence of meeting the prerequisites set forth in the Federal Motor Carrier Safety Regulations (49 CFR § 380.111) for the substitute for LCV driver training and is qualified to operate the LCVs indicated below:

YES NO

☐   ☐   **LCV Doubles**

☐   ☐   **LCV Triples**

DRIVER NAME (First name, MI, Last name)	
Commercial Driver's License Number	STATE
ADDRESS OF DRIVER (Street Address, City, State and Zip Code)	
FULL NAME OF MOTOR CARRIER	Telephone Number
ADDRESS OF PRINCIPAL PLACE OF BUSINESS (Street Address, City, State, and Zip) Code)	
SIGNATURE OF MOTOR CARRIER OFFICIAL	DATE ISSUED

(e) An applicant may be grandfathered under this section only during the year following June 1, 2004.

§ 380.113 Employer responsibilities.

(a) No motor carrier shall:

(1) Allow, require, permit or authorize an individual to operate an LCV unless he/she meets the requirements in §§ 380.203 or 380.205 and has been issued the LCV driver-training certificate de-scribed in § 380.401. This provision does not apply to individuals who are eligible for the substitute for driver training provision in § 380.111.

(2) Allow, require, permit, or authorize an individual to operate an LCV which the LCV driver-training certificate, CDL, and CDL endorsement(s) do not authorize the driver to operate. This provision applies to individuals

employed by or under contract to the motor carrier.

(b) A motor carrier that employs or has under contract LCV drivers shall provide evidence of the certifications required by § 380.401 or § 380.111 of this part when requested by an authorized FMCSA, State, or local official in the course of a compliance review.

Subpart B—LCV Driver-Training Program

§ 380.201 General requirements.

(a) The LCV Driver-Training Program that is described in the appendix to this part requires training using an LCV Double or LCV Triple and must include the following general categories of instruction:

(1) Orientation;

(2) Basic operation;

(3) Safe operating practices;

(4) Advanced operations; and

(5) Nondriving activities.

(b) The LCV Driver-Training Program must include the minimum topics of training set forth in the appendix to this part and behind-the-wheel instruction that is designed to provide an opportunity to develop the skills outlined under the Proficiency Development unit of the training program.

§ 380.203 LCV Doubles.

(a) To qualify for the training necessary to operate an LCV Double, a driver-student shall, during the 6 months immediately preceding application for training, have:

(1) A valid Class A CDL with a double/triple trailer endorsement;

(2) Driving experience in a Group A vehicle as described in § 383.91 of this subchapter. Evidence of driving experience shall be an employer's written statement that the driver has, for at least 6 months immediately preceding application, operated a Group A vehicle while under his/her employ;

(3) No more than one driver's license;

(4) No suspension, revocation, or cancellation of his/her CDL;

(5) No convictions for a major offense, as defined in § 383.51(b) of this subchapter, while operating a CMV;

(6) No convictions for a railroad-highway grade crossing offense, as defined

in § 383.51(d) of this subchapter, while operating a CMV;

(7) No convictions for violating an out-of-service order as defined in § 383.51(e) of this subchapter;

(8) No more than one conviction for a serious traffic violation, as defined in § 383.5 of this subchapter, while operating a CMV; and

(9) No convictions for a violation of State or local law relating to motor vehicle traffic control arising in connection with any traffic crash while operating a CMV.

(b) Driver-students meeting the preliminary requirements in paragraph (a) of this section shall successfully complete a training program that meets the minimum unit requirements for LCV Doubles as set forth in the appendix to this part.

(c) Driver-students who successfully complete the Driver Training Program for LCV Doubles shall be issued a certificate, in accordance with subpart D of this part, indicating the driver is qualified to operate an LCV Double.

§ 380.205 LCV Triples.

(a) To qualify for the training necessary to operate an LCV Triple, a driver-student shall, during the 6 months immediately preceding application for training, have:

(1) A valid Class A CDL with a double/triple trailer endorsement;

(2) Experience operating the vehicle listed under paragraph (a)(2)(i) or (a)(2)(ii) of this section. Evidence of driving experience shall be an employer's written statement that the driver has, during the 6 months immediately preceding application, operated the applicable vehicle(s):

(i) Group A truck-tractor/semi-trailer combination as described in § 383.91 of this subchapter; or

(ii) Group A truck-tractor/semi-trailer/trailer combination that operates at a gross vehicle weight of 80,000 pounds or less;

(3) No more than one driver's license;

(4) No suspension, revocation, or cancellation of his/her CDL;

(5) No convictions for a major offense, as defined in § 383.51(b) of this subchapter, while operating a CMV;

(6) No convictions for a railroad-highway grade crossing offense, as defined

in § 383.51(d) of this subchapter, while operating a CMV;

(7) No convictions for violating an out-of-service order, as defined in § 383.51(e) of this subchapter;

(8) No more than one conviction for a serious traffic violation, as defined in § 383.5 of this subchapter, while operating a CMV; and

(9) No convictions for a violation of State or local law relating to motor vehicle traffic control arising in connection with any traffic crash, while operating a CMV.

(b) Driver-students meeting the preliminary requirements in paragraph (a) of this section shall successfully complete a training program that meets the minimum unit requirements for LCV Triples as set forth in the appendix to this part.

(c) Driver-students who successfully complete the Driver Training Program for LCV Triples shall be issued a certificate, in accordance with subpart D of this part, indicating the driver is qualified to operate an LCV Triple.

Subpart C—LCV Driver-Instructor Requirements

§ 380.301 General requirements.

There are two types of LCV driver-instructors: Classroom instructors and Skills instructors. Except as provided in § 380.303, you must meet the conditions under paragraph (a) or paragraph (b) of this section to qualify as an LCV driver-instructor.

(a) *Classroom instructor.* To qualify as an LCV Classroom instructor, a person shall:

(1) Have audited the driver-training course that he/she intends to instruct.

(2) If employed by a training institution, meet all State requirements for a vocational instructor.

(b) *Skills instructor.* To qualify as an LCV skills instructor, a person shall:

(1) Provide evidence of successful completion of the Driver-Training Program requirements, as set forth in subpart B of this part, when requested by employers and/or an authorized FMCSA, State, or local official in the course of a compliance review. The Driver-Training Program must be for the operation of CMVs representative

of the subject matter that he/she will teach.

(2) If employed by a training institution, meet all State requirements for a vocational instructor;

(3) Possess a valid Class A CDL with all endorsements necessary to operate the CMVs applicable to the subject matter being taught (LCV Doubles and/or LCV Triples, including any specialized variation thereof, such as a tank vehicle, that requires an additional endorsement); and

(4) Have at least 2 years' CMV driving experience in a vehicle representative of the type of driver training to be provided (LCV Doubles or LCV Triples).

§ 380.303 Substitute for instructor requirements.

(a) *Classroom instructor.* The requirements specified under § 380.301(a) of this part for a qualified LCV driver-instructor are waived for a classroom instructor-candidate who has 2 years of recent satisfactory experience teaching the classroom portion of a program similar in content to that set forth in the appendix to this part.

(b) *Skills instructor.* The requirements specified under § 380.301(b) of this part for a qualified LCV driver-instructor are waived for a skills instructor-candidate who:

(1) Meets the conditions of § 380.111(b);

(2) Has CMV driving experience during the previous 2 years in a vehicle representative of the type of LCV that is the subject of the training course to be provided;

(3) Has experience during the previous 2 years in teaching the operation of the type of LCV that is the subject of the training course to be provided; and

(4) If employed by a training institution, meets all State requirements for a vocational instructor.

§ 380.305 Employer responsibilities.

(a) No motor carrier shall: (1) Knowingly allow, require, permit or authorize a driver-instructor in its employ, or under contract to the motor carrier, to provide LCV driver training unless such person is a qualified LCV driver-instructor under the requirements of this subpart; or

(2) Contract with a training institution to provide LCV driver training unless the institution:

(i) Uses instructors who are qualified LCV driver-instructors under the requirements of this subpart;

(ii) Is accredited by an accrediting institution recognized by the U.S. Department of Education;

(iii) Is in compliance with all applicable State training school requirements; and

(iv) Identifies drivers certified under §380.401 of this part, when requested by employers and/or an authorized FMCSA, State, or local official in the course of a compliance review.

(b) A motor carrier that employs or has under contract qualified LCV driver-instructors shall provide evidence of the certifications required by §380.301 or §380.303 of this part, when requested by an authorized FMCSA, State, or local official in the course of a compliance review.

Subpart D—Driver-Training Certification

§380.401 Certification document.

(a) A student who successfully completes LCV driver training shall be issued a Driver-Training Certificate that is substantially in accordance with the following form.

Longer Combination Vehicle (LCV) Driver-Training Certificate

I certify that _____ has presented evidence of meeting the training prerequisites set forth in the Federal Motor Carrier Safety Regulations (49 CFR §§ 380.203(a) and 380.205(a)) for LCV training, and has successfully completed the LCV Driver-Training Course(s) indicated below:

YES NO
☐ ☐   **LCV Doubles** _____
                                   Date Training Completed

☐ ☐   **LCV Triples** _____
                                   Date Training Completed

I certify that the indicated LCV Driver-Training course(s) was provided by a qualified LCV driver-instructor as defined under 49 CFR § 380.105 and meet(s) the minimum requirements set forth in 49 CFR part 380, subparts A and B.

DRIVER NAME (First Name, MI, Last Name)	
Commercial Driver's License Number	STATE
ADDRESS OF DRIVER (Street Address, City, State and Zip Code)	
FULL NAME OF TRAINING ENTITY	Telephone Number
BUSINESS ADDRESS (Street Address, City, State, and Zip Code)	
SIGNATURE OF TRAINING CERTIFYING OFFICIAL	DATE ISSUED

(b) An LCV driver must provide a copy of the Driver-Training Certificate to his/her employer to be filed in the Driver Qualification File.

Subpart E—Entry-Level Driver Training Requirements

SOURCE: 69 FR 29404, May 21, 2004, unless otherwise noted.

§ 380.501 Applicability.

All entry-level drivers who drive in interstate commerce and are subject to the CDL requirements of part 383 of this chapter must comply with the rules of this subpart, except drivers who are subject to the jurisdiction of the Federal Transit Administration or who are otherwise exempt under § 390.3(f) of this subchapter.

§ 380.502 Definitions.

(a) The definitions in part 383 of this chapter apply to this part, except where otherwise specifically noted.

(b) As used in this subpart:

Entry-level driver is a driver with less than one year of experience operating a CMV with a CDL in interstate commerce.

Entry-level driver training is training the CDL driver receives in driver qualification requirements, hours of service of drivers, driver wellness, and whistle blower protection as appropriate to the entry-level driver's current position in addition to passing the CDL test.

§ 380.503 Entry-level driver training requirements.

Entry-level driver training must include instruction addressing the following four areas:

(a) *Driver qualification requirements.* The Federal rules on medical certification, medical examination procedures, general qualifications, responsibilities, and disqualifications based on various offenses, orders, and loss of driving privileges (part 391, subparts B and E of this subchapter).

(b) *Hours of service of drivers.* The limitations on driving hours, the requirement to be off-duty for certain periods of time, record of duty status preparation, and exceptions (part 395 of this subchapter). Fatigue countermeasures as a means to avoid crashes.

(c) *Driver wellness.* Basic health maintenance including diet and exercise. The importance of avoiding excessive use of alcohol.

(d) *Whistleblower protection.* The right of an employee to question the safety practices of an employer without the employee's risk of losing a job or being subject to reprisals simply for stating a safety concern (29 CFR part 1978).

§ 380.505 Proof of training.

An employer who uses an entry-level driver must ensure the driver has received a training certificate containing all the information contained in § 380.513 from the training provider.

§ 380.507 Driver responsibilities.

Each entry-level driver must receive training required by § 380.503.

§ 380.509 Employer responsibilities.

(a) Each employer must ensure each entry-level driver who first began operating a CMV requiring a CDL in interstate commerce after July 20, 2003, receives training required by § 380.503.

(b) Each employer must place a copy of the driver's training certificate in the driver's personnel or qualification file.

(c) All records required by this subpart shall be maintained as required by § 390.31 of this subchapter and shall be made available for inspection at the employer's principal place of business within two business days after a request has been made by an authorized representative of the Federal Motor Carrier Safety Administration.

§ 380.511 Employer recordkeeping responsibilities.

The employer must keep the records specified in § 380.505 for as long as the employer employs the driver and for one year thereafter.

§ 380.513 Required information on the training certificate.

The training provider must provide a training certificate or diploma to the entry-level driver. If an employer is the training provider, the employer must provide a training certificate or diploma to the entry-level driver. The certificate or diploma must contain the following seven items of information:

(a) Date of certificate issuance.

(b) Name of training provider.

(c) Mailing address of training provider.

(d) Name of driver.

(e) A statement that the driver has completed training in driver qualification requirements, hours of service of drivers, driver wellness, and whistle blower protection requirements substantially in accordance with the following sentence:

I certify _____ has completed training requirements set forth in the Federal Motor Carrier Safety Regulations for entry-level driver training in accordance with 49 CFR 380.503.

(f) The printed name of the person attesting that the driver has received the required training.

(g) The signature of the person attesting that the driver has received the required training.

APPENDIX TO PART 380—LCV DRIVER TRAINING PROGRAMS, REQUIRED KNOWLEDGE AND SKILLS

The following table lists topics of instruction required for drivers of longer combination vehicles pursuant to 49 CFR part 380, subpart B. The training courses for operators of LCV Doubles and LCV Triples must be distinct and tailored to address their unique operating and handling characteristics. Each course must include the minimum topics of instruction, including behind-the-wheel training designed to provide an opportunity to develop the skills outlined under the Proficiency Development unit of the training program. Only a skills instructor may administer behind-the-wheel training involving the operation of an LCV or one of its components. A classroom instructor may administer only instruction that does not involve the operation of an LCV or one of its components.

TABLE TO THE APPENDIX—COURSE TOPICS FOR LCV DRIVERS

Section 1: Orientation

1.1	LCVs in Trucking
1.2	Regulatory Factors
1.3	Driver Qualifications
1.4	Vehicle Configuration Factors

Section 2: Basic Operation

2.1	Coupling and Uncoupling
2.2	Basic Control and Handling
2.3	Basic Maneuvers
2.4	Turning, Steering and Tracking

TABLE TO THE APPENDIX—COURSE TOPICS FOR LCV DRIVERS—Continued

2.5	Proficiency Development

Section 3: Safe Operating Practices

3.1	Interacting with Traffic
3.2	Speed and Space Management
3.3	Night Operations
3.4	Extreme Driving Conditions
3.5	Security Issues
3.6	Proficiency Development

Section 4: Advanced Operations

4.1	Hazard Perception
4.2	Hazardous Situations
4.3	Maintenance and Troubleshooting

Section 5: Non-Driving Activities

5.1	Routes and Trip Planning
5.2	Cargo and Weight Considerations

SECTION 1—ORIENTATION

The units in this section must provide an orientation to the training curriculum and must cover the role LCVs play within the motor carrier industry, the factors that affect their operations, and the role that drivers play in the safe operation of LCVs.

Unit 1.1—LCVs in Trucking. This unit must provide an introduction to the emergence of LCVs in trucking and must serve as an orientation to the course content. Emphasis must be placed upon the role the driver plays in transportation.

Unit 1.2—Regulatory factors. This unit must provide instruction addressing the Federal, State, and local governmental bodies that propose, enact, and implement the laws, rules, and regulations that affect the trucking industry. Emphasis must be placed on those regulatory factors that affect LCVs, including 23 CFR 658.23 and Appendix C to part 658.

Unit 1.3—Driver qualifications. This unit must provide classroom instruction addressing the Federal and State laws, rules, and regulations that define LCV driver qualifications. It also must include a discussion on medical examinations, drug and alcohol tests, certification, and basic health and wellness issues. Emphasis must be placed upon topics essential to physical and mental health maintenance, including (1) diet, (2) exercise, (3) avoidance of alcohol and drug abuse, and caution in the use of prescription and nonprescription drugs, (4) the adverse effects of driver fatigue, and (5) effective fatigue countermeasures. Driver-trainees who have successfully completed the Entry-level training segments at §380.503(a) and (c) are considered to have satisfied the requirements of Unit 1.3.

Unit 1.4—Vehicle configuration factors. This unit must provide classroom instruction addressing the key vehicle components used in the configuration of longer combination vehicles. It also must familiarize the driver-trainee with various vehicle combinations, as well as provide instruction about unique characteristics and factors associated with LCV configurations.

SECTION 2—BASIC OPERATION

The units in this section must cover the interaction between the driver and the vehicle. They must teach driver-trainees how to couple and uncouple LCVs, ensure the vehicles are in proper operating condition, and control the motion of LCVs under various road and traffic conditions.

During the driving exercises at off-highway locations required by this section, the driver-trainee must first familiarize himself/herself with basic operating characteristics of an LCV. Utilizing an LCV, students must be able to perform the skills learned in each unit to a level of proficiency required to permit safe transition to on-street driving.

Unit 2.1—Coupling and uncoupling. This unit must provide instruction addressing the procedures for coupling and uncoupling LCVs. While vehicle coupling and uncoupling procedures are common to all truck-tractor/semi-trailer operations, some factors are peculiar to LCVs. Emphasis must be placed upon preplanning and safe operating procedures.

Unit 2.2—Basic control and handling. This unit must provide an introduction to basic vehicular control and handling as it applies to LCVs. This must include instruction addressing brake performance, handling characteristics and factors affecting LCV stability while braking, turning, and cornering. Emphasis must be placed upon safe operating procedures.

Unit 2.3—Basic maneuvers. This unit must provide instruction addressing the basic vehicular maneuvers that will be encountered by LCV drivers. This must include instruction relative to backing, lane positioning and path selection, merging situations, and parking LCVs. Emphasis must be placed upon safe operating procedures as they apply to brake performance and directional stability while accelerating, braking, merging, cornering, turning, and parking.

Unit 2.4—Turning, steering, and tracking. This unit must provide instruction addressing turning situations, steering maneuvers, and the tracking of LCV trailers. This must include instruction related to trailer sway and off-tracking. Emphasis must be placed on maintaining directional stability.

Unit 2.5—Proficiency development: basic operations. The purpose of this unit is to enable driver-students to gain the proficiency in basic operation needed to safely undertake on-street instruction in the Safe Operations Practices section of the curriculum.

The activities of this unit must consist of driving exercises that provide practice for the development of basic control skills and mastery of basic maneuvers. Driver-students practice skills and maneuvers learned in the Basic Control and Handling; Basic Maneuvers; and Turning, Steering and Tracking units. A series of basic exercises is practiced at off-highway locations until students develop sufficient proficiency for transition to on-street driving.

Once the driver-student's skills have been measured and found adequate, the driver-student must be allowed to move to on-the-street driving.

Nearly all activity in this unit will take place on the driving range or on streets or roads that have low-density traffic conditions.

SECTION 3—SAFE OPERATING PRACTICES

The units in this section must cover the interaction between student drivers, the vehicle, and the traffic environment. They must teach driver-students how to apply their basic operating skills in a way that ensures their safety and that of other road users under various road, weather, and traffic conditions.

Unit 3.1—Interacting with traffic. This unit must provide instruction addressing the principles of visual search, communication, and sharing the road with other traffic. Emphasis must be placed upon visual search, mirror usage, signaling and/or positioning the vehicle to communicate, and understanding the special situations encountered by LCV drivers in various traffic situations.

Unit 3.2—Speed and space management. This unit must provide instruction addressing the principles of speed and space management. Emphasis must be placed upon maintaining safe vehicular speed and appropriate space surrounding the vehicle under various traffic and road conditions. Particular attention must be placed upon understanding the special situations encountered by LCVs in various traffic situations.

Unit 3.3—Night operations. This unit must provide instruction addressing the principles of Night Operations. Emphasis must be placed upon the factors affecting operation of LCVs at night. Night driving presents specific factors that require special attention on the part of the driver. Changes in vehicle safety inspection, vision, communications, speed management, and space management are needed to deal with the special problems night driving presents.

Unit 3.4—Extreme driving conditions. This unit must provide instruction addressing the

160

driving of LCVs under extreme driving conditions. Emphasis must be placed upon the factors affecting the operation of LCVs in cold, hot, and inclement weather and in the mountains and desert. Changes in basic driving habits are needed to deal with the specific problems presented by these extreme driving conditions.

Unit 3.5—Security issues. This unit must include a discussion of security requirements imposed by the Department of Homeland Security, Transportation Security Administration; the U.S. Department of Transportation, Research and Special Programs Administration; and any other State or Federal agency with responsibility for highway or motor carrier security.

Unit 3.6—Proficiency development. This unit must provide driver-students an opportunity to refine, within the on-street traffic environment, their vehicle handling skills learned in the first three sections. Driver-student performance progress must be closely monitored to determine when the level of proficiency required for carrying out the basic traffic maneuvers of stopping, turning, merging, straight driving, curves, lane changing, passing, driving on hills, driving through traffic restrictions, and parking has been attained. The driver-student must also be assessed for regulatory compliance with all traffic laws.

Nearly all activity in this unit will take place on public roadways in a full range of traffic environments applicable to this vehicle configuration. This must include urban and rural uncontrolled roadways, expressways or freeways, under light, moderate, and heavy traffic conditions. There must be a brief classroom session to familiarize driver-students with the type of on-street maneuvers they will perform and how their performance will be rated.

The instructor must assess the level of skill development of the driver-student and must increase in difficulty, based upon the level of skill attained, the types of maneuvers, roadways and traffic conditions to which the driver-student is exposed.

SECTION 4—ADVANCED OPERATIONS

The units in this section must introduce higher level skills that can be acquired only after the more fundamental skills and knowledge taught in sections two and three have been mastered. They must teach the perceptual skills necessary to recognize potential hazards, and must demonstrate the procedures needed to handle an LCV when faced with a hazard.

The Maintenance and Trouble-shooting Unit must provide instruction that addresses how to keep the vehicle in safe and efficient operating condition. The purpose of this unit is to teach the correct way to perform simple maintenance tasks, and how to troubleshoot and report those vehicle discrepancies or deficiencies that must be repaired by a qualified mechanic.

Unit 4.1—Hazard perception. This unit must provide instruction addressing the principles of recognizing hazards in sufficient time to reduce the severity of the hazard and neutralize a possible emergency situation. While hazards are present in all motor vehicle traffic operations, some are peculiar to LCV operations. Emphasis must be placed upon hazard recognition, visual search, and response to possible emergency-producing situations encountered by LCV drivers in various traffic situations.

Unit 4.2—Hazardous situations. This unit must address dealing with specific procedures appropriate for LCV emergencies. These must include evasive steering, emergency braking, off-road recovery, brake failures, tire blowouts, rearward amplification, hydroplaning, skidding, jackknifing and the rollover phenomenon. The discussion must include a review of unsafe acts and the role they play in producing hazardous situations.

Unit 4.3—Maintenance and trouble-shooting. This unit must introduce driver-students to the basic servicing and checking procedures for the various vehicle components and provide knowledge of conducting preventive maintenance functions, making simple emergency repairs, and diagnosing and reporting vehicle malfunctions.

SECTION 5—NON-DRIVING ACTIVITIES

The units in this section must cover activities that are not directly related to the vehicle itself but must be performed by an LCV driver. The units in this section must ensure these activities are performed in a manner that ensures the safety of the driver, vehicle, cargo, and other road users.

Unit 5.1—Routes and trip planning. This unit must address the importance of and requirements for planning routes and trips. This must include classroom discussion of Federal and State requirements for a number of topics including permits, vehicle size and weight limitations, designated highways, local access, the reasonable access rule, staging areas, and access zones.

Unit 5.2—Cargo and weight considerations. This unit must address the importance of proper cargo documentation, loading, securing and unloading cargo, weight distribution, load sequencing and trailer placement. Emphasis must be placed on the importance of axle weight distribution, as well as on trailer placement and its effect on vehicle handling.

PART 381—WAIVERS, EXEMPTIONS, AND PILOT PROGRAMS

Subpart A—General

Sec.
381.100 What is the purpose of this part?

AUTHORITY: 49 U.S.C. 31136(e) and 31315; and 49 CFR 1.73.

SOURCE: 63 FR 67608, Dec. 8, 1998, unless otherwise noted.

EDITORIAL NOTE: Nomenclature changes to part 381 appear at 66 FR 49872, Oct. 1, 2001.

Subpart A—General

§ 381.100 What is the purpose of this part?

This part prescribes the rules and procedures for requesting waivers and applying for exemptions from those provisions of the Federal Motor Carrier Safety Regulations (FMCSRs) which were issued on the authority of 49 U.S.C. 31136 or chapter 313, and the initiation and administration of pilot programs.

§ 381.105 Who is required to comply with the rules in this part?

(a) You must comply with the rules in this part if you are going to request a waiver or apply for an exemption.

(b) You should follow the instructions in subpart D of this part if you would like to recommend the agency initiate a pilot program.

§ 381.110 What definitions are applicable to this part?

Commercial motor vehicle means any motor vehicle that meets the definition of "commercial motor vehicle" found at 49 CFR 382.107 concerning controlled substances and alcohol use and testing, 49 CFR 383.5 concerning commercial driver's license standards, or 49 CFR 390.5 concerning parts 390 through 399 of the FMCSRs.

Federal Motor Carrier Safety Administrator (the Administrator) means the chief executive of the Federal Motor Carrier Safety Administration, an agency within the Department of Transportation.

FMCSRs means Federal Motor Carrier Safety Regulations (49 CFR parts

382 and 383, §§385.21 and 390.21, parts 391 through 393, 395, 396, and 399).

You means an individual or motor carrier or other entity that is, or will be, responsible for the operation of a CMV(s). The term includes a motor carrier's agents, officers and representatives as well as employees responsible for hiring, supervising, training, assigning, or dispatching of drivers and employees concerned with the installation, inspection, and maintenance of motor vehicle equipment and/or accessories. *You* also includes any interested party who would like to suggest or recommend that the FMCSA initiate a pilot program.

Subpart B—Procedures for Requesting Waivers

§381.200 What is a waiver?

(a) A waiver is temporary regulatory relief from one or more FMCSR given to a person subject to the regulations, or a person who intends to engage in an activity that would be subject to the regulations.

(b) A waiver provides the person with relief from the regulations for up to three months.

(c) A waiver is intended for unique, non-emergency events and is subject to conditions imposed by the Administrator.

(d) Waivers may only be granted from one or more of the requirements contained in the following parts and sections of the FMCSRs:

(1) Part 382—Controlled Substances and Alcohol Use and Testing;

(2) Part 383—Commercial Driver's License Standards; Requirements and Penalties;

(3) §390.19 Motor Carrier Identification Report;

(4) §390.21 Marking of commercial motor vehicles;

(5) Part 391—Qualifications of Drivers;

(6) Part 392—Driving of Commercial Motor Vehicles;

(7) Part 393—Parts and Accessories Necessary for Safe Operation;

(8) Part 395—Hours of Service of Drivers;

(9) Part 396—Inspection, Repair, and Maintenance (except §396.25); and

(10) Part 399—Step, Handhold and Deck Requirements.

§381.205 How do I determine when I may request a waiver?

(a) You may request a waiver if one or more FMCSR would prevent you from using or operating CMVs, or make it unreasonably difficult to do so, during a unique, non-emergency event that will take no more than three months to complete.

(b) Before you decide to request a waiver, you should carefully review the regulation to determine whether there are any practical alternatives already available that would allow your use or operation of CMVs during the event. You should also determine whether you need a waiver from all of the requirements in one or more parts of the regulations, or whether a more limited waiver of certain sections within one or more of the parts of the regulations would provide an acceptable level of regulatory relief. For example, if you need relief from one of the recordkeeping requirements concerning driver qualifications, you should not request relief from all of the requirements of part 391.

§381.210 How do I request a waiver?

(a) You must send a written request (for example, a typed or handwritten (printed) letter), which includes all of the information required by this section, to the Administrator, Federal Motor Carrier Safety Administration, 1200 New Jersey Ave., SE., Washington, DC 20590–0001.

(b) You must identify the person who would be covered by the waiver. The application for a waiver must include:

(1) Your name, job title, mailing address, and daytime telephone number;

(2) The name of the individual, motor carrier, or other entity that would be responsible for the use or operation of CMVs during the unique, non-emergency event;

(3) Principal place of business for the motor carrier or other entity (street address, city, State, and zip code); and

(4) The USDOT identification number for the motor carrier, if applicable.

(c) You must provide a written statement that:

(1) Describes the unique, non-emergency event for which the waiver would be used, including the time period during which the waiver is needed;

(2) Identifies the regulation that you believe needs to be waived;

(3) Provides an estimate of the total number of drivers and CMVs that would be operated under the terms and conditions of the waiver; and

(4) Explains how you would ensure that you could achieve a level of safety that is equivalent to, or greater than, the level of safety that would be obtained by complying with the regulation.

[72 FR 67608, Dec. 8, 1998, as amended at 72 FR 55699, Oct. 1, 2007]

§ 381.215 **What will the FMCSA do after the agency receives my request for a waiver?**

(a) The Federal Motor Carrier Safety Administration will review your request and make a recommendation to the Administrator. The final decision whether to grant or deny the application for a waiver will be made by the Administrator.

(b) After a decision is signed by the Administrator, you will be sent a copy of the document, which will include the terms and conditions for the waiver or the reason for denying the application for a waiver.

§ 381.220 **How long will it take the agency to respond to my request for a waiver?**

You should receive a response from the agency within 60 calendar days from the date the Administrator receives your request. However, depending on the complexity of the issues discussed in your application, and the availability of staff to review the material, a final decision may take up to 120 days.

§ 381.225 **Who should I contact if I have questions about the information I am required to submit to the FMCSA or about the status of my request for a waiver?**

You should contact the Federal Motor Carrier Safety Administration, Office of Bus and Truck Standards and Operations (MC–PS), 1200 New Jersey Ave., SE., Washington, DC 20590–0001.

[63 FR 67608, Dec. 8, 1998, as amended at 72 FR 55699, Oct. 1, 2007]

Subpart C—Procedures for Applying for Exemptions

§ 381.300 **What is an exemption?**

(a) An exemption is temporary regulatory relief from one or more FMCSR given to a person or class of persons subject to the regulations, or who intend to engage in an activity that would make them subject to the regulations.

(b) An exemption provides the person or class of persons with relief from the regulations for up to two years, and may be renewed.

(c) Exemptions may only be granted from one or more of the requirements contained in the following parts and sections of the FMCSRs:

(1) Part 382—Controlled Substances and Alcohol Use and Testing;

(2) Part 383—Commercial Driver's License Standards; Requirements and Penalties;

(3) Part 391—Qualifications of Drivers;

(4) Part 392—Driving of Commercial Motor Vehicles;

(5) Part 393—Parts and Accessories Necessary for Safe Operation;

(6) Part 395—Hours of Service of Drivers;

(7) Part 396—Inspection, Repair, and Maintenance (except for § 396.25); and

(8) Part 399—Step, Handhold and Deck Requirements.

§ 381.305 **How do I determine when I may apply for an exemption?**

(a) You may apply for an exemption if one or more FMCSR prevents you from implementing more efficient or effective operations that would maintain a level of safety equivalent to, or greater than, the level achieved without the exemption.

(b) Before you decide to apply for an exemption you should carefully review the regulation to determine whether there are any practical alternatives already available that would allow you to conduct your motor carrier operations. You should also determine whether you need an exemption from all of the requirements in one or more parts of the regulations, or whether a more limited exemption from certain sections within one or more parts of the regulations would provide an acceptable level of regulatory relief. For example, if you need regulatory relief from one of the recordkeeping requirements concerning driver qualifications, you should not request regulatory relief from all of the requirements of part 391.

§ 381.310 How do I apply for an exemption?

(a) You must send a written request (for example, a typed or handwritten (printed) letter), which includes all of the information required by this section, to the Administrator, Federal Motor Carrier Safety Administration, 1200 New Jersey Ave., SE., Washington, DC 20590–0001.

(b) You must identify the person or class of persons who would be covered by the exemption. The application for an exemption must include:

(1) Your name, job title, mailing address, and daytime telephone number;

(2) The name of the individual or motor carrier that would be responsible for the use or operation of CMVs;

(3) Principal place of business for the motor carrier (street address, city, State, and zip code); and

(4) The USDOT identification number for the motor carrier.

(c) You must provide a written statement that:

(1) Describes the reason the exemption is needed, including the time period during which it is needed;

(2) Identifies the regulation from which you would like to be exempted;

(3) Provides an estimate of the total number of drivers and CMVs that would be operated under the terms and conditions of the exemption;

(4) Assesses the safety impacts the exemption may have;

(5) Explains how you would ensure that you could achieve a level a safety that is equivalent to, or greater than, the level of safety that would be obtained by complying with the regulation; and

(6) Describes the impacts (e.g., inability to test innovative safety management control systems, etc.) you could

experience if the exemption is not granted by the FMCSA.

(d) Your application must include a copy of all research reports, technical papers, and other publications and documents you reference.

[63 FR 67608, Dec. 8, 1998, as amended at 72 FR 55700, Oct. 1, 2007]

§ 381.315 What will the FMCSA do after the agency receives my application for an exemption?

(a) The Federal Motor Carrier Safety Administration will review your application and prepare, for the Administrator's signature, a FEDERAL REGISTER notice requesting public comment on your application for an exemption. The notice will give the public an opportunity to review your request and your safety assessment or analysis (required by § 381.310) and any other relevant information known to the agency.

(b) After a review of the comments received in response to the FEDERAL REGISTER notice described in paragraph (a) of this section, the Federal Motor Carrier Safety Administration will make a recommendation(s) to the Administrator to either to grant or deny the exemption. Notice of the Administrator's decision will be published in the FEDERAL REGISTER.

(c)(1) If the exemption is granted, the notice will identify the provisions of the FMCSRs from which you will be exempt, the effective period, and all terms and conditions of the exemption.

(2) If the exemption is denied, the notice will explain the reason for the denial.

(d) A copy of your application for an exemption and all comments received in response to the FEDERAL REGISTER notice will be included in a public docket and be available for review by interested parties.

(1) Interested parties may view the information contained in the docket by visiting the Department of Transportation, Docket Management Facility, 1200 New Jersey Ave., SE., Washington, DC 20590–0001. All information in the exemption docket will be available for examination at this address from 10 a.m. to 5 p.m., e.t., Monday through Friday, except Federal holidays.

(2) Internet users can access all information received by the Department of

Transportation, Docket Management Facility by using the Federal Docket Management System using the uniform resources locator (URL): *http://www.regulations.gov*. It is available 24 hours each day, 365 days each year. Please follow the instructions online for more information and help.

[63 FR 67608, Dec. 8, 1998, as amended at 72 FR 55700, Oct. 1, 2007]

§ 381.320 How long will it take the agency to respond to my application for an exemption?

The agency will attempt to issue a final decision within 180 days of the date it receives your application. However, if you leave out important details or other information necessary for the FMCSA to prepare a meaningful request for public comments, the agency will attempt to issue a final decision within 180 days of the date it receives the additional information.

§ 381.325 Who should I contact if I have questions about the information I am required to submit to the FMCSA or about the status of my application for an exemption?

You should contact the Federal Motor Carrier Safety Administration, Office of Bus and Truck Standards and Operations (MC–PS), 1200 New Jersey Ave., SE., Washington, DC 20590–0001.

[63 FR 67608, Dec. 8, 1998, as amended at 72 FR 55700, Oct. 1, 2007]

§ 381.330 What am I required to do if the FMCSA grants my application for an exemption?

(a) You must comply with all the terms and conditions of the exemption.

(b) The FMCSA will immediately revoke your exemption if:

(1) You fail to comply with the terms and conditions of the exemption;

(2) The exemption has resulted in a lower level of safety than was maintained before the exemption was granted; or

(3) Continuation of the exemption is determined by the FMCSA to be inconsistent with the goals and objectives of the FMCSRs.

Subpart D—Initiation of Pilot Programs

§ 381.400 What is a pilot program?

(a) A pilot program is a study in which temporary regulatory relief from one or more FMCSR is given to a person or class of persons subject to the regulations, or a person or class of persons who intend to engage in an activity that would be subject to the regulations.

(b) During a pilot program, the participants would be given an exemption from one or more sections or parts of the regulations for a period of up to three years.

(c) A pilot program is intended for use in collecting specific data for evaluating alternatives to the regulations or innovative approaches to safety while ensuring that the safety performance goals of the regulations are satisfied.

(d) The number of participants in the pilot program must be large enough to ensure statistically valid findings.

(e) Pilot programs must include an oversight plan to ensure that participants comply with the terms and conditions of participation, and procedures to protect the health and safety of study participants and the general public.

(f) Exemptions for pilot programs may be granted only from one or more of the requirements contained in the following parts and sections of the FMCSRs:

(1) Part 382—Controlled Substances and Alcohol Use and Testing;

(2) Part 383—Commercial Driver's License Standards; Requirements and Penalties;

(3) Part 391—Qualifications of Drivers;

(4) Part 392—Driving of Commercial Motor Vehicles;

(5) Part 393—Parts and Accessories Necessary for Safe Operation;

(6) Part 395—Hours of Service of Drivers;

(7) Part 396—Inspection, Repair, and Maintenance (except for § 396.25); and

(8) Part 399—Step, Handhold and Deck Requirements.

§381.405 Who determines whether a pilot program should be initiated?

(a) Generally, pilot programs are initiated by the FMCSA when the agency determines that there may be an effective alternative to one or more of the requirements in the FMCSRs, but does not have sufficient research data to support the development of a notice of proposed rulemaking to change the regulation.

(b) You may request the FMCSA to initiate a pilot program. However, the decision of whether to propose a pilot program will be made at the discretion of the FMCSA. The FMCSA is not required to publish a notice in the FEDERAL REGISTER requesting public comment on your ideas or suggestions for pilot programs.

§381.410 What may I do if I have an idea or suggestion for a pilot program?

(a) You may send a written statement (for example, a typed or handwritten (printed) letter) to the Administrator, Federal Motor Carrier Safety Administration, 1200 New Jersey Ave., SE., Washington, DC 20590–0001.

(b) You should identify the persons or class of persons who would be covered by the pilot program exemptions. Your letter should include:

(1) Your name, job title, mailing address, and daytime telephone number;

(2) The name of the individuals or motor carrier that would be responsible for the use or operation of CMVs covered by the pilot program, if there are motor carriers that have expressed an interest in participating in the program;

(3) Principal place of business for the motor carrier (street address, city, State, and zip code); and

(4) The USDOT identification number for the motor carrier.

(c) You should provide a written statement that:

(1) Presents your estimate of the potential benefits to the motor carrier industry, the FMCSA, and the general public if the pilot program is conducted, and describes how you developed your estimate;

(2) Estimates of the amount of time that would be needed to conduct the pilot program (e.g., the time needed to complete the collection and analysis of data);

(3) Identifies the regulation from which the participants would need to be exempted;

(4) Recommends a reasonable number of participants necessary to yield statistically valid findings;

(5) Provides ideas or suggestions for a monitoring plan to ensure that participants comply with the terms and conditions of participation;

(6) Provides ideas or suggestions for a plan to protect the health and safety of study participants and the general public.

(7) Assesses the safety impacts the pilot program exemption may have; and

(8) Provides recommendations on how the safety measures in the pilot project would be designed to achieve a level a safety that is equivalent to, or greater than, the level of safety that would be obtained by complying with the regulation.

(d) Your recommendation should include a copy of all research reports, technical papers, publications and other documents you reference.

[63 FR 67608, Dec. 8, 1998, as amended at 72 FR 55700, Oct. 1, 2007]

§381.415 Who should I contact if I have questions about the information to be included in my suggestion?

You should contact the Federal Motor Carrier Safety Administration, Office of Bus and Truck Standards and Operations (MC–PS), 1200 New Jersey Ave., SE., Washington, DC 20590–0001.

[63 FR 67608, Dec. 8, 1998, as amended at 72 FR 55700, Oct. 1, 2007]

§381.420 What will the FMCSA do after the agency receives my suggestion for a pilot program?

(a) The Federal Motor Carrier Safety Administration will review your suggestion for a pilot program and make a recommendation to the Administrator. The final decision whether to propose the development of a pilot program based upon your recommendation will be made by the Administrator.

(b) You will be sent a copy of the Administrator's decision. If the pilot program is approved, the agency will follow the administrative procedures contained in subpart E of this part.

Subpart E—Administrative Procedures for Pilot Programs

§ 381.500 What are the general requirements the agency must satisfy in conducting a pilot program?

(a) The FMCSA may conduct pilot programs to evaluate alternatives to regulations, or innovative approaches, concerning motor carrier, CMV, and driver safety.

(b) Pilot programs may include exemptions from the regulations listed in § 381.400(f) of this part.

(c) Pilot programs must, at a minimum, include all of the program elements listed in § 381.505.

(d) The FMCSA will publish in the FEDERAL REGISTER a detailed description of each pilot program, including the exemptions to be considered, and provide notice and an opportunity for public comment before the effective date of the pilot program.

§ 381.505 What are the minimum elements required for a pilot program?

(a) *Safety measures.* Before granting exemptions for a pilot program, the FMCSA will ensure that the safety measures in a pilot program are designed to achieve a level of safety that is equivalent to, or greater than, the level of safety that would be achieved by complying with the regulations.

(b) *Pilot program plan.* Before initiating a pilot program, the FMCSA will ensure that there is a pilot program plan which includes the following elements:

(1) A scheduled duration of three years or less;

(2) A specific data collection and safety analysis plan that identifies a method of comparing the safety performance for motor carriers, CMVs, and drivers operating under the terms and conditions of the pilot program, with the safety performance of motor carriers, CMVs, and drivers that comply with the regulation;

(3) A reasonable number of participants necessary to yield statistically valid findings;

(4) A monitoring plan to ensure that participants comply with the terms and conditions of participation in the pilot program;

(5) Adequate safeguards to protect the health and safety of study participants and the general public; and

(6) A plan to inform the States and the public about the pilot program and to identify approved participants to enforcement personnel and the general public.

§ 381.510 May the FMCSA end a pilot program before its scheduled completion date?

The FMCSA will immediately terminate a pilot program if there is reason to believe the program is not achieving a level of safety that is at least equivalent to the level of safety that would be achieved by complying with the regulations.

§ 381.515 May the FMCSA remove approved participants from a pilot program?

The Administrator will immediately revoke participation in a pilot program of a motor carrier, CMV, or driver for failure to comply with the terms and conditions of the pilot program, or if continued participation is inconsistent with the goals and objectives of the safety regulations.

§ 381.520 What will the FMCSA do with the results from a pilot program?

At the conclusion of each pilot program, the FMCSA will report to Congress the findings and conclusions of the program and any recommendations it considers appropriate, including suggested amendments to laws and regulations that would enhance motor carrier, CMV, and driver safety and improve compliance with the FMCSRs.

Subpart F—Preemption of State Rules

§ 381.600 Do waivers, exemptions, and pilot programs preempt State laws and regulations?

Yes. During the time period that a waiver, exemption, or pilot program authorized by this part is in effect, no State shall enforce any law or regulation that conflicts with or is inconsistent with the waiver, exemption, or pilot program with respect to a person operating under the waiver or exemption or participating in the pilot program.

PART 382—CONTROLLED SUBSTANCES AND ALCOHOL USE AND TESTING

Subpart A—General

AUTHORITY: 49 U.S.C. 31133, 31136, 31301 *et seq.*, 31502; and 49 CFR 1.73.

SOURCE: 66 FR 43103, Aug. 17, 2001, unless otherwise noted.

Subpart A—General

§ 382.101 Purpose.

The purpose of this part is to establish programs designed to help prevent accidents and injuries resulting from the misuse of alcohol or use of controlled substances by drivers of commercial motor vehicles.

§ 382.103 Applicability.

(a) This part applies to every person and to all employers of such persons who operate a commercial motor vehicle in commerce in any State, and is subject to:

(1) The commercial driver's license requirements of part 383 of this subchapter;

(2) The Licencia Federal de Conductor (Mexico) requirements; or

(3) The commercial drivers license requirements of the Canadian National Safety Code.

(b) An employer who employs himself/herself as a driver must comply with both the requirements in this part that apply to employers and the requirements in this part that apply to drivers. An employer who employs only himself/herself as a driver shall implement a random alcohol and controlled substances testing program of two or more covered employees in the random testing selection pool.

(c) The exceptions contained in § 390.3(f) of this subchapter do not apply to this part. The employers and drivers identified in § 390.3(f) of this subchapter must comply with the requirements of this part, unless otherwise specifically provided in paragraph (d) of this section.

(d) *Exceptions.* This part shall not apply to employers and their drivers:

(1) Required to comply with the alcohol and/or controlled substances testing requirements of part 655 of this title (Federal Transit Administration alcohol and controlled substances testing regulations); or

(2) Who a State must waive from the requirements of part 383 of this subchapter. These individuals include active duty military personnel; members of the reserves; and members of the national guard on active duty, including personnel on full-time national guard duty, personnel on part-time national guard training and national guard military technicians (civilians who are required to wear military uniforms), and active duty U.S. Coast Guard personnel; or

(3) Who a State has, at its discretion, exempted from the requirements of part 383 of this subchapter. These individuals may be:

(i) Operators of a farm vehicle which is:

(A) Controlled and operated by a farmer;

(B) Used to transport either agricultural products, farm machinery, farm supplies, or both to or from a farm;

(C) Not used in the operations of a common or contract motor carrier; and

(D) Used within 241 kilometers (150 miles) of the farmer's farm.

(ii) Firefighters or other persons who operate commercial motor vehicles which are necessary for the preservation of life or property or the execution of emergency governmental functions, are equipped with audible and visual signals, and are not subject to normal traffic regulation.

§ 382.105 Testing procedures.

Each employer shall ensure that all alcohol or controlled substances testing conducted under this part complies with the procedures set forth in part 40 of this title. The provisions of part 40 of this title that address alcohol or controlled substances testing are made applicable to employers by this part.

§ 382.107 Definitions.

Words or phrases used in this part are defined in §§ 386.2 and 390.5 of this subchapter, and § 40.3 of this title, except as provided in this section—

Actual knowledge for the purpose of subpart B of this part, means actual knowledge by an employer that a driver has used alcohol or controlled substances based on the employer's direct observation of the employee, information provided by the driver's previous employer(s), a traffic citation for driving a CMV while under the influence of alcohol or controlled substances or an employee's admission of alcohol or controlled substance use, except as provided in § 382.121. Direct observation as used in this definition means observation of alcohol or controlled substances use and does not include observation of employee behavior or physical characteristics sufficient to warrant reasonable suspicion testing under § 382.307.

Alcohol means the intoxicating agent in beverage alcohol, ethyl alcohol, or other low molecular weight alcohols including methyl and isopropyl alcohol.

Alcohol concentration (or content) means the alcohol in a volume of breath expressed in terms of grams of alcohol per 210 liters of breath as indicated by an evidential breath test under this part.

Alcohol use means the drinking or swallowing of any beverage, liquid mixture or preparation (including any medication), containing alcohol.

Commerce means:

(1) Any trade, traffic or transportation within the jurisdiction of the United States between a place in a State and a place outside of such State, including a place outside of the United States; and

(2) Trade, traffic, and transportation in the United States which affects any trade, traffic, and transportation described in paragraph (1) of this definition.

Commercial motor vehicle means a motor vehicle or combination of motor vehicles used in commerce to transport passengers or property if the vehicle—

(1) Has a gross combination weight rating of 11,794 or more kilograms (26,001 or more pounds) inclusive of a towed unit with a gross vehicle weight rating of more than 4,536 kilograms (10,000 pounds); or

(2) Has a gross vehicle weight rating of 11,794 or more kilograms (26,001 or more pounds); or

(3) Is designed to transport 16 or more passengers, including the driver; or

(4) Is of any size and is used in the transportation of materials found to be hazardous for the purposes of the Hazardous Materials Transportation Act (49 U.S.C. 5103(b)) and which require the motor vehicle to be placarded under the Hazardous Materials Regulations (49 CFR part 172, subpart F).

Confirmation (or confirmatory) drug test means a second analytical procedure performed on a urine specimen to identify and quantify the presence of a specific drug or drug metabolite.

Confirmation (or confirmatory) validity test means a second test performed on a urine specimen to further support a validity test result.

Confirmed drug test means a confirmation test result received by an MRO from a laboratory.

Consortium/Third party administrator (C/TPA) means a service agent that provides or coordinates one or more drug and/or alcohol testing services to DOT-regulated employers. C/TPAs typically provide or coordinate the provision of a number of such services and perform administrative tasks concerning the operation of the employers' drug and alcohol testing programs. This term includes, but is not limited to, groups of employers who join together to administer, as a single entity, the DOT drug and alcohol testing programs of its members (e.g., having a combined random testing pool). C/TPAs are not "employers" for purposes of this part.

Controlled substances mean those substances identified in §40.85 of this title.

Designated employer representative (DER) is an individual identified by the employer as able to receive communications and test results from service agents and who is authorized to take immediate actions to remove employees from safety-sensitive duties and to make required decisions in the testing and evaluation processes. The individual must be an employee of the company. Service agents cannot serve as DERs.

Disabling damage means damage which precludes departure of a motor vehicle from the scene of the accident in its usual manner in daylight after simple repairs.

(1) *Inclusions.* Damage to motor vehicles that could have been driven, but would have been further damaged if so driven.

(2) *Exclusions.* (i) Damage which can be remedied temporarily at the scene of the accident without special tools or parts.

(ii) Tire disablement without other damage even if no spare tire is available.

(iii) Headlight or taillight damage.

(iv) Damage to turn signals, horn, or windshield wipers which make them inoperative.

DOT Agency means an agency (or "operating administration") of the United States Department of Transportation administering regulations requiring alcohol and/or drug testing (14 CFR parts 61, 63, 65, 121, and 135; 49 CFR parts 199, 219, 382, and 655), in accordance with part 40 of this title.

Driver means any person who operates a commercial motor vehicle. This includes, but is not limited to: Full time, regularly employed drivers; casual, intermittent or occasional drivers; leased drivers and independent owner-operator contractors.

Employer means a person or entity employing one or more employees (including an individual who is self-employed) that is subject to DOT agency regulations requiring compliance with this part. The term, as used in this part, means the entity responsible for overall implementation of DOT drug and alcohol program requirements, including individuals employed by the entity who take personnel actions resulting from violations of this part and any applicable DOT agency regulations. Service agents are not employers for the purposes of this part.

Licensed medical practitioner means a person who is licensed, certified, and/or registered, in accordance with applicable Federal, State, local, or foreign laws and regulations, to prescribe controlled substances and other drugs.

Performing (a safety-sensitive function) means a driver is considered to be performing a safety-sensitive function during any period in which he or she is actually performing, ready to perform, or immediately available to perform any safety-sensitive functions.

Positive rate for random drug testing means the number of verified positive results for random drug tests conducted under this part plus the number of refusals of random drug tests required by this part, divided by the total number of random drug tests results (*i.e.*, positives, negatives, and refusals) under this part.

Refuse to submit (to an alcohol or controlled substances test) means that a driver:

(1) Fail to appear for any test (except a pre-employment test) within a reasonable time, as determined by the employer, consistent with applicable DOT agency regulations, after being directed to do so by the employer. This includes the failure of an employee (including an owner-operator) to appear for a test when called by a C/TPA (see § 40.61(a) of this title);

(2) Fail to remain at the testing site until the testing process is complete. Provided, that an employee who leaves the testing site before the testing process commences (see § 40.63(c) of this title) a pre-employment test is not deemed to have refused to test;

(3) Fail to provide a urine specimen for any drug test required by this part or DOT agency regulations. Provided, that an employee who does not provide a urine specimen because he or she has left the testing site before the testing process commences (see § 40.63(c) of this title) for a pre-employment test is not deemed to have refused to test;

(4) In the case of a directly observed or monitored collection in a drug test, fails to permit the observation or monitoring of the driver's provision of a specimen (see §§ 40.67(l) and 40.69(g) of this title);

(5) Fail to provide a sufficient amount of urine when directed, and it has been determined, through a required medical evaluation, that there

was no adequate medical explanation for the failure (see § 40.193(d)(2) of this title);

(6) Fail or declines to take a second test the employer or collector has directed the driver to take;

(7) Fail to undergo a medical examination or evaluation, as directed by the MRO as part of the verification process, or as directed by the DER under § 40.193(d) of this title. In the case of a pre-employment drug test, the employee is deemed to have refused to test on this basis only if the pre-employment test is conducted following a contingent offer of employment;

(8) Fail to cooperate with any part of the testing process (e.g., refuse to empty pockets when so directed by the collector, behave in a confrontational way that disrupts the collection process); or

(9) Is reported by the MRO as having a verified adulterated or substituted test result.

Safety-sensitive function means all time from the time a driver begins to work or is required to be in readiness to work until the time he/she is relieved from work and all responsibility for performing work. Safety-sensitive functions shall include:

(1) All time at an employer or shipper plant, terminal, facility, or other property, or on any public property, waiting to be dispatched, unless the driver has been relieved from duty by the employer;

(2) All time inspecting equipment as required by §§ 392.7 and 392.8 of this subchapter or otherwise inspecting, servicing, or conditioning any commercial motor vehicle at any time;

(3) All time spent at the driving controls of a commercial motor vehicle in operation;

(4) All time, other than driving time, in or upon any commercial motor vehicle except time spent resting in a sleeper berth (a berth conforming to the requirements of § 393.76 of this subchapter);

(5) All time loading or unloading a vehicle, supervising, or assisting in the loading or unloading, attending a vehicle being loaded or unloaded, remaining in readiness to operate the vehicle, or in giving or receiving receipts for shipments loaded or unloaded; and

(6) All time repairing, obtaining assistance, or remaining in attendance upon a disabled vehicle.

Screening test (or initial test) means:

(1) In drug testing, a test to eliminate "negative" urine specimens from further analysis or to identify a specimen that requires additional testing for the presence of drugs.

(2) In alcohol testing, an analytical procedure to determine whether an employee may have a prohibited concentration of alcohol in a breath or saliva specimen.

Stand-down means the practice of temporarily removing an employee from the performance of safety-sensitive functions based only on a report from a laboratory to the MRO of a confirmed positive test for a drug or drug metabolite, an adulterated test, or a substituted test, before the MRO has completed verification of the test results.

Violation rate for random alcohol testing means the number of 0.04 and above random alcohol confirmation test results conducted under this part plus the number of refusals of random alcohol tests required by this part, divided by the total number of random alcohol screening tests (including refusals) conducted under this part.

[66 FR 43103, Aug. 17, 2001, as amended at 68 FR 75458, Dec. 31, 2003]

§382.109 Preemption of State and local laws.

(a) Except as provided in paragraph (b) of this section, this part preempts any State or local law, rule, regulation, or order to the extent that:

(1) Compliance with both the State or local requirement in this part is not possible; or

(2) Compliance with the State or local requirement is an obstacle to the accomplishment and execution of any requirement in this part.

(b) This part shall not be construed to preempt provisions of State criminal law that impose sanctions for reckless conduct leading to actual loss of life, injury, or damage to property, whether the provisions apply specifically to transportation employees, employers, or the general public.

§382.111 Other requirements imposed by employers.

Except as expressly provided in this part, nothing in this part shall be construed to affect the authority of employers, or the rights of drivers, with respect to the use of alcohol, or the use of controlled substances, including authority and rights with respect to testing and rehabilitation.

§382.113 Requirement for notice.

Before performing each alcohol or controlled substances test under this part, each employer shall notify a driver that the alcohol or controlled substances test is required by this part. No employer shall falsely represent that a test is administered under this part.

§382.115 Starting date for testing programs.

(a) All domestic-domiciled employers must implement the requirements of this part on the date the employer begins commercial motor vehicle operations.

(b) All foreign-domiciled employers must implement the requirements of this part on the date the employer begins commercial motor vehicle operations in the United States.

§382.117 Public interest exclusion.

No employer shall use the services of a service agent who is subject to public interest exclusion in accordance with 49 CFR part 40, Subpart R.

§382.119 Stand-down waiver provision.

(a) Employers are prohibited from standing employees down, except consistent with a waiver from the Federal Motor Carrier Safety Administration as required under this section.

(b) An employer subject to this part who seeks a waiver from the prohibition against standing down an employee before the MRO has completed the verification process shall follow the procedures in 49 CFR 40.21. The employer must send a written request, which includes all of the information required by that section to the Administrator, Federal Motor Carrier Safety Administration, 1200 New Jersey Ave., SE., Washington, DC 20590–0001.

(c) The final decision whether to grant or deny the application for a waiver will be made by the Administrator or the Administrator's designee.

(d) After a decision is signed by the Administrator or the Administrator's designee, the employer will be sent a copy of the decision, which will include the terms and conditions for the waiver or the reason for denying the application for a waiver.

(e) Questions regarding waiver applications should be directed to the Federal Motor Carrier Safety Administration, Office of Enforcement and Compliance (MC–EC), 1200 New Jersey Ave., SE., Washington, DC 20590–0001.

[66 FR 43103, Aug. 17, 2001, as amended at 72 FR 55700, Oct. 1, 2007]

§ 382.121 Employee admission of alcohol and controlled substances use.

(a) Employees who admit to alcohol misuse or controlled substances use are not subject to the referral, evaluation and treatment requirements of this part and part 40 of this title, provided that:

(1) The admission is in accordance with a written employer-established voluntary self-identification program or policy that meets the requirements of paragraph (b) of this section;

(2) The driver does not self-identify in order to avoid testing under the requirements of this part;

(3) The driver makes the admission of alcohol misuse or controlled substances use prior to performing a safety sensitive function (i.e., prior to reporting for duty); and

(4) The driver does not perform a safety sensitive function until the employer is satisfied that the employee has been evaluated and has successfully completed education or treatment requirements in accordance with the self-identification program guidelines.

(b) A qualified voluntary self-identification program or policy must contain the following elements:

(1) It must prohibit the employer from taking adverse action against an employee making a voluntary admission of alcohol misuse or controlled substances use within the parameters of the program or policy and paragraph (a) of this section;

(2) It must allow the employee sufficient opportunity to seek evaluation, education or treatment to establish control over the employee's drug or alcohol problem;

(3) It must permit the employee to return to safety sensitive duties only upon successful completion of an educational or treatment program, as determined by a drug and alcohol abuse evaluation expert, i.e., employee assistance professional, substance abuse professional, or qualified drug and alcohol counselor;

(4) It must ensure that:

(i) Prior to the employee participating in a safety sensitive function, the employee shall undergo a return to duty test with a result indicating an alcohol concentration of less than 0.02; and/or

(ii) Prior to the employee participating in a safety sensitive function, the employee shall undergo a return to duty controlled substance test with a verified negative test result for controlled substances use; and

(5) It may incorporate employee monitoring and include non-DOT follow-up testing.

Subpart B—Prohibitions

§ 382.201 Alcohol concentration.

No driver shall report for duty or remain on duty requiring the performance of safety-sensitive functions while having an alcohol concentration of 0.04 or greater. No employer having actual knowledge that a driver has an alcohol concentration of 0.04 or greater shall permit the driver to perform or continue to perform safety-sensitive functions.

§ 382.205 On-duty use.

No driver shall use alcohol while performing safety-sensitive functions. No employer having actual knowledge that a driver is using alcohol while performing safety-sensitive functions shall permit the driver to perform or continue to perform safety-sensitive functions.

§ 382.207 Pre-duty use.

No driver shall perform safety-sensitive functions within four hours after using alcohol. No employer having actual knowledge that a driver has used alcohol within four hours shall permit a driver to perform or continue to perform safety-sensitive functions.

§382.209 Use following an accident.

No driver required to take a post-accident alcohol test under §382.303 shall use alcohol for eight hours following the accident, or until he/she undergoes a post-accident alcohol test, whichever occurs first.

§382.211 Refusal to submit to a required alcohol or controlled substances test.

No driver shall refuse to submit to a post-accident alcohol or controlled substances test required under §382.303, a random alcohol or controlled substances test required under §382.305, a reasonable suspicion alcohol or controlled substances test required under §382.307, or a follow-up alcohol or controlled substances test required under §382.311. No employer shall permit a driver who refuses to submit to such tests to perform or continue to perform safety-sensitive functions.

§382.213 Controlled substances use.

(a) No driver shall report for duty or remain on duty requiring the performance of safety-sensitive functions when the driver uses any controlled substance, except when the use is pursuant to the instructions of a licensed medical practitioner, as defined in §382.107, who has advised the driver that the substance will not adversely affect the driver's ability to safely operate a commercial motor vehicle.

(b) No employer having actual knowledge that a driver has used a controlled substance shall permit the driver to perform or continue to perform a safety-sensitive function.

(c) An employer may require a driver to inform the employer of any therapeutic drug use.

§382.215 Controlled substances testing.

No driver shall report for duty, remain on duty or perform a safety-sensitive function, if the driver tests positive or has adulterated or substituted a test specimen for controlled substances. No employer having actual knowledge that a driver has tested positive or has adulterated or substituted a test specimen for controlled substances shall permit the driver to perform or continue to perform safety-sensitive functions.

Subpart C—Tests Required

§382.301 Pre-employment testing.

(a) Prior to the first time a driver performs safety-sensitive functions for an employer, the driver shall undergo testing for controlled substances as a condition prior to being used, unless the employer uses the exception in paragraph (b) of this section. No employer shall allow a driver, who the employer intends to hire or use, to perform safety-sensitive functions unless the employer has received a controlled substances test result from the MRO or C/TPA indicating a verified negative test result for that driver.

(b) An employer is not required to administer a controlled substances test required by paragraph (a) of this section if:

(1) The driver has participated in a controlled substances testing program that meets the requirements of this part within the previous 30 days; and

(2) While participating in that program, either:

(i) Was tested for controlled substances within the past 6 months (from the date of application with the employer), or

(ii) Participated in the random controlled substances testing program for the previous 12 months (from the date of application with the employer); and

(3) The employer ensures that no prior employer of the driver of whom the employer has knowledge has records of a violation of this part or the controlled substances use rule of another DOT agency within the previous six months.

(c)(1) An employer who exercises the exception in paragraph (b) of this section shall contact the controlled substances testing program(s) in which the driver participates or participated and shall obtain and retain from the testing program(s) the following information:

175

(i) Name(s) and address(es) of the program(s).

(ii) Verification that the driver participates or participated in the program(s).

(iii) Verification that the program(s) conforms to part 40 of this title.

(iv) Verification that the driver is qualified under the rules of this part, including that the driver has not refused to be tested for controlled substances.

(v) The date the driver was last tested for controlled substances.

(vi) The results of any tests taken within the previous six months and any other violations of subpart B of this part.

(2) An employer who uses, but does not employ a driver more than once a year to operate commercial motor vehicles must obtain the information in paragraph (c)(1) of this section at least once every six months. The records prepared under this paragraph shall be maintained in accordance with § 382.401. If the employer cannot verify that the driver is participating in a controlled substances testing program in accordance with this part and part 40 of this title, the employer shall conduct a pre-employment controlled substances test.

(d) An employer may, but is not required to, conduct pre-employment alcohol testing under this part. If an employer chooses to conduct pre-employment alcohol testing, it must comply with the following requirements:

(1) It must conduct a pre-employment alcohol test before the first performance of safety-sensitive functions by every covered employee (whether a new employee or someone who has transferred to a position involving the performance of safety-sensitive functions).

(2) It must treat all safety-sensitive employees performing safety-sensitive functions the same for the purpose of pre-employment alcohol testing (i.e., it must not test some covered employees and not others).

(3) It must conduct the pre-employment tests after making a contingent offer of employment or transfer, subject to the employee passing the pre-employment alcohol test.

(4) It must conduct all pre-employment alcohol tests using the alcohol testing procedures of 49 CFR part 40 of this title.

(5) It must not allow a covered employee to begin performing safety-sensitive functions unless the result of the employee's test indicates an alcohol concentration of less than 0.04.

§ 382.303 Post-accident testing.

(a) As soon as practicable following an occurrence involving a commercial motor vehicle operating on a public road in commerce, each employer shall test for alcohol for each of its surviving drivers:

(1) Who was performing safety-sensitive functions with respect to the vehicle, if the accident involved the loss of human life; or

(2) Who receives a citation within 8 hours of the occurrence under State or local law for a moving traffic violation arising from the accident, if the accident involved:

(i) Bodily injury to any person who, as a result of the injury, immediately receives medical treatment away from the scene of the accident; or

(ii) One or more motor vehicles incurring disabling damage as a result of the accident, requiring the motor vehicle to be transported away from the scene by a tow truck or other motor vehicle.

(b) As soon as practicable following an occurrence involving a commercial motor vehicle operating on a public road in commerce, each employer shall test for controlled substances for each of its surviving drivers:

(1) Who was performing safety-sensitive functions with respect to the vehicle, if the accident involved the loss of human life; or

(2) Who receives a citation within thirty-two hours of the occurrence under State or local law for a moving traffic violation arising from the accident, if the accident involved:

(i) Bodily injury to any person who, as a result of the injury, immediately receives medical treatment away from the scene of the accident; or

(ii) One or more motor vehicles incurring disabling damage as a result of the accident, requiring the motor vehicle to be transported away from the scene by a tow truck or other motor vehicle.

(c) The following table notes when a post-accident test is required to be con- ducted by paragraphs (a)(1), (a)(2), (b)(1), and (b)(2) of this section:

TABLE FOR §382.303(A) AND (B)

Type of accident involved	Citation issued to the CMV driver	Test must be performed by employer
i. Human fatality	YES	YES
	NO	YES
ii. Bodily injury with immediate medical treatment away from the scene	YES	YES
	NO	NO
iii. Disabling damage to any motor vehicle requiring tow away	YES	YES
	NO	NO

(d)(1) *Alcohol tests.* If a test required by this section is not administered within two hours following the accident, the employer shall prepare and maintain on file a record stating the reasons the test was not promptly administered. If a test required by this section is not administered within eight hours following the accident, the employer shall cease attempts to administer an alcohol test and shall prepare and maintain the same record. Records shall be submitted to the FMCSA upon request.

(2) *Controlled substance tests.* If a test required by this section is not administered within 32 hours following the accident, the employer shall cease attempts to administer a controlled substances test, and prepare and maintain on file a record stating the reasons the test was not promptly administered. Records shall be submitted to the FMCSA upon request.

(e) A driver who is subject to post-accident testing shall remain readily available for such testing or may be deemed by the employer to have refused to submit to testing. Nothing in this section shall be construed to require the delay of necessary medical attention for injured people following an accident or to prohibit a driver from leaving the scene of an accident for the period necessary to obtain assistance in responding to the accident, or to obtain necessary emergency medical care.

(f) An employer shall provide drivers with necessary post-accident information, procedures and instructions, prior to the driver operating a commercial motor vehicle, so that drivers will be able to comply with the requirements of this section.

(g)(1) The results of a breath or blood test for the use of alcohol, conducted by Federal, State, or local officials having independent authority for the test, shall be considered to meet the requirements of this section, provided such tests conform to the applicable Federal, State or local alcohol testing requirements, and that the results of the tests are obtained by the employer.

(2) The results of a urine test for the use of controlled substances, conducted by Federal, State, or local officials having independent authority for the test, shall be considered to meet the requirements of this section, provided such tests conform to the applicable Federal, State or local controlled substances testing requirements, and that the results of the tests are obtained by the employer.

(h) *Exception.* This section does not apply to:

(1) An occurrence involving only boarding or alighting from a stationary motor vehicle; or

(2) An occurrence involving only the loading or unloading of cargo; or

(3) An occurrence in the course of the operation of a passenger car or a multi-purpose passenger vehicle (as defined in §571.3 of this title) by an employer unless the motor vehicle is transporting passengers for hire or hazardous materials of a type and quantity that require the motor vehicle to be marked or placarded in accordance with §177.823 of this title.

177

§ 382.305 Random testing.

(a) Every employer shall comply with the requirements of this section. Every driver shall submit to random alcohol and controlled substance testing as required in this section.

(b)(1) Except as provided in paragraphs (c) through (e) of this section, the minimum annual percentage rate for random alcohol testing shall be 10 percent of the average number of driver positions.

(2) Except as provided in paragraphs (f) through (h) of this section, the minimum annual percentage rate for random controlled substances testing shall be 50 percent of the average number of driver positions.

(c) The FMCSA Administrator's decision to increase or decrease the minimum annual percentage rate for alcohol testing is based on the reported violation rate for the entire industry. All information used for this determination is drawn from the alcohol management information system reports required by § 382.403. In order to ensure reliability of the data, the FMCSA Administrator considers the quality and completeness of the reported data, may obtain additional information or reports from employers, and may make appropriate modifications in calculating the industry violation rate. In the event of a change in the annual percentage rate, the FMCSA Administrator will publish in the FEDERAL REGISTER the new minimum annual percentage rate for random alcohol testing of drivers. The new minimum annual percentage rate for random alcohol testing will be applicable starting January 1 of the calendar year following publication in the FEDERAL REGISTER.

(d)(1) When the minimum annual percentage rate for random alcohol testing is 25 percent or more, the FMCSA Administrator may lower this rate to 10 percent of all driver positions if the FMCSA Administrator determines that the data received under the reporting requirements of § 382.403 for two consecutive calendar years indicate that the violation rate is less than 0.5 percent.

(2) When the minimum annual percentage rate for random alcohol testing is 50 percent, the FMCSA Adminis-

trator may lower this rate to 25 percent of all driver positions if the FMCSA Administrator determines that the data received under the reporting requirements of § 382.403 for two consecutive calendar years indicate that the violation rate is less than 1.0 percent but equal to or greater than 0.5 percent.

(e)(1) When the minimum annual percentage rate for random alcohol testing is 10 percent, and the data received under the reporting requirements of § 382.403 for that calendar year indicate that the violation rate is equal to or greater than 0.5 percent, but less than 1.0 percent, the FMCSA Administrator will increase the minimum annual percentage rate for random alcohol testing to 25 percent for all driver positions.

(2) When the minimum annual percentage rate for random alcohol testing is 25 percent or less, and the data received under the reporting requirements of § 382.403 for that calendar year indicate that the violation rate is equal to or greater than 1.0 percent, the FMCSA Administrator will increase the minimum annual percentage rate for random alcohol testing to 50 percent for all driver positions.

(f) The FMCSA Administrator's decision to increase or decrease the minimum annual percentage rate for controlled substances testing is based on the reported positive rate for the entire industry. All information used for this determination is drawn from the controlled substances management information system reports required by § 382.403. In order to ensure reliability of the data, the FMCSA Administrator considers the quality and completeness of the reported data, may obtain additional information or reports from employers, and may make appropriate modifications in calculating the industry positive rate. In the event of a change in the annual percentage rate, the FMCSA Administrator will publish in the FEDERAL REGISTER the new minimum annual percentage rate for controlled substances testing of drivers. The new minimum annual percentage rate for random controlled substances testing will be applicable starting January 1 of the calendar year following publication in the FEDERAL REGISTER.

(g) When the minimum annual percentage rate for random controlled substances testing is 50 percent, the FMCSA Administrator may lower this rate to 25 percent of all driver positions if the FMCSA Administrator determines that the data received under the reporting requirements of §382.403 for two consecutive calendar years indicate that the positive rate is less than 1.0 percent.

(h) When the minimum annual percentage rate for random controlled substances testing is 25 percent, and the data received under the reporting requirements of §382.403 for any calendar year indicate that the reported positive rate is equal to or greater than 1.0 percent, the FMCSA Administrator will increase the minimum annual percentage rate for random controlled substances testing to 50 percent of all driver positions.

(i)(1) The selection of drivers for random alcohol and controlled substances testing shall be made by a scientifically valid method, such as a random number table or a computer-based random number generator that is matched with drivers' Social Security numbers, payroll identification numbers, or other comparable identifying numbers.

(2) Each driver selected for random alcohol and controlled substances testing under the selection process used, shall have an equal chance of being tested each time selections are made.

(3) Each driver selected for testing shall be tested during the selection period.

(j)(1)To calculate the total number of covered drivers eligible for random testing throughout the year, as an employer, you must add the total number of covered drivers eligible for testing during each random testing period for the year and divide that total by the number of random testing periods. Covered employees, and only covered employees, are to be in an employer's random testing pool, and all covered drivers must be in the random pool. If you are an employer conducting random testing more often than once per month (e.g., daily, weekly, bi-weekly) you do not need to compute this total number of covered drivers rate more than on a once per month basis.

(2) As an employer, you may use a service agent (e.g., a C/TPA) to perform random selections for you, and your covered drivers may be part of a larger random testing pool of covered employees. However, you must ensure that the service agent you use is testing at the appropriate percentage established for your industry and that only covered employees are in the random testing pool.

(k)(1) Each employer shall ensure that random alcohol and controlled substances tests conducted under this part are unannounced.

(2) Each employer shall ensure that the dates for administering random alcohol and controlled substances tests conducted under this part are spread reasonably throughout the calendar year.

(l) Each employer shall require that each driver who is notified of selection for random alcohol and/or controlled substances testing proceeds to the test site immediately; provided, however, that if the driver is performing a safety-sensitive function, other than driving a commercial motor vehicle, at the time of notification, the employer shall instead ensure that the driver ceases to perform the safety-sensitive function and proceeds to the testing site as soon as possible.

(m) A driver shall only be tested for alcohol while the driver is performing safety-sensitive functions, just before the driver is to perform safety-sensitive functions, or just after the driver has ceased performing such functions.

(n) If a given driver is subject to random alcohol or controlled substances testing under the random alcohol or controlled substances testing rules of more than one DOT agency for the same employer, the driver shall be subject to random alcohol and/or controlled substances testing at the annual percentage rate established for the calendar year by the DOT agency regulating more than 50 percent of the driver's function.

(o) If an employer is required to conduct random alcohol or controlled substances testing under the alcohol or controlled substances testing rules of more than one DOT agency, the employer may—

179

(1) Establish separate pools for random selection, with each pool containing the DOT-covered employees who are subject to testing at the same required minimum annual percentage rate; or

(2) Randomly select such employees for testing at the highest minimum annual percentage rate established for the calendar year by any DOT agency to which the employer is subject.

[66 FR 43103, Aug. 17, 2001, as amended at 67 FR 61821, Oct. 2, 2002; 68 FR 75459, Dec. 31, 2003]

§ 382.307 Reasonable suspicion testing.

(a) An employer shall require a driver to submit to an alcohol test when the employer has reasonable suspicion to believe that the driver has violated the prohibitions of subpart B of this part concerning alcohol. The employer's determination that reasonable suspicion exists to require the driver to undergo an alcohol test must be based on specific, contemporaneous, articulable observations concerning the appearance, behavior, speech or body odors of the driver.

(b) An employer shall require a driver to submit to a controlled substances test when the employer has reasonable suspicion to believe that the driver has violated the prohibitions of subpart B of this part concerning controlled substances. The employer's determination that reasonable suspicion exists to require the driver to undergo a controlled substances test must be based on specific, contemporaneous, articulable observations concerning the appearance, behavior, speech or body odors of the driver. The observations may include indications of the chronic and withdrawal effects of controlled substances.

(c) The required observations for alcohol and/or controlled substances reasonable suspicion testing shall be made by a supervisor or company official who is trained in accordance with § 382.603. The person who makes the determination that reasonable suspicion exists to conduct an alcohol test shall not conduct the alcohol test of the driver.

(d) Alcohol testing is authorized by this section only if the observations required by paragraph (a) of this section are made during, just preceding, or just after the period of the work day that the driver is required to be in compliance with this part. A driver may be directed by the employer to only undergo reasonable suspicion testing while the driver is performing safety-sensitive functions, just before the driver is to perform safety-sensitive functions, or just after the driver has ceased performing such functions.

(e)(1) If an alcohol test required by this section is not administered within two hours following the determination under paragraph (a) of this section, the employer shall prepare and maintain on file a record stating the reasons the alcohol test was not promptly administered. If an alcohol test required by this section is not administered within eight hours following the determination under paragraph (a) of this section, the employer shall cease attempts to administer an alcohol test and shall state in the record the reasons for not administering the test.

(2) Notwithstanding the absence of a reasonable suspicion alcohol test under this section, no driver shall report for duty or remain on duty requiring the performance of safety-sensitive functions while the driver is under the influence of or impaired by alcohol, as shown by the behavioral, speech, and performance indicators of alcohol misuse, nor shall an employer permit the driver to perform or continue to perform safety-sensitive functions, until:

(i) An alcohol test is administered and the driver's alcohol concentration measures less than 0.02; or

(ii) Twenty four hours have elapsed following the determination under paragraph (a) of this section that there is reasonable suspicion to believe that the driver has violated the prohibitions in this part concerning the use of alcohol.

(3) Except as provided in paragraph (e)(2) of this section, no employer shall take any action under this part against a driver based solely on the driver's behavior and appearance, with respect to alcohol use, in the absence of an alcohol test. This does not prohibit an employer with independent authority of this part from taking any action otherwise consistent with law.

(f) A written record shall be made of the observations leading to an alcohol or controlled substances reasonable suspicion test, and signed by the supervisor or company official who made the observations, within 24 hours of the observed behavior or before the results of the alcohol or controlled substances tests are released, whichever is earlier.

§382.309 Return-to-duty testing.

The requirements for return-to-duty testing must be performed in accordance with 49 CFR part 40, subpart O.

§382.311 Follow-up testing.

The requirements for follow-up testing must be performed in accordance with 49 CFR part 40, subpart O.

Subpart D—Handling of Test Results, Records Retention, and Confidentiality

§382.401 Retention of records.

(a) *General requirement.* Each employer shall maintain records of its alcohol misuse and controlled substances use prevention programs as provided in this section. The records shall be maintained in a secure location with controlled access.

(b) *Period of retention.* Each employer shall maintain the records in accordance with the following schedule:

(1) *Five years.* The following records shall be maintained for a minimum of five years:

(i) Records of driver alcohol test results indicating an alcohol concentration of 0.02 or greater,

(ii) Records of driver verified positive controlled substances test results,

(iii) Documentation of refusals to take required alcohol and/or controlled substances tests,

(iv) Driver evaluation and referrals,

(v) Calibration documentation,

(vi) Records related to the administration of the alcohol and controlled substances testing programs, and

(vii) A copy of each annual calendar year summary required by §382.403.

(2) *Two years.* Records related to the alcohol and controlled substances collection process (except calibration of evidential breath testing devices).

(3) *One year.* Records of negative and canceled controlled substances test results (as defined in part 40 of this title) and alcohol test results with a concentration of less than 0.02 shall be maintained for a minimum of one year.

(4) *Indefinite period.* Records related to the education and training of breath alcohol technicians, screening test technicians, supervisors, and drivers shall be maintained by the employer while the individual performs the functions which require the training and for two years after ceasing to perform those functions.

(c) *Types of records.* The following specific types of records shall be maintained. "Documents generated" are documents that may have to be prepared under a requirement of this part. If the record is required to be prepared, it must be maintained.

(1) Records related to the collection process:

(i) Collection logbooks, if used;

(ii) Documents relating to the random selection process;

(iii) Calibration documentation for evidential breath testing devices;

(iv) Documentation of breath alcohol technician training;

(v) Documents generated in connection with decisions to administer reasonable suspicion alcohol or controlled substances tests;

(vi) Documents generated in connection with decisions on post-accident tests;

(vii) Documents verifying existence of a medical explanation of the inability of a driver to provide adequate breath or to provide a urine specimen for testing; and

(viii) A copy of each annual calendar year summary as required by §382.403.

(2) Records related to a driver's test results:

(i) The employer's copy of the alcohol test form, including the results of the test;

(ii) The employer's copy of the controlled substances test chain of custody and control form;

(iii) Documents sent by the MRO to the employer, including those required by part 40, subpart G, of this title;

(iv) Documents related to the refusal of any driver to submit to an alcohol or controlled substances test required by this part;

(v) Documents presented by a driver to dispute the result of an alcohol or controlled substances test administered under this part; and

(vi) Documents generated in connection with verifications of prior employers' alcohol or controlled substances test results that the employer:

(A) Must obtain in connection with the exception contained in § 382.301, and

(B) Must obtain as required by § 382.413.

(3) Records related to other violations of this part.

(4) Records related to evaluations:

(i) Records pertaining to a determination by a substance abuse professional concerning a driver's need for assistance; and

(ii) Records concerning a driver's compliance with recommendations of the substance abuse professional.

(5) Records related to education and training:

(i) Materials on alcohol misuse and controlled substance use awareness, including a copy of the employer's policy on alcohol misuse and controlled substance use;

(ii) Documentation of compliance with the requirements of § 382.601, including the driver's signed receipt of education materials;

(iii) Documentation of training provided to supervisors for the purpose of qualifying the supervisors to make a determination concerning the need for alcohol and/or controlled substances testing based on reasonable suspicion;

(iv) Documentation of training for breath alcohol technicians as required by § 40.213(a) of this title; and

(v) Certification that any training conducted under this part complies with the requirements for such training.

(6) Administrative records related to alcohol and controlled substances testing:

(i) Agreements with collection site facilities, laboratories, breath alcohol technicians, screening test technicians, medical review officers, consortia, and third party service providers;

(ii) Names and positions of officials and their role in the employer's alcohol and controlled substances testing program(s);

(iii) Semi-annual laboratory statistical summaries of urinalysis required by § 40.111(a) of this title; and

(iv) The employer's alcohol and controlled substances testing policy and procedures.

(d) *Location of records.* All records required by this part shall be maintained as required by § 390.31 of this subchapter and shall be made available for inspection at the employer's principal place of business within two business days after a request has been made by an authorized representative of the Federal Motor Carrier Safety Administration.

(e) *OMB control number.* (1) The information collection requirements of this part have been reviewed by the Office of Management and Budget pursuant to the Paperwork Reduction Act of 1995 (44 U.S.C. 3501 et seq.) and have been assigned OMB control number 2126-0012.

(2) The information collection requirements of this part are found in the following sections: Sections 382.105, 382.113, 382.301, 382.303, 382.305, 382.307, 382.401, 382.403, 382.405, 382.409, 382.411, 382.601, 382.603.

[66 FR 43103, Aug. 17, 2001, as amended at 67 FR 61821, Oct. 2, 2002; 68 FR 75459, Dec. 31, 2003]

§ 382.403 Reporting of results in a management information system.

(a) An employer shall prepare and maintain a summary of the results of its alcohol and controlled substances testing programs performed under this part during the previous calendar year, when requested by the Secretary of Transportation, any DOT agency, or any State or local officials with regulatory authority over the employer or any of its drivers.

(b) If an employer is notified, during the month of January, of a request by the Federal Motor Carrier Safety Administration to report the employer's annual calendar year summary information, the employer shall prepare and submit the report to the FMCSA by March 15 of that year. The employer shall ensure that the annual summary report is accurate and received by March 15 at the location that the FMCSA specifies in its request. The employer must use the Management

Information System (MIS) form and instructions as required by 49 CFR part 40 (at §40.26 and appendix H to part 40). The employer may also use the electronic version of the MIS form provided by the DOT. The Administrator may designate means (*e.g.*, electronic program transmitted via the Internet), other than hard-copy, for MIS form submission. For information on the electronic version of the form, see: *http://www.fmcsa.dot.gov/safetyprogs/drugs/engtesting.htm.*

(c) When the report is submitted to the FMCSA by mail or electronic transmission, the information requested shall be typed, except for the signature of the certifying official. Each employer shall ensure the accuracy and timeliness of each report submitted by the employer or a consortium.

(d) If you have a covered employee who performs multi-DOT agency functions (*e.g.*, an employee drives a commercial motor vehicle and performs pipeline maintenance duties for the same employer), count the employee only on the MIS report for the DOT agency under which he or she is randomly tested. Normally, this will be the DOT agency under which the employee performs more than 50% of his or her duties. Employers may have to explain the testing data for these employees in the event of a DOT agency inspection or audit.

(e) A service agent (*e.g.*, *Consortia/Third party administrator* as defined in 49 CFR 382.107) may prepare the MIS report on behalf of an employer. However, a company official (*e.g.*, *Designated employer representative*) must certify the accuracy and completeness of the MIS report, no matter who prepares it.

[66 FR 43103, Aug. 17, 2001, as amended at 68 FR 75459, Dec. 31, 2003]

§382.405 Access to facilities and records.

(a) Except as required by law or expressly authorized or required in this section, no employer shall release driver information that is contained in records required to be maintained under §382.401.

(b) A driver is entitled, upon written request, to obtain copies of any records pertaining to the driver's use of alcohol or controlled substances, including any records pertaining to his or her alcohol or controlled substances tests. The employer shall promptly provide the records requested by the driver. Access to a driver's records shall not be contingent upon payment for records other than those specifically requested.

(c) Each employer shall permit access to all facilities utilized in complying with the requirements of this part to the Secretary of Transportation, any DOT agency, or any State or local officials with regulatory authority over the employer or any of its drivers.

(d) Each employer shall make available copies of all results for employer alcohol and/or controlled substances testing conducted under this part and any other information pertaining to the employer's alcohol misuse and/or controlled substances use prevention program, when requested by the Secretary of Transportation, any DOT agency, or any State or local officials with regulatory authority over the employer or any of its drivers.

(e) When requested by the National Transportation Safety Board as part of an accident investigation, employers shall disclose information related to the employer's administration of a post-accident alcohol and/or controlled substance test administered following the accident under investigation.

(f) Records shall be made available to a subsequent employer upon receipt of a written request from a driver. Disclosure by the subsequent employer is permitted only as expressly authorized by the terms of the driver's request.

(g) An employer may disclose information required to be maintained under this part pertaining to a driver to the decision maker in a lawsuit, grievance, or administrative proceeding initiated by or on behalf of the individual, and arising from a positive DOT drug or alcohol test or a refusal to test (including, but not limited to, adulterated or substituted test results) of this part (including, but not limited to, a worker's compensation, unemployment compensation, or other proceeding relating to a benefit sought by the driver). Additionally, an employer may disclose information in criminal or civil actions in accordance with § 40.323(a)(2) of this title.

(h) An employer shall release information regarding a driver's records as directed by the specific written consent of the driver authorizing release of the information to an identified person. Release of such information by the person receiving the information is permitted only in accordance with the terms of the employee's specific written consent as outlined in § 40.321(b) of this title.

§ 382.407 Medical review officer notifications to the employer.

Medical review officers shall report the results of controlled substances tests to employers in accordance with the requirements of part 40, Subpart G, of this title.

§ 382.409 Medical review officer record retention for controlled substances.

(a) A medical review officer or third party administrator shall maintain all dated records and notifications, identified by individual, for a minimum of five years for verified positive controlled substances test results.

(b) A medical review officer or third party administrator shall maintain all dated records and notifications, identified by individual, for a minimum of one year for negative and canceled controlled substances test results.

(c) No person may obtain the individual controlled substances test results retained by a medical review officer or third party administrator, and no medical review officer or third party administrator shall release the individual controlled substances test results of any driver to any person, without first obtaining a specific, written authorization from the tested driver. Nothing in this paragraph (c) shall prohibit a medical review officer or third party administrator from releasing, to the employer or to officials of the Secretary of Transportation, any DOT agency, or any State or local officials with regulatory authority over the controlled substances testing program under this part, the information delineated in part 40, Subpart G, of this title.

§ 382.411 Employer notifications.

(a) An employer shall notify a driver of the results of a pre-employment controlled substances test conducted under this part, if the driver requests such results within 60 calendar days of being notified of the disposition of the employment application. An employer shall notify a driver of the results of random, reasonable suspicion and post-accident tests for controlled substances conducted under this part if the test results are verified positive. The employer shall also inform the driver which controlled substance or substances were verified as positive.

(b) The designated employer representative shall make reasonable efforts to contact and request each driver who submitted a specimen under the employer's program, regardless of the driver's employment status, to contact and discuss the results of the controlled substances test with a medical review officer who has been unable to contact the driver.

(c) The designated employer representative shall immediately notify the medical review officer that the driver has been notified to contact the medical review officer within 72 hours.

§ 382.413 Inquiries for alcohol and controlled substances information from previous employers.

Employers shall request alcohol and controlled substances information from previous employers in accordance with the requirements of § 40.25 of this title.

Subpart E—Consequences for Drivers Engaging in Substance Use-Related Conduct

§ 382.501 Removal from safety-sensitive function.

(a) Except as provided in subpart F of this part, no driver shall perform safety-sensitive functions, including driving a commercial motor vehicle, if the driver has engaged in conduct prohibited by subpart B of this part or an alcohol or controlled substances rule of another DOT agency.

(b) No employer shall permit any driver to perform safety-sensitive functions; including driving a commercial motor vehicle, if the employer has determined that the driver has violated this section.

(c) For purposes of this subpart, commercial motor vehicle means a commercial motor vehicle in commerce as defined in §382.107, and a commercial motor vehicle in interstate commerce as defined in part 390 of this subchapter.

§382.503 Required evaluation and testing.

No driver who has engaged in conduct prohibited by subpart B of this part shall perform safety-sensitive functions, including driving a commercial motor vehicle, unless the driver has met the requirements of part 40, subpart O, of this title. No employer shall permit a driver who has engaged in conduct prohibited by subpart B of this part to perform safety-sensitive functions, including driving a commercial motor vehicle, unless the driver has met the requirements of part 40, subpart O, of this title.

§382.505 Other alcohol-related conduct.

(a) No driver tested under the provisions of subpart C of this part who is found to have an alcohol concentration of 0.02 or greater but less than 0.04 shall perform or continue to perform safety-sensitive functions for an employer, including driving a commercial motor vehicle, nor shall an employer permit the driver to perform or continue to perform safety-sensitive functions, until the start of the driver's next regularly scheduled duty period, but not less than 24 hours following administration of the test.

(b) Except as provided in paragraph (a) of this section, no employer shall take any action under this part against a driver based solely on test results showing an alcohol concentration less than 0.04. This does not prohibit an employer with authority independent of this part from taking any action otherwise consistent with law.

§382.507 Penalties.

Any employer or driver who violates the requirements of this part shall be subject to the civil and/or criminal penalty provisions of 49 U.S.C. 521(b).

In addition, any employer or driver who violates the requirements of 49 CFR part 40 shall be subject to the civil and/or criminal penalty provisions of 49 U.S.C. 521(b).

Subpart F—Alcohol Misuse and Controlled Substances Use Information, Training, and Referral

§382.601 Employer obligation to promulgate a policy on the misuse of alcohol and use of controlled substances.

(a) *General requirements.* Each employer shall provide educational materials that explain the requirements of this part and the employer's policies and procedures with respect to meeting these requirements.

(1) The employer shall ensure that a copy of these materials is distributed to each driver prior to the start of alcohol and controlled substances testing under this part and to each driver subsequently hired or transferred into a position requiring driving a commercial motor vehicle.

(2) Each employer shall provide written notice to representatives of employee organizations of the availability of this information.

(b) *Required content.* The materials to be made available to drivers shall include detailed discussion of at least the following:

(1) The identity of the person designated by the employer to answer driver questions about the materials;

(2) The categories of drivers who are subject to the provisions of this part;

(3) Sufficient information about the safety-sensitive functions performed by those drivers to make clear what period of the work day the driver is required to be in compliance with this part;

(4) Specific information concerning driver conduct that is prohibited by this part;

(5) The circumstances under which a driver will be tested for alcohol and/or controlled substances under this part, including post-accident testing under §382.303(d);

(6) The procedures that will be used to test for the presence of alcohol and

controlled substances, protect the driver and the integrity of the testing processes, safeguard the validity of the test results, and ensure that those results are attributed to the correct driver, including post-accident information, procedures and instructions required by § 382.303(d);

(7) The requirement that a driver submit to alcohol and controlled substances tests administered in accordance with this part;

(8) An explanation of what constitutes a refusal to submit to an alcohol or controlled substances test and the attendant consequences;

(9) The consequences for drivers found to have violated subpart B of this part, including the requirement that the driver be removed immediately from safety-sensitive functions, and the procedures under part 40, subpart O, of this title;

(10) The consequences for drivers found to have an alcohol concentration of 0.02 or greater but less than 0.04;

(11) Information concerning the effects of alcohol and controlled substances use on an individual's health, work, and personal life; signs and symptoms of an alcohol or a controlled substances problem (the driver's or a co-worker's); and available methods of intervening when an alcohol or a controlled substances problem is suspected, including confrontation, referral to any employee assistance program and or referral to management.

(c) *Optional provision.* The materials supplied to drivers may also include information on additional employer policies with respect to the use of alcohol or controlled substances, including any consequences for a driver found to have a specified alcohol or controlled substances level, that are based on the employer's authority independent of this part. Any such additional policies or consequences must be clearly and obviously described as being based on independent authority.

(d) *Certificate of receipt.* Each employer shall ensure that each driver is required to sign a statement certifying that he or she has received a copy of these materials described in this section. Each employer shall maintain the original of the signed certificate and may provide a copy of the certificate to the driver.

§ 382.603 Training for supervisors.

Each employer shall ensure that all persons designated to supervise drivers receive at least 60 minutes of training on alcohol misuse and receive at least an additional 60 minutes of training on controlled substances use. The training will be used by the supervisors to determine whether reasonable suspicion exists to require a driver to undergo testing under § 382.307. The training shall include the physical, behavioral, speech, and performance indicators of probable alcohol misuse and use of controlled substances. Recurrent training for supervisory personnel is not required.

§ 382.605 Referral, evaluation, and treatment.

The requirements for referral, evaluation, and treatment must be performed in accordance with 49 CFR part 40, Subpart O.

PART 383—COMMERCIAL DRIVER'S LICENSE STANDARDS; REQUIREMENTS AND PENALTIES

Subpart A—General

Subpart B—Single License Requirement

Subpart C—Notification Requirements and Employer Responsibilities

Subpart D—Driver Disqualifications and Penalties

AUTHORITY: 49 U.S.C. 521, 31136, 31301 *et seq.*, and 31502; secs. 214 and 215 of Pub. L. 106–159, 113 Stat. 1766, 1767; sec. 1012(b) of Pub. L. 107–56; 115 Stat. 397; sec. 4140 of Pub. L. 109–59, 119 Stat. 1144, 1726; and 49 CFR 1.73.

SOURCE: 52 FR 20587, June 1, 1987, unless otherwise noted.

EDITORIAL NOTE: Nomenclature changes to part 383 appear at 66 FR 49872, Oct. 1, 2001.

Subpart A—General

§ 383.1 Purpose and scope.

(a) The purpose of this part is to help reduce or prevent truck and bus accidents, fatalities, and injuries by requiring drivers to have a single commercial motor vehicle driver's license and by disqualifying drivers who operate commercial motor vehicles in an unsafe manner.

(b) This part:

(1) Prohibits a commercial motor vehicle driver from having more than one commercial motor vehicle driver's license;

(2) Requires a driver to notify the driver's current employer and the driver's State of domicile of certain convictions;

(3) Requires that a driver provide previous employment information when applying for employment as an operator of a commercial motor vehicle;

(4) Prohibits an employer from allowing a person with a suspended license to operate a commercial motor vehicle;

(5) Establishes periods of disqualification and penalties for those persons convicted of certain criminal and other offenses and serious traffic violations, or subject to any suspensions, revocations, or cancellations of certain driving privileges;

(6) Establishes testing and licensing requirements for commercial motor vehicle operators;

(7) Requires States to give knowledge and skills tests to all qualified applicants for commercial drivers' licenses which meet the Federal standard;

(8) Sets forth commercial motor vehicle groups and endorsements;

(9) Sets forth the knowledge and skills test requirements for the motor vehicle groups and endorsements;

(10) Sets forth the Federal standards for procedures, methods, and minimum passing scores for States and others to use in testing and licensing commercial motor vehicle operators; and

(11) Establishes requirements for the State issued commercial license documentation.

[52 FR 20587, June 1, 1987, as amended at 53 FR 27648, July 21, 1988; 54 FR 40787, Oct. 3, 1989]

§ 383.3 **Applicability.**

(a) The rules in this part apply to every person who operates a commercial motor vehicle (CMV) in interstate, foreign, or intrastate commerce, to all employers of such persons, and to all States.

(b) The exceptions contained in § 390.3(f) of this subchapter do not apply to this part. The employers and drivers identified in § 390.3(f) must comply with the requirements of this part, unless otherwise provided in this section.

(c) *Exception for certain military drivers.* Each State must exempt from the requirements of this part individuals who operate CMVs for military purposes. This exception is applicable to active duty military personnel; members of the military reserves; member of the national guard on active duty, including personnel on full-time national guard duty, personnel on part-time national guard training, and national guard military technicians (civilians who are required to wear military uniforms); and active duty U.S. Coast Guard personnel. This exception is not applicable to U.S. Reserve technicians.

(d) *Exception for farmers, firefighters, emergency response vehicle drivers, and drivers removing snow and ice.* A State may, at its discretion, exempt individuals identified in paragraphs (d)(1), (d)(2), and (d)(3) of this section from the requirements of this part. The use of this waiver is limited to the driver's home State unless there is a reciprocity agreement with adjoining States.

(1) Operators of a farm vehicle which is:

(i) Controlled and operated by a farmer, including operation by employees or family members;

(ii) Used to transport either agricultural products, farm machinery, farm supplies, or both to or from a farm;

(iii) Not used in the operations of a common or contract motor carrier; and

(iv) Used within 241 kilometers (150 miles) of the farmer's farm.

(2) Firefighters and other persons who operate CMVs which are necessary to the preservation of life or property or the execution of emergency governmental functions, are equipped with audible and visual signals and are not subject to normal traffic regulation. These vehicles include fire trucks, hook and ladder trucks, foam or water transport trucks, police SWAT team vehicles, ambulances, or other vehicles that are used in response to emergencies.

(3)(i) A driver, employed by an eligible unit of local government, operating a commercial motor vehicle within the boundaries of that unit for the purpose of removing snow or ice from a roadway by plowing, sanding, or salting, if

(A) The properly licensed employee who ordinarily operates a commercial motor vehicle for these purposes is unable to operate the vehicle; or

(B) The employing governmental entity determines that a snow or ice emergency exists that requires additional assistance.

(ii) This exemption shall not preempt State laws and regulations concerning the safe operation of commercial motor vehicles.

(e) *Restricted commercial drivers license (CDL) for certain drivers in the State of Alaska.* (1) The State of Alaska may, at its discretion, waive only the following requirements of this part and issue a CDL to each driver that meets the conditions set forth in paragraphs (e) (2) and (3) of this section:

(i) The knowledge tests standards for testing procedures and methods of subpart H, but must continue to administer knowledge tests that fulfill the content requirements of subpart G for *all* applicants;

(ii) All the skills test requirements; and

(iii) The requirement under § 383.153(a)(4) to have a photograph on the license document.

(2) Drivers of CMVs in the State of Alaska must operate exclusively over roads that meet *both* of the following criteria to be eligible for the exception in paragraph (e)(1) of this section:

(i) Such roads are not connected by land highway or vehicular way to the land-connected State highway system; and

(ii) Such roads are not connected to any highway or vehicular way with an average daily traffic volume greater than 499.

(3) Any CDL issued under the terms of this paragraph must carry two restrictions:

(i) Holders may not operate CMVs over roads other than those specified in paragraph (e)(2) of this section; and

(ii) The license is not valid for CMV operation outside the State of Alaska.

(f) *Restricted CDL for certain drivers in farm-related service industries.* (1) A State may, at its discretion, waive the required knowledge and skills tests of subpart H of this part and issue restricted CDLs to employees of these designated farm-related service industries:

(i) Agri-chemical businesses;

(ii) Custom harvesters;

(iii) Farm retail outlets and suppliers;

(iv) Livestock feeders.

(2) A restricted CDL issued pursuant to this paragraph shall meet all the requirements of this part, except subpart H of this part. A restricted CDL issued pursuant to this paragraph shall be accorded the same reciprocity as a CDL meeting all of the requirements of this part. The restrictions imposed upon the issuance of this restricted CDL shall not limit a person's use of the CDL in a non-CMV during either validated or non-validated periods, nor shall the CDL affect a State's power to administer its driver licensing program for operators of vehicles other than CMVs.

(3) A State issuing a CDL under the terms of this paragraph must restrict issuance as follows:

(i) Applicants must have a good driving record as defined in this paragraph. Drivers who have not held any motor vehicle operator's license for at least one year shall not be eligible for this CDL. Drivers who have between one and two years of driving experience must demonstrate a good driving record for their entire driving history. Drivers with more than two years of driving experience must have a good driving record for the two most recent years. For the purposes of this para-

graph, the term *good driving record* means that an applicant:

(A) Has not had more than one license (except in the instances specified in §383.21);

(B) Has not had *any* license suspended, revoked, or canceled;

(C) Has not had *any* conviction for any type of motor vehicle for the disqualifying offenses contained in §383.51(b);

(D) Has not had *any* conviction for any type of motor vehicle for serious traffic violations; and

(E) Has not had *any* conviction for a violation of State or local law relating to motor vehicle traffic control (other than a parking violation) arising in connection with any traffic accident, and has no record of an accident in which he/she was at fault.

(ii) Restricted CDLs shall have the same renewal cycle as unrestricted CDLs, but shall be limited to the seasonal period or periods as defined by the State of licensure, provided that the total number of calendar days in any 12-month period for which the restricted CDL is valid does not exceed 180. If a State elects to provide for more than one seasonal period, the restricted CDL is valid for commercial motor vehicle operation only during the currently approved season, and must be revalidated for each successive season. Only one seasonal period of validity may appear on the license document at a time. The good driving record must be confirmed prior to any renewal or revalidation.

(iii) Restricted CDL holders are limited to operating Group B and C vehicles, as described in subpart F of this part.

(iv) Restricted CDLs shall not be issued with *any* endorsements on the license document. Only the limited tank vehicle and hazardous materials endorsement privileges that the restricted CDL automatically confers and are described in paragraph (f)(3)(v) of this section are permitted.

(v) Restricted CDL holders may not drive vehicles carrying any placardable quantities of hazardous materials, except for diesel fuel in quantities of 3,785 liters (1,000 gallons) or less; liquid fertilizers (i.e., plant nutrients) in vehicles or implements of husbandry in

189

total quantities of 11,355 liters (3,000 gallons) or less; and solid fertilizers (i.e., solid plant nutrients) that are not transported with any organic substance.

(vi) Restricted CDL holders may not hold an unrestricted CDL at the same time.

(vii) Restricted CDL holders may not operate a commercial motor vehicle beyond 241 kilometers (150 miles) from the place of business or the farm currently being served.

(g) *Restricted CDL for certain drivers in the pyrotechnic industry.* (1) A State may, at its discretion, waive the required hazardous materials knowledge tests of subpart H of this part and issue restricted CDLs to part-time drivers operating commercial motor vehicles transporting less than 227 kilograms (500 pounds) of fireworks classified as DOT Class 1.3G explosives.

(2) A State issuing a CDL under the terms of this paragraph must restrict issuance as follows:

(i) The GVWR of the vehicle to be operated must be less than 4,537 kilograms (10,001 pounds);

(ii) If a State believes, at its discretion, that the training required by §172.704 of this title adequately prepares part-time drivers meeting the other requirements of this paragraph to deal with fireworks and the other potential dangers posed by fireworks transportation and use, the State may waive the hazardous materials knowledge tests of subpart H of this part. The State may impose any requirements it believes is necessary to ensure itself that a driver is properly trained pursuant to §172.704 of this title.

(iii) A restricted CDL document issued pursuant to this paragraph shall have a statement clearly imprinted on the face of the document that is substantially similar as follows: "For use as a CDL only during the period from June 30 through July 6 for purposes of transporting less than 227 kilograms (500 pounds) of fireworks classified as DOT Class 1.3G explosives in a vehicle with a GVWR of less than 4,537 kilograms (10,001 pounds).

(3) A restricted CDL issued pursuant to this paragraph shall meet all the requirements of this part, except those specifically identified. A restricted CDL issued pursuant to this paragraph shall be accorded the same reciprocity as a CDL meeting all of the requirements of this part. The restrictions imposed upon the issuance of this restricted CDL shall not limit a person's use of the CDL in a non-CMV during either validated or non-validated periods, nor shall the CDL affect a State's power to administer its driver licensing program for operators of vehicles other than CMVs.

(4) Restricted CDLs shall have the same renewal cycle as unrestricted CDLs, but shall be limited to the seasonal period of June 30 through July 6 of each year or a lesser period as defined by the State of licensure.

(5) Persons who operate commercial motor vehicles during the period from July 7 through June 29 for purposes of transporting less than 227 kilograms (500 pounds) of fireworks classified as DOT Class 1.3G explosives in a vehicle with a GVWR of less than 4,537 kilograms (10,001 pounds) and who also operate such vehicles for the same purposes during the period June 30 through July 6 shall not be issued a restricted CDL pursuant to this paragraph.

[61 FR 9564, Mar. 8, 1996, as amended at 61 FR 14679, Apr. 3, 1996; 62 FR 1296, Jan. 9, 1997; 67 FR 49755, July 31, 2002; 67 FR 61821, Oct. 2, 2002]

§ 383.5 Definitions.

As used in this part:

Administrator means the Federal Motor Carrier Safety Administrator, the chief executive of the Federal Motor Carrier Safety Administration, an agency within the Department of Transportation.

Alcohol or *alcoholic beverage* means: (a) Beer as defined in 26 U.S.C. 5052(a), of the Internal Revenue Code of 1954, (b) wine of not less than one-half of one per centum of alcohol by volume, or (c) distilled spirits as defined in section 5002(a)(8), of such Code.

Alcohol concentration (AC) means the concentration of alcohol in a person's blood or breath. When expressed as a percentage it means grams of alcohol per 100 milliliters of blood or grams of alcohol per 210 liters of breath.

Alien means any person not a citizen or national of the United States.

CDL downgrade means either:

(1) A State allows the driver to change his or her self-certification to interstate, but operating exclusively in transportation or operation excepted from part 391, as provided in §§390.3(f), 391.2, 391.68 or 398.3 of this chapter;

(2) A State allows the driver to change his or her self-certification to intrastate only, if the driver qualifies under that State's physical qualification requirements for intrastate only;

(3) A State allows the driver to change his or her certification to intrastate, but operating exclusively in transportation or operations excepted from all or part of the State driver qualification requirements, or

(4) A State removes the CDL privilege from the driver license.

CDL driver means a person holding a CDL or a person required to hold a CDL.

CDLIS driver record means the electronic record of the individual CDL driver's status and history stored by the State-of-Record as part of the Commercial Driver's License Information System (CDLIS) established under 49 U.S.C. 31309.

Commerce means (a) any trade, traffic or transportation within the jurisdiction of the United States between a place in a State and a place outside of such State, including a place outside of the United States and (b) trade, traffic, and transportation in the United States which affects any trade, traffic, and transportation described in paragraph (a) of this definition.

Commercial driver's license (CDL) means a license issued to an individual by a State or other jurisdiction of domicile, in accordance with the standards contained in this part, which authorizes the individual to operate a class of a commercial motor vehicle.

Commercial driver's license information system (CDLIS) means the CDLIS established by FMCSA pursuant to section 12007 of the Commercial Motor Vehicle Safety Act of 1986.

Commercial learner's permit (CLP) means a permit issued to an individual by a State or other jurisdiction of domicile, in accordance with the standards contained in this part, which, when carried with a valid driver's license issued by the same State or juris-diction, authorizes the individual to operate a class of a commercial motor vehicle when accompanied by a holder of a valid CDL for purposes of behind-the-wheel training. When issued to a CDL holder, a CLP serves as authorization for accompanied behind-the-wheel training in a CMV for which the holder's current CDL is not valid.

Commercial motor vehicle (CMV) means a motor vehicle or combination of motor vehicles used in commerce to transport passengers or property if the motor vehicle—

(1) Has a gross combination weight rating or gross combination weight of 11,794 kilograms or more (26,001 pounds or more), whichever is greater, inclusive of a towed unit(s) with a gross vehicle weight rating or gross vehicle weight of more than 4,536 kilograms (10,000 pounds), whichever is greater; or

(2) Has a gross vehicle weight rating or gross vehicle weight of 11,794 or more kilograms (26,001 pounds or more), whichever is greater; or

(3) Is designed to transport 16 or more passengers, including the driver; or

(4) Is of any size and is used in the transportation of *hazardous materials* as defined in this section.

Controlled substance has the meaning such term has under 21 U.S.C. 802(6) and includes all substances listed on schedules I through V of 21 CFR 1308 (§§1308.11 through 1308.15), as they may be amended by the United States Department of Justice.

Conviction means an unvacated adjudication of guilt, or a determination that a person has violated or failed to comply with the law in a court of original jurisdiction or by an authorized administrative tribunal, an unvacated forfeiture of bail or collateral deposited to secure the person's appearance in court, a plea of guilty or nolo contendere accepted by the court, the payment of a fine or court cost, or violation of a condition of release without bail, regardless of whether or not the penalty is rebated, suspended, or probated.''

Disqualification means any of the following three actions:

(1) The suspension, revocation, or cancellation of a CLP or CDL by the State or jurisdiction of issuance.

(2) Any withdrawal of a person's privileges to drive a CMV by a State or other jurisdiction as the result of a violation of State or local law relating to motor vehicle traffic control (other than parking, vehicle weight or vehicle defect violations).

(3) A determination by the FMCSA that a person is not qualified to operate a commercial motor vehicle under part 391 of this subchapter.

Driver applicant means an individual who applies to a State or other jurisdiction to obtain, transfer, upgrade, or renew a CDL or to obtain or renew a CLP.

Driver's license means a license issued by a State or other jurisdiction, to an individual which authorizes the individual to operate a motor vehicle on the highways.

Driving a commercial motor vehicle while under the influence of alcohol means committing any one or more of the following acts in a CMV—

(a) Driving a CMV while the person's alcohol concentration is 0.04 or more;

(b) Driving under the influence of alcohol, as prescribed by State law; or

(c) Refusal to undergo such testing as is required by any State or jurisdiction in the enforcement of §383.51(b) or §392.5(a)(2) of this subchapter.

Electronic device includes, but is not limited to, a cellular telephone; personal digital assistant; pager; computer; or any other device used to input, write, send, receive, or read text.

Eligible unit of local government means a city, town, borough, county, parish, district, or other public body created by or pursuant to State law which has a total population of 3,000 individuals or less.

Employee means any operator of a commercial motor vehicle, including full time, regularly employed drivers; casual, intermittent or occasional drivers; leased drivers and independent, owner-operator contractors (while in the course of operating a commercial motor vehicle) who are either directly employed by or under lease to an employer.

Employer means any person (including the United States, a State, District of Columbia or a political subdivision of a State) who owns or leases a commercial motor vehicle or assigns employees to operate such a vehicle.

Endorsement means an authorization to an individual's CLP or CDL required to permit the individual to operate certain types of commercial motor vehicles.

Fatality means the death of a person as a result of a motor vehicle accident.

Felony means an offense under State or Federal law that is punishable by death or imprisonment for a term exceeding 1 year.

Foreign means outside the fifty United States and the District of Columbia.

Gross combination weight rating (GCWR) means the value specified by the manufacturer as the loaded weight of a combination (articulated) vehicle. In the absence of a value specified by the manufacturer, GCWR will be determined by adding the GVWR of the power unit and the total weight of the towed unit and any load thereon.

Gross vehicle weight rating (GVWR) means the value specified by the manufacturer as the loaded weight of a single vehicle.

Hazardous materials means any material that has been designated as hazardous under 49 U.S.C. 5103 and is required to be placarded under subpart F of 49 CFR part 172 or any quantity of a material listed as a select agent or toxin in 42 CFR part 73.

Imminent hazard means the existence of a condition relating to hazardous material that presents a substantial likelihood that death, serious illness, severe personal injury, or a substantial endangerment to health, property, or the environment may occur before the reasonably foreseeable completion date of a formal proceeding begun to lessen the risk of that death, illness, injury or endangerment.

Manual transmission (also known as a stick shift, stick, straight drive or standard transmission) means a transmission utilizing a driver-operated clutch that is activated by a pedal or lever and a gear-shift mechanism operated either by hand or foot. All other transmissions, whether semi-automatic or automatic, will be considered automatic for the purposes of the standardized restriction code.

Motor vehicle means a vehicle, machine, tractor, trailer, or semitrailer propelled or drawn by mechanical power used on highways, except that such term does not include a vehicle, machine, tractor, trailer, semitrailer operated exclusively on a rail.

Non-CDL means any other type of motor vehicle license, such as an automobile driver's license, a chauffeur's license, or a motorcycle license.

Non-CMV means a motor vehicle or combination of motor vehicles not defined by the term "commercial motor vehicle (CMV)" in this section.

Non-domiciled CLP or Non-domiciled CDL means a CLP or CDL, respectively, issued by a State or other jurisdiction under either of the following two conditions:

(1) To an individual domiciled in a foreign country meeting the requirements of § 383.23(b)(1).

(2) To an individual domiciled in another State meeting the requirements of § 383.23(b)(2).

Out-of-service order means a declaration by an authorized enforcement officer of a Federal, State, Canadian, Mexican, or local jurisdiction that a driver, a commercial motor vehicle, or a motor carrier operation, is out-of-service pursuant to §§ 386.72, 392.5, 395.13, 396.9, or compatible laws, or the North American Uniform Out-of-Service Criteria.

Representative vehicle means a motor vehicle which represents the type of motor vehicle that a driver applicant operates or expects to operate.

School bus means a CMV used to transport pre-primary, primary, or secondary school students from home to school, from school to home, or to and from school-sponsored events. School bus does not include a bus used as a common carrier.

State means a State of the United States and the District of Columbia.

State of domicile means that State where a person has his/her true, fixed, and permanent home and principal residence and to which he/she has the intention of returning whenever he/she is absent.

Tank vehicle means any commercial motor vehicle that is designed to transport any liquid or gaseous materials within a tank or tanks having an individual rated capacity of more than 119 gallons and an aggregate rated capacity of 1,000 gallons or more that is either permanently or temporarily attached to the vehicle or the chassis. A commercial motor vehicle transporting an empty storage container tank, not designed for transportation, with a rated capacity of 1,000 gallons or more that is temporarily attached to a flatbed trailer is not considered a tank vehicle.

Texting means manually entering alphanumeric text into, or reading text from, an electronic device.

(1) This action includes, but is not limited to, short message service, e-mailing, instant messaging, a command or request to access a World Wide Web page, or engaging in any other form of electronic text retrieval or entry, for present or future communication.

(2) Texting does not include:

(i) Reading, selecting, or entering a telephone number, an extension number, or voicemail retrieval codes and commands into an electronic device for the purpose of initiating or receiving a phone call or using voice commands to initiate or receive a telephone call;

(ii) Inputting, selecting, or reading information on a global positioning system or navigation system; or

(iii) Using a device capable of performing multiple functions (e.g., fleet management systems, dispatching devices, smart phones, citizens band radios, music players, etc.) for a purpose that is not otherwise prohibited in this part.

Third party skills test examiner means a person employed by a third party tester who is authorized by the State to administer the CDL skills tests specified in subparts G and H of this part.

Third party tester means a person (including, but not limited to, another State, a motor carrier, a private driver training facility or other private institution, or a department, agency or instrumentality of a local government) authorized by the State to employ skills test examiners to administer the CDL skills tests specified in subparts G and H of this part.

United States means the 50 States and the District of Columbia.

193

Vehicle means a motor vehicle unless otherwise specified.

Vehicle group means a class or type of vehicle with certain operating characteristics.

[52 FR 20587, June 1, 1987, as amended at 53 FR 27648, July 21, 1988; 53 FR 39050, Oct. 4, 1988; 54 FR 40787, Oct. 3, 1989; 59 FR 26028, May 18, 1994; 61 FR 9566, Mar. 8, 1996; 61 FR 14679, Apr. 3, 1996; 62 FR 37151, July 11, 1997; 67 FR 49756, July 31, 2002; 68 FR 23849, May 5, 2003; 73 FR 73123, Dec. 1, 2008; 75 FR 59134, Sept. 27, 2010; 76 FR 26878, May 9, 2011]

§ 383.7 Validity of CDL issued by decertified State.

A CDL issued by a State prior to the date the State is notified by the Administrator, in accordance with the provisions of § 384.405 of this subchapter, that the State is prohibited from issuing CDLs, will remain valid until its stated expiration date.

[67 FR 49756, July 31, 2002]

Subpart B—Single License Requirement

§ 383.21 Number of drivers' licenses.

No person who operates a commercial motor vehicle shall at any time have more than one driver's license.

[64 FR 48110, Sept. 2, 1999]

§ 383.23 Commercial driver's license.

(a) *General rule.* (1) No person shall operate a commercial motor vehicle unless such person has taken and passed written and driving tests for a CLP or CDL that meet the Federal standards contained in subparts F, G, and H of this part for the commercial motor vehicle that person operates or expects to operate.

(2) Except as provided in paragraph (b) of this section, no person may legally operate a CMV unless such person possesses a CDL which meets the standards contained in subpart J of this part, issued by his/her State or jurisdiction of domicile.

(b) *Exception.* (1) If a CMV operator is not domiciled in a foreign jurisdiction that the Administrator has determined tests drivers and issues CDLs in accordance with, or under standards similar to, the standards contained in subparts F, G, and H of this part,[1] the person may obtain a Non-domiciled CLP or Non-domiciled CDL from a State that does comply with the testing and licensing standards contained in such subparts F, G, and H of this part, so long as that person meets the requirements of § 383.71(f).

(2) If an individual is domiciled in a State while that State is prohibited from issuing CDLs in accordance with § 384.405 of this subchapter, that individual is eligible to obtain a Non-domiciled CLP or Non-domiciled CDL from any State that elects to issue a Non-domiciled CDL and which complies with the testing and licensing standards contained in subparts F, G, and H of this part, so long as that person meets the requirements of § 383.71(f).

(3) If an individual possesses a CLP, as defined in § 383.5, the individual is authorized to operate a class of CMV as provided by the CLP in accordance with § 383.25.

[76 FR 26878, May 9, 2011]

§ 383.25 Commercial learner's permit (CLP).

(a) A CLP is considered a valid CDL for purposes of behind-the-wheel training on public roads or highways, if all of the following minimum conditions are met:

(1) The CLP holder is at all times accompanied by the holder of a valid CDL who has the proper CDL group and endorsement(s) necessary to operate the CMV. The CDL holder must at all times be physically present in the front seat of the vehicle next to the CLP

---

[1] Effective December 29, 1988, the Administrator determined that commercial driver's licenses issued by Canadian Provinces and Territories in conformity with the Canadian National Safety Code are in accordance with the standards of this part. Effective November 21, 1991, the Administrator determined that the new Licencias Federales de Conductor issued by the United Mexican States are in accordance with the standards of this part. Therefore, under the single license provision of § 383.21, a driver holding a commercial driver's license issued under the Canadian National Safety Code or a new Licencia Federal de Conductor issued by Mexico is prohibited from obtaining a non-domiciled CDL, or any other type of driver's license, from a State or other jurisdiction in the United States.

holder or, in the case of a passenger vehicle, directly behind or in the first row behind the driver and must have the CLP holder under observation and direct supervision.

(2) The CLP holder holds a valid driver's license issued by the same jurisdiction that issued the CLP.

(3) The CLP holder must have taken and passed a general knowledge test that meets the Federal standards contained in subparts F, G, and H of this part for the commercial motor vehicle that person operates or expects to operate.

(4) The CLP holder must be 18 years of age or older.

(5) Endorsements:

(i) A CLP holder with a passenger (P) endorsement must have taken and passed the P endorsement knowledge test. A CLP holder with a P endorsement is prohibited from operating a CMV carrying passengers, other than Federal/State auditors and inspectors, test examiners, other trainees, and the CDL holder accompanying the CLP holder as prescribed by paragraph (a)(1) of this section. The P endorsement must be class specific.

(ii) A CLP holder with a school bus (S) endorsement must have taken and passed the S endorsement knowledge test. A CLP holder with an S endorsement is prohibited from operating a school bus with passengers other than Federal/State auditors and inspectors, test examiners, other trainees, and the CDL holder accompanying the CLP holder as prescribed by paragraph (a)(1) of this section.

(iii) A CLP holder with a tank vehicle (N) endorsement must have taken and passed the N endorsement knowledge test. A CLP holder with an N endorsement may only operate an empty tank vehicle and is prohibited from operating any tank vehicle that previously contained hazardous materials that has not been purged of any residue.

(iv) All other Federal endorsements are prohibited on a CLP.

(6) The CLP holder does not operate a commercial motor vehicle transporting hazardous materials as defined in §383.5.

(b) The CLP must be a separate document from the CDL or non-CDL.

(c) The CLP must be valid for no more than 180 days from the date of issuance. The State may renew the CLP for an additional 180 days without requiring the CLP holder to retake the general and endorsement knowledge tests.

(d) The issuance of a CLP is a precondition to the initial issuance of a CDL. The issuance of a CLP is also a precondition to the upgrade of a CDL if the upgrade requires a skills test.

(e) The CLP holder is not eligible to take the CDL skills test in the first 14 days after initial issuance of the CLP.

[76 FR 26879, May 9, 2011]

Subpart C—Notification Requirements and Employer Responsibilities

§383.31 Notification of convictions for driver violations.

(a) Each person who operates a commercial motor vehicle, who has a commercial driver's license issued by a State or jurisdiction, and who is convicted of violating, in any type of motor vehicle, a State or local law relating to motor vehicle traffic control (other than a parking violation) in a State or jurisdiction other than the one which issued his/her license, shall notify an official designated by the State or jurisdiction which issued license, of such conviction. The notification must be made within 30 days after the date that the person has been convicted.

(b) Each person who operates a commercial motor vehicle, who has a commercial driver's license issued by a State or jurisdiction, and who is convicted of violating, in any type of motor vehicle, a State or local law relating to motor vehicle traffic control (other than a parking violation), shall notify his/her current employer of such conviction. The notification must be made within 30 days after the date that the person has been convicted. If the driver is not currently employed, he/she must notify the State or jurisdiction which issued the license according to §383.31(a).

(c) *Notification.* The notification to the State official and employer must be made in writing and contain the following information:

(1) Driver's full name;

(2) Driver's license number;

(3) Date of conviction;

(4) The specific criminal or other offense(s), serious traffic violation(s), and other violation(s) of State or local law relating to motor vehicle traffic control, for which the person was convicted and any suspension, revocation, or cancellation of certain driving privileges which resulted from such conviction(s);

(5) Indication whether the violation was in a commercial motor vehicle;

(6) Location of offense; and

(7) Driver's signature.

[52 FR 20587, June 1, 1987, as amended at 54 FR 40787, Oct. 3, 1989]

§ 383.33 Notification of driver's license suspensions.

Each employee who has a driver's license suspended, revoked, or canceled by a State or jurisdiction, who loses the right to operate a commercial motor vehicle in a State or jurisdiction for any period, or who is disqualified from operating a commercial motor vehicle for any period, shall notify his/her current employer of such suspension, revocation, cancellation, lost privilege, or disqualification. The notification must be made before the end of the business day following the day the employee received notice of the suspension, revocation, cancellation, lost privilege, or disqualification.

[54 FR 40788, Oct. 3, 1989]

§ 383.35 Notification of previous employment.

(a) Any person applying for employment as an operator of a commercial motor vehicle shall provide at the time of application for employment, the information specified in paragraph (c) of this section.

(b) All employers shall request the information specified in paragraph (c) of this section from all persons applying for employment as a commercial motor vehicle operator. The request shall be made at the time of application for employment.

(c) The following employment history information for the 10 years preceding the date the application is submitted shall be presented to the prospective employer by the applicant:

(1) A list of the names and addresses of the applicant's previous employers for which the applicant was an operator of a commercial motor vehicle;

(2) The dates the applicant was employed by these employers; and

(3) The reason for leaving such employment.

(d) The applicant shall certify that all information furnished is true and complete.

(e) An employer may require an applicant to provide additional information.

(f) Before an application is submitted, the employer shall inform the applicant that the information he/she provides in accordance with paragraph (c) of this section may be used, and the applicant's previous employers may be contacted for the purpose of investigating the applicant's work history.

§ 383.37 Employer responsibilities.

No employer may knowingly allow, require, permit, or authorize a driver to operate a CMV in the United States in any of the following circumstances:

(a) During any period in which the driver does not have a current CLP or CDL or does not have a CLP or CDL with the proper class or endorsements. An employer may not use a driver to operate a CMV who violates any restriction on the driver's CLP or CDL.

(b) During any period in which the driver has a CLP or CDL disqualified by a State, has lost the right to operate a CMV in a State, or has been disqualified from operating a CMV.

(c) During any period in which the driver has more than one CLP or CDL.

(d) During any period in which the driver, or the CMV he/she is driving, or the motor carrier operation, is subject to an out-of-service order.

(e) In violation of a Federal, State, or local law or regulation pertaining to railroad-highway grade crossings.

[76 FR 26879, May 9, 2011]

Subpart D—Driver Disqualifications and Penalties

§383.51 Disqualification of drivers.

(a) *General.* (1) A person required to have a CLP or CDL who is disqualified must not drive a CMV.

(2) An employer must not knowingly allow, require, permit, or authorize a driver who is disqualified to drive a CMV.

(3) A holder of a CLP or CDL is subject to disqualification sanctions designated in paragraphs (b) and (c) of this section, if the holder drives a CMV or non-CMV and is convicted of the violations listed in those paragraphs.

(4) *Determining first and subsequent violations.* For purposes of determining first and subsequent violations of the offenses specified in this subpart, each conviction for any offense listed in Tables 1 through 4 to this section resulting from a separate incident, whether committed in a CMV or non-CMV, must be counted.

(5) The disqualification period must be in addition to any other previous periods of disqualification.

(6) *Reinstatement after lifetime disqualification.* A State may reinstate any driver disqualified for life for offenses described in paragraphs (b)(1) through (8) of this section (Table 1 to §383.51) after 10 years, if that person has voluntarily entered and successfully completed an appropriate rehabilitation program approved by the State. Any person who has been reinstated in accordance with this provision and who is subsequently convicted of a disqualifying offense described in paragraphs (b)(1) through (8) of this section (Table 1 to §383.51) must not be reinstated.

(b) *Disqualification for major offenses.* Table 1 to §383.51 contains a list of the offenses and periods for which a person who is required to have a CLP or CDL is disqualified, depending upon the type of vehicle the driver is operating at the time of the violation, as follows:

TABLE 1 TO §383.51

If a driver operates a motor vehicle and is convicted of:	For a first conviction or refusal to be tested while operating a CMV, a person required to have a CLP or CDL and a CLP or CDL holder must be disqualified from operating a CMV for * * *	For a first conviction or refusal to be tested while operating a non-CMV, a CLP or CDL holder must be disqualified from operating a CMV for * * *	For a first conviction or refusal to be tested while operating a CMV transporting hazardous materials required to be placarded under the Hazardous Materials Regulations (49 CFR part 172, subpart F), a person required to have a CLP or CDL and a CLP or CDL holder must be disqualified from operating a CMV for * * *	For a second conviction or refusal to be tested in a separate incident of any combination of offenses in this Table while operating a CMV, a person required to have a CLP or CDL and a CLP or CDL holder must be disqualified from operating a CMV for * * *	For a second conviction or refusal to be tested in a separate incident of any combination of offenses in this Table while operating a non-CMV, a CLP or CDL holder must be disqualified from operating a CMV for * * *
(1) Being under the influence of alcohol as prescribed by State law * * *.	1 year	1 year	3 years	Life	Life.
(2) Being under the influence of a controlled substance * * *.	1 year	1 year	3 years	Life	Life.
(3) Having an alcohol concentration of 0.04 or greater while operating a CMV * * *.	1 year	Not applicable ...	3 years	Life	Not applicable.
(4) Refusing to take an alcohol test as required by a State or jurisdiction under its implied consent laws or regulations as defined in §383.72 of this part * * *.	1 year	1 year	3 years	Life	Life.

TABLE 1 TO § 383.51—Continued

If a driver operates a motor vehicle and is convicted of:	For a first conviction or refusal to be tested while operating a CMV, a person required to have a CLP or CDL and a CLP or CDL holder must be disqualified from operating a CMV for * * *	For a first conviction or refusal to be tested while operating a non-CMV, a CLP or CDL holder must be disqualified from operating a CMV for * * *	For a first conviction or refusal to be tested while operating a CMV transporting hazardous materials required to be placarded under the Hazardous Materials Regulations (49 CFR part 172, subpart F), a person required to have a CLP or CDL and a CLP or CDL holder must be disqualified from operating a CMV for * * *	For a second conviction or refusal to be tested in a separate incident of any combination of offenses in this Table while operating a CMV, a person required to have a CLP or CDL and a CLP or CDL holder must be disqualified from operating a CMV for * * *	For a second conviction or refusal to be tested in a separate incident of any combination of offenses in this Table while operating a non-CMV, a CLP or CDL holder must be disqualified from operating a CMV for * * *
(5) Leaving the scene of an accident * * *.	1 year	1 year	3 years	Life	Life.
(6) Using the vehicle to commit a felony, other than a felony described in paragraph (b)(9) of this table * * *.	1 year	1 year	3 years	Life	Life.
(7) Driving a CMV when, as a result of prior violations committed operating a CMV, the driver's CDL is revoked, suspended, or canceled, or the driver is disqualified from operating a CMV.	1 year	Not applicable ...	3 years	Life	Not applicable.
(8) Causing a fatality through the negligent operation of a CMV, including but not limited to the crimes of motor vehicle manslaughter, homicide by motor vehicle and negligent homicide.	1 year	Not applicable ...	3 years	Life	Not applicable.
(9) Using the vehicle in the commission of a felony involving manufacturing, distributing, or dispensing a controlled substance * * *.	Life-not eligible for 10-year reinstatement.	Life-not eligible for 10-year reinstatement.	Life-not eligible for 10-year reinstatement.	Life-not eligible for 10-year reinstatement.	Life-not eligible for 10-year reinstatement

(c) *Disqualification for serious traffic violations.* Table 2 to § 383.51 contains a list of the offenses and the periods for which a person who is required to have a CLP or CDL is disqualified, depending upon the type of vehicle the driver is operating at the time of the violation, as follows:

TABLE 2 TO §383.51

If the driver operates a motor vehicle and is convicted of:	For a second conviction of any combination of offenses in this Table in a separate incident within a 3-year period while operating a CMV, a person required to have a CLP or CDL and a CLP or CDL holder must be disqualified from operating a CMV for * * *	For a second conviction of any combination of offenses in this Table in a separate incident within a 3-year period while operating a non-CMV, a CLP or CDL holder must be disqualified from operating a CMV, if the conviction results in the revocation, cancellation, or suspension of the CLP or CDL holder's license or non-CMV driving privileges, for * * *	For a third or subsequent conviction of any combination of offenses in this Table in a separate incident within a 3-year period while operating a CMV, a person required to have a CLP or CDL and a CLP or CDL holder must be disqualified from operating a CMV for * * *	For a third or subsequent conviction of any combination of offenses in this Table in a separate incident within a 3-year period while operating a non-CMV, a CLP or CDL holder must be disqualified from operating a CMV, if the conviction results in the revocation, cancellation, or suspension of the CLP or CDL holder's license or non-CMV driving privileges, for * * *
(1) Speeding excessively, involving any speed of 24.1 kmph (15 mph) or more above the posted speed limit.	60 days	60 days	120 days	120 days.
(2) Driving recklessly, as defined by State or local law or regulation, including but, not limited to, offenses of driving a motor vehicle in willful or wanton disregard for the safety of persons or property.	60 days	60 days	120 days	120 days.
(3) Making improper or erratic traffic lane changes.	60 days	60 days	120 days	120 days.
(4) Following the vehicle ahead too closely.	60 days	60 days	120 days	120 days.
(5) Violating State or local law relating to motor vehicle traffic control (other than a parking violation) arising in connection with a fatal accident.	60 days	60 days	120 days	120 days.
(6) Driving a CMV without obtaining a CDL.	60 days	Not applicable	120 days	Not applicable.
(7) Driving a CMV without a CDL in the driver's possession[1].	60 days	Not applicable	120 days	Not applicable.
(8) Driving a CMV without the proper class of CDL and/or endorsements for the specific vehicle group being operated or for the passengers or type of cargo being transported.	60 days	Not applicable	120 days	Not applicable.
(9) Violating a State or local law or ordinance on motor vehicle traffic control prohibiting texting while driving.[2]	60 days	Not applicable	120 days	Not applicable.

[1] Any individual who provides proof to the enforcement authority that issued the citation, by the date the individual must appear in court or pay any fine for such a violation, that the individual held a valid CDL on the date the citation was issued, shall not be guilty of this offense.

[2] Driving, for the purpose of this disqualification, means operating a commercial motor vehicle, with the motor running, including while temporarily stationary because of traffic, a traffic control device, or other momentary delays. Driving does not include operating a commercial motor vehicle with or without the motor running when the driver has moved the vehicle to the side of, or off, a highway, as defined in 49 CFR 390.5, and has halted in a location where the vehicle can safely remain stationary.

(d) *Disqualification for railroad-high-way grade crossing offenses.* Table 3 to § 383.51 contains a list of the offenses and the periods for which a person who is required to have a CLP or CDL is disqualified, when the driver is operating a CMV at the time of the violation, as follows:

TABLE 3 TO § 383.51

If the driver is convicted of operating a CMV in violation of a Federal, State or local law because * * *.	For a first conviction a person required to have a CLP or CDL and a CLP or CDL holder must be disqualified from operating a CMV for * * *.	For a second conviction of any combination of offenses in this Table in a separate incident within a 3-year period, a person required to have a CLP or CDL and a CLP or CDL holder must be disqualified from operating a CMV for * * *.	For a third or subsequent conviction of any combination of offenses in this Table in a separate incident within a 3-year period, a person required to have a CLP or CDL and a CLP or CDL holder must be disqualified from operating a CMV for * * *
(1) The driver is not required to always stop, but fails to slow down and check that tracks are clear of an approaching train * * *.	No less than 60 days	No less than 120 days	No less than 1 year.
(2) The driver is not required to always stop, but fails to stop before reaching the crossing, if the tracks are not clear * * *.	No less than 60 days	No less than 120 days	No less than 1 year.
(3) The driver is always required to stop, but fails to stop before driving onto the crossing * * *.	No less than 60 days	No less than 120 days	No less than 1 year.
(4) The driver fails to have sufficient space to drive completely through the crossing without stopping * * *.	No less than 60 days	No less than 120 days	No less than 1 year.
(5) The driver fails to obey a traffic control device or the directions of an enforcement official at the crossing * * *.	No less than 60 days	No less than 120 days	No less than 1 year.
(6) The driver fails to negotiate a crossing because of insufficient undercarriage clearance * * *.	No less than 60 days	No less than 120 days	No less than 1 year.

(e) *Disqualification for violating out-of-service orders.* Table 4 to § 383.51 contains a list of the offenses and periods for which a person who is required to have a CLP or CDL is disqualified when the driver is operating a CMV at the time of the violation, as follows:

TABLE 4 TO § 383.51

If the driver operates a CMV and is convicted of * * *	For a first conviction while operating a CMV, a person required to have a CLP or CDL and a CLP or CDL holder must be disqualified from operating a CMV for * * *	For a second conviction in a separate incident within a 10-year period while operating a CMV, a person required to have a CLP or CDL and a CLP or CDL holder must be disqualified from operating a CMV for * * *	For a third or subsequent conviction in a separate incident within a 10-year period while operating a CMV, a person required to have a CLP or CDL and a CLP or CDL holder must be disqualified from operating a CMV for * * *
(1) Violating a driver or vehicle out-of-service order while transporting nonhazardous materials.	No less than 180 days or more than 1 year.	No less than 2 years or more than 5 years.	No less than 3 years or more than 5 years.
(2) Violating a driver or vehicle out-of-service order while transporting hazardous materials required to be placarded under part 172, subpart F of this title, or while operating a vehicle designed to transport 16 or more passengers, including the driver.	No less than 180 days or more than 2 years.	No less than 3 years or more than 5 years.	No less than 3 years or more than 5 years.

200

[67 FR 49756, July 31, 2002, as amended at 68 FR 4396, Jan. 29, 2003; 72 FR 36787, July 5, 2007; 75 FR 59134, Sept. 27, 2010; 76 FR 26879, May 9, 2011]

§ 383.52 Disqualification of drivers determined to constitute an imminent hazard.

(a) The Assistant Administrator or his/her designee must disqualify from operating a CMV any driver whose driving is determined to constitute an imminent hazard, as defined in § 383.5.

(b) The period of the disqualification may not exceed 30 days unless the FMCSA complies with the provisions of paragraph (c) of this section.

(c) The Assistant Administrator or his/her delegate may provide the driver an opportunity for a hearing after issuing a disqualification for a period of 30 days or less. The Assistant Administrator or his/her delegate must provide the driver notice of a proposed disqualification period of more than 30 days and an opportunity for a hearing to present a defense to the proposed disqualification. A disqualification imposed under this paragraph may not exceed one year in duration. The driver, or a representative on his/her behalf, may file an appeal of the disqualification issued by the Assistant Administrator's delegate with the Assistant Administrator, Adjudications Counsel (MC–CC), Federal Motor Carrier Safety Administration, 1200 New Jersey Ave., SE., Washington, DC 20590–0001.

(d) Any disqualification imposed in accordance with the provisions of this section must be transmitted by the FMCSA to the jurisdiction where the driver is licensed and must become a part of the driver's record maintained by that jurisdiction.

(e) A driver who is simultaneously disqualified under this section and under other provisions of this subpart, or under State law or regulation, shall serve those disqualification periods concurrently.

[67 FR 49759, July 31, 2002, as amended at 72 FR 55700, Oct. 1, 2007]

§ 383.53 Penalties.

(a) *General rule.* Any person who violates the rules set forth in subparts B and C of this part may be subject to civil or criminal penalties as provided for in 49 U.S.C. 521(b).

(b) *Special penalties pertaining to violation of out-of-service orders—*(1) *Driver violations.* A driver who is convicted of violating an out-of-service order shall be subject to a civil penalty of not less than $2,500 for a first conviction and not less than $5,000 for a second or subsequent conviction, in addition to disqualification under § 383.51(e).

(2) *Employer violations.* An employer who is convicted of a violation of § 383.37(c) shall be subject to a civil penalty of not less than $2,750 nor more than $25,000.

(c) *Special penalties pertaining to railroad-highway grade crossing violations.* An employer who is convicted of a violation of § 383.37(d) must be subject to a civil penalty of not more than $10,000.

[59 FR 26028, May 18, 1994, as amended at 64 FR 48111, Sept. 2, 1999; 67 FR 49759, July 31, 2002; 72 FR 36788, July 5, 2007]

Subpart E—Testing and Licensing Procedures

SOURCE: 53 FR 27649, July 21, 1988, unless otherwise noted.

§ 383.71 Driver application and certification procedures.

(a) *Commercial Learner's Permit.* Prior to obtaining a CLP, a person must meet the following requirements:

(1) *Commercial learner's permit applications submitted prior to July 8, 2014.* CLPs issued prior to July 8, 2014 for limited time periods according to State requirements, shall be considered valid commercial drivers' licenses for purposes of behind-the-wheel training on public roads or highways, if the following minimum conditions are met:

(i) The learner's permit holder is at all times accompanied by the holder of a valid CDL;

(ii) He/she either holds a valid automobile driver's license, or has passed such vision, sign/symbol, and knowledge tests as the State issuing the learner's permit ordinarily administers to applicants for automotive drivers' licenses; and

(iii) He/she does not operate a commercial motor vehicle transporting hazardous materials as defined in § 383.5.

(2) *Commercial learner's permit applications submitted on or after July 8, 2014.* Any person applying for a CLP on or after July 8, 2014 must meet the following conditions:

(i) The person must be 18 years of age or older and provide proof of his/her age.

(ii) The person must have taken and passed a general knowledge test that meets the Federal standards contained in subparts F, G, and H of this part for the commercial motor vehicle group that person operates or expects to operate.

(iii) The person must certify that he/she is not subject to any disqualification under § 383.51, or any license disqualification under State law, and that he/she does not have a driver's license from more than one State or jurisdiction.

(iv) The person must provide to the State of issuance the information required to be included on the CLP as specified in subpart J of this part.

(v) The person must provide to the State proof of citizenship or lawful permanent residency as specified in Table 1 of this section or obtain a Non-domiciled CLP as specified in paragraph (f) of this section.

(vi) The person must provide proof that the State to which application is made is his/her State of domicile, as the term is defined in § 383.5. Acceptable proof of domicile is a document with the person's name and residential address within the State, such as a government issued tax form.

(vii) The person must provide the names of all States where the applicant has been licensed to drive any type of motor vehicle during the previous 10 years.

(viii) A person seeking a passenger (P), school bus (S) or tank vehicle (N) endorsement must have taken and passed the endorsement knowledge test for the specific endorsement.

(ix) The person must provide the State the certification contained in paragraph (b)(1) of this section.

(b) *Initial Commercial Driver's License.* Prior to obtaining a CDL, a person must meet all of the following requirements:

(1)(i) *Initial Commercial Driver's License applications submitted prior to January 30, 2012.* Any person applying for a CDL prior to January 30, 2012, must meet the requirements set forth in paragraphs (b)(2) through (10) of this section, and make the following applicable certification in paragraph (b)(1)(i)(A), (B), or (C) of this section:

(A) A person who operates or expects to operate in interstate or foreign commerce, or is otherwise subject to 49 CFR part 391, must certify that he/she meets the qualification requirements contained in part 391 of this title; or

(B) A person who operates or expects to operate in interstate commerce, but is not subject to part 391 due to an exception under § 390.3(f) or an exemption under § 391.2, must certify that he/she is not subject to part 391.

(C) A person who operates or expects to operate entirely in intrastate commerce and is not subject to part 391, is subject to State driver qualification requirements and must certify that he/she is not subject to part 391.

(ii) *Initial Commercial Driver's License applications submitted on or after January 30, 2012.* Any person applying for a CDL on or after January 30, 2012, must meet the requirements set forth in paragraphs (b)(2) through (10), and (h) of this section, and make one of the following applicable certifications in paragraph (b)(1)(ii)(A), (B), (C), or (D) of this section:

(A) *Non-excepted interstate.* A person must certify that he/she operates or expects to operate in interstate commerce, is both subject to and meets the qualification requirements under 49 CFR part 391, and is required to obtain a medical examiner's certificate by § 391.45 of this chapter;

(B) *Excepted interstate.* A person must certify that he/she operates or expects to operate in interstate commerce, but engages exclusively in transportation or operations excepted under 49 CFR 390.3(f), 391.2, 391.68, or 398.3 from all or parts of the qualification requirements of 49 CFR part 391, and is therefore not required to obtain a medical examiner's certificate by 49 CFR 391.45 of this chapter;

(C) *Non-excepted intrastate.* A person must certify that he/she operates only in intrastate commerce and therefore is subject to State driver qualification requirements; or

(D) *Excepted intrastate.* A person must certify that he/she operates in intrastate commerce, but engages exclusively in transportation or operations excepted from all or parts of the State driver qualification requirements.

(2) The person must pass a driving or skills test in accordance with the standards contained in subparts F, G, and H of this part taken in a motor vehicle that is representative of the type of motor vehicle the person operates or expects to operate; or provide evidence that he/she has successfully passed a driving test administered by an authorized third party.

(3) The person must certify that the motor vehicle in which the person takes the driving skills test is representative of the type of motor vehicle that person operates or expects to operate.

(4) The person must provide the State the information required to be included on the CDL as specified in subpart J of this part.

(5) The person must certify that he/she is not subject to any disqualifica-

tion under § 383.51, or any license disqualification under State law, and that he/she does not have a driver's license from more than one State or jurisdiction.

(6) The person must surrender his/her non-CDL driver's licenses and CLP to the State.

(7) The person must provide the names of all States where he/she has previously been licensed to drive any type of motor vehicle during the previous 10 years.

(8) If the person is applying for a hazardous materials endorsement, he/she must comply with Transportation Security Administration requirements codified in 49 CFR part 1572. A lawful permanent resident of the United States requesting a hazardous materials endorsement must additionally provide his/her U.S. Citizenship and Immigration Services (USCIS) Alien registration number.

(9) The person must provide proof of citizenship or lawful permanent residency as specified in Table 1 of this section, or be registered under paragraph (f) of this section.

TABLE 1 TO § 383.71—LIST OF ACCEPTABLE PROOFS OF CITIZENSHIP OR LAWFUL PERMANENT RESIDENCY

Status	Proof of status
U.S. Citizen	• Valid, unexpired U.S. Passport.
	• Certified copy of a birth certificate filed with a State Office of Vital Statistics or equivalent agency in the individual's State of birth, Puerto Rico, the Virgin Islands, Guam, American Samoa or the Commonwealth of the Northern Mariana Islands.
	• Consular Report of Birth Abroad (CRBA) issued by the U.S. Department of State.
	• Certificate of Naturalization issued by the U.S. Department of Homeland Security (DHS).
	• Certificate of Citizenship issued by DHS.
Lawful Permanent Resident	• Valid, unexpired Permanent Resident Card, issued by USCIS or INS.

(10) The person must provide proof that the State to which application is made is his/her State of domicile, as the term is defined in § 383.5. Acceptable proof of domicile is a document with the person's name and residential address within the State, such as a government issued tax form.

(c) *License transfer.* When applying to transfer a CDL from one State of domicile to a new State of domicile, an applicant must apply for a CDL from the new State of domicile within no more

than 30 days after establishing his/her new domicile. The applicant must:

(1) Provide to the new State of domicile the certifications contained in paragraphs (b)(1) and (5) of this section;

(2) Provide to the new State of domicile updated information as specified in subpart J of this part;

(3) If the applicant wishes to retain a hazardous materials endorsement, he/she must comply with the requirements specified in paragraph (b)(8) of

this section and State requirements as specified in § 383.73(c)(4);

(4) Surrender the CDL from the old State of domicile to the new State of domicile; and

(5) Provide the names of all States where the applicant has previously been licensed to drive any type of motor vehicle during the previous 10 years.

(6) Provide to the State proof of citizenship or lawful permanent residency as specified in Table 1 of this section, or be registered under paragraph (f) of this section.

(7) Provide proof to the State that this is his/her State of domicile, as the term is defined in § 383.5. Acceptable proof of domicile is a document with the person's name and residential address within the State, such as a government issued tax form.

(d) *License renewal.* When applying for a renewal of a CDL, all applicants must:

(1) Provide to the State certifications contained in paragraphs (b)(1) and (5) of this section;

(2) Provide to the State updated information as specified in subpart J of this part; and

(3) If a person wishes to retain a hazardous materials endorsement, he/she must comply with the requirements specified in paragraph (b)(8) of this section and pass the test specified in § 383.121 for such endorsement.

(4) Provide the names of all States where the applicant has previously been licensed to drive any type of motor vehicle during the previous 10 years.

(5) Provide to the State proof of citizenship or lawful permanent residency as specified in Table 1 of this section, or be registered under paragraph (f) of this section.

(6) Provide proof to the State that this is his/her State of domicile, as the term is defined in § 383.5. Acceptable proof of domicile is a document, such as a government issued tax form, with the person's name and residential address within the State.

(e) *License upgrades.* When applying for a CDL or an endorsement authorizing the operation of a CMV not covered by the current CDL, all applicants must:

(1) Provide the certifications specified in paragraph (b) of this section;

(2) Pass all the knowledge tests in accordance with the standards contained in subparts F, G, and H of this part and all the skills tests specified in paragraph (b)(2) of this section for the new vehicle group and/or different endorsements;

(3) Comply with the requirements specified in paragraph (b)(8) of this section to obtain a hazardous materials endorsement; and

(4) Surrender the previous CDL.

(f) *Non-domiciled CLP and CDL.* (1) A person must obtain a Non-domiciled CLP or CDL:

(i) If the applicant is domiciled in a foreign jurisdiction, as defined in § 383.5, and the Administrator has not determined that the commercial motor vehicle operator testing and licensing standards of that jurisdiction meet the standards contained in subparts G and H of this part.

(ii) If the applicant is domiciled in a State that is prohibited from issuing CLPs and CDLs in accordance with § 384.405 of this subchapter. That person is eligible to obtain a Non-domiciled CLP or CDL from any State that elects to issue a Non-domiciled CLP or CDL and that complies with the testing and licensing standards contained in subparts F, G, and H of this part.

(2) An applicant for a Non-domiciled CLP and CDL must do both of the following:

(i) Complete the requirements to obtain a CLP contained in paragraph (a) of this section or a CDL contained in paragraph (b) of this section. *Exception:* An applicant domiciled in a foreign jurisdiction must provide an unexpired employment authorization document (EAD) issued by USCIS or an unexpired foreign passport accompanied by an approved I–94 form documenting the applicant's most recent admittance into the United States. No proof of domicile is required.

(ii) After receipt of the Non-domiciled CLP or CDL, and for as long as it is valid, notify the State which issued the Non-domiciled CLP or CDL of any adverse action taken by any jurisdiction or governmental agency, foreign or domestic, against his/her driving privileges. Such adverse actions include, but are not be limited to, license disqualification or disqualification from operating a commercial motor vehicle for the convictions described in §383.51. Notifications must be made within the time periods specified in §383.33.

(3) An applicant for a Non-domiciled CLP or CDL is not required to surrender his/her foreign license.

(g) *Existing CLP and CDL Holder's Self-Certification.* Every person who holds a CLP or CDL must provide to the State on or after January 30, 2012, but not later than January 30, 2014, the certification contained in §383.71(b)(1)(ii).

(h) *Medical Certification Documentation Required by the State.* An applicant or CLP or CDL holder who certifies to non-excepted, interstate driving operations according to §383.71(b)(1)(ii)(A) must comply with applicable requirements in paragraphs (h)(1) through (3) of this section:

(1) New CLP and CDL applicants. After January 30, 2012, a new CLP or CDL applicant who certifies that he/she will operate CMVs in non-excepted, interstate commerce must provide the State with an original or copy (as required by the State) of a medical examiner's certificate prepared by a medical examiner, as defined in §390.5 of this chapter, and the State will post a certification status of "certified" on the Commercial Driver's License Information System (CDLIS) driver record for the driver;

(2) Existing CLP and CDL holders. By January 30, 2014, provide the State with an original or copy (as required by the State) of a current medical examiner's certificate prepared by a medical examiner, as defined in 49 CFR 390.5, and the State will post a certification status of "certified" on CDLIS driver record for the driver. If the non-excepted, interstate CLP or CDL holder fails to provide the State with a current medical examiner's certificate, the State will post a certification status of "not-certified" in the CDLIS driver record for the driver, and initiate a CLP or CDL downgrade following State procedures in accordance with section 383.73(j)(4); and

(3) Maintaining the medical certification status of "certified." In order to maintain a medical certification status of "certified," after January 30, 2012, a CLP or CDL holder who certifies that he/she will operate CMVs in non-excepted, interstate commerce must provide the State with an original or copy (as required by the State) of each subsequently issued medical examiner's certificate.

[76 FR 26881, May 9, 2011]

§383.72 Implied consent to alcohol testing.

Any person who holds a CLP or CDL or is required to hold a CLP or CDL is considered to have consented to such testing as is required by any State or jurisdiction in the enforcement of §§383.51(b), Table 1, item (4) and 392.5(a)(2) of this subchapter. Consent is implied by driving a commercial motor vehicle.

[76 FR 26883, May 9, 2011]

§383.73 State procedures.

(a) *Commercial Learner's Permit.* (1) Prior to July 8, 2014. When issuing a CLP to a person prior to July 8, 2014, a State must meet the requirements in §383.71(a)(1):

(2) On or after July 8, 2014. Prior to issuing a CLP to a person on or after July 8, 2014, a State must:

(i) Require the applicant to make the certifications, pass the tests, and provide the information as described in §383.71(a)(2);

(ii) Initiate and complete a check of the applicant's driving record as described in paragraph (b)(3) of this section.

(iii) Make a CLP valid for no more than 180 days from the date of issuance and provide for renewal of a CLP for no more than an additional 180 days without the CLP holder having to retake the general and endorsement knowledge tests;

(iv) Allow only a group-specific passenger (P) and school bus (S) endorsement and tank vehicle (N) endorsement on a CLP, provided the applicant has taken and passed the knowledge test for the specified endorsement. All other Federal endorsements are prohibited on a CLP; and

205

(v) Complete the Social Security Number verification required by paragraph (g) of this section.

(vi) Require compliance with the standards for providing proof of citizenship or lawful permanent residency specified in § 383.71(b)(9) and proof of State of domicile specified in § 383.71(a)(2)(vi).

(vii) Beginning January 30, 2012, for drivers who certified their type of driving according to § 383.71(b)(1)(ii)(A) (non-excepted interstate) and, if the CLP applicant submits a current medical examiner's certificate, date-stamp the medical examiner's certificate, and post all required information from the medical examiner's certificate to the CDLIS driver record in accordance with paragraph (o) of this section.

(b) *Initial CDL.* Prior to issuing a CDL to a person, a State must:

(1) Require the driver applicant to certify, pass tests, and provide information as described in § 383.71(b);

(2) Check that the vehicle in which the applicant takes his/her test is representative of the vehicle group the applicant has certified that he/she operates or expects to operate;

(3) Initiate and complete a check of the applicant's driving record to ensure that the person is not subject to any disqualification under § 383.51, or any license disqualification under State law, and that the person does not have a driver's license from more than one State or jurisdiction. The record check must include, but is not limited to, the following:

(i) A check of the applicant's driving record as maintained by his/her current State of licensure, if any;

(ii) A check with the CDLIS to determine whether the driver applicant already has been issued a CDL, whether the applicant's license has been disqualified, or if the applicant has been disqualified from operating a commercial motor vehicle;

(iii) A check with the Problem Driver Pointer System (PDPS) to determine whether the driver applicant has:

(A) Been disqualified from operating a motor vehicle (other than a commercial motor vehicle);

(B) Had a license (other than CDL) disqualified for cause in the 3-year period ending on the date of application; or

(C) Been convicted of any offenses contained in 49 U.S.C. 30304(a)(3);

(iv) A request for the applicant's complete driving record from all States where the applicant was previously licensed over the last 10 years to drive any type of motor vehicle. *Exception:* A State is only required to make the request for the complete driving record specified in this paragraph for initial issuance of a CLP, transfer of CDL from another State or for drivers renewing a CDL for the first time after September 30, 2002, provided a notation is made on the driver's record confirming that the driver record check required by this paragraph has been made and noting the date it was done;

(v) Beginning January 30, 2012, a check that the medical certification status of a driver that self-certified according to § 383.71(b)(1)(ii)(A) of this chapter (non-excepted interstate) is "certified;"

(4) Require the driver applicant to surrender his/her non-CDL driver's license and CLP;

(5) Beginning January 30, 2012, for drivers who certified their type of driving according to § 383.71(b)(1)(ii)(A) (non-excepted interstate) and, if the CDL driver submits a current medical examiner's certificate, date-stamp the medical examiner's certificate, and post all required information from the medical examiner's certificate to the CDLIS driver record in accordance with paragraph (o) of this section.

(6) Require compliance with the standards for providing proof of citizenship or lawful permanent residency specified in § 383.71(b)(9) and proof of State of domicile specified in § 383.71(b)(10). *Exception:* A State is only required to check the proof of citizenship or legal presence specified in this paragraph for initial issuance of a CLP or Non-domiciled CDL, transfer of CDL from another State or for drivers renewing a CDL or Non-domiciled CDL for the first time after July 8, 2011, provided a notation is made on the driver's record confirming that the proof of citizenship or legal presence check required by this paragraph has been made and noting the date it was done;

(7) If not previously done, complete the Social Security Number verification required by paragraph (g) of this section;

(8) For persons applying for a hazardous materials endorsement, require compliance with the standards for such endorsement specified in §§ 383.71(b)(8) and 383.141; and

(9) Make the CDL valid for no more than 8 years from the date of issuance.

(c) *License transfers.* Prior to issuing a CDL to a person who has a CDL from another State, a State must:

(1) Require the driver applicant to make the certifications contained in § 383.71(b)(1) and (5);

(2) Complete a check of the driver applicant's record as contained in paragraph (b)(3) of this section;

(3) Request and receive updates of information specified in subpart J of this part;

(4) If such applicant wishes to retain a hazardous materials endorsement, require compliance with standards for such endorsement specified in §§ 383.71(b)(8) and 383.141 and ensure that the driver has, within the 2 years preceding the transfer, either:

(i) Passed the test for such endorsement specified in § 383.121; or

(ii) Successfully completed a hazardous materials test or training that is given by a third party and that is deemed by the State to substantially cover the same knowledge base as that described in § 383.121;

(5) If not previously done, complete the Social Security Number verification required by paragraph (g) of this section;

(6) Require the applicant to surrender the CDL issued by the applicant's previous State of domicile;

(7) Require compliance with the standards for providing proof of citizenship or lawful permanent residency specified in § 383.71(b)(9) and proof of State of domicile specified in § 383.71(b)(10). *Exception:* A State is only required to check the proof of citizenship or legal presence specified in this paragraph for initial issuance of a CLP or Non-domiciled CDL, transfer of CDL from another State or for drivers renewing a CDL or Non-domiciled CDL for the first time after July 8, 2011, provided a notation is made on the driver's record confirming that the proof of citizenship or legal presence check required by this paragraph has been made and noting the date it was done;

(8) Beginning January 30, 2012, verify from the CDLIS driver record that the medical certification status of driver is "certified" for those who certified according to § 383.71(b)(1)(ii)(A). *Exception:* A driver who certified according to § 383.71(b)(1)(ii)(A) that he/she plans to operate in non-excepted interstate commerce may present a current medical examiner's certificate issued prior to January 30, 2012. The medical examiner's certificate provided by the driver must be posted to the CDLIS driver record in accordance with paragraph (o) of this section and:

(9) Make the CDL valid for no more than 8 years from the date of issuance.

(d) *License Renewals.* Prior to renewing any CDL a State must:

(1) Require the driver applicant to make the certifications contained in § 383.71(b);

(2) Complete a check of the driver applicant's record as contained in paragraph (b)(3) of this section;

(3) Request and receive updates of information specified in subpart J of this part;

(4) If such applicant wishes to retain a hazardous materials endorsement, require the driver to pass the test specified in § 383.121 and comply with the standards specified in §§ 383.71(b)(8) and 383.141 for such endorsement;

(5) If not previously done, complete the Social Security Number verification required by paragraph (g) of this section;

(6) Make the renewal of the CDL valid for no more than 8 years from the date of issuance;

(7) Require compliance with the standards for providing proof of citizenship or lawful permanent residency specified in § 383.71(b)(9) and proof of State of domicile specified in § 383.71(b)(10); and

(8) Beginning January 30, 2012, verify from the CDLIS driver record that the medical certification status is "certified" for drivers who self-certified according to § 383.71(b)(1)(ii)(A). *Exception:* A driver who certified according to § 383.71(b)(1)(ii)(A) may present a current medical examiner's certificate

issued prior to January 30, 2012. The medical examiner's certificate provided by the driver must be posted to the CDLIS driver record in accordance with paragraph (o) of this section.

(e) *License upgrades.* Prior to issuing an upgrade of a CDL, a State must:

(1) Require such driver applicant to provide certifications, pass tests, and meet applicable hazardous materials standards specified in § 383.71(e);

(2) Complete a check of the driver applicant's record as described in paragraph (b)(3) of this section;

(3) If not previously done, complete the Social Security Number verification required by paragraph (g) of this section;

(4) Require the driver applicant to surrender his/her previous CDL;

(5) Require compliance with the standards for providing proof of citizenship or lawful permanent residency specified in § 383.71(b)(9) and proof of State of domicile specified in § 383.71(b)(10);

(6) Beginning January 30, 2012, verify from the CDLIS driver record that the medical certification status is "certified" for drivers who self-certified according to § 383.71(b)(1)(ii)(A). *Exception:* A driver who certified according to § 383.71(b)(1)(ii)(A) may present a current medical examiner's certificate issued prior to January 30, 2011. The medical examiner's certificate provided by the driver must be posted to the CDLIS driver record in accordance with paragraph (o) of this section and:

(7) Make the CDL valid for no more than 8 years from the date of issuance.

(f) *Non-domiciled CLP and CDL.* (1) A State may only issue a Non-domiciled CLP or CDL to a person who meets one of the circumstances described in § 383.71(f)(1).

(2) State procedures for the issuance of a non-domiciled CLP and CDL, for any modifications thereto, and for notifications to the CDLIS must at a minimum be identical to those pertaining to any other CLP or CDL, with the following exceptions:

(i) If the applicant is requesting a transfer of his/her Non-domiciled CDL, the State must obtain the Non-domiciled CDL currently held by the applicant and issued by another State;

(ii) The State must add the word "non-domiciled" to the face of the CLP or CDL, in accordance with § 383.153(b); and

(iii) The State must have established, prior to issuing any Non-domiciled CLP or CDL, the practical capability of disqualifying the holder of any Non-domiciled CLP or CDL, by withdrawing or disqualifying his/her Non-domiciled CLP or CDL as if the Non-domiciled CLP or CDL were a CLP or CDL issued to a person domiciled in the State.

(3) The State must require compliance with the standards for providing proof of legal presence specified in § 383.71(b)(9) and § 383.71(f)(2)(i).

(g) *Social Security Number verification.* (1) Prior to issuing a CLP or a CDL to a person the State must verify the name, date of birth, and Social Security Number provided by the applicant with the information on file with the Social Security Administration. The State is prohibited from issuing, renewing, upgrading, or transferring a CLP or CDL if the Social Security Administration database does not match the applicant-provided data.

(2) *Exception.* A State is only required to perform the Social Security Number verification specified in this paragraph for initial issuance of a CLP, transfer of CDL from another State or for drivers renewing a CDL for the first time after July 8, 2011 who have not previously had their Social Security Number information verified, provided a notation is made on the driver's record confirming that the verification required by this paragraph has been made and noting the date it was done.

(h) *License issuance.* After the State has completed the procedures described in paragraphs (a) through (g) of this section, as applicable, it may issue a CLP or CDL to the driver applicant. The State must notify the operator of the CDLIS of such issuance, transfer, renewal, or upgrade within the 10-day period beginning on the date of license issuance.

(i) *Surrender procedure.* A State may return a surrendered license to a driver after physically marking it so that it cannot be mistaken for a valid document. Simply punching a hole in the expiration date of the document is insufficient. A document perforated with the word "VOID" is considered invalidated.

(j) *Penalties for false information.* If a State determines, in its check of an applicant's license status and record prior to issuing a CLP or CDL, or at any time after the CLP or CDL is issued, that the applicant has falsified information contained in subpart J of this part, in any of the certifications required in §383.71(b) or (g), or in any of the documents required to be submitted by §383.71(h), the State must at a minimum disqualify the person's CLP or CDL or his/her pending application, or disqualify the person from operating a commercial motor vehicle for a period of at least 60 consecutive days.

(k) *Drivers convicted of fraud related to the testing and issuance of a CLP or CDL.* (1) The State must have policies in effect that result, at a minimum, in the disqualification of the CLP or CDL of a person who has been convicted of fraud related to the issuance of that CLP or CDL. The application of a person so convicted who seeks to renew, transfer, or upgrade the fraudulently obtained CLP or CDL must also, at a minimum, be disqualified. The State must record any such withdrawal in the person's driving record. The person may not reapply for a new CDL for at least 1 year.

(2) If a State receives credible information that a CLP- or CDL-holder is suspected, but has not been convicted, of fraud related to the issuance of his/her CLP or CDL, the State must require the driver to re-take the skills and/or knowledge tests. Within 30 days of receiving notification from the State that re-testing is necessary, the affected CLP- or CDL-holder must make an appointment or otherwise schedule to take the next available test. If the CLP- or CDL-holder fails to make an appointment within 30 days, the State must disqualify his/her CLP or CDL. If the driver fails either the knowledge or skills test or does not take the test, the State must disqualify his/her CLP or CDL. Once a CLP- or CDL-holder's CLP or CDL has been disqualified, he/she must reapply for a CLP or CDL under State procedures applicable to all CLP and CDL applicants.

(l) *Reciprocity.* A State must allow any person who has a valid CLP, CDL, Non-domiciled CLP, or Non-domiciled CDL and who is not disqualified from operating a CMV, to operate a CMV in the State.

(m) *Document verification.* The State must require at least two persons within the driver licensing agency to check and verify all documents involved in the licensing process for the initial issuance, renewal, upgrade, or transfer of a CLP or CDL. The documents being checked and verified must include, at a minimum, those provided by the applicant to prove legal presence and domicile, the information filled out on the application form, and knowledge and skills test scores. *Exception:* For offices with only one staff member, the documents must be checked and verified by a supervisor before issuance or, when a supervisor is not available, copies must be made of the documents used to prove legal presence and domicile and a supervisor must verify the documents and the filled out application form and test scores within one business day of issuance of the CLP or CDL.

(n) *Computer system controls.* The State must establish computer system controls that will:

(1) Prevent the issuance of an initial, renewed, upgraded, or transferred CLP or CDL when the results of transactions indicate the applicant is unqualified. These controls, at a minimum, must be established for the following transactions: State, CDLIS, and PDPS driver record checks; Social Security Number verification; and knowledge and skills test scores verification.

(2) Suspend the issuance process whenever State, CDLIS, and/or PDPS driver record checks return suspect results. The State must demonstrate that it has a system to detect and prevent fraud when a driver record check returns suspect results. At a minimum, the system must ensure that:

(i) The results are not connected to a violation of any State or local law relating to motor vehicle traffic control (other than parking, vehicle weight, or vehicle defect violations);

(ii) The name of the persons performing the record check and authorizing the issuance, and the justification for the authorization are documented by the State; and

(iii) The person performing the record check and the person authorizing the issuance are not the same.

(o) *Medical recordkeeping*—(1) *Status of CDL holder.* Beginning January 30, 2012, for each operator of a commercial motor vehicle required to have a CLP or CDL, the current licensing State must:

(i) Post the driver's self-certification of type of driving under § 383.71(b)(1)(ii),

(ii) Retain the original or a copy of the medical certificate of any driver required to provide documentation of physical qualification for 3 years beyond the date the certificate was issued, and

(iii) Post the information from the medical examiner's certificate within 10 calendar days to the CDLIS driver record, including:

(A) Medical examiner's name;

(B) Medical examiner's telephone number;

(C) Date of medical examiner's certificate issuance;

(D) Medical examiner's license number and the State that issued it;

(E) Medical examiner's National Registry identification number (if the National Registry of Medical Examiners, mandated by 49 U.S.C. 31149(d), requires one);

(F) The indicator of medical certification status, i.e., "certified" or "not-certified";

(G) Expiration date of the medical examiner's certificate;

(H) Existence of any medical variance on the medical certificate, such as an exemption, Skill Performance Evaluation (SPE) certification, or grandfather provisions;

(I) Any restrictions (e.g., corrective lenses, hearing aid, required to have possession of an exemption letter or SPE certificate while on-duty, etc.); and

(J) Date the medical examiner's certificate information was posted to the CDLIS driver record.

(2) *Status update.* Beginning January 30, 2012, the State must, within 10 calendar days of the driver's medical certification status expiring or a medical variance expiring or being rescinded, update the medical certification status of that driver as "not-certified."

(3) *Variance update.* Beginning January 30, 2012, within 10 calendar days of receiving information from FMCSA regarding issuance or renewal of a medical variance for a driver, the State must update the CDLIS driver record to include the medical variance information provided by FMCSA.

(4) *Downgrade.* (i) Beginning January 30, 2012, if a driver's medical certification or medical variance expires, or FMCSA notifies the State that a medical variance was removed or rescinded, the State must:

(A) Notify the CLP or CDL holder of his/her CLP or CDL "not-certified" medical certification status and that the CMV privileges will be removed from the CLP or CDL unless the driver submits a current medical certificate and/or medical variance, or changes his/her self-certification to driving only in excepted or intrastate commerce (if permitted by the State);

(B) Initiate established State procedures for downgrading the CLP or CDL. The CLP or CDL downgrade must be completed and recorded within 60 days of the driver's medical certification status becoming "not-certified" to operate a CMV.

(ii) Beginning January 30, 2014, if a driver fails to provide the State with the certification contained in § 383.71(b)(1)(ii), or a current medical examiner's certificate if the driver self-certifies according to § 383.71(b)(1)(ii)(A) that he/she is operating in non-excepted interstate commerce as required by § 383.71(h), the State must mark that CDLIS driver record as "not-certified" and initiate a CLP or CDL downgrade following State procedures in accordance with paragraph (o)(4)(i)(B) of this section.

(5) FMCSA Medical Programs is designated as the keeper of the list of State contacts for receiving medical variance information from FMCSA. Beginning January 30, 2012, States are responsible for insuring their medical variance contact information is always up-to-date with FMCSA's Medical Programs.

[76 FR 26883, May 9, 2011]

§383.75 Third party testing.

(a) *Third party tests.* A State may authorize a third party tester to administer the skills tests as specified in subparts G and H of this part, if the following conditions are met:

(1) The skills tests given by the third party are the same as those that would otherwise be given by the State using the same version of the skills tests, the same written instructions for test applicants, and the same scoring sheets as those prescribed in subparts G and H of this part;

(2) The State must conduct an on-site inspection of each third party tester at least once every 2 years, with a focus on examiners with irregular results such as unusually high or low pass/fail rates;

(3) The State must issue the third party tester a CDL skills testing certificate upon the execution of a third party skills testing agreement.

(4) The State must issue each third party CDL skills test examiner a skills testing certificate upon successful completion of a formal skills test examiner training course prescribed in §384.228.

(5) The State must, at least once every 2 years, do one of the following for each third party examiner:

(i) Have State employees covertly take the tests administered by the third party as if the State employee were a test applicant;

(ii) Have State employees co-score along with the third party examiner during CDL skills tests to compare pass/fail results; or

(iii) Re-test a sample of drivers who were examined by the third party to compare pass/fail results;

(6) The State must take prompt and appropriate remedial action against a third party tester that fails to comply with State or Federal standards for the CDL testing program, or with any other terms of the third party contract;

(7) A skills tester that is also a driver training school is prohibited from administering a skills test to an applicant who was trained by that training school. *Exception:* When the nearest alternative third party tester or State skills testing facility is over 50 miles from the training school, the SDLA may allow the training school to skills test the applicant it trained provided the individual skills test examiner did not train the applicant; and

(8) The State has an agreement with the third party containing, at a minimum, provisions that:

(i) Allow the FMCSA, or its representative, and the State to conduct random examinations, inspections, and audits of its records, facilities, and operations without prior notice;

(ii) Require that all third party skills test examiners meet the qualification and training standards of §384.228;

(iii) Allow the State to do any of the following:

(A) Have State employees covertly take the tests administered by the third party as if the State employee were a test applicant;

(B) Have State employees co-score along with the third party examiner during CDL skills tests to compare pass/fail results; or

(C) Have the State re-test a sample of drivers who were examined by the third party;

(iv) Reserve unto the State the right to take prompt and appropriate remedial action against a third party tester that fails to comply with State or Federal standards for the CDL testing program, or with any other terms of the third party contract;

(v) Require the third party tester to initiate and maintain a bond in an amount determined by the State to be sufficient to pay for re-testing drivers in the event that the third party or one or more of its examiners is involved in fraudulent activities related to conducting skills testing for applicants for a CDL.

(vi) Require the third party tester to use only CDL skills examiners who have successfully completed a formal CDL skills test examiner training course as prescribed by the State and have been certified by the State as a CDL skills examiner qualified to administer CDL skills tests;

(vii) Require the third party tester to use designated road test routes that have been approved by the State;

(viii) Require the third party tester to submit a schedule of CDL skills testing appointments to the State no later

211

than two business days prior to each test; and

(ix) Require the third party tester to maintain copies of the following records at its principal place of business:

(A) A copy of the State certificate authorizing the third party tester to administer a CDL skills testing program for the classes and types of commercial motor vehicles listed;

(B) A copy of each third party examiner's State certificate authorizing the third party examiner to administer CDL skills tests for the classes and types of commercial motor vehicles listed;

(C) A copy of the current third party agreement;

(D) A copy of each completed CDL skills test scoring sheet for the current year and the past two calendar years;

(E) A copy of the third party tester's State-approved road test route(s); and

(F) A copy of each third party examiner's training record.

(b) *Proof of testing by a third party.* The third party tester must notify the State driver licensing agency through secure electronic means when a driver applicant passes skills tests administered by the third party tester.

(c) *Minimum number of tests conducted.* The State must revoke the skills testing certification of any examiner who does not conduct skills test examinations of at least 10 different applicants per calendar year. *Exception:* Examiners who do not meet the 10-test minimum must either take the refresher training specified in § 384.228 of this chapter or have a State examiner ride along to observe the third party examiner successfully administer at least one skills test.

[76 FR 26886, May 9, 2011]

§ 383.77 Substitute for driving skills tests for drivers with military CMV experience.

At the discretion of a State, the driving skills test as specified in § 383.113 may be waived for a CMV driver with military CMV experience who is currently licensed at the time of his/her application for a CDL, and substituted with an applicant's driving record in combination with certain driving experience. The State shall impose conditions and limitations to restrict the applicants from whom a State may accept alternative requirements for the skills test described in § 383.113. Such conditions must require at least the following:

(a) An applicant must certify that, during the two-year period immediately prior to applying for a CDL, he/she:

(1) Has not had more than one license (except for a military license);

(2) Has not had any license suspended, revoked, or cancelled;

(3) Has not had any convictions for any type of motor vehicle for the disqualifying offenses contained in § 383.51(b);

(4) Has not had more than one conviction for any type of motor vehicle for serious traffic violations contained in § 383.51(c); and

(5) Has not had had any conviction for a violation of military, State or local law relating to motor vehicle traffic control (other than a parking violation) arising in connection with any traffic accident, and has no record of an accident in which he/she was at fault; and

(b) An applicant must provide evidence and certify that he/she:

(1) Is regularly employed or was regularly employed within the last 90 days in a military position requiring operation of a CMV;

(2) Was exempted from the CDL requirements in § 383.3(c); and

(3) Was operating a vehicle representative of the CMV the driver applicant operates or expects to operate, for at least the 2 years immediately preceding discharge from the military.

[76 FR 26887, May 9, 2011]

§ 383.79 Skills testing of out-of-State students.

(a) A State may administer its skills test, in accordance with subparts F, G, and H of this part, to a person who has taken training in that State and is to be licensed in another United States jurisdiction (i.e., his/her State of domicile). Such test results must be transmitted electronically directly from the testing State to the licensing State in an efficient and secure manner.

(b) The State of domicile of a CDL applicant must accept the results of a skills test administered to the applicant by any other State, in accordance with subparts F, G, and H of this part, in fulfillment of the applicant's testing requirements under §383.71, and the State's test administration requirements under §383.73.

[76 FR 26887, May 9, 2011]

Subpart F—Vehicle Groups and Endorsements

SOURCE: 53 FR 27651, July 21, 1988, unless otherwise noted.

§383.91 Commercial motor vehicle groups.

(a) *Vehicle group descriptions.* Each driver applicant must possess and be tested on his/her knowledge and skills, described in subpart G of this part, for the commercial motor vehicle group(s) for which he/she desires a CDL. The commercial motor vehicle groups are as follows:

(1) Combination vehicle (Group A)— Any combination of vehicles with a gross combination weight rating (GCWR) of 11,794 kilograms or more (26,001 pounds or more) provided the GVWR of the vehicle(s) being towed is in excess of 4,536 kilograms (10,000 pounds).

(2) Heavy Straight Vehicle (Group B)—Any single vehicle with a GVWR of 11,794 kilograms or more (26,001 pounds or more), or any such vehicle towing a vehicle not in excess of 4,536 kilograms (10,000 pounds) GVWR.

(3) Small Vehicle (Group C)—Any single vehicle, or combination of vehicles, that meets neither the definition of Group A nor that of Group B as contained in this section, but that either is designed to transport 16 or more passengers including the driver, or is used in the transportation of materials found to be hazardous for the purposes of the Hazardous Materials Transportation Act and which require the motor vehicle to be placarded under the Hazardous Materials Regulations (49 CFR part 172, subpart F).

(b) *Representative vehicle.* For purposes of taking the driving test in accordance with §383.113, a representative vehicle for a given vehicle group contained in §383.91(a), is any commercial motor vehicle which meets the definition of that vehicle group.

(c) *Relation between vehicle groups.* Each driver applicant who desires to operate in a different commercial motor vehicle group from the one which his/her CDL authorizes shall be required to retake and pass all related tests, except the following:

(1) A driver who has passed the knowledge and skills tests for a combination vehicle (Group A) may operate a heavy straight vehicle (Group B) or a small vehicle (Group C), provided that he/she possesses the requisite endorsement(s); and

(2) A driver who has passed the knowledge and skills tests for a heavy straight vehicle (Group B) may operate any small vehicle (Group C), provided that he/she possesses the requisite endorsement(s).

(d) *Vehicle group illustration.* Figure 1 illustrates typical vehicles within each of the vehicle groups defined in this section.

Figure 1
VEHICLE GROUPS AS ESTABLISHED BY FHWA (SECTION 383.91)

[Note: Certain types of vehicles, such as passenger and doubles/triples, will require an endorsement. Please consult text for particulars.]

Group: *Description:

A   Any combination of vehicles with a GCWR of 26,001 or more pounds provided the GVWR of the vehicle(s) being towed is in excess of 10,000 pounds. (Holders of a Group A license may, with any appropriate endorsements, operate all vehicles within Groups B and C.)

         Examples include but are not limited to:

B   Any single vehicle with a GVWR of 26,001 or more pounds, or any such vehicle towing a vehicle not in excess of 10,000 pounds GVWR. (Holders of a Group B license may, with any appropriate endorsements, operate all vehicles within Group C.)

         Examples include but are not limited to:

C   Any single vehicle, or combination of vehicles, that does not meet the definition of Group A or Group B as contained herein, but that either is designed to transport 16 or more passengers including the driver, or is placarded for hazardous materials.

         Examples include but are not limited to:

*
 The representative vehicle for the skills test must meet the written description for that group. The silhouettes typify, but do not fully cover, the types of vehicles falling within each group.

[53 FR 27651, July 21, 1988, as amended at 54 FR 47989, Nov. 20, 1989; 61 FR 9566, Mar. 8, 1996]

§383.93 Endorsements.

(a) *General.* (1) In addition to passing the knowledge and skills tests described in subpart G of this part, all persons who operate or expect to operate the type(s) of motor vehicles described in paragraph (b) of this section must pass specialized tests to obtain each endorsement. The State shall issue CDL endorsements only to drivers who successfully complete the tests.

(2) The only endorsements allowed on a CLP are the following:

(i) Passenger (P);

(ii) School bus (S); and

(iii) Tank vehicle (N).

(3) The State must use the codes listed in §383.153 when placing endorsements on a CLP or CDL.

(b) *Endorsement descriptions.* An operator must obtain State-issued endorsements to his/her CDL to operate commercial motor vehicles which are:

(1) Double/triple trailers;

(2) Passenger vehicles;

(3) Tank vehicles;

(4) Used to transport hazardous materials as defined in §383.5, or

(5) School buses.

(c) *Endorsement testing requirements.* The following tests are required for the endorsements contained in paragraph (b) of this section:

(1) *Double/Triple Trailers*—a knowledge test;

(2) *Passenger*—a knowledge and a skills test;

(3) *Tank vehicle*—a knowledge test;

(4) *Hazardous Materials*—a knowledge test; and

(5) *School bus*—a knowledge and a skills test.

[53 FR 27651, July 21, 1988, as amended at 67 FR 49760, July 31, 2002; 68 FR 23850, May 5, 2003; 76 FR 26887, May 9, 2011]

§383.95 Restrictions.

(a) *Air brake.* (1) If an applicant either fails the air brake component of the knowledge test, or performs the skills test in a vehicle not equipped with air brakes, the State must indicate on the CLP or CDL, if issued, that the person is restricted from operating a CMV equipped with any type of air brakes.

(2) For the purposes of the skills test and the restriction, air brakes include any braking system operating fully or partially on the air brake principle.

(b) *Full air brake.* (1) If an applicant performs the skills test in a vehicle equipped with air over hydraulic brakes, the State must indicate on the CDL, if issued, that the person is restricted from operating a CMV equipped with any braking system operating fully on the air brake principle.

(2) For the purposes of the skills test and the restriction, air over hydraulic brakes includes any braking system operating partially on the air brake and partially on the hydraulic brake principle.

(c) *Manual transmission.* (1) If an applicant performs the skills test in a vehicle equipped with an automatic transmission, the State must indicate on the CDL, if issued, that the person is restricted from operating a CMV equipped with a manual transmission.

(2) For the purposes of the skills test and the restriction, an automatic transmission includes any transmission other than a manual transmission as defined in §383.5.

(d) *Tractor-trailer.* If an applicant performs the skills test in a combination vehicle for a Group A CDL with the power unit and towed unit connected with a pintle hook or other non-fifth wheel connection, the State must indicate on the CDL, if issued, that the person is restricted from operating a tractor-trailer combination connected by a fifth wheel that requires a Group A CDL.

(e) *Group A passenger vehicle.* If an applicant applying for a passenger endorsement performs the skills test in a passenger vehicle requiring a Group B CDL, the State must indicate on the CDL, if issued, that the person is restricted from operating a passenger vehicle requiring a Group A CDL.

(f) *Group A and B passenger vehicle.* If an applicant applying for a passenger endorsement performs the skills test in a passenger vehicle requiring a Group C CDL, the State must indicate on the CDL, if issued, that the person is restricted from operating a passenger vehicle requiring a Group A or B CDL.

(g) *Medical variance restrictions.* If the State is notified according to §383.73(o)(3) that the driver has been issued a medical variance, the State must indicate the existence of such a medical variance on the CDLIS driver record and the CDL document, if issued, using the restriction code "V" to indicate there is information about a medical variance on the CDLIS driver record. NOTE: In accordance with the agreement between Canada and the United States (see footnote to § 391.41 of this chapter), drivers with a medical variance restriction code on their CDL are restricted from operating a CMV in the other country.

[76 FR 26887, May 9, 2011]

Subpart G—Required Knowledge and Skills

SOURCE: 53 FR 27654, July 21, 1988, unless otherwise noted.

§ 383.110   General requirement.

All drivers of CMVs must have the knowledge and skills necessary to operate a CMV safely as contained in this subpart. The specific types of items that a State must include in the knowledge and skills tests that it administers to CDL applicants are included in this subpart.

[76 FR 26888, May 9, 2011]

§ 383.111   Required knowledge.

(a) All CMV operators must have knowledge of the following 20 general areas:

(1) *Safe operations regulations.* Driver-related elements of the regulations contained in parts 391, 392, 393, 395, 396, and 397 of this subchapter, such as:

(i) Motor vehicle inspection, repair, and maintenance requirements;

(ii) Procedures for safe vehicle operations;

(iii) The effects of fatigue, poor vision, hearing impairment, and general health upon safe commercial motor vehicle operation;

(iv) The types of motor vehicles and cargoes subject to the requirements contained in part 397 of this subchapter; and

(v) The effects of alcohol and drug use upon safe commercial motor vehicle operations.

(2) *Safe vehicle control systems.* The purpose and function of the controls and instruments commonly found on CMVs.

(3) *CMV safety control systems.* (i) Proper use of the motor vehicle's safety system, including lights, horns, side and rear-view mirrors, proper mirror adjustments, fire extinguishers, symptoms of improper operation revealed through instruments, motor vehicle operation characteristics, and diagnosing malfunctions.

(ii) CMV drivers must have knowledge of the correct procedures needed to use these safety systems in an emergency situation, e.g., skids and loss of brakes.

(4) *Basic control.* The proper procedures for performing various basic maneuvers, including:

(i) Starting, warming up, and shutting down the engine;

(ii) Putting the vehicle in motion and stopping;

(iii) Backing in a straight line; and

(iv) Turning the vehicle, e.g., basic rules, off tracking, right/left turns and right curves.

(5) *Shifting.* The basic shifting rules and terms for common transmissions, including:

(i) Key elements of shifting, e.g., controls, when to shift, and double clutching;

(ii) Shift patterns and procedures; and

(iii) Consequences of improper shifting.

(6) *Backing.* The procedures and rules for various backing maneuvers, including:

(i) Backing principles and rules; and

(ii) Basic backing maneuvers, e.g., straight-line backing, and backing on a curved path.

(7) *Visual search.* The importance of proper visual search, and proper visual search methods, including:

(i) Seeing ahead and to the sides;

(ii) Use of mirrors; and

(iii) Seeing to the rear.

(8) *Communication.* The principles and procedures for proper communications and the hazards of failure to signal properly, including:

(i) Signaling intent, e.g., signaling when changing direction in traffic;

(ii) Communicating presence, e.g., using horn or lights to signal presence; and

(iii) Misuse of communications.

(9) *Speed management.* The importance of understanding the effects of speed, including:

(i) Speed and stopping distance;

(ii) Speed and surface conditions;

(iii) Speed and the shape of the road;

(iv) Speed and visibility; and

(v) Speed and traffic flow.

(10) *Space management.* The procedures and techniques for controlling the space around the vehicle, including:

(i) The importance of space management;

(ii) Space cushions, e.g., controlling space ahead/to the rear;

(iii) Space to the sides; and

(iv) Space for traffic gaps.

(11) *Night operation.* Preparations and procedures for night driving, including:

(i) Night driving factors, e.g., driver factors (vision, glare, fatigue, inexperience);

(ii) Roadway factors (low illumination, variation in illumination, unfamiliarity with roads, other road users, especially drivers exhibiting erratic or improper driving); and

(iii) Vehicle factors (headlights, auxiliary lights, turn signals, windshields and mirrors).

(12) *Extreme driving conditions.* The basic information on operating in extreme driving conditions and the hazards encountered in such conditions, including:

(i) Bad weather, e.g., snow, ice, sleet, high wind;

(ii) Hot weather; and

(iii) Mountain driving.

(13) *Hazard perceptions.* The basic information on hazard perception and clues for recognition of hazards, including:

(i) Road characteristics; and

(ii) Road user activities.

(14) *Emergency maneuvers.* The basic information concerning when and how to make emergency maneuvers, including:

(i) Evasive steering;

(ii) Emergency stop;

(iii) Off road recovery;

(iv) Brake failure; and

(v) Blowouts.

(15) *Skid control and recovery.* The information on the causes and major types of skids, as well as the procedures for recovering from skids.

(16) *Relationship of cargo to vehicle control.* The principles and procedures for the proper handling of cargo, including:

(i) Consequences of improperly secured cargo, drivers' responsibilities, and Federal/State and local regulations;

(ii) Principles of weight distribution; and

(iii) Principles and methods of cargo securement.

(17) *Vehicle inspections.* The objectives and proper procedures for performing vehicle safety inspections, as follows:

(i) The importance of periodic inspection and repair to vehicle safety.

(ii) The effect of undiscovered malfunctions upon safety.

(iii) What safety-related parts to look for when inspecting vehicles, e.g., fluid leaks, interference with visibility, bad tires, wheel and rim defects, braking system defects, steering system defects, suspension system defects, exhaust system defects, coupling system defects, and cargo problems.

(iv) Pre-trip/enroute/post-trip inspection procedures.

(v) Reporting findings.

(18) *Hazardous materials.* Knowledge of the following:

(i) What constitutes hazardous material requiring an endorsement to transport;

(ii) Classes of hazardous materials;

(iii) Labeling/placarding requirements; and

(iv) Need for specialized training as a prerequisite to receiving the endorsement and transporting hazardous cargoes.

(19) *Mountain driving.* Practices that are important when driving upgrade and downgrade, including:

(i) Selecting a safe speed;

(ii) Selecting the right gear; and

(iii) Proper braking techniques.

(20) *Fatigue and awareness.* Practices that are important to staying alert and safe while driving, including:

(i) Being prepared to drive;

(ii) What to do when driving to avoid fatigue;

(iii) What to do when sleepy while driving; and

(iv) What to do when becoming ill while driving.

(b) *Air brakes.* All CMV drivers operating vehicles equipped with air brakes must have knowledge of the following 7 areas:

(1) General air brake system nomenclature;

(2) The dangers of contaminated air supply (dirt, moisture, and oil);

(3) Implications of severed or disconnected air lines between the power unit and the trailer(s);

(4) Implications of low air pressure readings;

(5) Procedures to conduct safe and accurate pre-trip inspections, including knowledge about:

(i) Automatic fail-safe devices;

(ii) System monitoring devices; and

(iii) Low pressure warning alarms.

(6) Procedures for conducting en route and post-trip inspections of air-actuated brake systems, including:

(i) Ability to detect defects that may cause the system to fail;

(ii) Tests that indicate the amount of air loss from the braking system within a specified period, with and without the engine running; and

(iii) Tests that indicate the pressure levels at which the low air pressure warning devices and the tractor protection valve should activate.

(7) General operating practices and procedures, including:

(i) Proper braking techniques;

(ii) Antilock brakes;

(iii) Emergency stops; and

(iv) Parking brake.

(c) *Combination vehicles.* All CMV drivers operating combination vehicles must have knowledge of the following 3 areas:

(1) Coupling and uncoupling—The procedures for proper coupling and uncoupling a tractor to a semi-trailer;

(2) Vehicle inspection—The objectives and proper procedures that are unique for performing vehicle safety inspections on combination vehicles; and

(3) General operating practices and procedures, including:

(i) Safely operating combination vehicles; and

(ii) Air brakes.

[76 FR 26888, May 9, 2011]

§ 383.113   Required skills.

(a) *Pre-trip vehicle inspection skills.* Applicants for a CDL must possess the following basic pre-trip vehicle inspection skills for the vehicle class that the driver operates or expects to operate:

(1) *All test vehicles.* Applicants must be able to identify each safety-related part on the vehicle and explain what needs to be inspected to ensure a safe operating condition of each part, including:

(i) Engine compartment;

(ii) Cab/engine start;

(iii) Steering;

(iv) Suspension;

(v) Brakes;

(vi) Wheels;

(vii) Side of vehicle;

(viii) Rear of vehicle; and

(ix) Special features of tractor trailer, school bus, or coach/transit bus, if this type of vehicle is being used for the test.

(2) *Air brake equipped test vehicles.* Applicants must demonstrate the following skills with respect to inspection and operation of air brakes:

(i) Locate and verbally identify air brake operating controls and monitoring devices;

(ii) Determine the motor vehicle's brake system condition for proper adjustments and that air system connections between motor vehicles have been properly made and secured;

(iii) Inspect the low pressure warning device(s) to ensure that they will activate in emergency situations;

(iv) With the engine running, make sure that the system maintains an adequate supply of compressed air;

(v) Determine that required minimum air pressure build up time is within acceptable limits and that required alarms and emergency devices automatically deactivate at the proper pressure level; and

(vi) Operationally check the brake system for proper performance.

(b) *Basic vehicle control skills.* All applicants for a CDL must possess and demonstrate the following basic motor vehicle control skills for the vehicle class that the driver operates or expects to operate:

(1) Ability to start, warm up, and shut down the engine;

(2) Ability to put the motor vehicle in motion and accelerate smoothly, forward and backward;

(3) Ability to bring the motor vehicle to a smooth stop;

(4) Ability to back the motor vehicle in a straight line, and check path and clearance while backing;

(5) Ability to position the motor vehicle to negotiate safely and then make left and right turns;

(6) Ability to shift as required and select appropriate gear for speed and highway conditions; and

(7) Ability to back along a curved path.

(c) *Safe on-road driving skills.* All applicants for a CDL must possess and demonstrate the following safe on-road driving skills for their vehicle class:

(1) Ability to use proper visual search methods;

(2) Ability to signal appropriately when changing direction in traffic;

(3) Ability to adjust speed to the configuration and condition of the roadway, weather and visibility conditions, traffic conditions, and motor vehicle, cargo and driver conditions;

(4) Ability to choose a safe gap for changing lanes, passing other vehicles, as well as for crossing or entering traffic;

(5) Ability to position the motor vehicle correctly before and during a turn to prevent other vehicles from passing on the wrong side, as well as to prevent problems caused by off-tracking;

(6) Ability to maintain a safe following distance depending on the condition of the road, visibility, and vehicle weight;

(7) Ability to adjust operation of the motor vehicle to prevailing weather conditions including speed selection, braking, direction changes, and following distance to maintain control; and

(8) Ability to observe the road and the behavior of other motor vehicles, particularly before changing speed and direction.

(d) *Test area.* Skills tests shall be conducted in on-street conditions or under a combination of on-street and off-street conditions.

(e) *Simulation technology.* A State may utilize simulators to perform skills testing, but under no cir-cumstances as a substitute for the required testing in on-street conditions.

[76 FR 26889, May 9, 2011]

§383.115 Requirements for double/triple trailers endorsement.

In order to obtain a double/triple trailers endorsement each applicant must have knowledge covering:

(a) Procedures for assembly and hookup of the units;

(b) Proper placement of heaviest trailer;

(c) Handling and stability characteristics including off-tracking, response to steering, sensory feedback, braking, oscillatory sway, rollover in steady turns, and yaw stability in steady turns;

(d) Potential problems in traffic operations, including problems the motor vehicle creates for other motorists due to slower speeds on steep grades, longer passing times, possibility for blocking entry of other motor vehicles on freeways, splash and spray impacts, aerodynamic buffeting, view blockages, and lateral placement; and

(e) Operating practices and procedures not otherwise specified.

[76 FR 26890, May 9, 2011]

§383.117 Requirements for passenger endorsement.

An applicant for the passenger endorsement must satisfy both of the following additional knowledge and skills test requirements.

(a) *Knowledge test.* All applicants for the passenger endorsement must have knowledge covering the following topics:

(1) Proper procedures for loading/unloading passengers;

(2) Proper use of emergency exits, including push-out windows;

(3) Proper responses to such emergency situations as fires and unruly passengers;

(4) Proper procedures at railroad-highway grade crossings and draw-bridges;

(5) Proper braking procedures; and

(6) Operating practices and procedures not otherwise specified.

(b) *Skills test.* To obtain a passenger endorsement applicable to a specific vehicle class, an applicant must take his/her skills test in a passenger vehicle satisfying the requirements of that vehicle group as defined in § 383.91.

[76 FR 26890, May 9, 2011]

§ 383.119 Requirements for tank vehicle endorsement.

In order to obtain a tank vehicle endorsement, each applicant must have knowledge covering the following:

(a) Causes, prevention, and effects of cargo surge on motor vehicle handling;

(b) Proper braking procedures for the motor vehicle when it is empty, full, and partially full;

(c) Differences in handling of baffled/compartmented tank interiors versus non-baffled motor vehicles;

(d) Differences in tank vehicle type and construction;

(e) Differences in cargo surge for liquids of varying product densities;

(f) Effects of road grade and curvature on motor vehicle handling with filled, half-filled, and empty tanks;

(g) Proper use of emergency systems;

(h) For drivers of DOT specification tank vehicles, retest and marking requirements; and

(i) Operating practices and procedures not otherwise specified.

[76 FR 26890, May 9, 2011]

§ 383.121 Requirements for hazardous materials endorsement.

In order to obtain a hazardous materials endorsement, each applicant must have such knowledge as is required of a driver of a hazardous materials laden vehicle, from information contained in 49 CFR parts 171, 172, 173, 177, 178, and 397, on the following:

(a) Hazardous materials regulations including:

(1) Hazardous materials table;

(2) Shipping paper requirements;

(3) Marking;

(4) Labeling;

(5) Placarding requirements;

(6) Hazardous materials packaging;

(7) Hazardous materials definitions and preparation;

(8) Other regulated material (e.g., ORM–D);

(9) Reporting hazardous materials accidents; and

(10) Tunnels and railroad crossings.

(b) Hazardous materials handling including:

(1) Forbidden materials and packages;

(2) Loading and unloading materials;

(3) Cargo segregation;

(4) Passenger carrying buses and hazardous materials;

(5) Attendance of motor vehicles;

(6) Parking;

(7) Routes;

(8) Cargo tanks; and

(9) "Safe havens."

(c) Operation of emergency equipment including:

(1) Use of equipment to protect the public;

(2) Special precautions for equipment to be used in fires;

(3) Special precautions for use of emergency equipment when loading or unloading a hazardous materials laden motor vehicle; and

(4) Use of emergency equipment for tank vehicles.

(d) Emergency response procedures including:

(1) Special care and precautions for different types of accidents;

(2) Special precautions for driving near a fire and carrying hazardous materials, and smoking and carrying hazardous materials;

(3) Emergency procedures; and

(4) Existence of special requirements for transporting Class 1.1 and 1.2 explosives.

(e) Operating practices and procedures not otherwise specified.

[76 FR 26890, May 9, 2011]

§ 383.123 Requirements for a school bus endorsement.

(a) An applicant for the school bus endorsement must satisfy the following three requirements:

(1) *Qualify for passenger vehicle endorsement.* Pass the knowledge and skills test for obtaining a passenger vehicle endorsement.

(2) *Knowledge test.* Must have knowledge covering the following topics:

(i) Loading and unloading children, including the safe operation of stop signal devices, external mirror systems, flashing lights, and other warning and passenger safety devices required for school buses by State or Federal law or regulation.

(ii) Emergency exits and procedures for safely evacuating passengers in an emergency.

(iii) State and Federal laws and regulations related to safely traversing railroad-highway grade crossings; and

(iv) Operating practices and procedures not otherwise specified.

(3) *Skills test.* Must take a driving skills test in a school bus of the same vehicle group (see §383.91(a)) as the school bus applicant will drive.

(b) *Exception.* Knowledge and skills tests administered before September 30, 2002 and approved by FMCSA as meeting the requirements of this section, meet the requirements of paragraphs (a)(2) and (3) of this section

[76 FR 26891, May 9, 2011]

Subpart H—Tests

SOURCE: 53 FR 27657, July 21, 1988, unless otherwise noted.

§383.131   Test manuals.

(a) *Driver information manual.* (1) A State must provide an FMCSA pre-approved driver information manual to a CLP or CDL applicant. The manual must be comparable to the American Association of Motor Vehicle Administrators' (AAMVA's) "2005 CDL Test System (July 2010 Version) Model Commercial Driver Manual", which FMCSA has approved and provides to all State Driver Licensing Agencies. The driver information manual must include:

(i) Information on how to obtain a CDL and endorsements;

(ii) Information on the requirements described in §383.71, the implied consent to alcohol testing described in §383.72, the procedures and penalties contained in §383.51(b) to which a CLP or CDL holder is exposed for refusal to comply with such alcohol testing, State procedures described in §383.73, and other appropriate driver information contained in subpart E of this part;

(iii) Information on vehicle groups and endorsements as specified in subpart F of this part;

(iv) The substance of the knowledge and skills that drivers must have, as outlined in subpart G of this part for the different vehicle groups and endorsements; and

(v) Details of testing procedures, including the purpose of the tests, how to respond, and directions for taking the tests.

(2) A State may include any additional State-specific information related to the CDL testing and licensing process.

(b) *Examiner information manual.* (1) A State must provide an FMCSA pre-approved examiner information manual that conforms to model requirements in paragraphs (b)(1)(i–xi) of this section to all knowledge and skills test examiners. To be pre-approved by FMCSA, the examiner information manual must be comparable to AAMVA's "2005 CDL Test System (July 2010 Version) Model CDL Examiner's Manual," which FMCSA has approved and provides to all State Driver Licensing Agencies. The examiner information manual must include:

(i) Information on driver application procedures contained in §383.71, State procedures described in §383.73, and other appropriate driver information contained in subpart E of this part;

(ii) Details on information that must be given to the applicant;

(iii) Details on how to conduct the knowledge and skills tests;

(iv) Scoring procedures and minimum passing scores for the knowledge and skills tests;

(v) Information for selecting driving test routes for the skills tests;

(vi) List of the skills to be tested;

(vii) Instructions on where and how the skills will be tested;

(viii) How performance of the skills will be scored;

(ix) Causes for automatic failure of skills tests;

(x) Standardized scoring sheets for the skills tests; and

(xi) Standardized driving instructions for the applicants.

(2) A State may include any additional State-specific information related to the CDL testing process.

[76 FR 26891, May 9, 2011]

§383.133   Test methods.

(a) All tests must be constructed in such a way as to determine if the applicant possesses the required knowledge and skills contained in subpart G of this part for the type of motor vehicle or endorsement the applicant wishes to obtain.

(b) Knowledge tests:

(1) States must use the FMCSA pre-approved pool of test questions to develop knowledge tests for each vehicle group and endorsement. The pool of questions must be comparable to those in AAMVA's "2005 CDL Test System (July 2010 Version) 2005 Test Item Summary Forms," which FMCSA has approved and provides to all State Driver Licensing Agencies.

(2) The State method of generating knowledge tests must conform to the requirements in paragraphs (b)(2)(i) through (iv) of this section and be pre-approved by FMCSA. The State method of generating knowledge tests must be comparable to the requirements outlined in AAMVA's "2005 CDL Test System (July 2010 Version) 2005 Requirements Document For Use In Developing Computer-Generated Multiple-Choice CDL Knowledge Tests", which FMCSA has approved and provides to all State Driver Licensing Agencies to develop knowledge tests for each vehicle group and endorsement. These requirements include:

(i) The total difficulty level of the questions used in each version of a test must fall within a set range;

(ii) Twenty-five percent of the questions on a test must be new questions that were not contained in the previous version of the test;

(iii) Identical questions from the previous version of the test must be in a different location on the test and the three possible responses to the questions must be in a different order; and

(iv) Each test must contain a set number of questions with a prescribed number of questions from each of the knowledge areas.

(3) Each knowledge test must be valid and reliable so as to ensure that driver applicants possess the knowledge required under § 383.111. The knowledge tests may be administered in written form, verbally, or in automated format and can be administered in a foreign language, provided no interpreter is used in administering the test.

(4) A State must use a different version of the test when an applicant retakes a previously failed test.

(c) Skills tests:

(1) A State must develop, administer and score the skills tests based solely on the information and standards contained in the driver and examiner manuals referred to in § 383.131(a) and (b).

(2) A State must use the standardized scores and instructions for administering the tests contained in the examiner manual referred to in § 383.131(b).

(3) An applicant must complete the skills tests in a representative vehicle to ensure that the applicant possess the skills required under § 383.113. In determining whether the vehicle is a representative vehicle for the skills test and the group of CDL for which the applicant is applying, the vehicle's gross vehicle weight rating or gross combination weight rating must be used, not the vehicle's actual gross vehicle weight or gross combination weight.

(4) Skills tests must be conducted in on-street conditions or under a combination of on-street and off-street conditions.

(5) Interpreters are prohibited during the administration of skills tests. Applicants must be able to understand and respond to verbal commands and instructions in English by a skills test examiner. Neither the applicant nor the examiner may communicate in a language other than English during the skills test.

(6) The skills test must be administered and successfully completed in the following order: Pre-trip inspection, basic vehicle control skills, on-road skills. If an applicant fails one segment of the skills test:

(i) The applicant cannot continue to the next segment of the test; and

(ii) Scores for the passed segments of the test are only valid during initial issuance of the CLP. If the CLP is renewed, all three segments of the skills test must be retaken.

(d) Passing scores for the knowledge and skills tests must meet the standards contained in § 383.135.

[76 FR 26891, May 9, 2011]

§383.135 Passing knowledge and skills tests.

(a) *Knowledge tests.* (1) To achieve a passing score on each of the knowledge tests, a driver applicant must correctly answer at least 80 percent of the questions.

(2) If a driver applicant who fails the air brake portion of the knowledge test (scores less than 80 percent correct) is issued a CLP or CDL, an air brake restriction must be indicated on the CLP or CDL as required in §383.95(a).

(3) A driver applicant who fails the combination vehicle portion of the knowledge test (scores less than 80 percent correct) must not be issued a Group A CLP or CDL.

(b) *Skills Tests.* (1) To achieve a passing score on each segment of the skills test, the driver applicant must demonstrate that he/she can successfully perform all of the skills listed in §383.113 and attain the scores listed in Appendix A of the examiner manual referred to in §383.131(b) for the type of vehicle being used in the test.

(2) A driver applicant who does not obey traffic laws, causes an accident during the test, or commits any other offense listed as a reason for automatic failure in the standards contained in the driver and examiner manuals referred to in §§383.131(a) and (b), must automatically fail the test.

(3) If a driver applicant who performs the skills test in a vehicle not equipped with any type of air brake system is issued a CDL, an air brake restriction must be indicated on the license as required in §383.95(a).

(4) If a driver applicant who performs the skills test in a vehicle equipped with air over hydraulic brakes is issued a CDL, a full air brake restriction must be indicated on the license as required in §383.95(b).

(5) If a driver applicant who performs the skills test in a vehicle equipped with an automatic transmission is issued a CDL, a manual transmission restriction must be indicated on the license as required in §383.95(c).

(6) If a driver applicant who performs the skills test in a combination vehicle requiring a Group A CDL equipped with any non-fifth wheel connection is issued a CDL, a tractor-trailer restric-

tion must be indicated on the license as required in §383.95(d).

(7) If a driver applicant wants to remove any of the restrictions in paragraphs (b)(3) through (5) of this section, the applicant does not have to retake the complete skills test. The State may administer a modified skills test that demonstrates that the applicant can safely and effectively operate the vehicle's full air brakes, air over hydraulic brakes, and/or manual transmission. In addition, to remove the air brake or full air brake restriction, the applicant must successfully perform the air brake pre-trip inspection and pass the air brake knowledge test.

(8) If a driver applicant wants to remove the tractor-trailer restriction in paragraph (b)(6) of this section, the applicant must retake all three skills tests in a representative tractor-trailer.

(c) *State recordkeeping.* States must record and retain the knowledge and skills test scores of tests taken by driver applicants. The test scores must either be made part of the driver history record or be linked to the driver history record in a separate file.

[76 FR 26892, May 9, 2011]

Subpart I—Requirement for Transportation Security Administration approval of hazardous materials endorsement issuances

§383.141 General.

(a) *Applicability date.* Beginning on the date(s) listed in 49 CFR 1572.13(b), this section applies to State agencies responsible for issuing hazardous materials endorsements for a CDL, and applicants for such endorsements.

(b) *Prohibition.* A State may not issue, renew, upgrade, or transfer a hazardous materials endorsement for a CDL to any individual authorizing that individual to operate a commercial motor vehicle transporting a hazardous material in commerce unless the Transportation Security Administration has determined that the individual does not pose a security risk warranting denial of the endorsement.

(c) *Individual notification.* At least 60 days prior to the expiration date of the

CDL or hazardous materials endorsement, a State must notify the holder of a hazardous materials endorsement that the individual must pass a Transportation Security Administration security threat assessment process as part of any application for renewal of the hazardous materials endorsement. The notice must advise a driver that, in order to expedite the security screening process, he or she should file a renewal application as soon as possible, but not later than 30 days before the date of expiration of the endorsement. An individual who does not successfully complete the Transportation Security Administration security threat assessment process referenced in paragraph (b) of this section may not be issued a hazardous materials endorsement.

(d) *Hazardous materials endorsement renewal cycle.* Each State must require that hazardous materials endorsements be renewed every 5 years or less so that individuals are subject to a Transportation Security Administration security screening requirement referenced in paragraph (b) of this section at least every 5 years.

[68 FR 24850, May 5, 2003, as amended at 68 FR 63033, Nov. 7, 2003; 69 FR 51393, Aug. 19, 2004; 70 FR 22271, Apr. 29, 2005]

Subpart J—Commercial Learner's Permit and Commercial Driver's License Documents

SOURCE: 53 FR 27657, July 21, 1988, unless otherwise noted.

§ 383.151 General.

(a) The CDL must be a document that is easy to recognize as a CDL.

(b) The CLP must be a separate document from the CDL or non-CDL.

(c) At a minimum, the CDL and the CLP must contain the information specified in § 383.153.

[76 FR 26892, May 9, 2011]

§ 383.153 Information on the CLP and CDL documents and applications.

(a) *Commercial Driver's License.* All CDLs must contain all of the following information:

(1) The prominent statement that the license is a "Commercial Driver's License" or "CDL," except as specified in paragraph (c) of this section.

(2) The full name, signature, and mailing or residential address in the licensing State of the person to whom such license is issued.

(3) Physical and other information to identify and describe such person including date of birth (month, day, and year), sex, and height.

(4) Color photograph, digitized color image, or black and white laser engraved photograph of the driver. The State may issue a temporary CDL without a photo or image, if it is valid for no more than 60 days.

(5) The driver's State license number.

(6) The name of the State which issued the license.

(7) The date of issuance and the date of expiration of the license.

(8) The group or groups of commercial motor vehicle(s) that the driver is authorized to operate, indicated as follows:

(i) A for Combination Vehicle;

(ii) B for Heavy Straight Vehicle; and

(iii) C for Small Vehicle.

(9) The endorsement(s) for which the driver has qualified, if any, indicated as follows:

(i) T for double/triple trailers;

(ii) P for passenger;

(iii) N for tank vehicle;

(iv) H for hazardous materials;

(v) X for a combination of tank vehicle and hazardous materials endorsements;

(vi) S for school bus; and

(vii) At the discretion of the State, additional codes for additional groupings of endorsements, as long as each such discretionary code is fully explained on the front or back of the CDL document.

(10) The restriction(s) placed on the driver from operating certain equipment or vehicles, if any, indicated as follows:

(i) L for No Air brake equipped CMV;

(ii) Z for No Full air brake equipped CMV;

(iii) E for No Manual transmission equipped CMV;

(iv) O for No Tractor-trailer CMV;

(v) M for No Class A passenger vehicle;

(vi) N for No Class A and B passenger vehicle;

(vii) K for Intrastate only;

(viii) V for medical variance; and

(ix) At the discretion of the State, additional codes for additional restrictions, as long as each such restriction code is fully explained on the front or back of the CDL document.

(b) *Commercial Learner's Permit.* (1) A CLP must not contain a photograph, digitized image or other visual representation of the driver.

(2) All CLPs must contain all of the following information:

(i) The prominent statement that the permit is a "Commercial Learner's Permit" or "CLP," except as specified in paragraph (c) of this section, and that it is invalid unless accompanied by the underlying driver's license issued by the same jurisdiction.

(ii) The full name, signature, and mailing or residential address in the permitting State of the person to whom the permit is issued.

(iii) Physical and other information to identify and describe such person including date of birth (month, day, and year), sex, and height.

(iv) The driver's State license number.

(v) The name of the State which issued the permit.

(vi) The date of issuance and the date of expiration of the permit.

(vii) The group or groups of commercial motor vehicle(s) that the driver is authorized to operate, indicated as follows:

(A) A for Combination Vehicle;

(B) B for Heavy Straight Vehicle; and

(C) C for Small Vehicle.

(viii) The endorsement(s) for which the driver has qualified, if any, indicated as follows:

(A) *P for passenger endorsement.* A CLP holder with a P endorsement is prohibited from operating a CMV carrying passengers, other than Federal/State auditors and inspectors, test examiners, other trainees, and the CDL holder accompanying the CLP holder as prescribed by §CFR 383.25(a)(1) of this part;

(B) *S for school bus endorsement.* A CLP holder with an S endorsement is prohibited from operating a school bus with passengers other than Federal/State auditors and inspectors, test examiners, other trainees, and the CDL

holder accompanying the CLP holder as prescribed by §383.25(a)(1) of this part; and

(C) *N for tank vehicle endorsement.* A CLP holder with an N endorsement may only operate an empty tank vehicle and is prohibited from operating any tank vehicle that previously contained hazardous materials that has not been purged of any residue.

(ix) The restriction(s) placed on the driver, if any, indicated as follows:

(A) P for No passengers in CMV bus;

(B) X for No cargo in CMV tank vehicle;

(C) L for No Air brake equipped CMV;

(D) V for medical variance;

(E) M for No Class A passenger vehicle;

(F) N for No Class A and B passenger vehicle;

(G) K for Intrastate only.

(H) Any additional jurisdictional restrictions that apply to the CLP driving privilege.

(c) If the CLP or CDL is a Non-domiciled CLP or CDL, it must contain the prominent statement that the license or permit is a "Non-domiciled Commercial Driver's License," "Non-domiciled CDL," "Non-domiciled Commercial Learner's Permit," or "Non-domiciled CLP," as appropriate. The word "Non-domiciled" must be conspicuously and unmistakably displayed, but may be noncontiguous with the words "Commercial Driver's License," "CDL," "Commercial Learner's Permit," or "CLP."

(d) If the State has issued the applicant an air brake restriction as specified in §383.95, that restriction must be indicated on the CLP or CDL.

(e) Except in the case of a Non-domiciled CLP or CDL holder who is domiciled in a foreign jurisdiction:

(1) A driver applicant must provide his/her Social Security Number on the application of a CLP or CDL.

(2) The State must provide the Social Security Number to the CDLIS.

(3) The State must not display the Social Security Number on the CLP or CDL.

(f) The State may issue a multipart CDL provided that:

(1) Each document is explicitly tied to the other document(s) and to a single driver's record.

(2) The multipart license document includes all of the data elements specified in this section.

(g) Current CDL holders are not required to be retested to determine whether they need any of the new restrictions for no full air brakes, no manual transmission and no tractor-trailer. These new restrictions only apply to CDL applicants who take skills tests on or after July 8, 2014 (including those applicants who previously held a CDL before the new restrictions went into effect).

(h) On or after July 8, 2014 current CLP and CDL holders who do not have the standardized endorsement and restriction codes and applicants for a CLP or CDL are to be issued CLPs and CDLs with the standardized codes upon initial issuance, renewal, upgrade or transfer.

[76 FR 26892, May 9, 2011; 76 FR 39018, July 5, 2011]

§ 383.155 Tamperproofing requirements.

States must make the CLP and CDL tamperproof to the maximum extent practicable. At a minimum, a State must use the same tamperproof method used for noncommercial drivers' licenses.

[76 FR 26893, May 9, 2011]

PART 384—STATE COMPLIANCE WITH COMMERCIAL DRIVER'S LICENSE PROGRAM

Subpart A—General

Subpart B—Minimum Standards for Substantial Compliance by States

Subpart C—Procedures for Determining State Compliance

Subpart D—Consequences of State Noncompliance

AUTHORITY: 49 U.S.C. 31136, 31301 *et seq.*, and 31502; secs. 103 and 215 of Pub. L. 106–159, 113 Stat. 1753, 1767; and 49 CFR 1.73.

SOURCE: 59 FR 26039, May 18, 1994, unless otherwise noted.

EDITORIAL NOTE: Nomenclature changes to part 384 appear at 66 FR 49872, Oct. 1, 2001.

Subpart A—General

§384.101 Purpose and scope.

(a) *Purpose.* The purpose of this part is to ensure that the States comply with the provisions of section 12009(a) of the Commercial Motor Vehicle Safety Act of 1986 (49 U.S.C. 31311(a)).

(b) *Scope.* This part:

(1) Includes the minimum standards for the actions States must take to be in substantial compliance with each of the 22 requirements of 49 U.S.C. 31311(a);

(2) Establishes procedures for determinations to be made of such compliance by States; and

(3) Specifies the consequences of State noncompliance.

[62 FR 37152, July 11, 1997]

§384.103 Applicability.

The rules in this part apply to all States.

§384.105 Definitions.

(a) The definitions in part 383 of this title apply to this part, except where otherwise specifically noted.

(b) As used in this part:

CDLIS motor vehicle record (CDLIS MVR) means a report generated from the CDLIS driver record meeting the requirements for access to CDLIS information and provided by States to users authorized in §384.225(e)(3) and (4), subject to the provisions of the Driver Privacy Protection Act, 18 U.S.C. 2721–2725.

Issue and *issuance* mean initial issuance, transfer, renewal, or upgrade of a CLP or CDL and Non-domiciled CLP or CDL, as described in §383.73 of this subchapter.

Licensing entity means the agency of State government that is authorized to issue drivers' licenses.

Year of noncompliance means any Federal fiscal year during which—

(1) A State fails to submit timely certification as prescribed in subpart C of this part; or

(2) The State does not meet one or more of the standards of subpart B of this part, based on a final determination by the FMCSA under §384.307(c) of this part.

[59 FR 26039, May 18, 1994, as amended at 73 FR 73125, Dec. 1, 2008; 76 FR 26893, May 9, 2011]

§384.107 Matter incorporated by reference.

(a) *Incorporation by reference.* This part includes references to certain matter or materials. The text of the materials is not included in the regulations contained in this part. The materials are hereby made a part of the regulations in this part. The Director of the Office of the Federal Register has approved the materials incorporated by reference in accordance with 5 U.S.C. 552(a) and 1 CFR part 51. For materials subject to change, only the specific version approved by the Director of the Office of the Federal Register and specified in the regulation are incorporated. Material is incorporated as it exists on the date of the approval and a notice of any change in these materials will be published in the FEDERAL REGISTER.

(b) *Materials incorporated.* The AAMVA, Inc.'s "Commercial Driver License Information System (CDLIS) State Procedures Manual," Version 4.1.0, September 2007 ("CDLIS State Procedures Manual"), IBR approved for §§384.225(f) and 384.231(d).

(c) *Addresses.* (1) All of the materials incorporated by reference are available for inspection at:

(i) The Department of Transportation Library, 1200 New Jersey Ave., SE., Washington, DC 20590–0001; telephone is (202) 366–0746. These documents are also available for inspection and copying as provided in 49 CFR part 7.

(ii) The National Archives and Records Administration (NARA). For information on the availability of this material at NARA, call 202–741–6030, or go to: *http://www.archives.gov/ federal_register/ code_of_federal_regulations/ ibr_locations.html.*

(2) Information and copies of all of the materials incorporated by reference may be obtained by writing to: American Association of Motor Vehicle Administrators, Inc., 4301 Wilson Blvd,

Suite 400, Arlington, VA 22203; Web site is *http://www.aamva.org.*

[67 FR 49761, July 31, 2002, as amended at 72 FR 55700, Oct. 1, 2007; 73 FR 73125, Dec. 1, 2008]

Subpart B—Minimum Standards for Substantial Compliance by States

§ 384.201   Testing program.

(a) The State shall adopt and administer a program for testing and ensuring the fitness of persons to operate commercial motor vehicles (CMVs) in accordance with the minimum Federal standards contained in part 383 of this title.

(b) To obtain a copy of FMCSA pre-approved State Testing System referenced in §§ 383.131, 383.133 and 383.135, State Driver Licensing Agencies may contact: FMCSA, CDL Division, 1200 New Jersey Avenue, SE, Washington DC 20590.

[76 FR 26893, May 9, 2011]

§ 384.202   Test standards.

No State shall authorize a person to operate a CMV unless such person passes a knowledge and driving skills test for the operation of a CMV in accordance with part 383 of this title.

§ 384.203   Driving while under the influence.

(a) The State must have in effect and enforce through licensing sanctions the disqualifications prescribed in § 383.51(b) of this subchapter for driving a CMV with a 0.04 alcohol concentration.

(b) Nothing in this section shall be construed to require a State to apply its criminal or other sanctions for driving under the influence to a person found to have operated a CMV with an alcohol concentration of 0.04, except licensing sanctions including suspension, revocation, or cancellation.

(c) A State that enacts and enforces through licensing sanctions the disqualifications prescribed in § 383.51(b) of this subchapter for driving a CMV with a 0.04 alcohol concentration and gives full faith and credit to the disqualification of CMV drivers by other States shall be deemed in substantial compliance with section 12009(a)(3) of the Commercial Motor Vehicle Safety Act of 1986 (49 U.S.C. 31311(a)(3)).

[67 FR 49761, July 31, 2002]

§ 384.204   CLP or CDL issuance and information.

(a) *General rule.* The State shall authorize a person to operate a CMV only by issuance of a CLP or CDL, unless an exception in § 383.3(c) or (d) applies, which contains, at a minimum, the information specified in part 383, subpart J, of this subchapter.

(b) *Exceptions—*(1) *Training.* The State may authorize a person who does not hold a CDL valid for the type of vehicle in which training occurs to undergo behind-the-wheel training in a CMV only by means of a CLP issued and used in accordance with § 383.25 of this subchapter.

(2) *Confiscation of CLP or CDL pending enforcement.* A State may allow a CLP or CDL holder whose CLP or CDL is held in trust by that State or any other State in the course of enforcement of the motor vehicle traffic code, but who has not been convicted of a disqualifying offense under § 383.51 of this subchapter based on such enforcement, to drive a CMV while holding a dated receipt for such CLP or CDL.

[76 FR 26894, May 9, 2011]

§ 384.205   CDLIS information.

Before issuing a CLP or a CDL to any person, the State must, within the period of time specified in § 384.232, perform the check of the Commercial Driver's License Information System (CDLIS) in accordance with § 383.73(b)(3)(ii) of this subchapter, and, based on that information, issue the license or, in the case of adverse information, promptly implement the disqualifications, licensing limitations, denials, and/or penalties that are called for in any applicable section(s) of this subpart.

[76 FR 26894, May 9, 2011]

§ 384.206   State record checks.

(a) *Issuing State's records.* (1) Before issuing, renewing, upgrading, or transferring a CLP or CDL to any person, the driver's State of record must, within the period of time specified in

§384.232, check its own driver records as follows:

(i) The driver record of the person in accordance with §383.73(b)(3)(i) of this chapter; and

(ii) For a driver who certifies that his/her type of driving is non-excepted, interstate commerce according to §383.71(b)(1)(ii)(A) of this chapter, the medical certification status information on the person's CDLIS driver record.

(2) Based on the findings of its own State record check, the State of record must do one of the following as appropriate:

(i) Issue, renew, upgrade, or transfer the applicant's CLP or CDL;

(ii) In the event the State obtains adverse information regarding the applicant, promptly implement the disqualifications, licensing limitations, denials, or penalties that are called for in any applicable section(s) of this subpart; or

(iii) In the event there is no information regarding the driver's self-certification for driving type required by §383.71(b)(1)(ii), or for a driver who is required by §383.71(h) to be "certified," if the medical certification status of the individual is "non-certified," the State must deny the CDL action requested by the applicant and initiate a downgrade of the CDL, if required by §383.73(j)(4) of this chapter.

(b) *Other States' records.* (1) Before the initial or transfer issuance of a CLP or CDL to a person, and before renewing or upgrading a CLP or CDL held by any person, the issuing State must:

(i) Require the applicant to provide the names of all States where the applicant has previously been licensed to operate any type of motor vehicle during the previous 10 years.

(ii) Within the time period specified in §384.232, request the complete driver record from all States where the applicant was licensed within the previous 10 years to operate any type of motor vehicle.

(2) States receiving a request for the driver record of a person currently or previously licensed by the State must provide the information within 30 days.

(3) Based on the findings of the other State record checks, the issuing State must, in the case of adverse information regarding the applicant, promptly implement the disqualifications, licensing limitations, denials, or penalties that are called for in any applicable section(s) of this subpart.

[76 FR 26894, May 9, 2011]

§384.207 Notification of licensing.

Within the period defined in §383.73(h) of this subchapter, the State must:

(a) Notify the operator of the CDLIS of each CLP or CDL issuance;

(b) Notify the operator of the CDLIS of any changes in driver identification information; and

(c) In the case of transfer issuances, implement the Change State of Record transaction, as specified by the operator of the CDLIS, in conjunction with the previous State of record and the operator of the CDLIS.

[59 FR 26039, May 18, 1994, as amended at 76 FR 26894, May 9, 2011]

§384.208 Notification of disqualification.

(a) No later than 10 days after disqualifying a CLP or CDL licensed by another State, or disqualifying an out-of-State CLP or CDL holder's privilege to operate a commercial motor vehicle for at least 60 days, the State must notify the State that issued the license of the disqualification.

(b) The notification must include both the disqualification and the violation that resulted in the disqualification, revocation, suspension, or cancellation. The notification and the information it provides must be recorded on the CDLIS driver record.

[67 FR 49761, July 31, 2002, as amended at 73 FR 73125, Dec. 1, 2008; 76 FR 26894, May 9, 2011]

§384.209 Notification of traffic violations.

(a) *Required notification with respect to CLP or CDL holders.* Whenever a person who holds a CLP or CDL from another State is convicted of a violation of any State or local law relating to motor vehicle traffic control (other than parking, vehicle weight or vehicle defect violations), in any type of vehicle, the licensing entity of the State in which the conviction occurs must notify the licensing entity in the State where the driver is licensed of this conviction within the time period established in paragraph (c) of this section.

(b) *Required notification with respect to non-CDL holders.* Whenever a person who does not hold a CDL, but who is licensed to drive by another State, is convicted of a violation in a CMV of any State or local law relating to motor vehicle traffic control (other than a parking violation), the licensing entity of the State in which the conviction occurs must notify the licensing entity in the State where the driver is licensed of this conviction within the time period established in paragraph (c) of this section.

(c) *Time period for notification of traffic violations.* (1) Beginning on September 30, 2005, the notification must be made within 30 days of the conviction.

(2) Beginning on September 30, 2008, the notification must be made within 10 days of the conviction.

[67 FR 49761, July 31, 2002, as amended at 76 FR 26894, May 9, 2011]

§ 384.210   Limitation on licensing.

A State must not knowingly issue a CLP, a CDL, or a commercial special license or permit (including a provisional or temporary license) permitting a person to drive a CMV during a period in which:

(a) A person is disqualified from operating a CMV, as disqualification is defined in § 383.5 of this subchapter, or under the provisions of § 383.73(j) or § 384.231(b)(2) of this subchapter;

(b) The CLP or CDL holder's noncommercial driving privilege has been disqualified; or

(c) Any type of driver's license held by such person is disqualified by the State where the driver is licensed for any State or local law related to motor vehicle traffic control (other than parking, vehicle weight or vehicle defect violations).

[76 FR 26894, May 9, 2011]

§ 384.211   Surrender of old licenses.

The State may not initially issue, upgrade, or transfer a CDL to a person unless such person first surrenders any previously issued driver's license and CLP.

[76 FR 26894, May 9, 2011]

§ 384.212   Domicile requirement.

(a) The State may issue CDLs or CLPs only to persons for whom the State is the State of domicile as defined in § 383.5 of this subchapter; except that the State may issue a Non-domiciled CLP or CDL under the conditions specified in §§ 383.23(b), 383.71(f), and 383.73(f) of this subchapter.

(b) The State must require any person holding a CLP or CDL issued by another State to apply for a transfer CLP or CDL from the State within 30 days after establishing domicile in the State, as specified in § 383.71(c) of this subchapter.

[76 FR 26894, May 9, 2011]

§ 384.213   State penalties for drivers of CMVs.

The State must impose on drivers of CMVs appropriate civil and criminal penalties that are consistent with the penalties prescribed under part 383, subpart D, of this subchapter.

[67 FR 49761, July 31, 2002]

§ 384.214   Reciprocity.

The State must allow any person to operate a CMV in the State who is not disqualified from operating a CMV and who holds a CLP or CDL that is—

(a) Issued to him or her by his/her State or jurisdiction of domicile in accordance with part 383 of this subchapter;

(b) Not disqualified; and

(c) Valid, under the terms of part 383, subpart F, of this subchapter, for the type of vehicle being driven.

[76 FR 26895, May 9, 2011]

§ 384.215   First offenses.

(a) *General rule.* The State must disqualify from operating a CMV each person who is convicted, as defined in § 383.5 of this subchapter, in any State or jurisdiction, of a disqualifying offense specified in items (1) through (8) of Table 1 to § 383.51 of this subchapter, for no less than one year.

(b) *Special rule for hazardous materials offenses.* If the offense under paragraph

(a) of this section occurred while the driver was operating a vehicle transporting hazardous materials required to be placarded under the Hazardous Materials Transportation Act (implementing regulations at 49 CFR 177.823), the State shall disqualify the person for no less than three years.

[59 FR 26039, May 18, 1994, as amended at 67 FR 49762, July 31, 2002]

§384.216 Second offenses.

(a) *General rule.* The State must disqualify for life from operating a CMV each person who is convicted, as defined in §383.5 of this subchapter, in any State or jurisdiction, of a subsequent offense as described in Table 1 to §383.51 of this subchapter.

(b) *Special rule for certain lifetime disqualifications.* A driver disqualified for life under Table 1 to §383.51 may be reinstated after 10 years by the driver's State of residence if the requirements of §383.51(a)(5) have been met.

[67 FR 49762, July 31, 2002]

§384.217 Drug offenses.

The State must disqualify from operating a CMV for life any person who is convicted, as defined in §383.5 of this subchapter, in any State or jurisdiction of a first offense of using a CMV (or, in the case of a CLP or CDL holder, a CMV or a non-CMV) in the commission of a felony described in item (9) of Table 1 to §383.51 of this subchapter. The State shall not apply the special rule in §384.216(b) to lifetime disqualifications imposed for controlled substance felonies as detailed in item (9) of Table 1 to §383.51 of this subchapter.

[76 FR 26895, May 9, 2011]

§384.218 Second serious traffic violation.

The State must disqualify from operating a CMV for a period of not less than 60 days each person who, in a three-year period, is convicted, as defined in §383.5 of this subchapter, in any State(s) or jurisdiction(s), of two serious traffic violations as specified in Table 2 to §383.51.

[67 FR 49762, July 31, 2002]

§384.219 Third serious traffic violation.

The State must disqualify from operating a CMV for a period of not less than 120 days each person who, in a three-year period, is convicted, as defined in §383.5 of this subchapter, in any State(s) or jurisdiction(s), of three serious traffic violations as specified in Table 2 to §383.51. This disqualification period must be in addition to any other previous period of disqualification.

[67 FR 49762, July 31, 2002]

§384.220 Problem Driver Pointer System information.

Before issuing a CLP or CDL to any person, the State must, within the period of time specified in §384.232, perform the check of the Problem Driver Pointer System in accordance with §383.73(b)(3)(iii) of this subchapter, and, based on that information, promptly implement the disqualifications, licensing limitations, and/or penalties that are called for in any applicable section(s) of this subpart.

[76 FR 26895, May 9, 2011]

§384.221 Out-of-service regulations (intoxicating beverage).

The State shall adopt, and enforce on operators of CMVs as defined in §§383.5 and 390.5 of this title, the provisions of §392.5 (a) and (c) of this title in accordance with the Motor Carrier Safety Assistance Program as contained in 49 CFR part 350 and applicable policy and guidelines.

§384.222 Violation of out-of-service orders.

The State must have and enforce laws and/or regulations applicable to drivers of CMVs and their employers, as defined in §383.5 of this subchapter, which meet the minimum requirements of §§383.37(c), Table 4 to 383.51, and 383.53(b) of this subchapter.

[67 FR 49762, July 31, 2002]

§384.223 Railroad-highway grade crossing violation.

The State must have and enforce laws and/or regulations applicable to CMV drivers and their employers, as defined in §383.5 of this subchapter, which meet the minimum requirements of §§ 383.37(d), Table 3 to 383.51, and 383.53(c) of this subchapter.

[67 FR 49762, July 31, 2002]

§ 384.224 Noncommercial motor vehicle violations.

The State must have and enforce laws and/or regulations applicable to drivers of non-CMVs, as defined in § 383.5 of this subchapter, which meet the minimum requirements of Tables 1 and 2 to § 383.51 of this subchapter.

[67 FR 49762, July 31, 2002]

§ 384.225 CDLIS driver recordkeeping.

The State must:

(a) *CLP or CDL holder.* Post and maintain as part of the CDLIS driver record:

(1) All convictions, disqualifications and other licensing actions for violations of any State or local law relating to motor vehicle traffic control (other than parking, vehicle weight, or vehicle defect violations) committed in any type of vehicle.

(2) The following medical certification status information:

(i) Driver self-certification for the type of driving operations provided in accordance with § 383.71(b)(1)(ii) of this chapter, and

(ii) Information from medical certification recordkeeping in accordance with § 383.73(o) of this chapter.

(b) *A person required to have a CLP or CDL.* Record and maintain as part of the CDLIS driver record all convictions, disqualifications and other licensing actions for violations of any State or local law relating to motor vehicle traffic control (other than parking, vehicle weight, or vehicle defect violations) committed while the driver was operating a CMV.

(c) Make CDLIS driver record information required by this section available to the users designated in paragraph (e) of this section, or to their authorized agent, within 10 days of:

(1) Receiving the conviction or disqualification information from another State; or

(2) The date of the conviction, if it occurred in the same State.

(d) Retain on the CDLIS driver record record all convictions, disqualifications and other licensing actions for violations for at least 3 years or longer as required under § 384.231(d).

(e) Only the following users or their authorized agents may receive the designated information:

(1) States—All information on all CDLIS driver records.

(2) Secretary of Transportation—All information on all CDLIS driver records.

(3) Driver—All information on that driver's CDLIS driver record obtained on the CDLIS Motor Vehicle Record from the State according to its procedures.

(4) Motor Carrier or Prospective Motor Carrier—After notification to a driver, all information on that driver's, or prospective driver's, CDLIS driver record obtained on the CDLIS Motor Vehicle Record from the State according to its procedures.

(f) The content of the report provided a user authorized by paragraph (e) of this section from the CDLIS driver record, or from a copy of this record maintained for use by the National Law Enforcement Telecommunications System, must be comparable to the report that would be generated by a CDLIS State-to-State request for a CDLIS driver history, as defined in the "CDLIS State Procedures Manual" (incorporated by reference, see § 384.107(b)), and must include the medical certification status information of the driver in paragraph (a)(2) of this section. This does not preclude authorized users from requesting a CDLIS driver status.

[67 FR 49762, July 31, 2002, as amended at 73 FR 73125, Dec. 1, 2008; 76 FR 26895, May 9, 2011]

§ 384.226 Prohibition on masking convictions.

The State must not mask, defer imposition of judgment, or allow an individual to enter into a diversion program that would prevent a CLP or CDL holder's conviction for any violation, in any type of motor vehicle, of a State or local traffic control law (other than parking, vehicle weight, or vehicle defect violations) from appearing on the

CDLIS driver record, whether the driver was convicted for an offense committed in the State where the driver is licensed or another State.

[76 FR 26895, May 9, 2011]

§384.227 Record of digital image or photograph.

The State must:

(a) Record the digital color image or photograph or black and white laser engraved photograph that is captured as part of the application process and placed on the licensing document of every person who is issued a CDL, as required under §383.153. The digital color image or photograph or black and white laser engraved photograph must either be made part of the driver history or be linked to the driver history in a separate file.

(b) Check the digital color image or photograph or black and white laser engraved photograph on record whenever the CDL applicant or holder appears in person to renew, upgrade, or transfer a CDL and when a duplicate CDL is issued.

(c) Check the digital color image or photograph or black and white laser engraved photograph on record whenever the CLP applicant or holder appears in person to renew, upgrade, or transfer a CLP and when a duplicate CLP is issued. If no digital color image or photograph or black and white laser engraved photograph exists on record, the State must check the photograph or image on the base-license presented with the CLP application.

[76 FR 26895, May 9, 2011]

§384.228 Examiner training and record checks.

For all State and third party CDL test examiners, the State must meet the following 10 requirements:

(a) Establish examiner training standards for initial and refresher training that provides CDL test examiners with a fundamental understanding of the objectives of the CDL testing program, and with all of the knowledge and skills necessary to serve as a CDL test examiner and assist jurisdictions in meeting the Federal CDL testing requirements.

(b) Require all State knowledge and skills test examiners to successfully complete a formal CDL test examiner training course and examination before certifying them to administer CDL knowledge and skills tests.

(c) The training course for CDL knowledge test examiners must cover at least the following three units of instruction:

(1) Introduction to CDL Licensing System:

(i) The Commercial Motor Vehicle Safety Act of 1986.

(ii) Drivers covered by CDL program.

(iii) CDL vehicle classification.

(iv) CDL endorsements and restrictions.

(2) Overview of the CDL tests:

(i) CDL test, classifications, and endorsements.

(ii) Different examinations.

(iii) Representative vehicles.

(iv) Validity and reliability.

(v) Test maintenance.

(3) Knowledge tests:

(i) General knowledge tests.

(ii) Specialized knowledge tests.

(iii) Selecting the appropriate tests and test forms.

(iv) Knowledge test administration.

(d) The training course for CDL skills test examiners must cover at least the following five units of instruction:

(1) Introduction to CDL Licensing System:

(i) The Commercial Motor Vehicle Safety Act of 1986.

(ii) Drivers covered by CDL program.

(iii) CDL vehicle classification.

(iv) CDL endorsements and restrictions.

(2) Overview of the CDL tests:

(i) CDL test, classifications, and endorsements.

(ii) Different examinations.

(iii) Representative vehicles.

(iv) Validity and reliability.

(v) Test maintenance.

(3) Vehicle inspection test:

(i) Test overview.

(ii) Description of safety rules.

(iii) Test scoring procedures.

(iv) Scoring standards.

(v) Calculating final score.

(4) Basic control skills testing:

(i) Setting up the basic control skills course.

(ii) Description of safety rules.

(iii) General scoring procedures.

(iv) Administering the test.

(v) Calculating the score.

(5) Road test:

(i) Setting up the road test.

(ii) Required maneuvers.

(iii) Administering the road test.

(iv) Calculating the score.

(e) Require all third party skills test examiners to successfully complete a formal CDL test examiner training course and examination before certifying them to administer CDL skills tests. The training course must cover at least the five units of instruction in paragraph (d) of this section.

(f) Require State and third party CDL test examiners to successfully complete a refresher training course and examination every four years to maintain their CDL test examiner certification. The refresher training course must cover at least the following:

(1) For CDL knowledge test examiners, the three units of training described in paragraph (c) of this section.

(2) For CDL skills test examiners, the five units of training described in paragraph (d) of this section.

(3) Any State specific material and information related to administering CDL knowledge and skills tests.

(4) Any new Federal CDL regulations, updates to administering the tests, and new safety related equipment on the vehicles.

(g) Complete nationwide criminal background check of all skills test examiners prior to certifying them to administer CDL skills tests.

(h) Complete annual nationwide criminal background check of all test examiners.

(i) Maintain a record of the results of the criminal background check and CDL examiner test training and certification of all CDL test examiners.

(j) Rescind the certification to administer CDL tests of all test examiners who:

(1) Do not successfully complete the required refresher training every four years; or

(2) Do not pass annual nationwide criminal background checks. Criteria for not passing the criminal background check must include at least the following:

(i) Any felony conviction within the last 10 years; or

(ii) Any conviction involving fraudulent activities.

(k) The six units of training described in paragraphs (c) and (d) of this section may be supplemented with State-specific material and information related to administering CDL knowledge and skills tests.

[76 FR 26895, May 9, 2011]

§ 384.229 Skills test examiner auditing and monitoring.

To ensure the integrity of the CDL skills testing program, the State must:

(a) At least once every 2 years, conduct unannounced, on-site inspections of third party testers' and examiners' records, including comparison of the CDL skills test results of applicants who are issued CDLs with the CDL scoring sheets that are maintained in the third party testers' files. For third party testers and examiners who were granted the training and skills testing exception under section 383.75(a)(7), the record checks must be performed at least once every year;

(b) At least once every two years, conduct covert and overt monitoring of examinations performed by State and third party CDL skills test examiners. For third party testers and examiners who were granted the training and skills testing exception under § 383.75(a)(7), the covert and overt monitoring must be performed at least once every year;

(c) Establish and maintain a database to track pass/fail rates of applicants tested by each State and third party CDL skills test examiner, in order to focus covert and overt monitoring on examiners who have unusually high pass or failure rates;

(d) Establish and maintain a database of all third party testers and examiners, which at a minimum tracks the dates and results of audits and monitoring actions by the State, the dates third party testers were certified by the State, and name and identification number of each third party CDL skills test examiner;

(e) Establish and maintain a database of all State CDL skills examiners, which at a minimum tracks the dates and results of monitoring action by the

State, and the name and identification number of each State CDL skills examiner; and

(f) Establish and maintain a database that tracks skills tests administered by each State and third party CDL skills test examiner's name and identification number.

[76 FR 26896, May 9, 2011]

§384.230 [Reserved]

§384.231 Satisfaction of State disqualification requirement.

(a) *Applicability.* The provisions of §§384.203, 384.206(b), 384.210, 384.213, 384.215 through 384.219, 384.221 through 384.224, and 384.231 of this part apply to the State of licensure of the person affected by the provision. The provisions of §384.210 of this part also apply to any State to which a person makes application for a transfer CDL.

(b) *Required action*—(1) *CLP or CDL holders.* A State must satisfy the requirement of this subpart that the State disqualify a person who holds a CLP or a CDL by, at a minimum, disqualifying the person's CLP or CDL for the applicable period of disqualification.

(2) *A person required to have a CLP or CDL.* A State must satisfy the requirement of this subpart that the State disqualify a person required to have a CLP or CDL who is convicted of an offense or offenses necessitating disqualification under §383.51 of this subchapter. At a minimum, the State must implement the limitation on licensing provisions of §384.210 and the timing and recordkeeping requirements of paragraphs (c) and (d) of this section so as to prevent such a person from legally obtaining a CLP or CDL from any State during the applicable disqualification period(s) specified in this subpart.

(c) *Required timing.* The State must disqualify a driver as expeditiously as possible.

(d) *Recordkeeping requirements.* The State must conform to the requirements of the CDLIS State Procedures Manual (incorporated by reference in §384.107(b).) These requirements include the maintenance of such driver records and driver identification data on the CDLIS as the FMCSA finds are necessary to the implementation and enforcement of the disqualifications called for in §§384.215 through 384.219, and 384.221 through 384.224 of this part.

[67 FR 49762, July 31, 2002, as amended at 73 FR 73126, Dec. 1, 2008; 76 FR 26896, May 9, 2011]

§384.232 Required timing of record checks.

The State shall perform the record checks prescribed in §§384.205, 384.206, and 384.220, no earlier than 10 days prior to issuance for licenses issued before October 1, 1995. For licenses issued after September 30, 1995, the State shall perform the record checks no earlier than 24 hours prior to issuance if the license is issued to a driver who does not currently possess a valid CDL from the same State and no earlier than 10 days prior to issuance for all other drivers.

§384.233 Background records checks.

(a) The State shall comply with Transportation Security Administration requirements concerning background records checks for drivers seeking to obtain, renew, transfer or upgrade a hazardous materials endorsement in 49 CFR Part 1572, to the extent those provisions impose requirements on the State.

(b) The State shall comply with each requirement of 49 CFR 383.141.

[68 FR 23850, May 5, 2003]

§384.234 Driver medical certification recordkeeping.

The State must meet the medical certification recordkeeping requirements of §§383.73(a)(5) and (j) of this chapter.

[73 FR 73126, Dec. 1, 2008]

Subpart C—Procedures for Determining State Compliance

§384.301 Substantial compliance-general requirements.

(a) To be in substantial compliance with 49 U.S.C. 31311(a), a State must meet each and every standard of subpart B of this part by means of the demonstrable combined effect of its statutes, regulations, administrative procedures and practices, organizational structures, internal control mechanisms, resource assignments (facilities, equipment, and personnel), and enforcement practices.

(b)(1) A State must come into substantial compliance with the requirements of subpart B of this part in effect as of September 30, 2002 as soon as practical, but, unless otherwise specifically provided in this part, not later than September 30, 2005.

(2) *Exception.* A State must come into substantial compliance with 49 CFR 383.123 not later than September 30, 2006.

(c) A State must come into substantial compliance with the requirements of subpart B of this part in effect as of September 4, 2007 as soon as practical but, unless otherwise specifically provided in this part, not later than September 4, 2010.

(d) A State must come into substantial compliance with the requirements of subpart B of this part in effect as of January 30, 2009, as soon as practical, but not later than January 30, 2012.

(e) A State must come into substantial compliance with the requirements of subpart B of this part in effect as of October 27, 2010 as soon as practical, but not later than October 28, 2013.

(f) A State must come into substantial compliance with the requirements of subpart B of this part in effect as of July 8, 2011, as soon as practical but, unless otherwise specifically provided in this part, not later than July 8, 2014.

[67 FR 49763, July 31, 2002, as amended at 70 FR 56593, Sept. 28, 2005; 72 FR 36788, July 5, 2007; 73 FR 73126, Dec. 1, 2008; 75 FR 59135, Sept. 27, 2010; 76 FR 26896, May 9, 2011; 76 FR 39018, July 5, 2011]

§ 384.303 [Reserved]

§ 384.305 State certifications for Federal fiscal years after FY 1994.

(a) *Certification requirement.* Prior to January 1 of each Federal fiscal year after FY 1994, each State shall review its compliance with this part and certify to the Federal Motor Carrier Safety Administrator as prescribed in paragraph (b) of this section. The certification shall be submitted as a signed original and four copies to the State Director or Officer-in-Charge, Federal

Motor Carrier Safety Administration, located in that State.

(b) *Certification content.* The certification shall consist of a statement signed by the Governor of the State, or by an official designated by the Governor, and reading as follows: "I (name of certifying official), (position title), of the State (Commonwealth) of ____ , do hereby certify that the State (Commonwealth) has continuously been in substantial compliance with all requirements of 49 U.S.C. 31311(a), as defined in 49 CFR 384.301, since [the first day of the current Federal fiscal year], and contemplates no changes in statutes, regulations, or administrative procedures, or in the enforcement thereof, which would affect such substantial compliance through [the last date of the current Federal fiscal year]."

(Approved by the Office of Management and Budget under control number 2125–0542)

[59 FR 26039, May 18, 1994, as amended at 62 FR 37152, July 11, 1997]

§ 384.307 FMCSA program reviews of State compliance.

(a) *FMCSA Program Reviews.* Each State's CDL program will be subject to review to determine whether or not the State meets the general requirement for substantial compliance in § 384.301. The State must cooperate with the review and provide any information requested by the FMCSA.

(b) *Preliminary FMCSA determination and State response.* If, after review, a preliminary determination is made either that the State has not submitted the required annual self-certification or that the State does not meet one or more of the minimum standards for substantial compliance under subpart B of this part, the State will be informed accordingly.

(c) *Reply.* The State will have up to 30 calendar days to respond to the preliminary determination. The State's reply must explain what corrective action it either has implemented or intends to implement to correct the deficiencies cited in the notice or, alternatively, why the FMCSA preliminary determination is incorrect. The State must provide documentation of corrective action as required by the agency. Corrective action must be adequate to correct the deficiencies noted in the program review and be implemented on a schedule mutually agreed upon by the agency and the State. Upon request by the State, an informal conference will be provided during this time.

(d) *Final FMCSA determination.* If, after reviewing a timely response by the State to the preliminary determination, a final determination is made that the State is not in compliance with the affected standard, the State will be notified of the final determination. In making its final determination, the FMCSA will take into consideration the corrective action either implemented or planned to be implemented in accordance with the mutually agreed upon schedule.

(e) *State's right to judicial review.* Any State aggrieved by an adverse decision under this section may seek judicial review under 5 U.S.C. Chapter 7.

[67 FR 49763, July 31, 2002]

§384.309 Results of compliance determination.

(a) A State shall be determined not substantially in compliance with 49 U.S.C. 31311(a) for any fiscal year in which it:

(1) Fails to submit the certification as prescribed in this subpart; or

(2) Does not meet one or more of the standards of subpart B of this part, as established in a final determination by the FMCSA under §384.307(c).

(b) A State shall be in substantial compliance with 49 U.S.C. 31311(a) for any fiscal year in which neither of the eventualities in paragraph (a) of this section occurs.

[62 FR 37152, July 11, 1997]

Subpart D—Consequences of State Noncompliance

§384.401 Withholding of funds based on noncompliance.

(a) *Following the first year of noncompliance.* An amount up to 5 percent of the Federal-aid highway funds required to be apportioned to any State under each of sections 104(b)(1), (b)(3), and (b)(4) of title 23 U.S.C. shall be withheld from a State on the first day of the fiscal year following such State's

first year of noncompliance under this part.

(b) *Following second and subsequent year(s) of noncompliance.* An amount up to 10 percent of the Federal-aid highway funds required to be apportioned to any State under each of sections 104(b)(1), (b)(3), and (b)(4) of title 23 U.S.C. shall be withheld from a State on the first day of the fiscal year following such State's second or subsequent year(s) of noncompliance under this part.

[72 FR 36788, July 5, 2007]

§384.403 Availability of funds withheld for noncompliance.

(a) Federal-aid highway funds withheld from a State under §384.401(a)(1) or (b)(1) shall not thereafter be available for apportionment to the State.

(b) MCSAP funds withheld from a State under §384.401(a)(2) or (b)(2) remain available until June 30 of the fiscal year in which they were withheld. If before June 30 the State submits a document signed by the Governor or his or her delegate certifying, and the FMCSA determines, that the State is now in substantial compliance with the standards of subpart B of this part, the withheld funds shall be restored to the State. After June 30, unrestored funds shall lapse and be allocated in accordance with §350.313 of this subchapter to all States currently in substantial compliance with subpart B of this part.

[67 FR 49763, July 31, 2002]

§384.405 Decertification of State CDL program.

(a) *Prohibition on CLP or CDL transactions.* The Administrator may prohibit a State found to be in substantial noncompliance from performing any of the following CLP or CDL transactions:

(1) Initial issuance.

(2) Renewal.

(3) Transfer.

(4) Upgrade.

(b) *Conditions considered in making decertification determination.* The Administrator will consider, but is not limited to, the following five conditions in determining whether the CDL program of a State in substantial noncompliance should be decertified:

(1) The State computer system does not check the Commercial Driver's License Information System (CDLIS) and/or National Driver Registry Problem Driver Pointer System (PDPS) as required by § 383.73 of this subchapter when issuing, renewing, transferring, or upgrading a CLP or CDL.

(2) The State does not disqualify drivers convicted of disqualifying offenses in commercial motor vehicles.

(3) The State does not transmit convictions for out-of-State drivers to the State where the driver is licensed.

(4) The State does not properly administer knowledge and/or skills tests to CLP or CDL applicants or drivers.

(5) The State fails to submit a corrective action plan for a substantial compliance deficiency or fails to implement a corrective action plan within the agreed time frame.

(c) *Standard for considering deficiencies.* The deficiencies described in paragraph (b) of this section must affect a substantial number of either CLP and CDL applicants or drivers.

(d) *Decertification: Preliminary determination.* If the Administrator finds that a State is in substantial noncompliance with subpart B of this part, as indicated by the factors specified in paragraph (b) of this section, among other things, the FMCSA will inform the State that it has made a preliminary determination of noncompliance and that the State's CDL program may therefore be decertified. Any response from the State, including factual or legal arguments or a plan to correct the noncompliance, must be submitted within 30 calendar days after receipt of the preliminary determination.

(e) *Decertification: Final determination.* If, after considering all material submitted by the State in response to the FMCSA preliminary determination, the Administrator decides that substantial noncompliance exists, which warrants decertification of the CDL program, he/she will issue a decertification order prohibiting the State from issuing CLPs and CDLs until such time as the Administrator determines that the condition(s) causing the decertification has (have) been corrected.

(f) *Recertification of a State.* The Governor of the decertified State or his/her designated representative must submit a certification and documentation that the condition causing the decertification has been corrected. If the FMCSA determines that the condition causing the decertification has been satisfactorily corrected, the Administrator will issue a recertification order, including any conditions that must be met in order to begin issuing CLPs and CDLs in the State.

(g) *State's right to judicial review.* Any State aggrieved by an adverse decision under this section may seek judicial review under 5 U.S.C. Chapter 7.

(h) *Validity of previously issued CLPs or CDLs.* A CLP or CDL issued by a State prior to the date the State is prohibited from issuing CLPs or CDLs in accordance with provisions of paragraph (a) of this section, will remain valid until its stated expiration date.

[76 FR 26896, May 9, 2011]

§ 384.407 Emergency CDL grants.

The FMCSA may provide grants of up to $1,000,000 per State from funds made available under 49 U.S.C. 31107(a), to assist States whose CDL programs may fail to meet the compliance requirements of subpart B of this part, but which are determined by the FMCSA to be making a good faith effort to comply with these requirements.

[67 FR 49764, July 31, 2002]

PART 385—SAFETY FITNESS PROCEDURES

Subpart A—General

AUTHORITY: 49 U.S.C. 113, 504, 521(b), 5105(e), 5109, 13901–13905, 31133, 31135, 31136, 31137(a), 31144, 31148, and 31502; Sec. 113(a), Pub. L. 103–

311; Sec. 408, Pub. L. 104–88; Sec. 350, Pub. L. 107–87; and 49 CFR 1.73.

SOURCE: 53 FR 50968, Dec. 19, 1988, unless otherwise noted.

EDITORIAL NOTE: Nomenclature changes to part 385 appear at 66 FR 49872, Oct. 1, 2001.

Subpart A—General

§ 385.1 Purpose and scope.

(a) This part establishes FMCSA's procedures to determine the safety fitness of motor carriers, to assign safety ratings, to direct motor carriers to take remedial action when required, and to prohibit motor carriers determined to be unfit from operating a CMV.

(b) This part establishes the safety assurance program for a new entrant motor carrier initially seeking to register with FMCSA to conduct interstate operations. It also describes the consequences that will occur if the new entrant fails to maintain adequate basic safety management controls.

(c) This part establishes the safety permit program for a motor carrier to transport the types and quantities of hazardous materials listed in § 385.403.

(d) The provisions of this part apply to all motor carriers subject to the requirements of this subchapter, except non-business private motor carriers of passengers.

(e) Subpart F of this part establishes procedures to perform a roadability review of intermodal equipment providers to determine their compliance with the applicable Federal Motor Carrier Safety Regulations (FMCSRs).

[65 FR 50934, Aug. 22, 2000, as amended at 67 FR 31982, May 13, 2002; 69 FR 39366, June 30, 2004; 73 FR 76818, Dec. 17, 2008; 75 FR 17240, Apr. 5, 2010]

§ 385.3 Definitions and acronyms.

Applicable safety regulations or requirements means 49 CFR chapter III, subchapter B—Federal Motor Carrier Safety Regulations or, if the carrier is an intrastate motor carrier subject to the hazardous materials safety permit requirements in subpart E of this part, the equivalent State standards; and 49 CFR chapter I, subchapter C—Hazardous Materials Regulations.

CMV means a commercial motor vehicle as defined in § 390.5 of this subchapter.

Commercial motor vehicle shall have the same meaning as described in § 390.5 of this subchapter, except that this definition will also apply to intrastate motor vehicles subject to the hazardous materials safety permit requirements of subpart E of this part.

FMCSA means the Federal Motor Carrier Safety Administration.

FMCSRs mean Federal Motor Carrier Safety Regulations (49 CFR parts 350–399).

HMRs means the Hazardous Materials Regulations (49 CFR parts 100–178).

Motor carrier operations in commerce means commercial motor vehicle transportation operations either—

(1) In interstate commerce, or

(2) Affecting interstate commerce.

New entrant is a motor carrier not domiciled in Mexico that applies for a United States Department of Transportation (DOT) identification number in order to initiate operations in interstate commerce.

New entrant registration is the registration (US DOT number) granted a new entrant before it can begin interstate operations in an 18-month monitoring period. A safety audit must be performed on a new entrant's operations within 18 months after receipt of its US DOT number and it must be found to have adequate basic safety management controls to continue operating in interstate commerce at the end of the 18-month period.

Preventable accident on the part of a motor carrier means an accident (1) that involved a commercial motor vehicle, and (2) that could have been averted but for an act, or failure to act, by the motor carrier or the driver.

Reviews. For the purposes of this part:

(1) *Compliance review* means an onsite examination of motor carrier operations, such as drivers' hours of service, maintenance and inspection, driver qualification, commercial drivers license requirements, financial responsibility, accidents, hazardous materials, and other safety and transportation records to determine whether a motor carrier meets the safety fitness standard. A compliance review may be conducted in response to a request to change a safety rating, to investigate potential violations of safety regulations by motor carriers, or to investigate complaints or other evidence of safety violations. The compliance review may result in the initiation of an enforcement action.

(2) *Safety audit* means an examination of a motor carrier's operations to provide educational and technical assistance on safety and the operational requirements of the FMCSRs and applicable HMRs and to gather critical safety data needed to make an assessment of the carrier's safety performance and basic safety management controls. Safety audits do not result in safety ratings.

(3) *Safety management controls* means the systems, policies programs, practices, and procedures used by a motor carrier to ensure compliance with applicable safety and hazardous materials regulations which ensure the safe movement of products and passengers through the transportation system, and to reduce the risk of highway accidents and hazardous materials incidents resulting in fatalities, injuries, and property damage.

(4) *Roadability review* means an onsite examination of the intermodal equipment provider's compliance with the applicable FMCSRs.

RSPA means the Research and Special Programs Administration.

Safety fitness determination means the final determination by FMCSA that a motor carrier meets the safety fitness standard under § 385.5.

Safety rating or *rating* means a rating of "Satisfactory," "Conditional" or "Unsatisfactory," which the FMCSA assigns to a motor carrier using the factors prescribed in § 385.7, as computed under the Safety Fitness Rating Methodology (SFRM) set forth in Appendix B to this part and based on the carrier's demonstration of adequate safety management controls under § 385.5(a). A safety rating of "Satisfactory" or "Conditional" is necessary, but not sufficient, to meet the overall safety fitness standard under § 385.5.

(1) *Satisfactory safety rating* means that a motor carrier has in place and

functioning safety management controls adequate to meet that portion of the safety fitness standard prescribed in § 385.5(a). Safety management controls are adequate for this purpose if they are appropriate for the size and type of operation of the particular motor carrier.

(2) *Conditional safety rating* means a motor carrier does not have adequate safety management controls in place to ensure compliance with that portion of the safety fitness standard prescribed in § 385.5(a), which could result in occurrences listed in § 385.5(a)(1) through (a)(11).

(3) *Unsatisfactory safety rating* means a motor carrier does not have adequate safety management controls in place to ensure compliance with that portion of the safety fitness standard prescribed in § 385.5(a), and this has resulted in occurrences listed in § 385.5(a)(1) through (a)(11).

(4) *Unrated carrier* means that the FMCSA has not assigned a safety rating to the motor carrier.

[53 FR 50968, Dec. 19, 1988, as amended at 56 FR 40805, Aug. 16, 1991; 62 FR 60042, Nov. 6, 1997; 67 FR 12779, Mar. 19, 2002; 67 FR 31983, May 13, 2002; 69 FR 39367, June 30, 2004; 72 FR 36788, July 5, 2007; 73 FR 76818, Dec. 17, 2008; 75 FR 17240, Apr. 5, 2010]

§ 385.4 Matter incorporated by reference.

(a) *Incorporation by reference.* Part 385 includes references to certain matter or materials, as listed in paragraph (b) of this section. The text of the materials is not included in the regulations contained in part 385. The materials are hereby made a part of the regulations in part 385. The Director of the Federal Register has approved the materials incorporated by reference in accordance with 5 U.S.C. 552(a) and 1 CFR part 51. For materials subject to change, only the specific version in the regulation is incorporated. Material is incorporated as it exists on the date of the approval and a notice of any changes in these materials will be published in the FEDERAL REGISTER.

(b) *Matter or materials referenced in part 385.* The matter or materials in this paragraph are incorporated by reference in the corresponding sections noted.

(1) "North American Standard Out-of-Service Criteria and Level VI Inspection Procedures and Out-of-Service Criteria for Commercial Highway Vehicles Transporting Transuranics and Highway Route Controlled Quantities of Radioactive Materials as defined in 49 CFR Part 173.403," January 1, 2004. Information and copies may be obtained from the Commercial Vehicle Safety Alliance, 1101 17th Street, NW., Suite 803, Washington, DC 20036. Phone number (202) 775–1623.

(2) All of the materials incorporated by reference are available for inspection at: Federal Motor Carrier Safety Administration, Office of Enforcement and Compliance (MC–EC), 1200 New Jersey Ave., SE., Washington, DC 20590–0001; and the National Archives and Records Administration (NARA). For information on the availability of this material at NARA, call (202) 741–6030, or go to: *http://www.archives.gov/federal_register/code_of_federal_regulations/ibr_locations.html.*

[69 FR 39367, June 30, 2004, as amended at 72 FR 55700, Oct. 1, 2007]

§ 385.5 Safety fitness standard.

A motor carrier must meet the safety fitness standard set forth in this section. Intrastate motor carriers subject to the hazardous materials safety permit requirements of subpart E of this part must meet the equivalent State requirements. To meet the safety fitness standard, the motor carrier must demonstrate the following:

(a) It has adequate safety management controls in place, which function effectively to ensure acceptable compliance with applicable safety requirements to reduce the risk associated with:

(1) Commercial driver's license standard violations (part 383 of this chapter),

(2) Inadequate levels of financial responsibility (part 387 of this chapter),

(3) The use of unqualified drivers (part 391 of this chapter),

(4) Improper use and driving of motor vehicles (part 392 of this chapter),

(5) Unsafe vehicles operating on the highways (part 393 of this chapter),

(6) Failure to maintain accident registers and copies of accident reports (part 390 of this chapter),

(7) The use of fatigued drivers (part 395 of this chapter),

(8) Inadequate inspection, repair, and maintenance of vehicles (part 396 of this chapter),

(9) Transportation of hazardous materials, driving and parking rule violations (part 397 of this chapter),

(10) Violation of hazardous materials regulations (parts 170 through 177 of this title), and

(11) Motor vehicle accidents, as defined in §390.5 of this chapter, and hazardous materials incidents.

(b) The motor carrier has complied with all requirements contained in any remedial directive issued under subpart J of this part.

[75 FR 17241, Apr. 5, 2010]

§385.7 Factors to be considered in determining a safety rating.

The factors to be considered in determining the safety fitness and assigning a safety rating include information from safety reviews, compliance reviews and any other data. The factors may include all or some of the following:

(a) Adequacy of safety management controls. The adequacy of controls may be questioned if their degree of formalization, automation, etc., is found to be substantially below the norm for similar carriers. Violations, accidents or incidents substantially above the norm for similar carriers will be strong evidence that management controls are either inadequate or not functioning properly.

(b) Frequency and severity of regulatory violations.

(c) Frequency and severity of driver/vehicle regulatory violations identified during roadside inspections of motor carrier operations in commerce and, if the motor carrier operates in the United States, of operations in Canada and Mexico.

(d) Number and frequency of out-of-service driver/vehicle violations of motor carrier operations in commerce and, if the motor carrier operates in the United States, of operations in Canada and Mexico.

(e) Increase or decrease in similar types of regulatory violations discovered during safety or compliance reviews.

(f) For motor carrier operations in commerce and (if the motor carrier operates in the United States) in Canada and Mexico: Frequency of accidents; hazardous materials incidents; accident rate per million miles; indicators of preventable accidents; and whether such accidents, hazardous materials incidents, and preventable accident indicators have increased or declined over time.

(g) Number and severity of violations of CMV and motor carrier safety rules, regulations, standards, and orders that are both issued by a State, Canada, or Mexico and compatible with Federal rules, regulations, standards, and orders.

[53 FR 50968, Dec. 19, 1988, as amended at 58 FR 33776, June 21, 1993; 72 FR 36788, July 5, 2007]

§385.9 Determination of a safety rating.

(a) Following a compliance review of a motor carrier operation, FMCSA, using the factors prescribed in §385.7 as computed under the Safety Fitness Rating Methodology set forth in appendix B to this part, shall determine whether the present operations of the motor carrier are consistent with that portion of the safety fitness standard set forth in §385.5(a), and assign a safety rating accordingly.

(b) Unless otherwise specifically provided in this part, a safety rating will be issued to a motor carrier within 30 days following the completion of a compliance review.

[62 FR 60042, Nov. 6, 1997, as amended at 75 FR 17241, Apr. 5, 2010]

§385.11 Notification of safety rating and safety fitness determination.

(a) The FMCSA will provide a motor carrier written notice of any safety rating resulting from a compliance review as soon as practicable, but not later than 30 days after the review. The notice will take the form of a letter issued from the FMCSA's headquarters office and will include a list of FMCSR and HMR compliance deficiencies which the motor carrier must correct.

(b) If the safety rating is "satisfactory" or improves a previous "unsatisfactory" safety rating, it is final and

243

becomes effective on the date of the notice.

(c) In all other cases, a notice of a proposed safety rating will be issued. It becomes the final safety rating after the following time periods:

(1) For motor carriers transporting hazardous materials in quantities requiring placarding or transporting passengers by CMV—45 days after the date of the notice.

(2) For all other motor carriers operating CMVs—60 days after the date of the notice.

(d) A proposed safety rating of "unsatisfactory" is a notice to the motor carrier that the FMCSA has made a preliminary determination that the motor carrier is "unfit" to continue operating in interstate commerce, and that the prohibitions in § 385.13 will be imposed after 45 or 60 days if necessary safety improvements are not made.

(e) A motor carrier may request the FMCSA to perform an administrative review of a proposed or final safety rating. The process and the time limits are described in § 385.15.

(f) A motor carrier may request a change to a proposed or final safety rating based upon its corrective actions. The process and the time limits are described in § 385.17.

(g) If a motor carrier is subject to a remedial directive and proposed determination of unfitness under subpart J of this part, the notice of remedial directive will constitute the notice of safety fitness determination. If FMCSA has not issued a notice of remedial directive and proposed determination of unfitness under subpart J of this part, a notice of a proposed or final safety rating will constitute the notice of safety fitness determination.

[65 FR 50934, Aug. 22, 2000, as amended at 75 FR 17241, Apr. 5, 2010]

§ 385.13 Unsatisfactory rated motor carriers; prohibition on transportation; ineligibility for Federal contracts.

(a) Generally, a motor carrier rated "unsatisfactory" is prohibited from operating a CMV. Information on motor carriers, including their most current safety rating, is available from the FMCSA on the Internet at *http://*

www.safersys.org, or by telephone at (800) 832–5660.

(1) Motor carriers transporting hazardous materials in quantities requiring placarding, and motor carriers transporting passengers in a CMV, are prohibited from operating a CMV in motor carrier operations in commerce beginning on the 46th day after the date of the FMCSA notice of proposed "unsatisfactory" rating.

(2) All other motor carriers rated as a result of reviews completed on or after November 20, 2000, are prohibited from operating a CMV in motor carrier operations in commerce beginning on the 61st day after the date of the FMCSA notice of proposed "unsatisfactory" rating. If FMCSA determines that the motor carrier is making a good-faith effort to improve its safety fitness, FMCSA may allow the motor carrier to operate for up to 60 additional days.

(b) A Federal agency must not use a motor carrier that holds an "unsatisfactory" rating to transport passengers in a CMV or to transport hazardous materials in quantities requiring placarding.

(c) A Federal agency must not use a motor carrier for other CMV transportation if that carrier holds an "unsatisfactory" rating which became effective on or after January 22, 2001.

(d) *Penalties.* (1) If a proposed "unsatisfactory" safety rating becomes final, FMCSA will issue an order placing out of service the motor carrier's operations in commerce. The out-of-service order shall apply both to the motor carrier's operations in interstate commerce *and to its operations affecting interstate commerce.*

(2) If a motor carrier's intrastate operations are declared out of service by a State, FMCSA must issue an order placing out of service the carrier's operations in interstate commerce. The following conditions apply:

(i) The State that issued the intrastate out-of-service order participates in the Motor Carrier Safety Assistance Program and uses the FMCSA safety rating methodology provided in this part; and

(ii) The motor carrier has its principal place of business in the State that issued the out-of-service order.

(iii) The order prohibiting the motor carrier from operating a CMV in interstate commerce shall remain in effect until the State determines that the carrier is fit.

(3) Any motor carrier that operates CMVs in violation of this section is subject to the penalty provisions of 49 U.S.C. 521(b) and appendix B to part 386 of the FMCSRs.

(e) *Revocation of operating authority.* If a proposed "unsatisfactory" safety rating or a proposed determination of unfitness becomes final, the FMCSA will, following notice, issue an order revoking the operating authority of the owner or operator. For purposes of this section, the term "operating authority" means the registration required under 49 U.S.C. 13902 and § 392.9a of this subchapter. Any motor carrier that operates CMVs after revocation of its operating authority will be subject to the penalty provisions listed in 49 U.S.C. 14901.

[65 FR 50934, Aug. 22, 2000, as amended at 72 FR 36788, July 5, 2007; 72 FR 55700, Oct. 1, 2007; 75 FR 17241, Apr. 5, 2010]

§ 385.14 Motor carriers, brokers, and freight forwarders delinquent in paying civil penalties: prohibition on transportation.

(a) A CMV owner or operator that has failed to pay civil penalties imposed by the FMCSA, or has failed to abide by a payment plan, may be prohibited from operating CMVs in interstate commerce under 49 CFR 386.83.

(b) A broker, freight forwarder, or for-hire motor carrier that has failed to pay civil penalties imposed by the FMCSA, or has failed to abide by a payment plan, may be prohibited from operating in interstate commerce, and its registration may be suspended under the provisions of 49 CFR 386.84.

[65 FR 78427, Dec. 15, 2000]

§ 385.15 Administrative review.

(a) A motor carrier may request the FMCSA to conduct an administrative review if it believes FMCSA has committed an error in assigning its proposed safety rating in accordance with § 385.11(c) or its final safety rating in accordance with § 385.11(b).

(b) The motor carrier's request must explain the error it believes the FMCSA committed in issuing the safety rating. The motor carrier must include a list of all factual and procedural issues in dispute, and any information or documents that support its argument.

(c) The motor carrier must submit its request in writing to the Chief Safety Officer, Federal Motor Carrier Safety Administration, 1200 New Jersey Ave., SE., Washington, DC 20590–0001.

(1) If a motor carrier has received a notice of a proposed "unsatisfactory" safety rating, it should submit its request within 15 days from the date of the notice. This time frame will allow the FMCSA to issue a written decision before the prohibitions outlined in § 385.13 (a)(1) and (2) take effect. Failure to petition within this 15-day period may prevent the FMCSA from issuing a final decision before such prohibitions take effect.

(2) A motor carrier must make a request for an administrative review within 90 days of the date of the proposed safety rating issued under § 385.11 (c) or a final safety rating issued under § 385.11 (b), or within 90 days after denial of a request for a change in rating under § 385.17(i).

(d) The FMCSA may ask the motor carrier to submit additional data and attend a conference to discuss the safety rating. If the motor carrier does not provide the information requested, or does not attend the conference, the FMCSA may dismiss its request for review.

(e) The FMCSA will notify the motor carrier in writing of its decision following the administrative review. The FMCSA will complete its review:

(1) Within 30 days after receiving a request from a hazardous materials or passenger motor carrier that has received a proposed or final "unsatisfactory" safety rating.

(2) Within 45 days after receiving a request from any other motor carrier that has received a proposed or final "unsatisfactory" safety rating.

(f) The decision constitutes final agency action.

(g) Any motor carrier may request a rating change under the provisions of § 385.17.

[65 FR 50935, Aug. 22, 2000, as amended at 72 FR 55701, Oct. 1, 2007; 75 FR 17241, Apr. 5, 2010]

§ 385.17 Change to safety rating based upon corrective actions.

(a) A motor carrier that has taken action to correct the deficiencies that resulted in a proposed or final rating of "conditional" or "unsatisfactory" may request a rating change at any time.

(b) A motor carrier must make this request in writing to the FMCSA Service Center for the geographic area where the carrier maintains its principal place of business. The addresses and geographical boundaries of the Service Centers are listed in § 390.27 of this chapter.

(c) The motor carrier must base its request upon evidence that it has taken corrective actions and that its operations currently meet the safety standard and factors specified in §§ 385.5 and 385.7. The request must include a written description of corrective actions taken, and other documentation the carrier wishes the FMCSA to consider.

(d) The FMCSA will make a final determination on the request for change based upon the documentation the motor carrier submits, and any additional relevant information.

(e) The FMCSA will perform reviews of requests made by motor carriers with a proposed or final "unsatisfactory" safety rating in the following time periods after the motor carrier's request:

(1) Within 30 days for motor carriers transporting passengers in CMVs or placardable quantities of hazardous materials.

(2) Within 45 days for all other motor carriers.

(f) The filing of a request for change to a proposed or final safety rating under this section does not stay the 45-day period specified in § 385.13(a)(1) for motor carriers transporting passengers or hazardous materials. If the motor carrier has submitted evidence that corrective actions have been taken pursuant to this section and the FMCSA cannot make a final determination within the 45-day period, the period before the proposed safety rating becomes final may be extended for up to 10 days at the discretion of the FMCSA.

(g) FMCSA may allow a motor carrier (except a motor carrier transporting passengers or a motor carrier transporting hazardous materials in quantities requiring placarding) with a proposed rating of "unsatisfactory" to continue its motor carrier operations in commerce for up to 60 days beyond the 60 days specified in the proposed rating, if FMCSA determines that the motor carrier is making a good faith effort to improve its safety status. This additional period would begin on the 61st day after the date of the notice of proposed "unsatisfactory" rating.

(h) If the FMCSA determines that the motor carrier has taken the corrective actions required and that its operations currently meet the safety standard and factors specified in §§ 385.5 and 385.7, the agency will notify the motor carrier in writing of its upgraded safety rating.

(i) If the FMCSA determines that the motor carrier has not taken all the corrective actions required, or that its operations still fail to meet the safety standard and factors specified in §§ 385.5 and 385.7, the agency will notify the motor carrier in writing.

(j) Any motor carrier whose request for change is denied in accordance with paragraph (i) of this section may request administrative review under the procedures of § 385.15. The motor carrier must make the request within 90 days of the denial of the request for a rating change. If the proposed rating has become final, it shall remain in effect during the period of any administrative review.

(k) An upgraded safety rating based upon corrective action under this section will have no effect on an otherwise applicable notice of remedial directive, or proposed determination of unfitness issued in accordance with subpart J of this part.

(l) A motor carrier may not request a rescission of a determination of unfitness issued under subpart J of this part based on corrective action.

[65 FR 50935, Aug. 22, 2000, as amended at 72 FR 36788, July 5, 2007; 75 FR 17241, Apr. 5, 2010]

§385.19 Safety fitness information.

(a) Final safety ratings, remedial directives, and safety fitness determinations will be made available to other Federal and State agencies in writing, telephonically, or by remote computer access.

(b) The final safety rating, any applicable remedial directive(s), and the safety fitness determination pertaining to a motor carrier will be made available to the public upon request. Any person requesting information under this paragraph must provide FMCSA with the motor carrier's name, principal office address, and, if known, the USDOT Number or the Interstate Commerce Commission MC (ICCMC) docket number if any.

(c) Requests should be addressed to the Federal Motor Carrier Safety Administration, Office of Information Technology (MC–RI), 1200 New Jersey Ave., SE., Washington, DC 20590–0001. The information can also be found at the SAFER website: *http:// www.safersys.org.*

(d) Oral requests by telephone to (800) 832–5660 will be given an oral response.

[62 FR 60043, Nov. 6, 1997, as amended at 66 FR 49872, Oct. 1, 2001; 72 FR 55701, Oct. 1, 2007; 75 FR 17241, Apr. 5, 2010]

Subpart B—Safety Monitoring System for Mexico-Domiciled Carriers

Source: 67 FR 12771, Mar. 19, 2002, unless otherwise noted.

§385.101 Definitions

Compliance review means a compliance review as defined in §385.3 of this part.

Provisional certificate of registration means the registration under §368.6 of this subchapter that the FMCSA grants to a Mexico-domiciled motor carrier to provide interstate transportation of property within the United States solely within the municipalities along the United States-Mexico border and the commercial zones of such municipalities. It is provisional because it will be revoked if the registrant does not demonstrate that it is exercising basic safety management controls during the safety monitoring period established in this subpart.

Provisional operating authority means the registration under §365.507 of this subchapter that the FMCSA grants to a Mexico-domiciled motor carrier to provide interstate transportation within the United States beyond the municipalities along the United States-Mexico border and the commercial zones of such municipalities. It is provisional because it will be revoked if the registrant is not assigned a Satisfactory safety rating following a compliance review conducted during the safety monitoring period established in this subpart.

Safety audit means an examination of a motor carrier's operations to provide educational and technical assistance on safety and the operational requirements of the FMCSRs and applicable HMRs and to gather critical safety data needed to make an assessment of the carrier's safety performance and basic safety management controls. Safety audits do not result in safety ratings.

§385.103 Safety monitoring system.

(a) *General.* Each Mexico-domiciled carrier operating in the United States will be subject to an oversight program to monitor its compliance with applicable Federal Motor Carrier Safety Regulations (FMCSRs), Federal Motor Vehicle Safety Standards (FMVSSs), and Hazardous Materials Regulations (HMRs).

(b) *Roadside monitoring.* Each Mexico-domiciled carrier that receives provisional operating authority or a provisional Certificate of Registration will be subject to intensified monitoring through frequent roadside inspections.

(c) *CVSA decal.* Each Mexico-domiciled carrier granted provisional operating authority under part 365 of this subchapter must have on every commercial motor vehicle it operates in the United States a current decal attesting to a satisfactory inspection by a Commercial Vehicle Safety Alliance (CVSA) inspector.

(d) *Safety audit.* The FMCSA will conduct a safety audit on a Mexico-domiciled carrier within 18 months after the FMCSA issues the carrier a provisional Certificate of Registration under part 368 of this subchapter.

(e) *Compliance review.* The FMCSA will conduct a compliance review on a Mexico-domiciled carrier within 18 months after the FMCSA issues the carrier provisional operating authority under part 365 of this subchapter.

§ 385.105   Expedited action.

(a) A Mexico-domiciled motor carrier committing any of the following violations identified through roadside inspections, or by any other means, may be subjected to an expedited safety audit or compliance review, or may be required to submit a written response demonstrating corrective action:

(1) Using drivers not possessing, or operating without, a valid Licencia Federal de Conductor. An invalid Licencia Federal de Conductor includes one that is falsified, revoked, expired, or missing a required endorsement.

(2) Operating vehicles that have been placed out of service for violations of the Commercial Vehicle Safety Alliance (CVSA) North American Standard Out-of-Service Criteria, without making the required repairs.

(3) Involvement in, due to carrier act or omission, a hazardous materials incident within the United States involving:

(i) A highway route controlled quantity of a Class 7 (radioactive) material as defined in § 173.403 of this title;

(ii) Any quantity of a Class 1, Division 1.1, 1.2, or 1.3 explosive as defined in § 173.50 of this title; or

(iii) Any quantity of a poison inhalation hazard Zone A or B material as defined in § 173.115, § 173.132, or § 173.133 of this title.

(4) Involvement in, due to carrier act or omission, two or more hazardous material incidents occurring within the United States and involving any hazardous material not listed in paragraph (a)(3) of this section and defined in chapter I of this title.

(5) Using a driver who tests positive for controlled substances or alcohol or who refuses to submit to required controlled substances or alcohol tests.

(6) Operating within the United States a motor vehicle that is not insured as required by part 387 of this chapter.

(7) Having a driver or vehicle out-of-service rate of 50 percent or more based upon at least three inspections occurring within a consecutive 90-day period.

(b) Failure to respond to an agency demand for a written response demonstrating corrective action within 30 days will result in the suspension of the carrier's provisional operating authority or provisional Certificate of Registration until the required showing of corrective action is submitted to the FMCSA.

(c) A satisfactory response to a written demand for corrective action does not excuse a carrier from the requirement that it undergo a safety audit or compliance review, as appropriate, during the provisional registration period.

§ 385.107   The safety audit.

(a) The criteria used in a safety audit to determine whether a Mexico-domiciled carrier exercises the necessary basic safety management controls are specified in Appendix A to this part.

(b) If the FMCSA determines, based on the safety audit, that the Mexico-domiciled carrier has adequate basic safety management controls, the FMCSA will provide the carrier written notice of this finding as soon as practicable, but not later than 45 days after the completion of the safety audit. The carrier's Certificate of Registration will remain provisional and the carrier's on-highway performance will continue to be closely monitored for the remainder of the 18-month provisional registration period.

(c) If the FMCSA determines, based on the safety audit, that the Mexico-domiciled carrier's basic safety management controls are inadequate, it will initiate a suspension and revocation proceeding in accordance with § 385.111 of this subpart.

(d) The safety audit is also used to assess the basic safety management controls of Mexico-domiciled applicants for provisional operating authority to operate beyond United States municipalities and commercial zones on the United States-Mexico border under §365.507 of this subchapter.

§385.109 The compliance review.

(a) The criteria used in a compliance review to determine whether a Mexico-domiciled carrier granted provisional operating authority under §365.507 of this subchapter exercises the necessary basic safety management controls are specified in Appendix B to this part.

(b) *Satisfactory rating.* If the FMCSA assigns a Mexico-domiciled carrier a Satisfactory rating following a compliance review conducted under this subpart, the FMCSA will provide the carrier written notice as soon as practicable, but not later than 45 days after the completion of the compliance review. The carrier's operating authority will remain in provisional status and its on-highway performance will continue to be closely monitored for the remainder of the 18-month provisional registration period.

(c) *Conditional rating.* If the FMCSA assigns a Mexico-domiciled carrier a Conditional rating following a compliance review conducted under this subpart, it will initiate a revocation proceeding in accordance with §385.111 of this subpart. The carrier's provisional operating authority will not be suspended prior to the conclusion of the revocation proceeding.

(d) *Unsatisfactory rating.* If the FMCSA assigns a Mexico-domiciled carrier an Unsatisfactory rating following a compliance review conducted under this subpart, it will initiate a suspension and revocation proceeding in accordance with §385.111 of this subpart.

§385.111 Suspension and revocation of Mexico-domiciled carrier registration.

(a) If a carrier is assigned an "Unsatisfactory" safety rating following a compliance review conducted under this subpart, or a safety audit conducted under this subpart determines that a carrier does not exercise the basic safety management controls necessary to ensure safe operations, the FMCSA will provide the carrier written notice, as soon as practicable, that its registration will be suspended effective 15 days from the service date of the no-

tice unless the carrier demonstrates, within 10 days of the service date of the notice, that the compliance review or safety audit contains material error.

(b) For purposes of this section, material error is a mistake or series of mistakes that resulted in an erroneous safety rating or an erroneous determination that the carrier does not exercise the necessary basic safety management controls.

(c) If the carrier demonstrates that the compliance review or safety audit contained material error, its registration will not be suspended. If the carrier fails to show a material error in the safety audit, the FMCSA will issue an Order:

(1) Suspending the carrier's provisional operating authority or provisional Certificate of Registration and requiring it to immediately cease all further operations in the United States; and

(2) Notifying the carrier that its provisional operating authority or provisional Certificate of Registration will be revoked unless it presents evidence of necessary corrective action within 30 days from the service date of the Order.

(d) If a carrier is assigned a "Conditional" rating following a compliance review conducted under this subpart, the provisions of subparagraphs (a) through (c) of this section will apply, except that its provisional registration will not be suspended under paragraph (c)(1) of this section.

(e) If a carrier subject to this subpart fails to provide the necessary documents for a safety audit or compliance review upon reasonable request, or fails to submit evidence of the necessary corrective action as required by §385.105 of this subpart, the FMCSA will provide the carrier with written notice, as soon as practicable, that its registration will be suspended 15 days from the service date of the notice unless it provides all necessary documents or information. This suspension will remain in effect until the necessary documents or information are produced and:

(1) A safety audit determines that the carrier exercises basic safety management controls necessary for safe operations;

(2) The carrier is rated Satisfactory or Conditional after a compliance review; or

(3) The FMCSA determines, following review of the carrier's response to a demand for corrective action under § 385.105, that the carrier has taken the necessary corrective action.

(f) If a carrier commits any of the violations specified in § 385.105(a) of this subpart after the removal of a suspension issued under this section, the suspension will be automatically reinstated. The FMCSA will issue an Order requiring the carrier to cease further operations in the United States and demonstrate, within 15 days from the service date of the Order, that it did not commit the alleged violation(s). If the carrier fails to demonstrate that it did not commit the violation(s), the FMCSA will issue an Order revoking its provisional operating authority or provisional Certificate of Registration.

(g) If the FMCSA receives credible evidence that a carrier has operated in violation of a suspension order issued under this section, it will issue an Order requiring the carrier to show cause, within 10 days of the service date of the Order, why its provisional operating authority or provisional Certificate of Registration should not be revoked. If the carrier fails to make the necessary showing, the FMCSA will revoke its registration.

(h) If a Mexico-domiciled motor carrier operates a commercial motor vehicle in violation of a suspension or out-of-service order, it is subject to the penalty provisions in 49 U.S.C. 521(b)(2)(A), not to exceed $10,000 for each offense.

(i) Notwithstanding any provision of this subpart, a carrier subject to this subpart is also subject to the suspension and revocation provisions of 49 U.S.C. 13905 for repeated violations of DOT regulations governing its motor carrier operations.

§ 385.113 Administrative review.

(a) A Mexico-domiciled motor carrier may request the FMCSA to conduct an administrative review if it believes the FMCSA has committed an error in assigning a safety rating or suspending or revoking the carrier's provisional operating authority or provisional Certificate of Registration under this subpart.

(b) The carrier must submit its request in writing, in English, to the Associate Administrator for Enforcement and Program Delivery (MC–E), Federal Motor Carrier Safety Administration, 1200 New Jersey Ave., SE., Washington, DC 20590–0001.

(c) The carrier's request must explain the error it believes the FMCSA committed in assigning the safety rating or suspending or revoking the carrier's provisional operating authority or provisional Certificate of Registration and include any information or documents that support its argument.

(d) The FMCSA will complete its administrative review no later than 10 days after the carrier submits its request for review. The Associate Administrator's decision will constitute the final agency action.

[67 FR 12771, Mar. 19, 2002, as amended at 72 FR 55701, Oct. 1, 2007]

§ 385.115 Reapplying for provisional registration.

(a) A Mexico-domiciled motor carrier whose provisional operating authority or provisional Certificate of Registration has been revoked may reapply under part 365 or 368 of this subchapter, as appropriate, no sooner than 30 days after the date of revocation.

(b) The Mexico-domiciled motor carrier will be required to initiate the application process from the beginning. The carrier will be required to demonstrate how it has corrected the deficiencies that resulted in revocation of its registration and how it will ensure that it will have adequate basic safety management controls. It will also have to undergo a pre-authorization safety audit if it applies for provisional operating authority under part 365 of this subchapter.

§ 385.117 Duration of safety monitoring system.

(a) Each Mexico-domiciled carrier subject to this subpart will remain in the safety monitoring system for at least 18 months from the date FMCSA issues its provisional Certificate of Registration or provisional operating authority, except as provided in paragraphs (c) and (d) of this section.

(b) If, at the end of this 18-month period, the carrier's most recent safety audit or safety rating was Satisfactory and no additional enforcement or safety improvement actions are pending under this subpart, the Mexico-domiciled carrier's provisional operating authority or provisional Certificate of Registration will become permanent.

(c) If, at the end of this 18-month period, the FMCSA has not been able to conduct a safety audit or compliance review, the carrier will remain in the safety monitoring system until a safety audit or compliance review is conducted. If the results of the safety audit or compliance review are satisfactory, the carrier's provisional operating authority or provisional Certificate of Registration will become permanent.

(d) If, at the end of this 18-month period, the carrier's provisional operating authority or provisional Certificate of Registration is suspended under §385.111(a) of this subpart, the carrier will remain in the safety monitoring system until the FMCSA either:

(1) Determines that the carrier has taken corrective action; or

(2) Completes measures to revoke the carrier's provisional operating authority or provisional Certificate of Registration under §385.111(c) of this subpart.

§385.119 Applicability of safety fitness and enforcement procedures.

At all times during which a Mexico-domiciled motor carrier is subject to the safety monitoring system in this subpart, it is also subject to the general safety fitness procedures established in subpart A of this part and to compliance and enforcement procedures applicable to all carriers regulated by the FMCSA.

Subpart C—Certification of Safety Auditors, Safety Investigators, and Safety Inspectors

Source: 67 FR 12779, Mar. 19, 2002, unless otherwise noted.

§385.201 Who is qualified to perform a review of a motor carrier or an intermodal equipment provider?

(a) An FMCSA employee, or a State or local government employee funded through the Motor Carrier Safety Assistance Program (MCSAP), who was qualified to perform a compliance review before June 17, 2002, may perform a compliance review, safety audit, roadability review, or roadside inspection if he or she complies with §385.203(b).

(b) A person who was not qualified to perform a compliance review before June 17, 2002, may perform a compliance review, safety audit, roadability review, or roadside inspection after complying with the requirements of §385.203(a).

[73 FR 76818, Dec. 17, 2008]

§385.203 What are the requirements to obtain and maintain certification?

(a) After June 17, 2002, a person who is not qualified under §385.201(a) may not perform a compliance review, safety audit, roadability review, or roadside inspection unless he or she has been certified by FMCSA or a State or local agency applying the FMCSA standards after successfully completing classroom training and examinations on the FMCSRs and HMRs as described in detail on the FMCSA website (*www.fmcsa.dot.gov*). These employees must also comply with the maintenance of certification/qualification requirements of paragraph (b) of this section.

(b) *Maintenance of certification/qualification.* A person may not perform a compliance review, safety audit, roadability review, or roadside inspection unless he or she meets the quality-control and periodic re-training requirements adopted by the FMCSA to ensure the maintenance of high standards and familiarity with amendments to the FMCSRs and HMRs. These maintenance of certification/qualification requirements are described in detail on the FMCSA website (*www.fmcsa.dot.gov*).

(c) The requirements of paragraphs (a) and (b) of this section for training, performance and maintenance of certification/qualification, which are described on the FMCSA website

251

(*www.fmcsa.dot.gov*), are also available in hard copy from the Federal Motor Carrier Safety Administration, Professional Development and Training Division (MC–MHT), 4600 N. Fairfax Drive, Suite 700, Arlington, Virginia 22203.

[67 FR 12779, Mar. 19, 2002, as amended at 72 FR 55701, Oct. 1, 2007; 73 FR 76819, Dec. 17, 2008]

§ 385.205 How can a person who has lost his or her certification be recertified?

He or she must successfully complete the requirements of § 385.203(a) and (b).

Subpart D—New Entrant Safety Assurance Program

SOURCE: 67 FR 31983, May 13, 2002, unless otherwise noted.

§ 385.301 What is a motor carrier required to do before beginning interstate operations?

(a) Before a motor carrier of property or passengers begins interstate operations, it must register with the FMCSA and receive a USDOT number. In addition, for-hire motor carriers must obtain operating authority from FMCSA following the registration procedures described in 49 CFR part 365, unless providing transportation exempt from 49 CFR part 365 registration requirements.

(b) This subpart applies to motor carriers domiciled in the United States and Canada.

(c) A Mexico-domiciled motor carrier of property or passengers must register with the FMCSA by following the registration procedures described in 49 CFR part 365 or 368, as appropriate. The regulations in this subpart do not apply to Mexico-domiciled carriers.

§ 385.303 How does a motor carrier register with the FMCSA?

A motor carrier may contact the FMCSA by internet (*www.fmcsa.dot.gov*); or Washington, DC headquarters by mail at, Federal Motor Carrier Safety Administration, 1200 New Jersey Ave., SE., Washington, DC 20590–0001; fax (703) 280–4003; or telephone 1–800–832–5660, and request the application materials for a new entrant motor carrier.

[67 FR 31983, May 13, 2002, as amended at 72 FR 55701, Oct. 1, 2007]

§ 385.305 What happens after the FMCSA receives a request for new entrant registration?

(a) The requester for new entrant registration will be directed to the FMCSA Internet website (*www.fmcsa.dot.gov*) to secure and/or complete the application package online.

(b) The application package will contain the following:

(1) Educational and technical assistance material regarding the requirements of the FMCSRs and HMRs, if applicable.

(2) The Form MCS–150, The Motor Carrier Identification Report.

(3) Application forms to obtain operating authority under 49 CFR 365, as appropriate.

(c) Upon completion of the application forms, the new entrant will be issued a USDOT number.

(d) For-hire motor carriers, unless providing transportation exempt from 49 CFR part 365 registration requirements, must also comply with the procedures established in 49 CFR part 365 to obtain operating authority before operating in interstate commerce.

[67 FR 31983, May 13, 2002, as amended at 73 FR 76488, Dec. 16, 2008]

§ 385.306 What are the consequences of furnishing misleading information or making a false statement in connection with the registration process?

A carrier that furnishes false or misleading information, or conceals material information in connection with the registration process, is subject to the following actions:

(a) Revocation of registration.

(b) Assessment of the civil and/or criminal penalties prescribed in 49 U.S.C. 521 and 49 U.S.C. chapter 149.

[73 FR 76488, Dec. 16, 2008]

§ 385.307 What happens after a motor carrier begins operations as a new entrant?

After a new entrant satisfies all applicable pre-operational requirements, it will be subject to the new entrant safety monitoring procedures for a period of 18 months. During this 18-month period:

(a) The new entrant's roadside safety performance will be closely monitored to ensure the new entrant has basic safety management controls that are operating effectively.

(b) A safety audit will be conducted on the new entrant, once it has been in operation for enough time to have sufficient records to allow the agency to evaluate the adequacy of its basic safety management controls. This period will generally be at least 3 months.

(c) All records and documents required for the safety audit shall be made available for inspection upon request by an individual certified under FMCSA regulations to perform safety audits.

[67 FR 31983, May 13, 2002, as amended at 73 FR 76488, Dec. 16, 2008]

§ 385.308 What may cause an expedited action?

(a) A new entrant that commits any of the following actions, identified through roadside inspections or by any other means, may be subjected to an expedited safety audit or a compliance review or may be required to submit a written response demonstrating corrective action:

(1) Using a driver not possessing a valid commercial driver's license to operate a commercial vehicle as defined under § 383.5 of this chapter. An invalid commercial driver's license includes one that is falsified, revoked, expired, or missing a required endorsement.

(2) Operating a vehicle placed out of service for violations of the Federal Motor Carrier Safety Regulations or compatible State laws and regulations without taking necessary corrective action.

(3) Being involved in, through action or omission, a hazardous materials reportable incident, as described under 49 CFR 171.15 or 171.16, involving—

(i) A highway route controlled quantity of certain radioactive materials (Class 7).

(ii) Any quantity of certain explosives (Class 1, Division 1.1, 1.2, or 1.3).

(iii) Any quantity of certain poison inhalation hazard materials (Zone A or B).

(4) Being involved in, through action or omission, two or more hazardous materials reportable incidents as described under 49 CFR 171.15 or 171.16, involving hazardous materials other than those listed above.

(5) Using a driver who tests positive for controlled substances or alcohol or who refuses to submit to required controlled substances or alcohol tests.

(6) Operating a commercial motor vehicle without the levels of financial responsibility required under part 387 of this subchapter.

(7) Having a driver or vehicle out-of-service rate of 50 percent or more based upon at least three inspections occurring within a consecutive 90-day period.

(b) If a new entrant that commits any of the actions listed in paragraph (a) of this section:

(1) Has not had a safety audit or compliance review, FMCSA will schedule the new entrant for a safety audit as soon as practicable.

(2) Has had a safety audit or compliance review, FMCSA will send the new entrant a notice advising it to submit evidence of corrective action within 30 days of the service date of the notice.

(c) FMCSA may schedule a compliance review of a new entrant that commits any of the actions listed in paragraph (a) of this section at any time if it determines the violation warrants a thorough review of the new entrant's operation.

(d) Failure to respond within 30 days of the notice to an Agency demand for a written response demonstrating corrective action will result in the revocation of the new entrant's registration.

[73 FR 76488, Dec. 16, 2008]

§ 385.309 What is the purpose of the safety audit?

The purpose of a safety audit is to:

(a) Provide educational and technical assistance to the new entrant; and

(b) Gather safety data needed to make an assessment of the new entrant's safety performance and adequacy of its basic safety management controls.

253

§ 385.311 What will the safety audit consist of?

The safety audit will consist of a review of the new entrant's safety management systems and a sample of required records to assess compliance with the FMCSRs, applicable HMRs and related record-keeping requirements as specified in appendix A of this part. The areas for review include, but are not limited to, the following:

(a) Driver qualification;

(b) Driver duty status;

(c) Vehicle maintenance;

(d) Accident register; and

(e) Controlled substances and alcohol use and testing requirements.

§ 385.313 Who will conduct the safety audit?

An individual certified under the FMCSA regulations to perform safety audits will conduct the safety audit.

§ 385.315 Where will the safety audit be conducted?

The safety audit will generally be conducted at the new entrant's business premises.

§ 385.317 Will a safety audit result in a safety fitness determination by the FMCSA?

A safety audit will not result in a safety fitness determination. Safety fitness determinations follow completion of a compliance review.

§ 385.319 What happens after completion of the safety audit?

(a) Upon completion of the safety audit, the auditor will review the findings with the new entrant.

(b) *Pass.* If FMCSA determines the safety audit discloses the new entrant has adequate basic safety management controls, the Agency will provide the new entrant written notice as soon as practicable, but not later than 45 days after completion of the safety audit, that it has adequate basic safety management controls. The new entrant's safety performance will continue to be closely monitored for the remainder of the 18-month period of new entrant registration.

(c) *Fail.* If FMCSA determines the safety audit discloses the new entrant's basic safety management controls are inadequate, the Agency will provide the new entrant written notice, as soon as practicable, but not later than 45 days after the completion of the safety audit, that its USDOT new entrant registration will be revoked and its operations placed out-of-service unless it takes the actions specified in the notice to remedy its safety management practices.

(1) *60-day corrective action requirement.* All new entrants, except those specified in paragraph (c)(2) of this section, must take the specified actions to remedy inadequate safety management practices within 60 days of the date of the notice.

(2) *45-day corrective action requirement.* The new entrants listed below must take the specified actions to remedy inadequate safety management practices within 45 days of the date of the notice:

(i) A new entrant that transports passengers in a CMV designed or used to transport between 9 and 15 passengers (including the driver) for direct compensation.

(ii) A new entrant that transports passengers in a CMV designed or used to transport more than 15 passengers (including the driver).

(iii) A new entrant that transports hazardous materials in a CMV as defined in paragraph (4) of the definition of a ''Commercial Motor Vehicle'' in § 390.5 of this subchapter.

[73 FR 76489, Dec. 16, 2008]

§ 385.321 What failures of safety management practices disclosed by the safety audit will result in a notice to a new entrant that its USDOT new entrant registration will be revoked?

(a) *General.* The failures of safety management practices consist of a lack of basic safety management controls as described in Appendix A of this part or failure to comply with one or more of the regulations set forth in paragraph (b) of this section and will result in a notice to a new entrant that its USDOT new entrant registration will be revoked.

(b) *Automatic failure of the audit.* A new entrant will automatically fail a safety audit if found in violation of any one of the following 16 regulations:

TABLE TO § 385.321—VIOLATIONS THAT WILL RESULT IN AUTOMATIC FAILURE OF THE NEW ENTRANT SAFETY AUDIT

Violation	Guidelines for determining automatic failure of the safety audit
1. § 382.115(a)/§ 382.115(b)—Failing to implement an alcohol and/or controlled substances testing program (domestic and foreign motor carriers, respectively).	Single occurrence.
2. § 382.201—Using a driver known to have an alcohol content of 0.04 or greater to perform a safety-sensitive function.	Single occurrence.
3. § 382.211—Using a driver who has refused to submit to an alcohol or controlled substances test required under part 382.	Single occurrence.
4. § 382.215—Using a driver known to have tested positive for a controlled substance.	Single occurrence.
5. § 382.305—Failing to implement a random controlled substances and/ or alcohol testing program.	Single occurrence.
6. § 383.3(a)/§ 383.23(a)—Knowingly using a driver who does not possess a valid CDL.	Single occurrence.
7. § 383.37(a)—Knowingly allowing, requiring, permitting, or authorizing an employee with a commercial driver's license which is suspended, revoked, or canceled by a State or who is disqualified to operate a commercial motor vehicle.	Single occurrence.
8. § 383.51(a)—Knowingly allowing, requiring, permitting, or authorizing a driver to drive who is disqualified to drive a commercial motor vehicle.	Single occurrence. This violation refers to a driver operating a CMV as defined under § 383.5.
9. § 387.7(a)—Operating a motor vehicle without having in effect the required minimum levels of financial responsibility coverage.	Single occurrence.
10. § 387.31(a)—Operating a passenger carrying vehicle without having in effect the required minimum levels of financial responsibility.	Single occurrence.
11. § 391.15(a)—Knowingly using a disqualified driver	Single occurrence.
12. § 391.11(b)(4)—Knowingly using a physically unqualified driver	Single occurrence. This violation refers to a driver operating a CMV as defined under § 390.5.
13. § 395.8(a)—Failing to require a driver to make a record of duty status.	Requires a violation threshold (51% or more of examined records) to trigger automatic failure.
14. § 396.9(c)(2)—Requiring or permitting the operation of a commercial motor vehicle declared "out-of-service" before repairs are made.	Single occurrence.
15. § 396.11(c)—Failing to correct out-of-service defects listed by driver in a driver vehicle inspection report before the vehicle is operated again.	Single occurrence.
16. § 396.17(a)—Using a commercial motor vehicle not periodically inspected.	Requires a violation threshold (51% or more of examined records) to trigger automatic failure.

[73 FR 76489, Dec. 16, 2008]

§ 385.323 May FMCSA extend the period under § 385.319(c) for a new entrant to take corrective action to remedy its safety management practices?

(a) FMCSA may extend the 60-day period in § 385.319(c)(1) for up to an additional 60 days provided FMCSA determines the new entrant is making a good faith effort to remedy its safety management practices.

(b) FMCSA may extend the 45-day period in § 385.319(c)(2) for up to an additional 10 days if the new entrant has submitted evidence that corrective actions have been taken pursuant to § 385.319(c) and the Agency needs additional time to determine the adequacy of the corrective action.

[73 FR 76490, Dec. 16, 2008]

§ 385.325 What happens after a new entrant has been notified under § 385.319(c) to take corrective action to remedy its safety management practices?

(a) If the new entrant provides evidence of corrective action acceptable to the FMCSA within the time period provided in § 385.319(c), including any extension of that period authorized under § 385.323, the FMCSA will provide written notification to the new entrant that its DOT new entrant registration will not be revoked and it may continue operations.

(b) If a new entrant, after being notified that it is required to take corrective action to improve its safety management practices, fails to submit a written response demonstrating corrective action acceptable to FMCSA within the time specified in § 385.319, and any extension of that period authorized under § 385.323, FMCSA will revoke its new entrant registration and issue an out-of-service order effective on:

(1) Day 61 from the notice date for new entrants subject to § 385.319(c)(1).

(2) Day 46 from the notice date for new entrants subject to § 385.319(c)(2).

(3) If an extension has been granted under § 385.323, the day following the expiration of the extension date.

(c) The new entrant may not operate in interstate commerce on or after the effective date of the out-of-service order.

[67 FR 31983, May 13, 2002, as amended at 73 FR 76490, Dec. 16, 2008]

§ 385.327 May a new entrant request an administrative review of a determination of a failed safety audit?

(a) If a new entrant receives a notice under § 385.319(c) that its new entrant registration will be revoked, it may request FMCSA to conduct an administrative review if it believes FMCSA has committed an error in determining that its basic safety management controls are inadequate. The request must:

(1) Be made to the Field Administrator of the appropriate FMCSA Service Center.

(2) Explain the error the new entrant believes FMCSA committed in its determination.

(3) Include a list of all factual and procedural issues in dispute and any information or documents that support the new entrant's argument.

(b) FMCSA may request that the new entrant submit additional data and attend a conference to discuss the issues(s) in dispute. If the new entrant does not attend the conference or does not submit the requested data, FMCSA may dismiss the new entrant's request for review.

(c) A new entrant must submit a request for an administrative review within one of the following time periods:

(1) If it does not submit evidence of corrective action under § 385.319(c), within 90 days after the date it is notified that its basic safety management controls are inadequate.

(2) If it submits evidence of corrective action under § 385.319(c), within 90 days after the date it is notified that its corrective action is insufficient and

its basic safety management controls remain inadequate.

(d) If a new entrant wants to assure that FMCSA will be able to issue a final written decision before the prohibitions outlined in § 385.325(c) take effect, the new entrant must submit its request no later than 15 days from the date of the notice that its basic safety management controls are inadequate. Failure to submit the request within this 15-day period may result in revocation of new entrant registration and issuance of an out-of-service order before completion of administrative review.

(e) FMCSA will complete its review and notify the new entrant in writing of its decision within:

(1) 45 days after receiving a request for review from a new entrant that is subject to § 385.319(c)(1).

(2) 30 days after receiving a request for review from a new entrant that is subject to § 385.319(c)(2).

(f) The Field Administrator's decision constitutes the final Agency action.

(g) Notwithstanding this subpart, a new entrant is subject to the suspension and revocation provisions of 49 U.S.C. 13905 for violations of DOT regulations governing motor carrier operations.

[73 FR 76490, Dec. 16, 2008]

§ 385.329 May a new entrant that has had its USDOT new entrant registration revoked and its operations placed out of service reapply?

(a) A new entrant whose USDOT new entrant registration has been revoked, and whose operations have been placed out of service by FMCSA, may reapply for new entrant registration no sooner than 30 days after the date of revocation.

(b) If the USDOT new entrant registration was revoked because of a failed safety audit, the new entrant must do all of the following:

(1) Submit an updated MCS–150.

(2) Submit evidence that it has corrected the deficiencies that resulted in revocation of its registration and will otherwise ensure that it will have basic safety management controls in effect.

(3) Begin the 18-month new entrant monitoring cycle again as of the date the re-filed application is approved.

(c) If the USDOT new entrant registration was revoked because FMCSA found that the new entrant had failed to submit to a safety audit, it must do all of the following:

(1) Submit an updated MCS–150.

(2) Begin the 18-month new entrant monitoring cycle again as of the date the re-filed application is approved.

(3) Submit to a safety audit.

(d) If the new entrant is a for-hire carrier subject to the registration provisions under 49 U.S.C. 13901 and also has had its operating authority revoked, it must re-apply for operating authority as set forth in part 365 of this chapter.

[73 FR 76490, Dec. 16, 2008]

§ 385.331 What happens if a new entrant operates a CMV after having been issued an order placing its interstate operations out of service?

A new entrant that operates a CMV in violation of an out-of-service order is subject to the penalty provisions in 49 U.S.C. 521(b)(2)(A) for each offense as adjusted for inflation by 49 CFR part 386, appendix B.

[73 FR 76491, Dec. 16, 2008]

§ 385.333 What happens at the end of the 18-month safety monitoring period?

(a) If a safety audit has been performed within the 18-month period, and the new entrant is not currently subject to an order placing its operations out-of-service under § 385.325(b) or under a notice ordering it to take specified actions to remedy its safety management controls under § 385.319(c), the FMCSA will remove the new entrant designation and notify the new entrant in writing that its registration has become permanent. Thereafter, the FMCSA will evaluate the motor carrier on the same basis as any other carrier.

(b) If a new entrant is determined to be ''unfit'' after a compliance review its new entrant registration will be revoked. (See § 385.13)

(c) A new entrant that has reached the conclusion of the 18-month period but is under an order to correct its safety management practices under § 385.319(c) will have its new entrant registration removed following FMCSA's determination that the specified actions have been taken to remedy its safety management practices. The motor carrier will be notified in writing that its new entrant designation is removed and that its registration has become permanent. Thereafter, the FMCSA will evaluate the motor carrier on the same basis as any other carrier.

(d) If a safety audit or compliance review has not been performed by the end of the 18-month monitoring period through no fault of the motor carrier, the carrier will be permitted to continue operating as a new entrant until a safety audit or compliance review is performed and a final determination is made regarding the adequacy of its safety management controls. Based on the results of the safety audit or compliance review, the FMCSA will either:

(1) Remove the new entrant designation and notify the new entrant in writing that its registration has become permanent; or

(2) Revoke the new entrant registration in accordance with § 385.319(c).

§ 385.335 If the FMCSA conducts a compliance review on a new entrant, will the new entrant also be subject to a safety audit?

If the FMCSA conducts a compliance review on a new entrant that has not previously been subject to a safety audit and issues a safety fitness determination, the new entrant will not have to undergo a safety audit under this subpart. However, the new entrant will continue to be subject to the 18-month safety-monitoring period prior to removal of the new entrant designation.

§ 385.337 What happens if a new entrant refuses to permit a safety audit to be performed on its operations?

(a) If a new entrant refuses to permit a safety audit to be performed on its operations, FMCSA will provide the carrier with written notice that its registration will be revoked and its operations placed out of service unless the new entrant agrees in writing, within 10 days from the service date of the notice, to permit the safety audit to be performed. The refusal to permit a safety audit to be performed may subject the new entrant to the penalty provisions of 49 U.S.C. 521(b)(2)(A), as adjusted for inflation by 49 CFR part 386, appendix B.

(b) If the new entrant does not agree to undergo a safety audit as specified in paragraph (a) of this section, its registration will be revoked and its interstate operations placed out of service effective on the 11th day from the service date of the notice issued under paragraph (a) of this section.

[67 FR 31983, May 13, 2002, as amended at 73 FR 76491, Dec. 16, 2008]

Subpart E—Hazardous Materials Safety Permits

SOURCE: 69 FR 39367, June 30, 2004, unless otherwise noted.

§ 385.401 What is the purpose and scope of this subpart?

(a) This subpart contains the requirements for obtaining and maintaining a safety permit to transport certain hazardous materials. No one may transport the materials listed in § 385.403 without a safety permit required by this subpart.

(b) This subpart includes:

(1) Definitions of terms used in this subpart;

(2) The list of hazardous materials that require a safety permit if transported in commerce;

(3) The requirements and procedures a carrier must follow in order to be issued a safety permit and maintain a safety permit;

(4) The procedures for a motor carrier to follow to initiate an administrative review of a denial, suspension, or revocation of a safety permit.

§ 385.402 What definitions are used in this subpart?

(a) The definitions in parts 390 and 385 of this chapter apply to this subpart, except where otherwise specifically noted.

(b) As used in this part,

Hazardous material has the same meaning as under § 171.8 of this title: A substance or material that the Secretary of Transportation has determined is capable of posing an unreason-able risk to health, safety, and property when transported in commerce, and has designated as hazardous under Sec. 5103 of Federal hazardous materials transportation law (49 U.S.C. 5103). The term includes hazardous substances, hazardous wastes, marine pollutants, elevated temperature materials, materials designated as hazardous in the Hazardous Materials Table (see § 172.101 of this title), and materials that meet the defining criteria for hazard classes and divisions in part 173 of this title.

Hazmat employee has the same meaning as under § 171.8 of this title: A person who is employed by a hazmat employer as defined under § 171.8 of this title, and who in the course of employment directly affects hazardous materials transportation safety. This term includes an owner-operator of a motor vehicle that transports hazardous materials in commerce. This term includes an individual who, during the course of employment:

(1) Loads, unloads, or handles hazardous materials;

(2) Manufactures, tests, reconditions, repairs, modifies, marks, or otherwise represents containers, drums, or packaging as qualified for use in the transportation of hazardous materials;

(3) Prepares hazardous materials for transportation;

(4) Is responsible for the safe transportation of hazardous materials; or

(5) Operates a vehicle used to transport hazardous materials.

Liquefied natural gas (LNG) means a Division 2.1 liquefied natural gas material that is transported in a liquid state with a methane content of 85 percent or more.

Safety permit means a document issued by FMCSA that contains a permit number and confers authority to transport in commerce the hazardous materials listed in § 385.403.

Shipment means the offering or loading of hazardous materials at one loading facility using one transport vehicle, or the transport of that transport vehicle.

§ 385.403 Who must hold a safety permit?

After the date following January 1, 2005, that a motor carrier is required to

258

file a Motor Carrier Identification Report Form (MCS–150) according to the schedule set forth in §390.19(a) of this chapter, the motor carrier may not transport in interstate or intrastate commerce any of the following hazardous materials, in the quantity indicated for each, unless the motor carrier holds a safety permit:

(a) A highway route-controlled quantity of a Class 7 (radioactive) material, as defined in §173.403 of this title;

(b) More than 25 kg (55 pounds) of a Division 1.1, 1.2, or 1.3 (explosive) material or an amount of a Division 1.5 (explosive) material requiring placarding under part 172 of this title;

(c) More than one liter (1.08 quarts) per package of a "material poisonous by inhalation," as defined in §171.8 of this title, that meets the criteria for "hazard zone A," as specified in §173.116(a) or §173.133(a) of this title;

(d) A "material poisonous by inhalation," as defined in §171.8 of this title, that meets the criteria for "hazard zone B," as specified in §173.116(a) or §173.133(a) of this title in a bulk packaging (capacity greater than 450 L [119 gallons]);

(e) A "material poisonous by inhalation," as defined in §171.8 of this title, that meets the criteria for "hazard zone C," or "hazard zone D," as specified in §173.116(a) of this title, in a packaging having a capacity equal to or greater than 13,248 L (3,500) gallons; or

(f) A shipment of compressed or refrigerated liquefied methane or liquefied natural gas, or other liquefied gas with a methane content of at least 85 percent, in a bulk packaging having a capacity equal to or greater than 13,248 L (3,500 gallons).

§385.405 How does a motor carrier apply for a safety permit?

(a) *Application form(s).* (1) To apply for a new safety permit or renewal of the safety permit, a motor carrier must complete and submit Form MCS–150B, Combined Motor Carrier Identification Report and HM Permit Application.

(2) The Form MCS-150B will also satisfy the requirements for obtaining and renewing a USDOT Number; there is no need to complete Form MCS-150, Motor Carrier Identification Report.

(b) *Where to get forms and instructions.* The forms listed in paragraph (a) of this section, and instructions for completing the forms, may be obtained on the Internet at *http:// www.fmcsa.dot.gov*, or by contacting FMCSA at Federal Motor Carrier Safety Administration, Office of Information Technology (MC–RI), 1200 New Jersey Ave., SE., Washington, DC 20590–0001, Telephone: 1-800-832-5660.

(c) *Signature and certification.* An official of the motor carrier must sign and certify that the information is correct on each form the motor carrier submits.

(d) *Updating information on Form MCS–150B.* A motor carrier holding a safety permit must report to FMCSA any change in the information on its Form MCS–150B within 30 days of the change. The motor carrier must use Form MCS–150B to report the new information (contact information in paragraph (b) of this section).

[69 FR 39367, June 30, 2004, as amended at 72 FR 55701, Oct. 1, 2007; 73 FR 76491, Dec. 16, 2008]

§385.407 What conditions must a motor carrier satisfy for FMCSA to issue a safety permit?

(a) *Motor carrier safety performance.* (1) The motor carrier:

(i) Must be in compliance with any remedial directive issued under subpart J of this part, and

(ii) Must have a "Satisfactory" safety rating assigned by either FMCSA, under the Safety Fitness Procedures of this part, or the State in which the motor carrier has its principal place of business, if the State has adopted and implemented safety fitness procedures that are equivalent to the procedures in subpart A of this part.

(2) FMCSA will not issue a safety permit to a motor carrier that:

(i) Does not certify that it has a satisfactory security program as required in §385.407(b);

(ii) Has a crash rate in the top 30 percent of the national average as indicated in FMCSA Motor Carrier Management Information System (MCMIS); or

(iii) Has a driver, vehicle, hazardous materials, or total out-of-service rate in the top 30 percent of the national average as indicated in the MCMIS.

(b) *Satisfactory security program.* The motor carrier must certify that it has a satisfactory security program, including:

(1) A security plan meeting the requirements of part 172, subpart I of this title, and addressing how the carrier will ensure the security of the written route plan required by this part;

(2) A communications plan that allows for contact between the commercial motor vehicle operator and the motor carrier to meet the periodic contact requirements in § 385.415(c)(1); and

(3) Successful completion by all hazmat employees of the security training required in § 172.704(a)(4) and (a)(5) of this title.

(c) *Registration with the Research and Special Programs Administration (RSPA).* The motor carrier must be registered with RSPA in accordance with part 107, subpart G of this title.

[69 FR 39367, June 30, 2004, as amended at 75 FR 17241, Apr. 5, 2010]

§ 385.409 When may a temporary safety permit be issued to a motor carrier?

(a) *Temporary safety permit.* If a motor carrier does not meet the criteria in § 385.407(a), FMCSA may issue it a temporary safety permit. To obtain a temporary safety permit a motor carrier must certify on Form MCS–150B that it is operating in full compliance with the HMRs; with the FMCSRs, and/or comparable State regulations, whichever is applicable; and with the minimum financial responsibility requirements in part 387 of this chapter or in State regulations, whichever is applicable.

(b) FMCSA will not issue a temporary safety permit to a motor carrier that:

(1) Does not certify that it has a satisfactory security program as required in § 385.407(b);

(2) Has a crash rate in the top 30 percent of the national average as indicated in the FMCSA's MCMIS; or

(3) Has a driver, vehicle, hazardous materials, or total out-of-service rate in the top 30 percent of the national average as indicated in the MCMIS.

(c) A temporary safety permit shall be valid for 180 days after the date of issuance or until the motor carrier is assigned a new safety rating, whichever occurs first.

(1) A motor carrier that receives a Satisfactory safety rating will be issued a safety permit (see § 385.421).

(2) A motor carrier that receives a less than Satisfactory safety rating is ineligible for a safety permit and will be subject to revocation of its temporary safety permit.

(d) If a motor carrier has not received a safety rating within the 180-day time period, FMCSA will extend the effective date of the temporary safety permit for an additional 60 days, provided the motor carrier demonstrates that it is continuing to operate in full compliance with the FMCSRs and HMRs.

§ 385.411 Must a motor carrier obtain a safety permit if it has a State permit?

Yes. However, if FMCSA is able to verify that a motor carrier has a safety permit issued by a State under a program that FMCSA has determined to be equivalent to the provisions of this subpart, FMCSA will immediately issue a safety permit to the motor carrier upon receipt of an application in accordance with § 385.405, without further inspection or investigation.

§ 385.413 What happens if a motor carrier receives a proposed safety rating that is less than Satisfactory?

(a) If a motor carrier does not already have a safety permit, it will not be issued a safety permit (including a temporary safety permit) unless and until a Satisfactory safety rating is issued to the motor carrier.

(b) If a motor carrier holds a safety permit (including a temporary safety permit), the safety permit will be subject to revocation or suspension (see § 385.421).

§ 385.415 What operational requirements apply to the transportation of a hazardous material for which a permit is required?

(a) *Information that must be carried in the vehicle.* During transportation, the following must be maintained in each commercial motor vehicle that transports a hazardous material listed in §385.403 and must be made available to an authorized official of a Federal, State, or local government agency upon request.

(1) A copy of the safety permit or another document showing the permit number, provided that document clearly indicates the number is the FMCSA Safety Permit number;

(2) A written route plan that meets the requirements of §397.101 of this chapter for highway route-controlled Class 7 (radioactive) materials or §397.67 of this chapter for Division 1.1, 1.2, and 1.3 (explosive) materials; and

(3) The telephone number, including area code or country code, of an employee of the motor carrier or representative of the motor carrier who is familiar with the routing of the permitted material. The motor carrier employee or representative must be able to verify that the shipment is within the general area for the expected route for the permitted material. The telephone number, when called, must be answered directly by the motor carrier or its representative at all times while the permitted material is in transportation including storage incidental to transportation. Answering machines are not sufficient to meet this requirement.

(b)(1) *Inspection of vehicle transporting Class 7 (radioactive) materials.* Before a motor carrier may transport a highway route controlled quantity of a Class 7 (radioactive) material, the motor carrier must have a pre-trip inspection performed on each motor vehicle to be used to transport a highway route controlled quantity of a Class 7 (radioactive) material, in accordance with the requirements of the "North American Standard Out-of-Service Criteria and Level VI Inspection Procedures and Out-of-Service Criteria for Commercial Highway Vehicles Transporting Transuranics and Highway Route Controlled Quantities of Radioactive Materials as defined in 49 CFR Part 173.403," January 1, 2004, which is incorporated by reference. The Director of the Federal Register has approved the materials incorporated by reference in accordance with 5 U.S.C. 552(a) and 1 CFR part 51. Information

and copies may be obtained from the Commercial Vehicle Safety Alliance, 1101 17th Street, NW, Suite 803, Washington, DC 20036. Phone number (202) 775–1623.

(2) All materials incorporated by reference are available for inspection at the Federal Motor Carrier Safety Administration, Office of Enforcement and Compliance (MC–EC), 1200 New Jersey Ave., SE., Washington, DC 20590–0001; and the National Archives and Records Administration (NARA). For information on the availability of this material at NARA, call (202) 741–6030, or go to: *http://www.archives.gov/ federal_register/ code_of_federal_regulations/ ibr_locations.html.*

(c) *Additional requirements.* A motor carrier transporting hazardous materials requiring a permit under this part must also meet the following requirements:

(1) The operator of a motor vehicle used to transport a hazardous material listed in §385.403 must follow the communications plan required in §385.407(b)(2) to make contact with the carrier at the beginning and end of each duty tour, and at the pickup and delivery of each permitted load. Contact may be by telephone, radio or via an electronic tracking or monitoring system. The motor carrier or driver must maintain a record of communications for 6 months after the initial acceptance of a shipment of hazardous material for which a safety permit is required. The record of communications must contain the name of the driver, identification of the vehicle, permitted material(s) being transported, and the date, location, and time of each contact required under this section.

(2) The motor carrier should contact the Transportation Security Administration's Transportation Security Coordination Center (703–563–3236 or 703–563–3237) at any time the motor carrier suspects its shipment of a hazardous material listed in §385.403 is lost, stolen or otherwise unaccounted for.

[69 FR 39367, June 30, 2004, as amended at 72 FR 55701, Oct. 1, 2007]

§ 385.417 Is a motor carrier's safety permit number available to others?

Upon request, a motor carrier must provide the number of its safety permit to a person who offers a hazardous material listed in § 385.403 for transportation in commerce. A motor carrier's permit number will also be available to the public on the FMCSA Safety and Fitness Electronic Records System at *http://www.safersys.org.*

§ 385.419 How long is a safety permit effective?

Unless suspended or revoked, a safety permit (other than a temporary safety permit) is effective for two years, except that:

(a) A safety permit will be subject to revocation if a motor carrier fails to submit a renewal application (Form MCS–150B) in accordance with the schedule set forth for filing Form MCS–150 in § 390.19(a) of this chapter; and

(b) An existing safety permit will remain in effect pending FMCSA's processing of an application for renewal if a motor carrier submits the required application (Form MS–150B) in accordance with the schedule set forth in § 390.19(a)(2) and (a)(3) of this chapter.

§ 385.421 Under what circumstances will a safety permit be subject to revocation or suspension by FMCSA?

(a) *Grounds.* A safety permit will be subject to revocation or suspension by FMCSA for the following reasons:

(1) A motor carrier fails to submit a renewal application (Form MCS–150B) in accordance with the schedule set forth in § 390.19(a)(2) and (a)(3) of this chapter;

(2) A motor carrier provides any false or misleading information on its application (Form MCS–150B) or as part of updated information it is providing on Form MCS–150B (see § 385.405(d)).

(3) A motor carrier is issued a final safety rating that is less than Satisfactory;

(4) A motor carrier fails to maintain a satisfactory security plan as set forth in § 385.407(b);

(5) A motor carrier fails to comply with applicable requirements in the FMCSRs, the HMRs, or compatible State requirements governing the transportation of hazardous materials, in a manner showing that the motor carrier is not fit to transport the hazardous materials listed in § 385.403;

(6) A motor carrier fails to comply with an out-of-service order;

(7) A motor carrier fails to comply with any other order issued under the FMCSRs, the HMRs, or compatible State requirements governing the transportation of hazardous materials, in a manner showing that the motor carrier is not fit to transport the hazardous materials listed in § 385.403;

(8) A motor carrier fails to maintain the minimum financial responsibility required by § 387.9 of this chapter or an applicable State requirement;

(9) A motor carrier fails to maintain current hazardous materials registration with the Research and Special Programs Administration; or

(10) A motor carrier loses its operating rights or has its registration suspended in accordance with § 386.83 or § 386.84 of this chapter for failure to pay a civil penalty or abide by a payment plan.

(b) *Determining whether a safety permit is revoked or suspended.* A motor carrier's safety permit will be suspended the first time any of the conditions specified in paragraph (a) of this section are found to apply to the motor carrier. A motor carrier's safety permit will be revoked if any of the conditions specified in paragraph (a) of this section are found to apply to the motor carrier and the carrier's safety permit has been suspended in the past for any of the reasons specified in paragraph (a) of this section.

(c) *Effective date of suspension or revocation.* A suspension or revocation of a safety permit is effective:

(1) Immediately after FMCSA determines that an imminent hazard exists, after FMCSA issues a final safety rating that is less than Satisfactory, or after a motor carrier loses its operating rights or has its registration suspended for failure to pay a civil penalty or abide by a payment plan;

(2) Thirty (30) days after service of a written notification that FMCSA proposes to suspend or revoke a safety permit, if the motor carrier does not submit a written request for administrative review within that time period; or

(3) As specified in § 385.423(c), when the motor carrier submits a written request for administrative review of FMCSA's proposal to suspend or revoke a safety permit.

(4) A motor carrier whose safety permit has been revoked will not be issued a replacement safety permit or temporary safety permit for 365 days from the time of revocation.

§ 385.423 Does a motor carrier have a right to an administrative review of a denial, suspension, or revocation of a safety permit?

A motor carrier has a right to an administrative review pursuant to the following procedures and conditions:

(a) *Less than Satisfactory safety rating.* If a motor carrier is issued a proposed safety rating that is less than Satisfactory, it has the right to request (1) an administrative review of a proposed safety rating, as set forth in § 385.15, and (2) a change to a proposed safety rating based on corrective action, as set forth in § 385.17. After a motor carrier has had an opportunity for administrative review of, or change to, a proposed safety rating, FMCSA's issuance of a final safety rating constitutes final agency action, and a motor carrier has no right to further administrative review of FMCSA's denial, suspension, or revocation of a safety permit when the motor carrier has been issued a final safety rating that is less than Satisfactory.

(b) *Failure to pay civil penalty or abide by payment plan.* If a motor carrier is notified that failure to pay a civil penalty will result in suspension or termination of its operating rights, it has the right to an administrative review of that proposed action in a show cause proceeding, as set forth in § 386.83(b) or § 386.84(b) of this chapter. The decision by FMCSA's Chief Safety Officer in the show cause proceeding constitutes final agency action, and a motor carrier has no right to further administrative review of FMCSA's denial, suspension, or revocation of a safety permit when the motor carrier has lost its operating rights or had its registration suspended for failure to pay a civil penalty or abide by a payment plan.

(c) *Other grounds.* Under circumstances other than those set forth in paragraphs (a) and (b) of this section, a motor carrier may submit a written request for administrative review within 30 days after service of a written notification that FMCSA has denied a safety permit, that FMCSA has immediately suspended or revoked a safety permit, or that FMCSA has proposed to suspend or revoke a safety permit. The rules for computing time limits for service and requests for extension of time in §§ 386.5, 386.6, and 386.8 of this chapter apply to the proceedings on a request for administrative review under this section.

(1) The motor carrier must send or deliver its written request for administrative review to FMCSA Chief Safety Officer, with a copy to FMCSA Chief Counsel, at the following addresses:

(i) Chief Safety Officer, Federal Motor Carrier Safety Administration, 1200 New Jersey Ave., SE., Washington, DC 20590–0001 Attention: Adjudications Counsel (MC–CC).

(ii) Chief Counsel (MC–CC), Federal Motor Carrier Safety Administration, 1200 New Jersey Ave., SE., Washington, DC 20590–0001.

(2) A request for administrative review must state the specific grounds for review and include all information, evidence, and arguments upon which the motor carrier relies to support its request for administrative review.

(3) Within 30 days after service of a written request for administrative review, the Office of the Chief Counsel shall submit to the Chief Safety Officer a written response to the request for administrative review. The Office of the Chief Counsel must serve a copy of its written response on the motor carrier requesting administrative review.

(4) The Chief Safety Officer may decide a motor carrier's request for administrative review on the written submissions, hold a hearing personally, or refer the request to an administrative law judge for a hearing and recommended decision. The Chief Safety Officer or administrative law judge is authorized to specify, and must notify the parties of, specific procedural rules to be followed in the proceeding (which may include the procedural rules in part 386 of this chapter that are considered appropriate).

263

(5) If a request for administrative review is referred to an administrative law judge, the recommended decision of the administrative law judge becomes the final decision of the Chief Safety Officer 45 days after service of the recommended decision is served, unless either the motor carrier or the Office of the Chief Counsel submits a petition for review to the Chief Safety Officer (and serves a copy of its petition on the other party) within 15 days after service of the recommended decision. In response to a petition for review of a recommended decision of an administrative law judge:

(i) The other party may submit a written reply within 15 days of service of the petition for review.

(ii) The Chief Safety Officer may adopt, modify, or set aside the recommended decision of an administrative law judge, and may also remand the petition for review to the administrative law judge for further proceedings.

(6) The Chief Safety Officer will issue a final decision on any request for administrative review when:

(i) The request for administrative review has not been referred to an administrative law judge;

(ii) A petition for review of a recommended decision by an administrative law judge has not been remanded to the administrative law judge for further proceedings; or

(iii) An administrative law judge has held further proceedings on a petition for review and issued a supplementary recommended decision.

(7) The decision of the Chief Safety Officer (including a recommended decision of an administrative law judge that becomes the decision of the Chief Safety Officer under paragraph (c)(5) of this section) constitutes final agency action, and there is no right to further administrative reconsideration or review.

(8) Any appeal of a final agency action under this section must be taken to an appropriate United States Court of Appeals. Unless the Court of Appeals issues a stay pending appeal, the final agency action shall not be suspended while the appeal is pending.

[69 FR 39367, June 30, 2004, as amended at 72 FR 55701, Oct. 1, 2007]

Subpart F—Intermodal Equipment Providers

SOURCE: 73 FR 76819, Dec. 17, 2008, unless otherwise noted.

§ 385.501   Roadability review.

(a) FMCSA will perform roadability reviews of intermodal equipment providers, as defined in § 390.5 of this chapter.

(b) FMCSA will evaluate the results of the roadability review using the criteria in appendix A to this part as they relate to compliance with parts 390, 393, and 396 of this chapter.

§ 385.503   Results of roadability review.

(a) FMCSA will not assign a safety rating to an intermodal equipment provider based on the results of a roadability review. However, FMCSA may cite the intermodal equipment provider for violations of parts 390, 393, and 396 of this chapter and may impose civil penalties resulting from the roadability review.

(b) FMCSA may prohibit the intermodal equipment provider from tendering specific items of intermodal equipment determined to constitute an "imminent hazard" (See § 386.72(b)(1) of this chapter).

(c) FMCSA may prohibit an intermodal equipment provider from tendering any intermodal equipment from a particular location or multiple locations if the agency determines the intermodal equipment provider's failure to comply with the FMCSRs constitutes an imminent hazard under § 386.72(b)(1).

Subpart G [Reserved]

Subpart H—Special Rules for New Entrant Non-North America-Domiciled Carriers

SOURCE: 73 FR 76491, Dec. 16, 2008, unless otherwise noted.

§ 385.601   Scope of rules.

The rules in this subpart govern the application by a non-North America-domiciled motor carrier to provide transportation of property and passengers in interstate commerce in the United States.

§385.603 Application.

(a) Each applicant applying under this subpart must submit an application that consists of:

(1) Form OP–1(NNA)—Application for U.S. Department of Transportation (USDOT) Registration by Non-North America-Domiciled Motor Carriers;

(2) Form MCS–150—Motor Carrier Identification Report; and

(3) A notification of the means used to designate process agents, either by submission in the application package of Form BOC–3—Designation of Agents—Motor Carriers, Brokers and Freight Forwarders or a letter stating that the applicant will use a process agent service that will submit the Form BOC–3 electronically.

(b) FMCSA will only process an application if it meets the following conditions:

(1) The application must be completed in English;

(2) The information supplied must be accurate, complete, and include all required supporting documents and applicable certifications in accordance with the instructions to Form OP–1(NNA), Form MCS–150 and Form BOC–3;

(3) The application must include the filing fee payable to the FMCSA in the amount set forth at 49 CFR 360.3(f)(1); and

(4) The application must be signed by the applicant.

(c) An applicant must submit the application to the address provided in Form OP–1(NNA).

(d) An applicant may obtain the application forms from any FMCSA Division Office or download them from the FMCSA Web site at: *http://www.fmcsa.dot.gov/forms/forms.htm.*

§385.605 New entrant registration driver's license and drug and alcohol testing requirements.

(a) A non-North America-domiciled motor carrier must use only drivers who possess a valid commercial driver's license—a CDL, Canadian Commercial Driver's License, or Mexican Licencia de Federal de Conductor—to operate its vehicles in the United States.

(b) A non-North America-domiciled motor carrier must subject each of the drivers described in paragraph (a) of this section to drug and alcohol testing as prescribed under part 382 of this subchapter.

§385.607 FMCSA action on the application.

(a) FMCSA will review and act on each application submitted under this subpart in accordance with the procedures set out in this part.

(b) FMCSA will validate the accuracy of information and certifications provided in the application by checking, to the extent available, data maintained in databases of the governments of the country where the carrier's principal place of business is located and the United States.

(c) *Pre-authorization safety audit.* Every non-North America-domiciled motor carrier that applies under this part must satisfactorily complete an FMCSA-administered safety audit before FMCSA will grant new entrant registration to operate in the United States. The safety audit is a review by FMCSA of the carrier's written procedures and records to validate the accuracy of information and certifications provided in the application and determine whether the carrier has established or exercises the basic safety management controls necessary to ensure safe operations. FMCSA will evaluate the results of the safety audit using the criteria in the Appendix to this subpart.

(d) An application of a non-North America-domiciled motor carrier requesting for-hire operating authority under part 365 of this subchapter may be protested under §365.109(b). Such a carrier will be granted new entrant registration after successful completion of the pre-authorization safety audit and the expiration of the protest period, provided the application is not protested. If a protest to the application is filed with FMCSA, new entrant registration will be granted only if FMCSA denies or rejects the protest.

(e) If FMCSA grants new entrant registration to the applicant, it will assign a distinctive USDOT Number that identifies the motor carrier as authorized to operate in the United States. In order to initiate operations in the United States, a non-North America-domiciled motor carrier with new entrant registration must:

(1) Have its surety or insurance provider file proof of financial responsibility in the form of certificates of insurance, surety bonds, and endorsements, as required by § 387.7(e)(2), § 387.31(e)(2), and § 387.301 of this subchapter, as applicable; and

(2) File a hard copy of, or have its process agent(s) electronically submit, Form BOC–3—Designation of Agents—Motor Carriers, Brokers and Freight Forwarders, as required by part 366 of this subchapter.

(f) A non-North America-domiciled motor carrier must comply with all provisions of the safety monitoring system in part 385, subpart I of this subchapter, including successfully passing North American Standard commercial motor vehicle inspections at least every 90 days and having safety decals affixed to each commercial motor vehicle operated in the United States as required by § 385.703(c) of this subchapter.

(g) FMCSA may not re-designate a non-North America-domiciled carrier's registration from new entrant to permanent prior to 18 months after the date its USDOT Number is issued and subject to successful completion of the safety monitoring system for non-North America-domiciled carriers set out in part 385, subpart I of this subchapter. Successful completion includes obtaining a Satisfactory safety rating as the result of a compliance review.

§ 385.609 Requirement to notify FMCSA of change in applicant information.

(a)(1) A motor carrier subject to this subpart must notify FMCSA of any changes or corrections to the information the Form BOC–3—Designation of Agents—Motor Carriers, Brokers and Freight Forwarders that occur during the application process or after having been granted new entrant registration.

(2) A motor carrier subject to this subpart must notify FMCSA of any changes or corrections to the information in Section I, IA or II of Form OP–1(NNA)—Application for U.S. Department of Transportation (USDOT) Registration by Non-North America-Domiciled Motor Carriers that occurs during the application process or after having been granted new entrant registration.

(3) A motor carrier must notify FMCSA in writing within 45 days of the change or correction to information under paragraphs (a)(1) or (a)(2) of this section.

(b) If a motor carrier fails to comply with paragraph (a) of this section, FMCSA may suspend or revoke its new entrant registration until it meets those requirements.

APPENDIX TO SUBPART H OF PART 385—EXPLANATION OF PRE-AUTHORIZATION SAFETY AUDIT EVALUATION CRITERIA FOR NON-NORTH AMERICA-DOMICILED MOTOR CARRIERS

I. GENERAL

(a) FMCSA will perform a safety audit of each non-North America-domiciled motor carrier before granting the carrier new entrant registration to operate within the United States.

(b) FMCSA will conduct the safety audit at a location specified by the FMCSA. All records and documents must be made available for examination within 48 hours after a request is made. Saturdays, Sundays, and Federal holidays are excluded from the computation of the 48-hour period.

(c) The safety audit will include:

(1) Verification of available performance data and safety management programs;

(2) Verification of a controlled substances and alcohol testing program consistent with part 40 of this title;

(3) Verification of the carrier's system of compliance with hours-of-service rules in part 395 of this subchapter, including recordkeeping and retention;

(4) Verification of proof of financial responsibility;

(5) Review of available data concerning the carrier's safety history, and other information necessary to determine the carrier's preparedness to comply with the Federal Motor Carrier Safety Regulations, parts 382 through 399 of this subchapter, and the Federal Hazardous Material Regulations, parts 171 through 180 of this title;

(6) Inspection of available commercial motor vehicles to be used under new entrant registration, if any of these vehicles have not received a decal required by § 385.703(c) of this subchapter;

(7) Evaluation of the carrier's safety inspection, maintenance, and repair facilities

or management systems, including verification of records of periodic vehicle inspections;

(8) Verification of drivers' qualifications, including confirmation of the validity of the CDL, Canadian Commercial Driver's License, or Mexican Licencia de Federal de Conductor, as applicable, of each driver the carrier intends to assign to operate under its new entrant registration; and

(9) An interview of carrier officials to review safety management controls and evaluate any written safety oversight policies and practices.

(d) To successfully complete the safety audit, a non-North America-domiciled motor carrier must demonstrate to FMCSA that it has the required elements in paragraphs I (c)(2), (3), (4), (7), and (8) of this appendix and other basic safety management controls in place which function adequately to ensure minimum acceptable compliance with the applicable safety requirements. FMCSA developed "safety audit evaluation criteria," which uses data from the safety audit and roadside inspections to determine that each applicant for new entrant registration has basic safety management controls in place.

(e) The safety audit evaluation process developed by FMCSA is used to:

(1) Evaluate basic safety management controls and determine if each non-North America-domiciled carrier and each driver is able to operate safely in the United States; and

(2) Identify motor carriers and drivers who are having safety problems and need improvement in their compliance with the FMCSRs and the HMRs, before FMCSA issues new entrant registration to operate within the United States.

II. Source of the Data for the Safety Audit Evaluation Criteria

(a) The FMCSA's evaluation criteria are built upon the operational tool known as the safety audit. FMCSA developed this tool to assist auditors, inspectors, and investigators in assessing the adequacy of a non-North America-domiciled carrier's basic safety management controls.

(b) The safety audit is a review of a non-North America-domiciled motor carrier's operation and is used to:

(1) Determine if a carrier has the basic safety management controls required by 49 U.S.C. 31144; and

(2) In the event that a carrier is found not to be in compliance with applicable FMCSRs and HMRs, educate the carrier on how to comply with U.S. safety rules.

(c) Documents such as those contained in driver qualification files, records of duty status, vehicle maintenance records, drug and alcohol testing records, and other records are reviewed for compliance with the FMCSRs and HMRs. Violations are cited on the safety audit. Performance-based information, when available, is utilized to evaluate the carrier's compliance with the vehicle regulations. Recordable accident information is also collected.

III. Overall Determination of the Carrier's Basic Safety Management Controls

(a) The carrier will not receive new entrant registration if FMCSA cannot:

(1) Verify a controlled substances and alcohol testing program consistent with part 40 of this title;

(2) Verify a system of compliance with the hours-of-service rules of this subchapter, including recordkeeping and retention;

(3) Verify proof of financial responsibility;

(4) Verify records of periodic vehicle inspections; and

(5) Verify the qualifications of each driver the carrier intends to assign to operate commercial motor vehicles in the United States, as required by parts 383 and 391 of this subchapter, including confirming the validity of each driver's CDL, Canadian Commercial Driver's License, or Mexican Licencia de Federal de Conductor, as appropriate.

(b) If FMCSA confirms each item under paragraphs III (a)(1) through (5) of this appendix, the carrier will receive new entrant registration, unless FMCSA finds the carrier has inadequate basic safety management controls in at least three separate factors described in part IV of this appendix. If FMCSA makes such a determination, the carrier's application for new entrant registration will be denied.

IV. Evaluation of Regulatory Compliance

(a) During the safety audit, FMCSA gathers information by reviewing a motor carrier's compliance with "acute" and "critical" regulations of the FMCSRs and HMRs.

(b) Acute regulations are those where noncompliance is so severe as to require immediate corrective actions by a motor carrier regardless of the overall basic safety management controls of the motor carrier.

(c) Critical regulations are those where noncompliance relates to management and/or operational controls. These are indicative of breakdowns in a carrier's management controls.

(d) The list of the acute and critical regulations, which are used in determining if a carrier has basic safety management controls in place, is included in Appendix B, VII, List of Acute and Critical Regulations to part 385 of this subchapter.

(e) Noncompliance with acute and critical regulations are indicators of inadequate safety management controls and usually higher than average accident rates.

(f) Parts of the FMCSRs and the HMRs having similar characteristics are combined together into six regulatory areas called "factors." The regulatory factors, evaluated on the adequacy of the carrier's safety management controls, are:

(1) Factor 1—General: Parts 387 and 390;

(2) Factor 2—Driver: Parts 382, 383, and 391;

(3) Factor 3—Operational: Parts 392 and 395;

(4) Factor 4—Vehicle; Parts 393, 396 and inspection data for the last 12 months;

(5) Factor 5—Hazardous Materials: Parts 171, 177, 180 and 397; and

(6) Factor 6—Accident: Recordable Accident Rate per Million Miles.

(g) For each instance of noncompliance with an acute regulation, 1.5 points will be assessed.

(h) For each instance of noncompliance with a critical regulation, 1 point will be assessed.

(i) Vehicle Factor. (1) When at least three vehicle inspections are recorded in the Motor Carrier Management Information System (MCMIS) during the twelve months before the safety audit or performed at the time of the review, the Vehicle Factor (part 396) will be evaluated on the basis of the Out-of-Service (OOS) rates and noncompliance with acute and critical regulations. The results of the review of the OOS rate will affect the Vehicle Factor as follows:

(i) If the motor carrier has had at least three roadside inspections in the twelve months before the safety audit, and the vehicle OOS rate is 34 percent or higher, one point will be assessed against the carrier. That point will be added to any other points assessed for discovered noncompliance with acute and critical regulations of part 396 of this chapter to determine the carrier's level of safety management control for that factor.

(ii) If the motor carrier's vehicle OOS rate is less than 34 percent, or if there are less than three inspections, the determination of the carrier's level of safety management controls will only be based on discovered noncompliance with the acute and critical regulations of part 396 of this chapter.

(2) Roadside inspection information is retained in the MCMIS and is integral to evaluating a motor carrier's ability to successfully maintain its vehicles, thus preventing being placed OOS during a roadside inspection. Each safety audit will continue to have the requirements of part 396 of this chapter, Inspection, Repair, and Maintenance, reviewed as indicated by the above explanation.

(j) Accident Factor. (1) In addition to the five regulatory factors, a sixth factor is included in the process to address the accident history of the motor carrier. This factor is the recordable accident rate, which the carrier has experienced during the past 12 months. Recordable accident, as defined in 49 CFR 390.5, means an accident involving a commercial motor vehicle operating on a public road in interstate or intrastate commerce which results in a fatality; a bodily injury to a person who, as a result of the injury, immediately receives medical treatment away from the scene of the accident; or one or more motor vehicles incurring disabling damage as a result of the accident requiring the motor vehicle to be transported away from the scene by a tow truck or other motor vehicle.

(2) [Reserved]

(3) The recordable accident rate will be used in determining the carrier's basic safety management controls in Factor 6, Accident. It will be used only when a carrier incurs two or more recordable accidents within the 12 months before the safety audit. An urban carrier (a carrier operating entirely within a radius of 100 air miles) with a recordable rate per million miles greater than 1.7 will be deemed to have inadequate basic safety management controls for the accident factor. All other carriers with a recordable accident rate per million miles greater than 1.5 will be deemed to have inadequate basic safety management controls for the accident factor. The rates are the result of roughly doubling the United States national average accident rate in Fiscal Years 1994, 1995, and 1996.

(4) FMCSA will continue to consider preventability when a new entrant contests the evaluation of the accident factor by presenting compelling evidence that the recordable rate is not a fair means of evaluating its accident factor. Preventability will be determined according to the following standard: "If a driver, who exercises normal judgment and foresight, could have foreseen the possibility of the accident that in fact occurred, and avoided it by taking steps within his/her control which would not have risked causing another kind of mishap, the accident was preventable."

(k) Factor Ratings. (1) The following table shows the five regulatory factors, parts of the FMCSRs and HMRs associated with each factor, and the accident factor. Each carrier's level of basic safety management controls with each factor is determined as follows:

(i) Factor 1—General: Parts 390 and 387;

(ii) Factor 2—Driver: Parts 382, 383, and 391;

(iii) Factor 3—Operational: Parts 392 and 395;

(iv) Factor 4—Vehicle: Parts 393, 396 and the Out of Service Rate;

(v) Factor 5—Hazardous Materials: Part 171, 177, 180 and 397; and

(vi) Factor 6—Accident: Recordable Accident Rate per Million Miles;

(2) For paragraphs IV (k)(1)(i) through (v) of this appendix (Factors 1 through 5), if the combined violations of acute and/or critical regulations for each factor is equal to three or more points, the carrier is determined not

Federal Motor Carrier Safety Administration, DOT   § 385.705

to have basic safety management controls for that individual factor.

(3) For paragraph IV (k)(1)(vi) of this appendix, if the recordable accident rate is greater than 1.7 recordable accidents per million miles for an urban carrier (1.5 for all other carriers), the carrier is determined to have inadequate basic safety management controls.

(l) Notwithstanding FMCSA verification of the items listed in paragraphs III (a)(1) through (5) of this appendix, if the safety audit determines the carrier has inadequate basic safety management controls in at least three separate factors described in paragraph III of this appendix, the carrier's application for new entrant registration will be denied. For example, FMCSA evaluates a carrier finding:

(1) One instance of noncompliance with a critical regulation in part 387 scoring one point for Factor 1;

(2) Two instances of noncompliance with acute regulations in part 382 scoring three points for Factor 2;

(3) Three instances of noncompliance with critical regulations in part 396 scoring three points for Factor 4; and

(4) Three instances of noncompliance with acute regulations in parts 171 and 397 scoring four and one-half (4.5) points for Factor 5.

Under this example, the carrier will not receive new entrant registration because it scored three or more points for Factors 2, 4, and 5 and FMCSA determined the carrier had inadequate basic safety management controls in at least three separate factors.

Subpart I—Safety Monitoring System for Non-North American Carriers

SOURCE: 73 FR 76494, Dec. 16, 2008, unless otherwise noted.

§ 385.701 Definitions.

The following definitions apply to this subpart:

Compliance review means a compliance review as defined in § 385.3 of this part.

New entrant registration means the provisional registration under subpart H of this part that FMCSA grants to a non-North America-domiciled motor carrier to provide interstate transportation within the United States. It will be revoked if the registrant is not assigned a Satisfactory safety rating following a compliance review conducted during the safety monitoring period established in this subpart.

Non-North America-domiciled motor carrier means a motor carrier of property or passengers whose principal place of business is located in a country other than the United States, Canada or Mexico.

§ 385.703 Safety monitoring system.

(a) *General.* Each non-North America-domiciled carrier new entrant will be subject to an oversight program to monitor its compliance with applicable Federal Motor Carrier Safety Regulations (FMCSRs), Federal Motor Vehicle Safety Standards (FMVSSs), and Hazardous Materials Regulations (HMRs).

(b) *Roadside monitoring.* Each non-North America-domiciled carrier new entrant will be subject to intensified monitoring through frequent roadside inspections.

(c) *Safety decal.* Each non-North America-domiciled carrier must have on every commercial motor vehicle it operates in the United States a current decal attesting to a satisfactory North American Standard Commercial Vehicle inspection by a certified FMCSA or State inspector pursuant to 49 CFR 350.201(k). This requirement applies during the new entrant operating period and for three years after the carrier's registration becomes permanent following removal of its new entrant designation.

(d) *Compliance review.* FMCSA will conduct a compliance review on a non-North America-domiciled carrier within 18 months after FMCSA issues the carrier a USDOT Number.

§ 385.705 Expedited action.

(a) A non-North America-domiciled motor carrier committing any of the following actions identified through roadside inspections, or by any other means, may be subjected to an expedited compliance review, or may be required to submit a written response demonstrating corrective action:

(1) Using a driver not possessing, or operating without, a valid CDL, Canadian Commercial Driver's License, or Mexican Licencia Federal de Conductor. An invalid commercial driver's license includes one that is falsified, revoked, expired, or missing a required endorsement.

269

(2) Operating a vehicle placed out of service for violations of the Federal Motor Carrier Safety Regulations without taking the necessary corrective action.

(3) Being involved in, through action or omission, a hazardous materials reportable incident, as described under 49 CFR 171.15 or 171.16, within the United States involving—

(i) A highway route controlled quantity of certain radioactive materials (Class 7).

(ii) Any quantity of certain explosives (Class 1, Division 1.1, 1.2, or 1.3).

(iii) Any quantity of certain poison inhalation hazard materials (Zone A or B).

(4) Being involved in, through action or omission, two or more hazardous materials reportable incidents, as described under 49 CFR 171.15 or 171.16, occurring within the United States and involving any hazardous material not listed in paragraph (a)(3) of this section.

(5) Using a driver who tests positive for controlled substances or alcohol or who refuses to submit to required controlled substances or alcohol tests.

(6) Operating within the United States a commercial motor vehicle without the levels of financial responsibility required under part 387 of this subchapter.

(7) Having a driver or vehicle out-of-service rate of 50 percent or more based upon at least three inspections occurring within a consecutive 90-day period.

(b) Failure to respond to an Agency demand for a written response demonstrating corrective action within 30 days will result in the suspension of the carrier's new entrant registration until the required showing of corrective action is submitted to the FMCSA.

(c) A satisfactory response to a written demand for corrective action does not excuse a carrier from the requirement that it undergo a compliance review during the new entrant registration period.

§ 385.707 The compliance review.

(a) The criteria used in a compliance review to determine whether a non-North America-domiciled new entrant exercises the necessary basic safety management controls are specified in appendix B to this part.

(b) *Satisfactory Rating.* If FMCSA assigns a non-North America-domiciled carrier a Satisfactory rating following a compliance review conducted under this subpart, FMCSA will provide the carrier written notice as soon as practicable, but not later than 45 days after the completion of the compliance review. The carrier's registration will remain in provisional status and its on-highway performance will continue to be closely monitored for the remainder of the 18-month new entrant registration period.

(c) *Conditional Rating.* If FMCSA assigns a non-North America-domiciled carrier a Conditional rating following a compliance review conducted under this subpart, it will initiate a revocation proceeding in accordance with § 385.709 of this subpart. The carrier's new entrant registration will not be suspended prior to the conclusion of the revocation proceeding.

(d) *Unsatisfactory Rating.* If FMCSA assigns a non-North America-domiciled carrier an Unsatisfactory rating following a compliance review conducted under this subpart, it will initiate a suspension and revocation proceeding in accordance with § 385.709 of this subpart.

§ 385.709 Suspension and revocation of non-North America-domiciled carrier registration.

(a) If a carrier is assigned an "Unsatisfactory" safety rating following a compliance review conducted under this subpart, FMCSA will provide the carrier written notice, as soon as practicable, that its registration will be suspended effective 15 days from the service date of the notice unless the carrier demonstrates, within 10 days of the service date of the notice, that the compliance review contains material error.

(b) For purposes of this section, material error is a mistake or series of mistakes that resulted in an erroneous safety rating.

(c) If the carrier demonstrates that the compliance review contained material error, its new entrant registration will not be suspended. If the carrier fails to show a material error in the compliance review, FMCSA will issue an Order:

(1) Suspending the carrier's new entrant registration and requiring it to immediately cease all further operations in the United States; and

(2) Notifying the carrier that its new entrant registration will be revoked unless it presents evidence of necessary corrective action within 30 days from the service date of the Order.

(d) If a carrier is assigned a "Conditional" rating following a compliance review conducted under this subpart, the provisions of paragraphs (a) through (c) of this section will apply, except that its new entrant registration will not be suspended under paragraph (c)(1) of this section.

(e) If a carrier subject to this subpart fails to provide the necessary documents for a compliance review upon reasonable request, or fails to submit evidence of the necessary corrective action as required by §385.705 of this subpart, FMCSA will provide the carrier with written notice, as soon as practicable, that its new entrant registration will be suspended 15 days from the service date of the notice unless it provides all necessary documents or information. This suspension will remain in effect until the necessary documents or information is produced and:

(1) The carrier is rated Satisfactory after a compliance review; or

(2) FMCSA determines, following review of the carrier's response to a demand for corrective action under §385.705, that the carrier has taken the necessary corrective action.

(f) If a carrier commits any of the actions specified in §385.705(a) of this subpart after the removal of a suspension issued under this section, the suspension will be automatically reinstated. FMCSA will issue an Order requiring the carrier to cease further operations in the United States and demonstrate, within 15 days from the service date of the Order, that it did not commit the alleged action(s). If the carrier fails to demonstrate that it did not commit the action(s), FMCSA will issue an Order revoking its new entrant registration.

(g) If FMCSA receives credible evidence that a carrier has operated in violation of a suspension order issued under this section, it will issue an Order requiring the carrier to show cause, within 10 days of the service date of the Order, why its new entrant registration should not be revoked. If the carrier fails to make the necessary showing, FMCSA will revoke its registration.

(h) If a non-North America-domiciled motor carrier operates a commercial motor vehicle in violation of a suspension or out-of-service order, it is subject to the penalty provisions in 49 U.S.C. 521(b)(2)(A), as adjusted by inflation, not to exceed amounts for each offense under part 386, Appendix B of this subchapter.

(i) Notwithstanding any provision of this subpart, a carrier subject to this subpart is also subject to the suspension and revocation provisions of 49 U.S.C. 13905 for repeated violations of DOT regulations governing its motor carrier operations.

§385.711 Administrative review.

(a) A non-North America-domiciled motor carrier may request FMCSA to conduct an administrative review if it believes FMCSA has committed an error in assigning a safety rating or suspending or revoking the carrier's new entrant registration under this subpart.

(b) The carrier must submit its request in writing, in English, to the Associate Administrator for Enforcement and Program Delivery, Federal Motor Carrier Safety Administration, 1200 New Jersey Avenue, SE., Washington DC 20590.

(c) The carrier's request must explain the error it believes FMCSA committed in assigning the safety rating or suspending or revoking the carrier's new entrant registration and include any information or documents that support its argument.

(d) FMCSA will complete its administrative review no later than 10 days after the carrier submits its request for review. The Associate Administrator's decision will constitute the final Agency action.

§ 385.713 Reapplying for new entrant registration.

(a) A non-North America-domiciled motor carrier whose provisional new entrant registration has been revoked may reapply for new entrant registration no sooner than 30 days after the date of revocation.

(b) If the provisional new entrant registration was revoked because the new entrant failed to receive a Satisfactory rating after undergoing a compliance review, the new entrant must do all of the following:

(1) Submit an updated MCS–150.

(2) Submit evidence that it has corrected the deficiencies that resulted in revocation of its registration and will otherwise ensure that it will have basic safety management controls in effect.

(3) Successfully complete a pre-authorization safety audit in accordance with § 385.607(c) of this part.

(4) Begin the 18-month new entrant monitoring cycle again as of the date the re-filed application is approved.

(c) If the provisional new entrant registration was revoked because FMCSA found that the new entrant had failed to submit to a compliance review, it must do all of the following:

(1) Submit an updated MCS–150.

(2) Successfully complete a pre-authorization safety audit in accordance with § 385.607(c) of this Part.

(3) Begin the 18-month new entrant monitoring cycle again as of the date the re-filed application is approved.

(4) Submit to a compliance review upon request.

(d) If the new entrant is a for-hire carrier subject to the registration provisions under 49 U.S.C. 13901 and also has had its operating authority revoked, it must re-apply for operating authority as set forth in part 365 of this subchapter.

§ 385.715 Duration of safety monitoring system.

(a) Each non-North America-domiciled carrier subject to this subpart will remain in the safety monitoring system for at least 18 months from the date FMCSA issues its new entrant registration, except as provided in paragraphs (c) and (d) of this section.

(b) If, at the end of this 18-month period, the carrier's most recent safety rating was Satisfactory and no additional enforcement or safety improvement actions are pending under this subpart, the non-North America-domiciled carrier's new entrant registration will become permanent.

(c) If, at the end of this 18-month period, FMCSA has not been able to conduct a compliance review, the carrier will remain in the safety monitoring system until a compliance review is conducted. If the results of the compliance review are satisfactory, the carrier's new entrant registration will become permanent.

(d) If, at the end of this 18-month period, the carrier's new entrant registration is suspended under § 385.709(a) of this subpart, the carrier will remain in the safety monitoring system until FMCSA either:

(1) Determines that the carrier has taken corrective action; or

(2) Completes measures to revoke the carrier's new entrant registration under § 385.709(c) of this subpart.

§ 385.717 Applicability of safety fitness and enforcement procedures.

At all times during which a non-North America-domiciled motor carrier is subject to the safety monitoring system in this subpart, it is also subject to the general safety fitness procedures established in subpart A of this part and to compliance and enforcement procedures applicable to all carriers regulated by the FMCSA.

Subpart J—Remedial Directives

SOURCE: 75 FR 17241, Apr. 5, 2010, unless otherwise noted.

§ 385.801 Purpose and scope.

(a) This subpart establishes procedures for FMCSA's issuance of notices of remedial directives and proposed determinations of unfitness.

(b) This subpart establishes the circumstances under which FMCSA will direct motor carriers (including owner-operators leased to motor carriers, regardless of whether the owner-operator has separate operating authority under part 365), in accordance with § 385.1(a), to install electronic on-board recorders (EOBRs) in their commercial motor vehicles as a remedy for threshold rate violations, as defined by §385.803, of the part 395 hours-of-service regulations listed in appendix C to this part.

(c) This subpart establishes the procedures by which motor carriers may challenge FMCSA's issuance of proposed determinations of unfitness and remedial directives.

(d) The provisions of this subpart apply to all motor carriers subject to the requirements of part 395 of this chapter.

§385.803 Definitions and acronyms.

(a) The definitions in subpart A of this part and part 390 of this chapter apply to this subpart, except where otherwise specifically noted.

(b) As used in this subpart, the following terms have the meaning specified:

Appendix C regulation means any of the regulations listed in appendix C to part 385 of this chapter.

Appendix C violation means a violation of any of the regulations listed in appendix C to part 385 of this chapter.

Electronic on-board recording device (EOBR) means an electronic device that is capable of recording a driver's duty hours of service and duty status accurately and automatically and that meets the requirements of §395.16 of this chapter.

Final determination for purposes of part 385, subpart J means:

(1) An adjudication under this subpart upholding a notice of remedial directive and proposed unfitness determination;

(2) The expiration of the period for filing a request for administrative review of remedial directive and proposed unfitness determination under this subpart; or

(3) The entry of a settlement agreement stipulating that the carrier is subject to mandatory EOBR installation, use, and maintenance requirements.

Motor carrier includes owner-operators leased to carriers subject to a remedial directive, regardless of whether the owner-operator has separate operating authority under part 365 of this chapter.

Proposed determination of unfitness or *proposed unfitness determination* means a determination by FMCSA that a

motor carrier will not meet the safety fitness standard under §385.5 on a specified future date unless the carrier takes the actions necessary to comply with the terms of a remedial directive issued under this subpart.

Remedial directive means a mandatory instruction from FMCSA to take one or more specified action(s) as a condition of demonstrating safety fitness under 49 U.S.C. 31144(b).

Threshold rate violation for the purposes of this subpart means a violation rate for any appendix C regulation equal to or greater than 10 percent of the number of records reviewed.

§385.805 Events triggering issuance of remedial directive and proposed determination of unfitness.

A motor carrier subject to 49 CFR part 395 will be subject to a remedial directive and proposed unfitness determination in accordance with this subpart for threshold rate violations of any appendix C regulation or regulations that have been documented during a compliance review. A remedial directive and proposed unfitness determination will be issued if a compliance review conducted on the motor carrier resulted in a final determination of one or more threshold rate violations of any appendix C regulation are discovered.

§385.807 Notice and issuance of remedial directive.

(a) Following the close of the compliance review described in §385.805, FMCSA will issue the motor carrier a written notice of remedial directive and proposed determination of unfitness. FMCSA will issue the notice and proposed determination as soon as practicable, but not later than 30 days after the close of the review.

(b) The remedial directive will state that the motor carrier is required to install and maintain EOBRs compliant with §395.16 of this chapter in all of the motor carrier's CMVs and to use the EOBRS to record its drivers' hours of service pursuant to §395.16. The motor carrier shall provide proof of the installation to FMCSA in accordance with §385.811 within the following time periods:

(1) Motor carriers transporting hazardous materials in quantities requiring placarding, and motor carriers transporting passengers in a CMV, must install EOBRs and provide proof of the installation by the 45th day after the date of the notice of remedial directive.

(2) All other motor carriers must install EOBRs and provide proof of installation by the 60th day after the date of FMCSA's notice of remedial directive. If FMCSA determines the motor carrier is making a good-faith effort to comply with the terms of the remedial directive, FMCSA may allow the motor carrier to operate for up to 60 additional days.

(3) A motor carrier may challenge the notice of remedial directive and proposed determination of unfitness in accordance with § 385.817.

[75 FR 17241, Apr. 5, 2010, as amended at 75 FR 55491, Sept. 13, 2010]

§ 385.809 [Reserved]

§ 385.811 Proof of compliance with remedial directive.

(a) Motor carriers subject to a remedial directive to install EOBRs under this section must provide proof of EOBR installation by one of the following:

(1) Submitting all of the carrier's CMVs for visual and functional inspection by FMCSA or qualified State enforcement personnel.

(2) Transmitting to the FMCSA service center for the geographic area where the carrier maintains its principal place of business all of the following documentation:

(i) Receipts for all necessary EOBR purchases.

(ii) Receipts for the installation work.

(iii) Digital or other photographic evidence depicting the installed devices in the carrier's CMVs.

(iv) Documentation of the EOBR serial number for the specific device corresponding to each CMV in which the device has been installed.

(3) If no receipt is submitted for an installed device or the installation work in accordance with paragraph (a)(2) of this section, the carrier must submit a written statement explaining who installed the devices, how many devices were installed, the manufacturer and model numbers of the devices installed, and the vehicle identification numbers of the CMVs in which the devices were installed.

(b) Visual and functional EOBR inspections may be performed at any FMCSA roadside inspection station or at the roadside inspection or weigh station facility of any State that receives Motor Carrier Safety Assistance Program funds under 49 U.S.C. 31102 and that provides such inspection services. The carrier may also request such inspections be performed at its principal place of business.

(c) Motor carriers issued remedial directives pursuant to this section must install in all of their CMVs EOBRs meeting the standards set forth in 49 CFR 395.16. Such motor carriers must maintain and use the EOBRs to verify compliance with part 395 for a period of 2 years following the issuance of the remedial directive. In addition to any other requirements imposed by the FMCSRs, during the period of time the carrier is subject to a remedial directive the carrier must maintain all records and reports generated by the EOBRs and, upon demand, produce those records to FMCSA personnel.

(d) *Malfunctioning devices.* Motor carriers subject to remedial directives shall maintain EOBRs installed in their CMVs in good working order. Such carriers must cause any malfunctioning EOBR to be repaired or replaced within 14 days from the date the carrier becomes aware of the malfunction. During this repair or replacement period, carriers subject to a remedial directive under this part must prepare a paper record of duty status pursuant to § 395.8 of this chapter as a temporary replacement for the non-functioning EOBR unit. All other provisions of the remedial directive will continue to apply during the repair and replacement period. Failure to comply with the terms of this paragraph may subject the affected CMV and/or driver to an out-of-service order pursuant to § 396.9(c) and § 395.13 of this chapter, respectively. Repeated violations of this paragraph may subject the motor carrier to the provisions of § 385.819.

§385.813 Issuance and conditional rescission of proposed unfitness determination.

(a) Simultaneously with the notice of remedial directive, FMCSA will issue a proposed unfitness determination. The proposed unfitness determination will explain that, if the motor carrier fails to comply with the terms of the remedial directive, the carrier will be unfit under the fitness standard in §385.5, prohibited from engaging in interstate operations and intrastate operations affecting interstate commerce, and, in the case of a carrier registered under 49 U.S.C. 13902, have its registration revoked.

(b) FMCSA will conditionally rescind the proposed determination of unfitness upon the motor carrier's submission of sufficient proof of EOBR installation in accordance with §385.811.

(c) During the period the remedial directive is in effect, FMCSA may reinstate the proposed unfitness determination and immediately prohibit the motor carrier from operating in interstate commerce and intrastate operations affecting interstate commerce if the motor carrier violates the provisions of the remedial directive.

§385.815 Exemption for AOBRD users.

(a) Upon written request by the motor carrier, FMCSA will grant an exception from the requirements of remedial directives under this section to motor carriers that already had installed in all commercial motor vehicles, at the time of the compliance review immediately preceding the issuance of the notice of remedial directive, AOBRDs compliant with 49 CFR 395.15 of this chapter.

(b) The carrier will be permitted to continue using the previously installed devices if the carrier can satisfactorily demonstrate to FMCSA that the carrier and its employees understand how to use the AOBRDs and the information derived from them.

(c) The carrier must either use and maintain the AOBRDs currently in its CMVs or install new devices compliance with §395.16 of this chapter.

(d) Although FMCSA may suspend enforcement for noncompliance with the remedial directive, the directive will remain in effect; and the hours-of-service compliance of any motor carrier so exempted, will be subject to ongoing FMCSA oversight.

(e) The exemption granted under this section shall not apply to CMVs manufactured on or after June 4, 2012.

[75 FR 17241, Apr. 5, 2010, as amended at 75 FR 55491, Sept. 13, 2010]

§385.817 Administrative review.

(a) A motor carrier may request FMCSA to conduct an administrative review if the carrier believes FMCSA has committed an error in issuing a notice of remedial directive under §385.807 and proposed unfitness determination under §385.813. Administrative reviews of notices of remedial directive and proposed unfitness determinations are limited to findings in the compliance review immediately preceding the notice.

(b) The motor carrier's request must explain the error it believes FMCSA committed in issuing the notice of remedial directive and proposed unfitness determination. The motor carrier must include a list of all factual and procedural issues in dispute and any information or documents that support its argument.

(c) The motor carrier must submit its request in writing to the Assistant Administrator, Federal Motor Carrier Safety Administration, 1200 New Jersey Avenue, SE., Washington, DC 20590. The motor carrier must submit on the same day a copy of the request to FMCSA counsel in the FMCSA service center for the geographic area where the carrier maintains its principal place of business.

(1) If a motor carrier has received a notice of remedial directive and proposed unfitness determination, the carrier should submit its request in writing within 15 days from the date of the notice. This timeframe will allow FMCSA to issue a written decision before the prohibitions outlined in §385.819(a) take effect. If the carrier submits its request for administrative review within 15 days of the issuance of the notice of remedial directive and proposed unfitness determination, FMCSA will stay the finality of the proposed unfitness determination until the Agency has ruled on the carrier's request. Failure to submit the request

within this 15-day period may prevent FMCSA from ruling on the request before the prohibitions take effect.

(2) A motor carrier must make a request for an administrative review within 90 days after the date of the notice of remedial directive and proposed determination of unfitness under § 385.807.

(d) FMCSA may request the motor carrier to submit additional data or attend a conference to discuss the request for review. If the motor carrier does not provide the information requested, or does not attend the conference, FMCSA may dismiss its request for review.

(e) FMCSA will notify the motor carrier in writing of its decision following the administrative review. FMCSA will complete its review:

(1) Within 30 days after receiving a request from a hazardous materials or passenger motor carrier that has received a proposed unfitness determination;

(2) Within 45 days after receiving a request from any other motor carrier that has received a proposed unfitness determination;

(3) With respect to requests for administrative review of notices of remedial directive, as soon as practicable but not later than 60 days after receiving the request.

(f) The decision regarding a proposed unfitness determination constitutes final Agency action.

(g) The provisions of this section will not affect procedures for administrative review of proposed or final safety ratings in accordance with § 385.15 or for requests for changes to safety ratings based upon corrective action in accordance with § 385.17.

§ 385.819 Effect of failure to comply with remedial directive.

(a) A motor carrier that fails or refuses to comply with the terms of a remedial directive issued under this subpart, including a failure or refusal to provide proof of EOBR installation in accordance with § 385.811, does not meet the safety fitness standard set forth in § 385.5(b). With respect to such carriers, the proposed determination of unfitness issued in accordance with § 385.813 becomes final, and the motor carrier is prohibited from operating, as follows:

(1) Motor carriers transporting hazardous materials in quantities requiring placarding and motor carriers transporting passengers in a CMV are prohibited from operating CMVs in interstate commerce and in operations that affect interstate commerce beginning on the 46th day after the date of FMCSA's notice of remedial directive and proposed unfitness determination. A motor carrier subject to the registration requirements of 49 U.S.C. 13901 will have its registration revoked on the 46th day after the date of FMCSA's notice of remedial directive and proposed unfitness determination.

(2) All other motor carriers are prohibited from operating a CMV in interstate commerce and in operations that affect interstate commerce beginning on the 61st day after the date of FMCSA's notice of remedial directive and proposed unfitness determination. A motor carrier subject to the registration requirements of 49 U.S.C. 13901 will have its registration revoked on the 61st day after the date of FMCSA's notice of remedial directive and proposed unfitness determination. If FMCSA determines the motor carrier is making a good-faith effort to satisfy the terms of the remedial directive, FMCSA may allow the motor carrier to operate for up to 60 additional days.

(b) If a proposed unfitness determination becomes a final determination, FMCSA will issue an order prohibiting the motor carrier from operating in interstate commerce. If the motor carrier is required to register under 49 U.S.C. 13901, FMCSA will revoke the motor carrier's registration on the dates specified in § 385.819(a)(1) and (a)(2).

(c) If FMCSA has prohibited a motor carrier from operating in interstate commerce under paragraph (a) of this section and, if applicable, revoked the carrier's registration, and the motor carrier subsequently complies with the terms and conditions of the remedial directive and provides proof of EOBR installation under § 385.811, the carrier may request FMCSA to lift the prohibition on operations at any time after the prohibition becomes effective. The request should be submitted in writing in accordance with § 385.817(c).

(d) A Federal Agency must not use for CMV transportation a motor carrier that FMCSA has determined is unfit.

(e) *Penalties.* If a proposed unfitness determination becomes a final determination, FMCSA will issue an order prohibiting the motor carrier from operating in interstate commerce and any intrastate operations that affect interstate commerce and, if applicable, revoking its registration. Any motor carrier that operates a CMV in violation of this section will be subject to the penalty provisions listed in 49 U.S.C. 521(b).

APPENDIX A TO PART 385—EXPLANATION OF SAFETY AUDIT EVALUATION CRITERIA

I. GENERAL

(a) Section 210 of the Motor Carrier Safety Improvement Act (49 U.S.C. 31144) directed the Secretary to establish a procedure whereby each owner and each operator granted new authority must undergo a safety review within 18 months after the owner or operator begins operations. The Secretary was also required to establish the elements of this safety review, including basic safety management controls. The Secretary, in turn, delegated this to the FMCSA.

(b) To meet the safety standard, a motor carrier must demonstrate to the FMCSA that it has basic safety management controls in place which function adequately to ensure minimum acceptable compliance with the applicable safety requirements. A "safety audit evaluation criteria" was developed by the FMCSA, which uses data from the safety audit and roadside inspections to determine that each owner and each operator applicant for new entrant registration, provisional operating authority, or provisional Certificate of Registration has basic safety management controls in place. The term "safety audit" is the equivalent to the "safety review" required by Sec. 210. Using "safety audit" avoids any possible confusion with the safety reviews previously conducted by the agency that were discontinued on September 30, 1994.

(c) The safety audit evaluation process developed by the FMCSA is used to:

1. Evaluate basic safety management controls and determine if each owner and each operator is able to operate safely in interstate commerce; and

2. Identify owners and operators who are having safety problems and need improvement in their compliance with the FMCSRs

and the HMRs, before they are granted permanent registration.

II. SOURCE OF THE DATA FOR THE SAFETY AUDIT EVALUATION CRITERIA

(a) The FMCSA's evaluation criteria are built upon the operational tool known as the safety audit. This tool was developed to assist auditors and investigators in assessing the adequacy of a new entrant's basic safety management controls.

(b) The safety audit is a review of a Mexico-domiciled or new entrant motor carrier's operation and is used to:

1. Determine if a carrier has the basic safety management controls required by 49 U.S.C. 31144;

2. Meet the requirements of Section 350 of the DOT Appropriations Act; and

3. In the event that a carrier is found not to be in compliance with applicable FMCSRs and HMRs, the safety audit can be used to educate the carrier on how to comply with U.S. safety rules.

(c) Documents such as those contained in the driver qualification files, records of duty status, vehicle maintenance records, and other records are reviewed for compliance with the FMCSRs and HMRs. Violations are cited on the safety audit. Performance-based information, when available, is utilized to evaluate the carrier's compliance with the vehicle regulations. Recordable accident information is also collected.

III. DETERMINING IF THE CARRIER HAS BASIC SAFETY MANAGEMENT CONTROLS

(a) During the safety audit, the FMCSA gathers information by reviewing a motor carrier's compliance with "acute" and "critical" regulations of the FMCSRs and HMRs.

(b) Acute regulations are those where noncompliance is so severe as to require immediate corrective actions by a motor carrier regardless of the overall basic safety management controls of the motor carrier.

(c) Critical regulations are those where noncompliance relates to management and/or operational controls. These are indicative of breakdowns in a carrier's management controls.

(d) The list of the acute and critical regulations, which are used in determining if a carrier has basic safety management controls in place, is included in Appendix B, VII. List of Acute and Critical Regulations.

(e) Noncompliance with acute and critical regulations are indicators of inadequate safety management controls and usually higher than average accident rates.

(f) Parts of the FMCSRs and the HMRs having similar characteristics are combined together into six regulatory areas called "factors." The regulatory factors, evaluated on the basis of the adequacy of the carrier's safety management controls, are:

1. Factor 1—General: Parts 387 and 390;

2. Factor 2—Driver: Parts 382, 383 and 391;

3. Factor 3—Operational: Parts 392 and 395;

4. Factor 4—Vehicle: Part 393, 396 and inspection data for the last 12 months;

5. Factor 5—Hazardous Materials: Parts 171, 177, 180 and 397; and

6. Factor 6—Accident: Recordable Accident Rate per Million Miles.

(g) For each instance of noncompliance with an acute regulation, 1.5 points will be assessed.

(h) For each instance of noncompliance with a critical regulation, 1 point will be assessed.

(i) FMCSA also gathers information on compliance with applicable household goods and Americans with Disabilities Act of 1990 requirements, but failure to comply with these requirements does not affect the determination of the adequacy of basic safety management controls.

A. Vehicle Factor

(a) When at least three vehicle inspections are recorded in the Motor Carrier Management Information System (MCMIS) during the twelve months before the safety audit or performed at the time of the review, the Vehicle Factor (Part 396) will be evaluated on the basis of the Out-of-Service (OOS) rates and noncompliance with acute and critical regulations. The results of the review of the OOS rate will affect the Vehicle Factor as follows:

1. If the motor carrier has had at least three roadside inspections in the twelve months before the safety audit, and the vehicle OOS rate is 34 percent or higher, one point will be assessed against the carrier. That point will be added to any other points assessed for discovered noncompliance with acute and critical regulations of part 396 to determine the carrier's level of safety management control for that factor; and

2. If the motor carrier's vehicle OOS rate is less than 34 percent, or if there are less than three inspections, the determination of the carrier's level of safety management controls will only be based on discovered noncompliance with the acute and critical regulations of part 396.

(b) Over two million inspections occur on the roadside each year. This vehicle inspection information is retained in the MCMIS and is integral to evaluating motor carriers' ability to successfully maintain their vehicles, thus preventing them from being placed OOS during roadside inspections. Each safety audit will continue to have the requirements of part 396, Inspection, Repair, and Maintenance, reviewed as indicated by the above explanation.

B. The Accident Factor

(a) In addition to the five regulatory factors, a sixth factor is included in the process to address the accident history of the motor carrier. This factor is the recordable accident rate, which the carrier has experienced during the past 12 months. Recordable accident, as defined in 49 CFR 390.5, means an accident involving a commercial motor vehicle operating on a public road in interstate or intrastate commerce which results in a fatality; a bodily injury to a person who, as a result of the injury, immediately receives medical treatment away from the scene of the accident; or one or more motor vehicles incurring disabling damage as a result of the accident requiring the motor vehicle to be transported away from the scene by a tow truck or other motor vehicle.

(b) Experience has shown that urban carriers, those motor carriers operating entirely within a radius of less than 100 air miles (normally urban areas), have a higher exposure to accident situations because of their environment and normally have higher accident rates.

(c) The recordable accident rate will be used in determining the carrier's basic safety management controls in Factor 6, Accident. It will be used only when a carrier incurs two or more recordable accidents within the 12 months before the safety audit. An urban carrier (a carrier operating entirely within a radius of 100 air miles) with a recordable rate per million miles greater than 1.7 will be deemed to have inadequate basic safety management controls for the accident factor. All other carriers with a recordable accident rate per million miles greater than 1.5 will be deemed to have inadequate basic safety management controls for the accident factor. The rates are the result of roughly doubling the national average accident rate in Fiscal Years 1994, 1995, and 1996.

(d) The FMCSA will continue to consider preventability when a new entrant contests the evaluation of the accident factor by presenting compelling evidence that the recordable rate is not a fair means of evaluating its accident factor. Preventability will be determined according to the following standard: "If a driver, who exercises normal judgment and foresight, could have foreseen the possibility of the accident that in fact occurred, and avoided it by taking steps within his/her control which would not have risked causing another kind of mishap, the accident was preventable."

C. Factor Ratings

For Factors 1 through 5, if the combined violations of acute and or critical regulations for each factor is equal to three or more points, the carrier is determined not to have basic safety management controls for that individual factor.

If the recordable accident rate is greater than 1.7 recordable accidents per million miles for an urban carrier (1.5 for all other carriers), the carrier is determined to have inadequate basic safety management controls.

IV. OVERALL DETERMINATION OF THE CARRIER'S BASIC SAFETY MANAGEMENT CONTROLS

(a) If the carrier is evaluated as having inadequate basic safety management controls in at least three separate factors, the carrier will be considered to have inadequate safety management controls in place and corrective action will be necessary in order to avoid having its new entrant registration, provisional operating authority, or provisional Certificate of Registration revoked.

(b) For example, FMCSA evaluates a carrier finding:

(1) One instance of noncompliance with a critical regulation in part 387 scoring one point for Factor 1;

(2) Two instances of noncompliance with acute regulations in part 382 scoring three points for Factor 2;

(3) Three instances of noncompliance with critical regulations in part 396 scoring three points for Factor 4; and

(4) Three instances of noncompliance with acute regulations in parts 171 and 397 scoring four and one-half (4.5) points for Factor 5.

(c) In this example, the carrier scored three or more points for Factors 2, 4 and 5 and FMCSA determined the carrier had inadequate basic safety management controls in at least three separate factors. FMCSA will require corrective action in order to avoid having the carrier's new entrant registration revoked, or having the provisional operating authority or provisional Certificate of Registration suspended and possibly revoked.

[67 FR 12773, Mar. 19, 2002, as amended a6 67 FR 31985, May 13, 2002; 73 FR 76496, Dec. 16, 2008]

APPENDIX B TO PART 385—EXPLANATION OF SAFETY RATING PROCESS

(a) Section 215 of the Motor Carrier Safety Act of 1984 (49 U.S.C. 31144) directed the Secretary of Transportation to establish a procedure to determine the safety fitness of owners and operators of commercial motor vehicles operating in interstate or foreign commerce. The Secretary, in turn, delegated this responsibility to the Federal Motor Carrier Safety Administration (FMCSA).

(b) As directed, FMCSA promulgated a safety fitness regulation, entitled "Safety Fitness Procedures," which established a procedure to determine the safety fitness of motor carriers through the assignment of safety ratings and established a "safety fitness standard" that a motor carrier must meet to obtain a "Satisfactory" safety rating. FMCSA later amended the safety fitness standard to add a distinct requirement that motor carriers also be in compliance with applicable remedial directives.

(c) To meet the safety fitness standard, a motor carrier must meet two requirements. First, the carrier must demonstrate to FMCSA it has adequate safety management controls in place that function effectively to ensure acceptable compliance with the applicable safety requirements. (*See* §385.5(a)). A "safety fitness rating methodology" (SFRM) developed by FMCSA uses data from compliance reviews (CRs) and roadside inspections to rate motor carriers. Second, a motor carrier must also be in compliance with any applicable remedial directives issued in accordance with subpart J. This second requirement is set forth in §385.5(b).

(d) The safety rating process developed by FMCSA is used to:

1. Evaluate the first component of the safety fitness standard, under §385.5(a), and assign one of three safety ratings (Satisfactory, Conditional, or Unsatisfactory) to motor carriers operating in interstate commerce. This process conforms to §385.5(a), Safety fitness standard, and §385.7, Factors to be considered in determining a safety rating.

2. Identify motor carriers needing improvement in their compliance with the Federal Motor Carrier Safety Regulations (FMCSRs) and applicable Hazardous Materials Regulations (HMRs). These are carriers rated Unsatisfactory or Conditional.

(e) The hazardous materials safety permit requirements of part 385, subpart E apply to intrastate motor carriers. Intrastate motor carriers that are subject to the hazardous materials safety permit requirements in subpart E will be rated using equivalent State requirements whenever the FMCSRs are referenced in this appendix.

(f) The safety rating will be determined by applying the SFRM equally to all of a company's motor carrier operations in commerce, including if applicable its operations in Canada and/or Mexico.

I. SOURCE OF DATA FOR RATING METHODOLOGY

(a) The FMCSA's rating process is built upon the operational tool known as the CR. This tool was developed to assist Federal and State safety specialists in gathering pertinent motor carrier compliance and accident information.

(b) The CR is an in-depth examination of a motor carrier's operations and is used (1) to rate unrated motor carriers, (2) to conduct a follow-up investigation on motor carriers rated *unsatisfactory* or *conditional* as a result of a previous review, (3) to investigate complaints, or (4) in response to a request by a motor carrier to reevaluate its safety rating. Documents such as those contained in driver qualification files, records of duty status, vehicle maintenance records, and other records are thoroughly examined for compliance with the FMCSRs and HMRs. Violations are cited on the CR document. Performance-based information, when available, is utilized to evaluate the carrier's compliance with the vehicle regulations. Recordable accident information is also collected.

II. CONVERTING CR INFORMATION INTO A SAFETY RATING

(a) The FMCSA gathers information through an in-depth examination of the motor carrier's compliance with identified "acute" or "critical" regulations of the FMCSRs and HMRs.

(b) Acute regulations are those identified as such where noncompliance is so severe as to require immediate corrective actions by a motor carrier regardless of the overall safety posture of the motor carrier. An example of an acute regulation is §383.37(b), allowing, requiring, permitting, or authorizing an employee with more than one Commercial Driver's License (CDL) to operate a commercial motor vehicle. Noncompliance with §383.37(b) is usually discovered when the motor carrier's driver qualification file reflects that the motor carrier had knowledge of a driver with more than one CDL, and still permitted the driver to operate a commercial motor vehicle. If the motor carrier did not have such knowledge or could not reasonably be expected to have such knowledge, then a violation would not be cited.

(c) Critical regulations are those identified as such where noncompliance relates to management and/or operational controls. These are indicative of breakdowns in a carrier's management controls. An example of a critical regulation is §395.3(a)(1), requiring or permitting a property-carrying commercial motor vehicle driver to drive more than 11 hours.

(d) The list of the acute and critical regulations which are used in determining safety ratings is included at the end of this document.

(e) Noncompliance with acute regulations and patterns of non-compliance with critical regulations are quantitatively linked to inadequate safety management controls and usually higher than average accident rates. The FMCSA has used noncompliance with acute regulations and patterns of noncompliance with critical regulations since 1989 to determine motor carriers' adherence to the Safety fitness standard in §385.5.

(f) The regulatory factors, evaluated on the basis of the adequacy of the carrier's safety management controls, are (1) Parts 387 and 390; (2) Parts 382, 383 and 391; (3) Parts 392 and 395; (4) Parts 393 and 396 when there are less than three vehicle inspections in the last 12 months to evaluate; and (5) Parts 397, 171, 177 and 180.

(g) For each instance of noncompliance with an acute regulation or each pattern of noncompliance with a critical regulation during the CR, one point will be assessed. A pattern is more than one violation. When a number of documents are reviewed, the number of violations required to meet a pattern is equal to at least 10 percent of those examined.

(h) However, each pattern of noncompliance with a critical regulation relative to Part 395, Hours of Service of Drivers, will be assessed two points.

A. Vehicle Factor

(a) When a total of *three or more inspections are recorded in the Motor Carrier Management Information System (MCMIS) during the twelve months prior to the CR or performed at the time of the review*, the Vehicle Factor (Parts 393 and 396) will be evaluated on the basis of the Out-of-Service (OOS) rates and noncompliance with acute regulations and/or a pattern of noncompliance with critical regulations. The results of the review of the OOS rate will affect the Vehicle Factor rating as follows:

1. If a motor carrier has three or more roadside vehicle inspections in the twelve months prior to the carrier review, or three vehicles inspected at the time of the review, or a combination of the two totaling three or more, and the vehicle OOS rate is 34 percent or greater, the initial factor rating will be *conditional*. The requirements of Part 396, Inspection, Repair, and Maintenance, will be examined during each review. The results of the examination could lower the factor rating to *unsatisfactory* if noncompliance with an acute regulation or a pattern of noncompliance with a critical regulation is discovered. If the examination of the Part 396 requirements reveals no such problems with the systems the motor carrier is required to maintain for compliance, the Vehicle Factor remains *conditional*.

2. If a carrier's vehicle OOS rate is less than 34 percent, the initial factor rating will be *satisfactory*. If noncompliance with an acute regulation or a pattern of noncompliance with a critical regulation is discovered during the examination of Part 396 requirements, the factor rating will be lowered to *conditional*. If the examination of Part 396 requirements discovers no such problems with the systems the motor carrier is required to maintain for compliance, the Vehicle Factor remains *satisfactory*.

(b) Nearly two million vehicle inspections occur on the roadside each year. This vehicle inspection information is retained in the MCMIS and is integral to evaluating motor carriers' ability to successfully maintain their vehicles, thus preventing them from being placed OOS during roadside inspections. Since many of the roadside inspections are targeted to visibly defective vehicles and since there are a limited number of inspections for many motor carriers, the use of that data is limited. Each CR will continue to have the requirements of Part 396, Inspection, Repair, and Maintenance, reviewed as indicated by the above explanation.

B. Accident Factor

(a) In addition to the five regulatory rating factors, a sixth factor is included in the process to address the accident history of the motor carrier. This factor is the recordable accident rate for the past 12 months. A recordable accident, consistent with the definition for "accident" in 49 CFR 390.5, means an occurrence involving a commercial motor vehicle on a highway in motor carrier operations in commerce or within Canada or Mexico (if the motor carrier also operates in the United States) that results in a fatality; in bodily injury to a person who, as a result of the injury, immediately receives medical treatment away from the scene of the accident; or in one or more motor vehicles incurring disabling damage that requires the motor vehicle to be transported away from the scene by a tow truck or other motor vehicle.

(b) Recordable accidents per million miles were computed for each CR performed in Fiscal Years 1994, 1995 and 1996. The national average for all carriers rated was 0.747, and .839 for carriers operating entirely within the 100 air mile radius.

(c) Experience has shown that urban carriers, those motor carriers operating primarily within a radius of less than 100 air miles (normally in urban areas) have a higher exposure to accident situations because of their environment and normally have higher accident rates.

(d) The recordable accident rate will be used to rate Factor 6, Accident. It will be used only when a motor carrier incurs two or more recordable accidents occurred within the 12 months prior to the CR. An urban carrier (a carrier operating entirely within a radius of 100 air miles) with a recordable accident rate greater than 1.7 will receive an *unsatisfactory* rating for the accident factor. All other carriers with a recordable accident rate greater than 1.5 will receive an *unsatisfactory* factor rating. The rates are a result of roughly doubling the national average accident rate for each type of carrier rated in Fiscal Years 1994, 1995 and 1996.

(e) The FMCSA will continue to consider preventability when a motor carrier contests a rating by presenting compelling evidence that the recordable rate is not a fair means of evaluating its accident factor. Preventability will be determined according to the following standard: "If a driver, who exercises normal judgment and foresight could have foreseen the possibility of the accident that in fact occurred, and avoided it by taking steps within his/her control which would

not have risked causing another kind of mishap, the accident was preventable."

C. Factor Ratings

(a) Parts of the FMCSRs and the HMRs having similar characteristics are combined together into five regulatory areas called "factors."

(b) The following table shows the five regulatory factors, parts of the FMCSRs and HMRs associated with each factor, and the accident factor. Factor Ratings are determined as follows:

FACTORS

Factor 1 General=Parts 387 and 390
Factor 2 Driver=Parts 382, 383 and 391
Factor 3 Operational=Parts 392 and 395
Factor 4 Vehicle=Parts 393 and 396
Factor 5 Haz. Mat.=Parts 397, 171, 177 and 180
Factor 6 Accident Factor=Recordable Rate
"Satisfactory"—if the acute and/or critical=0 points
"Conditional"—if the acute and/or critical=1 point
"Unsatisfactory"—if the acute and/or critical=2 or more points

III. SAFETY RATING

A. Rating Table

(a) The ratings for the six factors are then entered into a rating table which establishes the motor carrier's safety rating.

(b) The FMCSA has developed a computerized rating formula for assessing the information obtained from the CR document and is using that formula in assigning a safety rating.

MOTOR CARRIER SAFETY RATING TABLE

Factor ratings		Overall Safety rating
Unsatisfactory	Conditional	
0	2 or fewer	Satisfactory
0	more than 2	Conditional
1	2 or fewer	Conditional
1	more than 2	Unsatisfactory
2 or more	0 or more	Unsatisfactory

B. Proposed Safety Rating

(a) The proposed safety rating will appear on the CR. The following appropriate information will appear after the last entry on the CR, MCS–151, part B.

"Your proposed safety rating is SATISFACTORY."

OR

"Your proposed safety rating is CONDITIONAL." The proposed safety rating will become the final safety rating 45 days after you receive this notice.

OR

"Your proposed safety rating is UNSATIS-FACTORY." The proposed safety rating will become the final safety rating 45 days after you receive this notice

(b) Proposed safety ratings of *conditional* or *unsatisfactory* will list the deficiencies discovered during the CR for which corrective actions must be taken.

(c) Proposed *unsatisfactory* safety ratings will indicate that, if the *unsatisfactory* rating becomes final, the motor carrier will be subject to the provision of §385.13, which prohibits motor carriers rated *unsatisfactory* from transporting hazardous materials requiring placarding or more than 15 passengers, including the driver.

IV. ASSIGNMENT OF FINAL RATING/MOTOR CARRIER NOTIFICATION

When the official rating is determined in Washington, D.C., the FMCSA notifies the motor carrier in writing of its safety rating as prescribed in §385.11. A proposed *conditional* safety rating (which is an improvement of an existing *unsatisfactory* rating) becomes effective as soon as the official safety rating from Washington, D.C. is issued, and the carrier may also avail itself of relief under the §385.15, Administrative Review and §385.17, Change to safety rating based on corrective actions.

V. MOTOR CARRIER RIGHTS TO A CHANGE IN THE SAFETY RATING

Under §§385.15 and 385.17, motor carriers have the right to petition for a review of their ratings *if there are factual or procedural disputes,* and to request another review after corrective actions have been taken. They are the procedural avenues a motor carrier which believes its safety rating to be in error may exercise, and the means to request another review after corrective action has been taken.

VI. CONCLUSION

(a) FMCSA believes this "safety fitness rating methodology" is a reasonable approach to assignment of a safety rating, as required by the safety fitness regulations (§385.9), that most closely reflects the motor carrier's current level of compliance with the safety fitness standard in §385.5(a). This methodology has the capability to incorporate regulatory changes as they occur.

(b) Improved compliance with the regulations leads to an improved rating, which in turn increases safety. This increased safety is our regulatory goal.

VII. LIST OF ACUTE AND CRITICAL REGULATIONS.

§382.115(a) Failing to implement an alcohol and/or controlled substances testing program (domestic motor carrier) (acute).

§382.115(b) Failing to implement an alcohol and/or controlled substances testing program (foreign motor carrier) (acute).

§382.201 Using a driver known to have an alcohol concentration of 0.04 or greater (acute).

§382.211 Using a driver who has refused to submit to an alcohol or controlled substances test required under part 382 (acute).

§382.213(b) Using a driver known to have used a controlled substance (acute).

§382.215 Using a driver known to have tested positive for a controlled substance (acute).

§382.301(a) Using a driver before the motor carrier has received a negative pre-employment controlled substance test result (critical).

§382.303(a) Failing to conduct post accident testing on driver for alcohol (critical).

§382.303(b) Failing to conduct post accident testing on driver for controlled substances (critical).

§382.305 Failing to implement a random controlled substances and/or an alcohol testing program (acute).

§382.305(b)(1) Failing to conduct random alcohol testing at an annual rate of not less than the applicable annual rate of the average number of driver positions (critical).

§382.305(b)(2) Failing to conduct random controlled substances testing at an annual rate of not less than the applicable annual rate of the average number of driver positions (critical).

§382.309(a) Using a driver who has not undergone a return-to-duty alcohol test with a result indicating an alcohol concentration of less than 0.02 (acute).

§382.309(b) Using a driver who has not undergone a return-to-duty controlled substances test with a result indicating a verified negative result for controlled substances (acute).

§382.503 Allowing a driver to perform safety sensitive function, after engaging in conduct prohibited by subpart B, without being evaluated by substance abuse professional, as required by §382.605 (critical).

§382.505(a) Using a driver within 24 hours after being found to have an alcohol concentration of 0.02 or greater but less than 0.04 (acute).

§382.605(c)(1) Using a driver who has not undergone a return-to-duty alcohol test with a result indicating an alcohol concentration of less than .02 or with verified negative test result, after engaging in conduct prohibited by part 382 subpart B (acute).

§ 382.605(c)(2)(ii) Failing to subject a driver who has been identified as needing assistance to at least six unannounced follow-up alcohol and/or controlled substance tests in the first 12 months following the driver's return to duty (critical).

§ 383.23(a) Operating a commercial motor vehicle without a valid commercial driver's license (critical).

§ 383.37(a) Knowingly allowing, requiring, permitting, or authorizing an employee who does not have a current CLP or CDL, who does not have a CLP or CDL with the proper class or endorsements, or who operates a CMV in violation of any restriction on the CLP or CDL to operate a CMV (acute).

§ 383.37(b) Knowingly allowing, requiring, permitting, or authorizing an employee with a commercial driver's license which is suspended, revoked, or canceled by a state or who is disqualified to operate a commercial motor vehicle (acute).

§ 383.37(c) Knowingly allowing, requiring, permitting, or authorizing an employee with more than one commercial driver's license to operate a commercial motor vehicle (acute).

§ 383.51(a) Knowingly allowing, requiring, permitting, or authorizing a driver to drive who is disqualified to drive a commercial motor vehicle (acute).

§ 387.7(a) Operating a motor vehicle without having in effect the required minimum levels of financial responsibility coverage (acute).

§ 387.7(d) Failing to maintain at principal place of business required proof of financial responsibility (critical).

§ 387.31(a) Operating a passenger carrying vehicle without having in effect the required minimum levels of financial responsibility (acute).

§ 387.31(d) Failing to maintain at principal place of business required proof of financial responsibility for passenger carrying vehicles (critical).

§ 390.15(b)(2) Failing to maintain copies of all accident reports required by State or other governmental entities or insurers (critical).

§ 390.35 Making, or causing to make fraudulent or intentionally false statements or records and/or reproducing fraudulent records (acute).

§ 391.11(b)(4) Using a physically unqualified driver (acute).

§ 391.15(a) Using a disqualified driver (acute).

§ 391.45(a) Using a driver not medically examined and certified (critical).

§ 391.45(b)(1) Using a driver not medically examined and certified during the preceding 24 months (critical).

§ 391.51(a) Failing to maintain driver qualification file on each driver employed (critical).

§ 391.51(b)(2) Failing to maintain inquiries into driver's driving record in driver's qualification file (critical).

§ 391.51(b)(7) Failing to maintain medical examiner's certificate in driver's qualification file (critical).

§ 392.2 Operating a motor vehicle not in accordance with the laws, ordinances, and regulations of the jurisdiction in which it is being operated (critical).

§ 392.4(b) Requiring or permitting a driver to drive while under the influence of, or in possession of, a narcotic drug, amphetamine, or any other substance capable of rendering the driver incapable of safely operating a motor vehicle (acute).

§ 392.5(b)(1) Requiring or permitting a driver to drive a motor vehicle while under the influence of, or in possession of, an intoxicating beverage (acute).

§ 392.5(b)(2) Requiring or permitting a driver who shows evidence of having consumed an intoxicating beverage within 4 hours to operate a motor vehicle (acute).

§ 392.6 Scheduling a run which would necessitate the vehicle being operated at speeds in excess of those prescribed (critical).

§ 392.9(a)(1) Requiring or permitting a driver to drive without the vehicle's cargo being properly distributed and adequately secured (critical).

§ 395.1(h)(1)(i) Requiring or permitting a property-carrying commercial motor vehicle driver to drive more than 15 hours (Driving in Alaska) (critical).

§ 395.1(h)(1)(ii) Requiring or permitting a property-carrying commercial motor vehicle driver to drive after having been on duty 20 hours (Driving in Alaska) (critical).

§ 395.1(h)(1)(iii) Requiring or permitting a property-carrying commercial motor vehicle driver to drive after having been on duty more than 70 hours in 7 consecutive days (Driving in Alaska) (critical).

§ 395.1(h)(1)(iv) Requiring or permitting a property-carrying commercial motor vehicle driver to drive after having been on duty more than 80 hours in 8 consecutive days (Driving in Alaska) (critical).

§ 395.1(h)(2)(i) Requiring or permitting a passenger-carrying commercial motor vehicle driver to drive more than 15 hours (Driving in Alaska) (critical).

§ 395.1(h)(2)(ii) Requiring or permitting a passenger-carrying commercial motor vehicle driver to drive after having been on duty 20 hours (Driving in Alaska) (critical).

§ 395.1(h)(2)(iii) Requiring or permitting a passenger-carrying commercial motor vehicle driver to drive after having been on duty more than 70 hours in 7 consecutive days (Driving in Alaska) (critical).

§ 395.1(h)(2)(iv) Requiring or permitting a passenger-carrying commercial motor vehicle driver to drive after having been on duty more than 80 hours in 8 consecutive days (Driving in Alaska) (critical).

§ 395.1(o) Requiring or permitting a property-carrying commercial motor vehicle driver to drive after having been on duty 16 consecutive hours (critical).

§ 395.3(a)(1) Requiring or permitting a property-carrying commercial motor vehicle driver to drive more than 11 hours (critical).

§ 395.3(a)(2) Requiring or permitting a property-carrying commercial motor vehicle driver to drive after the end of the 14th hour after coming on duty (critical).

§ 395.3(b)(1) Requiring or permitting a property-carrying commercial motor vehicle driver to drive after having been on duty more than 60 hours in 7 consecutive days (critical).

§ 395.3(b)(2) Requiring or permitting a property-carrying commercial motor vehicle driver to drive after having been on duty more than 70 hours in 8 consecutive days (critical).

§ 395.3(c)(1) Requiring or permitting a property-carrying commercial motor vehicle driver to restart a period of 7 consecutive days without taking an off-duty period of 34 or more consecutive hours (critical).

§ 395.3(c)(2) Requiring or permitting a property-carrying commercial motor vehicle driver to restart a period of 8 consecutive days without taking an off-duty period of 34 or more consecutive hours (critical).

§ 395.5(a)(1) Requiring or permitting a passenger-carrying commercial motor vehicle driver to drive more than 10 hours (critical).

§ 395.5(a)(2) Requiring or permitting a passenger-carrying commercial motor vehicle driver to drive after having been on duty 15 hours (critical).

§ 395.5(b)(1) Requiring or permitting a passenger-carrying commercial motor vehicle driver to drive after having been on duty more than 60 hours in 7 consecutive days (critical).

§ 395.5(b)(2) Requiring or permitting a passenger-carrying commercial motor vehicle driver to drive after having been on duty more than 70 hours in 8 consecutive days (critical).

§ 395.8(a) Failing to require driver to make a record of duty status (critical).

§ 395.8(e) False reports of records of duty status (critical).

§ 395.8(i) Failing to require driver to forward within 13 days of completion, the original of the record of duty status (critical).

§ 395.8(k)(1) Failing to preserve driver's record of duty status for 6 months (critical).

§ 395.8(k)(1) Failing to preserve driver's records of duty status supporting documents for 6 months (critical).

§ 396.3(b) Failing to keep minimum records of inspection and vehicle maintenance (critical).

§ 396.9(c)(2) Requiring or permitting the operation of a motor vehicle declared "out-of-service" before repairs were made (acute).

§ 396.11(a) Failing to require driver to prepare driver vehicle inspection report (critical).

§ 396.11(c) Failing to correct Out-of-Service defects listed by driver in a driver vehicle inspection report before the vehicle is operated again (acute).

§ 396.17(a) Using a commercial motor vehicle not periodically inspected (critical).

§ 396.17(g) Failing to promptly repair parts and accessories not meeting minimum periodic inspection standards (acute).

§ 397.5(a) Failing to ensure a motor vehicle containing Division 1.1, 1.2, or 1.3 (explosive) material is attended at all times by its driver or a qualified representative (acute).

§ 397.7(a)(1) Parking a motor vehicle containing Division 1.1, 1.2, or 1.3 materials within 5 feet of traveled portion of highway or street (critical).

§ 397.7(b) Parking a motor vehicle containing hazardous material(s) other than Division 1.1, 1.2, or 1.3 materials within 5 feet of traveled portion of highway or street (critical).

§ 397.13(a) Permitting a person to smoke or carry a lighted cigarette, cigar or pipe within 25 feet of a motor vehicle containing Class 1 materials, Class 5 materials, or flammable materials classified as Division 2.1, Class 3, Divisions 4.1 and 4.2 (critical).

§ 397.19(a) Failing to furnish driver of motor vehicle transporting Division 1.1, 1.2, or 1.3 (explosive) materials with a copy of the rules of part 397 and/or emergency response instructions (critical).

§ 397.67(d) Requiring or permitting the operation of a motor vehicle containing explosives in Class 1, Divisions 1.1, 1.2, or 1.3 that is not accompanied by a written route plan (critical).

§ 397.101(d) Requiring or permitting the operation of a motor vehicle containing highway route-controlled quantity, as defined in § 173.403, of radioactive materials that is not accompanied by a written route plan.

§ 171.15 Carrier failing to give immediate telephone notice of an incident involving hazardous materials (critical).

§ 171.16 Carrier failing to make a written report of an incident involving hazardous materials (critical).

§ 172.313(a) Accepting for transportation or transporting a package containing a poisonous-by-inhalation material that is not marked with the words "Inhalation Hazard" (acute).

§ 172.704(a)(4) Failing to provide security awareness training (critical).

§ 172.704(a)(5) Failing to provide in-depth security awareness training (critical).

§ 172.800(b) Transporting HM without a security plan (acute).

§ 172.800(b) Transporting HM without a security plan that conforms to Subpart I requirements (acute).

§ 172.800(b) Failure to adhere to a required security plan (acute).

§ 172.802(b) Failure to make copies of security plan available to hazmat employees (critical).

§ 173.24(b)(1) Accepting for transportation or transporting a package that has an identifiable release of a hazardous material to the environment (acute).

§ 173.421(a) Accepting for transportation or transporting a Class 7 (radioactive) material described, marked, and packaged as a limited quantity when the radiation level on the surface of the package exceeds 0.005mSv/hour (0.5 mrem/hour) (acute).

§ 173.431(a) Accepting for transportation or transporting in a Type A packaging a greater quantity of Class 7 (radioactive) material than authorized (acute).

§ 173.431(b) Accepting for transportation or transporting in a Type B packaging a greater quantity of Class 7 (radioactive) material than authorized (acute).

§ 173.441(a) Accepting for transportation or transporting a package containing Class 7 (radioactive) material with external radiation exceeding allowable limits (acute).

§ 173.442(b) Accepting for transportation or transporting a package containing Class 7 (radioactive) material when the temperature of the accessible external surface of the loaded package exceeds 50 °C (122 °F) in other than an exclusive use shipment, or 85 °C (185 °F) in an exclusive use shipment (acute).

§ 173.443(a) Accepting for transportation or transporting a package containing Class 7 (radioactive) material with removable contamination on the external surfaces of the package in excess of permissible limits (acute).

§ 177.800(c) Failing to instruct a category of employees in hazardous materials regulations (critical).

§ 177.801 Accepting for transportation or transporting a forbidden material (acute).

§ 177.835(a) Loading or unloading a Class 1 (explosive) material with the engine running (acute).

§ 177.835(c) Accepting for transportation or transporting Division 1.1, 1.2, or 1.3 (explosive) materials in a motor vehicle or combination of vehicles that is not permitted (acute).

§ 177.835(j) Transferring Division 1.1, 1.2, or 1.3 (explosive) materials between containers or motor vehicles when not permitted (acute).

§ 177.817(a) Transporting a shipment of hazardous materials not accompanied by a properly prepared shipping paper (critical).

§ 177.817(e) Failing to maintain proper accessibility of shipping papers (critical).

§ 177.823(a) Moving a transport vehicle containing hazardous material that is not properly marked or placarded (critical).

§ 177.841(e) Transporting a package bearing a poison label in the same transport vehicle with material marked or known to be foodstuff, feed, or any edible material intended for consumption by humans or animals unless an exception in § 177.841(e)(i) or (ii) is met (acute).

§ 180.407(a) Transporting a shipment of hazardous material in cargo tank that has not been inspected or retested in accordance with § 180.407 (critical).

§ 180.407(c) Failing to periodically test and inspect a cargo tank (critical).

§ 180.415 Failing to mark a cargo tank which passed an inspection or test required by § 180.407 (critical).

§ 180.417(a)(1) Failing to retain cargo tank manufacturer's data report certificate and related papers, as required (critical).

§ 180.417(a)(2) Failing to retain copies of cargo tank manufacturer's certificate and related papers (or alternative report) as required (critical).

[62 FR 60043, Nov. 6, 1997, as amended at 63 FR 62959, Nov. 10, 1998; 65 FR 11907, Mar. 7, 2000; 68 FR 22513, Apr. 28, 2003; 70 FR 50070, Aug. 25, 2005; 72 FR 36789, July 5, 2007; 72 FR 71269, Dec. 17, 2007; 75 FR 17244, Apr. 5, 2010; 76 FR 26897, May 9, 2011]

APPENDIX C TO PART 385—REGULATIONS PERTAINING TO REMEDIAL DIRECTIVES IN PART 385, SUBPART J

§ 395.1(h)(1)(i) Requiring or permitting a property-carrying commercial motor vehicle driver to drive more than 15 hours (Driving in Alaska).

§ 395.1(h)(1)(ii) Requiring or permitting a property-carrying commercial motor vehicle driver to drive after having been on duty 20 hours (Driving in Alaska).

§ 395.1(h)(1)(iii) Requiring or permitting a property-carrying commercial motor vehicle driver to drive after having been on duty more than 70 hours in 7 consecutive days (Driving in Alaska).

§ 395.1(h)(1)(iv) Requiring or permitting a property-carrying commercial motor vehicle driver to drive after having been on duty more than 80 hours in 8 consecutive days (Driving in Alaska).

§ 395.1(h)(2)(i) Requiring or permitting a passenger-carrying commercial motor vehicle driver to drive more than 15 hours (Driving in Alaska).

§ 395.1(h)(2)(ii) Requiring or permitting a passenger-carrying commercial motor vehicle driver to drive after having been on duty 20 hours (Driving in Alaska).

§ 395.1(h)(2)(iii) Requiring or permitting a passenger-carrying commercial motor vehicle driver to drive after having been on duty more than 70 hours in 7 consecutive days (Driving in Alaska).

§ 395.1(h)(2)(iv) Requiring or permitting a passenger-carrying commercial motor vehicle driver to drive after having been on duty more than 80 hours in 8 consecutive days (Driving in Alaska).

§ 395.1(o) Requiring or permitting a property-carrying commercial motor vehicle driver to drive after having been on duty 16 consecutive hours.

§ 395.3(a)(1) Requiring or permitting a property-carrying commercial motor vehicle driver to drive more than 11 hours.

§ 395.3(a)(2) Requiring or permitting a property-carrying commercial motor vehicle driver to drive after the end of the 14th hour after coming on duty.

§ 395.3(b)(1) Requiring or permitting a property-carrying commercial motor vehicle driver to drive after having been on duty more than 60 hours in 7 consecutive days.

§ 395.3(b)(2) Requiring or permitting a property-carrying commercial motor vehicle driver to drive after having been on duty more than 70 hours in 8 consecutive days.

§ 395.3(c)(1) Requiring or permitting a property-carrying commercial motor vehicle driver to restart a period of 7 consecutive days without taking an off-duty period of 34 or more consecutive hours.

§ 395.3(c)(2) Requiring or permitting a property-carrying commercial motor vehicle driver to restart a period of 8 consecutive days without taking an off-duty period of 34 or more consecutive hours.

§ 395.5(a)(1) Requiring or permitting a passenger-carrying commercial motor vehicle driver to drive more than 10 hours.

§ 395.5(a)(2) Requiring or permitting a passenger-carrying commercial motor vehicle driver to drive after having been on duty 15 hours.

§ 395.5(b)(1) Requiring or permitting a passenger-carrying commercial motor vehicle driver to drive after having been on duty more than 60 hours in 7 consecutive days.

§ 395.5(b)(2) Requiring or permitting a passenger-carrying commercial motor vehicle driver to drive after having been on duty more than 70 hours in 8 consecutive days.

§ 395.8(a) Failing to require driver to make a record of duty status.

§ 395.8(e) False reports of records of duty status.

§ 395.8(i) Failing to require driver to forward within 13 days of completion, the original of the record of duty status.

§ 395.8(k)(1) Failing to preserve driver's record of duty status for 6 months.

§ 395.8(k)(1) Failing to preserve driver's records of duty status supporting documents for 6 months.

[75 FR 17244, Apr. 5, 2010]

PART 386—RULES OF PRACTICE FOR MOTOR CARRIER, INTERMODAL EQUIPMENT PROVIDER, BROKER, FREIGHT FORWARDER, AND HAZARDOUS MATERIALS PROCEEDINGS

Subpart A—Scope of Rules; Definitions and General Provisions

Subpart B—Commencement of Proceedings, Pleadings

Subpart C—Settlement Agreements

Subpart D—General Rules and Hearings

AUTHORITY: 49 U.S.C. 113, chapters 5, 51, 59, 131–141, 145–149, 311, 313, and 315; Sec. 204, Pub. L. 104–88, 109 Stat. 803, 941 (49 U.S.C. 701 note); Sec. 217, Pub. L. 105–159, 113 Stat. 1748, 1767; Sec. 206, Pub. L. 106–159, 113 Stat. 1763; subtitle B, title IV of Pub. L. 109–59; and 49 CFR 1.45 and 1.73.

SOURCE: 50 FR 40306, Oct. 2, 1985, unless otherwise noted.

EDITORIAL NOTE: Nomenclature changes to part 386 appear at 65 FR 7755, Feb. 16, 2000, and 66 FR 49873, Oct. 1, 2001.

Subpart A—Scope of Rules; Definitions and General Provisions

§386.1 Scope of the rules in this part.

(a) The rules in this part govern proceedings before the Assistant Administrator, who also acts as the Chief Safety Officer of the Federal Motor Carrier Safety Administration (FMCSA), under applicable provisions of the Federal Motor Carrier Safety Regulations (FMCSRs) (49 CFR parts 350–399), including the commercial regulations (49 CFR parts 360–379), and the Hazardous Materials Regulations (49 CFR parts 171–180).

(b) The purpose of the proceedings is to enable the Assistant Administrator:

(1) To determine whether a motor carrier, intermodal equipment provider (as defined in §390.5 of this chapter), property broker, freight forwarder, or its agents, employees, or any other person subject to the jurisdiction of FMCSA, has failed to comply with the provisions or requirements of applicable statutes and the corresponding regulations; and

(2) To issue an appropriate order to compel compliance with the statute or regulation, assess a civil penalty, or both, if such violations are found.

[73 FR 76819, Dec. 17, 2008]

§386.2 Definitions.

Abate or abatement means to discontinue regulatory violations by refraining from or taking actions identified in a notice to correct noncompliance.

Administration means the Federal Motor Carrier Safety Administration.

Administrative adjudication means a process or proceeding to resolve contested claims in conformity with the Administrative Procedure Act, 5 U.S.C. 554–558.

Administrative law judge means an administrative law judge appointed pursuant to the provisions of 5 U.S.C. 3105.

Agency means the Federal Motor Carrier Safety Administration.

Agency Counsel means the attorney who prosecutes a civil penalty matter on behalf of the Field Administrator.

Assistant Administrator means the Assistant Administrator of the Federal Motor Carrier Safety Administration.

The Assistant Administrator is the Chief Safety Officer of the agency pursuant to 49 U.S.C. 113(e). Decisions of the Assistant Administrator in motor carrier, broker, freight forwarder, and hazardous materials proceedings under this part are administratively final.

Broker means a person who, for compensation, arranges or offers to arrange the transportation of property by an authorized motor carrier. A motor carrier, or person who is an employee or bona fide agent of a carrier, is not a broker within the meaning of this section when it arranges or offers to arrange the transportation of shipments which it is authorized to transport and which it has accepted and legally bound itself to transport.

Civil forfeiture proceedings means proceedings to collect civil penalties for violations under the Commercial Motor Vehicle Safety Act of 1986 (49 U.S.C. Chapter 313); the Hazardous Materials Transportation Act of 1975, as amended (49 U.S.C. Chapter 51); the Motor Carrier Safety Act of 1984 (49 U.S.C. Chapter 311, Subchapter III); section 18 of the Bus Regulatory Reform Act of 1982 (49 U.S.C. 31138); section 30 of the Motor Carrier Act of 1980 (49 U.S.C. 31139); and the ICC Termination Act of 1995 (49 U.S.C. Chapters 131–149).

Civil penalty proceedings means proceedings to collect civil penalties for violations of regulations and statutes within the jurisdiction of FMCSA.

Claimant means the representative of the Federal Motor Carrier Safety Administration authorized to make claims.

Commercial regulations means statutes and regulations that apply to persons providing or arranging transportation for compensation subject to the Secretary's jurisdiction under 49 U.S.C. Chapter 135. The statutes are codified in Part B of Subtitle IV, Title 49, U.S.C. (49 U.S.C. 13101 through 14913). The regulations include those issued by the Federal Motor Carrier Safety Administration or its predecessors under authority provided in 49 U.S.C. 13301 or a predecessor statute.

Decisionmaker means the Assistant Administrator of FMCSA, acting in the capacity of the decisionmaker or any person to whom the Assistant Adminis-

trator has delegated his/her authority in a civil penalty proceeding. As used in this subpart, the Agency decisionmaker is the official authorized to issue a final decision and order of the Agency in a civil penalty proceeding.

Default means an omission or failure to perform a legal duty within the time specified for action, failure to reply to a Notice of Claim within the time required, or failure to submit a reply in accordance with the requirements of this part. A default may result in issuance of a Final Agency Order or additional penalties against the defaulting party.

Department means the U.S. Department of Transportation.

Dockets means the U.S. Department of Transportation's docket management system, which is the central repository for original copies of all documents filed before the agency decisionmaker.

Driver qualification proceeding means a proceeding commenced under 49 CFR 391.47 or by issuance of a letter of disqualification.

Federal Motor Carrier Commercial Regulations (FMCCRs) means statutes and regulations applying to persons providing or arranging transportation for compensation subject to the Secretary's jurisdiction under 49 U.S.C. Chapter 135. The statutes are codified in Part B of Subtitle IV, Title 49 U.S.C. (49 U.S.C. 13101 through 14913). The regulations include those issued by FMCSA or its predecessors under authority provided in 49 U.S.C. 13301 or a predecessor statute.

Field Administrator means the head of an FMCSA Service Center who has been delegated authority to initiate compliance and enforcement actions on behalf of FMCSA.

Final Agency Order means the final action by FMCSA issued pursuant to this part by the appropriate Field Administrator (for default judgments under § 386.14) or the Assistant Administrator, or settlement agreements which become the Final Agency Order pursuant to 386.22, or decisions of the Administrative Law Judge, which become the Final Agency Order pursuant to 386.61 or binding arbitration awards. A person who fails to perform the actions directed in the Final Agency

Order commits a violation of that order and is subject to an additional penalty as prescribed in subpart G of this part.

FMCSRs means the Federal Motor Carrier Safety Regulations.

Formal hearing means an evidentiary hearing on the record in which parties have the opportunity to conduct discovery, present relevant evidence, and cross-examine witnesses.

Freight forwarder means a person holding itself out to the general public (other than as an express, pipeline, rail, sleeping car, motor, or water carrier) to provide transportation of property for compensation in interstate commerce, and in the ordinary course of its business:

(1) Performs or provides for assembling, consolidating, break-bulk, and distribution of shipments;

(2) Assumes responsibility for transportation from place of receipt to destination; and

(3) Uses for any part of the transportation a carrier subject to FMCSA jurisdiction.

Hearing officer means a neutral Agency employee designated by the Assistant Administrator to preside over an informal hearing.

HMRs means Hazardous Materials Regulations.

Informal hearing means a hearing in which the parties have the opportunity to present relevant evidence to a neutral Hearing Officer, who will prepare findings of fact and recommendations for the Agency decisionmaker. The informal hearing will not be on the transcribed record and discovery will not be allowed. Parties will have the opportunity to discuss their case and present testimony and evidence before the Hearing Officer without the formality of a formal hearing.

Mail means U.S. first class mail, U.S. registered or certified mail, or use of a commercial delivery service.

Motor carrier means a motor carrier, motor private carrier, or motor carrier of migrant workers as defined in 49 U.S.C. 13102 and 31501.

Notice of Claim (NOC) means the initial document issued by FMCSA to assert a civil penalty for alleged violations of the FMCSRs, HMRs, or FMCCRs.

Notice of Violation (NOV) means a document alleging a violation of the FMCSRs, HMRs, or FMCCRs, for which corrective action, other than payment of a civil penalty, is recommended.

Person means any individual, partnership, association, corporation, business trust, or any other organized group of individuals.

Reply means a written response to a Notice of Claim, admitting or denying the allegations contained within the Notice of Claim. In addition, the reply provides the mechanism for determining whether the respondent seeks to pay, settle, contest, or seek binding arbitration of the claim. *See* §386.14. If contesting the allegations, the reply must also set forth all known affirmative defenses and factors in mitigation of the claim.

Petitioner means a party petitioning to overturn a determination in a driver qualification proceeding.

Respondent means a party against whom relief is sought or claim is made.

Secretary means the Secretary of Transportation.

Submission of written evidence without hearing means the submission of written evidence and legal argument to the Agency decisionmaker, or his/her representative, in lieu of a formal or informal hearing.

[50 FR 40306, Oct. 2, 1985, as amended at 53 FR 2036, Jan. 26, 1988; 56 FR 10182, Mar. 11, 1991; 65 FR 7755, Feb. 16, 2000; 65 FR 78427, Dec. 15, 2000; 67 FR 61821, Oct. 2, 2002; 70 FR 28748, May 18, 2005; 72 FR 55701, Oct. 1, 2007]

§386.3 Separation of functions.

(a) Civil penalty proceedings will be prosecuted by Agency Counsel who represent the Field Administrator. In Notices of Violation, the Field Administrator will be represented by Agency Counsel.

(b) An Agency employee, including those listed in paragraph (c) of this section, engaged in the performance of investigative or prosecutorial functions in a civil penalty proceeding may not, in that case or a factually related case, discuss or communicate the facts or issues involved with the Agency decisionmaker, Administrative Law Judge, Hearing Officer or others listed in paragraph (d) of this section, except as counsel or a witness in the public proceedings. This prohibition also includes the staff of those covered by this section.

(c) The Deputy Chief Counsel, Assistant Chief Counsel for Enforcement and Litigation, and attorneys in the Enforcement and Litigation Division serve as enforcement counsel in the prosecution of all cases brought under this part.

(d) The Chief Counsel, the Special Counsel to the Chief Counsel, and attorneys serving as Adjudications Counsel advise the Agency decisionmaker regarding all cases brought under this Part.

(e) Nothing in this part shall preclude agency decisionmakers or anyone advising an agency decisionmaker from taking part in a determination to launch an investigation or issue a complaint, or similar preliminary decision.

[70 FR 28479, May 18, 2005]

§ 386.4 Appearances and rights of parties.

(a) A party may appear in person, by counsel, or by other representative, as the party elects, in a proceeding under this subpart.

(b) A person representing a party must file a notice of appearance in the proceeding, in the manner provided in § 386.7 of this subpart. The notice of appearance must list the name, address, telephone number, and facsimile number of the person designated to represent the party. A copy of the notice of appearance must be served on each party, in the manner provided in § 386.6 of this subpart. The notice of appearance must be filed and served before the representative can participate in the proceeding. Any changes in an attorney or representative's contact information must be served and filed according to §§ 386.6 and 386.7 in a timely manner.

(c) A separate notice of appearance must be filed by a representative in each case. Blanket appearances on behalf of a party will not be accepted.

[70 FR 28479, May 18, 2005]

§ 386.5 Form of filings and extensions of time.

(a) *Form.* Each document must be typewritten or legibly handwritten.

(b) *Contents.* Unless otherwise specified in this part, each document must contain a short, plain statement of the facts on which the person's case rests and a brief statement of the action requested in the document. Except by prior order, all contents will be made publicly available.

(c) *Length.* Except for the Notice of Claim and reply, motions, briefs, and other filings may not exceed 20 pages except as permitted by Order following a motion to exceed the page limitation based upon good cause shown. Exhibits or attachments in support of the relevant filing are not included in the page limit.

(d) *Paper and margins.* Filed documents must be printed on 8½″ by 11″ paper with a one-inch margin on all four sides of text, to include pagination and footnotes.

(e) *Spacing, and font size for typewritten documents.* Typewritten documents will use the following line format: single-spacing for the caption and footnotes, and double-spacing for the main text. All printed matter must appear in at least 12-point font, including footnotes.

(f) *Extensions of time.* Only those requests showing good cause will be granted. No motion for continuance or postponement of a hearing date filed within 15 days of the date set for a hearing will be granted unless accompanied by an affidavit showing extraordinary circumstances warrant a continuance. Unless directed otherwise by the Agency decisionmaker before whom a matter is pending, the parties may stipulate to reasonable extensions of time by filing the stipulation in the official docket and serving copies on all parties on the certificate of service. Motions for extensions of time must be filed in accordance with § 386.6 and served in accordance with § 386.7. A copy must also be served upon the person presiding over the proceeding at the time of the filing.

[70 FR 28479, May 18, 2005]

§386.6 Service.

(a) *General.* All documents must be served upon the party or the party's designated agent for service of process. If a notice of appearance has been filed in the specific case in question in accordance with §386.4, service is to be made on the party's attorney of record or its designated representative.

(b) *Type of service.* A person may serve documents by personal delivery utilizing governmental or commercial entities, U.S. mail, commercial mail delivery, and upon prior written consent of the parties, facsimile. Written consent for facsimile service must specify the facsimile number where service will be accepted. When service is made by facsimile, a copy will also be served by any other method permitted by this section. Facsimile service occurs when transmission is complete.

(c) *Certificate of service.* A certificate of service will accompany all documents served in a proceeding under this Part. The certificate must show the date and manner of service, be signed by the person making service, and list the persons served in accordance with §386.7.

(d) *Date of service.* A document will be considered served on the date of personal delivery; or if mailed, the mailing date shown on the certificate of service, the date shown on the postmark if there is no certificate of service, or other mailing date shown by other evidence if there is no certificate of service or postmark.

(e) *Valid service.* A properly addressed document, sent in accordance with this subpart, which was returned, unclaimed, or refused, is deemed to have been served in accordance with this subpart. The service will be considered valid as of the date and the time the document was mailed, or the date personal delivery of the document was refused. Service by delivery after 5 p.m. in the time zone in which the recipient will receive delivery is deemed to have been made on the next day that is not a Saturday, Sunday, or legal holiday.

(f) *Presumption of service.* There shall be a presumption of service if the document is served where a party or a person customarily receives mail or at the address designated in the entry of appearance. If an entry of appearance has been filed on behalf of the party, service is effective upon service of a document to its representative.

[70 FR 28480, May 18, 2005]

§386.7 Filing of documents.

Address and method of filing. A person serving or tendering a document for filing must personally deliver or mail one copy of each document to all parties and counsel or their designated representative of record if represented. A signed original and one copy of each document submitted for the consideration of the Assistant Administrator, an Administrative Law Judge, or Hearing Officer must be personally delivered or mailed to: Department of Transportation Docket Management Facility, 1200 New Jersey Ave., SE., Washington, DC 20590–0001. A person will serve a copy of each document on each party in accordance with §386.6 of this subpart.

[70 FR 28480, May 18, 2005, as amended at 72 FR 55701, Oct. 1, 2007]

§386.8 Computation of time.

(a) *Generally.* In computing any time period set out in these rules or in an order issued hereunder, the time computation begins with the day following the act, event, or default. The last day of the period is included unless it is a Saturday, Sunday, or legal Federal holiday in which case the time period will run to the end of the next day that is not a Saturday, Sunday, or legal Federal holiday. All Saturdays, Sundays, and legal Federal holidays except those falling on the last day of the period will be computed.

(b) *Date of entry of orders.* In computing any period of time involving the date of the entry of an order, the date of entry is the date the order is served.

(c) *Computation of time for delivery by mail.* (1) Service of all documents is deemed effected at the time of mailing.

(2) Documents are not deemed filed until received by Dockets.

(3) Whenever a party has a right or a duty to act or to make any response within a prescribed period after service

by mail, or on a date certain after service by mail, 5 days will be added to the prescribed period.

[70 FR 28480, May 18, 2005]

Subpart B—Commencement of Proceedings, Pleadings

§ 386.11 Commencement of proceedings.

(a) *Driver qualification proceedings.* These proceedings are commenced by the issuance of a determination by the Director, Office of Truck and Bus Standards and Operations, in a case arising under § 391.47 of this chapter or by the issuance of a letter of disqualification.

(1) Such determination and letters must be accompanied by the following:

(i) A citation of the regulation under which the action is being taken;

(ii) A copy of all documentary evidence relied on or considered in taking such action, or in the case of voluminous evidence a summary of such evidence;

(iii) Notice to the driver and motor carrier involved in the case that they may petition for review of the action;

(iv) Notice that a hearing will be granted if the Assistant Administrator determines there are material factual issues in dispute;

(v) Notice that failure to petition for review will constitute a waiver of the right to contest the action; and

(vi) Notice that the burden or proof will be on the petitioner in cases arising under § 391.47 of this chapter.

(2) At any time before the close of hearing, upon application of a party, the letter or determination may be amended at the discretion of the administrative law judge upon such terms as he/she approves.

(b) *Notice of Violation.* The Agency may issue a Notice of Violation as a means of notifying any person subject to the rules in this part that it has received information (*i.e.*, from an investigation, audit, or any other source) wherein it has been alleged the person has violated provisions of the FMCSRs, HMRs, or FMCCRs. The notice of violation serves as an informal mechanism to address compliance deficiencies. If the alleged deficiency is not addressed to the satisfaction of the Agency, formal enforcement action may be taken in accordance with paragraph (c) of this section. A notice of violation is not a prerequisite to the issuance of a Notice of Claim. The notice of violation will address the following issues, as appropriate:

(1) The specific alleged violations.

(2) Any specific actions the Agency determines are appropriate to remedy the identified problems.

(3) The means by which the notified person can inform the Agency that it has received the notice of violation and either has addressed the alleged violation or does not agree with the Agency's assertions in the notice of violation.

(4) Any other relevant information.

(c) *Civil penalty proceedings.* These proceedings are commenced by the issuance of a Notice of Claim.

(1) Each Notice of Claim must contain the following:

(i) A statement setting forth the facts alleged.

(ii) A statement of the provisions of law allegedly violated by the respondent.

(iii) The proposed civil penalty and notice of the maximum amount authorized to be claimed under statute.

(iv) The time, form, and manner whereby the respondent may pay, contest, or otherwise seek resolution of the claim.

(2) In addition to the information required by paragraph (c)(1) of this section, the Notice of Claim may contain such other matters as the Agency deems appropriate.

(3) In proceedings for collection of civil penalties for violations of the motor carrier safety regulations under the Motor Carrier Safety Act of 1984, the Agency may require the respondent to post a copy of the Notice of Claim in such place or places and for such duration as the Agency may determine appropriate to aid in the enforcement of the law and regulations.

[50 FR 40306, Oct. 2, 1985, as amended at 53 FR 2036, Jan. 26, 1988; 56 FR 10182, Mar. 11, 1991; 65 FR 7756, Feb. 16, 2000; 70 FR 28480, May 18, 2005]

§386.12 Complaint.

(a) *Complaint of substantial violation.* Any person may file a written complaint with the Assistant Administrator alleging that a substantial violation of any regulation issued under the Motor Carrier Safety Act of 1984 is occurring or has occurred within the preceding 60 days. A substantial violation is one which could reasonably lead to, or has resulted in, serious personal injury or death. Each complaint must be signed by the complainant and must contain:

(1) The name, address, and telephone number of the person who files it;

(2) The name and address of the alleged violator and, with respect to each alleged violator, the specific provisions of the regulations that the complainant believes were violated; and

(3) A concise but complete statement of the facts relied upon to substantiate each allegation, including the date of each alleged violation.

(b) *Action on complaint of substantial violation.* Upon the filing of a complaint of a substantial violation under paragraph (a) of this section, the Assistant Administrator shall determine whether it is nonfrivolous and meets the requirements of paragraph (a) of this section. If the Assistant Administrator determines the complaint is nonfrivolous and meets the requirements of paragraph (a), he/she shall investigate the complaint. The complainant shall be timely notified of findings resulting from such investigation. The Assistant Administrator shall not be required to conduct separate investigations of duplicative complaints. If the Assistant Administrator determines the complaint is frivolous or does not meet the requirements of the paragraph (a), he/she shall dismiss the complaint and notify the complainant in writing of the reasons for such dismissal.

(c) Notwithstanding the provisions of section 552 of title 5, United States Code, the Assistant Administrator shall not disclose the identity of complainants unless it is determined that such disclosure is necessary to prosecute a violation. If disclosure becomes necessary, the Assistant Administrator shall take every practical means within the Assistant Administrator's authority to assure that the complainant is not subject to harassment, intimidation, disciplinary action, discrimination, or financial loss as a result of such disclosure.

[50 FR 40306, Oct. 2, 1985, as amended at 70 FR 28481, May 18, 2005]

§386.13 Petitions to review and request for hearing: Driver qualification proceedings.

(a) Within 60 days after service of the determination under §391.47 of this chapter or the letter of disqualification, the driver or carrier may petition to review such action. Such petitions must be submitted to the Assistant Administrator and must contain the following:

(1) Identification of what action the petitioner wants overturned;

(2) Copies of all evidence upon which petitioner relies in the form set out in §386.49;

(3) All legal and other arguments which the petitioner wishes to make in support of his/her position;

(4) A request for oral hearing, if one is desired, which must set forth material factual issues believed to be in dispute;

(5) Certification that the reply has been filed in accordance with §386.31; and

(6) Any other pertinent material.

(b) Failure to submit a petition as specified in paragraph (a) of this section shall constitute a waiver of the right to petition for review of the determination or letter of disqualification. In these cases, the determination or disqualification issued automatically becomes the final decision of the Assistant Administrator 30 days after the time to submit the reply or petition to review has expired, unless the Assistant Administrator orders otherwise.

(c) If the petition does not request a hearing, the Assistant Administrator may issue a final decision and order based on the evidence and arguments submitted.

§386.14 Reply.

(a) *Time for reply to the Notice of Claim.* Respondent must serve a reply to the Notice of Claim in writing within 30 days following service of the Notice of Claim. The reply is to be served in accordance with § 386.6 upon the Service Center indicated in the Notice of Claim.

(b) *Options for reply.* The respondent must reply to the Notice of Claim within the time allotted by choosing one of the following:

(1) Paying the full amount asserted in the Notice of Claim in accordance with § 386.18 of this part;

(2) Contesting the claim by requesting administrative adjudication pursuant to paragraph (d) of this section; or

(3) Seeking binding arbitration in accordance with the Agency's program. Although the amount of the proposed penalty may be disputed, referral to binding arbitration is contingent upon an admission of liability that the violations occurred.

(c) *Failure to answer the Notice of Claim.* (1) Respondent's failure to answer the Notice of Claim in accordance with paragraph (a) may result in the issuance of a Notice of Default and Final Agency Order by the Field Administrator. The Notice of Default and Final Agency Order will declare respondent to be in default and further declare the Notice of Claim, including the civil penalty proposed in the Notice of Claim, to be the Final Agency Order in the proceeding. The Final Agency Order will be effective five days following service of the Notice of Default and Final Agency Order.

(2) The default constitutes an admission of all facts alleged in the Notice of Claim and a waiver of respondent's opportunity to contest the claim. The default will be reviewed by the Assistant Administrator in accordance with § 386.64(b), and the Final Agency Order may be vacated where a respondent demonstrates excusable neglect, a meritorious defense, or due diligence in seeking relief.

(3) Failure to pay the civil penalty as directed in a Final Agency Order constitutes a violation of that order, subjecting the respondent to an additional penalty as prescribed in Subpart G of this part.

(d) *Request for administrative adjudication.* The respondent may contest the claim and request administrative adju-

dication pursuant to paragraph (b)(2) of this section. An administrative adjudication is a process to resolve contested claims before the Assistant Administrator, Administrative Law Judge, or Hearing Officer. Once an administrative adjudication option is elected, it is binding on the respondent.

(1) *Contents.* In addition to the general requirements of this section, the reply must be in writing and state the grounds for contesting the claim and must raise any affirmative defenses the respondent intends to assert. Specifically, the reply:

(i) Must admit or deny each separately stated and numbered allegation of violation in the claim. A statement that the person is without sufficient knowledge or information to admit or deny will have the effect of a denial. Any allegation in the claim not specifically denied in the reply is deemed admitted. A mere general denial of the claim is insufficient and may result in a default being entered by the Agency decisionmaker upon motion by the Field Administrator.

(ii) Must include all known affirmative defenses, including those relating to jurisdiction, limitations, and procedure.

(iii) Must state which one of the following options respondent seeks:

(A) To submit written evidence without hearing; or

(B) An informal hearing; or

(C) A formal hearing.

(2) [Reserved]

[70 FR 28481, May 18, 2005]

§ 386.15 [Reserved]

§ 386.16 Action on replies to the Notice of Claim.

(a) *Requests to submit written evidence without a hearing.* Where respondent has elected to submit written evidence in accordance with § 386.14(d)(1)(iii)(A):

(1) Agency Counsel must serve all written evidence and argument in support of the Notice of Claim no later than 60 days following service of respondent's reply. The written evidence and argument must be served on the Assistant Administrator in accordance with §§ 386.6 and 386.7. The submission must include all pleadings, notices, and other filings in the case to date.

(2) Respondent will, not later than 45 days following service of Agency Counsel's written evidence and argument, serve its written evidence and argument on the Assistant Administrator in accordance with §§ 386.6 and 386.7.

(3) Agency Counsel may file a written response to respondent's submission. Any such submission must be filed within 20 days of service of respondent's submission.

(4) All written evidence submitted by the parties must conform to the requirements of § 386.49.

(5) Following submission of evidence and argument as outlined in this section, the Assistant Administrator may issue a Final Agency Order and order based on the evidence and arguments submitted, or may issue any other order as may be necessary to adjudicate the matter.

(b) *Requests for hearing.* (1) If a request for a formal or informal hearing has been filed, the Assistant Administrator will determine whether there exists a dispute of a material fact at issue in the matter. If so, the matter will be set for hearing in accordance with respondent's reply. If it is determined that there does not exist a dispute of a material fact at issue in the matter, the Assistant Administrator may issue a decision based on the written record, or may request the submission of further evidence or argument.

(2) If a respondent requests a formal or informal hearing in its reply, the Field Administrator must serve upon the Assistant Administrator and respondent a notice of consent or objection with a basis to the request within 60 days of service of respondent's reply. Failure to serve an objection within the time allotted may result in referral of the matter to hearing.

(3) *Requests for formal hearing.* Following the filing of an objection with basis, the Field Administrator must serve a motion for Final Agency Order pursuant to § 386.36 unless otherwise ordered by the Assistant Administrator. The motion must set forth the reasons why the Field Administrator is entitled to judgment as a matter of law. Respondent must, within 45 days of service of the motion for Final Agency Order, submit and serve a response to the Field Administrator's motion.

After reviewing the record, the Assistant Administrator will either set the matter for hearing by referral to the Office of Hearings or issue a Final Agency Order based upon the submissions.

(4) *Requests for informal hearing.* (i) If the Field Administrator objects with basis to a request for an informal hearing, he/she must serve the objection, a copy of the Notice of Claim, and a copy of respondent's reply, on the respondent and Assistant Administrator, pursuant to paragraph (b)(2) of this section. Based upon the Notice of Claim, the reply, and the objection with basis, the Assistant Administrator will issue an order granting or denying the request for informal hearing.

(A) *Informal hearing granted.* If the request for informal hearing is granted by the Assistant Administrator, a Hearing Officer will be assigned to hear the matter and will set forth the date, time and location for hearing. No further motions will be entertained, and no discovery will be allowed. At hearing, all parties may present evidence, written and oral, to the Hearing Officer, following which the Hearing Officer will issue a report to the Assistant Administrator containing findings of fact and recommending a disposition of the matter. The report will serve as the sole record of the proceedings. The Assistant Administrator may issue a Final Agency Order adopting the report, or issue other such orders as he/she may deem appropriate. By participating in an informal hearing, respondent waives its right to a formal hearing.

(B) *Informal hearing denied.* If the request for informal hearing is denied, the Field Administrator must serve a motion for Final Agency Order pursuant to § 386.36, unless otherwise directed by the Assistant Administrator. The motion must set forth the reasons why the Field Administrator is entitled to judgment as a matter of law. Respondent must, within 45 days of service of the motion for Final Agency Order, submit and serve a response to the Field Administrator's motion. After reviewing the record, the Assistant Administrator will set the matter for formal hearing by referral to the Office of Hearings, or will issue a Final

Agency Order based upon the submissions.

(C) Nothing in this section shall limit the Assistant Administrator's authority to refer any matter for formal hearing, even in instances where respondent seeks only an informal hearing.

[70 FR 28481, May 18, 2005]

§ 386.17 Intervention.

After the matter is called for hearing and before the date set for the hearing to begin, any person may petition for leave to intervene. The petition is to be served on the administrative law judge. The petition must set forth the reasons why the petitioner alleges he/she is entitled to intervene. The petition must be served on all parties in accordance with § 386.31. Any party may file a response within 10 days of service of the petition. The administrative law judge shall then determine whether to permit or deny the petition. The petition will be allowed if the administrative law judge determines that the final decision could directly and adversely affect the petitioner or the class he/she represents, and if the petitioner may contribute materially to the disposition of the proceedings and his/her interest is not adequately represented by existing parties. Once admitted, a petitioner is a party for the purpose of all subsequent proceedings.

§ 386.18 Payment of the claim.

(a) Payment of the full amount claimed may be made at any time before issuance of a Final Agency Order. After the issuance of a Final Agency Order, claims are subject to interest, penalties, and administrative charges in accordance with 31 U.S.C. 3717; 49 CFR part 89; and 31 CFR 901.9.

(b) If respondent elects to pay the full amount as its response to the Notice of Claim, payment must be served upon the Field Administrator at the Service Center designated in the Notice of Claim within 30 days following service of the Notice of Claim. No written reply is necessary if respondent elects the payment option during the 30-day reply period. Failure to serve full payment within 30 days of service of the Notice of Claim when this option has been chosen may constitute a default and may result in the Notice of Claim, including the civil penalty assessed by the Notice of Claim, becoming the Final Agency Order in the proceeding pursuant to § 386.14(c).

(c) Unless objected to in writing, submitted at the time of payment, payment of the full amount in response to the Notice of Claim constitutes an admission by the respondent of all facts alleged in the Notice of Claim. Payment waives respondent's opportunity to further contest the claim, and will result in the Notice of Claim becoming the Final Agency Order.

[70 FR 28482, May 18, 2005]

Subpart C—Settlement Agreements

§ 386.22 Settlement agreements and their contents.

(a) *Settlement agreements.* (1) When negotiations produce an agreement as to the amount or terms of payment of a civil penalty or the terms and conditions of an order, a settlement agreement shall be drawn and signed by the respondent and the Field Administrator or his/her designee. Such settlement agreement must contain the following:

(i) The statutory basis of the claim;

(ii) A brief statement of the violations;

(iii) The amount claimed and the amount paid;

(iv) The date, time, and place and form of payment;

(v) A statement that the agreement is not binding on the Agency until executed by the Field Administrator or his/her designee;

(vi) A statement that failure to pay in accordance with the terms of the agreement or to comply with the terms of the agreement may result in the reinstatement of any penalties held in abeyance and may also result in the loss of any reductions in civil penalties asserted in the Notice of Claim, in which case the original amount asserted will be due immediately; and

(vii) A statement that the agreement is the Final Agency Order.

(2) A settlement agreement may contain any conditions, actions, or provisions agreed by the parties to redress

the violations cited in the Notice of Claim or notice of violation.

(3) A settlement agreement accepted and approved by the Assistant Administrator or Administrative Law Judge is a Final Agency Order which is binding on all parties according to its terms. Consent to a settlement agreement which has not yet been approved by the Assistant Administrator or Administrative Law Judge may not be withdrawn for a period of 30 days.

(b) *Civil penalty proceedings not before agency decisionmaker.* When the parties have agreed to a settlement at any time prior to the case coming before the Agency decisionmaker, the parties may execute an appropriate agreement for disposing of the case. The agreement does not require approval by the Agency decisionmaker. The agreement becomes the Final Agency Order upon execution by the Field Administrator or his/her designee.

(c) *Civil penalty proceedings before agency decisionmaker.* When a respondent has agreed to a settlement of a civil penalty before a Final Agency Order has been issued, the parties may execute an appropriate agreement for disposal of the case by consent for the consideration of the Assistant Administrator. The agreement is filed with the Assistant Administrator, who may accept it, reject it and direct that proceedings in the case continue, or take such other action as he/she deems appropriate. If the Assistant Administrator accepts the agreement, he/she shall enter an order in accordance with its terms. The settlement agreement becomes the Final Agency Order as of the date the Assistant Administrator enters an order accepting the settlement agreement.

(d) *Civil penalty proceedings before Administrative Law Judge (ALJ).* When a respondent has agreed to a settlement of a civil penalty before the hearing is concluded, the parties may execute an appropriate agreement for disposing of the case by consent for the consideration of the ALJ. The agreement is filed with the ALJ who may accept it, reject it, and direct that proceedings in the case continue, or take such other action as he/she deems appropriate. If the ALJ accepts the agreement, he/she shall enter an order in accordance with

its terms. The settlement agreement becomes the Final Agency Order as per §386.61.

(e) *Civil penalty proceedings before Hearing Officer.* When a respondent has agreed to a settlement of a civil penalty before the hearing is concluded, the parties may execute an appropriate agreement for disposal of the case for the consideration of the Hearing Officer. The agreement is filed with the Hearing Officer, who, within 20 days of receipt, will make a report and recommendation to the Assistant Administrator who may accept it, reject it, and direct that proceedings in the case continue, or take such other action as he/she deems appropriate. If the Assistant Administrator accepts the agreement, he/she will enter an order in accordance with its terms. The settlement agreement becomes the Final Agency Order as of the date the Assistant Administrator enters an order accepting the settlement agreement.

[70 FR 28482, May 18, 2005]

Subpart D—General Rules and Hearings

§386.31 Official notice.

Upon notification to all parties, the Assistant Administrator or Administrative Law Judge may take official notice of any fact or document not appearing in evidence in the record. Any party objecting to the official notice must file an objection within 10 days after service of the notice. If a Final Agency Order has been issued, and the decision rests on a material and disputable fact of which the Agency decisionmaker has taken official notice, a party may challenge the action of official notice in accordance with §386.64 of this part.

[70 FR 28483, May 18, 2005]

§386.34 Motions.

(a) *General.* An application for an order or ruling not otherwise covered by these rules shall be by motion. All motions filed prior to the calling of the matter for a hearing shall be to the Assistant Administrator. All motions filed after the matter is called for hearing shall be to the administrative law judge.

(b) *Form.* Unless made during hearing, motions shall be made in writing, shall state with particularity the grounds for relief sought, and shall be accompanied by affidavits or other evidence relied upon.

(c) *Answers.* Except when a motion is filed during a hearing, any party may file an answer in support or opposition to a motion, accompanied by affidavits or other evidence relied upon. Such answers shall be served within 20 days after the motion is served or within such other time as the Assistant Administrator or administrative law judge may set.

(d) *Argument.* Oral argument or briefs on a motion may be ordered by the Assistant Administrator or the administrative law judge.

(e) *Disposition.* Motions may be ruled on immediately or at any other time specified by the administrative law judge or the Assistant Administrator.

(f) *Suspension of time.* The pendency of a motion shall not affect any time limits set in these rules unless expressly ordered by the Assistant Administrator or administrative law judge.

[50 FR 40306, Oct. 2, 1985. Redesignated and amended at 70 FR 28483, May 18, 2005]

§ 386.35 Motions to dismiss and motions for a more definite statement.

(a) Motions to dismiss must be made within the time set for reply or petition to review, except motions to dismiss for lack of jurisdiction, which may be made at any time.

(b) Motions for a more definite statement may be made in lieu of a reply. The motion must point out the defects complained of and the details desired. If the motion is granted, the pleading complained of must be remedied within 15 days of the granting of the motion or it will be stricken. If the motion is denied, the party who requested the more definite statement must file his/her pleading within 10 days after the denial.

[50 FR 40306, Oct. 2, 1985. Redesignated at 70 FR 28483, May 18, 2005]

§ 386.36 Motions for final agency order.

(a) *Generally.* Unless otherwise provided in this section, the motion and answer will be governed by § 386.34. Either party may file a motion for final order. The motion must be served in accordance with §§ 386.6 and 386.7. If the matter is still pending before the service center, upon filing, the matter is officially transferred from the service center to the Agency decisionmaker, who will then preside over the matter.

(b) *Form and content.* (1) Movant's filing must contain a motion and memorandum of law, which may be separate or combined and must include all responsive pleadings, notices, and other filings in the case to date.

(2) The motion for final order must be accompanied by written evidence in accordance with § 386.49.

(3) The motion will state with particularity the grounds upon which it is based and the substantial matters of law to be argued. A Final Agency Order may be issued if, after reviewing the record in a light most favorable to the non-moving party, the Agency decisionmaker determines no genuine issue exists as to any material fact.

(c) *Answer to Motion.* The non-moving party will, within 45 days of service of the motion for final order, submit and serve a response to rebut movant's motion.

[70 FR 28483, May 18, 2005]

§ 386.37 Discovery.

(a) Parties may obtain discovery by one or more of the following methods: Depositions upon oral examination or written questions; written interrogatories; request for production of documents or other evidence for inspection and other purposes; physical and mental examinations; and requests for admission.

(b) Discovery may not commence until the matter is pending before the Assistant Administrator or referred to the Office of Hearings.

(c) Except as otherwise provided in these rules, in the Administrative Procedure Act, 5 U.S.C. 551 *et seq.*, or by the Assistant Administrator or Administrative Law Judge, in the absence of specific Agency provisions or regulations, the Federal Rules of Civil Procedure may serve as guidance in administrative adjudications.

[70 FR 28483, May 18, 2005]

§386.38 Scope of discovery.

(a) Unless otherwise limited by order of the Assistant Administrator or, in cases that have been called for a hearing, the administrative law judge, in accordance with these rules, the parties may obtain discovery regarding any matter, not privileged, which is relevant to the subject matter involved in the proceeding, including the existence, description, nature, custody, condition, and location of any books, documents, or other tangible things and the identity and location of persons having knowledge of any discoverable matter.

(b) It is not ground for objection that information sought will not be admissible at the hearing if the information sought appears reasonably calculated to lead to the discovery of admissible evidence.

(c) A party may obtain discovery of documents and tangible things otherwise discoverable under paragraph (a) of this section and prepared in anticipation of or for the hearing by or for another party's representative (including his or her attorney, consultant, surety, indemnitor, insurer, or agent) only upon a showing that the party seeking discovery has substantial need of the materials in the preparation of his or her case and that he or she is unable without undue hardship to obtain the substantial equivalent of the materials by other means. In ordering discovery of such materials when the required showing has been made, the Assistant Administrator or the administrative law judge shall protect against disclosure of the mental impressions, conclusions, opinions, or legal theories of an attorney or other representative of a party concerning the proceeding.

§386.39 Protective orders.

Upon motion by a party or other person from whom discovery is sought, and for good cause shown, the Assistant Administrator or the administrative law judge, if one has been appointed, may make any order which justice requires to protect a party or person from annoyance, embarrassment, oppression, or undue burden or expense, including one or more of the following:

(a) The discovery not be had;

(b) The discovery may be had only on specified terms and conditions, including a designation of the time or place;

(c) The discovery may be had only by a method of discovery other than that selected by the party seeking discovery;

(d) Certain matters not relevant may not be inquired into, or that the scope of discovery be limited to certain matters;

(e) Discovery be conducted with no one present except persons designated by the Assistant Administrator or the administrative law judge; or

(f) A trade secret or other confidential research, development, or commercial information may not be disclosed or be disclosed only in a designated way.

§386.40 Supplementation of responses.

A party who has responded to a request for discovery with a response that was complete when made is under no duty to supplement his/her response to include information thereafter acquired, except as follows:

(a) A party is under a duty to supplement timely his/her response with respect to any question directly addressed to:

(1) The identity and location of persons having knowledge of discoverable matters; and

(2) The identity of each person expected to be called as an expert witness at the hearing, the subject matter on which he or she is expected to testify and the substance of his or her testimony.

(b) A party is under a duty to amend timely a prior response if he or she later obtains information upon the basis of which:

(1) he or she knows the response was incorrect when made; or

(2) he or she knows that the response though correct when made is no longer true and the circumstances are such that a failure to amend the response is in substance a knowing concealment.

(c) A duty to supplement responses may be imposed by order of the Assistant Administrator or the administrative law judge or agreement of the parties.

§ 386.41 Stipulations regarding discovery.

Unless otherwise ordered, a written stipulation entered into by all the parties and filed with the Assistant Administrator or the administrative law judge, if one has been appointed, may:

(a) Provide that depositions be taken before any person, at any time or place, upon sufficient notice, and in any manner, and when so taken may be used like other depositions, and

(b) Modify the procedures provided by these rules for other methods of discovery.

§ 386.42 Written interrogatories to parties.

(a) Without leave, any party may serve upon any other party written interrogatories to be answered by the party to whom the interrogatories are directed; or, if that party is a public or private corporation or partnership or association or governmental agency, by any officer or agent, who will furnish the information available to that party.

(b) The maximum number of interrogatories served will not exceed 30, including all subparts, unless the Assistant Administrator or Administrative Law Judge permits a larger number on motion and for good cause shown. Other interrogatories may be added without leave, so long as the total number of approved and additional interrogatories does not exceed 30.

(c) Each interrogatory shall be answered separately and fully in writing under oath unless it is objected to, in which event the grounds for objection shall be stated and signed by the party, or counsel for the party, if represented, making the response. The party to whom the interrogatories are directed shall serve the answers and any objections within 30 days after the service of the interrogatories, or within such shortened or longer period as the Assistant Administrator or the Administrative Law Judge may allow.

(d) Motions to compel may be made in accordance with § 386.45.

(e) A notice of discovery must be served on the Assistant Administrator or, in cases that have been referred to the Office of Hearings, on the Administrative Law Judge. A copy of the interrogatories, answers, and all related pleadings must be served on all parties to the proceeding.

(f) An interrogatory otherwise proper is not necessarily objectionable merely because an answer to the interrogatory involves an opinion or contention that relates to fact or the application of law to fact, but the Assistant Administrator or Administrative Law Judge may order that such an interrogatory need not be answered until after designated discovery has been completed or until a prehearing conference or other later time.

[70 FR 28483, May 18, 2005]

§ 386.43 Production of documents and other evidence; entry upon land for inspection and other purposes; and physical and mental examination.

(a) Any party may serve on any other party a request to:

(1) Produce and permit the party making the request, or a person acting on his or her behalf, to inspect and copy any designated documents, or to inspect and copy, test, or sample any tangible things which are in the possession, custody, or control of the party upon whom the request is served; or

(2) Permit entry upon designated land or other property in the possession or control of the party upon whom the request is served for the purpose of inspection and measuring, photographing, testing, or for other purposes as stated in paragraph (a)(1) of this section.

(3) Submit to a physical or mental examination by a physician.

(b) The request may be served on any party without leave of the Assistant Administrator or administrative law judge.

(c) The request shall:

(1) Set forth the items to be inspected either by individual item or category;

(2) Describe each item or category with reasonable particularity;

(3) Specify a reasonable time, place, and manner of making the inspection and performing the related acts;

(4) Specify the time, place, manner, conditions, and scope of the physical or mental examination and the person or persons by whom it is to be made. A report of examining physician shall be

made in accordance with Rule 35(b) of the Federal Rules of Civil Procedure, title 28, U.S. Code, as amended.

(d) The party upon whom the request is served shall serve on the party submitting the request a written response within 30 days after service of the request.

(e) The response shall state, with respect to each item or category:

(1) That inspection and related activities will be permitted as requested; or

(2) That objection is made in whole or in part, in which case the reasons for objection shall be stated.

(f) A copy of each request for production and each written response shall be served on all parties and filed with the Assistant Administrator or the administrative law judge, if one has been appointed.

§386.44 Request for admissions.

(a) *Request for admission.* (1) Any party may serve upon any other party a request for admission of any relevant matter or the authenticity of any relevant document. Copies of any document about which an admission is requested must accompany the request.

(2) Each matter for which an admission is requested shall be separately set forth and numbered. The matter is admitted unless within 15 days after service of the request, the party to whom the request is directed serves upon the party requesting the admission a written answer signed by the party or his/her attorney.

(3) Each answer must specify whether the party admits or denies the matter. If the matter cannot be admitted or denied, the party shall set out in detail the reasons.

(4) A party may not issue a denial or fail to answer on the ground that he/she lacks knowledge unless he/she has made reasonable inquiry to ascertain information sufficient to allow him/her to admit or deny.

(5) A party may file an objection to a request for admission within 10 days after service. Such motion shall be filed with the administrative law judge if one has been appointed, otherwise it shall be filed with the Assistant Administrator. An objection must explain in detail the reasons the party should not answer. A reply to the objection may be served by the party requesting the admission within 10 days after service of the objection. It is not sufficient ground for objection to claim that the matter about which an admission is requested presents an issue of fact for hearing.

(b) *Effect of admission.* Any matter admitted is conclusively established unless the Assistant Administrator or administrative law judge permits withdrawal or amendment. Any admission under this rule is for the purpose of the pending action only and may not be used in any other proceeding.

(c) If a party refuses to admit a matter or the authenticity of a document which is later proved, the party requesting the admission may move for an award of expenses incurred in making the proof. Such a motion shall be granted unless there was a good reason for failure to admit.

§386.45 Motion to compel discovery.

(a) If a deponent fails to answer a question propounded or a party upon whom a request is made pursuant to §§386.42 through 386.44, or a party upon whom interrogatories are served fails to respond adequately or objects to the request, or any part thereof, or fails to permit inspection as requested, the discovering party may move the Assistant Administrator or the administrative law judge, if one has been appointed, for an order compelling a response or inspection in accordance with the request.

(b) The motion shall set forth:

(1) The nature of the questions or request;

(2) The response or objections of the party upon whom the request was served; and

(3) Arguments in support of the motion.

(c) For purposes of this section, an evasive answer or incomplete answer or response shall be treated as a failure to answer or respond.

(d) In ruling on a motion made pursuant to this section, the Assistant Administrator or the administrative law judge, if one has been appointed, may make and enter a protective order such as he or she is authorized to enter on a motion made pursuant to §386.39(a).

§ 386.46 Depositions.

(a) *When, how, and by whom taken.* (1) The deposition of any witness may be taken at reasonable times subsequent to the appointment of an Administrative Law Judge. Prior to referral to the Office of Hearings, a party may petition the Assistant Administrator, in accordance with § 386.37, for leave to conduct a deposition based on good cause shown.

(2) Depositions may be taken by oral examination or upon written interrogatories before any person having power to administer oaths.

(3) The parties may stipulate in writing or the Administrative Law Judge may upon motion order that a deposition be taken by telephone or other remote electronic means.

(4) If a subpoena duces tecum is to be served on the person to be examined, the designation of the materials to be produced as set forth in the subpoena shall be attached to, or included in, the notice.

(5) If the deposition is to be recorded by videotape or audiotape, the notice shall specify the method of recording.

(b) *Application.* Any party desiring to take the deposition of a witness must indicate to the witness and all other parties the time when, the place where, and the name and post office address of the person before whom the deposition is to be taken; the name and address of each witness; and the subject matter concerning which each such witness is expected to testify.

(c) *Notice.* A party desiring to take a deposition must give notice to the witness and all other parties. Notice must be in writing. Notice of the deposition must be given not less than 20 days from when the deposition is to be taken if the deposition is to be held within the continental United States and not less than 30 days from when the deposition is to be taken if the deposition is to be held elsewhere, unless a shorter time is agreed to by the parties or by leave of the Assistant Administrator or Administrative Law Judge by motion for good cause shown.

(d) *Depositions upon written questions.* Within 14 days after the notice and written questions are served, a party may serve cross-questions upon all other parties. Within 7 days after being served with cross-questions, a party may serve redirect questions upon all other parties. Within 7 days after being served with redirect questions, a party may serve recross questions upon all other parties. The Assistant Administrator or Administrative Law Judge may enlarge or shorten the time for cause shown.

(e) *Taking and receiving in evidence.* Each witness testifying upon deposition must be sworn, and any other party must be given the right to cross-examine. The questions propounded and the answers to them, together with all objections made, must be reduced to writing; read by or to, and subscribed by the witness; and certified by the person administering the oath. The person who took the deposition must seal the deposition transcript in an envelope and file it in accordance with § 386.7. Subject to objections to the questions and answers as were noted at the time of taking the deposition and which would have been valid if the witness were personally present and testifying, the deposition may be read and offered in evidence by the party taking it as against any party who was present or represented at the taking of the deposition or who had due notice of it.

(f) *Witness limit.* No party may seek deposition testimony of more than five witnesses without leave of the Agency decisionmaker for good cause shown. Individual depositions are not to exceed 8 hours for any one witness.

(g) *Motion to terminate or limit examination.* During the taking of a deposition, a party or deponent may request suspension of the deposition on grounds of bad faith in the conduct of the examination, oppression of a deponent or party or improper questions propounded. The deposition will then be adjourned. The objecting party or deponent must, however, immediately move for a ruling on his or her objections to the deposition conduct or proceedings before the Assistant Administrator or Administrative Law Judge, who then may limit the scope or manner of the taking of the deposition.

[70 FR 28484, May 18, 2005]

§386.47 Use of deposition at hearings.

(a) *Generally.* At the hearing, any part or all of a deposition, so far as admissible under the rules of evidence, may be used against any party who was present or represented at the taking of the deposition or who had due notice thereof in accordance with any one of the following provisions:

(1) Any deposition may be used by any party for the purpose of contradicting or impeaching the testimony of the deponent as a witness.

(2) The deposition of expert witnesses, particularly the deposition of physicians, may be used by any party for any purpose, unless the Assistant Administrator or administrative law judge rules that such use would be unfair or a violation of due process.

(3) The deposition of a party or of anyone who at the time of taking the deposition was an officer, director, or duly authorized agent of a public or private organization, partnership, or association which is a party, may be used by any other party for any purpose.

(4) The deposition of a witness, whether or not a party, may be used by any party for any purpose if the presiding officer finds:

(i) That the witness is dead; or

(ii) That the witness is out of the United States or more than 100 miles from the place of hearing unless it appears that the absence of the witness was procured by the party offering the deposition; or

(iii) That the witness is unable to attend to testify because of age, sickness, infirmity, or imprisonment; or

(iv) That the party offering the deposition has been unable to procure the attendance of the witness by subpoena; or

(v) Upon application and notice, that such exceptional circumstances exist as to make it desirable, in the interest of justice and with due regard to the importance of presenting the testimony of witnesses orally in open hearing, to allow the deposition to be used.

(5) If only part of a deposition is offered in evidence by a party, any other party may require him or her to introduce all of it which is relevant to the part introduced, and any party may introduce any other parts.

(b) *Objections to admissibility.* Except as provided in this paragraph, objection may be made at the hearing to receiving in evidence any deposition or part thereof for any reason which would require the exclusion of the evidence if the witness were then present and testifying.

(1) Objections to the competency of a witness or to the competency, relevancy or materiality of testimony are not waived by failure to make them before or during the taking of the deposition, unless the ground of the objection is one which might have been obviated or removed if presented at that time.

(2) Errors and irregularities occurring at the oral examination in the manner of taking the deposition, in the form of the questions or answers, in the oath or affirmation, or in the conduct of parties and errors of any kind which might be obviated, removed, or cured if promptly presented, are waived unless reasonable objection thereto is made at the taking of the deposition.

(3) Objections to the form or written interrogatories are waived unless served in writing upon the party propounding them.

(c) *Effect of taking using depositions.* A party shall not be deemed to make a person his or her own witness for any purpose by taking his or her deposition. The introduction in evidence of the deposition or any part thereof for any purpose other than that of contradicting or impeaching the deponent makes the deponent the witness of the party introducing the deposition, but this shall not apply to the use by any other party of a deposition as described in paragraph (a)(2) of this section. At the hearing, any party may rebut any relevant evidence contained in a deposition whether introduced by him or her or by any other party.

§386.48 Medical records and physicians' reports.

In cases involving the physical qualifications of drivers, copies of all physicians' reports, test results, and other medical records that a party intends to rely upon shall be served on all other parties at least 30 days prior to the date set for a hearing. Except as waived by the Director, Office of Truck and Bus Standards and Operations, reports, test results and medical records not served under this rule shall be excluded from evidence at any hearing.

[50 FR 40306, Oct. 2, 1985, as amended at 53 FR 2036, Jan. 26, 1988; 65 FR 7756, Feb. 16, 2000]

§ 386.49 **Form of written evidence.**

All written evidence should be submitted in the following forms:

(a) A written statement of a person having personal knowledge of the facts alleged, or

(b) Documentary evidence in the form of exhibits attached to a written statement identifying the exhibit and giving its source.

[70 FR 28484, May 18, 2005]

§ 386.51 **Amendment and withdrawal of pleadings.**

(a) Except in instances covered by other rules, anytime more than 15 days prior to the hearing, a party may amend his/her pleadings by serving the amended pleading on the Assistant Administrator or the administrative law judge, if one has been appointed, and on all parties. Within 15 days prior to the hearing, an amendment shall be allowed only at the discretion of the Administrative law judge. When an amended pleading is filed, other parties may file a response and objection within 10 days.

(b) A party may withdraw his/her pleading any time more than 15 days prior to the hearing by serving a notice of withdrawal on the Assistant Administrator or the Administrative Law Judge. Within 15 days prior to the hearing a withdrawal may be made only at the discretion of the Assistant Administrator or the Administrative Law Judge. The withdrawal will be granted absent a finding that the withdrawal will result in injustice, prejudice, or irreparable harm to the non-moving party, or is otherwise contrary to the public interest.

[50 FR 40306, Oct. 2, 1985, as amended at 70 FR 28484, May 18, 2005]

§ 386.52 **Appeals from interlocutory rulings.**

(a) *General.* Unless otherwise provided in this subpart, a party may not appeal a ruling or decision of the Administrative Law Judge to the Assistant Administrator until the Administrative Law Judge's decision has been entered on the record. A decision or order of the Assistant Administrator on the interlocutory appeal does not constitute a Final Agency Order for the purposes of judicial review under § 386.67.

(b) *Interlocutory appeal for cause.* If a party files a written request for an interlocutory appeal for cause with the Administrative Law Judge, or orally requests an interlocutory appeal for cause, the proceedings are stayed until the Administrative Law Judge issues a decision on the request. If the Administrative Law Judge grants the request, the proceedings are stayed until the Assistant Administrator issues a decision on the interlocutory appeal. The Administrative Law Judge must grant an interlocutory appeal for cause if a party shows that delay of the appeal would be detrimental to the public interest or would result in undue prejudice to any party.

(c) [Reserved]

(d) *Procedure.* A party must file a notice of interlocutory appeal, with any supporting documents, with the Assistant Administrator, and serve copies on each party and the Administrative Law Judge, not later than 10 days after the Administrative Law Judge's oral decision has been issued, or a written decision has been served. A party must file a reply brief, if any, with the Assistant Administrator and serve a copy of the reply brief on each party, not later than 10 days after service of the appeal brief. The Assistant Administrator will render a decision on the interlocutory appeal, within a reasonable time after receipt of the interlocutory appeal.

(e) The Assistant Administrator may reject frivolous, repetitive, or dilatory appeals, and may issue an order precluding one or more parties from making further interlocutory appeals, and may order such further relief as required.

[70 FR 28484, May 18, 2005]

§ 386.53 **Subpoenas, witness fees.**

(a) Applications for the issuance of subpoenas must be submitted to the Assistant Administrator, or in cases that have been called for a hearing, to the administrative law judge. The application must show the general relevance and reasonable scope of the evidence sought. Any person served with a subpoena may, within 7 days after service, file a motion to quash or modify. The motion must be filed with the official who approved the subpoena. The filing of a motion shall stay the effect of the subpoena until a decision is reached.

(b) Witnesses shall be entitled to the same fees and mileage as are paid witnesses in the courts of the United States. The fees shall be paid by the party at whose instance the witness is subpoenaed or appears.

(c) Paragraph (a) of this section shall not apply to the Administrator or employees of the FMCSA or to the production of documents in their custody. Applications for the attendance of such persons or the production of such documents at a hearing shall be made to the Assistant Administrator or administrative law judge, if one is appointed, and shall set forth the need for such evidence and its relevancy.

§386.54 Administrative Law Judge.

(a) *Powers of an Administrative Law Judge.* The Administrative Law Judge may take any action and may prescribe all necessary rules and regulations to govern the conduct of the proceedings to ensure a fair and impartial hearing, and to avoid delay in the disposition of the proceedings. In accordance with the rules in this subchapter, an Administrative Law Judge may do the following:

(1) Give notice of and hold prehearing conferences and hearings.

(2) Administer oaths and affirmations.

(3) Issue subpoenas authorized by law.

(4) Rule on offers of proof.

(5) Receive relevant and material evidence.

(6) Regulate the course of the administrative adjudication in accordance with the rules of this subchapter and the Administrative Procedure Act.

(7) Hold conferences to settle or simplify the issues by consent of the parties.

(8) Dispose of procedural motions and requests, except motions that under this part are made directly to the Assistant Administrator.

(9) Issue orders permitting inspection and examination of lands, buildings, equipment, and any other physical thing and the copying of any document.

(10) Make findings of fact and conclusions of law, and issue decisions.

(11) To take any other action authorized by these rules and permitted by law.

(b) *Limitations on the power of the Administrative Law Judge.* The Administrative Law Judge is bound by the procedural requirements of this part and the precedent opinions of the Agency. This section does not preclude an Administrative Law Judge from barring a person from a specific proceeding based on a finding of obstreperous or disruptive behavior in that proceeding.

(c) *Disqualification.* The Administrative Law Judge may disqualify himself or herself at any time, either at the request of any party or upon his or her own initiative. Assignments of Administrative Law Judges are made by the Chief Administrative Law Judge upon the request of the Assistant Administrator. Any request for a change in such assignment, including disqualification, will be considered only for good cause which would unduly prejudice the proceeding.

[70 FR 28485, May 18, 2005]

§386.55 Prehearing conferences.

(a) *Convening.* At any time before the hearing begins, the administrative law judge, on his/her own motion or on motion by a party, may direct the parties or their counsel to participate with him/her in a prehearing conference to consider the following:

(1) Simplification and clarification of the issues;

(2) Necessity or desirability of amending pleadings;

(3) Stipulations as to the facts and the contents and authenticity of documents;

(4) Issuance of and responses to subpoenas;

(5) Taking of depositions and the use of depositions in the proceedings;

305

(6) Orders for discovery, inspection and examination of premises, production of documents and other physical objects, and responses to such orders;

(7) Disclosure of the names and addresses of witnesses and the exchange of documents intended to be offered in evidence; and

(8) Any other matter that will tend to simplify the issues or expedite the proceedings.

(b) *Order.* The administrative law judge shall issue an order which recites the matters discussed, the agreements reached, and the rulings made at the prehearing conference. The order shall be served on the parties and filed in the record of the proceedings.

§ 386.56 Hearings.

(a) As soon as practicable after his/her appointment, the administrative law judge shall issue an order setting the date, time, and place for the hearing. The order shall be served on the parties and become a part of the record of the proceedings. The order may be amended for good cause shown.

(b) *Conduct of hearing.* The administrative law judge presides over the hearing. Hearings are open to the public unless the administrative law judge orders otherwise.

(c) *Evidence.* Except as otherwise provided in these rules and the Administrative Procedure Act, 5 U.S.C. 551 *et seq.,* the Federal Rules of Evidence shall be followed.

(d) *Information obtained by investigation.* Any document, physical exhibit, or other material obtained by the Administration in an investigation under its statutory authority may be disclosed by the Administration during the proceeding and may be offered in evidence by counsel for the Administration.

(e) *Record.* The hearing shall be stenographically transcribed and reported. The transcript, exhibits, and other documents filed in the proceedings shall constitute the official record of the proceedings. A copy of the transcript and exhibits will be made available to any person upon payment of prescribed costs.

§ 386.57 Proposed findings of fact, conclusions of law.

The administrative law judge shall afford the parties reasonable opportunity to submit proposed findings of fact, conclusions of law, and supportng reasons therefor. If the administrative law judge orders written proposals and arguments, each proposed finding must include a citation to the specific portion of the record relied on to support it. Written submissions, if any, must be served within the time period set by the administrative law judge.

§ 386.58 Burden of proof.

(a) *Enforcement cases.* The burden of proof shall be on the Administration in enforcement cases.

(b) *Conflict of medical opinion.* The burden of proof in cases arising under § 391.47 of this chapter shall be on the party petitioning for review under § 386.13(a).

Subpart E—Decision

§ 386.61 Decision.

(a) *Administrative Law Judge* After receiving the proposed findings of fact, conclusions of law, and arguments of the parties, the administrative law judge shall issue a decision. If the proposed findings of fact, conclusions of law, and arguments were oral, he/she may issue an oral decision. The decision of the administrative law judge becomes the final decision of the Assistant Administrator 45 days after it is served unless a petition or motion for review is filed under § 386.62. The decision shall be served on all parties and on the Assistant Administrator.

(b) *Hearing Officer.* The Hearing Officer will prepare a report to the Assistant Administrator containing findings of fact and recommended disposition of the matter within 45 days after the conclusion of the hearing. The Assistant Administrator will issue a Final Agency Order adopting the report, or may make other such determinations as appropriate. The Assistant Administrator's decision to adopt a Hearing Officer's report may be reviewed in accordance with § 386.64.

[50 FR 40306, Oct. 2, 1985, as amended at 70 FR 28485, May 18, 2005]

§386.62 Review of administrative law judge's decision.

(a) All petitions to review must be accompanied by exceptions and briefs. Each petition must set out in detail objections to the initial decision and shall state whether such objections are related to alleged errors of law or fact. It shall also state the relief requested. Failure to object to any error in the initial decision shall waive the right to allege such error in subsequent proceedings.

(b) Reply briefs may be filed within 30 days after service of the appeal brief.

(c) No other briefs shall be permitted except upon request of the Assistant Administrator.

(d) Copies of all briefs must be served on all parties.

(e) No oral argument will be permitted except on order of the Assistant Administrator.

§386.63 Decision on review.

Upon review of a decision, the Assistant Administrator may adopt, modify, or set aside the administrative law judge's findings of fact and conclusions of law. He/she may also remand proceedings to the administrative law judge with instructions for such further proceedings as he/she deems appropriate. If not remanded, the Assistant Administrator shall issue a final order disposing of the proceedings, and serve it on all parties.

§386.64 Reconsideration.

(a) Within 20 days following service of the Final Agency Order, any party may petition the Assistant Administrator for reconsideration of the order. If a civil penalty was imposed, the filing of a petition for reconsideration stays the entire action, unless the Assistant Administrator orders otherwise.

(b) In the event a Notice of Default and Final Agency Order is issued by the Field Administrator as a result of the respondent's failure to reply in accordance with §386.14(a), the only issue that will be considered upon reconsideration is whether a default has occurred under §386.14(c). The Final Agency Order may be vacated where a respondent can demonstrate excusable neglect, a meritorious defense, or due diligence in seeking relief.

(c) Either party may serve an answer to a petition for reconsideration within 30 days of the service date of the petition.

(d) Following the close of the 30-day period, the Assistant Administrator will rule on the petition.

(e) The ruling on the petition will be the Final Agency Order. A petition for reconsideration of the Assistant Administrator's ruling will not be permitted.

[70 FR 28485, May 18, 2005]

§386.65 Failure to comply with final order.

If, within 30 days of receipt of a final agency order issued under this part, the respondent does not submit in writing his/her acceptance of the terms of an order directing compliance, or, where appropriate, pay a civil penalty, or file an appeal under §386.67, the case may be referred to the Attorney General with a request that an action be brought in the appropriate United States District Court to enforce the terms of a compliance order or collect the civil penalty.

§386.66 Motions for rehearing or for modification.

(a) No motion for rehearing or for modification of an order shall be entertained for 1 year following the date the Assistant Administrator's order goes into effect. After 1 year, any party may file a motion with the Assistant Administrator requesting a rehearing or modification of the order. The motion must contain the following:

(1) A copy of the order about which the change is requested;

(2) A statement of the changed circumstances justifying the request; and

(3) Copies of all evidence intended to be relied on by the party submitting the motion.

(b) Upon receipt of the motion, the Assistant Administrator may make a decision denying the motion or modifying the order in whole or in part. He/she may also, prior to making his/her decision, order such other proceedings under these rules as he/she deems necessary and may request additional information from the party making the motion.

§ 386.67 Judicial review.

(a) Any party to the underlying proceeding, who, after an administrative adjudication, is adversely affected by a Final Agency Order issued under 49 U.S.C. 521 may, within 30 days of service of the Final Agency Order, petition for review of the order in the United States Court of Appeals in the circuit where the violation is alleged to have occurred, or where the violator has its principal place of business or residence, or in the United States Court of Appeals for the District of Columbia Circuit.

(b) Judicial review will be based on a determination of whether the findings and conclusions in the Final Agency Order were supported by substantial evidence or were otherwise not in accordance with law. No objection that has not been raised before the Agency will be considered by the court, unless reasonable grounds existed for failure or neglect to do so. The commencement of proceedings under this section will not, unless ordered by the court, operate as a stay of the Final Agency Order of the Agency.

[70 FR 28485, May 18, 2005]

Subpart F—Injunctions and Imminent Hazards

§ 386.71 Injunctions.

Whenever it is determined that a person has engaged, or is about to engage, in any act or practice constituting a violation of section 31502 of title 49, United States Code; of the Motor Carrier Safety Act of 1984; the Hazardous Materials Transportation Act; or any regulation or order issued under that section or those Acts for which the Federal Motor Carrier Safety Administrator exercises enforcement responsibility, the Chief Counsel may request the United States Attorney General to bring an action in the appropriate United States District Court for such relief as is necessary or appropriate, including mandatory or prohibitive injunctive relief, interim equitable relief,

and punitive damages, as provided by section 213(c) of the Motor Carrier Safety Act of 1984 and section 111(a) of the Hazardous Materials Transportation Act (49 U.S.C. 507(c) 5122).

[70 FR 28485, May 18, 2005]

§ 386.72 Imminent hazard.

(a) Whenever it is determined that an imminent hazard exists as a result of the transportation by motor vehicle of a particular hazardous material, the Chief Counsel or Deputy Chief Counsel of the FMCSA may bring, or request the United States Attorney General to bring, an action in the appropriate United States District Court for an order suspending or restricting the transportation by motor vehicle of the hazardous material or for such other order as is necessary to eliminate or ameliorate the imminent hazard, as provided by 49 U.S.C. 5122. In this paragraph, "imminent hazard" means the existence of a condition that presents a substantial likelihood that death, serious illness, severe personal injury, or a substantial endangerment to health, property, or the environment may occur before a notice of investigation proceeding, or other administrative hearing or formal proceeding, to abate the risk of harm can be completed.

(b)(1) Whenever it is determined that a violation of 49 U.S.C. 31502 or the Motor Carrier Safety Act of 1984, as amended, or the Commercial Motor Vehicle Safety Act of 1986, as amended, or a regulation issued under such section or Acts, or a combination of such violations, poses an imminent hazard to safety, the Director of the Office of Enforcement and Compliance or a Division Administrator, or his or her delegate, shall order:

(i) A commercial motor vehicle or employee operating such vehicle out-of-service, or order an employer to cease all or part of the employer's commercial motor vehicle operations, as provided by 49 U.S.C. 521(b)(5);

(ii) An intermodal equipment provider's specific vehicle or equipment out-of-service, or order an intermodal equipment provider to cease all or part of its operations, as provided by 49 U.S.C. 521(b)(5) and 49 U.S.C. 31151(a)(3)(I).

(2) In making any such order, no restrictions shall be imposed on any vehicle, terminal or facility, employee, employer or intermodal equipment provider beyond that required to abate the hazard.

(3) In this paragraph (b), *imminent hazard* means any condition of vehicle, intermodal equipment, or commercial motor vehicle operations that substantially increases the likelihood of serious injury or death if not discontinued immediately.

(4) Upon the issuance of an order under paragraph (b)(1) of this section, the motor carrier employer, intermodal equipment provider or driver employee shall comply immediately with such order. Opportunity for review shall be provided in accordance with 5 U.S.C. 554, except that such review shall occur not later than 10 days after issuance of such order, as provided by section 213(b) of the Motor Carrier Safety Act of 1984 (49 U.S.C. 521(b)(5)). An order to an employer or intermodal equipment provider to cease all or part of its operations shall not prevent vehicles in transit at the time the order is served from proceeding to their immediate destinations, unless any such vehicle or its driver is specifically ordered out-of-service forthwith. However, vehicles and drivers proceeding to their immediate destination shall be subject to compliance upon arrival.

(5) For purposes of this section, the term *immediate destination* is the next scheduled stop of the vehicle already in motion where the cargo on board can be safely secured.

(6) Failure to comply immediately with an order issued under this section shall subject the motor carrier employer, intermodal equipment provider, or driver to penalties prescribed in subpart G of this part.

[50 FR 40306, Oct. 2, 1985, as amended at 53 FR 2036, Jan. 26, 1988; 53 FR 50970, Dec. 19, 1988; 56 FR 10184, Mar. 11, 1991; 65 FR 7756, Feb. 16, 2000; 65 FR 58664, Oct. 2, 2000; 73 FR 76819, Dec. 17, 2008]

Subpart G—Penalties

SOURCE: 56 FR 10184, Mar. 11, 1991, unless otherwise noted.

§386.81 General.

(a) The amounts of civil penalties that can be assessed for regulatory violations subject to the proceedings in this subchapter are established in the statutes granting enforcement powers. The determination of the actual civil penalties assessed in each proceeding is based on those defined limits or minimums and consideration of information available at the time the claim is made concerning the nature, gravity of the violation and, with respect to the violator, the degree of culpability, history of prior offenses, ability to pay, effect on ability to continue to do business, and such other matters as justice and public safety may require. In addition to these factors, a civil penalty assessed under 49 U.S.C. 14901(a) and (d) concerning household goods is also based on the degree of harm caused to a shipper and whether the shipper has been adequately compensated before institution of the civil penalty proceeding. In adjudicating the claims and orders under the administrative procedures herein, additional information may be developed regarding these factors that may affect the final amount of the claim.

(b) When assessing penalties for violations of notices and orders or settling claims based on these assessments, consideration will be given to good faith efforts to achieve compliance with the terms of the notices and orders.

[56 FR 10184, Mar. 11, 1991, as amended at 65 FR 7756, Feb. 16, 2000]

§386.82 Civil penalties for violations of notices and orders.

(a) Additional civil penalties are chargeable for violations of notices and orders which are issued under civil forfeiture proceedings pursuant to 49 U.S.C. 521(b). These notices and orders are as follows:

(1) Notice to abate—§386.11 (b)(2) and (c)(1)(iv);

(2) Notice to post—§386.11(b)(3);

(3) Final order—§386.14, §386.17, §386.22, and §386.61; and

(4) Out-of-service order—§386.72(b)(1).

(b) A schedule of these additional penalties is provided in the appendix A to this part. All the penalties are maximums, and discretion will be retained to meet special circumstances by setting penalties for violations of notices and orders, in some cases, at less than the maximum.

(c) Claims for penalties provided in this section and in the appendix A to this part shall be made through the civil forfeiture proceedings contained in this part. The issues to be decided in such proceedings will be limited to whether violations of notices and orders occurred as claimed and the appropriate penalty for such violations. Nothing contained herein shall be construed to authorize the reopening of a matter already finally adjudicated under this part.

[56 FR 10184, Mar. 11, 1991, as amended at 67 FR 61821, Oct. 2, 2002; 70 FR 28486, May 18, 2005]

§ 386.83 Sanction for failure to pay civil penalties or abide by payment plan; operation in interstate commerce prohibited.

(a)(1) *General rule.* (i) A CMV owner or operator that fails to pay a civil penalty in full within 90 days after the date specified for payment by FMCSA's final agency order, is prohibited from operating in interstate commerce starting on the next (i.e., the 91st) day. The prohibition continues until the FMCSA has received full payment of the penalty.

(ii) An intermodal equipment provider that fails to pay a civil penalty in full within 90 days after the date specified for payment by FMCSA's final agency order, is prohibited from tendering intermodal equipment to motor carriers for operation in interstate commerce starting on the next (i.e., the 91st) day. The prohibition continues until the FMCSA has received full payment of the penalty.

(2) *Civil penalties paid in installments.* The FMCSA Service Center may allow a CMV owner or operator, or an intermodal equipment provider, to pay a civil penalty in installments. If the CMV owner or operator, or intermodal equipment provider, fails to make an installment payment on schedule, the payment plan is void and the entire debt is payable immediately. A CMV owner or operator, or intermodal

equipment provider, that fails to pay the full outstanding balance of its civil penalty within 90 days after the date of the missed installment payment, is prohibited from operating in interstate commerce on the next (i.e., the 91st) day. The prohibition continues until the FMCSA has received full payment of the entire penalty.

(3) *Appeals to Federal Court.* If the CMV owner or operator, or intermodal equipment provider, appeals the final agency order to a Federal Circuit Court of Appeals, the terms and payment due date of the final agency order are not stayed unless the Court so directs.

(b) *Show cause proceeding.* (1) FMCSA will notify a CMV owner or operator, or intermodal equipment provider, in writing if it has not received payment within 45 days after the date specified for payment by the final agency order or the date of a missed installment payment. The notice will include a warning that failure to pay the entire penalty within 90 days after payment was due, will result in the CMV owner or operator, or an intermodal equipment provider, being prohibited from operating in interstate commerce.

(2) The notice will order the CMV owner or operator, or intermodal equipment provider, to show cause why it should not be prohibited from operating in interstate commerce on the 91st day after the date specified for payment. The prohibition may be avoided only by submitting to the Chief Safety Officer:

(i) Evidence that the respondent has paid the entire amount due; or

(ii) Evidence that the respondent has filed for bankruptcy under chapter 11, title 11, United States Code. Respondents in bankruptcy must also submit the information required by paragraph (d) of this section.

(3) The notice will be delivered by certified mail or commercial express service. If the principal place of business of a CMV owner or operator, or an intermodal equipment provider, is in a foreign country, the notice will be delivered to the designated agent of the CMV owner or operator or intermodal equipment provider.

(c) A CMV owner or operator, or intermodal equipment provider, that continues to operate in interstate commerce in violation of this section may be subject to additional sanctions under paragraph IV(h) of appendix A to part 386.

(d) This section does not apply to any person who is unable to pay a civil penalty because the person is a debtor in a case under 11 U.S.C. chapter 11. CMV owners or operators, or intermodal equipment providers, in bankruptcy proceedings under chapter 11 must provide the following information in their response to the FMCSA:

(1) The chapter of the Bankruptcy Code under which the bankruptcy proceeding is filed (i.e., chapter 7 or 11);

(2) The bankruptcy case number;

(3) The court in which the bankruptcy proceeding was filed; and

(4) Any other information requested by the agency to determine a debtor's bankruptcy status.

[73 FR 76819, Dec. 17, 2008, as amended at 74 FR 68708, Dec. 29, 2009]

§386.84 Sanction for failure to pay civil penalties or abide by payment plan; suspension or revocation of registration.

(a)(1) *General rule.* The registration of a broker, freight forwarder, or for-hire motor carrier that fails to pay a civil penalty in full within 90 days after the date specified for payment by the FMCSA's final agency order, will be suspended starting on the next (i.e., the 91st) day. The suspension continues until the FMCSA has received full payment of the penalty.

(2) *Civil penalties paid in installments.* The FMCSA Service Center may allow a respondent broker, freight forwarder, or for-hire motor carrier to pay a civil penalty in installments. If the respondent fails to make an installment payment on schedule, the payment plan is void and the entire debt is payable immediately. The registration of a respondent that fails to pay the remainder of its civil penalty in full within 90 days after the date of the missed installment payment, is suspended on the next (i.e., the 91st) day. The suspension continues until the FMCSA has received full payment of entire penalty.

(3) *Appeals to Federal Court.* If the respondent broker, freight forwarder, or for-hire motor carrier appeals the final agency order to a Federal Circuit Court of Appeals, the terms and payment due date of the final agency order are not stayed unless the Court so directs.

(b) *Show Cause Proceeding.* (1) The FMCSA will notify a respondent broker, freight forwarder, or for-hire motor carrier in writing if it has not received payment within 45 days after the date specified for payment by the final agency order or the date of a missed installment payment. The notice will include a warning that failure to pay the entire penalty within 90 days after payment was due, will result in the suspension of the respondent's registration.

(2) The notice will order the respondent to show cause why its registration should not be suspended on the 91st day after the date specified for payment. The prohibition may be avoided only by submitting to the Chief Safety Officer:

(i) Evidence that the respondent has paid the entire amount due; or

(ii) Evidence that the respondent has filed for bankruptcy under chapter 11, title 11, United States Code. Respondents in bankruptcy must also submit the information required by paragraph (d) of this section.

(3) The notice will be delivered by certified mail or commercial express service. If a respondent's principal place of business is in a foreign country, it will be delivered to the respondent's designated agent.

(c) The registration of a broker, freight forwarder or for-hire motor carrier that continues to operate in interstate commerce in violation of this section after its registration has been suspended may be revoked after an additional notice and opportunity for a proceeding in accordance with 49 U.S.C. 13905(c). Additional sanctions may be imposed under paragraph IV (h) of appendix A to part 386.

(d) This section does not apply to any person who is unable to pay a civil penalty because the person is a debtor in a case under chapter 11, title 11, United States Code. Brokers, freight forwarders, or for-hire motor carriers in bankruptcy proceedings under chapter 11 must provide the following information in their response to the FMCSA:

(1) The chapter of the Bankruptcy Code under which the bankruptcy proceeding is filed (*i.e.*, chapter 7 or 11);

(2) The bankruptcy case number;

(3) The court in which the bankruptcy proceeding was filed; and

(4) Any other information requested by the agency to determine a debtor's bankruptcy status.

[65 FR 78428, Dec. 15, 2000]

APPENDIX A TO PART 386—PENALTY SCHEDULE; VIOLATIONS OF NOTICES AND ORDERS

I. Notice To Abate

Violation—Failure to cease violations of the regulations in the time prescribed in the notice. (The time within to comply with a notice to abate shall not begin to run with respect to contested violations, *i.e.*, where there are material issues in dispute under § 386.14, until such time as the violation has been established.)

Penalty reinstatement of any deferred assessment or payment of a penalty or portion thereof.

II. [Reserved]

III. Final Order

Violation—Failure to comply with Final Agency Order.

Penalty—Automatic reinstatement of any penalty previously reduced or held in abeyance and restoration of the full amount assessed in the Notice of Claim less any payments previously made.

IV. Out-of-Service Order

a. Violation—Operation of a commercial vehicle by a driver during the period the driver was placed out of service.

Penalty—Up to $2,100 per violation.

(For purposes of this violation, the term "driver" means an operator of a commercial motor vehicle, including an independent contractor who, while in the course of operating a commercial motor vehicle, is employed or used by another person.)

b. Violation—Requiring or permitting a driver to operate a commercial vehicle during the period the driver was placed out of service.

Penalty—Up to $16,000 per violation.

(This violation applies to motor carriers, including an independent contractor who is not a "driver," as defined under paragraph IVa above.)

c. Violation—Operation of a commercial motor vehicle or intermodal equipment by a driver after the vehicle or intermodal equipment was placed out-of-service and before the required repairs are made.

Penalty—$2,100 each time the vehicle or intermodal equipment is so operated.

(This violation applies to drivers as defined in IVa above.)

d. Violation—Requiring or permitting the operation of a commercial motor vehicle or intermodal equipment placed out-of-service before the required repairs are made.

Penalty—Up to $16,000 each time the vehicle or intermodal equipment is so operated after notice of the defect is received.

(This violation applies to intermodal equipment providers and motor carriers, including an independent owner-operator who is not a "driver," as defined in IVa above.)

e. Violation—Failure to return written certification of correction as required by the out-of-service order.

Penalty—Up to $750 per violation.

f. Violation—Knowingly falsifies written certification of correction required by the out-of-service order.

Penalty—Considered the same as the violations described in paragraphs IVc and IVd above, and subject to the same penalties.

NOTE: Falsification of certification may also result in criminal prosecution under 18 U.S.C. 1001.

g. Violation—Operating in violation of an order issued under § 386.72(b) to cease all or part of the employer's commercial motor vehicle operations or to cease all or part of an intermodal equipment provider's operations, i.e., failure to cease operations as ordered.

Penalty—Up to $16,000 per day the operation continues after the effective date and time of the order to cease.

h. Violation—Conducting operations during a period of suspension under § 386.83 or § 386.84 for failure to pay penalties.

Penalty—Up to $11,000 for each day that operations are conducted during the suspension period.

[56 FR 10184, Mar. 11, 1991, as amended at 63 FR 12414, Mar. 13, 1998; 65 FR 78429, Dec. 15, 2000; 68 FR 15383, Mar. 31, 2003; 70 FR 28486, May 18, 2005; 72 FR 55102, Sept. 28, 2007; 73 FR 76820, Dec. 17, 2008]

APPENDIX B TO PART 386— PENALTY SCHEDULE; VIOLATIONS AND MONETARY PENALTIES

The Debt Collection Improvement Act of 1996 [Public Law 104–134, title III, chapter 10, Sec. 31001, par. (s), 110 Stat. 1321–373] amended the Federal Civil Penalties Inflation Adjustment Act of 1990 to require agencies to adjust for inflation "each civil monetary penalty provided by law within the jurisdiction of the Federal agency * * *'' and to publish that regulation in the FEDERAL REGISTER. Pursuant to that authority, the inflation-adjusted civil penalties listed in paragraphs (a) through (h) of this appendix supersede the corresponding civil penalty amounts listed in title 49, United States Code.

What are the types of violations and maximum monetary penalties?

(a) Violations of the Federal Motor Carrier Safety Regulations (FMCSRs):

(1) *Recordkeeping.* A person or entity that fails to prepare or maintain a record required by parts 40, 382, 385, and 390–99 of this subchapter, or prepares or maintains a required record that is incomplete, inaccurate, or false, is subject to a maximum civil penalty of $1,000 for each day the violation continues, up to $10,000.

(2) *Knowing falsification of records.* A person or entity that knowingly falsifies, destroys, mutilates, or changes a report or record required by parts 382, 385, and 390–99 of this subchapter, knowingly makes or causes to be made a false or incomplete record about an operation or business fact or transaction, or knowingly makes, prepares, or preserves a record in violation of a regulation or order of the Secretary is subject to a maximum civil penalty of $10,000 if such action misrepresents a fact that constitutes a violation other than a reporting or recordkeeping violation.

(3) *Non-recordkeeping violations.* A person or entity that violates parts 382, 385, or 390–99 of this subchapter, except a recordkeeping requirement, is subject to a civil penalty not to exceed $11,000 for each violation.

(4) *Non-recordkeeping violations by drivers.* A driver who violates parts 382, 385, and 390–99 of this subchapter, except a recordkeeping violation, is subject to a civil penalty not to exceed $2,750.

(5) *Violation of 49 CFR 392.5.* A driver placed out of service for 24 hours for violating the alcohol prohibitions of 49 CFR 392.5(a) or (b) who drives during that period is subject to a civil penalty not to exceed $3,750 for each violation.

(b) *Commercial driver's license (CDL) violations.* Any person who violates 49 CFR part 383, subparts B, C, E, F, G, or H is subject to a civil penalty of $3,750.

(c) *Special penalties pertaining to violations of out-of-service orders by CDL-holders.* A CDL-holder who is convicted of violating an out-of-service order shall be subject to a civil penalty of not less than $2,100 nor more than $3,750. An employer of a CDL-holder who knowingly allows, requires, permits, or authorizes that employee to operate a CMV during any period in which the CDL-holder is subject to an out-of-service order, is subject to a civil penalty of not less than $3,750 or more than $16,000.

(d) *Financial responsibility violations.* A motor carrier that fails to maintain the levels of financial responsibility prescribed by Part 387 of this subchapter is subject to a maximum penalty of $16,000 for each violation. Each day of a continuing violation constitutes a separate offense.

(e) Violations of the Hazardous Materials Regulations (HMRs) and Safety Permitting Regulations found in subpart E of Part 385. This paragraph applies to violations by motor carriers, drivers, shippers and other persons who transport hazardous materials on the highway in commercial motor vehicles or cause hazardous materials to be so transported.

(1) All knowing violations of 49 U.S.C. chapter 51 or orders or regulations issued under the authority of that chapter applicable to the transportation or shipment of hazardous materials by commercial motor vehicle on highways are subject to a civil penalty of not less than $250 and not more than $50,000 for each violation. Each day of a continuing violation constitutes a separate offense.

(2) All knowing violations of 49 U.S.C. chapter 51 or orders or regulations issued under the authority of that chapter applicable to training related to the transportation or shipment of hazardous materials by commercial motor vehicle on highways are subject to a civil penalty of not less than $450 and not more than $50,000 for each violation.

(3) All knowing violations of 49 U.S.C. chapter 51 or orders, regulations, or exemptions issued under the authority of that chapter applicable to the manufacture, fabrication, marking, maintenance, reconditioning, repair, or testing of a packaging or container that is represented, marked, certified, or sold as being qualified for use in the transportation or shipment of hazardous materials by commercial motor vehicle on highways are subject to a civil penalty of not less than $250 and not more than $50,000 for each violation.

(4) Whenever regulations issued under the authority of 49 U.S.C. chapter 51 require compliance with the FMCSRs while transporting hazardous materials, any violations of the FMCSRs will be considered a violation of the HMRs and subject to a civil penalty of not less than $250 and not more than $50,000.

(5) If any violation subject to the civil penalties set out in paragraphs (e)(1) through (4) of this appendix results in death, serious illness, or severe injury to any person or in substantial destruction of property, the civil penalty may be increased to not more than $105,000 for each offense.

(f) *Operating after being declared unfit by assignment of a final "unsatisfactory" safety rating.* (1) A motor carrier operating a commercial motor vehicle in interstate commerce (except owners or operators of commercial motor vehicles designed or used to transport

313

hazardous materials for which placarding of a motor vehicle is required under regulations prescribed under 49 U.S.C. chapter 51) is subject, after being placed out of service because of receiving a final "unsatisfactory" safety rating, to a civil penalty of not more than $11,000 (49 CFR 385.13). Each day the transportation continues in violation of a final "unsatisfactory" safety rating constitutes a separate offense.

(2) A motor carrier operating a commercial motor vehicle designed or used to transport hazardous materials for which placarding of a motor vehicle is required under regulations prescribed under 49 U.S.C. chapter 51 is subject, after being placed out of service because of receiving a final "unsatisfactory" safety rating, to a civil penalty of not less than $250 and not more than $50,000 for each offense. If the violation results in death, serious illness, or severe injury to any person or in substantial destruction of property, the civil penalty may be increased to not more than $105,000 for each offense. Each day the transportation continues in violation of a final "unsatisfactory" safety rating constitutes a separate offense.

(g) *Violations of the commercial regulations (CRs).* Penalties for violations of the CRs are specified in 49 U.S.C. Chapter 149. These penalties relate to transportation subject to the Secretary's jurisdiction under 49 U.S.C. Chapter 135. Unless otherwise noted, a separate violation occurs for each day the violation continues.

(1) A person who fails to make a report, to specifically, completely, and truthfully answer a question, or to make, prepare, or preserve a record in the form and manner prescribed is liable for a minimum penalty of $650 per violation.

(2) A person who operates as a carrier or broker for the transportation of property in violation of the registration requirements of 49 U.S.C. 13901 is liable for a minimum penalty of $650 per violation.

(3) A person who operates as a motor carrier of passengers in violation of the registration requirements of 49 U.S.C. 13901 is liable for a minimum penalty of $2,200 per violation.

(4) A person who operates as a foreign motor carrier or foreign motor private carrier in violation of the provisions of 49 U.S.C. 13902 (c) is liable for a minimum penalty of $650 per violation.

(5) A person who operates as a foreign motor carrier or foreign motor private carrier without authority, before the implementation of the land transportation provisions of the North American Free Trade Agreement, outside the boundaries of a commercial zone along the United States-Mexico border is liable for a maximum penalty of $11,000 for an intentional violation and a maximum penalty of $32,500 for a pattern of intentional violations.

(6) A person who operates as a motor carrier or broker for the transportation of hazardous wastes in violation of the registration provisions of 49 U.S.C. 13901 is liable for a maximum penalty of $22,000 per violation.

(7) A motor carrier or freight forwarder of household goods, or their receiver or trustee, that does not comply with any regulation relating to the protection of individual shippers is liable for a minimum penalty of $1,100 per violation.

(8) A person—

(i) Who falsifies, or authorizes an agent or other person to falsify, documents used in the transportation of household goods by motor carrier or freight forwarder to evidence the weight of a shipment or

(ii) Who charges for services which are not performed or are not reasonably necessary in the safe and adequate movement of the shipment is liable for a minimum penalty of $2,200 for the first violation and $6,500 for each subsequent violation.

(9) A person who knowingly accepts or receives from a carrier a rebate or offset against the rate specified in a tariff required under 49 U.S.C. 13702 for the transportation of property delivered to the carrier commits a violation for which the penalty is equal to three times the amount accepted as a rebate or offset and three times the value of other consideration accepted or received as a rebate or offset for the six-year period before the action is begun.

(10) A person who offers, gives, solicits, or receives transportation of property by a carrier at a different rate than the rate in effect under 49 U.S.C. 13702 is liable for a maximum penalty of $110,000 per violation. When acting in the scope of his/her employment, the acts or omissions of a person acting for or employed by a carrier or shipper are considered to be the acts and omissions of that carrier or shipper, as well as that person.

(11) Any person who offers, gives, solicits, or receives a rebate or concession related to motor carrier transportation subject to jurisdiction under subchapter I of 49 U.S.C. Chapter 135, or who assists or permits another person to get that transportation at less than the rate in effect under 49 U.S.C. 13702, commits a violation for which the penalty is $200 for the first violation and $275 for each subsequent violation.

(12) A freight forwarder, its officer, agent, or employee, that assists or willingly permits a person to get service under 49 U.S.C. 13531 at less than the rate in effect under 49 U.S.C. 13702 commits a violation for which the penalty is up to $650 for the first violation and up to $2,200 for each subsequent violation.

(13) A person who gets or attempts to get service from a freight forwarder under 49 U.S.C. 13531 at less than the rate in effect under 49 U.S.C. 13702 commits a violation for which the penalty is up to $650 for the first

violation and up to $2,200 for each subsequent violation.

(14) A person who knowingly authorizes, consents to, or permits a violation of 49 U.S.C. 14103 relating to loading and unloading motor vehicles or who knowingly violates subsection (a) of 49 U.S.C. 14103 is liable for a penalty of not more than $11,000 per violation.

(15) A person, or an officer, employee, or agent of that person, who tries to evade regulation under Part B of Subtitle IV, Title 49, U.S.C., for carriers or brokers is liable for a penalty of $220 for the first violation and at least $275 for a subsequent violation.

(16) A person required to make a report to the Secretary, answer a question, or make, prepare, or preserve a record under Part B of Subtitle IV, Title 49, U.S.C., or an officer, agent, or employee of that person, is liable for a maximum penalty of $6,500 per violation if it does not make the report, does not completely and truthfully answer the question within 30 days from the date the Secretary requires the answer, does not make or preserve the record in the form and manner prescribed, falsifies, destroys, or changes the report or record, files a false report or record, makes a false or incomplete entry in the record about a business related fact, or prepares or preserves a record in violation of a regulation or order of the Secretary.

(17) A motor carrier, water carrier, freight forwarder, or broker, or their officer, receiver, trustee, lessee, employee, or other person authorized to receive information from them, who discloses information identified in 49 U.S.C. 14908 without the permission of the shipper or consignee is liable for a maximum penalty of $2,200.

(18) A person who violates a provision of Part B, Subtitle IV, Title 49, U.S.C., or a regulation or order under Part B, or who violates a condition of registration related to transportation that is subject to jurisdiction under subchapter I or III or Chapter 135, or who violates a condition of registration of a foreign motor carrier or foreign motor private carrier under section 13902, is liable for a penalty of $650 for each violation if another penalty is not provided in 49 U.S.C. Chapter 149.

(19) A violation of Part B, Subtitle IV, Title 49, U.S.C., committed by a director, officer, receiver, trustee, lessee, agent, or employee of a carrier that is a corporation is also a violation by the corporation to which the penalties of Chapter 149 apply. Acts and omissions of individuals acting in the scope of their employment with a carrier are considered to be the actions and omissions of the carrier as well as the individual.

(20) In a proceeding begun under 49 U.S.C. 14902 or 14903, the rate that a carrier publishes, files, or participates in under section 13702 is conclusive proof against the carrier, its officers, and agents that it is the legal rate for the transportation or service. Departing, or offering to depart, from that published or filed rate is a violation of 49 U.S.C. 14902 and 14903.

(21) A person—

(i) Who knowingly and willfully fails, in violation of a contract, to deliver to, or unload at, the destination of a shipment of household goods in interstate commerce for which charges have been estimated by the motor carrier transporting such goods, and for which the shipper has tendered a payment in accordance with part 375, subpart G of this chapter, is liable for a civil penalty of not less than $10,000 for each violation. Each day of a continuing violation constitutes a separate offense.

(ii) Who is a carrier or broker and is found to be subject to the civil penalties in paragraph (i) of this appendix may also have his or her carrier and/or broker registration suspended for not less than 12 months and not more than 36 months under 49 U.S.C. chapter 139. Such suspension of a carrier or broker shall extend to and include any carrier or broker having the same ownership or operational control as the suspended carrier or broker.

(22) A broker for transportation of household goods who makes an estimate of the cost of transporting any such goods before entering into an agreement with a motor carrier to provide transportation of household goods subject to FMCSA jurisdiction is liable to the United States for a civil penalty of not less than $10,000 for each violation.

(23) A person who provides transportation of household goods subject to jurisdiction under 49 U.S.C. chapter 135, subchapter I, or provides broker services for such transportation, without being registered under 49 U.S.C. chapter 139 to provide such transportation or services as a motor carrier or broker, as the case may be, is liable to the United States for a civil penalty of not less than $25,000 for each violation.

(h) *Copying of records and access to equipment, lands, and buildings.* A person subject to 49 U.S.C. chapter 51 or a motor carrier, broker, freight forwarder, or owner or operator of a commercial motor vehicle subject to part B of subtitle VI of title 49 U.S.C. who fails to allow promptly, upon demand, the Federal Motor Carrier Safety Administration or an employee designated by the Federal Motor Carrier Safety Administration to inspect and copy any record or inspect and examine equipment, lands, buildings, and other property, in accordance with 49 U.S.C. 504(c), 5121(c), and 14122(b), is subject to a civil penalty of not more than $1,000 for each offense. Each day of a continuing violation constitutes a separate offense, except that the total of all civil penalties against any violator for all offenses related to a single violation shall not exceed $10,000.

[63 FR 12414, Mar. 13, 1998, as amended at 65 FR 7756, Feb. 16,, 2000; 67 FR 61821, Oct. 2, 2002; 68 FR 15383, Mar. 31, 2003; 69 FR 39371, June 30, 2004; 70 FR 28486, May 18, 2005; 72 FR 36789, July 5, 2007; 72 FR 55102, Sept. 28, 2007; 75 FR 72998, Nov. 29, 2010]

PART 387—MINIMUM LEVELS OF FINANCIAL RESPONSIBILITY FOR MOTOR CARRIERS

Subpart A—Motor Carriers of Property

Subpart B—Motor Carriers of Passengers

Subpart C—Surety Bonds and Policies of Insurance for Motor Carriers and Property Brokers

Subpart D—Surety Bonds and Policies of Insurance for Freight Forwarders

AUTHORITY: 49 U.S.C. 13101, 13301, 13906, 14701, 31138, 31139, and 31144; and 49 CFR 1.73.

EDITORIAL NOTE: Nomenclature changes to part 387 appear at 66 FR 49873, Oct. 1, 2001.

Subpart A—Motor Carriers of Property

§ 387.1 Purpose and scope.

This subpart prescribes the minimum levels of financial responsibility required to be maintained by motor carriers of property operating motor vehicles in interstate, foreign, or intrastate commerce. The purpose of these regulations is to create additional incentives to motor carriers to maintain and operate their vehicles in a safe manner and to assure that motor carriers maintain an appropriate level of financial responsibility for motor vehicles operated on public highways.

[46 FR 30982, June 11, 1981, as amended at 48 FR 52683, Nov. 21, 1983]

§ 387.3 Applicability.

(a) This subpart applies to for-hire motor carriers operating motor vehicles transporting property in interstate or foreign commerce.

(b) This subpart applies to motor carriers operating motor vehicles transporting hazardous materials, hazardous substances, or hazardous wastes in interstate, foreign, or intrastate commerce.

(c) *Exception.* (1) The rules in this part do not apply to a motor vehicle that has a gross vehicle weight rating (GVWR) of less than 10,001 pounds. This exception does not apply if the vehicle is used to transport any quantity of a

Division 1.1, 1.2, or 1.3 material, any quantity of a Division 2.3, Hazard Zone A, or Division 6.1, Packing Group I, Hazard Zone A, or to a highway route controlled quantity of a Class 7 material as it is defined in 49 CFR 173.403, in interstate or foreign commerce.

(2) The rules in this part do not apply to the transportation of non-bulk oil, non-bulk hazardous materials, substances, or wastes in intrastate commerce, except that the rules in this part do apply to the transportation of a highway route controlled quantity of a Class 7 material as defined in 49 CFR 173.403, in intrastate commerce.

[46 FR 30982, June 11, 1981; 46 FR 45612, Sept. 14, 1981, as amended at 48 FR 5559, Feb. 7, 1983; 48 FR 52683, Nov. 21, 1983; 49 FR 38290, Sept. 28, 1984; 59 FR 63923, Dec. 12, 1994; 73 FR 76496, Dec. 16, 2008]

§ 387.5 Definitions.

As used in this subpart—

Accident includes continuous or repeated exposure to the same conditions resulting in public liability which the insured neither expected nor intended.

Bodily injury means injury to the body, sickness, or disease including death resulting from any of these.

Cancellation of insurance the withdrawal of insurance coverage by either the insurer or the insured.

Endorsement an amendment to an insurance policy.

Environmental restoration restitution for the loss, damage, or destruction of natural resources arising out of the accidental discharge, dispersal, release or escape into or upon the land, atmosphere, watercourse, or body of water of any commodity transported by a motor carrier. This shall include the cost of removal and the cost of necessary measure taken to minimize or mitigate damage to human health, the natural environment, fish, shellfish, and wildlife.

Evidence of security a surety bond or a policy of insurance with the appropriate endorsement attached.

Financial responsibility the financial reserves (e.g., insurance policies or surety bonds) sufficient to satisfy liability amounts set forth in this subpart covering public liability.

For-hire carriage means the business of transporting, for compensation, the goods or property of another.

In bulk—the transportation, as cargo, of property, except Division 1.1, 1.2, or 1.3 materials, and Division 2.3, Hazard Zone A gases, in containment systems with capacities in excess of 3500 water gallons.

In bulk (Division 1.1, 1.2, and 1.3 explosives)—the transportation, as cargo, of any Division 1.1, 1.2, or 1.3 materials in any quantity.

In bulk (Division 2.3, Hazard Zone A or Division 6.1, Packing Group I, Hazard Zone A materials)—the transportation, as cargo, of any Division 2.3, Hazard Zone A, or Division 6.1, packing Group I, Hazard Zone A material, in any quantity.

Insured and principal—the motor carrier named in the policy of insurance, surety bond, endorsement, or notice of cancellation, and also the fiduciary of such motor carrier.

Insurance premium the monetary sum an insured pays an insurer for acceptance of liability for public liability claims made against the insured.

Motor carrier means a for-hire motor carrier or a private motor carrier. The term includes, but is not limited to, a motor carrier's agent, officer, or representative; an employee responsible for hiring, supervising, training, assigning, or dispatching a driver; or an employee concerned with the installation, inspection, and maintenance of motor vehicle equipment and/or accessories.

Property damage means damage to or loss of use of tangible property.

Public liability liability for bodily injury or property damage and includes liability for environmental restoration.

State means a State of the United States, the District of Columbia, Puerto Rico, the Virgin Islands, American Samoa, Guam, and the Northern Mariana Islands.

[46 FR 30982, June 11, 1981; 46 FR 45612, Sept. 14, 1981; 47 FR 12801, Mar. 25, 1982, as amended at 48 FR 52683, Nov. 21, 1983; 51 FR 33856, Sept. 23, 1986; 53 FR 12160, Apr. 13, 1988; 59 FR 63923, Dec. 12, 1994; 62 FR 16709, Apr. 8, 1997; 63 FR 33275, June 18, 1998]

§ 387.7 Financial responsibility required.

(a) No motor carrier shall operate a motor vehicle until the motor carrier has obtained and has in effect the minimum levels of financial responsibility as set forth in § 387.9 of this subpart.

(b)(1) Policies of insurance, surety bonds, and endorsements required under this section shall remain in effect continuously until terminated. Cancellation may be effected by the insurer or the insured motor carrier giving 35 days' notice in writing to the other. The 35 days' notice shall commence to run from the date the notice is mailed. Proof of mailing shall be sufficient proof of notice.

(2) *Exception.* Policies of insurance and surety bonds may be obtained for a finite period of time to cover any lapse in continuous compliance.

(3) *Exception.* A Mexico-domiciled motor carrier operating solely in municipalities in the United States on the U.S.-Mexico international border or within the commercial zones of such municipalities with a Certificate of Registration issued under part 368 may meet the minimum financial responsibility requirements of this subpart by obtaining insurance coverage, in the required amounts, for periods of 24 hours or longer, from insurers that meet the requirements of § 387.11 of this subpart. A Mexican motor carrier so insured must have available for inspection in each of its vehicles copies of the following documents:

(i) The Certificate of Registration;

(ii) The required insurance endorsement (Form MCS–90); and

(iii) An insurance identification card, binder, or other document issued by an authorized insurer which specifies both the effective date and the expiration date of the temporary insurance coverage authorized by this exception.

Mexican motor carriers insured under this exception are also exempt from the notice of cancellation requirements stated on Form MCS–90.

(c) Policies of insurance and surety bonds required under this section may be replaced by other policies of insurance or surety bonds. The liability of the retiring insurer or surety, as to events after the termination date, shall be considered as having terminated on the effective date of the replacement policy of insurance or surety bond or at the end of the 35 day cancellation period required in paragraph (b) of this section, whichever is sooner.

(d) Proof of the required financial responsibility shall be maintained at the motor carrier's principal place of business. The proof shall consist of—

(1) "Endorsement(s) for Motor Carrier Policies of Insurance for Public Liability Under Sections 29 and 30 of the Motor Carrier Act of 1980" (Form MCS–90) issued by an insurer(s);

(2) A "Motor Carrier Surety Bond for Public Liability Under Section 30 of the Motor Carrier Act of 1980" (Form MCS–82) issued by a surety; or

(3) A written decision, order, or authorization of the Federal Motor Carrier Safety Administration authorizing a motor carrier to self-insure under § 387.309, provided the motor carrier maintains a satisfactory safety rating as determined by the Federal Motor Carrier Safety Administration under part 385 of this chapter.

(e)(1) The proof of minimum levels of financial responsibility required by this section shall be considered public information and be produced for review upon reasonable request by a member of the public.

(2) In addition to maintaining proof of financial responsibility as required by paragraph (d) of this section, non-North America-domiciled private and for-hire motor carriers shall file evidence of financial responsibility with FMCSA in accordance with the requirements of subpart C of this part.

(f) All vehicles operated within the United States by motor carriers domiciled in a contiguous foreign country, shall have on board the vehicle a legible copy, in English, of the proof of the required financial responsibility (Form MCS–90 or MCS–82) used by the motor carrier to comply with paragraph (d) of this section.

(g) Any motor vehicle in which there is no evidence of financial responsibility required by paragraph (f) of this section shall be denied entry into the United States.

[46 FR 30982, June 11, 1981; 46 FR 45612, Sept. 14, 1981, as amended at 48 FR 5559, Feb. 7, 1983; 48 FR 52683, Nov. 21, 1983; 51 FR 22083, June 18, 1986; 54 FR 49092, Nov. 29, 1989; 59 FR 63923, Dec. 12, 1994; 67 FR 12661, Mar. 19, 2002; 73 FR 76496, Dec. 16, 2008]

§387.9 Financial responsibility, minimum levels.

The minimum levels of financial responsibility referred to in §387.7 of this subpart are hereby prescribed as follows:

SCHEDULE OF LIMITS—PUBLIC LIABILITY

Type of carriage	Commodity transported	January 1, 1985
(1) For-hire (In interstate or foreign commerce, with a gross vehicle weight rating of 10,001 or more pounds).	Property (nonhazardous)	$750,000
(2) For-hire and Private (In interstate, foreign, or intrastate commerce, with a gross vehicle weight rating of 10,001 or more pounds).	Hazardous substances, as defined in 49 CFR 171.8, transported in cargo tanks, portable tanks, or hopper-type vehicles with capacities in excess of 3,500 water gallons; or in bulk Division 1.1, 1.2 and 1.3 materials. Division 2.3, Hazard Zone A, or Division 6.1, Packing Group I, Hazard Zone A material; in bulk Division 2.1 or 2.2; or highway route controlled quantities of a Class 7 material, as defined in 49 CFR 173.403.	5,000,000
(3) For-hire and Private (In interstate or foreign commerce, in any quantity; or in intrastate commerce, in bulk only; with a gross vehicle weight rating of 10,001 or more pounds).	Oil listed in 49 CFR 172.101; hazardous waste, hazardous materials, and hazardous substances defined in 49 CFR 171.8 and listed in 49 CFR 172.101, but not mentioned in (2) above or (4) below.	1,000,000
(4) For-hire and Private (In interstate or foreign commerce, with a gross vehicle weight rating of less than 10,001 pounds).	Any quantity of Division 1.1, 1.2, or 1.3 material; any quantity of a Division 2.3, Hazard Zone A, or Division 6.1, Packing Group I, Hazard Zone A material; or highway route controlled quantities of a Class 7 material as defined in 49 CFR 173.403.	5,000,000

[73 FR 76946, Dec. 16, 2008]

§387.11 State authority and designation of agent.

A policy of insurance or surety bond does not satisfy the financial responsibility requirements of this subpart unless the insurer or surety furnishing the policy or bond is—

(a) Legally authorized to issue such policies or bonds in each State in which the motor carrier operates; or

(b) Legally authorized to issue such policies or bonds in the State in which the motor carrier has its principal place of business or domicile, and is willing to designate a person upon whom process, issued by or under the authority of any court having jurisdiction of the subject matter, may be served in any proceeding at law or equity brought in any State in which the motor carrier operates; or

(c) Legally authorized to issue such policies or bonds in any State of the United States and eligible as an excess or surplus lines insurer in any State in which business is written, and is willing to designate a person upon whom process, issued by or under the authority of any court having jurisdiction of the subject matter, may be served in any proceeding at law or equity brought in any State in which the motor carrier operates.

(d) A Canadian insurance company legally authorized to issue a policy of insurance in the Province or Territory of Canada in which the Canadian motor carrier has its principal place of business or domicile, and that is willing to designate a person upon whom process, issued by or under the authority of any court having jurisdiction over the subject matter, may be served in any proceeding at law or equity brought in any State in which the motor carrier operates.

[46 FR 30982, June 11, 1981, as amended at 48 FR 52683, Nov. 21, 1983; 75 FR 38430, July 2, 2010]

§ 387.13 Fiduciaries.

The coverage of fiduciaries shall attach at the moment of succession of such fiduciaries.

[46 FR 30982, June 11, 1981]

§ 387.15 Forms.

Endorsements for policies of insurance (Illustration I) and surety bonds (Illustration II) must be in the form prescribed by the FMCSA and approved by the OMB. Endorsements to policies of insurance and surety bonds shall specify that coverage thereunder will remain in effect continuously until terminated, as required in § 387.7 of this subpart. The continuous coverage requirement does not apply to Mexican motor carriers insured under § 387.7(b)(3) of this subpart. The endorsement and surety bond shall be issued in the exact name of the motor carrier.

ILLUSTRATION I

Form MCS–90 (3/82)
Form Approved
OMB No. 2125–0074

ENDORSEMENT FOR MOTOR CARRIER POLICIES OF INSURANCE FOR PUBLIC LIABILITY UNDER SECTIONS 29 AND 30 OF THE MOTOR CARRIER ACT OF 1980

Issued to _____
of _____
Dated at _____
this _____ day of _____,
19 __
Amending Policy No. _____
Effective Date _____
Name of Insurance Company _____
    Countersigned by _____
        Authorized Company Representative

The policy to which this endorsement is attached provides primary or excess insurance, as indicated by "X", for the limits shown:

☐ This insurance is primary and the company shall not be liable for amounts in excess of $_____ for each accident.

☐ This insurance is excess and the company shall not be liable for amounts in excess of $_____ for each accident in excess of the underlying limit of $_____ for each accident.

Whenever required by the FMCSA the company agrees to furnish the FMCSA a duplicate of said policy and all its endorsements. The company also agrees, upon telephone request by an authorized representative of FMCSA, to verify that the policy is in force as of a particular date. The telephone number to call is: _____

Cancellation of this endorsement may be effected by the company or the insured by giving (1) thirty-five (35) days notice in writing to the other party (said 35 days notice to commence from the date the notice is mailed, proof of mailing shall be sufficient proof of notice), and (2) if the insured is subject to the FMCSA's jurisdiction, by providing thirty (30) days notice to the FMCSA (said 30 days notice to commence from the date the notice is received by the FMCSA at its office in Washington, DC).

DEFINITIONS AS USED IN THIS ENDORSEMENT

Accident includes continuous or repeated exposure to conditions which results in bodily injury, property damage, or environmental damage which the insured neither expected or intended.

Motor Vehicle means a land vehicle, machine, truck, tractor, trailer, or semitrailer propelled or drawn by mechanical power and used on a highway for transporting property, or any combination thereof.

Bodily Injury means injury to the body, sickness, or disease to any person, including death resulting from any of these.

Environmental Restoration means restitution for the loss, damage, or destruction of natural resources arising out of the accidental discharge, dispersal, release or escape into or upon the land, atmosphere, watercourse, or body of water, of any commodity transported by a motor carrier. This shall include the cost of removal and the cost of necessary measures taken to minimize or mitigate damage to human health, the natural environment, fish, shellfish, and wildlife.

Property Damage means damage to or loss of use of tangible property.

Public Liability means liability for bodily injury, property damage, and environmental restoration.

The insurance policy to which this endorsement is attached provides automobile liability insurance and is amended to assure compliance by the insured, within the limits stated herein, as a motor carrier of property, with sections 29 and 30 of the Motor Carrier Act of 1980 and the rules and regulations of the Federal Motor Carrier Safety Administration.

In consideration of the premium stated in the policy to which this endorsement is attached, the insurer (the company) agrees to pay, within the limits of liability described herein, any final judgment recovered against the insured for public liability resulting from negligence in the operation, maintenance or use of motor vehicles subject to the financial responsibility requirements of sections 29 and 30 of the Motor Carrier Act of 1980 regardless of whether or not each motor vehicle is specifically described in the policy and whether or not such negligence occurs on any route or in any territory authorized to be served by the insured or elsewhere. Such insurance as is afforded, for public liability, does not apply to injury to or death of the insured's employees while engaged in the course of their employment, or property transported by the insured, designated as cargo. It is understood and agreed that no condition, provision, stipulation, or limitation contained in the policy, this endorsement, or any other endorsement thereon, or violation thereof, shall relieve the company from liability or from the payment of any final judgment, within the limits of liability herein described, irrespective of the financial condition, insolvency or bankruptcy of the insured. However, all terms, conditions, and limitations in the policy to which the endorsement is attached shall remain in full force and effect as binding between the insured and the company. The insured agrees to reimburse the company for any payment made by the company on account of any accident, claim, or suit involving a breach of the terms of the policy, and for any payment that the company would not have been obligated to make under the provisions of the policy except for the agreement contained in this endorsement.

It is further understood and agreed that, upon failure of the company to pay any final judgment recovered against the insured as provided herein, the judgment creditor may maintain an action in any court of competent jurisdiction against the company to compel such payment.

The limits of the company's liability for the amounts prescribed in this endorsement apply separately to each accident and any payment under the policy because of any one accident shall not operate to reduce the liability of the company for the payment of final judgments resulting from any other accident.

ILLUSTRATION II

Form MCS–82 (4/83)

(Form approved by Office of Management and Budget under control no. 2125–0075)

MOTOR CARRIER PUBLIC LIABILITY SURETY BOND UNDER SECTIONS 29 AND 30 OF THE MOTOR CARRIER ACT OF 1980

Parties	Surety company and principal place of business address	Motor carrier principal, FMCSA Docket No. and principal place of business
	....	....
	....	....
	....	....

Purpose—This is an agreement between the Surety and the Principal

under which the Surety, its successors and assignes, agree to be responsible for the payment of any final judgment or judgments against the Principal for public liability, property damage, and environmental restoration liability claims in the sums prescribed herein; subject to the governing provisions and the following conditions.

Governing provisions—(1) Sections 29 and 30 of the Motor Carrier Act of 1980 (49 U.S.C. 13906).

(2) Rules and regulations of the Federal Motor Carrier Safety Administration.

Conditions—The Principal is or intends to become a motor carrier of property subject to the applicable governing provisions relating to financial responsibility for the protection of the public.

This bond assures compliance by the Principal with the applicable governing provisions, and shall inure to the benefit of any person or persons who shall recover a final judgment or judgments against the Principal for public liability, property damage, or environmental restoration liability claims (excluding injury to or death of the Principal's employees while engaged in the course of their employment, and loss of or damange to property of the principal, and the cargo transported by the Principal). If every final judgment shall be paid for such claims resulting from the negligent operation, maintenance, or use of motor vehicles in transportation subject to the applicable governing provisions, then this obligation shall be void, otherwise it will remain in full effect.

Within the limits described herein, the Surety extends to such losses regardless of whether such motor vehicles are specifically described herein and whether occurring on the route or in the territory authorized to be served by the Principal or elsewhere.

The liability of the Surety on each motor vehicle subject to the financial responsibility requirements of Section's 29 and 30 of the Motor Carrier Act of 1980 for each accident shall not exceed $ _____ , and shall be a continuing one notwithstanding any recovery hereunder.

The surety agrees, upon telephone request by an authorized representative of the FMCSA, to verify that the surety bond is in force as of a particular date. The telephone number is:

_____

This bond is effective from _____ (12:01 a.m., standard time, at the address of the Principal as stated herein) and shall countine in force until terminated as described herein. The principal or the Surety may at any time terminate this bond by giving (1) thirty five (35) days notice in writing to the other party (said 35 day notice to commence from the date the notice is mailed, proof of mailing shall be sufficient proof of notice), and (2) if the Principal is subject to the FMCSA's jurisdiction, by providing thirty (30) days notice to the FMCSA (said 30 days notice to commence from the date notice is received by the FMCSA at its office in Washington, DC). The Surety shall not be liable for the payment of any judgment or judgments against the Principal for public liability, property damage, or environmental restoration claims resulting from accidents which occur after the termination of this bond as described herein, but such termination shall not affect the liability of the Surety for the payment of any such judgment or judgments resulting from accidents which occur during the time the bond is in effect.

(AFFIX CORPORATE SEAL)

Date _____
Surety _____
City _____
State _____
By _____

ACKNOWLEDGEMENT OF SURETY

State of _____
County of _____

On this _____ day of _____, 19___, before me personally came _____, who, being by me duly sworn, did depose and say that he/she resides in _____; that he/she is the _____ of the _____, the corporation described in and which executed the foregoing instrument; that he/she knows the seal of said corporation, that the seal affixed to said instrument is such corporate seal, that it was so affixed by order of the board of directors of said corporation, that he/she signed his/her name thereto by like order, and he/she duly acknowledged to me that he/she executed the same for and on behalf of said corporation.

(OFFICIAL SEAL)

Title of official administering oath _____
Surety Company File No. _____

[46 FR 30982, June 11, 1981, as amended at 48 FR 52683, Nov. 21, 1983; 49 FR 27292, July 2, 1984; 49 FR 38290, Sept. 28, 1984; 51 FR 33856, Sept. 23, 1986; 53 FR 12160, Apr. 13, 1988; 54 FR 49092, Nov. 29, 1989; 59 FR 63924, Dec. 12, 1994]

§ 387.17 Violation and penalty.

Any person (except an employee who acts without knowledge) who knowingly violates the rules of this subpart shall be liable to the United States for civil penalty of no more than $11,000 for each violation, and if any such violation is a continuing one, each day of violation will constitute a separate offense. The amount of any such penalty shall be assessed by the FMCSA's Administrator, by written notice. In determining the amount of such penalty, the Administrator, or his/her authorized delegate shall take into account the nature, circumstances, extent, the gravity of the violation committed and, with respect to the person found to have committed such violation, the degree of culpability, any history of prior offenses, ability to pay, effect on ability to continue to do business, and such other matters as justice may require.

[59 FR 63924, Dec. 12, 1994]

Subpart B—Motor Carriers of Passengers

SOURCE: 48 FR 52683, Nov. 21, 1983, unless otherwise noted.

§ 387.25 Purpose and scope.

This subpart prescribes the minimum levels of financial responsibility required to be maintained by for-hire motor carriers of passengers operating motor vehicles in interstate or foreign commerce. The purpose of these regulations is to create additional incentives to carriers to operate their vehicles in a safe manner and to assure that they maintain adequate levels of financial responsibility.

§ 387.27 Applicability.

(a) This subpart applies to for-hire motor carriers transporting passengers in interstate or foreign commerce.

(b) *Exception.* The rules in this subpart do not apply to—

(1) A motor vehicle transporting only school children and teachers to or from school;

(2) A motor vehicle providing taxicab service and having a seating capacity of less than 7 passengers and not operated on a regular route or between specified points;

(3) A motor vehicle carrying less than 16 individuals in a single daily round trip to commute to and from work; and

(4) A motor vehicle operated by a motor carrier under contract providing transportation of preprimary, primary, and secondary students for extracurricular trips organized, sponsored, and paid by a school district.

[48 FR 52683, Nov. 21, 1983, as amended at 63 FR 33275, June 18, 1998]

§387.29 Definitions.

As used in this subpart—

Accident includes continuous or repeated exposure to the same conditions resulting in public liability which the insured neither expected nor intended.

Bodily injury means injury to the body, sickness, or disease including death resulting from any of these.

Endorsement an amendment to an insurance policy.

Financial responsibility the financial reserves (e.g., insurance policies or surety bonds) sufficient to satisfy liability amounts set forth in this subpart covering public liability.

For-hire carriage means the business of transporting, for compensation, passengers and their property, including any compensated transportation of the goods or property of another.

Insured and principal the motor carrier named in the policy of insurance, surety bond, endorsement, or notice of cancellation, and also the fiduciary of such motor carrier.

Insurance premium the monetary sum an insured pays an insurer for acceptance of liability for public liability claims made against the insured.

Motor carrier means a for-hire motor carrier. The term includes, but is not limited to, a motor carrier's agent, officer, or representative; an employee responsible for hiring, supervising, training, assigning, or dispatching a driver; or an employee concerned with the installation, inspection, and maintenance of motor vehicle equipment and/or accessories.

Property damage means damage to or loss of use of tangible property.

Public liability liability for bodily injury or property damage.

Seating capacity any plan view location capable of accommodating a person at least as large as a 5th percentile adult female, if the overall seat configuration and design and vehicle design is such that the position is likely to be used as a seating position while the vehicle is in motion, except for auxiliary seating accommodations such as temporary or folding jump seats. Any bench or split bench seat in a passenger car, truck or multi-purpose passenger vehicle with a gross vehicle weight rating less than 10,000 pounds, having greater than 50 inches of hip room (measured in accordance with SEA Standards J1100(a)) shall have not less than three designated seating positions, unless the seat design or vehicle design is such that the center position cannot be used for seating.

[48 FR 52683, Nov. 21, 1983, as amended at 63 FR 33276, June 18, 1998]

§387.31 Financial responsibility required.

(a) No motor carrier shall operate a motor vehicle transporting passengers until the motor carrier has obtained and has in effect the minimum levels of financial responsibility as set forth in §387.33 of this subpart.

(b) Policies of insurance, surety bonds, and endorsements required under this section shall remain in effect continuously until terminated.

(1) Cancellation may be effected by the insurer or the insured motor carrier giving 35 days notice in writing to the other. The 35 days notice shall commence to run from the date the notice is mailed. Proof of mailing shall be sufficient proof of notice.

(2) *Exception.* Policies of insurance and surety bonds may be obtained for a finite period of time to cover any lapse in continuous compliance.

(3) *Exception.* Mexican motor carriers may meet the minimum financial responsibility requirements of this subpart by obtaining insurance coverage,

in the required amounts, for periods of 24 hours or longer, from insurers that meet the requirements of § 387.35 of this subpart. A Mexican motor carrier so insured must have available for inspection in each of its vehicles copies of the following documents:

(i) The required insurance endorsement (Form MCS–90B); and

(ii) An insurance identification card, binder, or other document issued by an authorized insurer which specifies both the effective date and the expiration date of the temporary insurance coverage authorized by this exception.

Mexican motor carriers insured under this exception are also exempt from the notice of cancellation requirements stated on Form MCS–90B.

(c) Policies of insurance and surety bonds required under this section may be replaced by other policies of insurance or surety bonds. The liability of retiring insurer or surety, as to events after the termination date, shall be considered as having terminated on the effective date of the replacement policy of insurance or surety bond or at the end or the 35 day cancellation period required in paragraph (b) of this section, whichever is sooner.

(d) Proof of the required financial responsibility shall be maintained at the motor carrier's principal place of business. The proof shall consist of—

(1) "Endorsement(s) for Motor Carriers of Passengers Policies of Insurance for Public Liability Under Section 18 of the Bus Regulatory Reform Act of 1982" (Form MCS–90B) issued by an insurer(s); or

(2) A "Motor Carrier of Passengers Surety Bond for Public Liability Under Section 18 of the Bus Regulatory Reform Act of 1982" (Form MCS–82B) issued by a surety.

(e)(1) The proof of minimum levels of financial responsibility required by this section shall be considered public information and be produced for review upon reasonable request by a member of the public.

(2) In addition to maintaining proof of financial responsibility as required by paragraph (d) of this section, non-North America-domiciled private and for-hire motor carriers shall file evidence of financial responsibility with

FMCSA in accordance with the requirements of subpart C of this part.

(f) All passenger carrying vehicles operated within the United States by motor carriers domiciled in a contiguous foreign country, shall have on board the vehicle a legible copy, in English, of the proof of the required financial responsibility (Forms MCS–90B or MCS–82B) used by the motor carrier to comply with paragraph (d) of this section.

(g) Any motor vehicle in which there is no evidence of financial responsibility required by paragraph (f) of this section shall be denied entry into the United States.

[48 FR 52683, Nov. 21, 1983, as amended at 50 FR 7062, Feb. 20, 1985; 54 FR 49092, Nov. 29, 1989; 60 FR 38743, July 28, 1995; 73 FR 76496, Dec. 16, 2008]

§ 387.33 Financial responsibility, minimum levels.

The minimum levels of financial responsibility referred to in § 387.31 of this subpart are hereby prescribed as follows:

SCHEDULE OF LIMITS

Public Liability

For-hire motor carriers of passengers operating in interstate or foreign commerce.

Vehicle seating capacity	Effective dates	
	Nov. 19, 1983	Nov. 19, 1985
(1) Any vehicle with a seating capacity of 16 passengers or more	$2,500,000	$5,000,000
(2) Any vehicle with a seating capacity of 15 passengers or less [1]	750,000	1,500,000

[1] Except as provided in § 387.27(b).

§ 387.35 State authority and designation of agent.

A policy of insurance or surety bond does not satisfy the financial responsibility requirements of this subpart unless the insurer or surety furnishing the policy or bond is—

(a) Legally authorized to issue such policies or bonds in each State in which the motor carrier operates, or

(b) Legally authorized to issue such policies or bonds in the State in which the motor carrier has its principal place of business or domicile, and is willing to designate a person upon whom process, issued by or under the authority of any court having jurisdiction of the subject matter, may be served in any proceeding at law or equity brought in any State in which the motor carrier operates; or

(c) Legally authorized to issue such policies or bonds in any State of the United States and eligible as an excess or surplus lines insurer in any State in which business is written, and is willing to designate a person upon whom process, issued by or under the authority of any court having jurisdiction of the subject matter, may be served in any proceeding at law or equity brought in any State in which the motor carrier operates.

(d) A Canadian insurance company legally authorized to issue a policy of insurance in the Province or Territory of Canada in which a Canadian motor carrier has its principal place of business or domicile, and that is willing to designate a person upon whom process, issued by or under the authority of any court having jurisdiction over the subject matter, may be served in any proceeding at law or equity brought in any

State in which the motor carrier operates.

[48 FR 52683, Nov. 21, 1983, as amended at 75 FR 38430, July 2, 2010]

§387.37 Fiduciaries.

The coverage of fiduciaries shall attach at the moment of succession of such fiduciaries.

§387.39 Forms.

Endorsements for policies of insurance (Illustration I) and surety bonds (Illustration II) must be in the form prescribed by the FMCSA and approved by the OMB. Endorsements to policies of insurance and surety bonds shall specify that coverage thereunder will remain in effect continuously until terminated, as required in §387.31 of this subpart. The continuous coverage requirement does not apply to Mexican motor carriers insured under §387.31(b)(3) of this subpart. The endorsement and surety bond shall be issued in the exact name of the motor carrier.

U.S. Department
of Transportation
Federal Motor Carrier
Safety Administration

**ENDORSEMENT FOR
MOTOR CARRIER POLICIES OF INSURANCE FOR PUBLIC LIABILITY
UNDER SECTION 18 OF THE BUS REGULATORY REFORM ACT OF 1982**

Form Approved:
OMB No.: 2126-0008

Issued to _____ of _____
Dated at _____ this _____ day of _____, 20 _____
Amending Policy No. _____ Effective Date _____
Name of Insurance Company _____

Countersigned by _____
Authorized Company Representative

The policy to which this endorsement is attached provides primary or excess insurance, as indicated by "[X]," for the limits shown:

[ ] This insurance is primary and the company shall not be liable for amounts in excess of $_____ for each accident.

[ ] This insurance is excess and the company shall not be liable for amounts in excess of $_____ for each accident in excess of the underlying limit of $_____ for each accident.
Whenever required by the Federal Motor Carrier Safety Administration (FMCSA), the company agrees to furnish the FMCSA a duplicate of said policy and all its endorsements. The company also agrees, upon telephone request by an authorized representative of the FMCSA , to verify that the policy is in force as of a particular date. The telephone number to call is: _____ .

Cancellation of this endorsement may be effected by the company of the insured by giving (1) thirty-five (35) days notice in writing to the other party (said 35 days notice to commence from the date the notice is mailed, proof of mailing shall be sufficient proof of notice), and (2) if the insured is subject to the FMCSA's registration requirements, by providing thirty (30) days notice to the FMCSA (said 30 days notice to commence from the date the notice is received by the FMCSA at its office in Washington, D.C.).

DEFINITIONS AS USED IN THIS ENDORSEMENT

Accident includes continuous or repeated exposure to conditions which result in Public Liability which the insured neither expected nor intended.
Bodily Injury means injury to the body, sickness, or disease to any person, including death resulting from any of these.

Motor Carrier means a for-hire carrier of passengers by motor vehicle.
Property Damage means damage to or loss of use of tangible property
Public Liability means liability for bodily injury or property damage.

The insurance policy to which this endorsement is attached provides automobile liability insurance and is amended to assure compliance by the insured, within the limits stated herein, as a for-hire motor carrier of passengers with Section 18 of the Bus Regulatory Reform Act of 1982 and the rules and regulations of the Federal Motor Carrier Safety Administration.

In consideration of the premium stated in the policy to which this endorsement is attached, the insurer (the company) agrees to pay, within the limits of liability described herein, any final judgment received against the insured for public liability resulting from negligence in the operation, maintenance or use of motor vehicles subject to financial responsibility requirements of Section 18 of the Bus Regulatory Reform Act of 1982 regardless of whether or not each motor vehicle is specifically described in the policy and whether or not such negligence occurs on any route or in any territory authorized to be served by the insured or elsewhere. Such insurance as is afforded, for public liability, does not apply to injury to or death of the insured's employees while engaged in the course of their employment, or property transported by the insured, designated as cargo. It is understood and agreed that no condition, provision, stipulation, or limitation contained in the policy, this endorsement, or any other endorsement thereon, or violation thereof, shall relieve the company from liability or from the payment of any final judgment, within the limits of liability herein described, irrespective of the financial condition, insolvency or bankruptcy of the insured.

However, all terms, conditions, and limitations in the policy to which the endorsement is attached shall remain in full force and effect as binding between the insured and the company. The insured agrees to reimburse the company for any payment made by the company on account of any accident, claim, or suit involving a breach of the terms of the policy, and for any payment that the company would not have been obligated to make under the provisions of the policy except for the agreement contained in this endorsement.

It is further understood and agreed that, upon failure of the company to pay any final judgment recovered against the insured as provided herein, the judgment creditor may maintain an action in any court of competent jurisdiction against the company to compel such payment.

The limits of the company's liability for the amounts prescribed in this endorsement apply separately to each accident and any payment under the policy because of any one accident shall not operate to reduce the liability of the company for the payment of final judgments resulting] from any other accident.

The Bus Regulatory Reform Act of 1982 requires limits of financial responsibility according to vehicle seating capacity, it is the MOTOR CARRIER'S obligation to obtain the required limits of financial responsibility. THE SCHEDULE OF LIMITS SHOWN ON THE REVERSE SIDE DOES NOT PROVIDE COVERAGE. The limits shown in the schedule are for information purposes only.

SCHEDULE OF LIMITS

PUBLIC LIABILITY
For-hire motor carriers of passengers operating in interstate or foreign commerce

Vehicle Seating Capacity	Effective Dates	
	Nov. 19, 1983	Nov. 19, 1985
(1) Any vehicle with a seating capacity of 16 passengers or more.	$2,500,000	$5,000,000
(2) Any vehicle with a seating capacity of 15 passengers or less.	$ 750,000	$1,500,000

Form MCS-90B
(6/2003)

U.S. Department
of Transportation
Federal Motor Carrier
Safety Administration

Form Approved:
OMB No.: 2126-0008

MOTOR CARRIER PUBLIC LIABILITY SURETY BOND
UNDER SECTION 18 OF THE BUS REGULATORY REFORM ACT OF 1982

PARTIES

Surety Company and Principal
Place of Business Address

Motor Carrier Principal, FMCSA Docket No.,
and Principal Place of Business Address

_____   _____
_____   _____
_____   _____
_____   _____

PURPOSE   This is an agreement between the Surety and the Principal under which the Surety, its successors and assignees, agree to be responsible for the payment of any final judgment or judgments against the Principal for public liability and property damage claims in the sums prescribed herein, subject to the governing provisions and following conditions.

GOVERNING   (1) Section 18 of the Bus Regulatory Reform Act of 1982
PROVISIONS   (2) Rules and regulations of the Federal Motor Carrier Safety Administration (FMCSA)

CONDITIONS   The Principal is or intends to become a motor carrier of passengers subject to the applicable governing provisions relating to financial responsibility for the protection of the public.

This bond assures ensures compliance by the Principal with the applicable governing provisions, and shall inure to the benefit of any person or persons who shall recover a final judgment or judgments against the Principal for public liability or property damage claims (excluding injury to or death of the Principal's employees while engaged in the course of their employment, and loss of or damage to property of the Principal, and the cargo transported by the Principal). If every final judgment shall be paid for such claims resulting from the negligent operation, maintenance, or use of motor vehicles in transportation subject to the applicable governing provisions, then this obligation shall be void, otherwise it will remain in full effect.

Within the limits described herein, the Surety extends to such losses regardless of whether such motor vehicles are specifically described herein and whether occurring on the route or in the territory authorized to be served by the Principal or elsewhere.

The liability of the Surety for each motor vehicle subject to the applicable governing provisions for each accident shall not exceed $_____, and shall be a continuing one notwithstanding any recovery thereunder.

The surety agrees, upon telephone request by an authorized representative of the FMCSA, to verify that the surety bond is in force as of a particular date. The telephone number to call is
_____

This bond is effective from _____ (12:01 a.m., standard time, at the address of the Principal as stated herein) and shall continue in force until terminated as described herein. The Principal or the Surety may at any time terminate this bond by giving (1) thirty-five (35) days notice in writing to the other party (said 35 days notice to commence from the date the notice is mailed, proof of mailing shall be sufficient proof of notice), and (2) if the Principal is subject to the FMCSA's registration requirements, by providing thirty (30) days notice to the FMCSA (said 30 days notice to commence from the date notice is received by the FMCSA at its office in Washington, D.C.). The Surety shall not be liable for the payment of any judgment or judgments against the Principal for public liability or property damage claims resulting from accidents which occur after the termination of this bond as described herein, but such termination shall not affect the liability of the Surety from the payment of any such judgment or judgments resulting from accidents which occur during the time the bond is in effect.

_____
Date

(AFFIX CORPORATE SEAL)

_____
Surety

_____   _____
City   State

By _____

ACKNOWLEDGMENT OF SURETY

STATE OF _____   COUNTY OF _____

On this _____ day of _____, 20___, before me personally came _____,
who, being by me duly sworn, did depose and say that he resides in _____; that he/she
is _____ of the _____, the corporation described in and which executed the foregoing instrument; that
he knows the seal of said corporation; that the seal affixed to said instrument is such corporate seal; that it was so affixed by order of the board of directors of said
corporation; that he signed his name thereto by like order, and he duly acknowledged to me that he executed the same for and on behalf of said corporation.

_____
_____
Title of official administering oath

(OFFICIAL SEAL)

Surety Company File No. _____
Form MCS-82B
(6/2003)

(Approved by the Office of Management and Budget under control number 2125–0518)

[48 FR 52683, Nov. 21, 1983, as amended at 49 FR 22326, May 29, 1984; 54 FR 49093, Nov. 29, 1989; 67 FR 61821, 61822, Oct. 2, 2002]

§ 387.41 Violation and penalty.

Any person (except an employee who acts without knowledge) who knowingly violates the rules of this subpart shall be liable to the United States for civil penalty of no more than $11,000 for each violation, and if any such violation is a continuing one, each day of violation will constitute a separate offense. The amount of any such penalty shall be assessed by the Administrator or his/her designee, by written notice. In determining the amount of such penalty, the Administrator or his/her designee shall take into account the nature, circumstances, extent, the gravity of the violation committed and, with respect to the person found to have committed such violation, the degree of culpability, any history of prior offenses, ability to pay, effect on ability to continue to do business, and such other matters as justice may require.

[53 FR 47543, Nov. 23, 1988]

Subpart C—Surety Bonds and Policies of Insurance for Motor Carriers and Property Brokers

CROSS REFERENCE: Prescribed forms relating to this part are listed in 49 CFR part 1003.

SOURCE: 32 FR 20032, Dec. 20, 1967, unless otherwise noted. Redesignated at 61 FR 54709, Oct. 21, 1996.

§ 387.301 Surety bond, certificate of insurance, or other securities.

(a) *Public liability.* (1) No common or contract carrier or foreign (Mexican) motor private carrier or foreign motor carrier transporting exempt commodities subject to Subtitle IV, part B, chapter 135 of title 49 of the U.S. Code shall engage in interstate or foreign commerce, and no certificate or permit shall be issued to such a carrier or remain in force unless and until there shall have been filed with and accepted by the FMCSA surety bonds, certificates of insurance, proof of qualifications as self-insurer, or other securities or agreements, in the amounts prescribed in § 387.303, conditioned to pay any final judgment recovered against such motor carrier for bodily injuries to or the death of any person resulting from the negligent operation, mainte-

nance or use of motor vehicles in transportation subject to Subtitle IV, part B, chapter 135 of title 49 of the U.S. Code, or for loss of or damage to property of others, or, in the case of motor carriers of property operating freight vehicles described in § 387.303(b)(2) of this part, for environmental restoration.

(2) Motor Carriers of property which are subject to the conditions set forth in paragraph (a)(1) of this section and transport the commodities described in § 387.303(b)(2), are required to obtain security in the minimum limits prescribed in § 387.303(b)(2).

(b) *Household goods motor carriers-cargo insurance.* No household goods motor carrier subject to subtitle IV, part B, chapter 135 of title 49 of the U.S. Code shall engage in interstate or foreign commerce, nor shall any certificate be issued to such a household goods motor carrier or remain in force unless and until there shall have been filed with and accepted by the FMCSA, a surety bond, certificate of insurance, proof of qualifications as a self-insurer, or other securities or agreements in the amounts prescribed in § 387.303, conditioned upon such carrier making compensation to individual shippers for all property belonging to individual shippers and coming into the possession of such carrier in connection with its transportation service. The terms ''household goods motor carrier'' and ''individual shipper'' are defined in part 375 of this subchapter.

(c) *Continuing compliance required.* Such security as is accepted by the FMCSA in accordance with the requirements of section 13906 of title 49 of the U.S. Code, shall remain in effect at all times.

[48 FR 51780, Nov. 14, 1983, as amended at 60 FR 63981, Dec. 13, 1995; 62 FR 49941, Sept. 24, 1997; 75 FR 35328, June 22, 2010]

§ 387.303 Security for the protection of the public: Minimum limits.

(a) *Definitions.* (1) *Primary security* means public liability coverage provided by the insurance or surety company responsible for the first dollar of coverage.

(2) *Excess security* means public liability coverage above the primary security, or above any additional underlying security, up to and including the required minimum limits set forth in paragraph (b)(2) of this section.

(b)(1) Motor carriers subject to §387.301(a)(1) are required to have security for the required minimum limits as follows:

Passenger Carriers: Kind of Equipment	
Vehicle seating capacity	Minimum limit
(i) Any vehicle with a seating capacity of 16 passengers or more	$5,000,000
(ii) Any vehicle designed or used to transport more than 8 passengers (including the driver) for compensation	1,500,000

(2) Motor carriers subject to §387.301(a)(2) are required to have security for the required minimum limits as follows:

Kind of equipment	Commodity transported	July 1, 1983*	July 1, 1984*
(a) Freight Vehicles of 10,001 Pounds or More GVWR.	Property (non-hazardous)	$500,000	$750,000
(b) Freight Vehicles of 10,001 Pounds or More GVWR.	Hazardous substances, as defined in §171.8, transported in cargo tanks, portable tanks, or hopper-type vehicles with capacities in excess of 3,500 water gallons, or in bulk Class A or B explosives, poison gas (Poison A) liquefied compressed gas or compressed gas, or highway route controlled quantity radioactive materials as defined in §173.455.	1,000,000	5,000,000
(c) Freight Vehicles of 10,001 Pounds or More GVWR.	Oil listed in §172.101; hazardous waste, hazardous materials and hazardous substances defined in §171.8 and listed in §172.101, but not mentioned in (b) above or (d) below.	500,000	1,000,000
(d) Freight Vehicles Under 10,001 Pounds GVWR.	Any quantity of Class A or B explosives; any quantity of poison gas (Poison A); or highway route controlled quantity radioactive materials as defined in §173.455.	1,000,000	5,000,000

*NOTE: The effective date of the current required minimum limit in §387.303(b)(2) was January 6, 1983, in accordance with the requirements of Pub. L. 97–424, 96 Stat. 2097.

(3) Motor carriers subject to the minimum limits governed by this section, which are also subject to Department of Transportation limits requirements, are at no time required to have security for more than the required minimum limits established by the Secretary of Transportation in the applicable provisions of 49 CFR Part 387—Minimum Levels of Financial Responsibility for Motor Carriers.

(4) *Foreign motor carriers and foreign motor private carriers.* Foreign motor carriers and foreign motor private carriers (Mexican), subject to the requirements of 49 U.S.C. 13902(c) and 49 CFR part 368 regarding obtaining certificates of registration from the FMCSA, must meet our minimum financial responsibility requirements by obtaining insurance coverage, in the required amounts, for periods of 24 hours or longer, from insurance or surety companies, that meet the requirements of 49 CFR 387.315. These carriers must have available for inspection, in each vehicle operating in the United States, copies of the following documents:

(i) The certificate of registration;

(ii) The required insurance endorsement (Form MCS–90); and

(iii) An insurance identification card, binder, or other document issued by an authorized insurer which specifies both the effective date and the expiration date of the insurance coverage.

Notwithstanding the provisions of §387.301(a)(1), the filing of evidence of insurance is not required as a condition to the issuance of a certificate of registration. Further, the reference to continuous coverage at §387.313(a)(6) and the reference to cancellation notice at §387.313(d) are not applicable to these carriers.

(c) *Household goods motor carriers: Cargo liability.* Security required to compensate individual shippers for loss or damage to property belonging to them and coming into the possession of household goods motor carriers in connection with their transportation service;

(1) For loss of or damage to household goods carried on any one motor vehicle—$5,000,

(2) For loss of or damage to or aggregate of losses or damages of or to household goods occurring at any one time and place—$10,000.

[47 FR 55944, Dec. 14, 1982, as amended at 48 FR 43333, Sept. 23, 1983; 48 FR 45775, Oct. 7, 1983; 48 FR 51780, Nov. 14, 1983; 49 FR 1991, Jan. 17, 1984; 49 FR 27767, July 6, 1984; 50 FR 40030, Oct. 1, 1985; 53 FR 36984, Sept. 23, 1988; 54 FR 52034, Dec. 20, 1989; 55 FR 47338, Nov. 13, 1990; 62 FR 49941, Sept. 24, 1997; 67 FR 61824, Oct. 2, 2002; 68 FR 56198, Sept. 30, 2003; 72 FR 55701, Oct. 1, 2007; 75 FR 35328, June 22, 2010]

§ 387.305 Combination vehicles.

The following combinations will be regarded as one motor vehicle for purposes of this part, (a) a tractor and trailer or semitrailer when the tractor is engaged solely in drawing the trailer or semitrailer, and (b) a truck and trailer when both together bear a single load.

§ 387.307 Property broker surety bond or trust fund.

(a) *Security.* (1) A property broker must have a surety bond or trust fund in effect for $10,000. The FMCSA will not issue a property broker license until a surety bond or trust fund for the full limits of liability prescribed herein is in effect. The broker license shall remain valid or effective only as long as a surety bond or trust fund remains in effect and shall ensure the financial responsibility of the broker.

(2) A household goods broker must have a surety bond or trust fund in effect for $25,000 on and after January 1, 2012. The FMCSA will not issue a household goods broker license until a surety bond or trust fund for the full limits of liability prescribed herein is in effect. The household goods broker license remains valid or effective only as long as a surety bond or trust fund remains in effect and ensures the financial responsibility of the household goods broker. The compliance date for paragraph (a)(2) is January 1, 2012.

(b) *Evidence of security.* Evidence of a surety bond must be filed using the FMCSA's prescribed Form BMC 84. Evidence of a trust fund with a financial institution must be filed using the FMCSA's prescribed Form BMC 85. The surety bond or the trust fund shall ensure the financial responsibility of the broker by providing for payments to shippers or motor carriers if the broker fails to carry out its contracts, agreements, or arrangements for the supplying of transportation by authorized motor carriers.

(c) *Financial institution*—when used in this section and in forms prescribed under this section, where not otherwise distinctly expressed or manifestly incompatible with the intent thereof, shall mean—Each agent, agency, branch or office within the United States of any person, as defined by the ICC Termination Act, doing business in one or more of the capacities listed below:

(1) An insured bank (as defined in section 3(h) of the Federal Deposit Insurance Act (12 U.S.C. 1813(h));

(2) A commercial bank or trust company;

(3) An agency or branch of a foreign bank in the United States;

(4) An insured institution (as defined in section 401(a) of the National Housing Act (12 U.S.C. 1724(a));

(5) A thrift institution (savings bank, building and loan association, credit union, industrial bank or other);

(6) An insurance company;

(7) A loan or finance company; or

(8) A person subject to supervision by any state or federal bank supervisory authority.

(d) *Forms and Procedures*—(1) *Forms for broker surety bonds and trust agreements.* Form BMC–84 broker surety bond will be filed with the FMCSA for the full security limits under subsection (a); or Form BMC–85 broker trust fund agreement will be filed with the FMCSA for the full security limits under paragraph (a) of this section.

(2) *Broker surety bonds and trust fund agreements in effect continuously.* Surety bonds and trust fund agreements shall specify that coverage thereunder will remain in effect continuously until terminated as herein provided.

(i) *Cancellation notice.* The surety bond and the trust fund agreement may be cancelled as only upon 30 days' written notice to the FMCSA, on prescribed Form BMC 36, by the principal or surety for the surety bond, and on prescribed Form BMC 85, by the trustor/broker or trustee for the trust fund agreement. The notice period commences upon the actual receipt of the notice at the FMCSA's Washington, DC office.

(ii) *Termination by replacement.* Broker surety bonds or trust fund agreements which have been accepted by the FMCSA under these rules may be replaced by other surety bonds or trust fund agreements, and the liability of the retiring surety or trustee under such surety bond or trust fund agreements shall be considered as having terminated as of the effective date of the replacement surety bond or trust fund agreement. However, such termination shall not affect the liability of the surety or the trustee hereunder for the payment of any damages arising as the result of contracts, agreements or arrangements made by the broker for the supplying of transportation prior to the date such termination becomes effective.

(3) *Filing and copies.* Broker surety bonds and trust fund agreements must be filed with the FMCSA in duplicate.

[53 FR 10396, Mar. 31, 1988, as amended at 75 FR 72998, Nov. 29, 2010]

§ 387.309 Qualifications as a self-insurer and other securities or agreements.

(a) *As a self-insurer.* The FMCSA will consider and will approve, subject to appropriate and reasonable conditions, the application of a motor carrier to qualify as a self-insurer, if the carrier furnishes a true and accurate statement of its financial condition and other evidence that establishes to the satisfaction of the FMCSA the ability of the motor carrier to satisfy its obligation for bodily injury liability, property damage liability, or cargo liability. Application Guidelines: In addition to filing Form BMC 40, applicants for authority to self-insure against bodily injury and property damage claims should submit evidence that will allow the FMCSA to determine:

(1) The adequacy of the tangible net worth of the motor carrier in relation to the size of operations and the extent of its request for self-insurance authority. Applicant should demonstrate that it will maintain a net worth that will ensure that it will be able to meet its statutory obligations to the public to indemnify all claimants in the event of loss.

(2) *The existence of a sound self-insurance program.* Applicant should demonstrate that it has established, and will maintain, an insurance program that will protect the public against all claims to the same extent as the minimum security limits applicable to applicant under § 387.303 of this part. Such a program may include, but not be limited to, one or more of the following: Irrevocable letters of credit; irrevocable trust funds; reserves; sinking funds; third-party financial guarantees, parent company or affiliate sureties; excess insurance coverage; or other similar arrangements.

(3) *The existence of an adequate safety program.* Applicant must submit evidence of a current "satisfactory" safety rating by the United States Department of Transportation. Non-rated carriers need only certify that they have not been rated. Applications by carriers with a less than satisfactory rating will be summarily denied. Any self-insurance authority granted by the FMCSA will automatically expire 30 days after a carrier receives a less than satisfactory rating from DOT.

(4) *Additional information.* Applicant must submit such additional information to support its application as the FMCSA may require.

(b) *Other securities or agreements.* The FMCSA also will consider applications for approval of other securities or agreements and will approve any such application if satisfied that the security or agreement offered will afford the security for protection of the public contemplated by 49 U.S.C. 13906.

[48 FR 51780, Nov. 14, 1983 and 51 FR 15008, Apr. 22, 1986, as amended at 52 FR 3815, Feb. 6, 1987; 62 FR 49941, Sept. 24, 1997; 68 FR 56199, Sept. 30, 2003]

§ 387.311 Bonds and certificates of insurance.

(a) *Public liability.* Each Form BMC 82 surety bond filed with the FMCSA must be for the full limits of liability required under § 387.303(b)(1). Form MCS–82 surety bonds and other forms of similar import prescribed by the Department of Transportation, may be aggregated to comply with the minimum security limits required under § 387.303(b)(1) or § 387.303(b)(2). Each Form BMC 91 certificate of insurance filed with the FMCSA will always represent the full security minimum limits required for the particular carrier, while it remains in force, under § 387.303(b)(1) or § 387.303(b)(2), whichever is applicable. Any previously executed Form BMC 91 filed before the current revision which is left on file with the FMCSA after the effective date of this regulation, and not canceled within 30 days of that date will be deemed to certify the same coverage limits as would the filing of a revised Form BMC 91. Each Form BMC 91X certificate of insurance filed with the FMCSA will represent the full security limits under § 387.303(b)(1) or § 387.303(b)(2) or the specific security limits of coverage as indicated on the face of the form. If the filing reflects aggregation, the certificate must show clearly whether the insurance is primary or, if excess coverage, the amount of underlying coverage as well as amount of the maximum limits of coverage.* Each Form BMC 91MX certificate of insurance filed with the FMCSA will represent the security limits of coverage as indicated on the face of the form. The Form BMC 91MX must show clearly whether the insurance is primary or, if excess coverage, the amount of underlying coverage as well as amount of the maximum limits of coverage.

(b) *Cargo liability.* Each form BMC 83 surety bond filed with the FMCSA must be for the full limits of liability required under § 387.303(c). Each Form BMC 34 certificate of insurance filed with the FMCSA will represent the full security limits under § 387.303(c) or the specific security limits of coverage as indicated on the face of the form. If the filing reflects aggregation, the certificate must show clearly whether the insurance is primary or, if excess coverage, the amount of underlying coverage as well as amount of the maximum limits of coverage.

(c) Each policy of insurance in connection with the certificate of insurance which is filed with the FMCSA,

*NOTE: Aggregation to meet the requirement of § 387.303(b)(1) will not be allowed until the completion of our rulemaking in Ex Parte No. MC–5 (Sub-No. 2), *Motor Carrier and Freight Forwarder Insurance Procedures and Minimum Amounts of Liability.*

shall be amended by attachment of the appropriate endorsement prescribed by the FMCSA and the certificate of insurance filed must accurately reflect that endorsement.

[47 FR 55944, Dec. 14, 1982, as amended at 48 FR 43332, Sept. 23, 1983; 48 FR 51781, Nov. 14, 1983; 50 FR 40030, Oct. 1, 1985; 62 FR 49941, Sept. 24, 1997; 68 FR 56199, Sept. 30, 2003]

§ 387.313 Forms and procedures.

(a) *Forms for endorsements, certificates of insurance and others*—(1) *In form prescribed.* Endorsements for policies of insurance and surety bonds, certificates of insurance, applications to qualify as a self-insurer, or for approval of other securities or agreements, and notices of cancellation must be in the form prescribed and approved by the FMCSA.

(2) *Aggregation of Insurance.*** When insurance is provided by more than one insurer in order to aggregate security limits for carriers operating only freight vehicles under 10,000 pounds Gross Vehicle Weight Rating, as defined in § 387.303(b)(1), a separate *Form BMC 90,* with the specific amounts of underlying and limits of coverage shown thereon or appended thereto, and *Form BMC 91X* certificate is required of each insurer.

For aggregation of insurance for all other carriers to cover security limits under § 387.303 (b)(1) or (b)(2), a separate Department of Transportation prescribed form endorsement and *Form BMC 91X* certificate is required of each insurer. When insurance is provided by more than one insurer to aggregate coverage for security limits under § 387.303(c) a separate Form BMC 32 endorsement and Form BMC 34 certificate of insurance is required for each insurer.

For aggregation of insurance for foreign motor private carriers of nonhazardous commodities to cover security

**NOTE: See NOTE for Rule 387.311. Also, it should be noted that DOT is considering prescribing adaptations of the Form MCS 90 endorsement and the Form MCS 82 surety bond for use by passenger carriers and Rules §§ 387.311 and 387.313 have been written sufficiently broad to provide for this contingency when new forms are prescribed by that Agency.

limits under §387.303(b)(4), a separate Form BMC 90 with the specific amounts of underlying and limits of coverage shown thereon or appended thereto, or Department of Transportation prescribed form endorsement, and Form BMC 91MX certificate is required for each insurer.

(3) *Use of Certificates and Endorsements in BMC Series.* Form BMC 91 certificates of insurance will be filed with the FMCSA for the full security limits under §387.303 (b)(1) or (b)(2).

Form BMC 91X certificate of insurance will be filed to represent full coverage or any level of aggregation for the security limits under §387.303 (b)(1) or (b)(2).

Form BMC 90 endorsement will be used with each filing of *Form BMC 91* or *Form 91X* certificate with the FMCSA which certifies to coverage not governed by the requirements of the Department of Transportation. *Form BMC 32* endorsement and *Form BMC 34* certificate of insurance and *Form BMC 83* surety bonds are used for the limits of cargo liability under §387.303(c).

Form BMC 91MX certificate of insurance will be filed to represent any level of aggregation for the security limits under §387.303(b)(4).

(4) *Use of Endorsements in MCS Series.* When Security limits certified under §387.303 (b)(1) or (b)(2) involves coverage also required by the Department of Transportation a *Form MCS endorsement* prescribed by the Department of Transportation such as, and including, the *Form MCS 90* endorsement is required.

(5) *Surety bonds.* When surety bonds are used rather than certificates of insurance, *Form BMC 82* is required for the security limits under §387.303(b)(1) not subject to regulation by the Department of Transportation, and *Form MCS 82*, or any form of similar import prescribed by the Department of Transportation, is used for the security limits subject also to minimum coverage requirements of the Department of Transportation.

(6) *Surety bonds and certificates in effect continuously.* Surety bonds and certificates of insurance shall specify that coverage thereunder will remain in effect continuously until terminated as herein provided, except: (1) When filed expressly to fill prior gaps or lapses in coverage or to cover grants of emergency temporary authority of unusually short duration and the filing clearly so indicates, or (2) in special or unusual circumstances, when special permission is obtained for filing certificates of insurance or surety bonds on terms meeting other particular needs of the situation.

(b) *Filing and copies.* Certificates of insurance, surety bonds, and notices of cancellation must be filed with the FMCSA in triplicate.

(c) *Name of insured.* Certificates of insurance and surety bonds shall be issued in the full and correct name of the individual, partnership, corporation or other person to whom the certificate, permit, or license is, or is to be, issued. In the case of a partnership, all partners shall be named.

(d) *Cancellation notice.* Except as provided in paragraph (e) of this section, surety bonds, certificates of insurance and other securities or agreements shall not be cancelled or withdrawn until 30 days after written notice has been submitted to the FMCSA at its offices in Washington, DC, on the prescribed form (Form BMC–35, Notice of Cancellation Motor Carrier Policies of Insurance under 49 U.S.C. 13906, and BMC–36, Notice of Cancellation Motor Carrier and Broker Surety Bonds, as appropriate) by the insurance company, surety or sureties, motor carrier, broker or other party thereto, as the case may be, which period of thirty (30) days shall commence to run from the date such notice on the prescribed form is actually received by the FMCSA.

(e) *Termination by replacement.* Certificates of insurance or surety bonds which have been accepted by the FMCSA under these rules may be replaced by other certificates of insurance, surety bonds or other security, and the liability of the retiring insurer or surety under such certificates of insurance or surety bonds shall be considered as having terminated as of the effective date of the replacement certificate of insurance, surety bond or other security, provided the said replacement certificate, bond or other security is acceptable to the FMCSA

333

under the rules and regulations in this part.

(f) *Termination of Forms BMC–32 and BMC–34 for motor carriers transporting property other than household goods.* Form BMC–32 endorsements and Form BMC–34 certificates of insurance issued to motor carriers transporting property other than household goods that have been accepted by the FMCSA under these rules will expire on March 21, 2011.

[47 FR 55944, Dec. 14, 1982, as amended at 48 FR 43334, Sept. 23, 1983; 48 FR 51781, Nov. 14, 1983; 50 FR 40030, Oct. 1, 1985; 51 FR 34623, Sept. 30, 1986; 62 FR 49941, Sept. 24, 1997; 75 FR 35328, June 22, 2010]

§ 387.315 Insurance and surety companies.

A certificate of insurance or surety bond will not be accepted by the FMCSA unless issued by an insurance or surety company that is authorized (licensed or admitted) to issue bonds or underlying insurance policies:

(a) In each state in which the motor carrier is authorized by the FMCSA to operate, or

(b) In the state in which the motor carrier has its principal place of business or domicile, and will designate in writing upon request by the FMCSA, a person upon whom process, issued by or under the authority of a court of competent jurisdiction, may be served in any proceeding at law or equity brought in any state in which the carrier operates, or

(c) In any state, and is eligible as an excess or surplus lines insurer in any state in which business is written, and will make the designation of process agent described in paragraph (b) of this section.

(d) In the Province or Territory of Canada in which a Canadian motor carrier has its principal place of business or domicile, and will designate in writing upon request by FMCSA, a person upon whom process, issued by or under the authority of a court of competent jurisdiction, may be served in any proceeding at law or equity brought in any State in which the carrier operates.

[56 FR 28111, June 19, 1991, as amended at 75 FR 38430, July 2, 2010]

§ 387.317 Refusal to accept, or revocation by the FMCSA of surety bonds, etc.

The FMCSA may, at any time, refuse to accept or may revoke its acceptance of any surety bond, certificate of insurance, qualifications as a self-insurer, or other securities or agreements if, in its judgment such security does not comply with these sections or for any reason fails to provide satisfactory or adequate protection for the public. Revocation of acceptance of any certificate of insurance, surety bond or other security shall not relieve the motor carrier from compliance with § 387.301(d).

[47 FR 55945, Dec. 14, 1982, as amended at 62 FR 49942, Sept. 24, 1997]

§ 387.319 Fiduciaries.

(a) *Definitions.* The terms "insured" and "principal" as used in a certificate of insurance, surety bond, and notice of cancellation, filed by or for a motor carrier, include the motor carrier and its fiduciary as of the moment of succession. The term "fiduciary" means any person authorized by law to collect and preserve property of incapacitated, financially disabled, bankrupt, or deceased holders of operating rights, and assignees of such holders.

(b) *Insurance coverage in behalf of fiduciaries to apply concurrently.* The coverage furnished under the provisions of this section on behalf of fiduciaries shall not apply subsequent to the effective date of other insurance, or other security, filed with and approved by the FMCSA in behalf of such fiduciaries. After the coverage provided in this section shall have been in effect thirty (30) days, it may be cancelled or withdrawn within the succeeding period of thirty (30) days by the insurer, the insured, the surety, or the principal upon ten (10) days' notice in writing to the FMCSA at its office in Washington, DC, which period of ten (10) days shall commence to run from the date such notice is actually received by the FMCSA. After such coverage has been in effect for a total of sixty (60) days, it may be cancelled or withdrawn only in accordance with § 1043.7.

[32 FR 20032, Dec. 20, 1967, as amended at 47 FR 49596, Nov. 1, 1982; 47 FR 55945, Dec. 14, 1982; 55 FR 11197, Mar. 27, 1990]

§387.321 Operations in foreign commerce.

No motor carrier may operate in the United States in the course of transportation between places in a foreign country or between a place in one foreign country and a place in another foreign country unless and until there shall have been filed with and accepted by the FMCSA a certificate of insurance, surety bond, proof of qualifications as a self-insurer, or other securities or agreements in the amount prescribed in §387.303(b), conditioned to pay any final judgment recovered against such motor carrier for bodily injuries to or the death of any person resulting from the negligent operation, maintenance, or use of motor vehicles in transportation between places in a foreign country or between a place in one foreign country and a place in another foreign country, insofar as such transportation takes place in the United States, or for loss of or damage to property of others. The security for the protection of the public required by this section shall be maintained in effect at all times and shall be subject to the provisions of §§387.309 through 387.319. The requirements of §387.315(a) shall be satisfied if the insurance or surety company, in addition to having been approved by the FMCSA, is legally authorized to issue policies or surety bonds in at least one of the States in the United States, or one of the Provinces in Canada, and has filed with the FMCSA the name and address of a person upon whom legal process may be served in each State in or through which the motor carrier operates. Such designation may from time to time be changed by like designation similarly filed, but shall be maintained during the effectiveness of any certificate of insurance or surety bond issued by the company, and thereafter with respect to any claims arising during the effectiveness of such certificate or bond. The term "motor carrier" as used in this section shall not include private carriers or carriers operating under the partial exemption from regulation in 49 U.S.C. 13503 and 13506.

[47 FR 55945, Dec. 14, 1982, as amended at 62 FR 49942, Sept. 24, 1997]

§387.323 Electronic filing of surety bonds, trust fund agreements, certificates of insurance and cancellations.

(a) Insurers may, at their option and in accordance with the requirements and procedures set forth in paragraphs (a) through (d) of this section, file forms BMC 34, BMC 35, BMC 36, BMC 82, BMC 83, BMC 84, BMC 85, BMC 91, and BMC 91X electronically, in lieu of using the prescribed printed forms.

(b) Each insurer must obtain authorization to file electronically by registering with the FMCSA. An individual account number and password for computer access will be issued to each registered insurer.

(c) Filings may be transmitted online via the Internet at: *http://fhwa-li.volpe.dot.gov* or via American Standard Code Information Interchange (ASCII). All ASCII transmission must be in fixed format, i.e., all records must have the same number of fields and same length. The record layouts for ASCII electronic transactions are described in the following table:

ELECTRONIC INSURANCE FILING TRANSACTIONS

Field name	Number of positions	Description	Required F=filing C=cancel B=both	Start field	End field
Record type	1 Numeric	1=Filing 2=Cancellation	B	1	1
Insurer number	8 Text	FMCSA Assigned Insurer Number (Home Office) With Suffix (Issuing Office), If Different, e.g. 12345–01.	B	2	9
Filing type	1 Numeric	1 = BI&PD 2 = Cargo 3 = Bond 4 = Trust Fund	B	10	10
FMCSA docket number	8 Text	FMCSA Assigned MC or FF Number, e.g., MC000045.	B	11	18

ELECTRONIC INSURANCE FILING TRANSACTIONS—Continued

Field name	Number of positions	Description	Required F=filing C=cancel B=both	Start field	End field
Insured legal name	120 Text	Legal Name	B	19	138
Insured d/b/a name	60 Text	Doing Business As Name If Different From Legal Name.	B	139	198
Insured address	35 Text	Either street or mailing address	B	199	233
Insured city	30 Text	....	B	234	263
Insured state	2 Text	....	B	264	265
Insured zip code	9 Numeric	(Do not include dash if using 9 digit code).	B	266	274
Insured country	2 Text	(Will default to US)	B	275	276
Form code	10 Text	BMC–91, BMC–91X, BMC–34, BMC–35, etc.	B	277	286
Full, primary or excess coverage.	1 Text	If BMC–91X, P or E = indicator of primary or excess policy; 1 = Full under § 387.303(b)(1); 2 = Full under § 387.303(b)(2).	F	287	287
Limit of liability	5 Numeric	$ in Thousands	F	288	292
Underlying limit of liability.	5 Numeric	$ in Thousands (will default to $000 if Primary).	F	293	297
Effective date	8 Text	MM/DD/YY Format for both Filing or Cancellation.	B	298	305
Policy number	25 Text	Surety companies may enter bond number.	B	306	330

(d) All registered insurers agree to furnish upon request to the FMCSA a duplicate original of any policy (or policies) and all endorsements, surety bond, trust fund agreement, or other filing.

[60 FR 16810, Apr. 3, 1995, as amended at 62 FR 49942, Sept. 24, 1997; 66 FR 49873, Oct. 1, 2001]

Subpart D—Surety Bonds and Policies of Insurance for Freight Forwarders

SOURCE: 55 FR 11201, Mar. 27, 1990, unless otherwise noted. Redesignated at 61 FR 54710, Oct. 21, 1996.

§ 387.401 Definitions.

(a) *Freight forwarder* means a person holding itself out to the general public (other than as an express, pipeline, rail, sleeping car, motor, or water carrier) to provide transportation of property for compensation in interstate commerce, and in the ordinary course of its business:

(1) Performs or provides for assembling, consolidating, break-bulk, and distribution of shipments; and

(2) Assumes responsibility for transportation from place of receipt to destination; and

(3) Uses for any part of the transportation a carrier subject to FMCSA jurisdiction.

(b) *Household goods freight forwarder* (HHGFF) means a freight forwarder of household goods, unaccompanied baggage, or used automobiles.

(c) *Motor vehicle* means any vehicle, machine, tractor, trailer, or semitrailer propelled or drawn by mechanical power and used to transport property, but does not include any vehicle, locomotive, or car operated exclusively on a rail or rails. The following combinations will be regarded as one motor vehicle:

(1) A tractor that draws a trailer or semitrailer; and

(2) A truck and trailer bearing a single load.

§ 387.403 General requirements.

(a) *Cargo.* A household goods freight forwarder may not operate until it has filed with FMCSA an appropriate surety bond, certificate of insurance, qualifications as a self-insurer, or other securities or agreements, in the amounts prescribed in § 387.405, for loss of or damage to household goods.

(b) *Public liability.* A HHGFF may not perform transfer, collection, and delivery service until it has filed with the FMCSA an appropriate surety bond, certificate of insurance, qualifications as a self-insurer, or other securities or agreements, in the amounts prescribed at §387.405, conditioned to pay any final judgment recovered against such HHGFF for bodily injury to or the death of any person, or loss of or damage to property (except cargo) of others, or, in the case of freight vehicles described at 49 CFR 387.303(b)(2), for environmental restoration, resulting from the negligent operation, maintenance, or use of motor vehicles operated by or under its control in performing such service.

[55 FR 11201, Mar. 27, 1990. Redesignated at 61 FR 54710, Oct. 21, 1996, as amended at 62 FR 49942, Sept. 24, 1997; 75 FR 35328, June 22, 2010]

§387.405 Limits of liability.

The minimum amounts for cargo and public liability security are identical to those prescribed for motor carriers at 49 CFR 387.303.

[55 FR 11201, Mar. 27, 1990. Redesignated at 61 FR 54710, Oct. 21, 1996, as amended at 62 FR 49942, Sept. 24, 1997]

§387.407 Surety bonds and certificates of insurance.

(a) The limits of liability under §387.405 may be provided by aggregation under the procedures at 49 CFR part 387, subpart C.

(b) Each policy of insurance used in connection with a certificate of insurance filed with the FMCSA shall be amended by attachment of the appropriate endorsement prescribed by the FMCSA (or the Department of Transportation, where applicable).

[55 FR 11201, Mar. 27, 1990. Redesignated at 61 FR 54710, Oct. 21, 1996, as amended at 62 FR 49942, Sept. 24, 1997]

§387.409 Insurance and surety companies.

A certificate of insurance or surety bond will not be accepted by the FMCSA unless issued by an insurance or surety company that is authorized (licensed or admitted) to issue bonds or underlying insurance policies:

(a) In each state in which the freight forwarder is authorized by the FMCSA to perform service, or

(b) In the state in which the freight forwarder has its principal place of business or domicile, and will designate in writing upon request by the FMCSA, a person upon whom process, issued by or under the authority of a court of competent jurisdiction, may be served in any proceeding at law or equity brought in any state in which the freight forwarder performs service; or

(c) In any state, and is eligible as an excess or surplus lines insurer in any state in which business is written, and will make the designation of process agent prescribed in paragraph (b) of this section.

(d) In the Province or Territory of Canada in which a Canadian freight forwarder has its principal place of business or domicile, and will designate in writing upon request by FMCSA, a person upon whom process, issued by or under the authority of a court of competent jurisdiction, may be served in any proceeding at law or equity brought in any State in which the freight forwarder operates.

[56 FR 28111, June 19, 1991, as amended at 75 FR 38430, July 2, 2010]

§387.411 Qualifications as a self-insurer and other securities or agreements.

(a) *Self-insurer.* The FMCSA will approve the application of a freight forwarder to qualify as a self-insurer if it is able to meet its obligations for bodily-injury, property-damage, and cargo liability without adversely affecting its business.

(b) *Other securities and agreements.* The FMCSA will grant applications for approval of other securities and agreements if the public will be protected as contemplated by 49 U.S.C. 13906(c).

[55 FR 11201, Mar. 27, 1990. Redesignated at 61 FR 54710, Oct. 21, 1996, as amended at 62 FR 49942, Sept. 24, 1997]

§387.413 Forms and procedure.

(a) *Forms.* Endorsements for policies of insurance, surety bonds, certificates of insurance, applications to qualify as a self-insurer or for approval of other securities or agreements, and notices of cancellation must be in the form prescribed at 49 CFR part 387, subpart C.

(b) *Procedure.* Certificates of insurance, surety bonds, and notices of cancellation must be filed with the FMCSA in triplicate.

(c) *Names.* Certificates of insurance and surety bonds shall be issued in the full name (including any trade name) of the individual, partnership (all partners named), corporation, or other person holding or to be issued the permit.

(d) *Cancellation.* Except as provided in paragraph (e) of this section, certificates of insurance, surety bonds, and other securities and agreements shall not be cancelled or withdrawn until 30 days after the FMCSA receives written notice from the insurance company, surety, freight forwarder, or other party, as the case may be.

(e) *Termination by replacement.* Certificates of insurance or surety bonds may be replaced by other certificates of insurance, surety bonds, or other security, and the liability of the retiring insurer or surety shall be considered as having terminated as of the replacement's effective date, if acceptable to the FMCSA.

(f) *Termination of Forms BMC–32 and BMC–34 for freight forwarders of property other than household goods.* Form BMC–32 endorsements and Form BMC–34 certificates of insurance issued to freight forwarders of property other than household goods that have been accepted by the FMCSA under these rules will expire on March 21, 2011.

[55 FR 11201, Mar. 27, 1990. Redesignated at 61 FR 54710, Oct. 21, 1996, as amended at 62 FR 49942, Sept. 24, 1997; 75 FR 35329, June 22, 2010]

§ 387.415 Acceptance and revocation by the FMCSA.

The FMCSA may at any time refuse to accept or may revoke its acceptance of any surety bond, certificate of insurance, qualifications as a self-insurer, or other security or agreement that does not comply with these rules or fails to provide adequate public protection.

§ 387.417 Fiduciaries.

(a) *Interpretations.* The terms "insured" and "principal" as used in a certificate of insurance, surety bond, and notice of cancellation, filed by or for a freight forwarder, include the freight forwarder and its fiduciary (as defined at 49 CFR 387.319(a)) as of the moment of succession.

(b) *Span of security coverage.* The coverage furnished for a fiduciary shall not apply after the effective date of other insurance or security, filed with and accepted by the FMCSA for such fiduciary. After the coverage shall have been in effect 30 days, it may be cancelled or withdrawn within the succeeding 30 days by the insurer, the insured, the surety, or the principal 10 days after the FMCSA receives written notice. After such coverage has been in effect 60 days, it may be cancelled or withdrawn only in accordance with § 387.413(d).

[55 FR 11201, Mar. 27, 1990. Redesignated at 61 FR 54710, Oct. 21, 1996, as amended at 62 FR 49942, Sept. 24, 1997]

§ 387.419 Electronic filing of surety bonds, certificates of insurance and cancellations.

Insurers may, at their option and in accordance with the requirements and procedures set forth at 49 CFR 387.323, file certificates of insurance, surety bonds, and other securities and agreements electronically.

[60 FR 16811, Apr. 3, 1995, as amended at 62 FR 49942, Sept. 24, 1997]

PART 388—COOPERATIVE AGREEMENTS WITH STATES

AUTHORITY: 49 U.S.C. 113 and 502; 49 CFR 1.73.

SOURCE: 33 FR 19725, Dec. 25, 1968, unless otherwise noted.

EDITORIAL NOTE: Nomenclature changes to part 388 appear at 66 FR 49873, Oct. 1, 2001.

§388.1 Eligibility.

Any State may agree with the Federal Motor Carrier Safety Administration to enforce the safety laws and regulations of said State and the United States concerning motor carrier transportation by filing with the Administrator at Administrator, Federal Motor Carrier Safety Administration, 1200 New Jersey Ave., SE., Washington, DC 20590–0001, a written acceptance of the terms herein.

[33 FR 19725, Dec. 25, 1968, as amended at 72 FR 55702, Oct. 1, 2007]

§388.2 Extent of acceptance.

The written acceptance may be in letter form, signed by competent authority of said State charged with regulations of motor carrier saftey and hazardous materials transportation and shall specify the terms herein pertaining to the obligations of a State in which said State will participate. To the extent that a State agrees to participate in the terms herein, officials of the Federal Motor Carrier Safety Administration will reciprocate.

§388.3 Cancellation.

Cancellation or withdrawal, in whole or in part, from any agreement made under this chapter may be effected by written notice from either party indicating the effective date of said cancellation or withdrawal.

§388.4 Exchange of information.

(a) *Federal Motor Carrier Safety Administration furnishing information to State.* Information that comes to the attention of an employee of the Federal Motor Carrier Safety Administration in the course of his/her official duties of investigation, inspection, or examination of the property, equipment, and records of a motor carrier or others, pursuant to 49 U.S.C. 504(c), and that is believed to be a violation of any law or regulation of the State pertaining to unsafe motor carrier operations and practices, shall be communicated to the appropriate State authority by an official of the Federal Motor Carrier Safety Administration.

(b) *State furnishing information to Federal Motor Carrier Safety Administration.* Information that comes to the attention of a duly authorized agent of the State in the course of his/her official duties of investigation, inspection, or examination of the property, equipment, and records of a motor carrier or others, and that is believed to be a violation of any provision of the safety or hazardous materials laws of the United States concerning highway transportation or the regulations of the Federal Motor Carrier Safety Administration thereunder, shall be communicated to the Field Administrator.

[51 FR 12621, Apr. 14, 1986, as amended at 67 FR 61824, Oct. 2, 2002]

§388.5 Requests for assistance.

(a) *State request for Federal Motor Carrier Safety Administration assistance.* Upon written request of the appropriate State authority, the officials of the Federal Motor Carrier Safety Administration for that State shall, as time, personnel, and funds permit, obtain evidence for use by said State in the enforcement of its laws and regulations concerning unsafe motor carrier operations. Evidence obtained in this manner shall be transmitted to the appropriate State authority together with the name and address of an agent or employee, if any, having knowledge of the facts, who shall be made available when necessary to testify as a witness in an enforcement proceeding or other action.

(b) *Federal Motor Carrier Safety Administration request for State assistance.* Upon written request from a Regional Director of Motor Carriers, the appropriate State authority, shall, as time, personnel, and funds permit, obtain evidence in the State for use by the Federal Motor Carrier Safety Administration in its enforcement of the safety and hazardous materials laws and regulations of the United States concerning highway transportation. Evidence obtained in this manner shall be transmitted to the Field Administrator, together with the name and address of an agent or employee, if any, having knowledge of the facts, who shall be made available when necessary to testify as a witness in an enforcement proceeding or other action.

[33 FR 19725, Dec. 25, 1968, as amended at 51 FR 12621, Apr. 14, 1986; 60 FR 38743, July 28, 1995; 67 FR 61824, Oct. 2, 2002]

§ 388.6 Joint investigation, inspection, or examination.

Upon agreement by the Field Administrator and the appropriate State authority, there will be conducted a joint investigation, inspection, or examination of the property, equipment, or records of motor carriers or others, for the enforcement of the safety and hazardous materials laws and regulations of the United States and the State concerning highway transportation. The said Field Administrator and the appropriate State authority shall decide as to the location and time, the objectives sought, and the identity of the person who will supervise the joint effort and make the necessary decisions. Any agent or employee of either agency who has personal knowledge of pertinent facts shall be made available when necessary to testify as a witness in an enforcement proceeding or other action.

[33 FR 19725, Dec. 25, 1968, as amended at 51 FR 12621, Apr. 14, 1986; 67 FR 61824, Oct. 2, 2002]

§ 388.7 Joint administrative activities related to enforcement of safety and hazardous materials laws and regulations.

To facilitate the interchange of information and evidence, and the conduct of joint investigation and administrative action, the Field Administrator and the appropriate State authority shall, when warranted, schedule joint conferences of staff members of both agencies. Information shall be exchanged as to the nature and extent of the authority and capabilities of the respective agencies to enforce the safety and hazardous materials laws and regulations of the State or of the United States concerning motor carrier transportation. The Federal Motor Carrier Safety Administration and the State (or appropriate State authority) shall use their best efforts to inform each other of changes in their rules and regulations and cooperate with and assist each other in conducting training schools for Federal and State enforcement officials engaged in such duties.

[33 FR 19725, Dec. 25, 1968, as amended at 51 FR 12621, Apr. 14, 1986; 67 FR 61824, Oct. 2, 2002]

§ 388.8 Supplemental agreements.

The terms specified in this part may be supplemented from time to time by specific agreement between the Federal Motor Carrier Safety Administration and the appropriate State authority in order to further implement the provisions of 49 U.S.C. 502.

[51 FR 12621, Apr. 14, 1986]

PART 389—RULEMAKING PROCEDURES—FEDERAL MOTOR CARRIER SAFETY REGULATIONS

Subpart A—General

Sec.
389.1 Applicability.
389.3 Definitions.
389.5 Regulatory docket.
389.7 Records.

Subpart B—Procedures for Adoption of Rules

389.11 General.
389.13 Initiation of rule making.
389.15 Contents of notices of proposed rule making.
389.17 Participation by interested persons.
389.19 Petitions for extension of time to comment.
389.21 Contents of written comments.
389.23 Consideration of comments received.
389.25 Additional rule making proceedings.
389.27 Hearings.
389.29 Adoption of final rules.
389.31 Petitions for rule making.
389.33 Processing of petition.
389.35 Petitions for reconsideration.
389.37 Proceedings on petitions for reconsideration.
389.39 Direct final rulemaking procedures

AUTHORITY: 49 U.S.C. 113, 501 et seq., subchapters I and III of chapter 311, chapter 313, and 31502; 42 U.S.C 4917; and 49 CFR 1.73

SOURCE: 35 FR 9209, June 12, 1970, unless otherwise noted.

EDITORIAL NOTE: Nomenclature changes to part 389 appear at 66 FR 49873, Oct. 1, 2001.

Subpart A—General

§ 389.1 Applicability.

This part prescribes rulemaking procedures that apply to the issuance, amendment and revocation of rules under an Act.

[62 FR 37152, July 11, 1997]

§389.3 Definitions.

Act means statutes granting the Secretary authority to regulate motor carrier safety.

Administrator means the Federal Motor Carrier Safety Administrator.

[62 FR 37152, July 11, 1997]

§389.5 Regulatory docket.

(a) Information and data deemed relevant by the Administrator relating to rulemaking actions, including notices of proposed rulemaking; comments received in response to notices; petitions for rulemaking and reconsideration; denials of petitions for rulemaking and reconsideration; records of additional rule making proceedings under §389.25; and final rules are maintained at headquarters, Federal Motor Carrier Safety Administration, 1200 New Jersey Ave., SE., Washington, DC 20590–0001.

(b) Except for material ordered withheld from the public under section 552(b) of title 5 of the United States Code, any person may examine docketed material in the Department of Transportation Docket Management Facility in the following ways:

(1) At headquarters at any time during regular business hours. Copies may be obtained upon payment of a fee.

(2) On the Web site *regulations.gov*, at any time, by using the uniform resources locator (URL) *http:// www.regulations.gov*. Copies may be downloaded or printed.

[72 FR 55702, Oct. 1, 2007]

§389.7 Records.

Records of the Administrator relating to rule making proceedings are available for inspection as provided in section 552(b) of title 5 of the United States Code and part 7 of the regulations of the Secretary of Transportation (part 7 of this title; 32 FR 9284 *et seq.*).

[35 FR 9209, June 12, 1970, as amended at 53 FR 2036, Jan. 26, 1988]

Subpart B—Procedures for Adoption of Rules

§389.11 General.

Except as provided in §389.39, Direct final rulemaking procedures, unless the Administrator, for good cause, finds a rule is impractical, unnecessary, or contrary to the public interest, and incorporates such a finding and a brief statement for the reason for it in the rule, a notice of proposed rulemaking must be issued, and interested persons are invited to participate in the rulemaking proceedings involving rules under an Act.

[75 FR 29916, May 28, 2010]

§389.13 Initiation of rule making.

The Administrator initiates rule making on his/her own motion. However, in so doing, he/she may, in his/her discretion, consider the recommendations of his/her staff or other agencies of the United States or of other interested persons.

[35 FR 9209, June 12, 1970, as amended at 53 FR 2036, Jan. 26, 1988]

§389.15 Contents of notices of proposed rule making.

(a) Each notice of proposed rule making is published in the FEDERAL REGISTER, unless all persons subject to it are named and are personally served with a copy of it.

(b) Each notice, whether published in the FEDERAL REGISTER or personally served, includes:

(1) A statement of the time, place, and nature of the proposed rule making proceeding;

(2) A reference to the authority under which it is issued;

(3) A description of the subjects and issues involved or the substance and terms of the proposed rule;

(4) A statement of the time within which written comments must be submitted; and

(5) A statement of how and to what extent interested persons may participate in the proceeding.

§389.17 Participation by interested persons.

(a) Any interested person may participate in rule making proceedings by submitting comments in writing containing information, views, or arguments.

341

(b) In his/her discretion, the Administrator may invite any interested person to participate in the rule making procedures described in § 389.25.

[35 FR 9209, June 12, 1970, as amended at 53 FR 2036, Jan. 26, 1988]

§ 389.19 Petitions for extension of time to comment.

A petition for extension of the time to submit comments must be received in duplicate not later than three (3) days before expiration of the time stated in the notice. The filing of the petition does not automatically extend the time for petitioner's comments. Such a petition is granted only if the petitioner shows good cause for the extension, and if the extension is consistent with the public interest. If an extension is granted, it is granted to all persons, and it is published in the FEDERAL REGISTER.

§ 389.21 Contents of written comments.

All written comments must be in English and submitted in five (5) legible copies, unless the number of copies is specified in the notice. Any interested person must submit as part of his/her written comments all material that he/she considers relevant to any statement of fact made by him/her. Incorporation of material by reference is to be avoided. However, if such incorporation is necessary, the incorporated material shall be identified with respect to document and page.

§ 389.23 Consideration of comments received.

All timely comments are considered before final action is taken on a rule making proposal. Late filed comments may be considered as far as practicable.

§ 389.25 Additional rule making proceedings.

The Administrator may initiate any further rule making proceedings that he/she finds necessary or desirable. or example, interested persons may be invited to make oral arguments, to participate in conferences between the Administrator or his/her representative at which minutes of the conference are kept, to appear at informal hearings presided over by officials designated by the Administrator at which a transcript or minutes are kept, or participate in any other proceeding to assure informed administrative action and to protect the public interest.

[35 FR 9209, June 12, 1970, as amended at 53 FR 2036, Jan. 26, 1988]

§ 389.27 Hearings.

(a) Sections 556 and 557 of title 5, United States Code, do not apply to hearings held under this part. Unless otherwise specified, hearings held under this part are informal, non-adversary, fact-finding procedures at which there are no formal pleadings or adverse parties. Any rule issued in a case in which an informal hearing is held is not necessarily based exclusively on the record of the hearing.

(b) The Administrator designates a representative to conduct any hearing held under this part. The Chief Counsel of the Federal Motor Carrier Safety Administration designates a member of his/her staff to serve as legal officer at the hearing.

[35 FR 9209, June 12, 1970, as amended at 53 FR 2036, Jan. 26, 1988]

§ 389.29 Adoption of final rules.

Final rules are prepared by representatives of the office concerned and the Office of the Chief Counsel. The rule is then submitted to the Administrator for his/her consideration. If the Administrator adopts the rule, it is published in the FEDERAL REGISTER, unless all persons subject to it are named and are personally served with a copy of it.

[35 FR 9209, June 12, 1970, as amended at 53 FR 2036, Jan. 26, 1988]

§ 389.31 Petitions for rule making.

(a) Any interested person may petition the Administrator to establish, amend, or repeal a rule.

(b) Each petition filed under this section must:

(1) Be submitted in duplicate to the Administrator, Federal Motor Carrier Safety Administration, 1200 New Jersey Ave., SE., Washington, DC 20590–0001;

(2) Set forth the text or substance of the rule or amendment proposed, or specify the rule that the petitioner

seeks to have repealed, as the case may be;

(3) Explain the interest of the petitioner in the action requested;

(4) Contain any information and arguments available to the petitioner to support the action sought.

[35 FR 9209, June 12, 1970, as amended at 45 FR 46424, July 10, 1980; 53 FR 2036, Jan. 26, 1988; 72 FR 55702, Oct. 1, 2007]

§389.33 Processing of petition.

(a) Unless the Administrator otherwise specifies, no public hearing, argument, or other proceeding is held directly on a petition before its disposition under this section.

(b) *Grants.* If the Administrator determines that the petition contains adequate justification, he/she initiates rule making action under this Subpart B.

(c) *Denials.* If the Administrator determines that the petition does not justify rule making, he/she denies the petition.

(d) *Notification.* Whenever the Administrator determines that a petition should be granted or denied, the Office of the Chief Counsel prepares a notice of that grant or denial for issuance to the petitioner, and the Administrator issues it to the petitioner.

[35 FR 9209, June 12, 1970, as amended at 53 FR 2036, Jan. 26, 1988]

§389.35 Petitions for reconsideration.

(a) Any interested person may petition the Administrator for reconsideration of any rule issued under this part. The petition must be in English and submitted in five (5) legible copies to the Administrator, Federal Motor Carrier Safety Administration, 1200 New Jersey Ave., SE., Washington, DC 20590–0001, and received not later than thirty (30) days after publication of the rule in the FEDERAL REGISTER. Petitions filed after that time will be considered as petitions filed under §389.31. The petition must contain a brief statement of the complaint and an explanation as to why compliance with the rule is not practicable, is unreasonable, or is not in the public interest.

(b) If the petitioner requests the consideration of additional facts, he/she must state the reason they were not

presented to the Administrator within the prescribed time.

(c) The Administrator does not consider repetitious petitions.

(d) Unless the Administrator otherwise provides, the filing of a petition under this section does not stay the effectiveness of the rule.

[35 FR 9209, June 12, 1970, as amended at 53 FR 2036, Jan. 26, 1988; 72 FR 55702, Oct. 1, 2007]

§389.37 Proceedings on petitions for reconsideration.

The Administrator may grant or deny, in whole or in part, any petition for reconsideration without further proceedings. In the event he/she determines to reconsider any rule, he/she may issue a final decision on reconsideration without further proceedings, or he/she may provide such opportunity to submit comment or information and data as he/she deems appropriate. Whenever the Administrator determines that a petition should be granted or denied, he/she prepares a notice of the grant or denial of a petition for reconsideration, for issuance to the petitioner, and issues it to the petitioner. The Administrator may consolidate petitions relating to the same rule.

[35 FR 9209, June 12, 1970, as amended at 53 FR 2036, Jan. 26, 1988]

§389.39 Direct final rulemaking procedures

A direct final rule makes regulatory changes and states that those changes will take effect on a specified date unless FMCSA receives an adverse comment or notice of intent to file an adverse comment by the date specified in the direct final rule published in the FEDERAL REGISTER.

(a) *Types of actions appropriate for direct final rulemaking.* Rules that the Administrator determines to be non-controversial and unlikely to result in adverse public comments may be published in the final rule section of the FEDERAL REGISTER as direct final rules. These include non-controversial rules that:

(1) Make non-substantive clarifications or corrections to existing rules;

(2) Incorporate by reference the latest or otherwise updated versions of technical or industry standards;

(3) Affect internal FMCSA procedures such as filing requirements and rules governing inspection and copying of documents;

(4) Update existing forms; and

(5) Make minor changes to rules regarding statistics and reporting requirements, such as a change in reporting period (for example, from quarterly to annually) or eliminating a type of data collection no longer necessary.

(b) *Adverse comment.* An adverse comment is a comment that FMCSA judges to be critical of the rule, to suggest that the rule should not be adopted, or to suggest that a change should be made to the rule. Under the direct final rule process, FMCSA does not consider the following types of comments to be adverse:

(1) Comments recommending another rule change, unless the commenter states that the direct final rule will be ineffective without the change;

(2) Comments outside the scope of the rule and comments suggesting that the rule's policy or requirements should or should not be extended to other Agency programs outside the scope of the rule;

(3) Comments in support of the rule; or

(4) Comments requesting clarification.

(c) *Confirmation of effective date.* FMCSA will publish a confirmation rule document in the FEDERAL REGISTER, if it has not received an adverse comment or notice of intent to file an adverse comment by the date specified in the direct final rule. The confirmation rule document tells the public the effective date of the rule.

(d) *Withdrawal of a direct final rule.* (1) If FMCSA receives an adverse comment or a notice of intent to file an adverse comment within the comment period, it will publish a rule document in the FEDERAL REGISTER, before the effective date of the direct final rule, advising the public and withdrawing the direct final rule.

(2) If FMCSA withdraws a direct final rule because of an adverse comment, the Agency may issue a notice of proposed rulemaking if it decides to pursue the rulemaking.

[75 FR 29916, May 28, 2010]

PART 390—FEDERAL MOTOR CARRIER SAFETY REGULATIONS; GENERAL

Subpart A—General Applicability and Definitions

AUTHORITY: 49 U.S.C. 508, 13301, 13902, 31132, 31133, 31136, 31144, 31151, 31502, 31504; sec. 204, Pub. L. 104–88, 109 Stat. 803, 941 (49 U.S.C. 701 note); sec. 114, Pub. L. 103–311, 108 Stat. 1673, 1677; sec. 212, 217, 229, Pub. L. 106–159, 113 Stat. 1748, 1766, 1767, 1773; sec. 4136, Pub. L. 109–59, 119 Stat. 1144, 1745 and 49 CFR 1.73.

SOURCE: 53 FR 18052, May 19, 1988, unless otherwise noted.

EDITORIAL NOTE: Nomenclature changes to part 390 appear at 66 FR 49873, Oct. 1, 2001.

Subpart A—General Applicability and Definitions

§390.1 Purpose.

This part establishes general applicability, definitions, general requirements and information as they pertain to persons subject to this chapter.

§390.3 General applicability.

(a) The rules in subchapter B of this chapter are applicable to all employers, employees, and commercial motor vehicles, which transport property or passengers in interstate commerce.

(b) The rules in part 383, Commercial Driver's License Standards; Requirements and Penalties, are applicable to every person who operates a commercial motor vehicle, as defined in §383.5 of this subchapter, in interstate or intrastate commerce and to all employers of such persons.

(c) The rules in part 387, Minimum Levels of Financial Responsibility for Motor Carriers, are applicable to motor carriers as provided in §387.3 or §387.27 of this subchapter.

(d) *Additional requirements.* Nothing in subchapter B of this chapter shall be construed to prohibit an employer from requiring and enforcing more stringent requirements relating to safety of operation and employee safety and health.

(e) *Knowledge of and compliance with the regulations.* (1) Every employer shall be knowledgeable of and comply with all regulations contained in this subchapter which are applicable to that motor carrier's operations.

(2) Every driver and employee shall be instructed regarding, and shall comply with, all applicable regulations contained in this subchapter.

(3) All motor vehicle equipment and accessories required by this subchapter shall be maintained in compliance with all applicable performance and design criteria set forth in this subchapter.

(f) *Exceptions.* Unless otherwise specifically provided, the rules in this subchapter do not apply to—

(1) All school bus operations as defined in §390.5 except for the provisions of §§391.15(e) and 392.80;

(2) Transportation performed by the Federal government, a State, or any political subdivision of a State, or an agency established under a compact between States that has been approved by the Congress of the United States;

(3) The occasional transportation of personal property by individuals not for compensation nor in the furtherance of a commercial enterprise;

(4) The transportation of human corpses or sick and injured persons;

(5) The operation of fire trucks and rescue vehicles while involved in emergency and related operations;

(6) The operation of commercial motor vehicles designed or used to transport between 9 and 15 passengers (including the driver), not for direct compensation, provided the vehicle does not otherwise meet the definition of a commercial motor vehicle except for the texting provisions of §§391.15(e) and 392.80, and except that motor carriers operating such vehicles are required to comply with §§390.15, 390.19, and 390.21(a) and (b)(2).

(7) Either a driver of a commercial motor vehicle used primarily in the transportation of propane winter heating fuel or a driver of a motor vehicle used to respond to a pipeline emergency, if such regulations would prevent the driver from responding to an emergency condition requiring immediate response as defined in §390.5.

(g) *Motor carriers that transport hazardous materials in intrastate commerce.* The rules in the following provisions of subchapter B of this chapter apply to motor carriers that transport hazardous materials in intrastate commerce and to the motor vehicles that transport hazardous materials in intrastate commerce:

(1) Part 385, subparts A and E, for carriers subject to the requirements of §385.403 of this chapter.

(2) Part 386, Rules of practice for motor carrier, broker, freight forwarder, and hazardous materials proceedings, of this chapter.

(3) Part 387, Minimum Levels of Financial Responsibility for Motor Carriers, to the extent provided in § 387.3 of this chapter.

(4) Section 390.19, Motor carrier identification report, and § 390.21, Marking of CMVs, for carriers subject to the requirements of § 385.403 of this chapter. Intrastate motor carriers operating prior to January 1, 2005, are excepted from § 390.19(a)(1).

(h) *Intermodal equipment providers.* On and after December 17, 2009, the rules in the following provisions of subchapter B of this chapter apply to intermodal equipment providers:

(1) Subpart F, Intermodal Equipment Providers, of Part 385, Safety Fitness Procedures.

(2) Part 386, Rules of Practice for Motor Carrier, Intermodal Equipment Provider, Broker, Freight Forwarder, and Hazardous Materials Proceedings.

(3) Part 390, Federal Motor Carrier Safety Regulations; General, except § 390.15(b) concerning accident registers.

(4) Part 393, Parts and Accessories Necessary for Safe Operation.

(5) Part 396, Inspection, Repair, and Maintenance.

[53 FR 18052, May 19, 1988, as amended at 54 FR 12202, Mar. 24, 1989; 58 FR 33776, June 21, 1993; 59 FR 8752, Feb. 23, 1994; 59 FR 67554, Dec. 29, 1994; 62 FR 1296, Jan. 9, 1997; 63 FR 33276, June 18, 1998; 64 FR 48516, Sept. 3, 1999; 66 FR 2766, Jan. 11, 2001; 68 FR 47875, Aug. 12, 2003; 69 FR 39372, June 30, 2004; 72 FR 36790, July 5, 2007; 73 FR 76820, Dec. 17, 2008; 75 FR 5002, Feb. 1, 2010; 75 FR 59135, Sept. 27, 2010]

§ 390.5   Definitions.

Unless specifically defined elsewhere, in this subchapter:

Accident means—

(1) Except as provided in paragraph (2) of this definition, an occurrence involving a commercial motor vehicle operating on a highway in interstate or intrastate commerce which results in:

(i) A fatality;

(ii) Bodily injury to a person who, as a result of the injury, immediately receives medical treatment away from the scene of the accident; or

(iii) One or more motor vehicles incurring disabling damage as a result of the accident, requiring the motor vehicle(s) to be transported away from the scene by a tow truck or other motor vehicle.

(2) The term accident does not include:

(i) An occurrence involving only boarding and alighting from a stationary motor vehicle; or

(ii) An occurrence involving only the loading or unloading of cargo.

Alcohol concentration (AC) means the concentration of alcohol in a person's blood or breath. When expressed as a percentage it means grams of alcohol per 100 milliliters of blood or grams of alcohol per 210 liters of breath.

Bus means any motor vehicle designed, constructed, and or used for the transportation of passengers, including taxicabs.

Business district means the territory contiguous to and including a highway when within any 600 feet along such highway there are buildings in use for business or industrial purposes, including but not limited to hotels, banks, or office buildings which occupy at least 300 feet of frontage on one side or 300 feet collectively on both sides of the highway.

Charter transportation of passengers means transportation, using a bus, of a group of persons who pursuant to a common purpose, under a single contract, at a fixed charge for the motor vehicle, have acquired the exclusive use of the motor vehicle to travel together under an itinerary either specified in advance or modified after having left the place of origin.

Commercial motor vehicle means any self-propelled or towed motor vehicle used on a highway in interstate commerce to transport passengers or property when the vehicle—

(1) Has a gross vehicle weight rating or gross combination weight rating, or gross vehicle weight or gross combination weight, of 4,536 kg (10,001 pounds) or more, whichever is greater; or

(2) Is designed or used to transport more than 8 passengers (including the driver) for compensation; or

(3) Is designed or used to transport more than 15 passengers, including the

driver, and is not used to transport passengers for compensation; or

(4) Is used in transporting material found by the Secretary of Transportation to be hazardous under 49 U.S.C. 5103 and transported in a quantity requiring placarding under regulations prescribed by the Secretary under 49 CFR, subtitle B, chapter I, subchapter C.

Conviction means an unvacated adjudication of guilt, or a determination that a person has violated or failed to comply with the law in a court of original jurisdiction or by an authorized administrative tribunal, an unvacated forfeiture of bail or collateral deposited to secure the person's appearance in court, a plea of guilty or nolo contendere accepted by the court, the payment of a fine or court cost, or violation of a condition of release without bail, regardless of whether or not the penalty is rebated, suspended, or probated.

Direct assistance means transportation and other relief services provided by a motor carrier or its driver(s) incident to the immediate restoration of essential services (such as, electricity, medial care, sewer, water, telecommunications, and telecommunication transmissions) or essential supplies (such as, food and fuel). It does not include transportation related to long-term rehabilitation of damaged physical infrastructure or routine commercial deliveries after the initial threat to life and property has passed.

Direct compensation means payment made to the motor carrier by the passengers or a person acting on behalf of the passengers for the transportation services provided, and not included in a total package charge or other assessment for highway transportation services.

Disabling damage means damage which precludes departure of a motor vehicle from the scene of the accident in its usual manner in daylight after simple repairs.

(1) *Inclusions.* Damage to motor vehicles that could have been driven, but would have been further damaged if so driven.

(2) *Exclusions.* (i) Damage which can be remedied temporarily at the scene of the accident without special tools or parts.

(ii) Tire disablement without other damage even if no spare tire is available.

(iii) Headlamp or taillight damage.

(iv) Damage to turn signals, horn, or windshield wipers which makes them inoperative.

Driveaway-towaway operation means an operation in which an empty or unladen motor vehicle with one or more sets of wheels on the surface of the roadway is being transported:

(1) Between vehicle manufacturer's facilities;

(2) Between a vehicle manufacturer and a dealership or purchaser;

(3) Between a dealership, or other entity selling or leasing the vehicle, and a purchaser or lessee;

(4) To a motor carrier's terminal or repair facility for the repair of disabling damage (as defined in §390.5) following a crash; or

(5) To a motor carrier's terminal or repair facility for repairs associated with the failure of a vehicle component or system; or

(6) By means of a saddle-mount or tow-bar.

Driver means any person who operates any commercial motor vehicle.

Driving a commercial motor vehicle while under the influence of alcohol means committing any one or more of the following acts in a CMV: Driving a CMV while the person's alcohol concentration is 0.04 or more; driving under the influence of alcohol, as prescribed by State law; or refusal to undergo such testing as is required by any State or jurisdiction in the enforcement of Table 1 to §383.51 or §392.5(a)(2) of this subchapter.

Electronic device includes, but is not limited to, a cellular telephone; personal digital assistant; pager; computer; or any other device used to input, write, send, receive, or read text.

Emergency means any hurricane, tornado, storm (e.g. thunderstorm, snowstorm, icestorm, blizzard, sandstorm, etc.), high water, wind-driven water, tidal wave, tsunami, earthquake, volcanic eruption, mud slide, drought, forest fire, explosion, blackout or other occurrence, natural or man-made,

347

which interrupts the delivery of essential services (such as, electricity, medical care, sewer, water, telecommunications, and telecommunication transmissions) or essential supplies (such as, food and fuel) or otherwise immediately threatens human life or public welfare, provided such hurricane, tornado, or other event results in:

(1) A declaration of an emergency by the President of the United States, the Governor of a State, or their authorized representatives having authority to declare emergencies; by the FMCSA Field Administrator for the geographical area in which the occurrence happens; or by other Federal, State or local government officials having authority to declare emergencies, or

(2) A request by a police officer for tow trucks to move wrecked or disabled motor vehicles.

Emergency condition requiring immediate response means any condition that, if left unattended, is reasonably likely to result in immediate serious bodily harm, death, or substantial damage to property. In the case of transportation of propane winter heating fuel, such conditions shall include (but are not limited to) the detection of gas odor, the activation of carbon monoxide alarms, the detection of carbon monoxide poisoning, and any real or suspected damage to a propane gas system following a severe storm or flooding. An "emergency condition requiring immediate response" does not include requests to refill empty gas tanks. In the case of a pipeline emergency, such conditions include (but are not limited to) indication of an abnormal pressure event, leak, release or rupture.

Emergency relief means an operation in which a motor carrier or driver of a commercial motor vehicle is providing direct assistance to supplement State and local efforts and capabilities to save lives or property or to protect public health and safety as a result of an emergency as defined in this section.

Employee means any individual, other than an employer, who is employed by an employer and who in the course of his or her employment directly affects commercial motor vehicle safety. Such term includes a driver of a commercial motor vehicle (including an independent contractor while in the course of operating a commercial motor vehicle), a mechanic, and a freight handler. Such term does not include an employee of the United States, any State, any political subdivision of a State, or any agency established under a compact between States and approved by the Congress of the United States who is acting within the course of such employment.

Employer means any person engaged in a business affecting interstate commerce who owns or leases a commercial motor vehicle in connection with that business, or assigns employees to operate it, but such terms does not include the United States, any State, any political subdivision of a State, or an agency established under a compact between States approved by the Congress of the United States.

Exempt intracity zone means the geographic area of a municipality or the commercial zone of that municipality described in appendix F to subchapter B of this chapter. The term "exempt intracity zone" does not include any municipality or commercial zone in the State of Hawaii. For purposes of § 391.62, a driver may be considered to operate a commercial motor vehicle wholly within an exempt intracity zone notwithstanding any common control, management, or arrangement for a continuous carriage or shipment to or from a point without such zone.

Exempt motor carrier means a person engaged in transportation exempt from economic regulation by the Federal Motor Carrier Safety Administration (FMCSA) under 49 U.S.C. 13506. "Exempt motor carriers" are subject to the safety regulations set forth in this subchapter.

Farm vehicle driver means a person who drives only a commercial motor vehicle that is—

(a) Controlled and operated by a farmer as a private motor carrier of property;

(b) Being used to transport either—

(1) Agricultural products, or

(2) Farm machinery, farm supplies, or both, to or from a farm;

(c) Not being used in the operation of a for-hire motor carrier;

348

(d) Not carrying hazardous materials of a type or quantity that requires the commercial motor vehicle to be placarded in accordance with §177.823 of this subtitle; and

(e) Being used within 150 air-miles of the farmer's farm.

Farmer means any person who operates a farm or is directly involved in the cultivation of land, crops, or livestock which—

(a) Are owned by that person; or

(b) Are under the direct control of that person.

Fatality means any injury which results in the death of a person at the time of the motor vehicle accident or within 30 days of the accident.

Federal Motor Carrier Safety Administrator means the chief executive of the Federal Motor Carrier Safety Administration, an agency within the Department of Transportation.

For-hire motor carrier means a person engaged in the transportation of goods or passengers for compensation.

Gross combination weight rating (GCWR) means the value specified by the manufacturer as the loaded weight of a combination (articulated) motor vehicle. In the absence of a value specified by the manufacturer, GCWR will be determined by adding the GVWR of the power unit and the total weight of the towed unit and any load thereon.

Gross vehicle weight rating (GVWR) means the value specified by the manufacturer as the loaded weight of a single motor vehicle.

Hazardous material means a substance or material which has been determined by the Secretary of Transportation to be capable of posing an unreasonable risk to health, safety, and property when transported in commerce, and which has been so designated.

Hazardous substance means a material, and its mixtures or solutions, that is identified in the appendix to §172.101, List of Hazardous Substances and Reportable Quantities, of this title when offered for transportation in one package, or in one transport motor vehicle if not packaged, and when the quantity of the material therein equals or exceeds the reportable quantity (RQ). This definition does not apply to petroleum products that are lubricants or fuels, or to mixtures or solutions of

hazardous substances if in a concentration less than that shown in the table in §171.8 of this title, based on the reportable quantity (RQ) specified for the materials listed in the appendix to §172.101.

Hazardous waste means any material that is subject to the hazardous waste manifest requirements of the EPA specified in 40 CFR part 262 or would be subject to these requirements absent an interim authorization to a State under 40 CFR part 123, subpart F.

Highway means any road, street, or way, whether on public or private property, open to public travel. "Open to public travel" means that the road section is available, except during scheduled periods, extreme weather or emergency conditions, passable by four-wheel standard passenger cars, and open to the general public for use without restrictive gates, prohibitive signs, or regulation other than restrictions based on size, weight, or class of registration. Toll plazas of public toll roads are not considered restrictive gates.

Interchange means the act of providing intermodal equipment to a motor carrier pursuant to an intermodal equipment interchange agreement for the purpose of transporting the equipment for loading or unloading by any person or repositioning the equipment for the benefit of the equipment provider, but it does not include the leasing of equipment to a motor carrier for primary use in the motor carrier's freight hauling operations.

Intermodal equipment means trailing equipment that is used in the intermodal transportation of containers over public highways in interstate commerce, including trailers and chassis.

Intermodal equipment interchange agreement means the Uniform Intermodal Interchange and Facilities Access Agreement (UIIFA) or any other written document executed by an intermodal equipment provider or its agent and a motor carrier or its agent, the primary purpose of which is to establish the responsibilities and liabilities of both parties with respect to the interchange of the intermodal equipment.

Intermodal equipment provider means any person that interchanges intermodal equipment with a motor carrier pursuant to a written interchange agreement or has a contractual responsibility for the maintenance of the intermodal equipment.

Interstate commerce means trade, traffic, or transportation in the United States—

(1) Between a place in a State and a place outside of such State (including a place outside of the United States);

(2) Between two places in a State through another State or a place outside of the United States; or

(3) Between two places in a State as part of trade, traffic, or transportation originating or terminating outside the State or the United States.

Intrastate commerce means any trade, traffic, or transportation in any State which is not described in the term "interstate commerce."

Medical examiner means a person who is licensed, certified, and/or registered, in accordance with applicable State laws and regulations, to perform physical examinations. The term includes but is not limited to, doctors of medicine, doctors of osteopathy, physician assistants, advanced practice nurses, and doctors of chiropractic.

Medical variance means a driver has received one of the following from FMCSA that allows the driver to be issued a medical certificate:

(1) An exemption letter permitting operation of a commercial motor vehicle pursuant to part 381, subpart C, of this chapter or § 391.64 of this chapter;

(2) A skill performance evaluation certificate permitting operation of a commercial motor vehicle pursuant to § 391.49 of this chapter.

Motor carrier means a for-hire motor carrier or a private motor carrier. The term includes a motor carrier's agents, officers and representatives as well as employees responsible for hiring, supervising, training, assigning, or dispatching of drivers and employees concerned with the installation, inspection, and maintenance of motor vehicle equipment and/or accessories. For purposes of subchapter B, this definition includes the terms *employer*, and *exempt motor carrier.*

Motor vehicle means any vehicle, machine, tractor, trailer, or semitrailer propelled or drawn by mechanical power and used upon the highways in the transportation of passengers or property, or any combination thereof determined by the Federal Motor Carrier Safety Administration, but does not include any vehicle, locomotive, or car operated exclusively on a rail or rails, or a trolley bus operated by electric power derived from a fixed overhead wire, furnishing local passenger transportation similar to street-railway service.

Motor vehicle record means the report of the driving status and history of a driver generated from the driver record, provided to users, such as, drivers or employers, and subject to the provisions of the Driver Privacy Protection Act, 18 U.S.C. 2721–2725.

Multiple-employer driver means a driver, who in any period of 7 consecutive days, is employed or used as a driver by more than one motor carrier.

Operating authority means the registration required by 49 U.S.C. 13902, 49 CFR part 365, 49 CFR part 368, and 49 CFR 392.9a.

Operator—See driver.

Other terms—Any other term used in this subchapter is used in its commonly accepted meaning, except where such other term has been defined elsewhere in this subchapter. In that event, the definition therein given shall apply.

Out-of-service order means a declaration by an authorized enforcement officer of a Federal, State, Canadian, Mexican, or local jurisdiction that a driver, a commercial motor vehicle, or a motor carrier operation is out of service pursuant to 49 CFR 386.72, 392.5, 392.9a, 395.13, or 396.9, or compatible laws, or the North American Standard Out-of-Service Criteria.

Person means any individual, partnership, association, corporation, business trust, or any other organized group of individuals.

Previous employer means any DOT regulated person who employed the driver in the preceding 3 years, including any possible current employer.

Principal place of business means the single location designated by the motor carrier, normally its headquarters, for purposes of identification under this subchapter. The motor carrier must make records required by parts 382, 387, 390, 391, 395, 396, and 397 of this subchapter available for inspection at this location within 48 hours (Saturdays, Sundays, and Federal holidays excluded) after a request has been made by a special agent or authorized representative of the Federal Motor Carrier Safety Administration.

Private motor carrier means a person who provides transportation of property or passengers, by commercial motor vehicle, and is not a for-hire motor carrier.

Private motor carrier of passengers (business) means a private motor carrier engaged in the interstate transportation of passengers which is provided in the furtherance of a commercial enterprise and is not available to the public at large.

Private motor carrier of passengers (nonbusiness) means private motor carrier involved in the interstate transportation of passengers that does not otherwise meet the definition of a private motor carrier of passengers (business).

Radar detector means any device or mechanism to detect the emission of radio microwaves, laser beams or any other future speed measurement technology employed by enforcement personnel to measure the speed of commercial motor vehicles upon public roads and highways for enforcement purposes. Excluded from this definition are radar detection devices that meet both of the following requirements:

(1) Transported outside the driver's compartment of the commercial motor vehicle. For this purpose, the *driver's* compartment of a passenger-carrying CMV shall include all space designed to accommodate both the driver and the passengers; and

(2) Completely inaccessible to, inoperable by, and imperceptible to the driver while operating the commercial motor vehicle.

Regional Director of Motor Carriers means the Field Administrator, Federal Motor Carrier Safety Administration, for a given geographical area of the United States.

Residential district means the territory adjacent to and including a highway which is not a business district and for a distance of 300 feet or more along the highway is primarily improved with residences.

School bus means a passenger motor vehicle which is designed or used to carry more than 10 passengers in addition to the driver, and which the Secretary determines is likely to be significantly used for the purpose of transporting preprimary, primary, or secondary school students to such schools from home or from such schools to home.

School bus operation means the use of a school bus to transport only school children and/or school personnel from home to school and from school to home.

Secretary means the Secretary of Transportation.

Single-employer driver means a driver who, in any period of 7 consecutive days, is employed or used as a driver solely by a single motor carrier. This term includes a driver who operates a commercial motor vehicle on an intermittent, casual, or occasional basis.

Special agent See appendix B to subchapter B—Special agents.

State means a State of the United States and the District of Columbia and includes a political subdivision of a State.

Texting means manually entering alphanumeric text into, or reading text from, an electronic device.

(1) This action includes, but is not limited to, short message service, e-mailing, instant messaging, a command or request to access a World Wide Web page, or engaging in any other form of electronic text retrieval or electronic text entry for present or future communication.

(2) Texting does not include:

(i) Reading, selecting, or entering a telephone number, an extension number, or voicemail retrieval codes and commands into an electronic device for the purpose of initiating or receiving a phone call or using voice commands to initiate or receive a telephone call;

(ii) Inputting, selecting or reading information on a global positioning system or navigation system; or

351

(iii) Using a device capable of performing multiple functions (e.g., fleet management systems, dispatching devices, smart phones, citizens band radios, music players, etc.) for a purpose that is not otherwise prohibited in part 392.

Trailer includes:

(a) *Full trailer* means any motor vehicle other than a pole trailer which is designed to be drawn by another motor vehicle and so constructed that no part of its weight, except for the towing device, rests upon the self-propelled towing motor vehicle. A semitrailer equipped with an auxiliary front axle (converter dolly) shall be considered a full trailer.

(b) *Pole trailer* means any motor vehicle which is designed to be drawn by another motor vehicle and attached to the towing motor vehicle by means of a "reach" or "pole," or by being "boomed" or otherwise secured to the towing motor vehicle, for transporting long or irregularly shaped loads such as poles, pipes, or structural members, which generally are capable of sustaining themselves as beams between the supporting connections.

(c) *Semitrailer* means any motor vehicle, other than a pole trailer, which is designed to be drawn by another motor vehicle and is constructed so that some part of its weight rests upon the self-propelled towing motor vehicle.

Truck means any self-propelled commercial motor vehicle except a truck tractor, designed and/or used for the transportation of property.

Truck tractor means a self-propelled commercial motor vehicle designed and/or used primarily for drawing other vehicles.

United States means the 50 States and the District of Columbia.

[53 FR 18052, May 19, 1988]

EDITORIAL NOTE: For FEDERAL REGISTER citations affecting § 390.5, see the List of CFR Sections Affected, which appears in the Finding Aids section of the printed volume and at www.fdsys.gov.

§ 390.7 Rules of construction.

(a) In part 325 of subchapter A and in this subchapter, unless the context requires otherwise:

(1) Words imparting the singular include the plural;

(2) Words imparting the plural include the singular;

(3) Words imparting the present tense include the future tense.

(b) In this subchapter the word—

(1) *Officer* includes any person authorized by law to perform the duties of the office;

(2) *Writing* includes printing and typewriting;

(3) *Shall* is used in an imperative sense;

(4) *Must* is used in an imperative sense;

(5) *Should* is used in a recommendatory sense;

(6) *May* is used in a permissive sense; and

(7) *Includes* is used as a word of inclusion, not limitation.

[53 FR 18052, May 19, 1988, as amended at 60 FR 38744, July 28, 1995]

Subpart B—General Requirements and Information

§ 390.9 State and local laws, effect on.

Except as otherwise specifically indicated, subchapter B of this chapter is not intended to preclude States or subdivisions thereof from establishing or enforcing State or local laws relating to safety, the compliance with which would not prevent full compliance with these regulations by the person subject thereto.

§ 390.11 Motor carrier to require observance of driver regulations.

Whenever in part 325 of subchapter A or in this subchapter a duty is prescribed for a driver or a prohibition is imposed upon the driver, it shall be the duty of the motor carrier to require observance of such duty or prohibition. If the motor carrier is a driver, the driver shall likewise be bound.

§ 390.13 Aiding or abetting violations.

No person shall aid, abet, encourage, or require a motor carrier or its employees to violate the rules of this chapter.

§390.15 Assistance in investigations and special studies.

(a) Each motor carrier and intermodal equipment provider must do the following:

(1) Make all records and information pertaining to an accident available to an authorized representative or special agent of the Federal Motor Carrier Safety Administration, an authorized State or local enforcement agency representative, or authorized third party representative within such time as the request or investigation may specify.

(2) Give an authorized representative all reasonable assistance in the investigation of any accident, including providing a full, true, and correct response to any question of the inquiry.

(b) For accidents that occur after April 29, 2003, motor carriers must maintain an accident register for three years after the date of each accident. For accidents that occurred on or prior to April 29, 2003, motor carriers must maintain an accident register for a period of one year after the date of each accident. Information placed in the accident register must contain at least the following:

(1) A list of accidents as defined at §390.5 of this chapter containing for each accident:

(i) Date of accident.

(ii) City or town, or most near, where the accident occurred and the State where the accident occurred.

(iii) Driver Name.

(iv) Number of injuries.

(v) Number of fatalities.

(vi) Whether hazardous materials, other than fuel spilled from the fuel tanks of motor vehicle involved in the accident, were released.

(2) Copies of all accident reports required by State or other governmental entities or insurers.

(Approved by the Office of Management and Budget under control number 2126–0009)

[69 FR 16719, Mar. 30, 2004, as amended at 73 FR 76821, Dec. 17, 2008]

§390.16 [Reserved]

§390.17 Additional equipment and accessories.

Nothing in this subchapter shall be construed to prohibit the use of additional equipment and accessories, not inconsistent with or prohibited by this subchapter, provided such equipment and accessories do not decrease the safety of operation of the commercial motor vehicles on which they are used.

[53 FR 18052, May 19, 1988, as amended at 60 FR 38744, July 28, 1995. Redesignated at 65 FR 35296, June 2, 2000]

§390.19 Motor carrier, hazardous material shipper, and intermodal equipment provider identification reports.

(a) *Applicability.* Each motor carrier and intermodal equipment provider must file Form MCS–150, Form MCS–150B or Form MCS–150C with FMCSA as follows:

(1) A U.S.-, Canada-, Mexico-, or non-North America-domiciled motor carrier conducting operations in interstate commerce must file a Motor Carrier Identification Report, Form MCS–150.

(2) A motor carrier conducting operations in intrastate commerce and requiring a Safety Permit under 49 CFR part 385, subpart E of this chapter must file the Combined Motor Carrier Identification Report and HM Permit Application, Form MCS–150B.

(3) Each intermodal equipment provider that offers intermodal equipment for transportation in interstate commerce must file an Intermodal Equipment Provider Identification Report, Form MCS–150C.

(b) *Filing schedule.* Each motor carrier or intermodal equipment provider must file the appropriate form under paragraph (a) of this section at the following times:

(1) Before it begins operations; and

(2) Every 24 months, according to the following schedule:

USDOT number ending in	Must file by last day of
1	January.
2	February.
3	March.
4	April.
5	May.
6	June.
7	July.
8	August.
9	September.
0	October.

(3) If the next-to-last digit of its USDOT Number is odd, the motor carrier or intermodal equipment provider

353

shall file its update in every odd-numbered calendar year. If the next-to-last digit of the USDOT Number is even, the motor carrier or intermodal equipment provider shall file its update in every even-numbered calendar year.

(c) *Availability of forms.* The forms described under paragraph (a) of this section and complete instructions are available from the FMCSA Web site at *http://www.fmcsa.dot.gov* (Keyword "MCS–150," or "MCS–150B," or "MCS–150C"); from all FMCSA Service Centers and Division offices nationwide; or by calling 1–800–832–5660.

(d) *Where to file.* The required form under paragraph (a) of this section must be filed with FMCSA Office of Information Management. The form may be filed electronically according to the instructions at the Agency's Web site, or it may be sent to Federal Motor Carrier Safety Administration, Office of Information Management, MC–RIO, 1200 New Jersey Avenue, SE., Washington, DC 20590.

(e) *Special instructions for for-hire motor carriers.* A for-hire motor carrier should submit the Form MCS–150, or Form MCS–150B, along with its application for operating authority (Form OP–1, OP–1(MX), OP–1(NNA) or OP–2), to the appropriate address referenced on that form, or may submit it electronically or by mail separately to the address mentioned in paragraph (d) of this section.

(f) Only the legal name or a single trade name of the motor carrier or intermodal equipment provider may be used on the forms under paragraph (a) of this section (Form MCS–150, MCS–150B, or MCS–150C).

(g) A motor carrier or intermodal equipment provider that fails to file the form required under paragraph (a) of this section, or furnishes misleading information or makes false statements upon the form, is subject to the penalties prescribed in 49 U.S.C. 521(b)(2)(B).

(h)(1) Upon receipt and processing of the form described in paragraph (a) of this section, FMCSA will issue the motor carrier or intermodal equipment provider an identification number (USDOT Number).

(2) The following applicants must additionally pass a pre-authorization safety audit as described below before being issued a USDOT Number:

(i) A Mexico-domiciled motor carrier seeking to provide transportation of property or passengers in interstate commerce between Mexico and points in the United States beyond the municipalities and commercial zones along the United States-Mexico international border must pass the pre-authorization safety audit under § 365.507 of this subchapter. The Agency will not issue a USDOT Number until expiration of the protest period provided in § 365.115 of this subchapter or—if a protest is received—after FMCSA denies or rejects the protest.

(ii) A non-North America-domiciled motor carrier seeking to provide transportation of property or passengers in interstate commerce within the United States must pass the pre-authorization safety audit under § 385.607(c) of this subchapter. The Agency will not issue a USDOT Number until expiration of the protest period provided in § 365.115 of this subchapter or—if a protest is received—after FMCSA denies or rejects the protest.

(3) The motor carrier must display the number on each self-propelled CMV, as defined in § 390.5, along with the additional information required by § 390.21.

(4) The intermodal equipment provider must identify each unit of interchanged intermodal equipment by its assigned USDOT number.

(i) A motor carrier that registers its vehicles in a State that participates in the Performance and Registration Information Systems Management (PRISM) program (authorized under section 4004 of the Transportation Equity Act for the 21st Century [(Public Law 105–178, 112 Stat. 107]) is exempt from the requirements of this section, provided it files all the required information with the appropriate State office.

[73 FR 76821, Dec. 17, 2008]

§ 390.21   Marking of self-propelled CMVs and intermodal equipment.

(a) *General.* Every self-propelled CMV subject to subchapter B of this chapter must be marked as specified in paragraphs (b), (c), and (d) of this section, and each unit of intermodal equipment interchanged or offered for interchange to a motor carrier by an intermodal equipment provider subject to subchapter B of this chapter must be marked as specified in paragraph (g) of this section.

(b) *Nature of marking.* The marking must display the following information:

(1) The legal name or a single trade name of the motor carrier operating the self-propelled CMV, as listed on the motor carrier identification report (Form MCS–150) and submitted in accordance with §390.19.

(2) The identification number issued by FMCSA to the motor carrier or intermodal equipment provider, preceded by the letters "USDOT."

(3) If the name of any person other than the operating carrier appears on the CMV, the name of the operating carrier must be followed by the information required by paragraphs (b)(1), and (2) of this section, and be preceded by the words "operated by."

(4) Other identifying information may be displayed on the vehicle if it is not inconsistent with the information required by this paragraph.

(5) Each motor carrier shall meet the following requirements pertaining to its operation:

(i) All CMVs that are part of a motor carrier's existing fleet on July 3, 2000, and which are marked with an ICCMC number must come into compliance with paragraph (b)(2) of this section by July 3, 2002.

(ii) All CMVs that are part of a motor carrier's existing fleet on July 3, 2000, and which are not marked with the legal name or a single trade name on both sides of their CMVs, as shown on the Motor Carrier Identification Report, Form MCS–150, must come into compliance with paragraph (b)(1) of this section by July 5, 2005.

(iii) All CMVs added to a motor carrier's fleet on or after July 3, 2000, must meet the requirements of this section before being put into service and operating on public ways.

(c) *Size, shape, location, and color of marking.* The marking must—

(1) Appear on both sides of the self-propelled CMV;

(2) Be in letters that contrast sharply in color with the background on which the letters are placed;

(3) Be readily legible, during daylight hours, from a distance of 50 feet (15.24 meters) while the CMV is stationary; and

(4) Be kept and maintained in a manner that retains the legibility required by paragraph (c)(3) of this section.

(d) *Construction and durability.* The marking may be painted on the CMV or may consist of a removable device, if that device meets the identification and legibility requirements of paragraph (c) of this section, and such marking must be maintained as required by paragraph (c)(4) of this section.

(e) *Rented CMVs.* A motor carrier operating a self-propelled CMV under a rental agreement having a term not in excess of 30 calendar days meets the requirements of this section if:

(1) The CMV is marked in accordance with the provisions of paragraphs (b) through (d) of this section; or

(2) The CMV is marked as set forth in paragraph (e)(2)(i) through (iv) of this section:

(i) The legal name or a single trade name of the lessor is displayed in accordance with paragraphs (c) and (d) of this section.

(ii) The lessor's identification number preceded by the letters "USDOT" is displayed in accordance with paragraphs (c) and (d) of this section; and

(iii) The rental agreement entered into by the lessor and the renting motor carrier conspicuously contains the following information:

(A) The name and complete physical address of the principal place of business of the renting motor carrier;

(B) The identification number issued the renting motor carrier by the FMCSA, preceded by the letters "USDOT," if the motor carrier has been issued such a number. In lieu of the identification number required in this paragraph, the following may be shown in the rental agreement:

(*1*) Information which indicates whether the motor carrier is engaged in "interstate" or "intrastate" commerce; and

(*2*) Information which indicates whether the renting motor carrier is

355

transporting hazardous materials in the rented CMV;

(C) The sentence: "This lessor cooperates with all Federal, State, and local law enforcement officials nationwide to provide the identity of customers who operate this rental CMV"; and

(iv) The rental agreement entered into by the lessor and the renting motor carrier is carried on the rental CMV during the full term of the rental agreement. See the leasing regulations at 49 CFR 376 for information that should be included in all leasing documents.

(f) *Driveaway services.* In driveaway services, a removable device may be affixed on both sides or at the rear of a single driven vehicle. In a combination driveaway operation, the device may be affixed on both sides of any one unit or at the rear of the last unit. The removable device must display the legal name or a single trade name of the motor carrier and the motor carrier's USDOT number.

(g) *Intermodal equipment.* (1) The requirements for marking intermodal equipment apply to each intermodal equipment provider, as defined in § 390.5, that interchanges or offers for interchange intermodal equipment to a motor carrier.

(2) Each unit of intermodal equipment interchanged or offered for interchange to a motor carrier by an intermodal equipment provider subject to subchapter B of this chapter must identify the intermodal equipment provider.

(3) The intermodal equipment provider must be identified by its legal name or a single trade name and the identification number issued by FMCSA, preceded by the letters "USDOT."

(4) The intermodal equipment must be identified as follows, using any one of the following methods:

(i) The identification marking must appear on the curb side of the item of equipment. It must be in letters that contrast sharply in color with the background on which the letters are placed. The letters must be readily legible, during daylight hours, from a distance of 50 feet (15.24 meters) while the CMV is stationary; and be kept and

maintained in a manner that retains this legibility; or

(ii) The identification marking must appear on a label placed upon the curb side of the item of equipment. The label must be readily visible and legible to an inspection official during daylight hours when the vehicle is stationary. The label must be a color that contrasts sharply with the background on which it is placed, and the letters must also contrast sharply in color with the background of the label. The label must be kept and maintained in a manner that retains this legibility; or

(iii) The USDOT number of the intermodal equipment provider must appear on the interchange agreement so that it is clearly identifiable to an inspection official. The interchange agreement must include additional information to identify the specific item of intermodal equipment (such as the VIN and 4-character SCAC code and 6-digit unique identifying number); or

(iv) The identification marking must be shown on a document placed in a weathertight compartment affixed to the frame of the item of intermodal equipment. The color of the letters used in the document must contrast sharply in color with the background of the document. The document must include additional information to identify the specific item of intermodal equipment (such as the VIN and 4-character SCAC code and 6-digit unique identifying number).

(v) The USDOT number of the intermodal equipment provider is maintained in a database that is available via real-time internet and telephonic access. The database must:

(A) Identify the name and USDOT number of the intermodal equipment provider responsible for the intermodal equipment, in response to an inquiry that includes:

(i) Standard Carrier Alpha Code (SCAC) plus trailing digits, or

(ii) License plate number and State of license, or

(iii) Vehicle Identification Number (VIN) of the item of intermodal equipment.

(B) Offer read-only access for inquiries on individual items of intermodal equipment, without requiring advance user registration, a password, or a usage fee.

[65 FR 35296, June 2, 2000, as amended at 73 FR 76821, Dec. 17, 2008; 74 FR 68708, Dec. 29, 2009]

§390.23 Relief from regulations.

(a) Parts 390 through 399 of this chapter shall not apply to any motor carrier or driver operating a commercial motor vehicle to provide emergency relief during an emergency, subject to the following time limits:

(1) *Regional emergencies.* (i) The exemption provided by paragraph (a)(1) of this section is effective only when:

(A) An emergency has been declared by the President of the United States, the Governor of a State, or their authorized representatives having authority to declare emergencies; or

(B) The FMCSA Field Administrator has declared that a regional emergency exists which justifies an exemption from parts 390 through 399 of this chapter.

(ii) Except as provided in §390.25, this exemption shall not exceed the duration of the motor carrier's or driver's direct assistance in providing emergency relief, or 30 days from the date of the initial declaration of the emergency or the exemption from the regulations by the FMCSA Field Administrator, whichever is less.

(2) *Local emergencies.* (i) The exemption provided by paragraph (a)(2) of this section is effective only when:

(A) An emergency has been declared by a Federal, State or local government official having authority to declare an emergency; or

(B) The FMCSA Field Administrator has declared that a local emergency exists which justifies an exemption from parts 390 through 399 of this chapter.

(ii) This exemption shall not exceed the duration of the motor carrier's or driver's direct assistance in providing emergency relief, or 5 days from the date of the initial declaration of the emergency or the exemption from the regulations by the FMCSA Field Administrator, whichever is less.

(3) *Tow trucks responding to emergencies.* (i) The exemption provided by paragraph (a)(3) of this section is effective only when a request has been made by a Federal, State or local police offi-

cer for tow trucks to move wrecked or disabled motor vehicles.

(ii) This exemption shall not exceed the length of the motor carrier's or driver's direct assistance in providing emergency relief, or 24 hours from the time of the initial request for assistance by the Federal, State or local police officer, whichever is less.

(b) Upon termination of direct assistance to the regional or local emergency relief effort, the motor carrier or driver is subject to the requirements of parts 390 through 399 of this chapter, with the following exception: A driver may return empty to the motor carrier's terminal or the driver's normal work reporting location without complying with parts 390 through 399 of this chapter. However, a driver who informs the motor carrier that he or she needs immediate rest must be permitted at least 10 consecutive hours off duty before the driver is required to return to such terminal or location. Having returned to the terminal or other location, the driver must be relieved of all duty and responsibilities. Direct assistance terminates when a driver or commercial motor vehicle is used in interstate commerce to transport cargo not destined for the emergency relief effort, or when the motor carrier dispatches such driver or commercial motor vehicle to another location to begin operations in commerce.

(c) When the driver has been relieved of all duty and responsibilities upon termination of direct assistance to a regional or local emergency relief effort, no motor carrier shall permit or require any driver used by it to drive nor shall any such driver drive in commerce until:

(1) The driver has met the requirements of §§395.3(a) and 395.5(a) of this chapter; and

(2) The driver has had at least 34 consecutive hours off-duty when:

(i) The driver has been on duty for more than 60 hours in any 7 consecutive days at the time the driver is relieved of all duty if the employing motor carrier does not operate every day in the week, or

(ii) The driver has been on duty for more than 70 hours in any 8 consecutive days at the time the driver is relieved of all duty if the employing motor carrier operates every day in the week.

[57 FR 33647, July 30, 1992, as amended at 60 FR 38744, July 28, 1995; 68 FR 22514, Apr. 28, 2003; 70 FR 50070, Aug. 25, 2005]

§ 390.25 Extension of relief from regulations—emergencies.

The FMCSA Field Administrator may extend the 30-day time period of the exemption contained in § 390.23(a)(1), but not the 5-day time period contained in § 390.23(a)(2) or the 24-hour period contained in § 390.23(a)(3). Any motor carrier or driver seeking to extend the 30-day limit shall obtain approval from the FMCSA Field Administrator in the region in which the motor carrier's principal place of business is located before the expiration of the 30-day period. The motor carrier or driver shall give full details of the additional relief requested. The FMCSA Field Administrator shall determine if such relief is necessary taking into account both the severity of the ongoing emergency and the nature of the relief services to be provided by the carrier or driver. If the FMCSA Field Administrator approves an extension of the exemption, he or she shall establish a new time limit and place on the motor carrier or driver any other restrictions deemed necessary.

[57 FR 33647, July 30, 1992]

§ 390.27 Locations of motor carrier safety service centers.

Service center	Territory included	Location of office
Eastern	CT, DC, DE, MA, MD, ME, NJ, NH, NY, PA, PR, RI, VA, VT, Virgin Islands, WV.	802 Cromwell Park Drive, Suite N, Glen Burnie, MD 21061.
Midwestern	IA, IL, IN, KS, MI, MO, MN, NE, OH, WI	19900 Governors Drive, Suite 210, Olympia Fields, IL 60461–1021.
Southern	AL, AR, FL, GA, KY, LA, MS, NC, OK, SC, TN, TX	1800 Century Boulevard, Suite 1700, Atlanta, GA 30345–3220.
Western	American Samoa, AK, AZ, CA, CO, Guam, HI, ID, Mariana Islands, MT, ND, NM, NV, OR, SD, UT, WA, WY.	Golden Hills Office Centre, 12600 West Colfax Avenue, Suite B–300, Lakewood, CO 80215.

NOTE 1: Canadian carriers, for information regarding proper service center, contact a FMCSA division (State) office in AK, ME, MI, MT, NY, ND, VT, or WA.

NOTE 2: Mexican carriers, for information regarding proper service center, contact a FMCSA division (State) office in AZ, CA, NM, or TX.

[65 FR 35297, June 2, 2000, as amended at 67 FR 61824, Oct. 2, 2002; 67 FR 63019, Oct. 9, 2002; 72 FR 55702, Oct. 1, 2007]

§ 390.29 Location of records or documents.

(a) A motor carrier with multiple offices or terminals may maintain the records and documents required by this subchapter at its principal place of business, a regional office, or driver work-reporting location unless otherwise specified in this subchapter.

(b) All records and documents required by this subchapter which are maintained at a regional office or driver work-reporting location shall be made available for inspection upon request by a special agent or authorized representative of the Federal Motor Carrier Safety Administration at the motor carrier's principal place of business or other location specified by the agent or representative within 48 hours after a request is made. Saturdays, Sundays, and Federal holidays are excluded from the computation of the 48-hour period of time.

[63 FR 33276, June 18, 1998]

§ 390.31 Copies of records or documents.

(a) All records and documents required to be maintained under this subchapter must be preserved in their original form for the periods specified, unless the records and documents are suitably photographed and the microfilm is retained in lieu of the original record for the required retention period.

(b) To be acceptable in lieu of original records, photographic copies of records must meet the following minimum requirements:

(1) Photographic copies shall be no less readily accessible than the original record or document as normally filed or preserved would be and suitable means or facilities shall be available to locate, identify, read, and reproduce such photographic copies.

(2) Any significant characteristic, feature or other attribute of the original record or document, which photography in black and white will not preserve, shall be clearly indicated before the photograph is made.

(3) The reverse side of printed forms need not be copied if nothing has been added to the printed matter common to all such forms, but an identified specimen of each form shall be on the film for reference.

(4) Film used for photographing copies shall be of permanent record-type meeting in all respects the minimum specifications of the National Bureau of Standards, and all processes recommended by the manufacturer shall be observed to protect it from deterioration or accidental destruction.

(5) Each roll of film shall include a microfilm of a certificate or certificates stating that the photographs are direct or facsimile reproductions of the original records. Such certificate(s) shall be executed by a person or persons having personal knowledge of the material covered thereby.

(c) All records and documents required to be maintained under this subchapter may be destroyed after they have been suitably photographed for preservation.

(d) *Exception.* All records except those requiring a signature may be maintained through the use of computer technology provided the motor carrier can produce, upon demand, a computer printout of the required data.

§390.33 Commercial motor vehicles used for purposes other than defined.

Whenever a commercial motor vehicle of one type is used to perform the functions normally performed by a commercial motor vehicle of another type, the requirements of this subchapter and part 325 of subchapter A shall apply to the commercial motor vehicle and to its operation in the same manner as though the commercial motor vehicle were actually a commercial motor vehicle of the latter type. *Example:* If a commercial motor vehicle other than a bus is used to perform the functions normally performed by a bus, the regulations pertaining to buses and to the transportation of passengers shall apply to that commercial motor vehicle.

[53 FR 18052, May 19, 1988, as amended at 60 FR 38744, July 28, 1995]

§390.35 Certificates, reports, and records: Falsification, reproduction, or alteration.

No motor carrier, its agents, officers, representatives, or employees shall make or cause to make—

(a) A fraudulent or intentionally false statement on any application, certificate, report, or record required by part 325 of subchapter A or this subchapter;

(b) A fraudulent or intentionally false entry on any application, certificate, report, or record required to be used, completed, or retained, to comply with any requirement of this subchapter or part 325 of subchapter A; or

(c) A reproduction, for fraudulent purposes, of any application, certificate, report, or record required by this subchapter or part 325 of subchapter A.

§390.37 Violation and penalty.

Any person who violates the rules set forth in this subchapter or part 325 of subchapter A may be subject to civil or criminal penalties.

Subpart C—Requirements and Information for Intermodal Equipment Providers and for Motor Carriers Operating Intermodal Equipment

SOURCE: 73 FR 76822, Dec. 17, 2008, unless otherwise noted.

§ 390.40 What responsibilities do intermodal equipment providers have under the Federal Motor Carrier Safety Regulations (49 CFR parts 350–399)?

An intermodal equipment provider must—

(a) Identify its operations to the FMCSA by filing the Form MCS–150C required by § 390.19.

(b) Mark its intermodal equipment with the USDOT number as required by § 390.21 before tendering the equipment to a motor carrier.

(c) Systematically inspect, repair, and maintain, or cause to be systematically inspected, repaired, and maintained, in a manner consistent with § 396.3(a)(1), as applicable, all intermodal equipment intended for interchange with a motor carrier.

(d) Provide intermodal equipment intended for interchange that is in safe and proper operating condition.

(e) Maintain a system of driver vehicle inspection reports submitted to the intermodal equipment provider as required by § 396.11 of this chapter.

(f) Maintain a system of inspection, repair, and maintenance records as required by § 396.12 of this chapter for equipment intended for interchange with a motor carrier.

(g) Periodically inspect equipment intended for interchange, as required under § 396.17 of this chapter.

(h) At facilities at which the intermodal equipment provider makes intermodal equipment available for interchange, have procedures in place, and provide sufficient space, for drivers to perform a pre-trip inspection of tendered intermodal equipment.

(i) At facilities at which the intermodal equipment provider makes intermodal equipment available for interchange, develop and implement procedures to repair any equipment damage, defects, or deficiencies identified as part of a pre-trip inspection, or replace the equipment, prior to the driver's departure. The repairs or replacement must be made after being notified by a driver of such damage, defects, or deficiencies.

(j) Refrain from placing intermodal equipment in service on the public highways if that equipment has been found to pose an imminent hazard, as defined in § 386.72(b)(1) of this chapter.

[73 FR 76822, Dec. 17, 2008, as amended at 74 FR 68708, Dec. 29, 2009]

§ 390.42 What are the responsibilities of drivers and motor carriers operating intermodal equipment?

(a) Before operating intermodal equipment over the road, the driver accepting the equipment must inspect the equipment components listed in § 392.7(b) of this subchapter and be satisfied they are in good working order.

(b) A driver or motor carrier transporting intermodal equipment must report to the intermodal equipment provider, or its designated agent, any known damage, defects, or deficiencies in the intermodal equipment at the time the equipment is returned to the provider or the provider's designated agent. If no damage, defects, or deficiencies are discovered by the driver, the report shall so indicate. The report must include, at a minimum, the items in § 396.11(a)(2) of this chapter.

§ 390.44 What are the procedures to correct the safety record of a motor carrier or an intermodal equipment provider?

(a) *An intermodal equipment provider or its agent* may electronically file questions or concerns at *http:// dataqs.fmcsa.dot.gov* about Federal and State data that reference the provider. This includes safety violations alleging that the components, parts, or accessories of intermodal chassis or trailers listed in § 392.7(b) of this chapter were not in good working order when inspected at roadside. An intermodal equipment provider should not be held responsible for such violations because a motor carrier indicated pursuant to § 392.7(b) that these components, parts, or accessories had no safety defects at the time of the pre-trip inspection.

(b) *A motor carrier or its agent* may electronically file questions or concerns at *http://dataqs.fmcsa.dot.gov* about Federal and State data that reference the motor carrier. This includes safety violations alleging that any components, parts, or accessories of intermodal chassis or trailers, except those listed in § 392.7(b) of this chapter, were not in good working order when inspected at roadside. Such violations will not be used by FMCSA in making a safety fitness determination of a motor carrier (unless there is evidence that the driver or motor carrier caused or substantially contributed to the violations) because the driver could not readily detect these violations during a pre-trip inspection performed in accordance with § 392.7(b).

(c) *An intermodal equipment provider, or its agent*, may request FMCSA to investigate a motor carrier believed to be in noncompliance with responsibilities under 49 U.S.C. 31151 or the implementing regulations in this subchapter regarding interchange of intermodal equipment by contacting the appropriate FMCSA Field Office.

(d) *A motor carrier or its agent* may request FMCSA to investigate an intermodal equipment provider believed to be in noncompliance with responsibilities under 49 U.S.C. 31151 or the implementing regulations in this subchapter regarding interchange of intermodal equipment by contacting the appropriate FMCSA Field Office.

§ 390.46 Are State and local laws and regulations on the inspection, repair, and maintenance of intermodal equipment preempted by the Federal Motor Carrier Safety Regulations?

(a) *General.* As provided by 49 U.S.C. 31151(d), a law, regulation, order, or other requirement of a State, a political subdivision of a State, or a tribal organization relating to the inspection, repair, and maintenance of intermodal equipment is preempted if such law, regulation, order, or other requirement exceeds or is inconsistent with a requirement imposed by the Federal Motor Carrier Safety Regulations.

(b) *Pre-existing State requirements*—(1) *In general.* Pursuant to 49 U.S.C. 31151(e)(1), unless otherwise provided in paragraph (b)(2) of this section, a State requirement for the periodic inspection of intermodal chassis by intermodal equipment providers that was in effect on January 1, 2005, shall remain in effect only until June 17, 2009.

(2) *Nonpreemption determinations*—(i) *In general.* Pursuant to 49 U.S.C. 31151(e)(2), and notwithstanding paragraph (a) of this section, a State requirement described in paragraph (b)(1)

of this section is not preempted if the Administrator determines that the State requirement is as effective as the FMCSA final rule and does not unduly burden interstate commerce.

(ii) *Application required.* Paragraph (b)(2)(i) of this section applies to a State requirement only if the State applies to the Administrator for a determination with respect to the requirement before the effective date of the final rule (June 17, 2009). The Administrator will make a determination with respect to any such application within 6 months after the date on which the Administrator receives the application.

(iii) *Amended State requirements.* If a State amends a regulation for which it previously received a nonpreemption determination from the Administrator under paragraph (b)(2)(i) of this section, it must apply for a determination of nonpreemption for the amended regulation. Any amendment to a State requirement not preempted under this subsection because of a determination by the Administrator may not take effect unless it is submitted to the Agency before the effective date of the amendment, and the Administrator determines that the amendment would not cause the State requirement to be less effective than the FMCSA final rule on "Requirements for Intermodal Equipment Providers and Motor Carriers and Drivers Operating Intermodal Equipment" and would not unduly burden interstate commerce.

PART 391—QUALIFICATIONS OF DRIVERS AND LONGER COMBINATION VEHICLE (LCV) DRIVER INSTRUCTORS

Subpart A—General

AUTHORITY: 49 U.S.C. 322, 504, 508, 31133, 31136, and 31502; sec. 4007(b) of Pub. L. 102–240, 105 Stat. 2152; sec. 114 of Pub. L. 103–311, 108 Stat. 1673, 1677; sec. 215 of Pub. L. 106–159, 113 Stat. 1767; and 49 CFR 1.73.

SOURCE: 35 FR 6460, Apr. 22, 1970, unless otherwise noted.

EDITORIAL NOTE: Nomenclature changes to part 391 appear at 66 FR 49873, Oct. 1, 2001.

Subpart A—General

§ 391.1   Scope of the rules in this part; additional qualifications; duties of carrier-drivers.

(a) The rules in this part establish minimum qualifications for persons who drive commercial motor vehicles as, for, or on behalf of motor carriers. The rules in this part also establish minimum duties of motor carriers with respect to the qualifications of their drivers.

(b) A motor carrier who employs himself/herself as a driver must comply with both the rules in this part that apply to motor carriers and the rules in this part that apply to drivers.

[35 FR 6460, Apr. 22, 1970, as amended at 53 FR 18057, May 19, 1988; 60 FR 38744, July 28, 1995]

§ 391.2   General exceptions.

(a) *Farm custom operation.* The rules in this part except for § 391.15(e) do not apply to a driver who drives a commercial motor vehicle controlled and operated by a person engaged in custom-harvesting operations, if the commercial motor vehicle is used to—

(1) Transport farm machinery, supplies, or both, to or from a farm for custom-harvesting operations on a farm; or

(2) Transport custom-harvested crops to storage or market.

(b) *Apiarian industries.* The rules in this part except for § 391.15(e) do not apply to a driver who is operating a commercial motor vehicle controlled and operated by a beekeeper engaged in the seasonal transportation of bees.

(c) *Certain farm vehicle drivers.* The rules in this part except for § 391.15(e) do not apply to a farm vehicle driver except a farm vehicle driver who drives an articulated (combination) commercial motor vehicle, as defined in § 390.5. For limited exemptions for farm vehicle drivers of articulated commercial motor vehicles, see § 391.67.

[75 FR 59135, Sept. 27, 2010]

Subpart B—Qualification and Disqualification of Drivers

§391.11 General qualifications of drivers.

(a) A person shall not drive a commercial motor vehicle unless he/she is qualified to drive a commercial motor vehicle. Except as provided in §391.63, a motor carrier shall not require or permit a person to drive a commercial motor vehicle unless that person is qualified to drive a commercial motor vehicle.

(b) Except as provided in subpart G of this part, a person is qualified to drive a motor vehicle if he/she—

(1) Is at least 21 years old;

(2) Can read and speak the English language sufficiently to converse with the general public, to understand highway traffic signs and signals in the English language, to respond to official inquiries, and to make entries on reports and records;

(3) Can, by reason of experience, training, or both, safely operate the type of commercial motor vehicle he/she drives;

(4) Is physically qualified to drive a commercial motor vehicle in accordance with subpart E—Physical Qualifications and Examinations of this part;

(5) Has a currently valid commercial motor vehicle operator's license issued only by one State or jurisdiction;

(6) Has prepared and furnished the motor carrier that employs him/her with the list of violations or the certificate as required by §391.27;

(7) Is not disqualified to drive a commercial motor vehicle under the rules in §391.15; and

(8) Has successfully completed a driver's road test and has been issued a certificate of driver's road test in accordance with §391.31, or has presented an operator's license or a certificate of road test which the motor carrier that employs him/her has accepted as equivalent to a road test in accordance with §391.33.

[35 FR 6460, Apr. 22, 1970, as amended at 35 FR 17420, Nov. 13, 1970; 35 FR 19181, Dec. 18, 1970; 36 FR 222, Jan. 7, 1971, 36 FR 24220, Dec. 22, 1971; 45 FR 46424, July 10, 1980; 52 FR 20589, June 1, 1987; 59 FR 60323, Nov. 23, 1994; 60 FR 38744, 38745, July 28, 1995; 63 FR 33276, June 18, 1998]

§391.13 Responsibilities of drivers.

In order to comply with the requirements of §§392.9(a) and 393.9 of this subchapter, a motor carrier shall not require or permit a person to drive a commercial motor vehicle unless the person—

(a) Can, by reason of experience, training, or both, determine whether the cargo he/she transports (including baggage in a passenger-carrying commercial motor vehicle) has been properly located, distributed, and secured in or on the commercial motor vehicle he/she drives;

(b) Is familiar with methods and procedures for securing cargo in or on the commercial motor vehicle he/she drives.

[63 FR 33277, June 18, 1998]

§391.15 Disqualification of drivers.

(a) *General.* A driver who is disqualified shall not drive a commercial motor vehicle. A motor carrier shall not require or permit a driver who is disqualified to drive a commercial motor vehicle.

(b) *Disqualification for loss of driving privileges.* (1) A driver is disqualified for the duration of the driver's loss of his/her privilege to operate a commercial motor vehicle on public highways, either temporarily or permanently, by reason of the revocation, suspension, withdrawal, or denial of an operator's license, permit, or privilege, until that operator's license, permit, or privilege is restored by the authority that revoked, suspended, withdrew, or denied it.

(2) A driver who receives a notice that his/her license, permit, or privilege to operate a commercial motor vehicle has been revoked, suspended, or withdrawn shall notify the motor carrier that employs him/her of the contents of the notice before the end of the

business day following the day the driver received it.

(c) *Disqualification for criminal and other offenses*—(1) *General rule.* A driver who is convicted of (or forfeits bond or collateral upon a charge of) a disqualifying offense specified in paragraph (c)(2) of this section is disqualified for the period of time specified in paragraph (c)(3) of this section, if—

(i) The offense was committed during on-duty time as defined in § 395.2(a) of this subchapter or as otherwise specified; and

(ii) The driver is employed by a motor carrier or is engaged in activities that are in furtherance of a commercial enterprise in interstate, intrastate, or foreign commerce;

(2) *Disqualifying offenses.* The following offenses are disqualifying offenses:

(i) Driving a commercial motor vehicle while under the influence of alcohol. This shall include:

(A) Driving a commercial motor vehicle while the person's alcohol concentration is 0.04 percent or more;

(B) Driving under the influence of alcohol, as prescribed by State law; or

(C) Refusal to undergo such testing as is required by any State or jurisdiction in the enforcement of § 391.15(c)(2)(i) (A) or (B), or § 392.5(a)(2).

(ii) Driving a commercial motor vehicle under the influence of a 21 CFR 1308.11 *Schedule I* identified controlled substance, an amphetamine, a narcotic drug, a formulation of an amphetamine, or a derivative of a narcotic drug;

(iii) Transportation, possession, or unlawful use of a 21 CFR 1308.11 *Schedule I* identified controlled substance, amphetamines, narcotic drugs, formulations of an amphetamine, or derivatives of narcotic drugs while the driver is on duty, as the term on-duty time is defined in § 395.2 of this subchapter;

(iv) Leaving the scene of an accident while operating a commercial motor vehicle; or

(v) A felony involving the use of a commercial motor vehicle.

(3) *Duration of disqualification*—(i) *First offenders.* A driver is disqualified for 1 year after the date of conviction or forfeiture of bond or collateral if, during the 3 years preceding that date,

the driver was not convicted of, or did not forfeit bond or collateral upon a charge of an offense that would disqualify the driver under the rules of this section. Exemption. The period of disqualification is 6 months if the conviction or forfeiture of bond or collateral soley concerned the transportation or possession of substances named in paragraph (c)(2)(iii) of this section.

(ii) *Subsequent offenders.* A driver is disqualified for 3 years after the date of his/her conviction or forfeiture of bond or collateral if, during the 3 years preceding that date, he/she was convicted of, or forfeited bond or collateral upon a charge of, an offense that would disqualify him/her under the rules in this section.

(d) *Disqualification for violation of out-of-service orders*—(1) *General rule.* A driver who is convicted of violating an out-of-service order is disqualified for the period of time specified in paragraph (d)(2) of this section.

(2) *Duration of disqualification for violation of out-of-service orders*—(i) *First violation.* A driver is disqualified for not less than 90 days nor more than one year if the driver is convicted of a first violation of an out-of-service order.

(ii) *Second violation.* A driver is disqualified for not less than one year nor more than five years if, during any 10-year period, the driver is convicted of two violations of out-of-service orders in separate incidents.

(iii) *Third or subsequent violation.* A driver is disqualified for not less than three years nor more than five years if, during any 10-year period, the driver is convicted of three or more violations of out-of-service orders in separate incidents.

(iv) *Special rule for hazardous materials and passenger offenses.* A driver is disqualified for a period of not less than 180 days nor more than two years if the driver is convicted of a first violation of an out-of-service order while transporting hazardous materials required to be placarded under the Hazardous Materials Transportation Act (49 U.S.C. 5101 *et seq.*), or while operating commercial motor vehicles designed to transport more than 15 passengers, including the driver. A driver is disqualified for a period of not less than three years nor more than five years if, during any 10-year period, the driver is convicted of any subsequent violations of out-of-service orders, in separate incidents, while transporting hazardous materials required to be placarded under the Hazardous Materials Transportation Act, or while operating commercial motor vehicles designed to transport more than 15 passengers, including the driver.

(e) *Disqualification for violation of prohibition of texting while driving a commercial motor vehicle—*

(1) *General rule.* A driver who is convicted of violating the prohibition of texting in §392.80(a) of this chapter is disqualified for the period of time specified in paragraph (e)(2) of this section.

(2) *Duration.* Disqualification for violation of prohibition of texting while driving a commercial motor vehicle—

(i) *Second violation.* A driver is disqualified for 60 days if the driver is convicted of two violations of §392.80(a) of this chapter in separate incidents during any 3-year period.

(ii) *Third or subsequent violation.* A driver is disqualified for 120 days if the driver is convicted of three or more violations of §392.80(a) of this chapter in separate incidents during any 3-year period.

[37 FR 24902, Nov. 23, 1972, as amended at 49 FR 44215, Nov. 5, 1984; 51 FR 8200, Mar. 10, 1986; 53 FR 18057, May 19, 1988; 53 FR 39051, Oct. 4, 1988; 54 FR 40788, Oct. 3, 1989; 59 FR 26028, May 18, 1994; 60 FR 38744, 38745, July 28, 1995; 62 FR 37152, July 11, 1997; 63 FR 33277, June 18, 1998; 75 FR 59136, Sept. 27, 2010]

Subpart C—Background and Character

§391.21 Application for employment.

(a) Except as provided in subpart G of this part, a person shall not drive a commercial motor vehicle unless he/she has completed and furnished the motor carrier that employs him/her with an application for employment that meets the requirements of paragraph (b) of this section.

(b) The application for employment shall be made on a form furnished by the motor carrier. Each application form must be completed by the applicant, must be signed by him/her, and must contain the following information:

(1) The name and address of the employing motor carrier;

(2) The applicant's name, address, date of birth, and social security number;

(3) The addresses at which the applicant has resided during the 3 years preceding the date on which the application is submitted;

(4) The date on which the application is submitted;

(5) The issuing State, number, and expiration date of each unexpired commercial motor vehicle operator's license or permit that has been issued to the applicant;

(6) The nature and extent of the applicant's experience in the operation of motor vehicles, including the type of equipment (such as buses, trucks, truck tractors, semitrailers, full trailers, and pole trailers) which he/she has operated;

(7) A list of all motor vehicle accidents in which the applicant was involved during the 3 years preceding the date the application is submitted, specifying the date and nature of each accident and any fatalities or personal injuries it caused;

(8) A list of all violations of motor vehicle laws or ordinances (other than violations involving only parking) of which the applicant was convicted or forfeited bond or collateral during the 3 years preceding the date the application is submitted;

(9) A statement setting forth in detail the facts and circumstances of any denial, revocation, or suspension of any license, permit, or privilege to operate a motor vehicle that has been issued to the applicant, or a statement that no such denial, revocation, or suspension has occurred;

(10)(i) A list of the names and addresses of the applicant's employers during the 3 years preceding the date the application is submitted,

(ii) The dates he or she was employed by that employer,

(iii) The reason for leaving the employ of that employer,

(iv) After October 29, 2004, whether the (A) Applicant was subject to the FMCSRs while employed by that previous employer,

(B) Job was designated as a safety sensitive function in any DOT regulated mode subject to alcohol and controlled substances testing requirements as required by 49 CFR part 40;

(11) For those drivers applying to operate a commercial motor vehicle as defined by Part 383 of this subchapter, a list of the names and addresses of the applicant's employers during the 7-year period preceding the 3 years contained in paragraph (b)(10) of this section for which the applicant was an operator of a commercial motor vehicle, together with the dates of employment and the reasons for leaving such employment; and

(12) The following certification and signature line, which must appear at the end of the application form and be signed by the applicant:

This certifies that this application was completed by me, and that all entries on it and information in it are true and complete to the best of my knowledge.

_____
                                           (Date)

_____
                          (Applicant's signature)

(c) A motor carrier may require an applicant to provide information in addition to the information required by paragraph (b) of this section on the application form.

(d) Before an application is submitted, the motor carrier must inform the applicant that the information he/she provides in accordance with paragraph (b)(10) of this section may be used, and the applicant's previous employers will be contacted, for the purpose of investigating the applicant's safety performance history information as required by paragraphs (d) and (e) of § 391.23. The prospective employer must also notify the driver in writing of his/her due process rights as specified in § 391.23(i) regarding information received as a result of these investigations.

[35 FR 6460, Apr. 22, 1970, as amended at 35 FR 17420, Nov. 13, 1970; 52 FR 20589, June 1, 1987; 60 FR 38744, July 28, 1995; 69 FR 16719, Mar. 30, 2004]

§ 391.23 Investigation and inquiries.

(a) Except as provided in subpart G of this part, each motor carrier shall make the following investigations and inquiries with respect to each driver it employs, other than a person who has been a regularly employed driver of the motor carrier for a continuous period which began before January 1, 1971:

(1) An inquiry to each State where the driver held or holds a motor vehicle operator's license or permit during the preceding 3 years to obtain that driver's motor vehicle record.

(2) An investigation of the driver's safety performance history with Department of Transportation regulated employers during the preceding three years.

(b) A copy of the motor vehicle record(s) obtained in response to the inquiry or inquiries to each State required by paragraph (a)(1) of this section must be placed in the driver qualification file within 30 days of the date the driver's employment begins and be retained in compliance with § 391.51. If no motor vehicle record is received from the State or States required to submit this response, the motor carrier must document a good faith effort to obtain such information, and certify that no record exists for that driver in that State or States. The inquiry to the State driver licensing agency or agencies must be made in the form and manner each agency prescribes.

(c)(1) Replies to the investigations of the driver's safety performance history required by paragraph (a)(2) of this section, or documentation of good faith efforts to obtain the investigation data, must be placed in the driver investigation history file, after October 29, 2004, within 30 days of the date the driver's employment begins. Any period of time required to exercise the driver's due process rights to review the information received, request a previous employer to correct or include a rebuttal, is separate and apart from this 30-day requirement to document investigation of the driver safety performance history data.

(2) The investigation may consist of personal interviews, telephone interviews, letters, or any other method for investigating that the carrier deems appropriate. Each motor carrier must make a written record with respect to each previous employer contacted, or good faith efforts to do so. The record must include the previous employer's

name and address, the date the previous employer was contacted, or the attempts made, and the information received about the driver from the previous employer. Failures to contact a previous employer, or of them to provide the required safety performance history information, must be documented. The record must be maintained pursuant to §391.53.

(3) Prospective employers should report failures of previous employers to respond to an investigation to the FMCSA following procedures specified at §386.12 of this chapter and keep a copy of such reports in the Driver Investigation file as part of documenting a good faith effort to obtain the required information.

(4) *Exception.* For drivers with no previous employment experience working for a DOT regulated employer during the preceding three years, documentation that no investigation was possible must be placed in the driver history investigation file, after October 29, 2004, within the required 30 days of the date the driver's employment begins.

(d) The prospective motor carrier must investigate, at a minimum, the information listed in this paragraph from all previous employers of the applicant that employed the driver to operate a CMV within the previous three years. The investigation request must contain specific contact information on where the previous motor carrier employers should send the information requested.

(1) General driver identification and employment verification information.

(2) The data elements as specified in §390.15(b)(1) of this chapter for accidents involving the driver that occurred in the three-year period preceding the date of the employment application.

(i) Any accidents as defined by §390.5 of this chapter.

(ii) Any accidents the previous employer may wish to provide that are retained pursuant to §390.15(b)(2), or pursuant to the employer's internal policies for retaining more detailed minor accident information.

(e) In addition to the investigations required by paragraph (d) of this section, the prospective motor carrier employers must investigate the information listed below in this paragraph from all previous DOT regulated employers that employed the driver within the previous three years from the date of the employment application, in a safety-sensitive function that required alcohol and controlled substance testing specified by 49 CFR part 40.

(1) Whether, within the previous three years, the driver had violated the alcohol and controlled substances prohibitions under subpart B of part 382 of this chapter, or 49 CFR part 40.

(2) Whether the driver failed to undertake or complete a rehabilitation program prescribed by a substance abuse professional (SAP) pursuant to §382.605 of this chapter, or 49 CFR part 40, subpart O. If the previous employer does not know this information (*e.g.,* an employer that terminated an employee who tested positive on a drug test), the prospective motor carrier must obtain documentation of the driver's successful completion of the SAP's referral directly from the driver.

(3) For a driver who had successfully completed a SAP's rehabilitation referral, and remained in the employ of the referring employer, information on whether the driver had the following testing violations subsequent to completion of a §382.605 or 49 CFR part 40, subpart O referral:

(i) Alcohol tests with a result of 0.04 or higher alcohol concentration;

(ii) Verified positive drug tests;

(iii) Refusals to be tested (including verified adulterated or substituted drug test results).

(f) A prospective motor carrier employer must provide to the previous employer the driver's written consent meeting the requirements of §40.321(b) for the release of the information in paragraph (e) of this section. If the driver refuses to provide this written consent, the prospective motor carrier employer must not permit the driver to operate a commercial motor vehicle for that motor carrier.

(g) After October 29, 2004, previous employers must:

(1) Respond to each request for the DOT defined information in paragraphs (d) and (e) of this section within 30 days after the request is received. If there is no safety performance history

367

information to report for that driver, previous motor carrier employers are nonetheless required to send a response confirming the non-existence of any such data, including the driver identification information and dates of employment.

(2) Take all precautions reasonably necessary to ensure the accuracy of the records.

(3) Provide specific contact information in case a driver chooses to contact the previous employer regarding correction or rebuttal of the data.

(4) Keep a record of each request and the response for one year, including the date, the party to whom it was released, and a summary identifying what was provided.

(5) *Exception.* Until May 1, 2006, carriers need only provide information for accidents that occurred after April 29, 2003.

(h) The release of information under this section may take any form that reasonably ensures confidentiality, including letter, facsimile, or e-mail. The previous employer and its agents and insurers must take all precautions reasonably necessary to protect the driver safety performance history records from disclosure to any person not directly involved in forwarding the records, except the previous employer's insurer, except that the previous employer may not provide any alcohol or controlled substances information to the previous employer's insurer.

(i)(1) The prospective employer must expressly notify drivers with Department of Transportation regulated employment during the preceding three years—via the application form or other written document prior to any hiring decision—that he or she has the following rights regarding the investigative information that will be provided to the prospective employer pursuant to paragraphs (d) and (e) of this section:

(i) The right to review information provided by previous employers;

(ii) The right to have errors in the information corrected by the previous employer and for that previous employer to re-send the corrected information to the prospective employer;

(iii) The right to have a rebuttal statement attached to the alleged erroneous information, if the previous employer and the driver cannot agree on the accuracy of the information.

(2) Drivers who have previous Department of Transportation regulated employment history in the preceding three years, and wish to review previous employer-provided investigative information must submit a written request to the prospective employer, which may be done at any time, including when applying, or as late as 30 days after being employed or being notified of denial of employment. The prospective employer must provide this information to the applicant within five (5) business days of receiving the written request. If the prospective employer has not yet received the requested information from the previous employer(s), then the five-business days deadline will begin when the prospective employer receives the requested safety performance history information. If the driver has not arranged to pick up or receive the requested records within thirty (30) days of the prospective employer making them available, the prospective motor carrier may consider the driver to have waived his/her request to review the records.

(j)(1) Drivers wishing to request correction of erroneous information in records received pursuant to paragraph (i) of this section must send the request for the correction to the previous employer that provided the records to the prospective employer.

(2) After October 29, 2004, the previous employer must either correct and forward the information to the prospective motor carrier employer, or notify the driver within 15 days of receiving a driver's request to correct the data that it does not agree to correct the data. If the previous employer corrects and forwards the data as requested, that employer must also retain the corrected information as part of the driver's safety performance history record and provide it to subsequent prospective employers when requests for this information are received. If the previous employer corrects the data and forwards it to the prospective motor carrier employer, there is no need to notify the driver.

(3) Drivers wishing to rebut information in records received pursuant to paragraph (i) of this section must send the rebuttal to the previous employer with instructions to include the rebuttal in that driver's safety performance history.

(4) After October 29, 2004, within five business days of receiving a rebuttal from a driver, the previous employer must:

(i) Forward a copy of the rebuttal to the prospective motor carrier employer;

(ii) Append the rebuttal to the driver's information in the carrier's appropriate file, to be included as part of the response for any subsequent investigating prospective employers for the duration of the three-year data retention requirement.

(5) The driver may submit a rebuttal initially without a request for correction, or subsequent to a request for correction.

(6) The driver may report failures of previous employers to correct information or include the driver's rebuttal as part of the safety performance information, to the FMCSA following procedures specified at §386.12.

(k)(1) The prospective motor carrier employer must use the information described in paragraphs (d) and (e) of this section only as part of deciding whether to hire the driver.

(2) The prospective motor carrier employer, its agents and insurers must take all precautions reasonably necessary to protect the records from disclosure to any person not directly involved in deciding whether to hire the driver. The prospective motor carrier employer may not provide any alcohol or controlled substances information to the prospective motor carrier employer's insurer.

(l)(1) No action or proceeding for defamation, invasion of privacy, or interference with a contract that is based on the furnishing or use of information in accordance with this section may be brought against—

(i) A motor carrier investigating the information, described in paragraphs (d) and (e) of this section, of an individual under consideration for employment as a commercial motor vehicle driver,

(ii) A person who has provided such information; or

(iii) The agents or insurers of a person described in paragraph (l)(1)(i) or (ii) of this section, except insurers are not granted a limitation on liability for any alcohol and controlled substance information.

(2) The protections in paragraph (l)(1) of this section do not apply to persons who knowingly furnish false information, or who are not in compliance with the procedures specified for these investigations.

(m)(1) The motor carrier must obtain an original or copy of the medical examiner's certificate issued in accordance with §391.43, and any medical variance on which the certification is based, and place the records in the driver qualification file, before allowing the driver to operate a CMV.

(2) *Exception.* For drivers required to have a commercial driver's license under part 383 of this chapter:

(i) Beginning January 30, 2012, using the CDLIS motor vehicle record obtained from the current licensing State, the motor carrier must verify and document in the driver qualification file the following information before allowing the driver to operate a CMV:

(A) The type of operation the driver self-certified that he or she will perform in accordance with §§383.71(a)(1)(ii) and 383.71(g) of this chapter, and

(B) *Exception.* If the driver provided the motor carrier with a copy of the current medical examiner's certificate that was submitted to the State in accordance with §383.73(a)(5) of this chapter, the motor carrier may use a copy of that medical examiner's certificate as proof of the driver's medical certification for up to 15 days after the date it was issued.

(ii) Until January 30, 2014, if a driver operating in non-excepted, interstate commerce has no medical certification status information on the CDLIS MVR obtained from the current State driver licensing agency, the employing motor carrier may accept a medical examiner's certificate issued to that driver prior to January 30, 2012, and place a copy of it in the driver qualification

369

file before allowing the driver to operate a CMV in interstate commerce.

(Approved by the Office of Management and Budget under control number 2126–0004)

[35 FR 6460, Apr. 22, 1970, as amended at 35 FR 17420, Nov. 13, 1970; 69 FR 16720, Mar. 30, 2004; 72 FR 55703, Oct. 1, 2007; 73 FR 73126, Dec. 1, 2008; 75 FR 28502, May 21, 2010]

§ 391.25 Annual inquiry and review of driving record.

(a) Except as provided in subpart G of this part, each motor carrier shall, at least once every 12 months, make an inquiry to obtain the motor vehicle record of each driver it employs, covering at least the preceding 12 months, to the appropriate agency of every State in which the driver held a commercial motor vehicle operator's license or permit during the time period.

(b) Except as provided in subpart G of this part, each motor carrier shall, at least once every 12 months, review the motor vehicle record of each driver it employs to determine whether that driver meets minimum requirements for safe driving or is disqualified to drive a commercial motor vehicle pursuant to § 391.15.

(1) The motor carrier must consider any evidence that the driver has violated any applicable Federal Motor Carrier Safety Regulations in this subchapter or Hazardous Materials Regulations (49 CFR chapter I, subchapter C).

(2) The motor carrier must consider the driver's accident record and any evidence that the driver has violated laws governing the operation of motor vehicles, and must give great weight to violations, such as speeding, reckless driving, and operating while under the influence of alcohol or drugs, that indicate that the driver has exhibited a disregard for the safety of the public.

(c) *Recordkeeping.* (1) A copy of the motor vehicle record required by paragraph (a) of this section shall be maintained in the driver's qualification file.

(2) A note, including the name of the person who performed the review of the driving record required by paragraph (b) of this section and the date of such review, shall be maintained in the driver's qualification file.

[63 FR 33277, June 18, 1998, as amended at 73 FR 73127, Dec. 1, 2008]

§ 391.27 Record of violations.

(a) Except as provided in subpart G of this part, each motor carrier shall, at least once every 12 months, require each driver it employs to prepare and furnish it with a list of all violations of motor vehicle traffic laws and ordinances (other than violations involving only parking) of which the driver has been convicted or on account of which he/she has forfeited bond or collateral during the preceding 12 months.

(b) Each driver shall furnish the list required in accordance with paragraph (a) of this section. If the driver has not been convicted of, or forfeited bond or collateral on account of, any violation which must be listed, he/she shall so certify.

(c) The form of the driver's list or certification shall be prescribed by the motor carrier. The following form may be used to comply with this section:

DRIVER'S CERTIFICATION

I certify that the following is a true and complete list of traffic violations (other than parking violations) for which I have been convicted or forfeited bond or collateral during the past 12 months.

Date of conviction   Offense

Location   Type of motor vehicle operated

If no violations are listed above, I certify that I have not been convicted or forfeited bond or collateral on account of any violation required to be listed during the past 12 months.

(Date of certification) (Driver's signature)

(Motor carrier's name)

(Motor carrier's address)

(Reviewed by: Signature) (Title)

(d) The motor carrier shall retain the list or certificate required by this section, or a copy of it, in its files as part of the driver's qualification file.

(e) Drivers who have provided information required by § 383.31 of this subchapter need not repeat that information in the annual list of violations required by this section.

[35 FR 6460, Apr. 22, 1970, as amended at 35 FR 17420, Nov. 13, 1970; 52 FR 20589, June 1, 1987; 60 FR 38745, July 28, 1995]

Subpart D—Tests

§391.31 Road test.

(a) Except as provided in subpart G, a person shall not drive a commercial motor vehicle unless he/she has first successfully completed a road test and has been issued a certificate of driver's road test in accordance with this section.

(b) The road test shall be given by the motor carrier or a person designated by it. However, a driver who is a motor carrier must be given the test by a person other than himself/herself. The test shall be given by a person who is competent to evaluate and determine whether the person who takes the test has demonstrated that he/she is capable of operating the commercial motor vehicle, and associated equipment, that the motor carrier intends to assign him/her.

(c) The road test must be of sufficient duration to enable the person who gives it to evaluate the skill of the person who takes it at handling the commercial motor vehicle, and associated equipment, that the motor carriers intends to assign to him/her. As a minimum, the person who takes the test must be tested, while operating the type of commercial motor vehicle the motor carrier intends to assign him/her, on his/her skill at performing each of the following operations:

(1) The pretrip inspection required by §392.7 of this subchapter;

(2) Coupling and uncoupling of combination units, if the equipment he/she may drive includes combination units;

(3) Placing the commercial motor vehicle in operation;

(4) Use of the commercial motor vehicle's controls and emergency equipment;

(5) Operating the commercial motor vehicle in traffic and while passing other motor vehicles;

(6) Turning the commercial motor vehicle;

(7) Braking, and slowing the commercial motor vehicle by means other than braking; and

(8) Backing and parking the commercial motor vehicle.

(d) The motor carrier shall provide a road test form on which the person who gives the test shall rate the performance of the person who takes it at each operation or activity which is a part of the test. After he/she completes the form, the person who gave the test shall sign it.

(e) If the road test is successfully completed, the person who gave it shall complete a certificate of driver's road test in substantially the form prescribed in paragraph (f) of this section.

(f) The form for the certificate of driver's road test is substantially as follows:

CERTIFICATION OF ROAD TEST

Driver's name _____
Social Security No _____
Operator's or Chauffeur's License No _____
State _____
Type of power unit _____ Type of trailer(s) _____
If passenger carrier, type of bus _____

This is to certify that the above-named driver was given a road test under my supervision on _____ , 20___ , consisting of approximately _____ miles of driving.

It is my considered opinion that this driver possesses sufficient driving skill to operate safely the type of commercial motor vehicle listed above.

_____
(Signature of examiner)

_____
(Title)

_____
(Organization and address of examiner)

(g) A copy of the certificate required by paragraph (e) of this section shall be given to the person who was examined. The motor carrier shall retain in the driver qualification file of the person who was examined—

(1) The original of the signed road test form required by paragraph (d) of this section; and

(2) The original, or a copy of, the certificate required by paragraph (e) of this section.

[35 FR 6460, Apr. 22, 1970, as amended at 36 FR 223, Jan. 7, 1971; 59 FR 8752, Feb. 23, 1994; 60 FR 38744, July 28, 1995]

§391.33 Equivalent of road test.

(a) In place of, and as equivalent to, the road test required by §391.31, a person who seeks to drive a commercial motor vehicle may present, and a motor carrier may accept—

(1) A valid Commercial Driver's License as defined in §383.5 of this subchapter, but not including double/triple trailer or tank vehicle endorsements,

which has been issued to him/her to operate specific categories of commercial motor vehicles and which, under the laws of that State, licenses him/her after successful completion of a road test in a commercial motor vehicle of the type the motor carrier intends to assign to him/her; or

(2) A copy of a valid certificate of driver's road test issued to him/her pursuant to § 391.31 within the preceding 3 years.

(b) If a driver presents, and a motor carrier accepts, a license or certificate as equivalent to the road test, the motor carrier shall retain a legible copy of the license or certificate in its files as part of the driver's qualification file.

(c) A motor carrier may require any person who presents a license or certificate as equivalent to the road test to take a road test or any other test of his/her driving skill as a condition to his/her employment as a driver.

[35 FR 6460, Apr. 22, 1970, as amended at 60 FR 38744, July 28, 1995; 63 FR 33277, June 18, 1998]

Subpart E—Physical Qualifications and Examinations

§ 391.41 Physical qualifications for drivers.

(a)(1)(i) A person subject to this part must not operate a commercial motor vehicle unless he or she is medically certified as physically qualified to do so, and, except as provided in paragraph (a)(2) of this section, when on-duty has on his or her person the original, or a copy, of a current medical examiner's certificate that he or she is physically qualified to drive a commercial motor vehicle. NOTE: Effective December 29, 1991, the FMCSA Administrator determined that the new Licencia Federal de Conductor issued by the United Mexican States is recognized as proof of medical fitness to drive a CMV. The United States and Canada entered into a Reciprocity Agreement, effective March 30, 1999, recognizing that a Canadian commercial driver's license is proof of medical fitness to drive a CMV. Therefore, Canadian and Mexican CMV drivers are not required to have in their possession a medical examiner's certificate if the driver has been issued, and possesses, a valid commercial driver license issued by the United Mexican States, or a Canadian Province or Territory and whose license and medical status, including any waiver or exemption, can be electronically verified. Drivers from any of the countries who have received a medical authorization that deviates from the mutually accepted compatible medical standards of the resident country are not qualified to drive a CMV in the other countries. For example, Canadian drivers who do not meet the medical fitness provisions of the Canadian National Safety Code for Motor Carriers, but are issued a waiver by one of the Canadian Provinces or Territories, are not qualified to drive a CMV in the United States. In addition, U.S. drivers who received a medical variance from FMCSA are not qualified to drive a CMV in Canada.

(ii) A person who qualifies for the medical examiner's certificate by virtue of having obtained a medical variance from FMCSA, in the form of an exemption letter or a skill performance evaluation certificate, must have on his or her person a copy of the variance documentation when on-duty.

(2) *CDL exception.* (i) Beginning January 30, 2012, a driver required to have a commercial driver's license under part 383 of this chapter, and who submitted a current medical examiner's certificate to the State in accordance with § 383.71(h) of this chapter documenting that he or she meets the physical qualification requirements of this part, no longer needs to carry on his or her person the medical examiner's certificate specified at § 391.43(h), or a copy. If there is no medical certification information on that driver's CDLIS motor vehicle record defined at 49 CFR 384.105, a current medical examiner's certificate issued prior to January 30, 2012, will be accepted until January 30, 2014. After January 30, 2014, a driver may use a copy of the current medical examiner's certificate that was submitted to the State for up to 15 days after the date it was issued as proof of medical certification.

(ii) A CDL holder required by § 383.71(h) to obtain a medical examiner's certificate, who obtained such by virtue of having obtained a medical variance from FMCSA, must continue to have in his or her possession the original or copy of that medical variance documentation at all times when on-duty.

(3) A person is physically qualified to drive a commercial motor vehicle if:

(i) That person meets the physical qualification standards in paragraph (b) of this section and has complied with the medical examination requirements in §391.43; or

(ii) That person obtained from FMCSA a medical variance from the physical qualification standards in paragraph (b) of this section and has complied with the medical examination requirement in §391.43.

(b) A person is physically qualified to drive a commercial motor vehicle if that person—

(1) Has no loss of a foot, a leg, a hand, or an arm, or has been granted a skill performance evaluation certificate pursuant to §391.49;

(2) Has no impairment of:

(i) A hand or finger which interferes with prehension or power grasping; or

(ii) An arm, foot, or leg which interferes with the ability to perform normal tasks associated with operating a commercial motor vehicle; or any other significant limb defect or limitation which interferes with the ability to perform normal tasks associated with operating a commercial motor vehicle; or has been granted a skill performance evaluation certificate pursuant to §391.49.

(3) Has no established medical history or clinical diagnosis of diabetes mellitus currently requiring insulin for control;

(4) Has no current clinical diagnosis of myocardial infarction, angina pectoris, coronary insufficiency, thrombosis, or any other cardiovascular disease of a variety known to be accompanied by syncope, dyspnea, collapse, or congestive cardiac failure.

(5) Has no established medical history or clinical diagnosis of a respiratory dysfunction likely to interfere with his/her ability to control and drive a commercial motor vehicle safely;

(6) Has no current clinical diagnosis of high blood pressure likely to interfere with his/her ability to operate a commercial motor vehicle safely;

(7) Has no established medical history or clinical diagnosis of rheumatic, arthritic, orthopedic, muscular, neuromuscular, or vascular disease which interferes with his/her ability to control and operate a commercial motor vehicle safely;

(8) Has no established medical history or clinical diagnosis of epilepsy or any other condition which is likely to cause loss of consciousness or any loss of ability to control a commercial motor vehicle;

(9) Has no mental, nervous, organic, or functional disease or psychiatric disorder likely to interfere with his/her ability to drive a commercial motor vehicle safely;

(10) Has distant visual acuity of at least 20/40 (Snellen) in each eye without corrective lenses or visual acuity separately corrected to 20/40 (Snellen) or better with corrective lenses, distant binocular acuity of at least 20/40 (Snellen) in both eyes with or without corrective lenses, field of vision of at least 70° in the horizontal Meridian in each eye, and the ability to recognize the colors of traffic signals and devices showing standard red, green, and amber;

(11) First perceives a forced whispered voice in the better ear at not less than 5 feet with or without the use of a hearing aid or, if tested by use of an audiometric device, does not have an average hearing loss in the better ear greater than 40 decibels at 500 Hz, 1,000 Hz, and 2,000 Hz with or without a hearing aid when the audiometric device is calibrated to American National Standard (formerly ASA Standard) Z24.5—1951.

(12)(i) Does not use a controlled substance identified in 21 CFR 1308.11 *Schedule I*, an amphetamine, a narcotic, or any other habit-forming drug.

(ii) *Exception.* A driver may use such a substance or drug, if the substance or drug is prescribed by a licensed medical practitioner who:

(A) Is familiar with the driver's medical history and assigned duties; and

(B) Has advised the driver that the prescribed substance or drug will not adversely affect the driver's ability to safely operate a commercial motor vehicle; and

(13) Has no current clinical diagnosis of alcoholism.

[35 FR 6460, Apr. 22, 1970, as amended at 35 FR 17420, Nov. 13, 1970; 36 FR 223, Jan. 7, 1971; 36 FR 12857, July 8, 1971; 43 FR 56900, Dec. 5, 1978; 55 FR 3554, Feb. 1, 1990; 60 FR 38744, July 28, 1995; 62 FR 37152, July 11, 1997; 65 FR 59369, Oct. 5, 2000; 67 FR 61824, Oct. 2, 2002; 73 FR 73127, Dec. 1, 2008, 75 FR 28502, May 21, 2010]

§ 391.43 Medical examination; certificate of physical examination.

(a) Except as provided by paragraph (b) of this section, the medical examination shall be performed by a licensed medical examiner as defined in § 390.5 of this subchapter.

(b) A licensed optometrist may perform so much of the medical examination as pertains to visual acuity, field of vision, and the ability to recognize colors as specified in paragraph (10) of § 391.41(b).

(c) Medical examiners shall:

(1) Be knowledgeable of the specific physical and mental demands associated with operating a commercial motor vehicle and the requirements of this subpart, including the medical advisory criteria prepared by the FMCSA as guidelines to aid the medical examiner in making the qualification determination; and

(2) Be proficient in the use of and use the medical protocols necessary to adequately perform the medical examination required by this section.

(d) Any driver authorized to operate a commercial motor vehicle within an exempt intracity zone pursuant to § 391.62 of this part shall furnish the examining medical examiner with a copy of the medical findings that led to the issuance of the first certificate of medical examination which allowed the driver to operate a commercial motor vehicle wholly within an exempt intracity zone.

(e) Any driver operating under a limited exemption authorized by § 391.64 shall furnish the medical examiner with a copy of the annual medical findings of the endocrinologist, ophthalmologist or optometrist, as required under that section. If the medical examiner finds the driver qualified under the limited exemption in § 391.64, such

fact shall be noted on the Medical Examiner's Certificate.

(f) The medical examination shall be performed, and its results shall be recorded, substantially in accordance with the following instructions and examination form. Existing forms may be used until current printed supplies are depleted or until September 30, 2004, whichever occurs first.

INSTRUCTIONS FOR PERFORMING AND RECORDING PHYSICAL EXAMINATIONS

The medical examiner must be familiar with 49 CFR 391.41, Physical qualifications for drivers, and should review these instructions before performing the physical examination. Answer each question "yes" or "no" and record numerical readings where indicated on the physical examination form.

The medical examiner must be aware of the rigorous physical, mental, and emotional demands placed on the driver of a commercial motor vehicle. In the interest of public safety, the medical examiner is required to certify that the driver does not have any physical, mental, or organic condition that might affect the driver's ability to operate a commercial motor vehicle safely.

General information. The purpose of this history and physical examination is to detect the presence of physical, mental, or organic conditions of such a character and extent as to affect the driver's ability to operate a commercial motor vehicle safely. The examination should be conducted carefully and should at least include all of the information requested in the following form. History of certain conditions may be cause for rejection. Indicate the need for further testing and/or require evaluation by a specialist. Conditions may be recorded which do not, because of their character or degree, indicate that certification of physical fitness should be denied. However, these conditions should be discussed with the driver and he/she should be advised to take the necessary steps to insure correction, particularly of those conditions which, if neglected, might affect the driver's ability to drive safely.

General appearance and development. Note marked overweight. Note any postural defect, perceptible limp, tremor, or other conditions that might be caused by alcoholism, thyroid intoxication or other illnesses.

Head-eyes. When other than the Snellen chart is used, the results of such test must be expressed in values comparable to the standard Snellen test. If the driver wears corrective lenses for driving, these should be worn while driver's visual acuity is being tested. If contact lenses are worn, there should be sufficient evidence of good tolerance of and adaptation to their use. Indicate the driver's need to wear corrective lenses to meet the vision standard on the Medical Examiner's Certificate by checking the box, "Qualified only when wearing corrective lenses." In recording distance vision use 20 feet as normal. Report all vision as a fraction with 20 as the numerator and the smallest type read at 20 feet as the denominator. Monocular drivers are not qualified to operate commercial motor vehicles in interstate commerce.

Ears. Note evidence of any ear disease, symptoms of aural vertigo, or Meniere's Syndrome. When recording hearing, record distance from patient at which a forced whispered voice can first be heard. For the whispered voice test, the individual should be stationed at least 5 feet from the examiner with the ear being tested turned toward the examiner. The other ear is covered. Using the breath which remains after a normal expiration, the examiner whispers words or random numbers such as 66, 18, 23, etc. The examiner should not use only sibilants (s-sounding test materials). The opposite ear should be tested in the same manner. If the individual fails the whispered voice test, the audiometric test should be administered. For the audiometric test, record decibel loss at 500 Hz, 1,000 Hz, and 2,000 Hz. Average the decibel loss at 500 Hz, 1,000 Hz and 2,000 Hz and record as described on the form. If the individual fails the audiometric test and the whispered voice test has not been administered, the whispered voice test should be performed to determine if the standard applicable to that test can be met.

Throat. Note any irremediable deformities likely to interfere with breathing or swallowing.

Heart. Note murmurs and arrhythmias, and any history of an enlarged heart, congestive heart failure, or cardiovascular disease that is accompanied by syncope, dyspnea, or collapse. Indicate onset date, diagnosis, medication, and any current limitation. An electrocardiogram is required when findings so indicate.

Blood pressure (BP). If a driver has hypertension and/or is being medicated for hypertension, he or she should be recertified more frequently. An individual diagnosed with Stage 1 hypertension (BP is 140/90–159/99) may be certified for one year. At recertification, an individual with a BP equal to or less than 140/90 may be certified for one year; however, if his or her BP is greater than 140/90 but less than 160/100, a one-time certificate for 3 months can be issued. An individual diagnosed with Stage 2 (BP is 160/100–179/109) should be treated and a one-time certificate for 3-month certification can be issued. Once the driver has reduced his or her BP to equal to or less than 140/90, he or she may be recertified annually thereafter. An individual diagnosed with Stage 3 hypertension (BP equal to or greater than 180/110) should not be certified until his or her BP is reduced to 140/90 or less, and may be recertified every 6 months.

Lungs. Note abnormal chest wall expansion, respiratory rate, breath sounds including wheezes or alveolar rales, impaired respiratory function, dyspnea, or cyanosis. Abnormal finds on physical exam may require further testing such as pulmonary tests and/or x-ray of chest.

Abdomen and Viscera. Note enlarged liver, enlarged spleen, abnormal masses, bruits, hernia, and significant abdominal wall muscle weakness and tenderness. If the diagnosis suggests that the condition might interfere with the control and safe operation of a commercial motor vehicle, further testing and evaluation is required.

Genital-urinary and rectal examination. A urinalysis is required. Protein, blood or sugar in the urine may be an indication for further testing to rule out any underlying medical problems. Note hernias. A condition causing discomfort should be evaluated to determine the extent to which the condition might interfere with the control and safe operation of a commercial motor vehicle.

Neurological. Note impaired equilibrium, coordination, or speech pattern; paresthesia; asymmetric deep tendon reflexes; sensory or positional abnormalities; abnormal patellar and Babinski's reflexes; ataxia. Abnormal neurological responses may be an indication for further testing to rule out an underlying medical condition. Any neurological condition should be evaluated for the nature and severity of the condition, the degree of limitation present, the likelihood of progressive limitation, and the potential for sudden incapacitation. In instances where the medical examiner has determined that more frequent monitoring of a condition is appropriate, a certificate for a shorter period should be issued.

Spine, musculoskeletal. Previous surgery, deformities, limitation of motion, and tenderness should be noted. Findings may indicate additional testing and evaluation should be conducted.

Extremities. Carefully examine upper and lower extremities and note any loss or impairment of leg, foot, toe, arm, hand, or finger. Note any deformities, atrophy, paralysis, partial paralysis, clubbing, edema, or hypotonia. If a hand or finger deformity exists, determine whether prehension and power grasp are sufficient to enable the driver to maintain steering wheel grip and to control other vehicle equipment during routine and emergency driving operations. If a foot or leg deformity exists, determine whether sufficient mobility and strength exist to enable the driver to operate pedals properly. In the case of any loss or impairment to an extremity which may interfere

375

with the driver's ability to operate a commercial motor vehicle safely, the medical examiner should state on the medical certificate "medically unqualified unless accompanied by a Skill Performance Evaluation Certificate." The driver must then apply to the Field Service Center of the FMCSA, for the State in which the driver has legal residence, for a Skill Performance Evaluation Certificate under § 391.49.

Laboratory and other testing. Other test(s) may be indicated based upon the medical history or findings of the physical examination.

Diabetes. If insulin is necessary to control a diabetic driver's condition, the driver is not qualified to operate a commercial motor vehicle in interstate commerce. If mild diabetes is present and it is controlled by use of an oral hypoglycemic drug and/or diet and exercise, it should not be considered disqualifying. However, the driver must remain under adequate medical supervision.

Upon completion of the examination, the medical examiner must date and sign the form, provide his/her full name, office address and telephone number. The completed medical examination form shall be retained on file at the office of the medical examiner.

Medical Examination Report
FOR COMMERCIAL DRIVER FITNESS DETERMINATION

649-F (6045)

1. DRIVER'S INFORMATION — Driver completes this section

Driver's Name (Last, First, Middle)	Social Security No.	Birthdate M / D / Y	Age	Sex ☐ M ☐ F	New Certification ☐ Recertification ☐ Follow-up ☐	Date of Exam

Address	City, State, Zip Code	Work Tel: ( ) Home Tel: ( )	Driver License No.	License Class ☐ A ☐ C ☐ B ☐ D ☐ Other	State of Issue

2. HEALTH HISTORY — Driver completes this section, but medical examiner is encouraged to discuss with driver.

Yes No

☐☐ Any illness or injury in the last 5 years?
☐☐ Head/Brain injuries, disorders or illnesses
☐☐ Seizures, epilepsy
  ☐ medication _____

☐☐ Eye disorders or impaired vision (except corrective lenses)
☐☐ Ear disorders, loss of hearing or balance
☐☐ Heart disease or heart attack; other cardiovascular condition
  ☐ medication _____

☐☐ Heart surgery (valve replacement/bypass, angioplasty, pacemaker) ☐ medication _____
☐☐ High blood pressure
☐☐ Muscular disease
☐☐ Shortness of breath

Yes No

☐☐ Lung disease, emphysema, asthma, chronic bronchitis
☐☐ Kidney disease, dialysis
☐☐ Liver disease
☐☐ Digestive problems
☐☐ Diabetes or elevated blood sugar controlled by:
  ☐ diet
  ☐ pills
  ☐ insulin
☐☐ Nervous or psychiatric disorders, e.g., severe depression
  ☐ medication _____
☐☐ Loss of, or altered consciousness

Yes No

☐☐ Fainting, dizziness
☐☐ Sleep disorders, pauses in breathing while asleep, daytime sleepiness, loud snoring

☐☐ Stroke or paralysis
☐☐ Missing or impaired hand, arm, foot, leg, finger, toe
☐☐ Spinal injury or disease

☐☐ Chronic low back pain

☐☐ Regular, frequent alcohol use
☐☐ Narcotic or habit forming drug use

For any YES answer, indicate onset date, diagnosis, treating physician's name and address, and any current limitation. List all medications (including over-the-counter medications) used regularly or recently.

_____

I certify that the above information is complete and true. I understand that inaccurate, false or missing information may invalidate the examination and my Medical Examiner's Certificate.

Driver's Signature _____ Date _____

Medical Examiner's Comments on Health History (The medical examiner must review and discuss with the driver any "yes" answers and potential hazards of medications, including over-the-counter medications, while driving. This discussion must be documented below.)

_____

377

3. TESTING (Medical Examiner completes Section 3 through 7)

Name: Last, _____ First, _____ Middle, _____

3. VISION

Standard: At least 20/40 acuity (Snellen) in each eye with or without correction. At least 70 degrees peripheral in horizontal meridian measured in each eye. The use of corrective lenses should be noted on the Medical Examiner's Certificate.

INSTRUCTIONS: When other than the Snellen chart is used, give test results in Snellen-comparable values. In recording distance vision, use 20 feet as normal. Report visual acuity as a ratio with 20 as numerator and the smallest type read at 20 feet as denominator. If the applicant wears corrective lenses, these should be worn while visual acuity is being tested. If the driver habitually wears contact lenses, or intends to do so while driving, sufficient evidence of good tolerance and adaptation to their use must be obvious. *Monocular drivers are not qualified.*

Numerical readings must be provided.

ACUITY	UNCORRECTED	CORRECTED	HORIZONTAL FIELD OF VISION	
Right Eye	20/	20/	Right Eye	°
Left Eye	20/	20/	Left Eye	°
Both Eyes	20/	20/		

Applicant can recognize and distinguish among traffic control signals and devices showing standard red, green, and amber colors? ☐ Yes ☐ No

Applicant meets visual acuity requirement only when wearing:
☐ Corrective Lenses

Monocular Vision: ☐ Yes ☐ No

Complete next line only if vision testing is done by an opthalmologist or optometrist

Date of Examination _____ Name of Ophthalmologist or Optometrist (print) _____ Tel. No. _____ License No./ State of Issue _____ Signature _____

4. HEARING

Standard: a) Must first perceive forced whispered voice > 5 ft., with or without hearing aid, or **b)** average hearing loss in better ear ≤ 40 dB

☐ Check if hearing aid and used for tests. ☐ Check if hearing aid required to meet standard.

INSTRUCTIONS: To convert audiometric test results from ISO to ANSI, -14 dB from ISO for 500Hz, -10dB for 1,000 Hz, -8.5 dB for 2000 Hz. To average, add the readings for 3 frequencies tested and divide by 3.

Numerical readings must be recorded.

			Right Ear			Left Ear		
a) Record distance from individual at which forced whispered voice can first be heard.	Right ear \Feet	Left Ear \Feet	500 Hz	1000 Hz	2000 Hz	500 Hz	1000 Hz	2000 Hz
b) If audiometer is used, record hearing loss in decibels. (acc. to ANSI Z24.5.1951)			Average:			Average:		

5. BLOOD PRESSURE/ PULSE RATE

Numerical readings must be recorded. Medical Examiner should take at least two readings to confirm BP.

Blood Pressure	Systolic	Diastolic	Reading	Category	Expiration Date	Recertification
			140-159/90-99	Stage 1	1 year	1 year if ≤140/90. One-time certificate for 3 months if 141-159/91-99.
Driver qualified if ≤140/90.			160-179/100-109	Stage 2	One-time certificate for 3 months.	1 year from date of exam if ≤140/90
Pulse Rate: ☐ Regular ☐ Irregular			≥180/110	Stage 3	6 months from date of exam if ≤140/90	6 months if ≤140/90
Record Pulse Rate:						

6. LABORATORY AND OTHER TEST FINDINGS

Numerical readings must be recorded.

Urinalysis is required. Protein, blood or sugar in the urine may be an indication for further testing to rule out any underlying medical problem.

URINE SPECIMEN	SP. GR.	PROTEIN	BLOOD	SUGAR

Other Testing (Describe and record)

7. PHYSICAL EXAMINATION

Height. _____ (in.) Weight. _____ (lbs.) Name. _____ Last, _____ First, _____ Middle,

The presence of a certain condition may not necessarily disqualify a driver, particularly if the condition is controlled adequately, is not likely to worsen or is readily amenable to treatment. Even if a condition does not disqualify a driver, the medical examiner may consider deferring the driver temporarily. Also, the driver should be advised to take the necessary steps to correct the condition as soon as possible particularly if the condition, if neglected, could result in more serious illness that might affect driving.

Check YES if there are any abnormalities. Check NO if the body system is normal. Discuss any YES answers in detail in the space below, and indicate whether it would affect the driver's ability to operate a commercial motor vehicle safely. Enter applicable item number before each comment. If organic disease is present, note that it has been compensated for. See *Instructions to the Medical Examiner* for guidance.

BODY SYSTEM	CHECK FOR:	YES*	NO	BODY SYSTEM	CHECK FOR:	YES*	NO
1. General Appearance	Marked overweight, tremor, signs of alcoholism, problem drinking, or drug abuse.			7. Abdomen and Viscera	Enlarged liver, enlarged spleen, masses, bruits, hernia, significant abdominal wall muscle weakness.		
2. Eyes	Pupillary equality, reaction to light, accommodation, ocular motility, ocular muscle imbalance, extraocular movement, nystagmus, exophthalmos. Ask about retinopathy, cataracts, aphakia, glaucoma, macular degeneration and refer to a specialist if appropriate.			8. Vascular System	Abnormal pulse and amplitude, carotid or arterial bruits, varicose veins.		
3. Ears	Scarring of tympanic membrane, occlusion of external canal, perforated eardrums.			9. Genito-urinary System	Hernias.		
4. Mouth and Throat	Irremediable deformities likely to interfere with breathing or swallowing.			10. Extremities- Limb impaired. Driver may be subject to SPE certificate if otherwise qualified.	Loss or impairment of leg, foot, toe, arm, hand, finger. Perceptible limp, deformities, atrophy, weakness, paralysis, clubbing, edema, hypotonia. Insufficient grasp and prehension in upper limb to maintain steering wheel grip. Insufficient mobility and strength in lower limb to operate pedals properly.		
5. Heart	Murmurs, extra sounds, enlarged heart, pacemaker, implantable defibrillator.			11. Spine, other musculoskeletal	Previous surgery, deformities, limitation of motion, tenderness.		
6. Lungs and chest, not including breast examination	Abnormal chest wall expansion, abnormal respiratory rate, abnormal breath sounds including wheezes or alveolar rales, impaired respiratory function, cyanosis. Abnormal findings on physical exam may require further testing such as pulmonary tests and/ or xray of chest.			12. Neurological	Impaired equilibrium, coordination or speech pattern, asymmetric deep tendon reflexes, sensory or positional abnormalities, abnormal patellar and Babinski's reflexes, ataxia.		

*COMMENTS:

_____

Note certification status here. See Instructions to the Medical Examiner for guidance.

☐ Meets standards in 49 CFR 391.41; qualifies for 2 year certificate
☐ Does not meet standards
☐ Meets standards, but periodic monitoring required due to _____
   Driver qualified only for: ☐3 months ☐6 months ☐1 year ☐ Other

☐ Wearing corrective lense
☐ Wearing hearing aid
☐ Accompanied by a _____ waiver/ exemption. Driver must present exemption at time of certification.
☐ Skill Performance Evaluation (SPE) Certificate
☐ Driving within an exempt intracity zone (See 49 CFR 391.62)
☐ Qualified by operation of 49 CFR 391.64

Medical Examiner's signature _____
Medical Examiner's name _____
Address _____
Telephone Number _____

Temporarily disqualified due to (condition or medication): _____

Return to medical examiner's office for follow up on _____

If meets standards, complete a Medical Examiner's Certificate as stated in 49 CFR 391.43(h). (Driver must carry certificate when operating a commercial vehicle.)

49 CFR 391.41 Physical Qualifications for Drivers

THE DRIVER'S ROLE

Responsibilities, work schedules, physical and emotional demands, and lifestyle among commercial drivers vary by the type of driving that they do. Some of the main types of drivers include the following: turn around or short relay (drivers return to their home base each evening); long relay (drivers drive 9-11 hours and then have at least a 10-hour off-duty period); straight through haul (cross country drivers); and team drivers (drivers share the driving by alternating their 5-hour driving periods and 5-hour rest periods.)

The following factors may be involved in a driver's performance of duties: abrupt schedule changes and rotating work schedules, which may result in irregular sleep patterns and a driver beginning a trip in a fatigued condition; long hours; extended time away from family and friends, which may result in lack of social support; tight pickup and delivery schedules, with irregularity in work, rest, and eating patterns, adverse road, weather and traffic conditions, which may cause delays and lead to hurriedly loading or unloading cargo in order to compensate for the lost time; and environmental conditions such as excessive vibration, noise, and extremes in temperature. Transporting passengers or hazardous materials may add to the demands on the commercial driver.

There may be duties in addition to the driving task for which a driver is responsible and needs to be fit. Some of these responsibilities are: coupling and uncoupling trailer(s) from the tractor, loading and unloading trailer(s) (sometimes a driver may lift a heavy load or unload as much as 50,000 lbs. of freight after sitting for a long period of time without any stretching period); inspecting the operating condition of tractor and/or trailer(s) before, during and after delivery of cargo; lifting, installing, and removing heavy tire chains; and, lifting heavy tarpaulins to cover open top trailers. The above tasks demand agility, the ability to bend and stoop, the ability to maintain a crouching position to inspect the underside of the vehicle, frequent entering and exiting of the cab, and the ability to climb ladders on the tractor and/or trailer(s).

In addition, a driver must have the perceptual skills to monitor a sometimes complex driving situation, the judgment skills to make quick decisions, when necessary, and the manipulative skills to control an oversize steering wheel, shift gears using a manual transmission, and maneuver a vehicle in crowded areas.

§391.45 PHYSICAL QUALIFICATIONS FOR DRIVERS

(a) A person shall not drive a commercial motor vehicle unless he is physically qualified to do so and, except as provided in §391.67, has on his person the original, or a photographic copy, of a medical examiner's certificate that he is physically qualified to drive a commercial motor vehicle.

(b) A person is physically qualified to drive a motor vehicle if that person:

(1) Has no loss of a foot, a leg, a hand, or an arm, or has been granted a Skill Performance Evaluation (SPE) Certificate (formerly Limb Waiver Program) pursuant to §391.49.

(2) Has no impairment of: (i) A hand or finger which interferes with prehension or power grasping; or (ii) An arm, foot, or leg which interferes with the ability to perform normal tasks associated with operating a commercial motor vehicle; or any other significant limb defect or limitation which interferes with the ability to perform normal tasks associated with operating a commercial motor vehicle; or has been granted a SPE Certificate pursuant to §391.49.

(3) Has no established medical history or clinical diagnosis of diabetes mellitus currently requiring insulin for control;

(4) Has no current clinical diagnosis of myocardial infarction, angina pectoris, coronary insufficiency, thrombosis, or any other cardiovascular disease of a variety known to be accompanied by syncope, dyspnea, collapse, or congestive cardiac failure.

(5) Has no established medical history or clinical diagnosis of a respiratory dysfunction likely to interfere with his ability to control and drive a commercial motor vehicle safely.

(6) Has no current clinical diagnosis of high blood pressure likely to interfere with his ability to operate a commercial motor vehicle safely.

(7) Has no established medical history or clinical diagnosis of rheumatic, arthritic, orthopedic, muscular, neuromuscular, or vascular disease which interferes with his ability to control and operate a commercial motor vehicle safely.

(8) Has no established medical history or clinical diagnosis of epilepsy or any other condition which is likely to cause loss of consciousness or any loss of ability to control a commercial motor vehicle;

(9) Has no mental, nervous, organic, or functional disease or psychiatric disorder likely to interfere with his ability to drive a commercial motor vehicle safely;

(10) Has distant visual acuity of at least 20/40 (Snellen) in each eye without corrective lenses or visual acuity separately corrected to 20/40 (Snellen) or better with corrective lenses, distant binocular acuity of at least 20/40 (Snellen) in both eyes with or without corrective lenses, field of vision of at least 70 degrees in the horizontal meridian in each eye, and the ability to recognize the colors of traffic signals and devices showing standard red, green and amber;

(11) First perceives a forced whispered voice in the better ear not less than 5 feet with or without the use of a hearing aid, or, if tested by use of an audiometric device, does not have an average hearing loss in the better ear greater than 40 decibels at 500 Hz, 1,000 Hz and 2,000 Hz with or without a hearing device when the audiometric device is calibrated to the American National Standard (formerly ASA Standard) Z24.5-1951;

(12) (i) Does not use a controlled substance identified in 21 CFR 1308.11 Schedule I, an amphetamine, a narcotic, or any other habit-forming drug. (ii) Exception: A driver may use such a substance or drug, if the substance or drug is prescribed by a licensed medical practitioner who: (A) Is familiar with the driver's medical history and assigned duties; and (B) Has advised the driver that the prescribed substance or drug will not adversely affect the driver's ability to safely operate a commercial motor vehicle; and

(13) Has no current clinical diagnosis of alcoholism.

INSTRUCTIONS TO THE MEDICAL EXAMINER

Federal Motor Carrier Safety Regulations
-Advisory Criteria-

General Information

The purpose of this examination is to determine a driver's physical qualification to operate a commercial motor vehicle (CMV) in interstate commerce according to the requirements in 49 CFR 391.41-49. Therefore, the medical examiner must be knowledgeable of these requirements and guidelines developed by the FMCSA to assist the medical examiner in making the qualification determination. The medical examiner should be familiar with the driver's responsibilities and work environment and is referred to the section on the form, **The Driver's Role**.

In addition to reviewing the **Health History** section with the driver and conducting the physical examination, the medical examiner should discuss common prescriptions and over-the-counter medications may have effects and hazards of these medications while driving. Educate the driver to read warning labels on all medications. History of certain conditions may be cause for rejection, particularly if required by regulation, or may indicate the need for additional laboratory tests or more stringent examination perhaps by a medical specialist. These decisions are usually made by the medical examiner in light of the driver's job responsibilities, work schedule and potential for the conditions to render the driver unsafe.

Medical conditions should be recorded even if they are not cause for denial, and they should be discussed with the driver to encourage appropriate remedial care. This advice is especially needed when a condition, if neglected, could develop into a serious illness that could affect driving.

If the medical examiner determines that the driver is fit to drive and is also able to perform non-driving responsibilities as may be required, the medical examiner signs the medical certificate which the driver must carry with his/her license. The certificate must be dated. **Under current regulations, the certificate is valid for two years, unless the driver has a medical condition that does not prohibit driving but does require more frequent monitoring.** In such situations, the medical certificate should be issued for a shorter length of time. The physical examination should be done carefully and at least as complete as is indicated by the attached form. Contact the FMCSA at (202) 366-1790 for further information (a vision exemption, qualifying drivers under 49 CFR 391.64, etc.).

Interpretation of Medical Standards

Since the issuance of the regulations for physical qualifications of commercial drivers, the Federal Motor Carrier Safety Administration (FMCSA) has published recommendations called Advisory Criteria to help medical examiners in determining whether a driver meets the physical qualifications for commercial driving. These recommendations have been condensed to provide information to medical examiners that (1) is directly relevant to the physical examination and (2) is not already included in the medical examination form. The specific regulation is printed in italics and it's reference by section is highlighted.

Loss of Limb:
§391.41(b)(1)

A person is physically qualified to drive a commercial motor vehicle if that person:

Has no loss of a foot, leg, hand or an arm, or has been granted a Skill Performance Evaluation (SPE) Certificate pursuant to Section 391.49.

Limb Impairment:
§391.41(b)(2)

A person is physically qualified to drive a commercial motor vehicle if that person:

Has no impairment of: (i) A hand or finger which interferes with prehension or power grasping; or (ii) An arm, foot, or leg which interferes with the ability to perform normal tasks associated with operating a commercial motor vehicle; or (iii) Any other significant limb defect or limitation which interferes with the ability to perform normal tasks associated with operating a commercial motor vehicle; or (iv) Has been granted a Skill Performance Evaluation (SPE) Certificate pursuant to Section 391.49.

A person who suffers loss of a foot, leg, hand or arm or whose limb impairment in any way interferes with the safe performance of normal tasks associated with operating a commercial motor vehicle is subject to the Skill Performance Evaluation Certification Program pursuant to section 391.49 assuming the person is otherwise qualified.

With the advancement of technology, medical aids and equipment modifications have been developed to compensate for certain disabilities. The SPE Certification Program (formerly the Limb Waiver Program) was designed to allow persons with the loss of a foot or limb or with functional impairment to qualify under the Federal Motor Carrier Safety Regulations (FMCSRs) by use of prosthetic devices or equipment modifications which enable them to safely operate a commercial motor vehicle. Since there are no medical aids equivalent to the original body or limb, certain risks are still present, and thus restrictions may be included on individual SPE certificates when a State Director for the FMCSA determines they are necessary to be consistent with safety and public interest.

If the driver is found otherwise medically qualified (§391.41(b)(3) through (13)), the medical examiner must check on the medical certificate that the driver is qualified only if accompanied by a SPE certificate. The driver and the employing motor carrier are subject to appropriate penalty if the driver operates a motor vehicle in interstate or foreign commerce without a curent SPE certificate for his/her physical disability.

Diabetes
§391.41(b)(3)

A person is physically qualified to drive a commercial motor vehicle if that person:

Has no established medical history or clinical diagnosis of diabetes mellitus currently requiring insulin for control.

Diabetes mellitus is a disease which, on occasion, can result in a loss of consciousness or disorientation in time and space. Individuals who require insulin for control have conditions which can get out of control by the use of too much or too little insulin, or food intake not consistent with the insulin dosage. Incapacitation may occur from symptoms of hyperglycemic or hypoglycemic reactions (drowsiness, semiconsciousness, diabetic coma or insulin shock).

The administration of insulin is, within itself, a complicated process requiring insulin, syringe, needle, alcohol sponge and a sterile technique. Factors related to long-haul commercial motor vehicle operations, such as fatigue, lack of sleep, poor diet, emotional conditions, stress, and concomitant illness, compound the dangers. Hypoglycemic drugs, taken orally, are sometimes prescribed for diabetic individuals to help stimulate natural body production of insulin. If the condition can be controlled by the use of oral medication and diet, then an individual may be qualified under the present rule. CMV drivers who do not meet the Federal diabetes standard may call (202) 366-1790 for an application for a diabetes exemption.

(See Conference Report on Diabetic Disorders and Commercial Drivers and Insulin-Using Commercial Motor Vehicle Drivers at:
http://www.fmcsa.dot.gov/rulesreg/medreports.htm)

Cardiovascular Condition
§391.41(b)(4)

A person is physically qualified to drive a commercial motor vehicle if that person:

Has no current clinical diagnosis of myocardial infarction, angina pectoris, coronary insufficiency, thrombosis or any other cardiovascular disease of a variety known to be accompanied by syncope, dyspnea, collapse or congestive cardiac failure.

The term "has no current clinical diagnosis of" is specifically designed to encompass: "a clinical diagnosis of: (1) a current cardiovascular condition, or (2) a cardiovascular condition which has not fully stabilized regardless of the time limit. The term "known to be "accompanied by" is designed to include a clinical diagnosis of a cardiovascular disease (1) which is accompanied by symptoms of syncope, dyspnea, collapse or congestive cardiac failure, and/or (2) which is likely to cause syncope, dyspnea, collapse or congestive cardiac failure.

It is the intent of the FMCSRs to render unqualified, a driver who has a current cardiovascular disease which is accompanied by and/or likely to cause symptoms of syncope, dyspnea, collapse, or congestive cardiac failure. However, the subjective decision of whether the nature and severity of an individual's condition will likely cause symptoms of cardiovascular insufficiency is on an individual basis and qualification rests with the medical examiner and the motor carrier. In those cases where there is an occurrence of cardiovascular insufficiency (myocardial infarction, thrombosis, etc.), it is suggested before a driver is certified that he or she have a normal resting and stress electrocardiogram (ECG), no residual complications and is taking no medication likely to interfere with safe driving.

Coronary artery bypass surgery and pacemaker implantation are remedial procedures and thus, not unqualifying. Implantable cardioverter defibrillators are disqualifying due to risk of syncope. Coumadin is a medical treatment which can improve the health and safety of the driver and should not, by its use, medically disqualify the commercial driver. The emphasis should be on the underlying medical condition(s) which require treatment and the general health of the driver. The FMCSA should be contacted at (202) 366-1790 for additional recommendations regarding the physical qualification of drivers on coumadin.

(See Cardiovascular Advisory Panel Guidelines for the Medical examination of Commercial Motor Vehicle Drivers at: http://www.fmcsa.dot.gov/rulesregs/medreports.htm)

Respiratory Dysfunction
§391.41(b)(5)
A person is physically qualified to drive a commercial motor vehicle if that person:
Has no established medical history or clinical diagnosis of a respiratory dysfunction likely to interfere with ability to control and drive a commercial motor vehicle safely.
Since a driver must be alert at all times, any change in his or her mental state is in direct conflict with highway safety. Even the slightest impairment in respiratory function under emergency conditions (when greater oxygen supply is necessary for performance) may be detrimental to safe driving.

There are many conditions that interfere with oxygen exchange and may result in incapacitation, including emphysema, chronic asthma, carcinoma, tuberculosis, chronic bronchitis and sleep apnea. If the medical examiner detects a respiratory dysfunction, that in any way is likely to interfere with the driver's ability to safely control and drive a commercial motor vehicle, the driver must be referred to a specialist for further evaluation and therapy. Anticoagulation therapy for deep vein thrombosis and/or pulmonary thromboembolism is not unqualifying once optimum dose is achieved, provided lower extremity venous examinations remain normal and the treating physician gives a favorable recommendation.

(See Conference on Pulmonary/Respiratory Disorders and Commercial Drivers at: http://www.fmcsa.dot.gov/rulesregs/medreports.htm

Hypertension
§391.41(b)(6)
A person is physically qualified to drive a commercial motor vehicle if that person:
Has no current clinical diagnosis of high blood pressure likely to interfere with ability to operate a commercial motor vehicle safely.

Hypertension alone is unlikely to cause sudden collapse; however, the likelihood increases when target organ damage, particularly cerebral vascular disease, is present. This regulatory criteria is based on FMCSA's Cardiovascular Advisory Guidelines for the Examination of CMV Drivers, which used the Sixth Report of the Joint National Committee on Detection, Evaluation, and Treatment of High Blood Pressure (1997).

Stage 1 hypertension corresponds to a systolic BP of 140-159 mmHg and/or a diastolic BP of 90-99 mmHg. The driver with a BP in this range is at low risk for hypertension-related acute incapacitation and may be medically certified to drive for a one-year period. Certification examinations should be done annually thereafter and should be at or less than 140/90. If less than 160/100, certification may be extended one time for 3 months.

A blood pressure of 160-179 systolic and/or 100-109 diastolic is considered Stage 2 hypertension, and the driver is not necessarily unqualified during evaluation and institution of treatment. The driver is given a one time certification of three months to reduce his or her blood pressure to less than or equal to 140/90. A blood pressure in this range is an absolute indication for anti-hypertensive drug therapy. Provided treatment is well tolerated and the driver demonstrates a BP value of 140/90 or less, he or she may be certified for one year from date of the initial exam. The driver is certified annually thereafter.

A blood pressure at or greater than 180 (systolic) and 110 (diastolic) is considered Stage 3, high risk for an acute BP-related event. The driver may not be qualified, even temporarily, until reduced to 140/90 or less and treatment is well tolerated. The driver may be certified for 6 months and biannually (every 6 months) thereafter if at recheck BP is 140/90 or less.

Annual recertification is recommended if the medical examiner does not know the severity of hypertension prior to treatment.

An elevated blood pressure finding should be confirmed by at least two subsequent measurements on different days.

Treatment includes nonpharmacologic and pharmacologic modalities as well as counseling to reduce other risk factors. Most antihypertensive medications also have side effects, the importance of which must be judged on an individual basis. Individuals must be alerted to the hazards of these medications while driving. Side effects of somnolence or syncope are particularly undesirable in commercial drivers.

Secondary hypertension is based on the above stages. Evaluation is warranted if patient is persistently hypertensive on maximal or near-maximal doses of 2-3 pharmacologic agents. Some causes of secondary hypertension may be amenable to surgical intervention or specific pharmacologic disease.
(See Cardiovascular Advisory Panel Guidelines for the Medical Examination of Commercial Motor Vehicle Drivers at: http://www.fmcsa.dot.gov/rulesregs/medreports.htm)

Rheumatic, Arthritic, Orthopedic, Muscular, Neuromuscular or Vascular Disease §391.41(b)(7)
A person is physically qualified to drive a commercial motor vehicle if that person:
Has no established medical history or clinical diagnosis of rheumatic, arthritic, orthopedic, muscular, neuromuscular or vascular disease which interferes with the ability to control and operate a commercial motor vehicle safely.

Certain diseases are known to have acute episodes of transient muscle weakness, poor muscular coordination (ataxia), abnormal sensations (paresthesia), decreased muscular tone (hypotonia), visual disturbances and pain which may be suddenly incapacitating. With each recurring episode, these symptoms may become more pronounced and remain for longer periods of time. Other diseases have more insidious onsets and display symptoms of muscle wasting (atrophy), swelling and paresthesia which may not suddenly incapacitate a person but may restrict his/her movements and eventually interfere with the ability to safely operate a motor vehicle. In many instances these diseases are degenerative in nature or may result in deterioration of the involved area.

Once the individual has been diagnosed as having a rheumatic, arthritic, orthopedic, muscular, neuromuscular or vascular disease, then he/she has an established history of that disease. The physician, when examining an individual, should consider the following: (1) the nature and severity of the individual's condition (such as sensory loss or loss of strength); (2) the degree of limitation present (such as range of motion); (3) the likelihood of progressive limitation (not always present initially but may manifest itself over time); and (4) the likelihood of sudden incapacitation. If severe functional impairment exists, the driver does not qualify. In cases where more frequent monitoring is required, a certificate for a shorter period of time may be issued. (See Conference on Neurological Disorders and Commercial Drivers at: http://www.fmcsa.dot.gov/rulesregs/medreports.htm)

Epilepsy

§391.41(b)(8)

A person is physically qualified to drive a commercial motor vehicle if that person:

Has no established medical history or clinical diagnosis of epilepsy or any other condition which is likely to cause loss of consciousness or any loss of ability to control a motor vehicle.

Epilepsy is a chronic functional disease characterized by seizures or episodes that occur without warning, resulting in loss of voluntary control which may lead to loss of consciousness and/or seizures. Therefore, the following drivers cannot be qualified: (1) a driver who has a medical history of epilepsy; (2) a driver who has a current clinical diagnosis of epilepsy; or (3) a driver who is taking antiseizure medication.

If an individual has had a sudden episode of a nonepileptic seizure or loss of consciousness of unknown cause which did not require antiseizure medication, the decision as to whether that person's condition will likely cause loss of consciousness or loss of ability to control a motor vehicle is made on an individual basis by the medical examiner in consultation with the treating physician. Before certification is considered, it is suggested that a 6 month waiting period elapse from the time of the episode. Following the waiting period, it is suggested that the individual have a complete neurological examination. If the results of the examination are negative and antiseizure medication is not required, then the driver may be qualified.

In those individual cases where a driver has a seizure or an episode of loss of consciousness that resulted from a known medical condition (e.g., drug reaction, high temperature, acute infectious disease, dehydration or acute metabolic disturbance), certification should be deferred until the driver has fully recovered from that condition and has no existing residual complications, and not taking antiseizure medication.

Drivers with a history of epilepsy/seizures off antiseizure medication and seizure-free for 10 years may be qualified to drive a CMV in interstate commerce. Interstate drivers with a history of a single unprovoked seizure may be qualified to drive a CMV in interstate commerce if seizure-free and off antiseizure medication for a 5-year period or more.

(See Conference on Neurological Disorders and Commercial Drivers at:

http://www.fmcsa.dot.gov/rulesregs/medreports.htm)

Mental Disorders

§391.41(b)(9)

A person is physically qualified to drive a commercial motor vehicle if that person:

Has no mental, nervous, organic or functional disease or psychiatric disorder likely to interfere with ability to drive a motor vehicle safely.

Emotional or adjustment problems contribute directly to an individual's level of memory, reasoning, attention, and judgment. These problems often underlie physical disorders. A variety of functional disorders can cause drowsiness, dizziness, confusion, weakness or paralysis that may lead to incoordination, inattention, loss of functional control and susceptibility to accidents while driving. Physical fatigue, headache, impaired coordination, recurring physical ailments and chronic "nagging" pain may be present to such a degree that certification for commercial driving is inadvisable. Somatic and psychosomatic complaints should be thoroughly examined when determining an individual's overall fitness to drive. Disorders of a periodically incapacitating nature, even in the early stages of development, may warrant disqualification.

Many bus and truck drivers have documented that "nervous trouble" related to neurotic, personality, or emotional or adjustment problems is responsible for a significant fraction of their preventable accidents. The degree to which an individual is able to appreciate, evaluate and adequately respond to environmental strain and emotional stress is critical when assessing an individual's mental alertness and flexibility to cope with the stresses of commercial motor vehicle driving.

When examining the driver, it should be kept in mind that individuals who live under chronic emotional upsets may have deeply ingrained maladaptive or erratic behavior patterns. Excessively antagonistic, instinctive, impulsive, openly aggressive, paranoid or severely depressed behavior greatly interfere with the driver's ability to drive safely. These individuals who are highly susceptible to frequent states of emotional instability (schizophrenia, affective psychoses, paranoia, anxiety or depressive neuroses) may warrant disqualification. Careful consideration should be given to the side effects and interactions of medications in the overall qualification determination. See Psychiatric Conference Report for specific recommendations on the use of medications and potential hazards for driving.

(See Conference on Psychiatric Disorders and Commercial Drivers at:

http://www.fmcsa.dot.gov/rulesregs/medreports.htm)

Vision

§391.41(b)(10)

A person is physically qualified to drive a commercial motor vehicle if that person:

Has distant visual acuity of at least 20/40 (Snellen) in each eye with or without corrective lenses or visual acuity separately corrected to 20/40 (Snellen) or better with corrective lenses, distant binocular acuity of at least 20/40 (Snellen) in both eyes with or without corrective lenses, field of vision of at least 70 degrees in the horizontal meridian in each eye, and the ability to recognize the colors of traffic signals and devices showing standard red, green, and amber.

The term "ability to recognize the colors of" is interpreted to mean if a person can recognize and distinguish among traffic control signals and devices showing standard red, green and amber, he or she meets the minimum standard, even though he or she may have some type of color perception deficiency. If certain color perception tests are administered, (such as Ishihara, Pseudoisochromatic, Yarn) and doubtful findings are discovered, a controlled test using signal red, green and amber may be employed to determine the driver's ability to recognize these colors.

Contact lenses are permissible if there is sufficient evidence to indicate that the driver has good tolerance and is well adapted to their use. Use of a contact lens in one eye for distance visual acuity and another lens in the other eye for near vision is not acceptable, nor telescopic lenses acceptable for the driving of commercial motor vehicles.

If an individual meets the criteria by the use of glasses or contact lenses, the following statement shall appear on the Medical Examiner's Certificate: "Qualified only if wearing corrective lenses."

CMV drivers who do not meet the Federal vision standard may call (202) 366-1790 for an application for a vision exemption.

(See Visual Disorders and Commercial Drivers at:

http://www.fmcsa.dot.gov/rulesregs/medreports.htm)

Hearing

§391.41(b)(11)

A person is physically qualified to drive a commercial motor vehicle if that person:

First perceives a forced whispered voice in the better ear at not less than 5 feet with or without the use of a hearing aid, or, if tested by use of an audiometric device, does not have an average hearing loss in the better ear greater than 40 decibels at 500 Hz, 1,000 Hz, and 2,000 Hz with or without a hearing aid when the audiometric device is calibrated to American National Standard (formerly ASA Standard) Z24.5-1951.

Since the prescribed standard under the FMCSRs is the American Standards Association (ANSI), it may be necessary to convert the audiometric results from the ISO standard to the ANSI standard. Instructions are included on the Medical Examination report form.

If an individual meets the criteria by using a hearing aid, the driver must wear that hearing aid and have it in operation at all times while driving. Also, the driver must be in possession of a spare power source for the hearing aid.

For the whispered voice test, the individual should be stationed at least 5 feet from the examiner. The other ear is covered. Using the breath which remains after a normal expiration, the examiner whispers words or random numbers such as 66, 18,

23, etc. The examiner should not use only sibilants (s sounding materials). The opposite ear should be tested in the same manner. If the individual fails the whispered voice test, the audiometric test should be administered.

If an individual meets the criteria by the use of a hearing aid, the following statement must appear on the Medical Examiner's Certificate "Qualified only when wearing a hearing aid."

(See Hearing Disorders and Commercial Motor Vehicle Drivers at: http://www.fmcsa.dot.gov/rulesregs/medreports.htm)

Drug Use
§391.41(b)(12)
A person is physically qualified to drive a commercial motor vehicle if that person:

Does not use a controlled substance identified in 21 CFR 1308.11, Schedule I, an amphetamine, a narcotic, or any other habit-forming drug.

Exception: A driver may use such a substance or drug, if the substance or drug is prescribed by a licensed medical practitioner who is familiar with the driver's medical history and assigned duties; and has advised the driver that the prescribed substance or drug will not adversely affect the driver's ability to safely operate a commercial motor vehicle.

This exception does not apply to methadone. The intent of the medical certification process is to medically evaluate a driver to ensure that the driver has no medical condition which interferes with the safe performance of driving tasks on a public road. If a driver uses a Schedule I drug or other substance, an amphetamine, a narcotic, or any other habit-forming drug, it may be cause for the driver to be found medically unqualified. Motor carriers are encouraged to obtain a practitioner's written statement about the effects on transportation safety of the use of a particular drug.

A test for controlled substances is not required as part of this biennial certification process. The FMCSA or the driver's employer should be contacted directly for information on controlled substances and alcohol testing under Part 382 of the FMCSRs.

The term "uses" is designed to encompass instances of prohibited drug use determined by a physician through established medical means. This may or may not involve body fluid testing. If body fluid testing takes place, positive test results should be confirmed by a second test of greater specificity. The term "habit-forming" is intended to include any drug or medication generally recognized as capable of becoming habitual, and which may impair the user's ability to operate a commercial motor vehicle safely.

The driver is medically unqualified for the duration of the prohibited drug(s) use and until a second examination shows the driver is free from the prohibited drug(s) use. Recertification may involve a substance abuse evaluation, the successful completion of a drug rehabilitation program, and a negative drug test result. Additionally, given that the certification period is normally two years, the examiner has the option to certify for a period of less than 2 years if this examiner determines more frequent monitoring is required.

(See Conference on Neurological Disorders and Commercial Drivers and Conference on Psychiatric Disorders and Commercial Drivers at: http://www.fmcsa.dot.gov/rulesregs/medreports.htm)

Alcoholism
§391.41(b)(13)
A person is physically qualified to drive a commercial motor vehicle if that person:

Has no current clinical diagnosis of alcoholism.

The term "current clinical diagnosis of" is specifically designed to encompass a current alcoholic illness or those instances where the individual's physical condition has not fully stabilized, regardless of the time element. If an individual shows signs of having an alcohol-use problem, he or she should be referred to a specialist. After counseling and/or treatment, he or she may be considered for certification.

(g)(1) If the medical examiner finds that the person examined is physically qualified to operate a commercial motor vehicle in accordance with § 391.41(b), the medical examiner should complete a certificate in the form prescribed in paragraph (h) of this section and furnish the original to the person who was examined. The examiner may provide a copy to a prospective or current employing motor carrier who requests it.

(2) For all drivers examined, the medical examiner should retain a copy of the Medical Examination Report at

least 3 years from the date of the examination. If the driver was certified as physically qualified, then the medical examiner should also retain the medical certificate as well for at least 3-years from the date the certificate was issued.

(h) The medical examiner's certificate shall be substantially in accordance with the following form. Existing forms may be used until current printed supplies are depleted or until November 6, 2001, whichever occurs first.

MEDICAL EXAMINER'S CERTIFICATE

I certify that I have examined _____ in accordance with the Federal Motor Carrier Safety Regulations (49 CFR 391.41-391.49) and with knowledge of the driving duties, I find this person is qualified; and, if applicable, only when:

☐ wearing corrective lenses

☐ wearing hearing aid

☐ accompanied by a _____ waiver/exemption

☐ driving within an exempt intracity zone (49 CFR 391.62)

☐ accompanied by a Skill Performance Evaluation Certificate (SPE)

☐ Qualified by operation of 49 CFR 391.64

The information I have provided regarding this physical examination is true and complete. A complete examination form with any attachment embodies my findings completely and correctly, and is on file in my office.

SIGNATURE OF MEDICAL EXAMINER _____

TELEPHONE _____   DATE _____

MEDICAL EXAMINER'S NAME (PRINT) _____

☐ MD   ☐ DO   ☐ Chiropractor

☐ Physician   ☐ Advanced
   Assistant   Practice
                        Nurse

MEDICAL EXAMINER'S LICENSE OR CERTIFICATE NO. / ISSUING STATE _____

SIGNATURE OF DRIVER _____

DRIVER'S LICENSE NO. _____   STATE _____

ADDRESS OF DRIVER _____

MEDICAL CERTIFICATE EXPIRATION DATE _____

[35 FR 6460, Apr. 22, 1970]

EDITORIAL NOTE: For FEDERAL REGISTER citations affecting § 391.43, see the List of CFR Sections Affected, which appears in the Finding Aids section of the printed volume and at www.fdsys.gov.

§391.45 Persons who must be medically examined and certified.

Except as provided in §391.67, the following persons must be medically examined and certified in accordance with §391.43 as physically qualified to operate a commercial motor vehicle:

(a) Any person who has not been medically examined and certified as physically qualified to operate a commercial motor vehicle;

(b)(1) Any driver who has not been medically examined and certified as qualified to operate a commercial motor vehicle during the preceding 24 months; or

(2) Any driver authorized to operate a commercial motor vehicle only with an exempt intracity zone pursuant to §391.62, or only by operation of the exemption in §391.64, if such driver has not been medically examined and certified as qualified to drive in such zone during the preceding 12 months; and

(c) Any driver whose ability to perform his/her normal duties has been impaired by a physical or mental injury or disease.

[35 FR 6460, Apr. 22, 1970, as amended at 36 FR 223, Jan. 7, 1971; 54 FR 12202, Mar. 24, 1989; 61 FR 13347, Mar. 26, 1996]

§391.47 Resolution of conflicts of medical evaluation.

(a) *Applications.* Applications for determination of a driver's medical qualifications under standards in this part will only be accepted if they conform to the requirements of this section.

(b) *Content.* Applications will be accepted for consideration only if the following conditions are met.

(1) The application must contain the name and address of the driver, motor carrier, and all physicians involved in the proceeding.

(2) The applicant must submit proof that there is a disagreement between the physician for the driver and the physician for the motor carrier concerning the driver's qualifications.

(3) The applicant must submit a copy of an opinion and report including results of all tests of an impartial medical specialist in the field in which the medical conflict arose. The specialist should be one agreed to by the motor carrier and the driver.

(i) In cases where the driver refuses to agree on a specialist and the applicant is the motor carrier, the applicant must submit a statement of his/her agreement to submit the matter to an impartial medical specialist in the field, proof that he/she has requested the driver to submit to the medical specialist, and the response, if any, of the driver to his/her request.

(ii) In cases where the motor carrier refuses to agree on a medical specialist, the driver must submit an opinion and test results of an impartial medical specialist, proof that he/she has requested the motor carrier to agree to submit the matter to the medical specialist and the response, if any, of the motor carrier to his/her request.

(4) The applicant must include a statement explaining in detail why the decision of the medical specialist identified in paragraph (b)(3) of this section, is unacceptable.

(5) The applicant must submit proof that the medical specialist mentioned in paragraph (b)(3) of this section was provided, prior to his/her determination, the medical history of the driver and an agreed-upon statement of the work the driver performs.

(6) The applicant must submit the medical history and statement of work provided to the medical specialist under paragraph (b)(5) of this section.

(7) The applicant must submit all medical records and statements of the physicians who have given opinions on the driver's qualifications.

(8) The applicant must submit a description and a copy of all written and documentary evidence upon which the party making application relies in the form set out in 49 CFR 386.37.

(9) The application must be accompanied by a statement of the driver that he/she intends to drive in interstate commerce not subject to the commercial zone exemption or a statement of the carrier that he/she has used or intends to use the driver for such work.

(10) The applicant must submit three copies of the application and all records.

(c) *Information.* The Director, Office of Bus and Truck Standards and Operations (MC-PSDPSD) may request further information from the applicant if he/she determines that a decision cannot be made on the evidence submitted. If the applicant fails to submit the information requested, the Director may refuse to issue a determination.

(d)(1) *Action.* Upon receiving a satisfactory application the Director, Office of Bus and Truck Standards and Operations (MC-PSDPSD) shall notify the parties (the driver, motor carrier, or any other interested party) that the application has been accepted and that a determination will be made. A copy of all evidence received shall be attached to the notice.

(2) *Reply.* Any party may submit a reply to the notification within 15 days after service. Such reply must be accompanied by all evidence the party wants the Director, Office of Bus and Truck Standards and Operations (MC-PSDPSD) to consider in making his/her determination. Evidence submitted should include all medical records and test results upon which the party relies.

(3) *Parties.* A party for the purposes of this section includes the motor carrier and the driver, or anyone else submitting an application.

(e) *Petitions to review, burden of proof.* The driver or motor carrier may petition to review the Director's determination. Such petition must be submitted in accordance with § 386.13(a) of this chapter. The burden of proof in such a proceeding is on the petitioner.

(f) *Status of driver.* Once an application is submitted to the Director, Office of Bus and Truck Standards and Operations (MC-PSDPSD), the driver shall be deemed disqualified until such time as the Director, Office of Bus and Truck Standards and Operations (MC-PSDPSD) makes a determination, or until the Director, Office of Bus and Truck Standards and Operations (MC-PSDPSD) orders otherwise.

(49 U.S.C. 304, 322; 18 U.S.C. 831–835; Pub. L. 93–633, 88 Stat. 8156 (49 U.S.C. 1801, *et seq.*); 49 CFR 1.48, 301.60)

[42 FR 18081, Apr. 5, 1977, as amended at 42 FR 53966, Oct. 4, 1977; 60 FR 38746, July 28, 1995]

§ 391.49 Alternative physical qualification standards for the loss or impairment of limbs.

(a) A person who is not physically qualified to drive under § 391.41(b)(1) or (b)(2) and who is otherwise qualified to drive a commercial motor vehicle, may drive a commercial motor vehicle, if the Division Administrator, FMCSA, has granted a Skill Performance Evaluation (SPE) Certificate to that person.

(b) *SPE certificate—*(1) *Application.* A letter of application for an SPE certificate may be submitted jointly by the person (driver applicant) who seeks an SPE certificate and by the motor carrier that will employ the driver applicant, if the application is accepted.

(2) *Application address.* The application must be addressed to the applicable field service center, FMCSA, for the State in which the co-applicant motor carrier's principal place of business is located. The address of each, and the States serviced, are listed in § 390.27 of this chapter.

(3) *Exception.* A letter of application for an SPE certificate may be submitted unilaterally by a driver applicant. The application must be addressed to the field service center, FMCSA, for the State in which the driver has legal residence. The driver applicant must comply with all the requirements of paragraph (c) of this section except those in (c)(1)(i) and (iii). The driver applicant shall respond to the requirements of paragraphs (c)(2)(i) to (v) of this section, if the information is known.

(c) A letter of application for an SPE certificate shall contain:

(1) Identification of the applicant(s):

(i) Name and complete address of the motor carrier coapplicant;

(ii) Name and complete address of the driver applicant;

(iii) The U.S. DOT Motor Carrier Identification Number, if known; and

(iv) A description of the driver applicant's limb impairment for which SPE certificate is requested.

(2) Description of the type of operation the driver will be employed to perform:

(i) State(s) in which the driver will operate for the motor carrier co-applicant (if more than 10 States, designate general geographic area only);

(ii) Average period of time the driver will be driving and/or on duty, per day;

(iii) Type of commodities or cargo to be transported;

(iv) Type of driver operation (*i.e.,* sleeper team, relay, owner operator, etc.); and

(v) Number of years experience operating the type of commercial motor vehicle(s) requested in the letter of application and total years of experience operating all types of commercial motor vehicles.

(3) Description of the commercial motor vehicle(s) the driver applicant intends to drive:

(i) Truck, truck tractor, or bus make, model, and year (if known);

(ii) Drive train;

(A) Transmission type (automatic or manual—if manual, designate number of forward speeds);

(B) Auxiliary transmission (if any) and number of forward speeds; and

(C) Rear axle (designate single speed, 2 speed, or 3 speed).

(iii) Type of brake system;

(iv) Steering, manual or power assisted;

(v) Description of type of trailer(s) (*i.e.,* van, flatbed, cargo tank, drop frame, lowboy, or pole);

(vi) Number of semitrailers or full trailers to be towed at one time;

(vii) For commercial motor vehicles designed to transport passengers, indicate the seating capacity of commercial motor vehicle; and

(viii) Description of any modification(s) made to the commercial motor vehicle for the driver applicant; attach photograph(s) where applicable.

(4) Otherwise qualified:

(i) The coapplicant motor carrier must certify that the driver applicant is otherwise qualified under the regulations of this part;

(ii) In the case of a unilateral application, the driver applicant must certify that he/she is otherwise qualified under the regulations of this part.

(5) Signature of applicant(s):

(i) Driver applicant's signature and date signed;

(ii) Motor carrier official's signature (if application has a coapplicant), title, and date signed. Depending upon the motor carrier's organizational structure (corporation, partnership, or proprietorship), the signer of the application shall be an officer, partner, or the proprietor.

(d) The letter of application for an SPE certificate shall be accompanied by:

(1) A copy of the results of the medical examination performed pursuant to §391.43;

(2) A copy of the medical certificate completed pursuant to §391.43(h);

(3) A medical evaluation summary completed by either a board qualified or board certified physiatrist (doctor of physical medicine) or orthopedic surgeon. The coapplicant motor carrier or the driver applicant shall provide the physiatrist or orthopedic surgeon with a description of the job-related tasks the driver applicant will be required to perform;

(i) The medical evaluation summary for a driver applicant disqualified under §391.41(b)(1) shall include:

(A) An assessment of the functional capabilities of the driver as they relate to the ability of the driver to perform normal tasks associated with operating a commercial motor vehicle; and

(B) A statement by the examiner that the applicant is capable of demonstrating precision prehension (*e.g.,* manipulating knobs and switches) and power grasp prehension (*e.g.,* holding and maneuvering the steering wheel) with each upper limb separately. This requirement does not apply to an individual who was granted a waiver, absent a prosthetic device, prior to the publication of this amendment.

(ii) The medical evaluation summary for a driver applicant disqualified under §391.41(b)(2) shall include:

(A) An explanation as to how and why the impairment interferes with the ability of the applicant to perform normal tasks associated with operating a commercial motor vehicle;

(B) An assessment and medical opinion of whether the condition will likely remain medically stable over the lifetime of the driver applicant; and

(C) A statement by the examiner that the applicant is capable of demonstrating precision prehension (*e.g.*, manipulating knobs and switches) and power grasp prehension (*e.g.*, holding and maneuvering the steering wheel) with each upper limb separately. This requirement does not apply to an individual who was granted an SPE certificate, absent an orthotic device, prior to the publication of this amendment.

(4) A description of the driver applicant's prosthetic or orthotic device worn, if any;

(5) Road test:

(i) A copy of the driver applicant's road test administered by the motor carrier coapplicant and the certificate issued pursuant to § 391.31(b) through (g); or

(ii) A unilateral applicant shall be responsible for having a road test administered by a motor carrier or a person who is competent to administer the test and evaluate its results.

(6) Application for employment:

(i) A copy of the driver applicant's application for employment completed pursuant to § 391.21; or

(ii) A unilateral applicant shall be responsible for submitting a copy of the last commercial driving position's employment application he/she held. If not previously employed as a commercial driver, so state.

(7) A copy of the driver applicant's SPE certificate of certain physical defects issued by the individual State(s), where applicable; and

(8) A copy of the driver applicant's State Motor Vehicle Driving Record for the past 3 years from each State in which a motor vehicle driver's license or permit has been obtained.

(e) *Agreement.* A motor carrier that employs a driver with an SPE certificate agrees to:

(1) File promptly (within 30 days of the involved incident) with the Medical Program Specialist, FMCSA service center, such documents and information as may be required about driving activities, accidents, arrests, license suspensions, revocations, or withdrawals, and convictions which involve the driver applicant. This applies whether the driver's SPE certificate is a unilateral one or has a coapplicant motor carrier;

(i) A motor carrier who is a coapplicant must file the required documents with the Medical Program Specialist, FMCSA for the State in which the carrier's principal place of business is located; or

(ii) A motor carrier who employs a driver who has been issued a unilateral SPE certificate must file the required documents with the Medical Program Specialist, FMCSA service center, for the State in which the driver has legal residence.

(2) Evaluate the driver with a road test using the trailer the motor carrier intends the driver to transport or, in lieu of, accept a certificate of a trailer road test from another motor carrier if the trailer type(s) is similar, or accept the trailer road test done during the Skill Performance Evaluation if it is a similar trailer type(s) to that of the prospective motor carrier. Job tasks, as stated in paragraph (e)(3) of this section, are not evaluated in the Skill Performance Evaluation;

(3) Evaluate the driver for those non-driving safety related job tasks associated with whatever type of trailer(s) will be used and any other nondriving safety related or job related tasks unique to the operations of the employing motor carrier; and

(4) Use the driver to operate the type of commercial motor vehicle defined in the SPE certificate only when the driver is in compliance with the conditions and limitations of the SPE certificate.

(f) The driver shall supply each employing motor carrier with a copy of the SPE certificate.

(g) The State Director, FMCSA, may require the driver applicant to demonstrate his or her ability to safely operate the commercial motor vehicle(s) the driver intends to drive to an agent of the State Director, FMCSA. The SPE certificate form will identify the power unit (bus, truck, truck tractor) for which the SPE certificate has been granted. The SPE certificate forms will also identify the trailer type used in the Skill Performance Evaluation; however, the SPE certificate is not limited to that specific trailer type. A driver may use the SPE certificate with other trailer types if a successful trailer road test is completed in accordance with paragraph (e)(2) of this section. Job tasks, as stated in paragraph (e)(3) of this section, are not evaluated during the Skill Performance Evaluation.

(h) The State Director, FMCSA, may deny the application for SPE certificate or may grant it totally or in part and issue the SPE certificate subject to such terms, conditions, and limitations as deemed consistent with the public interest. The SPE certificate is valid for a period not to exceed 2 years from date of issue, and may be renewed 30 days prior to the expiration date.

(i) The SPE certificate renewal application shall be submitted to the Medical Program Specialist, FMCSA service center, for the State in which the driver has legal residence, if the SPE certificate was issued unilaterally. If the SPE certificate has a coapplicant, then the renewal application is submitted to the Medical Program Specialist, FMCSA field service center, for the State in which the coapplicant motor carrier's principal place of business is located. The SPE certificate renewal application shall contain the following:

(1) Name and complete address of motor carrier currently employing the applicant;

(2) Name and complete address of the driver;

(3) Effective date of the current SPE certificate;

(4) Expiration date of the current SPE certificate;

(5) Total miles driven under the current SPE certificate;

(6) Number of accidents incurred while driving under the current SPE certificate, including date of the accident(s), number of fatalities, number of injuries, and the estimated dollar amount of property damage;

(7) A current medical examination report;

(8) A medical evaluation summary pursuant to paragraph (d)(3) of this section, if an unstable medical condition exists. All handicapped conditions classified under §391.41(b)(1) are considered unstable. Refer to paragraph (d)(3)(ii) of this section for the condition under §391.41(b)(2) which may be considered medically stable.

(9) A copy of driver's current State motor vehicle driving record for the pe-

riod of time the current SPE certificate has been in effect;

(10) Notification of any change in the type of tractor the driver will operate;

(11) Driver's signature and date signed; and

(12) Motor carrier coapplicant's signature and date signed.

(j)(1) Upon granting an SPE certificate, the State Director, FMCSA, will notify the driver applicant and co-applicant motor carrier (if applicable) by letter. The terms, conditions, and limitations of the SPE certificate will be set forth. A motor carrier shall maintain a copy of the SPE certificate in its driver qualification file. A copy of the SPE certificate shall be retained in the motor carrier's file for a period of 3 years after the driver's employment is terminated. The driver applicant shall have the SPE certificate (or a legible copy) in his/her possession whenever on duty.

(2) Upon successful completion of the skill performance evaluation, the State Director, FMCSA, for the State where the driver applicant has legal residence, must notify the driver by letter and enclose an SPE certificate substantially in the following form:

Skill Performance Evaluation Certificate

Name of Issuing Agency: _____
Agency Address: _____
Telephone Number: ( ) _____

Issued Under 49 CFR 391.49, subchapter B of the Federal Motor Carrier Safety Regulations

Driver's Name: _____
Effective Date: _____
SSN: _____
DOB: _____
Expiration Date: _____
Address: _____
_____

Driver Disability: _____
Check One: _ New _ Renewal
Driver's License: _____
(State)   (Number)

In accordance with 49 CFR 391.49, subchapter B of the Federal Motor Carrier Safety Regulations (FMCSRs), the driver application for a skill performance evaluation (SPE) certificate is hereby granted authorizing the above-named driver to operate in interstate or foreign commerce under the provisions set forth below. This certificate is granted for the period shown above, not to exceed 2 years, subject to periodic review as may be found necessary. This certificate may be renewed upon submission of a renewal application. Continuation of this certificate is dependent upon strict adherence by the above-named driver to the provisions set forth below and compliance with the FMCSRs. Any failure to comply with provisions herein may be cause for cancellation.

CONDITIONS: As a condition of this certificate, reports of all accidents, arrests, suspensions, revocations, withdrawals of driver licenses or permits, and convictions involving the above-named driver shall be reported in writing to the Issuing Agency by the EMPLOYING MOTOR CARRIER within 30 days after occurrence.

LIMITATIONS:

1. Vehicle Type (power unit):* _____

2. Vehicle modification(s): _____

3. Prosthetic or Orthotic device(s) (Required to be Worn While Driving): _____

4. Additional Provision(s): _____

NOTICE: To all MOTOR CARRIERS employing a driver with an SPE certificate. This certificate is granted for the operation of the *power unit only*. It is the responsibility of the employing motor carrier to evaluate the driver with a road test using the trailer type(s) the motor carrier intends the driver to transport, or in lieu of, accept the trailer road test done during the SPE if it is a similar trailer type(s) to that of the prospective motor carrier. Also, it is the responsibility of the employing motor carrier to evaluate the driver for those non-driving safety-related job tasks associated with the type of trailer(s) utilized, as well as, any other non-driving safety-related or job-related tasks unique to the operations of the employing motor carrier.

The SPE of the above named driver was given by a Skill Performance Evaluation Program Specialist. It was successfully completed utilizing the above named power unit and _____ (trailer, if applicable)

The tractor or truck had a _____ transmission.

Please read the *NOTICE* paragraph above.

Name: _____
Signature: _____
Title: _____
Date: _____

(k) The State Director, FMCSA, may revoke an SPE certificate after the person to whom it was issued is given notice of the proposed revocation and has been allowed a reasonable opportunity to appeal.

(l) Falsifying information in the letter of application, the renewal application, or falsifying information required by this section by either the applicant or motor carrier is prohibited.

[65 FR 25287, May 1, 2000, as amended at 65 FR 59380, Oct. 5, 2000; 67 FR 61824, Oct. 2, 2002]

Subpart F—Files and Records

§ 391.51   General requirements for driver qualification files.

(a) Each motor carrier shall maintain a driver qualification file for each driver it employs. A driver's qualification file may be combined with his/her personnel file.

(b) The qualification file for a driver must include:

(1) The driver's application for employment completed in accordance with § 391.21;

(2) A copy of the motor vehicle record received from each State record pursuant to § 391.23(a)(1);

(3) The certificate of driver's road test issued to the driver pursuant to § 391.31(e), or a copy of the license or certificate which the motor carrier accepted as equivalent to the driver's road test pursuant to § 391.33;

(4) The motor vehicle record received from each State driver licensing agency to the annual driver record inquiry required by § 391.25(a);

(5) A note relating to the annual review of the driver's driving record as required by § 391.25(c)(2);

(6) A list or certificate relating to violations of motor vehicle laws and ordinances required by § 391.27;

(7)(i) The medical examiner's certificate as required by § 391.43(g) or a legible copy of the certificate.

(ii) *Exception.* For CDL holders, beginning January 30, 2012, if the CDLIS motor vehicle record contains medical certification status information, the motor carrier employer must meet this requirement by obtaining the CDLIS motor vehicle record defined at § 384.105 of this chapter. That record must be obtained from the current licensing State and placed in the driver qualification file. After January 30, 2014, a non-excepted, interstate CDL holder without medical certification status information on the CDLIS motor vehicle record is designated "not-certified" to operate a CMV in interstate commerce. After January 30, 2014, a motor carrier may use a copy of the driver's current medical examiner's certificate that was submitted to the State for up to 15 days from the date it was issued as proof of medical certification.

(iii) If that driver obtained the medical certification based on having obtained a medical variance from FMCSA, the motor carrier must also include a copy of the medical variance documentation in the driver qualification file in accordance with §391.51(b)(8); and

(8) A Skill Performance Evaluation Certificate obtained from a Field Administrator, Division Administrator, or State Director issued in accordance with §391.49; or the Medical Exemption document, issued by a Federal medical program in accordance with part 381 of this chapter.

(c) Except as provided in paragraph (d) of this section, each driver's qualification file shall be retained for as long as a driver is employed by that motor carrier and for three years thereafter.

(d) The following records may be removed from a driver's qualification file three years after the date of execution:

(1) The motor vehicle record received from each State driver licensing agency to the annual driver record inquiry required by §391.25(a);

(2) The note relating to the annual review of the driver's driving record as required by §391.25(c)(2);

(3) The list or certificate relating to violations of motor vehicle laws and ordinances required by §391.27;

(4) The medical examiner's certificate required by §391.43(g), a legible copy of the certificate, or for CDL drivers any CDLIS MVR obtained as required by §391.51(b)(7)(ii); and

(5) Any medical variance issued by FMCSA, including a Skill Performance Evaluation Certificate issued in accordance with §391.49; or the Medical Exemption letter issued by a Federal medical program in accordance with part 381 of this chapter.

(Approved by the Office of Management and Budget under control number 2126–004)

[63 FR 33277, June 18, 1998, as amended at 69 FR 16721, Mar. 30, 2004; 73 FR 73127, Dec. 1, 2008; 75 FR 28502, May 21, 2010]

§391.53 Driver investigation history file.

(a) After October 29, 2004, each motor carrier must maintain records relating to the investigation into the safety performance history of a new or prospective driver pursuant to paragraphs (d) and (e) of §391.23. This file must be maintained in a secure location with controlled access.

(1) The motor carrier must ensure that access to this data is limited to those who are involved in the hiring decision or who control access to the data. In addition, the motor carrier's insurer may have access to the data, except the alcohol and controlled substances data.

(2) This data must only be used for the hiring decision.

(b) The file must include:

(1) A copy of the driver's written authorization for the motor carrier to seek information about a driver's alcohol and controlled substances history as required under §391.23(d).

(2) A copy of the response(s) received for investigations required by paragraphs (d) and (e) of §391.23 from each previous employer, or documentation of good faith efforts to contact them. The record must include the previous employer's name and address, the date the previous employer was contacted, and the information received about the driver from the previous employer. Failures to contact a previous employer, or of them to provide the required safety performance history information, must be documented.

(c) The safety performance histories received from previous employers for a driver who is hired must be retained for as long as the driver is employed by that motor carrier and for three years thereafter.

(d) A motor carrier must make all records and information in this file available to an authorized representative or special agent of the Federal Motor Carrier Safety Administration, an authorized State or local enforcement agency representative, or an authorized third party, upon request or as part of any inquiry within the time period specified by the requesting representative.

(Approved by the Office of Management and Budget under control number 2126–004)

[69 FR 16721, Mar. 30, 2004]

§ 391.55 LCV Driver-Instructor qualification files.

(a) Each motor carrier must maintain a qualification file for each LCV driver-instructor it employs or uses. The LCV driver-instructor qualification file may be combined with his/her personnel file.

(b) The LCV driver-instructor qualification file must include the information in paragraphs (b)(1) and (b)(2) of this section for a skills instructor or the information in paragraph (b)(1) of this section for a classroom instructor, as follows:

(1) Evidence that the instructor has met the requirements of 49 CFR 380.301 or 380.303;

(2) A photographic copy of the individual's currently valid CDL with the appropriate endorsements.

[69 FR 16738, Mar. 30, 2004; 69 FR 28846, May 19, 2004]

Subpart G—Limited Exemptions

§ 391.61 Drivers who were regularly employed before January 1, 1971.

The provisions of § 391.21 (relating to applications for employment), § 391.23 (relating to investigations and inquiries), and § 391.33 (relating to road tests) do not apply to a driver who has been a single-employer driver (as defined in § 390.5 of this subchapter) of a motor carrier for a continuous period which began before January 1, 1971, as long as he/she continues to be a single-employer driver of that motor carrier.

[63 FR 33278, June 18, 1998]

§ 391.62 Limited exemptions for intracity zone drivers.

The provisions of §§ 391.11(b)(1) and 391.41(b)(1) through (b)(11) do not apply to a person who:

(a) Was otherwise qualified to operate and operated a commercial motor vehicle in a municipality or exempt intracity zone thereof throughout the one-year period ending November 18, 1988;

(b) Meets all the other requirements of this section;

(c) Operates wholly within the exempt intracity zone (as defined in 49 CFR 390.5);

(d) Does not operate a vehicle used in the transportation of hazardous materials in a quantity requiring placarding under regulations issued by the Secretary under 49 U.S.C. chapter 51.; and

(e) Has a medical or physical condition which:

(1) Would have prevented such person from operating a commercial motor vehicle under the Federal Motor Carrier Safety Regulations contained in this subchapter;

(2) Existed on July 1, 1988, or at the time of the first required physical examination after that date; and

(3) The examining physician has determined this condition has not substantially worsened since July 1, 1988, or at the time of the first required physical examination after that date.

[61 FR 13346, Mar. 26, 1996; 61 FR 17253, Apr. 19, 1996]

§ 391.63 Multiple-employer drivers.

(a) If a motor carrier employs a person as a multiple-employer driver (as defined in § 390.5 of this subchapter), the motor carrier shall comply with all requirements of this part, except that the motor carrier need not—

(1) Require the person to furnish an application for employment in accordance with § 391.21;

(2) Make the investigations and inquiries specified in § 391.23 with respect to that person;

(3) Perform the annual driving record inquiry required by § 391.25(a);

(4) Perform the annual review of the person's driving record required by § 391.25(b); or

(5) Require the person to furnish a record of violations or a certificate in accordance with § 391.27.

(b) Before a motor carrier permits a multiple-employer driver to drive a commercial motor vehicle, the motor carrier must obtain his/her name, his/her social security number, and the identification number, type and issuing

State of his/her commercial motor vehicle operator's license. The motor carrier must maintain this information for three years after employment of the multiple-employer driver ceases.

(Approved by the Office of Management and Budget under control number 2125–0081)

[63 FR 33278, June 18, 1998]

§391.64 Grandfathering for certain drivers participating in vision and diabetes waiver study programs.

(a) The provisions of §391.41(b)(3) do not apply to a driver who was a participant in good standing on March 31, 1996, in a waiver study program concerning the operation of commercial motor vehicles by insulin-controlled diabetic drivers; *provided:*

(1) The driver is physically examined every year, including an examination by a board-certified/eligible endocrinologist attesting to the fact that the driver is:

(i) Otherwise qualified under §391.41;

(ii) Free of insulin reactions (an individual is free of insulin reactions if that individual does not have severe hypoglycemia or hypoglycemia unawareness, and has less than one documented, symptomatic hypoglycemic reaction per month);

(iii) Able to and has demonstrated willingness to properly monitor and manage his/her diabetes; and

(iv) Not likely to suffer any diminution in driving ability due to his/her diabetic condition.

(2) The driver agrees to and complies with the following conditions:

(i) A source of rapidly absorbable glucose shall be carried at all times while driving;

(ii) Blood glucose levels shall be self-monitored one hour prior to driving and at least once every four hours while driving or on duty prior to driving using a portable glucose monitoring device equipped with a computerized memory;

(iii) Submit blood glucose logs to the endocrinologist or medical examiner at the annual examination or when otherwise directed by an authorized agent of the FMCSA;

(iv) Provide a copy of the endocrinologist's report to the medical examiner at the time of the annual medical examination; and

(v) Provide a copy of the annual medical certification to the employer for retention in the driver's qualification file and retain a copy of the certification on his/her person while driving for presentation to a duly authorized Federal, State or local enforcement official.

(b) The provisions of §391.41(b)(10) do not apply to a driver who was a participant in good standing on March 31, 1996, in a waiver study program concerning the operation of commercial motor vehicles by drivers with visual impairment in one eye; *provided:*

(1) The driver is physically examined every year, including an examination by an ophthalmologist or optometrist attesting to the fact that the driver:

(i) Is otherwise qualified under §391.41; and

(ii) Continues to measure at least 20/40 (Snellen) in the better eye.

(2) The driver provides a copy of the ophthalmologist or optometrist report to the medical examiner at the time of the annual medical examination.

(3) The driver provides a copy of the annual medical certification to the employer for retention in the driver's qualification file and retains a copy of the certification on his/her person while driving for presentation to a duly authorized federal, state or local enforcement official.

[61 FR 13346, Mar. 26, 1996]

§391.65 Drivers furnished by other motor carriers.

(a) A motor carrier may employ a driver who is not a regularly employed driver of that motor carrier without complying with the generally applicable driver qualification file requirements in this part, if—

(1) The driver is regularly employed by another motor carrier; and

(2) The motor carrier which regularly employs the driver certifies that the driver is fully qualified to drive a commercial motor vehicle in a written statement which—

(i) Is signed and dated by an officer or authorized employee of the regularly employing carrier;

(ii) Contains the driver's name and signature;

(iii) Certifies that the driver has been regularly employed as defined in §390.5;

(iv) Certifies that the driver is fully qualified to drive a commercial motor vehicle under the rules in part 391 of the Federal Motor Carrier Safety Regulations;

(v) States the expiration date of the driver's medical examiner's certificate;

(vi) Specifies an expiration date for the certificate, which shall be not longer than 2 years or, if earlier, the expiration date of the driver's current medical examiner's certificate; and

(vii) After April 1, 1977, is substantially in accordance with the following form:

_____
(Name of driver)

_____
(SS No.)

(Signature of driver)

I certify that the above named driver, as defined in § 390.5 is regularly driving a commercial motor vehicle operated by the below named carrier and is fully qualified under part 391, Federal Motor Carrier Safety Regulations. His/her current medical examiner's certificate expires on _____ (Date)
This certificate expires:

_____
(Date not later than expiration date of medical certificate)

Issued on _____ (date)

Issued by _____
(Name of carrier)

_____
(Address)

_____
(Signature)

_____
(Title)

(b) A motor carrier that obtains a certificate in accordance with paragraph (a)(2) of this section shall:

(1) Contact the motor carrier which certified the driver's qualifications under this section to verify the validity of the certificate. This contact may be made in person, by telephone, or by letter.

(2) Retain a copy of that certificate in its files for three years.

(c) A motor carrier which certifies a driver's qualifications under this section shall be responsible for the accuracy of the certificate. The certificate is no longer valid if the driver leaves the employment of the motor carrier which issued the certificate or is no longer qualified under the rules in this part.

[41 FR 36656, Aug. 31, 1976, as amended at 53 FR 18057, May 19, 1988; 60 FR 38745, July 28, 1995; 63 FR 33278, June 18, 1998; 67 FR 61824, Oct. 2, 2002]

§ 391.67 Farm vehicle drivers of articulated commercial motor vehicles.

The following rules in this part do not apply to a farm vehicle driver (as defined in § 390.5 of this subchapter) who is 18 years of age or older and who drives an articulated commercial motor vehicle:

(a) Section 391.11(b)(1), (b)(6) and (b)(8) (relating to general qualifications of drivers);

(b) Subpart C (relating to disclosure of, investigation into, and inquiries about the background, character, and driving record of drivers);

(c) Subpart D (relating to road tests); and

(d) Subpart F (relating to maintenance of files and records).

[63 FR 33278, June 18, 1998]

§ 391.68 Private motor carrier of passengers (nonbusiness).

The following rules in this part do not apply to a private motor carrier of passengers (nonbusiness) and its drivers:

(a) Section 391.11(b)(1), (b)(6) and (b)(8) (relating to general qualifications of drivers);

(b) Subpart C (relating to disclosure of, investigation into, and inquiries about the background, character, and driving record of, drivers);

(c) So much of §§ 391.41 and 391.45 as require a driver to be medically examined and to have a medical examiner's certificate on his/her person; and

(d) Subpart F (relating to maintenance of files and records).

[63 FR 33278, June 18, 1998]

§ 391.69 Private motor carrier of passengers (business).

The provisions of § 391.21 (relating to applications for employment), § 391.23 (relating to investigations and inquiries), and § 391.31 (relating to road tests) do not apply to a driver who was a single-employer driver (as defined in § 390.5 of this subchapter) of a private motor carrier of passengers (business) as of July 1, 1994, so long as the driver continues to be a single-employer driver of that motor carrier.

[63 FR 33278, June 18, 1998]

§ 391.71 [Reserved]

PART 392—DRIVING OF COMMERCIAL MOTOR VEHICLES

Subpart A—General

Subpart B—Driving of Commercial Motor Vehicles

Subpart C—Stopped Commercial Motor Vehicles

Subpart D—Use of Lighted Lamps and Reflectors

Subpart E—License Revocation; Duties of Driver

Subpart F—Fueling Precautions

Subpart G—Prohibited Practices

Subpart H—Limiting the Use of Electronic Devices

AUTHORITY: 49 U.S.C. 13902, 31136, 31151, 31502; and 49 CFR 1.73.

SOURCE: 33 FR 19732, Dec. 25, 1968, unless otherwise noted.

EDITORIAL NOTE: Nomenclature changes to part 392 appear at 66 FR 49874, Oct. 1, 2001.

Subpart A—General

§ 392.1 Scope of the rules in this part.

Every motor carrier, its officers, agents, representatives, and employees responsible for the management, maintenance, operation, or driving of commercial motor vehicles, or the hiring, supervising, training, assigning, or dispatching of drivers, shall be instructed in and comply with the rules in this part.

[53 FR 18057, May 19, 1988, as amended at 60 FR 38746, July 28, 1995]

§ 392.2 Applicable operating rules.

Every commercial motor vehicle must be operated in accordance with the laws, ordinances, and regulations of the jurisdiction in which it is being operated. However, if a regulation of the Federal Motor Carrier Safety Administration imposes a higher standard of care than that law, ordinance or regulation, the Federal Motor Carrier Safety Administration regulation must be complied with.

[35 FR 7800, May 21, 1970, as amended at 60 FR 38746, July 28, 1995]

§ 392.3   Ill or fatigued operator.

No driver shall operate a commercial motor vehicle, and a motor carrier shall not require or permit a driver to operate a commercial motor vehicle, while the driver's ability or alertness is so impaired, or so likely to become impaired, through fatigue, illness, or any other cause, as to make it unsafe for him/her to begin or continue to operate the commercial motor vehicle. However, in a case of grave emergency where the hazard to occupants of the commercial motor vehicle or other users of the highway would be increased by compliance with this section, the driver may continue to operate the commercial motor vehicle to the nearest place at which that hazard is removed.

[35 FR 7800, May 21, 1970, as amended at 60 FR 38746, July 28, 1995]

§ 392.4   Drugs and other substances.

(a) No driver shall be on duty and possess, be under the influence of, or use, any of the following drugs or other substances:

(1) Any 21 CFR 1308.11 *Schedule I* substance;

(2) An amphetamine or any formulation thereof (including, but not limited, to "pep pills," and "bennies");

(3) A narcotic drug or any derivative thereof; or

(4) Any other substance, to a degree which renders the driver incapable of safely operating a motor vehicle.

(b) No motor carrier shall require or permit a driver to violate paragraph (a) of this section.

(c) Paragraphs (a) (2), (3), and (4) do not apply to the possession or use of a substance administered to a driver by or under the instructions of a licensed medical practitioner, as defined in § 382.107 of this subchapter, who has advised the driver that the substance will not affect the driver's ability to safely operate a motor vehicle.

(d) As used in this section, "possession" does not include possession of a substance which is manifested and transported as part of a shipment.

[61 FR 9567, Mar. 8, 1996, as amended at 62 FR 37153, July 11, 1997]

§ 392.5   Alcohol prohibition.

(a) No driver shall—

(1) Use alcohol, as defined in § 382.107 of this subchapter, or be under the influence of alcohol, within 4 hours before going on duty or operating, or having physical control of, a commercial motor vehicle; or

(2) Use alcohol, be under the influence of alcohol, or have any measured alcohol concentration or detected presence of alcohol, while on duty, or operating, or in physical control of a commercial motor vehicle; or

(3) Be on duty or operate a commercial motor vehicle while the driver possesses wine of not less than one-half of one per centum of alcohol by volume, beer as defined in 26 U.S.C. 5052(a), of the Internal Revenue Code of 1954, and distilled spirits as defined in section 5002(a)(8), of such Code. However, this does not apply to possession of wine, beer, or distilled spirits which are:

(i) Manifested and transported as part of a shipment; or

(ii) Possessed or used by bus passengers.

(b) No motor carrier shall require or permit a driver to—

(1) Violate any provision of paragraph (a) of this section; or

(2) Be on duty or operate a commercial motor vehicle if, by the driver's general appearance or conduct or by other substantiating evidence, the driver appears to have used alcohol within the preceding four hours.

(c) Any driver who is found to be in violation of the provisons of paragraph (a) or (b) of this section shall be placed out-of-service immediately for a period of 24 hours.

(1) The 24-hour out-of-service period will commence upon issuance of an out-of-service order.

(2) No driver shall violate the terms of an out-of-service order issued under this section.

(d) Any driver who is issued an out-of-service order under this section shall:

(1) Report such issuance to his/her employer within 24 hours; and

(2) Report such issuance to a State official, designated by the State which issued his/her driver's license, within 30 days unless the driver chooses to request a review of the order. In this

case, the driver shall report the order to the State official within 30 days of an affirmation of the order by either the Division Administrator or State Director for the geographical area or the Administrator.

(e) Any driver who is subject to an out-of-service order under this section may petition for review of that order by submitting a petition for review in writing within 10 days of the issuance of the order to the Division Administrator or State Director for the geographical area in which the order was issued. The Division Administrator or State Director may affirm or reverse the order. Any driver adversely affected by such order of the Regional Director of Motor Carriers may petition the Administrator for review in accordance with 49 CFR 386.13.

(49 U.S.C. 304, 1655; 49 CFR 1.48(b) and 301.60)

[47 FR 47837, Oct. 28, 1982, as amended at 52 FR 27201, July 20, 1987; 59 FR 7515, Feb. 15, 1994; 61 FR 9567, Mar. 8, 1996]

§392.6 Schedules to conform with speed limits.

No motor carrier shall schedule a run nor permit nor require the operation of any commercial motor vehicle between points in such period of time as would necessitate the commercial motor vehicle being operated at speeds greater than those prescribed by the jurisdictions in or through which the commercial motor vehicle is being operated.

[33 FR 19732, Dec. 25, 1968, as amended at 60 FR 38746, July 28, 1995]

§392.7 Equipment, inspection and use.

(a) No commercial motor vehicle shall be driven unless the driver is satisfied that the following parts and accessories are in good working order, nor shall any driver fail to use or make use of such parts and accessories when and as needed:

Service brakes, including trailer brake connections.
Parking (hand) brake.
Steering mechanism.
Lighting devices and reflectors.
Tires.
Horn.
Windshield wiper or wipers.
Rear-vision mirror or mirrors.
Coupling devices.

(b) Drivers preparing to transport intermodal equipment must make an inspection of the following components, and must be satisfied they are in good working order before the equipment is operated over the road. Drivers who operate the equipment over the road shall be deemed to have confirmed the following components were in good working order when the driver accepted the equipment:

—Service brake components that are readily visible to a driver performing as thorough a visual inspection as possible without physically going under the vehicle, and trailer brake connections
—Lighting devices, lamps, markers, and conspicuity marking material
—Wheels, rims, lugs, tires
—Air line connections, hoses, and couplers
—King pin upper coupling device
—Rails or support frames
—Tie down bolsters
—Locking pins, clevises, clamps, or hooks
—Sliders or sliding frame lock

[33 FR 19732, Dec. 25, 1968, as amended at 60 FR 38746, July 28, 1995; 73 FR 76823, Dec. 17, 2008; 74 FR 68708, Dec. 29, 2009]

§392.8 Emergency equipment, inspection and use.

No commercial motor vehicle shall be driven unless the driver thereof is satisfied that the emergency equipment required by §393.95 of this subchapter is in place and ready for use; nor shall any driver fail to use or make use of such equipment when and as needed.

[49 FR 38290, Sept. 28, 1984, as amended at 60 FR 38746, July 28, 1995]

§392.9 Inspection of cargo, cargo securement devices and systems.

(a) *General.* A driver may not operate a commercial motor vehicle and a motor carrier may not require or permit a driver to operate a commercial motor vehicle unless—

(1) The commercial motor vehicle's cargo is properly distributed and adequately secured as specified in §§393.100 through 393.136 of this subchapter.

(2) The commercial motor vehicle's tailgate, tailboard, doors, tarpaulins, spare tire and other equipment used in its operation, and the means of fastening the commercial motor vehicle's cargo, are secured; and

(3) The commercial motor vehicle's cargo or any other object does not obscure the driver's view ahead or to the right or left sides (except for drivers of self-steer dollies), interfere with the free movement of his/her arms or legs, prevent his/her free and ready access to accessories required for emergencies, or prevent the free and ready exit of any person from the commercial motor vehicle's cab or driver's compartment.

(b) *Drivers of trucks and truck tractors.* Except as provided in paragraph (b)(4) of this section, the driver of a truck or truck tractor must—

(1) Assure himself/herself that the provisions of paragraph (a) of this section have been complied with before he/she drives that commercial motor vehicle;

(2) Inspect the cargo and the devices used to secure the cargo within the first 50 miles after beginning a trip and cause any adjustments to be made to the cargo or load securement devices as necessary, including adding more securement devices, to ensure that cargo cannot shift on or within, or fall from the commercial motor vehicle; and

(3) Reexamine the commercial motor vehicle's cargo and its load securement devices during the course of transportation and make any necessary adjustment to the cargo or load securement devices, including adding more securement devices, to ensure that cargo cannot shift on or within, or fall from, the commercial motor vehicle. Reexamination and any necessary adjustments must be made whenever—

(i) The driver makes a change of his/her duty status; or

(ii) The commercial motor vehicle has been driven for 3 hours; or

(iii) The commercial motor vehicle has been driven for 150 miles, whichever occurs first.

(4) The rules in this paragraph (b) do not apply to the driver of a sealed commercial motor vehicle who has been ordered not to open it to inspect its cargo or to the driver of a commercial motor vehicle that has been loaded in a manner that makes inspection of its cargo impracticable.

[67 FR 61224, Sept. 27, 2002, as amended at 72 FR 55703, Oct. 1, 2007]

§ 392.9a   Operating authority.

(a) *Operating authority required.* A motor vehicle providing transportation requiring operating authority must not be operated—

(1) Without the required operating authority or

(2) Beyond the scope of the operating authority granted.

(b) *Penalties.* Every motor vehicle providing transportation requiring operating authority shall be ordered out of service if it is determined that the motor carrier responsible for the operation of such a vehicle is operating in violation of paragraph (a) of this section. In addition, the motor carrier may be subject to penalties in accordance with 49 U.S.C. 14901.

(c) *Administrative review.* Upon issuance of the out-of-service order under paragraph (b) of this section, the driver shall comply immediately with such order. Opportunity for review shall be provided in accordance with 5 U.S.C. 554 not later than 10 days after issuance of such order.

[71 FR 50867, Aug. 28, 2006]

Subpart B—Driving of Commercial Motor Vehicles

§ 392.10   Railroad grade crossings; stopping required.

(a) Except as provided in paragraph (b) of this section, the driver of a commercial motor vehicle specified in paragraphs (a) (1) through (6) of this section shall not cross a railroad track or tracks at grade unless he/she first: Stops the commercial motor vehicle within 50 feet of, and not closer than 15 feet to, the tracks; thereafter listens and looks in each direction along the tracks for an approaching train; and ascertains that no train is approaching. When it is safe to do so, the driver may drive the commercial motor vehicle across the tracks in a gear that permits the commercial motor vehicle to complete the crossing without a change of gears. The driver must not shift gears while crossing the tracks.

(1) Every bus transporting passengers,

(2) Every commercial motor vehicle transporting any quantity of a Division 2.3 chlorine.

(3) Every commercial motor vehicle which, in accordance with the regulations of the Department of Transportation, is required to be marked or placarded with one of the following classifications:

(i) Division 1.1

(ii) Division 1.2, or Division 1.3

(iii) Division 2.3 Poison gas

(iv) Division 4.3

(v) Class 7

(vi) Class 3 Flammable

(vii) Division 5.1

(viii) Division 2.2

(ix) Division 2.3 Chlorine

(x) Division 6.1 Poison

(xi) Division 2.2 Oxygen

(xii) Division 2.1

(xiii) Class 3 Combustible liquid

(xiv) Division 4.1

(xv) Division 5.1

(xvi) Division 5.2

(xvii) Class 8

(xviii) Division 1.4

(4) Every cargo tank motor vehicle, whether loaded or empty, used for the transportation of any hazardous material as defined in the Hazardous Materials Regulations of the Department of Transportation, parts 107 through 180 of this title.

(5) Every cargo tank motor vehicle transporting a commodity which at the time of loading has a temperature above its flashpoint as determined by §173.120 of this title.

(6) Every cargo tank motor vehicle, whether loaded or empty, transporting any commodity under exemption in accordance with the provisions of subpart B of part 107 of this title.

(b) A stop need not be made at:

(1) A streetcar crossing, or railroad tracks used exclusively for industrial switching purposes, within a business district, as defined in §390.5 of this chapter.

(2) A railroad grade crossing when a police officer or crossing flagman directs traffic to proceed,

(3) A railroad grade crossing controlled by a functioning highway traffic signal transmitting a green indication which, under local law, permits the commercial motor vehicle to proceed across the railroad tracks without slowing or stopping.

(4) An abandoned railroad grade crossing which is marked with a sign indicating that the rail line is abandoned,

(5) An industrial or spur line railroad grade crossing marked with a sign reading ''Exempt.'' Such ''Exempt'' signs shall be erected only by or with the consent of the appropriate State or local authority.

(Sec. 12, 80 Stat. 931; 49 U.S.C. 1651 note; 49 U.S.C. 304, 1655; 49 CFR 1.48(b) and 301.60)

[33 FR 19732, Dec. 25, 1968, as amended at 35 FR 7801, May 21, 1970; 38 FR 1589, Jan. 16, 1973; 40 FR 44555, Sept. 29, 1975; 45 FR 46424, July 10, 1980; 47 FR 47837, Oct. 28, 1982; 59 FR 63924, Dec. 12, 1994; 60 FR 38746, 38747, July 28, 1995]

§392.11 Railroad grade crossings; slowing down required.

Every commercial motor vehicle other than those listed in §392.10 shall, upon approaching a railroad grade crossing, be driven at a rate of speed which will permit said commercial motor vehicle to be stopped before reaching the nearest rail of such crossing and shall not be driven upon or over such crossing until due caution has been taken to ascertain that the course is clear.

[33 FR 19732, Dec. 25, 1968, as amended at 60 FR 38747, July 28, 1995]

§§392.12–392.13 [Reserved]

§392.14 Hazardous conditions; extreme caution.

Extreme caution in the operation of a commercial motor vehicle shall be exercised when hazardous conditions, such as those caused by snow, ice, sleet, fog, mist, rain, dust, or smoke, adversely affect visibility or traction. Speed shall be reduced when such conditions exist. If conditions become sufficiently dangerous, the operation of the commercial motor vehicle shall be discontinued and shall not be resumed until the commercial motor vehicle can be safely operated. Whenever compliance with the foregoing provisions of this rule increases hazard to passengers, the commercial motor vehicle may be operated to the nearest point at which the safety of passengers is assured.

[33 FR 19732, Dec. 25, 1968, as amended at 60 FR 38747, July 28, 1995]

§ 392.15 [Reserved]

§ 392.16 Use of seat belts.

A commercial motor vehicle which has a seat belt assembly installed at the driver's seat shall not be driven unless the driver has properly restrained himself/herself with the seat belt assembly.

[35 FR 10860, July 3, 1970, as amended at 60 FR 38747, July 28, 1995]

§ 392.18 [Reserved]

Subpart C—Stopped Commercial Motor Vehicles

§§ 392.20–392.21 [Reserved]

§ 392.22 Emergency signals; stopped commercial motor vehicles.

(a) *Hazard warning signal flashers.* Whenever a commercial motor vehicle is stopped upon the traveled portion of a highway or the shoulder of a highway for any cause other than necessary traffic stops, the driver of the stopped commercial motor vehicle shall immediately activate the vehicular hazard warning signal flashers and continue the flashing until the driver places the warning devices required by paragraph (b) of this section. The flashing signals shall be used during the time the warning devices are picked up for storage before movement of the commercial motor vehicle. The flashing lights may be used at other times while a commercial motor vehicle is stopped in addition to, but not in lieu of, the warning devices required by paragraph (b) of this section.

(b) *Placement of warning devices*—(1) *General rule.* Except as provided in paragraph (b)(2) of this section, whenever a commercial motor vehicle is stopped upon the traveled portion or the shoulder of a highway for any cause other than necessary traffic stops, the driver shall, as soon as possible, but in any event within 10 minutes, place the warning devices required by § 393.95 of this subchapter, in the following manner:

(i) One on the traffic side of and 4 paces (approximately 3 meters or 10 feet) from the stopped commercial motor vehicle in the direction of approaching traffic;

(ii) One at 40 paces (approximately 30 meters or 100 feet) from the stopped commercial motor vehicle in the center of the traffic lane or shoulder occupied by the commercial motor vehicle and in the direction of approaching traffic; and

(iii) One at 40 paces (approximately 30 meters or 100 feet) from the stopped commercial motor vehicle in the center of the traffic lane or shoulder occupied by the commercial motor vehicle and in the direction away from approaching traffic.

(2) *Special rules*—(i) *Fusees and liquid-burning flares.* The driver of a commercial motor vehicle equipped with only fusees or liquid-burning flares shall place a lighted fusee or liquid-burning flare at each of the locations specified in paragraph (b)(1) of this section. There shall be at least one lighted fusee or liquid-burning flare at each of the prescribed locations, as long as the commercial motor vehicle is stopped. Before the stopped commercial motor vehicle is moved, the driver shall extinguish and remove each fusee or liquid-burning flare.

(ii) *Daylight hours.* Except as provided in paragraph (b)(2)(iii) of this section, during the period lighted lamps are not required, three bidirectional reflective triangles, or three lighted fusees or liquid-burning flares shall be placed as specified in paragraph (b)(1) of this section within a time of 10 minutes. In the event the driver elects to use only fusees or liquid-burning flares in lieu of bidirectional reflective triangles or red flags, the driver must ensure that at least one fusee or liquid-burning flare remains lighted at each of the prescribed locations as long as the commercial motor vehicle is stopped or parked.

(iii) *Business or residential districts.* The placement of warning devices is not required within the business or residential district of a municipality, except during the time lighted lamps are required and when street or highway lighting is insufficient to make a commercial motor vehicle clearly discernable at a distance of 500 feet to persons on the highway.

(iv) *Hills, curves, and obstructions.* If a commercial motor vehicle is stopped within 500 feet of a curve, crest of a hill, or other obstruction to view, the driver shall place the warning signal required by paragraph (b)(1) of this section in the direction of the obstruction to view a distance of 100 feet to 500 feet from the stopped commercial motor vehicle so as to afford ample warning to other users of the highway.

(v) *Divided or one-way roads.* If a commercial motor vehicle is stopped upon the traveled portion or the shoulder of a divided or one-way highway, the driver shall place the warning devices required by paragraph (b)(1) of this section, one warning device at a distance of 200 feet and one warning device at a distance of 100 feet in a direction toward approaching traffic in the center of the lane or shoulder occupied by the commercial motor vehicle. He/she shall place one warning device at the traffic side of the commercial motor vehicle within 10 feet of the rear of the commercial motor vehicle.

(vi) *Leaking, flammable material.* If gasoline or any other flammable liquid, or combustible liquid or gas seeps or leaks from a fuel container or a commercial motor vehicle stopped upon a highway, no emergency warning signal producing a flame shall be lighted or placed except at such a distance from any such liquid or gas as will assure the prevention of a fire or explosion.

[37 FR 17175, Aug. 25, 1972, as amended at 40 FR 10685, Mar. 7, 1975; 47 FR 47837, Oct. 28, 1982; 48 FR 57139, Dec. 23, 1983; 59 FR 34711, July 6, 1994; 60 FR 38747, July 28, 1995; 63 FR 33279, June 18, 1998]

§392.24 Emergency signals; flame-producing.

No driver shall attach or permit any person to attach a lighted fusee or other flame-producing emergency signal to any part of a commercial motor vehicle.

[33 FR 19732, Dec. 25, 1968, as amended at 60 FR 38747, July 28, 1995]

§392.25 Flame producing devices.

No driver shall use or permit the use of any flame-producing emergency signal for protecting any commercial motor vehicle transporting Division 1.1, Division 1.2, or Division 1.3 explosives; any cargo tank motor vehicle used for the transportation of any Class 3 or Division 2.1, whether loaded or empty; or any commercial motor vehicle using compressed gas as a motor fuel. In lieu thereof, emergency reflective triangles, red electric lanterns, or red emergency reflectors shall be used, the placement of which shall be in the same manner as prescribed in §392.22(b).

[59 FR 63925, Dec. 12, 1994, as amended at 60 FR 38747, July 28, 1995]

Subpart D—Use of Lighted Lamps and Reflectors

§§392.30–392.32 [Reserved]

§392.33 Obscured lamps or reflective devices/material.

(a) No commercial motor vehicle shall be driven when any of the lamps or reflective devices/material required by subpart B of part 393 of this title are obscured by the tailboard, or by any part of the load or its covering, by dirt, or other added vehicle or work equipment or otherwise.

(b) *Exception.* The conspicuity treatments on the front end protection devices of the trailer may be obscured by part of the load being transported.

[70 FR 48025, Aug. 15, 2005]

Subpart E—License Revocation; Duties of Driver

§§392.40–392.41 [Reserved]

Subpart F—Fueling Precautions

§392.50 Ignition of fuel; prevention.

No driver or any employee of a motor carrier shall:

(a) Fuel a commercial motor vehicle with the engine running, except when it is necessary to run the engine to fuel the commercial motor vehicle;

(b) Smoke or expose any open flame in the vicinity of a commercial motor vehicle being fueled;

(c) Fuel a commercial motor vehicle unless the nozzle of the fuel hose is continuously in contact with the intake pipe of the fuel tank;

(d) Permit, insofar as practicable, any other person to engage in such activities as would be likely to result in fire or explosion.

[33 FR 19732, Dec. 25, 1968, as amended at 60 FR 38747, July 28, 1995]

§ 392.51 Reserve fuel; materials of trade.

Small amounts of fuel for the operation or maintenance of a commercial motor vehicle (including its auxiliary equipment) may be designated as materials of trade (see 49 CFR 171.8).

(a) The aggregate gross weight of all materials of trade on a motor vehicle may not exceed 200 kg (440 pounds).

(b) Packaging for gasoline must be made of metal or plastic and conform to requirements of 49 CFR Parts 171, 172, 173, and 178 or requirements of the Occupational Safety and Health Administration contained in 29 CFR 1910.106.

(c) For Packing Group II (including gasoline), Packing Group III (including aviation fuel and fuel oil), or ORM-D, the material is limited to 30 kg (66 pounds) or 30 L (8 gallons).

(d) For diesel fuel, the capacity of the package is limited to 450 L (119 gallons).

(e) A Division 2.1 material in a cylinder is limited to a gross weight of 100 kg (220 pounds). (A Division 2.1 material is a flammable gas, including liquefied petroleum gas, butane, propane, liquefied natural gas, and methane).

[63 FR 33279, June 18, 1998]

§ 392.52 [Reserved]

Subpart G—Prohibited Practices

§ 392.60 Unauthorized persons not to be transported.

(a) Unless specifically authorized in writing to do so by the motor carrier under whose authority the commercial motor vehicle is being operated, no driver shall transport any person or permit any person to be transported on any commercial motor vehicle other than a bus. When such authorization is issued, it shall state the name of the person to be transported, the points where the transportation is to begin and end, and the date upon which such

authority expires. No written authorization, however, shall be necessary for the transportation of:

(1) Employees or other persons assigned to a commercial motor vehicle by a motor carrier;

(2) Any person transported when aid is being rendered in case of an accident or other emergency;

(3) An attendant delegated to care for livestock.

(b) This section shall not apply to the operation of commercial motor vehicles controlled and operated by any farmer and used in the transportation of agricultural commodities or products thereof from his/her farm or in the transportation of supplies to his/her farm.

[60 FR 38747, July 28, 1995]

§ 392.61 [Reserved]

§ 392.62 Safe operation, buses.

No person shall drive a bus and a motor carrier shall not require or permit a person to drive a bus unless—

(a) All standees on the bus are rearward of the standee line or other means prescribed in § 393.90 of this subchapter;

(b) All aisle seats in the bus conform to the requirements of § 393.91 of this subchapter; and

(c) Baggage or freight on the bus is stowed and secured in a manner which assures—

(1) Unrestricted freedom of movement to the driver and his proper operation of the bus;

(2) Unobstructed access to all exits by any occupant of the bus; and

(3) Protection of occupants of the bus against injury resulting from the falling or displacement of articles transported in the bus.

[63 FR 33278, June 18, 1998]

§ 392.63 Towing or pushing loaded buses.

No disabled bus with passengers aboard shall be towed or pushed; nor shall any person use or permit to be used a bus with passengers aboard for the purpose of towing or pushing any disabled motor vehicle, except in such circumstances where the hazard to passengers would be increased by observance of the foregoing provisions of this section, and then only in traveling to the nearest point where the safety of the passengers is assured.

[33 FR 19732, Dec. 25, 1968, as amended at 60 FR 38747, July 28, 1995]

§ 392.64 Riding within closed commercial motor vehicles without proper exits.

No person shall ride within the closed body of any commercial motor vehicle unless there are means on the inside thereof of obtaining exit. Said means shall be in such condition as to permit ready operation by the occupant.

[33 FR 19732, Dec. 25, 1968, as amended at 60 FR 38747, July 28, 1995]

§ 392.65 [Reserved]

§ 392.66 Carbon monoxide; use of commercial motor vehicle when detected.

(a) No person shall dispatch or drive any commercial motor vehicle or permit any passengers thereon, when the following conditions are known to exist, until such conditions have been remedied or repaired:

(1) Where an occupant has been affected by carbon monoxide;

(2) Where carbon monoxide has been detected in the interior of the commercial motor vehicle;

(3) When a mechanical condition of the commercial motor vehicle is discovered which would be likely to produce a hazard to the occupants by reason of carbon monoxide.

(b) [Reserved]

[60 FR 38747, July 28, 1995]

§ 392.67 Heater, flame-producing; on commercial motor vehicle in motion.

No open flame heater used in the loading or unloading of the commodity transported shall be in operation while the commercial motor vehicle is in motion.

[33 FR 19732, Dec. 25, 1968, as amended at 60 FR 38747, July 28, 1995]

§§ 392.68–392.69 [Reserved]

§ 392.71 Radar detectors; use and/or possession.

(a) No driver shall use a radar detector in a commercial motor vehicle, or operate a commercial motor vehicle that is equipped with or contains any radar detector.

(b) No motor carrier shall require or permit a driver to violate paragraph (a) of this section.

[58 FR 67375, Dec. 21, 1993]

Subpart H—Limiting the Use of Electronic Devices

§ 392.80 Prohibition against texting.

(a) *Prohibition.* No driver shall engage in texting while driving.

(b) *Motor carriers.* No motor carrier shall allow or require its drivers to engage in texting while driving.

(c) *Definition.* For the purpose of this section only, *driving* means operating a commercial motor vehicle, with the motor running, including while temporarily stationary because of traffic, a traffic control device, or other momentary delays. Driving does not include operating a commercial motor vehicle with or without the motor running when the driver moved the vehicle to the side of, or off, a highway, as defined in 49 CFR 390.5, and halted in a location where the vehicle can safely remain stationary.

(d) *Exceptions—*(1) *School bus operations and vehicles designed or used to transport 9 to 15 passengers, including the driver, not for direct compensation.* The provisions of § 390.3(f)(1) and (6) are not applicable to this section.

(2) *Emergency use.* Texting while driving is permissible by drivers of a commercial motor vehicle when necessary to communicate with law enforcement officials or other emergency services.

[75 FR 59136, Sept. 27, 2010]

PART 393—PARTS AND ACCESSORIES NECESSARY FOR SAFE OPERATION

Subpart A—General

Subpart J—Frames, Cab and Body Components, Wheels, Steering, and Suspension Systems

AUTHORITY: 49 U.S.C. 322, 31136, 31151 and
31502; sec. 1041(b), Pub. L. 102–240, 105 Stat.
1914, 1993 (1991); and 49 CFR 1.73.

EFFECTIVE DATE NOTE: At 76 FR 56321,
Sept. 13, 2011, the authority citation for part
393 was revised, effective Oct. 13, 2011. For
the convenience of the user, the revised text
is set forth as follows:
AUTHORITY: 49 U.S.C. 31136, 31151, and
31502; Sec. 1041(b) of Pub. L. 102–240, 105 Stat.
1914, 1993 (1991); and 49 CFR 1.73.

SOURCE: 33 FR 19735, Dec. 25, 1968, unless
otherwise noted.

EDITORIAL NOTE: Nomenclature changes to
part 393 appear at 66 FR 49874, Oct. 1, 2001.

Subpart A—General

SOURCE: 53 FR 49384, Dec. 7, 1988, unless
otherwise noted.

§393.1 Scope of the rules in this part.

(a) The rules in this part establish
minimum standards for commercial
motor vehicles as defined in §390.5 of
this title. Only motor vehicles (as defined in §390.5) and combinations of
motor vehicles which meet the definition of a commercial motor vehicle are
subject to the requirements of this
part. All requirements that refer to
motor vehicles with a GVWR below
4,536 kg (10,001 pounds) are applicable
only when the motor vehicle or combination of motor vehicles meets the
definition of a commercial motor vehicle.

(b)(1) Every motor carrier and its employees must be knowledgeable of and
comply with the requirements and
specifications of this part.

(2) Every intermodal equipment provider and its employees or agents responsible for the inspection, repair, and
maintenance of intermodal equipment
interchanged to motor carriers must be
knowledgeable of and comply with the
applicable requirements and specifications of this part.

(c) No motor carrier may operate a
commercial motor vehicle, or cause or
permit such vehicle to be operated, unless it is equipped in accordance with
the requirements and specifications of
this part.

(d) No intermodal equipment provider may operate intermodal equipment, or cause or permit such equipment to be operated, unless it is
equipped in accordance with the requirements and specifications of this
part.

[70 FR 48025, Aug. 15, 2005, as amended at 73
FR 76823, Dec. 17, 2008]

§393.3 Additional equipment and accessories.

Nothing contained in this subchapter
shall be construed to prohibit the use
of additional equipment and accessories, not inconsistent with or prohibited by this subchapter, provided such
equipment and accessories do not decrease the safety of operation of the
motor vehicles on which they are used.

§393.5 Definitions.

As used in this part, the following
words and terms are construed to
mean:

Aggregate working load limit. The summation of the working load limits or
restraining capacity of all devices used
to secure an article of cargo on a vehicle.

Agricultural commodity trailer. A trailer that is designed to transport bulk agricultural commodities in off-road harvesting sites and to a processing plant or storage location, as evidenced by skeletal construction that accommodates harvest containers, a maximum length of 28 feet, and an arrangement of air control lines and reservoirs that minimizes damage in field operations.

Air brake system. A system, including an air-over-hydraulic brake subsystem, that uses air as a medium for transmitting pressure or force from the driver control to the service brake, but does not include a system that uses compressed air or vacuum only to assist the driver in applying muscular force to hydraulic or mechanical components.

Air-over-hydraulic brake subsystem. A subsystem of the air brake system that uses compressed air to transmit a force from the driver control to a hydraulic brake system to actuate the service brakes.

Anchor point. Part of the structure, fitting or attachment on a vehicle or article of cargo to which a tiedown is attached.

Antilock Brake System or *ABS* means a portion of a service brake system that automatically controls the degree of rotational wheel slip during braking by:

(1) Sensing the rate of angular rotation of the wheels;

(2) Transmitting signals regarding the rate of wheel angular rotation to one or more controlling devices which interpret those signals and generate responsive controlling output signals; and

(3) Transmitting those controlling signals to one or more modulators which adjust brake actuating forces in response to those signals.

Article of cargo. A unit of cargo, other than a liquid, gas, or aggregate that lacks physical structure (e.g., grain, gravel, etc.) including articles grouped together so that they can be handled as a single unit or unitized by wrapping, strapping, banding or edge protection device(s).

Auxiliary driving lamp. A lighting device mounted to provide illumination forward of the vehicle which supplements the upper beam of a standard headlighting system. It is not intended for use alone or with the lower beam of a standard headlamp system.

Bell pipe concrete. Pipe whose flanged end is of larger diameter than its barrel.

Blocking. A structure, device or another substantial article placed against or around an article of cargo to prevent horizontal movement of the article of cargo.

Boat trailer. A trailer designed with cradle-type mountings to transport a boat and configured to permit launching of the boat from the rear of the trailer.

Bracing. A structure, device, or another substantial article placed against an article of cargo to prevent it from tipping, that may also prevent it from shifting.

Brake. An energy conversion mechanism used to stop, or hold a vehicle stationary.

Brake power assist unit. A device installed in a hydraulic brake system that reduces the operator effort required to actuate the system, but which if inoperative does not prevent the operator from braking the vehicle by a continued application of muscular force on the service brake control.

Brake power unit. A device installed in a brake system that provides the energy required to actuate the brakes, either directly or indirectly through an auxiliary device, with the operator action consisting only of modulating the energy application level.

Brake tubing/hose. Metallic brake tubing, nonmetallic brake tubing and brake hose are conduits or lines used in a brake system to transmit or contain the medium (fluid or vacuum) used to apply the motor vehicle's brakes.

Chassis. The load-supporting frame of a commercial motor vehicle, exclusive of any appurtenances which might be added to accommodate cargo.

Clearance Lamps. Lamps that provide light to the front or rear, mounted on the permanent structure of the vehicle, such that they indicate the overall width of the vehicle.

Container chassis trailer. A semitrailer of skeleton construction limited to a bottom frame, one or more axles, specially built and fitted with locking devices for the transport of intermodal cargo containers, so that when the chassis and container are assembled, the units serve the same function as an over the road trailer.

Converter dolly. A motor vehicle consisting of a chassis equipped with one or more axles, a fifth wheel and/or equivalent mechanism, and drawbar, the attachment of which converts a semitrailer to a full trailer.

Crib-type log trailer means a trailer equipped with stakes, bunks, a front-end structure, and a rear structure to restrain logs. The stakes prevent movement of the logs from side to side on the vehicle while the front-end and rear structures prevent movement of the logs from front to back on the vehicle.

Curb weight. The weight of a motor vehicle with standard equipment, maximum capacity of fuel, oil, and coolant; and, if so equipped, air conditioning and additional weight of optional engine. Curb weight does not include the driver.

Dunnage. All loose materials used to support and protect cargo.

Dunnage bag. An inflatable bag intended to fill otherwise empty space between articles of cargo, or between articles of cargo and the wall of the vehicle.

Edge protector. A device placed on the exposed edge of an article to distribute tiedown forces over a larger area of cargo than the tiedown itself, to protect the tie-down and/or cargo from damage, and to allow the tiedown to slide freely when being tensioned.

Electric brake system. A system that uses electric current to actuate the service brake.

Emergency brake. A mechanism designed to stop a motor vehicle after a failure of the service brake system.

Emergency brake system. A mechanism designed to stop a vehicle after a single failure occurs in the service brake system of a part designed to contain compressed air or brake fluid or vacuum (except failure of a common valve, manifold brake fluid housing or brake chamber housing).

Fifth wheel. A device mounted on a truck tractor or similar towing vehicle

(e.g., converter dolly) which interfaces with and couples to the upper coupler assembly of a semitrailer.

Frame vehicle. A vehicle with skeletal structure fitted with one or more bunk units for transporting logs. A bunk unit consists of U-shaped front and rear bunks that together cradle logs. The bunks are welded, gusseted or otherwise firmly fastened to the vehicle's main beams, and are an integral part of the vehicle.

Friction mat. A device placed between the deck of a vehicle and article of cargo, or between articles of cargo, intended to provide greater friction than exists naturally between these surfaces.

Front fog lamp. A lighting device whose beam provides downward illumination forward of the vehicle and close to the ground, and is to be used only under conditions of rain, snow, dust, smoke or fog. A pair of fog lamps may be used alone, with parking, tail, side, marker, clearance and identification lamps, or with a lower beam headlamp at the driver's discretion in accordance with state and local use law.

Fuel tank fitting. Any removable device affixed to an opening in the fuel tank with the exception of the filler cap.

g. The acceleration due to gravity, 32.2 ft/sec^2 (9.81 m/sec^2).

Grommet. A device that serves as a support and protection to that which passes through it.

Hazard warning signal. Lamps that flash simultaneously to the front and rear, on both the right and left sides of a commercial motor vehicle, to indicate to an approaching driver the presence of a vehicular hazard.

Head lamps. Lamps used to provide general illumination ahead of a motor vehicle.

Heater. Any device or assembly of devices or appliances used to heat the interior of any motor vehicle. This includes a catalytic heater which must meet the requirements of § 177.834(1)(2) of this title when Class 3 (flammable liquid) or Division 2.1 (flammable gas) is transported.

Heavy hauler trailer. A trailer which has one or more of the following characteristics, but which is not a container chassis trailer:

(1) Its brake lines are designed to adapt to separation or extension of the vehicle frame; or

(2) Its body consists only of a platform whose primary cargo-carrying surface is not more than 1,016 mm (40 inches) above the ground in an unloaded condition, except that it may include sides that are designed to be easily removable and a permanent "front-end structure" as that term is used in § 393.106 of this title.

Hook-lift container. A specialized container, primarily used to contain and transport materials in the waste, recycling, construction/demolition and scrap industries, which is used in conjunction with specialized vehicles, in which the container is loaded and unloaded onto a tilt frame body by an articulating hook-arm.

Hydraulic brake system. A system that uses hydraulic fluid as a medium for transmitting force from a service brake control to the service brake, and that may incorporate a brake power assist unit, or a brake power unit.

Identification lamps. Lamps used to identify certain types of commercial motor vehicles.

Integral securement system. A system on certain roll-on/roll-off containers and hook-lift containers and their related transport vehicles in which compatible front and rear hold down devices are mated to provide securement of the complete vehicle and its articles of cargo.

Lamp. A device used to produce artificial light.

Length of a manufactured home. The largest exterior length in the traveling mode, including any projections which contain interior space. Length does not include bay windows, roof projections, overhangs, or eaves under which there is no interior space, nor does it include drawbars, couplings or hitches.

License plate lamp. A lamp used to illuminate the license plate on the rear of a motor vehicle.

Longwood. All logs that are not shortwood, i.e., are over 4.9 m (16 feet) long. Such logs are usually described as long logs or treelength.

Low chassis vehicle. (1) A trailer or semitrailer manufactured on or after January 26, 1998, having a chassis which extends behind the rearmost point of the rearmost tires and which has a lower rear surface that meets the guard width, height, and rear surface requirements of § 571.224 in effect on the date of manufacture, or a subsequent edition.

(2) A motor vehicle, not described by paragraph (1) of this definition, having a chassis which extends behind the rearmost point of the rearmost tires and which has a lower rear surface that meets the guard configuration requirements of § 393.86(b)(1).

Manufactured home means a structure, transportable in one or more sections, which in the traveling mode, is eight body feet or more in width or forty body feet or more in length, or, when erected on site, is three hundred twenty or more square feet, and which is built on a permanent chassis and designed to be used as a dwelling with or without a permanent foundation when connected to the required utilities, and includes the plumbing, heating, air-conditioning, and electrical systems contained therein. Calculations used to determine the number of square feet in a structure will be based on the structure's exterior dimensions measured at the largest horizontal projections when erected on site. These dimensions will include all expandable rooms, cabinets, and other projections containing interior space, but do not include bay windows. This term includes all structures which meet the *above* requirements except the size requirements and with respect to which the manufacturer voluntarily files a certification pursuant to 24 CFR 3282.13 and complies with the standards set forth in 24 CFR part 3280.

Metal coil means an article of cargo comprised of elements, mixtures, compounds, or alloys commonly known as metal, metal foil, metal leaf, forged metal, stamped metal, metal wire, metal rod, or metal chain that are packaged as a roll, coil, spool, wind, or wrap, including plastic or rubber coated electrical wire and communications cable

Multi-piece windshield. A windshield consisting of two or more windshield glazing surface areas.

Parking brake system. A mechanism designed to prevent the movement of a stationary motor vehicle.

Play. Any free movement of components.

Pulpwood trailer. A trailer or semitrailer that is designed exclusively for harvesting logs or pulpwood and constructed with a skeletal frame with no means for attachment of a solid bed, body, or container.

Rail vehicle. A vehicle whose skeletal structure is fitted with stakes at the front and rear to contain logs loaded crosswise.

Rear extremity. The rearmost point on a motor vehicle that falls above a horizontal plane located 560 mm (22 inches) above the ground and below a horizontal plane located 1,900 mm (75 inches) above the ground when the motor vehicle is stopped on level ground; unloaded; its fuel tanks are full; the tires (and air suspension, if so equipped) are inflated in accordance with the manufacturer's recommendations; and the motor vehicle's cargo doors, tailgate, or other permanent structures are positioned as they normally are when the vehicle is in motion. Nonstructural protrusions such as taillamps, rubber bumpers, hinges and latches are excluded from the determination of the rearmost point.

Reflective material. A material conforming to Federal Specification L-S-300, "Sheeting and Tape, Reflective; Non-exposed Lens, Adhesive Backing," (September 7, 1965) meeting the performance standard in either Table 1 or Table 1A of SAE Standard J594f, "Reflex Reflectors" (January, 1977).

Reflex reflector. A device which is used on a vehicle to give an indication to an approaching driver by reflected lighted from the lamps on the approaching vehicle.

Saddle-mount. A device, designed and constructed as to be readily demountable, used in driveaway-towaway operations to perform the functions of a conventional fifth wheel:

(1) *Upper-half.* *Upper-half* of a "saddle-mount" means that part of the device which is securely attached to the towed vehicle and maintains a fixed position relative thereto, but does not include the "king-pin;"

(2) *Lower-half.* *Lower-half* of a "saddle-mount" means that part of the device which is securely attached to the towing vehicle and maintains a fixed position relative thereto but does not include the "king-pin;" and

(3) *King-pin.* *King-pin* means that device which is used to connect the "upper-half" to the "lower-half" in such manner as to permit relative movement in a horizontal plane between the towed and towing vehicles.

Service brake system. A primary brake system used for slowing and stopping a vehicle.

Shoring bar. A device placed transversely between the walls of a vehicle and cargo to prevent cargo from tipping or shifting.

Shortwood. All logs typically up to 4.9 m (16 feet) long. Such logs are often described as cut-up logs, cut-to-length logs, bolts or pulpwood. Shortwood may be loaded lengthwise or crosswise, though that loaded crosswise is usually no more than 2.6 m (102 inches) long.

Sided vehicle. A vehicle whose cargo compartment is enclosed on all four sides by walls of sufficient strength to contain articles of cargo, where the walls may include latched openings for loading and unloading, and includes vans, dump bodies, and a sided intermodal container carried by a vehicle.

Side extremity. The outermost point on a side of the motor vehicle that is above a horizontal plane located 560 mm (22 inches) above the ground, below a horizontal plane located 1,900 mm (75 inches) above the ground, and between a transverse vertical plane tangent to the rear extremity of the vehicle and a transverse vertical plane located 305 mm (12 inches) forward of that plane when the vehicle is unloaded; its fuel tanks are full; and the tires (and air suspension, if so equipped) are inflated in accordance with the manufacturer's recommendations. Non-structural protrusions such as taillights, hinges and latches are excluded from the determination of the outermost point.

Side marker lamp (Intermediate). A lamp mounted on the side, on the permanent structure of the motor vehicle that provides light to the side to indicate the approximate middle of the vehicle, when the motor vehicle is 9.14 meters (30 feet) or more in length.

Side marker lamps. Lamps mounted on the side, on the permanent structure of the motor vehicle as near as practicable to the front and rear of the vehicle, that provide light to the side to indicate the overall length of the motor vehicle.

Special purpose vehicle. (1) A trailer or semitrailer manufactured on or after January 26, 1998, having work-performing equipment that, while the motor vehicle is in transit, resides in or moves through the area that could be occupied by the horizontal member of the rear impact guard, as defined by the guard width, height and rear surface requirements of § 571.224 (paragraphs S5.1.1 through S5.1.3), in effect on the date of manufacture, or a subsequent edition.

(2) A motor vehicle, not described by paragraph (1) of this definition, having work-performing equipment that, while the motor vehicle is in transit, resides in or moves through the area that could be occupied by the horizontal member of the rear impact guard, as defined by the guard width, height and rear surface requirements of § 393.86(b)(1).

Split service brake system. A brake system consisting of two or more subsystems actuated by a single control designed so that a leakage-type failure of a pressure component in a single subsystem (except structural failure of a housing that is common to two or more subsystems) shall not impair the operation of any other subsystem.

Steering wheel lash. The condition in which the steering wheel may be turned through some part of a revolution without associated movement of the front wheels.

Stop lamps. Lamps shown to the rear of a motor vehicle to indicate that the service brake system is engaged.

Surge brake. A self-contained, permanently closed hydraulic brake system for trailers that relies on inertial forces, developed in response to the braking action of the towing vehicle, applied to a hydraulic device mounted on or connected to the tongue of the trailer, to slow down or stop the towed vehicle.

Tail lamps. Lamps used to designate the rear of a motor vehicle.

Tiedown. A combination of securing devices which forms an assembly that attaches articles of cargo to, or restrains articles of cargo on, a vehicle or trailer, and is attached to anchor point(s).

Tow bar. A strut or column-like device temporarily attached between the rear of a towing vehicle and the front of the vehicle being towed.

Tractor-pole trailer. A combination vehicle that carries logs lengthwise so that they form the body of the vehicle. The logs are supported by a bunk located on the rear of the tractor, and another bunk on the skeletal trailer. The tractor bunk may rotate about a vertical axis, and the trailer may have a fixed, scoping, or cabled reach, or other mechanical freedom, to allow it to turn.

Trailer kingpin. A pin (with a flange on its lower end) which extends vertically from the front of the underside of a semitrailer and which locks into a fifth wheel.

Turn signals. Lamps used to indicate a change in direction by emitting a flashing light on the side of a motor vehicle towards which a turn will be made.

Upper coupler assembly. A structure consisting of an upper coupler plate, king-pin and supporting framework which interfaces with and couples to a fifth wheel.

Upper coupler plate. A plate structure through which the king-pin neck and collar extend. The bottom surface of the plate contacts the fifth wheel when coupled.

Vacuum brake system. A system that uses a vacuum and atmospheric pressure for transmitting a force from the driver control to the service brake, not including a system that uses vacuum only to assist the driver in applying muscular force to hydraulic or mechanical components.

Void filler. Material used to fill a space between articles of cargo and the structure of the vehicle that has sufficient strength to prevent movement of the articles of cargo.

Well. The depression formed between two cylindrical articles of cargo when they are laid with their eyes horizontal and parallel against each other.

Wheels back vehicle. (1) A trailer or semitrailer manufactured on or after January 26, 1998, whose rearmost axle is permanently fixed and is located such that the rearmost surface of the tires (of the size recommended by the vehicle manufacturer for the rear axle) is not more than 305 mm (12 inches) forward of the transverse vertical plane tangent to the rear extremity of the vehicle.

(2) A motor vehicle, not described by paragraph (1) of this definition, whose rearmost axle is permanently fixed and is located such that the rearmost surface of the tires (of the size recommended by the vehicle manufacturer for the rear axle) is not more than 610 mm (24 inches) forward of the transverse vertical plane tangent to the rear extremity of the vehicle.

Width of a manufactured home. The largest exterior width in the traveling mode, including any projections which contain interior space. Width does not include bay windows, roof projections, overhangs, or eaves under which there is no interior space.

Windshield. The principal forward facing glazed surface provided for forward vision in operating a motor vehicle.

Working load limit (WLL). The maximum load that may be applied to a component of a cargo securement system during normal service, usually assigned by the manufacturer of the component.

[53 FR 49384, Dec. 7, 1988, as amended at 63 FR 8339, Feb. 18, 1998; 63 FR 24465, May 4, 1998; 64 FR 47707, Sept. 1, 1999; 67 FR 61224, Sept. 27, 2002; 68 FR 56208, Sept. 30, 2003; 70 FR 48026, Aug. 15, 2005; 71 FR 35832, June 22, 2006; 72 FR 9870, Mar. 6, 2007]

§393.7 Matter incorporated by reference.

(a) *Incorporation by reference.* Part 393 includes references to certain matter or materials, as listed in paragraph (b) of this section. The text of the materials is not included in the regulations contained in part 393. The materials are hereby made a part of the regulations in part 393. The Director of the Federal Register has approved the materials incorporated by reference in accordance with 5 U.S.C. 552(a) and 1 CFR part 51. For materials subject to change, only the specific version approved by the Director of the Federal Register and specified in the regulation are incorporated. Material is incorporated as it exists on the date of the approval and a notice of any change in these materials will be published in the FEDERAL REGISTER.

(b) *Matter or materials referenced in part 393.* The matter or materials listed in this paragraph are incorporated by reference in the corresponding sections noted.

(1) Auxiliary Upper Beam Lamps, Society of Automotive Engineers (SAE) J581, July 2004, incorporation by reference approved for §393.24(b).

(2) Front Fog Lamp, SAE J583, August 2004, incorporation by reference approved for §393.24(b).

(3) Stop Lamps for Use on Motor Vehicles Less Than 2032 mm in Overall Width, SAE J586, March 2000, incorporation by reference approved for §393.25(c).

(4) Stop Lamps and Front- and Rear-Turn Signal Lamps for Use on Motor Vehicles 2032 mm or more in Overall Width, SAE J2261, January 2002, incorporated by reference approved for §393.25 (c).

(5) Tail Lamps (Rear Position Lamps) for Use on Motor Vehicles Less Than 2032 mm in Overall Width, SAE J585, March 2000, incorporation by reference approved for §393.25(c).

(6) Tail Lamps (Rear Position Lamps) for Use on Vehicles 2032 mm or More in Overall Width, SAE J2040, March 2002, incorporation by reference approved for §393.25(c).

(7) Turn Signal Lamps for Use on Motor Vehicles Less Than 2032 mm in Overall Width, SAE J588, March 2000, incorporation by reference approved for §393.25(c).

(8) Sidemarker Lamps for Use on Road Vehicles Less Than 2032 mm in Overall Width, SAE J592, August 2000, incorporation by reference approved for §393.25(c).

(9) Directional Flashing Optical Warning Devices for Authorized Emergency, Maintenance, and Service Vehicles, SAE J595, January 2005, incorporation by reference approved for §393.25(e).

(10) Optical Warning Devices for Authorized Emergency, Maintenance, and Service Vehicles, SAE J845, May 1997,

incorporation by reference approved for § 393.25(e).

(11) Gaseous Discharge Warning Lamp for Authorized Emergency, Maintenance, and Service Vehicles, SAE J1318, May 1998, incorporation by reference approved for § 393.25(e).

(12) Reflex Reflectors, SAE J594, December 2003, incorporation by reference approved for § 393.26(c).

(13) Standard Specification for Retroreflective Sheeting for Traffic Control, American Society of Testing and Materials, ASTM D 4956–04, 2004, incorporation by reference approved for § 393.26(c).

(14) Automobile, Truck, Truck-Tractor, Trailer, and Motor Coach Wiring, SAE J1292, October 1981, incorporation by reference approved for § 393.28.

(15) Long Stroke Air Brake Actuator Marking, SAE J1817, July 2001, incorporation by reference approved for § 393.47(e).

(16) American National Standard for Safety Glazing Materials for Glazing Motor Vehicles and Motor Vehicle Equipment Operating on Land Highways-Safety Standard, SAE Z26.1–1996, August 1997, incorporation by reference approved for § 393.62(d).

(17) Specification for Sound Level Meters, American National Standards Institute, S1.4–1983, incorporation by reference approved for § 393.94(c).

(18) Standard Specification for Strapping, Flat Steel and Seals, American Society for Testing and Materials (ASTM), D3953–97, February 1998, incorporation by reference approved for § 393.104(e).

(19) Welded Steel Chain Specifications, National Association of Chain Manufacturers, September 28, 2005, incorporation by reference approved for § 393.104(e).

(20) Recommended Standard Specification for Synthetic Web Tiedowns, Web Sling and Tiedown Association, WSTDA-T1, 1998, incorporation by reference approved for § 393.104(e).

(21) Wire Rope Users Manual, 2nd Edition, Wire Rope Technical Board November 1985, incorporation by reference approved for § 393.104(e).

(22) Cordage Institute rope standards approved for incorporation into § 393.104(e):

(i) PETRS–2, Polyester Fiber Rope, 3-Strand and 8-Strand Constructions, January 1993;

(ii) PPRS–2, Polypropylene Fiber Rope, 3-Strand and 8-Strand Constructions, August 1992;

(iii) CRS–1, Polyester/Polypropylene Composite Rope Specifications, Three-Strand and Eight-Strand Standard Construction, May 1979;

(iv) NRS–1, Nylon Rope Specifications, Three-Strand and Eight-Strand Standard Construction, May 1979; and

(v) C–1, Double Braided Nylon Rope Specifications DBN, January 1984.

(c) *Availability.* The materials incorporated by reference are available as follows:

(1) Standards of the Underwriters Laboratories, Inc. Information and copies may be obtained by writing to: Underwriters Laboratories, Inc., 333 Pfingsten Road, Northbrook, Illinois 60062.

(2) Specifications of the American Society for Testing and Materials. Information and copies may be obtained by writing to: American Society for Testing and Materials, 100 Barr Harbor Drive, West Conshohocken, Pennsylvania 19428–2959.

(3) Specifications of the National Association of Chain Manufacturers. Information and copies may be obtained by writing to: National Association of Chain Manufacturers, P.O. Box 22681, Lehigh Valley, Pennsylvania 18002–2681.

(4) Specifications of the Web Sling and Tiedown Association. Information and copies may be obtained by writing to: Web Sling and Tiedown Association, Inc., 5024–R Campbell Boulevard, Baltimore, Maryland 21236–5974.

(5) Manuals of the Wire Rope Technical Board. Information and copies may be obtained by writing to: Wire Rope Technical Committee, P.O. Box 849, Stevensville, Maryland 21666.

(6) Standards of the Cordage Institute. Information and copies may be obtained by writing to: Cordage Institute, 350 Lincoln Street, # 115, Hingham, Massachusetts 02043.

(7) Standards of the Society of Automotive Engineers (SAE). Information and copies may be obtained by writing to: Society of Automotive Engineers, Inc., 400 Commonwealth Drive, Warrendale, Pennsylvania 15096.

(8) Standards of the American National Standards Institute (ANSI). Information and copies may be obtained by writing to: American National Standards Institute, 25 West 43rd Street, New York, New York 10036.

(9) [Reserved].

(10) All of the materials incorporated by reference are available for inspection at:

(i) Federal Motor Carrier Safety Administration, Office of Bus and Truck Standards and Operations (MC–PS), 1200 New Jersey Ave., SE., Washington, DC 20590–0001; and

(ii) The National Archives and Records Administration (NARA). For information on the availability of this material at NARA, call 202–741–6030, or go to: *http://www.archives.gov/federal_register/code_of_federal_regulations/ibr_locations.html.*

[67 FR 61225, Sept. 27, 2002, as amended at 70 FR 48027, Aug. 15, 2005; 71 FR 35832, June 22, 2006; 72 FR 55703, Oct. 1, 2007]

Subpart B—Lamps, Reflective Devices, and Electrical Wiring

§393.9 Lamps operable, prohibition of obstructions of lamps and reflectors.

(a) All lamps required by this subpart shall be capable of being operated at all times. This paragraph shall not be construed to require that any auxiliary or additional lamp be capable of operating at all times.

(b) Lamps and reflective devices/material required by this subpart must not be obscured by the tailboard, or by any part of the load, or its covering by dirt, or other added vehicle or work equipment, or otherwise. Exception: The conspicuity treatments on the front end protection devices may be obscured by part of the load being transported.

[70 FR 48027, Aug. 15, 2005]

§393.11 Lamps and reflective devices.

(a)(1) *Lamps and reflex reflectors.* Table 1 specifies the requirements for lamps, reflective devices and associated equipment by the type of commercial motor vehicle. The diagrams in this section illustrate the position of the lamps, reflective devices and associated equipment specified in Table 1. All commercial motor vehicles manufactured on or after December 25, 1968, must, at a minimum, meet the applicable requirements of 49 CFR 571.108 (FMVSS No. 108) in effect at the time of manufacture of the vehicle. Commercial motor vehicles manufactured before December 25, 1968, must, at a minimum, meet the requirements of subpart B of part 393 in effect at the time of manufacture.

(2) *Exceptions:* Pole trailers and trailer converter dollies must meet the part 393 requirements for lamps, reflective devices and electrical equipment in effect at the time of manufacture. Trailers which are equipped with conspicuity material which meets the requirements of §393.11(b) are not required to be equipped with the reflex reflectors listed in Table 1 if—

(i) The conspicuity material is placed at the locations where reflex reflectors are required by Table 1; and

(ii) The conspicuity material when installed on the motor vehicle meets the visibility requirements for the reflex reflectors.

(b) *Conspicuity Systems.* Each trailer of 2,032 mm (80 inches) or more overall width, and with a GVWR over 4,536 kg (10,000 pounds), manufactured on or after December 1, 1993, except pole trailers and trailers designed exclusively for living or office use, shall be equipped with either retroreflective sheeting that meets the requirements of FMVSS No. 108 (S5.7.1), reflex reflectors that meet the requirements FMVSS No. 108 (S5.7.2), or a combination of retroreflective sheeting and reflex reflectors that meet the requirements of FMVSS No. 108 (S5.7.3). The conspicuity system shall be installed and located as specified in FMVSS No. 108 [S5.7.1.4 (for retroreflective sheeting), S5.7.2.2 (for reflex reflectors), S5.7.3 (for a combination of sheeting and reflectors)] and have certification and markings as required by S5.7.1.5 (for retroreflective tape) and S5.7.2.3 (for reflex reflectors).

(c) *Prohibition on the use of amber stop lamps and tail lamps.* No commercial motor vehicle may be equipped with an amber stop lamp, a tail lamp, or other lamp which is optically combined with an amber stop lamp or tail lamp.

TABLE 1 OF §393.11—REQUIRED LAMPS AND REFLECTORS ON COMMERCIAL MOTOR VEHICLES

Item on the vehicle	Quantity	Color	Location	Position	Height above the road surface in millimeters (mm) (with English units in parenthesis) measured from the center of the lamp at curb weight	Vehicles for which the devices are required
Headlamps	2	White	Front	On the front at the same height, with an equal number at each side of the vertical center line as far apart as practicable.	Not less than 559 mm (22 inches) nor more than 1,372 mm (54 inches).	A, B, C
Turn signal (front). See footnotes #2 and 12.	2	Amber	At or near the front.	One on each side of the vertical centerline at the same height and as far apart as practicable.	Not less than 381 mm (15 inches) nor more than 2,108 mm (83 inches).	A, B, C
Identification lamps (front). See footnote #1.	3	Amber	Front	As close as practicable to the top of the vehicle, at the same height, and as close as practicable to the vertical centerline of the vehicle (or the vertical centerline of the cab where different from the centerline of the vehicle) with lamp centers spaced not less than 152 mm (6 inches) or more than 305 mm (12 inches) apart. Alternatively, the front lamps may be located as close as practicable to the top of the cab.	All three on the same level as close as practicable to the top of the motor vehicle.	B, C
Tail lamps. See footnotes #5 and 11	2	Red	Rear	One lamp on each side of the vertical centerline at the same height and as far apart as practicable.	Both on the same level between 381 mm (15 inches) and 1,829 mm (72 inches).	A, B, C, D, E, F, G, H

417

TABLE 1 OF § 393.11—REQUIRED LAMPS AND REFLECTORS ON COMMERCIAL MOTOR VEHICLES

Item on the vehicle	Quantity	Color	Location	Position	Height above the road surface in millimeters (mm) (with English units in parenthesis) measured from the center of the lamp at curb weight	Vehicles for which the devices are required
Stop lamps. See footnotes #5 and 13	2	Red	Rear	One lamp on each side of the vertical center-line at the same height and as far apart as practicable.	Both on the same level between 381 mm (15 inches) and 1,829 mm (72 inches).	A, B, C, D, E, F, G
Clearance lamps. See footnotes #8, 9, 10, 15 & 17.	2	Amber	One on each side of the front of the vehicle.	One on each side of the vertical centerline to in-dicate overall width.	Both on the same level as high as practicable.	B, C, D, G, H
	2	Red	One on each side of the rear of the vehicle.	One on each side of the vertical centerline to in-dicate overall width.	Both on the same level as high as practicable.	B, D, G, H
Reflex reflector, intermediate (side)	2	Amber	One on each side.	At or near the midpoint between the front and rear side marker lamps, if the length of the vehicle is more than 9,144 mm (30 feet).	Between 381 mm (15inches) and 1,524 (60 inches).	A, B, D, F, G
Reflex reflector (rear). See footnotes #5, 6, and 8.	2	Red	Rear	One on each side of the vertical centerline, as far apart as practicable and at the same height.	Both on the same level, between 381 mm (15 inches) and 1,524 mm (60 inches).	A, B, C, D, E, F, G
Reflex reflector (rear side).	2	Red	One on each side (rear).	As far to the rear as practicable.	Both on the same level, between 381 mm (15 inches) and 1,524 mm (60 inches).	A, B, D, F, G
Reflex reflector (front side). See foot-note #16.	2	Amber	One on each side (front).	As far to the front as practicable.	Between 381 mm (15 inches) and 1,524 mm (60 inches).	A, B, C, D, F, G
License plate lamp (rear). See foot-note #11.	1	White	At rear license plate to illu-minate the plate from the top or side.		No requirements	A, B, C, D, F, G
Side marker lamp (front). See foot-note #16.	2	Amber	One on each side.	As far to the front as practicable.	Not less than 381 mm (15 inches).	A, B, C, D, F

418

Type of lamp or reflector	No.	Color	Location	Position	Height above road surface	Combination
Side marker lamp intermediate	2	Amber	One on each side.	At or near the midpoint between the front and rear side marker lamps, if the length of the vehicle is more than 9.144 mm (30 feet).	Not less tan 381 mm (15 inches).	A, B, D, F, G
Side marker lamp (rear). See footnotes #4 and 8.	2	Red	One on each side.	As far to the rear as practicable.	Not less than 381 mm (15 inches), and on the rear of trailers not more than 1.524 mm (60 inches).	A, B, D, F, G
Turn signal (rear). See footnotes #5 and 12.	2	Amber or red	Rear	One lamp on each side of the vertical center-line as far apart as practicable.	Both on the same level, between 381 mm (15 inches) and 2,108 mm (83 inches).	A, B, C, D, E, F, G
Identification lamp (rear). See footnotes #3, 7, and 15.	3	Red	Rear	One as close as practicable to the vertical centerline. One on each side with lamp centers spaced not less than 152 mm (6 inches) or more than 305 mm (12 inches) apart.	All three on the same level as close as practicable to the top of the vehicle.	B, D, G
Vehicular hazard warning signal flasher lamps. See footnotes #5 and 12.	2	Amber	Front	One lamp on each side of the vertical center-line, as far apart as practicable.	Both on the same level, between 381 mm (15 inches) and 2,108 mm (83 inches).	A, B, C
	2	Amber or red	Rear	One lamp on each side of the vertical center-line, as far apart as practicable.	Both on the same level, between 381 mm (15 inches) and 2,108 mm (83 inches).	A, B, C, D, E, F, G
Backup lamp. See footnote #14.	1 or 2	White	Rear		No requirement	A, B, C
Parking lamp	2	Amber or white	Front	One lamp on each side of the vertical center-line, as far apart as practicable.	Both on the same level, between 381 mm (15 inches) and 2,108 mm (83 inches).	A

Legend: Types of commercial motor vehicles shown in the last column of Table 1.
A. Buses and trucks less than 2,032 mm (80 inches) in overall width.
B. Buses and trucks 2,032 mm (80 inches) or more in overall width.
C. Truck tractors.
D. Semitrailers and full trailers 2,032 mm (80 inches) or more in overall width except converter dollies.
E. Converter dolly.
F. Semitrailers and full trailers less than 2,032 mm (80 inches) in overall width.
G. Pole trailers.
H. Projecting loads.

Note: Lamps and reflectors may be combined as permitted by §393.22 and S5.4 of 49 CFR 571.108. Equipment combinations.
Footnote—1 Identification lamps may be mounted on the vertical centerline of the cab where different from the centerline of the vehicle, except where the cab is not more than 42 inches wide at the front roofline, then a single lamp at the center of the cab shall be deemed to comply with the requirements for identification lamps. No part of the identification lamps or their mountings may extend below the top of the vehicle windshield.

419

Footnote—2 Unless the turn signals on the front are so constructed (double-faced) and located as to be visible to passing drivers, two turn signals are required on the rear of the truck tractor, one at each side as far apart as practicable.

Footnote—3 The identification lamps need not be visible or lighted if obscured by a vehicle in the same combination.

Footnote—4 Any semitrailer or full trailer manufactured on or after March 1, 1979, shall be equipped with rear side-marker lamps at a height of not less than 381 mm (15 inches), and on the rear of trailers not more than 1,524 mm (60 inches) above the road surface, as measured from the center of the lamp on the vehicle at curb weight.

Footnote—5 Each converter dolly, when towed singly by another vehicle and not as part of a full trailer, shall be equipped with one stop lamp, one tail lamp, and two reflectors (one on each side of the vertical centerline, as far apart as practicable) on the rear. Each converter dolly shall be equipped with rear turn signals and vehicular hazard warning signal flasher lamps when towed singly by another vehicle and not as part of a full trailer, if the converter dolly obscures the turn signals at the rear of the towing vehicle.

Footnote—6 Pole trailers shall be equipped with two reflex reflectors on the rear, one on each side of the vertical centerline as far apart as practicable, to indicate the extreme width of the trailer.

Footnote—7 Pole trailers, when towed by motor vehicles with rear identification lamps meeting the requirements of § 393.11 and mounted at a height greater than the load being transported on the pole trailer, are not required to have rear identification lamps.

Footnote—8 Pole trailers shall have on the rearmost support for the load: (1) two front clearance lamps, one on each side of the vehicle, both on the same level and as high as practicable to indicate the overall width of the pole trailer; (2) two rear clearance lamps, one on each side of the vehicle, both on the same level and as high as practicable to indicate the overall width of the pole trailer; (3) two rear side marker lamps, one on each side of the vehicle, both on the same level, not less than 375 mm (15 inches) above the road surface; (4) two rear reflex reflectors, one on each side, both on the same level, not less than 375 mm (15 inches) above the road surface to indicate maximum width of the pole trailer; and (5) one red reflector on each side of the rearmost support for the load. Lamps and reflectors may be combined as allowed in § 393.22.

Footnote—9 Any motor vehicle transporting a load which extends more than 102 mm (4 inches) beyond the overall width of the motor vehicle shall be equipped with the following lamps in addition to other required lamps when operated during the hours when headlamps are required to be used:

(1) The foremost edge of that portion of the load which projects beyond the side of the vehicle shall be marked (at its outermost extremity) with an amber lamp visible from the front and side.

(2) The rearmost edge of that portion of the load which projects beyond the side of the vehicle shall be marked (at its outermost extremity) with a red lamp visible from the rear and side.

(3) If the projecting load does not measure more than 914 mm (3 feet) from front to rear, it shall be marked with an amber lamp visible from the front, both sides, and rear, except that if the projection is located at or near the rear it shall be marked by a red lamp visible from front, side, and rear.

Footnote—10 Projections beyond rear of motor vehicles. Motor vehicles transporting loads which extend more than 1,219 mm (4 feet) beyond the rear of the motor vehicle, or which have tailboards or tailgates extending more than 1,219 mm (4 feet) beyond the body, shall have these projections marked as follows when the vehicle is operated during the hours when headlamps are required to be used:

(1) On each side of the projecting load, one red side marker lamp, visible from the side, located so as to indicate maximum overhang.

(2) On the rear of the projecting load, two red lamps, visible from the rear, one at each side; and two red reflectors visible from the rear, one at each side, located so as to indicate maximum width.

Footnote—11 To be illuminated when tractor headlamps are illuminated.

Footnote—12 Every bus, truck, and truck tractor shall be equipped with a signaling system that, in addition to signaling turning movements, shall have a switch or combination of switches that will cause the two front turn signals and the two rear signals to flash simultaneously as a vehicular traffic signal warning, required by § 392–22(a). The system shall be capable of flashing simultaneously with the ignition of the vehicle on or off.

Footnote—13 To be actuated upon application of service brakes.

Footnote—14 Backup lamp required to operate when bus, truck, or truck tractor is in reverse.

Footnote—15

(1) For the purposes of Section 393.11, the term "overall width" refers to the nominal design dimension of the widest part of the vehicle, exclusive of the signal lamps, marker lamps, outside rearview mirrors, flexible fender extensions, and mud flaps.

(2) Clearance lamps may be mounted at a location other than on the front and rear if necessary to indicate the overall width of a vehicle, or for protection from damage during normal operation of the vehicle.

(3) On a trailer, the front clearance lamps may be mounted at a height below the extreme height if mounting at the extreme height results in the lamps failing to mark the overall width of the trailer.

(4) On a truck tractor, clearance lamps mounted on the cab may be located to indicate the width of the cab, rather than the width of the vehicle.

(5) When the rear identification lamps are mounted at the extreme height of a vehicle, rear clearance lamps are not required to be located as close as practicable to the top of the vehicle.

Footnote—16 A trailer subject to this part that is less than 1829 mm (6 feet) in overall length, including the trailer tongue, need not be equipped with front side marker lamps and front side reflex reflectors.

Footnote—17 A boat trailer subject to this part whose overall width is 2032 mm (80 inches) or more need not be equipped with both front and rear clearance lamps provided an amber (front) and red (rear) clearance lamp is located at or near the midpoint on each side so as to indicate its extreme width.

Figure 1 - Truck Tractor Illustration for § 393.11

Figure 2 - Straight Truck Illustration for § 393.11

Figure 3 - Straight Truck Illustration for § 393.11

Figure 4 - Straight Truck Illustration for § 393.11

Figure 5 - Straight Truck Illustration for § 393.11

Figure 6 - Straight Truck Illustration for § 393.11

Figure 7 - Bus Illustration for § 393.11

LEGEND FOR FIGURES 1 THROUGH 7 - 49 CFR 393.11
TRUCK & BUS VEHICLE ILLUSTRATIONS
(DOES NOT APPLY TO FIGURES 8 THROUGH 18 FOR TRAILERS)

Area	Equipment
①	Headlamps - Lower Beam
	Headlamps - Upper Beam
	Parking Lamps - Attention: *Required only on vehicles less than 2032mm wide*
	Front Turn Signal/Hazard Warning Lamps
②	Front Clearance Lamps - Attention: *Required for vehicles 2032mm wide or wider*
③	Front Identification Lamps (ID)
④a	Front Side Marker Lamps
④b	Front Side Reflex Reflectors
⑤a	Rear Side Marker Lamps - *Not required on Truck Tractors*
⑤b	Rear Side Reflex Reflectors - *Not required on Truck Tractors*
⑥	Rear Clearance Lamps Attention: *Required for vehicles 2032mm wide or wider, but not required on Truck Tractors*
⑦	Rear Identification Lamps (ID) Attention: *Required for vehicles 2032mm wide or wider, but not required on Truck Tractors*
⑧	Tail Lamps
	Stop Lamps
	Rear Turn Signal/Hazard Warning Lamps
	Rear Reflex Reflectors
⑨	Backup Lamp
⑩	License Plate Lamp
⑪	Center High Mounted Stop Lamp Attention: *Required for vehicles less than 2032mm wide and 4536kg*

ADDITIONAL EQUIPMENT FOR SPECIFIC TRUCKS AND BUS VEHICLES

Area	Equipment
⑫a	Intermediate Side Marker Lamps
⑫b	Intermediate Side Reflex Relectors

TRUCK TRACTORS

	DESCRIPTION
Area	Conspicuity Treatment
⑬	Rear Upper Body Marking
⑭	Rear Marking

Figure 8 - Semi-Trailer Illustration for § 393.11

Figure 9 - Semi-Trailer Illustration for § 393.11

Figure 10 - Semi-Trailer Illustration for § 393.11

Figure 11 - Container Chassis Illustration for § 393.11

Front

Rear

Figure 12 - Pole Trailer Illustration for § 393.11
- All Vehicle Widths

Front of Vehicle

**Rear of Vehicle
(Including Truck Cab)**

Figure 13 - Converter Dolly Illustration for § 393.11

Side View of Dolly   **Rear**

Figure 14 - Semi-Trailer Illustration for § 393.11

Figure 15 - Semi-Trailer Illustration for § 393.11

Figure 16 - Semi-Trailer Illustration for § 393.11

Figure 17 - Semi-Trailer Illustration for § 393.11

Figure 18 - Semi-Trailer Illustration for § 393.11

LEGEND FOR FIGURES 8 THROUGH 18 - 49 CFR 393.11
TRAILER ILLUSTRATIONS
(DOES NOT APPLY TO FIGURES 1 THROUGH 7 FOR TRUCKS & BUSES)

Area	Equipment
1	Tail Lamps
	Stop Lamps
	Rear Turn Signal Lamps
	Rear Reflex Reflectors
2	License Plate Lamp (s)
3	Rear Side Marker Lamps
	Rear Side Reflex Reflectors
4a	Front Side Marker Lamps
4b	Front Side Reflex Reflectors

ADDITIONAL EQUIPMENT FOR TRAILERS EXCEEDING THE FOLLOWING PARAMETERS

LENGTH 9.1 m (30 ft.) OR LONGER

Area	Equipment
5a	Intermediate Side Marker Lamps
5b	Intermediate Side Reflex Reflectors

WIDTH 2.032 m (80 in.) OR WIDER

Area	Equipment
6	Rear Clearance Lamps
7	Rear Identification Lamps
8	Front Clearance Lamps

WIDTH 2.032 m (80 in.) OR WIDER AND GVWR 4,536 kg (10,000 lb.) OR MORE

Area	DESCRIPTION Conspicuity Treatment
9	Rear Upper Body Marking
10	Bumper Bar Marking
11	Rear Lower Body Marking
12	Side Marking

[70 FR 48027, Aug. 15, 2005, as amended at 72 FR 32014, June 11, 2007; 72 FR 33562, June 18, 2007]

§ 393.13 **Retroreflective sheeting and reflex reflectors, requirements for semitrailers and trailers manufactured before December 1, 1993.**

(a) *Applicability.* All trailers and semitrailers manufactured prior to December 1, 1993, which have an overall width of 2,032 mm (80 inches) or more and a gross vehicle weight rating of 4,536 kg (10,001 pounds) or more, except trailers that are manufactured exclusively for use as offices or dwellings, pole trailers (as defined in §390.5 of this subchapter), and trailers transported in a driveaway-towaway operation, must be equipped with retroreflective sheeting or an array of reflex reflectors that meet the requirements of this section. Motor carriers operating trailers, other than container chassis (as defined in §393.5), have until June 1, 2001, to comply with the requirements of this section. Motor carriers operating container chassis have until December 1, 2001, to comply with the requirements of this section.

(b) *Retroreflective sheeting and reflex reflectors.* Motor carriers are encouraged to retrofit their trailers with a conspicuity system that meets all of the requirements applicable to trailers manufactured on or after December 1, 1993, including the use of retroreflective sheeting or reflex reflectors in a red and white pattern (see Federal Motor Vehicle Safety Standard No. 108 (49 CFR 571.108), S5.7, *Conspicuity systems*). Motor carriers which do not retrofit their trailers to meet the requirements of FMVSS No. 108, for example by using an alternative color pattern, must comply with the remainder of this paragraph and with paragraph (c) or (d) of this section. Retroreflective sheeting or reflex reflectors in colors or color combinations other than red and white may be used on the sides or lower rear area of the semitrailer or trailer until June 1, 2009. The alternate color or color combination must be uniform along the sides and lower rear area of the trailer. The retroreflective sheeting or reflex reflectors on the upper rear area of the trailer must be white and conform to the requirements of FMVSS No. 108 (S5.7). Red retroreflective sheeting or reflex reflectors shall not be used along the sides of the trailer unless it is used as part of a red and white pattern. Retroreflective sheeting shall have a width of at least 50 mm (2 inches).

(c) *Locations for retroreflective sheeting*—(1) *Sides.* Retroreflective sheeting shall be applied to each side of the trailer or semitrailer. Each strip of retroreflective sheeting shall be positioned as horizontally as practicable, beginning and ending as close to the front and rear as practicable. The strip need not be continuous but the sum of the length of all of the segments shall be at least half of the length of the trailer and the spaces between the segments of the strip shall be distributed as evenly as practicable. The centerline for each strip of retroreflective sheeting shall be between 375 mm (15 inches) and 1,525 mm (60 inches) above the road surface when measured with the trailer empty or unladen, or as close as practicable to this area. If necessary to clear rivet heads or other similar obstructions, 50 mm (2 inches) wide retroreflective sheeting may be separated into two 25 mm (1 inch) wide strips of the same length and color, separated by a space of not more than 25 mm (1 inch).

(2) *Lower rear area.* The rear of each trailer and semitrailer must be equipped with retroreflective sheeting. Each strip of retroreflective sheeting shall be positioned as horizontally as practicable, extending across the full width of the trailer, beginning and ending as close to the extreme edges as practicable. The centerline for each of the strips of retroreflective sheeting shall be between 375 mm (15 inches) and 1,525 mm (60 inches) above the road surface when measured with the trailer empty or unladen, or as close as practicable to this area.

(3) *Upper rear area.* Two pairs of white strips of retroreflective sheeting, each pair consisting of strips 300 mm (12 inches) long, must be positioned horizontally and vertically on the right and left upper corners of the rear of the body of each trailer and semitrailer, as close as practicable to the top of the trailer and as far apart as practicable. If the perimeter of the body, as viewed from the rear, is not square or rectangular, the strips may be applied along the perimeter, as close as practicable to the uppermost and outermost areas

433

of the rear of the body on the left and right sides.

(d) *Locations for reflex reflectors*—(1) *Sides.* Reflex reflectors shall be applied to each side of the trailer or semitrailer. Each array of reflex reflectors shall be positioned as horizontally as practicable, beginning and ending as close to the front and rear as practicable. The array need not be continuous but the sum of the length of all of the array segments shall be at least half of the length of the trailer and the spaces between the segments of the strip shall be distributed as evenly as practicable. The centerline for each array of reflex reflectors shall be between 375 mm (15 inches) and 1,525 mm (60 inches) above the road surface when measured with the trailer empty or unladen, or as close as practicable to this area. The center of each reflector shall not be more than 100 mm (4 inches) from the center of each adjacent reflector in the segment of the array. If reflex reflectors are arranged in an alternating color pattern, the length of reflectors of the first color shall be as close as practicable to the length of the reflectors of the second color.

(2) *Lower rear area.* The rear of each trailer and semitrailer must be equipped with reflex reflectors. Each array of reflex reflectors shall be positioned as horizontally as practicable, extending across the full width of the trailer, beginning and ending as close to the extreme edges as practicable. The centerline for each array of reflex reflectors shall be between 375 mm (15 inches) and 1,525 mm (60 inches) above the road surface when measured with the trailer empty or unladen, or as close as practicable to this area. The center of each reflector shall not be more than 100 mm (4 inches) from the center of each adjacent reflector in the segment of the array.

(3) *Upper rear area.* Two pairs of white reflex reflector arrays, each pair at least 300 mm (12 inches) long, must be positioned horizontally and vertically on the right and left upper corners of the rear of the body of each trailer and semitrailer, as close as practicable to the top of the trailer and as far apart as practicable. If the perimeter of the body, as viewed from the rear, is not square or rectangular, the arrays may

be applied along the perimeter, as close as practicable to the uppermost and outermost areas of the rear of the body on the left and right sides. The center of each reflector shall not be more than 100 mm (4 inches) from the center of each adjacent reflector in the segment of the array.

[64 FR 15605, Mar. 31, 1999, as amended at 66 FR 30339, June 6, 2001]

§ 393.17 **Lamps and reflectors—combinations in driveaway-towaway operation.**

A combination of motor vehicles engaged in driveaway-towaway operation must be equipped with operative lamps and reflectors conforming to the rules in this section.

(a) The towing vehicle must be equipped as follows:

(1) On the front, there must be at least two headlamps, an equal number at each side, two turn signals, one at each side, and two clearance lamps, one at each side.

(2) On each side, there must be at least one side-marker lamp, located near the front of the vehicle.

(3) On the rear, there must be at least two tail lamps, one at each side, and two stop lamps, one at each side.

(b) Except as provided in paragraph (c) of this section, the rearmost towed vehicle of the combination (including the towed vehicle or a tow-bar combination, the towed vehicle of a single saddle-mount combination, and the rearmost towed vehicle of a double or triple saddle-mount combination) or, in the case of a vehicle full-mounted on a saddle-mount vehicle, either the full-mounted or the rearmost saddle-mounted vehicle must be equipped as follows:

(1) On each side, there must be at least one side-marker lamp, located near the rear of the vehicle.

(2) On the rear, there must be at least two tail lamps, two stop lamps, two turn signals, two clearance lamps, and two reflectors, one of each type at each side. In addition, if any vehicle in the combination is 80 inches or more in overall width, there must be three identification lamps on the rear.

(c) If the towed vehicle in a combination is a mobile structure trailer, it must be equipped in accordance with the following lighting devices. For the purposes of this part, *mobile structure trailer* means a trailer that has a roof and walls, is at least 10 feet wide, and can be used off road for dwelling or commercial purposes.

(1) When the vehicle is operated in accordance with the terms of a special permit prohibiting operation during the times when lighted lamps are required under §392.30, it must have on the rear—

(i) Two stop lamps, one on each side of the vertical centerline, at the same height, and as far apart as practicable;

(ii) Two tail lamps, one on each side of the vertical centerline, at the same height, and as far apart as practicable;

(iii) Two red reflex reflectors, one on each side of the vertical centerline, at the same height, and as far apart as practicable; and

(iv) Two turn signal lamps, one on each side of the vertical centerline, at the same height, and as far apart as practicable.

(2) At all other times, the vehicle must be equipped as specified in paragraph (b) of this section.

(d) An intermediate towed vehicle in a combination consisting of more than two vehicles (including the first saddle-mounted vehicle of a double saddle-mount combination and the first and second saddle-mount vehicles of a triple saddle-mount combination) must have one side-marker lamp on each side, located near the rear of the vehicle.

Figure 19 - Single-Saddle-Mount Diagram
to Illustrate § 393.17

Front of Towing Vehicle

Rear of Towed Vehicle

Each Side of Vehicle

Lamps may be combined as permitted by § 393.22. The color of
exterior lighting devices and reflectors shall conform to requirements of § 393.11

Figure 20 - Double-Saddle-Mount Diagram
to Illustrate § 393.17

Front of Towing Vehicle

Rear of Towed Vehicle

Each Side of Vehicle

Lamps may be combined as permitted by § 393.22. The color of
exterior lighting devices and reflectors shall conform to requirements of § 393.11

Figure 21 - Tow-bar Diagram to Illustrate § 393.17

Front of Towing Vehicle   Rear of Towing Vehicle

Each Side of Vehicle

Lamps may be combined as permitted by § 393.22. The color of
exterior lighting devices and reflectors shall conform to requirements of § 393.11

(49 U.S.C. 304, 1655; 49 CFR 1.48(b) and 301.60)

[40 FR 36126, Aug. 19, 1975, as amended at 47 FR 47837, Oct. 28, 1982; 70 FR 48044, Aug. 15, 2005]

§ 393.19 Hazard warning signals.

The hazard warning signal operating unit on each commercial motor vehicle shall operate independently of the ignition or equivalent switch, and when activated, cause all turn signals required by § 393.11 to flash simultaneously.

[70 FR 48046, Aug. 15, 2005]

§ 393.20 [Reserved]

§ 393.22 Combination of lighting devices and reflectors.

(a) *Permitted combinations.* Except as provided in paragraph (b) of this section, two or more lighting devices and reflectors (whether or not required by the rules in this part) may be combined optically if—

(1) Each required lighting device and reflector conforms to the applicable rules in this part; and

(2) Neither the mounting nor the use of a nonrequired lighting device or reflector impairs the effectiveness of a required lighting device or reflector or causes that device or reflector to be inconsistent with the applicable rules in this part.

(b) *Prohibited combinations.* (1) A turn signal lamp must not be combined optically with either a head lamp or other lighting device or combination of lighting devices that produces a greater intensity of light than the turn signal lamp.

(2) A turn signal lamp must not be combined optically with a stop lamp unless the stop lamp function is always deactivated when the turn signal function is activated.

(3) A clearance lamp must not be combined optically with a tail lamp or identification lamp.

[39 FR 26908, July 24, 1974]

§ 393.23 Power supply for lamps.

All required lamps must be powered by the electrical system of the motor vehicle with the exception of battery powered lamps used on projecting loads.

[70 FR 48046, Aug. 15, 2005]

§ 393.24 Requirements for head lamps, auxiliary driving lamps and front fog lamps.

(a) *Headlamps.* Every bus, truck and truck tractor shall be equipped with headlamps as required by § 393.11(a). The headlamps shall provide an upper and lower beam distribution of light, selectable at the driver's will and be steady-burning. The headlamps shall be marked in accordance with FMVSS No. 108. Auxiliary driving lamps and/or front fog lamps may not be used to satisfy the requirements of this paragraph.

(b) *Auxiliary driving lamps and front fog lamps.* Commercial motor vehicles may be equipped with auxiliary driving lamps and/or front fog lamps for use in conjunction with, but not in lieu of the required headlamps. Auxiliary driving lamps shall meet SAE Standard J581 Auxiliary Upper Beam Lamps, July 2004, and front fog lamps shall meet SAE Standard J583 Front Fog Lamp, August 2004. (See § 393.7 for information on the incorporation by reference and availability of these documents.)

(c) *Mounting.* Headlamps shall be mounted and aimable in accordance with FMVSS No. 108. Auxiliary driving lamps and front fog lamps shall be mounted so that the beams are aimable and the mounting shall prevent the aim of the lighting device from being disturbed while the vehicle is operating on public roads.

(d) *Aiming.* Headlamps, auxiliary driving lamps and front fog lamps shall be aimed to meet the aiming specifications in FMVSS No. 108 (49 CFR 571.108), SAE J581, and SAE J583, respectively.

[70 FR 48046, Aug. 15, 2005]

§ 393.25 Requirements for lamps other than head lamps.

(a) *Mounting.* All lamps shall be securely mounted on a rigid part of the vehicle. Temporary lamps must be securely mounted to the load and are not required to be mounted to a permanent part of the vehicle.

(b) *Visibility.* Each lamp shall be located so that it meets the visibility requirements specified by FMVSS No. 108 in effect at the time of manufacture of the vehicle. Vehicles which were not subject to FMVSS No. 108 at the time of manufacture shall have each lamp located so that it meets the visibility requirements specified in the SAE standards listed in paragraph (c) of this section. If motor vehicle equipment (*e.g.*, mirrors, snow plows, wrecker booms, backhoes, and winches) prevents compliance with this paragraph by any required lamp, an auxiliary lamp or device meeting the requirements of this paragraph shall be provided. This shall not be construed to apply to lamps on one unit which are obscured by another unit of a combination of vehicles.

(c) *Specifications.* All required lamps (except marker lamps on projecting loads, lamps which are temporarily attached to vehicles transported in driveaway-towaway operations, and lamps on converter dollies and pole trailers) on vehicles manufactured on or after December 25, 1968, shall, at a minimum, meet the applicable requirements of FMVSS No. 108 in effect on the date of manufacture of the vehicle. Marker lamps on projecting loads, all lamps which are temporarily attached to vehicles transported in driveaway-towaway operations, and all lamps on converter dollies and pole trailers must meet the following applicable SAE standards: J586—Stop Lamps for Use on Motor Vehicles Less Than 2032 mm in Overall Width, March 2000; J2261 Stop

439

Lamps and Front- and Rear-Turn Signal Lamps for Use on Motor Vehicles 2032 mm or More in Overall Width, January 2002; J585—Tail Lamps (Rear Position Lamps) for Use on Motor Vehicles Less Than 2032 mm in Overall Width, March 2000; J588—Turn Signal Lamps for Use on Motor Vehicles Less Than 2032 mm in Overall Width, March 2000; J2040—Tail Lamps (Rear Position Lamps) for Use on Vehicles 2032 mm or More in Overall Width, March 2002; J592—Sidemarker Lamps for Use on Road Vehicles Less Than 2032 mm in Overall Width, August 2000. (See § 393.7 for information on the incorporation by reference and availability of these documents.)

(d) (Reserved)

(e) *Lamps to be steady-burning.* All exterior lamps (both required lamps and any additional lamps) shall be steady-burning with the exception of turn signal lamps; hazard warning signal lamps; school bus warning lamps; amber warning lamps or flashing warning lamps on tow trucks and commercial motor vehicles transporting oversized loads; and warning lamps on emergency and service vehicles authorized by State or local authorities. Lamps combined into the same shell or housing with a turn signal are not required to be steady burning while the turn signal is in use. Amber warning lamps must meet SAE J845—Optical Warning Devices for Authorized Emergency, Maintenance and Service Vehicles, May 1997. Amber flashing warning lamps must meet SAE J595—Directional Flashing Optical Warning Devices for Authorized Emergency, Maintenance and Service Vehicles, January 2005. Amber gaseous discharge warning lamps must meet SAE J1318 Gaseous Discharge Warning Lamp for Authorized Emergency, Maintenance, and Service Vehicles, May 1998. (See § 393.7(b) for information on the incorporation by reference and availability of these documents.)

(f) *Stop lamp operation.* The stop lamps on each vehicle shall be activated upon application of the service brakes. The stop lamps are not required to be activated when the emergency feature of the trailer brakes is used or when the stop lamp is optically combined with the turn signal and the turn signal is in use.

[70 FR 48047, Aug. 15, 2005]

§ 393.26 Requirements for reflectors.

(a) *Mounting.* Reflex reflectors shall be mounted at the locations required by § 393.11. In the case of motor vehicles so constructed that requirement for a 381 mm (15-inch) minimum height above the road surface is not practical, the reflectors shall be mounted as close as practicable to the required mounting height range. All permanent reflex reflectors shall be securely mounted on a rigid part of the vehicle. Temporary reflectors on projecting loads must be securely mounted to the load and are not required to be permanently mounted to a part of the vehicle. Temporary reflex reflectors on vehicles transported in driveaway-towaway operations must be firmly attached.

(b) *Specifications.* All required reflex reflectors (except reflex reflectors on projecting loads, vehicles transported in a driveaway-towaway operation, converter dollies and pole trailers) on vehicles manufactured on or after December 25, 1968, shall meet the applicable requirements of FMVSS No. 108 in effect on the date of manufacture of the vehicle. Reflex reflectors on projecting loads, vehicles transported in a driveaway-towaway operation, and all reflex reflectors on converter dollies and pole trailers must conform to SAE J594—Reflex Reflectors, December 2003.

(c) *Substitute material for side reflex reflectors.* Reflective material conforming to ASTM D 4956-04, Standard Specification for Retroreflective Sheeting for Traffic Control, may be used in lieu of reflex reflectors if the material as used on the vehicle, meets the performance standards in either Table I of SAE J594 or Table IA of SAE J594—Reflex Reflectors, December 2003. (See § 393.7(b) for information on the incorporation by reference and availability of these documents.)

(d) *Use of additional retroreflective surfaces.* Additional retroreflective surfaces may be used in conjunction with, but not in lieu of the reflex reflectors required in subpart B of part 393, and the substitute material for side reflex reflectors allowed by paragraph (c) of this section, provided:

(1) Designs do not resemble traffic control signs, lights, or devices, except that straight edge striping resembling a barricade pattern may be used.

(2) Designs do not tend to distort the length and/or width of the motor vehicle.

(3) Such surfaces shall be at least 3 inches from any required lamp or reflector unless of the same color as such lamp or reflector.

(4) No red color shall be used on the front of any motor vehicle, except for display of markings or placards required by §177.823 of this title.

(5) Retroreflective license plates required by State or local authorities may be used.

[33 FR 19735, Dec. 25, 1968, as amended at 35 FR 3167, Feb. 19, 1970; 53 FR 49397, Dec. 7, 1988; 70 FR 48047, Aug. 15, 2005]

§393.27 [Reserved]

§393.28 Wiring systems.

Electrical wiring shall be installed and maintained to conform to SAE J1292—Automobile, Truck, Truck-Tractor, Trailer, and Motor Coach Wiring, October 1981, except the jumper cable plug and receptacle need not conform to SAE J560. The reference to SAE J1292 shall not be construed to require circuit protection on trailers. (See §393.7(b) for information on the incorporation by reference and availability of this document.)

[70 FR 48047, Aug. 15, 2005]

§393.29 [Reserved]

§393.30 Battery installation.

Every storage battery on every vehicle, unless located in the engine compartment, shall be covered by a fixed part of the motor vehicle or protected by a removable cover or enclosure. Removable covers or enclosures shall be substantial and shall be securely latched or fastened. The storage battery compartment and adjacent metal parts which might corrode by reason of battery leakage shall be painted or coated with an acid-resisting paint or coating and shall have openings to provide ample battery ventilation and drainage. Wherever the cable to the starting motor passes through a metal compartment, the cable shall be protected against grounding by an acid and waterproof insulating bushing. Wherever a battery and a fuel tank are both placed under the driver's seat, they shall be partitioned from each other, and each compartment shall be provided with an independent cover, ventilation, and drainage.

§§393.31–393.33 [Reserved]

Subpart C—Brakes

§393.40 Required brake systems.

(a) Each commercial motor vehicle must have brakes adequate to stop and hold the vehicle or combination of motor vehicles. Each commercial motor vehicle must meet the applicable service, parking, and emergency brake system requirements provided in this section.

(b) *Service brakes*—(1) *Hydraulic brake systems.* Motor vehicles equipped with hydraulic brake systems and manufactured on or after September 2, 1983, must, at a minimum, have a service brake system that meets the requirements of FMVSS No. 105 in effect on the date of manufacture. Motor vehicles which were not subject to FMVSS No. 105 on the date of manufacture must have a service brake system that meets the applicable requirements of §§393.42, 393.48, 393.49, 393.51, and 393.52 of this subpart.

(2) *Air brake systems.* Buses, trucks and truck-tractors equipped with air brake systems and manufactured on or after March 1, 1975, and trailers manufactured on or after January 1, 1975, must, at a minimum, have a service brake system that meets the requirements of FMVSS No. 121 in effect on the date of manufacture. Motor vehicles which were not subject to FMVSS No. 121 on the date of manufacture must have a service brake system that meets the applicable requirements of §§393.42, 393.48, 393.49, 393.51, and 393.52 of this subpart.

(3) *Vacuum brake systems.* Motor vehicles equipped with vacuum brake systems must have a service brake system that meets the applicable requirements of §§393.42, 393.48, 393.49, 393.51, and 393.52 of this subpart.

(4) *Electric brake systems.* Motor vehicles equipped with electric brake systems must have a service brake system that meets the applicable requirements of §§ 393.42, 393.48, 393.49 and 393.52 of this subpart.

(5) *Surge brake systems.* Motor vehicles equipped with surge brake systems must have a service brake system that meets the applicable requirements of §§ 393.42, 393.48, 393.49, and 393.52 of this subpart.

(c) *Parking brakes.* Each commercial motor vehicle must be equipped with a parking brake system that meets the applicable requirements of § 393.41.

(d) *Emergency brakes—partial failure of service brakes—*(1) *Hydraulic brake systems.* Motor vehicles manufactured on or after September 2, 1983, and equipped with a split service brake system must, at a minimum, meet the partial failure requirements of FMVSS No. 105 in effect on the date of manufacture.

(2) *Air brake systems.* Buses, trucks and truck tractors manufactured on or after March 1, 1975, and trailers manufactured on or after January 1, 1975, must be equipped with an emergency brake system which, at a minumum, meets the requirements of FMVSS No. 121 in effect on the date of manufacture.

(3) *Vehicles not subject to FMVSS Nos. 105 and 121 on the date of manufacture.* Buses, trucks and truck tractors not subject to FMVSS Nos. 105 or 121 on the date of manufacture must meet the requirements of § 393.40(e). Trailers not subject to FMVSS No. 121 at the time of manufacture must meet the requirements of § 393.43.

(e) *Emergency brakes, vehicles manufactured on or after July 1, 1973.* (1) A bus, truck, truck tractor, or a combination of motor vehicles manufactured on or after July 1, 1973, and not covered under paragraphs (d)(1) or (d)(2) of this section, must have an emergency brake system which consists of emergency features of the service brake system or an emergency system separate from the service brake system. The emergency brake system must meet the applicable requirements of §§ 393.43 and 393.52.

(2) A control by which the driver applies the emergency brake system must be located so that the driver can operate it from the normal seating position while restrained by any seat belts with which the vehicle is equipped. The emergency brake control may be combined with either the service brake control or the parking brake control. However, all three controls may not be combined.

(f) *Interconnected systems.* (1) If the brake systems required by § 393.40(a) are interconnected in any way, they must be designed, constructed, and maintained so that in the event of a failure of any part of the operating mechanism of one or more of the systems (except the service brake actuation pedal or valve), the motor vehicle will have operative brakes and, for vehicles manufactured on or after July 1, 1973, be capable of meeting the requirements of § 393.52(b).

(2) A motor vehicle to which the requirements of FMVSS No. 105 (S5.1.2), dealing with partial failure of the service brake, applied at the time of manufacture meets the requirements of § 393.40(f)(1) if the motor vehicle is maintained in conformity with FMVSS No. 105 and the motor vehicle is capable of meeting the requirements of § 393.52(b), except in the case of a structural failure of the brake master cylinder body.

(3) A bus is considered to meet the requirements of § 393.40(f)(1) if it meets the requirements of § 393.44 and § 393.52(b).

[70 FR 48048, Aug. 15, 2005, as amended at 72 FR 9870, Mar. 6, 2007]

§ 393.41 Parking brake system.

(a) *Hydraulic-braked vehicles manufactured on or after September 2, 1983.* Each truck and bus (other than a school bus) with a GVWR of 4,536 kg (10,000 pounds) or less which is subject to this part and school buses with a GVWR greater than 4,536 kg (10,000 pounds) shall be equipped with a parking brake system as required by FMVSS No. 571.105 (S5.2) in effect at the time of manufacture. The parking brake shall be capable of holding the vehicle or combination of vehicles stationary under any condition of loading in which it is found on a public road (free of ice and snow). Hydraulic-braked vehicles which were not subject to the parking brake requirements of FMVSS No. 571.105 (S5.2) must be equipped with a parking brake system that meets the requirements of paragraph (c) of this section.

(b) *Air-braked power units manufactured on or after March 1, 1975, and air-braked trailers manufactured on or after January 1, 1975.* Each air-braked bus, truck and truck tractor manufactured on and after March 1, 1975, and each air-braked trailer except an agricultural commodity trailer, converter dolly, heavy hauler trailer or pulpwood trailer, shall be equipped with a parking brake system as required by FMVSS No. 121 (S5.6) in effect at the time of manufacture. The parking brake shall be capable of holding the vehicle or combination of vehicles stationary under any condition of loading in which it is found on a public road (free of ice and snow). An agricultural commodity trailer, heavy hauler or pulpwood trailer shall carry sufficient chocking blocks to prevent movement when parked.

(c) *Vehicles not subject to FMVSS Nos. 105 and 121 on the date of manufacture.* (1) Each singly driven motor vehicle not subject to parking brake requirements of FMVSS Nos. 105 or 121 at the time of manufacturer, and every combination of motor vehicles must be equipped with a parking brake system adequate to hold the vehicle or combination on any grade on which it is operated, under any condition of loading in which it is found on a public road (free of ice and snow).

. (2) The parking brake system shall, at all times, be capable of being applied by either the driver's muscular effort or by spring action. If other energy is used to apply the parking brake, there must be an accumulation of that energy isolated from any common source and used exclusively for the operation of the parking brake.

Exception: This paragraph shall not be applicable to air-applied, mechanically-held parking brake systems which meet the parking brake requirements of FMVSS No. 121 (S5.6).

(3) The parking brake system shall be held in the applied position by energy other than fluid pressure, air pressure, or electric energy. The parking brake system shall not be capable of being re-

leased unless adequate energy is available to immediately reapply the parking brake with the required effectiveness.

[70 FR 48048, Aug. 15, 2005]

§393.42 Brakes required on all wheels.

(a) Every commercial motor vehicle shall be equipped with brakes acting on all wheels.

(b) *Exception.* (1) Trucks or truck tractors having three or more axles and manufactured before July 25, 1980, are not required to have brakes on the front wheels. However, these vehicles must meet the requirements of §393.52.

(2) Motor vehicles being towed in a driveaway-towaway operation are not required to have operative brakes provided the combination of vehicles meets the requirements of §393.52. This exception is not applicable to:

(i) Any motor vehicle towed by means of a tow-bar when another motor vehicle is full-mounted on the towed vehicle; and

(ii) Any combination of motor vehicles utilizing three or more saddle-mounts.

(3) Any semitrailer or pole trailer (laden or unladen) with a gross weight of 1,361 kg (3,000 pounds) or less which is subject to this part is not required to be equipped with brakes if the axle weight of the towed vehicle does not exceed 40 percent of the sum of the axle weights of the towing vehicle.

(4) Any full trailer or four-wheel pole trailer (laden or unladen) with a gross weight of 1,361 kg (3,000 pounds) or less which is subject to this part is not required to be equipped with brakes if the sum of the axle weights of the towed vehicle does not exceed 40 percent of the sum of the axle weights of the towing vehicle.

(5) Brakes are not required on the steering axle of a three-axle dolly which is steered by a co-driver.

(6) Loaded housemoving dollies, specialized trailers and dollies used to transport industrial furnaces, reactors, and similar motor vehicles are not required to be equipped with brakes, provided the speed at which the combination of vehicles will be operated does not exceed 32 km/hour (20 mph) and brakes on the combination of vehicles

are capable of stopping the combination within 12.2 meters (40 feet) from the speed at which the vehicle is being operated or 32 km/hour (20 mph), whichever is less.

Figure 22 - Illustrations of Brake Requirements for Light-Duty Trailers in § 393.42

(Semitrailer or 2-wheel pole trailer of 1,360 kilograms (3,000 pounds) gross weight or less must be equipped with brakes if W-3 is greater than 40 percent of the sum of W-1 and W-2.)

(Full trailer or 4-wheel pole trailer of 1,360 kilograms (3,000 pounds) gross weight or less must be equipped with brakes if the sum of W-3 and W-4 is greater than 40 percent of the sum of W-1 and W-2.)

[52 FR 2803, Jan. 27, 1987, as amended at 53 FR 49398, Dec. 7, 1988; 54 FR 48617, Nov. 24, 1989; 59 FR 25574, May 17, 1994; 61 FR 1843, Jan. 24, 1996; 70 FR 48049, Aug. 15, 2005]

EFFECTIVE DATE NOTE: At 76 FR 56321, Sept. 13, 2011, § 393.42 was amended by revising paragraphs (a) and (b)(2), effective October 13, 2011 . For the convenience of the user, the revised text is set forth as follows:

§ 393.42 Brakes required on all wheels.

(a) Every commercial motor vehicle shall be equipped with brakes acting on all wheels. This requirement also applies to certain motor vehicles being towed in a driveaway-towaway operation, as follows:

(1) Any motor vehicle towed by means of a tow-bar when another motor vehicle is full-mounted on the towed vehicle; and

(2) Any saddlemount configuration with a fullmount.

(b) * * *

(2) Motor vehicles being towed in a driveaway-towaway operation (including the last truck of triple saddle-mount combinations (see § 393.71(a)(3)) are not required to

444

have operative brakes provided the combination of vehicles meets the requirements of §393.52.

* * * * *

§393.43 Breakaway and emergency braking.

(a) *Towing vehicle protection system.* Every motor vehicle, if used to tow a trailer equipped with brakes, shall be equipped with a means for providing that in the case of a breakaway of the trailer, the service brakes on the towing vehicle will be capable of stopping the towing vehicle. For air braked towing units, the tractor protection valve or similar device shall operate automatically when the air pressure on the towing vehicle is between 138 kPa and 310 kPa (20 psi and 45 psi).

(b) *Emergency brake requirements, air brakes.* Every truck or truck tractor equipped with air brakes, when used for towing other vehicles equipped with air brakes, shall be equipped with two means of activating the emergency features of the trailer brakes. One of these means shall operate automatically in the event of reduction of the towing vehicle air supply to a fixed pressure which shall not be lower than 20 pounds per square inch nor higher than 45 pounds per square inch. The other means shall be a manually controlled device readily operable by a person seated in the driving seat. Its emergency position or method of operation shall be clearly indicated. In no instance may the manual means be so arranged as to permit its use to prevent operation of the automatic means. The automatic and manual means required by this section may be, but are not required to be, separate.

(c) *Emergency brake requirements, vacuum brakes.* Every truck tractor and truck when used for towing other vehicles equipped with vacuum brakes, shall have, in addition to the single control required by §393.49 to operate all brakes of the combination, a second manual control device which can be used to operate the brakes on the towed vehicles in emergencies. Such second control shall be independent of brake air, hydraulic, and other pressure, and independent of other controls, unless the braking system be so arranged that failure of the pressure on which the second control depends will cause the towed vehicle brakes to be applied automatically. The second control is not required by this rule to provide modulated or graduated braking.

(d) *Breakaway braking requirements for trailers.* Every trailer required to be equipped with brakes shall have brakes which apply automatically and immediately upon breakaway from the towing vehicle. With the exception of trailers having three or more axles, all brakes with which the trailer is required to be equipped must be applied upon breakaway from the towing vehicle. The brakes must remain in the applied position for at least 15 minutes.

(e) *Emergency valves.* Air brake systems installed on towed vehicles shall be so designed, by the use of "no-bleed-back" relay emergency valves or equivalent devices, that the supply reservoir used to provide air for brakes shall be safeguarded against backflow of air to the towing vehicle upon reduction of the towing vehicle air pressure.

(f) *Exception.* The requirements of paragraphs (b), (c) and (d) of this section shall not be applicable to commercial motor vehicles being transported in driveaway-towaway operations.

[53 FR 49384, Dec. 7, 1988, as amended at 70 FR 48050, Aug. 15, 2005]

§393.44 Front brake lines, protection.

On every bus, if equipped with air brakes, the braking system shall be so constructed that in the event any brake line to any of the front wheels is broken, the driver can apply the brakes on the rear wheels despite such breakage. The means used to apply the brakes may be located forward of the driver's seat as long as it can be operated manually by the driver when the driver is properly restrained by any seat belt assembly provided for use. Every bus shall meet this requirement or comply with the regulations in effect at the time of its manufacture.

[53 FR 49400, Dec. 7, 1988]

§393.45 Brake tubing and hoses; hose assemblies and end fittings.

(a) *General construction requirements for tubing and hoses, assemblies, and end fittings.* All brake tubing and hoses, brake hose assemblies, and brake hose end fittings must meet the applicable requirements of FMVSS No. 106 (49 CFR 571.106).

(b) *Brake tubing and hose installation.* Brake tubing and hose must—

(1) Be long and flexible enough to accommodate without damage all normal motions of the parts to which it is attached;

(2) Be secured against chaffing, kinking, or other mechanical damage; and

(3) Be installed in a manner that prevents it from contacting the vehicle's exhaust system or any other source of high temperatures.

(c) *Nonmetallic brake tubing.* Coiled nonmetallic brake tubing may be used for connections between towed and towing motor vehicles or between the frame of a towed vehicle and the unsprung subframe of an adjustable axle of the motor vehicle if—

(1) The coiled tubing has a straight segment (pigtail) at each end that is at least 51 mm (2 inches) in length and is encased in a spring guard or similar device which prevents the tubing from kinking at the fitting at which it is attached to the vehicle; and

(2) The spring guard or similar device has at least 51 mm (2 inches) of closed coils or similar surface at its interface with the fitting and extends at least 38 mm (1½ inches) into the coiled segment of the tubing from its straight segment.

(d) *Brake tubing and hose connections.* All connections for air, vacuum, or hydraulic braking systems shall be installed so as to ensure an attachment free of leaks, constrictions or other conditions which would adversely affect the performance of the brake system.

[70 FR 48050, Aug. 15, 2005]

§ 393.46 [Reserved]

§ 393.47 Brake actuators, slack adjusters, linings/pads and drums/rotors.

(a) *General requirements.* Brake components must be constructed, installed and maintained to prevent excessive fading and grabbing. The means of attachment and physical characteristics must provide for safe and reliable stopping of the commercial motor vehicle.

(b) *Brake chambers.* The service brake chambers and spring brake chambers on each end of an axle must be the same size.

(c) *Slack adjusters.* The effective length of the slack adjuster on each end of an axle must be the same.

(d) *Linings and pads.* The thickness of the brake linings or pads shall meet the applicable requirements of this paragraph—

(1) *Steering axle brakes.* The brake lining/pad thickness on the steering axle of a truck, truck-tractor or bus shall not be less than 4.8 mm (³⁄₁₆ inch) at the shoe center for a shoe with a continuous strip of lining; less than 6.4 mm (¼ inch) at the shoe center for a shoe with two pads; or worn to the wear indicator if the lining is so marked, for air drum brakes. The steering axle brake lining/pad thickness shall not be less than 3.2 mm (⅛ inch) for air disc brakes, or 1.6 mm (¹⁄₁₆ inch) or less for hydraulic disc, drum and electric brakes.

(2) *Non-steering axle brakes.* An air braked commercial motor vehicle shall not be operated with brake lining/pad thickness less than 6.4 mm (¼ inch) or to the wear indicator if the lining is so marked (measured at the shoe center for drum brakes); or less than 3.2 mm (⅛ inch) for disc brakes. Hydraulic or electric braked commercial motor vehicles shall not be operated with a lining/pad thickness less than 1.6 mm (¹⁄₁₆ inch) (measured at the shoe center) for disc or drum brakes.

(e) *Clamp and roto-chamber brake actuator readjustment limits.* The pushrod travel for clamp and roto-chamber type actuators must be less than 80 percent of the rated strokes listed in SAE J1817—Long Stroke Air Brake Actuator Marking, July 2001 (See § 393.7 (b) for information on incorporation by reference and availability of this document), or 80 percent of the rated stroke marked on the brake chamber by the chamber manufacturer, or the readjustment limit marked on the brake chamber by the chamber manufacturer. The pushrod travel for Type 16 and 20 long stroke clamp type brake actuators must be less than 51 mm (2 inches) or 80 percent of the rated stroke marked on the brake chamber by the chamber manufacturer, or the readjustment limit marked on the brake chamber by the chamber manufacturer.

(f) *Wedge brake adjustment.* The movement of the scribe mark on the lining shall not exceed 1.6 mm (1⁄16 inch).

(g) *Drums and rotors.* The thickness of the drums or rotors shall not be less than the limits established by the brake drum or rotor manufacturer.

[70 FR 48051, Aug. 15, 2005]

§ 393.48 Brakes to be operative.

(a) *General rule.* Except as provided in paragraphs (b), (c), and (d) of this section, all brakes with which a motor vehicle is equipped must at all times be capable of operating.

(b) *Devices to reduce or remove front-wheel braking effort.* A commercial motor vehicle may be equipped with a device to reduce the front wheel braking effort (or in the case of a three-axle truck or truck tractor manufactured before March 1, 1975, a device to remove the front-wheel braking effort) if that device meets the applicable requirements of paragraphs (b)(1) and (2) of this section.

(1) *Manually operated devices.* Manually operated devices to reduce or remove front-wheel braking effort may only be used on buses, trucks, and truck tractors manufactured before March 1, 1975. Such devices must not be used unless the vehicle is being operated under adverse conditions such as wet, snowy, or icy roads.

(2) *Automatic devices.* Automatic devices must not reduce the front-wheel braking force by more than 50 percent of the braking force available when the automatic device is disconnected (regardless of whether or not an antilock system failure has occurred on any axle). The device must not be operable by the driver except upon application of the control that activates the braking system. The device must not be operable when the brake control application pressure exceeds 85 psig (for vehicles equipped with air brakes) or 85 percent of the maximum system pressure (for vehicles which are not equipped with air brakes).

(c) *Exception.* Paragraph (a) of this section does not apply to—

(1) A towed vehicle with disabling damage as defined in § 390.5;

(2) A vehicle which is towed in a driveaway-towaway operation and is included in the exemption to the requirement for brakes on all wheels, § 393.42(b);

(3) Unladen converter dollies with a gross weight of 1,361 kg (3,000 lbs) or less, and manufactured prior to March 1, 1998;

(4) The steering axle of a three-axle dolly which is steered by a co-driver;

(5) Loaded house moving dollies, specialized trailers and dollies used to transport industrial furnaces, reactors, and similar motor vehicles provided the speed at which the combination of vehicles will be operated does not exceed 32 km/hour (20 mph) and brakes on the combination of vehicles are capable of stopping the combination within 12.2 meters (40 feet) from the speed at which the vehicle is being operated or 32 km/hour (20 mph), whichever is less.

(6) Raised lift axles. Brakes on lift axles need not be capable of being operated while the lift axle is raised. However, brakes on lift axles must be capable of being applied whenever the lift axle is lowered and the tires contact the roadway.

(d) *Surge brakes.* (1) Surge brakes are allowed on:

(i) Any trailer with a gross vehicle weight rating (GVWR) of 12,000 pounds or less, when its GVWR does not exceed 1.75 times the GVWR of the towing vehicle; and

(ii) Any trailer with a GVWR greater than 12,000 pounds, but less than 20,001 pounds, when its GVWR does not exceed 1.25 times the GVWR of the towing vehicle.

(2) The gross vehicle weight (GVW) of a trailer equipped with surge brakes may be used instead of its GVWR to calculate compliance with the weight ratios specified in paragraph (d)(1) of this section when the trailer manufacturer's GVWR label is missing.

(3) The GVW of a trailer equipped with surge brakes must be used to calculate compliance with the weight ratios specified in paragraph (d)(1) of this section when the trailer's GVW exceeds its GVWR.

(4) The surge brakes must meet the requirements of § 393.40.

[70 FR 48051, Aug. 15, 2005, as amended at 72 FR 9870, Mar. 6, 2007]

§ 393.49 Control valves for brakes.

(a) *General rule.* Except as provided in paragraphs (b) and (c) of this section, every motor vehicle manufactured after June 30, 1953, which is equipped with power brakes, must have the braking system so arranged that one application valve must when activated cause all of the service brakes on the motor vehicle or combination motor vehicle to operate. This requirement must not be construed to prohibit motor vehicles from being equipped with an additional valve to be used to operate the brakes on a trailer or trailers or as required for busses in § 393.44.

(b) *Driveaway-Towaway Exception.* This section is not applicable to driveaway-towaway operations unless the brakes on such operations are designed to be operated by a single valve.

(c) *Surge brake exception.* This requirement is not applicable to trailers equipped with surge brakes that satisfy the conditions specified in § 393.48(d).

[72 FR 9871, Mar. 6, 2007]

§ 393.50 Reservoirs required.

(a) *Reservoir capacity for air-braked power units manufactured on or after March 1, 1975, and air-braked trailers manufactured on or after January 1, 1975.* Buses, trucks, and truck-tractors manufactured on or after March 1, 1975, and air-braked trailers manufactured on or after January 1, 1975, must meet the reservoir requirements of FMVSS No. 121, S5.1.2, in effect on the date of manufacture.

(b) *Reservoir capacity for air-braked vehicles not subject to FMVSS No. 121 on the date of manufacture and all vacuum braked vehicles.* Each motor vehicle using air or vacuum braking must have either reserve capacity, or a reservoir, that would enable the driver to make a full service brake application with the engine stopped without depleting the air pressure or vacuum below 70 percent of that indicated by the air or vacuum gauge immediately before the brake application is made. For the purposes of this paragraph, a full service brake application means depressing the brake pedal or treadle valve to the limit of its travel.

(c) *Safeguarding of air and vacuum.* Each service reservoir system on a motor vehicle shall be protected against a loss of air pressure or vacuum due to a failure or leakage in the system between the service reservoir and the source of air pressure or vacuum, by check valves or equivalent devices whose proper functioning can be checked without disconnecting any air or vacuum line, or fitting.

(d) *Drain valves for air braked vehicles.* Each reservoir must have a condensate drain valve that can be manually operated. Automatic condensate drain valves may be used provided (1) they may be operated manually, or (2) a manual means of draining the reservoirs is retained.

[70 FR 48052, Aug. 15, 2005]

§ 393.51 Warning signals, air pressure and vacuum gauges.

(a) *General Rule.* Every bus, truck and truck tractor, except as provided in paragraph (f), must be equipped with a signal that provides a warning to the driver when a failure occurs in the vehicle's service brake system. The warning signal must meet the applicable requirements of paragraphs (b), (c), (d) or (e) of this section.

(b) *Hydraulic brakes.* Vehicles manufactured on or after September 1, 1975, must meet the brake system indicator lamp requirements of FMVSS No. 571.105 (S5.3) applicable to the vehicle on the date of manufacture. Vehicles manufactured on or after July 1, 1973 but before September 1, 1975, or to which FMVSS No. 571.105 was not applicable on the date of manufacture, must have a warning signal which operates before or upon application of the brakes in the event of a hydraulic-type complete failure of a partial system. The signal must be either visible within the driver's forward field of view or audible. The signal must be continuous. (NOTE: FMVSS No. 105 was applicable to trucks and buses from September 1, 1975 to October 12, 1976, and from September 1, 1983, to the present. FMVSS No. 105 was not applicable to trucks and buses manufactured between October 12, 1976, and September 1, 1983. Motor carriers have the option of equipping those vehicles to meet either the indicator lamp requirements of FMVSS No. 105, or the indicator lamp requirements specified in this paragraph for vehicles which were not subject to FMVSS No. 105 on the date of manufacture.)

(c) *Air brakes.* A commercial motor vehicle (regardless of the date of manufacture) equipped with service brakes activated by compressed air (air brakes) or a commercial motor vehicle towing a vehicle with service brakes activated by compressed air (air brakes) must be equipped with a pressure gauge and a warning signal. Trucks, truck tractors, and buses manufactured on or after March 1, 1975, must, at a minimum, have a pressure gauge and a warning signal which meets the requirements of FMVSS No. 121 (S5.1.4 for the pressure gauge and S5.1.5 for the warning signal) applicable to the vehicle on the date of manufacture of the vehicle. Power units to which FMVSS No. 571.121 was not applicable on the date of manufacture of the vehicle must be equipped with—

(1) A pressure gauge, visible to a person seated in the normal driving position, which indicates the air pressure (in kilopascals (kPa) or pounds per square inch (psi)) available for braking; and

(2) A warning signal that is audible or visible to a person in the normal driving position and provides a continuous warning to the driver whenever the air pressure in the service reservoir system is at 379 kPa (55 psi) and below, or one-half of the compressor governor cutout pressure, whichever is less.

(d) *Vacuum brakes.* A commercial motor vehicle (regardless of the date it was manufactured) having service brakes activated by vacuum or a vehicle towing a vehicle having service brakes activated by vacuum must be equipped with—

(1) A vacuum gauge, visible to a person seated in the normal driving position, which indicates the vacuum (in millimeters or inches of mercury) available for braking; and

(2) A warning signal that is audible or visible to a person in the normal driving position and provides a continuous warning to the driver whenever the vacuum in the vehicle's supply reservoir is less than 203 mm (8 inches) of mercury.

(e) *Hydraulic brakes applied or assisted by air or vacuum.* Each vehicle equipped with hydraulically activated service brakes which are applied or assisted by compressed air or vacuum, and to which FMVSS No. 105 was not applicable on the date of manufacture, must be equipped with a warning signal that conforms to paragraph (b) of this section for the hydraulic portion of the system; paragraph (c) of this section for the air assist/air applied portion; or paragraph (d) of this section for the vacuum assist/vacuum applied portion. This paragraph shall not be construed as requiring air pressure gauges or vacuum gauges, only warning signals.

(f) *Exceptions.* The rules in paragraphs (c), (d) and (e) of this section do not apply to property carrying commercial motor vehicles which have less than three axles and (1) were manufactured before July 1, 1973, and (2) have a manufacturer's gross vehicle weight rating less than 4,536 kg (10,001 pounds).

[70 FR 48052, Aug. 15, 2005]

§393.52 Brake performance.

(a) Upon application of its service brakes, a motor vehicle or combination of motor vehicles must under any condition of loading in which it is found on a public highway, be capable of—

(1) Developing a braking force at least equal to the percentage of its gross weight specified in the table in paragraph (d) of this section;

(2) Decelerating to a stop from 20 miles per hour at not less than the rate specified in the table in paragraph (d) of this section; and

(3) Stopping from 20 miles per hour in a distance, measured from the point at which movement of the service brake pedal or control begins, that is not greater than the distance specified in the table in paragraph (d) of this section; or, for motor vehicles or motor vehicle combinations that have a GVWR or GVW greater than 4,536 kg (10,000 pounds),

(4) Developing only the braking force specified in paragraph (a)(1) of this section and the stopping distance specified in paragraph (a)(3) of this section, if braking force is measured by a performance-based brake tester which meets the requirements of functional specifications for performance-based brake testers for commercial motor vehicles, where braking force is the sum

449

of the braking force at each wheel of the vehicle or vehicle combination as a percentage of gross vehicle or combination weight.

(b) Upon application of its emergency brake system and with no other brake system applied, a motor vehicle or combination of motor vehicles must, under any condition of loading in which it is found on a public highway, be capable of stopping from 20 miles per hour in a distance, measured from the point at which movement of the emergency brake control begins, that is not greater than the distance speci-

fied in the table in paragraph (d) of this section.

(c) Conformity to the stopping-distance requirements of paragraphs (a) and (b) of this section shall be determined under the following conditions:

(1) Any test must be made with the vehicle on a hard surface that is substantially level, dry, smooth, and free of loose material.

(2) The vehicle must be in the center of a 12-foot-wide lane when the test begins and must not deviate from that lane during the test.

(d) Vehicle brake performance table:

Type of motor vehicle	Service brake systems			Emergency brake systems
	Braking force as a percentage of gross vehicle or combination weight	Deceleration in feet per second per second	Application and braking distance in feet from initial speed of 20 mph	Application and braking distance in feet from initial speed of 20 mph
A. Passenger-carrying vehicles:				
(1) Vehicles with a seating capacity of 10 persons or less, including driver, and built on a passenger car chassis	65.2	21	20	54
(2) Vehicles with a seating capacity of more than 10 persons, including driver, and built on a passenger car chassis; vehicles built on a truck or bus chassis and having a manufacturer's GVWR of 10,000 pounds or less	52.8	17	25	66
(3) All other passenger-carrying vehicles	43.5	14	35	85
B. Property-carrying vehicles:				
(1) Single unit vehicles having a manufacturer's GVWR of 10,000 pounds or less	52.8	17	25	66
(2) Single unit vehicles having a manufacturer's GVWR of more than 10,000 pounds, except truck tractors. Combinations of a 2-axle towing vehicle and trailer having a GVWR of 3,000 pounds or less. All combinations of 2 or less vehicles in drive-away or tow-away operation	43.5	14	35	85
(3) All other property-carrying vehicles and combinations of property-carrying vehicles	43.5	14	40	90

Notes: (a) There is a definite mathematical relationship between the figures in columns 2 and 3. If the decelerations set forth in column 3 are divided by 32.2 feet per-second per-second, the figures in column 2 will be obtained. (For example, 21 divided by 32.2 equals 65.2 percent.) Column 2 is included in the tabulation because certain brake testing devices utilize this factor.

(b) The decelerations specified in column 3 are an indication of the effectiveness of the basic brakes, and as measured in practical brake testing are the the maximum decelerations attained at some time during the stop. These decelerations as measured in brake tests cannot be used to compute the values in column 4 because the deceleration is not sustained at the same rate over the entire period of the stop. The deceleration increases from zero to a maximum during a period of brake system application and brake-force buildup. Also, other factors may cause the deceleration to decrease after reaching a maximum. The added distance that results because maximum deceleration is not sustained is included in the figures in column 4 but is not indicated by the usual brake-testing devices for checking deceleration.

(c) The distances in column 4 and the decelerations in column 3 are not directly related. "Brake-system application and braking distance in feet" (column 4) is a definite measure of the overall effectiveness of the braking system, being the distance traveled between the point at which the driver starts to move the braking controls and the point at which the vehicle comes to rest. It includes distance traveled while the brakes are being applied and distance traveled while the brakes are retarding the vehicle.

(d) The distance traveled during the period of brake-system application and brake-force buildup varies with vehicle type, being negligible for many passenger cars and greatest for combinations of commercial vehicles. This fact accounts for the variation from 20 to 40 feet in the values in column 4 for the various classes of vehicles.

(e) The terms "GVWR" and "GVW" refer to the manufacturer's gross vehicle weight rating and the actual gross vehicle weight, respectively.

[36 FR 20298, Oct. 20, 1971, as amended at 37 FR 5251, Mar. 11, 1972; 37 FR 11336, June 7, 1972; 68 FR 51777, Aug. 9, 2002]

§ 393.53 Automatic brake adjusters and brake adjustment indicators.

(a) *Automatic brake adjusters (hydraulic brake systems).* Each commercial motor vehicle manufactured on or after October 20, 1993, and equipped with a hydraulic brake system, shall meet the automatic brake adjustment system requirements of Federal Motor Vehicle Safety Standard No. 105 (49 CFR 571.105, S5.1) applicable to the vehicle at the time it was manufactured.

(b) *Automatic brake adjusters (air brake systems).* Each commercial motor vehicle manufactured on or after October 20, 1994, and equipped with an air brake system shall meet the automatic brake adjustment system requirements of Federal Motor Vehicle Safety Standard No. 121 (49 CFR 571.121, S5.1.8) applicable to the vehicle at the time it was manufactured.

(c) *Brake adjustment indicator (air brake systems).* On each commercial motor vehicle manufactured on or after October 20, 1994, and equipped with an air brake system which contains an external automatic adjustment mechanism and an exposed pushrod, the condition of service brake under-adjustment shall be displayed by a brake adjustment indicator conforming to the requirements of Federal Motor Vehicle Safety Standard No. 121 (49 CFR 571.121, S5.1.8) applicable to the vehicle at the time it was manufactured.

[60 FR 46245, Sept. 6, 1995]

§ 393.55 Antilock brake systems.

(a) *Hydraulic brake systems.* Each truck and bus manufactured on or after March 1, 1999 (except trucks and buses engaged in driveaway-towaway operations), and equipped with a hydraulic brake system, shall be equipped with an antilock brake system that meets the requirements of Federal Motor Vehicle Safety Standard (FMVSS) No. 105 (49 CFR 571.105, S5.5).

(b) *ABS malfunction indicators for hydraulic braked vehicles.* Each hydraulic braked vehicle subject to the requirements of paragraph (a) of this section shall be equipped with an ABS malfunction indicator system that meets the requirements of FMVSS No. 105 (49 CFR 571.105, S5.3).

(c) *Air brake systems.* (1) Each truck tractor manufactured on or after March 1, 1997 (except truck tractors engaged in driveaway-towaway operations), shall be equipped with an antilock brake system that meets the requirements of FMVSS No. 121 (49 CFR 571.121, S5.1.6.1(b)).

(2) Each air braked commercial motor vehicle other than a truck tractor, manufactured on or after March 1, 1998 (except commercial motor vehicles engaged in driveaway-towaway operations), shall be equipped with an antilock brake system that meets the requirements of FMVSS No. 121 (49 CFR 571.121, S5.1.6.1(a) for trucks and buses, S5.2.3 for semitrailers, converter dollies and full trailers).

(d) *ABS malfunction circuits and signals for air braked vehicles.* (1) Each truck tractor manufactured on or after March 1, 1997, and each single-unit air braked vehicle manufactured on or after March 1, 1998, subject to the requirements of paragraph (c) of this section, shall be equipped with an electrical circuit that is capable of signaling a malfunction that affects the generation or transmission of response or control signals to the vehicle's antilock brake system (49 CFR 571.121, S5.1.6.2(a)).

(2) Each truck tractor manufactured on or after March 1, 2001, and each single-unit vehicle that is equipped to tow another air-braked vehicle, subject to the requirements of paragraph (c) of this section, shall be equipped with an electrical circuit that is capable of transmitting a malfunction signal from the antilock brake system(s) on the towed vehicle(s) to the trailer ABS malfunction lamp in the cab of the towing vehicle, and shall have the means for connection of the electrical circuit to the towed vehicle. The ABS malfunction circuit and signal shall meet the requirements of FMVSS No. 121 (49 CFR 571.121, S5.1.6.2(b)).

(3) Each semitrailer, trailer converter dolly, and full trailer manufactured on or after March 1, 2001, and subject to the requirements of paragraph (c)(2) of this section, shall be equipped with an electrical circuit that is capable of signaling a malfunction in the trailer's antilock brake system,

and shall have the means for connection of this ABS malfunction circuit to the towing vehicle. In addition, each trailer manufactured on or after March 1, 2001, subject to the requirements of paragraph (c)(2) of this section, that is designed to tow another air-brake equipped trailer shall be capable of transmitting a malfunction signal from the antilock brake system(s) of the trailer(s) it tows to the vehicle in front of the trailer. The ABS malfunction circuit and signal shall meet the requirements of FMVSS No. 121 (49 CFR 571.121, S5.2.3.2).

(e) *Exterior ABS malfunction indicator lamps for trailers.* Each trailer (including a trailer converter dolly) manufactured on or after March 1, 1998, and subject to the requirements of paragraph (c)(2) of this section, shall be equipped with an ABS malfunction indicator lamp which meets the requirements of FMVSS No. 121 (49 CFR 571.121, S5.2.3.3).

[63 FR 24465, May 4, 1998, as amended at 75 FR 57396, Sept. 21, 2010]

Subpart D—Glazing and Window Construction

§ 393.60 Glazing in specified openings.

(a) *Glazing material.* Glazing material used in windshields, windows, and doors on a motor vehicle manufactured on or after December 25, 1968, shall at a minimum meet the requirements of Federal Motor Vehicle Safety Standard (FMVSS) No. 205 in effect on the date of manufacture of the motor vehicle. The glazing material shall be marked in accordance with FMVSS No. 205 (49 CFR 571.205, S6).

(b) *Windshields required.* Each bus, truck and truck-tractor shall be equipped with a windshield. Each windshield or portion of a multi-piece windshield shall be mounted using the full periphery of the glazing material.

(c) *Windshield condition.* With the exception of the conditions listed in paragraphs (c)(1), (c)(2), and (c)(3) of this section, each windshield shall be free of discoloration or damage in the area extending upward from the height of the top of the steering wheel (excluding a 51 mm (2 inch) border at the top of the windshield) and extending from a 25

mm (1 inch) border at each side of the windshield or windshield panel. *Exceptions:*

(1) Coloring or tinting which meets the requirements of paragraph (d) of this section;

(2) Any crack that is not intersected by any other cracks;

(3) Any damaged area which can be covered by a disc 19 mm (¾ inch) in diameter if not closer than 76 mm (3 inches) to any other similarly damaged area.

(d) *Coloring or tinting of windshields and windows.* Coloring or tinting of windshields and the windows to the immediate right and left of the driver is allowed, provided the parallel luminous transmittance through the colored or tinted glazing is not less than 70 percent of the light at normal incidence in those portions of the windshield or windows which are marked as having a parallel luminous transmittance of not less than 70 percent. The transmittance restriction does not apply to other windows on the commercial motor vehicle.

(e) *Prohibition on obstructions to the driver's field of view*—(1) *Devices mounted at the top of the windshield.* Antennas, transponders, and similar devices must not be mounted more than 152 mm (6 inches) below the upper edge of the windshield. These devices must be located outside the area swept by the windshield wipers, and outside the driver's sight lines to the road and highway signs and signals.

(2) *Decals and stickers mounted on the windshield.* Commercial Vehicle Safety Alliance (CVSA) inspection decals, and stickers and/or decals required under Federal or State laws may be placed at the bottom or sides of the windshield provided such decals or stickers do not extend more than 115 mm (4½ inches) from the bottom of the windshield and are located outside the area swept by the windshield wipers, and outside the driver's sight lines to the road and highway signs or signals.

[63 FR 1387, Jan. 9, 1998]

§ 393.61 Truck and truck tractor window construction.

Each truck and truck tractor (except trucks engaged in armored car service) shall have at least one window on each side of the driver's compartment. Each window must have a minimum area of 1,290 cm² (200 in²) formed by a rectangle 33 cm by 45 cm (13 inches by 17¾ inches). The maximum radius of the corner arcs shall not exceed 152 mm (6 inches). The long axis of the rectangle shall not make an angle of more than 45 degrees with the surface on which the unladen vehicle stands. If the cab is designed with a folding door or doors or with clear openings where doors or windows are customarily located, no windows shall be required in those locations.

[70 FR 48052, Aug. 15, 2005]

§ 393.62 Emergency exits for buses.

(a) *Buses manufactured on or after September 1, 1994.* Each bus with a GVWR of 4,536 kg (10,000 pounds) or less must meet the emergency exit requirements of FMVSS No. 217 (S5.2.2.3) in effect on the date of manufacture. Each bus with a GVWR of more than 4,536 kg (10,000 pounds) must have emergency exits which meet the applicable emergency exit requirements of FMVSS No. 217 (S5.2.2 or S5.2.3) in effect on the date of manufacture.

(b) *Buses manufactured on or after September 1, 1973, but before September 1, 1994.* (1) Each bus (including a school bus used in interstate commerce for non-school bus operations) with a GVWR of more than 4,536 kg (10,000 lbs) must meet the requirements of FMVSS No. 217, S5.2.2 in effect on the date of manufacture.

(2) Each bus (including a school bus used in interstate commerce for non-school bus operations) with a GVWR of 4,536 kg (10,000 lbs) or less must meet the requirements of FMVSS No. 217, S5.2.2.3 in effect on the date of manufacture.

(c) *Buses manufactured before September 1, 1973.* For each seated passenger space provided, inclusive of the driver there shall be at least 432 cm² (67 square inches) of glazing if such glazing is not contained in a push-out window; or, at least 432 cm² (67 square inches) of free opening resulting from opening of a push-out type window. No area shall be included in this minimum prescribed area unless it will provide an unobstructed opening of at least 1,290 cm² (200 in²) formed by a rectangle 33 cm by 45 cm (13 inches by 17¾ inches).

The maximum radius of the corner arcs shall not exceed 152 mm (6 inches). The long axis of the rectangle shall not make an angle of more than 45 degrees with the surface on which the unladen vehicle stands. The area shall be measured either by removal of the glazing if not of the push-out type, or of the movable sash if of the push-out type. The exit must comply with paragraph (d) of this section. Each side of the bus must have at least 40 percent of emergency exit space required by this paragraph.

(d) *Laminated safety glass/push-out window requirements for buses manufactured before September 1, 1973.* Emergency exit space used to satisfy the requirements of paragraph (c) of this section must have laminated safety glass or push-out windows designed and maintained to yield outward to provide a free opening.

(1) *Safety glass.* Laminated safety glass must meet Test No. 25, Egress, of American National Standard for Safety Glazing Materials for Glazing Motor Vehicles and Motor Vehicle Equipment Operating on Land Highways—Safety Standards ANSI/SAE Z26.1/96, August 1997. (See § 393.7 (b) for information on incorporation by reference and availability of this document.)

(2) *Push-out windows.* Each push-out window shall be releasable by operating no more than two mechanisms and allow manual release of the exit by a single occupant. For mechanisms which require rotary or straight (parallel to the undisturbed exit surface) motions to operate the exit, no more than 89 Newtons (20 pounds) of force shall be required to release the exit. For exits which require a straight motion perpendicular to the undisturbed exit surface, no more than 267 Newtons (60 pounds) shall be required to release the exit.

(e) *Emergency exit identification.* Each bus and each school bus used in interstate commerce for non-school bus operations, manufactured on or after September 1, 1973, shall meet the applicable emergency exit identification or marking requirements of FMVSS No. 217, S5.5, in effect on the date of manufacture. The emergency exits and doors on all buses (including school buses used in interstate commerce for non-school bus operations) must be marked

454

"Emergency Exit" or "Emergency Door" followed by concise operating instructions describing each motion necessary to unlatch or open the exit located within 152 mm (6 inches) of the release mechanism.

(f) *Exception for the transportation of prisoners.* The requirements of this section do not apply to buses used exclusively for the transportation of prisoners.

[70 FR 48052, Aug. 15, 2005]

§393.63 [Reserved]

Subpart E—Fuel Systems

AUTHORITY: Sec. 204, Interstate Commerce Act, as amended, 49 U.S.C. 304; sec. 6, Department of Transportation Act, 49 U.S.C. 1655; delegation of authority at 49 CFR 1.48 and 389.4.

§393.65 All fuel systems.

(a) *Application of the rules in this section.* The rules in this section apply to systems for containing and supplying fuel for the operation of motor vehicles or for the operation of auxiliary equipment installed on, or used in connection with, motor vehicles.

(b) *Location.* Each fuel system must be located on the motor vehicle so that—

(1) No part of the system extends beyond the widest part of the vehicle;

(2) No part of a fuel tank is forward of the front axle of a power unit;

(3) Fuel spilled vertically from a fuel tank while it is being filled will not contact any part of the exhaust or electrical systems of the vehicle, except the fuel level indicator assembly;

(4) Fill pipe openings are located outside the vehicle's passenger compartment and its cargo compartment;

(5) A fuel line does not extend between a towed vehicle and the vehicle that is towing it while the combination of vehicles is in motion; and

(6) No part of the fuel system of a bus manufactured on or after January 1, 1973, is located within or above the passenger compartment.

(c) *Fuel tank installation.* Each fuel tank must be securely attached to the motor vehicle in a workmanlike manner.

(d) *Gravity or syphon feed prohibited.* A fuel system must not supply fuel by gravity or syphon feed directly to the carburetor or injector.

(e) *Selection control valve location.* If a fuel system includes a selection control valve which is operable by the driver to regulate the flow of fuel from two or more fuel tanks, the valve must be installed so that either—

(1) The driver may operate it while watching the roadway and without leaving his/her driving position; or

(2) The driver must stop the vehicle and leave his/her seat in order to operate the valve.

(f) *Fuel lines.* A fuel line which is not completely enclosed in a protective housing must not extend more than 2 inches below the fuel tank or its sump. Diesel fuel crossover, return, and withdrawal lines which extend below the bottom of the tank or sump must be protected against damage from impact. Every fuel line must be—

(1) Long enough and flexible enough to accommodate normal movements of the parts to which it is attached without incurring damage; and

(2) Secured against chafing, kinking, or other causes of mechanical damage.

(g) *Excess flow valve.* When pressure devices are used to force fuel from a fuel tank, a device which prevents the flow of fuel from the fuel tank if the fuel feed line is broken must be installed in the fuel system.

[36 FR 15445, Aug. 14, 1971, as amended at 37 FR 4341, Mar. 2, 1972; 37 FR 28752, Dec. 29, 1972]

§393.67 Liquid fuel tanks.

(a) *Application of the rules in this section.* The rules in this section apply to tanks containing or supplying fuel for the operation of commercial motor vehicles or for the operation of auxiliary equipment installed on, or used in connection with commercial motor vehicles.

(1) A liquid fuel tank manufactured on or after January 1, 1973, and a side-mounted gasoline tank must conform to all rules in this section.

(2) A diesel fuel tank manufactured before January 1, 1973, and mounted on a bus must conform to the rules in paragraphs (c)(7)(iii) and (d)(2) of this section.

455

(3) A diesel fuel tank manufactured before January 1, 1973, and mounted on a vehicle other than a bus must conform to the rules in paragraph (c)(7)(iii) of this section.

(4) A gasoline tank, other than a side-mounted gasoline tank, manufactured before January 1, 1973, and mounted on a bus must conform to the rules in paragraphs (c) (1) through (10) and (d)(2) of this section.

(5) A gasoline tank, other than a side-mounted gasoline tank, manufactured before January 1, 1973, and mounted on a vehicle other than a bus must conform to the rules in paragraphs (c) (1) through (10), inclusive, of this section.

(6) Private motor carrier of passengers. Motor carriers engaged in the private transportation of passengers may continue to operate a commercial motor vehicle which was not subject to this section or 49 CFR 571.301 at the time of its manufacture, provided the fuel tank of such vehicle is maintained to the original manufacturer's standards.

(7) Motor vehicles that meet the fuel system integrity requirements of 49 CFR 571.301 are exempt from the requirements of this subpart, as they apply to the vehicle's fueling system.

(b) *Definitions.* As used in this section—

(1) The term *liquid fuel tank* means a fuel tank designed to contain a fuel that is liquid at normal atmospheric pressures and temperatures.

(2) A *side-mounted* fuel tank is a liquid fuel tank which—

(i) If mounted on a truck tractor, extends outboard of the vehicle frame and outside of the plan view outline of the cab; or

(ii) If mounted on a truck, extends outboard of a line parallel to the longitudinal centerline of the truck and tangent to the outboard side of a front tire in a straight ahead position. In determining whether a fuel tank on a truck or truck tractor is side-mounted, the fill pipe is not considered a part of the tank.

(c) *Construction of liquid fuel tanks—* (1) *Joints.* Joints of a fuel tank body must be closed by arc-, gas-, seam-, or spot-welding, by brazing, by silver soldering, or by techniques which provide heat resistance and mechanical securement at least equal to those specifically named. Joints must not be closed solely by crimping or by soldering with a lead-based or other soft solder.

(2) *Fittings.* The fuel tank body must have flanges or spuds suitable for the installation of all fittings.

(3) *Threads.* The threads of all fittings must be Dryseal American Standard Taper Pipe Thread or Dryseal SAE Short Taper Pipe Thread, specified in Society of Automotive Engineers Standard J476, as contained in the 1971 edition of the "SAE Handbook," except that straight (nontapered) threads may be used on fittings having integral flanges and using gaskets for sealing. At least four full threads must be in engagement in each fitting.

(4) *Drains and bottom fittings.* (i) Drains or other bottom fittings must not extend more than three-fourths of an inch below the lowest part of the fuel tank or sump.

(ii) Drains or other bottom fittings must be protected against damage from impact.

(iii) If a fuel tank has drains the drain fittings must permit substantially complete drainage of the tank.

(iv) Drains or other bottom fittings must be installed in a flange or spud designed to accommodate it.

(5) *Fuel withdrawal fittings.* Except for diesel fuel tanks, the fittings through which fuel is withdrawn from a fuel tank must be located above the normal level of fuel in the tank when the tank is full.

(6) [Reserved]

(7) *Fill pipe.* (i) Each fill pipe must be designed and constructed to minimize the risk of fuel spillage during fueling operations and when the vehicle is involved in a crash.

(ii) For diesel-fueled vehicles, the fill pipe and vents of a fuel tank having a capacity of more than 94.75 L (25 gallons) of fuel must permit filling the tank with fuel at a rate of at least 75.8 L/m (20 gallons per minute) without fuel spillage.

(iii) For gasoline- and methanol-fueled vehicles with a GVWR of 3,744 kg (8,500 pounds) or less, the vehicle must permit filling the tank with fuel dispensed at the applicable fill rate required by the regulations of the Environmental Protection Agency under 40 CFR 80.22.

(iv) For gasoline- and methanol-fueled vehicles with a GVWR of 14,000 pounds (6,400 kg) or less, the vehicle must comply with the applicable fuel-spitback prevention and onboard refueling vapor recovery regulations of the Environmental Protection Agency under 40 CFR part 86.

(v) Each fill pipe must be fitted with a cap that can be fastened securely over the opening in the fill pipe. Screw threads or a bayonet-type point are methods of conforming to the requirements of paragraph (c) of this section.

(8) *Safety venting system.* A liquid fuel tank with a capacity of more than 25 gallons of fuel must have a venting system which, in the event the tank is subjected to fire, will prevent internal tank pressure from rupturing the tank's body, seams, or bottom opening (if any).

(9) *Pressure resistance.* The body and fittings of a liquid fuel tank with a capacity of more than 25 gallons of fuel must be capable of withstanding an internal hydrostatic pressure equal to 150 percent of the maximum internal pressure reached in the tank during the safety venting systems test specified in paragraph (d)(1) of this section.

(10) *Air vent.* Each fuel tank must be equipped with a nonspill air vent (such as a ball check). The air vent may be combined with the fill-pipe cap or safety vent, or it may be a separate unit installed on the fuel tank.

(11) *Markings.* If the body of a fuel tank is readily visible when the tank is installed on the vehicle, the tank must be plainly marked with its liquid capacity. The tank must also be plainly marked with a warning against filling it to more than 95 percent of its liquid capacity.

(12) *Overfill restriction.* A liquid fuel tank manufactured on or after January 1, 1973, must be designed and constructed so that—

(i) The tank cannot be filled, in a normal filling operation, with a quantity of fuel that exceeds 95 percent of the tank's liquid capacity; and

(ii) When the tank is filled, normal expansion of the fuel will not cause fuel spillage.

(d) *Liquid fuel tank tests.* Each liquid fuel tank must be capable of passing the tests specified in paragraphs (d)(1) and (2) of this section. The specified tests are a measure of performance only. Alternative procedures which assure that equipment meets the required performance standards may be used. .

(1) *Safety venting system test*—(i) *Procedure.* Fill the tank three-fourths full with fuel, seal the fuel feed outlet, and invert the tank. When the fuel temperature is between 50 °F. and 80 °F., apply an enveloping flame to the tank so that the temperature of the fuel rises at a rate of not less than 6 °F. and not more than 8 °F. per minute.

(ii) *Required performance.* The safety venting system required by paragraph (c)(8) of this section must activate before the internal pressure in the tank exceeds 50 pounds per square inch, gauge, and the internal pressure must not thereafter exceed the pressure at which the system activated by more than five pounds per square inch despite any further increase in the temperature of the fuel.

(2) *Leakage test*—(i) *Procedure.* Fill the tank to capacity with fuel having a temperature between 50 °F. and 80 °F. With the fill-pipe cap installed, turn the tank through an angle of 150° in any direction about any axis from its normal position.

(ii) *Required performance.* Neither the tank nor any fitting may leak more than a total of one ounce by weight of fuel per minute in any position the tank assumes during the test.

(e) *Side-mounted liquid fuel tank tests.* Each side-mounted liquid fuel tank must be capable of passing the tests specified in paragraphs (e)(1) and (2) of this section and the test specified in paragraphs (d)(1) and (2) of this section. The specified tests are a measure of performance only. Alternative procedures which assure that equipment meets the required performance criteria may be used.

(1) *Drop test*—(i) *Procedure.* Fill the tank with a quantity of water having a weight equal to the weight of the maximum fuel load of the tank and drop

the tank 30 feet onto an unyielding surface so that it lands squarely on one corner.

(ii) *Required performance.* Neither the tank nor any fitting may leak more than a total of 1 ounce by weight of water per minute.

(2) *Fill-pipe test*—(i) *Procedure.* Fill the tank with a quantity of water having a weight equal to the weight of the maximum fuel load of the tank and drop the tank 10 feet onto an unyielding surface so that it lands squarely on its fill-pipe.

(ii) *Required performance.* Neither the tank nor any fitting may leak more than a total of 1 ounce by weight of water per minute.

(f) *Certification and markings.* Each liquid fuel tank shall be legibly and permanently marked by the manufacturer with the following minimum information:

(1) The month and year of manufacture,

(2) The manufacturer's name on tanks manufactured on and after July 1, 1989, and means of identifying the facility at which the tank was manufactured, and

(3) A certificate that it conforms to the rules in this section applicable to the tank. The certificate must be in the form set forth in either of the following:

(i) If a tank conforms to all rules in this section pertaining to side-mounted fuel tanks: "Meets all FMCSA side-mounted tank requirements."

(ii) If a tank conforms to all rules in this section pertaining to tanks which are not side-mounted fuel tanks: "Meets all FMCSA requirements for non-side-mounted fuel tanks."

(iii) The form of certificate specified in paragraph (f)(3) (i) or (ii) of this section may be used on a liquid fuel tank manufactured before July 11, 1973, but it is not mandatory for liquid fuel tanks manufactured before March 7, 1989. The form of certification manufactured on or before March 7, 1989, must meet the requirements in effect at the time of manufacture.

(4) *Exception.* The following previously exempted vehicles are *not* required to carry the certification and marking specified in paragraphs (f)(1) through (3) of this section:

(i) Ford vehicles with GVWR over 10,000 pounds identified as follows: The vehicle identification numbers (VINs) contain A, K, L, M, N, W, or X in the fourth position.

(ii) GM G-Vans (Chevrolet Express and GMC Savanna) and full-sized C/K trucks (Chevrolet Silverado and GMC Sierra) with GVWR over 10,000 pounds identified as follows: The VINs contain either a "J" or a "K" in the fourth position. In addition, the seventh position of the VINs on the G-Van will contain a "1."

[36 FR 15445, Aug. 14, 1971, as amended at 37 FR 4341, Mar. 2, 1972; 37 FR 28753, Dec. 29, 1972; 45 FR 46424, July 10, 1980; 53 FR 49400, Dec. 7, 1988; 59 FR 8753, Feb. 23, 1994; 69 FR 31305, June 3, 2004; 70 FR 48053, Aug. 15, 2005]

§ 393.68 Compressed natural gas fuel containers.

(a) *Applicability.* The rules in this section apply to compressed natural gas (CNG) fuel containers used for supplying fuel for the operation of commercial motor vehicles or for the operation of auxiliary equipment installed on, or used in connection with commercial motor vehicles.

(b) *CNG containers manufactured on or after March 26, 1995.* Any motor vehicle manufactured on or after March 26, 1995, and equipped with a CNG fuel tank must meet the CNG container requirements of FMVSS No. 304 (49 CFR 571.304) in effect at the time of manufacture of the vehicle.

(c) *Labeling.* Each CNG fuel container shall be permanently labeled in accordance with the requirements of FMVSS No. 304, S7.4.

[70 FR 48053, Aug. 15, 2005]

§ 393.69 Liquefied petroleum gas systems.

(a) A fuel system that uses liquefied petroleum gas as a fuel for the operation of a motor vehicle or for the operation of auxiliary equipment installed on, or used in connection with, a motor vehicle must conform to the "Standards for the Storage and Handling of Liquefied Petroleum Gases" of the National Fire Protection Association, Battery March Park, Quincy, MA 02269, as follows:

(1) A fuel system installed before December 31, 1962, must conform to the 1951 edition of the Standards.

(2) A fuel system installed on or after December 31, 1962, and before January 1, 1973, must conform to Division IV of the June 1959 edition of the Standards.

(3) A fuel system installed on or after January 1, 1973, and providing fuel for propulsion of the motor vehicle must conform to Division IV of the 1969 edition of the Standards.

(4) A fuel system installed on or after January 1, 1973, and providing fuel for the operation of auxiliary equipment must conform to Division VII of the 1969 edition of the Standards.

(b) When the rules in this section require a fuel system to conform to a specific edition of the Standards, the fuel system may conform to the applicable provisions in a later edition of the Standards specified in this section.

(c) The tank of a fuel system must be marked to indicate that the system conforms to the Standards.

[36 FR 15445, Aug. 14, 1971, as amended at 37 FR 4342, Mar. 2, 1972; 41 FR 53031, Dec. 3, 1976; 53 FR 49400, Dec. 7, 1988]

Subpart F—Coupling Devices and Towing Methods

§393.70 Coupling devices and towing methods, except for driveaway-towaway operations.

(a) *Tracking.* When two or more vehicles are operated in combination, the coupling devices connecting the vehicles shall be designed, constructed, and installed, and the vehicles shall be designed and constructed, so that when the combination is operated in a straight line on a level, smooth, paved surface, the path of the towed vehicle will not deviate more than 3 inches to either side of the path of the vehicle that tows it.

(b) *Fifth wheel assemblies*—(1) *Mounting*—(i) *Lower half.* The lower half of a fifth wheel mounted on a truck tractor or converter dolly must be secured to the frame of that vehicle with properly designed brackets, mounting plates or angles and properly tightened bolts of adequate size and grade, or devices that provide equivalent security. The installation shall not cause cracking, warping, or deformation of the frame. The installation must include a device for positively preventing the lower half of the fifth wheel from shifting on the frame to which it is attached.

(ii) *Upper half.* The upper half of a fifth wheel must be fastened to the motor vehicle with at least the same security required for the installation of the lower half on a truck tractor or converter dolly.

(2) *Locking.* Every fifth wheel assembly must have a locking mechanism. The locking mechanism, and any adapter used in conjunction with it, must prevent separation of the upper and lower halves of the fifth wheel assembly unless a positive manual release is activated. The release may be located so that the driver can operate it from the cab. If a motor vehicle has a fifth wheel designed and constructed to be readily separable, the fifth wheel locking devices shall apply automatically on coupling.

(3) *Location.* The lower half of a fifth wheel shall be located so that, regardless of the condition of loading, the relationship between the kingpin and the rear axle or axles of the towing motor vehicle will properly distribute the gross weight of both the towed and towing vehicles on the axles of those vehicles, will not unduly interfere with the steering, braking, and other maneuvering of the towing vehicle, and will not otherwise contribute to unsafe operation of the vehicles comprising the combination. The upper half of a fifth wheel shall be located so that the weight of the vehicles is properly distributed on their axles and the combination of vehicles will operate safely during normal operation.

(c) *Towing of full trailers.* A full trailer must be equipped with a tow-bar and a means of attaching the tow-bar to the towing and towed vehicles. The tow-bar and the means of attaching it must—

(1) Be structurally adequate for the weight being drawn;

(2) Be properly and securely mounted;

(3) Provide for adequate articulation at the connection without excessive slack at that location; and

(4) Be provided with a locking device that prevents accidental separation of the towed and towing vehicles. The

mounting of the trailer hitch (pintle hook or equivalent mechanism) on the towing vehicle must include reinforcement or bracing of the frame sufficient to produce strength and rigidity of the frame to prevent its undue distortion.

(d) *Safety devices in case of tow-bar failure or disconnection.* Every full trailer and every converter dolly used to convert a semitrailer to a full trailer must be coupled to the frame, or an extension of the frame, of the motor vehicle which tows it with one or more safety devices to prevent the towed vehicle from breaking loose in the event the tow-bar fails or becomes disconnected. The safety device must meet the following requirements:

(1) The safety device must not be attached to the pintle hook or any other device on the towing vehicle to which the tow-bar is attached. However, if the pintle hook or other device was manufactured prior to July 1, 1973, the safety device may be attached to the towing vehicle at a place on a pintle hook forging or casting if that place is independent of the pintle hook.

(2) The safety device must have no more slack than is necessary to permit the vehicles to be turned properly.

(3) The safety device, and the means of attaching it to the vehicles, must have an ultimate strength of not less than the gross weight of the vehicle or vehicles being towed.

(4) The safety device must be connected to the towed and towing vehicles and to the tow-bar in a manner which prevents the tow-bar from dropping to the ground in the event it fails or becomes disconnected.

(5) Except as provided in paragraph (d)(6) of this section, if the safety device consists of safety chains or cables, the towed vehicle must be equipped with either two safety chains or cables or with a bridle arrangement of a single chain or cable attached to its frame or axle at two points as far apart as the configuration of the frame or axle permits. The safety chains or cables shall be either two separate pieces, each equipped with a hook or other means for attachment to the towing vehicle, or a single piece leading along each side of the tow-bar from the two points of attachment on the towed vehicle and arranged into a bridle with a single means of attachment to be connected to the towing vehicle. When a single length of cable is used, a thimble and twin-base cable clamps shall be used to form the forward bridle eye. The hook or other means of attachment to the towing vehicle shall be secured to the chains or cables in a fixed position.

(6) If the towed vehicle is a converter dolly with a solid tongue and without a hinged tow-bar or other swivel between the fifth wheel mounting and the attachment point of the tongue eye or other hitch device—

(i) Safety chains or cables, when used as the safety device for that vehicle, may consist of either two chains or cables or a single chain or cable used alone;

(ii) A single safety device, including a single chain or cable used alone as the safety device, must be in line with the centerline of the trailer tongue; and

(iii) The device may be attached to the converter dolly at any point to the rear of the attachment point of the tongue eye or other hitch device.

(7) Safety devices other than safety chains or cables must provide strength, security of attachment, and directional stability equal to, or greater than, safety chains or cables installed in accordance with paragraphs (d) (5) and (6) of this section.

(8)(i) When two safety devices, including two safety chains or cables, are used and are attached to the towing vehicle at separate points, the points of attachment on the towing vehicle shall be located equally distant from, and on opposite sides of, the longitudinal centerline of the towing vehicle.

(ii) Where two chains or cables are attached to the same point on the towing vehicle, and where a bridle or a single chain or cable is used, the point of attachment must be on the longitudinal centerline or within 152 mm (6 inches) to the right of the longitudinal centerline of the towing vehicle.

(iii) A single safety device, other than a chain or cable, must also be attached to the towing vehicle at a point on the longitudinal centerline or within 152 mm (6 inches) to the right of the longitudinal centerline of the towing vehicle.

[37 FR 21439, Oct. 11, 1972, as amended at 70 FR 48053, Aug. 15, 2005]

§ 393.71 Coupling devices and towing methods, driveaway-towaway operations.

(a) *Number in combination.* (1) No more than three saddle-mounts may be used in any combination.

(2) No more than one tow-bar or ball-and-socket type coupling device may be used in any combination.

(3) When motor vehicles are towed by means of triple saddle-mounts, the towed vehicles shall have brakes acting on all wheels which are in contact with the roadway.

(b) *Carrying vehicles on towing vehicle.* (1) When adequately and securely attached by means equivalent in security to that provided in paragraph (j)(2) of this section, a motor vehicle or motor vehicles may be full-mounted on the structure of a towing vehicle engaged in any driveaway-towaway operation.

(2) No motor vehicle or motor vehicles may be full-mounted on a towing vehicle unless the relationship of such full-mounted vehicles to the rear axle or axles results in proper distribution of the total gross weight of the vehicles and does not unduly interfere with the steering, braking, or maneuvering of the towing vehicle, or otherwise contribute to the unsafe operation of the vehicles comprising the combination.

(3) Saddle-mounted vehicles must be arranged such that the gross weight of the vehicles is properly distributed to prevent undue interference with the steering, braking, or maneuvering of the combination of vehicles.

(c) *Carrying vehicles on towed vehicles.* (1) When adequately and securely attached by means equivalent in security to that provided in paragraph (j)(2) of this section, a motor vehicle or motor vehicles may be full-mounted on the structure of towed vehicles engaged in any driveaway-towaway operation.

(2) No motor vehicle shall be full-mounted on a motor vehicle towed by means of a tow-bar unless the towed vehicle is equipped with brakes and is provided with means for effective application of brakes acting on all wheels and is towed on its own wheels.

(3) No motor vehicle or motor vehicles shall be full-mounted on a motor vehicle towed by means of a saddle-mount unless the center line of the kingpin or equivalent means of attachment of such towed vehicle shall be so located on the towing vehicle that the relationship to the rear axle or axles results in proper distribution of the total gross weight of the vehicles and does not unduly interfere with the steering, braking, or maneuvering of the towing vehicle or otherwise contribute to the unsafe operation of vehicles comprising the combination; and unless a perpendicular to the ground from the center of gravity of the full-mounted vehicles lies forward of the center line of the rear axle of the saddle-mounted vehicle.

(4) If a motor vehicle towed by means of a double saddle-mount has any vehicle full-mounted on it, such saddle-mounted vehicle shall at all times while so loaded have effective brakes acting on those wheels which are in contact with the roadway.

(d) *Bumper tow-bars on heavy vehicles prohibited.* Tow-bars of the type which depend upon the bumpers as a means of transmitting forces between the vehicles shall not be used to tow a motor vehicle weighing more than 5,000 pounds.

(e) *Front wheels of saddle-mounted vehicles restrained.* A motor vehicle towed by means of a saddle-mount shall have the motion of the front wheels restrained if under any condition of turning of such wheels they will project beyond the widest part of either the towed or towing vehicle.

(f) *Vehicles to be towed in forward position.* Unless the steering mechanism is adequately locked in a straight-forward position, all motor vehicles towed by means of a saddle-mount shall be towed with the front end mounted on the towing vehicle.

(g) *Means required for towing.* No motor vehicles or combination of motor vehicles shall be towed in driveaway-towaway operations by means other than a tow-bar, ball-and-socket type coupling device, saddle-mount connections which meet the requirements of this section, or in the case of a semi-trailer equipped with an upper coupler assembly, a fifth-wheel meeting the requirements of § 393.70.

(h) *Requirements for tow-bars.* Tow-bars shall comply with the following requirements:

(1) *Tow-bars, structural adequacy and mounting.* Every tow-bar shall be structurally adequate and properly installed and maintained. To insure that it is structurally adequate, it must, at least, meet the requirements of the following table:

Gross weight of towed vehicle (pounds)[1]	Longitudinal strength in tension and compression[2]		Strength as a beam (in any direction concentrated load at center)[2,3]
	All tow-bars	New tow-bars acquired and used by a motor carrier after Sept. 30, 1948	
	Pounds		
Less than 5,000	3,000	6,500	3,000
5,000 and over	....	....	....
Less than 10,000	6,000	([1])	([1])
10,000 and over	....	....	....
Less than 15,000	9,000	([1])	([1])

[1] The required strength of tow-bars for towed vehicles of 15,000 pounds and over gross weight and of new tow-bars acquired and used after Sept. 30, 1948, for towed vehicles of 5,000 pounds and over gross weight shall be computed by means of the following formulae: Longitudinal strength=gross weight of towed vehicle × 1.3. Strength as a beam=gross weight of towed vehicle × 0.6.

[2] In testing, the whole unit shall be tested with all clamps, joints, and pins so mounted and fastened as to approximate conditions of actual operation.

[3] This test shall be applicable only to tow-bars which are, in normal operation, subjected to a bending movement such as tow-bars for house trailers.

(2) *Tow-bars, jointed.* The tow-bar shall be so constructed as to freely permit motion in both horizontal and vertical planes between the towed and towing vehicles. The means used to provide the motion shall be such as to prohibit the transmission of stresses under normal operation between the towed and towing vehicles, except along the longitudinal axis of the tongue or tongues.

(3) *Tow-bar fastenings.* The means used to transmit the stresses to the chassis or frames of the towed and towing vehicles may be either temporary structures or bumpers or other integral parts of the vehicles: *Provided, however,* That the means used shall be so constructed, installed, and maintained that when tested as an assembly, failure in such members shall not occur when the weakest new tow-bar which is permissible under paragraph (h)(1) of

this section is subjected to the tests given therein.

(4) *Means of adjusting length.* On tow-bars, adjustable as to length, the means used to make such adjustment shall fit tightly and not result in any slackness or permit the tow-bar to bend. With the tow-bar supported rigidly at both ends and with a load of 50 pounds at the center, the sag, measured at the center, in any direction shall not exceed 0.25 inch under any condition of adjustment as to length.

(5) *Method of clamping.* Adequate means shall be provided for securely fastening the tow-bar to the towed and towing vehicles.

(6) *Tow-bar connection to steering mechanism.* The tow-bar shall be provided with suitable means of attachment to and actuation of the steering mechanism, if any, of the towed vehicle. The attachment shall provide for sufficient angularity of movement of the front wheels of the towed vehicle so that it may follow substantially in the path of the towing vehicle without cramping the tow-bar. The tow-bar shall be provided with suitable joints to permit such movement.

(7) *Tracking.* The tow-bar shall be so designed, constructed, maintained, and mounted as to cause the towed vehicle to follow substantially in the path of the towing vehicle. Tow-bars of such design on in our condition as to permit the towed vehicle to deviate more than 3 inches to either side of the path of a towing vehicle moving in a straight line as measured from the center of the towing vehicle are prohibited.

(8) *Passenger car-trailer type couplings.* Trailer couplings used for driveaway-towaway operations of passenger car trailers shall conform to Society of Automotive Engineers Standard No. J684c, "Trailer Couplings and Hitches—Automotive Type," July 1970.[1]

(9) *Marking tow-bars.* Every tow-bar acquired and used in driveaway-towaway operations by a motor carrier shall be plainly marked with the following certification of the manufacturer thereof (or words of equivalent meaning):

This tow-bar complies with the requirements of the Federal Motor Carrier Safety

_____
[1] See footnote 1 to § 393.24(c).

462

Administration for (maximum gross weight for which tow-bar is manufactured) vehicles.

Allowable Maximum Gross Weight

Manufactured _____

(month and year)

by _____

(name of manufacturer)

Tow-bar certification manufactured before the effective date of this regulation must meet requirements in effect at the time of manufacture.

(10) *Safety devices in case of tow-bar failure or disconnection.* (i) The towed vehicle shall be connected to the towing vehicle by a safety device to prevent the towed vehicle from breaking loose in the event the tow-bar fails or becomes disconnected. When safety chains or cables are used as the safety device for that vehicle, at least two safety chains or cables meeting the requirements of paragraph (h)(10)(ii) of this section shall be used. The tensile strength of the safety device and the means of attachment to the vehicles shall be at least equivalent to the corresponding longitudinal strength for tow-bars required in the table of paragraph (h)(1) of this section. If safety chains or cables are used as the safety device, the required strength shall be the combined strength of the combination of chains and cables.

(ii) If chains or cables are used as the safety device, they shall be crossed and attached to the vehicles near the points of bumper attachments to the chassis of the vehicles. The length of chain used shall be no more than necessary to permit free turning of the vehicles. The chains shall be attached to the tow-bar at the point of crossing or as close to that point as is practicable.

(iii) A safety device other than safety chains or cables must provide strength, security of attachment, and directional stability equal to, or greater than, that provided by safety chains or cables installed in accordance with paragraph (h)(10)(ii) of this section. A safety device other than safety chains or cables must be designed, constructed, and installed so that, if the tow-bar fails or becomes disconnected, the tow-bar will not drop to the ground.

(i) [Reserved]

(j) *Requirements for upper-half of saddle-mounts.* The upper-half of any sad-

dle-mount shall comply with the following requirements:

(1) *Upper-half connection to towed vehicle.* The upper-half shall be securely attached to the frame or axle of the towed vehicle by means of U-bolts or other means providing at least equivalent security.

(2) *U-bolts or other attachments.* U-bolts used to attach the upper half to the towed vehicle shall be made of steel rod, free of defects, so shaped as to avoid at any point a radius of less than 1 inch: *Provided, however,* That a lesser radius may be utilized if the U-bolt is so fabricated as not to cause more than 5 percent reduction in cross-sectional area at points of curvature, in which latter event the minimum radius shall be one-sixteenth inch. U-bolts shall have a diameter not less than required by the following table:

DIAMETER OF U-BOLTS IN INCHES

Weight in pounds of heaviest towed vehicle	Double or triple saddle-mount			
	Front mount	Middle or front mount	Rear mount	Single saddle-mount [1]
Up to 5,000	0.625	0.5625	0.500	0.500
5,000 and over	0.6875	0.625	0.5625	0.5625

[1] The total weight of all the vehicles being towed shall govern. If other devices are used to accomplish the same purposes as U-bolts they shall have at least equivalent strength of U-bolts made of mild steel. Cast iron shall not be used for clamps or any other holding devices.

(3) *U-bolts and points of support, location.* The distance between the most widely separated U-bolts shall not be less than 9 inches. The distance between the widely separated points where the upper-half supports the towed vehicle shall not be less than 9 inches, except that saddle-mounts employing ball and socket joints shall employ a device which clamps the axle of the towed vehicle throughout a length of not less than 5 inches.

(4) *Cradle-type upper-halves, specifications.* Upper-halves of the cradle-type using vertical members to restrain the towed vehicle from relative movement in the direction of motion of the vehicles shall be substantially constructed and adequate for the purpose. Such cradle-mounts shall be equipped with at least one bolt or equivalent means to provide against relative vertical movement between the upper-half and the towed vehicle. Bolts, if used, shall be at

463

least one-half inch in diameter. Devices using equivalent means shall have at least equivalent strength. The means used to provide against relative vertical motion between the upper-half and the towed vehicle shall be such as not to permit a relative motion of over one-half inch. The distance between the most widely separated points of support between the upper-half and the towed vehicle shall be at least 9 inches.

(5) *Lateral movement of towed vehicle.* (i) Towed vehicles having a straight axle or an axle having a drop of less than 3 inches, unless the saddle-mount is constructed in accordance with paragraph (m)(2) of this section, shall be securely fastened by means of chains or cables to the upper-half so as to insure against relative lateral motion between the towed vehicle and the upper-half. The chains or cables shall be at least ³⁄₁₆-inch diameter and secured by bolts of at least equal diameter.

(ii) Towed vehicles with an axle with a drop of 3 inches or more, or connected by a saddle-mount constructed in accordance with paragraph (m)(2) of this section, need not be restrained by chains or cables provided that the upper-half is so designed as to provide against such relative motion.

(iii) Chains or cables shall not be required if the upper-half is so designed as positively to provide against lateral movement of the axle.

(k) *Requirements for lower half of saddle-mounts.* The lower half of any saddle-mount shall comply with the following requirements:

(1) *U-bolts or other attachments.* U-bolts used to attach the lower half to the towing vehicle shall be made of steel rod, free of defects, so shaped as to avoid at any point a radius of less than 1 inch: *Provided, however,* That a lesser radius may be utilized if the U-bolt is so fabricated as not to cause more than 5 percent reduction in cross-sectional area at points of curvature, in which latter event the minimum radius shall be one-sixteenth inch. U-bolts shall have a total cross-sectional area not less than as required by the following table:

TOTAL CROSS-SECTIONAL AREA OF U-BOLTS IN SQUARE INCHES

Weight in pounds of heaviest towed vehicle	Double or triple saddle-mount			Single saddle-mount [1]
	Front mount	Middle or front mount	Rear mount	
Up to 5,000	1.2	1.0	0.8	0.8
5,000 and over	1.4	1.2	1.0	1.0

[1] The total weight of all the vehicles being towed shall govern. If other devices are used to accomplish the same purposes as U-bolts they shall have at least equivalent strength of U-bolts made of mild steel. Cast iron shall not be used for clamps or any other holding devices.

(2) *Shifting.* Adequate provision shall be made by design and installation to provide against relative movement between the lower-half and the towing vehicle especially during periods of rapid acceleration and deceleration. To insure against shifting, designs of the tripod type shall be equipped with adequate and securely fastened hold-back chains or similar devices.

(3) *Swaying.* (i) Adequate provision shall be made by design and installation to provide against swaying or lateral movement of the towed vehicle relative to the towing vehicle. To insure against swaying, lower-halves designed with cross-members attached to but separable from vertical members shall have such cross-members fastened to the vertical members by at least two bolts on each side. Such bolts shall be of at least equivalent cross-sectional area as those required for U-bolts for the corresponding saddle-mount as given in the table in paragraph (k)(1) of this section. The minimum distance between the most widely separated points of support of the cross-member by the vertical member shall be three inches as measured in a direction parallel to the longitudinal axis of the towing vehicle.

(ii) The lower-half shall have a bearing surface on the frame of the towing vehicle of such dimensions that the pressure exerted by the lower-half upon the frame of the towing vehicle shall not exceed 200 pounds per square inch under any conditions of static loading. Hardwood blocks or blocks of other suitable material, such as hard rubber, aluminum or brakelining, if used between the lower half and the frame of the towing vehicle shall be at least ½ inch thick, 3 inches wide, and a combined length of 6 inches.

(iii) Under no condition shall the highest point of support of the towed vehicle by the upper-half be more than 24 inches, measured vertically, above the top of the frame of the towing vehicle, measured at the point where the lower-half rests on the towing vehicle.

(4) *Wood blocks.* (i) Hardwood blocks of good quality may be used to build up the height of the front end of the towed vehicle, provided that the total height of such wood blocks shall not exceed 8 inches and not over two separate pieces are placed upon each other to obtain such height; however, hardwood blocks, not over 4 in number, to a total height not to exceed 14 inches, may be used if the total cross-sectional area of the U-bolts used to attach the lower-half of the towing vehicle is at least 50 percent greater than that required by the table contained in paragraph (k)(1) of this section, or, if other devices are used in lieu of U-bolts, they shall provide for as great a resistance to bending as is provided by the larger U-bolts above prescribed.

(ii) Hardwood blocks must be at least 4 inches in width and the surfaces between blocks or block and lower-half or block and upper-half shall be planed and so installed and maintained as to minimize any tendency of the towed vehicle to sway or rock.

(5) *Cross-member, general requirements.* The cross-member, which is that part of the lower-half used to distribute the weight of the towed vehicle equally to each member of the frame of the towing vehicle, if used, shall be struc-turally adequate and properly installed and maintained adequately to perform this function.

(6) *Cross-member, use of wood.* No materials, other than suitable metals, shall be used as the cross-member, and wood may not be used structurally in any manner that will result in its being subject to tensile stresses. Wood may be used in cross-members if supported throughout its length by suitable metal cross-members.

(7) *Lower half strength.* The lower half shall be capable of supporting the loads given in the following table. For the purpose of test, the saddle-mount shall be mounted as normally operated and the load applied through the upper half:

MINIMUM TEST LOAD IN POUNDS

Weight in pounds of heaviest towed vehicle	Double or triple saddle-mount			Single saddle-mount [1]
	Front mount	Middle or front mount	Rear mount	
Up to 5,000	15,000	10,000	5,000	5,000
5,000 and over	30,000	20,000	10,000	10,000

[1] The total weight of all the vehicles being towed shall govern.

(l) *Requirements for kingpins of saddle-mounts.* The kingpin of any saddle-mount shall comply with the following requirements:

(1) *Kingpin size.* (i) Kingpins shall be constructed of steel suitable for the purpose, free of defects, and having a diameter not less than required by the following table:

DIAMETER OF SOLID KINGPIN IN INCHES

Weight in pounds of heaviest towed vehicle	Double or triple saddle-mount						Single saddle-mount [1]	
	Front mount		Middle or front mount		Rear mount			
	Mild steel	H.T.S. [2]	Mild steel	H.T.S. [2]	Mild steel	H.T.S. [2]	Mild steel	H.T.S.
Up to 5,000	1.125	1.000	1.000	0.875	0.875	0.750	0.875	0.750
5,000 and over	1.500	1.125	1.250	1.000	1.000	0.875	1.000	0.875

[1] The total weight of all the vehicles being towed shall govern.
[2] High-tensile steel is steel having a minimum ultimate strength of 65,000 pounds per square inch.

(ii) If a ball and socket joint is used in place of a kingpin, the diameter of the neck of the ball shall be at least equal to the diameter of the corresponding solid kingpin given in the above table. If hollow kingpins are used, the metallic cross-sectional area shall be at least equal to the cross-sectional area of the corresponding solid kingpin.

(2) *Kingpin fit.* If a kingpin bushing is not used, the king-pin shall fit snugly

465

into the upper and lower-halves but shall not bind. Those portions of the upper or lower-halves in moving contact with the kingpin shall be smoothly machined with no rough or sharp edges. The bearing surface thus provided shall not be less in depth than the radius of the kingpin.

(3) *Kingpin bushing on saddle-mounts.* The kingpin of all new saddle-mounts acquired and used shall be snugly enclosed in a bushing at least along such length of the kingpin as may be in moving contact with either the upper or lower-halves. The bearing surface thus provided shall not be less in depth than the radius of the kingpin.

(4) *Kingpin to restrain vertical motion.* The kingpin shall be so designed and installed as to restrain the upper-half from moving in a vertical direction relative to the lower-half.

(m) *Additional requirements for saddle-mounts.* Saddle-mounts shall comply with the following requirements:

(1) *Bearing surface between upper and lower-halves.* The upper and lower-halves shall be so constructed and connected that the bearing surface between the two halves shall not be less than 16 square inches under any conditions of angularity between the towing and towed vehicles: *Provided, however,* That saddle-mounts using a ball and socket joint shall have a ball of such dimension that the static bearing load shall not exceed 800 pounds per square inch, based on the projected cross-sectional area of the ball: *And further provided,* That saddle-mounts having the upper-half supported by ball, taper, or roller-bearings shall not have such bearings loaded beyond the limits prescribed for such bearings by the manufacturer thereof. The upper-half shall rest evenly and smoothly upon the lower-half and the contact surfaces shall be lubricated and maintained so that there shall be a minimum of frictional resistance between the parts.

(2) *Saddle-mounts, angularity.* All saddle-mounts acquired and used shall provide for angularity between the towing and towed vehicles due to vertical curvatures of the highway. Such means shall not depend upon either the looseness or deformation of the parts of either the saddle-mount or the vehicles to provide for such angularity.

(3) *Tracking.* The saddle-mount shall be so designed, constructed, maintained, and installed that the towed vehicle or vehicles will follow substantially in the path of the towing vehicle without swerving. Towed vehicles shall not deviate more than 3 inches to either side of the path of the towing vehicle when moving in a straight line.

(4) *Prevention of frame bending.* Where necessary, provision shall be made to prevent the bending of the frame of the towing vehicle by insertion of suitable blocks inside the frame channel to prevent kinking. The saddle-mount shall not be so located as to cause deformation of the frame by reason of cantilever action.

(5) *Extension of frame.* No saddle-mount shall be located at a point to the rear of the frame of a towing vehicle.

(6) *Nuts, secured.* All nuts used on bolts, U-bolts, king-pins, or in any other part of the saddle-mount shall be secured against accidental disconnection by means of cotter-keys, lock-washers, double nuts, safety nuts, or equivalent means. Parts shall be so designed and installed that nuts shall be fully engaged.

(7) *Inspection of all parts.* The saddle-mount shall be so designed that it may be disassembled and each separate part inspected for worn, bent, cracked, broken, or missing parts.

(8) *Saddle-mounts, marking.* Every new saddle-mount acquired and used in driveaway-towaway operations by a motor carrier shall have the upper-half and the lower-half separately marked with the following certification of the manufacturer thereof (or words of equivalent meaning).

This saddle-mount complies with the requirements of the Federal Motor Carrier Safety Administration for vehicles up to 5,000 pounds (or over 5,000 pounds):

Manufactured _____
      (Month and year)
by _____
      (Name of manufacturer)

(n) *Requirements for devices used to connect motor vehicles or parts of motor vehicles together to form one vehicle—(1) Front axle attachment.* The front axle of one motor vehicle intended to be coupled with another vehicle as defined in paragraph (g)(2)(ii) of this section shall be attached with U-bolts meeting the requirements of paragraph (j)(2) of this section.

(2) *Rear axle attachment.* The rear axle of one vehicle shall be coupled to the frame of the other vehicle by means of a connecting device which when in place forms a rectangle. The device shall be composed of two pieces, top and bottom. The device shall be made of 4-inch by ½-inch steel bar bent to shape and shall have the corners reinforced with a plate at least 3 inches by ½ inch by 8 inches long. The device shall be bolted together with ¾-inch bolts and at least three shall be used on each side. Wood may be used as spacers to keep the frames apart and it shall be at least 4 inches square.

(Sec. 12, 80 Stat. 931; 49 U.S.C. 1651 note; section 6 of the Department of Transportation Act, 49 U.S.C. 1655, and the delegations of authority at 49 CFR 1.48 and 389.4)

[33 FR 19735, Dec. 25, 1968, as amended at 35 FR 10907, July 7, 1970; 37 FR 21440, Oct. 11, 1972; 53 FR 49400, Dec. 7, 1988; 70 FR 48054, Aug. 15, 2005]

EFFECTIVE DATE NOTE: At 76 FR 56322, Sept. 13, 2011, §393.71 was amended by revising paragraphs (a)(3) and (c)(4), effective October 13, 2011. For the convenience of the user, the revised text is set forth as follows:

§393.71 Coupling devices and towing methods, driveaway-towaway operations.

(a) * * *

(3) When motor vehicles are towed by means of triple saddle-mounts, all but the final towed vehicle must have brakes acting on all wheels in contact with the roadway.

*   *   *   *   *

(c) * * *

(4) If a motor vehicle towed by means of a saddle-mount has any vehicle full-mounted on it, the saddle-mounted vehicle must at all times while so loaded have effective brakes acting on all wheels in contact with the roadway.

*   *   *   *   *

Subpart G—Miscellaneous Parts and Accessories

§393.75 Tires.

(a) No motor vehicle shall be operated on any tire that—

(1) Has body ply or belt material exposed through the tread or sidewall,

(2) Has any tread or sidewall separation,

(3) Is flat or has an audible leak, or

(4) Has a cut to the extent that the ply or belt material is exposed.

(b) Any tire on the front wheels of a bus, truck, or truck tractor shall have a tread groove pattern depth of at least $\frac{4}{32}$ of an inch when measured at any point on a major tread groove. The measurements shall not be made where tie bars, humps, or fillets are located.

(c) Except as provided in paragraph (b) of this section, tires shall have a tread groove pattern depth of at least $\frac{2}{32}$ of an inch when measured in a major tread groove. The measurement shall not be made where tie bars, humps or fillets are located.

(d) No bus shall be operated with regrooved, recapped or retreaded tires on the front wheels.

(e) A regrooved tire with a load-carrying capacity equal to or greater than 2,232 kg (4,920 pounds) shall not be used on the front wheels of any truck or truck tractor.

(f) *Tire loading restrictions (except on manufactured homes).* No motor vehicle (except manufactured homes, which are governed by paragraph (g) of this section) shall be operated with tires that carry a weight greater than that marked on the sidewall of the tire or, in the absence of such a marking, a weight greater than that specified for the tires in any of the publications of any of the organizations listed in Federal Motor Vehicle Safety Standard No. 119 (49 CFR 571.119, S5.1(b)) unless:

(1) The vehicle is being operated under the terms of a special permit issued by the State; and

(2) The vehicle is being operated at a reduced speed to compensate for the tire loading in excess of the manufacturer's rated capacity for the tire. In no case shall the speed exceed 80 km/hr (50 mph).

(g)(1) *Tire loading restrictions for manufactured homes built before January 1,*

2002. Manufactured homes that are labeled pursuant to 24 CFR 3282.362(c)(2)(i) before January 1, 2002, must not be transported on tires that are loaded more than 18 percent over the load rating marked on the sidewall of the tire or, in the absence of such a marking, more than 18 percent over the load rating specified in any of the publications of any of the organizations listed in FMVSS No. 119 (49 CFR 571.119, S5.1(b)). Manufactured homes labeled before January 1, 2002, transported on tires overloaded by 9 percent or more must not be operated at speeds exceeding 80 km/hr (50 mph).

(2) *Tire loading restrictions for manufactured homes built on or after January 1, 2002.* Manufactured homes that are labeled pursuant to 24 CFR 3282.362(c)(2)(i) on or after January 1, 2002, must not be transported on tires loaded beyond the load rating marked on the sidewall of the tire or, in the absence of such a marking, the load rating specified in any of the publications of any of the organizations listed in FMVSS No. 119 (49 CFR 571.119, S5.1(b)).

(h) *Tire inflation pressure.* (1) No motor vehicle shall be operated on a tire which has a cold inflation pressure less than that specified for the load being carried.

(2) If the inflation pressure of the tire has been increased by heat because of the recent operation of the vehicle, the cold inflation pressure shall be estimated by subtracting the inflation buildup factor shown in Table 1 from the measured inflation pressure.

TABLE 1—INFLATION PRESSURE MEASUREMENT CORRECTION FOR HEAT

Average speed of vehicle in the previous hour	Minimum inflation pressure buildup	
	Tires with 1,814 kg (4,000 lbs.) maximum load rating or less	Tires with over 1,814 kg (4,000 lbs.) load rating
66–88.5 km/hr (41–55 mph).	34.5 kPa (5 psi) ...	103.4 kPa (15 psi).

[34 FR 9344, June 13, 1969, as amended at 40 FR 44557, Sept. 29, 1975; 41 FR 36657, Aug. 31, 1976; 44 FR 25455, May 1, 1979; 44 FR 47938, Aug. 16, 1979; 53 FR 18057, May 19, 1988; 53 FR 49401, Dec. 7, 1988; 63 FR 8339, Feb. 18, 1998; 65 FR 70220, Nov. 21, 2000; 66 FR 67694, Dec. 31, 2001; 70 FR 48054, Aug. 15, 2005]

§ 393.76 Sleeper berths.

(a) *Dimensions—*(1) *Size.* A sleeper berth must be at least the following size:

Date of installation on motor vehicle	Length measured on center-line of longitudinal axis (inches)	Width measured on center-line of transverse axis (inches)	Height measured from highest point of top of mattress (inches) [1]
Before January 1, 1953	72	18	18
After December 31, 1952, and before October 1, 1975 ...	75	21	21
After September 30, 1975	75	24	24

[1] In the case of a sleeper berth which utilizes an adjustable mechanical suspension system, the required clearance can be measured when the suspension system is adjusted to the height to which it would settle when occupied by a driver.

(2) *Shape.* A sleeper berth installed on a motor vehicle on or after January 1, 1953 must be of generally rectangular shape, except that the horizontal corners and the roof corners may be rounded to radii not exceeding 10½ inches.

(3) *Access.* A sleeper berth must be constructed so that an occupant's ready entrance to, and exit from, the sleeper berth is not unduly hindered.

(b) *Location.* (1) A sleeper berth must not be installed in or on a semitrailer or a full trailer other than a house trailer.

(2) A sleeper berth located within the cargo space of a motor vehicle must be securely compartmentalized from the remainder of the cargo space. A sleeper berth installed on or after January 1, 1953 must be located in the cab or immediately adjacent to the cab and must be securely fixed with relation to the cab.

(c) *Exit from the berth.* (1) Except as provided in paragraph (c)(2) of this section, there must be a direct and ready means of exit from a sleeper berth into the driver's seat or compartment. If the sleeper berth was installed on or after January 1, 1963, the exit must be a doorway or opening at least 18 inches high and 36 inches wide. If the sleeper berth was installed before January 1, 1963, the exit must have sufficient area to contain an ellipse having a major axis of 24 inches and a minor axis of 16 inches.

(2) A sleeper berth installed before January 1, 1953 must either:

(i) Conform to the requirements of paragraph (c)(1) of this section; or

(ii) Have at least two exits, each of which is at least 18 inches high and 21 inches wide, located at opposite ends of the vehicle and useable by the occupant without the assistance of any other person.

(d) *Communication with the driver.* A sleeper berth which is not located within the driver's compartment and has no direct entrance into the driver's compartment must be equipped with a means of communication between the occupant and the driver. The means of communication may consist of a telephone, speaker tube, buzzer, pull cord, or other mechanical or electrical device.

(e) *Equipment.* A sleeper berth must be properly equipped for sleeping. Its equipment must include:

(1) Adequate bedclothing and blankets; and

(2) Either:

(i) Springs and a mattress; or

(ii) An innerspring mattress; or

(iii) A cellular rubber or flexible foam mattress at least four inches thick; or

(iv) A mattress filled with a fluid and of sufficient thickness when filled to prevent "bottoming-out" when occupied while the vehicle is in motion.

(f) *Ventilation.* A sleeper berth must have louvers or other means of providing adequate ventilation. A sleeper berth must be reasonably tight against dust and rain.

(g) *Protection against exhaust and fuel leaks and exhaust heat.* A sleeper berth must be located so that leaks in the vehicle's exhaust system or fuel system do not permit fuel, fuel system gases, or exhaust gases to enter the sleeper berth. A sleeper berth must be located so that it will not be overheated or damaged by reason of its proximity to the vehicle's exhaust system.

(h) *Occupant restraint.* A motor vehicle manufactured on or after July 1, 1971, and equipped with a sleeper berth must be equipped with a means of preventing ejection of the occupant of the sleeper berth during deceleration of the vehicle. The restraint system must be designed, installed, and maintained to withstand a minimum total force of 6,000 pounds applied toward the front of the vehicle and parallel to the longitudinal axis of the vehicle.

[39 FR 14711, Apr. 26, 1974; 39 FR 17233, May 14, 1974, as amended at 53 FR 49401, Dec. 7, 1988]

§393.77 **Heaters.**

On every motor vehicle, every heater shall comply with the following requirements:

(a) *Prohibited types of heaters.* The installation or use of the following types of heaters is prohibited:

(1) *Exhaust heaters.* Any type of exhaust heater in which the engine exhaust gases are conducted into or through any space occupied by persons or any heater which conducts engine compartment air into any such space.

(2) *Unenclosed flame heaters.* Any type of heater employing a flame which is not fully enclosed, except that such heaters are not prohibited when used for heating the cargo of tank motor vehicles.

(3) *Heaters permitting fuel leakage.* Any type of heater from the burner of which there could be spillage or leakage of fuel upon the tilting or overturning of the vehicle in which it is mounted.

(4) *Heaters permitting air contamination.* Any heater taking air, heated or to be heated, from the engine compartment or from direct contact with any portion of the exhaust system; or any heater taking air in ducts from the outside atmosphere to be conveyed through the engine compartment, unless said ducts are so constructed and installed as to prevent contamination of the air so conveyed by exhaust or engine compartment gases.

(5) *Solid fuel heaters except wood charcoal.* Any stove or other heater employing solid fuel except wood charcoal.

(6) *Portable heaters.* Portable heaters shall not be used in any space occupied by persons except the cargo space of motor vehicles which are being loaded or unloaded.

(b) *Heater specifications.* All heaters shall comply with the following specifications:

(1) *Heating elements, protection.* Every heater shall be so located or protected

469

as to prevent contact therewith by occupants, unless the surface temperature of the protecting grilles or of any exposed portions of the heaters, inclusive of exhaust stacks, pipes, or conduits shall be lower than would cause contact burns. Adequate protection shall be afforded against igniting parts of the vehicle or burning occupants by direct radiation. Wood charcoal heaters shall be enclosed within a metal barrel, drum, or similar protective enclosure which enclosure shall be provided with a securely fastened cover.

(2) *Moving parts, guards.* Effective guards shall be provided for the protection of passengers or occupants against injury by fans, belts, or any other moving parts.

(3) *Heaters, secured.* Every heater and every heater enclosure shall be securely fastened to the vehicle in a substantial manner so as to provide against relative motion within the vehicle during normal usage or in the event the vehicle overturns. Every heater shall be so designed, constructed, and mounted as to minimize the likelihood of disassembly of any of its parts, including exhaust stacks, pipes, or conduits, upon overturn of the vehicle in or on which it is mounted. Wood charcoal heaters shall be secured against relative motion within the enclosure required by paragraph (c)(1) of this section, and the enclosure shall be securely fastened to the motor vehicle.

(4) *Relative motion between fuel tank and heater.* When either in normal operation or in the event of overturn, there is or is likely to be relative motion between the fuel tank for a heater and the heater, or between either of such units and the fuel lines between them, a suitable means shall be provided at the point of greatest relative motion so as to allow this motion without causing failure of the fuel lines.

(5) *Operating controls to be protected.* On every bus designed to transport more than 15 passengers, including the driver, means shall be provided to prevent unauthorized persons from tampering with the operating controls. Such means may include remote control by the driver; installation of controls at inaccessible places; control of adjustments by key or keys; enclosure of controls in a locked space, locking

of controls, or other means of accomplishing this purpose.

(6) *Heater hoses.* Hoses for all hot water and steam heater systems shall be specifically designed and constructed for that purpose.

(7) *Electrical apparatus.* Every heater employing any electrical apparatus shall be equipped with electrical conductors, switches, connectors, and other electrical parts of ample current-carrying capacity to provide against overheating; any electric motor employed in any heater shall be of adequate size and so located that it will not be overheated; electrical circuits shall be provided with fuses and/or circuit breakers to provide against electrical overloading; and all electrical conductors employed in or leading to any heater shall be secured against dangling, chafing, and rubbing and shall have suitable protection against any other condition likely to produce short or open circuits.

NOTE: Electrical parts certified as proper for use by Underwriters' Laboratories, Inc., shall be deemed to comply with the foregoing requirements.

(8) *Storage battery caps.* If a separate storage battery is located within the personnel or cargo space, such battery shall be securely mounted and equipped with nonspill filler caps.

(9) *Combustion heater exhaust construction.* Every heater employing the combustion of oil, gas, liquefied petroleum gas, or any other combustible material shall be provided with substantial means of conducting the products of combustion to the outside of the vehicle: *Provided, however,* That this requirement shall not apply to heaters used solely to heat the cargo space of motor vehicles where such motor vehicles or heaters are equipped with means specifically designed and maintained so that the carbon monoxide concentration will never exceed 0.2 percent in the cargo space. The exhaust pipe, stack, or conduit if required shall be sufficiently substantial and so secured as to provide reasonable assurance against leakage or discharge of products of combustion within the vehicle and, if necessary, shall be so insulated as to make unlikely the burning or charring of parts of the vehicle by radiation or by direct contact. The

place of discharge of the products of combustion to the atmosphere and the means of discharge of such products shall be such as to minimize the likelihood of their reentry into the vehicle under all operating conditions.

(10) *Combustion chamber construction.* The design and construction of any combustion-type heater except cargo space heaters permitted by the proviso of paragraph (c)(9) of this section and unenclosed flame heaters used for heating cargo of tank motor vehicles shall be such as to provide against the leakage of products of combustion into air to be heated and circulated. The material employed in combustion chambers shall be such as to provide against leakage because of corrosion, oxidation, or other deterioration. Joints between combustion chambers and the air chambers with which they are in thermal and mechanical contact shall be so designed and constructed as to prevent leakage between the chambers and the materials employed in such joints shall have melting points substantially higher than the maximum temperatures likely to be attained at the points of jointure.

(11) *Heater fuel tank location.* Every bus designed to transport more than 15 passengers, including the driver, with heaters of the combustion type shall have fuel tanks therefor located outside of and lower than the passenger space. When necessary, suitable protection shall be afforded by shielding or other means against the puncturing of any such tank or its connections by flying stones or other objects.

(12) *Heater, automatic fuel control.* Gravity or siphon feed shall not be permitted for heaters using liquid fuels. Heaters using liquid fuels shall be equipped with automatic means for shutting off the fuel or for reducing such flow of fuel to the smallest practicable magnitude, in the event of overturn of the vehicle. Heaters using liquefied petroleum gas as fuel shall have the fuel line equipped with automatic means at the source of supply for shutting off the fuel in the event of separation, breakage, or disconnection of any of the fuel lines between the supply source and the heater.

(13) *"Tell-tale" indicators.* Heaters subject to paragraph (c)(14) of this sec-

tion and not provided with automatic controls shall be provided with "tell-tale" means to indicate to the driver that the heater is properly functioning. This requirement shall not apply to heaters used solely for the cargo space in semitrailers or full trailers.

(14) *Shut-off control.* Automatic means, or manual means if the control is readily accessible to the driver without moving from the driver's seat, shall be provided to shut off the fuel and electrical supply in case of failure of the heater to function for any reason, or in case the heater should function improperly or overheat. This requirement shall not apply to wood charcoal heaters or to heaters used solely to heat the contents of cargo tank motor vehicles, but wood charcoal heaters must be provided with a controlled method of regulating the flow of combustion air.

(15) *Certification required.* Every combustion-type heater, except wood charcoal heaters, the date of manufacture of which is subsequent to December 31, 1952, and every wood charcoal heater, the date of manufacture of which is subsequent to September 1, 1953, shall be marked plainly to indicate the type of service for which such heater is designed and with a certification by the manufacturer that the heater meets the applicable requirements for such use. For example, "Meets I.C.C. Bus Heater Requirements," Meets I.C.C. Flue-Vented Cargo Space Heater Requirements," and after December 31, 1967, such certification shall read "Meets FMCSA Bus Heater Requirements," "Meets FMCSA Flue-Vented Cargo Space Heater Requirements," etc.

(i) *Exception.* The certification for a catalytic heater which is used in transporting flammable liquid or gas shall be as prescribed under §177.834(l) of this title.

[33 FR 19735, Dec. 25, 1968, as amended at 40 FR 51198, Nov. 4, 1975; 53 FR 49401, Dec. 7, 1988]

§393.78 Windshield wiping and washing systems.

(a) *Vehicles manufactured on or after December 25, 1968.* Each bus, truck, and truck-tractor manufactured on or after

December 25, 1968, must have a wind-shield wiping system that meets the requirements of FMVSS No. 104 (S4.1) in effect on the date of manufacture. Each of these vehicles must have a wind-shield washing system that meets the requirements of FMVSS No. 104 (S4.2.2) in effect on the date of manufacture.

(b) *Vehicles manufactured between June 30, 1953, and December 24, 1968.* Each truck, truck-tractor, and bus manufactured between June 30, 1953, and December 24, 1968, shall be equipped with a power-driven windshield wiping system with at least two wiper blades, one on each side of the centerline of the windshield. Motor vehicles which depend upon vacuum to operate the wind-shield wipers, shall have the wiper system constructed and maintained such that the performance of the wipers will not be adversely affected by a change in the intake manifold pressure.

(c) *Driveaway-towaway operations.* Windshield wiping and washing systems need not be in working condition while a commercial motor vehicle is being towed in a driveaway-towaway operation.

[70 FR 48054, Aug. 15, 2005]

§ 393.79   Windshield defrosting and defogging systems.

(a) *Vehicles manufactured on or after December 25, 1968.* Each bus, truck, and truck-tractor manufactured on or after December 25, 1968, must have a windshield defrosting and defogging system that meets the requirements of FMVSS No. 103 in effect on the date of manufacture.

(b) *Vehicles manufactured before December 25, 1968.* Each bus, truck, and truck-tractor shall be equipped with a means for preventing the accumulation of ice, snow, frost, or condensation that could obstruct the driver's view through the windshield while the vehicle is being driven.

[70 FR 48054, Aug. 15, 2005]

§ 393.80   Rear-vision mirrors.

(a) Every bus, truck, and truck tractor shall be equipped with two rear-vision mirrors, one at each side, firmly attached to the outside of the motor vehicle, and so located as to reflect to the driver a view of the highway to the rear, along both sides of the vehicle. All such regulated rear-vision mirrors and their replacements shall meet, as a minimum, the requirements of FMVSS No. 111 (49 CFR 571.111) in force at the time the vehicle was manufactured.

(b) *Exceptions.* (1) Mirrors installed on a vehicle manufactured prior to January 1, 1981, may be continued in service, provided that if the mirrors are replaced they shall be replaced with mirrors meeting, as a minimum, the requirements of FMVSS No. 111 (49 CFR 571.111) in force at the time the vehicle was manufactured.

(2) Only one outside mirror shall be required, which shall be on the driver's side, on trucks which are so constructed that the driver has a view to the rear by means of an interior mirror.

(3) In driveway-towaway operations, the driven vehicle shall have at least one mirror furnishing a clear view to the rear.

[48 FR 57139, Dec. 28, 1983]

§ 393.81   Horn.

Every bus, truck, truck-tractor, and every driven motor vehicle in driveaway-towaway operations shall be equipped with a horn and actuating elements which shall be in such condition as to give an adequate and reliable warning signal.

§ 393.82   Speedometer.

Each bus, truck, and truck-tractor must be equipped with a speedometer indicating vehicle speed in miles per hour and/or kilometers per hour. The speedometer must be accurate to within plus or minus 8 km/hr (5 mph) at a speed of 80 km/hr (50 mph).

[70 FR 48054, Aug. 15, 2005]

§ 393.83   Exhaust systems.

(a) Every motor vehicle having a device (other than as part of its cargo) capable of expelling harmful combustion fumes shall have a system to direct the discharge of such fumes. No part shall be located where its location would likely result in burning, charring, or damaging the electrical wiring, the fuel supply, or any combustible part of the motor vehicle.

(b) No exhaust system shall discharge to the atmosphere at a location immediately below the fuel tank or the fuel tank filler pipe.

(c) The exhaust system of a bus powered by a gasoline engine shall discharge to the atmosphere at or within 6 inches forward of the rearmost part of the bus.

(d) The exhaust system of a bus using fuels other than gasoline shall discharge to the atmosphere either:

(1) At or within 15 inches forward of the rearmost part of the vehicle; or

(2) To the rear of all doors or windows designed to be open, except windows designed to be opened solely as emergency exits.

(e) The exhaust system of every truck and truck tractor shall discharge to the atmosphere at a location to the rear of the cab or, if the exhaust projects above the cab, at a location near the rear of the cab.

(f) No part of the exhaust system shall be temporarily repaired with wrap or patches.

(g) No part of the exhaust system shall leak or discharge at a point forward of or directly below the driver/sleeper compartment. The exhaust outlet may discharge above the cab/sleeper roofline.

(h) The exhaust system must be securely fastened to the vehicle.

(i) Exhaust systems may use hangers which permit required movement due to expansion and contraction caused by heat of the exhaust and relative motion between engine and chassis of a vehicle.

[53 FR 49401, Dec. 7, 1988]

§393.84 Floors.

The flooring in all motor vehicles shall be substantially constructed, free of unnecessary holes and openings, and shall be maintained so as to minimize the entrance of fumes, exhaust gases, or fire. Floors shall not be permeated with oil or other substances likely to cause injury to persons using the floor as a traction surface.

[53 FR 49401, Dec. 7, 1988]

§393.85 [Reserved]

§393.86 Rear impact guards and rear end protection.

(a)(1) *General requirements for trailers and semitrailers manufactured on or after January 26, 1998.* Each trailer and semitrailer with a gross vehicle weight rating of 4,536 kg (10,000 pounds) or more, and manufactured on or after January 26, 1998, must be equipped with a rear impact guard that meets the requirements of Federal Motor Vehicle Safety Standard No. 223 (49 CFR 571.223) in effect at the time the vehicle was manufactured. When the rear impact guard is installed on the trailer or semitrailer, the vehicle must, at a minimum, meet the requirements of FMVSS No. 224 (49 CFR 571.224) in effect at the time the vehicle was manufactured. The requirements of paragraph (a) of this section do not apply to pole trailers (as defined in §390.5 of this chapter); pulpwood trailers, low chassis vehicles, special purpose vehicles, wheels back vehicles (as defined in §393.5); and trailers towed in driveaway-towaway operations (as defined in §390.5).

(2) *Impact guard width.* The outermost surfaces of the horizontal member of the guard must extend to within 100 mm (4 inches) of the side extremities of the vehicle. The outermost surface of the horizontal member shall not extend beyond the side extremity of the vehicle.

(3) *Guard height.* The vertical distance between the bottom edge of the horizontal member of the guard and the ground shall not exceed 560 mm (22 inches) at any point across the full width of the member. Guards with rounded corners may curve upward within 255 mm (10 inches) of the longitudinal vertical planes that are tangent to the side extremities of the vehicle.

(4) *Guard rear surface.* At any height 560 mm (22 inches) or more above the ground, the rearmost surface of the horizontal member of the guard must be within 305 mm (12 inches) of the rear extremity of the vehicle. This paragraph shall not be construed to prohibit the rear surface of the guard from extending beyond the rear extremity of

the vehicle. Guards with rounded corners may curve forward within 255 mm (10 inches) of the side extremity.

(5) *Cross-sectional vertical height.* The horizontal member of each guard must have a cross sectional vertical height of at least 100 mm (3.94 inches) at any point across the guard width.

(6) *Certification and labeling requirements for rear impact protection guards.* Each rear impact guard used to satisfy the requirements of paragraph (a)(1) of this section must be permanently marked or labeled as required by FMVSS No. 223 (49 CFR 571.223, S5.3). The label must be on the forward-facing surface of the horizontal member of the guard, 305 mm (12 inches) inboard of the right end of the guard. The certification label must contain the following information:

(i) The impact guard manufacturer's name and address;

(ii) The statement "Manufactured in ___ " (inserting the month and year that the guard was manufactured); and,

(iii) The letters "DOT", constituting a certification by the guard manufacturer that the guard conforms to all requirements of FMVSS No. 223.

(b)(1) *Requirements for motor vehicles manufactured after December 31, 1952 (except trailers or semitrailers manufactured on or after January 26, 1998).* Each motor vehicle manufactured after December 31, 1952, (except truck tractors, pole trailers, pulpwood trailers, or vehicles in driveaway-towaway operations) in which the vertical distance between the rear bottom edge of the body (or the chassis assembly if the chassis is the rearmost part of the vehicle) and the ground is greater than 76.2 cm (30 inches) when the motor vehicle is empty, shall be equipped with a rear impact guard(s). The rear impact guard(s) must be installed and maintained in such a manner that:

(i) The vertical distance between the bottom of the guard(s) and the ground does not exceed 76.2 cm (30 inches) when the motor vehicle is empty;

(ii) The maximum lateral distance between the closest points between guards, if more than one is used, does not exceed 61 cm (24 inches);

(iii) The outermost surfaces of the horizontal member of the guard are no

more than 45.7 cm (18 inches) from each side extremity of the motor vehicle;

(iv) The impact guard(s) are no more than 61 cm (24 inches) forward of the rear extremity of the motor vehicle.

(2) *Construction and attachment.* The rear impact guard(s) must be substantially constructed and attached by means of bolts, welding, or other comparable means.

(3) *Vehicle components and structures that may be used to satisfy the requirements of paragraph (b) of this section.* Low chassis vehicles, special purpose vehicles, or wheels back vehicles constructed and maintained so that the body, chassis, or other parts of the vehicle provide the rear end protection comparable to impact guard(s) conforming to the requirements of paragraph (b)(1) of this section shall be considered to be in compliance with those requirements.

[64 FR 47708, Sept. 1, 1999, as amended at 67 FR 61824, Oct. 2, 2002]

§ 393.87 Warning flags on projecting loads.

(a) Any commercial motor vehicle transporting a load which extends beyond the sides by more than 102 mm (4 inches) or more than 1,219 mm (4 feet) beyond the rear must have the extremities of the load marked with red or orange fluorescent warning flags. Each warning flag must be at least 457 mm (18 inches) square.

(b) *Position of flags.* There must be a single flag at the extreme rear if the projecting load is two feet wide or less. Two warning flags are required if the projecting load is wider than two feet. Flags must be located to indicate maximum width of loads which extend beyond the sides and/or rear of the vehicle.

[70 FR 48054, Aug. 15, 2005]

§ 393.88 Television receivers.

Any motor vehicle equipped with a television viewer, screen or other means of visually receiving a television broadcast shall have the viewer or screen located in the motor vehicle at a point to the rear of the back of the driver's seat if such viewer or screen is in the same compartment as the driver and the viewer or screen shall be so located as not to be visible to the driver, while he/she is driving the motor vehicle. The operating controls for the television receiver shall be so located that the driver cannot operate them without leaving the driver's seat.

§393.89 Buses, driveshaft protection.

Any driveshaft extending lengthways under the floor of the passenger compartment of a bus shall be protected by means of at least one guard or bracket at that end of the shaft which is provided with a sliding connection (spline or other such device) to prevent the whipping of the shaft in the event of failure thereof or of any of its component parts. A shaft contained within a torque tube shall not require any such device.

[33 FR 19735, Dec. 25, 1968, as amended at 53 FR 49402, Dec. 7, 1988]

§393.90 Buses, standee line or bar.

Except as provided below, every bus, which is designed and constructed so as to allow standees, shall be plainly marked with a line of contrasting color at least 2 inches wide or equipped with some other means so as to indicate to any person that he/she is prohibited from occupying a space forward of a perpendicular plane drawn through the rear of the driver's seat and perpendicular to the longitudinal axis of the bus. Every bus shall have clearly posted at or near the front, a sign with letters at least one-half inch high stating that it is a violation of the Federal Motor Carrier Safety Administration's regulations for a bus to be operated with persons occupying the prohibited area. The requirements of this section shall not apply to any bus being transported in driveaway-towaway operation or to any level of the bus other that the level in which the driver is located nor shall they be construed to prohibit any seated person from occupying permanent seats located in the prohibited area provided such seats are so located that persons sitting therein will not interfere with the driver's safe operation of the bus.

§393.91 Buses, aisle seats prohibited.

No bus shall be equipped with aisle seats unless such seats are so designed and installed as to automatically fold and leave a clear aisle when they are unoccupied. No bus shall be operated if any seat therein is not securely fastened to the vehicle.

[53 FR 49402, Dec. 7, 1988]

§393.92 [Reserved]

§393.93 Seats, seat belt assemblies, and seat belt assembly anchorages.

(a) *Buses*—(1) *Buses manufactured on or after January 1, 1965, and before July 1, 1971.* After June 30, 1972, every bus manufactured on or after January 1, 1965, and before July 1, 1971, must be equipped with a Type 1 or Type 2 seat belt assembly that conforms to Federal Motor Vehicle Safety Standard No. 209[1] (§571.209) installed at the driver's seat and seat belt assembly anchorages that conform to the location and geometric requirements of Federal Motor Vehicle Safety Standard No. 210[1] (§571.210) for that seat belt assembly.

(2) *Buses manufactured on or after July 1, 1971.* Every bus manufactured on or after July 1, 1971, must conform to the requirements of Federal Motor Vehicle Safety Standard No. 208[1] (§571.208) (relating to installation of seat belt assemblies) and Federal Motor Vehicle Safety Standard No. 210[1] (§571.210) (relating to installation of seat belt assembly anchorages).

(3) *Buses manufactured on or after January 1, 1972.* Every bus manufactured on or after January 1, 1972, must conform to the requirements of Federal Motor Vehicle Safety Standard No. 207[1] (§571.207) (relating to seating systems).

(b) *Trucks and truck tractors*—(1) *Trucks and truck tractors manufactured on and after January 1, 1965, and before July 1, 1971.* Except as provided in paragraph (d) of this section, after June 30, 1972, every truck and truck tractor manufactured on or after January 1, 1965, and before July 1, 1971, must be equipped with a Type 1 or Type 2 seat belt assembly that conforms to Federal Motor Vehicle Safety Standard No. 209

---

[1] Individual copies of Federal Motor Vehicle Safety Standards may be obtained from the National Highway Traffic Safety Administration, 1200 New Jersey Ave., SE., Washington, DC 20590–0001.

(§ 571.209) installed at the driver's seat and at the right front outboard seat, if the vehicle has one, and seat belt assembly anchorages that conform to the location and geometric requirements of Federal Motor Vehicle Safety Standard No. 210 (§ 571.210) for each seat belt assembly that is required by this subparagraph.

(2) *Trucks and truck tractors manufactured on or after July 1, 1971.* Every truck and truck tractor manufactured on or after July 1, 1971, except a truck or truck tractor being transported in driveaway-towaway operation and having an incomplete vehicle seating and cab configuration, must conform to the requirements of Federal Motor Vehicle Safety Standard No. 208[1] (§ 571.208) (relating to installation of seat belt assemblies) and Federal Motor Vehicle Safety Standard No. 210[1] (§ 571.210) (relating to installation of seat belt assembly anchorages).

(3) *Trucks and truck tractors manufactured on or after January 1, 1972.* Every truck and truck tractor manufactured on or after January 1, 1972, except a truck or truck tractor being transported in driveaway-towaway operation and having an incomplete vehicle seating and cab configuration, must conform to the requirements of Federal Motor Vehicle Safety Standard No. 207[1] (§ 571.207) (relating to seating systems).

(c) *Effective date of standards.* Whenever paragraph (a) or (b) of this section requires conformity to a Federal Motor Vehicle Safety Standard, the vehicle or equipment must conform to the version of the Standard that is in effect on the date the vehicle is manufactured or on the date the vehicle is modified to conform to the requirements of paragraph (a) or (b) of this section, whichever is later.

(d) Trucks and truck tractors manufactured on or after January 1, 1965, and before July 1, 1971, and operated in the State of Hawaii, must comply with the provisions of paragraph (b) of this section on and after January 1, 1976.

[35 FR 16839, Oct. 30, 1970, as amended at 39 FR 32561, Sept. 9, 1974; 40 FR 32336, Aug. 1, 1975; 72 FR 55703, Oct. 1, 2007]

---

[1] See footnote to § 393.93(a).

§ 393.94　Interior noise levels in power units.

(a) *Applicability of this section.* The interior noise level requirements apply to all trucks, truck-tractors, and buses.

(b) *General rule.* The interior sound level at the driver's seating position of a motor vehicle must not exceed 90 dB(A) when measured in accordance with paragraph (c) of this section.

(c) *Test procedure.* (1) Park the vehicle at a location so that no large reflecting surfaces, such as other vehicles, signboards, buildings, or hills, are within 50 feet of the driver's seating position.

(2) Close all vehicle doors, windows, and vents. Turn off all power-operated accessories.

(3) Place the driver in his/her normal seated position at the vehicle's controls. Evacuate all occupants except the driver and the person conducting the test.

(4) The sound level meters used to determine compliance with the requirements of this section must meet the American National Standards Institute *"Specification for Sound Level Meters,"* ANSI S1.4—1983. (See § 393.7(b) for information on the incorporation by reference and availability of this document.)

(5) Locate the microphone, oriented vertically upward, 6 inches to the right of, in the same plane as, and directly in line with, the driver's right ear.

(6) With the vehicle's transmission in neutral gear, accelerate its engine to either its maximum governed engine speed, if it is equipped with an engine governor, or its speed at its maximum rated horsepower, if it is not equipped with an engine governor. Stabilize the engine at that speed.

(7) Observe the A-weighted sound level reading on the meter for the stabilized engine speed condition. Record that reading, if the reading has not been influenced by extraneous noise sources such as motor vehicles operating on adjacent roadways.

(8) Return the vehicle's engine speed to idle and repeat the procedures specified in paragraphs (c) (6) and (7) of this

section until two maximum sound levels within 2 dB of each other are recorded. Numerically average those two maximum sound level readings.

(9) The average obtained in accordance with paragraph (c)(8) of this section is the vehicle's interior sound level at the driver's seating position for the purpose of determining whether the vehicle conforms to the rule in paragraph (b) of this section. However, a 2 dB tolerance over the sound level limitation specified in that paragraph is permitted to allow for variations in test conditions and variations in the capabilities of meters.

(10) If the motor vehicle's engine radiator fan drive is equipped with a clutch or similar device that automatically either reduces the rotational speed of the fan or completely disengages the fan from its power source in response to reduced engine cooling loads the vehicle may be parked before testing with its engine running at high idle or any other speed the operator may choose, for sufficient time but not more than 10 minutes, to permit the engine radiator fan to automatically disengage.

[38 FR 30881, Nov. 8, 1973, as amended at 40 FR 32336, Aug. 1, 1975; 41 FR 28268, July 9, 1976; 70 FR 48054, Aug. 15, 2005]

Subpart H—Emergency Equipment

§393.95 Emergency equipment on all power units.

Each truck, truck tractor, and bus (except those towed in driveaway-towaway operations) must be equipped as follows:

(a) *Fire extinguishers*—(1) *Minimum ratings.* (i) A power unit that is used to transport hazardous materials in a quantity that requires placarding (See §177.823 of this title) must be equipped with a fire extinguisher having an Underwriters' Laboratories rating of 10 B:C or more.

(ii) A power unit that is not used to transport hazardous materials must be equipped with either:

(A) A fire extinguisher having an Underwriters' Laboratories rating of 5 B:C or more; or

(B) Two fire extinguishers, each of which has an Underwriters' Laboratories rating of 4 B:C or more.

(2) *Labeling and marking.* Each fire extinguisher required by this section must be labeled or marked by the manufacturer with its Underwriters' Laboratories rating.

(3) *Visual Indicators.* The fire extinguisher must be designed, constructed, and maintained to permit visual determination of whether it is fully charged.

(4) *Condition, location, and mounting.* The fire extinguisher(s) must be filled and located so that it is readily accessible for use. The extinguisher(s) must be securely mounted to prevent sliding, rolling, or vertical movement relative to the motor vehicle.

(5) *Extinguishing agents.* The fire extinguisher must use an extinguishing agent that does not need protection from freezing. Extinguishing agents must comply with the toxicity provisions of the Environmental Protection Agency's Significant New Alternatives Policy (SNAP) regulations under 40 CFR Part 82, Subpart G.

(6) *Exception.* This paragraph (a) does not apply to the driven unit in a driveaway-towaway operation.

(b) *Spare fuses.* Power units for which fuses are needed to operate any required parts and accessories must have at least one spare fuse for each type/size of fuse needed for those parts and accessories.

(c)–(e) [Reserved]

(f) *Warning devices for stopped vehicles.* Except as provided in paragraph (g) of this section, one of the following options must be used:

(1) Three bidirectional emergency reflective triangles that conform to the requirements of Federal Motor Vehicle Safety Standard No. 125, §571.125 of this title; or

(2) At least 6 fusees or 3 liquid-burning flares. The vehicle must have as many additional fusees or liquid-burning flares as are necessary to satisfy the requirements of §392.22.

(3) Other warning devices may be used in addition to, but not in lieu of, the required warning devices, provided those warning devices do not decrease the effectiveness of the required warning devices.

(g) *Restrictions on the use of flame-producing devices.* Liquid-burning flares, fusees, oil lanterns, or any signal produced by a flame shall not be carried

477

on any commercial motor vehicle transporting Division 1.1, 1.2, 1.3 (explosives) hazardous materials; any cargo tank motor vehicle used for the transportation of Division 2.1 (flammable gas) or Class 3 (flammable liquid) hazardous materials whether loaded or empty; or any commercial motor vehicle using compressed gas as a motor fuel.

(h)–(i) [Reserved]

(j) *Requirements for fusees and liquid-burning flares.* Each fusee shall be capable of burning for 30 minutes, and each liquid-burning flare shall contain enough fuel to burn continuously for at least 60 minutes. Fusees and liquid-burning flares shall conform to the requirements of Underwriters Laboratories, Inc., UL No. 912, Highway Emergency Signals, Fourth Edition, July 30, 1979, (with an amendment dated November 9, 1981). (See § 393.7(c) for information on the incorporation by reference and availability of this document.) Each fusee and liquid-burning flare shall be marked with the UL symbol in accordance with the requirements of UL 912.

(k) *Requirements for red flags.* Red flags shall be not less than 12 inches square, with standards adequate to maintain the flags in an upright position.

(49 U.S.C. 304, 1655; 49 CFR 1.48(b) and 301.60)

[33 FR 19735, Dec. 25, 1968, as amended at 35 FR 13019, Aug. 15, 1970; 35 FR 14619, Sept. 18, 1970; 37 FR 17176, Aug. 25, 1972; 40 FR 10685, Mar. 7, 1975; 41 FR 53031, Dec. 3, 1976; 47 FR 47837, Oct. 28, 1982; 59 FR 34712, July 6, 1994; 67 FR 61225, Sept. 27, 2002; 70 FR 48054, Aug. 15, 2005; 72 FR 44036, Aug. 7, 2007]

Subpart I—Protection Against Shifting and Falling Cargo

Source: 67 FR 61225, Sept. 27, 2002, unless otherwise noted.

§ 393.100 Which types of commercial motor vehicles are subject to the cargo securement standards of this subpart, and what general requirements apply?

(a) *Applicability.* The rules in this subpart are applicable to trucks, truck tractors, semitrailers, full trailers, and pole trailers.

(b) *Prevention against loss of load.* Each commercial motor vehicle must, when transporting cargo on public roads, be loaded and equipped, and the cargo secured, in accordance with this subpart to prevent the cargo from leaking, spilling, blowing or falling from the motor vehicle.

(c) *Prevention against shifting of load.* Cargo must be contained, immobilized or secured in accordance with this subpart to prevent shifting upon or within the vehicle to such an extent that the vehicle's stability or maneuverability is adversely affected.

§ 393.102 What are the minimum performance criteria for cargo securement devices and systems?

(a) *Performance criteria*—(1) *Breaking strength.* Tiedown assemblies (including chains, wire rope, steel strapping, synthetic webbing, and cordage) and other attachment or fastening devices used to secure articles of cargo to, or in, commercial motor vehicles must be designed, installed, and maintained to ensure that the maximum forces acting on the devices or systems do not exceed the manufacturer's breaking strength rating under the following conditions, applied separately:

(i) 0.8 g deceleration in the forward direction;

(ii) 0.5 g acceleration in the rearward direction; and

(iii) 0.5 g acceleration in a lateral direction.

(2) *Working Load limit.* Tiedown assemblies (including chains, wire rope, steel strapping, synthetic webbing, and cordage) and other attachment or fastening devices used to secure articles of cargo to, or in, commercial motor vehicles must be designed, installed, and maintained to ensure that the forces acting on the devices or systems do not exceed the working load limit for the devices under the following conditions, applied separately:

(i) 0.435 g deceleration in the forward direction;

(ii) 0.5 g acceleration in the rearward direction; and

(iii) 0.25 g acceleration in a lateral direction.

(b) *Performance criteria for devices to prevent vertical movement of loads that are not contained within the structure of the vehicle.* Securement systems must provide a downward force equivalent to at least 20 percent of the weight of the article of cargo if the article is not fully contained within the structure of the vehicle. If the article is fully contained within the structure of the vehicle, it may be secured in accordance with Sec. 393.106(b).

(c) *Equivalent means of securement.* The means of securing articles of cargo are considered to meet the performance requirements of this section if the cargo is "

(1) Immobilized, such so that it cannot shift or tip to the extent that the vehicle's stability or maneuverability is adversely affected; or

(2) Transported in a sided vehicle that has walls of adequate strength, such that each article of cargo within the vehicle is in contact with, or sufficiently close to a wall or other articles, so that it cannot shift or tip to the extent that the vehicle's stability or maneuverability is adversely affected; or

(3) Secured in accordance with the applicable requirements of §§393.104 through 393.136.

[71 FR 35832, June 22, 2006]

§393.104 What standards must cargo securement devices and systems meet in order to satisfy the requirements of this subpart?

(a) *General.* All devices and systems used to secure cargo to or within a vehicle must be capable of meeting the requirements of §393.102.

(b) *Prohibition on the use of damaged securement devices.* All tiedowns, cargo securement systems, parts and components used to secure cargo must be in proper working order when used to perform that function with no damaged or weakened components, such as, but not limited to, cracks or cuts that will adversely affect their performance for cargo securement purposes, including reducing the working load limit.

(c) *Vehicle structures and anchor points.* Vehicle structures, floors, walls, decks, tiedown anchor points, headerboards, bulkheads, stakes, posts, and associated mounting pockets used to contain or secure articles of cargo must be strong enough to meet the performance criteria of §393.102, with no damaged or weakened components, such as, but not limited to, cracks or cuts that will adversely affect their performance for cargo securement purposes, including reducing the working load limit.

(d) *Material for dunnage, chocks, cradles, shoring bars, blocking and bracing.* Material used as dunnage or dunnage bags, chocks, cradles, shoring bars, or used for blocking and bracing, must not have damage or defects which would compromise the effectiveness of the securement system.

(e) *Manufacturing standards for tiedown assemblies.* Tiedown assemblies (including chains, wire rope, steel strapping, synthetic webbing, and cordage) and other attachment or fastening devices used to secure articles of cargo to, or in, commercial motor vehicles must conform to the following applicable standards:

An assembly component of . . .	Must conform to . . .
(1) Steel strapping [1,2]	Standard Specification for Strapping, Flat Steel and Seals, American Society for Testing and Materials (ASTM) D3953–97, February 1998. [4]
(2) Chain	National Association of Chain Manufacturers' Welded Steel Chain Specifications, dated September 28, 2005. [4]
(3) Webbing	Web Sling and Tiedown Association's Recommended Standard Specification for Synthetic Web Tiedowns, WSTDA-T1, 1998. [4]
(4) Wire rope [3]	Wire Rope Technical Board's Wire Rope Users Manual, 2nd Edition, November 1985. [4]
(5) Cordage	Cordage Institute rope standard: (i) PETRS–2, Polyester Fiber Rope, three-Strand and eight-Strand Constructions, January 1993. [4] (ii) PPRS–2, Polypropylene Fiber Rope, three-Strand and eight-Strand Constructions, August 1992; [4] (iii) CRS–1, Polyester/Polypropylene Composite Rope Specifications, three-Strand and eight-Strand Standard Construction, May 1979; [4] (iv) NRS–1, Nylon Rope Specifications, three-Strand and eight-Strand Standard Construction, May 1979; [4] and (v) C–1, Double Braided Nylon Rope Specifications DBN, January 1984. [4]

[1] Steel strapping not marked by the manufacturer with a working load limit will be considered to have a working load limit equal to one-fourth of the breaking strength listed in ASTM D3953–97.

[2] Steel strapping 25.4 mm (1 inch) or wider must have at least two pairs of crimps in each seal and, when an end-over-end lap joint is formed, must be sealed with at least two seals.

[3] Wire rope which is not marked by the manufacturer with a working load limit shall be considered to have a working load limit equal to one-fourth of the nominal strength listed in the manual.

[4] See § 393.7 for information on the incorporation by reference and availability of this document.

(f) *Use of tiedowns.* (1) Tiedowns and securing devices must not contain knots.

(2) If a tiedown is repaired, it must be repaired in accordance with the applicable standards in paragraph (e) of this section, or the manufacturer's instructions.

(3) Each tiedown must be attached and secured in a manner that prevents it from becoming loose, unfastening, opening or releasing while the vehicle is in transit.

(4) Edge protection must be used whenever a tiedown would be subject to abrasion or cutting at the point where it touches an article of cargo. The edge protection must resist abrasion, cutting and crushing.

[67 FR 61225, Sept. 27, 2002, as amended at 71 FR 35833, June 22, 2006]

§393.106 What are the general requirements for securing articles of cargo?

(a) *Applicability.* The rules in this section are applicable to the transportation of all types of articles of cargo, except commodities in bulk that lack structure or fixed shape (*e.g.,* liquids, gases, grain, liquid concrete, sand, gravel, aggregates) and are transported in a tank, hopper, box, or similar device that forms part of the structure of a commercial motor vehicle. The rules in this section apply to the cargo types covered by the commodity-specific rules of §393.116 through §393.136. The commodity-specific rules take precedence over the general requirements of this section when additional requirements are given for a commodity listed in those sections.

(b) *General.* Cargo must be firmly immobilized or secured on or within a vehicle by structures of adequate strength, dunnage or dunnage bags, shoring bars, tiedowns or a combination of these.

(c) *Cargo placement and restraint.* (1) Articles of cargo that are likely to roll must be restrained by chocks, wedges, a cradle or other equivalent means to prevent rolling. The means of preventing rolling must not be capable of becoming unintentionally unfastened or loose while the vehicle is in transit.

(2) Articles or cargo placed beside each other and secured by transverse tiedowns must either:

(i) Be placed in direct contact with each other, or

(ii) Be prevented from shifting towards each other while in transit.

(d) *Aggregate working load limit for tiedowns.* The aggregate working load limit of tiedowns used to secure an article or group of articles against movement must be at least one-half times the weight of the article or group of articles. The aggregate working load limit is the sum of:

(1) One-half the working load limit of each tiedown that goes from an anchor point on the vehicle to an anchor point on an article of cargo;

(2) One-half the working load limit of each tiedown that is attached to an anchor point on the vehicle, passes through, over, or around the article of cargo, and is then attached to an anchor point on the same side of the vehicle.

(3) The working load limit for each tiedown that goes from an anchor point on the vehicle, through, over, or around the article of cargo, and then attaches to another anchor point on the other side of the vehicle.

[67 FR 61225, Sept. 27, 2002, as amended at 68 FR 56208, Sept. 30, 2003; 71 FR 35833, June 22, 2006]

§393.108 How is the working load limit of a tiedown, or the load restraining value of a friction mat, determined?

(a) The working load limit (WLL) of a tiedown, associated connector or attachment mechanism is the lowest working load limit of any of its components (including tensioner), or the working load limit of the anchor points to which it is attached, whichever is less.

(b) The working load limits of tiedowns may be determined by using either the tiedown manufacturer's markings or by using the tables in this section. The working load limits listed in the tables are to be used when the tiedown material is not marked by the manufacturer with the working load limit. Tiedown materials which are marked by the manufacturer with working load limits that differ from the tables, shall be considered to have a working load limit equal to the value for which they are marked.

(c) Synthetic cordage (*e.g.*, nylon, polypropylene, polyester) which is not marked or labeled to enable identification of its composition or working load limit shall be considered to have a working load limit equal to that for polypropylene fiber rope.

(d) Welded steel chain which is not marked or labeled to enable identification of its grade or working load limit shall be considered to have a working load limit equal to that for grade 30 proof coil chain.

(e)(1) Wire rope which is not marked by the manufacturer with a working load limit shall be considered to have a working load limit equal to one-fourth

of the nominal strength listed in the Wire Rope Users Manual.

(2) Wire which is not marked or labeled to enable identification of its construction type shall be considered to have a working load limit equal to that for 6 × 37, fiber core wire rope.

(f) Manila rope which is not marked by the manufacturer with a working load limit shall be considered to have a working load limit based on its diameter as provided in the tables of working load limits.

(g) Friction mats which are not marked or rated by the manufacturer shall be considered to provide resistance to horizontal movement equal to 50 percent of the weight placed on the mat.

TABLES TO § 393.108
[Working Load Limits (WLL), Chain]

Size mm (inches)	WLL in kg (pounds)				
	Grade 30 proof coil	Grade 43 high test	Grade 70 trans-port	Grade 80 alloy	Grade 100 alloy
1. 7 (1/4)	580 (1,300)	1,180 (2,600)	1,430 (3,150)	1,570 (3,500)	1,950 (4,300)
2. 8 (5/16)	860 (1,900)	1,770 (3,900)	2,130 (4,700)	2,000 (4,500)	2,600 (5,700)
3. 10 (3/8)	1,200 (2,650)	2,450 (5,400)	2,990 (6,600)	3,200 (7,100)	4,000 (8,800)
4. 11 (7/16)	1,680 (3,700)	3,270 (7,200)	3,970 (8,750)		
5. 13 (1/2)	2,030 (4,500)	4,170 (9,200)	5,130 (11,300)	5,400 (12,000)	6,800 (15,000)
6. 16 (5/8)	3,130 (6,900)	5,910 (13,000)	7,170 (15,800)	8,200 (18,100)	10,300 (22,600)
Chain Mark Examples:					
Example 1	3	4	7	8	10
Example 2	30	43	70	80	100
Example 3	300	430	700	800	1000

SYNTHETIC WEBBING

Width mm (inches)	WLL kg (pounds)
45 (1¾)	790 (1,750)
50 (2)	910 (2,000)
75 (3)	1,360 (3,000)
100 (4)	1,810 (4,000)

WIRE ROPE (6 × 37, FIBER CORE)

Diameter mm (inches)	WLL kg (pounds)
7 (1/4)	640 (1,400)
8 (5/16)	950 (2,100)
10 (3/8)	1,360 (3,000)
11 (7/16)	1,860 (4,100)
13 (1/2)	2,400 (5,300)
16 (5/8)	3,770 (8,300)
20 (3/4)	4,940 (10,900)
22 (7/8)	7,300 (16,100)
25 (1)	9,480 (20,900)

MANILA ROPE

Diameter mm (inches)	WLL kg (pounds)
10 (3/8)	90 (205)

MANILA ROPE—Continued

Diameter mm (inches)	WLL kg (pounds)
11 (7/16)	120 (265)
13 (1/2)	150 (315)
16 (5/8)	210 (465)
20 (3/4)	290 (640)
25 (1)	480 (1,050)

POLYPROPYLENE FIBER ROPE WLL (3-STRAND AND 8-STRAND CONSTRUCTIONS)

Diameter mm (inches)	WLL kg (pounds)
10 (3/8)	180 (400)
11 (7/16)	240 (525)
13 (1/2)	280 (625)
16 (5/8)	420 (925)
20 (3/4)	580 (1,275)
25 (1)	950 (2,100)

POLYESTER FIBER ROPE WLL (3-STRAND AND 8-STRAND CONSTRUCTIONS)

Diameter mm (inches)	WLL kg (pounds)
10 (3/8)	250 (555)

POLYESTER FIBER ROPE WLL (3-STRAND AND 8-STRAND CONSTRUCTIONS)—Continued

Diameter mm (inches)	WLL kg (pounds)
11 (7/16)	340 (750)
13 (1/2)	440 (960)
16 (5/8)	680 (1,500)
20 (3/4)	850 (1,880)
25 (1)	1,500 (3,300)

NYLON ROPE

Diameter mm (inches)	WLL kg (pounds)
10 (3/8)	130 (278)
11 (7/16)	190 (410)
13 (1/2)	240 (525)
16 (5/8)	420 (935)
20 (3/4)	640 (1,420)
25 (1)	1,140 (2,520)

DOUBLE BRAIDED NYLON ROPE

Diameter mm (inches)	WLL kg (pounds)
10 (3/8)	150 (336)
11 (7/16)	230 (502)
13 (1/2)	300 (655)
16 (5/8)	510 (1,130)
20 (3/4)	830 (1,840)
25 (1)	1,470 (3,250)

STEEL STRAPPING

Width × thickness mm (inches)	WLL kg (pounds)
31.7 × .74 (1 1/4 × 0.029)	540 (1,190)
31.7 × .79 (1¼ × 0.031)	540 (1,190)
31.7 × .89 (1¼ × 0.035)	540 (1,190)
31.7 × 1.12 (1¼ × 0.044)	770 (1,690)
31.7 × 1.27 (1¼ × 0.05)	770 (1,690)
31.7 × 1.5 (1¼ × 0.057)	870 (1,925)
50.8 × 1.12 (2 × 0.044)	1,200 (2,650)
50.8 × 1.27 (2 × 0.05)	1,200 (2,650)

§393.110 What else do I have to do to determine the minimum number of tiedowns?

(a) When tiedowns are used as part of a cargo securement system, the minimum number of tiedowns required to secure an article or group of articles against movement depends on the length of the article(s) being secured, and the requirements of paragraphs (b) and (c) of this section. These requirements are in addition to the rules under §393.106.

(b) When an article is not blocked or positioned to prevent movement in the forward direction by a headerboard, bulkhead, other cargo that is positioned to prevent movement, or other appropriate blocking devices, it must be secured by at least:

(1) One tiedown for articles 5 feet (1.52 meters) or less in length, and 1,100 pounds (500 kg) or less in weight;

(2) Two tiedowns if the article is:

(i) 5 feet (1.52 meters) or less in length and more than 1,100 pounds (500 kg) in weight; or

(ii) Longer than 5 feet (1.52 meters) but less than or equal to 10 feet (3.04 meters) in length, irrespective of the weight.

(3) Two tiedowns if the article is longer than 10 feet (3.04 meters), and one additional tiedown for every 10 feet (3.04 meters) of article length, or fraction thereof, beyond the first 10 feet (3.04 meters) of length.

(c) If an individual article is blocked, braced, or immobilized to prevent movement in the forward direction by a headerboard, bulkhead, other articles which are adequately secured or by an appropriate blocking or immobilization method, it must be secured by at least one tiedown for every 3.04 meters (10 feet) of article length, or fraction thereof.

(d) *Special rule for special purpose vehicles.* The rules in this section do not apply to a vehicle transporting one or more articles of cargo such as, but not limited to, machinery or fabricated structural items (e.g., steel or concrete beams, crane booms, girders, and trusses, etc.) which, because of their design, size, shape, or weight, must be fastened by special methods. However, any article of cargo carried on that vehicle must be securely and adequately fastened to the vehicle.

[67 FR 61225, Sept. 27, 2002, as amended at 71 FR 35833, June 22, 2006]

§393.112 Must a tiedown be adjustable?

Each tiedown, or its associated connectors, or its attachment mechanisms must be designed, constructed, and maintained so the driver of an in-transit commercial motor vehicle can tighten them. However, this requirement does not apply to the use of steel strapping.

§393.114 What are the requirements for front end structures used as part of a cargo securement system?

(a) *Applicability.* The rules in this section are applicable to commercial motor vehicles transporting articles of cargo that are in contact with the front end structure of the vehicle. The front end structure on these cargo-carrying vehicles must meet the performance requirements of this section.

(b) *Height and width.* (1) The front end structure must extend either to a height of 4 feet above the floor of the vehicle or to a height at which it blocks forward movement of any item or article of cargo being carried on the vehicle, whichever is lower.

(2) The front end structure must have a width which is at least equal to the width of the vehicle or which blocks forward movement of any article of cargo being transported on the vehicle, whichever is narrower.

(c) *Strength.* The front end structure must be capable of withstanding the following horizontal forward static load:

(1) For a front end structure less than 6 feet in height, a horizontal forward static load equal to one-half (0.5) of the weight of the articles of cargo being transported on the vehicle uniformly distributed over the entire portion of the front end structure that is within 4 feet above the vehicle's floor or that is at or below a height above the vehicle's floor at which it blocks forward movement of any article of the vehicle's cargo, whichever is less; or

(2) For a front end structure 6 feet in height or higher, a horizontal forward static load equal to four-tenths (0.4) of the weight of the articles of cargo being transported on the vehicle uniformly distributed over the entire front end structure.

(d) *Penetration resistance.* The front end structure must be designed, constructed, and maintained so that it is capable of resisting penetration by any article of cargo that contacts it when the vehicle decelerates at a rate of 20 feet per second, per second. The front end structure must have no aperture large enough to permit any article of cargo in contact with the structure to pass through it.

(e) *Substitute devices.* The requirements of this section may be met by the use of devices performing the same functions as a front end structure, if the devices are at least as strong as, and provide protection against shifting

articles of cargo at least equal to, a front end structure which conforms to those requirements.

[67 FR 61225, Sept. 27, 2002, as amended at 71 FR 35833, June 22, 2006]

SPECIFIC SECUREMENT REQUIREMENTS
BY COMMODITY TYPE

§ 393.116 What are the rules for securing logs?

(a) *Applicability.* The rules in this section are applicable to the transportation of logs with the following exceptions:

(1) Logs that are unitized by banding or other comparable means may be transported in accordance with the general cargo securement rules of §§ 393.100 through 393.114.

(2) Loads that consist of no more than four processed logs may be transported in accordance with the general cargo securement rules of §§ 393.100 through 393.114.

(3) Firewood, stumps, log debris and other such short logs must be transported in a vehicle or container enclosed on both sides, front, and rear and of adequate strength to contain them. Longer logs may also be so loaded.

(b) *Components of a securement system.* (1) Logs must be transported on a vehicle designed and built, or adapted, for the transportation of logs. Any such vehicle must be fitted with bunks, bolsters, stakes or standards, or other equivalent means, that cradle the logs and prevent them from rolling.

(2) All vehicle components involved in securement of logs must be designed and built to withstand all anticipated operational forces without failure, accidental release or permanent deformation. Stakes or standards that are not permanently attached to the vehicle must be secured in a manner that prevents unintentional separation from the vehicle in transit.

(3) Tiedowns must be used in combination with the stabilization provided by bunks, stakes, and bolsters to secure the load unless the logs:

(i) are transported in a crib-type log trailer (as defined in 49 CFR 393.5), and

(ii) are loaded in compliance with paragraphs (b)(2) and (c) of this section.

(4) The aggregate working load limit for tiedowns used to secure a stack of logs on a frame vehicle, or a flatbed vehicle equipped with bunks, bolsters, or stakes must be at least one-sixth the weight of the stack of logs.

(c) *Use of securement system.* (1) Logs must be solidly packed, and the outer bottom logs must be in contact with and resting solidly against the bunks, bolsters, stakes or standards.

(2) Each outside log on the side of a stack of logs must touch at least two stakes, bunks, bolsters, or standards. If one end does not actually touch a stake, it must rest on other logs in a stable manner and must extend beyond the stake, bunk, bolster or standard.

(3) The center of the highest outside log on each side or end must be below the top of each stake, bunk or standard.

(4) Each log that is not held in place by contact with other logs or the stakes, bunks, or standards must be held in place by a tiedown. Additional tiedowns or securement devices must be used when the condition of the wood results in such low friction between logs that they are likely to slip upon each other.

(d) *Securement of shortwood logs loaded crosswise on frame, rail and flatbed vehicles.* In addition to the requirements of paragraphs (b) and (c) of this section, each stack of logs loaded crosswise must meet the following rules:

(1) In no case may the end of a log in the lower tier extend more than one-third of the log's total length beyond the nearest supporting structure on the vehicle.

(2) When only one stack of shortwood is loaded crosswise, it must be secured with at least two tiedowns. The tiedowns must attach to the vehicle frame at the front and rear of the load, and must cross the load in this direction.

(3) When two tiedowns are used, they must be positioned at approximately one-third and two-thirds of the length of the logs.

(4) A vehicle that is more than 10 meters (33 feet) long must be equipped with center stakes, or comparable devices, to divide it into sections approximately equal in length. Where a vehicle is so divided, each tiedown must secure the highest log on each side of the center stake, and must be fastened below these logs. It may be fixed at each end and tensioned from the middle, or fixed in the middle and tensioned from each end, or it may pass through a pulley or equivalent device in the middle and be tensioned from one end.

(5) Any structure or stake that is subjected to an upward force when the tiedowns are tensioned must be anchored to resist that force.

(6) If two stacks of shortwood are loaded side-by-side, in addition to meeting the requirements of paragraphs (d)(1) through (d)(5) of this section, they must be loaded so that:

(i) There is no space between the two stacks of logs;

(ii) The outside of each stack is raised at least 2.5 cm (1 in) within 10 cm (4 in) of the end of the logs or the side of the vehicle;

(iii) The highest log is no more than 2.44 m (8 ft) above the deck; and

(iv) At least one tiedown is used lengthwise across each stack of logs.

(e) *Securement of logs loaded lengthwise on flatbed and frame vehicles*—(1) *Shortwood.* In addition to meeting the requirements of paragraphs (b) and (c) of this section, each stack of shortwood loaded lengthwise on a frame vehicle or on a flatbed must be cradled in a bunk unit or contained by stakes and

(i) Secured to the vehicle by at least two tiedowns, or

(ii) If all the logs in any stack are blocked in the front by a front-end structure strong enough to restrain the load, or by another stack of logs, and blocked in the rear by another stack of logs or vehicle end structure, the stack may be secured with one tiedown. If one tiedown is used, it must be positioned about midway between the stakes, or

(iii) Be bound by at least two tiedown-type devices such as wire rope, used as wrappers that encircle the entire load at locations along the load that provide effective securement. If wrappers are being used to bundle the logs together, the wrappers are not required to be attached to the vehicle.

(2) *Longwood.* Longwood must be cradled in two or more bunks and must either:

(i) Be secured to the vehicle by at least two tiedowns at locations that provide effective securement, or

(ii) Be bound by at least two tiedown-type devices, such as wire rope, used as wrappers that encircle the entire load at locations along the load that provide effective securement. If a wrapper(s) is being used to bundle the logs together, the wrapper is not required to be attached to the vehicle.

(f) *Securement of logs transported on pole trailers.* (1) The load must be secured by at least one tiedown at each bunk, or alternatively, by at least two tiedowns used as wrappers that encircle the entire load at locations along the load that provide effective securement.

(2) The front and rear wrappers must be at least 3.04 meters (10 feet) apart.

(3) Large diameter single and double log loads must be immobilized with chock blocks or other equivalent means to prevent shifting.

(4) Large diameter logs that rise above bunks must be secured to the underlying load with at least two additional wrappers.

[67 FR 61225, Sept. 27, 2002, as amended at 71 FR 35833, June 22, 2006]

§ 393.118 What are the rules for securing dressed lumber or similar building products?

(a) *Applicability.* The rules in this section apply to the transportation of bundles of dressed lumber, packaged lumber, building products such as plywood, gypsum board or other materials of similar shape. Lumber or building products which are not bundled or packaged must be treated as loose items and transported in accordance with §§ 393.100 through 393.114 of this subpart. For the purpose of this section, "bundle" refers to packages of lumber, building materials or similar products which are unitized for securement as a single article of cargo.

(b) *Positioning of bundles.* Bundles must be placed side by side in direct contact with each other, or a means must be provided to prevent bundles from shifting towards each other.

(c) *Securement of bundles transported using no more than one tier.* Bundles carried on one tier must be secured in accordance with the general provisions of §§ 393.100 through 393.114.

(d) *Securement of bundles transported using more than one tier.* Bundles carried in more than one tier must be either:

(1) Blocked against lateral movement by stakes on the sides of the vehicle and secured by tiedowns laid out over the top tier, as outlined in the general provisions of §§ 393.100 through 393.114; or

(2) Restrained from lateral movement by blocking or high friction devices between tiers and secured by tiedowns laid out over the top tier, as outlined in the general provisions of §§ 393.100 through 393.114; or

(3) Placed directly on top of other bundles or on spacers and secured in accordance with the following:

(i) The length of spacers between bundles must provide support to all pieces in the bottom row of the bundle.

(ii) The width of individual spacers must be equal to or greater than the height.

(iii) If spacers are comprised of layers of material, the layers must be unitized or fastened together in a manner which ensures that the spacer performs as a single piece of material.

(iv) The arrangement of the tiedowns for the bundles must be:

(A) Secured by tiedowns over the top tier of bundles, in accordance with the general provisions of §§ 393.100 through 393.114 with a minimum of two tiedowns for bundles longer than 1.52 meters (5 ft); and

(B) Secured by tiedowns as follows:

(*1*) If there are 3 tiers, the middle and top bundles must be secured by tiedowns in accordance with the general provisions of §§ 393.100 through 393.114; or

(*2*)(*i*) If there are more than 3 tiers, then one of the middle bundles and the top bundle must be secured by tiedown devices in accordance with the general provision of §§ 393.100 through 393.114, and the maximum height for the middle tier that must be secured may not exceed 6 feet about the deck of the trailer; or

(*ii*) Otherwise, the second tier from the bottom must be secured in accordance with the general provisions of §§ 393.100 through 393.114; or

(4) Secured by tiedowns over each tier of bundles, in accordance with §§393.100 through 393.114 using a minimum of two tiedowns over each of the top bundles longer than 1.52 meters (5 ft), in all circumstances; or

(5) When loaded in a sided vehicle or container of adequate strength, dressed lumber or similar building products may be secured in accordance with the general provisions of §§393.100 through 393.114.

[67 FR 61225, Sept. 27, 2002, as amended at 71 FR 35834, June 22, 2006]

§393.120 What are the rules for securing metal coils?

(a) *Applicability.* The rules in this section apply to the transportation of one or more metal coils which, individually or grouped together, weigh 2268 kg (5000 pounds) or more. Shipments of metal coils that weigh less than 2268 kg (5000 pounds) may be secured in accordance with the provisions of §§393.100 through 393.114.

(b) *Securement of coils transported with eyes vertical on a flatbed vehicle, in a sided vehicle or intermodal container with anchor points*—(1) *An individual coil.* Each coil must be secured by tiedowns arranged in a manner to prevent the coils from tipping in the forward, rearward, and lateral directions. The restraint system must include the following:

(i) At least one tiedown attached diagonally from the left side of the vehicle or intermodal container (near the forwardmost part of the coil), across the eye of the coil, to the right side of the vehicle or intermodal container (near the rearmost part of the coil);

(ii) At least one tiedown attached diagonally from the right side of the vehicle or intermodal container (near the forwardmost part of the coil), across the eye of the coil, to the left side of the vehicle or intermodal container (near the rearmost part of the coil);

(iii) At least one tiedown attached transversely over the eye of the coil; and

(iv) Either blocking and bracing, friction mats or tiedowns must be used to prevent longitudinal movement in the forward direction.

(2) *Coils grouped in rows.* When coils are grouped and loaded side by side in a transverse or longitudinal row, the each row of coils must be secured by the following:

(i) At least one tiedown attached to the front of the row of coils, restraining against forward motion, and whenever practicable, making an angle no more than 45 degrees with the floor of the vehicle or intermodal container when viewed from the side of the vehicle or container;

(ii) At least one tiedown attached to the rear of the row of coils, restraining against rearward motion, and whenever practicable, making an angle no more than 45 degrees with the floor of the vehicle or intermodal container when viewed from the side of the vehicle or container;

(iii) At least one tiedown over the top of each coil or transverse row of coils, restraining against vertical motion. Tiedowns going over the top of a coil(s) must be as close as practicable to the eye of the coil and positioned to prevent the tiedown from slipping or becoming unintentionally unfastened while the vehicle is in transit; and

(iv) Tiedowns must be arranged to prevent shifting or tipping in the forward, rearward and lateral directions.

(c) *Securement of coils transported with eyes crosswise on a flatbed vehicle, in a sided vehicle or intermodal container with anchor points*—(1) *An individual coil.* Each coil must be secured by the following:

(i) A means (*e.g.,* timbers, chocks or wedges, a cradle, etc.) to prevent the coil from rolling. The means of preventing rolling must support the coil off the deck, and must not be capable of becoming unintentionally unfastened or loose while the vehicle is in transit. If timbers, chocks or wedges are used, they must be held in place by coil bunks or similar devices to prevent them from coming loose. The use of nailed blocking or cleats as the sole means to secure timbers, chocks or wedges, or a nailed wood cradle, is prohibited;

(ii) At least one tiedown through its eye, restricting against forward motion, and whenever practicable, making an angle no more than 45 degrees with the floor of the vehicle or intermodal container when viewed from the side of the vehicle or container; and

(iii) At least one tiedown through its eye, restricting against rearward motion, and whenever practicable, making an angle no more than 45 degrees with the floor of the vehicle or intermodal container when viewed from the side of the vehicle or container.

(2) *Prohibition on crossing of tiedowns when coils are transported with eyes crosswise.* Attaching tiedowns diagonally through the eye of a coil to form an X-pattern when viewed from above the vehicle is prohibited.

(d) *Securement of coils transported with eyes lengthwise on a flatbed vehicle, in a sided vehicle or intermodal container with anchor points*—(1) *An individual coil—option 1.* Each coil must be secured by:

(i) A means (*e.g.,* timbers, chocks or wedges, a cradle, etc.) to prevent the coil from rolling. The means of preventing rolling must support the coil off the deck, and must not be capable of becoming unintentionally unfastened or loose while the vehicle is in transit. If timbers, chocks or wedges are used, they must be held in place by coil bunks or similar devices to prevent them from coming loose. The use of nailed blocking or cleats as the sole means to secure timbers, chocks or wedges, or a nailed wood cradle, is prohibited;

(ii) At least one tiedown attached diagonally through its eye from the left side of the vehicle or intermodal container (near the forward-most part of the coil), to the right side of the vehicle or intermodal container (near the rearmost part of the coil), making an angle no more than 45 degrees, whenever practicable, with the floor of the vehicle or intermodal container when viewed from the side of the vehicle or container;

(iii) At least one tiedown attached diagonally through its eye, from the right side of the vehicle or intermodal container (near the forward-most part of the coil), to the left side of the vehicle or intermodal container (near the rearmost part of the coil), making an angle no more than 45 degrees, whenever practicable, with the floor of the vehicle or intermodal container when viewed from the side of the vehicle or container;

(iv) At least one tiedown attached transversely over the top of the coil; and

(v) Either blocking, or friction mats to prevent longitudinal movement.

(2) *An individual coil—option 2.* Each coil must be secured by:

(i) A means (*e.g.,* timbers, chocks or wedges, a cradle, etc.) to prevent the coil from rolling. The means of preventing rolling must support the coil off the deck, and must not be capable of becoming unintentionally unfastened or loose while the vehicle is in transit. If timbers, chocks or wedges are used, they must be held in place by coil bunks or similar devices to prevent them from coming loose. The use of nailed blocking or cleats as the sole means to secure timbers, chocks or wedges, or a nailed wood cradle, is prohibited;

(ii) At least one tiedown attached straight through its eye from the left side of the vehicle or intermodal container (near the forward-most part of the coil), to the left side of the vehicle or intermodal container (near the rearmost part of the coil), and, whenever practicable, making an angle no more than 45 degrees with the floor of the vehicle or intermodal container when viewed from the side of the vehicle or container;

(iii) At least one tiedown attached straight through its eye, from the right side of the vehicle or intermodal container (near the forward-most part of the coil), to the right side of the vehicle or intermodal container (near the rearmost part of the coil), and whenever practicable, making an angle no more than 45 degrees with the floor of the vehicle or intermodal container when viewed from the side of the vehicle or container;

(iv) At least one tiedown attached transversely over the top of the coil; and

(v) Either blocking or friction mats to prevent longitudinal movement.

(3) *An individual coil—option 3.* Each coil must be secured by:

(i) A means (*e.g.,* timbers, chocks or wedges, a cradle, etc.) to prevent the coil from rolling. The means of preventing rolling must support the coil off the deck, and must not be capable of becoming unintentionally unfastened or loose while the vehicle is in transit. If timbers, chocks or wedges are used, they must be held in place by coil bunks or similar devices to prevent them from coming loose. The use of nailed blocking or cleats as the sole means to secure timbers, chocks or wedges, or a nailed wood cradle, is prohibited;

(ii) At least one tiedown over the top of the coil, located near the forward-most part of the coil;

(iii) At least one tiedown over the top of the coil located near the rearmost part of the coil; and

(iv) Either blocking or friction mats to prevent longitudinal movement.he forward direction.

(4) *Rows of coils.* Each transverse row of coils having approximately equal outside diameters must be secured with:

(i) A means (*e.g.*, timbers, chocks or wedges, a cradle, etc.) to prevent each coil in the row of coils from rolling. The means of preventing rolling must support each coil off the deck, and must not be capable of becoming unintentionally unfastened or loose while the vehicle is in transit. If timbers, chocks or wedges are used, they must be held in place by coil bunks or similar devices to prevent them from coming loose. The use of nailed blocking or cleats as the sole means to secure timbers, chocks or wedges, or a nailed wood cradle, is prohibited;

(ii) At least one tiedown over the top of each coil or transverse row, located near the forward-most part of the coil;

(iii) At least one tiedown over the top of each coil or transverse row, located near the rearmost part of the coil; and

(iv) Either blocking, bracing or friction mats to prevent longitudinal movement.

(e) *Securement of coils transported in a sided vehicle without anchor points or an intermodal container without anchor points.* Metal coils transported in a vehicle with sides without anchor points or an intermodal container without anchor points must be loaded in a manner to prevent shifting and tipping. The coils may also be secured using a system of blocking and bracing, friction mats, tiedowns, or a combination of these to prevent any horizontal movement and tipping.

§ 393.122   **What are the rules for securing paper rolls?**

(a) *Applicability.* The rules in this section apply to shipments of paper rolls which, individually or together, weigh 2268 kg (5000 lb) or more. Shipments of paper rolls that weigh less than 2268 kg (5000 lb), and paper rolls that are unitized on a pallet, may either be secured in accordance with the rules in this section or the requirements of §§ 393.100 through 393.114.

(b) *Securement of paper rolls transported with eyes vertical in a sided vehicle.* (1) Paper rolls must be placed tightly against the walls of the vehicle, other paper rolls, or other cargo, to prevent movement during transit.

(2) If there are not enough paper rolls in the shipment to reach the walls of the vehicle, lateral movement must be prevented by filling the void, blocking, bracing, tiedowns or friction mats. The paper rolls may also be banded together.

(3) When any void behind a group of paper rolls, including that at the rear of the vehicle, exceeds the diameter of the paper rolls, rearward movement must be prevented by friction mats, blocking, bracing, tiedowns, or banding to other rolls.

(4)(i) If a paper roll is not prevented from tipping or falling sideways or rearwards by vehicle structure or other cargo, and its width is more than 2 times its diameter, it must be prevented from tipping or falling by banding it to other rolls, bracing, or tiedowns.

(ii) If the forwardmost roll(s) in a group of paper rolls has a width greater than 1.75 times its diameter and it is not prevented from tipping or falling forwards by vehicle structure or other cargo, then it must be prevented from tipping or falling forwards by banding it to other rolls, bracing, or tiedowns.

(iii) If the forwardmost roll(s) in a group of paper rolls has a width equal to or less than 1.75 times its diameter, and it is restrained against forward movement by friction mat(s) alone, then banding, bracing, or tiedowns are not required to prevent tipping or falling forwards.

489

(iv) If a paper roll or the forwardmost roll in a group of paper rolls has a width greater than 1.25 times its diameter, and it is not prevented from tipping or falling forwards by vehicle structure or other cargo, and it is not restrained against forward movement by friction mat(s) alone, then it must be prevented from tipping or falling by banding it to other rolls, bracing or tiedowns.

(5) If paper rolls are banded together, the rolls must be placed tightly against each other to form a stable group. The bands must be applied tightly, and must be secured so that they cannot fall off the rolls or to the deck.

(6) A friction mat used to provide the principal securement for a paper roll must protrude from beneath the roll in the direction in which it is providing that securement.

(c) *Securement of split loads of paper rolls transported with eyes vertical in a sided vehicle.* (1) If a paper roll in a split load is not prevented from forward movement by vehicle structure or other cargo, it must be prevented from forward movement by filling the open space, or by blocking, bracing, tiedowns, friction mats, or some combination of these.

(2) A friction mat used to provide the principal securement for a paper roll must protrude from beneath the roll in the direction in which it is providing that securement.

(d) *Securement of stacked loads of paper rolls transported with eyes vertical in a sided vehicle.* (1) Paper rolls must not be loaded on a layer of paper rolls beneath unless the lower layer extends to the front of the vehicle.

(2) Paper rolls in the second and subsequent layers must be prevented from forward, rearward or lateral movement by means as allowed for the bottom layer, or by use of a blocking roll from a lower layer.

(3) The blocking roll must be at least 38 mm (1.5 in) taller than other rolls, or must be raised at least 38 mm (1.5 in) using dunnage.

(4) A roll in the rearmost row of any layer raised using dunnage may not be secured by friction mats alone.

(e) *Securement of paper rolls transported with eyes crosswise in a sided vehicle.* (1) The paper rolls must be pre-

vented from rolling or shifting longitudinally by contact with vehicle structure or other cargo, by chocks, wedges or blocking and bracing of adequate size, or by tiedowns.

(2) Chocks, wedges or blocking must be held securely in place by some means in addition to friction, so they cannot become unintentionally unfastened or loose while the vehicle is in transit.

(3) The rearmost roll must not be secured using the rear doors of the vehicle or intermodal container, or by blocking held in place by those doors.

(4) If there is more than a total of 203 mm (8 in) of space between the ends of a paper roll, or a row of rolls, and the walls of the vehicle, void fillers, blocking, bracing, friction mats, or tiedowns must be used to prevent the roll from shifting towards either wall.

(f) *Securement of stacked loads of paper rolls transported with eyes crosswise in a sided vehicle.* (1) Rolls must not be loaded in a second layer unless the bottom layer extends to the front of the vehicle.

(2) Rolls must not be loaded in a third or higher layer unless all wells in the layer beneath are filled.

(3) The foremost roll in each upper layer, or any roll with an empty well in front of it, must be secured against forward movement by:

(i) Banding it to other rolls, or

(ii) Blocking against an adequately secured eye-vertical blocking roll resting on the floor of the vehicle which is at least 1.5 times taller than the diameter of the roll being blocked, or

(iii) Placing it in a well formed by two rolls on the lower row whose diameter is equal to or greater than that of the roll on the upper row.

(4) The rearmost roll in each upper layer must be secured by banding it to other rolls if it is located in either of the last two wells formed by the rearmost rolls in the layer below.

(5) Rolls must be secured against lateral movement by the same means allowed for the bottom layer when there is more than a total of 203 mm (8 in) of space between the ends of a paper roll, or a row of rolls, and the walls of the vehicle.

(g) *Securement of paper rolls transported with the eyes lengthwise in a sided vehicle.* (1) Each roll must be prevented from forward movement by contact with vehicle structure, other cargo, blocking or tiedowns.

(2) Each roll must be prevented from rearward movement by contact with other cargo, blocking, friction mats or tiedowns.

(3) The paper rolls must be prevented from rolling or shifting laterally by contact with the wall of the vehicle or other cargo, or by chocks, wedges or blocking of adequate size.

(4) Chocks, wedges or blocking must be held securely in place by some means in addition to friction, so they cannot become unintentionally unfastened or loose while the vehicle is in transit.

(h) *Securement of stacked loads of paper rolls transported with the eyes lengthwise in a sided vehicle.* (1) Rolls must not be loaded in a higher layer if another roll will fit in the layer beneath.

(2) An upper layer must be formed by placing paper rolls in the wells formed by the rolls beneath.

(3) A roll in an upper layer must be secured against forward and rearward movement by any of the means allowed for the bottom layer, by use of a blocking roll, or by banding to other rolls.

(i) *Securement of paper rolls transported on a flatbed vehicle or in a curtain-sided vehicle*—(1) *Paper rolls with eyes vertical or with eyes lengthwise.* (i) The paper rolls must be loaded and secured as described for a sided vehicle, and the entire load must be secured by tiedowns in accordance with the requirements of §§393.100 through 393.114.

(ii) Stacked loads of paper rolls with eyes vertical are prohibited.

(2) *Paper rolls with eyes crosswise.* (i) The paper rolls must be prevented from rolling or shifting longitudinally by contact with vehicle structure or other cargo, by chocks, wedges or blocking and bracing of adequate size, or by tiedowns.

(ii) Chocks, wedges or blocking must be held securely in place by some means in addition to friction so that they cannot become unintentionally unfastened or loose while the vehicle is in transit.

(iii) Tiedowns must be used in accordance with the requirements of §§393.100 through 393.114 to prevent lateral movement.

[67 FR 61225, Sept. 27, 2002, as amended at 71 FR 35834, June 22, 2006]

§393.124 What are the rules for securing concrete pipe?

(a) *Applicability.* (1) The rules in this section apply to the transportation of concrete pipe on flatbed trailers and vehicles, and lowboy trailers.

(2) Concrete pipe bundled tightly together into a single rigid article that has no tendency to roll, and concrete pipe loaded in a sided vehicle or container must be secured in accordance with the provisions of §§393.100 through 393.114.

(b) *General specifications for tiedowns.* (1) The aggregate working load limit of all tiedowns on any group of pipes must not be less than half the total weight of all the pipes in the group.

(2) A transverse tiedown through a pipe on an upper tier or over longitudinal tiedowns is considered to secure all those pipes beneath on which that tiedown causes pressure.

(c) *Blocking.* (1) Blocking may be one or more pieces placed symmetrically about the center of a pipe.

(2) One piece must extend at least half the distance from the center to each end of the pipe, and two pieces must be placed on the opposite side, one at each end of the pipe.

(3) Blocking must be placed firmly against the pipe, and must be secured to prevent it moving out from under the pipe.

(4) Timber blocking must have minimum dimensions of at least 10 × 15 cm (4 × 6 in).

(d) *Arranging the load*—(1) *Pipe of different diameter.* If pipe of more than one diameter are loaded on a vehicle, groups must be formed that consist of pipe of only one size, and each group must be separately secured.

(2) *Arranging a bottom tier.* The bottom tier must be arranged to cover the full length of the vehicle, or as a partial tier in one group or two groups.

(3) *Arranging an upper tier.* Pipe must be placed only in the wells formed by adjacent pipes in the tier beneath. A third or higher tier must not be started unless all wells in the tier beneath are filled.

(4) *Arranging the top tier.* The top tier must be arranged as a complete tier, a partial tier in one group, or a partial tier in two groups.

(5) *Arranging bell pipe.* (i) Bell pipe must be loaded on at least two longitudinal spacers of sufficient height to ensure that the bell is clear of the deck.

(ii) Bell pipe loaded in one tier must have the bells alternating on opposite sides of the vehicle.

(iii) The ends of consecutive pipe must be staggered, if possible, within the allowable width, otherwise they must be aligned.

(iv) Bell pipe loaded in more than one tier must have the bells of the bottom tier all on the same side of the vehicle.

(v) Pipe in every upper tier must be loaded with bells on the opposite side of the vehicle to the bells of the tier below.

(vi) If the second tier is not complete, pipe in the bottom tier which do not support a pipe above must have their bells alternating on opposite sides of the vehicle.

(a) *Securing pipe with an inside diameter up to 1,143 mm (45 in).* In addition to the requirements of paragraphs (b), (c) and (d) of this section, the following rules must be satisfied:

(1) *Stabilizing the bottom tier.* (i) The bottom tier must be immobilized longitudinally at each end by blocking, vehicle end structure, stakes, a locked pipe unloader, or other equivalent means.

(ii) Other pipe in the bottom tier may also be held in place by blocks and/or wedges; and

(iii) Every pipe in the bottom tier must also be held firmly in contact with the adjacent pipe by tiedowns though the front and rear pipes:

(A) At least one tiedown through the front pipe of the bottom tier must run aft at an angle not more than 45 degrees with the horizontal, whenever practicable.

(B) At least one tiedown through the rear pipe of the bottom tier must run forward at an angle not more than 45 degrees with the horizontal, whenever practicable.

(2) *Use of tiedowns.* (i) Each pipe may be secured individually with tiedowns through the pipe.

(ii) If each pipe is not secured individually with a tiedown, then:

(A) Either one 1/2-inch diameter chain or wire rope, or two 3/8-inch diameter chain or wire rope, must be placed longitudinally over the group of pipes;

(B) One transverse tiedown must be used for every 3.04 m (10 ft) of load length. The transverse tiedowns may be placed through a pipe, or over both longitudinal tiedowns between two pipes on the top tier.

(C) If the first pipe of a group in the top tier is not placed in the first well formed by pipes at the front of the tier beneath, it must be secured by an additional tiedown that runs rearward at an angle not more than 45 degrees to the horizontal, whenever practicable. This tiedown must pass either through the front pipe of the upper tier, or outside it and over both longitudinal tiedowns; and

(D) If the last pipe of a group in the top tier is not placed in the last well formed by pipes at the rear of the tier beneath, it must be secured by an additional tiedown that runs forward at an angle not more than 45 degrees to the horizontal, whenever practicable. This tiedown must pass either through the rear pipe of the upper tier or outside it and over both longitudinal tiedowns.

(f) *Securing large pipe, with an inside diameter over 1143 mm (45 in).* In addition to the requirements of paragraphs (b), (c) and (d) of this section, the following rules must be satisfied:

(1) The front pipe and the rear pipe must be immobilized by blocking, wedges, vehicle end structure, stakes, locked pipe unloader, or other equivalent means.

(2) Each pipe must be secured by tiedowns through the pipe:

(i) At least one tiedown through each pipe in the front half of the load, which includes the middle one if there is an odd number, and must run rearward at an angle not more than 45 degrees with the horizontal, whenever practicable.

(ii) At least one tiedown through each pipe in the rear half of the load, and must run forward at an angle not more than 45 degrees with the horizontal, whenever practicable, to hold each pipe firmly in contact with adjacent pipe; and

(iii) If the front or rear pipe is not also in contact with vehicle end structure, stakes, a locked pipe unloader, or other equivalent means, at least two tiedowns positioned as described in paragraphs (f)(2)(i) and (ii) of this section, must be used through that pipe.

(3) If only one pipe is transported, or if several pipes are transported without contact between other pipes, the requirements in this paragraph apply to each pipe as a single front and rear article.

§393.126 What are the rules for securing intermodal containers?

(a) *Applicability.* The rules in this section apply to the transportation of intermodal containers. Cargo contained within an intermodal container must be secured in accordance with the provisions of §§393.100 through 393.114 or, if applicable, the commodity specific rules of this part.

(b) *Securement of intermodal containers transported on container chassis vehicle(s).* (1) All lower corners of the intermodal container must be secured to the container chassis with securement devices or integral locking devices that cannot unintentionally become unfastened while the vehicle is in transit.

(2) The securement devices must restrain the container from moving more than 1.27 cm (1/2 in) forward, more than 1.27 cm (1/2 in) aft, more than 1.27 cm (1/2 in) to the right, more than 1.27 cm (1/2 in) to the left, or more than 2.54 cm (1 in) vertically.

(3) The front and rear of the container must be secured independently.

(c) *Securement of loaded intermodal containers transported on vehicles other than container chassis vehicle(s).* (1) All lower corners of the intermodal container must rest upon the vehicle, or the corners must be supported by a structure capable of bearing the weight of the container and that support structure must be independently secured to the motor vehicle.

(2) Each container must be secured to the vehicle by:

(i) Chains, wire ropes or integral devices which are fixed to all lower corners; or

(ii) Crossed chains which are fixed to all upper corners; and,

(3) The front and rear of the container must be secured independently. Each chain, wire rope, or integral locking device must be attached to the container in a manner that prevents it from being unintentionally unfastened while the vehicle is in transit.

(d) *Securement of empty intermodal containers transported on vehicles other than container chassis vehicle(s).* Empty intermodal containers transported on vehicles other than container chassis vehicles do not have to have all lower corners of the intermodal container resting upon the vehicle, or have all lower corners supported by a structure capable of bearing the weight of the empty container, provided:

(1) The empty intermodal container is balanced and positioned on the vehicle in a manner such that the container is stable before the addition of tiedowns or other securement equipment; and,

(2) The amount of overhang for the empty container on the trailer does not exceed five feet on either the front or rear of the trailer;

(3) The empty intermodal container must not interfere with the vehicle's maneuverability; and,

(4) The empty intermodal container is secured to prevent lateral, longitudinal, or vertical shifting.

[67 FR 61225, Sept. 27, 2002, as amended at 71 FR 35834, June 22, 2006]

§393.128 What are the rules for securing automobiles, light trucks and vans?

(a) *Applicability.* The rules in this section apply to the transportation of automobiles, light trucks, and vans which individually weigh 4,536 kg. (10,000 lb) or less. Vehicles which individually are heavier than 4,536 kg (10,000 lb) must be secured in accordance with the provisions of §393.130 of this part.

(b) *Securement of automobiles, light trucks, and vans.* (1) Automobiles, light trucks, and vans must be restrained at both the front and rear to prevent lateral, forward, rearward, and vertical movement using a minimum of two tiedowns.

(2) Tiedowns that are designed to be affixed to the structure of the automobile, light truck, or van must use

the mounting points on those vehicles that have been specifically designed for that purpose.

(3) Tiedowns that are designed to fit over or around the wheels of an automobile, light truck, or van must provide restraint in the lateral, longitudinal and vertical directions.

(4) Edge protectors are not required for synthetic webbing at points where the webbing comes in contact with the tires.

§ 393.130 What are the rules for securing heavy vehicles, equipment and machinery?

(a) *Applicability.* The rules in this section apply to the transportation of heavy vehicles, equipment and machinery which operate on wheels or tracks, such as front end loaders, bulldozers, tractors, and power shovels and which individually weigh 4,536 kg (10,000 lb.) or more. Vehicles, equipment and machinery which is lighter than 4,536 kg (10,000 lb.) may also be secured in accordance with the provisions of this section, with § 393.128, or in accordance with the provisions of §§ 393.100 through 393.114.

(b) *Preparation of equipment being transported.* (1) Accessory equipment, such as hydraulic shovels, must be completely lowered and secured to the vehicle.

(2) Articulated vehicles shall be restrained in a manner that prevents articulation while in transit.

(c) *Securement of heavy vehicles, equipment or machinery with crawler tracks or wheels.* (1) In addition to the requirements of paragraph (b) of this section, heavy equipment or machinery with crawler tracks or wheels must be restrained against movement in the lateral, forward, rearward, and vertical direction using a minimum of four tiedowns.

(2) Each of the tiedowns must be affixed as close as practicable to the front and rear of the vehicle, or mounting points on the vehicle that have been specifically designed for that purpose.

§ 393.132 What are the rules for securing flattened or crushed vehicles?

(a) *Applicability.* The rules in this section apply to the transportation of vehicles such as automobiles, light trucks, and vans that have been flattened or crushed.

(b) *Prohibition on the use of synthetic webbing.* The use of synthetic webbing to secure flattened or crushed vehicles is prohibited except that such webbing may be used to connect wire rope or chain to anchor points on the commercial motor vehicle. However, the webbing (regardless of whether edge protection is used) must not come into contact with the flattened or crushed cars.

(c) *Securement of flattened or crushed vehicles.* Flattened or crushed vehicles must be transported on vehicles which have:

(1) Containment walls or comparable means on four sides which extend to the full height of the load and which block against movement of the cargo in the forward, rearward and lateral directions; or

(2)(i) Containment walls or comparable means on three sides which extend to the full height of the load and which block against movement of the cargo in the direction for which there is a containment wall or comparable means, and

(ii) A minimum of two tiedowns are required per vehicle stack; or

(3)(i) Containment walls on two sides which extend to the full height of the load and which block against movement of the cargo in the forward and rearward directions, and

(ii) A minimum of three tiedowns are required per vehicle stack; or

(4) A minimum of four tiedowns per vehicle stack.

(5) In addition to the requirements of paragraphs (c)(2), (3), and (4), the following rules must be satisfied:

(i) Vehicles used to transport flattened or crushed vehicles must be equipped with a means to prevent liquids from leaking from the bottom of the vehicle, and loose parts from falling from the bottom and all four sides of the vehicle extending to the full height of the cargo.

(ii) The means used to contain loose parts may consist of structural walls, sides or sideboards, or suitable covering material, alone or in combinations.

(iii) The use of synthetic material for containment of loose parts is permitted.

[67 FR 61225, Sept. 27, 2002, as amended at 71 FR 35834, June 22, 2006]

§393.134 What are the rules for securing roll-on/roll-off or hook lift containers?

(a) *Applicability.* The rules in this section apply to the transportation of roll-on/roll-off or hook lift containers.

(b) *Securement of a roll-on/roll-off and hook lift container.* Each roll-on/roll-off and hook lift container carried on a vehicle which is not equipped with an integral securement system must be:

(1) Blocked against forward movement by the lifting device, stops, a combination of both or other suitable restraint mechanism;

(2) Secured to the front of the vehicle by the lifting device or other suitable restraint against lateral and vertical movement;

(3) Secured to the rear of the vehicle with at least one of the following mechanisms:

(i) One tiedown attached to both the vehicle chassis and the container chassis;

(ii) Two tiedowns installed lengthwise, each securing one side of the container to one of the vehicle's side rails; or

(iii) Two hooks, or an equivalent mechanism, securing both sides of the container to the vehicle chassis at least as effectively as the tiedowns in the two previous items.

(4) The mechanisms used to secure the rear end of a roll-on/roll off or hook lift container must be installed no more than two meters (6 ft 7 in) from the rear of the container.

(5) In the event that one or more of the front stops or lifting devices are missing, damaged or not compatible, additional manually installed tiedowns must be used to secure the container to the vehicle, providing the same level of securement as the missing, damaged or incompatible components.

§393.136 What are the rules for securing large boulders?

(a) *Applicability.* (1) The rules in this section are applicable to the transportation of any large piece of natural, irregularly shaped rock weighing in excess of 5,000 kg (11,000 lb.) or with a volume in excess of 2 cubic-meters on an open vehicle, or in a vehicle whose sides are not designed and rated to contain such cargo.

(2) Pieces of rock weighing more than 100 kg (220 lb.), but less than 5,000 kg (11,000 lb.) must be secured, either in accordance with this section, or in accordance with the provisions of §§393.100 through 393.114, including:

(i) Rock contained within a vehicle which is designed to carry such cargo; or

(ii) Secured individually by tiedowns, provided each piece can be stabilized and adequately secured.

(3) Rock which has been formed or cut to a shape and which provides a stable base for securement must also be secured, either in accordance with the provisions of this section, or in accordance with the provisions of §§393.100 through 393.114.

(b) *General requirements for the positioning of boulders on the vehicle.* (1) Each boulder must be placed with its flattest and/or largest side down.

(2) Each boulder must be supported on at least two pieces of hard wood blocking at least 10 cm × 10 cm (4 inches × 4 inches) side dimensions extending the full width of the boulder.

(3) Hardwood blocking pieces must be placed as symmetrically as possible under the boulder and should support at least three-fourths of the length of the boulder.

(4) If the flattest side of a boulder is rounded or partially rounded, so that the boulder may roll, it must be placed in a crib made of hardwood timber fixed to the deck of the vehicle so that the boulder rests on both the deck and the timber, with at least three well-separated points of contact that prevent its tendency to roll in any direction.

(5) If a boulder is tapered, the narrowest end must point towards the front of the vehicle.

(c) *General tiedown requirements.* (1) Only chain may be used as tiedowns to secure large boulders.

(2) Tiedowns which are in direct contact with the boulder should, where possible, be located in valleys or notches across the top of the boulder,

and must be arranged to prevent sliding across the rock surface.

(d) *Securement of a cubic shaped boulder.* In addition to the requirements of paragraphs (b) and (c) of this section, the following rules must be satisfied:

(1) Each boulder must be secured individually with at least two chain tiedowns placed transversely across the vehicle.

(2) The aggregate working load limit of the tiedowns must be at least half the weight of the boulder.

(3) The tiedowns must be placed as closely as possible to the wood blocking used to support the boulder.

(e) *Securement of a non-cubic shaped boulder—with a stable base.* In addition to the requirements of paragraphs (b) and (c) of this section, the following rules must be satisfied:

(1) The boulder must be secured individually with at least two chain tiedowns forming an "X" pattern over the boulder.

(2) The aggregate working load limit of the tiedowns must be at least half the weight of the boulder.

(3) The tiedowns must pass over the center of the boulder and must be attached to each other at the intersection by a shackle or other connecting device.

(f) *Securement of a non-cubic shaped boulder—with an unstable base.* In addition to the requirements of paragraphs (b) and (c) of this section, each boulder must be secured by a combination of chain tiedowns as follows:

(1) One chain must surround the top of the boulder (at a point between one-half and two-thirds of its height). The working load limit of the chain must be at least half the weight of the boulder.

(2) Four chains must be attached to the surrounding chain and the vehicle to form a blocking mechanism which prevents any horizontal movement. Each chain must have a working load limit of at least one-fourth the weight of the boulder. Whenever practicable, the angle of the chains must not exceed 45 degrees from the horizontal.

Subpart J—Frames, Cab and Body Components, Wheels, Steering, and Suspension Systems

Source: 53 FR 49402, Dec. 7, 1988, unless otherwise noted.

§ 393.201 Frames.

(a) The frame or chassis of each commercial motor vehicle shall not be cracked, loose, sagging or broken.

(b) Bolts or brackets securing the cab or the body of the vehicle to the frame must not be loose, broken, or missing.

(c) The frame rail flanges between the axles shall not be bent, cut or notched, except as specified by the manufacturer.

(d) Parts and accessories shall not be welded to the frame or chassis of a commercial motor vehicle except in accordance with the vehicle manufacturer's recommendations. Any welded repair of the frame must also be in accordance with the vehicle manufacturer's recommendations.

(e) No holes shall be drilled in the top or bottom rail flanges, except as specified by the manufacturer.

[53 FR 49402, Dec. 7, 1988, as amended at 70 FR 48055, Aug. 15, 2005]

§ 393.203 Cab and body components.

(a) The cab compartment doors or door parts used as an entrance or exist shall not be missing or broken. Doors shall not sag so that they cannot be properly opened or closed. No door shall be wired shut or otherwise secured in the closed position so that it cannot be readily opened. Exception: When the vehicle is loaded with pipe or bar stock that blocks the door and the cab has a roof exit.

(b) Bolts or brackets securing the cab or the body of the vehicle to the frame shall not be loose, broken, or missing.

(c) The hood must be securely fastened.

(d) All seats must be securely mounted.

(e) The front bumper must not be missing, loosely attached, or protruding beyond the confines of the vehicle so as to create a hazard.

§393.205 Wheels.

(a) Wheels and rims shall not be cracked or broken.

(b) Stud or bolt holes on the wheels shall shall not be elongated (out of round).

(c) Nuts or bolts shall not be missing or loose.

§393.207 Suspension systems.

(a) *Axles.* No axle positioning part shall be cracked, broken, loose or missing. All axles must be in proper alignment.

(b) *Adjustable axles.* Adjustable axle assemblies shall not have locking pins missing or disengaged.

(c) *Leaf springs.* No leaf spring shall be cracked, broken, or missing nor shifted out of position.

(d) *Coil springs.* No coil spring shall be cracked or broken.

(e) *Torsion bar.* No torsion bar or torsion bar suspension shall be cracked or broken.

(f) *Air suspensions.* The air pressure regulator valve shall not allow air into the suspension system until at least 55 psi is in the braking system. The vehicle shall be level (not tilting to the left or right). Air leakage shall not be greater than 3 psi in a 5-minute time period when the vehicle's air pressure gauge shows normal operating pressure.

(g) *Air suspension exhaust controls.* The air suspension exhaust controls must not have the capability to exhaust air from the suspension system of one axle of a two-axle air suspension trailer unless the controls are either located on the trailer, or the power unit and trailer combination are not capable of traveling at a speed greater than 10 miles per hour while the air is exhausted from the suspension system. This paragraph shall not be construed to prohibit—

(1) Devices that could exhaust air from both axle systems simultaneously; or

(2) Lift axles on multi-axle units.

[53 FR 49402, Dec. 7, 1988, as amended at 70 FR 48055, Aug. 15, 2005]

§393.209 Steering wheel systems.

(a) The steering wheel shall be secured and must not have any spokes cracked through or missing.

(b) *Steering wheel lash.* (1) The steering wheel lash shall not exceed the following parameters:

Steering wheel diameter	Manual steering system	Power steering system
406 mm or less (16 inches or less)	51 mm (2 inches)	108 mm (4¼ inches).
457 mm (18 inches)	57 mm (2¼ inches)	121 mm (4¾ inches).
483 mm (19 inches)	60 mm (2⅜ inches)	127 mm (5 inches).
508 mm (20 inches)	64 mm (2½ inches)	133 mm (5¼ inches).
533 mm (21 inches)	67 mm (2⅝ inches)	140 mm (5½ inches).
559 mm (22 inches)	70 mm (2¾ inches)	146 mm (5¾ inches).

(2) For steering wheel diameters not listed in paragraph (b)(1) of this section the steering wheel lash shall not exceed 14 degrees angular rotation for manual steering systems, and 30 degrees angular rotation for power steering systems.

(c) *Steering column.* The steering column must be securely fastened.

(d) *Steering system.* Universal joints and ball-and-socket joints shall not be worn, faulty or repaired by welding. The steering gear box shall not have loose or missing mounting bolts or cracks in the gear box or mounting brackets. The pitman arm on the steering gear output shaft shall not be loose. Steering wheels shall turn freely through the limit of travel in both directions.

(e) *Power steering systems.* All components of the power system must be in operating condition. No parts shall be loose or broken. Belts shall not be frayed, cracked or slipping. The system shall not leak. The power steering system shall have sufficient fluid in the reservoir.

[53 FR 49402, Dec. 7, 1988, as amended at 70 FR 48055, Aug. 15, 2005]

PART 394 [RESERVED]

PART 395—HOURS OF SERVICE OF DRIVERS

AUTHORITY: 49 U.S.C. 504, 31133, 31136, 31137, and 31502; sec. 113, Pub. L. 103–311, 108 Stat. 1673, 1676; sec. 229, Pub. L. 106–159 (as transferred by sec. 4115 and amended by secs. 4130–4132, Pub. L. 109–59, 119 Stat. 1144, 1726, 1743, 1744); sec. 4133, Pub. L. 109–59, 119 Stat. 1144, 1744; sec. 108, Pub. L. 110–432. 122 Stat. 4860–4866; and 49 CFR 1.73.

SOURCE: 33 FR 19758, Dec. 25, 1968, unless otherwise noted.

EDITORIAL NOTE: Nomenclature changes to part 395 appear at 66 FR 49874, Oct. 1, 2001.

§ 395.1 Scope of rules in this part.

(a) *General.* (1) The rules in this part apply to all motor carriers and drivers, except as provided in paragraphs (b) through (r) of this section.

(2) The exceptions from Federal requirements contained in paragraphs (l) and (m) of this section do not preempt State laws and regulations governing the safe operation of commercial motor vehicles.

(b) *Adverse driving conditions.* (1) Except as provided in paragraph (h)(2) of this section, a driver who encounters adverse driving conditions, as defined in § 395.2, and cannot, because of those conditions, safely complete the run within the maximum driving time permitted by § 395.3(a) or § 395.5(a) may drive and be permitted or required to drive a commercial motor vehicle for not more than 2 additional hours in order to complete that run or to reach a place offering safety for the occupants of the commercial motor vehicle and security for the commercial motor vehicle and its cargo. However, that driver may not drive or be permitted to drive—

(i) For more than 13 hours in the aggregate following 10 consecutive hours off duty for drivers of property-carrying commercial motor vehicles;

(ii) After the end of the 14th hour since coming on duty following 10 consecutive hours off duty for drivers of property-carrying commercial motor vehicles;

(iii) For more than 12 hours in the aggregate following 8 consecutive hours off duty for drivers of passenger-carrying commercial motor vehicles; or

(iv) After he/she has been on duty 15 hours following 8 consecutive hours off duty for drivers of passenger-carrying commercial motor vehicles.

(2) *Emergency conditions.* In case of any emergency, a driver may complete his/her run without being in violation of the provisions of the regulations in this part, if such run reasonably could have been completed absent the emergency.

(c) *Driver-salesperson.* The provisions of § 395.3(b) shall not apply to any driver-salesperson whose total driving time does not exceed 40 hours in any period of 7 consecutive days.

(d) *Oilfield operations.* (1) In the instance of drivers of commercial motor vehicles used exclusively in the transportation of oilfield equipment, including the stringing and picking up of pipe used in pipelines, and servicing of the field operations of the natural gas and oil industry, any period of 8 consecutive days may end with the beginning of any off-duty period of 24 or more successive hours.

(2) In the case of specially trained drivers of commercial motor vehicles which are specially constructed to service oil wells, on-duty time shall not include waiting time at a natural gas or oil well site; *provided*, that all such time shall be fully and accurately accounted for in records to be maintained by the motor carrier. Such records shall be made available upon request of the Federal Motor Carrier Safety Administration.

(e) *Short-haul operations*—(1) *100 air-mile radius driver.* A driver is exempt from the requirements of §395.8 if:

(i) The driver operates within a 100 air-mile radius of the normal work reporting location;

(ii) The driver, except a driver-salesperson, returns to the work reporting location and is released from work within 12 consecutive hours;

(iii)(A) A property-carrying commercial motor vehicle driver has at least 10 consecutive hours off duty separating each 12 hours on duty;

(B) A passenger-carrying commercial motor vehicle driver has at least 8 consecutive hours off duty separating each 12 hours on duty;

(iv)(A) A property-carrying commercial motor vehicle driver does not exceed 11 hours maximum driving time following 10 consecutive hours off-duty; or

(B) A passenger-carrying commercial motor vehicle driver does not exceed 10 hours maximum driving time following 8 consecutive hours off duty; and

(v) The motor carrier that employs the driver maintains and retains for a period of 6 months accurate and true time records showing:

(A) The time the driver reports for duty each day;

(B) The total number of hours the driver is on duty each day;

(C) The time the driver is released from duty each day; and

(D) The total time for the preceding 7 days in accordance with §395.8(j)(2) for drivers used for the first time or intermittently.

(2) *Operators of property-carrying commercial motor vehicles not requiring a commercial driver's license.* Except as provided in this paragraph, a driver is exempt from the requirements of §395.3 and §395.8 and ineligible to use the provisions of §395.1(e)(1), (g) and (o) if:

(i) The driver operates a property-carrying commercial motor vehicle for which a commercial driver's license is not required under part 383 of this subchapter;

(ii) The driver operates within a 150 air-mile radius of the location where the driver reports to and is released from work, *i.e.*, the normal work reporting location;

(iii) The driver returns to the normal work reporting location at the end of each duty tour;

(iv) The driver has at least 10 consecutive hours off duty separating each on-duty period;

(v) The driver does not drive more than 11 hours following at least 10 consecutive hours off-duty;

(vi) The driver does not drive:

(A) After the 14th hour after coming on duty on 5 days of any period of 7 consecutive days; and

(B) After the 16th hour after coming on duty on 2 days of any period of 7 consecutive days;

(vii) The driver does not drive:

(A) After having been on duty for 60 hours in 7 consecutive days if the employing motor carrier does not operate commercial motor vehicles every day of the week;

(B) After having been on duty for 70 hours in 8 consecutive days if the employing motor carrier operates commercial motor vehicles every day of the week;

(viii) Any period of 7 or 8 consecutive days may end with the beginning of any off-duty period of 34 or more consecutive hours.

(ix) The motor carrier that employs the driver maintains and retains for a period of 6 months accurate and true time records showing:

(A) The time the driver reports for duty each day;

(B) The total number of hours the driver is on duty each day;

(C) The time the driver is released from duty each day;

(D) The total time for the preceding 7 days in accordance with §395.8(j)(2) for drivers used for the first time or intermittently.

(f) *Retail store deliveries.* The provisions of §395.3 (a) and (b) shall not apply with respect to drivers of commercial motor vehicles engaged solely in making local deliveries from retail stores and/or retail catalog businesses to the ultimate consumer, when driving solely within a 100-air mile radius of the driver's work-reporting location, during the period from December 10 to December 25, both inclusive, of each year.

(g) *Sleeper berths*—(1) *Property-carrying commercial motor vehicle*—(i) *In*

499

General. A driver who operates a property-carrying commercial motor vehicle equipped with a sleeper berth, as defined in §§ 395.2 and 393.76 of this subchapter,

(A) Must, before driving, accumulate

(*1*) At least 10 consecutive hours off duty;

(*2*) At least 10 consecutive hours of sleeper-berth time;

(*3*) A combination of consecutive sleeper-berth and off-duty time amounting to at least 10 hours; or

(*4*) The equivalent of at least 10 consecutive hours off duty if the driver does not comply with paragraph (g)(1)(i)(A)(*1*), (*2*), or (*3*) of this section;

(B) May not drive more than 11 hours following one of the 10-hour off-duty periods specified in paragraph (g)(1)(i)(A)(*1*) through (*4*) of this section; and

(C) May not drive after the 14th hour after coming on duty following one of the 10-hour off-duty periods specified in paragraph (g)(1)(i)(A)(*1*) through (*4*) of this section; and

(D) Must exclude from the calculation of the 14-hour limit any sleeper berth period of at least 8 but less than 10 consecutive hours.

(ii) *Specific requirements.* The following rules apply in determining compliance with paragraph (g)(1)(i) of this section:

(A) The term "equivalent of at least 10 consecutive hours off duty" means a period of (*1*) At least 8 but less than 10 consecutive hours in a sleeper berth, and

(*2*) A separate period of at least 2 but less than 10 consecutive hours either in the sleeper berth or off duty, or any combination thereof.

(B) Calculation of the 11-hour driving limit includes all driving time; compliance must be re-calculated from the end of the first of the two periods used to comply with paragraph (g)(1)(ii)(A) of this section.

(C) Calculation of the 14-hour limit includes all time except any sleeper-berth period of at least 8 but less than 10 consecutive hours; compliance must be re-calculated from the end of the first of the two periods used to comply with the requirements of paragraph (g)(1)(ii)(A) of this section.

(2) *Specially trained driver of a specially constructed oil well servicing commercial motor vehicle at a natural gas or oil well location.* A specially trained driver who operates a commercial motor vehicle specially constructed to service natural gas or oil wells that is equipped with a sleeper berth, as defined in §§ 395.2 and 393.76 of this subchapter, or who is off duty at a natural gas or oil well location, may accumulate the equivalent of 10 consecutive hours off duty time by taking a combination of at least 10 consecutive hours of off-duty time, sleeper-berth time, or time in other sleeping accommodations at a natural gas or oil well location; or by taking two periods of rest in a sleeper berth, or other sleeping accommodation at a natural gas or oil well location, providing:

(i) Neither rest period is shorter than 2 hours;

(ii) The driving time in the period immediately before and after each rest period, when added together, does not exceed 11 hours;

(iii) The driver does not drive after the 14th hour after coming on duty following 10 hours off duty, where the 14th hour is calculated:

(A) By excluding any sleeper berth or other sleeping accommodation period of at least 2 hours which, when added to a subsequent sleeper berth or other sleeping accommodation period, totals at least 10 hours, and

(B) By including all on-duty time, all off-duty time not spent in the sleeper berth or other sleeping accommodations, all such periods of less than 2 hours, and any period not described in paragraph (g)(2)(iii)(A) of this section; and

(iv) The driver may not return to driving subject to the normal limits under § 395.3 without taking at least 10 consecutive hours off duty, at least 10 consecutive hours in the sleeper berth or other sleeping accommodations, or a combination of at least 10 consecutive hours off duty, sleeper berth time, or time in other sleeping accommodations.

(3) *Passenger-carrying commercial motor vehicles.* A driver who is driving a passenger-carrying commercial motor vehicle that is equipped with a sleeper berth, as defined in §§ 395.2 and 393.76 of

this subchapter, may accumulate the equivalent of 8 consecutive hours of off-duty time by taking a combination of at least 8 consecutive hours off-duty and sleeper berth time; or by taking two periods of rest in the sleeper berth, providing:

(i) Neither rest period is shorter than two hours;

(ii) The driving time in the period immediately before and after each rest period, when added together, does not exceed 10 hours;

(iii) The on-duty time in the period immediately before and after each rest period, when added together, does not include any driving time after the 15th hour; and

(iv) The driver may not return to driving subject to the normal limits under §395.5 without taking at least 8 consecutive hours off duty, at least 8 consecutive hours in the sleeper berth, or a combination of at least 8 consecutive hours off duty and sleeper berth time.

(h) *State of Alaska*—(1) *Property-carrying commercial motor vehicle.* The provisions of §395.3(a) and (b) do not apply to any driver who is driving a commercial motor vehicle in the State of Alaska. A driver who is driving a property-carrying commercial motor vehicle in the State of Alaska must not drive or be required or permitted to drive—

(i) More than 15 hours following 10 consecutive hours off duty; or

(ii) After being on duty for 20 hours or more following 10 consecutive hours off duty.

(iii) After having been on duty for 70 hours in any period of 7 consecutive days, if the motor carrier for which the driver drives does not operate every day in the week; or

(iv) After having been on duty for 80 hours in any period of 8 consecutive days, if the motor carrier for which the driver drives operates every day in the week.

(2) *Passenger-carrying commercial motor vehicle.* The provisions of §395.5 do not apply to any driver who is driving a passenger-carrying commercial motor vehicle in the State of Alaska. A driver who is driving a passenger-carrying commercial motor vehicle in the State of Alaska must not drive or be required or permitted to drive—

(i) More than 15 hours following 8 consecutive hours off duty;

(ii) After being on duty for 20 hours or more following 8 consecutive hours off duty;

(iii) After having been on duty for 70 hours in any period of 7 consecutive days, if the motor carrier for which the driver drives does not operate every day in the week; or

(iv) After having been on duty for 80 hours in any period of 8 consecutive days, if the motor carrier for which the driver drives operates every day in the week.

(3) A driver who is driving a commercial motor vehicle in the State of Alaska and who encounters adverse driving conditions (as defined in §395.2) may drive and be permitted or required to drive a commercial motor vehicle for the period of time needed to complete the run.

(i) After a property-carrying commercial motor vehicle driver completes the run, that driver must be off duty for at least 10 consecutive hours before he/she drives again; and

(ii) After a passenger-carrying commercial motor vehicle driver completes the run, that driver must be off duty for at least 8 consecutive hours before he/she drives again.

(i) *State of Hawaii.* The rules in §395.8 do not apply to a driver who drives a commercial motor vehicle in the State of Hawaii, if the motor carrier who employs the driver maintains and retains for a period of 6 months accurate and true records showing—

(1) The total number of hours the driver is on duty each day; and

(2) The time at which the driver reports for, and is released from, duty each day.

(j) *Travel time*—(1) When a property-carrying commercial motor vehicle driver at the direction of the motor carrier is traveling, but not driving or assuming any other responsibility to the carrier, such time must be counted as on-duty time unless the driver is afforded at least 10 consecutive hours off duty when arriving at destination, in which case he/she must be considered off duty for the entire period.

(2) When a passenger-carrying commercial motor vehicle driver at the direction of the motor carrier is traveling, but not driving or assuming any other responsibility to the carrier, such time must be counted as on-duty time unless the driver is afforded at least 8 consecutive hours off duty when arriving at destination, in which case he/she must be considered off duty for the entire period.

(k) *Agricultural operations.* The provisions of this part shall not apply to drivers transporting agricultural commodities or farm supplies for agricultural purposes in a State if such transportation:

(1) Is limited to an area within a 100 air-mile radius from the source of the commodities or the distribution point for the farm supplies, and

(2) Is conducted (except in the case of livestock feed transporters) during the planting and harvesting seasons within such State, as determined by the State.

(l) *Ground water well drilling operations.* In the instance of a driver of a commercial motor vehicle who is used primarily in the transportation and operations of a ground water well drilling rig, any period of 7 or 8 consecutive days may end with the beginning of any off-duty period of 24 or more successive hours.

(m) Construction materials and equipment. In the instance of a driver of a commercial motor vehicle who is used primarily in the transportation of construction materials and equipment, any period of 7 or 8 consecutive days may end with the beginning of any off-duty period of 24 or more successive hours.

(n) *Utility service vehicles.* The provisions of this part shall not apply to a driver of a utility service vehicle as defined in § 395.2.

(o) *Property-carrying driver.* A property-carrying driver is exempt from the requirements of § 395.3(a)(2) if:

(1) The driver has returned to the driver's normal work reporting location and the carrier released the driver from duty at that location for the previous five duty tours the driver has worked;

(2) The driver has returned to the normal work reporting location and the carrier releases the driver from duty within 16 hours after coming on duty following 10 consecutive hours off duty; and

(3) The driver has not taken this exemption within the previous 6 consecutive days, except when the driver has begun a new 7- or 8-consecutive day period with the beginning of any off-duty period of 34 or more consecutive hours as allowed by § 395.3(c).

(p) *Commercial motor vehicle transportation to or from a motion picture production site.* A driver of a commercial motor vehicle providing transportation of property or passengers to or from a theatrical or television motion picture production site is exempt from the requirements of § 395.3(a) if the driver operates within a 100 air-mile radius of the location where the driver reports to and is released from work, i.e., the normal work-reporting location. With respect to the maximum daily hours of service, such a driver may not drive—

(1) More than 10 hours following 8 consecutive hours off duty;

(2) For any period after having been on duty 15 hours following 8 consecutive hours off duty.

(3) If a driver of a commercial motor vehicle providing transportation of property or passengers to or from a theatrical or television motion picture production site operates beyond a 100 air-mile radius of the normal work-reporting location, the driver is subject to § 395.3(a), and paragraphs (p)(1) and (2) of this section do not apply.

(q) *Transporters of grapes during harvest period in the State of New York.* The provisions of this part shall not apply to drivers transporting grapes if such transportation:

(1) Is within the State of New York;

(2) Is west of Interstate 81;

(3) Is within a 150 air-mile radius of where the grapes were picked or distributed; and

(4) Is during the harvest period as defined by the State of New York. This provision expires September 30, 2009.

(r) *Railroad signal employees.* The provisions of this part shall not apply to a signal employee, as defined in § 395.2, who operates a commercial motor vehicle, is engaged in installing, repairing, or maintaining signal systems, is employed by a railroad carrier or a contractor or subcontractor to a railroad carrier, while regulated by the Federal Railroad Administration.

[57 FR 33647, July 30, 1992, as amended at 58 FR 33777, June 21, 1993; 60 FR 38748, July 28, 1995; 61 FR 14679, Apr. 3, 1996; 63 FR 33279, June 18, 1998; 68 FR 22515, Apr. 28, 2003; 68 FR 56211, Sept. 30, 2003; 70 FR 50071, Aug. 25, 2005; 72 FR 36790, July 5, 2007; 72 FR 55703, Oct. 1, 2007; 72 FR 71269, Dec. 17, 2007; 76 FR 25590, May 5, 2011]

§ 395.2 Definitions.

As used in this part, the following words and terms are construed to mean:

Adverse driving conditions means snow, sleet, fog, other adverse weather conditions, a highway covered with snow or ice, or unusual road and traffic conditions, none of which were apparent on the basis of information known to the person dispatching the run at the time it was begun.

Agricultural commodity means any agricultural commodity, nonprocessed food, feed, fiber, or livestock (including livestock as defined in sec. 602 of the Emergency Livestock Feed Assistance Act of 1988 [7 U.S.C. 1471] and insects).

Automatic on-board recording device means an electric, electronic, electromechanical, or mechanical device capable of recording driver's duty status information accurately and automatically as required by §395.15. The device must be integrally synchronized with specific operations of the commercial motor vehicle in which it is installed. At a minimum, the device must record engine use, road speed, miles driven, the date, and time of day.

CD–RW (Compact Disc—Re-Writeable) means an optical disc digital storage format that allows digital data to be erased and rewritten many times. The technical and physical specifications for CD–RW are described in the document Orange Book Part III: CD–RW, published by Royal Philips Electronics.

CMRS (Commercial Mobile Radio Services) An FCC designation for any carrier or licensee whose wireless network is connected to the public switched telephone network and/or is operated for profit. Another common term for these entities is cellular telephony providers.

Driver-salesperson means any employee who is employed solely as such by a private carrier of property by commercial motor vehicle, who is engaged both in selling goods, services, or the use of goods, and in delivering by commercial motor vehicle the goods sold or provided or upon which the services are performed, who does so entirely within a radius of 100 miles of the point at which he/she reports for duty, who devotes not more than 50 percent of his/her hours on duty to driving time. The term *selling goods* for purposes of this section shall include in all cases solicitation or obtaining of reorders or new accounts, and may also include other selling or merchandising activities designed to retain the customer or to increase the sale of goods or services, in addition to solicitation or obtaining of reorders or new accounts.

Driving time means all time spent at the driving controls of a commercial motor vehicle in operation.

Eight consecutive days means the period of 8 consecutive days beginning on any day at the time designated by the motor carrier for a 24-hour period.

802.11 is a set of communications and product compatibility standards for wireless local area networks (WLAN). The 802.11 standards are also known as WiFi by marketing convention.

Electronic on-board recording device (EOBR) means an electronic device that is capable of recording a driver's hours of service and duty status accurately and automatically and that meets the requirements of §395.16. The device must be integrally synchronized with specific operations of the commercial motor vehicle in which it is installed. The EOBR must record, at minimum, the information listed in §395.16(b).

Farm supplies for agricultural purposes means products directly related to the growing or harvesting of agricultural commodities during the planting and harvesting seasons within each State, as determined by the State, and livestock feed *at any time of the year.*

Ground water well drilling rig means any vehicle, machine, tractor, trailer, semi-trailer, or specialized mobile equipment propelled or drawn by mechanical power and used on highways to transport water well field operating equipment, including water well drilling and pump service rigs equipped to access ground water.

Integrally synchronized refers to an AOBRD or EOBR that receives and records the engine use status and distance traveled for the purpose of deriving on-duty driving status from a source or sources internal to the CMV.

Multiple stops means all stops made in any one village, town, or city may be computed as one.

On duty time means all time from the time a driver begins to work or is required to be in readiness to work until the time the driver is relieved from work and all responsibility for performing work. *On duty time* shall include:

(1) All time at a plant, terminal, facility, or other property of a motor carrier or shipper, or on any public property, waiting to be dispatched, unless the driver has been relieved from duty by the motor carrier;

(2) All time inspecting, servicing, or conditioning any commercial motor vehicle at any time;

(3) All driving time as defined in the term *driving time;*

(4) All time, other than *driving time,* in or upon any commercial motor vehicle except time spent resting in a *sleeper berth;*

(5) All time loading or unloading a commercial motor vehicle, supervising, or assisting in the loading or unloading, attending a commercial motor vehicle being loaded or unloaded, remaining in readiness to operate the commercial motor vehicle, or in giving or receiving receipts for shipments loaded or unloaded;

(6) All time repairing, obtaining assistance, or remaining in attendance upon a disabled commercial motor vehicle;

(7) All time spent providing a breath sample or urine specimen, including travel time to and from the collection site, in order to comply with the random, reasonable suspicion, post-accident, or follow-up testing required by part 382 of this subchapter when directed by a motor carrier;

(8) Performing any other work in the capacity, employ, or service of a motor carrier; and

(9) Performing any compensated work for a person who is not a motor carrier.

Seven consecutive days means the period of 7 consecutive days beginning on any day at the time designated by the motor carrier for a 24-hour period.

Signal employee, as defined in 49 U.S.C. 21101(4), means an individual who is engaged in installing, repairing, or maintaining signal systems.

Sleeper berth means a berth conforming to the requirements of § 393.76 of this chapter.

Transportation of construction materials and equipment means the transportation of construction and pavement materials, construction equipment, and construction maintenance vehicles, by a driver to or from an active construction site (a construction site between mobilization of equipment and materials to the site to the final completion of the construction project) within a 50 air mile radius of the normal work reporting location of the driver. This paragraph does not apply to the transportation of material found by the Secretary to be hazardous under 49 U.S.C. 5103 in a quantity requiring placarding under regulations issued to carry out such section.

Twenty-four-hour period means any 24-consecutive-hour period beginning at the time designated by the motor carrier for the terminal from which the driver is normally dispatched.

USB (Universal Serial Bus) is a serial bus interface standard for connecting electronic devices.

UTC (Coordinated Universal Time) is the international civil time standard, determined by using highly precise atomic clocks. It is the basis for civil standard time in the United States and its territories. UTC time refers to time kept on the Greenwich meridian (longitude zero), which is 5 hours ahead of Eastern Standard Time. UTC times are expressed in terms of a 24-hour clock. Standard time within any U.S. time zone is offset from UTC by a given number of hours determined by the time zone's distance from the Greenwich meridian.

Utility service vehicle means any commercial motor vehicle:

(1) Used in the furtherance of repairing, maintaining, or operating any

structures or any other physical facilities necessary for the delivery of public utility services, including the furnishing of electric, gas, water, sanitary sewer, telephone, and television cable or community antenna service;

(2) While engaged in any activity necessarily related to the ultimate delivery of such public utility services to consumers, including travel or movement to, from, upon, or between activity sites (including occasional travel or movement outside the service area necessitated by any utility emergency as determined by the utility provider); and

(3) Except for any occasional emergency use, operated primarily within the service area of a utility's subscribers or consumers, without regard to whether the vehicle is owned, leased, or rented by the utility.

[57 FR 33648, July 30, 1992, as amended at 59 FR 7515, Feb. 15, 1994; 59 FR 60324, Nov. 23, 1994; 60 FR 38748, July 28, 1995; 61 FR 14679, Apr. 3, 1996; 63 FR 33279, June 18, 1998; 72 FR 36790, July 5, 2007; 75 FR 17245, Apr. 5, 2010; 76 FR 25590, May 5, 2011]

§395.3 Maximum driving time for property-carrying vehicles.

Subject to the exceptions and exemptions in §395.1:

(a) No motor carrier shall permit or require any driver used by it to drive a property-carrying commercial motor vehicle, nor shall any such driver drive a property-carrying commercial motor vehicle:

(1) More than 11 cumulative hours following 10 consecutive hours off-duty;

(2) For any period after the end of the 14th hour after coming on duty following 10 consecutive hours off duty, except when a property-carrying driver complies with the provisions of §395.1(o) or §395.1(e)(2).

(b) No motor carrier shall permit or require a driver of a property-carrying commercial motor vehicle to drive, nor shall any driver drive a property-carrying commercial motor vehicle, regardless of the number of motor carriers using the driver's services, for any period after—

(1) Having been on duty 60 hours in any period of 7 consecutive days if the employing motor carrier does not oper-

ate commercial motor vehicles every day of the week; or

(2) Having been on duty 70 hours in any period of 8 consecutive days if the employing motor carrier operates commercial motor vehicles every day of the week.

(c)(1) Any period of 7 consecutive days may end with the beginning of any off-duty period of 34 or more consecutive hours; or

(2) Any period of 8 consecutive days may end with the beginning of any off-duty period of 34 or more consecutive hours.

[70 FR 50073, Aug. 25, 2005, as amended at 72 FR 71270, Dec. 17, 2007]

§395.5 Maximum driving time for passenger-carrying vehicles.

Subject to the exceptions and exemptions in §395.1:

(a) No motor carrier shall permit or require any driver used by it to drive a passenger-carrying commercial motor vehicle, nor shall any such driver drive a passenger-carrying commercial motor vehicle:

(1) More than 10 hours following 8 consecutive hours off duty; or

(2) For any period after having been on duty 15 hours following 8 consecutive hours off duty.

(b) No motor carrier shall permit or require a driver of a passenger-carrying commercial motor vehicle to drive, nor shall any driver drive a passenger-carrying commercial motor vehicle, regardless of the number of motor carriers using the driver's services, for any period after—

(1) Having been on duty 60 hours in any 7 consecutive days if the employing motor carrier does not operate commercial motor vehicles every day of the week; or

(2) Having been on duty 70 hours in any period of 8 consecutive days if the employing motor carrier operates commercial motor vehicles every day of the week.

[70 FR 50073, Aug. 25, 2005]

§395.7 [Reserved]

§395.8 Driver's record of duty status.

(a) Except for a private motor carrier of passengers (nonbusiness), every motor carrier shall require every driver

505

used by the motor carrier to record his/her duty status for each 24 hour period using the methods prescribed in either paragraph (a)(1) or (2) of this section.

(1) Every driver who operates a commercial motor vehicle shall record his/her duty status, in duplicate, for each 24-hour period. The duty status time shall be recorded on a specified grid, as shown in paragraph (g) of this section. The grid and the requirements of paragraph (d) of this section may be combined with any company forms. The previously approved format of the Daily Log, Form MCS–59 or the Multiday Log, MCS–139 and 139A, which meets the requirements of this section, may continue to be used.

(2) Every driver operating a commercial motor vehicle equipped with either an automatic on-board recording device meeting the requirements of § 395.15 or an electronic on-board recorder meeting the requirements of § 395.16 must record his or her duty status using the device installed in the vehicle. The requirements of this section shall not apply, except for paragraphs (e) and (k)(1) and (2) of this section.

(b) The duty status shall be recorded as follows:

(1) "Off duty" or "OFF."

(2) "Sleeper berth" or "SB" (only if a sleeper berth used).

(3) "Driving" or "D."

(4) "On-duty not driving" or "ON."

(c) For each change of duty status (e.g., the place of reporting for work, starting to drive, on-duty not driving and where released from work), the name of the city, town, or village, with State abbreviation, shall be recorded.

NOTE: If a change of duty status occurs at a location other than a city, town, or village, show one of the following: (1) The highway number and nearest milepost followed by the name of the nearest city, town, or village and State abbreviation, (2) the highway number and the name of the service plaza followed by the name of the nearest city, town, or village and State abbreviation, or (3) the highway numbers of the nearest two intersecting roadways followed by the name of the nerest city, town, or village and State abbreviation.

(d) The following information must be included on the form in addition to the grid:

(1) Date;

(2) Total miles driving today;

(3) Truck or tractor and trailer number;

(4) Name of carrier;

(5) Driver's signature/certification;

(6) 24-hour period starting time (e.g. midnight, 9:00 a.m., noon, 3:00 p.m.);

(7) Main office address;

(8) Remarks;

(9) Name of co-driver;

(10) Total hours (far right edge of grid);

(11) Shipping document number(s), or name of shipper and commodity;

(e) Failure to complete the record of duty activities of either this section, § 395.15 or § 395.16, failure to preserve a record of such duty activities, or making false reports in connection with such duty activities shall make the driver and/or the carrier liable to prosecution.

(f) The driver's activities shall be recorded in accordance with the following provisions:

(1) *Entries to be current.* Drivers shall keep their records of duty status current to the time shown for the last change of duty status.

(2) *Entries made by driver only.* All entries relating to driver's duty status must be legible and in the driver's own handwriting.

(3) *Date.* The month, day and year for the beginning of each 24-hour period shall be shown on the form containing the driver's duty status record.

(4) *Total miles driving today.* Total mileage driven during the 24-hour period shall be recorded on the form containing the driver's duty status record.

(5) *Commercial motor vehicle identification.* The driver shall show the number assigned by the motor carrier, or the license number and licensing State of each commercial motor vehicle operated during each 24-hour period on his/her record of duty status. The driver of an articulated (combination) commercial motor vehicle shall show the number assigned by the motor carrier, or the license number and licensing State of each motor vehicle used in each commercial motor vehicle combination operated during that 24-hour period on his/her record of duty status.

(6) *Name of motor carrier.* The name(s) of the motor carrier(s) for which work is performed shall be shown on the form containing the driver's record of

duty status. When work is performed for more than one motor carrier during the same 24-hour period, the beginning and finishing time, showing a.m. or p.m., worked for each motor carrier shall be shown after each motor carrier's name. Drivers of leased commercial motor vehicles shall show the name of the motor carrier performing the transportation.

(7) *Signature/certification.* The driver shall certify to the correctness of all entries by signing the form containing the driver's duty status record with his/her legal name or name of record. The driver's signature certifies that all entries required by this section made by the driver are true and correct.

(8) *Time base to be used.* (i) The driver's duty status record shall be prepared, maintained, and submitted using the time standard in effect at the driver's home terminal, for a 24-hour period beginning with the time specified by the motor carrier for that driver's home terminal.

(ii) The term "7 or 8 consecutive days" means the 7 or 8 consecutive 24-hour periods as designated by the carrier for the driver's home terminal.

(iii) The 24-hour period starting time must be identified on the driver's duty status record. One-hour increments must appear on the graph, be identified, and preprinted. The words "Midnight" and "Noon" must appear above or beside the appropriate one-hour increment.

(9) *Main office address.* The motor carrier's main office address shall be shown on the form containing the driver's duty status record.

(10) *Recording days off duty.* Two or more consecutive 24-hour periods off duty may be recorded on one duty status record.

(11) *Total hours.* The total hours in each duty status: ff duty other than in a sleeper berth; off duty in a sleeper berth; driving, and on duty not driving, shall be entered to the right of the grid, the total of such entries shall equal 24 hours.

(12) *Shipping document number(s) or name of shipper and commodity* shall be shown on the driver's record of duty status.

(g) *Graph grid.* The following graph grid must be incorporated into a motor carrier recordkeeping system which must also contain the information required in paragraph (d) of this section.

(h) *Graph grid preparation.* The graph grid may be used horizontally or vertically and shall be completed as follows:

(1) *Off duty.* Except for time spent resting in a sleeper berth, a continuous line shall be drawn between the appropriate time markers to record the period(s) of time when the driver is not on duty, is not required to be in readiness to work, or is not under any responsibility for performing work.

(2) *Sleeper berth.* A continuous line shall be drawn between the appropriate time markers to record the period(s) of time off duty resting in a sleeper berth, as defined in §395.2. (If a non-sleeper berth operation, sleeper berth need not be shown on the grid.)

(3) *Driving.* A continuous line shall be drawn between the appropriate time markers to record the period(s) of driving time, as defined in §395.2.

(4) *On duty not driving.* A continuous line shall be drawn between the appropriate time markers to record the period(s) of time on duty not driving specified in §395.2.

(5) *Location—remarks.* The name of the city, town, or village, with State abbreviation where each change of duty status occurs shall be recorded.

508

NOTE: If a change of duty status occurs at a location other than a city, town, or village, show one of the following: (1) The highway number and nearest milepost followed by the name of the nearest city, town, or village and State abbreviation, (2) the highway number and the name of the service plaza followed by the name of the nearest city, town, or village and State abbreviation, or (3) the highway numbers of the nearest two intersecting roadways followed by the name of the nearest city, town, or village and State abbreviation.

(i) *Filing driver's record of duty status.* The driver shall submit or forward by mail the original driver's record of duty status to the regular employing motor carrier within 13 days following the completion of the form.

(j) *Drivers used by more than one motor carrier.* (1) When the services of a driver are used by more than one motor carrier during any 24-hour period in effect at the driver's home terminal, the driver shall submit a copy of the record of duty status to each motor carrier. The record shall include:

(i) All duty time for the entire 24-hour period;

(ii) The name of each motor carrier served by the driver during that period; and

(iii) The beginning and finishing time, including a.m. or p.m., worked for each carrier.

(2) Motor carriers, when using a driver for the first time or intermittently, shall obtain from the driver a signed statement giving the total time on duty during the immediately preceding 7 days and the time at which the driver was last relieved from duty prior to beginning work for the motor carriers.

(k) *Retention of driver's record of duty status.* (1) Each motor carrier shall maintain records of duty status and all supporting documents for each driver it employs for a period of six months from the date of receipt.

(2) The driver shall retain a copy of each record of duty status for the previous 7 consecutive days which shall be in his/her possession and available for inspection while on duty.

NOTE: Driver's Record of Duty Status.

The graph grid, when incorporated as part of any form used by a motor carrier, must be of sufficient size to be legible.

The following executed specimen grid illustrates how a driver's duty status should be recorded for a trip from Richmond, Virginia, to Newark, New Jersey. The grid reflects the midnight to midnight 24 hour period.

Graph Grid (Midnight to Midnight Operation)

The driver in this instance reported for duty at the motor carrier's terminal. The driver reported for work at 6 a.m., helped load, checked with dispatch, made a pretrip inspection, and performed other duties until 7:30 a.m. when the driver began driving. At 9 a.m. the driver had a minor accident in Fredericksburg, Virginia, and spent one half hour handling details with the local police. The driver arrived at the company's Baltimore, Maryland, terminal at noon and went to lunch while minor repairs were made to the tractor. At 1 p.m. the driver resumed the trip and made a delivery in Philadelphia, Pennsylvania, between 3 p.m. and 3:30 p.m. at which time the driver started driving again. Upon arrival at Cherry Hill, New Jersey, at 4 p.m., the driver entered the sleeper berth

509

for a rest break until 5:45 p.m. at which time the driver resumed driving again. At 7 p.m. the driver arrived at the company's terminal in Newark, New Jersey. Between 7 p.m. and 8 p.m. the driver prepared the required paperwork including completing the driver's record of duty status, driver vehicle inspection report, insurance report for the Fredericksburg, Virginia accident, checked for the next day's dispatch, etc. At 8 p.m., the driver went off duty.

(Approved by the Office of Management and Budget under control number 2125–0016)

[47 FR 53389, Nov. 26, 1982, as amended at 49 FR 38290, Sept. 28, 1984; 49 FR 46147, Nov. 23, 1984; 51 FR 12622, Apr. 14, 1986; 52 FR 41721, Oct. 30, 1987; 53 FR 18058, May 19, 1988; 53 FR 38670, Sept. 30, 1988; 57 FR 33649, July 30, 1992; 58 FR 33777, June 21, 1993; 59 FR 8753, Feb. 23, 1994; 60 FR 38748, July 28, 1995; 62 FR 16709, Apr. 8, 1997; 63 FR 33279, June 18, 1998; 75 FR 17245, Apr. 5, 2010]

§ 395.10 [Reserved]

§ 395.11 Supporting documents for drivers using EOBRs.

(a) Motor carriers maintaining date, time and location data produced by a § 395.16-compliant EOBR need only maintain additional supporting documents (*e.g.*, driver payroll records, fuel receipts) that provide the ability to verify on-duty not driving activities and off-duty status according to the requirements of § 395.8(k).

(b) This section does not apply to motor carriers and owner-operators that have been issued a remedial directive to install, use, and maintain EOBRs.

[75 FR 17245, Apr. 5, 2010]

§ 395.12 [Reserved]

§ 395.13 Drivers declared out of service.

(a) *Authority to declare drivers out of service.* Every special agent of the Federal Motor Carrier Safety Administration (as defined in appendix B to this subchapter) is authorized to declare a driver out of service and to notify the motor carrier of that declaration, upon finding at the time and place of examination that the driver has violated the out of service criteria as set forth in paragraph (b) of this section.

(b) *Out of service criteria.* (1) No driver shall drive after being on duty in ex-

cess of the maximum periods permitted by this part.

(2) Every driver required to maintain a record of duty status under § 395.8 must have a record of duty status current on the day of examination and for the prior 7 consecutive days.

(3) *Exception.* A driver failing only to have possession of a record of duty status current on the day of examination and the prior day, but has completed records of duty status up to that time (previous 6 days), will be given the opportunity to make the duty status record current.

(4) No driver shall drive a CMV in violation of § 385.811(d) of this chapter.

(c) *Responsibilities of motor carriers.* (1) No motor carrier shall:

(i) Require or permit a driver who has been declared out of service to operate a commercial motor vehicle until that driver may lawfully do so under the rules in this part.

(ii) Require a driver who has been declared out of service for failure to prepare a record of duty status to operate a commercial motor vehicle until that driver has been off duty for the appropriate number of consecutive hours required by this part and is in compliance with this section. The appropriate consecutive hours off-duty may include sleeper berth time.

(2) A motor carrier shall complete the "Motor Carrier Certification of Action Taken" portion of the form MCS–63 (Driver-Vehicle Examination Report) and deliver the copy of the form either personally or by mail to the Division Administrator or State Director Federal Motor Carrier Safety Administration, at the address specified upon the form within 15 days following the date of examination. If the motor carrier mails the form, delivery is made on the date it is postmarked.

(d) *Responsibilities of the driver.* (1) No driver who has been declared out of service shall operate a commercial motor vehicle until that driver may lawfully do so under the rules of this part.

(2) No driver who has been declared out of service, for failing to prepare a record of duty status, shall operate a commercial motor vehicle until the

driver has been off duty for the appropriate number of consecutive hours required by this part and is in compliance with this section.

(3) A driver to whom a form has been tendered declaring the driver out of service shall within 24 hours thereafter deliver or mail the copy to a person or place designated by motor carrier to receive it.

(4) Section 395.13 does not alter the hazardous materials requirements prescribed in § 397.5 pertaining to attendance and surveillance of commercial motor vehicles.

[44 FR 34963, June 18, 1979, as amended at 47 FR 53392, Nov. 26, 1982; 51 FR 12622, Apr. 14, 1986; 53 FR 18058, May 19, 1988; 53 FR 38670, Sept. 30, 1988; 53 FR 47544, Nov. 23, 1988; 60 FR 38748, July 28, 1995; 68 FR 22516, Apr. 28, 2003; 70 FR 50073, Aug. 25, 2005; 75 FR 17245, Apr. 5, 2010]

§ 395.15 Automatic on-board recording devices.

(a) *Applicability and authority to use.* This section applies to automatic on-board recording devices (AOBRDs) used to record drivers' hours of service as specified by part 395.

(1) A motor carrier may require a driver to use an AOBRD to record the driver's hours of service in lieu of complying with the requirements of § 395.8 of this part. For commercial motor vehicles manufactured prior to June 4, 2012, manufacturers or motor carriers may install an electronic device to record hours of service if the device meets the requirements of either this section or § 395.16.

(2) Every driver required by a motor carrier to use an automatic on-board recording device shall use such device to record the driver's hours of service.

(b) *Information requirements.* (1) Automatic on-board recording devices shall produce, upon demand, a driver's hours of service chart, electronic display, or printout showing the time and sequence of duty status changes including the drivers' starting time at the beginning of each day.

(2) The device shall provide a means whereby authorized Federal, State, or local officials can immediately check the status of a driver's hours of service. This information may be used in conjunction with handwritten or printed records of duty status, for the previous 7 days.

(3) Support systems used in conjunction with on-board recorders at a driver's home terminal or the motor carrier's principal place of business must be capable of providing authorized Federal, State or local officials with summaries of an individual driver's hours of service records, including the information specified in § 395.8(d) of this part. The support systems must also provide information concerning on-board system sensor failures and identification of edited data. Such support systems should meet the information interchange requirements of the American National Standard Code for Information Interchange (ANSCII) (EIARS–232/CCITT V.24 port (National Bureau of Standards "Code for Information Interchange," FIPS PUB 1–1)).

(4) The driver shall have in his/her possession records of duty status for the previous 7 consecutive days available for inspection while on duty. These records shall consist of information stored in and retrievable from the automatic on-board recording device, handwitten records, computer generated records, or any combination thereof.

(5) All hard copies of the driver's record of duty status must be signed by the driver. The driver's signature certifies that the information contained thereon is true and correct.

(c) The duty status and additional information shall be recorded as follows:

(1) "Off duty" or "OFF", or by an identifiable code or character;

(2) "Sleeper berth" or "SB" or by an identifiable code or character (only if the sleeper berth is used);

(3) "Driving" or "D", or by an identifiable code or character; and

(4) "On-duty not driving" or "ON", or by an identifiable code or character.

(5) Date;

(6) Total miles driving today;

(7) Truck or tractor and trailer number;

(8) Name of carrier;

(9) Main office address;

(10) 24-hour period starting time (e.g., midnight, 9:00 a.m., noon, 3:00 p.m.)

(11) Name of co-driver;

(12) Total hours; and

(13) Shipping document number(s), or name of shipper and commodity.

(d) *Location of duty status change.* (1) For each change of duty status (e.g., the place and time of reporting for work, starting to drive, on-duty not driving and where released from work), the name of the city, town, or village, with State abbreviation, shall be recorded.

(2) Motor carriers are permitted to use location codes in lieu of the requirements of paragraph (d)(1) of this section. A list of such codes showing all possible location identifiers shall be carried in the cab of the commercial motor vehicle and available at the motor carrier's principal place of business. Such lists shall be made available to an enforcement official on request.

(e) *Entries made by driver only.* If a driver is required to make written entries relating to the driver's duty status, such entries must be legible and in the driver's own handwriting.

(f) *Reconstruction of records of duty status.* Drivers are required to note any failure of automatic on-board recording devices, and to reconstruct the driver's record of duty status for the current day, and the past 7 days, less any days for which the drivers have records, and to continue to prepare a handwritten record of all subsequent duty status until the device is again operational.

(g) *On-board information.* Each commercial motor vehicle must have on-board the commercial motor vehicle an information packet containing the following items:

(1) An instruction sheet describing in detail how data may be stored and retrieved from an automatic on-board recording system; and

(2) A supply of blank driver's records of duty status graph-grids sufficient to record the driver's duty status and other related information for the duration of the current trip.

(h) *Submission of driver's record of duty status.* (1) The driver shall submit, electronically or by mail, to the employing motor carrier, each record of the driver's duty status within 13 days following the completion of each record;

(2) The driver shall review and verify that all entries are accurate prior to submission to the employing motor carrier; and

(3) The submission of the record of duty status certifies that all entries made by the driver are true and correct.

(i) *Performance of recorders.* Motor carriers that use automatic on-board recording devices for recording their drivers' records of duty status in lieu of the handwritten record shall ensure that:

(1) A certificate is obtained from the manufacturer certifying that the design of the automatic on-board recorder has been sufficiently tested to meet the requirements of this section and under the conditions it will be used;

(2) The automatic on-board recording device permits duty status to be updated only when the commercial motor vehicle is at rest, except when registering the time a commercial motor vehicle crosses a State boundary;

(3) The automatic on-board recording device and associated support systems are, to the maximum extent practicable, tamperproof and do not permit altering of the information collected concerning the driver's hours of service;

(4) The automatic on-board recording device warns the driver visually and/or audibly that the device has ceased to function. Devices installed and operational as of October 31, 1988, and authorized to be used in lieu of the handwritten record of duty status by the FMCSA are exempted from this requirement.

(5) Automatic on-board recording devices with electronic displays shall have the capability of displaying the following:

(i) Driver's total hours of driving today;

(ii) The total hours on duty today;

(iii) Total miles driving today;

(iv) Total hours on duty for the 7 consecutive day period, including today;

(v) Total hours on duty for the prior 8 consecutive day period, including the present day; and

(vi) The sequential changes in duty status and the times the changes occurred for each driver using the device.

(6) The on-board recorder is capable of recording separately each driver's duty status when there is a multiple-driver operation;

(7) The on-board recording device/system identifies sensor failures and edited data when reproduced in printed form. Devices installed and operational as of October 31, 1988, and authorized to be used in lieu of the handwritten record of duty status by the FMCSA are exempted from this requirement.

(8) The on-board recording device is maintained and recalibrated in accordance with the manufacturer's specifications;

(9) The motor carrier's drivers are adequately trained regarding the proper operation of the device; and

(10) The motor carrier must maintain a second copy (back-up copy) of the electronic hours-of-service files, by month, in a different physical location than where the original data is stored.

(j) *Rescission of authority.* (1) The FMCSA may, after notice and opportunity to reply, order any motor carrier or driver to comply with the requirements of §395.8 of this part.

(2) The FMCSA may issue such an order if the FMCSA has determined that—

(i) The motor carrier has been issued a conditional or unsatisfactory safety rating by the FMCSA;

(ii) The motor carrier has required or permitted a driver to establish, or the driver has established, a pattern of exceeding the hours of service limitations of this part;

(iii) The motor carrier has required or permitted a driver to fail, or the driver has failed, to accurately and completely record the driver's hours of service as required in this section; or

(iv) The motor carrier or driver has tampered with or otherwise abused the automatic on-board recording device on any commercial motor vehicle.

[53 FR 38670, Sept. 30, 1988, as amended at 60 FR 38748, July 28, 1995; 68 FR 22516, Apr. 28, 2003; 70 FR 50073, Aug. 25, 2005; 75 FR 17245, Apr. 5, 2010]

§395.16 Electronic on-board recording devices.

(a) *Applicability and authority to use.* This section applies to electronic on-board recording devices (EOBRs) used to record the driver's hours of service as specified by part 395. Motor carriers subject to a remedial directive to install, use and maintain EOBRs, issued in accordance with 49 CFR part 385, subpart J, must comply with this section.

(1) A motor carrier may require a driver to use an EOBR to record the driver's hours of service in lieu of complying with the requirements of §395.8 of this part. For commercial motor vehicles manufactured after June 4, 2012, any electronic device installed in a CMV by a manufacturer or motor carrier to record hours of service must meet the requirements of this section.

(2) Every driver required by a motor carrier to use an EOBR shall use such device to record the driver's hours of service.

(b) *Information to be recorded.* An EOBR must record the following information:

(1) Name of driver and any co-driver(s), and corresponding driver identification information (such as a user ID and password). However, the name of the driver and any co-driver is not required to be transmitted as part of the downloaded file during a roadside inspection.

(2) Duty status.

(3) Date and time.

(4) Location of CMV.

(5) Distance traveled.

(6) Name and USDOT Number of motor carrier.

(7) 24-hour period starting time (*e.g.*, midnight, 9 a.m., noon, 3 p.m.).

(8) The multiday basis (7 or 8 days) used by the motor carrier to compute cumulative duty hours and driving time.

(9) Hours in each duty status for the 24-hour period, and total hours.

(10) Truck or tractor and trailer number.

(11) Shipping document number(s), or name of shipper and commodity.

(c) *Duty status categories.* An EOBR must use the following duty statuses:

(1) "Off duty" or "OFF".

(2) "Sleeper berth" or "SB", to be used only if sleeper berth is used.

(3) "Driving" or "D".

(4) "On-duty not driving" or "ON".

(d) *Duty status defaults.* (1) An EOBR must automatically record driving time. If the CMV is being used as a personal conveyance, the driver must affirmatively enter an annotation before the CMV begins to move.

(2) When the CMV is stationary for 5 minutes or more, the EOBR must default to on-duty not driving, and the driver must enter the proper duty status.

(3) An EOBR must record the results of power-on self-tests and diagnostic error codes.

(e) *Date and time.* (1) The date and time must be recorded on the EOBR output record as specified under paragraph (i) of this section at each change of duty status, and at intervals of no greater than 60 minutes when the CMV is in motion. The date and time must be displayed on the EOBR's visual output device.

(2) The date and time must be obtained, transmitted, and recorded in such a way that it cannot be altered by a motor carrier, driver, or third party.

(3) The driver's duty status record must be prepared, maintained, and submitted using the time standard in effect at the driver's home terminal, for a 24-hour period beginning with the time specified by the motor carrier for that driver's home terminal.

(4) The time must be coordinated to UTC and the absolute deviation shall not exceed 10 minutes at any time.

(f) *Location.* (1) Information used to determine the location of the CMV must be derived from a source not subject to alteration by the motor carrier or driver.

(2) The location description for the duty status change, and for intervening intervals while the CMV is in motion, must be sufficiently precise to enable Federal, State, and local enforcement personnel to quickly determine the vehicle's geographic location on a standard map or road atlas. The term "sufficiently precise," for purposes of this paragraph means the nearest city, town or village.

(3) When the CMV is in motion, location and time must be recorded at intervals no greater than 60 minutes. This recorded information must be capable of being made available in an output file format as specified in appendix A to this part, but does not need

to be displayed on the EOBR's visual output device.

(4) For each change of duty status (*e.g.,* the place and time of reporting for work, starting to drive, on-duty not driving, and where released from work), the name of the nearest city, town, or village, with State abbreviation, must be recorded.

(5) The EOBR must record location names using codes derived from satellite or terrestrial sources, or a combination of these. The location codes must correspond, at a minimum, to ANSI INCITS 446–2008, "American National Standard for Information Technology—Identifying Attributes for Named Physical and Cultural Geographic Features (Except Roads and Highways) of the United States, Its Territories, Outlying Areas, and Freely Associated Areas and the Waters of the Same to the Limit of the Twelve-Mile Statutory Zone (10/28/2008)," where "GNIS Feature Class" = "Populated Place" (incorporated by reference, *see* § 395.18. (For further information, *see also* the Geographic Names Information System (GNIS) at *http://geonames.usgs.gov/domestic/index.html*).

(g) *Distance traveled.* (1) Distance traveled must use units of miles or kilometers driving during each on-duty driving period and total for each 24-hour period for each driver operating the CMV.

(2) If the EOBR records units of distance in kilometers, it must provide a means to display the equivalent distance in miles.

(3) Distance traveled information obtained from a source internal to the CMV must be accurate to the distance traveled as measured by the CMV's odometer.

(h) *Review of information by driver.* (1) The EOBR must allow for the driver's review of each day's record before the driver submits the record to the motor carrier.

(2) The driver must review the information contained in the EOBR record and affirmatively note the review before submitting the record to the motor carrier.

(3) The driver may annotate only non-driving-status periods and the use of a CMV as a personal conveyance as described in paragraph (d)(1) of this

section. The driver must electronically confirm his or her intention to make any annotations. The annotation must not overwrite the original record.

(4) If the driver makes a written entry on a hardcopy output of an EOBR relating to his or her duty status, the entries must be legible and in the driver's own handwriting.

(i) *Information reporting requirements.* (1) An EOBR must make it possible for authorized Federal, State, or local officials to immediately check the status of a driver's hours of service.

(2) An EOBR must produce, upon demand, a driver's hours-of-service record in either electronic or printed form. It must also produce a digital file in the format described in appendix A to this part. The record must show the time and sequence of duty status changes including the driver's starting time at the beginning of each day. As an alternative, the EOBR must be able to provide a driver's hours-of-service record as described in paragraph (i)(6) of this section.

(3) This information may be used in conjunction with handwritten or printed records of duty status for the previous 7 days.

(4) Hours-of-service information must be made accessible to authorized Federal, State, or local safety assurance officials for their review without requiring the official to enter in or upon the CMV. The output record must conform to the file format specified in appendix A to this part.

(5) The driver must have in his or her possession records of duty status for the previous 7 consecutive days available for inspection while on duty. These records must consist of information stored in and retrievable from the EOBR, handwritten records, records available from motor carriers' support systems, other printed records, or any combination of these. Electronic records must be capable of one-way transfer through wired and wireless methods to portable computers used by roadside safety assurance officials and must provide files in the format specified in Appendix A to this part. Wired communication information interchange methods must comply with the "Universal Serial Bus Specification (Revision 2.0) incorporated by reference, *see* §395.18) and additional specifications in appendix A, paragraph 2.2 to this part. Wireless communication information interchange methods must comply with the requirements of the 802.11g–2003 standard as defined in the 802.11–2007 base standard "IEEE Standard for Information Technology—Telecommunications and information exchange between systems—Local and metropolitan area networks—Specific requirements: Part 11: Wireless LAN Medium Access Control (MAC) and Physical Layer (PHY) Specifications" (IEEE Std. 802.11–2007) (incorporated by reference, *see* §395.18), or CMRS.

(6) Support systems used in conjunction with EOBRs at a driver's home terminal or the motor carrier's principal place of business must be capable of providing authorized Federal, State, or local officials with summaries of an individual driver's hours of service records, including the information specified in §395.8(d). The support systems must also provide information concerning on-board system sensor failures and identification of amended and edited data. Support systems must provide a file in the format specified in appendix A to this part. The system must also be able to produce a copy of files on portable storage media (CD–RW, USB 2.0 drive) upon request of authorized safety assurance officials. The support system may be maintained by a third-party service provider on behalf of the motor carrier.

(j) *Driver identification.* For the driver to log into the EOBR, the EOBR must require the driver to enter information (such as a user ID and password) that identifies the driver or to provide other information (such as smart cards, biometrics) that identifies the driver.

(k) *Availability of records of duty status.* (1) An EOBR must be capable of producing duty status records for the current day and the previous 7 days from either the information stored in and retrievable from the EOBR or motor carrier support system records, or any combination of these.

(2) If an EOBR fails, the driver must do the following:

(i) Note the failure of the EOBR and inform the motor carrier within 2 days.

(ii) Reconstruct the record of duty status for the current day and the previous 7 days, less any days for which the driver has records.

(iii) Continue to prepare a handwritten record of all subsequent duty status until the device is again operational.

(iv) A brief (less than 5 minute) loss of connectivity between the EOBR and a location-tracking system or the motor carriers' support system is not considered an EOBR failure for the purpose of this section.

(1) *On-board information.* Each commercial motor vehicle must have onboard the commercial motor vehicle an information packet containing the following items:

(1) An instruction sheet describing how data may be stored and retrieved from the EOBR.

(2) A supply of blank driver's records of duty status graph-grids sufficient to record the driver's duty status and other related information for the duration of the current trip.

(m) *Submission of driver's record of duty status.* (1) The driver must submit electronically, to the employing motor carrier, each record of the driver's duty status.

(2) For motor carriers not subject to the remedies provisions of part 385 subpart J of this chapter, each record must be submitted within 13 days of its completion.

(3) For motor carriers subject to the remedies provisions of part 385 subpart J of this chapter, each record must be submitted within 3 days of its completion.

(4) The driver must review and verify that all entries are accurate prior to submission to the employing motor carrier.

(5) The submission of the record of duty status certifies that all entries made by the driver are true and correct.

(n) *EOBR display requirements.* An EOBR must have the capability of displaying all of the following information:

(1) The driver's name and EOBR login ID number on all EOBR records associated with that driver, including records in which the driver serves as a co-driver.

(2) The driver's total hours of driving during each driving period and the current duty day.

(3) The total hours on duty for the current duty day.

(4) Total miles or kilometers of driving during each driving period and the current duty day.

(5) Total hours on duty and driving time for the prior 7-consecutive-day period, including the current duty day.

(6) Total hours on duty and driving time for the prior 8-consecutive-day period, including the current duty day.

(7) The sequence of duty status for each day, and the time of day and location for each change of duty status, for each driver using the device.

(8) EOBR serial number or other identification, and identification number(s) of vehicle(s) operated that day.

(9) Remarks, including fueling, waypoints, loading and unloading times, unusual situations, or violations.

(10) Driver's override of an automated duty status change to driving if using the vehicle for personal conveyance or for yard movement.

(11) The EOBR may record other data as the motor carrier deems appropriate, including the date and time of crossing a State line for purposes of fuel-tax reporting.

(o) *Performance of recorders.* A motor carrier that uses an EOBR for recording a driver's records of duty status instead of the handwritten record must ensure the EOBR meets the following requirements:

(1) The EOBR must permit the driver to enter information into the EOBR only when the commercial motor vehicle is at rest.

(2) The EOBR and associated support systems must not permit alteration or erasure of the original information collected concerning the driver's hours of service, or alteration of the source data streams used to provide that information.

(3) The EOBR must be able to perform a power-on self-test, as well as a self-test at any point upon request of an authorized safety assurance official. The EOBR must provide an audible and visible signal as to its functional status. It must record the outcome of the self-test and its functional status as a

diagnostic event record in conformance with appendix A to this part.

(4) The EOBR must provide an audible and visible signal to the driver at least 30 minutes in advance of reaching the driving time limit and the on-duty limit for the 24-hour period.

(5) The EOBR must be able to track total weekly on-duty and driving hours over a 7- or 8-day consecutive period. The EOBR must be able to warn a driver at least 30 minutes in advance of reaching the weekly duty-/driving-hour limitation.

(6) The EOBR must warn the driver via an audible and visible signal that the device has ceased to function. "Ceasing to function" for the purpose of this paragraph does not include brief losses of communications signals during such time as, but not limited to, when the vehicle is traveling through a tunnel.

(7) The EOBR must record a code corresponding to the reason it has ceased to function and the date and time of that event.

(8) The audible signal must be capable of being heard and discerned by the driver when seated in the normal driving position, whether the CMV is in motion or parked with the engine operating. The visual signal must be visible to the driver when the driver is seated in the normal driving position.

(9) The EOBR must be capable of recording separately each driver's duty status when there is a multiple-driver operation.

(10) The EOBR device/system must identify sensor failures and edited and annotated data when downloaded or reproduced in printed form.

(11) The EOBR device/system must identify annotations made to all records, the date and time the annotations were made, and the identity of the person making them.

(12) If a driver or any other person annotates a record in an EOBR or an EOBR support system, the annotation must not overwrite the original contents of the record.

(p) *Motor carrier requirements.* (1) The motor carrier must not alter or erase, or permit or require alteration or erasure of, the original information collected concerning the driver's hours of service, the source data streams used to provide that information, or information contained in its EOBR support systems that use the original information and source data streams.

(2) The motor carrier must ensure the EOBR is calibrated, maintained, and recalibrated in accordance with the manufacturer's specifications; the motor carrier must retain records of these activities.

(3) The motor carrier's drivers and other personnel reviewing and using EOBRs and the information derived from them must be adequately trained regarding the proper operation of the device.

(4) The motor carrier must maintain a second copy (back-up copy) of the electronic hours-of-service files, by month, on a physical device different from that on which the original data are stored.

(5) The motor carrier must review the EOBR records of its drivers for compliance with part 395.

(6) If the motor carrier receives or discovers information concerning the failure of an EOBR, the carrier must document the failure in the hours-of-service record for that driver.

(q) *Manufacturer's self-certification.* (1) The EOBR and EOBR support systems must be certified by the manufacturer as evidence that they have been sufficiently tested to meet the requirements of §395.16 and appendix A to this part under the conditions in which they would be used.

(2) The exterior faceplate of the EOBR must be marked by the manufacturer with the text "USDOT-EOBR" as evidence that the device has been tested and certified as meeting the performance requirements of §395.16 and appendix A to this part.

[75 FR 17245, Apr. 5, 2010]

§395.18 Matter incorporated by reference.

(a) *Incorporation by reference.* Certain materials are incorporated by reference in part 395, with the approval of the Director of the Federal Register under 5 U.S.C. 552(a), and 1 CFR part 51. For materials subject to change, only the specific version approved by the Director of the Office of the Federal Register and specified in the regulation is incorporated. To enforce any edition other than that specified in this section, the Federal Motor Carrier Safety Administration must publish notice of change in the FEDERAL REGISTER and the material must be available to the public. All of the approved material is available for inspection at the National Archives and Records Administration (NARA). For information on the availability of this material at NARA, call 202–741–6030 or go to *http:// www.archives.gov/federal-register/cfr/ibr-locations.html.* Also, it is available for inspection at the Federal Motor Carrier Safety Administration, Office of Bus and Truck Standards and Operations (MC–PS), 1200 New Jersey Ave., SE., Washington, DC 20590–00001, (202) 366–4325, and is available from the sources listed in paragraphs (b) and (c) of this section.

(b) *Institute of Electrical and Electronic Engineers (IEEE).* 3 Park Avenue, New York, New York 10016–5997. Web page is *http://www.ieee.org/web/publications/ home;* telephone is (800) 678–4333.

(1) "IEEE Standard for Information Technology—Telecommunications and information exchange between systems—Local and metropolitan area networks—Specific requirements: Part 11: Wireless LAN Medium Access Control (MAC) and Physical Layer (PHY) Specifications," IEEE Computer Society, Sponsored by the LAN/MAN Standards Committee: June 12, 2007 (IEEE Std. 802.11–2007). Incorporation by reference approved for §395.16(i); and appendix A to part 395, paragraph 2.3.

(2) [Reserved]

(c) *Universal Serial Bus Implementers Forum (USBIF).* 3855 SW. 153rd Drive, Beaverton, Oregon 97006. Web page is *http://www.usb.org;* telephone is (503) 619–0426.

(1) "Universal Serial Bus Specification," Compaq, Hewlett-Packard, Intel, Lucent, Microsoft, NEC, Philips; April 27, 2000 (Revision 2.0). Incorporation by reference approved for §395.16(i) and Appendix A to part 395, paragraph 2.2.

(2) [Reserved]

(d) *American National Standards Institute (ANSI).* 11 West 42nd Street, New York, New York 10036. Web page is *http://webstore.ansi.org;* telephone is (212) 642–4900.

(1) "ANSI INCITS 446–2008, American National Standard for Information Technology—Identifying Attributes for Named Physical and Cultural Geographic Features (Except Roads and Highways) of the United States, Its Territories, Outlying Areas, and Freely Associated Areas and the Waters of the Same to the Limit of the Twelve-Mile Statutory Zone (10/28/2008)," (ANSI INCITS 446–2008). Incorporation by reference approved for §395.16(f); appendix A to part 395, paragraph 1.3, Table 2; and appendix A to part 395, paragraph 3.1.1.3. (For further information, *see also* the Geographic Names Information System (GNIS) at *http:// geonames.usgs.gov/domestic/index.html.*

(2) [Reserved]

[75 FR 17248, Apr. 5, 2010]

APPENDIX A TO PART 395—ELECTRONIC ON-BOARD RECORDER PERFORMANCE SPECIFICATIONS

1. Data Elements Dictionary for Electronic On-Board Recorders (EOBRs)

1.1 To facilitate the electronic transfer of records to roadside inspection personnel and compliance review personnel, and provide the ability of various third-party and proprietary EOBR devices to be interoperable, a consistent electronic file format and record layout for the electronic RODS data to be recorded are necessary. This EOBR data elements dictionary provides a standardized and consistent format for EOBR output data.

EOBR Data File Format

1.2 Regardless of the particular electronic file type (such as ASCII or XML) ultimately used for recording the electronic RODS produced by an EOBR, RODS data must be recorded according to a "flat file" database model format. A flat file is a simple database in which all information is stored in a plain text format with one database "record" per line. Each of these data records is divided into "fields" using delimiters (as in a comma-separate-values data file) or based on fixed column positions. Table 1 below presents the general concept of a flat data file consisting of data "fields" (columns) and data "records" (rows).

Table 1: Flat Data File Database Model

FIELDS ⟶

	Person First Name	Person Last Name	Driver PIN	Event Date	Event Time	Status Code
RECORDS	William	Smith	978354	20050718	12:11	D
	William	Smith	978354	20050718	15:17	SB
	William	Smith	978354	20050718	18:53	D
	William	Smith	978354	20050718	21:43	ON
	William	Smith	978354	20050718	22:14	OFF
	William	Smith	978354	20050719	06:25	ON
	William	Smith	978354	20050719	06:47	D
	William	Smith	978354	20050719	13:32	SB
	William	Smith	978354	20050719	15:27	D
	William	Smith	978354	20050719	20:04	SB

1.3 The data elements dictionary describes the data fields component of the above framework. Individual data records must be generated and recorded whenever there is a change in driver duty status, an EOBR diagnostic event (such as power-on/off, self test, etc.), or when one or more data fields of an existing data record are later amended. In the last case, the corrected record must be recorded and noted as "current" in the "Event Status Code" data field, with the original record maintained in its unedited form and noted as "historical" in the "Event Status Code" data field. The EOBR Data Elements Dictionary is described in Table 2. The event codes are listed in Table 3.

TABLE 2—EOBR DATA ELEMENTS DICTIONARY

Data element	Data element definition	Type	Length	Valid values and notes
Driver Identification Data				
Driver First Name	First name of the driver	A	35	See Note 1.
Driver Last Name	Last name, family name, or surname of the driver.	A	35	See Note 1.
Driver PIN/ID	Numeric identification number assigned to a driver by the motor carrier.	A	40	
Vehicle Identification Data				
Tractor Number	Motor carrier assigned identification number for tractor unit.	A	10	
Trailer Number	Motor carrier assigned identification number for trailer.	A	10	
Tractor VIN Number.	Unique vehicle ID number assigned by manufacturer according to US DOT regulations.	A	17	
Co-Driver Data				
Co-Driver First Name.	First name of the co-driver	A	35	See Note 1.
Co-Driver Last Name.	Last name, family name or surname of the co-driver.	A	35	See Note 1.
Co-Driver ID	Numeric identification number assigned to a driver by the motor carrier.	A	40	

519

TABLE 2—EOBR DATA ELEMENTS DICTIONARY—Continued

Data element	Data element definition	Type	Length	Valid values and notes
Company Identification Data				
Carrier USDOT Number.	USDOT Number of the motor carrier assigned by FMCSA.	N	8	
Carrier Name	Name or trade name of the motor carrier company appearing on the Form MCS-150.	A	120	
Shipment Data				
Shipping Document Number.	Shipping document number	A	40	
Event Data				
Event Sequence ID.	A serial identifier for an event that is unique to a particular vehicle and a particular day.	N	4	0001 through 9999.
Event Status Code	Character codes for the four driver duty status change events, State border crossing event, and diagnostic events.	A	3	OFF = Off Duty SB = Sleeper Berth D = On Duty Driving ON = On Duty Not Driving DG = Diagnostic.
Event Date	The date when an event occurred	N (Date)	8	UTC (universal time) recommended. Format: YYYYMMDD.
Event Time	The time when an event occurred	N (Time)	6	UTC (universal time) recommended. Format: HHMMSS (hours, minutes, seconds).
Event Latitude	Latitude of a location where an event occurred.	N	2,6	Decimal format: XX.XXXXXX.
Event Longitude ...	Longitude of a location where an event occurred.	N	3,6	Decimal format: XXX.XXXXXX.
Place Name	The location codes must correspond, at a minimum, to ANSI INCITS 446-2008, "American National Standard for Information Technology—Identifying Attributes for Named Physical and Cultural Geographic Features (Except Roads and Highways) of the United States, Its Territories, Outlying Areas, and Freely Associated Areas and the Waters of the Same to the Limit of the Twelve-Mile Statutory Zone (10/28/2008)," where "GNIS Feature Class" = "Populated Place" (incorporated by reference, see §395.18). (For further information, see also the Geographic Names Information System (GNIS) at *http://geonames.usgs.gov/domestic/index.html.*	N	5	Unique within a FIPS state code. Lookup list derived from GNIS.
Place Distance Miles.	Distance in miles to nearest populated place from the location where an event occurred.	N	4	
Total Vehicle Miles	Total vehicle miles (as noted on vehicle odometer or as measured by any other compliant means such as vehicle location system, *etc.*).	N	7	With total vehicle mileage recorded at the time of each event, vehicle miles traveled while driving, *etc.*, can be computed.
Event Update Status Code.	A status of an event, either Current (the most up-to-date update or edit) or Historical (the original record if the record has subsequently been updated or edited).	A	1	C = Current, H = Historical.
Diagnostic Event Code.	For diagnostic events (events where the "Event Status Code" is noted as "DG"), records the type of diagnostic performed (*e.g.*, power-on, self test, power-off, etc.).	A	2	(See Table 3).
Event Error Code	Error code associated with an event	A	2	(See Table 3).
Event Update Date	The date when an event record was last updated or edited.	N (Date)	8	UTC (universal time) recommended. Format: YYYYMMDD.
Event Update Time.	Then time when an event record was last updated or edited.	N (Time)	6	UTC (universal time) recommended. Format: HHMMSS (hours, minutes, seconds).

TABLE 2—EOBR DATA ELEMENTS DICTIONARY—Continued

Data element	Data element definition	Type	Length	Valid values and notes
Event Update Person ID.	An identifier of the person who last updated or edited a record.	A	40	
Event Update Text	A textual note related to the most recent record update or edit.	A	60	Brief narrative regarding reason for record update or edit.

NOTE 1: This element must not be included in the records downloaded from an EOBR or support system at roadside.

TABLE 3—EOBR DIAGNOSTIC EVENT CODES

Code class	Code	Brief description	Full description
General System Diagnostic	PWR_ON	Power on	EOBR initial power-on.
General System Diagnostic	PWROFF	Power off	EOBR power-off.
General System Diagnostic	TESTOK	test okay	EOBR self test successful.
General System Diagnostic	SERVIC	Service	EOBR Malfunction (return unit to factory for servicing).
General System Diagnostic	MEMERR	memory error	System memory error.
General System Diagnostic	LOWVLT	Low voltage	Low system supply voltage.
General System Diagnostic	BATLOW	battery low	Internal system battery backup low.
General System Diagnostic	CLKERR	clock error	EOBR system clock error (clock not set or defective).
General System Diagnostic	BYPASS	Bypass	EOBR system bypassed (RODS data not collected).
Data Storage Diagnostic	INTFUL	internal memory full	Internal storage memory full (requires download or transfer to external storage).
Data Storage Diagnostic	DATACC	Data accepted	System accepted driver data entry.
Data Storage Diagnostic	EXTFUL	external memory full.	External memory full (smartcard or other external data storage device full).
Data Storage Diagnostic	EXTERR	external data access error.	Access external storage device failed.
Data Storage Diagnostic	DLOADY	download yes	EOBR data download successful.
Data Storage Diagnostic	DLOADN	download no	Data download rejected (unauthorized request/wrong Password).
Driver Identification Issue	NODRID	no driver ID	No driver information in system and vehicle is in motion.
Driver Identification Issue	PINERR	PIN error	Driver PIN/identification number invalid.
Driver Identification Issue	DRIDRD	Driver ID read	Driver information successfully read from external storage device (transferred to EOBR).
Peripheral Device Issue	DPYERR	display error	EOBR display malfunction.
Peripheral Device Issue	KEYERR	keyboard error	EOBR keyboard/input device malfunction.
External Sensor Issue	NOLTLN	no latitude longitude.	No latitude and longitude from positioning sensor.
External Sensor Issue	NOTSYC	no time synchronization.	Unable to synchronize with external time reference input.
External Sensor Issue	COMERR	communications error.	Unable to communicate with external data link (to home office or wireless service provider).
External Sensor Issue	NO_ECM	no ECM data	No sensory information received from vehicle's Engine Control Module (ECM).
External Sensor Issue	ECM_ID	ECM ID number mismatch.	ECM identification/serial number mismatch (with preprogrammed information).

2. *Communications Standards for the Transmittal of Data Files From Electronic On-Board Recorders (EOBRs)*

2.1 EOBRs must produce and store RODS in accordance with the file format specified in this appendix and must be capable of a one-way transfer of these records through wired and wireless methods to authorized safety officials upon request.

2.2 *Wired.* EOBRs must be capable of transferring RODS using the "Universal Serial Bus Specification (Revision 2.0)" (incorporated by reference, see §395.18). Each EOBR device must implement a single USB compliant interface featuring a Type A connector. The USB interface must implement the Mass Storage class (08h) for driverless operation.

2.3 *Wireless.* EOBRs must be capable of transferring RODS using one of the following wireless standards:

2.3.1 802.11g–2003 standard as defined in the 802.11–2007 base standard for wireless communication "IEEE Standard for Information Technology—Telecommunications and information exchange between systems—Local and metropolitan area networks—Specific requirements: Part 11: Wireless LAN Medium Access Control (MAC) and Physical Layer (PHY) Specifications" (IEEE Std. 802.11–2007) (incorporated by reference, see §395.18).

2.3.2 Commercial Mobile Radio Services (*e.g.*, cellular).

3. *Certification of EOBRs To Assess Conformity With FMCSA Standards*

3.1 The following outcome-based performance requirements must be included in the self-certification testing conducted by EOBR manufacturers:

3.1.1 Location

3.1.1.1 The location description for the duty status change must be sufficiently precise to enable enforcement personnel to quickly determine the vehicle's geographic location at each change of duty status on a standard map or road atlas.

3.1.1.2 When the CMV is in motion, location and time must be recorded at intervals of no greater than 60 minutes. This recorded information must be available for an audit of EOBR data, but is not required to be displayed on the EOBR's visual output device.

3.1.1.3 Location codes derived from satellite or terrestrial sources, or a combination thereof must be used. The location codes must correspond, at minimum, to the GNIS maintained by the United States Geological Survey.

3.1.2 Distance traveled

3.1.2.1 Distance traveled may use units of miles or kilometers driving during each on-duty driving period and total for each 24-hour period for each driver operating the CMV.

3.1.2.2 If the EOBR records units of distance in kilometers, it must provide a means to display the equivalent distance in English units.

3.1.2.3 If the EOBR obtains distance-traveled information from a source internal to the CMV, the information must be accurate to the CMV's odometer.

3.1.3 Date and time

3.1.3.1 The date and time must be reported on the EOBR output record and display for each change of duty status and at such additional entries as specified under "Location."

3.1.3.2 The date and time must be obtained, transmitted, and recorded in such a way that it cannot be altered by a motor carrier or driver.

3.1.3.3 The time must be coordinated to the Universal Time Clock (UTC) and must not drift more than 60 seconds per month.

3.1.4 File format and communication protocols: The EOBR must produce and transfer a RODS file in the format and communication methods specified in sections 1.0 and 2.0 of this Appendix.

3.1.5 Environment

3.1.5.1 [Reserved]

3.1.5.2 Vibration and shock—The EOBR must meet industry standards for vibration stability and for preventing electrical shocks to device operators.

3.2 The EOBR and EOBR support systems must be certified by the manufacturer as evidence that their design has been sufficiently tested to meet the requirements of §395.16 under the conditions in which they would be used.

3.3 The exterior faceplate of EOBRs must be marked by the manufacturer with the text 'USDOT–EOBR' as evidence that the device has been tested and certified as meeting the performance requirements of §395.16.

[75 FR 17248, Apr. 5, 2010, as amended at 75 FR 55491, Sept. 13, 2010]

PART 396—INSPECTION, REPAIR, AND MAINTENANCE

396.21 Periodic inspection recordkeeping requirements.
396.23 Equivalent to periodic inspection.
396.25 Qualifications of brake inspectors.

AUTHORITY: 49 U.S.C. 31133, 31136, 31151, and 31502; and 49 CFR 1.73.

SOURCE: 44 FR 38526, July 2, 1979, unless otherwise noted.

EDITORIAL NOTE: Nomenclature changes to part 396 appear at 66 FR 49874, Oct. 1, 2001.

§396.1 Scope.

(a) Every motor carrier, its officers, drivers, agents, representatives, and employees directly concerned with the inspection or maintenance of commercial motor vehicles must be knowledgeable of and comply with the rules of this part.

(b) Every intermodal equipment provider, its officers, agents, representatives, and employees directly concerned with the inspection or maintenance of intermodal equipment interchanged or offered for interchange to motor carriers must be knowledgeable of and comply with the rules of this part.

[73 FR 76823, Dec. 17, 2008]

§396.3 Inspection, repair, and maintenance.

(a) *General.* Every motor carrier and intermodal equipment provider must systematically inspect, repair, and maintain, or cause to be systematically inspected, repaired, and maintained, all motor vehicles and intermodal equipment subject to its control.

(1) Parts and accessories shall be in safe and proper operating condition at all times. These include those specified in part 393 of this subchapter and any additional parts and accessories which may affect safety of operation, including but not limited to, frame and frame assemblies, suspension systems, axles and attaching parts, wheels and rims, and steering systems.

(2) Pushout windows, emergency doors, and emergency door marking lights in buses shall be inspected at least every 90 days.

(b) *Required records.* Motor carriers, except for a private motor carrier of passengers (nonbusiness), must maintain, or cause to be maintained, records for each motor vehicle they control for 30 consecutive days. Inter-modal equipment providers must maintain or cause to be maintained, records for each unit of intermodal equipment they tender or intend to tender to a motor carrier. These records must include:

(1) An identification of the vehicle including company number, if so marked, make, serial number, year, and tire size. In addition, if the motor vehicle is not owned by the motor carrier, the record shall identify the name of the person furnishing the vehicle;

(2) A means to indicate the nature and due date of the various inspection and maintenance operations to be performed;

(3) A record of inspection, repairs, and maintenance indicating their date and nature; and

(4) A record of tests conducted on pushout windows, emergency doors, and emergency door marking lights on buses.

(c) *Record retention.* The records required by this section shall be retained where the vehicle is either housed or maintained for a period of 1 year and for 6 months after the motor vehicle leaves the motor carrier's control.

[44 FR 38526, July 2, 1979, as amended at 48 FR 55868, Dec. 16, 1983; 53 FR 18058, May 19, 1988; 59 FR 8753, Feb. 23, 1994; 59 FR 60324, Nov. 23, 1994; 73 FR 75824, Dec. 17, 2008]

§396.5 Lubrication.

Every motor carrier shall ensure that each motor vehicle subject to its control is—

(a) Properly lubricated; and

(b) Free of oil and grease leaks.

§396.7 Unsafe operations forbidden.

(a) *General.* A motor vehicle shall not be operated in such a condition as to likely cause an accident or a breakdown of the vehicle.

(b) *Exemption.* Any motor vehicle discovered to be in an unsafe condition while being operated on the highway may be continued in operation only to the nearest place where repairs can safely be effected. Such operation shall be conducted only if it is less hazardous to the public than to permit the vehicle to remain on the highway.

§ 396.9 Inspection of motor vehicles in operation.

(a) *Personnel authorized to perform inspections.* Every special agent of the FMCSA (as defined in appendix B to this subchapter) is authorized to enter upon and perform inspections of a motor carrier's vehicles in operation and intermodal equipment in operation.

(b) *Prescribed inspection report.* The Driver Vehicle Examination Report shall be used to record results of motor vehicle inspections and results of intermodal equipment inspections conducted by authorized FMCSA personnel.

(c) *Motor vehicles declared "out of service."* (1) Authorized personnel shall declare and mark "out of service" any motor vehicle which by reason of its mechanical condition or loading would likely cause an accident or a breakdown. Authorized personnel may declare and mark "out of service" any motor vehicle not in compliance with § 385.811(d). An "Out of Service Vehicle" sticker shall be used to mark vehicles "out of service."

(2) No motor carrier or intermodal equipment provider shall require or permit any person to operate nor shall any person operate any motor vehicle or intermodal equipment declared and marked "out-of-service" until all repairs required by the "out-of-service notice" have been satisfactorily completed. The term *operate* as used in this section shall include towing the vehicle or intermodal equipment, except that vehicles or intermodal equipment marked "out-of-service" may be towed away by means of a vehicle using a crane or hoist. A vehicle combination consisting of an emergency towing vehicle and an "out-of-service" vehicle shall not be operated unless such combination meets the performance requirements of this subchapter except for those conditions noted on the Driver Vehicle Examination Report.

(3) No person shall remove the "Out-of-Service Vehicle" sticker from any motor vehicle or intermodal equipment prior to completion of all repairs required by the "out-of-service notice."

(d) *Motor carrier or intermodal equipment provider disposition.* (1) The driver of any motor vehicle, including a motor vehicle transporting intermodal equipment, who receives an inspection report shall deliver a copy to both the motor carrier operating the vehicle and the intermodal equipment provider upon his/her arrival at the next terminal or facility. If the driver is not scheduled to arrive at a terminal or facility of the motor carrier operating the vehicle or at a facility of the intermodal equipment provider within 24 hours, the driver shall immediately mail, fax, or otherwise transmit the report to the motor carrier and intermodal equipment provider.

(2) Motor carriers and intermodal equipment providers shall examine the report. Violations or defects noted thereon shall be corrected. Repairs of items of intermodal equipment placed out-of-service are also to be documented in the maintenance records for such equipment.

(3) Within 15 days following the date of the inspection, the motor carrier or intermodal equipment provider shall—

(i) Certify that all violations noted have been corrected by completing the "Signature of Carrier/Intermodal Equipment Provider Official, Title, and Date Signed" portions of the form; and

(ii) Return the completed roadside inspection form to the issuing agency at the address indicated on the form and retain a copy at the motor carrier's principal place of business, at the intermodal equipment provider's principal place of business, or where the vehicle is housed for 12 months from the date of the inspection.

[73 FR 76824, Dec. 17, 2008, as amended at 75 FR 17252, Apr. 5, 2010]

§ 396.11 Driver vehicle inspection report(s).

(a) *Report required*—(1) *Motor Carriers.* Every motor carrier shall require its drivers to report, and every driver shall prepare a report in writing at the completion of each day's work on each vehicle operated, except for intermodal equipment tendered by an intermodal equipment provider. The report shall cover at least the following parts and accessories:

—Service brakes including trailer brake connections
—Parking brake
—Steering mechanism

—Lighting devices and reflectors
—Tires
—Horn
—Windshield wipers
—Rear vision mirrors
—Coupling devices
—Wheels and rims
—Emergency equipment

(2) *Intermodal equipment providers.* Every intermodal equipment provider must have a process to receive driver reports of defects or deficiencies in the intermodal equipment operated. The driver must report on, and the process to receive reports must cover, at least the following parts and accessories:

—Brakes
—Lighting devices, lamps, markers, and conspicuity marking material
—Wheels, rims, lugs, tires
—Air line connections, hoses, and couplers
—King pin upper coupling device
—Rails or support frames
—Tie down bolsters
—Locking pins, clevises, clamps, or hooks
—Sliders or sliding frame lock

(b) *Report content.* The report shall identify the vehicle and list any defect or deficiency discovered by or reported to the driver which would affect the safety of operation of the vehicle or result in its mechanical breakdown. If no defect or deficiency is discovered by or reported to the driver, the report shall so indicate. In all instances, the driver shall sign the report. On two-driver operations, only one driver needs to sign the driver vehicle inspection report, provided both drivers agree as to the defects or deficiencies identified. If a driver operates more than one vehicle during the day, a report shall be prepared for each vehicle operated.

(c) *Corrective action.* Prior to requiring or permitting a driver to operate a vehicle, every motor carrier or its agent shall repair any defect or deficiency listed on the driver vehicle inspection report which would be likely to affect the safety of operation of the vehicle.

(1) Every motor carrier or its agent shall certify on the original driver vehicle inspection report which lists any defect or deficiency that the defect or deficiency has been repaired or that repair is unnecessary before the vehicle is operated again.

(2) Every motor carrier shall maintain the original driver vehicle inspec-

tion report, the certification of repairs, and the certification of the driver's review for three months from the date the written report was prepared.

(d) *Exceptions.* The rules in this section shall not apply to a private motor carrier of passengers (nonbusiness), a driveaway-towaway operation, or any motor carrier operating only one commercial motor vehicle.

[44 FR 38526, July 2, 1979, as amended at 45 FR 46425, July 10, 1980; 53 FR 18058, May 19, 1988; 59 FR 8753, Feb. 23, 1994; 63 FR 33279, June 18, 1998; 73 FR 76824, Dec. 17, 2008; 74 FR 68709, Dec. 29, 2009]

§ 396.12 Procedures for intermodal equipment providers to accept reports required by § 390.42(b) of this chapter.

(a) *System for reports.* Each intermodal equipment provider must establish a system for motor carriers and drivers to report to it any damage, defects, or deficiencies of intermodal equipment discovered by, or reported to, the motor carrier or driver which would—

(1) Affect the safety of operation of the intermodal equipment, or

(2) Result in its mechanical breakdown while transported on public roads.

(b) *Report content.* The system required by paragraph (a) of this section must include documentation of all of the following:

(1) Name of the motor carrier responsible for the operation of the intermodal equipment at the time the damage, defects, or deficiencies were discovered by, or reported to, the driver.

(2) Motor carrier's USDOT number; intermodal equipment provider's USDOT number, and a unique identifying number for the item of intermodal equipment.

(3) Date and time the report was submitted.

(4) All damage, defects, or deficiencies of the intermodal equipment reported to the equipment provider by the motor carrier or its driver. If no defect or deficiency in the intermodal equipment is discovered by the driver, the report shall so indicate.

(5) The signature of the driver who prepared the report.

(c) *Corrective action.* (1) Prior to allowing or permitting a motor carrier to transport a piece of intermodal equipment for which a motor carrier or driver has submitted a report about damage, defects or deficiencies, each intermodal equipment provider or its agent must repair the reported damage, defects, or deficiencies that are likely to affect the safety of operation of the vehicle.

(2) Each intermodal equipment provider or its agent must certify on the original driver's report which lists any damage, defects, or deficiencies of the intermodal equipment that the reported damage, defects, or deficiencies have been repaired, or that repair is unnecessary, before the vehicle is operated again.

(d) *Retention period for reports.* Each intermodal equipment provider must maintain all documentation required by this section, including the original driver report and the certification of repairs on all intermodal equipment, for a period of three months from the date that a motor carrier or its driver submits the report to the intermodal equipment provider or its agent.

[73 FR 76824, Dec. 17, 2008, as amended at 74 FR 68709, Dec. 29, 2009]

§ 396.13   Driver inspection.

Before driving a motor vehicle, the driver shall:

(a) Be satisfied that the motor vehicle is in safe operating condition;

(b) Review the last driver vehicle inspection report; and

(c) Sign the report, only if defects or deficiencies were noted by the driver who prepared the report, to acknowledge that the driver has reviewed it and that there is a certification that the required repairs have been performed. The signature requirement does not apply to listed defects on a towed unit which is no longer part of the vehicle combination.

[44 FR 76526, Dec. 27, 1979, as amended at 48 FR 55868, Dec. 16, 1983; 63 FR 33280, June 18, 1998]

§ 396.15   Driveaway-towaway operations and inspections.

(a) *General.* Effective December 7, 1989, every motor carrier, with respect to motor vehicles engaged in driveaway-towaway operations, shall comply with the requirements of this part. EXCEPTION: Maintenance records required by § 396.3, the vehicle inspection report required by § 396.11, and the periodic inspection required by § 396.17 of this part shall not be required for any vehicle which is part of the shipment being delivered.

(b) *Pre-trip inspection.* Before the beginning of any driveaway-towaway operation of motor vehicles in combination, the motor carrier shall make a careful inspection and test to ascertain that:

(1) The towbar or saddle-mount connections are properly secured to the towed and towing vehicle;

(2) They function adequately without cramping or binding of any of the parts; and

(3) The towed motor vehicle follows substantially in the path of the towing vehicle without whipping or swerving.

(c) *Post-trip inspection.* Motor carriers shall maintain practices to ensure that following completion of any trip in driveaway-towaway operation of motor vehicles in combination, and before they are used again, the towbars and saddle-mounts are disassembled and inspected for worn, bent, cracked, broken, or missing parts. Before reuse, suitable repair or replacement shall be made of any defective parts and the devices shall be properly reassembled.

[44 FR 38526, July 2, 1979, as amended at 53 FR 49410, Dec. 7, 1988; 53 FR 49968, Dec. 12, 1988]

§ 396.17   Periodic inspection.

(a) Every commercial motor vehicle must be inspected as required by this section. The inspection must include, at a minimum, the parts and accessories set forth in appendix G of this subchapter. The term *commercial motor vehicle* includes each vehicle in a combination vehicle. For example, for a tractor semitrailer, full trailer combination, the tractor, semitrailer, and the full trailer (including the converter dolly if so equipped) must each be inspected.

(b) Except as provided in § 396.23 and this paragraph, motor carriers must inspect or cause to be inspected all motor vehicles subject to their control. Intermodal equipment providers must inspect or cause to be inspected intermodal equipment that is interchanged or intended for interchange to motor carriers in intermodal transportation.

(c) A motor carrier must not use a commercial motor vehicle, and an intermodal equipment provider must not tender equipment to a motor carrier for interchange, unless each component identified in appendix G of this subchapter has passed an inspection in accordance with the terms of this section at least once during the preceding 12 months and documentation of such inspection is on the vehicle. The documentation may be:

(1) The inspection report prepared in accordance with §396.21(a), or

(2) Other forms of documentation, based on the inspection report (e.g., sticker or decal), which contains the following information:

(i) The date of inspection;

(ii) Name and address of the motor carrier, intermodal equipment provider, or other entity where the inspection report is maintained;

(iii) Information uniquely identifying the vehicle inspected if not clearly marked on the motor vehicle; and

(iv) A certification that the vehicle has passed an inspection in accordance with §396.17.

(d) A motor carrier may perform the required annual inspection for vehicles under the carrier's control which are not subject to an inspection under §396.23(b)(1). An intermodal equipment provider may perform the required annual inspection for intermodal equipment interchanged or intended for interchange to motor carriers that are not subject to an inspection under §396.23(b)(1).

(e) In lieu of the self-inspection provided for in paragraph (d) of this section, a motor carrier or intermodal equipment provider responsible for the inspection may choose to have a commercial garage, fleet leasing company, truck stop, or other similar commercial business perform the inspection as its agent, provided that business operates and maintains facilities appropriate for commercial vehicle inspections and it employs qualified inspectors, as required by §396.19.

(f) Vehicles passing roadside or periodic inspections performed under the auspices of any State government or equivalent jurisdiction or the FMCSA,

meeting the minimum standards contained in appendix G of this subchapter, will be considered to have met the requirements of an annual inspection for a period of 12 months commencing from the last day of the month in which the inspection was performed. If a vehicle is subject to a mandatory State inspection program, as provided in §396.23(b)(1), a roadside inspection may only be considered equivalent if it complies with the requirements of that program.

(g) It is the responsibility of the motor carrier or intermodal equipment provider to ensure that all parts and accessories on commercial motor vehicles intended for use in interstate commerce for which they are responsible are maintained at, or promptly repaired to, the minimum standards set forth in appendix G to this subchapter.

(h) Failure to perform properly the annual inspection required by this section shall cause the motor carrier or intermodal equipment provider to be subject to the penalty provisions of 49 U.S.C. 521(b).

[73 FR 76825, Dec. 17, 2008]

§ 396.19 Inspector qualifications.

(a) Motor carriers and intermodal equipment providers must ensure that individuals performing annual inspections under §396.17(d) or (e) are qualified as follows:

(1) Understand the inspection criteria set forth in part 393 and appendix G of this subchapter and can identify defective components;

(2) Are knowledgeable of and have mastered the methods, procedures, tools and equipment used when performing an inspection; and

(3) Are capable of performing an inspection by reason of experience, training, or both as follows:

(i) Successfully completed a Federal- or State-sponsored training program or have a certificate from a State or Canadian Province that qualifies the individuals to perform commercial motor vehicle safety inspections, or

(ii) Have a combination of training or experience totaling at least 1 year. Such training or experience may consist of:

(A) Participation in a commercial motor vehicle manufacturer-sponsored training program or similar commercial training program designed to train students in commercial motor vehicle operation and maintenance;

(B) Experience as a mechanic or inspector in a motor carrier or intermodal equipment maintenance program;

(C) Experience as a mechanic or inspector in commercial motor vehicle maintenance at a commercial garage, fleet leasing company, or similar facility; or

(D) Experience as a commercial motor vehicle inspector for a State, Provincial or Federal government.

(b) Motor carriers and intermodal equipment providers must retain evidence of that individual's qualifications under this section. They must retain this evidence for the period during which that individual is performing annual motor vehicle inspections for the motor carrier or intermodal equipment provider, and for one year thereafter. However, motor carriers and intermodal equipment providers do not have to maintain documentation of inspector qualifications for those inspections performed either as part of a State periodic inspection program or at the roadside as part of a random roadside inspection program.

[73 FR 76825, Dec. 17, 2008]

§ 396.21 Periodic inspection recordkeeping requirements.

(a) The qualified inspector performing the inspection shall prepare a report that:

(1) Identifies the individual performing the inspection;

(2) Identifies the motor carrier operating the vehicle or intermodal equipment provider intending to interchange the vehicle to a motor carrier;

(3) Identifies the date of the inspection;

(4) Identifies the vehicle inspected;

(5) Identifies the vehicle components inspected and describes the results of the inspection, including the identification of those components not meeting the minimum standards set forth in appendix G to this subchapter; and

(6) Certifies the accuracy and completeness of the inspection as complying with all the requirements of this section.

(b)(1) The original or a copy of the inspection report shall be retained by the motor carrier, intermodal equipment provider, or other entity that is responsible for the inspection for a period of fourteen months from the date of the inspection report. The original or a copy of the inspection report must be retained where the vehicle is either housed or maintained.

(2) The original or a copy of the inspection report must be available for inspection upon demand of an authorized Federal, State or local official.

(3) *Exception.* If the motor carrier operating the commercial motor vehicles did not perform the commercial motor vehicle's last annual inspection, or if an intermodal equipment provider did not itself perform the annual inspection on equipment intended for interchange to a motor carrier, the motor carrier or intermodal equipment provider is responsible for obtaining the original or a copy of the last annual inspection report upon demand of an authorized Federal, State, or local official.

[73 FR 76825, Dec. 17, 2008]

§ 396.23 Equivalent to periodic inspection.

(a) A motor carrier or an intermodal equipment provider may meet the requirements of § 396.17 through a State or other jurisdiction's roadside inspection program. The inspection must have been performed during the preceding 12 months. In using the roadside inspection, the motor carrier or intermodal equipment provider would need to retain a copy of an annual inspection report showing that the inspection was performed in accordance with the minimum periodic inspection standards set forth in appendix G to this subchapter. If the motor carrier operating the commercial vehicle is not the party directly responsible for its maintenance, the motor carrier must deliver the roadside inspection report to the responsible party in a timely manner. Before accepting such an inspection report, the motor carrier or intermodal equipment provider must ensure that the report complies with the requirements of § 396.21(a).

(b)(1) If a commercial motor vehicle is subject to a mandatory State inspection program which is determined by the Administrator to be as effective as §396.17, the motor carrier or intermodal equipment provider must meet the requirement of §396.17 through that State's inspection program. Commercial motor vehicle inspections may be conducted by State personnel, at State authorized commercial facilities, or by the motor carrier or intermodal equipment provider itself under the auspices of a State authorized self-inspection program.

(2) Should the FMCSA determine that a State inspection program, in whole or in part, is not as effective as §396.17, the motor carrier or intermodal equipment provider must ensure that the periodic inspection required by §396.17 is performed on all commercial motor vehicles under its control in a manner specified in §396.17.

[73 FR 76825, Dec. 17, 2008]

§396.25 **Qualifications of brake inspectors.**

(a) Motor carriers and intermodal equipment providers must ensure that all inspections, maintenance, repairs or service to the brakes of its commercial motor vehicles, are performed in compliance with the requirements of this section.

(b) For purposes of this section, *brake inspector* means any employee of a motor carrier or intermodal equipment provider who is responsible for ensuring that all brake inspections, maintenance, service, or repairs to any commercial motor vehicle, subject to the motor carrier's or intermodal equipment provider's control, meet the applicable Federal standards.

(c) No motor carrier or intermodal equipment provider may require or permit any employee who does not meet the minimum brake inspector qualifications of paragraph (d) of this section to be responsible for the inspection, maintenance, service or repairs of any brakes on its commercial motor vehicles.

(d) The motor carrier or intermodal equipment provider must ensure that each brake inspector is qualified as follows:

(1) Understands the brake service or inspection task to be accomplished and can perform that task; and

(2) Is knowledgeable of and has mastered the methods, procedures, tools and equipment used when performing an assigned brake service or inspection task; and

(3) Is capable of performing the assigned brake service or inspection by reason of experience, training, or both as follows:

(i) Has successfully completed an apprenticeship program sponsored by a State, a Canadian Province, a Federal agency or a labor union, or a training program approved by a State, Provincial or Federal agency, or has a certificate from a State or Canadian Province that qualifies the person to perform the assigned brake service or inspection task (including passage of Commercial Driver's License air brake tests in the case of a brake inspection); or

(ii) Has brake-related training or experience or a combination thereof totaling at least one year. Such training or experience may consist of:

(A) Participation in a training program sponsored by a brake or vehicle manufacturer or similar commercial training program designed to train students in brake maintenance or inspection similar to the assigned brake service or inspection tasks; or

(B) Experience performing brake maintenance or inspection similar to the assigned brake service or inspection task in a motor carrier or intermodal equipment provider maintenance program; or

(C) Experience performing brake maintenance or inspection similar to the assigned brake service or inspection task at a commercial garage, fleet leasing company, or similar facility.

(e) No motor carrier or intermodal equipment provider may employ any person as a brake inspector unless the evidence of the inspector's qualifications, required under this section, is maintained by the motor carrier or intermodal equipment provider at its principal place of business, or at the location at which the brake inspector is employed. The evidence must be maintained for the period during which the brake inspector is employed in that capacity and for one year thereafter. However, motor carriers and intermodal equipment providers do not have to maintain evidence of qualifications to inspect air brake systems for such inspections performed by persons who have passed the air brake knowledge and skills test for a Commercial Driver's License.

[73 FR 76825, Dec. 17, 2008]

PART 397—TRANSPORTATION OF HAZARDOUS MATERIALS; DRIVING AND PARKING RULES

Subpart A—General

AUTHORITY: 49 U.S.C. 322; 49 CFR 1.73. Subpart A also issued under 49 U.S.C. 5103, 31136, 31502, and 49 CFR 1.53. Subparts C, D, and E also issued under 49 U.S.C. 5112, 5125.

SOURCE: 36 FR 4876, Mar. 13, 1971, unless otherwise noted.

EDITORIAL NOTE: Nomenclature changes to part 397 appear at 66 FR 49874, Oct. 1, 2001.

Subpart A—General

§ 397.1 Application of the rules in this part.

(a) The rules in this part apply to each motor carrier engaged in the transportation of hazardous materials by a motor vehicle which must be marked or placarded in accordance with § 177.823 of this title and to—

(1) Each officer or employee of the motor carrier who performs supervisory duties related to the transportation of hazardous materials; and

(2) Each person who operates or who is in charge of a motor vehicle containing hazardous materials.

(b) Each person designated in paragraph (a) of this section must know and obey the rules in this part.

[36 FR 4876, Mar. 13, 1971, as amended at 36 FR 16067, Aug. 19, 1971; 53 FR 18058, May 19, 1988; 60 FR 38749, July 28, 1995]

§ 397.2 Compliance with Federal motor carrier safety regulations.

A motor carrier or other person to whom this part is applicable must comply with the rules in parts 390 through 397, inclusive, of this subchapter when he/she is transporting hazardous materials by a motor vehicle which must be marked or placarded in accordance with § 177.823 of this title.

[37 FR 18080, Sept. 7, 1972]

§397.3 State and local laws, ordinances, and regulations.

Every motor vehicle containing hazardous materials must be driven and parked in compliance with the laws, ordinances, and regulations of the jurisdiction in which it is being operated, unless they are at variance with specific regulations of the Department of Transportation which are applicable to the operation of that vehicle and which impose a more stringent obligation or restraint.

§397.5 Attendance and surveillance of motor vehicles.

(a) Except as provided in paragraph (b) of this section, a motor vehicle which contains a Division 1.1, 1.2, or 1.3 (explosive) material must be attended at all times by its driver or a qualified representative of the motor carrier that operates it.

(b) The rules in paragraph (a) of this section do not apply to a motor vehicle which contains Division 1.1, 1.2, or 1.3 material if all the following conditions exist—

(1) The vehicle is located on the property of a motor carrier, on the property of a shipper or consignee of the explosives, in a safe haven, or, in the case of a vehicle containing 50 pounds or less of a Division 1.1, 1.2, or 1.3 material, on a construction or survey site; and

(2) The lawful bailee of the explosives is aware of the nature of the explosives the vehicle contains and has been instructed in the procedures which must be followed in emergencies; and

(3) The vehicle is within the bailee's unobstructed field of view or is located in a safe haven.

(c) A motor vehicle which contains hazardous materials other than Division 1.1, 1.2, or 1.3, materials, and which is located on a public street or highway, or the shoulder of a public highway, must be attended by its driver. However, the vehicle need not be attended while its driver is performing duties which are incident and necessary to the driver's duties as the operator of the vehicle.

(d) For purposes of this section—

(1) A motor vehicle is attended when the person in charge of the vehicle is on the vehicle, awake, and not in a sleeper berth, or is within 100 feet of the vehicle and has it within his/her unobstructed field of view.

(2) A qualified representative of a motor carrier is a person who—

(i) Has been designated by the carrier to attend the vehicle;

(ii) Is aware of the nature of the hazardous materials contained in the vehicle he/she attends;

(iii) Has been instructed in the procedures he/she must follow in emergencies; and

(iv) Is authorized to move the vehicle and has the means and ability to do so.

(3) A safe haven in an area specifically approved in writing by local, State, or Federal governmental authorities for the parking of unattended vehicles containing Division 1.1, 1.2, or 1.3 materials.

(e) The rules in this section do not relieve the driver from any obligation imposed by law relating to the placing of warning devices when a motor vehicle is stopped on a public street or highway.

[59 FR 63925, Dec. 12, 1994]

§397.7 Parking.

(a) A motor vehicle which contains Division 1.1, 1.2, or 1.3 materials must not be parked under any of the following circumstances—

(1) On or within 5 feet of the traveled portion of a public street or highway;

(2) On private property (including premises of fueling or eating facility) without the knowledge and consent of the person who is in charge of the property and who is aware of the nature of the hazardous materials the vehicle contains; or

(3) Within 300 feet of a bridge, tunnel, dwelling, or place where people work, congregate, or assemble, except for brief periods when the necessities of operation require the vehicle to be parked and make it impracticable to park the vehicle in any other place.

(b) A motor vehicle which contains hazardous materials other than Division 1.1, 1.2, or 1.3 materials must not be parked on or within five feet of the traveled portion of public street or highway except for brief periods when the necessities of operation require the vehicle to be parked and make it impracticable to park the vehicle in any other place.

[59 FR 63925, Dec. 12, 1994]

§ 397.9 [Reserved]

§ 397.11 Fires.

(a) A motor vehicle containing hazardous materials must not be operated near an open fire unless its driver has first taken precautions to ascertain that the vehicle can safely pass the fire without stopping.

(b) A motor vehicle containing hazardous materials must not be parked within 300 feet of an open fire.

§ 397.13 Smoking.

No person may smoke or carry a lighted cigarette, cigar, or pipe on or within 25 feet of—

(a) A motor vehicle which contains Class 1 materials, Class 5 materials, or flammable materials classified as Division 2.1, Class 3, Divisions 4.1 and 4.2; or

(b) An empty tank motor vehicle which has been used to transport Class 3, flammable materials, or Division 2.1 flammable gases, which when so used, was required to be marked or placarded in accordance with the rules in § 177.823 of this title.

[59 FR 63925, Dec. 12, 1994]

§ 397.15 Fueling.

When a motor vehicle which contains hazardous materials is being fueled—

(a) Its engine must not be operating; and

(b) A person must be in control of the fueling process at the point where the fuel tank is filled.

§ 397.17 Tires.

(a) A driver must examine each tire on a motor vehicle at the beginning of each trip and each time the vehicle is parked.

(b) If, as the result of an examination pursuant to paragraph (a) of this section, or otherwise, a tire if found to be flat, leaking, or improperly inflated, the driver must cause the tire to be repaired, replaced, or properly inflated before the vehicle is driven. However, the vehicle may be driven to the nearest safe place to perform the required repair, replacement, or inflation.

(c) If, as the result of an examination pursuant to paragraph (a) of this section, or otherwise, a tire is found to be overheated, the driver shall immediately cause the overheated tire to be removed and placed at a safe distance from the vehicle. The driver shall not operate the vehicle until the cause of the overheating is corrected.

(d) Compliance with the rules in this section does not relieve a driver from the duty to comply with the rules in §§ 397.5 and 397.7.

§ 397.19 Instructions and documents.

(a) A motor carrier that transports Division 1.1, 1.2, or 1.3 (explosive) materials must furnish the driver of each motor vehicle in which the explosives are transported with the following documents:

(1) A copy of the rules in this part;

(2) [Reserved]

(3) A document containing instructions on procedures to be followed in the event of accident or delay. The documents must include the names and telephone numbers of persons (including representatives of carriers or shippers) to be contracted, the nature of the explosives being transported, and the precautions to be taken in emergencies such as fires, accidents, or leakages.

(b) A driver who receives documents in accordance with paragraph (a) of this section must sign a receipt for them. The motor carrier shall maintain the receipt for a period of one year from the date of signature.

(c) A driver of a motor vehicle which contains Division 1.1, 1.2, or 1.3 materials must be in possession of, be familiar with, and be in compliance with

(1) The documents specified in paragraph (a) of this section;

(2) The documents specified in § 177.817 of this title; and

(3) The written route plan specified in § 397.67.

[59 FR 63925, Dec. 12, 1994, as amended at 63 FR 33280, June 18, 1998]

Subpart B [Reserved]

Subpart C—Routing of Non-Radioactive Hazardous Materials

SOURCE: 59 FR 51830, Oct. 12, 1994, unless otherwise noted.

§397.61 Purpose and scope.

This subpart contains routing requirements and procedures that States and Indian tribes are required to follow if they establish, maintain, or enforce routing designations over which a nonradioactive hazardous material (NRHM) in a quantity which requires placarding may or may not be transported by a motor vehicle. It also provides regulations for motor carriers transporting placarded or marked NRHM and procedures for dispute resolutions regarding NRHM routing designations.

§397.63 Applicability.

The provisions of this subpart apply to any State or Indian tribe that establishes, maintains, or enforces any routing designations over which NRHM may or may not be transported by motor vehicle. They also apply to any motor carrier that transports or causes to be transported placarded or marked NRHM in commerce.

§397.65 Definitions.

For purposes of this subpart, the following definitions apply:

Administrator. The Federal Motor Carrier Safety Administrator, who is the chief executive of the Federal Motor Carrier Safety Administration, an agency within the United States Department of Transportation, or his/her designate.

Commerce. Any trade, traffic, or transportation in the United States which:

(1) Is between a place under the jurisdiction of a State or Indian tribe and any place outside of such jurisdiction; or

(2) Is solely within a place under the jurisdiction of a State or Indian tribe but which affects trade, traffic, or transportation described in subparagraph (a).

FMCSA. The Federal Motor Carrier Safety Administration, an agency within the Department of Transportation.

Hazardous material. A substance or material, including a hazardous substance, which has been determined by the Secretary of Transportation to be capable of posing an unreasonable risk to health, safety, or property when transported in commerce, and which has been so designated.

Indian tribe. Has the same meaning as contained in §4 of the Indian Self-Determination and Education Act, 25 U.S.C. 450b.

Motor carrier. A for-hire motor carrier or a private motor carrier of property. The term includes a motor carrier's agents, officers and representatives as well as employees responsible for hiring, supervising, training, assigning, or dispatching of drivers.

Motor vehicle. Any vehicle, machine, tractor, trailer, or semitrailer propelled or drawn by mechanical power and used upon the highways in the transportation of passengers or property, or any combination thereof.

NRHM. A non-radioactive hazardous material transported by motor vehicle in types and quantities which require placarding, pursuant to Table 1 or 2 of 49 CFR 172.504.

Political subdivision. A municipality, public agency or other instrumentality of one or more States, or a public corporation, board, or commission established under the laws of one or more States.

Radioactive material. Any material having a specific activity greater than 0.002 microcuries per gram (uCi/g), as defined in 49 CFR 173.403.

Routing agency. The State highway agency or other State agency designated by the Governor of that State, or an agency designated by an Indian tribe, to supervise, coordinate, and approve the NRHM routing designations for that State or Indian tribe.

Routing designations. Any regulation, limitation, restriction, curfew, time of travel restriction, lane restriction, routing ban, port-of-entry designation, or route weight restriction, applicable to the highway transportation of NRHM over a specific highway route or portion of a route.

Secretary. The Secretary of Transportation.

State. A State of the United States, the District of Columbia, the Commonwealth of Puerto Rico, the Commonwealth of the Northern Mariana Islands, the Virgin Islands, American Samoa or Guam.

§ 397.67 Motor carrier responsibility for routing.

(a) A motor carrier transporting NRHM shall comply with NRHM routing designations of a State or Indian tribe pursuant to this subpart.

(b) A motor carrier carrying hazardous materials required to be placarded or marked in accordance with 49 CFR 177.823 and not subject to a NRHM routing designations pursuant to this subpart, shall operate the vehicle over routes which do not go through or near heavily populated areas, places where crowds are assembled, tunnels, narrow streets, or alleys, except where the motor carrier determines that:

(1) There is no practicable alternative;

(2) A reasonable deviation is necessary to reach terminals, points of loading and unloading, facilities for food, fuel, repairs, rest, or a safe haven; or

(3) A reasonable deviation is required by emergency conditions, such as a detour that has been established by a highway authority, or a situation exists where a law enforcement official requires the driver to take an alternative route.

(c) Operating convenience is not a basis for determining whether it is practicable to operate a motor vehicle in accordance with paragraph (b) of this section.

(d) Before a motor carrier requires or permits a motor vehicle containing explosives in Class 1, Divisions 1.1, 1.2, 1.3, as defined in 49 CFR 173.50 and 173.53 respectively, to be operated, the carrier or its agent shall prepare a written route plan that complies with this section and shall furnish a copy to the driver. However, the driver may prepare the written plan as agent for the motor carrier when the trip begins at a location other than the carrier's terminal.

§ 397.69 Highway routing designations; preemption.

(a) Any State or Indian tribe that establishes or modifies a highway routing designation over which NRHM may or may not be transported on or after November 14, 1994, and maintains or enforces such designation, shall comply with the highway routing standards set forth in § 397.71 of this subpart. For purposes of this subpart, any highway routing designation affecting the highway transportation of NRHM, made by a political subdivision of a State is considered as one made by that State, and all requirements of this subpart apply.

(b) Except as provided in §§ 397.75 and 397.219, a NRHM route designation made in violation of paragraph (a) of this section is preempted pursuant to section 105(b)(4) of the Hazardous Materials Transportation Act (49 U.S.C. app. 1804(b)(4)). This provision shall become effective after November 14, 1996.

(c) A highway routing designation established by a State, political subdivision, or Indian tribe before November 14, 1994 is subject to preemption in accordance with the preemption standards in paragraphs (a)(1) and (a)(2) of § 397.203 of this subpart.

(d) A State, political subdivision, or Indian tribe may petition for a waiver of preemption in accordance with § 397.213 of this part.

§ 397.71 Federal standards.

(a) A State or Indian tribe shall comply with the Federal standards under paragraph (b) of this section when establishing, maintaining or enforcing specific NRHM routing designations over which NRHM may or may not be transported.

(b) The Federal standards are as follows:

(1) *Enhancement of public safety.* The State or Indian tribe shall make a finding, supported by the record to be developed in accordance with paragraphs (b)(2)(ii) and (b)(3)(iv) of this section, that any NRHM routing designation enhances public safety in the areas subject to its jurisdiction and in other areas which are directly affected by such highway routing designation. In making such a finding, the State or Indian tribe shall consider:

(i) The factors listed in paragraph (b)(9) of this section; and

(ii) The DOT "Guidelines for Applying Criteria to Designate Routes for Transporting Hazardous Materials," DOT/RSPA/OHMT–89–02, July 1989[1] or its most current version; or an equivalent routing analysis which adequately considers overall risk to the public.

(2) *Public participation.* Prior to the establishment of any NRHM routing designation, the State or Indian tribe shall undertake the following actions to ensure participation by the public in the routing process:

(i) The State or Indian tribe shall provide the public with notice of any proposed NRHM routing designation and a 30-day period in which to comment. At any time during this period or following review of the comments received, the State or Indian tribe shall decide whether to hold a public hearing on the proposed NRHM route designation. The public shall be given 30 days prior notice of the public hearing which shall be conducted as described in paragraph (b)(2)(ii) of this section. Notice for both the comment period and the public hearing, if one is held, shall be given by publication in at least two newspapers of general circulation in the affected area or areas and shall contain a complete description of the proposed routing designation, together with the date, time, and location of any public hearings. Notice for both the comment period and any public hearing may also be published in the official register of the State.

(ii) If it is determined that a public hearing is necessary, the State or Indian tribe shall hold at least one public hearing on the record during which the public will be afforded the opportunity to present their views and any information or data related to the proposed NRHM routing designation. The State shall make available to the public, upon payment of prescribed costs, copies of the transcript of the hearing, which shall include all exhibits and documents presented during the hearing or submitted for the record.

(3) *Consultation with others.* Prior to the establishment of any NRHM routing designation, the State or Indian tribe shall provide notice to, and consult with, officials of affected political subdivisions, States and Indian tribes, and any other affected parties. Such actions shall include the following:

(i) At least 60 days prior to establishing a routing designation, the State or Indian tribe shall provide notice, in writing, of the proposed routing designation to officials responsible for highway routing in all other affected States or Indian tribes. A copy of this notice may also be sent to all affected political subdivisions. This notice shall request approval, in writing, by those States or Indian tribes, of the proposed routing designations. If no response is received within 60 days from the day of receipt of the notification of the proposed routing designation, the routing designation shall be considered approved by the affected State or Indian tribe.

(ii) The manner in which consultation under this paragraph is conducted is left to the discretion of the State or Indian tribe.

(iii) The State or Indian tribe shall attempt to resolve any concern or disagreement expressed by any consulted official related to the proposed routing designation.

(iv) The State or Indian tribe shall keep a record of the names and addresses of the officials notified pursuant to this section and of any consultation or meeting conducted with these officials or their representatives. Such record shall describe any concern or disagreement expressed by the officials and any action undertaken to resolve such disagreement or address any concern.

(4) *Through routing.* In establishing any NRHM routing designation, the State or Indian tribe shall ensure through highway routing for the transportation of NRHM between adjacent areas. The term "through highway routing" as used in this paragraph means that the routing designation must ensure continuity of movement so as to not impede or unnecessarily delay the transportation of NRHM. The State or Indian tribe shall utilize the procedures established in paragraphs

[1] This document may be obtained from Federal Motor Carrier Safety Administration, Office of Enforcement and Compliance (MC–EC), 1200 New Jersey Ave., SE., Washington, DC 20590–0001.

(b)(2) and (b)(3) of this section in meeting these requirements. In addition, the State or Indian tribe shall make a finding, supported by a risk analysis conducted in accordance with paragraph (b)(1) of this section, that the routing designation enhances public safety. If the risk analysis shows—

(i) That the current routing presents at least 50 percent more risk to the public than the deviation under the proposed routing designation, then the proposed routing designation may go into effect.

(ii) That the current routing presents a greater risk but less than 50 percent more risk to the public than the deviation under the proposed routing restriction, then the proposed routing restriction made by a State or Indian tribe shall only go into effect if it does not force a deviation of more than 25 miles or result in an increase of more than 25 percent of that part of a trip affected by the deviation, whichever is shorter, from the most direct route through a jurisdiction as compared to the intended deviation.

(iii) That the current route has the same or less risk to the public than the deviation resulting from the proposed routing designation, then the routing designation shall not be allowed.

(5) *Agreement of other States; burden on commerce.* Any NRHM routing designation which affects another State or Indian tribe shall be established, maintained, or enforced only if:

(i) It does not unreasonably burden commerce, and

(ii) It is agreed to by the affected State or Indian tribe within 60 days of receipt of the notice sent pursuant to paragraph (b)(3)(i) of this section, or it is approved by the Administrator pursuant to § 397.75.

(6) *Timeliness.* The establishment of a NRHM routing designation by any State or Indian tribe shall be completed within 18 months of the notice given in either paragraph (b)(2) or (b)(3) of this section, whichever occurs first.

(7) *Reasonable routes to terminals and other facilities.* In establishing or providing for reasonable access to and from designated routes, the State or Indian tribe shall use the shortest practicable route considering the factors listed in paragraph (b)(9) of this section. In establishing any NRHM routing designation, the State or Indian tribe shall provide reasonable access for motor vehicles transporting NRHM to reach:

(i) Terminals,

(ii) Points of loading, unloading, pickup and delivery, and

(iii) Facilities for food, fuel, repairs, rest, and safe havens.

(8) *Responsibility for local compliance.* The States shall be responsible for ensuring that all of their political subdivisions comply with the provisions of this subpart. The States shall be responsible for resolving all disputes between such political subdivisions within their jurisdictions. If a State or any political subdivision thereof, or an Indian tribe chooses to establish, maintain, or enforce any NRHM routing designation, the Governor, or Indian tribe, shall designate a routing agency for the State or Indian tribe, respectively. The routing agency shall ensure that all NRHM routing designations within its jurisdiction comply with the Federal standards in this section. The State or Indian tribe shall comply with the public information and reporting requirements contained in § 397.73.

(9) *Factors to consider.* In establishing any NRHM routing designation, the State or Indian tribe shall consider the following factors:

(i) *Population density.* The population potentially exposed to a NRHM release shall be estimated from the density of the residents, employees, motorists, and other persons in the area, using United States census tract maps or other reasonable means for determining the population within a potential impact zone along a designated highway route. The impact zone is the potential range of effects in the event of a release. Special populations such as schools, hospitals, prisons, and senior citizen homes shall, among other things, be considered when determining the potential risk to the populations along a highway routing. Consideration shall be given to the amount of time during which an area will experience a heavy population density.

(ii) *Type of highway.* The characteristics of each alternative NRHM highway routing designation shall be compared.

Vehicle weight and size limits, underpass and bridge clearances, roadway geometrics, number of lanes, degree of access control, and median and shoulder structures are examples of characteristics which a State or Indian tribe shall consider.

(iii) *Types and quantities of NRHM.* An examination shall be made of the type and quantity of NRHM normally transported along highway routes which are included in a proposed NRHM routing designation, and consideration shall be given to the relative impact zone and risks of each type and quantity.

(iv) *Emergency response capabilities.* In consultation with the proper fire, law enforcement, and highway safety agencies, consideration shall be given to the emergency response capabilities which may be needed as a result of a NRHM routing designation. The analysis of the emergency response capabilities shall be based upon the proximity of the emergency response facilities and their capabilities to contain and suppress NRHM releases within the impact zones.

(v) *Results of consultation with affected persons.* Consideration shall be given to the comments and concerns of all affected persons and entities provided during public hearings and consultations conducted in accordance with this section.

(vi) *Exposure and other risk factors.* States and Indian tribes shall define the exposure and risk factors associated with any NRHM routing designations. The distance to sensitive areas shall be considered. Sensitive areas include, but are not limited to, homes and commercial buildings; special populations in hospitals, schools, handicapped facilities, prisons and stadiums; water sources such as streams and lakes; and natural areas such as parks, wetlands, and wildlife reserves.

(vii) *Terrain considerations.* Topography along and adjacent to the proposed NRHM routing designation that may affect the potential severity of an accident, the dispersion of the NRHM upon release and the control and clean up of NRHM if released shall be considered.

(viii) *Continuity of routes.* Adjacent jurisdictions shall be consulted to ensure routing continuity for NRHM across common borders. Deviations from the most direct route shall be minimized.

(ix) *Alternative routes.* Consideration shall be given to the alternative routes to, or resulting from, any NRHM route designation. Alternative routes shall be examined, reviewed, or evaluated to the extent necessary to demonstrate that the most probable alternative routing resulting from a routing designation is safer than the current routing.

(x) *Effects on commerce.* Any NRHM routing designation made in accordance with this subpart shall not create an unreasonable burden upon interstate or intrastate commerce.

(xi) *Delays in transportation.* No NRHM routing designations may create unnecessary delays in the transportation of NRHM.

(xii) *Climatic conditions.* Weather conditions unique to a highway route such as snow, wind, ice, fog, or other climatic conditions that could affect the safety of a route, the dispersion of the NRHM upon release, or increase the difficulty of controlling it and cleaning it up shall be given appropriate consideration.

(xiii) *Congestion and accident history.* Traffic conditions unique to a highway routing such as: traffic congestion; accident experience with motor vehicles, traffic considerations that could affect the potential for an accident, exposure of the public to any release, ability to perform emergency response operations, or the temporary closing of a highway for cleaning up any release shall be given appropriate consideration.

[36 FR 4876, Mar. 13, 1971, as amended at 72 FR 55703, Oct. 1, 2007]

§ 397.73 **Public information and reporting requirements.**

(a) *Public information.* Information on NRHM routing designations must be made available by the States and Indian tribes to the public in the form of maps, lists, road signs or some combination thereof. If road signs are used, those signs and their placements must comply with the provisions of the Manual on Uniform Traffic Control Devices,[2] published by the FMCSA, particularly the Hazardous Cargo signs identified as R14–2 and R14–3 shown in Section 2B–43 of that Manual.

(b) *Reporting and publishing requirements.* Each State or Indian tribe, through its routing agency, shall provide information identifying all NRHM routing designations which exist within their jurisdictions on November 14, 1994 to the Federal Motor Carrier Safety Administration, Office of Enforcement and Compliance (MC–EC), 1200 New Jersey Ave., SE., Washington, DC 20590–0001 by March 13, 1995. The State or Indian tribe shall include descriptions of these routing designations, along with the dates they were established. This information may also be published in each State's official register of State regulations. Information on any subsequent changes or new NRHM routing designations shall be furnished within 60 days after establishment to the FMCSA. This information will be available from the FMCSA, consolidated by the FMCSA, and published annually in whole or as updates in the FEDERAL REGISTER. Each State may also publish this information in its official register of State regulations.

(Approved by the Office of Management and Budget under control number 2125–0554)

[36 FR 4876, Mar. 13, 1971, as amended at 72 FR 55703, Oct. 1, 2007]

§ 397.75 Dispute resolution.

(a) *Petition.* One or more States or Indian tribes may petition the Administrator to resolve a dispute relating to an agreement on a proposed NRHM routing designation. In resolving a dispute under these provisions, the Administrator will provide the greatest level of safety possible without unreasonably burdening commerce, and ensure compliance with the Federal

standards established at § 397.71 of this subpart.

(b) *Filing.* Each petition for dispute resolution filed under this section must:

(1) Be submitted to the Administrator, Federal Motor Carrier Safety Administration, 1200 New Jersey Ave., SE., Washington, DC 20590–0001. Attention: Office of the Chief Counsel (MC–CC).

(2) Identify the State or Indian tribe filing the petition and any other State, political subdivision, or Indian tribe whose NRHM routing designation is the subject of the dispute.

(3) Contain a certification that the petitioner has complied with the notification requirements of paragraph (c) of this section, and include a list of the names and addresses of each State, political subdivision, or Indian tribe official who was notified of the filing of the petition.

(4) Clearly set forth the dispute for which resolution is sought, including a complete description of any disputed NRHM routing designation and an explanation of how the disputed routing designation affects the petitioner or how it impedes through highway routing. If the routing designation being disputed results in alternative routing, then a comparative risk analysis for the designated route and the resulting alternative routing shall be provided.

(5) Describe any actions taken by the State or Indian tribe to resolve the dispute.

(6) Explain the reasons why the petitioner believes that the Administrator should intervene in resolving the dispute.

(7) Describe any proposed actions that the Administrator should take to resolve the dispute and how these actions would provide the greatest level of highway safety without unreasonably burdening commerce and would ensure compliance with the Federal standards established in this subpart.

(c) *Notice.* (1) Any State or Indian tribe that files a petition for dispute resolution under this subpart shall mail a copy of the petition to any affected State, political subdivision, or

---

[2] This publication may be purchased from the Superintendent of Documents, U.S. Government Printing Office (GPO), Washington, D.C. 20402 and has Stock No. 050–001–81001–8. It is available for inspection and copying as prescribed in 49 CFR part 7, appendix D. See 23 CFR part 655, subpart F.

Indian tribe, accompanied by a statement that the State, political subdivision, or Indian tribe may submit comments regarding the petition to the Administrator within 45 days.

(2) By serving notice on any other State, political subdivision, or Indian tribe determined by the Administrator to be possibly affected by the issues in dispute or the resolution sought, or by publication in the FEDERAL REGISTER, the Administrator may afford those persons an opportunity to file written comments on the petition.

(3) Any affected State, political subdivision, or Indian tribe submitting written comments to the Administrator with respect to a petition filed under this section shall send a copy of the comments to the petitioner and certify to the Administrator as to having complied with this requirement. The Administrator may notify other persons participating in the proceeding of the comments and provide an opportunity for those other persons to respond.

(d) *Court actions.* After a petition for dispute resolution is filed in accordance with this section, no court action may be brought with respect to the subject matter of such dispute until a final decision has been issued by the Administrator or until the last day of the one-year period beginning on the day the Administrator receives the petition, whichever occurs first.

(e) *Hearings; alternative dispute resolution.* Upon receipt of a petition filed pursuant to paragraph (a) of this section, the Administrator may schedule a hearing to attempt to resolve the dispute and, if a hearing is scheduled, will notify all parties to the dispute of the date, time, and place of the hearing. During the hearing the parties may offer any information pertinent to the resolution of the dispute. If an agreement is reached, it may be stipulated by the parties, in writing, and, if the Administrator agrees, made part of the decision in paragraph (f) of this section. If no agreement is reached, the Administrator may take the matter under consideration and announce his or her decision in accordance with paragraph (f) of this section. Nothing in this section shall be construed as prohibiting the parties from settling

the dispute or seeking other methods of alternative dispute resolution prior to the final decision by the Administrator.

(f) *Decision.* The Administrator will issue a decision based on the petition, the written comments submitted by the parties, the record of the hearing, and any other information in the record. The decision will include a written statement setting forth the relevant facts and the legal basis for the decision.

(g) *Record.* The Administrator will serve a copy of the decision upon the petitioner and any other party who participated in the proceedings. A copy of each decision will be placed on file in the public docket. The Administrator may publish the decision or notice of the decision in the FEDERAL REGISTER.

[36 FR 4876, Mar. 13, 1971, as amended at 72 FR 55703, Oct. 1, 2007]

§397.77 Judicial review of dispute decision.

Any State or Indian tribe adversely affected by the Administrator's decision under §397.75 of this subpart may seek review by the appropriate district court of the United States under such proceeding only by filing a petition with such court within 90 days after such decision becomes final.

Subpart D—Routing of Class 7 (Radioactive) Materials

§397.101 Requirements for motor carriers and drivers.

(a) Except as provided in paragraph (b) of this section or in circumstances when there is only one practicable highway route available, considering operating necessity and safety, a carrier or any person operating a motor vehicle that contains a Class 7 (radioactive) material, as defined in 49 CFR 172.403, for which placarding is required under 49 CFR part 172 shall:

(1) Ensure that the motor vehicle is operated on routes that minimize radiological risk;

(2) Consider available information on accident rates, transit time, population density and activities, and the time of day and the day of week during which

transportation will occur to determine the level of radiological risk; and

(3) Tell the driver which route to take and that the motor vehicle contains Class 7 (radioactive) materials.

(b) Except as otherwise permitted in this paragraph and in paragraph (f) of this section, a carrier or any person operating a motor vehicle containing a highway route controlled quantity of Class 7 (radioactive) materials, as defined in 49 CFR 173.403(l), shall operate the motor vehicle only over preferred routes.

(1) For purposes of this subpart, a preferred route is an Interstate System highway for which an alternative route is not designated by a State routing agency; a State-designated route selected by a State routing agency pursuant to § 397.103; or both of the above.

(2) The motor carrier or the person operating a motor vehicle containing a highway route controlled quantity of Class 7 (radioactive) materials, as defined in 49 CFR 173.403(l) and (y), shall select routes to reduce time in transit over the preferred route segment of the trip. An Interstate System bypass or Interstate System beltway around a city, when available, shall be used in place of a preferred route through a city, unless a State routing agency has designated an alternative route.

(c) A motor vehicle may be operated over a route, other than a preferred route, only under the following conditions:

(1) The deviation from the preferred route is necessary to pick up or deliver a highway route controlled quantity of Class 7 (radioactive) materials, to make necessary rest, fuel or motor vehicle repair stops, or because emergency conditions make continued use of the preferred route unsafe or impossible;

(2) For pickup and delivery not over preferred routes, the route selected must be the shortest-distance route from the pickup location to the nearest preferred route entry location, and the shortest-distance route to the delivery location from the nearest preferred route exit location. Deviation from the shortest-distance pickup or delivery route is authorized if such deviation:

(i) Is based upon the criteria in paragraph (a) of this section to minimize the radiological risk; and

(ii) Does not exceed the shortest-distance pickup or delivery route by more than 25 miles and does not exceed 5 times the length of the shortest-distance pickup or delivery route.

(iii) Deviations from preferred routes, or pickup or delivery routes other than preferred routes, which are necessary for rest, fuel, or motor vehicle repair stops or because of emergency conditions, shall be made in accordance with the criteria in paragraph (a) of this section to minimize radiological risk, unless due to emergency conditions, time does not permit use of those criteria.

(d) A carrier (or a designated agent) who operates a motor vehicle which contains a package of highway route controlled quantity of Class 7 (radioactive) materials, as defined in 49 CFR 173.403(l), shall prepared a written route plan and supply a copy before departure to the motor vehicle driver and a copy to the shipper (before departure for exclusive use shipments, as defined in 49 CFR 173.403(i), or within fifteen working days following departure for all other shipments). Any variation between the route plan and routes actually used, and the reason for it, shall be reported in an amendment to the route plan delivered to the shipper as soon as practicable but within 30 days following the deviation. The route plan shall contain:

(1) A statement of the origin and destination points, a route selected in compliance with this section, all planned stops, and estimated departure and arrival times; and

(2) Telephone numbers which will access emergency assistance in each State to be entered.

(e) No person may transport a package of highway route controlled quantity of Class 7 (radioactive) materials on a public highway unless:

(1) The driver has received within the two preceding years, written training on:

(i) Requirements in 49 CFR parts 172, 173, and 177 pertaining to the Class 7 (radioactive) materials transported;

(ii) The properties and hazards of the Class 7 (radioactive) materials being transported; and

(iii) Procedures to be followed in case of an accident or other emergency.

(2) The driver has in his or her immediate possession a certificate of training as evidence of training required by this section, and a copy is placed in his or her qualification file (see § 391.51 of this subchapter), showing:

(i) The driver's name and operator's license number;

(ii) The dates training was provided;

(iii) The name and address of the person providing the training;

(iv) That the driver has been trained in the hazards and characteristics of highway route controlled quantity of Class 7 (radioactive) materials; and

(v) A statement by the person providing the training that information on the certificate is accurate.

(3) The driver has in his or her immediate possession the route plan required by paragraph (d) of this section and operates the motor vehicle in accordance with the route plan.

(f) A person may transport irradiated reactor fuel only in compliance with a plan if required under 49 CFR 173.22(c) that will ensure the physical security of the material. Variation for security purposes from the requirements of this section is permitted so far as necessary to meet the requirements imposed under such a plan, or otherwise imposed by the U.S. Nuclear Regulatory Commission in 10 CFR part 73.

(g) Except for packages shipped in compliance with the physical security requirements of the U.S. Nuclear Regulatory Commission in 10 CFR part 73, each carrier who accepts for transportation a highway route controlled quantity of Class 7 (radioactive) material (see 49 CFR 173.401(l)), must, within 90 days following the acceptance of the package, file the following information concerning the transportation of each such package with the Federal Motor Carrier Safety Administration, Office of Enforcement and Compliance (MC–EC), 1200 New Jersey Ave., SE., Washington, DC 20590–0001:

(1) The route plan required under paragraph (d) of this section, including all required amendments reflecting the routes actually used;

(2) A statement identifying the names and addresses of the shipper, carrier and consignee; and

(3) A copy of the shipping paper or the description of the Class 7 (radioactive) material in the shipment required by 49 CFR 172.202 and 172.203.

[57 FR 44131, Sept. 24, 1992, as amended at 66 FR 49874, Oct. 1, 2001; 72 FR 55703, Oct. 1, 2007]

§ 397.103 Requirements for State routing designations.

(a) The State routing agency, as defined in § 397.201(c), shall select routes to minimize radiological risk using "Guidelines for Selecting Preferred Highway Routes for Highway Route Controlled Quantity Shipments of Radioactive Materials," or an equivalent routing analysis which adequately considers overall risk to the public. Designations must be preceded by substantive consultation with affected local jurisdictions and with any other affected States to ensure consideration of all impacts and continuity of designated routes.

(b) State routing agencies may designate preferred routes as an alternative to, or in addition to, one or more Interstate System highways, including interstate system bypasses, or Interstate System beltways.

(c) A State-designated route is effective when—

(1) The State gives written notice by certified mail, return receipt requested, to the Federal Motor Carrier Safety Administration, Office of Enforcement and Compliance (MC–EC), 1200 New Jersey Ave., SE., Washington, DC 20590–0001. Attention: National Hazardous Materials Route Registry.

(2) Receipt thereof is acknowledged in writing by the FMCSA.

(d) A list of State-designated preferred routes and a copy of the "Guidelines for Selecting Preferred Highway Routes for Highway Route Controlled Quantity Shipments of Radioactive Materials" are available upon request to Federal Motor Carrier Safety Administration, Office of Enforcement and Compliance (MC–EC), 1200 New Jersey Ave., SE., Washington, DC 20590–0001.

[57 FR 44131, Sept. 24, 1992, as amended at 66 FR 49874, Oct. 1, 2001; 72 FR 55703, Oct. 1, 2007]

Subpart E—Preemption Procedures

SOURCE: 57 FR 44132, Sept. 24, 1992, unless otherwise noted.

§ 397.201 Purpose and scope of the procedures.

(a) This subpart prescribes procedures by which:

(1) Any person, including a State, political subdivision thereof, or Indian tribe, directly affected by any highway routing designation for hazardous materials may apply to the Administrator for a determination as to whether that highway routing designation is preempted under 49 U.S.C. 5125, or § 397.69 or § 397.203 of this part; and

(2) A State, political subdivision thereof, or Indian tribe may apply to the Administrator for a waiver of preemption with respect to any highway routing designation that the State, political subdivision thereof, or Indian tribe acknowledges to be preempted by 49 U.S.C. 5125, or § 397.69 or § 397.203 of this part, or that has been determined by a court of competent jurisdiction to be so preempted.

(b) Unless otherwise ordered by the Administrator, an application for a preemption determination which includes an application for a waiver of preemption will be treated and processed solely as an application for a preemption determination.

(c) For purposes of this part:

Act means 49 U.S.C. 5101 *et seq.*, formerly known as the Hazardous Materials Transportation Act.

Administrator means the Federal Highway Administrator, who is the chief executive of the Federal Motor Carrier Safety Administration, an agency of the United States Department of Transportation, or his/her designate.

Hazardous material means a substance or material, including a hazardous substance, which has been determined by the Secretary of Transportation to be capable of posing an unreasonable risk to health, safety, or property, when transported in commerce, and which has been so designated.

Indian tribe has the same meaning as contained in section 4 of the Indian Self-Determination and Education Act, 25 U.S.C. 450b.

Person means an individual, firm, co-partnership, corporation, company, association, joint-stock association, including any trustee, receiver, assignee, or similar representative thereof, or government, Indian tribe, or agency or instrumentality of any government or Indian tribe when it offers hazardous materials for transportation in commerce or transports hazardous materials in furtherance of a commercial enterprise, but such term does not include the United States Postal Service.

Political subdivision includes a municipality; a public agency or other instrumentality of one or more States, or a public corporation, board, or commission established under the laws of one or more States.

Routing agency means the State highway agency or other State agency designated by the Governor of a State, or an agency designated by an Indian tribe, to supervise, coordinate, and approve the highway routing designations for that State or Indian tribe. Any highway routing designation made by a political subdivision of a State shall be considered a designation made by that State.

Routing designation includes any regulation, limitation, restriction, curfew, time of travel restriction, lane restriction, routing ban, port-of-entry designation, or route weight restriction applicable to the highway transportation of hazardous materials over a specific highway route or portion of a route.

State means a State of the United States, the District of Columbia, the Commonwealth of Puerto Rico, the Commonwealth of the Northern Mariana Islands, the Virgin Islands, American Samoa, Guam, or any other territory or possession of the United States designated by the Secretary.

[57 FR 44132, Sept. 24, 1992, as amended at 59 FR 51834, Oct. 12, 1994]

§ 397.203 Standards for determining preemption.

(a) Any highway routing designation established, maintained, or enforced by a State, political subdivision thereof, or Indian tribe is preempted if—

(1) Compliance with both the highway routing designation and any requirement under the Act or of a regulation issued under the Act is not possible;

(2) The highway routing designation as applied or enforced creates an obstacle to the accomplishment and execution of the Act or the regulations issued under the Act; or

(3) The highway routing designation is preempted pursuant to §397.69(b) of this part.

(b) [Reserved]

[57 FR 44132, Sept. 24, 1992, as amended at 59 FR 51834, Oct. 12, 1994]

§397.205 Preemption application.

(a) Any person, including a State, political subdivision thereof, or Indian tribe directly affected by any highway routing designation of another State, political subdivision, or Indian tribe, may apply to the Administrator for a determination of whether that highway routing designation is preempted by the Act or §397.203 of this subpart. The Administrator shall publish notice of the application in the FEDERAL REGISTER.

(b) Each application filed under this section for a determination must:

(1) Be submitted to the Administrator, Federal Motor Carrier Safety Administration, 1200 New Jersey Ave., SE., Washington, DC 20590–0001. Attention: Office of the Chief Counsel, Enforcement and Litigation Division (MC–CCE);

(2) Set forth a detailed description of the highway routing designation of the State, political subdivision thereof, or Indian tribe for which the determination is sought;

(3) If applicable, specify the provisions of the Act or the regulations issued under the Act under which the applicant seeks preemption of the highway routing designation of the State, political subdivision thereof, or Indian tribe;

(4) Explain why the applicant believes the highway routing designation of the State, political subdivision thereof, or Indian tribe should or should not be preempted under the standards of §397.203; and

(5) State how the applicant is affected by the highway routing designation of the State, political subdivision thereof, or Indian tribe.

(c) The filing of an application for a determination under this section does not constitute grounds for noncompliance with any requirement of the Act or any regulation issued under the Act.

(d) Once the Administrator has published notice in the FEDERAL REGISTER of an application received under paragraph (a) of this section, no applicant for such determination may seek relief with respect to the same or substantially the same issue in any court until final action has been taken on the application or until 180 days after filing of the application, whichever occurs first. Nothing in this section shall be construed as prohibiting any person, including a State, political subdivision thereof, or Indian tribe, directly affected by any highway routing designation from seeking a determination of preemption in any court of competent jurisdiction in lieu of applying to the Administrator under paragraph (a) of this section.

[57 FR 44132, Sept. 24, 1992, as amended at 72 FR 55703, Oct. 1, 2007]

§397.207 Preemption notice.

(a) If the applicant is other than a State, political subdivision thereof, or Indian tribe, the applicant shall mail a copy of the application to the State, political subdivision thereof, or Indian tribe concerned, accompanied by a statement that comments may be submitted regarding the application to the Administrator within 45 days. The application filed with the Administrator must include a certification that the applicant has complied with this paragraph and must include the names and addresses of each official to whom a copy of the application was sent.

(b) The Administrator may afford interested persons an opportunity to file written comments on the application by serving notice on any persons readily identifiable by the Administrator as persons who will be affected by the ruling sought or by publication in the FEDERAL REGISTER.

(c) Each person submitting written comments to the Administrator with respect to an application filed under this section shall send a copy of the comments to the applicant and certify

543

to the Administrator that he or she has complied with this requirement. The Administrator may notify other persons participating in the proceeding of the comments and provide an opportunity for those other persons to respond.

§ 397.209 Preemption processing.

(a) The Administrator may initiate an investigation of any statement in an application and utilize in his or her evaluation any relevant facts obtained by that investigation. The Administrator may solicit and accept submissions from third persons relevant to an application and will provide the applicant an opportunity to respond to all third person submissions. In evaluating an application, the Administrator may consider any other source of information. The Administrator may convene a hearing or conference, if a hearing or conference will advance the evaluation of the application.

(b) The Administrator may dismiss the application without prejudice if:

(1) he or she determines that there is insufficient information upon which to base a determination; or

(2) he or she requests additional information from the applicant and it is not submitted.

§ 397.211 Preemption determination.

(a) Upon consideration of the application and other relevant information received, the Administrator issues a determination.

(b) Notwithstanding that an application for a determination has not been filed under § 397.205, the Administrator, on his or her own initiative, may issue a determination as to whether a particular highway routing designation of a State, political subdivision thereof, or Indian tribe is preempted under the Act or the regulations issued under the Act.

(c) The determination includes a written statement setting forth the relevant facts and the legal basis for the determination, and provides that any person aggrieved thereby may file a petition for reconsideration within 20 days in accordance with § 397.223.

(d) Unless the determination is issued pursuant to paragraph (b) of this section, the Administrator serves a copy of the determination upon the applicant. In all preemption determinations, the Administrator serves a copy of the determination upon any other person who participated in the proceeding or who is readily identifiable by the Administrator as affected by the determination. A copy of each determination is placed on file in the public docket. The Administrator may publish the determination or notice of the determination in the FEDERAL REGISTER.

(e) If no petition for reconsideration is filed within 20 days in accordance with § 397.223, a determination issued under this section constitutes the final agency decision as to whether a particular highway routing designation of a State, political subdivision thereof, or Indian tribe is preempted under the Act or regulations issued thereunder. The fact that a determination has not been issued under this section with respect to a particular highway routing designation of a State, political subdivision thereof, or Indian tribe carries no implication as to whether the requirement is preempted under the Act or regulations issued thereunder.

§ 397.213 Waiver of preemption application.

(a) Any State, political subdivision thereof, or Indian tribe may apply to the Administrator for a waiver of preemption with respect to any highway routing designation that the State, political subdivision thereof, or Indian tribe acknowledges to be preempted by the Act, § 397.203 of this subpart, or a court of competent jurisdiction. The Administrator may waive preemption with respect to such requirement upon a determination that such requirement—

(1) Affords an equal or greater level of protection to the public than is afforded by the requirements of the Act or regulations issued under the Act, and

(2) Does not unreasonably burden commerce.

(b) Each application filed under this section for a waiver of preemption determination must:

(1) Be submitted to the Administrator, Federal Motor Carrier Safety Administration, 1200 New Jersey Ave.,

SE., Washington, DC 20590–0001. Attention: Office of the Chief Counsel, Enforcement and Litigation Division (MC–CCE);

(2) Set forth a detailed description of the highway routing designation of the State, political subdivision thereof, or Indian tribe for which the determination is being sought;

(3) Include a copy of any relevant court order or determination issued pursuant to §397.211;

(4) Contain an express acknowledgment by the applicant that the highway routing designation of the State, political subdivision thereof, our Indian tribe is preempted under the Act or the regulations issued under the Act, unless it has been so determined by a court of competent jurisdiction or in a determination issued under this subpart;

(5) Specify each provision of the Act or the regulations issued under the Act that preempts the highway routing designation of the State, political subdivision thereof, or Indian tribe;

(6) State why the applicant believes that the highway routing designation of the State, political subdivision thereof, or Indian tribe affords an equal or greater level of protection to the public than is afforded by the requirements of the Act or the regulations issued under the Act;

(7) State why the applicant believes that the highway routing designation of the State, political subdivision thereof, or Indian tribe does not unreasonably burden commerce; and

(8) Specify what steps the State, political subdivision thereof, or Indian tribe is taking to administer and enforce effectively the preempted requirement.

[57 FR 44132, Sept. 24, 1992, as amended at 72 FR 55703, Oct. 1, 2007]

§397.215 Waiver notice.

(a) The applicant State, political subdivision thereof, or Indian tribe shall mail a copy of the application and any subsequent amendments or other documents relating to the application to each person whom the applicant reasonably ascertains will be affected by the determination sought. The copy of the application must be accompanied by a statement that the person may submit comments regarding the application to the Administrator within 45 days. The application filed with the Administrator must include a certification with the application has complied with this paragraph and must include the names and addresses of each person to whom the application was sent.

(b) Notwithstanding the provisions of paragraph (a) of this section, if the State, political subdivision thereof, or Indian tribe determines that compliance with paragraph (a) of this section would be impracticable, the applicant shall:

(1) Comply with the requirements of paragraph (a) of this section with regard to those persons whom it is reasonable and practicable to notify; and

(2) Include with the application filed with the Administrator a description of the persons or class or classes of persons to whom notice was not sent.

(c) The Administrator may require the applicant to provide notice in addition to that required by paragraphs (a) and (b) of this section, or may determine that the notice required by paragraph (a) of this section is not impracticable, or that notice should be published in the FEDERAL REGISTER.

(d) The Administrator may serve notice on any other persons readily identifiable by the Administrator as persons who will be affected by the determination sought and may afford those persons an opportunity to file written comments on the application.

(e) Any person submitting written comments to the Administrator with respect to an application filed under this section shall send a copy of the comments to the applicant. The person shall certify to the Administrator that he or she has complied with the requirements of this paragraph. The Administrator may notify other persons participating in the proceeding of the comments and provide an opportunity for those other persons to respond.

§397.217 Waiver processing.

(a) The Administrator may initiate an investigation of any statement in an application and utilize any relevant facts obtained by that investigation. The Administrator may solicit and accept submissions from third persons relevant to an application and will provide the applicant an opportunity to respond to all third person submissions. In evaluating an application, the Administrator may convene a hearing or conference, if a hearing or conference will advance the evaluation of the application.

(b) The Administrator may dismiss the application without prejudice if:

(1) he or she determines that there is insufficient information upon which to base a determination;

(2) Upon his or her request, additional information is not submitted by the applicant; or

(3) The applicant fails to provide the notice required by this subpart.

(c) Except as provided in this subpart, the Administrator will only consider an application for a waiver of preemption determination if:

(1) The applicant expressly acknowledges in its application that the highway routing designation of the State, political subdivision thereof, or Indian tribe for which the determination is sought is preempted by the Act or the regulations thereunder; or

(2) The highway routing designation of the State, political subdivision thereof, or Indian tribe has been determined by a court of competent jurisdiction or in a determination issued pursuant to § 397.211 to be preempted by the Act or the regulations issued thereunder.

(d) When the Administrator has received all substantive information necessary to process an application for a waiver of preemption determination, notice of that fact will be served upon the applicant. Additional notice to all other persons who received notice of the proceeding may be served by publishing a notice in the FEDERAL REGISTER.

§ 397.219 Waiver determination and order.

(a) Upon consideration of the application and other relevant information received or obtained during the proceeding, the Administrator issues an order setting forth his or her determination.

(b) The Administrator may issue a waiver of preemption order only if he or she finds that the requirement of the State, political subdivision thereof, or Indian tribe affords the public a level of safety at least equal to that afforded by the requirements of the Act and the regulations issued under the Act and does not unreasonably burden commerce. In determining whether the requirement of the State, political subdivision thereof, or Indian tribe unreasonably burdens commerce, the Administrator may consider the following factors:

(1) The extent to which increased costs and impairment of efficiency result from the highway routing designation of the State, political subdivision thereof, or Indian tribe;

(2) Whether the highway routing designation of the State, political subdivision thereof, or Indian tribe has a rational basis;

(3) Whether the highway routing designation of the State, political subdivision thereof, or Indian tribe achieves its stated purpose; and

(4) Whether there is need for uniformity with regard to the subject concerned and if so, whether the highway routing designation of the State, political subdivision thereof, or Indian tribe competes or conflicts with those of other States, political subdivisions thereof, or Indian tribes.

(c) The order includes a written statement setting forth the relevant facts and the legal basis for the determination, and provides that any person aggrieved by the order may file a petition for reconsideration in accordance with § 397.223.

(d) The Administrator serves a copy of the order upon the applicant, any other person who participated in the proceeding and upon any other person readily identifiable by the Administrator as one who may be affected by the order. A copy of each order is placed on file in the public docket. The Administrator may publish the order or notice of the order in the FEDERAL REGISTER.

(e) If no petition for reconsideration is filed within 20 days in accordance with § 397.223, an order issued under this section constitutes the final agency decision regarding whether a particular requirement of a State, political subdivision thereof, or Indian tribe is preempted under the Act or any regulations issued thereunder, or whether preemption is waived.

§397.221 Timeliness.

If the Administrator fails to take action on the application within 90 days of serving the notice required by §397.217(d), the applicant may treat the application as having been denied in all respects.

§397.223 Petition for reconsideration.

(a) Any person aggrieved by an order issued under §397.211 or §397.219 may file a petition for reconsideration with the Administrator. The petition must be filed within 20 days of service of the determination or order issued under the above sections.

(b) The petition must contain a concise statement of the basis for seeking reconsideration, including any specific factual or legal errors, or material information not previously available.

(c) The petitioner shall mail a copy of the petition to each person who participated, either as an applicant or routing, in the waiver of preemption proceeding, accompanied by a statement that the person may submit comments concerning the petition to the Administrator within 20 days. The petition filed with the Administrator must contain a certification that the petitioner has complied with this paragraph and include the names and addresses of all persons to whom a copy of the petition was sent.

(d) The Administrator's decision under this section constitutes the final agency decision. If no petition for reconsideration is filed under this section, then the determination issued under §397.211 or §397.219 becomes the final agency decision at the end of the 20 day period.

§397.225 Judicial review.

A party to a proceeding under §397.205(a), §397.213(a), or §397.223(a) may seek review by the appropriate district court of the United States of the decision of the Administrator under such proceeding only by filing a petition with such court within 60 days after the final agency decision.

PART 398—TRANSPORTATION OF MIGRANT WORKERS

Sec.
398.1 Definitions.
398.2 Applicability.
398.3 Qualifications of drivers or operators.
398.4 Driving of motor vehicles.
398.5 Parts and accessories necessary for safe operation.
398.6 Hours of service of drivers; maximum driving time.
398.7 Inspection and maintenance of motor vehicles.
398.8 Administration inspection of motor vehicles in operation.

AUTHORITY: 49 U.S.C. 13301, 13902, 31132, 31133, 31136, 31502, and 31504; sec. 204, Pub. L. 104–88, 109 Stat. 803, 941 (49 U.S.C. 701 note); sec. 212, Pub. L. 106–159, 113 Stat. 1748, 1766; and 49 CFR 1.73.

SOURCE: 33 FR 19765, Dec. 25, 1968, unless otherwise noted.

EDITORIAL NOTE: Nomenclature changes to part 398 appear at 66 FR 49874, Oct. 1, 2001.

§398.1 Definitions.

(a) *Migrant worker.* "Migrant worker" means any individual proceeding to or returning from employment in agriculture as defined in section 3(f) of the Fair Labor Standards Act of 1938, as amended (29 U.S.C. 203(f)) or section 3121(g) of the Internal Revenue Code of 1954 (26 U.S.C. 3121(g)).

(b) *Carrier of migrant workers by motor vehicle.* "Carrier of migrant worker by motor vehicle" means any person, including any "contract carrier by motor vehicle", but not including any "common carrier by motor vehicle", who or which transports in interstate or foreign commerce at any one time three or more migrant workers to or from their employment by any motor vehicle other than a passenger automobile or station wagon, except a migrant worker transporting himself/herself or his/her immediate family.

(c) *Motor carrier.* "Motor carrier" means any carrier of migrant workers by motor vehicle as defined in paragraph (b) of this section.

(d) *Motor vehicle.* "Motor vehicle" means any vehicle, machine, tractor, trailer, or semitrailer propelled or drawn by mechanical power and used upon the highways in the transportation of passengers or property, or any combination thereof, determined by the Administration, but does not include a passenger automobile or station wagon, any vehicle, locomotive, or car operated exclusively on a rail or rails, or a trolley bus operated by electric power derived from a fixed overhead wire, furnishing local passenger transportation in street-railway service.

(e) *Bus.* "Bus" means any motor vehicle designed, constructed, and used for the transportation of passengers: Except passenger automobiles or station wagons other than taxicabs.

(f) *Truck.* "Truck" means any self-propelled motor vehicle except a truck tractor, designed and constructed primarily for the transportation of property.

(g) *Truck tractor.* "Truck tractor" means a self-propelled motor vehicle designed and used primarily for drawing other vehicles and not so constructed as to carry a load other than a part of the weight of the vehicle and load so drawn.

(h) *Semitrailer.* "Semitrailer" means any motor vehicle other than a "pole trailer", with or without motive power designed to be drawn by another motor vehicle and so constructed that some part of its weight rests upon the towing vehicle.

(i) *Driver or operator.* "Driver or operator" means any person who drives any motor vehicle.

(j) *Highway.* "Highway" means the entire width between the boundary lines of every way publicly maintained when any part thereof is open to the use of the public for purposes of vehicular traffic.

§ 398.2 Applicability.

(a) *General.* The regulations prescribed in this part are applicable to carriers of migrant workers by motor vehicle, as defined in § 398.1(b), but only in the case of transportation of any migrant worker for a total distance of more than 75 miles (120.7 kilometers) in interstate commerce, as defined in 49 CFR 390.5.

(b) *Exception.* (1) The regulations prescribed in this part are not applicable to carriers of migrant workers by motor vehicle, as defined in § 398.1(b), when:

(i) The motor vehicle is designed or used to transport between 9 and 15 passengers (including the driver);

(ii) The motor carrier is directly compensated for the transportation service; and

(iii) The vehicle used to transport migrant workers is operated beyond a 75 air-mile radius (86.3 statute miles or 138.9 kilometers) from the driver's normal work-reporting location.

(2) Carriers of migrant workers by motor vehicle that operate vehicles, designed or used to transport between 9 and 15 passengers (including the driver) for direct compensation, in interstate commerce, must comply with the applicable requirements of 49 CFR parts 385, 390, 391, 392, 393, 395, and 396, when the motor vehicle is operated beyond a 75 air-mile radius (86.3 statute miles or 138.9 kilometers) from the driver's normal work-reporting location.

[68 FR 47875, Aug. 12, 2003]

§ 398.3 Qualifications of drivers or operators.

(a) *Compliance required.* Every motor carrier, and its officers, agents, representatives and employees who drive motor vehicles or are responsible for the hiring, supervision, training, assignment or dispatching of drivers shall comply and be conversant with the requirements of this part.

(b) *Minimum physical requirements.* No person shall drive, nor shall any motor carrier require or permit any person to drive, any motor vehicle unless such person possesses the following minimum qualifications:

(1) No loss of foot, leg, hand or arm,

(2) No mental, nervous, organic, or functional disease, likely to interfere with safe driving.

(3) No loss of fingers, impairment of use of foot, leg, fingers, hand or arm, or other structural defect or limitation, likely to interfere with safe driving.

(4) *Eyesight.* Visual acuity of at least 20/40 (Snellen) in each eye either without glasses or by correction with glasses; form field of vision in the horizontal meridian shall not be less than a total of 140 degrees; ability to distinguish colors red, green and yellow; drivers requiring correction by glasses shall wear properly prescribed glasses at all times when driving.

(5) *Hearing.* Hearing shall not be less than 10/20 in the better ear, for conversational tones, without a hearing aid.

(6) *Liquor, narcotics and drugs.* Shall not be addicted to the use of narcotics or habit forming drugs, or the excessive use of alcoholic beverages or liquors.

(7) *Initial and periodic physical examination of drivers.* No person shall drive nor shall any motor carrier require or permit any person to drive any motor vehicle unless within the immediately preceding 36 month period such person shall have been physically examined and shall have been certified in accordance with the provisions of paragraph (b)(8) of this section by a licensed doctor of medicine or osteopathy as meeting the requirements of this subsection.

(8) *Certificate of physical examination.* Every motor carrier shall have in its files at its principal place of business for every driver employed or used by it a legible certificate of a licensed doctor of medicine or osteopathy based on a physical examination as required by paragraph (b)(7) of this section or a legible photographically reproduced copy thereof, and every driver shall have in his/her possession while driving, such a certificate or a photographically reproduced copy thereof covering himself/herself.

(9) *Doctor's certificate.* The doctor's certificate shall certify as follows:

DOCTOR'S CERTIFICATE

(Driver of Migrant Workers)

This is to certify that I have this day examined _____ in accordance with §398.3(b) of the Federal Motor Carrier Safety Regulations of the Federal Motor Carrier Safety Administration and that I find him/her

Qualified under said rules □
Qualified only when wearing glasses □
I have kept on file in my office a completed examination.

_____
                                    (Date)

                                    (Place)
(Signature of examining doctor)
_____
                    (Address of doctor)
Signature of driver   _____
Address of driver   _____

(c) *Minimum age and experience requirements.* No person shall drive, nor shall any motor carrier require or permit any person to drive, any motor vehicle unless such person possesses the following minimum qualifications:

(1) *Age.* Minimum age shall be 21 years.

(2) *Driving skill.* Experience in driving some type of motor vehicle (including private automobiles) for not less than one year, including experience throughout the four seasons.

(3) *Knowledge of regulations.* Familiarity with the rules and regulations prescribed in this part pertaining to the driving of motor vehicles.

(4) *Knowledge of English.* Every driver shall be able to read and speak the English language sufficiently to understand highway traffic signs and signals and directions given in English and to respond to official inquiries.

(5) *Driver's permit.* Possession of a valid permit qualifying the driver to operate the type of vehicle driven by him/her in the jurisdiction by which the permit is issued.

[33 FR 19765, Dec. 25, 1968, as amended at 40 FR 44557, Sept. 29, 1975]

§398.4 Driving of motor vehicles.

(a) *Compliance required.* Every motor carrier shall comply with the requirements of this part, shall instruct its officers, agents, representatives and drivers with respect thereto, and shall take such measures as are necessary to insure compliance therewith by such persons. All officers, agents, representatives, drivers, and employees of motor carriers directly concerned with the management, maintenance, operation, or driving of motor vehicles, shall comply with and be conversant with the requirements of this part.

(b) *Driving rules to be obeyed.* Every motor vehicle shall be driven in accordance with the laws, ordinances, and regulations of the jurisdiction in which it is being operated, unless such laws, ordinances and regulations are at variance with specific regulations of this Administration which impose a greater affirmative obligation or restraint.

(c) *Driving while ill or fatigued.* No driver shall drive or be required or permitted to drive a motor vehicle while

549

his/her ability or alertness is so impaired through fatigue, illness, or any other cause as to make it unsafe for him/her to begin or continue to drive, except in case of grave emergency where the hazard to passengers would be increased by observance of this section and then only to the nearest point at which the safety of passengers is assured.

(d) *Alcoholic beverages.* No driver shall drive or be required or permitted to drive a motor vehicle, be in active control of any such vehicle, or go on duty or remain on duty, when under the influence of any alcoholic beverage or liquor, regardless of its alcoholic content, nor shall any driver drink any such beverage or liquor while on duty.

(e) *Schedules to conform with speed limits.* No motor carrier shall permit nor require the operation of any motor vehicle between points in such period of time as would necessitate the vehicle being operated at speeds greater than those prescribed by the jurisdictions in or through which the vehicle is being operated.

(f) *Equipment and emergency devices.* No motor vehicle shall be driven unless the driver thereof shall have satisfied himself/herself that the following parts, accessories, and emergency devices are in good working order; nor shall any driver fail to use or make use of such parts, accessories, and devices when and as needed:

Service brakes, including trailer brake connections.
   Parking (hand) brake.
   Steering mechanism.
Lighting devices and reflectors.
   Tires.
   Horn.
   Windshield wiper or wipers.
Rear-vision mirror or mirrors.
Coupling devices.
Fire extinguisher, at least one properly mounted.
Road warning devices, at least one red burning fusee and at least three flares (oil burning pot torches), red electric lanterns, or red emergency reflectors.

(g) *Safe loading*—(1) *Distribution and securing of load.* No motor vehicle shall be driven nor shall any motor carrier permit or require any motor vehicle to be driven if it is so loaded, or if the load thereon is so improperly distrib-

uted or so inadequately secured, as to prevent its safe operation.

(2) *Doors, tarpaulins, tailgates and other equipment.* No motor vehicle shall be driven unless the tailgate, tailboard, tarpaulins, doors, all equipment and rigging used in the operation of said vehicle, and all means of fastening the load, are securely in place.

(3) *Interference with driver.* No motor vehicle shall be driven when any object obscures his/her view ahead, or to the right or left sides, or to the rear, or interferes with the free movement of his/her arms or legs, or prevents his/her free and ready access to the accessories required for emergencies, or prevents the free and ready exit of any person from the cab or driver's compartment.

(4) *Property on motor vehicles.* No vehicle transporting persons and property shall be driven unless such property is stowed in a manner which will assure:

(i) Unrestricted freedom of motion to the driver for proper operation of the vehicle;

(ii) Unobstructed passage to all exits by any person; and

(iii) Adequate protection to passengers and others from injury as a result of the displacement or falling of such articles.

(5) *Maximum passengers on motor vehicles.* No motor vehicle shall be driven if the total number of passengers exceeds the seating capacity which will be permitted on seats prescribed in § 398.5(f) when that section is effective. All passengers carried on such vehicle shall remain seated while the motor vehicle is in motion.

(h) *Rest and meal stops.* Every carrier shall provide for reasonable rest stops at least once between meal stops. Meal stops shall be made at intervals not to exceed six hours and shall be for a period of not less than 30 minutes duration.

(i) *Kinds of motor vehicles in which workers may be transported.* Workers may be transported in or on only the following types of motor vehicles: A bus, a truck with no trailer attached, or a semitrailer attached to a truck-tractor provided that no other trailer is attached to the semitrailer. Closed vans without windows or means to assure ventilation shall not be used.

(j) *Limitation on distance of travel in trucks.* Any truck when used for the transportation of migrant workers, if such workers are being transported in excess of 600 miles, shall be stopped for a period of not less than eight consecutive hours either before or upon completion of 600 miles travel, and either before or upon completion of any subsequent 600 miles travel to provide rest for drivers and passengers.

(k) *Lighting devices and reflectors.* No motor vehicle shall be driven when any of the required lamps or reflectors are obscured by the tailboard, by any and all lighting devices required by subpart B of part 393 of this subchapter shall be lighted during darkness or at any other time when there is not sufficient light to render vehicles and persons visible upon the highway at a distance of 500 feet.

(l) *Ignition of fuel; prevention.* No driver or any employee of a motor carrier shall:

(1) Fuel a motor vehicle with the engine running, except when it is necessary to run the engine to fuel the vehicle;

(2) Smoke or expose any open flame in the vicinity of a vehicle being fueled;

(3) Fuel a motor vehicle unless the nozzle of the fuel hose is continuously in contact with the intake pipe of the fuel tank;

(4) Permit any other person to engage in such activities as would be likely to result in fire or explosion.

(m) *Reserve fuel.* No supply of fuel for the propulsion of any motor vehicle or for the operation of any accessory thereof shall be carried on the motor vehicle except in a properly mounted fuel tank or tanks.

(n) *Driving by unauthorized person.* Except in case of emergency, no driver shall permit a motor vehicle to which he/she is assigned to be driven by any person not authorized to drive such vehicle by the motor carrier in control thereof.

(o) *Protection of passengers from weather.* No motor vehicle shall be driven while transporting passengers unless the passengers therein are protected from inclement weather conditions such as rain, snow, or sleet, by

use of the top or protective devices required by § 398.5(f).

(p) *Unattended vehicles; precautions.* No motor vehicle shall be left unattended by the driver until the parking brake has been securely set, the wheels chocked, and all reasonable precautions have been taken to prevent the movement of such vehicle.

(q) *Railroad grade crossings; stopping required; sign on rear of vehicle.* Every motor vehicle shall, upon approaching any railroad grade crossing, make a full stop not more than 50 feet, nor less than 15 feet from the nearest rail of such railroad grade crossing, and shall not proceed until due caution has been taken to ascertain that the course is clear; except that a full stop need not be made at:

(1) A street car crossing within a business or residence district of a municipality;

(2) A railroad grade crossing where a police officer or a traffic-control signal (not a railroad flashing signal) directs traffic to proceed;

(3) An abandoned or exempted grade crossing which is clearly marked as such by or with the consent of the proper state authority, when such marking can be read from the driver's position.

All such motor vehicles shall display a sign on the rear reading, "This Vehicle Stops at Railroad Crossings."

[33 FR 19765, Dec. 25, 1968, as amended at 40 FR 44557, Sept. 29, 1975]

§ 398.5 Parts and accessories necessary for safe operation.

(a) *Compliance.* Every motor carrier and its officers, agents, drivers, representatives and employees directly concerned with the installation and maintenance of equipment and accessories shall comply and be conversant with the requirements and specifications of this part, and no motor carrier shall operate any motor vehicle, or cause or permit it to be operated, unless it is equipped in accordance with said requirements and specifications.

(b) *Lighting devices.* Every motor vehicle shall be equipped with the lighting devices and reflectors required by subpart B of part 393 of this subchapter.

(c) *Brakes.* Every motor vehicle shall be equipped with brakes as required by subpart C of part 393 of this subchapter, except § 393.44 of this subchapter, and shall satisfy the braking performance requirements contained therein.

(d) *Coupling devices; fifth wheel mounting and locking.* The lower half of every fifth wheel mounted on any truck-tractor or dolly shall be securely affixed to the frame thereof by U-bolts of adequate size, securely tightened, or by other means providing at least equivalent security. Such U-bolts shall not be of welded construction. The installation shall be such as not to cause cracking, warping, or deformation of the frame. Adequate meansshall be provided positively to prevent the shifting of the lower half of a fifth wheel on the frame to which it is attached. The upper half of every fifth wheel shall be fastened to the motor vehicle with at least the security required for the securing of the lower half to a truck-tractor or dolly. Locking means shall be provided in every fifth wheel mechanism including adapters when used, so that the upper and lower halves may not be separated without the operation of a positive manual release. A release mechanism operated by the driver from the cab shall be deemed to meet this requirement. On fifth wheels designed and constructed as to be readily separable, the fifth wheel locking devices shall apply automatically on coupling for any motor vehicle the date of manufacture of which is subsequent to December 31, 1952.

(e) *Tires.* Every motor vehicle shall be equipped with tires of adequate capacity to support its gross weight. No motor vehicle shall be operated on tires which have been worn so smooth as to expose any tread fabric or which have any other defect likely to cause failure. No vehicle shall be operated while transporting passengers while using any tire which does not have tread configurations on that part of the tire which is in contact with the road surface. No vehicle transporting passengers shall be operated with re-grooved, re-capped, or re-treaded tires on front wheels.

(f) *Passenger compartment.* Every motor vehicle transporting passengers, other than a bus, shall have a passenger compartment meeting the following requirements:

(1) *Floors.* A substantially smooth floor, without protruding obstructions more than two inches high, except as are necessary for securing seats or other devices to the floor, and without cracks or holes.

(2) *Sides.* Side walls and ends above the floor at least 60 inches high, by attachment of sideboards to the permanent body construction if necessary. Stake body construction shall be construed to comply with this requirement only if all six-inch or larger spaces between stakes are suitably closed to prevent passengers from falling off the vehicle.

(3) *Nails, screws, splinters.* The floor and the interior of the sides and ends of the passenger-carrying space shall be free of inwardly protruding nails, screws, splinters, or other projecting objects likely to be injurious to passengers or their apparel.

(4) *Seats.* On and after November 1, 1957, a seat shall be provided for each worker transported. The seats shall be: Securely attached to the vehicle during the course of transportation; not less than 16 inches nor more than 19 inches above the floor; at least 13 inches deep; equipped with backrests extending to a height of at least 36 inches above the floor, with at least 24 inches of space between the backrests or between the edges of the opposite seats when face to face; designed to provide at least 18 inches of seat for each passenger; without cracks more than two inches wide, and the exposed surfaces, if made of wood, planed or sanded smooth and free of splinters.

(5) *Protection from weather.* Whenever necessary to protect the passengers from inclement weather conditions, be equipped with a top at least 80 inches high above the floor and facilities for closing the sides and ends of the passenger-carrying compartment. Tarpaulins or other such removable devices for protection from the weather shall be secured in place.

(6) *Exit.* Adequate means of ingress and egress to and from the passenger space shall be provided on the rear or at the right side. Such means of ingress and egress shall be at least 18 inches wide. The top and the clear opening

shall be at least 60 inches high, or as high as the side wall of the passenger space if less than 60 inches. The bottom shall be at the floor of the passenger space.

(7) *Gates and doors.* Gates or doors shall be provided to close the means of ingress and egress and each such gate or door shall be equipped with at least one latch or other fastening device of such construction as to keep the gate or door securely closed during the course of transportation; and readily operative without the use of tools.

(8) *Ladders or steps.* Ladders or steps for the purpose of ingress or egress shall be used when necessary. The maximum verticle spacing of footholds shall not exceed 12 inches, except that the lowest step may be not more than 18 inches above the ground when the vehicle is empty.

(9) *Hand holds.* Hand holds or devices for similar purpose shall be provided to permit ingress and egress without hazard to passengers.

(10) *Emergency exit.* Vehicles with permanently affixed roofs shall be equipped with at least one emergency exit having a gate or door, latch and hand hold as prescribed in paragraphs (f) (7) and (9) of this section and located on a side or rear not equipped with the exit prescribed in paragraph (f)(6) of this section.

(11) *Communication with driver.* Means shall be provided to enable the passengers to communicate with the driver. Such means may include telephone, speaker tubes, buzzers, pull cords, or other mechanical or electrical means.

(g) *Protection from cold.* Every motor vehicle shall be provided with a safe means of protecting passengers from cold or undue exposure, but in no event shall heaters of the following types be used:

(1) *Exhaust heaters.* Any type of exhaust heater in which the engine exhaust gases are conducted into or through any space occupied by persons or any heater which conducts engine compartment air into any such space.

(2) *Unenclosed flame heaters.* Any type of heater employing a flame which is not fully enclosed.

(3) *Heaters permitting fuel leakage.* Any type of heater from the burner of which there could be spillage or leakage of fuel upon the tilting or overturning of the vehicle in which it is mounted.

(4) *Heaters permitting air contamination.* Any heater taking air, heated or to be heated, from the engine compartment or from direct contact with any portion of the exhaust system; or any heater taking air in ducts from the outside atmosphere to be conveyed through the engine compartment, unless said ducts are so constructed and installed as to prevent contamination of the air so conveyed by exhaust or engine compartment gases.

(5) Any heater not securely fastened to the vehicle.

§ 398.6 Hours of service of drivers; maximum driving time.

No person shall drive nor shall any motor carrier permit or require a driver employed or used by it to drive or operate for more than 10 hours in the aggregate (excluding rest stops and stops for meals) in any period of 24 consecutive hours, unless such driver be afforded eight consecutive hours rest immediately following the 10 hours aggregate driving. The term "24 consecutive hours" as used in this part means any such period starting at the time the driver reports for duty.

§ 398.7 Inspection and maintenance of motor vehicles.

Every motor carrier shall systematically inspect and maintain or cause to be systematically maintained, all motor vehicles and their accessories subject to its control, to insure that such motor vehicles and accessories are in safe and proper operating condition.

§ 398.8 Administration inspection of motor vehicles in operation.

(a) *Administration personnel authorized to perform inspections.* All persons designated as Special Agents of the Federal Motor Carrier Safety Administration, as detailed in appendix B of chapter III of this title, are authorized to enter upon and perform inspections of motor carrier's vehicles in operation.

(b) *Prescribed inspection report.* Form MCS 63, Driver-Equipment Compliance Check, shall be used to record findings from motor vehicles selected for final inspection by authorized Administration employees.

(c) *Motor vehicles declared "out of service"*. (1) Authorized Administration employees shall declare and mark "out of service" any motor vehicle which by reason of its mechanical condition or loading is so imminently hazardous to operate as to be likely to cause an accident or a breakdown. Form MCS 64, "Out of Service Vehicle" sticker shall be used to mark vehicles "out of service."

(2) No motor carrier shall require or permit any person to operate nor shall any person operate any motor vehicle declared and marked, "out of service" until all repairs required by the "out of service notice" on Form MCS 63 have been satisfactorily completed. The term operate as used in this section shall include towing the vehicle; provided, however, that vehicles marked "out of service" may be towed away by means of a vehicle using a crane or hoist; and provided further, that the vehicle combination consisting of the emergency towing vehicle and the "out of service" vehicle meets the performance requirements of § 393.52.

(3) No person shall remove the "Out of Service Vehicle" sticker from any motor vehicle prior to completion of all repairs required by the "out of service notice" on Form MCS 63.

(4) The person or persons completing the repairs required by the "out of service notice" shall sign the "Certification of Repairman" in accordance with the terms prescribed on Form MCS 63, entering the name of his/her shop or garage and the date and time the required repairs were completed. If the driver completes the required repairs, he/she shall sign and complete the "Certification of Repairman."

(d) *Motor carrier's disposition of Form MCS 63*. (1) Motor carriers shall carefully examine Forms MCS 63. Any and all violations or mechanical defects noted thereon shall be corrected. To the extent drivers are shown not to be in compliance with the Federal Motor Carrier Safety Regulations, appropriate corrective action shall be taken by the motor carrier.

(2) Motor carriers shall complete the "Motor Carrier Certification of Action Taken" on Form MCS 63 in accordance with the terms prescribed thereon. Motor carriers shall return Forms MCS 63 to the address indicated upon Form MCS 63 within fifteen (15) days following the date of the vehicle inspection.

[33 FR 19765, Dec. 25, 1968, as amended at 40 FR 44557, Sept. 29, 1975]

PART 399—EMPLOYEE SAFETY AND HEALTH STANDARDS

Subparts A–K [Reserved]

Subpart L—Step, Handhold, and Deck Requirements for Commercial Motor Vehicles

Sec.
399.201 Purpose and scope.
399.203 Applicability.
399.205 Definitions.
399.207 Truck and truck-tractor access requirements.
399.209 Test procedures.
399.211 Maintenance.

AUTHORITY: 49 U.S.C. 31502; and 49 CFR 1.73.

SOURCE: 44 FR 43732, July 26, 1979, unless otherwise noted.

EDITORIAL NOTE: Nomenclature changes to part 399 appear at 66 FR 49874, Oct. 1, 2001.

Subparts A–K [Reserved]

Subpart L—Step, Handhold, and Deck Requirements for Commercial Motor Vehicles

§ 399.201 Purpose and scope.

This subpart prescribes step, handhold, and deck requirements on commercial motor vehicles. These requirements are intended to enhance the safety of motor carrier employees.

§ 399.203 Applicability.

This subpart applies to all trucks and truck-tractors, having a high profile cab-over-engine (COE) configuration, for entrance, egress and back of cab access, manufactured on and after September 1, 1982.

[44 FR 43732, July 26, 1979, as amended at 46 FR 56799, Nov. 19, 1981]

§ 399.205 Definitions.

Cab-over-engine (COE) A truck or truck-tractor having all, or the front portion, of the engine under the cab.

COE—High profile A COE having the door sill step above the height of the front tires.

Deck plate A horizontal surface designed to provide a person with stable footing for the performance of work such as the connection and disconnection of air and electrical lines, gaining access to permanently-mounted equipment or machinery or for similar needs.

Door sill step Any step normally protected from the elements by the cab door when closed.

Effective peripheral grip Any shaped surface, free of sharp edges, in which a full grasp can be made to secure a handhold by a person.

Fingertip grasp A handhold surface which provides a person contact restricted to finger segments 1 and/or 2 only; or which limits wrap-around closure of finger segment 1 with the palm of the hand to 90 degrees as shown in Illustration I.

Finger Segments

Illustration I
Fingertip Grasp

Full grasp A handhold surface which provides a person contact with finger segments 2 and 3 and which provides space for finger segment 1 to wrap around toward the palm of the hand beyond the 90-degree surface restriction shown in Illustration I. The handhold need not require contact between fingers and thumb. For example, the hand position shown in Illustration II qualifies as full grasp.

Illustration II
Full Grasp

Ground The flat horizontal surface on which the tires of a motor vehicle rest.

Handhold That which qualifies as providing full grasp if a person is able to find a hand position on the handhold which allows more than fingertip grasp.

Handprint The surface area contacted by the hand when grasping a handhold. The size of this area is the width of the hand across the metacarpal and half the circumference of the handhold. The hand breadth of the typical person is 88.9 millimeters (3.5 inches).

Person Any individual within the 5th percentile female adult through the 95th percentile male adult of anthropometric measures as described by the 1962 Health Examination Survey, "Weight, Height and Selected Body Dimensions of Adults, United States 1960–1962" which is incorporated by reference. It is Public Health Service publication No. 1000–Series 11–No. 8 and is for sale from the U.S. Department of Commerce, National Technical Information Service, 5285 Port Royal Road, Springfield, Virginia 22161. When ordering use NTIS Accession No. PB 267174. It is also available for inspection at the National Archives and Records Administration (NARA). For information on the availability of this material at NARA, call 202–741–6030, or go to: *http:// www.archives.gov/federal_register/ code_of_federal_regulations/ ibr_locations.html*. This incorporation by reference was approved by the Director of the Federal Register on July 17, 1979. These materials are incorporated as they exist on the date of the approval and a notice of any change in these materials will be published in the FEDERAL REGISTER.

Slip resistant material Any material designed to minimize the accumulation of grease, ice, mud or other debris and afford protection from accidental slipping.

§ 399.207 Truck and truck-tractor access requirements.

(a) *General rule.* Any person entering or exiting the cab or accessing the rear portion of a high profile COE truck or truck-tractor shall be afforded sufficient steps and handholds, and/or deck plates to allow the user to have at least 3 limbs in contact with the truck or truck-tractor at any time. This rule applies to intermediate positions as well as transition between intermediate positions. To allow for changes in climbing sequence, the step design shall include, as a minimum, one intermediate step of sufficient size to accommodate two feet. *Exception.* If air and electrical connections necessary to couple or uncouple a truck-tractor from a trailer are accessible from the ground, no step, handholds or deck plates are required to permit access to the rear of the cab.

(b) *Performance requirements.* All high profile COE trucks or truck-tractors shall be equipped on each side of the vehicle where a seat is located, with a sufficient number of steps and handholds to conform with the requirements of paragraph (a) of this section and shall meet the performance requirements:

(1) *Vertical height.* All measurements of vertical height shall be made from ground level with the vehicle at unladen weight.

(2) *Distance between steps.* The distance between steps, up to and including the door sill step, shall provide any person a stable resting position which can be sustained without body motion and by exerting no more arm force than 35 percent of the person's body weight per grasp during all stages of entry and exit. This criterion applies to intermediate positions as well as transition between intermediate positions above ground level.

(i) When the ground provides the person foot support during entry or is the final step in the sequence during exit, and the step is 508 millimeters (20 inches) or more above ground, the stable resting position shall be achievable by the person using both hands to grasp the handhold(s) and requiring no more arm force than 35 percent of body weight per grasp.

(ii) The vertical height of the first step shall be no more than 609 millimeters (24 inches) from ground level.

(3) *Construction.* Each step or deck plate shall be of a slip resistant design which minimizes the accumulation of foreign material. Wherever practicable, a self-cleaning material should be used.

(4) *Foot accommodation.* Step depth or clearance and step width necessary to accommodate a climbing person are defined by using a minimum 127 millimeter (5 inch) diameter disc as shown in Illustration III.

(i) *Single foot accommodation.* The disc shall fit on a tread rung, or in a step recess, with no exterior overhang.

(ii) *Two-foot accommodation.* Two discs shall fit on a tread rung, or in a step recess, with no exterior overhang.

Single - foot Accommodation   **Two - foot Accommodaton**

Illustration III
Foot Accommodation

NOTE: The 127 millimeter (5 inch) disc is only intended to test for a minimum depth and width requirement. The step need not retain the disc at rest.

(5) *Step strength.* Each step must withstand a vertical static load of at least 204 kilograms (450 pounds) uniformly distributed over any 127 millimeter (5 inch) increment of step width.

(6) *Handhold location.* A handhold must be located within the reach of any person entering or exiting the vehicle.

(7) *Exterior mounting specifications for handholds.* Each handhold, affixed to the exterior of the vehicle, shall have at least 38 millimeters (1.5 inches) clearance between the handhold and the surface to which it is mounted for the distance between its mounting points.

(8) *Handhold size and shape.* Each handhold shall be free of sharp edges (minimum 1 millimeter [0.04 inch] radius) and have an effective peripheral grip length that permits full grasp by any person.

(9) *Handhold strength.* Each handhold shall withstand a horizontal static load of at least 114 kilograms (250 pounds) uniformly distributed over the area of a hand print and applied away from the mounting surface.

(10) *Deck plates.* Deck plates shall be on the rear of a truck-tractor as necessary to couple or uncouple air and/or electrical connections.

(11) *Deck plate strength.* Each deck plate shall be capable of withstanding the vertical static load of at least 205 kilograms (450 pounds) uniformly dis-

tributed over a 127 millimeter (5 inch) diameter disc.

§ 399.209 **Test procedures.**

(a) The force exerted on a handhold will be measured using a handheld spring scale or force transducer which can be attached to the vehicle and is free to rotate into alignment with a person's hand position.

(b) Hand grasp will be evaluated by observing the handgrip of any individual who conforms with the definition of "person" appearing in § 399.205 of this subpart.

§ 399.211 **Maintenance.**

All steps, handholds, and/or deck plates required by this subpart shall be adequately maintained to serve their intended function.

APPENDIX A TO SUBCHAPTER B OF CHAPTER III [RESERVED]

APPENDIX B TO SUBCHAPTER B OF CHAPTER III—SPECIAL AGENTS

CAUTIONARY NOTE: This appendix relates only to Federal authority to enforce the regulations in this subchapter. In its present form, it has no application for the States and is not to be included in any adoption of these regulations by State authorities as a condition of eligibility for grants under part 350 of this chapter.

1. *Authority.* Persons appointed as special agents of the Federal Motor Carrier Safety Administration ("Administration"), are authorized to enter upon, to inspect, and to examine any and all lands, buildings, and equipment of motor carriers and other persons subject to the Interstate Commerce

Act, the Department of Transportation Act, and other related Acts, and to inspect and copy any and all accounts, books, records, memoranda, correspondence, and other documents of such carriers and other persons.

2. *Compliance.* Motor carriers and other persons subject to these Acts shall submit their accounts, books, records, memoranda, correspondence, and other documents for inspection and copying, and they shall submit their lands, buildings, and equipment for examination and inspection, to any special agent of the Administration upon demand and display of an Administration credential identifying him/her as a special agent.

3. *Definition of Special Agent.* Special agents are Federal Motor Carrier Safety Administration (FMCSA) employees who are identified by credentials issued by the FMCSA authorizing them to enforce 42 U.S.C. 4917 and to exercise relevant authority of the Secretary of Transportation under 49 U.S.C. 113, chapters 5, 51, 57, 131–149, 311, 313, and 315 and other statutes, as delegated to FMCSA by 49 CFR 1.73, and under regulations issued on the authority of those statutes. Special agents are authorized to inspect and copy records and to inspect and examine land, buildings, and equipment in the manner and to the extent provided by law.

4. *Facsimile of the Administration Credential:*

UNITED STATES OF AMERICA

DEPARTMENT OF TRANSPORTATION FEDERAL MOTOR CARRIER SAFETY ADMINISTRATION

This is to certify that _____ whose photograph and signature appear hereon is duly accredited as _____ with authority to enter upon, to inspect, and examine lands, buildings, and equipment, and to inspect and copy records and papers of carriers and other persons, in performance of his/her duties under the Department of Transportation Act, related acts, and regulations of the Department.

By direction of the Secretary

(Certifying Authority)   (Bearer)

(49 U.S.C. 504, 5121, 14122, 31502 and 31503; and 49 CFR 1.73)

[35 FR 1016, Jan. 24, 1970 as amended at 36 FR 16067, Aug. 19, 1971; 43 FR 20011, May 10, 1978; 44 FR 46425, July 10, 1980; 49 FR 38290, Sept. 28, 1984; 60 FR 38749, July 28, 1995; 61 FR 1843, Jan. 24, 1996]

APPENDIXES C–E TO SUBCHAPTER B OF CHAPTER III [RESERVED]

APPENDIX F TO SUBCHAPTER B OF CHAPTER III—COMMERCIAL ZONES

"NOTE: The text of these definitions is identical to the text of 49 CFR Part 1048, revised as of October 1, 1975, which is no longer in print."

COMMERCIAL ZONES

Sec.
1 New York, N.Y.
2 Chicago, Ill.
3 St. Louis, Mo.-East St. Louis, Ill.
4 Washington, D.C.
5 Los Angeles, Calif., and contiguous and adjacent municipalities.
6 Philadelphia, Pa.
7 Cincinnati, Ohio
8 Kansas City, Mo.-Kansas City, Kans.
9 Boston, Mass.
10 Davenport, Iowa; Rock Island and Moline, Ill.
11 Commercial zones of municipalities in New Jersey within 5 miles of New York, N.Y.
12 Commercial zones of municipalities in Westchester and Nassau Counties, N.Y.
13 Tucson, Ariz.
14 Albuquerque, N. Mex.
18 Ravenswood, W. Va.
19 Lake Charles, La.
20 Syracuse, N.Y.
21 Baltimore, Md.
22 Cleveland, Ohio.
23 Detroit, Mich.
24 Seattle, Wash.
25 Albany, N.Y.
26 Minneapolis-St. Paul, Minn.
27 New Orleans, La.
28 Pittsburgh, Pa.
29 Portland, Oreg.
30 Vancouver, Wash.
31 Charleston, S.C.
32 Charleston, W. Va.
33 Memphis, Tenn.
34 Houston, Tex.
35 Pueblo, Colo.
36 Warren, Ohio
37 Louisville, Ky.
38 Sioux City, Iowa.
39 Beaumont, Tex.
40 Metropolitan Government of Nashville and Davidson County, Tenn.
41 Consolidated City of Indianapolis, Ind.
42 Lexington-Fayette Urban County, Ky.
43 Definitions.
44 Commercial zones determined generally, with exceptions.
45 Controlling distances and population data.

Section 1 New York, N.Y.

(a) The application of §372.241 Commercial Zones determined generally, with exceptions, is hereby extended to New York, N.Y.

(b) The exemption provided by section 203(b)(8) of the Interstate Commerce Act, of transportation by motor vehicle, in interstate or foreign commerce, performed wholly within the zone the limits of which are defined in paragraph (a) of this section, is hereby removed as to all such transportation except:

(1) Transportation which is performed wholly within the following territory: The area within the corporate limits of the cities of New York, Yonkers, Mount Vernon, North Pelham, Pelham, Pelham Manor, Great Neck Estates, Floral Park, and Valley Stream, N.Y., and Englewood, N.J.; the area within the borough limits of Alpine, Tenafly, Englewood Cliffs, Leonia, Fort Lee, Edgewater, Cliffside Park, Fairview, Palisades Park, and Ridgefield, Bergen County, N.J.; and that part of Hudson County, N.J., east of Newark Bay and the Hackensack River;

(2) Transportation which is performed in respect of a shipment which has had a prior, or will have a subsequent movement by water carrier, and which is performed wholly between points named in subparagraph (1) of this paragraph, on the one hand, and, on the other, those points in Newark and Elizabeth, N.J., identified as follows: All points in that area within the corporate limits of the cities of Newark and Elizabeth, N.J., west of Newark Bay and bounded on the south by the main line of the Central Railroad of New Jersey, on the west by the Newark & Elizabeth Branch of the Central Railroad Company of New Jersey, and on the north by the property line of the Penn Central Transportation Company.

(3) Transportation which is performed in respect of a shipment by rail carrier, and which is performed wholly between points named in subparagraph (1) of this paragraph, on the one hand, and, on the other,

(a) Those portions of Kearny, N.J., within an area bounded on the north by the main line of the Jersey City Branch of the Penn Central Transportation Co., on the south and east by Fish House Road and Pennsylvania Avenue, and on the west by the property line of the Penn Central Transportation Co. Truck-Train Terminal.

(b)(i) That portion of Newark, N.J., within an area bounded on the north by South Street and Delancey Street, on the east by Doremus Avenue, on the south by the freight right-of-way of the Penn Central Transportation Co. (Waverly Yard, Newark, N.J., to Greenville Piers, Jersey City, N.J., line), and on the west by the Penn Central Transportation Co.'s Hunter Street produce yard, and (ii) that portion of Newark, N.J., within an area bounded on the north by Poinier Street, on the east by Broad Steet, on the south by the passenger right-of-way of the Penn Central Transportation Co.'s main line and on the west by Frelinghuysen Avenue.

(c) That portion of Port Reading, N.J., within an area bounded on the east by the Arthur Kill, on the south by the right-of-way of the Reading Co., on the west by Cliff Road, and on the north by Woodbridge-Carteret Road, and

(d) That portion of Elizabeth, N.J., within an area bounded by a line extending from Newark Bay westward along Trumbull Street to its intersection with Division Street; thence northward along Trumbull Street to its intersection with East North Avenue; thence eastward along East North Avenue to its intersection with the New Jersey Turnpike, thence along the New Jersey Turnpike to the Elizabeth Channel; thence easterly along the Elizabeth Channel to Newark Bay; thence along the western shore of Newark Bay to the point of beginning.

Sec. 2 Chicago, Ill.

The zone adjacent to and commercially a part of Chicago, Ill., within which transportation by motor vehicle, in interstate or foreign commerce, not under a common control, management, or arrangement for a continuous carriage or shipment to or from a point beyond the zone is partially exempt from regulation under section 203(b)(8) of the Interstate Commerce Act (49 U.S.C. 303(b)(8)), includes and is comprised of all points as follows:

The area within the corporate limits of Chicago, Evanston, Oak Park, Cicero, Berwyn, River Forest, Willow Springs, Bridgeview, Hickory Hills, Worth, Homewood, and Lansing, Ill.; the area within the township limits of Niles, Maine, Leyden, Norwood Park, Proviso, Lyons, Riverside, Stickeny, Worth, Calumet, Bremen, and Thornton Townships, Cook County, Ill.; the area comprised of that part of Lemont Township, Cook County, and that part of Downers Grove Township, Du Page County, Ill., bounded by a line beginning at the intersection of Archer Avenue and the southern corporate limits of WillowSprings, Ill., and extending in a southwesterly direction along Archer Avenue to its junction with Chicago Joliet Road (Sag Lemont Highway), thence in a westerly direction over Chicago Joliet Road to its junction with Walker Road, thence directly north along an imaginary line to the southern shoreline of the Chicago Sanitary and Ship Canal, thence in a northeasterly direction along said shoreline to the corporate limits of Willow Springs, including points on the indicated portions of the highways specified; the area within Burr Ridge, Du Page County, bounded by a line beginning at the intersection of County Line Road and Frontage Road, thence southwesterly along Frontage Road to its intersection with Garfield Street, thence northerly along Garfield Street to its junction with 74th Street, thence westerly along an imaginary line to the junction of 74th Street and Grant Street, thence southerly along Grant Street to its junction with 75th Street, thence westerly along 75th Street to its junction with Brush

Hill Road, thence southerly along Brush Hill Road to its junction with Frontage Road, thence northeasterly along Frontage Road to its junction with County Line Road; and the area within the corporate limits of Hammond, Whiting, East Chicago, and Gary, Ind.

Sec. 3 St. Louis, Mo.-East St. Louis, Ill.

(a) The zone adjacent to and commercially a part of St. Louis, Mo.-East St. Louis, Ill, within which transportation by motor vehicle in interstate or foreign commerce, not under a common control, management or arrangement for a continuous carriage to or from a point beyond the zone is partially exempt from regulation under section 203(b)(8) of the Interstate Commerce Act (49 U.S.C. 303(b)(8)), includes and is comprised of all points as follows: (1) All points within the corporate limits of St. Louis, Mo.; (2) all points in St. Louis County, Mo., within a line drawn 0.5 mile south, west, and north of the following line: Beginning at the Jefferson Barracks Bridge across the Mississippi River and extending westerly along Missouri Highway 77 to its junction with U.S. Highway 61 Bypass, thence along U.S. Highway 61 Bypass to its junction with U.S. Highway 66, thence westerly along U.S. Highway 66 to its junction with Bowles Avenue, thence northerly along Bowles Avenue, actual or projected, to the Meramec River, thence easterly along the south bank of the Meramec River to a point directly south of the western boundary of Kirkwood, thence across the Meramec River to and along the western boundary of Kirkwood to Marshall Road, thence westerly along Marshall Road to its junction with Treecourt Avenue, thence northerly along Treecourt Avenue to its junction with Big Bend Road, thence easterly along Big Bend Road to the western boundry of Kirkwood, thence northerly along the western boundary of Kirkwood to its junction with Dougherty Ferry Road, thence westerly along Dougherty Ferry Road to its junction with Interstate Highway 244, thence northerly along InterstateHighway 244 to its junction with Manchester Road, thence easterly along Manchester Road to its junction with the northwest corner of Kirkwood, thence along the western and northern boundaries of Kirkwood to the western boundary of Huntleigh, Mo., thence along the western and northern boundaries of Huntleigh to its junction with Lindbergh Boulevard, thence northerly along Lindbergh Boulevard to its junction with Lackland Avenue, thence in a westerly direction along Lackland Avenue to its junction with the right-of-way of the proposed Circumferential Expressway (Interstate Highway 244), thence in a northerly direction along said right-of-way to its junction with the right-of-way of the Chicago, Rock Island and Pacific Railroad, thence in an easterly direction along said right-of-way to its junction with Dorsett Road, thence in an easterly direction along Dorsett Road to its junction with Lindbergh Boulevard, thence in a northerly direction along Lindbergh Boulevard to its junction with St. Charles Rock Road, thence westerly along St. Charles Rock Road to its junction with the Missouri River, thence northerly along the east shore of the Missouri River to its junction with the Norfolk and Western Railway Co. right-of-way, thence easterly along the southern boundary of the Norfolk and Western Railway Co. right-of-way to Lindbergh Boulevard, thence in an easterly direction along Lindbergh Boulevard to the western boundary of St. Ferdinand (Florissant), Mo., thence along the western, northern, and eastern boundaries of St. Ferdinand to junction Insterstate Highway 270, and thence along Interstate Highway 270 to the corporate limits of St. Louis (near Chain of Rocks Bridge); and (3) all points within the corporate limits of East St. Louis, Belleville, Granite City, Madison, Venice, Brooklyn, National City, Fairmont City, Washington Park, and Sauget, Ill.; that part of the village of Cahokia, Ill., bounded by Illinois Highway 3 on the east, First Avenue and Red House (Cargill) Road on the south and southwest, the east line of the right-of-way of the Alton and Southern Railroad on the west, and the corporate limits of Sauget, Ill., on the northwest and north; that part of Centerville, Ill., bounded by a line beginning at the junction of 26th Street and the corporate limit of East St. Louis, Ill., and extending northeasterly along 26th Street to its junction with BondAvenue, thence southeasterly along Bond Avenue to its junction with Owen Street, thence southwesterly along Owen Street to its junction with Church Road, thence southeasterly along Church Road to its junction with Illinois Avenue, thence southwesterly along Illinois Avenue to the southwesterly side of the right-of-way of the Illinois Central Railroad Co., thence along the southwesterly side of the right-of-way of the Illinois Central Railroad Co. to the corporate limits of East St. Louis, Ill, thence along the corporate limits of East St. Louis, Ill., to the point of beginning; and that area bounded by a line commencing at the intersection of the right-of-way of the Alton and Southern Railroad and the Madison, Ill., corporate limits near 19th Street, and extending east and south along said right-of-way to its intersection with the right-of-way of Illinois Terminal Railroad Co., thence southwesterly along the Illinois Terminal Railroad Co. right-of-way to its intersection with Illinois Highway 203, thence northwesterly along said highway to its intersection with the Madison, Ill., corporate boundary near McCambridge Avenue, thence northerly along the Madison, Ill., corporate boundary to the point of beginning.

(b) The exemption provided by section 203(b)(8) of the Interstate Commerce Act in respect of transportation by motor vehicle, in interstate or foreign commerce, between Belleville, Ill., on the one hand, and, on the other, any other point in the commercial zone, the limits of which are defined in paragraph (a) of this section, is hereby removed, and the said transportation is hereby subjected to all applicable provisions of the Interstate Commerce Act.

Sec. 4 Washington, DC.

The zone adjacent to and commercially a part of Washington, DC, within which transportation by motor vehicle, in interstate or foreign commerce, not under a common control, management, or arrangement for a continuous carriage to or from a point beyond the zone is partially exempt from regulation under section 203(b)(8) of the Interstate Commerce Act (49 U.S.A. 303(b)(8)) includes and it is comprised of all as follows:

Beginning at the intersection of Mac-Arthur Boulevard and Falls Road (Maryland Highway 189) and extending northeasterly along Falls Road to its junction with Scott Drive, thence west on Scott Drive to its junction with Viers Drive, thence west on Viers Drive to its junction with Glen Mill Road, thence northeast on Glen Mill Road to its junction with Maryland Highway 28, thence west on Maryland Highway 28 to its junction with Shady Grove Road, thence northeast on Shady Grove Road approximately 2.7 miles to Crabbs Branch, thence southeasterly along the course of Crabbs Branch to Rock Creek, thence southerly along the course of Rock Creek to Viers Mill Road (Maryland Highway 586), thence southeasterly along Viers Mill Road approximately 0.3 mile to its junction with Aspen Hill Road, thence northeasterly along Aspen Hill Road to its junction with Brookeville Road (Maryland Highway 97), thence southeasterly along Brookeville Road to its junction with Maryland Highway 183, thence northeasterly along Maryland Highway 183 to Colesville, Md., thence southeasterly along Beltsville Road to its junction with Powder Mill Road (Maryland Highway 212), thence easterly over Powder Mill Road to its junction with Montgomery Road, thence northeasterly along Montgomery Road, approximately 0.2 mile, to its junction with an unnumbered highway extending northeasterly to the north of Ammendale Normal Institute, thence along such unnumbered highway for a distance of about 2.2 miles to its junction somewhat north of Virginia Manor, Md., with an unnumbered highway extending easterly through Muirkirk, Md., thence along such unnumbered highway through Muirkirk to its junction, approximately 1.8 miles east of the Baltimore and Ohio Railroad, with an unnumbered highway, thence southwesterly along such unnumbered highway for a distance of about 0.5 mile to its junction with an unnumbered highway, thence southeasterly along such unnumbered highway through Springfield and Hillmeade, Md., to its junction with Defense Highway (U.S. Highway 50), thence southwesterly along Defense Highway approximately 0.8 mile to its junction with Enterprise Road (Maryland Highway 556), thence southerly over Enterprise Road to its junction with Central Avenue (Maryland Highway 214), thence westerly over Central Avenue about 0.5 mile to its crossing of Western Branch, thence southerly down the course of Western Branch to Maryland Highway 202, thence westerly approximately 0.3 mile along Maryland Highway 202 to its junction with White House Road, thence southwesterly along White House Road to its junction with Maryland Highway 221, thence southeasterly along Maryland Highway 221 to its junction with Maryland Highway 4, thence westerly along Maryland Highway 4 to the boundary of Andrews Air Force Base, thence south and west along said boundary to Brandywine Road (Maryland Highway 5), thence northwesterly along Maryland Highway 5 to its junction with Maryland Highway 337, thence southwesterly along Maryland Highway 337 to its junction with Maryland Highway 224, thence southerly along Maryland Highway 224 to a point opposite the mouth of Broad Creek, thence due west across the Potomac River to the west bank thereof, thence southerly along the west bank of the Potomac River to Gunston Cove, thence up the course of Gunston Cove to Pohick Creek, thence up the course of Pohick Creek to Virginia Highway 611, thence southwesterly along Virginia Highway 611 to the Fairfax-Prince William County line, thence along said county line to Virginia Highway 123, thence northerly along Virginia Highway 123 to its junction with Virginia Highway 636, thence northeasterly along Virginia Highway 636 to its junction with Virginia Highway 638, thence northwesterly along Virginia Highway 638 to its junction with Virginia Highway 620, thence westerly along Virginia Highway 620 to its junction with Virginia Highway 655, thence northeasterly along Virginia Highway 655 to its junction with U.S. Highway 211, thence westerly along U.S. Highway 211 to its junction with Virginia Highway 608, thence northerly along Virginia Highway 608 to its junction with U.S. Highway 50, thence westerly along U.S. Highway 50 to the Fairfax-Loudoun County line, thence northeasterly along said county line to its intersection with Dulles International Airport, thence along the southern, western, and northern boundaries of said airport to the Fairfax-Loudoun County line (at or near Dulles Airport Access Road), thence northeasterly along said county line to its junction with Virginia Highway 7, thence southeasterly along Virginia Highway 7 to its junction with Virginia Highway 193, thence along Virginia Highway 193 to its junction with Scott Run Creek, thence northerly down the course of Scott Run Creek to the Potomac River, thence due north across the river to MacArthur Boulevard to its junction with Maryland Highway 189, the point of beginning.

Sec. 5 Los Angeles, Calif., and contiguous and adjacent municipalities.

(a) The exemption provided by section 203(b)(8) of Part II of the Interstate Commerce Act to the extent it affects transportation by motor vehicle, in interstate or foreign commerce, performed wholly within Los Angeles, Calif., or wholly within any municipalitiy contiguous or adjacent to Los Angeles, Calif., or wholly a part of Los Angeles, as defined in paragraph (b) of this section, or wholly within the zone adjacent to and commercially a part of the San Pedro, Wilmington, and Terminal Island Districts of Los Angeles and Long Beach, as defined in paragraph (c) of this section, or wholly within the zone of any independent municipality contiguous or adjacent to Los Angeles, as determined under § 372.241, or otherwise, between any point in Los Angeles County, Calif., north of the line described below, on the one hand, and, on the other, any point in Los Angeles County, Calif., south thereof is hereby removed and the said transportation is hereby subjected to all the applicable provisions of the Interstate Commerce Act:

Beginning at the Pacific Ocean, and extending easterly along the northern and eastern corporate limits of Manhattan Beach to the northern corporate limits of Redondo Beach, thence along the northern and eastern corporate limits of Redondo Beach to the intersection of Inglewood Avenue and Redondo Beach Boulevard, thence along Redondo Beach Boulevard to the corporate limits of Torrance, thence along the northwestern and eastern corporate limits of Torrance to 182d Street, thence along 182d Street, Walnut, and Main Streets to Alondra Boulevard, thence along Alondra Boulevard to its intersection with Dwight Avenue, thence southerly along Dwight Avenue and an imaginary straight line extending southward to Greenleaf Boulevard, thence eastward along Greenleaf Boulevard to the northwestern corner of the corporate limits of Long Beach, thence along the northern and eastern corporate limits of Long Beach to Artesia Boulevard, thence east on Artesia Boulevard to the Los Angeles-Orange County line.

(b) For the purpose of administration and enforcement of Part II of the Interstate Commerce Act, the zone adjacent to and commercially a part of Los Angeles and contiguous municipalities (except the San Pedro, Wilmington, and Terminal Island districts of Los Angeles and Long Beach, Calif.), in which transportation by motor vehicle in interstate or foreign commerce, not under a common control, management, or arrangement for a continuous carriage or shipment to or from a point beyond the zone, will be partially exempt from regulation under section 203(b)(8) of the act, is hereby defined to includethe area of a line extending in a generally northwesterly and northerly direction from the intersection of Inglewood Avenue and Redondo Beach Boulevard along the eastern and northern corporate limits of Redondo Beach, Calif., to the eastern corporate limits of Manhattan Beach, Calif., thence along the eastern and northern corporate limits of Manhattan Beach to the Pacific Ocean, thence along the shoreline of the Pacific Ocean to the western corporate limits of Los Angeles at a point east of Topanga Canyon, and thence along the western corporate limits of Los Angeles to a point near Santa Susana Pass; south of a line extending in a generally easterly direction from a point near Santa Susana Pass along the northern corporate limits of Los Angeles to the eastern corporate limits of Burbank, Calif., thence along the eastern corporate limits of Burbank to the northern corporate limits of Glendale, Calif., and thence along the northern corporate limits of Glendale and Pasadena, Calif., to the northeastern corner of Pasadena; west of a line extending in a generally southerly and southwesterly direction from the northeastern corner of Pasadena along the eastern and a portion of the southern corporate limits of Pasadena to the eastern corporate limits of SanMarino, Calif., thence along the eastern corporate limits of San Marino and the eastern and a portion of the southern corporate limits of Alhambra, Calif., to the western corporate limits of Monterey Park, Calif., and the western corporate limits of Montebello, Calif., thence along the western corporate limits of Montebello, Calif., to the Rio Hondo, and the Los Angeles River to the northern corporate limits of Long Beach; and north of a line extending in a generally westerly direction from the Los Angeles River along the northern corporate limits of Long Beach and thence along Greenleaf Boulevard to its intersection with an imaginary straight line extending southward from Dwight Avenue, thence north on the imaginary straight line extending southward from Dwight Avenue, and thence northerly along Dwight Avenue to Alondra Boulevard, thence west along Alondra Boulevard, Main, Walnut, and 182d Streets to the eastern corporate limits of Torrance, thence along a portion of the eastern and the northwestern corporate limits of Torrance to Redondo Beach Boulevard, and thence along Redondo Beach Boulevard to Inglewood Avenue.

(c) For the purpose of administration and enforcement of Part II of the Interstate Commerce Act, the zone adjacent to and commercially a part of the San Pedro, Wilmington, and Terminal Island districts of Los Angeles and Long Beach in which transportation by motor vehicle in interstate or foreign commerce, not under a common control, management, or arrangement for a continuous carriage or shipment to or from a point beyond the zone, will be partially exempt from regulation under section 203(b)(8) of the act, is hereby defined to include the area east of a line extending in a generally northerly and northwesterly direction from the Pacific Ocean along the western corporate limits of Los Angeles to 258th Street, thence along 258th Street to the eastern corporate limits of Torrance, and thence along a portion of the eastern, and along the southern and western, corporate limits of Torrance to the northwestern corner of Torrance, south of a line extending in a generally easterly direction from the northwestern corner of Torrance along the northwestern and a portion of the eastern corporate limits of Torrance to 182d Street, thence along 182d, Walnut, Main, and Alondra Boulevard to its intersection with Dwight Avenue, thence southerly along Dwight Avenue and an imaginary straight line extending southward from Dwight Avenue to Greenleaf Boulevard and thence along Greenleaf Boulevard and the northern corporate limits of Long Beach to the northeastern corner of Long Beach; west of the eastern corporate limits of Long Beach; and north of the southern corporate limits of Long Beach and Los Angeles.

Sec. 6   Philadelphia, Pa.

The zone adjacent to and commercially a part of Philadelphia, Pa., within which transportation by motor vehicle, in interstate or foreign commerce, not under a common control, management, or arrangement for a continuous carriage or shipment to or from a point beyond such zone, is partially exempt from regulation under section 203(b)(8) of the Interstate Commerce Act (49 U.S.C. 303(b)(8)) includes and is comprised of all points as follows:

(a) The area within Pennsylvania included within the corporate limits of Philadelphia and Bensalem and Lower Southampton Townships in Bucks County; Conshohocken and West Conshohocken, Pa., and Lower Moreland, Abington, Cheltenham, Springfield, Whitemarsh, and Lower Merion Townships in Montgomery County; an area in Upper Dublin Township, Montgomery County, bounded by a line beginning at the intersection of Pennsylvania Avenue and Fort Washington Avenue and extending northeast along Fort Washington Avenue to its junction with Susquehanna Road, thence south-

east along Susquehanna Road to its junction with the right-of-way of the Pennsylvania Railroad Company, thence southwest along the right-of-way of the Pennsylvania Railroad Company to Pennsylvania Avenue, thence northwest along Pennsylvania Avenue to its junction with Fort Washington Avenue, the point of beginning; Haverford Township in Delaware County; and an area in Delaware County south and east of a line extending southward from the intersection of the western and northern boundaries of Upper Darby Township along Darby Creek to Bishop Avenue, thence south along Bishop Avenue to Baltimore Pike, thence west along Baltimore Pike to Pennsylvania Highway 320, thence south along Pennsylvania Highway 320 to the corporate limits of Chester, thence along the northern corporate limit of Chester in a westerly direction to the eastern boundary of Upper Chichester Township, thence south to the southern boundary of said township along the eastern boundary thereof, and thence west along the southern boundary of said township to the Delaware State line, and thence south along the Delaware State line to the Delaware River, and

(b) The area in New Jersey included in the corporate limits of Camden, Gloucester City, Woodlynne, Merchantville, and Palmyra Boroughs, and the area included in Pennsauken Township in Camden County.

Sec. 7   Cincinnati, Ohio.

The zone adjacent to and commercially a part of Cincinnati, Ohio, within which transportation by motor vehicle, in interstate or foreign commerce, not under a common control, management, or arrangement for a continuing carriage to or from a point beyond the zone is partially exempt from regulation under section 203(b)(8) of the Interstate Commerce Act (49 U.S.C. 203(b)(8)), includes and is comprised of all points as follows:

Addyston, Ohio.	Mariemont, Ohio.
Cheviot, Ohio.	North Bend, Ohio.
Cincinnati, Ohio.	Norwood, Ohio.
Cleves, Ohio.	St. Bernard, Ohio.
Elmwood Place, Ohio.	Covington, Ky.
	Newport, Ky.
Fairfax, Ohio.	Cold Spring, Ky.

That part of Ohio bounded by a line commencing at the intersection of the Colerain-Springfield Township line and corporate limits of Cincinnati, Ohio, and extending along said township line in a northerly direction to its intersection with the Butler-Hamilton County line, thence in an easterly direction along said county line to its intersection with Ohio Highway 4, thence in a northerly direction along Ohio Highway 4 to its intersection with Seward Road, thence in a northerly direction along said road to its intersection with Port Union Road, thence east along Port Union Road to the Fairfield

Township-Union Township line, thence northward along said township line to its intersection with the right-of-way of the Pennsylvania Railroad Co., thence southeasterly along the right-of-way of the Pennsylvania RailroadCo. to its intersection with Princeton-Glendale Road (Ohio Highway 747), thence southward along said road to its intersection with Mulhauser Road, thence in an easterly direction along said road to the terminus thereof west of the tracks of the Pennsylvania Railroad Co., thence continue in an easterly direction in a straight line to Allen Road, thence along the latter to the junction thereof with Cincinnati-Dayton Road, thence in a southerly direction along Cincinnati-Dayton Road, to the Butler, Hamilton County line, thence along said county line to the Warren-Hamilton County line in an easterly direction to the Symmes-Sycamore Township line, thence in a southerly direction along the Symmes-Sycamore Township line to its intersection with the Columbia Township line, thence in a westerly direction along Sycamore-Columbia Township line to Madeira Township, thence in a clockwise direction around the boundary of Madeira Township to the Sycamore-Columbia Township line, thence in a westerly direction along said township line to Silverton Township, thence in a southerly direction along said corporate limits to junction with Redbank Road, thence in a southerly direction over Redbank Road to the Cincinnati Corporate limits.

That part of Kenton County, Ky., lying on and north of a line commencing at the intersection of the Kenton-Boone County line and Dixie Highway (U.S. Highways 25 and 42), and extending over said highway to the corporate limits of Covington, Ky., including communities on the described line.

That part of Campbell County, Ky., lying on and north of a line commencing at the southern corporate limits of Newport, Ky., and extending along Licking Pike (Kentucky Highway 9) to junction with Johns Hill Road, thence along Johns Hill Road to junction with Alexandria Pike (U.S. Highway 27), thence northward along Alexandria Pike to junction with River Road (Kentucky Highway 445), thence over the latter to the Ohio River, including communities on the described line.

That part of Boone County, Ky., bounded by a line beginning at the Boone-Kenton County line west of Erlanger, Ky., and extending in a northwesterly direction along Donaldson Highway to its intersection with Zig-Zag Road, thence along Zig-Zag Road to its intersection with Kentucky Highway 18, thence along Kentucky Highway 18 to its intersection with Kentucky Highway 237, thence along Kentucky Highway 237 to its intersection with Kentucky Highway 20, and thence easterly along Kentucky Highway 20 to the Boone-Kenton County line.

That part of Boone and Kenton Counties, Ky., bounded by a line commencing at the intersection of the Boone-Kenton County line and U.S. Highway 42, and extending in a southwesterly direction along U.S. Highway 42 to its junction with Gunpowder Road, thence southerly along Gunpowder Road to its junction with Sunnybrook Road, thence easterly along Sunnybrook Road to its junction with Interstate Highway 75, thence in a straight line in a northeasterly direction to Richardson Road, thence in an easterly direction over Richardson Road to its junction with Kentucky State Route 1303, thence in a northerly direction over Kentucky State Route 1303 to the southern boundary of Edgewood, Kenton County, Ky.

Sec. 8 Kansas City, Mo.-Kansas City, Kans.

The zone adjacent to and commercially a part of Kansas City, Mo.-Kansas City, Kans., within which transportation by motor vehicle, in interstate or foreign commerce, not under a common control, management, or arrangement for a continuing carriage to or from a point beyond the zone is partially exempt from regulation under section 203(b)(8) of the Interstate Commerce Act (49 U.S.C. 303(b)(8)), includes and is comprised of all points as follows:

Beginning on the north side of the Missouri River at the western boundary line of Parkville, Mo., thence along the western and northern boundaries of Parkville to the Kansas City, Mo., corporate limits, thence along the western, northern, and eastern corporate limits of Kansas City, Mo., to its junction with U.S. Bypass 71 (near Liberty, Mo.), thence along U.S. Bypass 71 to Liberty, thence along the northern and eastern boundaries of Liberty to its junction with U.S. Bypass 71 south of Liberty, thence south along U.S. Bypass71 to its junction with the Independence, Mo., corporate limits, thence along the eastern Independence, Mo., corporate limits to its junction with Interstate Highway 70, thence along Interstate Highway 70 to its junction with the Blue Springs, Mo., corporate limits, thence along the western, northern, and eastern corporate limits of Blue Springs, Mo., to its junction with U.S. Highway 40, thence east along U.S. Highway 40 to its junction with Brizen-Dine Road, thence south along the southerly extension of Brizen-Dine Road to its junction with Missouri Highway AA, thence along Missouri Highway AA to its junction with the Blue Springs, Mo., corporate limits, thence along the southern and western corporate limits of Blue Springs, Mo., to its junction with U.S. Highway 40, thence west along U.S. Highway 40 to its junction with the Lee's Summit, Mo., corporate limits.

Thence along the eastern Lee's Summit corporate limits to the Jackson-Cass County line, thence west along Jackson-Cass County line to the eastern corporate limits of Belton, Mo., thence along the eastern, southern, and western corporate limits of Belton to the western boundary of Richards-Gebaur Air Force Base, thence along the western boundary of said Air Force Base to Missouri Highway 150, thence west along Missouri Highway 150 to the Kansas-Missouri State line, thence north along the Kansas-Missouri State line, to 110th Street, thence west along 110th Street to its junction with U.S. Highway 69, thence north along U.S. Highway 69 to its junction with 103d Street, thence west along 103d Street to its junction with Quivera Road (the corporate boundary of Lenexa, Kans.), thence along the eastern and southern boundaries of Lenexa to Black Bob Road, thence south along Black Bob Road to 119th Street, thence east along 119th Street to the corporate limits of Olathe, Kans., thence south and along the Olathe corporate limits to Schlagel Road, thence south along Schlagel Road to Olathe Morse Road, thence west along Olathe Morse Road to the northeast corner of Johnson County Airportr, thence south, west, and north along the boundaries of said airport to Pflumm Road, thence north along Pflumm Road to its junction with Olathe Martin City Road, thence west along Olathe Martin City Road to its junction with Murden Road, thence south along Murden Road to its junction with Olathe Morse Road (the corporate boundary of Olathe, Kans.), thence west and north along said corporate boundary to its intersection with U.S. Highway 56, thence southwest along U.S. Highway 56 to its junction with 159th Street.

Thence west along 159th Street to its junction with the Johnson County Industrial Airport, thence south, west, north and east along the boundaries of said airport to the point of beginning, on 159th Street, thence, east along 159th Street to its junction with U.S. Highway 56, thence northeast along U.S. Highway 56 to its junction with Parker Road, thence north along Parker Road to the northern boundary of Olathe, thence east and north along the northern corporate limits of Olathe to Pickering Road, thence north along Pickering Road to 107th Street (the corporate boundary of Lenexa, Kans.), thence along the western and northern boundaries of Lenexa to Pflumm Road, thence north along Pflumm Road to its junction with Kansas Highway 10, thence along Kansas Highway 10 to its junction with Kansas Highway 7, thence along an imaginary line due west across the Kansas River to the Wyandotte County-Leavenworth County line (142d Street) at Loring, Kans., thence westerly along County Route No. 82, a distance of three-fourths of a mile to the entrance of the facilities at Mid-Continent Underground Storage, Loring, thence from Loring in a northerly direction along Loring Lane and Lindwood Avenue to the southern boundary of Bonner Springs, Kans.

Thence along the southern, western, and northern boundaries of Bonner Springs to its intersection with Kansas Highway 7, thence southeast along Kansas Highway 7 to its junction with Kansas Highway 32, thence east on Kansas Highway 32 to the corporate boundary of Kansas City, Kans., thence north, west, and east along the corporate boundaries of Kansas City, Kans., to its junction with Cernech Road and Pomeroy Drive, thence northwesterly along Pomeroy Drive to its junction with 79th Street, thence along 79th Street to its junction with Walcotte Drive at Pomeroy, Kans., thence due west 1.3 miles to its junction with an unnamed road, thence north along such unnamed road to the entrance of Powell Port facility, thence due north to the southern bank of the Missouri River, thence east along the southern bank of Missouri River to a point directly across from the western boundary of Parkville, Mo., thence across the Missouri River to the point of beginning.

Sec. 9 Boston, Mass.

For the purpose of administration and enforcement of Part II of the Interstate Commerce Act, the zone adjacent to and commercially a part of Boston, Mass., and contiguous municipalities in which transportation by motor vehicle in interstate or foreign commerce, not under a common control, management, or arrangement for a continuous carriage or shipment to or from a point beyond the zone, will be partially exempt under section 203(b)(8) of the act from regulation, is hereby defined to include the following:

Boston, Mass.	Cambridge, Mass.
Winthrop, Mass.	Watertown, Mass.
Chelsea, Mass.	Brookline, Mass.
Revere, Mass.	Newton, Mass.
Everett, Mass.	Needham, Mass.
Malden, Mass.	Dedham, Mass.
Medford, Mass.	Milton, Mass.
Somerville, Mass.	Quincy, Mass.

Sec. 10 Davenport, Iowa; Rock Island and Moline, Ill.

For the purpose of administration and enforcement of Part II of the Interstate Commerce Act, the zones adjacent to and commercially a part of Davenport, Iowa, Rock Island and Moline, Ill., in which transportation by motor vehicle, in interstate or foreign commerce, not under a common control, management, or arrangement for a continuous carriage or shipment to or from a point beyond such municipalities or zones, will be partially exempt from regulation under section 203(b)(8) of the act (49 U.S.C. 303(b)(8) are hereby determined to be coextensive and to include and to be comprised of the following:

(a) All points within the corporate limits of the city of Davenport and the city of Bettendorf, and in Davenport Township, Iowa.

(b) All points north of Davenport Township within that portion of Sheridan Township, Iowa, bounded by a line as follows: Beginning at the points where U.S. Highway 61 crosses the Davenport-Sheridan Township line and extending northward along U.S. Highway 61 to the right-of-way of the Chicago, Milwaukee, St. Paul & Pacific Railroad Co., thence northwesterly along said right-of-way to its junction with the first east-west unnumbered highway, thence westerly approximately 0.25 mile to its junction with a north-south unnumbered highway, thence southerly along such unnumbered highway to the northeast corner of Mount Joy Airport, thence along the northern and western boundaries of said airport to the southwestern corner thereof, and thence south in a straight line to the northern boundary of Davenport Township.

(c)(1) That part of Iowa lying west of the municipal limits of Davenport south of Iowa Highway 22, north of the Mississippi River and east of the present western boundary of the Dewey Portland Cement Co., at Linwood, including points on such boundaries, and (2) that part of Iowa east of the municipal limits of Bettendorf, south of U.S. Highway 67, west of a private road running between U.S. Highway 67 and Riverside Power Plant of the Iowa-Illinois Gas & Electric Co., and north of the Mississippi River, including points on such boundaries.

(d) The municipalities of Carbon Cliff, Silvis, East Moline, Moline, Rock Island, and Milan, Ill., and that part of Illinois lying south or east of such municipalities, within a line as follows: Beginning at a point where Illinois Highway 84 crosses the southern municipal limits of Carbon Cliff and extending southerly along such highway to its junction with Colona Road, thence westerly along Colona Road to Bowlesburg Road, thence southerly on Bowlesburg Road to the southern boundary of Hampton Township, thence along the southern boundaries of Hampton and South Moline Townships to U.S. Highway 150, thence southerly along U.S. Highway 150 to the southern boundary of the Moline Airport, thence along the southern and western boundaries of the Moline Airport to Illinois Highway 92, and thence along Illinois Highway 92 to the corporate limits of Milan.

(e) All points in Illinois within one-half mile on each side of Rock Island County State Aid Route No. 9 extending southwesterly from the corporate limits of Milan for a distance of 1 mile, including points on such highway.

Sec. 11 Commercial zones of municipalities in New Jersey within 5 miles of New York, N.Y.

(a) The application of §372.241 is hereby extended to each municipality in New Jersey, any part of which is within 5 miles of the corporate limits of New York, N.Y.

(b) The exemption provided by section 203(b)(8) of the Interstate Commerce Act, of transportation by motor vehicle, in interstate or foreign commerce, performed wholly within any commercial zone, the limits of which are defined in paragraph (a) of this section, is hereby removed as to all such transportation except (1) transportation which is performed wholly between any two points in New Jersey, or (2) transportation which is performed wholly between points in New Jersey named in §372.201, on the one hand, and, on the other, points in New York named in §372.201.

Sec. 12 Commercial zones of municipalities in Westchester and Nassau Counties, N.Y.

(a) The application of §372.241 is hereby extended to each municipality in Westchester or Nassau Counties, N.Y.

(b) The exemption provided by section 203(b)(8) of the Interstate Commerce Act, of transportation by motor vehicle, in interstate or foreign commerce, performed wholly within any commercial zone, the limits of which are defined in paragraph (a) of this section, is hereby removed as to all such transportation except (1) transportation which is performed wholly between points in New York neither of which is New York City, NY, or (2) transportation which is performed wholly between points in Westchester or Nassau County named in §372.201, on the one hand, and, on the other, New York City, N.Y., or points in New Jersey named in §372.201.

Sec. 13 Tucson, Ariz.

That zone adjacent to and commercially a part of Tucson, Ariz., within which transportation by motor vehicle, in interstate or foreign commerce, not under a common control, management, or arrangement for a continuous carriage or shipment to or from a point beyond the zone, is partially exempt, under section 203(b)(8) of the Interstate Commerce Act (49 U.S.C. 303(b)(8)) from regulation, includes, and is comprised of, all points as follows:

(a) The municipality of Tucson, Ariz., itself.

(b) All points within a line drawn 5 miles beyond the corporate limits of Tucson, Ariz.

(c) All points in that area south of the line described in paragraph (b) of this section, bounded by a line as follows: Beginning at the point where the line described in paragraph (b) of this section, intersects Wilmot Road, thence south along Wilmot Road to junction Nogales Old Vail Connection, thence west along Nogales Old Vail Connection, actual or extended, to the Santa Cruz River, thence north along the east bank of the Santa Cruz River to its joinder with the line described in paragraph (b) of this section.

(d) All of any municipality any part of which is within the limits of the combined areas defined in paragraphs (b) and (c) of this section.

(e) All of any municipality wholly surrounded, or so surrounded except for a water boundary, by the city of Tucson or by any municipality included under the terms of paragraph (d) of this section.

Sec. 14 Albuquerque, N. Mex.

The zone adjacent to and commercially a part of Albuquerque, N. Mex., within which transportation by motor vehicle, in interstate or foreign commerce, not under a common control, management, or arrangement for a continuous carriage or shipment to or from a point beyond the zone, is partially exempt, under section 203(b)(8) of the Interstate Commerce Act (49 U.S.C. 303(b)(8)), from regulation, includes, and is comprised of, all points as follows:

(a) The municipality of Albuquerque, N. Mex., itself.

(b) All points within a line drawn 5 miles beyond the corporate limits of Albuquerque, N. Mex.

(c) All points in that area north of the line described in paragraph (b) of this section, bounded by a line as follows: Beginning at the intersection of the line described in paragraph (b) of this section and New Mexico Highway 528, extending in a northeasterly direction along New Mexico Highway 528 to its intersection with New Mexico Highway 44, thence easterly along New Mexico Highway 44 to its intersection with New Mexico Highway 422, thence southerly along New Mexico Highway 422 to its intersection with the line described in paragraph (b) of this section.

(d) All of any municipality any part of which is within the limits of the combined areas defined in paragraphs (b) and (c) of this section;

(e) All of any municipality wholly surrounded, or so surrounded except for a water boundary, by the city of Albuquerque, N. Mex., or by any municipality included under the terms of paragraph (b) of this section.

Sec. 18 Ravenswood, W. Va.

That zone adjacent to and commercially a part of Ravenswood, W. Va., within which transportation by motor vehicle, in interstate or foreign commerce, not under common control, management, or arrangement for a continuous carriage or shipment to or from a point beyond the zone, is partially exempt, under section 203(b)(8) of the Interstate Commerce Act (49 U.S.C. 303(b)(8)),

from regulation, includes, and is comprised of, all points as follows:

(a) The municipality of Ravenswood, W. Va., itself.

(b) All points within a line drawn 3 miles beyond the corporate limits of Ravenswood, W. Va., and

(c) All points in West Virginia in that area south and southwest of those described in paragraph (b) of this section, bounded by a line as follows: Beginning at the point where the Ohio River meets the line described in paragraph (b) of this section southwest of Ravenswood, thence southerly along the east bank of the Ohio River to the point where the mouth of the Lick Run River empties into the Ohio River; thence in a northeasterly direction along the northern bank of the Lick Run River to the point where it crosses West Virginia Highway 2 south of Ripley Landing, W. Va.; thence in a northerly direction along West Virginia Highway 2 to its intersection with the line described in paragraph (b) of this section west of Pleasant View, W. Va.

Sec. 19 Lake Charles, La.

That zone adjacent to and commercially a part of Lake Charles, La., within which transportation by motor vehicle, in interstate or foreign commerce, not under common control, management, or arrangement for a continuous carriage or shipment to or from a point beyond the zone, is partially exempt, under section 203(b)(8) of the Interstate Commerce Act (49 U.S.C. 303(b)(8)), from regulation, includes, and is comprised of, all points as follows:

(a) The municipality of Lake Charles La., itself;

(b) All points within a line drawn 4 miles beyond the corporate limits of Lake Charles, La.;

(c) All points in that area south and west of the line described in paragraph (b) of this section, bounded by a line, as follows: beginning at the point where the line described in paragraph (b) of this section intersects Louisiana Highway 385; thence south along Louisiana Highway 385 to its intersection with the Calcasieu-Cameron Parish line; thence west along the Calcasieu-Cameron Parish line to its intersection with Louisiana Highway 27; thence northerly along Louisiana Highway 27 to a point thereon 2 miles south of U.S. Highway 90; thence east along a line parallel to U.S. Highway 90 to Louisiana Highway 108; thence north along Louisiana Highway 108 to junction U.S. Highway 90; thence east along U.S. Highway 90 to the intersection thereof with the line described in paragraph (b) of this section;

(d) All of the municipality any part of which is within the limits of the combined areas in paragraphs (b) and (c) of this section; and

(e) All of any municipality wholly surrounded, or so surrounded except for a water boundary, by the City of Lake Charles or by any municipality included under the terms of paragraph (d) of this section.

Sec. 20 Syracuse, N.Y.

The zone adjacent to and commercially a part of Syracuse, N.Y., within which transportation by motor vehicle, in interstate or foreign commerce, not under a common control, management, or arrangement for a continuing carriage to or from a point beyond the zone is partially exempt from regulation under section 203(b)(8) of the Interstate Commerce Act (49 U.S.C. 303(b)(8)), includes and is comprised of all points as follows:

(a) The municipality of Syracuse, NY., itself;

(b) All other municipalities and unincorporated areas within 5 miles of the corporate limits of Syracuse, N.Y., and all of any other municipality any part of which lies within 5 miles of such corporate limits;

(c) Those points in the town of Geddes, Onondaga County, N.Y., which are not within 5 miles of the corporate limits of Syracuse, N.Y.;

(d) Those points in the towns of Van Buren and Lysander, Onondaga County, N.Y., not within 5 miles of the corporate limits of Syracuse, N.Y., and within an area bounded by a line beginning at the intersection of Van Buren Road with the line described in (b) above, thence northwesterly along Van Buren Road to its intersection with the cleared right-of-way of Niagara Mohawk Power Company, thence northwesterly and north along said right-of-way to its intersection between Church Road and Emerick Road, with the cleared right-of-way of New York State Power Authority, thence easterly along said clearedright-of-way to its intersection with the Seneca River, thence south along the Seneca River to its intersection, near Gaskin Road, with the cleared right-of-way of Niagara Mohawk Power Company, thence southwesterly along said cleared right-of-way to its intersection with the eastern limits of the Village of Baldwinsville, thence south along such Village limits to their intersection with a line of railroad presently operated by the Erie-Lackawanna Railroad Company, thence southeasterly along said line of railroad to its intersection with the Van-Buren Lysander Town line, thence southeasterly along the Van-Buren Lysander Town line to its intersection with the Van-Buren Geddes Town line, thence southeasterly along the Van-Buren Geddes Town line to the line described in (b) above.

Sec. 21 Baltimore, Md.

The zone adjacent to and commercially a part of Baltimore, Md., within which transportation by motor vehicle, in interstate or foreign commerce, not under a common control, management, or arrangement for a continuous carriage to or from a point beyond the zone is partially exempt from regulation under section 203(b)(8) of the Interstate Commerce Act (49 U.S.C. 303(b)(8)) includes and it is comprised of all as follows:

(a) The municipality of Baltimore itself;

(b) All points within a line drawn 5 miles beyond the boundaries of Baltimore;

(c) All points in that area east of the line described in paragraph (b) of this section bounded by a line as follows: Beginning at the point where the line described in paragraph (b) of this section crosses Dark Head Creek and extending in a southeasterly direction along the center of Dark Head Creek and beyond to a point off Wilson Point, thence in a northeasterly direction to and along the center of Frog Mortar Creek to Stevens Road, thence northerly along Stevens Road to Eastern Avenue, thence easterly along Eastern Avenue to Bengies Road, thence northwesterly along Bengies Road, to the right-of-way of the Penn Central Transportation Co., thence westerly along such right-of-way to the junction thereof with the line described in paragraph (b) of this section;

(d) All points in that area south of the line described in paragraph (b) of this section, bounded on the west by the right-of-way of the line of the Penn Central Transportation Co., extending between Stony Run and Severn, Md., and on the south by that part of Maryland Highway 176, extending easterly from the said railroad to its junction with the line described in paragraph (b) of this section;

(e) All points in that area southwest of the line described in paragraph (b) of this section, bounded by a line as follows: Beginning at the point where the line described in paragraph (b) of this section crosses the Baltimore-Washington Expressway and extending in a southwesterly direction along the Baltimore-Washington Expressway to its intersection with Maryland Highway 176, thence westerly along Maryland Highway 176 to its intersection with the Howard-Anne Arundel County line, thence southwesterly along said county line to its intersection with Maryland Highway 32, thence northwesterly along Maryland Highway 32 to its intersection with the Little Patuxent River, thence northerly along the Little Patuxent River to the intersection of its north fork and its east fork located approximately 1 mile north of the intersection of Maryland Highway 32 and Berger Road, thenceeasterly along the east fork of the Little Patuxent River to its intersection with Broken Land Parkway, thence southerly along Broken Land Parkway to its intersection with Snowden River Parkway, thence easterly along Snowden

River Parkway, to its intersection with relocated Maryland Highway 175, thence southeasterly along relocated Maryland Highway 175, to its intersection with Lark Brown Road, thence northeasterly along Lark Brown Road to its intersection with Maryland Highway 175, thence southerly along Maryland Highway 175 to its intersection with Interstate Highway 95, thence northeasterly along Interstate Highway 95 to its intersection with the line described in paragraph (b) of this section;

(f) All points in that area north of the line described in paragraph (b) of this section bounded by a line as follows: Beginning at the junction of the line described in paragraph (b) of this section and the Baltimore-Harrisburg Expressway (Interstate Highway 83), thence northerly along Interstate Highway 83 to its junction with Shawan Road, thence easterly along Shawan Road to its junction with York Road (Maryland Highway 45) and continuing to a point 1,500 feet east of Maryland Highway 45, thence southerly along a line 1,500 feet east of the parallel to Maryland Highway 45 to its junction with the line described in paragraph (b) of this section;

(g) All points in that area west of the line described in paragraph (b) of this section bounded by a line as follows: Beginning at the point where the line described in paragraph (b) of this section intersects U.S. Highway 40 west of Baltimore, Md., and extending in a westerly direction along U.S. Highway 40 to its intersection with St. John's Lane, thence southerly along St. John's Lane to its intersection with Maryland Highway 144, thence easterly along Maryland Highway 144 to its intersection with the line in paragraph (b) of this section;

(h) All of any municipality any part of which is within the limits of the combined areas defined in paragraphs (b), (c), (d), (e), (f), and (g) of this section;

(i) All of any municipality wholly surrounded, or surrounded except for a water boundary, by the city of Baltimore or by any municipality included under the terms of (h) above.

Sec. 22 Cleveland, Ohio

The zone adjacent to and commercially a part of Cleveland, Ohio, within which transportation by motor vehicle, in interstate or foreign commerce, not under a common control, management, or arrangement for a continuous carriage to or from a point beyond the zone is partially exempt from regulation under section 203(b)(8) of the Interstate Commerce Act (49 U.S.C. 303(b)(8)) includes and it is comprised of all as follows:

(a) All points in Cuyahoga County, Ohio, and

(b) All points in Wickliffe, Willoughby Hills, Waite Hill, Willoughby, Willowick, Eastlake, Lakeline, Timberlake, and Mentor, Lake County, Ohio.

Sec. 23 Detroit, Mich.

For the purpose of administration and enforcement of Part II of the Interstate Commerce Act, the zone adjacent to and commercially a part of Detroit, Mich., in which transportation by motor vehicle in interstate or foreign commerce, not under a common control, management, or arrangement for a continuous carriage or shipment to or from a point beyond the zone, will be partially exempt under section 203(b)(8) of the act (49 U.S.C. 303(b)(8)) from regulation, is hereby determined to include, and to be comprised of, all that area within a line as follows:

Beginning at a point on Lake St. Clair opposite the intersection of Fifteen Mile Road and Michigan Highway 29 and extending south and southwest along the shore of Lake St. Clair, to the Detroit River, thence along such River (east of Belle Isle) and Trenton Channel to a point opposite Sibley Road, thence west to and along Sibley Road to Waltz Road, thence north along Waltz Road to Wick Road, thence west along Wick Road to Cogswell Road, thence north along Cogswell Road to Van Born Road, thence east along Van Born Road to Newburgh Road, thence north along Newburgh Road to its junction with Halsted Road, thence north along Halsted Road to West Maple Road, thence east along West Maple Road to Telegraph Road, thence north along Telegraph Road to Sixteen Mile Road, thence east along Sixteen Mile Road to Utica Road, thence southeasterly along Utica Road to Fifteen Mile Road (also called East Maple Road), thence along Fifteen Mile Road and across Michigan Highway 29 to Lake St. Clair, the point of beginning.

Sec. 24 Seattle, Wash.

The zone adjacent to and commercially a part of Seattle, Wash., within which transportation by motor vehicle, in interstate or foreign commerce, not under common control, management, or arrangement for continuous carriage or shipments to or from a point beyond such zone, is partially exempt from regulation under section 203(b)(8) of the Interstate Commerce Act (49 U.S.C. 303(b)(8)) includes and is comprised of all points as follows:

(a) The municipality of Seattle itself.

(b) All points within a line drawn 5 miles beyond the municipal limits of Seattle, except points on Bainbridge Island, Vashon Island, and Blake Island.

(c) All points more than 5 miles beyond the municipal limits of Seattle (1) within a line as follows: Beginning at that point south of Seattle where the eastern shore of Puget

Sound intersects the line described in paragraph (b) of this section, thence southerly along the eastern shore of Puget Sound to Southwest 192d Street, thence easterly along Southwest 192d Street to the point where it again intersects the line described in paragraph (b) of this section; and (2) within a line as follows: Beginning at the junction of the southern corporate limits of Kent, Wash., and Washington Highway 181, and extending south along Washington Highway 181 to the northern corporate limits of Auburn, Wash., thence along the western, southern, and eastern corporate limits of Auburn to the junction of the northern corporate limits of Auburn and Washington Highway 167, thence northerly along Washington Highway 167 to its junction with the southern corporate limits of Kent, Wash., including all points on the highways named.

(d) All points more than 5 miles beyond the municipal limits of Seattle within a line as follows: Beginning at the junction of the northern corporate limits of Lynwood, Wash., and U.S. Highway 99, thence north along U.S. Highway 99 to its junction with Washington Highway 525, thence along Washington Highway 525 to its junction with West Casino Road, thence east along West Casino Road to the western boundary of the Everett facilities of the Boeing Co. at or near 4th Avenue West, thence along the western, northern and eastern boundaries of the facilities of the Boeing Co. to West Casino Road, thence east along West Casino Road to its junction with U.S. Highway 99, thence south along U.S. Highway 99 to 112th Street, thence easterly along 112th Street to its junction with Interstate Highway 5, thence southerly along Interstate Highway 5 to its intersection with the present zone limits, including all points on the named routes.

(e) All of any municipality any part of which is within the limits set forth in (b) above.

(f) All of any municipality wholly surrounded, or so surrounded except for a water boundary, by the city of Seattle or by any municipality included under the terms of (b) above.

Sec. 25 Albany, N.Y.

For the purpose of administration and enforcement of Part II of the Interstate Commerce Act, the zone adjacent to and commercially a part of Albany, N.Y., in which transportation by motor vehicle in interstate or foreign commerce, not under a common control, management, or arrangement for a continuous carriage or shipment to or from a point beyond the zone, will be partially exempt under section 203(b)(8) of the act (49 U.S.C. 303(b)(8)) from regulations, is hereby determined to include, and to be comprised of, the following:

(a) The municipality of Albany itself,

(b) All points within a line drawn 5 miles beyond the municipal limits of Albany,

(c) All points in that area more than 5 miles beyond the municipal limits of Albany bounded by a line as follows: Beginning at that point on Swatling Road (in the Town of Colonie) where it crosses the line described in (b) above and extending northerly along such road to the municipal limits of Cohoes, thence along the western and northern boundary of Cohoes to the Mohawk River, thence along such river to the northern boundary of the Town of Waterford, thence along the northern and eastern boundaries of the Town of Waterford to the northern boundary of the City of Troy (all of which city is included under the next following provision),

(d) All of any municipality any part of which is within the limits of the combined areas defined in (b) and (c) above, and

(e) All of any municipality wholly surrounded, or so surrounded except for a water boundary, by the municipality of Albany or by any other municipality included under the terms of (d) above.

Sec. 26 Minneapolis-St. Paul, Minn.

The zone adjacent to and commercially a part of Minneapolis-St. Paul, Minn, within which transportation by motor vehicle, in interstate or foreign commerce, not under a common control, management, or arrangement for a continuous carriage to or from a point beyond the zone is partially exempt from regulation under section 203(b)(8) of the Interstate Commerce Act (49 U.S.C. 303(b)(8)) includes and it is comprised of all as follows:

Beginning at the intersection of Minnesota Highway 36 and the Minnesota River and extending along the Minnesota River to the southwest corner of the city of Bloomington, thence north along the western boundaries of the city of Bloomington and the village of Edina to the southern boundary of the city of Hopkins, thence along the southern, western, and northern boundaries of the city of Hopkins to the western boundary of the city of St. Louis Park, thence north along the western boundaries of the city of St. Louis Park and the village of Golden Valley to the southeast corner of the village of Plymouth, thence west along the southern boundaries of Plymouth to Interstate Highway 494, thence north along Interstate Highway 494 to Minnesota Highway 55, thence southeast along Minnesota Highway 55 to the western boundary of the village of Golden Valley, thence north along the western boundaries of the villages of Golden Valley and New Hope to the northwestern corner of the village of New Hope, thence east along the northern boundary of the village of New Hope and the city of Crystal to the western boundary of the village of Brooklyn Center, thence north along the western boundary of the village of

Brooklyn Center to its northern boundary, thence east along such northernboundary to the Hennepin County-Anoka County line, thence north along such county line to the northwestern corner of the village of Spring Lake Park in Anoka County, thence east along the northern boundary of the village of Spring Lake Park to the northwest corner of Mounds View Township in Ramsey County, thence east and south along the northern and eastern boundaries of Mounds View Township to the northwestern corner of the village of Little Canada, thence east and south along the northern and eastern boundaries of Little Canada to the northwest corner of the village of Maplewood, thence east and south along the northern and eastern boundaries of the village of Maplewood to the northeastern corner of the village of North St. Paul, thence south along the eastern boundary of the village of North St. Paul to the southeast corner of such village, thence south along the eastern boundary of the village of Maplewood to the northeastern corner of the village of Newport, thence south and west along the eastern and southern boundaries of the village of Newport to U.S. Highway 61, thence southeasterly along U.S. Highway 61, to the eastern boundary of the village of St. Paul Park, thence along the eastern, southern, and western boundaries of the village of St. Paul Park to a point on the Mississippi River opposite the southeast corner of the original village of Inver Grove, thence westerly across the river and along the southern and western boundaries of the original village of Inver Grove to the northwestcorner of such village, thence due north to the southern boundary of South St. Paul, thence north and west along the western and southern boundaries of South St. Paul to the southeastern corner of West St. Paul, thence west along the southern boundary of West St. Paul to County Highway 63, thence south along County Highway 63 to its junction with County Highway 63A, thence west along County Highway 63A to its junction with Minnesota Highway 49, thence north along Minnesota Highway 49 to its junction with County Highway 28, thence west along County Highway 28 to its junction with Minnesota Highway 13, thence southwest along Minnesota Highway 13 to its junction with Minnesota Highway 36, thence north and northwest along Minnesota Highway 36 to the Minnesota River, the point of beginning.

Sec. 27 New Orleans, La.

The zone adjacent to and commercially a part of New Orleans, La., within which transportation by motor vehicle, in interstate or foreign commerce, not under common control, management, or arrangement for a continuous carriage or shipment to or from a point beyond the zone is partially exempt from regulation under section 203(b)(8) of the Interstate Commerce Act (49 U.S.C. 303(b)(8)), includes and is comprised of all points in the area bounded as follows:

Commencing at a point on the shore of Lake Pontchartrain where it is crossed by the Jefferson Parish-Orleans Parish line; thence easterly along the shore of Lake Pontchartrain to the Rigolets; thence through the Rigolets in an easterly direction to Lake Borgne; thence southwesterly along the shore of Lake Borgne to the Bayou Bienvenue; thence in a general westerly direction along the Bayou Bienvenue (which also constitutes the Orleans Parish-St. Bernard Parish line) to Paris Road; thence in a southerly direction along Paris Road to the Back Protection Levee; thence in a southeasterly direction along the Back Protection Levee (across Lake Borgne Canal) to a point 1 mile north of Louisiana Highway 46; thence in an easterly direction 1 mile north of Louisiana Highway 46 to longitude 89°50′ W.; thence south along longitude line 89°50′ W. (crossing Louisiana Highway 46 approximately three-eighths of a mile east of Toca) to Forty Arpent Canal; thence westerly, northwesterly, and southerly along Forty Arpent Canal to Scarsdale Canal; thence northwesterly along Scarsdale Canal and beyond it in the same direction to the middle of the Mississippi River; thence southerly along the middle of the Mississippi River to the Augusta Canal; thence in a westerly direction along the Augusta Canal to the Gulf Intracoastal Waterway; thence in a northerly direction along the middle of the Gulf Intracoastal Waterway (Harvey Canal) to the point where Lapalco Boulevard runs perpendicular to the Gulf Intracoastal Waterway (Harvey Canal); thence in a westerly direction along Lapalco Boulevard to its junction with Barataria Boulevard; thence north on Barartaria Boulevard to a point approximately 2 miles south of the MississippiRiver where a high tension transmission line crosses Barataria Boulevard; thence in a westerly direction following such transmission line to the intersection thereof with U.S. Highway 90; thence westerly along U.S. Highway 90 to the Jefferson Parish-St. Charles Parish line; thence north along such parish line to the middle of the Mississippi River; thence westerly along the middle of the Mississippi River to a point south of Almedia Road; thence north to Almedia Road; thence in a northerly direction along Almedia Road to its junction with Highway 61; thence north to the shore of Lake Pontchartrain; thence along the shore of Lake Pontchartrain in an easterly direction to the Jefferson Parish-Orleans Parish line, the point of beginning.

Sec. 28 Pittsburgh, Pa.

For the purpose of administration and enforcement of Part II of the Interstate Commerce Act, the zone adjacent to and commercially a part of Pittsburgh, Pa., in which transportation by motor vehicle in interstate or foreign commerce, not under a common control, management, or arrangement for a continuous carriage or shipment to or from a point beyond the zone, will be partially exempt under section 203(b)(8) of the act (49 U.S.C. 303(b)(8)) from regulation, is hereby determined to include, and to be comprised of, the following:

(a) All points in Allegheny County, Pa., except Forward, Elizabeth, South Versailles, Marshall (including the Borough of Bradford Woods), Pine Richland, West Deer and Fawn Townships and that part of Frazer Township north of a line made by extending easterly in a straight line the southern boundary of West Deer Township.

(b) Borough of Trafford situated in both Allegheny and Westmoreland Counties;

(c) Borough of Ambridge and Harmony Township located in Beaver County; and

(d) The City of New Kensington and Borough of Arnold in Westmoreland County.

Sec. 29 Portland, Oreg.

For the purpose of administration and enforcement of Part II of the Interstate Commerce Act, the zone adjacent to and commercially a part of Portland, Oreg., in which transportation by motor vehicle in interstate or foreign commerce, not under a common control, management, or arrangement for a continuous carriage or shipment to or from a point beyond the zone, will be partially exempt under section 203(b)(8) of the act (49 U.S.C. 303(b)(8)) from regulation, is hereby determined to include, and to be comprised of, the following:

(a) The municipality itself.

(b) All points in Oregon within a line drawn 5 miles beyond the corporate limits of Portland.

(c) All of any municipality any part of which is within the line described in (b) above.

(d) All of any municipality wholly surrounded, or so surrounded except for a water boundary, by the city of Portland or by any municipality included under the terms of (c) above.

Sec. 30 Vancouver, Wash.

For the purpose of administration and enforcement of Part II of the Interstate Commerce Act, the zone adjacent to and commercially a part of Vancouver, Wash., in which transportation by motor vehicle in interstate or foreign commerce, not under a common control, management, or arrangement for a continuous carriage or shipment to or from a point beyond the zone, will be par-tially exempt under section 203(b)(8) of the act (49 U.S.C. 303(b)(8)) from regulation, is hereby determined to include, and to be comprised of, the following:

(a) The municipality itself.

(b) All points in Washington within a line drawn 4 miles beyond the corporate limits of Vancouver.

(c) All of any municipality any part of which is within the line described in (b) above.

(d) All of any municipality wholly surrounded, or so surrounded except for a water boundary, by the City of Vancouver or by any municipality included under the terms of (c) above.

Sec. 31 Charleston, S.C.

The zone adjacent to and commercially a part of Charleston, S.C., within which transportation by motor vehicle, in interstate or foreign commerce, not under a common control, management, or arrangement for a continuous carriage or shipment to or from a point beyond the zone is partially exempt, under section 203(b)(8) of the Interstate Commerce Act (49 U.S.C. 303(b)(8)), from regulation, includes and is comprised of, all points and places as follows:

(a) The municipality of Charleston itself.

(b) All points within a line drawn 4 miles beyond the boundaries of Charleston.

(c) All points in that area north of the line described in paragraph (b) of this section, bounded by a line as follows: Beginning at the point where the line described in paragraph (b) of this section crosses Cooper River and extending in a northerly direction along the center of Cooper River to Goose Creek; thence north and west along the center of Goose Creek to the dam of the reservoir of the Charleston waterworks; thence northwesterly along the west bank of the Charleston waterworks reservoir for approximately one mile to an unnamed creek; thence westerly along the center of this unnamed creek for approximately one mile to U.S. Highway 52; thence northerly along U.S. Highway 52 to junction South Carolina Highway S-10-75; thence westerly along South Carolina Highway S-10-75 approximately one and one half miles to a point one quarter mile west of the track of the Southern Railway Company; thence southeasterly along a line one quarter of a mile west of, and parallel to, the track of the Southern Railway Company to the junction thereof with the line described in paragraph (b) of this section.

(d) All of any municipality any part of which is within the limits of the combined areas defined in paragraphs (1) and (c) of this section.

(e) All of any municipality wholly surrounded, or so surrounded except for a water boundary, by the city of Charleston or by any municipality included under the terms of paragraph (d) of this section.

Sec. 32 Charleston, W. Va.

That zone adjacent to and commercially a part of Charleston, W. Va., within which transportation by motor vehicle, in interstate or foreign commerce, not under a common control, management, or arrangement for a continuous carriage or shipment to or from a point beyond the zone, is partially exempt, under section 203(b)(8) of the Interstate Commerce Act (49 U.S.C. 303(b)(8)), from regulation, includes, and is comprised of, all points and places as follows:

(a) The municipality of Charleston, W. Va., itself.

(b) All points within a line drawn 4 miles beyond the corporate limits of Charleston, W. Va.

(c) All points in that area northwest of those described in (b) above, bounded by a line as follows: Beginning at a point on the line described in (b) above, one-half mile south of U.S. Highway 60 west of Charleston, thence westerly along a line one-half mile south of the junction of U.S. Highway 60 with West Virginia Highway 17 near 2¾ Mile Creek, thence westerly along a line one-half mile south of and parallel to West Virginia Highway 17 to the Coal River, thence north along the center of the Coal River to West Virginia Highway 17, thence northerly along West Virginia Highway 17 to Scary Creek, near Scary, W. Va., thence east along Scary Creek to the center of the Kanawha River, thence northerly along the center of the Kanawha River to a point opposite the mouth of Blake Creek (between Nitro and Poca, W. Va.), thence easterly along a straight line drawn through the junction of U.S. Highway 35 and West Virginia Highway 25 to a point one-half mile beyond said junction, thence southerly along a line one-half mile northeast of and parallel to West Virginia Highway 25 to the junction of the line described in (b) above.

(d) All points in that area southeast of those described in (b) above, bounded by a line as follows: Beginning at a point on the line described in (b) above one-half mile south of the Kanawha River, thence easterly along a line one-half mile south of, and parallel to, the Kanawha River to junction with a straight line intersecting the highway bridge at Chelyan, W. Va., thence northerly along said straight line across the Kanawha River to a point one-half mile north of the Kanawha River, thence westerly along a line one-half mile north of and parallel to the Kanawha River to the junction of the line described in (b) above.

(e) All of any municipality any part of which is within the limits of the combined areas defined in (b), (c), and (d) above.

Sec. 33 Memphis, Tenn.

That zone adjacent to and commercially a part of Memphis, Tenn., within which transportation by motor vehicle, in interstate or foreign commerce, not under a common control management, or arrangement for a continuous carriage or shipment to or from a point beyond the zone, is partially exempt, under section 203(b)(8) of the Interstate Commerce Act (49 U.S.C. 303(b)(8)) from regulation, includes, and is comprised of, all points as follows:

(a) The municipality of Memphis, Tenn., itself.

(b) All points within a line drawn 5 miles beyond the corporate limits of Memphis, Tenn.

(c) All points in that part of Shelby County, Tenn., north of the line described in paragraph (b) of this section, bounded by a line as follows: Beginning at the intersection of the line described in paragraph (b) of this section and U.S. Highway 51 north of Memphis, thence northeasterly along U.S. Highway 51 for approximately 3 miles to its intersection with Lucy Road, thence easterly along Lucy Road for approximately 1.4 miles to its intersection with Chase Road, thence northerly along Chase Road for approximately 0.6 mile to its intersection with Lucy Road thence easterly along Lucy Road for approximately 0.8 mile to its intersection with Main Road, thence southereasterly along Main Road approximately 0.3 mile to its intersection with Amherst Road, thence southerly and easterly along Amherst Road for approximately 0.8 mile to its intersection with Raleigh-Millington Road, thence southerly along Raleigh-Millington Road for approximately 2 miles to its intersection with the line described in paragraph (b) of this section north of Memphis;

(d) All of any municipality any part of which is within the limits of the combined areas described in paragraphs (b) and (c) of this section.

Sec. 34 Houston, Tex.

The zone adjacent to, and commercially a part of Houston, Tex., and contiguous municipalities in which transportation by motor vehicle, in interstate or foreign commerce, not under common control, management, or arrangement for a continuous carriage or shipment to or from a point beyond the zone, will be partially exempt under section 203(b)(8) of the act from regulation, is hereby defined to include the area which would result by application of the general formula promulgated in §372.241, and in addition thereto, the municipalities of Baytown, La Porte and Lomax, Tex.

573

Sec. 35 Pueblo, Colo.

The zone adjacent to and commercially a part of Pueblo, Colo., within which transportation by motor vehicle, in interstate or foreign commerce, not under a common control, management, or arrangement for a continuous carriage or shipment to or from a point beyond such zone is partially exempt from regulation under section 203(b)(8) of the Interstate Commerce Act (49 U.S.C. 303(b)(8)), includes and is comprised of all points as follows:

(a) the municipality of Pueblo, Colo., itself;

(b) All points within a line drawn 4 miles beyond the corporate limits of Pueblo, Colo.:

(c) All of the area known as the Pueblo Memorial Airport, consisting of about 3,500 acres, not within 4 miles of the corporate limits of Pueblo, Colo., and within an area located on the East of Pueblo, the nearest point being about 3.80 miles from the city limits of Pueblo, and bounded on the south by the tracks of the Santa Fe Railroad and the Missouri Pacific Railroad, and a public highway known as Baxter Road and designated as U.S. Highway 50 Bypass and Colorado Highway 96, with such property extending north, west, and east of the described southern base line.

Sec. 36 Warren, Ohio.

The zone adjacent to and commercially a part of Warren, Ohio, within which transportation by motor vehicle, in interstate or foreign commerce, not under a common control, management, or arrangement for a continuous carriage or shipment to or from a point beyond the zone, is partially exempt, under section 203(b)(8) of the Interstate Commerce Act (49 U.S.C. 303(b)(8)) from regulation includes, and is comprised of, all points as follows:

(a) The municipality of Warren, Ohio, itself.

(b) All points within a line drawn 4 miles beyond the corporate limits of Warren, Ohio.

(c) All points in that area, south of the line in paragraph (b) of this section, bounded by a line as follows: Beginning at the point where the line described in paragraph (b) of this section intersects Ellsworth-Baily Road, thence south along Ellsworth-Baily Road to the Ohio Turnpike, thence southeast along the Ohio Turnpike to New Hallock-Young Road, thence northeast along New Hallock-Young Road to Hallock-Young Road, thence east along Hallock-Young Road to junction Ohio Highway 45 (Salem-Warren Road), thence north along Ohio Highway 45 (Salem-Warren Road) to its intersection with the line described in paragraph (b) of this section.

Sec. 37 Louisville, Ky.

The zone adjacent to and commercially a part of Louisville, Ky., within which transportation by motor vehicle, in interstate or foreign commerce, not under a common control, management, or arrangement for a continuous carriage or shipment to or from a point beyond such zone, is partially exempt from regulation under section 203(b)(8) of the Interstate Commerce Act (49 U.S.C. 303(b)(8)) includes and is comprised of all points as follows:

(a) The municipality of Louisville, Ky., itself;

(b) All other municipalities and unincorporated areas within 5 miles of the corporate limits of Louisville, Ky., and all of any municipality any part of which lies within 5 miles of such corporate limits; and

(c) Those points not within 5 miles of the corporate limits of Louisville, Ky., and within an area bounded by a line beginning at the junction of Kentucky Highway 146 (La-Grange Road) and Kentucky Highway 1447 (Westport Road), thence over Kentucky Highway 146 to the junction of Kentucky Highway 146 and Kentucky Highway 841 (Jefferson Freeway), thence over Kentucky Highway 841 to the junction of Kentucky Highway 841 and Kentucky Highway 1447, thence over Kentucky Highway 1447 to junction Kentucky Highway 1447 and Kentucky Highway 146, the point of beginning, all within Jefferson County, Ky.

Sec. 38 Sioux City, Iowa.

The zone adjacent to and commercially a part of Sioux City, Iowa, within which transportation by motor vehicle, in interstate or foreign commerce, not under a common control, management, or arrangement for a continuous carriage or shipment to or from a point beyond such zone, is partially exempt from regulation under section 203(b)(8) of the Interstate Commerce Act (49 U.S.C. 303(b)(8)) includes and is comprised of all points as follows:

(a) The area which would result by application of the general formula promulgated in §372.241; and, in addition thereto,

(b) That area bounded by a line beginning at the intersection of Interstate Highway 29 and the line described in paragraph (a) of this section, and extending southeasterly along Interstate Highway 29 to its intersection with the Liberty-Lakeport Township, Iowa, line, thence westerly along the Liberty-Lakeport Township, Iowa, line to the Missouri River, thence northerly along the east bank of the Missouri River to its intersection with the line described in paragraph (a) of this section, thence along the line described in paragraph (a) of this section, to the point of beginning.

Sec. 39 Beaumont, Tex.

The zone adjacent to and commercially a part of Beaumont, Tex., within which transportation by motor vehicle, in interstate or foreign commerce, not under a common control, management, or arrangement for a continuous carriage or shipment to or from a point beyond such zone, is partially exempt from regulation under section 203(b)(8) of the Interstate Commerce Act (49 U.S.C. 303(b)(8)) includes and is comprised of all points as follows:

(a) The areas which would result by application of the general formula promulgated in §372.241 for Beaumont, Tex.; and in addition thereto,

(b) That area bounded by a line beginning at that point where the west bank of Hillebrandt Bayou intersects the line described in paragraph (a) of this section; thence along the west bank of Hillebrandt Bayou to its confluence with Taylors Bayou; thence in a southeasterly direction along the west and south banks of Taylors Bayou to its confluence with the Intracoastal Waterway; thence along the west and north banks of the Intra-coastal Waterway to its confluence with Sabine River and Sabine Lake at a point immediately east of Groves; thence in a northeasterly direction along the north and west banks of Sabine Lake and Sabine River to the Orange-Newton County line; thence westerly along said county line to the west right-of-way line of State Highway 87; thence southerly along the west right-of-way line of State Highway 87 to the north right-of-way line of Interstate Highway 10; thence westerly along the north right-of-way line of Interstate Highway 10 to intersection with the line described in paragraph (a) of this section; thence along the line described in paragraph (a) of this section, to the point of beginning.

Sec. 40 Metropolitian Government of Nashville and Davidson County, Tenn.

The zone adjacent to and commercially a part of the Metropolitan Government of Nashville and Davidson County, Tenn, within which transportation by motor vehicle, in interstate or foreign commerce, not under a common control, management, or arrangement for a continuous carriage or shipment to or from a point beyond the zone, is partially exempt from regulation under section 203(b)(8) of the Interstate Commerce Act (49 U.S.C. 303(b)(8)) includes and is comprised of all points as follows:

(a) The Metropolitan Government of Nashville and Davidson County itself.

(b) All of any municipality wholly surrounded, or so surrounded except for a water boundary, by the Metropolitan Government of Nashville and Davidson County.

Sec. 41 Consolidated City of Indianapolis, Ind.

The zone adjacent to and commercially a part of the Consolidated City of Indianapolis, Ind., within which transportation by motor vehicle, in interstate or foreign commerce, not under a common control, management, or arrangement for a continuous carriage or shipment to or from a point beyond the zone, is partially exempt from regulation under section 203(b)(8) of the Interstate Commerce Act (49 U.S.C. 303(b)(8) includes and is comprised of all points as follows:

(a) The Consolidated City of Indianapolis, Ind., itself.

(b) All of any municipality wholly surrounded or so surrounded except for a water boundary, by the Consolidated City of Indianapolis.

Sec. 42 Lexington-Fayette Urban County, Ky.

The zone adjacent to and commercially a part of Lexington-Fayette Urban County, Ky., within which transporation by motor vehicle, in interstate or foreign commerce, not under a common control, management, or arrangement for a continuous carriage or shipment to or from a point beyond the zone, is partially exempt from regulation under section 203(b)(8) of the Interstate Commerce Act (49 U.S.C. 303(b)(8)) includes and is comprised of all points as follows:

(a) Lexington-Fayette Urban County, Ky., itself.

(b) All other municipalities and unincorporated areas within 5 miles of the intersection of U.S. Highway 27 (Nicholasville Road) with the corporate boundary line between Jessamine County, Ky., and Lexington-Fayette Urban County, Ky.

Sec. 43 Definitions.

For the purposes of this part, the following terms are defined:

(a) "Municipality" means any city, town, village, or borough which has been created by special legislative act or which has been, otherwise, individually incorporated or chartered pursuant to general State laws, or which is recognized as such, under the Constitution or by the laws of the State in which located, and which has a local government. It does not include a town of the township or New England type.

(b) "Contiguous municipalities" means municipalities, as defined in paragraph (a) of this section, which have at some point a common municipal or corporate boundary.

(c) "Unincorporated area" means any area not within the corporate or municipal boundaries of any municipality as defined in paragraph (a) of this section.

Sec. 44   Commercial zones determined generally, with exceptions.

The commercial zone of each municipality in the United States, with the exceptions indicated in the note at the end of this section, within which the transportation of passengers or property, in interstate or foreign commerce, when not under a common control, management, or arrangement for a continuous carriage or shipment to or from a point without such zone, is exempt from all provisions of Part II, Interstate Commerce Act, except the provisions of section 204 relative to the qualifications and maximum hours of service of employees and safety of operation or standards of equipment shall be deemed to consist of:

(a) The municipality itself, hereinafter called the base municipality;

(b) All municipalities which are contiguous to the base municipality;

(c) All other municipalities and all unincorporated area within the United States which are adjacent to the base municipality as follows:

(1) When the base municipality has a population less than 2,500 all unincorporated areas within two miles of its corporate limits and all of any other municipality any part of which is within two miles of the corporate limits of the base municipality,

(2) When the base municipality has a population of 2,500 but less than 25,000, all unincorporated areas within 3 miles of its corporate limits and all of any other municipality any part of which is within 3 miles of the corporate limits of the base municipality,

(3) When the base municipality has a population of 25,000 but less than 100,000, all unincorporated areas within 4 miles of its corporate limits and all of any other municipality any part of which is within 4 miles of the corporate limits of the base municipality, and

(4) When the base municipality has a population of 100,000 or more, all unincorporated areas within 5 miles of its corporate limits and all of any other municipality any part of which is within 5 miles of the corporate limits of the base municipality, and

(d) All municipalities wholly surrounded, or so surrounded except for a water boundary, by the base municipality, by any municipality contiguous thereto, or by any municipality adjacent thereto which is included in the commercial zone of such base municipality under the provisions of paragraph (c) of this section.

NOTE: Except: Municipalities the commercial zones of which have been or are hereafter individually or specially determined.

Sec. 45   Controlling distances and population data.

In the application of § 372.241:

(a) Air-line distances or mileages about corporate limits of municipalities shall be used.

(b) The population of any municipality shall be deemed to be the highest figure shown for that municipality in any decennial census since (and including) the 1940 decennial census.

[53 FR 18058, May 19, 1988, as amended at 62 FR 49942, Sept. 24, 1997]

APPENDIX G TO SUBCHAPTER B OF CHAPTER III—MINIMUM PERIODIC INSPECTION STANDARDS

A vehicle does not pass an inspection if it has one of the following defects or deficiencies:

1. *Brake System.*

a. *Service brakes.* (1) Absence of braking action on any axle required to have brakes upon application of the service brakes (such as missing brakes or brake shoe(s) failing to move upon application of a wedge, S-cam, cam, or disc brake).

(2) Missing or broken mechanical components including: shoes, lining, pads, springs, anchor pins, spiders, cam rollers, push-rods, and air chamber mounting bolts.

(3) Loose brake components including air chambers, spiders, and cam shaft support brackets.

(4) Audible air leak at brake chamber (Example-ruptured diaphragm, loose chamber clamp, etc.).

(5) Readjustment limits. The maximum stroke at which brakes should be readjusted is given below. Any brake ¼″ or more past the readjustment limit or any two brakes less than ¼″ beyond the readjustment limit shall be cause for rejection. Stroke shall be measured with engine off and reservoir pressure of 80 to 90 psi with brakes fully applied.

BOLT TYPE BRAKE CHAMBER DATA

Type	Effective area (sq. in.)	Outside dia. (in.)	Maximum stroke at which brakes should be readjusted
A	12	6¹⁵⁄₁₆	1⅜
B	24	9³⁄₁₆	1¾
C	16	8¹⁄₁₆	1¾
D	6	5¼	1¼
E	9	6³⁄₁₆	1⅜
F	36	11	2¼
G	30	9⅞	2

ROTOCHAMBER DATA

Type	Effective area (sq. in.)	Outside dia. (in.)	Maximum stroke at which brakes should be readjusted
9	9	4⁹/₃₂	1½
12	12	4¹³/₁₆	1½
16	16	5¹³/₃₂	2
20	20	5¹⁵/₁₆	2
24	24	6¹³/₃₂	2
30	30	7¹/₁₆	2¼
36	36	7⅝	2¾
50	50	8⅞	3

CLAMP TYPE BRAKE CHAMBER DATA

Type	Effective area (sq. in.)	Outside dia. (in.)	Maximum stroke at which brakes should be readjusted
6	6	4½	1¼
9	9	5¼	1⅜
12	12	5¹¹/₁₆	1⅜
16	16	6⅜	1¾
20	20	6²⁵/₃₂	1¾
24	24	7⁷/₃₂	¹ 1¾
30	30	8³/₃₂	2
36	36	9	2¼

¹ (2″ for long stroke design).

Wedge Brake Data—Movement of the scribe mark on the lining shall not exceed ¹/₁₆ inch.

(6) Brake linings or pads.

(a) Lining or pad is not firmly attached to the shoe;

(b) Saturated with oil, grease, or brake fluid; or

(c) Non-steering axles: Lining with a thickness less than ¼ inch at the shoe center for air drum brakes, ¹/₁₆ inch or less at the shoe center for hydraulic and electric drum brakes, and less than ⅛ inch for air disc brakes.

(d) Steering axles: Lining with a thickness less than ¼ inch at the shoe center for drum brakes, less than ⅛ inch for air disc brakes and ¹/₁₆ inch or less for hydraulic disc and electric brakes.

(7) Missing brake on any axle required to have brakes.

(8) Mismatch across any power unit steering axle of:

(a) Air chamber sizes.

(b) Slack adjuster length.

b. *Parking Brake System.* No brakes on the vehicle or combination are applied upon actuation of the parking brake control, including driveline hand controlled parking brakes.

c. *Brake Drums or Rotors.*

(1) With any external crack or cracks that open upon brake application (do not confuse short hairline heat check cracks with flexural cracks).

(2) Any portion of the drum or rotor missing or in danger of falling away.

d. *Brake Hose.*

(1) Hose with any damage extending through the outer reinforcement ply. (Rubber impregnated fabric cover is not a reinforcement ply). (Thermoplastic nylon may have braid reinforcement or color difference between cover and inner tube. Exposure of second color is cause for rejection.

(2) Bulge or swelling when air pressure is applied.

(3) Any audible leaks.

(4) Two hoses improperly joined (such as a splice made by sliding the hose ends over a piece of tubing and clamping the hose to the tube).

(5) Air hose cracked, broken or crimped.

e. *Brake Tubing.*

(1) Any audible leak.

(2) Tubing cracked, damaged by heat, broken or crimped.

f. *Low Pressure Warning Device* missing, inoperative, or does not operate at 55 psi and below, or ½ the governor cut-out pressure, whichever is less.

g. *Tractor Protection Valve.* Inoperable or missing tractor protection valve(s) on power unit.

h. *Air Compressor.*

(1) Compressor drive belts in condition of impending or probable failure.

(2) Loose compressor mounting bolts.

(3) Cracked, broken or loose pulley.

(4) Cracked or broken mounting brackets, braces or adapters.

i. *Electric Brakes.*

(1) Absence of braking action on any wheel required to have brakes.

(2) Missing or inoperable breakaway braking device.

j. *Hydraulic Brakes. (Including Power Assist Over Hydraulic and Engine Drive Hydraulic Booster).*

(1) Master cylinder less than ¼ full.

(2) No pedal reserve with engine running except by pumping pedal.

(3) Power assist unit fails to operate.

(4) Seeping or swelling brake hose(s) under application of pressure.

(5) Missing or inoperative check valve.

(6) Has any visually observed leaking hydraulic fluid in the brake system.

(7) Has hydraulic hose(s) abraded (chafed) through outer cover-to-fabric layer.

(8) Fluid lines or connections leaking, restricted, crimped, cracked or broken.

(9) Brake failure or low fluid warning light on and/or inoperative.

k. *Vacuum Systems.* Any vacuum system which:

(1) Has insufficient vacuum reserve to permit one full brake application after engine is shut off.

(2) Has vacuum hose(s) or line(s) restricted, abraded (chafed) through outer cover to cord

577

ply, crimped, cracked, broken or has collapse of vacuum hose(s) when vacuum is applied.

(3) Lacks an operative low-vacuum warning device as required.

2. *Coupling devices.*

a. *Fifth Wheels.*

(1) Mounting to frame.

(a) Any fasteners missing or ineffective.

(b) Any movement between mounting components.

(c) Any mounting angle iron cracked or broken.

(2) Mounting plates and pivot brackets.

(a) Any fasteners missing or ineffective.

(b) Any welds or parent metal cracked.

(c) More than ⅜ inch horizontal movement between pivot bracket pin and bracket.

(d) Pivot bracket pin missing or not secured.

(3) Sliders.

(a) Any latching fasteners missing or ineffective.

(b) Any fore or aft stop missing or not securely attached.

(c) Movement more than ⅜ inch between slider bracket and slider base.

(d) Any slider component cracked in parent metal or weld.

(4) Lower coupler.

(a) Horizontal movement between the upper and lower fifth wheel halves exceeds ½ inch.

(b) Operating handle not in closed or locked position.

(c) Kingpin not properly engaged.

(d) Separation between upper and lower coupler allowing light to show through from side to side.

(e) Cracks in the fifth wheel plate.

Exceptions: Cracks in fifth wheel approach ramps and casting shrinkage cracks in the ribs of the body of a cast fifth wheel.

(f) Locking mechanism parts missing, broken, or deformed to the extent the kingpin is not securely held.

b. *Pintle Hooks.*

(1) Mounting to frame.

(a) Any missing or ineffective fasteners (a fastener is not considered missing if there is an empty hole in the device but no corresponding hole in the frame or vice versa).

(b) Mounting surface cracks extending from point of attachment (e.g., cracks in the frame at mounting bolt holes).

(c) Loose mounting.

(d) Frame cross member providing pintle hook attachment cracked.

(2) Integrity.

(a) Cracks anywhere in pintle hook assembly.

(b) Any welded repairs to the pintle hook.

(c) Any part of the horn section reduced by more than 20%.

(d) Latch insecure.

c. *Drawbar/Towbar Eye.*

(1) Mounting.

(a) Any cracks in attachment welds.

(b) Any missing or ineffective fasteners.

(2) Integrity.

(a) Any cracks.

(b) Any part of the eye reduced by more than 20%.

d. *Drawbar/Towbar Tongue.*

(1) Slider (power or manual).

(a) Ineffective latching mechanism

(b) Missing or ineffective stop.

(c) Movement of more than ¼ inch between slider and housing.

(d) Any leaking, air or hydraulic cylinders, hoses, or chambers (other than slight oil weeping normal with hydraulic seals).

(2) Integrity.

(a) Any cracks.

(b) Movement of ¼ inch between subframe and drawbar at point of attachment.

e. *Safety Devices.*

(1) Safety devices missing.

(2) Unattached or incapable of secure attachment.

(3) Chains and hooks.

(a) Worn to the extent of a measurable reduction in link cross section.

(b) Improper repairs including welding, wire, small bolts, rope and tape.

(4) Cable.

(a) Kinked or broken cable strands.

(b) Improper clamps or clamping.

f. *Saddle-Mounts.*

(1) Method of attachment.

(a) Any missing or ineffective fasteners.

(b) Loose mountings.

(c) Any cracks or breaks in a stress or load bearing member.

(d) Horizontal movement between upper and lower saddle-mount halves exceeds ¼ inch.

3. *Exhaust System.*

a. Any exhaust system determined to be leaking at a point forward of or directly below the driver/sleeper compartment.

b. A bus exhaust system leaking or discharging to the atmosphere:

(1) Gasoline powered—excess of 6 inches forward of the rearmost part of the bus.

(2) Other than gasoline powered—in excess of 15 inches forward of the rearmost part of the bus.

(3) Other than gasoline powered—forward of a door or window designed to be opened. (exception: Emergency exits).

c. No part of the exhaust system of any motor vehicle shall be so located as would be likely to result in burning, charring, or damaging the electrical wiring, the fuel supply, or any combustible part of the motor vehicle.

4. *Fuel System.*

a. A fuel system with a visable leak at any point.

b. A fuel tank filler cap missing.

c. A fuel tank not securely attached to the motor vehicle by reason of loose, broken or missing mounting bolts or brackets (some fuel tanks use springs or rubber bushings to permit movement).

5. *Lighting Devices.* All lighting devices and reflectors required by Section 393 shall be operable.

6. *Safe Loading.*

a. Part(s) of vehicle or condition of loading such that the spare tire or any part of the load or dunnage can fall onto the roadway.

b. Protection Against Shifting Cargo—Any vehicle without a front-end structure or equivalent device as required.

c. Container securement devices on intermodal equipment—All devices used to secure an intermodal container to a chassis, including rails or support frames, tiedown bolsters, locking pins, clevises, clamps, and hooks that are cracked, broken, loose, or missing.

7. *Steering Mechanism.*

a. *Steering Wheel Free Play (on vehicles equipped with power steering the engine must be running).*

Steering wheel diameter	Manual steering system	Power steering system
16″	2″	4½″
18″	2¼″	4¾″
20″	2½″	5¼″
22″	2¾″	5¾″

b. *Steering Column.*

(1) Any absence or looseness of U-bolt(s) or positioning part(s).

(2) Worn, faulty or obviously repair welded universal joint(s).

(3) Steering wheel not properly secured.

c. *Front Axle Beam and All Steering Components Other Than Steering Column.*

(1) Any crack(s).

(2) Any obvious welded repair(s).

d. *Steering Gear Box.*

(1) Any mounting bolt(s) loose or missing.

(2) Any crack(s) in gear box or mounting brackets.

e. *Pitman Arm.* Any looseness of the pitman arm on the steering gear output shaft.

f. *Power Steering.* Auxiliary power assist cylinder loose.

g. *Ball and Socket Joints.*

(1) Any movement under steering load of a stud nut.

(2) Any motion, other than rotational, between any linkage member and its attachment point of more than ¼ inch.

h. *Tie Rods and Drag Links.*

(1) Loose clamp(s) or clamp bolts(s) on tie rods or drag links.

(2) Any looseness in any threaded joint.

i. *Nuts.* Nut(s) loose or missing on tie rods, pitman arm, drag link, steering arm or tie rod arm.

j. *Steering System.* Any modification or other condition that interferes with free movement of any steering component.

8. *Suspension.*

a. Any U-bolt(s), spring hanger(s), or other axle positioning part(s) cracked, broken, loose or missing resulting in shifting of an axle from its normal position. (After a turn, lateral axle displacement is normal with some suspensions. Forward or rearward operation in a straight line will cause the axle to return to alignment).

b. *Spring Assembly.*

(1) Any leaves in a leaf spring assembly broken or missing.

(2) Any broken main leaf in a leaf spring assembly. (Includes assembly with more than one main spring).

(3) Coil spring broken.

(4) Rubber spring missing.

(5) One or more leaves displaced in a manner that could result in contact with a tire, rim, brake drum or frame.

(6) Broken torsion bar spring in a torsion bar suspension.

(7) Deflated air suspension, i.e., system failure, leak, etc.

c. *Torque, Radius or Tracking Components.* Any part of a torque, radius or tracking component assembly or any part used for attaching the same to the vehicle frame or axle that is cracked, loose, broken or missing. (Does not apply to loose bushings in torque or track rods.)

9. *Frame.*

a. *Frame Members.*

(1) Any cracked, broken, loose, or sagging frame member.

(2) Any loose or missing fasteners including fasteners attaching functional component such as engine, transmission, steering gear, suspension, body parts, and fifth wheel.

b. *Tire and Wheel Clearance.* Any condition, including loading, that causes the body or frame to be in contact with a tire or any part of the wheel assemblies.

c. (1) *Adjustable Axle Assemblies (Sliding Subframes).* Adjustable axle assembly with locking pins missing or not engaged.

10. *Tires.*

a. Any tire on any steering axle of a power unit.

(1) With less than ⁴⁄₃₂ inch tread when measured at any point on a major tread groove.

(2) Has body ply or belt material exposed through the tread or sidewall.

(3) Has any tread or sidewall separation.

(4) Has a cut where the ply or belt material is exposed.

(5) Labeled "Not for Highway Use" or displaying other marking which would exclude use on steering axle.

(6) A tube-type radial tire without radial tube stem markings. These markings include a red band around the tube stem, the word "radial" embossed in metal stems, or the word "radial" molded in rubber stems.

(7) Mixing bias and radial tires on the same axle.

579

(8) Tire flap protrudes through valve slot in rim and touches stem.

(9) Regrooved tire except motor vehicles used solely in urban or suburban service (see exception in 393.75(e)).

(10) Boot, blowout patch or other ply repair.

(11) Weight carried exceeds tire load limit. This includes overloaded tire resulting from low air pressure.

(12) Tire is flat or has noticeable (e.g., can be heard or felt) leak.

(13) Any bus equipped with recapped or retreaded tire(s).

(14) So mounted or inflated that it comes in contact with any part of the vehicle.

b. All tires other than those found on the steering axle of a power unit:

(1) Weight carried exceeds tire load limit. This includes overloaded tire resulting from low air pressure.

(2) Tire is flat or has noticeable (e.g., can be heard or felt) leak.

(3) Has body ply or belt material exposed through the tread or sidewall.

(4) Has any tread or sidewall separation.

(5) Has a cut where ply or belt material is exposed.

(6) So mounted or inflated that it comes in contact with any part of the vehicle. (This includes a tire that contacts its mate.)

(7) Is marked "Not for highway use" or otherwise marked and having like meaning.

(8) With less than $\frac{2}{32}$ inch tread when measured at any point on a major tread groove.

11. *Wheels and Rims.*

a. *Lock or Side Ring.* Bent, broken, cracked, improperly seated, sprung or mismatched ring(s).

b. *Wheels and rims.* Cracked or broken or has elongated bolt holes.

c. *Fasteners (both spoke and disc wheels).* Any loose, missing, broken, cracked, stripped or otherwise ineffective fasteners.

d. *Welds.*

(1) Any cracks in welds attaching disc wheel disc to rim.

(2) Any crack in welds attaching tubeless demountable rim to adapter.

(3) Any welded repair on aluminum wheel(s) on a steering axle.

(4) Any welded repair other than disc to rim attachment on steel disc wheel(s) mounted on the steering axle.

12. *Windshield Glazing.* (Not including a 2 inch border at the top, a 1 inch border at each side and the area below the topmost portion of the steering wheel.) Any crack, discoloration or vision reducing matter except: (1) coloring or tinting applied at time of manufacture; (2) any crack not over ¼ inch wide, if not intersected by any other crack; (3) any damaged area not more than ¾ inch in diameter, if not closer than 3 inches to any other such damaged area; (4) labels,

stickers, decalcomania, etc. (see 393.60 for exceptions).

13. *Windshield Wipers.* Any power unit that has an inoperative wiper, or missing or damaged parts that render it ineffective.

COMPARISON OF APPENDIX G, AND THE NEW NORTH AMERICAN UNIFORM DRIVER-VEHICLE INSPECTION PROCEDURE (NORTH AMERICAN COMMERCIAL VEHICLE CRITICAL SAFETY INSPECTION ITEMS AND OUT-OF-SERVICE CRITERIA)

The vehicle portion of the FMCSA's North American Uniform Driver-Vehicle Inspection Procedure (NAUD-VIP) requirements, CVSA's North American Commercial Vehicle Critical Safety Inspection Items and Out-Of-Service Criteria and appendix G of subchapter B are similar documents and follow the same inspection procedures. The same items are required to be inspected by each document. FMCSA's and CVSA's out-of-service criteria are intended to be used in random roadside inspections to identify critical vehicle inspection items and provide criteria for placing a vehicle(s) out-of-service. A vehicle(s) is placed out-of-service only when by reason of its mechanical condition or loading it is determined to be so imminently hazardous as to likely cause an accident or breakdown, or when such condition(s) would likely contribute to loss of control of the vehicle(s) by the driver. A certain amount of flexibility is given to the inspecting official whether to place the vehicle out-of-service at the inspection site or if it would be less hazardous to allow the vehicle to proceed to a repair facility for repair. The distance to the repair facility must not exceed 25 miles. The roadside type of inspection, however, does not necessarily mean that a vehicle has to be defect-free in order to continue in service.

In contrast, the appendix G inspection procedure requires that all items required to be inspected are in proper adjustment, are not defective and function properly prior to the vehicle being placed in service.

DIFFERENCES BETWEEN THE OUT-OF-SERVICE CRITERIA & FMCSA'S ANNUAL INSPECTION

1. *Brake System.*

The appendix G criteria rejects vehicles with any defective brakes, any air leaks, etc. The out-of-service criteria allows 20% defective brakes on non-steering axles and a certain latitude on air leaks before placing a vehicle out-of-service.

2. *Coupling Devices.*

Appendix G rejects vehicles with any fifth wheel mounting fastener missing or ineffective. The out-of-service criteria allows up to 20% missing or ineffective fasteners on frame mountings and pivot bracket mountings and 25% on slider latching fasteners. The out-of-service criteria also allows some latitude on cracked welds.

3. *Exhaust System.*

Appendix G follows Section 393.83 verbatim. The CVSA out-of-service criteria allows vehicles to exhaust forward of the dimensions given in Section 393.83 as long as the exhaust does not leak or exhaust under the chassis.

4. *Fuel System.*

Same for Appendix G and the out-of-service criteria.

5. *Lighting Devices.*

Appendix G requires all lighting devices required by Section 393 to be operative at all times. The out-of-service criteria only requires one stop light and functioning turn signals on the rear most vehicle of a combination vehicle to be operative at all times. In addition one operative head lamp and tail lamp are required during the hours of darkness.

6. *Safe Loading.*

Same for both Appendix G and the out-of-service criteria.

7. *Steering Mechanism*

Steering lash requirements of appendix G follows the new requirements of § 393.209.

8. *Suspension*

Appendix G follows the new requirements of § 393.207 which does not allow any broken leaves in a leaf spring assembly. The out-of-service criteria allows up to 25% broken or missing leaves before being placed out-of-service.

9. *Frame*

The out-of-service criteria allows a certain latitude in frame cracks before placing a vehicle out-of-service. Appendix G follows the new requirements of 393.201 which does not allow any frame cracks.

10. *Tires*

Appendix G follows the requirements of 393.75 which requires a tire tread depth of 1/32 inch on power unit steering axles and 2/32 inch on all other axles. The out-of-service criteria only requires 2/32 inch tire tread depth on power unit steering axles and 1/32 inch on all other axles.

11. *Wheel and Rims*

The out-of-service criteria allows a certain amount latitude for wheel and rim cracks and missing or defective fasteners. Appendix G meets the requirements of the new 393.205 which does not allow defective wheels and rims non-effective nuts and bolts.

12. *Windshield Glazing*

The out-of-service criteria places in a restricted service condition any vehicle that has a crack or discoloration in the windshield area lying within the sweep of the wiper on the drivers side and does not address the remaining area of the windshield. Appendix G addresses requirements for the whole windshield as specified in 393.60.

13. *Windshield Wipers*

Appendix G requires windshield wipers to be operative at all times. The out-of-service criteria only requires that the windshield wiper on the driver's side to be inspected during inclement weather.

[53 FR 49411, Dec. 7, 1988; 53 FR 49968, Dec. 12, 1988, as amended at 73 FR 76827, Dec. 17, 2008]

Title 49 —Transportation
Subtitle A —Office of the Secretary of Transportation

PART 40—PROCEDURES FOR TRANSPORTATION WORKPLACE DRUG AND ALCOHOL TESTING PROGRAMS

Authority: 49 U.S.C. 102, 301, 322, 5331, 20140, 31306, and 54101 *et seq.*

Source: 65 FR 79526, Dec. 19, 2000, unless otherwise noted.

Editorial Note: Nomenclature changes to part 40 appear at 73 FR 33329, June 12, 2008.

Subpart A—Administrative Provisions

§ 40.1 Who does this regulation cover?

(a) This part tells all parties who conduct drug and alcohol tests required by Department of Transportation (DOT) agency regulations how to conduct these tests and what procedures to use.

(b) This part concerns the activities of transportation employers, safety-sensitive transportation employees (including self-employed individuals, contractors and volunteers as covered by DOT agency regulations), and service agents.

(c) Nothing in this part is intended to supersede or conflict with the implementation of the Federal Railroad Administration's post-accident testing program (see 49 CFR 219.200).

§ 40.3 What do the terms used in this part mean?

In this part, the terms listed in this section have the following meanings:

Adulterated specimen. A specimen that has been altered, as evidenced by test results showing either a substance that is not a normal constituent for that type of specimen or showing an abnormal concentration of an endogenous substance.

Affiliate. Persons are affiliates of one another if, directly or indirectly, one controls or has the power to control the other, or a third party controls or has the power to control both. Indicators of control include, but are not limited to: interlocking management or ownership; shared interest among family members; shared facilities or equipment; or common use of employees. Following the issuance of a public interest exclusion, an organization having the same or similar management, ownership, or principal employees as the service agent concerning whom a public interest exclusion is in effect is regarded as an affiliate. This definition is used in connection with the public interest exclusion procedures of Subpart R of this part.

Air blank. In evidential breath testing devices (EBTs) using gas chromatography technology, a reading of the device's internal standard. In all other EBTs, a reading of ambient air containing no alcohol.

Alcohol. The intoxicating agent in beverage alcohol, ethyl alcohol or other low molecular weight alcohols, including methyl or isopropyl alcohol.

Alcohol concentration. The alcohol in a volume of breath expressed in terms of grams of alcohol per 210 liters of breath as indicated by a breath test under this part.

Alcohol confirmation test. A subsequent test using an EBT, following a screening test with a result of 0.02 or greater, that provides quantitative data about the alcohol concentration.

Alcohol screening device (ASD). A breath or saliva device, other than an EBT, that is approved by the National Highway Traffic Safety Administration (NHTSA) and appears on ODAPC's Web page for "Approved Screening Devices to Measure Alcohol in Bodily Fluids" because it conforms to the model specifications from NHTSA.

Alcohol screening test. An analytic procedure to determine whether an employee may have a prohibited concentration of alcohol in a breath or saliva specimen.

Alcohol testing site. A place selected by the employer where employees present themselves for the purpose of providing breath or saliva for an alcohol test.

Alcohol use. The drinking or swallowing of any beverage, liquid mixture or preparation (including any medication), containing alcohol.

Aliquot. A fractional part of a specimen used for testing. It is taken as a sample representing the whole specimen.

Alternate specimen. An authorized specimen, other than the type of specimen previously collected or attempted to be collected.

Breath Alcohol Technician (BAT). A person who instructs and assists employees in the alcohol testing process and operates an evidential breath testing device.

Cancelled test. A drug or alcohol test that has a problem identified that cannot be or has not been corrected, or which this part otherwise requires to be cancelled. A cancelled test is neither a positive nor a negative test.

Chain of custody. The procedure used to document the handling of the urine specimen from the time the employee gives the specimen to the collector until the specimen is destroyed. This procedure uses the Federal Drug Testing Custody and Control Form (CCF) as approved by the Office of Management and Budget.

Collection container. A container used to collect a specimen.

Collection site. A place selected by the employer where employees present themselves for the purpose of providing a specimen for a drug test.

Collector. A person who instructs and assists employees at a collection site, who receives and makes an initial inspection of the specimen provided by those employees, and who initiates and completes the CCF.

Commercial Driver's License Drug and Alcohol Clearinghouse (Clearinghouse). A database, administered by the Federal Motor Carrier Safety Administration, containing records of commercial motor vehicle drivers' violations of controlled substances and alcohol testing program requirements, as set forth in part 382 of this title, as well as their return-to-duty status.

Confirmatory drug test. A second analytical procedure performed on a different aliquot of the original specimen to identify and quantify a specific drug or drug metabolite.

Confirmatory validity test. A second test performed on a different aliquot of the original urine specimen to further support a validity test result.

Confirmed drug test. A confirmation test result received by an MRO from a laboratory.

Consortium/Third-party administrator (C/TPA). A service agent that provides or coordinates the provision of a variety of drug and alcohol testing services to employers. C/TPAs typically perform administrative tasks concerning the operation of the employers' drug and alcohol testing programs. This term includes, but is not limited to, groups of employers who join together to administer, as a single entity, the DOT drug and alcohol testing programs of its members. C/TPAs are not "employers" for purposes of this part.

Continuing education. Training for substance abuse professionals (SAPs) who have completed qualification training and are performing SAP functions, designed to keep SAPs current on changes and developments in the DOT drug and alcohol testing program.

Cutoff. The analytical value (*e.g.,* drug or drug metabolite concentration) used as the decision point to determine a result (*e.g.,* negative, positive, adulterated, invalid, or substituted) or the need for further testing.

Designated employer representative (DER). An employee authorized by the employer to take immediate action(s) to remove employees from safety-sensitive duties, or cause employees to be removed from these covered duties, and to make required decisions in the testing and evaluation processes. The DER also receives test results and other communications for the employer, consistent with the requirements of this part. Service agents cannot act as DERs.

Dilute specimen. A urine specimen with creatinine and specific gravity values that are lower than expected for human urine.

DOT, The Department, DOT Agency. These terms encompass all DOT agencies, including, but not limited to, the Federal Aviation Administration (FAA), the Federal Railroad Administration (FRA), the Federal Motor Carrier Safety Administration (FMCSA), the Federal Transit Administration (FTA), the National Highway Traffic Safety Administration (NHTSA), the Pipeline and Hazardous Materials Safety Administration (PHMSA), and the Office of the Secretary (OST). For purposes of this part, the United States Coast Guard

(USCG), in the Department of Homeland Security, is considered to be a DOT agency for drug testing purposes only since the USCG regulation does not incorporate Part 40 for its alcohol testing program. These terms include any designee of a DOT agency.

Drugs. The drugs for which tests are required under this part and DOT agency regulations are marijuana, cocaine, amphetamines, phencyclidine (PCP), and opioids.

Employee. Any person who is designated in a DOT agency regulation as subject to drug testing and/or alcohol testing. The term includes individuals currently performing safety-sensitive functions designated in DOT agency regulations and applicants for employment subject to pre-employment testing. For purposes of drug testing under this part, the term employee has the same meaning as the term "donor" as found on CCF and related guidance materials produced by the Department of Health and Human Services.

Employer. A person or entity employing one or more employees (including an individual who is self-employed) subject to DOT agency regulations requiring compliance with this part. The term includes an employer's officers, representatives, and management personnel. Service agents are not employers for the purposes of this part.

Error Correction Training. Training provided to BATs, collectors, and screening test technicians (STTs) following an error that resulted in the cancellation of a drug or alcohol test. Error correction training must be provided in person or by a means that provides real-time observation and interaction between the instructor and trainee.

Evidential Breath Testing Device (EBT). A device that is approved by the National Highway Traffic Safety Administration (NHTSA) for the evidential testing of breath at the .02 and .04 alcohol concentrations, and appears on ODAPC's Web page for "Approved Evidential Breath Measurement Devices" because it conforms with the model specifications available from NHTSA.

HHS. The Department of Health and Human Services or any designee of the Secretary, Department of Health and Human Services.

Initial drug test. The first test used to differentiate a negative specimen from one that requires further testing for drugs or drug metabolites.

Initial specimen validity test. The first test used to determine if a specimen is adulterated, diluted, substituted, or invalid.

Invalid result. The result reported by an HHS-certified in accordance with the criteria established by HHS when a positive, negative, adulterated, or substituted result cannot be established for a specific drug or specimen validity test.

Laboratory. Any U.S. laboratory certified by HHS under the National Laboratory Certification Program as meeting the minimum standards set by HHS; or, in the case of foreign laboratories, a laboratory approved for participation by DOT under this part.

Limit of Detection (LOD). The lowest concentration at which the analyte (*e.g.,* drug or drug metabolite) can be identified.

Limit of Quantitation (LOQ). For quantitative assays, the lowest concentration at which the identity and concentration of the analyte (*e.g.,* drug or drug metabolite) can be accurately established.

Medical Review Officer (MRO). A person who is a licensed physician and who is responsible for receiving and reviewing laboratory results generated by an employer's drug testing program and evaluating medical explanations for certain drug test results.

Negative result. The result reported by an HHS-certified laboratory to an MRO when a specimen contains no drug or the concentration of the drug is less than the cutoff concentration for the drug or drug class and the specimen is a valid specimen.

Non-negative specimen. A specimen that is reported as adulterated, substituted, positive (for drug(s) or drug metabolite(s)), or invalid.

Office of Drug and Alcohol Policy and Compliance (ODAPC). The office in the Office of the Secretary, DOT, that is responsible for coordinating drug and alcohol testing program matters within the Department and providing information concerning the implementation of this part.

Oral fluid specimen. A specimen that is collected from an employee's oral cavity and is a combination of physiological fluids produced primarily by the salivary glands. An oral fluid specimen is considered to be a direct observation collection for all purposes of this part.

Oxidizing adulterant. A substance that acts alone or in combination with other substances to oxidize drugs or drug metabolites to prevent the detection of the drug or drug metabolites, or affects the reagents in either the initial or confirmatory drug test.

Primary specimen. In drug testing, the specimen bottle that is opened and tested by a first laboratory to determine whether the employee has a drug or drug metabolite in his or her system; and for the purpose of specimen validity testing. The primary specimen is the portion of the donor's subdivided specimen designated as the primary ("A") specimen by the collector to distinguish it from the split ("B") specimen, as defined in this section.

Positive result. The result reported by an HHS-certified laboratory when a specimen contains a drug or drug metabolite equal to or greater than the cutoff concentrations.

Qualification Training. The training required in order for a collector, BAT, MRO, SAP, or STT to be qualified to perform their functions in the DOT drug and alcohol testing program. Qualification training may be provided by any appropriate means (*e.g.,* classroom instruction, internet application, CD-ROM, video).

Reconfirmed. The result reported for a split (Bottle B) specimen when the second HHS-certified laboratory corroborates the original result reported for the primary (Bottle A) specimen.

Refresher Training. The training required periodically for qualified collectors, BATs, and STTs to review basic requirements and provide instruction concerning changes in technology (*e.g.,* new testing methods that may be authorized) and amendments, interpretations, guidance, and issues concerning this part and DOT agency drug and alcohol testing regulations. Refresher training can be provided by any appropriate means (*e.g.,* classroom instruction, internet application, CD-ROM, video).

Rejected for testing. The result reported by an HHS-certified laboratory when no tests are performed for a specimen because of a fatal flaw or a correctable flaw that is not corrected.

Screening Test Technician (STT). A person who instructs and assists employees in the alcohol testing process and operates an ASD.

Secretary. The Secretary of Transportation or the Secretary's designee.

Service agent. Any person or entity, other than an employee of the employer, who provides services to employers and/or employees in connection with DOT drug and alcohol testing requirements. This includes, but is not limited to, collectors, BATs and STTs, laboratories, MROs, substance abuse professionals, and C/TPAs. To act as service agents, persons and organizations must meet DOT qualifications, if applicable. Service agents are not employers for purposes of this part.

Shipping container. A container that is used for transporting and protecting specimen bottles and associated documents from the collection site to the laboratory.

Specimen. Fluid, breath, or other material collected from an employee at the collection site for the purpose of a drug or alcohol test.

Specimen bottle. The bottle that, after being sealed and labeled according to the procedures in this part, is used to hold a primary ("A") or split ("B") specimen during transportation to the laboratory. In the context of oral fluid testing, it may be referred to as a "vial," "tube," or "bottle."

Split specimen. In drug testing, the specimen that is sent to a first laboratory and stored with its original seal intact, and which is transported to a second laboratory for retesting at the employee's request following MRO verification of the primary specimen as positive, adulterated or substituted.

Split specimen collection. A collection in which the single specimen collected is divided into two separate specimen bottles, the primary specimen (Bottle A) and the split specimen (Bottle B).

SSN or Employee ID No. This number serves as a unique identifier that must be used on the Federal Drug Testing Custody and Control Form (CCF) or Alcohol Testing Form (ATF) for a donor, on the MRO's reports, on SAP reports, or on other documents that are required under this part. For all purposes of this part, this term means: only the Commercial Driver's License (CDL) Number and State of issuance for drivers tested under the authority of the Federal Motor Carrier Safety Administration (FMCSA); and, for all drivers and other safety-sensitive employees tested under the authority of the other DOT agencies, this can be the individual's actual Social Security Number, a unique identifier issued by the employer, a State-issued identification card number, a State-issued driver's license number (including a CDL number) or any other State-issued or federally-issued identification number.

Stand-down. The practice of temporarily removing an employee from the performance of safety-sensitive functions based only on a report from a laboratory to the MRO of a confirmed positive test for a drug or drug metabolite, an adulterated test, or a substituted test, before the MRO has completed verification of the test result.

Substance Abuse Professional (SAP). A person who evaluates employees who have violated a DOT drug and alcohol regulation and makes recommendations concerning education, treatment, follow-up testing, and aftercare.

Substituted specimen. An employee's specimen not consistent with a normal human specimen, as determined by HHS (*e.g.,* a urine specimen, with creatinine and specific gravity values that are so diminished, or so divergent that they are not consistent with normal human urine).

Undiluted (neat) oral fluid. An oral fluid specimen to which no other solid or liquid has been added. For example: A collection device that uses a diluent (or other component, process, or method that modifies the volume of the testable specimen) must collect at least 1 mL of undiluted (neat) oral fluid.

Urine specimen. Urine collected from an employee at the collection site for the purpose of a drug test.

Verified test. A drug test result or validity testing result from an HHS-certified laboratory that has undergone review and final determination by the MRO.

[65 FR 79526, Dec. 19, 2000, as amended at 66 FR 41950, Aug. 9, 2001; 71 FR 49384, Aug. 23, 2006; 71 FR 55347, Sept. 22, 2006; 73 FR 35969, June 25, 2008; 75 FR 49861, Aug. 16, 2010; 76 FR 59577, Sept. 27, 2011; 80 FR 19553, Apr. 13, 2015; 81 FR 52365, Aug. 8, 2016; 82 FR 52243, Nov. 13, 2017; 88 FR 27636, May 2, 2023]

§ 40.5 Who issues authoritative interpretations of this regulation?

ODAPC and the DOT Office of General Counsel (OGC) provide written interpretations of the provisions of this part. These written DOT interpretations are the only official and authoritative interpretations concerning the provisions of this part. DOT agencies may incorporate ODAPC/OGC interpretations in written guidance they issue concerning drug and alcohol testing matters. Only Part 40 interpretations issued after August 1, 2001, are considered valid.

§ 40.7 How can you get an exemption from a requirement in this regulation?

(a) If you want an exemption from any provision of this part, you must request it in writing from the Office of the Secretary of Transportation, under the provisions and standards of 49 CFR part 5. You must send requests for an exemption to the following address: Department of Transportation, Deputy Assistant General Counsel for Regulation and Enforcement, 1200 New Jersey Avenue, SE., Washington, DC 20590.

(b) Under the standards of 49 CFR part 5, we will grant the request only if the request documents special or exceptional circumstances, not likely to be generally applicable and not contemplated in connection with the rulemaking that established this part, that make your compliance with a specific provision of this part impracticable.

(c) If we grant you an exemption, you must agree to take steps we specify to comply with the intent of the provision from which an exemption is granted.

(d) We will issue written responses to all exemption requests.

Subpart B—Employer Responsibilities

§ 40.11 What are the general responsibilities of employers under this regulation?

(a) As an employer, you are responsible for meeting all applicable requirements and procedures of this part.

(b) You are responsible for all actions of your officials, representatives, and agents (including service agents) in carrying out the requirements of the DOT agency regulations.

(c) All agreements and arrangements, written or unwritten, between and among employers and service agents concerning the implementation of DOT drug and alcohol testing requirements are deemed, as a matter of law, to require compliance with all applicable provisions of this part and DOT agency drug and alcohol testing regulations. Compliance with these provisions is a material term of all such agreements and arrangements.

§ 40.13 How do DOT drug and alcohol tests relate to non-DOT tests?

(a) DOT tests must be completely separate from non-DOT tests in all respects.

(b) DOT tests must take priority and must be conducted and completed before a non-DOT test is begun. When conducting a urine DOT drug test, you must discard any excess urine left over from a DOT test and collect a separate urine void for the subsequent non-DOT test.

(c) Except as provided in paragraph (d) of this section, you must not perform any tests on DOT specimens other than those tests specifically authorized by this part or DOT agency regulations. For example, you must not test a DOT specimen for additional drugs. In addition, a laboratory is prohibited from making a DOT specimen available for a DNA test or other types of specimen identity testing.

(d) When a DOT urine drug test collection is conducted as part of a physical examination required by DOT agency regulations, it is permissible to conduct medical tests related to this physical examination (*e.g.,* for glucose) on any specimen remaining in the collection container after the DOT portion has been sealed into the specimen bottles.

(e) A non-DOT drug or alcohol test administered, as part of a physical examination, is not a DOT drug or alcohol test for purposes of this part and/or related DOT agency drug and alcohol testing rules, if that test was performed to determine if an employee is medically qualified for a license or certificate. Consequently, the results of such a test do not have consequences under this part.

(f) No one is permitted to change or disregard the results of DOT tests based on the results of non-DOT tests. For example, as an employer you must not disregard a verified positive DOT drug test result because the employee presents a negative test result from a blood or urine specimen collected by the employee's physician or a DNA test result purporting to question the identity of the DOT specimen.

(g) As an employer, you must not use the CCF or the ATF in your non-DOT drug and alcohol testing programs. This prohibition includes the use of the DOT forms with references to DOT programs and agencies crossed out. You also must always use the CCF and ATF for all your DOT-mandated drug and alcohol tests.

(h) No one is permitted to conduct a DOT drug or alcohol test on an individual who is not a DOT-regulated employee, as defined by the DOT agency regulations.

[65 FR 79526, Dec. 19, 2000, as amended at 88 FR 27637, May 2, 2023]

§ 40.14 What collection information must employers provide to collectors?

As an employer, or an employer's service agent—for example a C/TPA, you must ensure the collector has the following information when conducting a urine specimen collection for you:

(a) Full name of the employee being tested.

(b) SSN or Employee ID No.

(c) Laboratory name and address (can be pre-printed on the CCF).

(d) Employer name, address, phone number, and fax number (can be pre-printed on the CCF at Step 1–A).

(e) DER information required at § 40.35 of this part.

(f) MRO name, address, phone number, and fax number (can be pre-printed on the CCF at Step 1–B).

(g) The DOT Agency which regulates the employee's safety-sensitive duties (the checkmark can pre-printed in the appropriate box on the CCF at Step 1–D).

(h) Test reason, as appropriate: Pre-employment; Random; Reasonable Suspicion/Reasonable Cause; Post-Accident; Return-to-Duty; and Follow-up.

(i) Whether the test is to be observed or not (see § 40.67 of this part).

(j) (Optional) C/TPA name, address, phone, and fax number (can be pre-printed on the CCF).

(k) Specimen type to be collected (*i.e.,* oral fluid or urine).

[75 FR 59107, Sept. 27, 2010, as amended at 88 FR 27637, May 2, 2023]

§ 40.15 May an employer use a service agent to meet DOT drug and alcohol testing requirements?

(a) As an employer, you may use a service agent to perform the tasks needed to comply with this part and DOT agency drug and alcohol testing regulations, consistent with the requirements of Subpart Q and other applicable provisions of this part.

(b) As an employer, you are responsible for ensuring that the service agents you use meet the qualifications set forth in this part (e.g., § 40.121 for MROs). You may require service agents to show you documentation that they meet the requirements of this part (e.g., documentation of MRO qualifications required by § 40.121(e)).

(c) You remain responsible for compliance with all applicable requirements of this part and other DOT drug and alcohol testing regulations, even when you use a service agent. If you violate this part or other DOT drug and alcohol testing regulations because a service agent has not provided services as our rules require, a DOT agency can subject you to sanctions. Your good faith use of a service agent is not a defense in an enforcement action initiated by a DOT agency in which your alleged noncompliance with this part or a DOT agency drug and alcohol regulation may have resulted from the service agent's conduct.

(d) As an employer, you must not permit a service agent to act as your DER.

§ 40.17 Is an employer responsible for obtaining information from its service agents?

Yes, as an employer, you are responsible for obtaining information required by this part from your service agents. This is true whether or not you choose to use a C/TPA as an intermediary in transmitting information to you. For example, suppose an applicant for a safety-sensitive job takes a pre-employment drug test, but there is a significant delay in your receipt of the test result from an MRO or C/TPA. You must not assume that "no news is good news" and permit the applicant to perform safety-sensitive duties before receiving the result. This is a violation of the Department's regulations.

§ 40.19 [Reserved]

§ 40.21 May an employer stand down an employee before the MRO has completed the verification process?

(a) As an employer, you are prohibited from standing employees down, except consistent with a waiver a DOT agency grants under this section.

(b) You may make a request to the concerned DOT agency for a waiver from the prohibition of paragraph (a) of this section. Such a waiver, if granted, permits you to stand an employee down following the MRO's receipt of a laboratory report of a confirmed positive test for a drug or drug metabolite, an adulterated test, or a substituted test pertaining to the employee.

(1) For this purpose, the concerned DOT agency is the one whose drug and alcohol testing rules apply to the majority of the covered employees in your organization. The concerned DOT agency uses its applicable procedures for considering requests for waivers.

(2) Before taking action on a waiver request, the concerned DOT agency coordinates with other DOT agencies that regulate the employer's other covered employees.

49 CFR Part 40 (up to date as of 3/05/2024)
Procedures for Transportation Workplace Drug and Alcohol Testing Programs

49 CFR 40.21(b)(3)

(3) The concerned DOT agency provides a written response to each employer that petitions for a waiver, setting forth the reasons for the agency's decision on the waiver request.

(c) Your request for a waiver must include, as a minimum, the following elements:

(1) Information about your organization:

(i) Your determination that standing employees down is necessary for safety in your organization and a statement of your basis for it, including any data on safety problems or incidents that could have been prevented if a stand-down procedure had been in place;

(ii) Data showing the number of confirmed laboratory positive, adulterated, and substituted test results for your employees over the two calendar years preceding your waiver request, and the number and percentage of those test results that were verified positive, adulterated, or substituted by the MRO;

(iii) Information about the work situation of the employees subject to stand-down, including a description of the size and organization of the unit(s) in which the employees work, the process through which employees will be informed of the stand-down, whether there is an in-house MRO, and whether your organization has a medical disqualification or stand-down policy for employees in situations other than drug and alcohol testing; and

(iv) A statement of which DOT agencies regulate your employees.

(2) Your proposed written company policy concerning stand-down, which must include the following elements:

(i) Your assurance that you will distribute copies of your written policy to all employees that it covers;

(ii) Your means of ensuring that no information about the confirmed positive, adulterated, or substituted test result or the reason for the employee's temporary removal from performance of safety-sensitive functions becomes available, directly or indirectly, to anyone in your organization (or subsequently to another employer) other than the employee, the MRO and the DER;

(iii) Your means of ensuring that all covered employees in a particular job category in your organization are treated the same way with respect to stand-down;

(iv) Your means of ensuring that a covered employee will be subject to stand-down only with respect to the actual performance of safety-sensitive duties;

(v) Your means of ensuring that you will not take any action adversely affecting the employee's pay and benefits pending the completion of the MRO's verification process. This includes continuing to pay the employee during the period of the stand-down in the same way you would have paid him or her had he or she not been stood down;

(vi) Your means of ensuring that the verification process will commence no later than the time an employee is temporarily removed from the performance of safety-sensitive functions and that the period of stand-down for any employee will not exceed five days, unless you are informed in writing by the MRO that a longer period is needed to complete the verification process; and

(vii) Your means of ensuring that, in the event that the MRO verifies the test negative or cancels it—

(A) You return the employee immediately to the performance of safety-sensitive duties;

49 CFR Part 40 (up to date as of 3/05/2024)
Procedures for Transportation Workplace Drug and Alcohol Testing Programs

49 CFR 40.21(c)(2)(vii)(B)

(B) The employee suffers no adverse personnel or financial consequences as a result;

(C) For a verified negative result, the employee will not be required to submit an alternate specimen for the same testing action. For a cancelled result, the employee could be required to submit an alternate specimen on a re-collection; and

(D) You maintain no individually identifiable record that the employee had a confirmed laboratory positive, adulterated, or substituted test result (*i.e.,* you maintain a record of the test only as a negative or cancelled test).

(d) The Administrator of the concerned DOT agency, or his or her designee, may grant a waiver request only if he or she determines that, in the context of your organization, there is a high probability that the procedures you propose will effectively enhance safety and protect the interests of employees in fairness and confidentiality.

    (1) The Administrator, or his or her designee, may impose any conditions he or she deems appropriate on the grant of a waiver.

    (2) The Administrator, or his or her designee, may immediately suspend or revoke the waiver if he or she determines that you have failed to protect effectively the interests of employees in fairness and confidentiality, that you have failed to comply with the requirements of this section, or that you have failed to comply with any other conditions the DOT agency has attached to the waiver.

(e) You must not stand employees down in the absence of a waiver, or inconsistent with the terms of your waiver. If you do, you are in violation of this part and DOT agency drug testing regulations, and you are subject to enforcement action by the DOT agency just as you are for other violations of this part and DOT agency rules.

[65 FR 79526, Dec. 19, 2000, as amended at 88 FR 27637, May 2, 2023]

§ 40.23 What actions do employers take after receiving verified test results?

(a) As an employer who receives a verified positive drug test result, you must immediately remove the employee involved from performing safety-sensitive functions. You must take this action upon receiving the initial report of the verified positive test result. Do not wait to receive the written report or the result of a split specimen test.

(b) As an employer who receives a verified adulterated or substituted drug test result, you must consider this a refusal to test and immediately remove the employee involved from performing safety-sensitive functions. You must take this action on receiving the initial report of the verified adulterated or substituted test result. Do not wait to receive the written report or the result of a split specimen test.

(c) As an employer who receives an alcohol test result of 0.04 or higher, you must immediately remove the employee involved from performing safety-sensitive functions. If you receive an alcohol test result of 0.02–0.039, you must temporarily remove the employee involved from performing safety-sensitive functions, as provided in applicable DOT agency regulations. Do not wait to receive the written report of the result of the test.

(d) As an employer, when an employee has a verified positive, adulterated, or substituted test result, or has otherwise violated a DOT agency drug and alcohol regulation, you must not return the employee to the performance of safety-sensitive functions until or unless the employee successfully completes the return-to-duty process of Subpart O of this part.

(e) As an employer who receives a drug test result indicating that the employee's specimen was dilute, take action as provided in § 40.197.

(f) As an employer who receives a drug test result indicating that the employee's test was cancelled because it was invalid and that a second collection must take place under direct observation—

(1) You must immediately direct the employee to provide a new specimen under direct observation (either an oral fluid specimen or a urine specimen under direct observation).

(2) You must not attach consequences to the finding that the test was invalid other than collecting a new specimen under direct observation.

(3) You must not give any advance notice of this test requirement to the employee.

(4) You must instruct the collector to note on the CCF the same reason (*e.g.*, random test, post-accident test) and DOT Agency (e.g., check DOT and FMCSA) as for the original collection.

(5) You must ensure that the collector conducts the collection under direct observation (either an oral fluid specimen or a urine specimen under direct observation).

(g) As an employer who receives a cancelled test result when a negative result is required (*e.g.*, pre-employment, return-to-duty, or follow-up test), you must direct the employee to provide another specimen immediately.

(h) As an employer, you may also be required to take additional actions required by DOT agency regulations (*e.g.*, FAA rules require some positive drug tests to be reported to the Federal Air Surgeon).

(i) As an employer, you must not alter a drug or alcohol test result transmitted to you by an MRO, BAT, or C/TPA.

[65 FR 79526, Dec. 19, 2000, as amended at 71 FR 49384, Aug. 23, 2006; 73 FR 35970, June 25, 2008; 75 FR 59107, Sept. 27, 2010; 88 FR 27637, May 2, 2023]

§ 40.25 Must an employer check on the drug and alcohol testing record of employees it is intending to use to perform safety-sensitive duties?

(a)

(1) Yes, as an employer, you must, after obtaining an employee's written consent, request the information about the employee listed in paragraphs (b) through (j) of this section. This requirement applies only to employees seeking to begin performing safety-sensitive duties for you for the first time (*i.e.*, a new hire, an employee transferring into a safety-sensitive position). If the employee refuses to provide this written consent, you must not permit the employee to perform safety-sensitive functions.

(2) If you are an employer regulated by FMCSA, you must comply with the requirements of this section by using the FMCSA's Drug and Alcohol Clearinghouse in accordance with 49 CFR 382.71(a). In addition, you must continue to comply with the requirements of this § 40.25 when checking an employee's testing history with employers regulated by a DOT operating administration other than FMCSA.

(3) If you are an employer regulated by FMCSA, with a prospective employee subject to drug and alcohol testing with a DOT agency other than FMCSA, you must continue to request the information about the employee listed in paragraphs (b) through (j) of this section. For example, if you are an employer

regulated by both FMCSA and PHMSA, and you are hiring an employee to perform functions regulated by both DOT agencies, then you must query FMCSA's Clearinghouse to satisfy FMCSA's requirements and you must request the information listed in paragraphs (b) through (j) of this section to satisfy PHMSA's requirements.

(b) You must request the information listed in this paragraph (b) from DOT-regulated employers who have employed the employee during any period during the two years before the date of the employee's application or transfer:

(1) Alcohol tests with a result of 0.04 or higher alcohol concentration;

(2) Verified positive drug tests;

(3) Refusals to be tested (including verified adulterated or substituted drug test results);

(4) Other violations of DOT agency drug and alcohol testing regulations; and

(5) With respect to any employee who violated a DOT drug and alcohol regulation, documentation of the employee's successful completion of DOT return-to-duty requirements (including follow-up tests). If the previous employer does not have information about the return-do-duty process (e.g., an employer who did not hire an employee who tested positive on a pre-employment test), you must seek to obtain this information from the employee.

(c) The information obtained from a previous employer includes any drug or alcohol test information obtained from previous employers under this section or other applicable DOT agency regulations.

(d) If feasible, you must obtain and review this information before the employee first performs safety-sensitive functions. If this is not feasible, you must obtain and review the information as soon as possible. However, you must not permit the employee to perform safety-sensitive functions after 30 days from the date on which the employee first performed safety-sensitive functions, unless you have obtained or made and documented a good faith effort to obtain this information.

(e) If you obtain information that the employee has violated a DOT agency drug and alcohol regulation, you must not use the employee to perform safety-sensitive functions unless you also obtain information that the employee has subsequently complied with the return-to-duty requirements of Subpart O of this part and DOT agency drug and alcohol regulations.

(f) You must provide to each of the employers from whom you request information under paragraph (b) of this section written consent for the release of the information cited in paragraph (a) of this section.

(g) The release of information under this section must be in any written form (e.g., fax, e-mail, letter) that ensures confidentiality. As the previous employer, you must maintain a written record of the information released, including the date, the party to whom it was released, and a summary of the information provided.

(h) If you are an employer from whom information is requested under paragraph (b) of this section, you must, after reviewing the employee's specific, written consent, immediately release the requested information to the employer making the inquiry.

(i) As the employer requesting the information required under this section, you must maintain a written, confidential record of the information you obtain or of the good faith efforts you made to obtain the information. You must retain this information for three years from the date of the employee's first performance of safety-sensitive duties for you.

(j) As the employer, you must also ask the employee whether he or she has tested positive, or refused to test, on any pre-employment drug or alcohol test administered by an employer to which the employee applied for, but did not obtain, safety-sensitive transportation work covered by DOT agency drug and alcohol testing rules during the past two years. If the employee admits that he or she had a positive test or a refusal to test, you must not use the employee to perform safety-sensitive functions for you, until and unless the employee documents successful completion of the return-to-duty process (see paragraphs (b)(5) and (e) of this section).

[65 FR 79526, Dec. 19, 2000, as amended at 88 FR 27637, May 2, 2023]

§ 40.26 What form must an employer use to report Management Information System (MIS) data to a DOT agency?

As an employer, when you are required to report MIS data to a DOT agency, you must use the U.S. Department of Transportation Drug and Alcohol Testing MIS Data Collection Form to report that data. You must use the form and instructions referenced at appendix J to part 40. You must submit the MIS report in accordance with rule requirements (*e.g.*, dates for submission; selection of companies required to submit, and method of reporting) established by the DOT agency regulating your operation.

[84 FR 16773, Apr. 23, 2019, as amended at 88 FR 27638, May 2, 2023]

§ 40.27 May an employer require an employee to sign a consent or release in connection with the DOT drug and alcohol testing program?

No, as an employer, you must not require an employee to sign a consent, release, waiver of liability, or indemnification agreement with respect to any part of the drug or alcohol testing process covered by this part (including, but not limited to, collections, laboratory testing, MRO and SAP services).

[66 FR 41950, Aug. 9, 2001]

Subpart C—Urine Collection Personnel

§ 40.31 Who may collect specimens for DOT drug testing?

(a) Collectors meeting the requirements of this subpart are the only persons authorized to collect urine specimens for DOT drug testing.

(b) A urine collector must meet training requirements of § 40.33.

(c) An oral fluid collector must meet the training requirements of § 40.35.

(d) To avoid the appearance of a conflict of interest, if you are the immediate supervisor of the employee being tested, you must not act as the collector when that employee is tested, unless no other collector is available and you are permitted to do so under DOT agency drug and alcohol regulations.

(e) You must not act as the collector for the employee being tested if you work for a HHS-certified laboratory (*e.g.*, as a technician or accessioner) and could link the employee with a urine specimen, drug testing result, or laboratory report.

(f) Employees are not permitted to be their own collector.

(1) An employee who is a qualified collector is not permitted to be their own collector; another qualified collector must perform the collection in accordance with this part.

(2) To avoid a potential conflict of interest, a collector must not be related to the employee being tested (*e.g.*, spouse, ex-spouse, relative) or a close personal friend.

[65 FR 79526, Dec. 19, 2000, as amended at 88 FR 27637, May 2, 2023]

§ 40.33 What training requirements must a collector meet for urine collection?

To be permitted to act as a urine collector in the DOT drug testing program, you must meet each of the requirements of this section:

(a) *Basic information.* You must be knowledgeable about this part, the current "DOT Urine Specimen Collection Procedures Guidelines," and DOT agency regulations applicable to the employers for whom you perform collections. DOT agency regulations, the DOT Urine Specimen Collection Procedures Guidelines, and other materials are available from ODAPC (Department of Transportation, 1200 New Jersey Avenue SE., Washington DC, 20590, 202–366–3784, or on the ODAPC Web site (*https://www.transportation.gov/odapc*). You must keep current on any changes to these materials. You must subscribe to the ODAPC list-serve at: *https://www.transportation.gov/odapc/get-odapc-email-updates*.

(b) *Qualification training.* You must receive qualification training meeting the requirements of this paragraph. Qualification training must provide instruction on the following subjects:

(1) All steps necessary to complete a collection correctly and the proper completion and transmission of the CCF;

(2) "Problem" collections (*e.g.*, situations like "shy bladder" and attempts to tamper with a specimen);

(3) Fatal flaws, correctable flaws, and how to correct problems in collections; and

(4) The collector's responsibility for maintaining the integrity of the collection process, ensuring the privacy of employees being tested, ensuring the security of the specimen, and avoiding conduct or statements that could be viewed as offensive or inappropriate;

(c) *Initial Proficiency Demonstration.* Following your completion of qualification training under paragraph (b) of this section, you must demonstrate proficiency in collections under this part by completing five consecutive error-free mock collections.

(1) The five mock collections must include two uneventful collection scenarios, one insufficient quantity of urine scenario, one temperature out of range scenario, and one scenario in which the employee refuses to sign the CCF and initial the specimen bottle tamper-evident seal.

(2) Another person must monitor and evaluate your performance, in person or by a means that provides real-time observation and interaction between the instructor and trainee, and attest in writing that the mock collections are "error-free." This person must be a qualified collector who has demonstrated necessary knowledge, skills, and abilities by—

(i) Regularly conducting DOT drug test collections for a period of at least a year;

(ii) Conducting collector training under this part for a year; or

(iii) Successfully completing a "train the trainer" course.

(d) You must meet the requirements of paragraphs (b) and (c) of this section before you begin to perform collector functions.

(e) *Refresher training.* No less frequently than every five years from the date on which you satisfactorily complete the requirements of paragraphs (b) and (c) of this section, you must complete refresher training that meets all the requirements of paragraphs (b) and (c) of this section.

(f) *Error correction training.* If you make a mistake in the collection process that causes a test to be cancelled (*i.e.,* a fatal or uncorrected flaw), you must undergo error correction training. This training must occur within 30 days of the date you are notified of the error that led to the need for retraining. Errors that cause cancellation but occur outside the collection process (*e.g.,* when a specimen is crushed or otherwise damaged during the transportation process, or is lost in transit), the cancellation would not be the result of an error by the collector during the collection process and does not require the collector to be retrained.

   (1) Error correction training must be provided and your proficiency documented in writing by a person who meets the requirements of paragraph (c)(2) of this section.

   (2) Error correction training is required to cover only the subject matter area(s) in which the error that caused the test to be cancelled occurred.

   (3) As part of the error correction training, you must demonstrate your proficiency in the collection procedures of this part by completing three consecutive error-free mock collections. The mock collections must include one uneventful scenario and two scenarios related to the area(s) in which your error(s) occurred. The person providing the training must monitor and evaluate your performance and attest in writing that the mock collections were "error-free."

(g) *Documentation.* You must maintain documentation showing that you currently meet all requirements of this section. You must provide this documentation on request to DOT agency representatives and to employers and C/TPAs who are using or negotiating to use your services.

[65 FR 79526, Dec. 19, 2000; 66 FR 3885, Jan. 17, 2001, as amended at 66 FR 41950, Aug. 9, 2001; 82 FR 52244, Nov. 13, 2017; 88 FR 27638, May 2, 2023]

§ 40.35 What training requirements must a collector meet for oral fluid collection?

To be permitted to act as an oral fluid collector in the DOT drug testing program, you must meet each of the requirements of this section:

(a) *Basic information.* You must be knowledgeable about this part, the current "DOT Oral Fluid Specimen Collection Procedures Guidelines," and DOT agency regulations applicable to the employers for whom you perform collections. DOT agency regulations, guidelines, and other materials are available from ODAPC (Department of Transportation, 1200 New Jersey Avenue SE, Washington DC, 20590, 202–366–3784, or on the ODAPC website (*https://www.transportation.gov/odapc*). You must keep current on any changes to these materials. You must subscribe to the ODAPC list-serve at: *https://www.transportation.gov/odapc/get-odapc-email-updates.*

(b) *Qualification training.* You must receive qualification training meeting the requirements of this paragraph (b). Qualification training must provide instruction on the following subjects:

   (1) Training on the testing procedures of this part;

(2) Training to proficiency in the operation of the particular oral fluid collection device(s) you will be using.

(3) All steps necessary to complete a collection correctly and the proper completion and transmission of the CCF;

(4) "Problem" collections (*e.g.*, situations like "dry mouth" and attempts to tamper with a specimen);

(5) Fatal flaws, correctable flaws, and how to correct problems in collections; and

(6) The collector's responsibility for maintaining the integrity of the collection process, ensuring the privacy of employees being tested, ensuring the security of the specimen, and avoiding conduct or statements that could be viewed as offensive or inappropriate.

(c) *Initial proficiency demonstration.* Following your completion of qualification training under paragraph (b) of this section, you must demonstrate proficiency in collections under this part by completing five consecutive error-free mock collections for each device you will use.

(1) The five mock collections for each device must include one uneventful collection scenario, one insufficient specimen quantity scenario; one scenario in which the employee has something in their mouth that might interfere with the collection; one scenario in which the employee attempts to tamper with the specimen; and one scenario in which the employee refuses to sign the CCF. For each of the five mock collections, the collector must check the expiration date of the device, show it to the employee, and record the date on the CCF used. The collector must ensure, when applying the labels, they do not cover the expiration dates.

(2) Another person must monitor and evaluate your performance, in person or by a means that provides real-time observation and interaction between you and the qualified collector, who must attest in writing that the mock collections are "error-free." This person must be a qualified collector who has demonstrated necessary knowledge, skills, and abilities by—

(i) Regularly conducting DOT drug test collections for a period of at least one year;

(ii) Conducting collector training under this part for at least one year; or

(iii) Successfully completing a "train the trainer" course.

(d) *Schedule for qualification training and initial proficiency demonstration.* You must meet the requirements of paragraphs (b) and (c) of this section before you begin to perform collector functions.

(e) *Refresher training.* No less frequently than every five years from the date on which you satisfactorily complete the requirements of paragraphs (b) and (c) of this section, you must complete refresher training that meets all the requirements of paragraphs (b) and (c).

(f) *Error correction training.* If you make a mistake in the collection process that causes a test to be cancelled (*i.e.*, a fatal or uncorrected flaw), you must undergo error correction training. This training must occur within 30 days of the date you are notified of the error that led to the need for retraining.

(1) Error correction training must be provided and your proficiency documented in writing by a person who meets the requirements of paragraph (c)(2) of this section.

(2) Error correction training is required to cover only the subject matter area(s) in which the error that caused the test to be cancelled occurred.

(3) As part of the error correction training, you must demonstrate your proficiency in the collection procedures of this part by completing three consecutive error-free mock collections. The mock collections must include one uneventful scenario and two scenarios related to the area(s) in which your error(s) occurred. The person providing the training must monitor and evaluate your performance and attest in writing that the mock collections were "error-free."

(g) *Documentation.* You must maintain documentation showing that you currently meet all requirements of this section. You must provide this documentation on request to DOT agency representatives and to employers and C/TPAs who are using or negotiating to use your services.

[88 FR 27638, May 2, 2023]

§ 40.36 What information about the DER must employers provide to collectors?

As an employer, you must provide to collectors the name and telephone number of the appropriate DER (and C/TPA, where applicable) to contact about any problems or issues that may arise during the testing process.

[65 FR 79526, Dec. 19, 2000. Redesignated at 88 FR 27639, May 2, 2023]

Subpart D—Collection Sites, Forms, Equipment and Supplies Used in DOT Urine and Oral Fluid Collections

§ 40.40 What form is used to document a DOT collection?

(a) The Federal Drug Testing Custody and Control Form (CCF) must be used to document every collection required by the DOT drug testing program. You may view this form on the Department's website (*https://www.transportation.gov/odapc*) or the HHS website (*https://www.workplace.samhsa.gov*).

(b) You must not use a non-Federal form or an expired CCF to conduct a DOT collection. As a laboratory, C/TPA or other party that provides CCFs to employers, collection sites, or other customers, you must not provide copies of an expired CCF to these participants. You must also affirmatively notify these participants that they must not use an expired CCF.

(c) As a participant in the DOT drug testing program, you are not permitted to modify or revise the CCF except as follows:

(1) You may include, in the area outside the border of the form, other information needed for billing or other purposes necessary to the collection process.

(2) The CCF must include the names, addresses, telephone numbers and any other appropriate contact information (*e.g.*, an email address of the employer and the MRO), including the DER's name and contact information. All of this information must be preprinted, typed, or handwritten. Fax numbers may be included but are not required. The MRO information must include the physician's name and address, as opposed to only a generic clinic, health care organization, company name, or post office box. This information is required, and an employer, collector, service agent or any other party is prohibited from omitting it. In addition, a C/TPA's name, address, telephone and fax numbers, and any other appropriate contact information should be included, but is not required. The employer may use a C/TPA's address in place of its own, but must continue to include its name, telephone and fax numbers, and any other appropriate contact information.

(3) As an employer you may preprint the box in Step 1–D of the CCF for the DOT agency under whose authority the test will occur.

(4) As a collector, you may use a CCF with your name, address, telephone number, and fax number preprinted, but under no circumstances may you sign the form before the collection event. If a collection takes place at a clinic, the actual address of the clinic should be used, not a corporate address of the collection company. If the collection takes place onsite at the employer, the employer's address must be noted as the collection site address. If the collection takes place in a "mobile unit" or at an accident site, the collector must enter the actual location address of the collection or as near an approximation as possible. The collector must ensure that the required collector telephone number is the number that the laboratory, MRO, or employer may use to directly contact the individual collector and/or the collector's supervisor during the collection site's business hours. The collector must not provide a number for a call center.

(5) When using an electronic CCF, you must establish adequate confidentiality and security measures to ensure that confidential employee records are not available to unauthorized persons. This includes protecting the physical security of records, access controls, and computer security measures to safeguard confidential data in electronic form.

(d) Under no circumstances may the CCF transmit personal identifying information about an employee (other than a SSN or Employee ID No.) to a laboratory.

(e) As an employer, you may use an equivalent foreign-language version of the CCF approved by ODAPC. You may use such a non-English language form only in a situation where both the employee and collector understand and can use the form in that language.

(f) An employer who uses an electronic CCF must ensure that the collection site, the primary and split laboratories, and MRO have compatible systems, and that the employee and any other program participants in the testing process will receive a legible copy of the CCF.

[65 FR 79526, Dec. 19, 2000, as amended at 66 FR 41950, Aug. 9, 2001; 75 FR 59107, Sept. 27, 2010; 76 FR 59577, Sept. 27, 2011; 80 FR 19553, Apr. 13, 2015; 82 FR 52244, Nov. 13, 2017. Redesignated and amended at 88 FR 27639, May 2, 2023]

§ 40.41 May employers use the CCF for non-Federal collections or non-Federal forms for DOT collections?

(a) No, as an employer, you are prohibited from using the CCF for non-Federal collections. You are also prohibited from using non-Federal forms for DOT collections. Doing either subjects you to enforcement action under DOT agency regulations.

(b)

(1) In the rare case where the collector, either by mistake or as the only means to conduct a test under difficult circumstances (e.g., post-accident or reasonable suspicion test with insufficient time to obtain the CCF), uses a non-Federal form for a DOT collection, the use of a non-Federal form does not present a reason for the laboratory to reject the specimen for testing or for an MRO to cancel the result.

(2) The use of the non-Federal form is a "correctable flaw." As an MRO, to correct the problem you must follow the procedures of § 40.205(b)(2).

49 CFR Part 40 (up to date as of 3/05/2024)
Procedures for Transportation Workplace Drug and Alcohol Testing Programs

49 CFR 40.42

[65 FR 79526, Dec. 19, 2000, as amended at 66 FR 41950, Aug. 9, 2001. Redesignated and amended at 88 FR 27639, June 1, 2023]

§ 40.42 Where does a urine collection for a DOT drug test take place?

(a) A urine collection for a DOT drug test must take place in a collection site meeting the requirements of this section.

(b) If you are operating a collection site, you must ensure that it meets the security requirements of § 40.43.

(c) If you are operating a collection site, you must have all necessary personnel, materials, equipment, facilities and supervision to provide for the collection, temporary storage, and shipping of urine specimens to a laboratory, and a suitable clean surface for writing.

(d) Your collection site must include a facility for urination described in either paragraph (e) or paragraph (f) of this section.

(e) The first, and preferred, type of facility for urination that a collection site may include is a single-toilet room, having a full-length privacy door, within which urination can occur.

   (1) No one but the employee may be present in the room during the collection, except for the observer in the event of a directly observed collection.

   (2) You must have a source of water for washing hands, that, if practicable, should be external to the closed room where urination occurs. If an external source is not available, you may meet this requirement by securing all sources of water and other substances that could be used for adulteration and substitution (*e.g.*, water faucets, soap dispensers) and providing moist towelettes outside the closed room.

(f) The second type of facility for urination that a collection site may include is a multistall restroom.

   (1) Such a site must provide substantial visual privacy (*e.g.*, a toilet stall with a partial-length door) and meet all other applicable requirements of this section.

   (2) If you use a multi-stall restroom, you must either—

      (i) Secure all sources of water and other substances that could be used for adulteration and substitution (*e.g.*, water faucets, soap dispensers) and place bluing agent in all toilets or secure the toilets to prevent access; or

      (ii) Conduct all collections in the facility as monitored collections (see § 40.69 for procedures). This is the only circumstance in which you may conduct a monitored collection.

   (3) No one but the employee may be present in the multistall restroom during the collection, except for the monitor in the event of a monitored collection or the observer in the event of a directly observed collection.

(g) A collection site may be in a medical facility, a mobile facility (*e.g.*, a van), a dedicated collection facility, or any other location meeting the requirements of this section.

[65 FR 79526, Dec. 19, 2000. Redesignated at 88 FR 27639, May 2, 2023]

§ 40.43 What steps must operators of collection sites and collectors take to protect the security and integrity of urine collections?

(a) Collectors and operators of collection sites must take the steps listed in this section to prevent unauthorized access that could compromise the integrity of collections.

(b) As a collector, you must do the following before each collection to deter tampering with specimens:

    (1) Secure any water sources or otherwise make them unavailable to employees (*e.g.*, turn off water inlet, tape handles to prevent opening faucets);

    (2) Ensure that the water in the toilet is blue;

    (3) Ensure that no soap, disinfectants, cleaning agents, or other possible adulterants are present;

    (4) Inspect the site to ensure that no foreign or unauthorized substances are present;

    (5) Tape or otherwise secure shut any movable toilet tank top, or put bluing in the tank;

    (6) Ensure that undetected access (*e.g.*, through a door not in your view) is not possible;

    (7) Secure areas and items (*e.g.*, ledges, trash receptacles, paper towel holders, under-sink areas) that appear suitable for concealing contaminants; and

    (8) Recheck items in paragraphs (b)(1) through (7) of this section following each collection to ensure the site's continued integrity.

(c) If the collection site uses a facility normally used for other purposes, like a public rest room or hospital examining room, you must, as a collector, also ensure before the collection that:

    (1) Access to collection materials and specimens is effectively restricted; and

    (2) The facility is secured against access during the procedure to ensure privacy to the employee and prevent distraction of the collector. Limited-access signs must be posted.

(d) As a collector, you must take the following additional steps to ensure security during the collection process:

    (1) To avoid distraction that could compromise security, you are limited to conducting a collection for only one employee at a time. However, during the time one employee is in the period for drinking fluids in a "shy bladder" situation (see § 40.193(b)), you may conduct a collection for another employee.

    (2) To the greatest extent you can, keep an employee's collection container within view of both you and the employee between the time the employee has urinated and the specimen is sealed.

    (3) Ensure you are the only person in addition to the employee who handles the specimen before it is poured into the bottles and sealed with tamper-evident seals.

    (4) In the time between when the employee gives you the specimen and when you seal the specimen, remain within the collection site.

    (5) Maintain personal control over each specimen and CCF throughout the collection process.

(e) If you are operating a collection site, you must implement a policy and procedures to prevent unauthorized personnel from entering any part of the site in which urine specimens are collected or stored.

(1) Only employees being tested, collectors and other collection site workers, DERs, employee and employer representatives authorized by the employer (*e.g.*, employer policy, collective bargaining agreement), and DOT agency representatives are authorized persons for purposes of this paragraph (e).

(2) Except for the observer in a directly observed collection or the monitor in the case of a monitored collection, you must not permit anyone to enter the urination facility in which employees provide specimens.

(3) You must ensure that all authorized persons are under the supervision of a collector at all times when permitted into the site.

(4) You or the collector may remove any person who obstructs, interferes with, or causes a delay in the collection process.

(f) If you are operating a collection site, you must minimize the number of persons handling specimens.

§ 40.44 What materials are used to collect urine specimens?

For each DOT drug test, you must use a collection kit meeting the requirements of Appendix A of this part.

[65 FR 79526, Dec. 19, 2000. Redesignated at 88 FR 27639, May 2, 2023]

§ 40.45 What materials are used to send urine specimens to the laboratory?

(a) Except as provided in paragraph (b) of this section, you must use a shipping container that adequately protects the specimen bottles from shipment damage in the transport of specimens from the collection site to the laboratory.

(b) You are not required to use a shipping container if a laboratory courier hand-delivers the specimens from the collection site to the laboratory.

[65 FR 79526, Dec. 19, 2000. Redesignated at 88 FR 27639, May 2, 2023]

§ 40.47 Where does an oral fluid collection for a DOT drug test take place?

(a) An oral fluid collection for a DOT drug test must take place in a collection site meeting the requirements of this section.

(b) If you are operating an oral fluid collection site:

(1) You must ensure that it meets the security requirements of § 40.48;

(2) The site may be a permanent or temporary facility located either at the work site or at a remote site;

(3) The site may be in a medical facility, a mobile facility (*e.g.*, a van), a dedicated collection facility, or any other location meeting the requirements of this section; and

(4) You must have all necessary personnel, materials, equipment, and facilities that include privacy and supervision to provide for the collection, temporary storage, and shipping of specimens to a laboratory, and a suitable clean surface for writing.

(c) If a collection site is not accessible and there is an immediate requirement to collect an oral fluid specimen (*e.g.*, an accident investigation), another site may be used for the collection, if the collection is performed by a collector who has been trained to collect oral fluid specimens in accordance with this part and the manufacturer's procedures for the collection device.

[88 FR 27640, May 2, 2023]

§ 40.48 What steps must operators of collection sites and collectors take to protect the security and integrity of oral fluid collections?

(a) Collectors and operators of collection sites must take the steps listed in this section to prevent unauthorized access that could compromise the integrity of collections.

(b) As a collector, you must do the following before each collection to deter tampering with specimens:

  (1) Ensure that access to collection materials and specimens is effectively restricted;

  (2) Ensure that undetected access (*e.g.*, through a door not in your view) is not possible; and

  (3) Ensure the security of the facility during the collection process to maintain privacy to the employee and prevent distraction of the collector. Limited-access signs must be posted.

(c) As a collector, you must take the following additional steps to ensure security during the collection process:

  (1) To avoid distraction that could compromise security, you are limited to conducting a collection for only one employee at a time. However, during the time one employee is in the period for drinking fluids in a "dry mouth" situation (*see* § 40.72(b)(1)), you may conduct a collection for another employee as long as the employee with "dry mouth" remains supervised.

  (2) To the greatest extent practicable, keep an employee's collection container within view of both you and the employee between the time the employee has provided the oral fluid specimen and the specimen is sealed.

  (3) Ensure you are the only person in addition to the employee who handles the specimen before it is sealed with tamper-evident seals.

  (4) In the time between when the employee gives you the specimen and when you seal the specimen, remain within the collection site.

  (5) Maintain personal control over each specimen and CCF throughout the collection process.

(d) If you are operating a collection site, you must implement a policy and procedures to prevent unauthorized personnel from entering any part of the site in which oral fluid specimens are collected or stored.

  (1) Only employees being tested, collectors and other collection site workers, DERs, employee and employer representatives authorized by the employer (*e.g.*, employer policy, collective bargaining agreement), and DOT agency representatives are authorized persons for purposes of this paragraph (d).

  (2) You must ensure that all authorized persons are under the supervision of a collector at all times when permitted into the site.

  (3) You or the collector may remove any person who obstructs, interferes with, or causes a delay in the collection process.

(e) If you are operating a collection site, you must minimize the number of persons handling specimens.

[88 FR 27640, May 2, 2023]

§ 40.49 What materials are used to collect oral fluid specimens?

For each DOT drug test, you must use a collection device meeting the requirements of appendix B of this part.

[88 FR 27640, May 2, 2023]

§ 40.51 What materials are used to send oral fluid specimens to the laboratory?

(a) Except as provided in paragraph (b) of this section, you must use a shipping container that adequately protects the specimen bottles from damage in the transport of specimens from the collection site to the laboratory.

(b) You are not required to use a shipping container if a laboratory courier hand-delivers the specimens from the collection site to the laboratory.

[88 FR 27640, May 2, 2023]

Subpart E—Specimen Collections

§ 40.61 What are the preliminary steps in the drug testing collection process?

As the collector, you must take the following steps before actually beginning a collection:

(a) When a specific time for an employee's test has been scheduled, or the collection site is at the employee's work site, and the employee does not appear at the collection site at the scheduled time, contact the DER to determine the appropriate interval within which the DER has determined the employee is authorized to arrive. If the employee's arrival is delayed beyond that time, you must notify the DER that the employee has not reported for testing, the DER must determine whether the employee has refused to test (*see* §§ 40.191(a)(1) and 40.355(i)). In a situation where a C/TPA has notified an owner/operator or other individual employee to report for testing (other than for a pre-employment test) and the employee does not appear, the C/TPA must determine whether the employee has refused to test (*see* §§ 40.191(a)(1) and 40.355(j)).

(b) Ensure that, when the employee enters the collection site, you begin the testing process without undue delay. For example, you must not wait because the employee says he or she is not ready or is unable to urinate or because an authorized employer or employee representative is delayed in arriving.

(1) If the employee is also going to take a DOT alcohol test, you must ensure, to the greatest extent practicable, that the alcohol test is completed before the drug testing collection process begins.

Example to paragraph (b)(1): An employee enters the test site for both a drug and an alcohol test. Normally, the collector would wait until the BAT had completed the alcohol test process before beginning the drug test process. However, there are some situations in which an exception to this normal practice would be reasonable. One such situation might be if several people were waiting for the BAT to conduct alcohol tests, but a drug testing collector in the same facility were free. Someone waiting might be able to complete a drug test without unduly delaying his or her alcohol test. Collectors and BATs should work together, however, to ensure that post-accident and reasonable suspicion alcohol tests happen as soon as possible (*e.g.,* by moving the employee to the head of the line for alcohol tests).

(2) If the employee needs medical attention (*e.g.,* an injured employee in an emergency medical facility who is required to have a post-accident test), do not delay this treatment to collect a specimen.

(3) You must not collect a specimen from an unconscious employee to conduct a drug test under this part.

(4) You must not catheterize a conscious employee for purposes of a urine test. However, you must inform an employee who normally voids through self-catheterization that the employee is required to provide a specimen in that manner. If an employee normally voids through self-catheterization, but declines to do so for the urine test, the collector should notify the DER of the circumstances, so that the actual employer can determine whether the situation constitutes a refusal to test by the employee.

(c) Require the employee to provide positive identification. You must see a photo ID issued by the employer (other than in the case of an owner-operator or other self-employed individual) or a Federal, state, or local government (*e.g.,* a driver's license). You may not accept faxes or photocopies of identification. Positive identification by an employer representative (not a co-worker or another employee being tested) is also acceptable. If the employee cannot produce positive identification, you must contact a DER to verify the identity of the employee.

(d) If the employee asks, provide your identification to the employee. Your identification must include your name and your employer's name, but does not have to include your picture, address, or telephone number.

(e) Explain the basic collection procedure to the employee, and notify the employee that instructions for completing the CCF can be found at the HHS (*https://www.samhsa.gov/workplace*) and DOT (*https://www.transportation.gov/odapc*) websites.

(f) Direct the employee to remove outer clothing (*e.g.,* coveralls, jacket, coat, hat) that could be used to conceal items or substances that could be used to tamper with a specimen. You must also direct the employee to leave these garments and any briefcase, purse, or other personal belongings with you or in a mutually agreeable location. You must advise the employee that failure to comply with your directions constitutes a refusal to test.

(1) If the employee asks for a receipt for any belongings left with you, you must provide one.

(2) You must allow the employee to keep his or her wallet.

(3) You must not ask the employee to remove other clothing (*e.g.,* shirts, pants, dresses, underwear), to remove all clothing, or to change into a hospital or examination gown (unless the urine collection is being accomplished simultaneously with a DOT agency-authorized medical examination).

(4) You must direct the employee to empty his or her pockets and display the items in them to ensure that no items are present which could be used to adulterate the specimen. If nothing is there that can be used to adulterate a specimen, the employee can place the items back into his or her pockets. As the employee, you must allow the collector to make this observation.

(5) If, in your duties under paragraph (f)(4) of this section, you find any material that could be used to tamper with a specimen, you must:

    (i) Determine if the material appears to be brought to the collection site with the intent to alter the specimen, and, if it is, either conduct a directly observed urine collection using direct observation procedures (*see* § 40.67) or an oral fluid specimen collection, make a note on the CCF and continue with collection process; or

    (ii) Determine if the material appears to be inadvertently brought to the collection site (*e.g.,* eye drops), secure and maintain it until the collection process is completed and conduct a normal (*i.e.,* unobserved) collection.

(g) You must instruct the employee not to list medications that he or she is currently taking on the CCF. (The employee may make notes of medications on the back of the employee copy of the form for his or her own convenience, but these notes must not be transmitted to anyone else.)

[65 FR 79526, Dec. 19, 2000, as amended at 88 FR 27640, May 2, 2023]

§ 40.63 What steps does the collector take in the collection process before the employee provides a urine specimen?

As the collector, you must take the following steps before the employee provides the urine specimen:

(a) Ensure all items under Step 1 of the CCF are complete and accurate (*e.g.,* if Step 1.D is not checked, put a check mark for the "Specify DOT Agency" under the authority of which the test will take place; if the address where the collection is actually taking place is not in Step 1.G, update that.)

(b) Instruct the employee to wash and dry his or her hands at this time. You must tell the employee not to wash his or her hands again until after delivering the specimen to you. You must not give the employee any further access to water or other materials that could be used to adulterate or dilute a specimen.

(c) Select, or allow the employee to select, an individually wrapped or sealed collection container from collection kit materials. Either you or the employee, with both of you present, must unwrap or break the seal of the collection container. You must not unwrap or break the seal on any specimen bottle at this time. You must not allow the employee to take anything from the collection kit into the room used for urination except the collection container.

(d) Direct the employee to go into the room used for urination, provide a specimen of at least 45 mL, not flush the toilet, and return to you with the specimen as soon as the employee has completed the void.

    (1) Except in the case of an observed or a monitored collection (see §§ 40.67 and 40.69), neither you nor anyone else may go into the room with the employee.

    (2) As the collector, you may set a reasonable time limit for voiding.

(e) You must pay careful attention to the employee during the entire collection process to note any conduct that clearly indicates an attempt to tamper with a specimen (*e.g.,* substitute urine in plain view or an attempt to bring into the collection site an adulterant or urine substitute). If you detect such conduct, you must require that a collection take place immediately under direct observation (*see* § 40.67) and complete Step 2 by noting the conduct in the "Remarks" line of the CCF and the fact that the collection was observed by checking the "Observed" box. You must also, as soon as possible, inform the DER and collection site supervisor that a collection took place under direct observation and the reason for doing so.

[65 FR 79526, Dec. 19, 2000, as amended at 75 FR 59107, Sept. 27, 2010; 88 FR 27641, May 2, 2023]

§ 40.65 What does the collector check for when the employee presents a urine specimen?

As a collector, you must check the following when the employee gives the collection container to you:

(a) *Sufficiency of specimen.* You must check to ensure that the specimen contains at least 45 mL of urine.

   (1) If it does not, you must follow "shy bladder" procedures (see § 40.193(b)).

   (2) When you follow "shy bladder" procedures, you must discard the original specimen, unless another problem (*i.e.*, temperature out of range, signs of tampering) also exists.

   (3) You are never permitted to combine urine collected from separate voids to create a specimen.

   (4) You must discard any excess urine.

(b) *Temperature.* You must check the temperature of the specimen no later than four minutes after the employee has given you the specimen.

   (1) The acceptable temperature range is 32–38 °C/90–100 °F.

   (2) You must determine the temperature of the specimen by reading the temperature strip attached to the collection container.

   (3) If the specimen temperature is within the acceptable range, you must mark the "Yes" box on the CCF (Step 2).

   (4) If the specimen temperature is outside the acceptable range, you must mark the "No" box and enter in the "Remarks" line (Step 2) your findings about the temperature.

   (5) If the specimen temperature is outside the acceptable range, you must immediately conduct a new urine collection using direct observation procedures (*see* § 40.67) or an oral fluid collection.

   (6) In a case where a specimen is collected under direct observation because of the temperature being out of range, you must process both the original specimen and the specimen collected using direct observation (including oral fluid) and send the two sets of specimens to their respective laboratories. This is true even in a case in which the original specimen has insufficient volume and the temperature is out of range. You must also, as soon as possible, inform the DER and collection site supervisor that a collection took place under direct observation and the reason for doing so.

   (7) In a case where the employee refuses to provide another specimen (see § 40.191(a)(3)) or refuses to provide another specimen under direct observation (see § 40.191(a)(4)), you must notify the DER. As soon as you have notified the DER, you must discard any specimen the employee has provided previously during the collection procedure.

(c) *Signs of tampering.* You must inspect the specimen for unusual color, presence of foreign objects or material, or other signs of tampering (*e.g.*, if you notice any unusual odor).

(1) If it is apparent from this inspection that the employee has tampered with the specimen (*e.g.,* blue dye in the specimen, excessive foaming when shaken, or smell of bleach), you must immediately conduct a new urine collection using direct observation procedures (*see* § 40.67) or an oral fluid collection.

(2) In a case where a specimen is collected under direct observation because of showing signs of tampering, you must process both the original specimen and the specimen collected using direct observation and send the two sets of specimens to the laboratory. This is true even in a case in which the original specimen has insufficient volume but it shows signs of tampering. You must also, as soon as possible, inform the DER and collection site supervisor that a collection took place under direct observation and the reason for doing so.

(3) In a case where the employee refuses to provide a specimen under direct observation (see § 40.191(a)(4)), you must discard any specimen the employee provided previously during the collection procedure. Then you must notify the DER as soon as practicable.

[65 FR 79526, Dec. 19, 2000, as amended at 66 FR 41950, Aug. 9, 2001; 88 FR 27641, May 2, 2023]

§ 40.67 When and how is a directly observed urine collection conducted?

(a) As an employer, you must direct an immediate collection under direct observation with no advance notice to the employee, if:

(1) The laboratory reported to the MRO that a specimen is invalid, and the MRO reported to you that there was not an adequate medical explanation for the result;

(2) The MRO reported to you that the original positive, adulterated, or substituted result had to be cancelled because the test of the split specimen could not be performed; or

(3) The laboratory reported to the MRO that the specimen was negative-dilute with a creatinine concentration greater than or equal to 2 mg/dL but less than or equal to 5 mg/dL, and the MRO reported the specimen to you as negative-dilute and that a second collection must take place under direct observation (see § 40.197(b)(1)).

(4) You realize a collection under direct observation was required but was not conducted or the service agent informs you that a direct observation should have been collected but was not (*see* paragraph (n) of this section).

(b) As an employer, you must direct a collection under direct observation of an employee if the drug test is a return-to-duty test or a follow-up test.

(c) As a collector, you must immediately conduct a collection under direct observation if:

(1) You are directed by the DER to do so (see paragraph (a) of this section); or

(2) You observed materials brought to the collection site or the employee's conduct clearly indicates an attempt to tamper with a specimen (see §§ 40.61(f)(5)(i) and 40.63(e)); or

(3) The temperature on the original specimen was out of range (*see* § 40.65(b)(5));

(4) The original specimen appeared to have been tampered with (*see* § 40.65(c)(1)); or

(5) The test reason is return-to-duty or follow-up.

(d)

49 CFR Part 40 (up to date as of 3/05/2024)
Procedures for Transportation Workplace Drug and Alcohol Testing Programs
49 CFR 40.67(d)(1)

   (1)   As the employer, you must explain to the employee the reason for a directly observed collection under paragraph (a) or (b) of this section.

   (2)   As the collector, you must explain to the employee the reason, if known, under this part for a directly observed collection.

(e)   As the collector, you must complete a new CCF for the directly observed collection.

   (1)   You must mark the "reason for test" block (Step 1) the same as for the first collection.

   (2)   You must check the "Observed, (Enter Remark)" box and enter the reason (see paragraphs (c)(2) through (4) of this section) in the "Remarks" line (Step 2).

(f)   In a case where two sets of specimens are being sent to the laboratory because of suspected tampering with the specimen at the collection site, enter on the "Remarks" line of the CCF (Step 2) for each specimen a notation to this effect (e.g., collection 1 of 2, or 2 of 2) and the specimen ID number of the other specimen.

(g)   As the collector, you must ensure that the observer is the same gender as the employee.

   (1)   You must never permit an opposite gender person to act as the observer.

   (2)   The observer can be a different person from the collector and need not be a qualified collector.

   (3)   If a same gender collector cannot be found or in circumstances of nonbinary or transgender employees:

      (i)   If the employer has a standing order to allow oral fluid testing in such situations, the collector will follow that order;

      (ii)   If there is no standing order from the employer, the collector must contact the DER and either conduct an oral fluid test if the collection site is able to do so, or send the employee to a collection site acceptable to the employer for the oral fluid test.

(h)   As the collector, if someone else is to observe the collection (e.g., in order to ensure a same gender observer), you must verbally instruct that person to follow procedures at paragraphs (i) and (j) of this section. If you, the collector, are the observer, you too must follow these procedures.

(i)   As the observer, you must request the employee to raise his or her shirt, blouse, or dress/skirt, as appropriate, above the waist; and lower clothing and underpants to show you, by turning around, that they do not have a prosthetic device. After you have determined that the employee does not have such a device, you may permit the employee to return clothing to its proper position for observed urination.

(j)   As the observer, you must watch the employee urinate into the collection container. Specifically, you are to watch the urine go from the employee's body into the collection container.

(k)   As the observer but not the collector, you must not take the collection container from the employee, but you must observe the specimen as the employee takes it to the collector.

(l)   As the collector, when someone else has acted as the observer, you must include the observer's name in the "Remarks" line of the CCF (Step 2).

(m)   As the employee, if you decline to allow a directly observed collection required or permitted under this section to occur, this is a refusal to test.

(n) As a service agent, when you learn that a directly observed collection should have been collected but was not, you must inform the employer that it must direct the employee to have an immediate recollection under direct observation.

[65 FR 79526, Dec. 19, 2000, as amended at 66 FR 41950, Aug. 9, 2001; 68 FR 31626, May 28, 2003; 69 FR 64867, Nov. 9, 2004; 73 FR 35970, June 25, 2008; 73 FR 50223, Aug. 26, 2008; 73 FR 62910, Oct. 22, 2008; 73 FR 70284, Nov. 20, 2008; 74 FR 37952, July 30, 2009; 82 FR 52244, Nov. 13, 2017; 88 FR 27641, May 2, 2023]

§ 40.69 How is a monitored urine collection conducted?

(a) As stated in § 40.42(f)(2), if you are conducting a urine collection in a multi-stall restroom and you cannot secure all sources of water and other substances that could be used for adulteration and substitution, you must conduct a monitored collection. This is the only circumstance in which you must conduct a monitored collection.

(b) As the collector, you must secure the room being used for the monitored collection so that no one except the employee and the monitor can enter it until after the collection has been completed.

(c) As the collector, you must ensure that the monitor is the same gender as the employee, unless the monitor is a medical professional (e.g., nurse, doctor, physician's assistant, technologist, or technician licensed or certified to practice in the jurisdiction in which the collection takes place). The monitor can be a different person from the collector and need not be a qualified collector.

(d) As the collector, if someone else is to monitor the collection (e.g., in order to ensure a same-gender monitor), you must verbally instruct that person to follow the procedures of paragraphs (d) and (e) of this section. If you, the collector, are the monitor, you must follow these procedures.

(e) As the monitor, you must not watch the employee urinate into the collection container. If you hear sounds or make other observations indicating an attempt to tamper with a specimen, there must be an additional collection under direct observation. *See* §§ 40.63(e), 40.65(c), and 40.67(c)(2)(3)).

(f) As the monitor, you must ensure that the employee takes the collection container directly to the collector as soon as the employee has exited the enclosure.

(g) As the collector, when someone else has acted as the monitor, you must note that person's name in the "Remarks" line of the CCF (Step 2).

(h) As the employee being tested, if you decline to permit a collection authorized under this section to be monitored, it is a refusal to test.

[65 FR 79526, Dec. 19, 2000, as amended at 66 FR 41951, Aug. 9, 2001; 88 FR 27641, May 2, 2023]

§ 40.71 How does the collector prepare the urine specimen?

(a) All collections under DOT agency drug testing regulations must be split specimen collections.

(b) As the collector, you must take the following steps, in order, after the employee brings the urine specimen to you. You must take these steps in the presence of the employee.

(1) After the collection, check the box on the CCF (Step 2) indicating that this was a "Urine" and "Split" specimen collection.

(2) You, not the employee, must first pour at least 30 mL of urine from the collection container into one specimen bottle, to be used for the primary specimen.

(3) You, not the employee, must then pour at least 15 mL of urine from the collection container into the second specimen bottle to be used for the split specimen.

(4) You, not the employee, must place and secure (*i.e.*, tighten or snap) the lids/caps on the bottles.

(5) You, not the employee, must seal the bottles by placing the tamper-evident bottle seals over the bottle caps/lids and down the sides of the bottles.

(6) You, not the employee, must then write the date on the tamper-evident bottle seals.

(7) You must then ensure that the employee initials the tamper-evident bottle seals for the purpose of certifying that the bottles contain the specimens he or she provided. If the employee fails or refuses to do so, you must note this in the "Remarks" line of the CCF (Step 2) and complete the collection process.

(8) You must discard any urine left over in the collection container after both specimen bottles have been appropriately filled and sealed. There is one exception to this requirement: you may use excess urine to conduct clinical tests (e.g., protein, glucose) if the collection was conducted in conjunction with a physical examination required by a DOT agency regulation. Neither you nor anyone else may conduct further testing (such as adulteration testing) on this excess urine and the employee has no legal right to demand that the excess urine be turned over to the employee.

[65 FR 79526, Dec. 19, 2000, as amended at 66 FR 41951, Aug. 9, 2001; 88 FR 27641, May 2, 2023]

§ 40.72 What steps does the collector take in the collection process before the employee provides an oral fluid specimen?

(a) The collector requests that the employee open the employee's mouth, and the collector inspects the oral cavity to ensure that it is free of any items that could impede or interfere with the collection of an oral fluid specimen (*e.g.*, candy, gum, food, or tobacco) or could be used to adulterate, substitute, or alter the specimen.

(1) If the collector finds indication(s) of anything identified above, the collector will ask the employee to lift their tongue and/or separate their cheek from their gum to permit full inspection. If this occurs, the employee may cleanse his or her hands, but must not decline the collector's request for further inspection.

(2) If the employee claims that he or she has a medical condition that prevents opening his or her mouth for inspection, the collector follows the procedure described in § 40.193(a).

(3) If the collector observes materials brought to the collection site or the employee's conduct clearly indicates an attempt to adulterate, substitute, or alter the specimen, the collector must terminate the collection, note the circumstances in the Remarks section of the CCF, and report the circumstances to the DER, so that the employer can decide whether to deem the situation a refusal in accordance with § 40.191(a).

(b) If an item is present that might impede or interfere with the collection of an oral fluid specimen, the collector must request the employee remove the item.

(1) If the employee removes any item that could impede or interfere with the collection of an oral fluid specimen, the employee has abnormally colored saliva, or the employee claims to have "dry mouth," then the collector must give the employee water, up to 8 ounces, to rinse their mouth. The employee may drink the water. The collector must then wait 10 minutes before beginning the specimen collection.

(2) If the employee refuses to remove the item or rinse, the collector must terminate the collection, note the circumstances in the Remarks section of the CCF, and report the information to the DER to test as described in § 40.191(a)(8) (failure to cooperate), so that the employer can decide whether to deem the situation a refusal.

(c) If there is nothing of concern in the oral cavity and no "dry mouth" condition, the collector starts a 10-minute wait period and proceeds with the steps below before beginning the specimen collection as described in § 40.73.

(d) During the 10-minute wait period:

(1) Review with the employee the procedures required for a successful oral fluid specimen collection as stated in the manufacturer's instructions for the specimen collection device.

(2) Complete all items under Step 1 of the CCF, and for clarification:

(i) In Step 1.D of the CCF, the collector must put a check mark for the "Specify DOT Agency" under whose authority the test will take place.

(ii) In Step 1.G of the CCF for the "Collection Site Address", the collector must provide the address where the collection took place.

(3) The collector will provide, or the employee may select, a specimen collection device that is clean, unused, and wrapped/sealed in original packaging.

(i) The collector will check the expiration date on the device or the package containing the device and show it to the employee.

(ii) The collector must not use the device after its expiration date.

(iii) The collector must open the specimen collection device in view of the employee.

(4) The collector will complete Step 2 of the CCF.

(i) Check "Oral Fluid",

(ii) For "Oral Fluid: Split Type" check "Subdivided", and

(iii) Check "Each Device Within Expiration Date?" after ensuring the device is within its expiration date.

(5) The collector will enter the Split Specimen Device Expiration Date in Step 4 of the CCF. Since the collector will use one oral fluid device that will collect a single specimen, which is then subdivided in the presence of the donor, only one entry in Step 4 is to be made for the device expiration date.

(6) The collector must instruct the employee to use hand sanitizer or wash and dry his or her hands.

(e) To the greatest extent practicable, the collector must keep the employee's unwrapped collection device within view of both the collector and the employee, between the time the employee has provided a specimen and the specimen is sealed.

[88 FR 27642, May 2, 2023]

§ 40.73 How is an oral fluid specimen collected?

(a) The collector must be present and maintain visual contact with the employee during the procedures outlined in this section.

(b) The collector must note any unusual behavior or appearance of the employee on the CCF. If the collector detects any conduct that clearly indicates an attempt to tamper with a specimen (*e.g.*, an attempt to bring into the collection site an adulterant or oral fluid substitute), the collector must terminate the collection and report the information to the DER so that the employer can decide whether to deem the situation a refusal.

(c) The employee and collector must complete the specimen collection in accordance with the manufacturer's instructions for the collection device.

　(1) Under the observation of the collector, the employee is responsible for positioning the specimen collection device for collection.

　(2) The collector must ensure the collection is performed correctly (*i.e.*, using the oral fluid device in the manner described by its manufacturer), that the collection device is working properly, and that a sufficient specimen volume is collected.

　(3) If the employee states that he or she is unable to provide an oral fluid specimen or provides an insufficient specimen during the collection process, the collector must continue to make one attempt to collect, after an insufficient specimen, the collector follows the procedure in § 40.193.

　(4) The collector must inspect the specimen for unusual color, presence of foreign objects or material, or other signs of tampering. If it is apparent from this inspection that the employee has tampered with the specimen, the collector must conduct a new collection.

　　(i) Document any unusual characteristics referenced above in the Remarks section of the CCF.

　　(ii) Proceed with obtaining the new oral fluid specimen from the donor. Note on the new CCF that this is another collection for the same testing event (*i.e.*, Document in the remarks section that this is Specimen 2 of 2 and include the Specimen ID number of the other specimen). Make the same notation on the CCF of the suspect specimen.

[88 FR 27642, May 2, 2023]

§ 40.74 How does the collector prepare the oral fluid specimens?

(a) The collector follows the manufacturer's instructions to package the split specimen collections.

(b) A volume of at least 1 mL of undiluted (neat) oral fluid is collected for the specimen designated as "Bottle A", and a volume of at least 1 mL of undiluted (neat) oral fluid is collected for the specimen designated as "Bottle B", or an otherwise sufficient amount of oral fluid is collected to permit an HHS-certified laboratory to analyze the specimen(s).

(c) In the presence of the employee, the collector places a tamper-evident seal from the CCF over the cap of each specimen container, taking care not to obstruct the expiration date on the collection containers. The collector must record the date of the collection on the tamper-evident seals, after they are affixed to the specimen containers.

(d) The collector instructs the employee to initial the tamper-evident seals on each specimen container. If the employee declines to do so, the collector must note this in the "Remarks" line of the CCF (Step 2) and complete the collection process.

[88 FR 27642, May 2, 2023]

§§ 40.75-40.78 [Reserved]

§ 40.79 How is the collection process completed?

(a) As the collector, when using the paper CCF, you must do the following things to complete the collection process. You must complete the steps called for in paragraphs (a)(1) through (7) of this section in the employee's presence.

   (1) Direct the employee to read and sign the certification statement on Copy 2 of the CCF and provide all information required in Step 5. If the employee declines to sign the CCF or to provide any of the required information, you must note this in the "Remarks" line (Step 2) of the CCF and complete the collection. If the employee declines to fill out any information, you must, as a minimum, print the employee's name in the appropriate place.

   (2) Complete the chain of custody on the CCF (Step 4) by printing your name (note: you may pre-print your name), recording the time and date of the collection, signing the statement, and entering the name of the delivery service transferring the specimen to the laboratory,

   (3) Ensure that all copies of the CCF are legible and complete.

   (4) Remove Copy 5 of the CCF and give it to the employee.

   (5) Place the specimen bottles and Copy 1 of the CCF in the appropriate pouches of the plastic bag.

   (6) Secure both pouches of the plastic bag.

   (7) Advise the employee that he or she may leave the collection site.

   (8) To prepare the sealed plastic bag containing the specimens and CCF for shipment you must:

      (i) Place the sealed plastic bag in a shipping container (*e.g.,* standard courier box) designed to minimize the possibility of damage during shipment. (More than one sealed plastic bag can be placed into a single shipping container if you are doing multiple collections.)

      (ii) Seal the container as appropriate.

      (iii) If a laboratory courier hand-delivers the specimens from the collection site to the laboratory, prepare the sealed plastic bag for shipment as directed by the courier service.

   (9) Send Copy 2 of the CCF to the MRO and Copy 4 to the DER. You must fax or otherwise transmit these copies to the MRO and DER within 24 hours or during the next business day. Keep Copy 3 for at least 30 days, unless otherwise specified by applicable DOT agency regulations.

(b) As a collector, when using other forms of the CCF as approved by the Office of Management and Budget, you must follow the procedures approved for that form.

(c) As a collector or collection site, you must ensure that each specimen you collect is shipped to a laboratory as quickly as possible, but in any case, within 24 hours or during the next business day.

[65 FR 79526, Dec. 19, 2000, as amended at 71 FR 49384, Aug. 23, 2006; 80 FR 19553, Apr. 13, 2015. Redesignated and amended at 88 FR 27641, 27643, May 2, 2023]

Subpart F—Drug Testing Laboratories

§ 40.81 What laboratories may be used for DOT drug testing?

(a) As a drug testing laboratory located in the U.S., you are permitted to participate in DOT drug testing only if you are certified by HHS under the National Laboratory Certification Program (NLCP) for each specimen testing methodology performed required under this part.

(b) As a drug testing laboratory located in Canada or Mexico which is not certified by HHS under the NLCP, you are permitted to participate in DOT drug testing only if:

(1) The DOT, based on a written recommendation from HHS, has approved your laboratory as meeting HHS laboratory certification standards or deemed your laboratory fully equivalent to a laboratory meeting HHS laboratory certification standards for all testing required under this part; or

(2) The DOT, based on a written recommendation from HHS, has recognized a Canadian or Mexican certifying organization as having equivalent laboratory certification standards and procedures to those of HHS, and the Canadian or Mexican certifying organization has certified your laboratory under those equivalent standards and procedures.

(c) As a laboratory participating in the DOT drug testing program, you must comply with the requirements of this part. You must also comply with all applicable requirements of HHS in testing DOT specimens, whether or not the HHS requirements are explicitly stated in this part.

(d) If DOT determines that you are in noncompliance with this part, you could be subject to PIE proceedings under Subpart R of this part. If the Department issues a PIE with respect to you, you are ineligible to participate in the DOT drug testing program even if you continue to meet the requirements of paragraph (a) or (b) of this section.

[65 FR 79526, Dec. 19, 2000, as amended at 88 FR 27643, May 2, 2023]

§ 40.82 What drugs do laboratories test for?

As a laboratory, you must test for the following five drugs or classes of drugs in a DOT drug test. You must not test "DOT specimens" for any other drugs.

(a) Marijuana metabolites.

(b) Cocaine metabolites.

(c) Amphetamines.

(d) Opioids.

(e) Phencyclidine (PCP).

[82 FR 52244, Nov. 13, 2017. Redesignated at 88 FR 27643, May 2, 2023]

§ 40.83 How do laboratories process incoming specimens?

As the laboratory, you must do the following when you receive a DOT specimen:

(a) You are authorized to receive only Copy 1 of the CCF. You are not authorized to receive other copies of the CCF or any copies of the alcohol testing form.

(b) You must comply with applicable provisions of the HHS Guidelines concerning accessioning and processing drug specimens.

(c) You must inspect each specimen and CCF for the following "fatal flaws":

    (1) There is no CCF;

    (2) In cases where a specimen has been collected, there is no specimen submitted with the CCF;

    (3) There is no printed collector's name and no collector's signature;

    (4) Two separate collections are performed using one CCF;

    (5) The specimen ID numbers on the specimen bottle and the CCF do not match;

    (6) The specimen bottle seal is broken or shows evidence of tampering, unless a split specimen can be redesignated (see paragraph (h) of this section);

    (7) There is an insufficient amount of specimen in the primary bottle for analysis, unless the specimens can be redesignated (see paragraph (h) of this section).

    (8) For an oral fluid collection, the collector used an expired device at the time of collection.

    (9) For an oral fluid collection, if the collector failed to enter the expiration date in Step 4 of the CCF and the laboratory is unable to determine the expiration date by inspecting Bottles A and B.

(d) When you find a specimen meeting the criteria of paragraph (c) of this section, you must document your findings and stop the testing process. Report the result in accordance with § 40.97(a)(3) .

(e) You must inspect each CCF for the presence of the collector's signature on the certification statement in Step 4 of the CCF. Upon finding that the signature is omitted, document the flaw and continue the testing process.

    (1) In such a case, you must retain the specimen for a minimum of 5 business days from the date on which you initiated action to correct the flaw.

    (2) You must then attempt to correct the flaw by following the procedures of § 40.205(b)(1).

    (3) If the flaw is not corrected, report the result as rejected for testing in accordance with § 40.97(a)(3).

(f) If you determine that the urine specimen temperature was not checked and the "Remarks" line did not contain an entry regarding the temperature being outside of range, you must then attempt to correct the problem by following the procedures of § 40.208.

    (1) In such a case, you must continue your efforts to correct the problem for five business days, before you report the result.

    (2) When you have obtained the correction, or five business days have elapsed, report the result in accordance with § 40.97(a).

(g) If you determine that a CCF that fails to meet the requirements of § 40.40(a) (e.g., a non-Federal form or an expired Federal form was used for the collection), you must attempt to correct the use of the improper form by following the procedures of § 40.205(b)(2).

 (1) In such a case, you must retain the specimen for a minimum of 5 business days from the date on which you initiated action to correct the problem.

 (2) If the problem(s) is not corrected, you must reject the test and report the result in accordance with § 40.97(a)(3).

(h) If the CCF is marked indicating that a split specimen collection was collected and if the split specimen does not accompany the primary, has leaked, or is otherwise unavailable for testing, you must still test the primary specimen and follow appropriate procedures outlined in § 40.175(b) regarding the unavailability of the split specimen for testing.

 (1) The primary specimen and the split specimen can be redesignated (*i.e.*, Bottle B is redesignated as Bottle A, and vice-versa) if:

  (i) The primary specimen appears to have leaked out of its sealed bottle and the laboratory believes a sufficient amount of specimen exists in the split specimen to conduct all appropriate primary laboratory testing; or

  (ii) The primary specimen is labeled as Bottle B, and the split specimen as Bottle A; or

  (iii) The laboratory opens the split specimen instead of the primary specimen, the primary specimen remains sealed, and the laboratory believes a sufficient amount of specimen exists in the split specimen to conduct all appropriate primary laboratory testing; or

  (iv) The primary specimen seal is broken but the split specimen remains sealed and the laboratory believes a sufficient amount of specimen exists in the split specimen to conduct all appropriate primary laboratory testing.

 (2) In situations outlined in paragraph (h)(1) of this section, the laboratory shall mark through the "A" and write "B," then initial and date the change. A corresponding change shall be made to the other bottle by marking through the "B" and writing "A," and initialing and dating the change.

(i) A notation shall be made on Copy 1 of the CCF (Step 5a) and on any laboratory internal chain of custody documents, as appropriate, for any fatal or correctable flaw.

[65 FR 79526, Dec. 19, 2000, as amended at 66 FR 41951, Aug. 9, 2001; 71 FR 49384, Aug. 23, 2006; 73 FR 35970, June 25, 2008; 75 FR 59107, Sept. 27, 2010; 82 FR 52244, Nov 13, 2017; 88 FR 27643, May 2, 2023]

§ 40.84 How long does the laboratory retain specimens after testing?

(a) As a laboratory testing the primary specimen, you must retain a specimen that was reported with positive, adulterated, substituted, or invalid results for a minimum of one year.

(b) You must keep such a specimen in secure, long-term, frozen storage in accordance with HHS requirements.

(c) Within the one-year period, the MRO, the employee, the employer, or a DOT agency may request in writing that you retain a specimen for an additional period of time (*e.g.*, for the purpose of preserving evidence for litigation or a safety investigation). If you receive such a request, you must comply with it. If you do not receive such a request, you may discard the specimen at the end of the year.

(d) If you have not sent the split specimen to another laboratory for testing, you must retain the split specimen for an employee's test for the same period of time that you retain the primary specimen and under the same storage conditions.

(e) As the laboratory testing the split specimen, you must meet the requirements of paragraphs (a) through (d) of this section with respect to the split specimen.

[65 FR 79526, Dec. 19, 2000. Redesignated at 88 FR 27643, May 2, 2023]

§ 40.85 What are the cutoff concentrations for urine drug tests?

(a) As a laboratory, you must use the cutoff concentrations displayed in the following table for initial and confirmatory drug tests. All cutoff concentrations are expressed in nanograms per milliliter (ng/mL). The table follows:

Initial test analyte	Initial test cutoff[1]	Confirmatory test analyte	Confirmatory test cutoff concentration
Marijuana metabolites (THCA)[2]	50 ng/mL[3]	THCA	15 ng/mL.
Cocaine metabolite (Benzoylecgonine)	150 ng/mL[3]	Benzoylecgonine	100 ng/mL.
Codeine/ Morphine	2000 ng/mL	Codeine Morphine	2000 ng/mL. 2000 ng/mL.
Hydrocodone/ Hydromorphone	300 ng/mL	Hydrocodone Hydromorphone	100 ng/mL. 100 ng/mL.
Oxycodone/ Oxymorphone	100 ng/mL	Oxycodone Oxymorphone	100 ng/mL. 100 ng/mL.
6-Acetylmorphine	10 ng/mL	6-Acetylmorphine	10 ng/mL.
Phencyclidine	25 ng/mL	Phencyclidine	25 ng/mL.
Amphetamine/ Methamphetamine	500 ng/mL	Amphetamine Methamphetamine	250 ng/mL. 250 ng/mL.
MDMA[4]/MDA[5]	500 ng/mL	MDMA MDA	250 ng/mL. 250 ng/mL.

[1] For grouped analytes (i.e., two or more analytes that are in the same drug class and have the same initial test cutoff):

Immunoassay: The test must be calibrated with one analyte from the group identified as the target analyte. The cross-reactivity of the immunoassay to the other analyte(s) within the group must be 80 percent or greater; if not, separate immunoassays must be used for the analytes within the group.

Alternate technology: Either one analyte or all analytes from the group must be used for calibration, depending on the technology. At least one analyte within the group must have a concentration equal to or greater than the initial test cutoff or, alternatively, the sum of the analytes present (i.e., equal to or greater than the laboratory's validated limit of quantification) must be equal to or greater than the initial test cutoff.

[2] An immunoassay must be calibrated with a target analyte.

[3] *Alternate technology (THCA and Benzoylecgonine):* When using an alternate technology initial test for the specific target analytes of THCA and Benzoylecgonine, the laboratory must use the same cutoff for the initial and confirmatory tests (i.e., 15 ng/mL for THCA and 100ng/mL for Benzoylecgonine).

[4] Methylenedioxymethamphetamine (MDMA).

[5] Methylenedioxyamphetamine (MDA).

(b) On an initial drug test, you must report a result below the cutoff concentration as negative. If the result is at or above the cutoff concentration, you must conduct a confirmation test.

(c) On a confirmation drug test, you must report a result below the cutoff concentration as negative and a result at or above the cutoff concentration as confirmed positive.

(d) You must report quantitative values for morphine or codeine at 15,000 ng/mL or above.

[65 FR 79526, Dec. 19, 2000, as amended at 75 FR 49862, Aug. 16, 2010; 77 FR 26473, May 4, 2012; 82 FR 52244, Nov. 13, 2017. Redesignated and amended at 88 FR 27643, May 2, 2023]

§ 40.86 What is urine validity testing, and are laboratories required to conduct it?

(a) Specimen validity testing is the evaluation of the specimen to determine if it is consistent with normal human urine. The purpose of validity testing is to determine whether certain adulterants or foreign substances were added to the urine, if the urine was diluted, or if the specimen was substituted.

(b) As a laboratory, you must conduct validity testing.

[65 FR 79526, Dec. 19, 2000, as amended at 66 FR 41951, Aug. 9, 2001; 73 FR 35970, June 25, 2008. Redesignated at 88 FR 27643, May 2, 2023]

§ 40.87 What validity tests must laboratories conduct on primary urine specimens?

As a laboratory, when you conduct validity testing under § 40.86, you must conduct it in accordance with the requirements of this section.

(a) You must determine the creatinine concentration on each primary specimen. You must also determine its specific gravity if you find the creatinine concentration to be less than 20 mg/dL.

(b) You must determine the pH of each primary specimen.

(c) You must perform one or more validity tests for oxidizing adulterants on each primary specimen.

(d) You must perform additional validity tests on the primary specimen when the following conditions are observed:

(1) Abnormal physical characteristics;

(2) Reactions or responses characteristic of an adulterant obtained during initial or confirmatory drug tests (*e.g.*, non-recovery of internal standards, unusual response); or

(3) Possible unidentified interfering substance or adulterant.

(e) If you determine that the specimen is invalid and HHS guidelines direct you to contact the MRO, you must contact the MRO and together decide if testing the primary specimen by another HHS certified laboratory would be useful in being able to report a positive or adulterated test result.

[65 FR 79526, Dec. 19, 2000, as amended at 69 FR 64867, Nov. 9, 2004. Redesignated and amended at 88 FR 27643, May 2, 2023]

§ 40.88 What criteria do laboratories use to establish that a urine specimen is dilute or substituted?

(a) As a laboratory, you must consider the primary specimen to be dilute when:

(1) The creatinine concentration is greater than or equal to 2 mg/dL but less than 20 mg/dL, and

(2) The specific gravity is greater than 1.0010 but less than 1.0030 on a single aliquot.

(b) As a laboratory, you must consider the primary specimen to be substituted when the creatinine concentration is less than 2 mg/dL and the specific gravity is less than or equal to 1.0010 or greater than or equal to 1.0200 on both the initial and confirmatory creatinine tests and on both the initial and confirmatory specific gravity tests on two separate aliquots.

[69 FR 64867, Nov. 9, 2004. Redesignated at 88 FR 27643, May 2, 2023]

§ 40.89 What are the adulterant cutoff concentrations for initial and confirmation urine tests?

(a) As a laboratory, you must use the cutoff concentrations for the initial and confirmation adulterant testing as required by the HHS Mandatory Guidelines and you must use two separate aliquots—one for the initial test and another for the confirmation test.

(b) As a laboratory, you must report results at or above the cutoffs (or for pH, at or above or below the values, as appropriate) as adulterated and provide the numerical value that supports the adulterated result.

[73 FR 35970, June 25, 2008. Redesignated at 88 FR 27643, May 2, 2023]

§ 40.90 What criteria do laboratories use to establish that a urine specimen is invalid?

(a) As a laboratory, you must use the invalid test result criteria for the initial and confirmation testing as required by the HHS Mandatory Guidelines, and you must use two separate aliquots—one for the initial test and another for the confirmation test.

(b) As a laboratory, for a specimen having an invalid result for one of the reasons outlined in the HHS Mandatory Guidelines, you must contact the MRO to discuss whether sending the specimen to another HHS certified laboratory for testing would be useful in being able to report a positive or adulterated result.

(c) As a laboratory, you must report invalid results in accordance with the invalid test result criteria as required by the HHS Guidelines and provide the numerical value that supports the invalid result, where appropriate, such as pH.

(d) As a laboratory, you must report the reason a test result is invalid.

[73 FR 35970, June 25, 2008. Redesignated at 88 FR 27643, May 2, 2023]

§ 40.91 What are the cutoff concentrations for oral fluid drug tests?

As a laboratory, you must use the cutoff concentrations displayed in the following table for initial and confirmatory drug tests for oral fluid specimens. All cutoff concentrations are expressed in nanograms per milliliter (ng/mL). The table follows:

Table 1 to § 40.91—Oral Fluid Testing Cutoff Concentrations

Initial test analyte	Initial test cutoff[1]	Confirmatory test analyte	Confirmatory test cutoff concentration
Marijuana (THC)[2]	4 ng/mL[3]	THC	2 ng/mL.
Cocaine/Benzoylecgonine	15 ng/mL	Cocaine Benzoylecgonine	8 ng/mL. 8 ng/mL.
Codeine/Morphine	30 ng/mL	Codeine Morphine	15 ng/mL. 15 ng/mL.
Hydrocodone/Hydromorphone	30 ng/mL	Hydrocodone Hydromorphone	15 ng/mL. 15 ng/mL.
Oxycodone/Oxymorphone	30 ng/mL	Oxycodone Oxymorphone	15 ng/mL. 15 ng/mL.
6-Acetylmorphine	4 ng/mL[3]	6-Acetylmorphine	2 ng/mL.
Phencyclidine	10 ng/mL	Phencyclidine	10 ng/mL.
Amphetamine/Methamphetamine	50 ng/mL	Amphetamine Methamphetamine	25 ng/mL. 25 ng/mL.
MDMA[4]/MDA[5]	50 ng/mL	MDMA MDA	25 ng/mL. 25 ng/mL.

[1] For grouped analytes (*i.e.,* two or more analytes that are in the same drug class and have the same initial test cutoff):

Immunoassay: The test must be calibrated with one analyte from the group identified as the target analyte. The cross reactivity of the immunoassay to the other analyte(s) within the group must be 80 percent or greater; if not, separate immunoassays must be used for the analytes within the group.

Alternate technology: Either one analyte or all analytes from the group must be used for calibration, depending on the technology. At least one analyte within the group must have a concentration equal to or greater than the initial test cutoff or, alternatively, the sum of the analytes present (*i.e.,* with concentrations equal to or greater than the laboratory's validated limit of quantification) must be equal to or greater than the initial test cutoff.

[2] An immunoassay must be calibrated with the target analyte.

[3] *Alternate technology (THC and 6-AM):* The confirmatory test cutoff must be used for an alternate technology initial test that is specific for the target analyte (*i.e.*, 2 ng/mL for THC, 2 ng/mL for 6-AM).

[4] Methylenedioxymethamphetamine (MDMA).

[5] Methylenedioxyamphetamine (MDA).

[88 FR 27643, May 2, 2023]

§ 40.92 What is oral fluid validity testing, and are laboratories required to conduct it?

(a) Specimen validity testing is the evaluation of the specimen to determine if it is consistent with normal human oral fluid. The purpose of validity testing is to determine whether certain adulterants or foreign substances were added to the oral fluid, if the oral fluid was altered.

(b) If a specimen exhibits abnormal characteristics (*e.g.*, unusual odor or color), causes reactions or responses characteristic of an adulterant during initial or confirmatory drug tests (*e.g.*, non-recovery of internal standard, unusual response), or contains an unidentified substance that interferes with the confirmatory analysis, then you may conduct validity testing.

(c) If you determine that the specimen is invalid and HHS guidelines direct you to contact the MRO, you must contact the MRO and together decide if testing the primary specimen by another HHS-certified laboratory would be useful in being able to report a positive or adulterated test result.

[88 FR 27643, May 2, 2023]

§ 40.93 What validity tests must laboratories conduct on primary oral fluid specimens?

As a laboratory, if you conduct validity testing under § 40.92, you must conduct it in accordance with the requirements of this section.

(a) You may test for a biomarker such as albumin or immunoglobulin G (IgG) or a test for a specific adulterant.

(b) You must follow the applicable HHS requirements for any additional validity testing.

[88 FR 27643, May 2, 2023]

§ 40.97 What do laboratories report and how do they report it?

(a) As a laboratory, when reporting a result of any kind, you must report the specimen type.

(b) You must also report the results for each primary specimen, which will fall into one of the following three categories. As a laboratory, you must report the actual results (and not the categories):

(1) *Category 1: Negative results.* As a laboratory, when you find a specimen to be negative, you must report the test result as being one of the following, as applicable:

(i) Negative, or

(ii) For urine only, negative-dilute, with numerical values for creatinine and specific gravity.

(2) *Category 2: Non-negative results.* As a laboratory, when you find a specimen to be non-negative, you must report the test result as being one or more of the following, as applicable:

    (i) Positive, with drug(s)/metabolite(s) noted, with numerical values for the drug(s) or drug metabolite(s).

    (ii) Adulterated, with adulterant(s) noted, with confirmatory test values (when applicable), and with remarks(s);

    (iii) For urine only, positive-dilute, with drug(s)/metabolite(s) noted, with numerical values for the drug(s) or drug metabolite(s) and with numerical values for creatinine and specific gravity;

    (iv) For urine only, substituted, with confirmatory test values for creatinine and specific gravity; or

    (v) For urine only, invalid result, with remark(s). Laboratories will report actual values for pH results.

    (vi) For oral fluid only, invalid result, with remark(s). Laboratories must report numerical values of the specimen validity test results that support a specimen reported as invalid.

(3) *Category 3: Rejected for testing.* As a laboratory, when you reject a specimen for testing, you must report the result as being Rejected for Testing, with remark(s).

(c) As a laboratory, you must report laboratory results directly, and only, to the MRO at his or her place of business. You must not report results to or through the DER or a service agent (*e.g.*, a C/TPA).

(1) Negative results: You must fax, courier, mail, or electronically transmit a legible image or copy of the fully completed Copy 1 of the CCF which has been signed by the certifying scientist, or you may provide the laboratory results report electronically (*i.e.*, computer data file).

    (i) If you elect to provide the laboratory results report, you must include the following elements, as a minimum, in the report format:

        (A) Laboratory name and address;

        (B) Employer's name (you may include I.D. or account number);

        (C) Medical review officer's name;

        (D) Specimen I.D. number;

        (E) SSN or Employee ID from Step 1C of the CCF, if provided;

        (F) Reason for test, if provided;

        (G) Collector's name and telephone number;

        (H) Date of the collection;

        (I) For oral fluid only, collection device expiration date;

        (J) Date received at the laboratory;

        (K) Date certifying scientist released the results;

        (L) Certifying scientist's name;

        (M) Results (*e.g.*, positive, adulterated) as listed in paragraph (a) of this section; and

        (N)   Remarks section, with an explanation of any situation in which a correctable flaw has been corrected.

     (ii)   You may release the laboratory results report only after review and approval by the certifying scientist. It must reflect the same test result information as contained on the CCF signed by the certifying scientist. The information contained in the laboratory results report must not contain information that does not appear on the CCF.

     (iii)   The results report may be transmitted through any means that ensures accuracy and confidentiality. You, as the laboratory, together with the MRO, must ensure that the information is adequately protected from unauthorized access or release, both during transmission and in storage (*e.g.,* see § 40.351).

   (2)   Non-negative and Rejected for Testing results: You must fax, courier, mail, or electronically transmit a legible image or copy of the fully completed Copy 1 of the CCF that has been signed by the certifying scientist. In addition, you may provide the electronic laboratory results report following the format and procedures set forth in paragraphs (b)(1)(i) and (ii) of this section.

  (d)   In transmitting laboratory results to the MRO, you, as the laboratory, together with the MRO, must ensure that the information is adequately protected from unauthorized access or release, both during transmission and in storage. If the results are provided by fax or other electronic means, the electronic communication must be accessible only to authorized individuals.

  (e)   You must transmit test results to the MRO in a timely manner, preferably the same day that review by the certifying scientist is completed.

  (f)

   (1)   You must provide quantitative values for confirmed positive drug test results to the MRO.

   (2)   You must provide numerical values that support the adulterated (when applicable) or substituted result, without a request from the MRO.

   (3)   You must also provide the MRO numerical values for creatinine and specific gravity for the negative-dilute urine test result, without a request from the MRO.

  (g)   You must provide quantitative values for confirmed positive morphine and/or codeine urine results at or below 15,000 ng/mL, and for confirmed positive morphine or codeine oral fluid results at or below 150 ng/mL.

[88 FR 27644, May 2, 2023]

§ 40.101 What relationship may a laboratory have with an MRO?

  (a)   As a laboratory, you may not enter into any relationship with an MRO that creates a conflict of interest or the appearance of a conflict of interest with the MRO's responsibilities for the employer. You may not derive any financial benefit by having an employer use a specific MRO.

  (b)   The following are examples of relationships between laboratories and MROs that the Department regards as creating conflicts of interest, or the appearance of such conflicts. This following list of examples is not intended to be exclusive or exhaustive:

   (1)   The laboratory employs an MRO who reviews test results produced by the laboratory;

(2) The laboratory has a contract or retainer with the MRO for the review of test results produced by the laboratory;

(3) The laboratory designates which MRO the employer is to use, gives the employer a slate of MROs from which to choose, or recommends certain MROs;

(4) The laboratory gives the employer a discount or other incentive to use a particular MRO;

(5) The laboratory has its place of business co-located with that of an MRO or MRO staff who review test results produced by the laboratory; or

(6) The laboratory permits an MRO, or an MRO's organization, to have a financial interest in the laboratory.

§ 40.107 Who may inspect laboratories?

As a laboratory, you must permit an inspection, with or without prior notice, by ODAPC, a DOT agency, or a DOT-regulated employer that contracts with the laboratory for drug testing under the DOT drug testing program, or the designee of such an employer.

§ 40.109 What documentation must the laboratory keep, and for how long?

(a) As a laboratory, you must retain all records pertaining to each employee urine specimen for a minimum of two years.

(b) As a laboratory, you must also keep for two years employer-specific data required in § 40.111.

(c) Within the two-year period, the MRO, the employee, the employer, or a DOT agency may request in writing that you retain the records for an additional period of time (e.g., for the purpose of preserving evidence for litigation or a safety investigation). If you receive such a request, you must comply with it. If you do not receive such a request, you may discard the records at the end of the two-year period.

§ 40.111 When and how must a laboratory disclose statistical summaries and other information it maintains?

(a) As a laboratory, you must transmit an aggregate statistical summary, by employer, of the data listed in appendix D of this part with respect to each specimen type for which you conduct tests to the employer on a semi-annual basis.

(1) The summary must not reveal the identity of any employee.

(2) In order to avoid sending data from which it is likely that information about an employee's test result can be readily inferred, you must not send a summary if the employer has fewer than five aggregate tests results.

(3) The summary must be sent by January 20 of each year for July 1 through December 31 of the prior year.

(4) The summary must also be sent by July 20 of each year for January 1 through June 30 of the current year.

(b) When the employer requests a summary in response to an inspection, audit, or review by a DOT agency, you must provide it unless the employer had fewer than five aggregate test results. In that case, you must send the employer a report indicating that not enough testing was conducted to warrant a summary. You may transmit the summary or report by hard copy, fax, or other electronic means.

(c) You must also release information to appropriate parties as provided in §§ 40.329 and 40.331.

(d) As a laboratory, you must transmit an aggregate statistical summary listed in appendix E of this part for each specimen type for which you conduct testing to DOT on a semi-annual basis. The summary must be sent by January 31 of each year for July 1 through December 31 of the prior year. It must be sent by July 31 of each year for January 1 through June 30 of the current year. If you withdraw or are removed from NLCP's laboratory certification during a reporting period, you must provide the aggregate statistical summary to the DOT-regulated employers and to ODAPC for the last reporting period in which you conducted DOT-regulated testing.

[65 FR 79526, Dec. 19, 2000, as amended at 73 FR 35971, June 25, 2008; 88 FR 27645, May 2, 2023]

§ 40.113 Where is other information concerning laboratories found in this regulation?

You can find more information concerning laboratories in several sections of this part:

§ 40.3—Definition.

§ 40.13—Prohibition on making specimens available for other purposes.

§ 40.31—Conflicts of interest concerning collectors.

§ 40.47—Laboratory rejections of test for improper form.

§ 40.125—Conflicts of interest concerning MROs.

§ 40.175—Role of first laboratory in split specimen tests.

§ 40.177—Role of second laboratory in split specimen tests (drugs).

§ 40.179—Role of second laboratory in split specimen tests (adulterants).

§ 40.181—Role of second laboratory in split specimen tests (substitution).

§§ 40.183–40.185—Transmission of split specimen test results to MRO.

§§ 40.201–40.205—Role in correcting errors.

§ 40.329—Release of information to employees.

§ 40.331—Limits on release of information.

§ 40.355—Role with respect to other service agents.

Subpart G—Medical Review Officers and the Verification Process

§ 40.121 Who is qualified to act as an MRO?

To be qualified to act as an MRO in the DOT drug testing program, you must meet each of the requirements of this section:

(a) *Credentials.* You must be a licensed physician (Doctor of Medicine or Osteopathy). If you are a licensed physician in any U.S., Canadian, or Mexican jurisdiction and meet the other requirements of this section, you are authorized to perform MRO services with respect to all covered employees, wherever they are located. For example, if you are licensed as an M.D. in one state or province in the U.S., Canada, or Mexico, you are not limited to performing MRO functions in that state or province, and you may perform MRO functions for employees in other states or provinces without becoming licensed to practice medicine in the other jurisdictions.

(b) *Basic knowledge.* You must be knowledgeable in the following areas:

   (1) You must be knowledgeable about and have clinical experience in controlled substances abuse disorders, including detailed knowledge of alternative medical explanations for laboratory confirmed drug test results.

   (2) You must be knowledgeable about issues relating to adulterated and substituted specimens as well as the possible medical causes of specimens having an invalid result.

   (3) You must be knowledgeable about this part, the DOT MRO Guidelines, and the DOT agency regulations applicable to the employers for whom you evaluate drug test results, and you must keep current on any changes to these materials. You must subscribe to the ODAPC list-serve at *https://www.transportation.gov/odapc/get-odapc-email-updates*. DOT agency regulations, DOT MRO Guidelines, and other materials are available from ODAPC (Department of Transportation, 1200 New Jersey Avenue SE, Washington, DC 20590, 202–366–3784), or on the ODAPC Web site (*http://www.transportation.gov/odapc*).

(c) *Qualification training.* You must receive qualification training meeting the requirements of this paragraph (c).

   (1) Qualification training must provide instruction on the following subjects:

      (i) Collection procedures for specimens;

      (ii) Chain of custody, reporting, and recordkeeping;

      (iii) Interpretation of drug and validity tests results;

      (iv) The role and responsibilities of the MRO in the DOT drug testing program;

      (v) The interaction with other participants in the program (*e.g.*, DERs, SAPs); and

      (vi) Provisions of this part and DOT agency rules applying to employers for whom you review test results, including changes and updates to this part and DOT agency rules, guidance, interpretations, and policies affecting the performance of MRO functions, as well as issues that MROs confront in carrying out their duties under this part and DOT agency rules.

(2) Following your completion of qualification training under paragraph (c)(1) of this section, you must satisfactorily complete an examination administered by a nationally-recognized MRO certification board or subspecialty board for medical practitioners in the field of medical review of DOT-mandated drug tests. The examination must comprehensively cover all the elements of qualification training listed in paragraph (c)(1) of this section.

(3) You must meet the requirements of paragraphs (a), (b), and (c) of this section before you begin to perform MRO functions.

(d) *Requalification training.* During each five-year period from the date on which you satisfactorily completed the examination under paragraph (c)(2) of this section, you must complete requalification training.

(1) This requalification training must meet the requirements of the qualification training under paragraph (c)(1) of this section.

(2) Following your completion of requalification training, you must satisfactorily complete an examination administered by a nationally-recognized MRO certification board or subspecialty board for medical practitioners in the field of medical review of DOT-mandated drug tests. The examination must comprehensively cover all the elements of qualification training listed in paragraph (c)(1) of this section.

(e) *Documentation.* You must maintain documentation showing that you currently meet all requirements of this section. You must provide this documentation on request to DOT agency representatives and to employers and C/TPAs who are using or negotiating to use your services.

[65 FR 79526, Dec. 19, 2000, as amended at 66 FR 41951, Aug. 9, 2001; 75 FR 49862, Aug. 16, 2010; 82 FR 52245, Nov. 13, 2017; 88 FR 27645, May 2, 2023]

§ 40.123 What are the MRO's responsibilities in the DOT drug testing program?

As an MRO, you have the following basic responsibilities:

(a) Acting as an independent and impartial "gatekeeper" and advocate for the accuracy and integrity of the drug testing process.

(b) Providing a quality assurance review of the drug testing process for the specimens under your purview. This includes, but is not limited to:

(1) Ensuring the review of the CCF on all specimen collections for the purposes of determining whether there is a problem that may cause a test to be cancelled (see §§ 40.199–40.203). As an MRO, you are not required to review laboratory internal chain of custody documentation. No one is permitted to cancel a test because you have not reviewed this documentation;

(2) Providing feedback to employers, collection sites and laboratories regarding performance issues where necessary; and

(3) Reporting to and consulting with the ODAPC or a relevant DOT agency when you wish DOT assistance in resolving any program issue. As an employer or service agent, you are prohibited from limiting or attempting to limit the MRO's access to DOT for this purpose and from retaliating in any way against an MRO for discussing drug testing issues with DOT.

(c) You must determine whether there is a legitimate medical explanation for confirmed positive, adulterated, substituted, and invalid results from the laboratory.

(d) While you provide medical review of employees' test results, this part does not deem that you have established a doctor-patient relationship with the employees whose tests you review.

(e) You must act to investigate and correct problems where possible and notify appropriate parties (*e.g.*, HHS, DOT, employers, service agents) where assistance is needed, (*e.g.*, cancelled or problematic tests, incorrect results).

(f) You must ensure the timely flow of test results and other information to employers.

(g) You must protect the confidentiality of the drug testing information.

(h) You must perform all your functions in compliance with this part and other DOT agency regulations.

[65 FR 79526, Dec. 19, 2000, as amended at 82 FR 52245, Nov. 13, 2017; 88 FR 27645, May 2, 2023]

§ 40.125 What relationship may an MRO have with a laboratory?

As an MRO, you may not enter into any relationship with an employer's laboratory that creates a conflict of interest or the appearance of a conflict of interest with your responsibilities to that employer. You may not derive any financial benefit by having an employer use a specific laboratory. For examples of relationships between laboratories and MROs that the Department views as creating a conflict of interest or the appearance of such a conflict, see § 40.101(b).

§ 40.127 What are the MRO's functions in reviewing negative test results?

As the MRO, you must do the following with respect to negative drug test results you receive from a laboratory, prior to verifying the result and releasing it to the DER:

(a) Review Copy 2 of the CCF to determine if there are any fatal or correctable errors that may require you to initiate corrective action or to cancel the test (see §§ 40.199 and 40.203).

(b) Review the negative laboratory test result and ensure that it is consistent with the information contained on the CCF.

(c) Before you report a negative test result, you must have in your possession the following documents:

   (1) Copy 2 of the CCF, a legible copy of it, or any other CCF copy containing the employee's signature; and

   (2) A legible copy (fax, photocopy, image) of Copy 1 of the CCF or the electronic laboratory results report that conveys the negative laboratory test result.

(d) If the copy of the documentation provided to you by the collector or laboratory appears unclear, you must request that the collector or laboratory send you a legible copy.

(e) On Copy 2 of the CCF, place a check mark in the "Negative" box (Step 6), provide your name, and sign, initial, or stamp and date the verification statement.

(f) Report the result in a confidential manner (see §§ 40.163–40.167).

(g) Staff under your direct, personal supervision may perform the administrative functions of this section for you, but only you can cancel a test. If you cancel a laboratory-confirmed negative result, check the "Test Cancelled" box (Step 6) on Copy 2 of the CCF, make appropriate annotation in the "Remarks" line, provide your name, and sign, initial or stamp and date the verification statement.

(1) On specimen results that are reviewed by your staff, you are responsible for assuring the quality of their work.

(2) You are required to personally review at least 5 percent of all CCFs reviewed by your staff on a quarterly basis, including all results that required a corrective action. However, you need not review more than 500 negative results of all specimen types combined in any quarter.

(3) Your review must, as a minimum, include the CCF, negative laboratory test result, any accompanying corrective documents, and the report sent to the employer. You must correct any errors that you discover. You must take action as necessary to ensure compliance by your staff with this part and document your corrective action. You must attest to the quality assurance review by initialing the CCFs that you review.

(4) You must make these CCFs easily identifiable and retrievable by you for review by DOT agencies.

[65 FR 79526, Dec. 19, 2000, as amended at 66 FR 41951, Aug. 9, 2001; 88 FR 27645, May 2, 2023]

§ 40.129 What are the MRO's functions in reviewing laboratory confirmed non-negative drug test results?

(a) As the MRO, you must do the following with respect to confirmed positive, adulterated, substituted, or invalid results you receive from a laboratory, before you verify the result and release it to the DER:

(1) Review Copy 2 of the CCF to determine if there are any fatal or correctable errors that may require you to cancel the test (see §§ 40.199 and 40.203). Staff under your direct, personal supervision may conduct this administrative review for you, but only you may verify or cancel a test.

(2) Review Copy 1 of the CCF and ensure that it is consistent with the information contained on Copy 2, that the test result is legible, and that the certifying scientist signed the form. You are not required to review any other documentation generated by the laboratory during their analysis or handling of the specimen (*e.g.*, the laboratory internal chain of custody).

(3) If the copy of the documentation provided to you by the collector or laboratory appears unclear, you must request that the collector or laboratory send you a legible copy.

(4) Except in the circumstances spelled out in § 40.133 , conduct a verification interview. This interview must include direct contact in person or by telephone between you and the employee. You may initiate the verification process based on the laboratory results report.

(5) Verify the test result, consistent with the requirements of §§ 40.135 through 40.145, 40.159, and 40.160, as:

(i) Negative; or

(ii) Cancelled; or

(iii) Positive, and/or refusal to test because of adulteration or substitution.

(b) Before you report a verified negative, positive, refusal to test because of adulteration or substitution, you must have in your possession the following documents:

(1) Copy 2 of the CCF, a legible copy of it, or any other CCF copy containing the employee's signature; and

(2)   A legible copy (fax, photocopy, image) of Copy 1 of the CCF, containing the certifying scientist's signature.

(c)   With respect to verified positive test results, place a checkmark in the "Positive" box in Step 6 on Copy 2 of the CCF, indicate the drug(s)/metabolite(s) verified positive, and sign and date the verification statement.

(d)   If you cancel a laboratory confirmed positive, adulterated, substituted, or invalid result, check the "test cancelled" box (Step 6) on Copy 2 of the CCF, make appropriate annotation in the "Remarks" line, sign, provide your name, and date the verification statement.

(e)   Report the result in a confidential manner (see §§ 40.163–40.167).

(f)   With respect to adulteration or substitution test results, check the "refusal to test because:" box (Step 6) on Copy 2 of the CCF, check the "Adulterated" or "Substituted" box, as appropriate, make appropriate annotation in the "Remarks" line, sign and date the verification statement.

(g)   As the MRO, your actions concerning reporting confirmed positive, adulterated, or substituted results to the employer before you have completed the verification process are also governed by the stand-down provisions of § 40.21 .

(1)   If an employer has a stand-down policy that meets the requirements of § 40.21 , you may report to the DER that you have received an employee's laboratory confirmed positive, adulterated, or substituted test result, consistent with the terms of the waiver the employer received. You must not provide any further details about the test result (e.g., the name of the drug involved).

(2)   If the employer does not have a stand-down policy that meets the requirements of § 40.21, you must not inform the employer that you have received an employee's laboratory confirmed positive, adulterated, or substituted test result until you verify the test result. For example, as an MRO employed directly by a company, you must not tell anyone on the company's staff or management that you have received an employee's laboratory confirmed test result.

[65 FR 79526, Dec. 19, 2000, as amended at 66 FR 41952, Aug. 9, 2001; 73 FR 35971, June 25, 2008; 75 FR 59107, Sept. 27, 2010; 88 FR 27645, May 2, 2023]

§ 40.131 How does the MRO or DER notify an employee of the verification process after receiving laboratory confirmed non-negative drug test results?

(a)   When, as the MRO, you receive a confirmed positive, adulterated, substituted, or invalid test result from the laboratory, you must contact the employee directly (i.e., actually talk to the employee), on a confidential basis, to determine whether the employee wants to discuss the test result. In making this contact, you must explain to the employee that, if he or she declines to discuss the result, you will verify the test as positive or as a refusal to test because of adulteration or substitution, as applicable.

(b)   As the MRO, staff under your personal supervision may conduct this initial contact for you.

(1)   This staff contact must be limited to scheduling the discussion between you and the employee and explaining the consequences of the employee's declining to speak with you (i.e., that the MRO will verify the test without input from the employee). If the employee declines to speak with you, the staff person must document the employee's decision, including the date and time.

(2)   A staff person must not gather any medical information or information concerning possible explanations for the test result.

49 CFR Part 40 (up to date as of 3/05/2024)
Procedures for Transportation Workplace Drug and Alcohol Testing Programs

49 CFR 40.131(b)(3)

(3) A staff person may advise an employee to have medical information (*e.g.*, prescriptions, information forming the basis of a legitimate medical explanation for a confirmed positive test result) ready to present at the interview with the MRO.

(4) Since you are required to speak personally with the employee, face-to-face or on the phone, your staff must not inquire if the employee wishes to speak with you.

(c) As the MRO, you or your staff must make reasonable efforts to reach the employee at the day and evening telephone numbers listed on the CCF. Reasonable efforts include, as a minimum, three attempts, spaced reasonably over a 24-hour period, to reach the employee at the day and evening telephone numbers listed on the CCF. If you or your staff cannot reach the employee directly after making these efforts, you or your staff must take the following steps:

(1) Document the efforts you made to contact the employee, including dates and times. If both phone numbers are incorrect (*e.g.*, disconnected, wrong number), you may take the actions listed in paragraph (c)(2) of this section without waiting the full 24-hour period.

(2) Contact the DER, instructing the DER to contact the employee.

(i) You must simply direct the DER to inform the employee to contact you.

(ii) You must not inform the DER that the employee has a confirmed positive, adulterated, substituted, or invalid test result.

(iii) You must document the dates and times of your attempts to contact the DER, and you must document the name of the DER you contacted and the date and time of the contact.

(d) As the DER, you must attempt to contact the employee immediately, using procedures that protect, as much as possible, the confidentiality of the MRO's request that the employee contact the MRO. If you successfully contact the employee (i.e., actually talk to the employee), you must document the date and time of the contact, and inform the MRO. You must inform the employee that he or she should contact the MRO immediately. You must also inform the employee of the consequences of failing to contact the MRO within the next 72 hours (see § 40.133(a)(2)).

(1) As the DER, you must not inform anyone else working for the employer that you are seeking to contact the employee on behalf of the MRO.

(2) If, as the DER, you have made all reasonable efforts to contact the employee but failed to do so, you may place the employee on temporary medically unqualified status or medical leave. Reasonable efforts include, as a minimum, three attempts, spaced reasonably over a 24-hour period, to reach the employee at the day and evening telephone numbers listed on the CCF.

(i) As the DER, you must document the dates and times of these efforts.

(ii) If, as the DER, you are unable to contact the employee within this 24-hour period, you must leave a message for the employee by any practicable means (*e.g.*, voice mail, e-mail, letter) to contact the MRO and inform the MRO of the date and time of this attempted contact.

[65 FR 79526, Dec. 19, 2000, as amended at 66 FR 41952, Aug. 9, 2001; 68 FR 31626, May 28, 2003; 69 FR 64867, Nov. 9, 2004]

§ 40.133 Without interviewing the employee, under what circumstances may the MRO verify a test result as positive, or as a refusal to test because of adulteration or substitution, or as cancelled because the test was invalid?

(a)   As the MRO, you normally may verify a confirmed positive test (for any drug or drug metabolite, including opiates), or as a refusal to test because of adulteration or substitution, only after interviewing the employee as provided in §§ 40.135–40.145 . However, there are three circumstances in which you may verify such a result without an interview:

   (1)   You may verify a test result as a positive or refusal to test, as applicable, if the employee expressly declines the opportunity to discuss the test with you. You must maintain complete documentation of this occurrence, including notation of informing, or attempting to inform, the employee of the consequences of not exercising the option to speak with the you.

   (2)   You may verify a test result as a positive or refusal to test, as applicable, if the DER has successfully made and documented a contact with the employee and instructed the employee to contact you and more than 72 hours have passed since the time the DER contacted the employee.

   (3)   You may verify a test result as a positive or refusal to test, as applicable, if neither you nor the DER, after making and documenting all reasonable efforts, has been able to contact the employee within ten days of the date on which the MRO receives the confirmed test result from the laboratory.

(b)   As the MRO, you may verify an invalid test result as cancelled (with instructions to recollect immediately under direct observation) without interviewing the employee, as provided at § 40.159:

   (1)   If the employee expressly declines the opportunity to discuss the test with you;

   (2)   If the DER has successfully made and documented a contact with the employee and instructed the employee to contact you and more than 72 hours have passed since the time the DER contacted the employee; or

   (3)   If neither you nor the DER, after making and documenting all reasonable efforts, has been able to contact the employee within ten days of the date on which you received the confirmed invalid test result from the laboratory.

(c)   As the MRO, after you verify a test result as a positive or as a refusal to test under this section, you must document the date and time and reason, following the instructions in § 40.163. For a cancelled test due to an invalid result under this section, you must follow the instructions in § 40.159(a)(5).

(d)   As the MRO, after you have verified a test result under this section and reported the result to the DER, you must allow the employee to present information to you within 60 days of the verification to document that serious illness, injury, or other circumstances unavoidably precluded contact with the MRO and/or DER in the times provided. On the basis of such information, you may reopen the verification, allowing the employee to present information concerning whether there is a legitimate medical explanation of the confirmed test result.

[65 FR 79526, Dec. 19, 2000, as amended at 73 FR 35971, June 25, 2008]

§ 40.135 What does the MRO tell the employee at the beginning of the verification interview?

(a) As the MRO, you must tell the employee that the laboratory has determined that the employee's test result was positive, adulterated, substituted, or invalid, as applicable. You must also tell the employee of the drugs for which his or her specimen tested positive, or the basis for the finding of adulteration or substitution.

(b) You must explain the verification interview process to the employee and inform the employee that your decision will be based on information the employee provides in the interview.

(c) You must explain that, if further medical evaluation is needed for the verification process, the employee must comply with your request for this evaluation and that failure to do so is equivalent of expressly declining to discuss the test result.

(d) As the MRO, you must warn an employee who has a confirmed positive, adulterated, substituted or invalid result that you are required to provide to third parties drug test result information and medical information affecting the performance of safety-sensitive duties that the employee gives you in the verification process without the employee's consent (see § 40.327).

   (1) You must give this warning to the employee before obtaining any medical information as part of the verification process.

   (2) For purposes of this paragraph (d), medical information includes information on medications or other substances affecting the performance of safety-sensitive duties that the employee reports using or medical conditions the employee reports having.

   (3) For purposes of this paragraph (d), the persons to whom this information may be provided include the employer, a SAP evaluating the employee as part of the return to duty process (see § 40.293(g)), DOT, another Federal safety agency (e.g., the NTSB), or any state safety agency as required by state law.

(e) You must also advise the employee that, before informing any third party about any medication the employee is using pursuant to a legally valid prescription consistent with the Controlled Substances Act, you will allow 5 business days from the date you report the verified negative result for the employee to have the prescribing physician contact you to determine if the medication can be changed to one that does not make the employee medically unqualified or does not pose a significant safety risk. If, in your reasonable medical judgment, a medical qualification issue or a significant safety risk remains after you communicate with the employee's prescribing physician or after 5 business days, whichever is shorter, you must follow § 40.327. If, as the MRO, you receive information that eliminates the medical qualification issue or significant safety risk, you must transmit this information to any third party to whom you previously provided information under § 40.327.

[65 FR 79526, Dec. 19, 2000, as amended at 66 FR 41952, Aug. 9, 2001; 82 FR 52245, Nov. 13, 2017; 88 FR 27645, May 2, 2023]

§ 40.137 On what basis does the MRO verify test results involving marijuana, cocaine, amphetamines, semi-synthetic opioids, or PCP?

(a) As the MRO, you must verify a confirmed positive test result for marijuana, cocaine, amphetamines, semi-synthetic opioids (i.e., hydrocodone, hydromorphone, oxycodone, and oxymorphone), and/or PCP unless the employee presents a legitimate medical explanation for the presence of the drug(s)/metabolite(s) in his or her system. In determining whether an employee's legally valid prescription consistent with the Controlled Substances Act for a substance in these categories constitutes a legitimate medical explanation, you must not question whether the prescribing physician should have prescribed the substance.

(b) You must offer the employee an opportunity to present a legitimate medical explanation in all cases.

(c) The employee has the burden of proof that a legitimate medical explanation exists. The employee must present information meeting this burden at the time of the verification interview. As the MRO, you have discretion to extend the time available to the employee for this purpose for up to five days before verifying the test result, if you determine that there is a reasonable basis to believe that the employee will be able to produce relevant evidence concerning a legitimate medical explanation within that time.

(d) If you determine that there is a legitimate medical explanation, you must verify the test result as negative. Otherwise, you must verify the test result as positive.

(e) In determining whether a legitimate medical explanation exists, you may consider the employee's use of a medication from a foreign country. You must exercise your professional judgment consistently with the following principles:

(1) There can be a legitimate medical explanation only with respect to a substance that is obtained legally in a foreign country.

(2) There can be a legitimate medical explanation only with respect to a substance that has a legitimate medical use. Use of a drug of abuse (e.g., heroin, PCP, marijuana) or any other substance (see § 40.151(f) and (g)) that cannot be viewed as having a legitimate medical use can never be the basis for a legitimate medical explanation, even if the substance is obtained legally in a foreign country.

(3) Use of the substance can form the basis of a legitimate medical explanation only if it is used consistently with its proper and intended medical purpose.

(4) Even if you find that there is a legitimate medical explanation under this paragraph (e) and verify a test negative, you may have a responsibility to raise fitness-for-duty considerations with the employer (see § 40.327).

[65 FR 79526, Dec. 19, 2000, as amended at 82 FR 52245, Nov. 13, 2017]

§ 40.139 On what basis does the MRO verify test results involving 6-acetylmorphine, codeine, and morphine?

As the MRO, you must proceed as follows when you receive a laboratory confirmed positive opiate result:

(a) If the laboratory confirms the presence of 6-acetylmorphine (6–AM) in the specimen, you must verify the test result positive.

(b) In the absence of 6–AM, if the laboratory confirms the presence of either morphine or codeine equal to or above 15,000 ng/mL (in urine) or equal to or above 150 ng/mL (in oral fluid), you must verify the test result as positive, unless the employee presents a legitimate medical explanation for the presence of the drug or drug metabolite in his or her system, as in the case of other drugs (see § 40.137). Consumption of food products (e.g., poppy seeds) must not be considered a legitimate medical explanation for the employee having morphine or codeine at these concentrations.

(c) For all other codeine and morphine positive results, you must verify a confirmed positive test result only if you determine that there is clinical evidence, in addition to the test, of unauthorized use of any opium, opiate, or opium derivative (*i.e.*, morphine, codeine, or heroin).

    (1) As an MRO, it is your responsibility to use your best professional and ethical judgement and discretion to determine whether there is clinical evidence of unauthorized use of opiates. Examples of information that you may consider in making this judgement include, but are not limited to, the following:

        (i) Recent needle tracks;

        (ii) Behavioral and psychological signs of acute opiate intoxication or withdrawal;

        (iii) Clinical history of unauthorized use recent enough to have produced the laboratory test result;

        (iv) Use of a medication from a foreign country. See § 40.137(e) for guidance on how to make this determination.

    (2) In order to establish the clinical evidence referenced in paragraphs (c)(1)(i) and (ii) of this section, personal observation of the employee is essential.

        (i) Therefore, you, as the MRO, must conduct, or cause another physician to conduct, a face-to-face examination of the employee.

        (ii) No face-to-face examination is needed in establishing the clinical evidence referenced in paragraph (c)(1)(iii) or (iv) of this section.

    (3) To be the basis of a verified positive result for codeine or morphine, the clinical evidence you find must concern a drug that the laboratory found in the specimen. (For example, if the test confirmed the presence of codeine, and the employee admits to unauthorized use of hydrocodone, you must not verify the test positive for codeine. The admission must be for the substance that was found through the actual drug test.)

    (4) As the MRO, you have the burden of establishing that there is clinical evidence of unauthorized use of opiates referenced in this paragraph (c). If you cannot make this determination (e.g., there is not sufficient clinical evidence or history), you must verify the test as negative. The employee does not need to show you that a legitimate medical explanation exists if no clinical evidence is established.

[77 FR 26473, May 4, 2012, as amended at 82 FR 52245, Nov. 13, 2017; 88 FR 27645, May 2, 2023]

§ 40.141 How does the MRO obtain information for the verification decision?

As the MRO, you must do the following as you make the determinations needed for a verification decision:

    (a) You must conduct a medical interview. You must review the employee's medical history and any other relevant biomedical factors presented to you by the employee. You may direct the employee to undergo further medical evaluation by you or another physician.

    (b) If the employee asserts that the presence of a drug or drug metabolite in his or her specimen results from taking prescription medication (*i.e.*, a legally valid prescription consistent with the Controlled Substances Act), you must review and take all reasonable and necessary steps to verify the authenticity of all medical records the employee provides.

(1) You may contact the employee's physician or other relevant medical personnel for further information.

    (i) If you decide to contact the employee's pharmacy to authenticate whether the prescription offered by the employee was filled by the pharmacy, you or staff under your operational control can contact the pharmacy.

    (ii) If you utilize staff to perform the inquiry in paragraph (b)(1)(i) of this section, you must ensure operational control over the hiring, firing, evaluation of the staff and you must oversee the performance of the function of contacting a pharmacy to authenticate specific prescription(s) (*e.g.,* outline or script what the staff will ask the pharmacy; occasionally monitor calls to assure quality control; or other methods to ensure the staff are properly conducting the calls with the pharmacies).

(2) You may request an HHS-certified laboratory with validated protocols (*see* § 40.81(c)) to conduct testing for D,L stereoisomers of amphetamine and methamphetamine or testing for tetrahydrocannabivarin (THC–V) when verifying lab results, as you determine necessary.

[65 FR 79526, Dec. 19, 2000, as amended at 82 FR 52245, Nov. 13, 2017; 88 FR 27645, May 2, 2023]

§ 40.143 [Reserved]

§ 40.145 On what basis does the MRO verify test results involving adulteration or substitution?

(a) As an MRO, when you receive a laboratory report that a specimen is adulterated or substituted, you must treat that report in the same way you treat the laboratory's report of a confirmed positive for a drug or drug metabolite.

(b) You must follow the same procedures used for verification of a confirmed positive test for a drug or drug metabolite (see §§ 40.129–40.135, 40.141, 40.151), except as otherwise provided in this section.

(c) In the verification interview, you must explain the laboratory findings to the employee and address technical questions or issues the employee may raise.

(d) You must offer the employee the opportunity to present a legitimate medical explanation for the laboratory findings with respect to presence of the adulterant in, or the creatinine and specific gravity findings for, the specimen.

(e) The employee has the burden of proof that there is a legitimate medical explanation.

    (1) To meet this burden in the case of an adulterated specimen, the employee must demonstrate that the adulterant found by the laboratory entered the specimen through physiological means.

    (2) To meet this burden in the case of a substituted specimen, the employee must demonstrate that he or she did produce or could have produced urine through physiological means, meeting the creatinine concentration criterion of less than 2 mg/dL and the specific gravity criteria of less than or equal to 1.0010 or greater than or equal to 1.0200 (see § 40.93(b)).

    (3) The employee must present information meeting this burden at the time of the verification interview. As the MRO, you have discretion to extend the time available to the employee for this purpose for up to five days before verifying the specimen, if you determine that there is a reasonable basis to believe that the employee will be able to produce relevant evidence supporting a legitimate medical explanation within that time.

(f) As the MRO or the employer, you are not responsible for arranging, conducting, or paying for any studies, examinations or analyses to determine whether a legitimate medical explanation exists.

(g) As the MRO, you must exercise your best professional judgment in deciding whether the employee has established a legitimate medical explanation.

(1) If you determine that the employee's explanation does not present a reasonable basis for concluding that there may be a legitimate medical explanation, you must report the test to the DER as a verified refusal to test because of adulteration or substitution, as applicable.

(2) If you believe that the employee's explanation may present a reasonable basis for concluding that there is a legitimate medical explanation, you must direct the employee to obtain, within the five-day period set forth in paragraph (e)(3) of this section, a further medical evaluation. This evaluation must be performed by a licensed physician (the "referral physician"), acceptable to you, with expertise in the medical issues raised by the employee's explanation. (The MRO may perform this evaluation if the MRO has appropriate expertise.)

(i) As the MRO or employer, you are not responsible for finding or paying a referral physician. However, on request of the employee, you must provide reasonable assistance to the employee's efforts to find such a physician. The final choice of the referral physician is the employee's, as long as the physician is acceptable to you.

(ii) As the MRO, you must consult with the referral physician, providing guidance to him or her concerning his or her responsibilities under this section. As part of this consultation, you must provide the following information to the referral physician:

(A) That the employee was required to take a DOT drug test, but the laboratory reported that the specimen was adulterated or substituted, which is treated as a refusal to test;

(B) The consequences of the appropriate DOT agency regulation for refusing to take the required drug test;

(C) That the referral physician must agree to follow the requirements of paragraphs (g)(3) through (g)(4) of this section; and

(D) That the referral physician must provide you with a signed statement of his or her recommendations.

(3) As the referral physician, you must evaluate the employee and consider any evidence the employee presents concerning the employee's medical explanation. You may conduct additional tests to determine whether there is a legitimate medical explanation. Any additional drug tests must be performed in an HHS-certified laboratory.

(4) As the referral physician, you must then make a written recommendation to the MRO about whether the MRO should determine that there is a legitimate medical explanation. As the MRO, you must seriously consider and assess the referral physician's recommendation in deciding whether there is a legitimate medical explanation.

(5) As the MRO, if you determine that there is a legitimate medical explanation, you must cancel the test and inform ODAPC in writing of the determination and the basis for it (e.g., referral physician's findings, evidence produced by the employee).

(6) As the MRO, if you determine that there is not a legitimate medical explanation, you must report the test to the DER as a verified refusal to test because of adulteration or substitution.

(h)   The following are examples of types of evidence an employee could present to support an assertion of a legitimate medical explanation for a substituted urine result.

  (1)   Medically valid evidence demonstrating that the employee is capable of physiologically producing urine meeting the creatinine and specific gravity criteria of § 40.93(b).

    (i)   To be regarded as medically valid, the evidence must have been gathered using appropriate methodology and controls to ensure its accuracy and reliability.

    (ii)   Assertion by the employee that his or her personal characteristics (*e.g.*, with respect to race, gender, weight, diet, working conditions) are responsible for the substituted result does not, in itself, constitute a legitimate medical explanation. To make a case that there is a legitimate medical explanation, the employee must present evidence showing that the cited personal characteristics actually result in the physiological production of urine meeting the creatinine and specific gravity criteria of § 40.93(b).

  (2)   Information from a medical evaluation under paragraph (g) of this section that the individual has a medical condition that has been demonstrated to cause the employee to physiologically produce urine meeting the creatinine and specific gravity criteria of § 40.93(b).

    (i)   A finding or diagnosis by the physician that an employee has a medical condition, in itself, does not constitute a legitimate medical explanation.

    (ii)   To establish there is a legitimate medical explanation, the employee must demonstrate that the cited medical condition actually results in the physiological production of urine meeting the creatinine and specific gravity criteria of § 40.93(b).

[65 FR 79526, Dec. 19, 2000, as amended at 68 FR 31626, May 28, 2003; 69 FR 64867, Nov. 9, 2004; 88 FR 27646, May 2, 2023]

§ 40.147 [Reserved]

§ 40.149 May the MRO change a verified drug test result?

(a)   As the MRO, you may change a verified test result only in the following situations:

  (1)   When you have reopened a verification that was done without an interview with an employee (see § 40.133(d)).

  (2)   If you receive information, not available to you at the time of the original verification, demonstrating that the laboratory made an error in identifying (*e.g.*, a paperwork mistake) or testing (*e.g.*, a false positive or negative) the employee's primary or split specimen. For example, suppose the laboratory originally reported a positive test result for Employee X and a negative result for Employee Y. You verified the test results as reported to you. Then the laboratory notifies you that it mixed up the two test results, and X was really negative and Y was really positive. You would change X's test result from positive to negative and contact Y to conduct a verification interview.

  (3)   If, within 60 days of the original verification decision—

    (i)   You receive information that could not reasonably have been provided to you at the time of the decision demonstrating that there is a legitimate medical explanation for the presence of drug(s)/metabolite(s) in the employee's specimen; or

    (ii)   You receive credible new or additional evidence that a legitimate medical explanation for an adulterated or substituted result exists.

Example to paragraph (a)(3): If the employee's physician provides you a valid prescription that he or she failed to find at the time of the original verification, you may change the test result from positive to negative if you conclude that the prescription provides a legitimate medical explanation for the drug(s)/ metabolite(s) in the employee's specimen.

   (4) If you receive the information in paragraph (a)(3) of this section after the 60-day period, you must consult with ODAPC prior to changing the result.

   (5) When you have made an administrative error and reported an incorrect result.

(b) If you change the result, you must immediately notify the DER in writing, as provided in §§ 40.163–40.165.

(c) You are the only person permitted to change a verified test result, such as a verified positive test result or a determination that an individual has refused to test because of adulteration or substitution. This is because, as the MRO, you have the sole authority under this part to make medical determinations leading to a verified test (e.g., a determination that there was or was not a legitimate medical explanation for a laboratory test result). For example, an arbitrator is not permitted to overturn the medical judgment of the MRO that the employee failed to present a legitimate medical explanation for a positive, adulterated, or substituted test result of his or her specimen.

[65 FR 79526, Dec. 19, 2000, as amended at 66 FR 41952, Aug. 9, 2001; 73 FR 35971, June 25, 2008]

§ 40.151 What are MROs prohibited from doing as part of the verification process?

As an MRO, you are prohibited from doing the following as part of the verification process:

(a) You must not consider any evidence (verbal or written information) from any drug tests that are not collected or tested in accordance with this part. For example, if an employee tells you he went to his own physician, provided a urine specimen, sent it to a laboratory, and received a negative test result, you are required to ignore this test result.

(b) It is not your function to make decisions about factual disputes between the employee and the collector concerning matters occurring at the collection site that are not reflected on the CCF (*e.g.,* concerning allegations that the collector left the area or left open collection containers where other people could access them.)

(c) It is not your function to determine whether the employer should have directed that a test occur. For example, if an employee tells you that the employer misidentified her as the subject of a random test, or directed her to take a reasonable suspicion or post-accident test without proper grounds under a DOT agency drug or alcohol regulation, you must inform the employee that you cannot play a role in deciding these issues.

(d) It is not your function to consider explanations of confirmed positive, adulterated, or substituted test results that would not, even if true, constitute a legitimate medical explanation. For example, an employee may tell you that someone slipped amphetamines into her drink at a party, that she unknowingly ingested a marijuana brownie, or that she traveled in a closed car with several people smoking crack. MROs are unlikely to be able to verify the facts of such passive or unknowing ingestion stories. Even if true, such stories do not present a legitimate medical explanation. Consequently, you must not declare a test as negative based on an explanation of this kind.

(e) You must not verify a test negative based on information that a physician recommended that the employee use a drug listed in Schedule I of the Controlled Substances Act. (*e.g.*, under a state law that purports to authorize such recommendations, such as the "medical marijuana" laws that some states have adopted).

(f) You must not accept an assertion of consumption or other use of a hemp or other non-prescription marijuana-related product as a basis for verifying a marijuana test negative. You also must not accept such an explanation related to consumption of coca teas as a basis for verifying a cocaine test result as negative. Consuming or using such a product is not a legitimate medical explanation.

(g) You must not accept an assertion that there is a legitimate medical explanation for the presence of PCP, 6−AM, MDMA, or MDA in a specimen.

(h) You must not accept, as a legitimate medical explanation for an adulterated specimen, an assertion that soap, bleach, or glutaraldehyde entered a specimen through physiological means. There are no physiological means through which these substances can enter a specimen.

(i) You must not accept, as a legitimate medical explanation for a substituted specimen, an assertion that an employee can produce a urine specimen for which the creatinine level is below the laboratory's limit of detection. There are no physiological means through which a person can produce a urine specimen having this characteristic.

[65 FR 79526, Dec. 19, 2000, as amended at 66 FR 41952, Aug. 9, 2001; 75 FR 49863, Aug. 16, 2010; 88 FR 27646, May 2, 2023]

§ 40.153 How does the MRO notify employees of their right to a test of the split specimen?

(a) As the MRO, when you have verified a drug test as positive for a drug or drug metabolite, or as a refusal to test because of adulteration or substitution, you must notify the employee of his or her right to have the split specimen tested. You must also notify the employee of the procedures for requesting a test of the split specimen.

(b) You must inform the employee that he or she has 72 hours from the time you provide this notification to him or her to request a test of the split specimen.

(c) You must tell the employee how to contact you to make this request. You must provide telephone numbers or other information that will allow the employee to make this request. As the MRO, you must have the ability to receive the employee's calls at all times during the 72 hour period (*e.g.*, by use of an answering machine with a "time stamp" feature when there is no one in your office to answer the phone).

(d) You must tell the employee that if he or she makes this request within 72 hours, the employer must ensure that the test takes place, and that the employee is not required to pay for the test from his or her own funds before the test takes place. You must also tell the employee that the employer may seek reimbursement for the cost of the test (see § 40.173).

(e) You must tell the employee that additional tests of the specimen *e.g.*, DNA tests) are not authorized.

§ 40.155 What does the MRO do when a negative or positive test result is also dilute?

(a) When the laboratory reports that a specimen is dilute, you must, as the MRO, report to the DER that the specimen, in addition to being negative or positive, is dilute.

(b) You must check the "dilute" box (Step 6) on Copy 2 of the CCF.

(c) When you report a dilute specimen to the DER, you must explain to the DER the employer's obligations and choices under § 40.197, to include the requirement for an immediate recollection under direct observation if the creatinine concentration of a negative-dilute specimen was greater than or equal to 2mg/dL but less than or equal to 5mg/dL.

(d) If the employee's recollection under direct observation, in paragraph (c) of this section, results in another negative-dilute, as the MRO, you must:

(1) Review the CCF to ensure that there is documentation that the recollection was directly observed.

(2) If the CCF documentation shows that the recollection was directly observed as required, report this result to the DER as a negative-dilute result.

(3) If CCF documentation indicates that the recollection was not directly observed as required, do not report a result but again explain to the DER that there must be an immediate recollection under direct observation.

[65 FR 79526, Dec. 19, 2000, as amended at 66 FR 41952, Aug. 9, 2001; 68 FR 31626, May 28, 2003; 69 FR 64867, Nov. 9, 2004; 73 FR 35971, June 25, 2008]

§ 40.157 [Reserved]

§ 40.159 What does the MRO do when a drug test result is invalid?

(a) As the MRO, when the laboratory reports that the test result is an invalid result, you must do the following:

(1) Discuss the laboratory results with a certifying scientist to determine if the primary specimen should be tested at another HHS-certified laboratory. If the laboratory did not contact you as required by §§ 40.91(e) and 40.96(b), you must contact the laboratory.

(2) If you and the laboratory have determined that no further testing is necessary, contact the employee and inform the employee that the specimen was invalid. In contacting the employee, use the procedures set forth in § 40.131.

(3) After explaining the limits of disclosure (see §§ 40.135(d) and 40.327), you must determine if the employee has a medical explanation for the invalid result. You must inquire about the medications the employee may have taken.

(4) If the employee gives an explanation that is acceptable, you must:

(i) Place a check mark in the "Test Cancelled" box (Step 6) on Copy 2 of the CCF and enter "Invalid Result" and "direct observation collection not required" on the "Remarks" line.

(ii) Report to the DER that the test is cancelled, the reason for cancellation, and that no further action is required unless a negative test result is required (i.e., pre-employment, return-to-duty, or follow-up tests).

(iii) If a negative test result is required and the medical explanation concerns a situation in which the employee has a permanent or long-term medical condition that precludes him or her from providing a valid specimen, as the MRO, you must follow the procedures outlined at § 40.160 for determining if there is clinical evidence that the individual is an illicit drug user.

(5) If the employee is unable to provide an explanation and/or a valid prescription for a medication that interfered with the immunoassay test but denies having adulterated the specimen, you must:

(i) Place a check mark in the "Test Cancelled" box (Step 6) on Copy 2 of the CCF and enter "Invalid Result" and "direct observation collection required" on the "Remarks" line.

(ii) Report to the DER that the test is cancelled, the reason for cancellation, and that a second collection must take place immediately under direct observation. Recommend to the employer that an alternate specimen should be collected if practicable (*e.g.,* oral fluid, if the specimen was urine).

(iii) Instruct the employer to ensure that the employee has the minimum possible advance notice that he or she must go to the collection site.

(6) When the test result is invalid because pH is greater than or equal to 9.0 but less than or equal to 9.5 and the employee has no other medical explanation for the pH, you should consider whether there is evidence of elapsed time and increased temperature that could account for the pH value.

(i) You are authorized to consider the temperature conditions that were likely to have existed between the time of collection and transportation of the specimen to the laboratory, and the length of time between the specimen collection and arrival at the laboratory.

(ii) You may talk with the collection site and laboratory to discuss time and temperature issues, including any pertinent information regarding specimen storage.

(iii) If you determine that time and temperature account for the pH value, you must cancel the test and take no further action, as provided at paragraph (a)(4) of this section.

(iv) If you determine that time and temperature fail to account for the pH value, you must cancel the test and direct another collection under direct observation, as provided at paragraph (a)(5) of this section.

(b) You may only report an invalid test result when you are in possession of a legible copy of Copy 1 of the CCF. In addition, you must have Copy 2 of the CCF, a legible copy of it, or any other copy of the CCF containing the employee's signature.

(c) If the employee admits to having adulterated or substituted the specimen, you must, on the same day, write and sign your own statement of what the employee told you. You must then report a refusal to test in accordance with § 40.163 .

(d) If the employee admits to using a drug, you must, on the same day, write and sign your own statement of what the employee told you. You must then report that admission to the DER for appropriate action under DOT Agency regulations. This test will be reported as cancelled with the reason noted.

(e) If the employee's recollection (required at paragraph (a)(5) of this section) results in another invalid result for the same reason as reported for the first specimen, as the MRO, you must:

(1) Review the CCF to ensure that there is documentation that the recollection was directly observed.

(2) If the CCF review indicates that the recollection was directly observed as required, document that the employee had another specimen with an invalid result for the same reason.

(3) Follow the recording and reporting procedures at (a)(4)(i) and (ii) of this section.

(4) If a negative result is required (i.e., pre-employment, return-to-duty, or follow-up tests), follow the procedures at § 40.160 for determining if there is clinical evidence that the individual is an illicit drug user.

(5) If the recollection was not directly observed as required, do not report a result but again explain to the DER that there must be an immediate recollection under direct observation.

(f) If the employee's recollection (required at paragraph (a)(5) of this section) results in another invalid result for a different reason than that reported for the first specimen, as the MRO, you must:

(1) Review the CCF to ensure that there is documentation that the recollection was directly observed.

(2) If the CCF review indicates that the recollection was directly observed as required, document that the employee had another specimen with an invalid result for a different reason.

(3) As the MRO, you should not contact the employee to discuss the result, but rather direct the DER to conduct an immediate recollection under direct observation without prior notification to the employee.

(4) If the CCF documentation indicates that the recollection was not directly observed as required, do not report a result but again explain to the DER that there must be an immediate recollection under direct observation.

(g) If, as the MRO, you receive a laboratory invalid result in conjunction with a positive, adulterated, and/or substituted result and you verify any of those results as being a positive and/or refusal to test, you do not report the invalid result unless the split specimen fails to reconfirm the result(s) of the primary specimen.

[65 FR 79526, Dec. 19, 2000, as amended at 73 FR 35972, June 25, 2008; 75 FR 49863, Aug. 16, 2010; 88 FR 27646, May 2, 2023]

§ 40.160 What does the MRO do when a valid test result cannot be produced and a negative result is required?

(a) If a valid test result cannot be produced and a negative result is required, (under § 40.159 (a)(5)(iii) and (e)(4)), as the MRO, you must determine if there is clinical evidence that the individual is currently an illicit drug user. You must make this determination by personally conducting, or causing to be conducted, a medical evaluation. In addition, if appropriate, you may also consult with the employee's physician to gather information you need to reach this determination.

(b) If you do not personally conduct the medical evaluation, as the MRO, you must ensure that one is conducted by a licensed physician acceptable to you.

(c) For purposes of this section, the MRO or the physician conducting the evaluation may conduct an alternative test (e.g., blood) as part of the medically appropriate procedures in determining clinical evidence of drug use.

(d) If the medical evaluation reveals no clinical evidence of drug use, as the MRO, you must report this to the employer as a negative test result with written notations regarding the medical examination. The report must also state why the medical examination was required (i.e., either the basis for the determination that a permanent or long-term medical condition exists or because the recollection under direct observation resulted in another invalid result for the same reason, as appropriate) and for the determination that no signs and symptoms of drug use exist.

(1) Check "Negative" (Step 6) on the CCF.

(2) Sign and date the CCF.

(e) If the medical evaluation reveals clinical evidence of drug use, as the MRO, you must report the result to the employer as a cancelled test with written notations regarding the results of the medical examination. The report must also state why the medical examination was required (i.e., either the basis for the determination that a permanent or long-term medical condition exists or because the recollection under direct observation resulted in another invalid result for the same reason, as appropriate) and state the reason for the determination that signs and symptoms of drug use exist. Because this is a cancelled test, it does not serve the purpose of an actual negative test result (i.e., the employer is not authorized to allow the employee to begin or resume performing safety-sensitive functions, because a negative test result is needed for that purpose).

[73 FR 35972, June 25, 2008]

§ 40.161 What does the MRO do when a drug test specimen is rejected for testing?

As the MRO, when the laboratory reports that the specimen is rejected for testing (*e.g.*, because of a fatal or uncorrected flaw), you must do the following:

(a) Place a check mark in the "Test Cancelled" box (Step 6) on Copy 2 (or a legible copy of Copy 3–5) of the CCF and enter the reason on the "Remarks" line. If you do not have Copy 2 (or a legible copy of Copy 3–5), then enter "Test Cancelled" and the reason for the cancellation on a report in the format required under § 40.163(c).

(b) Report to the DER that the test is cancelled and the reason for cancellation, and that no further action is required unless a negative test is required (*e.g.*, in the case of a pre-employment, return-to-duty, or follow-up test).

(c) You may only report a test cancelled because of a "rejected for testing" laboratory result when you are in possession of a legible copy of Copy 1 of the CCF. In addition, you must have Copy 2 of the CCF, a legible copy of it, or any other copy of the CCF containing the employee's signature. If you do not have Copy 2 (or a legible copy of Copy 3–5), then enter "Test Cancelled" and the reason for the cancellation on a report in the format required under § 40.163(c).

[65 FR 79526, Dec. 19, 2000, as amended at 88 FR 27646, May 2, 2023]

§ 40.162 What must MROs do with multiple verified results for the same testing event?

(a) If the testing event is one in which there was one specimen collection with multiple verified non-negative results, as the MRO, you must report them all to the DER. For example, if you verified the specimen as being positive for marijuana and cocaine and as being a refusal to test because the specimen was also adulterated, as the MRO, you should report the positives and the refusal to the DER.

(b) If the testing event was one in which two separate specimen collections (e.g., a specimen out of temperature range and the subsequent observed collection) were sent to the laboratory, as the MRO, you must:

(1) If both specimens were verified negative, report the result as negative.

(2) If either of the specimens was verified negative and the other was verified as one or more non-negative(s), report the non-negative result(s) only. For example, if you verified one specimen as negative and the other as a refusal to test because the second specimen was substituted, as the MRO you should report only the refusal to the DER.

(i) If the first specimen is reported as negative, but the result of the second specimen has not been reported by the laboratory, as the MRO, you should hold—not report—the result of the first specimen until the result of the second specimen is received.

(ii) If the first specimen is reported as non-negative, as the MRO, you should report the result immediately and not wait to receive the result of the second specimen.

(3) If both specimens were verified non-negative, report all of the non-negative results. For example, if you verified one specimen as positive and the other as a refusal to test because the specimen was adulterated, as the MRO, you should report the positive and the refusal results to the DER.

(c) As an exception to paragraphs (a) and (b) of this section, as the MRO, you must follow procedures at § 40.159(g) when any verified non-negative result is also invalid.

[73 FR 35972, June 25, 2008, as amended at 82 FR 52245, Nov. 13, 2017]

§ 40.163 How does the MRO report drug test results?

(a) As the MRO, it is your responsibility to report all drug test results to the employer.

(b) You may use a signed or stamped and dated legible photocopy of Copy 2 of the CCF to report test results.

(c) If you do not report test results using Copy 2 of the CCF for this purpose, you must provide a written report (e.g., a letter) for each test result. This report must, as a minimum, include the following information:

(1) Full name, as indicated on the CCF, of the employee tested;

(2) Specimen ID number from the CCF and the SSN or employee ID No.;

(3) Reason for the test, if indicated on the CCF (e.g., random, post-accident);

(4) Date of the collection;

(5) Date you received Copy 2 of the CCF;

(6) Result of the test (i.e., positive, negative, dilute, refusal to test, test cancelled) and the date the result was verified by the MRO;

(7) For verified positive tests, the drug(s)/metabolite(s) for which the test was positive;

(8) For cancelled tests, the reason for cancellation; and

(9) For refusals to test, the reason for the refusal determination (e.g., in the case of an adulterated test result, the name of the adulterant).

(d) As an exception to the reporting requirements of paragraph (b) and (c) of this section, the MRO may report negative results using an electronic data file.

(1) If you report negatives using an electronic data file, the report must contain, as a minimum, the information specified in paragraph (c) of this section, as applicable for negative test results.

(2) In addition, the report must contain your name, address, and phone number, the name of any person other than you reporting the results, and the date the electronic results report is released.

(e) If you use a written report as provided in paragraph (c) of this section to report results, you must retain a copy of the written report. If you use the electronic data file to report negatives, as provided in paragraph (d) of this section, you must retain a retrievable copy of that report in a format suitable for inspection and audit by a DOT representative. In either case, you must keep the completed Copy 2 of the CCF. When completing Copy 2, either the MRO must sign and date it (for both negatives and non-negatives) or MRO staff must stamp and date it (for negatives only).

(f) You must not use Copy 1 of the CCF to report drug test results.

(g) You must not provide quantitative values to the DER or C/TPA for drug or validity test results. However, you must provide the test information in your possession to a SAP who consults with you (see § 40.293(g)).

(h) You must maintain reports and records related to negatives and cancelled results for one year; you must maintain reports and records related to positives and refusals for five years, unless otherwise specified by applicable DOT agency regulations.

[66 FR 41952, Aug. 9, 2001, as amended at 75 FR 49863, Aug. 16, 2010; 75 FR 59107, Sept. 27, 2010; 76 FR 59578, Sept. 27, 2011; 88 FR 27646, May 2, 2023]

§ 40.165 To whom does the MRO transmit reports of drug test results?

(a) As the MRO, you must report all drug test results to the DER, except in the circumstances provided for in § 40.345 .

(b) If the employer elects to receive reports of results through a C/TPA, acting as an intermediary as provided in § 40.345 , you must report the results through the designated C/TPA.

§ 40.167 How are MRO reports of drug results transmitted to the employer?

As the MRO or C/TPA who transmits drug test results to the employer, you must comply with the following requirements:

(a) You must report the results in a confidential manner.

(b) You must transmit to the DER on the same day the MRO verifies the result or the next business day all verified positive test results, results requiring an immediate collection under direct observation, adulterated or substituted specimen results, and other refusals to test.

(1) Direct telephone contact with the DER is the preferred method of immediate reporting. Follow up your phone call with appropriate documentation (see § 40.163).

(2) You are responsible for identifying yourself to the DER, and the DER must have a means to confirm your identification.

(3) The MRO's report that you transmit to the employer must contain all of the information required by § 40.163 .

(c) You must transmit the MRO's report(s) of verified tests to the DER so that the DER receives it within two days of verification by the MRO.

(1) You must fax, courier, mail, or electronically transmit a legible image or copy of either the signed or stamped and dated Copy 2 or the written report (see § 40.163(b) and (c)).

(2) Negative results reported electronically (i.e., computer data file) do not require an image of Copy 2 or the written report.

(d) In transmitting test results, you or the C/TPA and the employer must ensure the security of the transmission and limit access to any transmission, storage, or retrieval systems.

(e) MRO reports are not subject to modification or change by anyone other than the MRO, as provided in § 40.149(c).

[65 FR 79526, Dec. 19, 2000, as amended at 66 FR 41953, Aug. 9, 2001]

§ 40.169 Where is other information concerning the role of MROs and the verification process found in this regulation?

You can find more information concerning the role of MROs in several sections of this part:

§ 40.3—Definition.

§§ 40.47–40.49—Correction of form and kit errors.

§ 40.67—Role in direct observation and other atypical test situations.

§ 40.83—Laboratory handling of fatal and correctable flaws.

§ 40.97—Laboratory handling of test results and quantitative values.

§ 40.99—Authorization of longer laboratory retention of specimens.

§ 40.101—Relationship with laboratories; avoidance of conflicts of interest.

§ 40.171—Request for test of split specimen.

§ 40.187—Action concerning split specimen test results.

§ 40.193—Role in "shy bladder" situations.

§ 40.195—Role in cancelling tests.

§§ 40.199–40.203—Documenting errors in tests.

§ 40.327—Confidentiality and release of information.

§ 40.347—Transfer of records.

§ 40.353—Relationships with service agents.

[65 FR 79526, Dec. 19, 2000, as amended at 82 FR 52245, Nov. 13, 2017]

Subpart H—Split Specimen Tests

§ 40.171 How does an employee request a test of a split specimen?

(a) As an employee, when the MRO has notified you that you have a verified positive drug test and/or refusal to test because of adulteration or substitution, you have 72 hours from the time of notification to request a test of the split specimen. The request may be verbal or in writing. If you make this request to the MRO within 72 hours, you trigger the requirements of this section for a test of the split specimen. There is no split specimen testing for an invalid result.

(b)

    (1) If, as an employee, you have not requested a test of the split specimen within 72 hours, you may present to the MRO information documenting that serious injury, illness, lack of actual notice of the verified test result, inability to contact the MRO (e.g., there was no one in the MRO's office and the answering machine was not working), or other circumstances unavoidably prevented you from making a timely request.

    (2) As the MRO, if you conclude from the employee's information that there was a legitimate reason for the employee's failure to contact you within 72 hours, you must direct that the test of the split specimen take place, just as you would when there is a timely request.

(c) When the employee makes a timely request for a test of the split specimen under paragraphs (a) and (b) of this section, you must, as the MRO, immediately provide written notice to the laboratory that tested the primary specimen, directing the laboratory to forward the split specimen to a second HHS-certified laboratory. You must also document the date and time of the employee's request.

[65 FR 79526, Dec. 19, 2000, as amended at 73 FR 35972, June 25, 2008]

§ 40.173 Who is responsible for paying for the test of a split specimen?

(a) As the employer, you are responsible for making sure (e.g., by establishing appropriate accounts with laboratories for testing split specimens) that the MRO, first laboratory, and second laboratory perform the functions noted in §§ 40.175–40.185 in a timely manner, once the employee has made a timely request for a test of the split specimen.

(b) As the employer, you must not condition your compliance with these requirements on the employee's direct payment to the MRO or laboratory or the employee's agreement to reimburse you for the costs of testing. For example, if you ask the employee to pay for some or all of the cost of testing the split specimen, and the employee is unwilling or unable to do so, you must ensure that the test takes place in a timely manner, even though this means that you pay for it.

(c) As the employer, you may seek payment or reimbursement of all or part of the cost of the split specimen from the employee (e.g., through your written company policy or a collective bargaining agreement). This part takes no position on who ultimately pays the cost of the test, so long as the employer ensures that the testing is conducted as required and the results released appropriately.

§ 40.175 What steps does the first laboratory take with a split specimen?

(a) As the laboratory at which the primary and split specimen first arrive, you must check to see whether the split specimen is available for testing.

(b) If the split specimen is unavailable or appears insufficient, you must then do the following:

(1) Continue the testing process for the primary specimen as you would normally. Report the results for the primary specimen without providing the MRO information regarding the unavailable split specimen.

(2) Upon receiving a letter from the MRO instructing you to forward the split specimen to another laboratory for testing, report to the MRO that the split specimen is unavailable for testing. Provide as much information as you can about the cause of the unavailability.

(c) As the laboratory that tested the primary specimen, you are not authorized to open the split specimen under any circumstances (except when the split specimen is redesignated as provided in § 40.83).

(d) When you receive written notice from the MRO instructing you to send the split specimen to another HHS-certified laboratory, you must forward the following items to the second laboratory:

(1) The split specimen in its original specimen bottle, with the seal intact;

(2) A copy of the MRO's written request; and

(3) A copy of Copy 1 of the CCF, which identifies the drug(s)/metabolite(s) or the validity criteria to be tested for.

(e) You must not send to the second laboratory any information about the identity of the employee. Inadvertent disclosure does not, however, cause a fatal flaw.

(f) This subpart does not prescribe who gets to decide which HHS-certified laboratory is used to test the split specimen. That decision is left to the parties involved.

§ 40.177 What does the second laboratory do with the split specimen when it is tested to reconfirm the presence of a drug or drug metabolite?

(a) As the laboratory testing the split specimen, you must test the split specimen for the drug(s)/drug metabolite(s) confirmed in the primary specimen.

(b) You must conduct this test without regard to the cutoff concentrations of § 40.85 or § 40.91, as applicable.

(c) If the test fails to reconfirm the presence of the drug(s)/drug metabolite(s) that were reported in the primary specimen, you must conduct validity tests in an attempt to determine the reason for being unable to reconfirm the presence of the drug(s)/metabolite(s). You should conduct the same validity tests as you would conduct on a primary specimen set forth in § 40.87 or § 40.93, as applicable.

(d) In addition, if the test fails to reconfirm the presence of the drug(s)/ drug metabolite(s) reported in the primary specimen, you may send the specimen or an aliquot of it for testing at another HHS-certified laboratory that has the capability to conduct another reconfirmation test.

[65 FR 79526, Dec. 19, 2000, as amended at 73 FR 35972, June 25, 2008; 88 FR 27646, May 2, 2023]

§ 40.179 What does the second laboratory do with the split specimen when it is tested to reconfirm an adulterated test result?

(a) As the laboratory testing the split specimen, you must test the split specimen for the adulterant detected in the primary specimen, using the confirmatory test for the adulterant and using criteria in § 40.89 or § 40.93, as applicable and confirmatory cutoff levels required by the HHS Mandatory Guidelines.

(b) In addition, if the test fails to reconfirm the adulterant result reported in the primary specimen, you may send the specimen or an aliquot of it for testing at another HHS-certified laboratory that has the capability to conduct another reconfirmation test.

[73 FR 35973, June 25, 2008, as amended at 88 FR 27646, May 2, 2023]

§ 40.181 What does the second laboratory do with the split specimen when it is tested to reconfirm a substituted test result?

As the laboratory testing a urine split specimen, you must test the split specimen using the confirmatory tests for creatinine and specific gravity, using the criteria set forth in § 40.88.

[88 FR 27646, May 2, 2023]

§ 40.183 What information do laboratories report to MROs regarding split specimen results?

(a) As the laboratory responsible for testing the split specimen, you must report split specimen test results by checking the "Reconfirmed" box and/or the "Failed to Reconfirm" box (Step 5(b)) on Copy 1 of the CCF, as appropriate, and by providing clarifying remarks using current HHS Mandatory Guidelines requirements.

(b) As the laboratory certifying scientist, enter your name, sign, and date the CCF.

[65 FR 79526, Dec. 19, 2000, as amended at 73 FR 35972, June 25, 2008]

§ 40.185 Through what methods and to whom must a laboratory report split specimen results?

(a) As the laboratory testing the split specimen, you must report laboratory results directly, and only, to the MRO at his or her place of business. You must not report results to or through the DER or another service agent (e.g., a C/TPA).

(b) You must fax, courier, mail, or electronically transmit a legible image or copy of the fully-completed Copy 1 of the CCF, which has been signed by the certifying scientist.

(c) You must transmit the laboratory result to the MRO immediately, preferably on the same day or next business day as the result is signed and released.

§ 40.187 What does the MRO do with split specimen laboratory results?

As the MRO, the split specimen laboratory results you receive will fall into five categories. You must take the following action, as appropriate, when a laboratory reports split specimen results to you.

(a) *Category 1:* The laboratory reconfirmed one or more of the primary specimen results. As the MRO, you must report to the DER and the employee the result(s) that was/were reconfirmed.

    (1) In the case of a reconfirmed positive test(s) for drug(s) or drug metabolite(s), the positive is the final result.

    (2) In the case of a reconfirmed adulterated or substituted result, the refusal to test is the final result.

    (3) In the case of a combination positive and refusal to test results, the final result is both positive and refusal to test.

49 CFR Part 40 (up to date as of 3/05/2024)
Procedures for Transportation Workplace Drug and Alcohol Testing Programs

49 CFR 40.187(b)

(b) *Category 2:* The laboratory failed to reconfirm all of the primary specimen results because, as appropriate, drug(s)/drug metabolite(s) were not detected; adulteration criteria were not met; and/or substitution criteria were not met. As the MRO, you must report to the DER and the employee that the test must be cancelled.

(1) As the MRO, you must inform ODAPC of the failure to reconfirm using the format in appendix F to this part.

(2) In a case where the split failed to reconfirm because the substitution criteria were not met and the split specimen creatinine concentration was equal to or greater than 2mg/dL but less than or equal to 5mg/dL, as the MRO, you must, in addition to step (b)(1) of this paragraph, direct the DER to ensure the immediate collection of another specimen from the employee under direct observation, with no notice given to the employee of this collection requirement until immediately before the collection.

(3) In a case where the split failed to reconfirm and the primary specimen's result was also invalid, direct the DER to ensure the immediate collection of another specimen from the employee under direct observation, with no notice given to the employee of this collection requirement until immediately before the collection.

(c) *Category 3:* The laboratory failed to reconfirm all of the primary specimen results, and also reported that the split specimen was invalid, adulterated, and/or substituted.

(1) In the case where the laboratory failed to reconfirm all of the primary specimen results and the split was reported as invalid, as the MRO, you must:

(i) Report to the DER and the employee that the test must be cancelled and the reason for the cancellation.

(ii) Direct the DER to ensure the immediate collection of another specimen from the employee under direct observation, with no notice given to the employee of this collection requirement until immediately before the collection.

(iii) Inform ODAPC of the failure to reconfirm using the format in appendix F to this part.

(2) In the case where the laboratory failed to reconfirm any of the primary specimen results, and the split was reported as adulterated and/or substituted, as the MRO, you must:

(i) Contact the employee and inform the employee that the laboratory has determined that his or her split specimen is adulterated and/or substituted, as appropriate.

(ii) Follow the procedures of § 40.145 to determine if there is a legitimate medical explanation for the laboratory finding of adulteration and/or substitution, as appropriate.

(iii) If you determine that there is a legitimate medical explanation for the adulterated and/or substituted test result, report to the DER and the employee that the test must be cancelled; and inform ODAPC of the failure to reconfirm using the format in appendix F to this part.

(iv) If you determine that there is not a legitimate medical explanation for the adulterated and/or substituted test result, you must take the following steps:

(A) Report the test to the DER and the employee as a verified refusal to test. Inform the employee that he or she has 72 hours to request a test of the primary specimen to determine if the adulterant found in the split specimen is also present in the primary specimen and/or to determine if the primary specimen meets appropriate substitution criteria.

(B) Except when the request is for a test of the primary specimen and is being made to the laboratory that tested the primary specimen, follow the procedures of §§ 40.153, 40.171, 40.173, 40.179, 40.181, and 40.185, as appropriate.

(C) As the laboratory that tests the primary specimen to reconfirm the presence of the adulterant found in the split specimen and/or to determine that the primary specimen meets appropriate substitution criteria, report your result to the MRO on a photocopy (faxed, mailed, scanned, couriered) of Copy 1 of the CCF.

(D) If the test of the primary specimen reconfirms the adulteration and/or substitution finding of the split specimen, as the MRO you must report the result as a refusal to test as provided in paragraph (a)(2) of this section.

(E) If the test of the primary specimen fails to reconfirm the adulteration and/or substitution finding of the split specimen, as the MRO you must cancel the test, following procedures in paragraph (b) of this section.

(d) *Category 4:* The laboratory failed to reconfirm one or more but not all of the primary specimen results, and also reported that the split specimen was invalid, adulterated, and/or substituted. As the MRO, in the case where the laboratory reconfirmed one or more of the primary specimen result(s), you must follow procedures in paragraph (a) of this section and:

(1) Report that the split was also reported as being invalid, adulterated, and/or substituted (as appropriate).

(2) Inform the DER to take action only on the reconfirmed result(s).

(e) *Category 5:* The split specimen was not available for testing or there was no split laboratory available to test the specimen. As the MRO, you must:

(1) Report to the DER and the employee that the test must be cancelled and the reason for the cancellation;

(2) Direct the DER to ensure the immediate recollection of another specimen from the employee under direct observation, with no notice given to the employee of this collection requirement until immediately before the collection; and

(3) Notify ODAPC of the failure to reconfirm using the format in appendix F to this part.

(f) For all split specimen results, as the MRO you must in Step 7 of Copy 2 of the CCF:

(1) Report split specimen test results by checking the "Reconfirmed" box and/or the "Failed to Reconfirm" box, or the "Test Cancelled" box, as appropriate.

(2) , Enter your name, sign, and date.

(3) Send a legible copy of Copy 2 of the CCF (or a signed and dated letter, see § 40.163) to the employer and keep a copy for your records. Transmit the document as provided in § 40.167.

[73 FR 35973, June 25, 2008, as amended at 75 FR 59108, Sept. 27, 2010; 88 FR 27646, May 2, 2023]

§ 40.189 Where is other information concerning split specimens found in this regulation?

You can find more information concerning split specimens in several sections of this part:

§ 40.3—Definition.

§ 40.65—Quantity of split specimen.

§ 40.67—Directly observed test when split specimen is unavailable.

§§ 40.71–40.73—Collection process for split specimens.

§ 40.83—Laboratory accessioning of split specimens.

§ 40.99—Laboratory retention of split specimens.

§ 40.153—MRO notice to employees on tests of split specimen.

§§ 40.193 and 40.201—MRO actions on insufficient or unavailable split specimens.

Appendix D to Part 40—Report format for split specimen failure to reconfirm.

[65 FR 79526, Dec. 19, 2000, as amended at 82 FR 52245, Nov. 13, 2017]

Subpart I—Problems in Drug Tests

§ 40.191 What is a refusal to take a DOT drug test, and what are the consequences?

(a) As an employee, you have refused to take a drug test if you:

(1) Fail to appear for any test (except a pre-employment test) within a reasonable time, as determined by the employer, consistent with applicable DOT agency regulations, after being directed to do so by the employer. This includes the failure of an employee (including an owner-operator) to appear for a test when called by a C/TPA (see § 40.61(a));

(2) Fail to remain at the testing site until the testing process is complete. Provided that an employee who leaves the collection site before the testing process commences (*see* § 40.63(c) or § 40.72(e), as applicable) for a pre-employment test is not deemed to have refused to test. The collector is not required to inform an employee that the failure to remain at the collection site is a refusal. If an employee leaves prior to the completion of the testing process, per § 40.355(i) the employer must decide whether the employee's actions constitute a refusal;

(3) Fail to provide a specimen for any drug test required by this part or DOT agency regulations. Provided that an employee who does not provide a specimen because he or she has left the testing site before the testing process commences (*see* § 40.63(c) or § 40.72(e), as applicable) for a pre-employment test is not deemed to have refused to test. The collector is not required to inform an

employee that the failure to remain at the collection site is a refusal. If an employee leaves prior to the completion of the testing process, per § 40.355(i) the employer must decide whether the employee's actions constitute a refusal;

(4) In the case of a directly observed or monitored urine collection in a drug test, fail to permit the observation or monitoring of an employee's provision of a specimen (*see* §§ 40.67(m) and 40.69(g));

(5) Fail to provide a sufficient amount of specimen when directed, and it has been determined, through a required medical evaluation, that there was no adequate medical explanation for the failure (*see* § 40.193(d)(2));

(6) Fail or decline to take an additional drug test the employer or collector has directed you to take (*see*, for instance, § 40.197(b) as applicable);

(7) Fail to undergo a medical examination or evaluation, as directed by the MRO as part of the verification process, or as directed by the DER under § 40.193(c). In the case of a pre-employment drug test, the employee is deemed to have refused to test on this basis only if the pre-employment test is conducted following a contingent offer of employment. If there was no contingent offer of employment, the MRO will cancel the test;

(8) Fail to cooperate with any part of the testing process (*e.g.*, refuse to empty pockets when directed by the collector, behave in a confrontational way that disrupts the collection process, fail to wash hands after being directed to do so by the collector, fail to remove objects from mouth, fail to permit inspection of the oral cavity, or fail to complete a rinse when requested);

(9) For an observed urine collection, fail to follow the observer's instructions to raise your clothing above the waist, lower clothing and underpants, and to turn around to permit the observer to determine if you have any type of prosthetic or other device that could be used to interfere with the collection process;

(10) Possess or wear a prosthetic or other device that could be used to interfere with the collection process; or

(11) Admit to the collector or MRO that you adulterated or substituted the specimen.

(b) As an employee, if the MRO reports that you have a verified adulterated or substituted test result, you have refused to take a drug test.

(c) As an employee, if you refuse to take a drug test, you incur the consequences specified under DOT agency regulations for a violation of those DOT agency regulations. The consequences specified under DOT agency regulations for a refusal cannot be overturned or set aside by an arbitration, grievance, State court or other non-Federal forum that adjudicates the personnel decisions the employer has taken against the employee.

(d) As a collector or an MRO, when an employee refuses to participate in the part of the testing process in which you are involved, you must terminate the portion of the testing process in which you are involved, document the refusal on the CCF (including, in the case of the collector, printing the employee's name on Copy 2 of the CCF), immediately notify the DER by any means (e.g., telephone or secure fax machine) that ensures that the refusal notification is immediately received. As a referral physician (e.g., physician evaluating a "shy bladder" condition or a claim of a legitimate medical explanation in a validity testing situation), you must notify the MRO, who in turn will notify the DER.

(1) As the collector, you must note the actions that may constitute a refusal in the "Remarks" line (Step 2), and sign and date the CCF. The collector does not make the final decision about whether the employee's conduct constitutes a refusal to test; the employer has the sole responsibility to decide whether a refusal occurred, as stated in § 40.355(i), the employer has a non-delegable duty to make the decision about whether the employee has refused to test.

(2) As the MRO, you must note the refusal by checking the "Refusal to Test" box in Step 6 on Copy 2 of the CCF, checking whether the specimen was adulterated or substituted and, if adulterated, noting the adulterant/reason. If there was another reason for the refusal, check "Other" in Step 6 on Copy 2 of the CCF, and note the reason next to the "Other" box and on the "Remarks" lines, as needed. You must then sign and date the CCF.

(e) As an employee, when you refuse to take a non-DOT test or to sign a non-DOT form, you have not refused to take a DOT test. There are no consequences under DOT agency regulations for refusing to take a non-DOT test.

[65 FR 79526, Dec. 19, 2000, as amended at 66 FR 41953, Aug. 9, 2001; 68 FR 31626, May 28, 2003; 71 FR 49384, Aug. 23, 2006; 73 FR 35974, June 25, 2008; 75 FR 59108, Sept. 27, 2010; 88 FR 27647, May 2, 2023]

§ 40.193 What happens when an employee does not provide a sufficient amount of specimen for a drug test?

(a) If an employee does not provide a sufficient amount of specimen to permit a drug test (*i.e.*, 45 mL of urine in a single void, or 2mL oral fluid in a single sampling, as applicable) you, as the collector, must provide another opportunity to the employee to do so. In accordance with the employer's instructions, this can be done using the same specimen type as the original collection or this can be done by a collector qualified to use an alternate specimen collection for this purpose.

(1) If you change to an alternate specimen collection at this point (*i.e.*, from urine to oral fluid; or from oral fluid to urine), the next collection begins under § 40.61(e) for urine or § 40.72 for oral fluid collection.

(i) If you proceed with an alternate specimen collection, discard the insufficient specimen and proceed with the next specimen collection.

(ii) If you proceed with an alternate specimen collection, discard the CCF for the insufficient specimen and begin a new CCF for the next specimen collection with a notation in the remarks section of the new CCF.

(b)

(1) As the collector, you must do the following when continuing with a urine specimen collection under this section:

(i) Discard the insufficient specimen, except where the insufficient specimen was out of temperature range or showed evidence of adulteration or tampering (*see* § 40.65(b) and (c)).

(ii) Urge the employee to drink up to 40 ounces of fluid, distributed reasonably through a period of up to three hours, or until the individual has provided a sufficient urine specimen, whichever occurs first. It is not a refusal to test if the employee declines to drink. Document on the Remarks line of the CCF (Step 2), and inform the employee of the time at which the three-hour period begins and ends.

(iii) If the employee refuses to make the attempt to provide a new urine specimen or leaves the collection site before the collection process is complete, you must discontinue the collection, note that fact on the "Remarks" line of the CCF (Step 2), and immediately notify the DER of the conduct as provided in § 40.191(e)(1); the employer decides whether the situation is deemed to be a refusal.

(iv) If the employee has not provided a sufficient specimen within three hours of the first unsuccessful attempt to provide the specimen, you must discontinue the collection, note the fact on the "Remarks" line of the CCF (Step 2), and immediately notify the DER. You must also discard any specimen the employee previously provided, including any specimen that is "out of temperature range" or shows signs of tampering. In the remarks section of the CCF that you will distribute to the MRO and DER, note the fact that the employee provided an "out of temperature range specimen" or "specimen that shows signs of tampering" and that it was discarded because the employee did not provide a second sufficient specimen.

(2) As the collector, you must do the following when continuing with an oral fluid specimen collection under this section:

(i) If the employee demonstrates an inability to provide a specimen after 15 minutes of using the collection device, and if the donor states that he or she could provide a specimen after drinking some fluids, urge the employee to drink (up to 8 ounces) and wait an additional 10 minutes before beginning the next specimen collection (a period of up to one hour must be provided, or until the donor has provided a sufficient oral fluid specimen, whichever occurs first). If the employee simply needs more time before attempting to provide an oral fluid specimen, the employee is not required to drink any fluids during the one-hour wait time. It is not a refusal to test if the employee declines to drink. The employee must remain at the collection site, in a monitored area designated by the collector, during the wait period.

(ii) If the employee has not provided a sufficient specimen within one hour of the first unsuccessful attempt to provide the specimen, you must discontinue the collection, note the fact on the "Remarks" line of the CCF (Step 2), and immediately notify the DER.

(3) Send Copy 2 of the CCF to the MRO and Copy 4 to the DER. You must send or fax these copies to the MRO and DER within 24 hours or the next business day.

(c) As the DER, if the collector informs you that the employee has not provided a sufficient amount of specimen (*see* paragraph (b) of this section), you must, after consulting with the MRO, direct the employee to obtain, within five days, an evaluation from a licensed physician, acceptable to the MRO, who has expertise in the medical issues raised by the employee's failure to provide a urine (*see* paragraph (b)(1) of this section) or oral fluid (*see* paragraph (b)(2) of this section) sufficient specimen, but not both. The evaluation and MRO determination required by this section only applies to the oral fluid or the urine insufficient specimen that was the final methodology at the collection site. (The MRO may perform this evaluation if the MRO has appropriate expertise.)

(1) As the MRO, if another physician will perform the evaluation, you must provide the other physician with the following information and instructions:

(i) That the employee was required to take a DOT drug test, but was unable to provide a sufficient amount of specimen to complete the test;

(ii) The consequences of the appropriate DOT agency regulation for refusing to take the required drug test;

(iii) That the referral physician must agree to follow the requirements of paragraphs (d) through (g) of this section.

(2) [Reserved]

(d) As the referral physician conducting this evaluation, you must recommend that the MRO make one of the following determinations:

(1) A medical condition has, or with a high degree of probability could have, precluded the employee from providing a sufficient amount of specimen. As the MRO, if you accept this recommendation, you must:

(i) Check "Test Cancelled" (Step 6) on the CCF; and

(ii) Sign and date the CCF.

(2) There is not an adequate basis for determining that a medical condition has, or with a high degree of probability could have, precluded the employee from providing a sufficient amount of specimen. As the MRO, if you accept this recommendation, you must:

(i) Check the "Refusal to Test" box and "Other" box in Step 6 on Copy 2 of the CCF and note the reason next to the "Other" box and on the "Remarks" lines, as needed.

(ii) Sign and date the CCF.

(e) For purposes of this paragraph, a medical condition includes an ascertainable physiological condition (e.g., a urinary system dysfunction in the case of a urine test or autoimmune disorder in the case of an oral fluid test), or a medically documented pre-existing psychological disorder, but does not include unsupported assertions of "situational anxiety" or dehydration.

(f) As the referral physician making the evaluation, after completing your evaluation, you must provide a written statement of your recommendations and the basis for them to the MRO. You must not include in this statement detailed information on the employee's medical condition beyond what is necessary to explain your conclusion.

(g) If, as the referral physician making this evaluation in the case of a pre-employment, return-to-duty, or follow-up test, you determine that the employee's medical condition is a serious and permanent or long-term disability that is highly likely to prevent the employee from providing a sufficient amount of specimen for a very long or indefinite period of time, you must set forth your determination and the reasons for it in your written statement to the MRO. As the MRO, upon receiving such a report, you must follow the requirements of § 40.195, where applicable.

(h) As the MRO, you must seriously consider and assess the referral physician's recommendations in making your determination about whether the employee has a medical condition that has, or with a high degree of probability could have, precluded the employee from providing a sufficient amount of specimen. You must report your determination to the DER in writing as soon as you make it.

(i) As the employer, when you receive a report from the MRO indicating that a test is cancelled as provided in paragraph (d)(1) of this section, you take no further action with respect to the employee. If the test reason was 'random', the employee remains in the random testing pool.

[88 FR 27647, May 2, 2023]

§ 40.195 What happens when an individual is unable to provide a sufficient amount of specimen

for a pre-employment, follow-up, or return-to-duty test because of a permanent or long-term medical condition?

(a) This section concerns a situation in which an employee has a medical condition that precludes him or her from providing a sufficient specimen for a pre-employment follow-up or return-to-duty test and the condition involves a permanent or long-term disability. As the MRO in this situation, you must do the following:

    (1) You must determine if there is clinical evidence that the individual is an illicit drug user. You must make this determination by personally conducting, or causing to be conducted, a medical evaluation and through consultation with the employee's physician and/or the physician who conducted the evaluation under § 40.193(d).

    (2) If you do not personally conduct the medical evaluation, you must ensure that one is conducted by a licensed physician acceptable to you.

    (3) For purposes of this section, the MRO or the physician conducting the evaluation may conduct an alternative test (*e.g.,* blood) as part of the medically appropriate procedures in determining clinical evidence of drug use.

(b) If the medical evaluation reveals no clinical evidence of drug use, as the MRO, you must report the result to the employer as a negative test with written notations regarding results of both the evaluation conducted under § 40.193(d) and any further medical examination. This report must state the basis for the determination that a permanent or long-term medical condition exists, making provision of a sufficient urine specimen impossible, and for the determination that no signs and symptoms of drug use exist.

    (1) Check "Negative" (Step 6) on the CCF.

    (2) Sign and date the CCF.

(c) If the medical evaluation reveals clinical evidence of drug use, as the MRO, you must report the result to the employer as a cancelled test with written notations regarding results of both the evaluation conducted under § 40.193(d) and any further medical examination. This report must state that a permanent or long-term medical condition exists, making provision of a sufficient urine specimen impossible, and state the reason for the determination that signs and symptoms of drug use exist. Because this is a cancelled test, it does not serve the purposes of a negative test (*i.e.,* the employer is not authorized to allow the employee to begin or resume performing safety-sensitive functions, because a negative test is needed for that purpose).

(d) For purposes of this section, permanent or long-term medical conditions are those physiological, anatomic, or psychological abnormalities documented as being present prior to the attempted collection, and considered not amenable to correction or cure for an extended period of time, if ever.

    (1) Examples would include destruction (any cause) of the glomerular filtration system leading to renal failure; unrepaired traumatic disruption of the urinary tract; or a severe psychiatric disorder focused on genito-urinary matters.

    (2) Acute or temporary medical conditions, such as cystitis, urethritis or prostatitis, though they might interfere with collection for a limited period of time, cannot receive the same exceptional consideration as the permanent or long-term conditions discussed in paragraph (d)(1) of this section.

[65 FR 79526, Dec. 19, 2000, as amended at 66 FR 41953, Aug. 9, 2001]

§ 40.197 What happens when an employer receives a report of a dilute urine specimen?

(a) As the employer, if the MRO informs you that a positive drug test was dilute, you simply treat the test as a verified positive test. You must not direct the employee to take another test based on the fact that the specimen was dilute.

(b) As an employer, if the MRO informs you that a negative test was dilute, take the following action:

(1) If the MRO directs you to conduct a recollection under direct observation (*i.e.*, because the creatinine concentration of the specimen was equal to or greater than 2mg/dL, but less than or equal to 5 mg/dL (*see* § 40.155(c)), you must do so immediately.

(2) Otherwise (*i.e.*, if the creatinine concentration of the dilute specimen is greater than 5 mg/dL), you may, but are not required to, direct the employee to take another test immediately.

(i) Such recollections must not be collected under direct observation, unless there is another basis for use of direct observation (see § 40.67 (b) and (c)).

(ii) You must treat all employees the same for this purpose. For example, you must not retest some employees and not others. You may, however, establish different policies for different types of tests (*e.g.*, conduct retests in pre-employment situations, but not in random test situations). You must inform your employees in advance of your decisions on these matters.

(c) The following provisions apply to all tests you direct an employee to take under paragraph (b) of this section:

(1) You must ensure that the employee is given the minimum possible advance notice that he or she must go to the collection site;

(2) You must treat the result of the test you directed the employee to take under paragraph (b) of this section—and not a prior test—as the test result of record, on which you rely for purposes of this part;

(3) If the result of the test you directed the employee to take under paragraph (b)(1) of this section is also negative and dilute, you are not permitted to make the employee take an additional test because the result was dilute.

(4) If the result of the test you directed the employee to take under paragraph (b)(2) of this section is also negative and dilute, you are not permitted to make the employee take an additional test because the result was dilute. Provided, however, that if the MRO directs you to conduct a recollection under direct observation under paragraph (b)(1) of this section, you must immediately do so.

(5) If the employee declines to take a test you directed him or her to take under paragraph (b) of this section, the employee has refused the test for purposes of this part and DOT agency regulations.

[68 FR 31626, May 28, 2003, as amended at 69 FR 64867, Nov. 9, 2004; 73 FR 35974, June 25, 2008]

§ 40.199 What problems always cause a drug test to be cancelled?

(a) As the MRO, when the laboratory discovers a "fatal flaw" during its processing of incoming specimens (see § 40.83), the laboratory will report to you that the specimen has been "Rejected for Testing" (with the reason stated). You must always cancel such a test.

(b) The following are "fatal flaws":

(1) There is no CCF;

49 CFR Part 40 (up to date as of 3/05/2024)
Procedures for Transportation Workplace Drug and Alcohol Testing Programs
49 CFR 40.199(b)(2)

(2) In cases where a specimen has been collected, there is no specimen submitted with the CCF;

(3) There is no printed collector's name and no collector's signature;

(4) Two separate collections are performed using one CCF;

(5) The specimen ID numbers on the specimen bottle and the CCF do not match;

(6) The specimen bottle seal is broken or shows evidence of tampering (and a split specimen cannot be re-designated, see § 40.83(h)); or

(7) Because of leakage or other causes, there is an insufficient amount of specimen in the primary specimen bottle for analysis and the specimens cannot be re-designated (see § 40.83(h)).

(8) For an oral fluid collection, the collector used an expired device at the time of collection.

(9) For an oral fluid collection, the collector failed to enter the expiration date in Step 4 of the CCF and the laboratory confirmed that the device was expired.

(c) You must report the result as provided in § 40.161.

[65 FR 79526, Dec. 19, 2000, as amended at 82 FR 52245, Nov. 13, 2017; 88 FR 27648, May 2, 2023]

§ 40.201 What problems always cause a drug test to be cancelled and may result in a requirement for another collection?

As the MRO, you must cancel a drug test when a laboratory reports that any of the following problems have occurred. You must inform the DER that the test was cancelled. You must also direct the DER to ensure that an additional collection occurs immediately, if required by the applicable procedures specified in paragraphs (a) through (e) of this section.

(a) The laboratory reports an "Invalid Result." You must follow applicable procedures in § 40.159 (recollection under direct observation may be required).

(b) The laboratory reports the result as "Rejected for Testing." You must follow applicable procedures in § 40.161 (a recollection may be required).

(c) The laboratory reports that the split specimen failed to reconfirm all of the primary specimen results because the drug(s)/drug metabolite(s) were not detected; adulteration criteria were not met; and/or substitution criteria were not met. You must follow the applicable procedures in § 40.187(b)—no recollection is required in this case, unless the split specimen creatinine concentration for a substituted primary specimen was greater than or equal to 2mg/dL but less than or equal to 5mg/ dL, or the primary specimen had an invalid result which was not reported to the DER. Both these cases require recollection under direct observation.

(d) The laboratory reports that the split specimen failed to reconfirm all of the primary specimen results, and that the split specimen was invalid. You must follow the procedures in § 40.187(c)(1)—recollection under direct observation is required in this case.

(e) The laboratory reports that the split specimen failed to reconfirm all of the primary specimen results because the split specimen was not available for testing or there was no split laboratory available to test the specimen. You must follow the applicable procedures in § 40.187(e)—recollection under direct observation is required in this case.

(f) The examining physician has determined that there is an acceptable medical explanation of the employee's failure to provide a sufficient amount of specimen. You must follow applicable procedures in § 40.193(d)(1) (no recollection is required in this case).

[65 FR 79526, Dec. 19, 2000, as amended at 73 FR 35974, June 25, 2008; 88 FR 27648, May 2, 2023]

§ 40.203 What problems cause a drug test to be cancelled unless they are corrected?

(a) As the MRO, when a laboratory discovers a "correctable flaw" during its processing of incoming specimens (see § 40.83), the laboratory will attempt to correct it. If the laboratory is unsuccessful in this attempt, it will report to you that the specimen has been "Rejected for Testing" (with the reason stated).

(b) The following is a "correctable flaw" that laboratories must attempt to correct: The collector's signature is omitted on the certification statement on the CCF.

(c) As the MRO, when you discover a "correctable flaw" during your review of the CCF, you must cancel the test unless the flaw is corrected.

(d) The following are correctable flaws that you must attempt to correct:

(1) The employee's signature is omitted from the certification statement, unless the employee's failure or refusal to sign is noted on the "Remarks" line of the CCF.

(2) The certifying scientist's signature is omitted on Copy 1 of the CCF for a positive, adulterated, substituted, or invalid test result.

(3) The collector uses a non-Federal form or an expired CCF for the test. This flaw may be corrected through the procedure set forth in § 40.205(b)(2), provided that the collection testing process has been conducted in accordance with the procedures in this part in an HHS-certified laboratory.

[65 FR 79526, Dec. 19, 2000, as amended at 66 FR 41954, Aug. 9, 2001; 75 FR 59108, Sept. 27, 2010; 76 FR 59578, Sept. 27, 2011; 82 FR 52246, Nov. 13, 2017]

§ 40.205 How are drug test problems corrected?

(a) As a collector, you have the responsibility of trying to successfully complete a collection procedure for each employee.

(1) If, during or shortly after the collection process, you become aware of any event that prevents the completion of a valid test or collection (*e.g.,* a procedural or paperwork error), you must try to correct the problem promptly, if doing so is practicable. You may conduct another collection as part of this effort.

(2) If another collection is necessary, you must begin the new collection procedure as soon as possible, using a new CCF and a new collection kit.

(b) If, as a collector, laboratory, MRO, employer, or other person implementing these drug testing regulations, you become aware of a problem that can be corrected (see § 40.203), but which has not already been corrected under paragraph (a) of this section, you must take all practicable action to correct the problem so that the test is not cancelled.

(1) If the problem resulted from the omission of required information, you must, as the person responsible for providing that information, supply in writing the missing information and a statement that it is true and accurate. For example, suppose you are a collector, and you forgot to make a notation on the "Remarks" line of the CCF that the employee did not sign the certification. You would, when the problem is called to your attention, supply a signed statement that the employee failed or refused to sign the certification and that your statement is true and accurate. You must supply this information on the same business day on which you are notified of the problem, transmitting it by fax or courier.

(2) If the problem is the use of a non-Federal form or an expired Federal form, you must provide a signed statement (i.e., a memorandum for the record). It must state that the incorrect form contains all the information needed for a valid DOT drug test, and that the incorrect form was used inadvertently or as the only means of conducting a test, in circumstances beyond your control. The statement must also list the steps you have taken to prevent future use of non-Federal forms or expired Federal forms for DOT tests. For this flaw to be corrected, the test of the specimen must have occurred at a HHS-certified laboratory where it was tested consistent with the requirements of this part. You must supply this information on the same business day on which you are notified of the problem, transmitting it by fax or courier.

(3) You must maintain the written documentation of a correction with the CCF.

(4) You must mark the CCF in such a way (e.g., stamp noting correction) as to make it obvious on the face of the CCF that you corrected the flaw.

(c) If the correction does not take place, as the MRO you must cancel the test.

[65 FR 79526, Dec. 19, 2000, as amended at 66 FR 41954, Aug. 9, 2001]

§ 40.207 What is the effect of a cancelled drug test?

(a) A cancelled drug test is neither positive nor negative.

(1) As an employer, you must not attach to a cancelled test the consequences of a positive test or other violation of a DOT drug testing regulation (e.g., removal from a safety-sensitive position).

(2) As an employer, you must not use a cancelled test for the purposes of a negative test to authorize the employee to perform safety-sensitive functions (i.e., in the case of a pre-employment, return-to-duty, or follow-up test).

(3) However, as an employer, you must not direct a recollection for an employee because a test has been cancelled, except in the situations cited in paragraph (a)(2) of this section or other provisions of this part that require another test to be conducted (e.g., §§ 40.159(a)(5) and 40.187(b)(2), (c)(1), and (e).

(b) A cancelled test does not count toward compliance with DOT requirements (e.g., being applied toward the number of tests needed to meet the employer's minimum random testing rate).

(c) A cancelled DOT test does not provide a valid basis for an employer to conduct a non-DOT test (i.e., a test under company authority).

(d) If a test is cancelled for a correctible flaw (i.e., § 40.203 or § 40.205), only the MRO who cancelled the test can reverse the cancellation and must do so within 60 days of the cancellation. After 60 days, the MRO who cancelled the test cannot reverse the cancellation without the permission of ODAPC. For example, if an MRO cancels a test because the MRO did not receive a copy of the CCF, but later receives a copy of the

CCF, the MRO may reverse the decision to cancel the test within 60 days. After 60 days, the MRO must contact ODAPC for permission to reverse the cancellation. An MRO must not reverse the cancellation of a test that the laboratory has reported as rejected for testing, as described in § 40.83(g). A laboratory is not authorized to reverse a cancellation due to a fatal flaw, as described in § 40.199.

[65 FR 79526, Dec. 19, 2000, as amended at 73 FR 35975, June 25, 2008; 88 FR 27648, May 2, 2023]

§ 40.208 What problems require corrective action but do not result in the cancellation of a test?

(a) If, as a laboratory, collector, employer, or other person implementing the DOT drug testing program, you become aware that any of the following omissions listed in paragraphs (a)(1) through (3) of this section occurred, you must take corrective action, including securing a memorandum for the record explaining the problem and taking appropriate action to ensure the problem does not recur:

(1) For a urine collection, the specimen temperature on the CCF was not checked and the "Remarks" line did not contain an entry regarding the temperature being out of range; or

(2) For an oral fluid collection, the collector failed to check the box in Step 2 of the CCF that indicates "Each Device was Within Expiration Date" but the collector entered the "Split Specimen Device Expiration Date" in Step 4 of the CCF.

(3) For an oral fluid collection, the collector erred by entering the expiration date as the "Primary/Single Specimen Device Expiration Date" instead of entering the date as the "Split Specimen Device Expiration Date" in Step 4 of the CCF.

(b) The errors listed in paragraph (a) of this section do not result in the cancellation of the test.

(c) As an employer or service agent, the errors listed in paragraph (a) of this section, even though not sufficient to cancel a drug test result, may subject you to enforcement action under DOT agency regulations or subpart R of this part.

[88 FR 27649, May 2, 2023]

§ 40.209 What procedural problems do not result in the cancellation of a test and do not require correction?

(a) As a collector, laboratory, MRO, employer or other person administering the drug testing process, you must document any errors in the testing process of which you become aware, even if they are not considered problems that will cause a test to be cancelled as listed in this subpart. Decisions about the ultimate impact of these errors will be determined by other administrative or legal proceedings, subject to the limitations of paragraph (b) of this section.

(b) No person concerned with the testing process may declare a test cancelled based on an error that does not have a significant adverse effect on the right of the employee to have a fair and accurate test. Matters that do not result in the cancellation of a test include, but are not limited to, the following:

(1) A minor administrative mistake (*e.g.*, the omission of the employee's middle initial, a transposition of numbers in the employee's SSN or Employee ID No., the omission of the DOT Agency in Step 1–D of the CCF.)

49 CFR Part 40 (up to date as of 3/05/2024)
Procedures for Transportation Workplace Drug and Alcohol Testing Programs
49 CFR 40.209(b)(2)

(2) An error that does not affect employee protections under this part (*e.g.*, the collector's failure to add bluing agent to the toilet bowl, which adversely affects only the ability of the collector to detect tampering with the specimen by the employee);

(3) The collection of a specimen by a collector who is required to have been trained (see § 40.33 or 40.35), but who has not met this requirement;

(4) A delay in the collection process (see § 40.61(a));

(5) Verification of a test result by an MRO who has the basic credentials to be qualified as an MRO (see § 40.121(a) through (b)) but who has not met training and/or documentation requirements (see § 40.121(c) through (e));

(6) The failure to directly observe or monitor a collection that the rule requires or permits to be directly observed or monitored, or the unauthorized use of direct observation or monitoring for a collection;

(7) The fact that a test was conducted in a facility that does not meet the requirements of § 40.42;

(8) If the specific name of the courier on the CCF is omitted or erroneous;

(9) Personal identifying information is inadvertently contained on the CCF (*e.g.*, the employee signs his or her name on Copy 1); or

(10) Claims that the employee was improperly selected for testing.

(11) The failure to use a new CCF for a second collection after an insufficient specimen was conducted under a different methodology (*e.g.*, failing to use a new CCF for an oral fluid test after an insufficient quantity of urine was produced on a urine test.)

(c) As an employer or service agent, these types of errors, even though not sufficient to cancel a drug test result, may subject you to enforcement action under DOT agency regulations or action under Subpart R of this part.

[65 FR 79526, Dec. 19, 2000, as amended at 66 FR 41954, Aug. 9, 2001; 75 FR 59108, Sept. 27, 2010; 88 FR 27649, May 2, 2023]

§ 40.210 What kinds of drug tests are permitted under the regulations?

Both urine and oral fluid specimens are authorized for collection and testing under this part. An employer can use one or the other, but not both at the beginning of the testing event. For example, if an employee is sent for a test, either a urine or oral fluid specimen can be collected, but not both simultaneously. However, if there is a problem in the collection that necessitates a second collection (*e.g.*, insufficient quantity of urine, temperature out of range, or insufficient saliva), then a different specimen type could be chosen by the employer (*i.e.*, through a standing order or a discussion with the collector) or its service agent (*i.e.*, if there is no standing order and the service agent cannot contact the DER) to complete the collection process for the testing event. Only urine and oral fluid specimens screened and confirmed at HHS-certified laboratories (see § 40.81) are allowed for drug testing under this part. Point-of-collection (POC) urine, POC oral fluid drug testing, hair testing, or instant tests are not authorized.

[88 FR 27649, May 2, 2023]

Subpart J—Alcohol Testing Personnel

§ 40.211 Who conducts DOT alcohol tests?

(a) Screening test technicians (STTs) and breath alcohol technicians (BATs) meeting their respective requirements of this subpart are the only people authorized to conduct DOT alcohol tests.

(b) An STT can conduct only alcohol screening tests, but a BAT can conduct alcohol screening and confirmation tests.

(c) As a BAT- or STT-qualified immediate supervisor of a particular employee, you may not act as the STT or BAT when that employee is tested, unless no other STT or BAT is available and DOT agency regulations do not prohibit you from doing so.

§ 40.213 What training requirements must STTs and BATs meet?

To be permitted to act as a BAT or STT in the DOT alcohol testing program, you must meet each of the requirements of this section:

(a) You must be knowledgeable about the alcohol testing procedures in this part and the current DOT guidance. Procedures and guidance are available from ODAPC (Department of Transportation, 1200 New Jersey Avenue SE., Washington, DC 20590, 202–366–3784, or on the ODAPC Web site, *http://www.transportation.gov/odapc*). You must keep current on any changes to these materials. You must subscribe to the ODAPC list-serve at (*https://www.transportation.gov/odapc/get-odapc-email-updates*).

(b) *Qualification training.* You must receive qualification training meeting the requirements of this paragraph (b).

  (1) Qualification training must be in accordance with the DOT Model BAT or STT Course, as applicable. The DOT Model Courses are available from ODAPC (Department of Transportation, 1200 New Jersey Avenue, SE., Washington DC, 20590, 202–366–3784, or on the ODAPC web site, *http://www.dot.gov/ost/dapc*). The training can also be provided using a course of instruction equivalent to the DOT Model Courses. On request, ODAPC will review BAT and STT instruction courses for equivalency.

  (2) Qualification training must include training to proficiency in using the alcohol testing procedures of this part and in the operation of the particular alcohol testing device(s) (*i.e.*, the ASD(s) or EBT(s)) you will be using.

  (3) The training must emphasize that you are responsible for maintaining the integrity of the testing process, ensuring the privacy of employees being tested, and avoiding conduct or statements that could be viewed as offensive or inappropriate.

  (4) The instructor must be an individual who has demonstrated necessary knowledge, skills, and abilities by regularly conducting DOT alcohol tests as an STT or BAT, as applicable, for a period of at least a year, who has conducted STT or BAT training, as applicable, under this part for a year, or who has successfully completed a "train the trainer" course.

(c) *Initial Proficiency Demonstration.* Following your completion of qualification training under paragraph (b) of this section, you must demonstrate proficiency in alcohol testing under this part by completing seven consecutive error-free mock tests (BATs) or five consecutive error-free tests (STTs).

(1) Another person must monitor and evaluate your performance, in person or by a means that provides real-time observation and interaction between the instructor and trainee, and attest in writing that the mock collections are "error-free." This person must be an individual who meets the requirements of paragraph (b)(4) of this section.

(2) These tests must use the alcohol testing devices (*e.g.*, EBT(s) or ASD(s)) that you will use as a BAT or STT.

(3) If you are an STT who will be using an ASD that indicates readings by changes, contrasts, or other readings in color, you must demonstrate as part of the mock test that you are able to discern changes, contrasts, or readings correctly.

(d) You must meet the requirements of paragraphs (b) and (c) of this section before you begin to perform STT or BAT functions.

(e) *Refresher training.* No less frequently than every five years from the date on which you satisfactorily complete the requirements of paragraphs (b) and (c) of this section, you must complete refresher training that meets all the requirements of paragraphs (b) and (c) of this section.

(f) *Error Correction Training.* If you make a mistake in the alcohol testing process that causes a test to be cancelled (*i.e.*, a fatal or uncorrected flaw), you must undergo error correction training. This training must occur within 30 days of the date you are notified of the error that led to the need for retraining.

(1) Error correction training must be provided and your proficiency documented in writing by a person who meets the requirements of paragraph (b)(4) of this section.

(2) Error correction training is required to cover only the subject matter area(s) in which the error that caused the test to be cancelled occurred.

(3) As part of the error correction training, you must demonstrate your proficiency in the alcohol testing procedures of this part by completing three consecutive error-free mock tests. The mock tests must include one uneventful scenario and two scenarios related to the area(s) in which your error(s) occurred. The person providing the training must monitor and evaluate your performance and attest in writing that the mock tests were error-free.

(g) *Documentation.* You must maintain documentation showing that you currently meet all requirements of this section. You must provide this documentation on request to DOT agency representatives and to employers and C/TPAs who are negotiating to use your services.

(h) *Other persons who may serve as BATs or STTs.*

(1) Anyone meeting the requirements of this section to be a BAT may act as an STT, provided that the individual has demonstrated initial proficiency in the operation of the ASD that he or she is using, as provided in paragraph (c) of this section.

(2) Law enforcement officers who have been certified by state or local governments to conduct breath alcohol testing are deemed to be qualified as BATs. They are not required to also complete the training requirements of this section in order to act as BATs. In order for a test conducted by such an officer to be accepted under DOT alcohol testing requirements, the officer must have been certified by a state or local government to use the EBT or ASD that was used for the test.

[65 FR 79526, Dec. 19, 2000, as amended at 66 FR 41954, Aug. 9, 2001; 75 FR 5244, Feb. 2, 2010; 82 FR 52246, Nov. 13, 2017]

§ 40.215 What information about the DER do employers have to provide to BATs and STTs?

As an employer, you must provide to the STTs and BATs the name and telephone number of the appropriate DER (and C/TPA, where applicable) to contact about any problems or issues that may arise during the testing process.

§ 40.217 Where is other information on the role of STTs and BATs found in this regulation?

You can find other information on the role and functions of STTs and BATs in the following sections of this part:

§ 40.3—Definitions.

§ 40.223—Responsibility for supervising employees being tested.

§§ 40.225–40.227—Use of the alcohol testing form.

§§ 40.241–40.245—Screening test procedures with ASDs and EBTs.

§§ 40.251–40.255—Confirmation test procedures.

§ 40.261—Refusals to test.

§§ 40.263–40.265—Insufficient saliva or breath.

§ 40.267—Problems requiring cancellation of tests.

§§ 40.269–40.271—Correcting problems in tests.

Subpart K—Testing Sites, Forms, Equipment and Supplies Used in Alcohol Testing

§ 40.221 Where does an alcohol test take place?

(a) A DOT alcohol test must take place at an alcohol testing site meeting the requirements of this section.

(b) If you are operating an alcohol testing site, you must ensure that it meets the security requirements of § 40.223.

(c) If you are operating an alcohol testing site, you must ensure that it provides visual and aural privacy to the employee being tested, sufficient to prevent unauthorized persons from seeing or hearing test results.

(d) If you are operating an alcohol testing site, you must ensure that it has all needed personnel, materials, equipment, and facilities to provide for the collection and analysis of breath and/or saliva samples, and a suitable clean surface for writing.

(e) If an alcohol testing site fully meeting all the visual and aural privacy requirements of paragraph (c) is not readily available, this part allows a reasonable suspicion or post-accident test to be conducted at a site that partially meets these requirements. In this case, the site must afford visual and aural privacy to the employee to the greatest extent practicable.

(f) An alcohol testing site can be in a medical facility, a mobile facility (*e.g.*, a van), a dedicated collection facility, or any other location meeting the requirements of this section.

§ 40.223 What steps must be taken to protect the security of alcohol testing sites?

(a) If you are a BAT, STT, or other person operating an alcohol testing site, you must prevent unauthorized personnel from entering the testing site.

    (1) The only people you are to treat as authorized persons are employees being tested, BATs, STTs, and other alcohol testing site workers, DERs, employee representatives authorized by the employer (*e.g.*, on the basis of employer policy or labor-management agreement), and DOT agency representatives.

    (2) You must ensure that all persons are under the supervision of a BAT or STT at all times when permitted into the site.

    (3) You may remove any person who obstructs, interferes with, or causes unnecessary delay in the testing process.

(b) As the BAT or STT, you must not allow any person other than you, the employee, or a DOT agency representative to actually witness the testing process (see §§ 40.241–40.255).

(c) If you are operating an alcohol testing site, you must ensure that when an EBT or ASD is not being used for testing, you store it in a secure place.

(d) If you are operating an alcohol testing site, you must ensure that no one other than BATs or other employees of the site have access to the site when an EBT is unsecured.

(e) As a BAT or STT, to avoid distraction that could compromise security, you are limited to conducting an alcohol test for only one employee at a time.

    (1) When an EBT screening test on an employee indicates an alcohol concentration of 0.02 or higher, and the same EBT will be used for the confirmation test, you are not allowed to use the EBT for a test on another employee before completing the confirmation test on the first employee.

    (2) As a BAT who will conduct both the screening and the confirmation test, you are to complete the entire screening and confirmation process on one employee before starting the screening process on another employee.

    (3) You are not allowed to leave the alcohol testing site while the testing process for a given employee is in progress, except to notify a supervisor or contact a DER for assistance in the case an employee or other person who obstructs, interferes with, or unnecessarily delays the testing process.

§ 40.225 What form is used for an alcohol test?

(a) The DOT Alcohol Testing Form (ATF) must be used for every DOT alcohol test. The ATF must be a three-part carbonless manifold form. The ATF is found in appendix I to this part. You may view this form on the ODAPC web site (*http://www.transportation.gov/odapc*).

(b) As an employer in the DOT alcohol testing program, you are not permitted to modify or revise the ATF except as follows:

    (1) You may include other information needed for billing purposes, outside the boundaries of the form.

    (2) You may use a ATF directly generated by an EBT which omits the space for affixing a separate printed result to the ATF, provided the EBT prints the result directly on the ATF.

(3) You may use an ATF that has the employer's name, address, and telephone number preprinted. In addition, a C/TPA's name, address, and telephone number may be included, to assist with negative results.

(4) You may use an ATF in which all pages are printed on white paper. You may modify the ATF by using colored paper, or have clearly discernable borders or designation statements on Copy 2 and Copy 3. When colors are used, they must be green for Copy 2 and blue for Copy 3.

(5) As a BAT or STT, you may add, on the "Remarks" line of the ATF, the name of the DOT agency under whose authority the test occurred.

(6) As a BAT or STT, you may use a ATF that has your name, address, and telephone number preprinted, but under no circumstances can your signature be preprinted.

(c) As an employer, you may use an equivalent foreign-language version of the ATF approved by ODAPC. You may use such a non-English language form only in a situation where both the employee and BAT/STT understand and can use the form in that language.

[65 FR 79526, Dec. 19, 2000, as amended at 66 FR 41954, Aug. 9, 2001; 75 FR 8529, Feb. 25, 2010; 75 FR 13009, Mar. 18, 2010; 82 FR 52246, Nov. 13, 2017; 88 FR 27649, May 2, 2023]

§ 40.227 May employers use the ATF for non-DOT tests, or non-DOT forms for DOT tests?

(a) No, as an employer, BAT, or STT, you are prohibited from using the ATF for non-DOT alcohol tests. You are also prohibited from using non-DOT forms for DOT alcohol tests. Doing either subjects you to enforcement action under DOT agency regulations.

(b) If the STT or BAT, either by mistake, or as the only means to conduct a test under difficult circumstances (*e.g.*, post-accident test with insufficient time to obtain the ATF), uses a non-DOT form for a DOT test, the use of a non-DOT form does not, in and of itself, require the employer or service agent to cancel the test. However, in order for the test to be considered valid, a signed statement must be obtained from the STT or BAT in accordance with § 40.271(b) .

§ 40.229 What devices are used to conduct alcohol screening tests?

ASDs listed on ODAPC's Web page for "Approved Screening Devices to Measure Alcohol in Bodily Fluids" and EBTs listed on ODAPC's Web page for "Approved Evidential Breath Measurement Devices" are the only devices you are allowed to use to conduct alcohol screening tests under this part. You may use an ASD for DOT alcohol tests only if there are instructions for its use in this part. An ASD can be used only for screening tests for alcohol, and must not be used for confirmation tests.

[82 FR 52246, Nov. 13, 2017]

§ 40.231 What devices are used to conduct alcohol confirmation tests?

(a) EBTs on ODAPC's Web page for "Approved Evidential Breath Measurement Devices" that meet the requirements of paragraph (b) of this section are the only devices you may use to conduct alcohol confirmation tests under this part.

(b) To conduct a confirmation test, you must use an EBT that has the following capabilities:

(1) Provides a printed triplicate result (or three consecutive identical copies of a result) of each breath test;

(2) Assigns a unique number to each completed test, which the BAT and employee can read before each test and which is printed on each copy of the result;

(3) Prints, on each copy of the result, the manufacturer's name for the device, its serial number, and the time of the test;

(4) Distinguishes alcohol from acetone at the 0.02 alcohol concentration level;

(5) Tests an air blank; and

(6) Performs an external calibration check.

[65 FR 79526, Dec. 19, 2000, as amended at 82 FR 52246, Nov. 13, 2017]

§ 40.233 What are the requirements for proper use and care of EBTs?

(a) As an EBT manufacturer, you must submit, for NHTSA approval, a quality assurance plan (QAP) for your EBT before ODAPC places the EBT on its Web page for "Approved Evidential Breath Measurement Devices."

(1) Your QAP must specify the methods used to perform external calibration checks on the EBT, the tolerances within which the EBT is regarded as being in proper calibration, and the intervals at which these checks must be performed. In designating these intervals, your QAP must take into account factors like frequency of use, environmental conditions (e.g., temperature, humidity, altitude) and type of operation (e.g., stationary or mobile).

(2) Your QAP must also specify the inspection, maintenance, and calibration requirements and intervals for the EBT.

(b) As the manufacturer, you must include, with each EBT, instructions for its use and care consistent with the QAP.

(c) As the user of the EBT (e.g., employer, service agent), you must do the following:

(1) You must follow the manufacturer's instructions (see paragraph (b) of this section), including performance of external calibration checks at the intervals the instructions specify.

(2) In conducting external calibration checks, you must use only calibration devices appearing on NHTSA's CPL for "Calibrating Units for Breath Alcohol Tests."

(3) If an EBT fails an external check of calibration, you must take the EBT out of service. You may not use the EBT again for DOT alcohol testing until it is repaired and passes an external calibration check.

(4) You must maintain records of the inspection, maintenance, and calibration of EBTs as provided in § 40.333(a)(3).

(5) You must ensure that inspection, maintenance, and calibration of the EBT are performed by its manufacturer or a maintenance representative certified either by the manufacturer or by a state health agency or other appropriate state agency.

[65 FR 79526, Dec. 19, 2000, as amended at 82 FR 52246, Nov. 13, 2017]

§ 40.235 What are the requirements for proper use and care of ASDs?

    (a) As an ASD manufacturer, you must submit, for NHTSA approval, a QAP for your ASD before NHTSA approves it and ODAPC places the device on its Web page for "Approved Screening Devices to Measure Alcohol in Bodily Fluids". Your QAP must specify the methods used for quality control checks, temperatures at which the ASD must be stored and used, the shelf life of the device, and environmental conditions (*e.g.*, temperature, altitude, humidity) that may affect the ASD's performance.

    (b) As a manufacturer, you must include with each ASD instructions for its use and care consistent with the QAP. The instructions must include directions on the proper use of the ASD, and, where applicable the time within which the device must be read, and the manner in which the reading is made.

    (c) As the user of the ADS (*e.g.*, employer, STT), you must follow the QAP instructions.

    (d) You are not permitted to use an ASD that does not pass the specified quality control checks or that has passed its expiration date.

    (e) As an employer, with respect to breath ASDs, you must also follow the device use and care requirements of § 40.233 .

[65 FR 79526, Dec. 19, 2000, as amended at 82 FR 52246, Nov. 13, 2017]

Subpart L—Alcohol Screening Tests

§ 40.241 What are the first steps in any alcohol screening test?

As the BAT or STT you will take the following steps to begin all alcohol screening tests, regardless of the type of testing device you are using:

    (a) When a specific time for an employee's test has been scheduled, or the collection site is at the employee's worksite, and the employee does not appear at the collection site at the scheduled time, contact the DER to determine the appropriate interval within which the DER has determined the employee is authorized to arrive. If the employee's arrival is delayed beyond that time, you must notify the DER that the employee has not reported for testing. In a situation where a C/TPA has notified an owner/operator or other individual employee to report for testing and the employee does not appear, the C/TPA must notify the employee that he or she has refused to test.

    (b) Ensure that, when the employee enters the alcohol testing site, you begin the alcohol testing process without undue delay. For example, you must not wait because the employee says he or she is not ready or because an authorized employer or employee representative is delayed in arriving.

        (1) If the employee is also going to take a DOT drug test, you must, to the greatest extent practicable, ensure that the alcohol test is completed before the urine collection process begins.

        (2) If the employee needs medical attention (*e.g.*, an injured employee in an emergency medical facility who is required to have a post-accident test), do not delay this treatment to conduct a test.

    (c) Require the employee to provide positive identification. You must see a photo ID issued by the employer (other than in the case of an owner-operator or other self-employer individual) or a Federal, state, or local government (*e.g.*, a driver's license). You may not accept faxes or photocopies of identification. Positive identification by an employer representative (not a co-worker or another employee being tested) is also acceptable. If the employee cannot produce positive identification, you must contact a DER to verify the identity of the employee.

(d) If the employee asks, provide your identification to the employee. Your identification must include your name and your employer's name but is not required to include your picture, address, or telephone number.

(e) Explain the testing procedure to the employee, including showing the employee the instructions on the back of the ATF.

(f) Complete Step 1 of the ATF.

(g) Direct the employee to complete Step 2 on the ATF and sign the certification. If the employee refuses to sign this certification, you must document this refusal on the "Remarks" line of the ATF and immediately notify the DER. This is a refusal to test.

§ 40.243 What is the procedure for an alcohol screening test using an EBT or non-evidential breath ASD?

As the BAT or STT, you must take the following steps:

(a) Select, or allow the employee to select, an individually wrapped or sealed mouthpiece from the testing materials.

(b) Open the individually wrapped or sealed mouthpiece in view of the employee and insert it into the device in accordance with the manufacturer's instructions.

(c) Instruct the employee to blow steadily and forcefully into the mouthpiece for at least six seconds or until the device indicates that an adequate amount of breath has been obtained.

(d) Show the employee the displayed test result.

(e) If the device is one that prints the test number, testing device name and serial number, time, and result directly onto the ATF, you must check to ensure that the information has been printed correctly onto the ATF.

(f) If the device is one that prints the test number, testing device name and serial number, time and result, but on a separate printout rather than directly onto the ATF, you must affix the printout of the information to the designated space on the ATF with tamper-evident tape or use a self-adhesive label that is tamper-evident.

(g) If the device is one that does not print the test number, testing device name and serial number, time, and result, or it is a device not being used with a printer, you must record this information in Step 3 of the ATF.

§ 40.245 What is the procedure for an alcohol screening test using a saliva ASD or a breath tube ASD?

(a) As the STT or BAT, you must take the following steps when using the saliva ASD:

(1) Check the expiration date on the device or on the package containing the device and show it to the employee. You may not use the device after its expiration date.

(2) Open an individually wrapped or sealed package containing the device in the presence of the employee.

(3) Offer the employee the opportunity to use the device. If the employee uses it, you must instruct the employee to insert it into his or her mouth and use it in a manner described by the device's manufacturer.

(4) If the employee chooses not to use the device, or in all cases in which a new test is necessary because the device did not activate (see paragraph (a)(7) of this section), you must insert the device into the employee's mouth and gather saliva in the manner described by the device's manufacturer. You must wear single-use examination or similar gloves while doing so and change them following each test.

(5) When the device is removed from the employee's mouth, you must follow the manufacturer's instructions regarding necessary next steps in ensuring that the device has activated.

(6)

    (i) If you were unable to successfully follow the procedures of paragraphs (a)(3) through (a)(5) of this section (e.g., the device breaks, you drop the device on the floor), you must discard the device and conduct a new test using a new device.

    (ii) The new device you use must be one that has been under your control or that of the employee before the test.

    (iii) You must note on the "Remarks" line of the ATF the reason for the new test. (Note: You may continue using the same ATF with which you began the test.)

    (iv) You must offer the employee the choice of using the device or having you use it unless the employee, in the opinion of the STT or BAT, was responsible (e.g., the employee dropped the device) for the new test needing to be conducted.

    (v) If you are unable to successfully follow the procedures of paragraphs (a)(3) through (a)(5) of this section on the new test, you must end the collection and put an explanation on the "Remarks" line of the ATF.

    (vi) You must then direct the employee to take a new test immediately, using an EBT for the screening test.

(7) If you are able to successfully follow the procedures of paragraphs (a)(3)–(a)(5) of this section, but the device does not activate, you must discard the device and conduct a new test, in the same manner as provided in paragraph (a)(6) of this section. In this case, you must place the device into the employee's mouth to collect saliva for the new test.

(8) You must read the result displayed on the device no sooner than the device's manufacturer instructs. In all cases the result displayed must be read within 15 minutes of the test. You must then show the device and it's reading to the employee and enter the result on the ATF.

(9) You must never re-use devices, swabs, gloves or other materials used in saliva testing.

(10) You must note the fact that you used a saliva ASD in Step 3 of the ATF.

(b) As the STT or BAT, you must take the following steps when using the breath tube ASD:

(1) Check the expiration date on the detector device and the electronic analyzer or on the package containing the device and the analyzer and show it to the employee. You must not use the device or the analyzer after their expiration date. You must not use an analyzer which is not specifically pre-calibrated for the device being used in the collection.

(2) Remove the device from the package and secure an inflation bag onto the appropriate end of the device, as directed by the manufacturer on the device's instructions.

(3) Break the tube's ampoule in the presence of the employee.

(4) Offer the employee the opportunity to use the device. If the employee chooses to use (*e.g.* hold) the device, instruct the employee to blow forcefully and steadily into the blowing end of device until the inflation bag fills with air (approximately 12 seconds).

(5) If the employee chooses not to hold the device, you must hold it and provide the use instructions in paragraph (b)(4) of this section.

(6) When the employee completes the breath process, take the device from the employee (or if you were holding it, remove it from the employee's mouth), remove the inflation bag, and prepare the device to be read by the analyzer in accordance with the manufacturer's directions.

(7)

    (i) If you were unable to successfully follow the procedures of paragraphs (b)(4) through (b)(6) of this section (*e.g.*, the device breaks apart, the employee did not fill the inflation bag), you must discard the device and conduct a new test using a new one.

    (ii) The new device you use must be one that has been under your control or that of the employer before the test.

    (iii) You must note on the "Remarks" line of the ATF the reason for the new test. (Note: You may continue using the same ATF with which you began the test.)

    (iv) You must offer the employee the choice of holding the device or having you hold it unless the employee, in the your opinion, was responsible (*e.g.*, the employee failed to fill the inflation bag) for the new test needing to be conducted.

    (v) If you are unable to successfully follow the procedures of paragraphs (b)(4) through (b)(6) of this section on the new test, you must end the collection and put an explanation on the "Remarks" line of the ATF.

    (vi) You must then direct the employee to take a new test immediately, using another type of ASD (*e.g.*, saliva device) or an EBT.

(8) If you were able to successfully follow the procedures of paragraphs (b)(4) through (b)(6) of this section and after having waited the required amount of time directed by the manufacturer for the detector device to incubate, you must place the device in the analyzer in accordance with the manufacturer's directions. The result must be read from the analyzer no earlier then the required incubation time of the device. In all cases, the result must be read within 15 minutes of the test.

(9) You must follow the manufacturer's instructions for determining the result of the test. You must show the analyzer result to the employee and record the result on Step 3 of the ATF.

(10) You must never re-use detector devices or any gloves used in breath tube testing. The inflation bag must be voided of air following removal from a device. Inflation bags and electronic analyzers may be re-used but only in accordance with the manufacturer's directions.

(11) You must note the fact that you used a breath tube device in Step 3 of the ATF.

[67 FR 61522, Oct. 1, 2002, as amended at 72 FR 1299, Jan. 11, 2007]

§ 40.247 What procedures does the BAT or STT follow after a screening test result?

(a) If the test result is an alcohol concentration of less than 0.02, as the BAT or STT, you must do the following:

    (1) Sign and date Step 3 of the ATF; and

    (2) Transmit the result to the DER in a confidential manner, as provided in § 40.255 .

(b) If the test result is an alcohol concentration of 0.02 or higher, as the BAT or STT, you must direct the employee to take a confirmation test.

    (1) If you are the BAT who will conduct the confirmation test, you must then conduct the test using the procedures beginning at § 40.251 .

    (2) If you are not the BAT who will conduct the confirmation test, direct the employee to take a confirmation test, sign and date Step 3 of the ATF, and give the employee Copy 2 of the ATF.

    (3) If the confirmation test will be performed at a different site from the screening test, you must take the following additional steps:

        (i) Advise the employee not to eat, drink, put anything (*e.g.*, cigarette, chewing gum) into his or her mouth, or belch;

        (ii) Tell the employee the reason for the waiting period required by § 40.251(a) (*i.e.*, to prevent an accumulation of mouth alcohol from leading to an artificially high reading);

        (iii) Explain that following your instructions concerning the waiting period is to the employee's benefit;

        (iv) Explain that the confirmation test will be conducted at the end of the waiting period, even if the instructions have not been followed;

        (v) Note on the "Remarks" line of the ATF that the waiting period instructions were provided;

        (vi) Instruct the person accompanying the employee to carry a copy of the ATF to the BAT who will perform the confirmation test; and

        (vii) Ensure that you or another BAT, STT, or employer representative observe the employee as he or she is transported to the confirmation testing site. You must direct the employee not to attempt to drive a motor vehicle to the confirmation testing site.

(c) If the screening test is invalid, you must, as the BAT or STT, tell the employee the test is cancelled and note the problem on the "Remarks" line of the ATF. If practicable, repeat the testing process (see § 40.271).

Subpart M—Alcohol Confirmation Tests

§ 40.251 What are the first steps in an alcohol confirmation test?

As the BAT for an alcohol confirmation test, you must follow these steps to begin the confirmation test process:

(a) You must carry out a requirement for a waiting period before the confirmation test, by taking the following steps:

(1) You must ensure that the waiting period lasts at least 15 minutes, starting with the completion of the screening test. After the waiting period has elapsed, you should begin the confirmation test as soon as possible, but not more than 30 minutes after the completion of the screening test.

    (i) If the confirmation test is taking place at a different location from the screening test (see § 40.247(b)(3)) the time of transit between sites counts toward the waiting period if the STT or BAT who conducted the screening test provided the waiting period instructions.

    (ii) If you cannot verify, through review of the ATF, that waiting period instructions were provided, then you must carry out the waiting period requirement.

    (iii) You or another BAT or STT, or an employer representative, must observe the employee during the waiting period.

(2) Concerning the waiting period, you must tell the employee:

    (i) Not to eat, drink, put anything (e.g., cigarette, chewing gum) into his or her mouth, or belch;

    (ii) The reason for the waiting period (i.e., to prevent an accumulation of mouth alcohol from leading to an artificially high reading);

    (iii) That following your instructions concerning the waiting period is to the employee's benefit; and

    (iv) That the confirmation test will be conducted at the end of the waiting period, even if the instructions have not been followed.

(3) If you become aware that the employee has not followed the instructions, you must note this on the "Remarks" line of the ATF.

(b) If you did not conduct the screening test for the employee, you must require positive identification of the employee, explain the confirmation procedures, and use a new ATF. You must note on the "Remarks" line of the ATF that a different BAT or STT conducted the screening test.

(c) Complete Step 1 of the ATF.

(d) Direct the employee to complete Step 2 on the ATF and sign the certification. If the employee refuses to sign this certification, you must document this refusal on the "Remarks" line of the ATF and immediately notify the DER. This is a refusal to test.

(e) Even if more than 30 minutes have passed since the screening test result was obtained, you must begin the confirmation test procedures in § 40.253, not another screening test.

(f) You must note on the "Remarks" line of the ATF the time that elapsed between the two events, and if the confirmation test could not begin within 30 minutes of the screening test, the reason why.

(g) Beginning the confirmation test procedures after the 30 minutes have elapsed does not invalidate the screening or confirmation tests, but it may constitute a regulatory violation subject to DOT agency sanction.

§ 40.253 What are the procedures for conducting an alcohol confirmation test?

As the BAT conducting an alcohol confirmation test, you must follow these steps in order to complete the confirmation test process:

(a) In the presence of the employee, you must conduct an air blank on the EBT you are using before beginning the confirmation test and show the reading to the employee.

(1) If the reading is 0.00, the test may proceed. If the reading is greater than 0.00, you must conduct another air blank.

(2) If the reading on the second air blank is 0.00, the test may proceed. If the reading is greater than 0.00, you must take the EBT out of service.

(3) If you take an EBT out of service for this reason, no one may use it for testing until the EBT is found to be within tolerance limits on an external check of calibration.

(4) You must proceed with the test of the employee using another EBT, if one is available.

(b) You must open a new individually wrapped or sealed mouthpiece in view of the employee and insert it into the device in accordance with the manufacturer's instructions.

(c) You must ensure that you and the employee read the unique test number displayed on the EBT.

(d) You must instruct the employee to blow steadily and forcefully into the mouthpiece for at least six seconds or until the device indicates that an adequate amount of breath has been obtained.

(e) You must show the employee the result displayed on the EBT.

(f) You must show the employee the result and unique test number that the EBT prints out either directly onto the ATF or onto a separate printout.

(g) If the EBT provides a separate printout of the result, you must attach the printout to the designated space on the ATF with tamper-evident tape, or use a self-adhesive label that is tamper-evident.

[65 FR 79526, Dec. 19, 2000, as amended at 66 FR 41954, Aug. 9, 2001]

§ 40.255 What happens next after the alcohol confirmation test result?

(a) After the EBT has printed the result of an alcohol confirmation test, you must, as the BAT, take the following additional steps:

(1) Sign and date Step 3 of the ATF.

(2) If the alcohol confirmation test result is lower than 0.02, nothing further is required of the employee. As the BAT, you must sign and date Step 3 of the ATF.

(3) If the alcohol confirmation test result is 0.02 or higher, direct the employee to sign and date Step 4 of the ATF. If the employee does not do so, you must note this on the "Remarks" line of the ATF. However, this is not considered a refusal to test.

(4) If the test is invalid, tell the employee the test is cancelled and note the problem on the "Remarks" line of the ATF. If practicable, conduct a re-test. (see § 40.271).

(5) Immediately transmit the result directly to the DER in a confidential manner.

(i) You may transmit the results using Copy 1 of the ATF, in person, by telephone, or by electronic means. In any case, you must immediately notify the DER of any result of 0.02 or greater by any means (*e.g.,* telephone or secure fax machine) that ensures the result is immediately received by the DER. You must not transmit these results through C/TPAs or other service agents.

(ii) If you do not make the initial transmission in writing, you must follow up the initial transmission with Copy 1 of the ATF.

(b) As an employer, you must take the following steps with respect to the receipt and storage of alcohol test result information:

    (1) If you receive any test results that are not in writing (*e.g.*, by telephone or electronic means), you must establish a mechanism to establish the identity of the BAT sending you the results.

    (2) You must store all test result information in a way that protects confidentiality.

Subpart N—Problems in Alcohol Testing

§ 40.261 What is a refusal to take an alcohol test, and what are the consequences?

(a) As an employee, you are considered to have refused to take an alcohol test if you:

    (1) Fail to appear for any test (except a pre-employment test) within a reasonable time, as determined by the employer, consistent with applicable DOT agency regulations, after being directed to do so by the employer. This includes the failure of an employee (including an owner-operator) to appear for a test when called by a C/TPA (see § 40.241(a));

    (2) Fail to remain at the testing site until the testing process is complete. Provided that an employee who leaves the collection site before the testing process commences (*see* § 40.243(a)) for a pre-employment test is not deemed to have refused to test. The BAT or STT is not required to inform an employee that the failure to remain at the collection site is a refusal. If an employee leaves prior to the completion of the testing process, per § 40.355(i) the employer must decide whether the employee's actions constitute a refusal;

    (3) Fail to provide an adequate amount of saliva or breath for any alcohol test required by this part or DOT agency regulations; *Provided* that an employee who does not provide an adequate amount of breath or saliva because he or she has left the testing site before the testing process commences (*see* § 40.243(a)) for a pre-employment test is not deemed to have refused to test. The BAT or STT is not required to inform an employee that the failure to remain at the collection site is a refusal. If an employee leaves prior to the completion of the testing process, per § 40.355(i) the employer must decide whether the employee's actions constitute a refusal;

    (4) Fail to provide a sufficient breath specimen, and the physician has determined, through a required medical evaluation, that there was no adequate medical explanation for the failure (see § 40.265(c));

    (5) Fail to undergo a medical examination or evaluation, as directed by the employer as part of the insufficient breath procedures outlined at § 40.265(c);

    (6) Fail to sign the certification at Step 2 of the ATF (see §§ 40.241(g) and 40.251(d)); or

    (7) Fail to cooperate with any part of the testing process.

(b) As an employee, if you refuse to take an alcohol test, you incur the same consequences specified under DOT agency regulations for a violation of those DOT agency regulations. The consequences specified under DOT agency regulations for a refusal cannot be overturned or set aside by an arbitration, grievance, State court or other non-Federal forum that adjudicates the personnel decisions the employer has taken against the employee.

(c)

(1) As a BAT or an STT, or as the physician evaluating a "shy lung" situation, when an employee refuses to test as provided in paragraph (a) of this section, you must terminate the portion of the testing process in which you are involved, document the refusal on the ATF (or in a separate document which you cause to be attached to the form), immediately notify the DER by any means (*e.g.*, telephone or secure fax machine) that ensures the refusal notification is immediately received. You must make this notification directly to the DER (not using a C/TPA as an intermediary).

(2) As the BAT or STT, you must note the actions that may constitute a refusal in the "Remarks" line (Step 3), and sign and date the ATF. The BAT or STT does not make the final decision about whether the employee's conduct constitutes a refusal to test; the employer has the sole responsibility to decide whether a refusal occurred, as stated in § 40.355(i), the employer has a non-delegable duty to make the decision about whether the employee has refused to test.

(d) As an employee, when you refuse to take a non-DOT test or to sign a non-DOT form, you have not refused to take a DOT test. There are no consequences under DOT agency regulations for such a refusal.

[65 FR 79526, Dec. 19, 2000, as amended at 66 FR 41954, Aug. 9, 2001; 88 FR 27649, May 2, 2023]

§ 40.263 What happens when an employee is unable to provide a sufficient amount of saliva for an alcohol screening test?

(a) As the STT, you must take the following steps if an employee is unable to provide sufficient saliva to complete a test on a saliva screening device (*e.g.*, the employee does not provide sufficient saliva to activate the device).

(1) You must conduct a new screening test using a new screening device.

(2) If the employee refuses to make the attempt to complete the new test, you must discontinue testing, note the fact on the "Remarks" line of the ATF, and immediately notify the DER. This is a refusal to test.

(3) If the employee has not provided a sufficient amount of saliva to complete the new test, you must note the fact on the "Remarks" line of the ATF and immediately notify the DER.

(b) As the DER, when the STT informs you that the employee has not provided a sufficient amount of saliva (see paragraph (a)(3) of this section), you must immediately arrange to administer an alcohol test to the employee using an EBT or other breath testing device.

§ 40.265 What happens when an employee is unable to provide a sufficient amount of breath for an alcohol test?

(a) If an employee does not provide a sufficient amount of breath to permit a valid breath test, you must take the steps listed in this section.

(b) As the BAT or STT, you must instruct the employee to attempt again to provide a sufficient amount of breath and about the proper way to do so.

(1) If the employee refuses to make the attempt, you must discontinue the test, note the fact on the "Remarks" line of the ATF, and immediately notify the DER. This is a refusal to test.

(2) If the employee again attempts and fails to provide a sufficient amount of breath, you may provide another opportunity to the employee to do so if you believe that there is a strong likelihood that it could result in providing a sufficient amount of breath.

(3)   When the employee's attempts under paragraph (b)(2) of this section have failed to produce a sufficient amount of breath, you must note the fact on the "Remarks" line of the ATF and immediately notify the DER.

(4)   If you are using an EBT that has the capability of operating manually, you may attempt to conduct the test in manual mode.

(5)   If you are qualified to use a saliva ASD and you are in the screening test stage, you may change to a saliva ASD only to complete the screening test.

(c)   As the employer, when the BAT or STT informs you that the employee has not provided a sufficient amount of breath, you must direct the employee to obtain, within five days, an evaluation from a licensed physician who is acceptable to you and who has expertise in the medical issues raised by the employee's failure to provide a sufficient specimen.

(1)   You are required to provide the physician who will conduct the evaluation with the following information and instructions:

(i)   That the employee was required to take a DOT breath alcohol test, but was unable to provide a sufficient amount of breath to complete the test;

(ii)   The consequences of the appropriate DOT agency regulation for refusing to take the required alcohol test;

(iii)   That the physician must provide you with a signed statement of his or her conclusions; and

(iv)   That the physician, in his or her reasonable medical judgment, must base those conclusions on one of the following determinations:

(A)   A medical condition has, or with a high degree of probability could have, precluded the employee from providing a sufficient amount of breath. The physician must not include in the signed statement detailed information on the employee's medical condition. In this case, the test is cancelled.

(B)   There is not an adequate basis for determining that a medical condition has, or with a high degree of probability could have, precluded the employee from providing a sufficient amount of breath. This constitutes a refusal to test.

(C)   For purposes of paragraphs (c)(1)(iv)(A) and (B) of this section, a medical condition includes an ascertainable physiological condition (*e.g.,* a respiratory system dysfunction) or a medically documented pre-existing psychological disorder, but does not include unsupported assertions of "situational anxiety" or hyperventilation.

(2)   As the physician making the evaluation, after making your determination, you must provide a written statement of your conclusions and the basis for them to the DER directly (and not through a C/TPA acting as an itermediary). You must not include in this statement detailed information on the employee's medical condition beyond what is necessary to explain your conclusion.

(3)   Upon receipt of the report from the examining physician, as the DER you must immediately inform the employee and take appropriate action based upon your DOT agency regulations.

§ 40.267 What problems always cause an alcohol test to be cancelled?

As an employer, a BAT, or an STT, you must cancel an alcohol test if any of the following problems occur. These are "fatal flaws." You must inform the DER that the test was cancelled and must be treated as if the test never occurred. These problems are:

(a) In the case of a screening test conducted on a saliva ASD or a breath tube ASD:

    (1) The STT or BAT reads the result either sooner than or later than the time allotted by the manufacturer and this Part (see § 40.245(a)(8) for the saliva ASD and § 40.245(b)(8) for the breath tube ASD).

    (2) The saliva ASD does not activate (*see* § 40.245(a)(7); or

    (3) The device is used for a test after the expiration date printed on the device or on its package (see § 40.245(a)(1) for the saliva ASD and § 40.245(b)(1) for the breath tube ASD).

    (4) The breath tube ASD is tested with an analyzer which has not been pre-calibrated for that device's specific lot (see § 40.245(b)(1)).

(b) In the case of a screening or confirmation test conducted on an EBT, the sequential test number or alcohol concentration displayed on the EBT is not the same as the sequential test number or alcohol concentration on the printed result (see § 40.253(c), (e) and (f)).

(c) In the case of a confirmation test:

    (1) The BAT conducts the confirmation test before the end of the minimum 15-minute waiting period (see § 40.251(a)(1));

    (2) The BAT does not conduct an air blank before the confirmation test (see § 40.253(a));

    (3) There is not a 0.00 result on the air blank conducted before the confirmation test (see § 40.253(a)(1) and (2));

    (4) The EBT does not print the result (see § 40.253(f)); or

    (5) The next external calibration check of the EBT produces a result that differs by more than the tolerance stated in the QAP from the known value of the test standard. In this case, every result of 0.02 or above obtained on the EBT since the last valid external calibration check is cancelled (see § 40.233(a)(1) and (c)(3)).

[65 FR 79526, Dec. 19, 2000, as amended at 67 FR 61522, Oct. 1, 2002; 71 FR 49384, Aug. 23, 2006; 72 FR 1299, Jan. 11, 2007]

§ 40.269 What problems cause an alcohol test to be cancelled unless they are corrected?

As a BAT or STT, or employer, you must cancel an alcohol test if any of the following problems occur, unless they are corrected. These are "correctable flaws." These problems are:

(a) The BAT or STT does not sign the ATF (see §§ 40.247(a)(1) and 40.255(a)(1)).

(b) The BAT or STT fails to note on the "Remarks" line of the ATF that the employee has not signed the ATF after the result is obtained (see § 40.255(a)(3)).

(c) The BAT or STT uses a non-DOT form for the test (see § 40.225(a)).

[65 FR 79526, Dec. 19, 2000, as amended at 71 FR 49384, Aug. 23, 2006]

§ 40.271 How are alcohol testing problems corrected?

(a) As a BAT or STT, you have the responsibility of trying to complete successfully an alcohol test for each employee.

    (1) If, during or shortly after the testing process, you become aware of any event that will cause the test to be cancelled (see § 40.267), you must try to correct the problem promptly, if practicable. You may repeat the testing process as part of this effort.

    (2) If repeating the testing process is necessary, you must begin a new test as soon as possible. You must use a new ATF, a new sequential test number, and, if needed, a new ASD and/or a new EBT. It is permissible to use additional technical capabilities of the EBT (*e.g.*, manual operation) if you have been trained to do so in accordance with § 40.213(c).

    (3) If repeating the testing process is necessary, you are not limited in the number of attempts to complete the test, provided that the employee is making a good faith effort to comply with the testing process.

    (4) If another testing device is not available for the new test at the testing site, you must immediately notify the DER and advise the DER that the test could not be completed. As the DER who receives this information, you must make all reasonable efforts to ensure that the test is conducted at another testing site as soon as possible.

(b) If, as an STT, BAT, employer or other service agent administering the testing process, you become aware of a "correctable flaw" (see § 40.269) that has not already been corrected, you must take all practicable action to correct the problem so that the test is not cancelled.

    (1) If the problem resulted from the omission of required information, you must, as the person responsible for providing that information, supply in writing the missing information and a signed statement that it is true and accurate. For example, suppose you are a BAT and you forgot to make a notation on the "Remarks" line of the ATF that the employee did not sign the certification. You would, when the problem is called to your attention, supply a signed statement that the employee failed or refused to sign the certification after the result was obtained, and that your signed statement is true and accurate.

    (2) If the problem is the use of a non-DOT form, you must, as the person responsible for the use of the incorrect form, certify in writing that the incorrect form contains all the information needed for a valid DOT alcohol test. You must also provide a signed statement that the incorrect form was used inadvertently or as the only means of conducting a test, in circumstances beyond your control, and the steps you have taken to prevent future use of non-DOT forms for DOT tests. You must supply this information on the same business day on which you are notified of the problem, transmitting it by fax or courier.

(c) If you cannot correct the problem, you must cancel the test.

§ 40.273 What is the effect of a cancelled alcohol test?

(a) A cancelled alcohol test is neither positive nor negative.

    (1) As an employer, you must not attach to a cancelled test the consequences of a test result that is 0.02 or greater (*e.g.*, removal from a safety-sensitive position).

(2) As an employer, you must not use a cancelled test in a situation where an employee needs a test result that is below 0.02 (*e.g.*, in the case of a return-to-duty or follow-up test to authorize the employee to perform safety-sensitive functions).

(3) As an employer, you must not direct a recollection for an employee because a test has been cancelled, except in the situations cited in paragraph (a)(2) of this section or other provisions of this part.

(b) A cancelled test does not count toward compliance with DOT requirements, such as a minimum random testing rate.

(c) When a test must be cancelled, if you are the BAT, STT, or other person who determines that the cancellation is necessary, you must inform the affected DER within 48 hours of the cancellation.

(d) A cancelled DOT test does not provide a valid basis for an employer to conduct a non-DOT test (*i.e.*, a test under company authority).

§ 40.275 What is the effect of procedural problems that are not sufficient to cancel an alcohol test?

(a) As an STT, BAT, employer, or a service agent administering the testing process, you must document any errors in the testing process of which you become aware, even if they are not "fatal flaws" or "correctable flaws" listed in this subpart. Decisions about the ultimate impact of these errors will be determined by administrative or legal proceedings, subject to the limitation of paragraph (b) of this section.

(b) No person concerned with the testing process may declare a test cancelled based on a mistake in the process that does not have a significant adverse effect on the right of the employee to a fair and accurate test. For example, it is inconsistent with this part to cancel a test based on a minor administrative mistake (*e.g.*, the omission of the employee's middle initial) or an error that does not affect employee protections under this part. Nor does the failure of an employee to sign in Step 4 of the ATF result in the cancellation of the test. Nor is a test to be cancelled on the basis of a claim by an employee that he or she was improperly selected for testing.

(c) As an employer, these errors, even though not sufficient to cancel an alcohol test result, may subject you to enforcement action under DOT agency regulations.

§ 40.277 Are alcohol tests other than saliva or breath permitted under these regulations?

No, other types of alcohol tests (*e.g.*, blood and urine) are not authorized for testing done under this part. Only saliva or breath for screening tests and breath for confirmation tests using approved devices are permitted.

Subpart O—Substance Abuse Professionals and the Return-to-Duty Process

§ 40.281 Who is qualified to act as a SAP?

To be permitted to act as a SAP in the DOT drug and alcohol testing program, you must meet each of the requirements of this section:

(a) *Credentials.* You must have one of the following credentials:

(1) You are a licensed physician (Doctor of Medicine or Osteopathy);

(2) You are a licensed or certified social worker;

(3)   You are a licensed or certified psychologist;

(4)   You are a licensed or certified employee assistance professional;

(5)   You are a state-licensed or certified marriage and family therapist; or

(6)   You are a drug and alcohol counselor certified by an organization listed at
       https://www.transportation.gov/odapc/sap.

(b)   *Basic knowledge.* You must be knowledgeable in the following areas:

(1)   You must be knowledgeable about and have clinical experience in the diagnosis and treatment of
       alcohol and controlled substances-related disorders.

(2)   You must be knowledgeable about the SAP function as it relates to employer interests in safety-
       sensitive duties.

(3)   You must be knowledgeable about this part, the DOT agency regulations applicable to the employers
       for whom you evaluate employees, and the DOT SAP Guidelines. You must keep current on any
       changes to these materials. You must subscribe to the ODAPC list-serve at
       https://www.transportation.gov/odapc/get-odapc-email-updates. DOT agency regulations, DOT SAP
       Guidelines, and other materials are available from ODAPC (Department of Transportation, 1200 New
       Jersey Avenue SE., Washington DC, 20590 (202–366–3784), or on the ODAPC Web site
       (*http://www.transportation.gov/odapc*).

(c)   *Qualification training.* You must receive qualification training meeting the requirements of this paragraph
       (c).

(1)   Qualification training must provide instruction on the following subjects:

(i)   Background, rationale, and coverage of the Department's drug and alcohol testing program;

(ii)   49 CFR Part 40 and DOT agency drug and alcohol testing rules;

(iii)   Key DOT drug testing requirements, including collections, laboratory testing, MRO review, and
         problems in drug testing;

(iv)   Key DOT alcohol testing requirements, including the testing process, the role of BATs and STTs,
         and problems in alcohol tests;

(v)   SAP qualifications and prohibitions;

(vi)   The role of the SAP in the return-to-duty process, including the initial employee evaluation,
         referrals for education and/or treatment, the follow-up evaluation, continuing treatment
         recommendations, and the follow-up testing plan;

(vii)   SAP consultation and communication with employers, MROs, and treatment providers;

(viii)   Reporting and recordkeeping requirements;

(ix)   Issues that SAPs confront in carrying out their duties under the program.

(2)   Following your completion of qualification training under paragraph (c)(1) of this section, you must
       satisfactorily complete an examination administered by a nationally-recognized professional or
       training organization. The examination must comprehensively cover all the elements of qualification
       training listed in paragraph (c)(1) of this section.

(3) You must meet the requirements of paragraphs (a), (b), and (c) of this section before you begin to perform SAP functions.

(d) *Continuing education.* During each three-year period from the date on which you satisfactorily complete the examination under paragraph (c)(2) of this section, you must complete continuing education consisting of at least 12 professional development hours (*e.g.,* CEUs) relevant to performing SAP functions.

(1) This continuing education must include material concerning new technologies, interpretations, recent guidance, rule changes, and other information about developments in SAP practice, pertaining to the DOT program, since the time you met the qualification training requirements of this section.

(2) Your continuing education activities must include documentable assessment tools to assist you in determining whether you have adequately learned the material.

(e) *Documentation.* You must maintain documentation showing that you currently meet all requirements of this section. You must provide this documentation on request to DOT agency representatives and to employers and C/TPAs who are using or contemplating using your services.

(f) *Limitation.* If you are an otherwise qualified SAP under this part, you must abide by the geographic limitations applicable to your credential when performing remote evaluations. You must not conduct an evaluation that exceeds your geographic limitations.

[65 FR 79526, Dec. 19, 2000, as amended at 69 FR 3022, Jan. 22, 2004; 71 FR 49384; Aug. 23, 2006; 71 FR 55347, Sept. 22, 2006; 82 FR 52246, Nov. 13, 2017; 88 FR 27649, May 2, 2023]

§ 40.283 How does a certification organization obtain recognition for its members as SAPs?

(a) If you represent a certification organization that wants DOT to authorize its certified drug and alcohol counselors to be added to § 40.281(a)(6), you may submit a written petition to DOT requesting a review of your petition for inclusion.

(b) You must obtain the National Commission for Certifying Agencies (NCCA) accreditation before DOT will act on your petition.

(c) You must also meet the minimum requirements of appendix G to this part before DOT will act on your petition.

[65 FR 79526, Dec. 19, 2000, as amended at 71 FR 49384, Aug. 23, 2006; 88 FR 27650, May 2, 2023]

§ 40.285 When is a SAP evaluation required?

(a) As an employee, when you have violated DOT drug and alcohol regulations, you cannot again perform any DOT safety-sensitive duties for any employer until and unless you complete the SAP evaluation, referral, and education/treatment process set forth in this subpart and in applicable DOT agency regulations. The first step in this process is a SAP evaluation.

(b) For purposes of this subpart, a verified positive DOT drug test result, a DOT alcohol test with a result indicating an alcohol concentration of 0.04 or greater, a refusal to test (including by adulterating or substituting a specimen) or any other violation of the prohibition on the use of alcohol or drugs under a DOT agency regulation constitutes a DOT drug and alcohol regulation violation.

[65 FR 79526, Dec. 19, 2000, as amended at 88 FR 27650, May 2, 2023]

§ 40.287 What information is an employer required to provide concerning SAP services to an employee who has a DOT drug and alcohol regulation violation?

As an employer, you must provide to each employee (including an applicant or new employee) who violates a DOT drug and alcohol regulation a listing of SAPs readily available to the employee and acceptable to you, with names, addresses, and telephone numbers. You cannot charge the employee any fee for compiling or providing this list. You may provide this list yourself or through a C/TPA or other service agent.

§ 40.289 Are employers required to provide SAP and treatment services to employees?

(a) As an employer, you are not required to provide a SAP evaluation or any subsequent recommended education or treatment for an employee who has violated a DOT drug and alcohol regulation.

(b) However, if you offer that employee an opportunity to return to a DOT safety-sensitive duty following a violation, you must, before the employee again performs that duty, ensure that the employee receives an evaluation by a SAP meeting the requirements of § 40.281 and that the employee successfully complies with the SAP's evaluation recommendations.

(c) Payment for SAP evaluations and services is left for employers and employees to decide and may be governed by existing management-labor agreements and health care benefits.

§ 40.291 What is the role of the SAP in the evaluation, referral, and treatment process of an employee who has violated DOT agency drug and alcohol testing regulations?

(a) As a SAP, you are charged with:

(1) Making a clinical assessment and evaluation to determine what assistance is needed by the employee to resolve problems associated with alcohol and/or drug use. At the SAP's discretion, this assessment or evaluation may be performed face-to-face in-person or remotely. If a SAP is not prohibited from using technology within the parameters of the SAP's State-issued license or other credential(s), a remote evaluation must be must be conducted in accordance with the following criteria:

(i) The technology must permit real-time audio and visual interaction between the SAP and the employee; and

(ii) The quality of the technology (e.g., speed of the internet connection and clarity of the video display) must be sufficient to allow the SAP to gather all the visual and audible information the SAP would otherwise gather in an in-person face-to-face interaction, while providing security to protect the confidentiality of the communications at the level expected by industry standards for remote substance abuse evaluations.

(2) Referring the employee to an appropriate education and/or treatment program;

(3) Conducting a follow-up evaluation to determine if the employee has actively participated in the education and/or treatment program and has demonstrated successful compliance with the initial assessment and evaluation recommendations. This assessment or evaluation may be performed face-to-face in-person or remotely. A face-to-face remote evaluation must meet the criteria in paragraphs (a)(1)(i) and (ii) of this section.

(4) Providing the DER with a follow-up drug and/or alcohol testing plan for the employee; and

    (5) Providing the employee and employer with recommendations for continuing education and/or treatment.

  (b) As a SAP, you are not an advocate for the employer or employee. Your function is to protect the public interest in safety by professionally evaluating the employee and recommending appropriate education/ treatment, follow-up tests, and aftercare.

[65 FR 79526, Dec. 19, 2000, as amended at 88 FR 27650, May 2, 2023]

§ 40.293 What is the SAP's function in conducting the initial evaluation of an employee?

As a SAP, for every employee who comes to you following a DOT drug and alcohol regulation violation, you must accomplish the following:

  (a) Provide a comprehensive assessment and clinical evaluation meeting the requirements of § 40.291(a)(1).

  (b) Recommend a course of education and/or treatment with which the employee must demonstrate successful compliance prior to returning to DOT safety-sensitive duty.

    (1) You must make such a recommendation for every individual who has violated a DOT drug and alcohol regulation.

    (2) You must make a recommendation for education and/or treatment that will, to the greatest extent possible, protect public safety in the event that the employee returns to the performance of safety-sensitive functions.

  (c) Appropriate education may include, but is not limited to, self-help groups (*e.g.,* Alcoholics Anonymous) and community lectures, where attendance can be independently verified, and bona fide drug and alcohol education courses.

  (d) Appropriate treatment may include, but is not limited to, in-patient hospitalization, partial in-patient treatment, out-patient counseling programs, and aftercare.

  (e) You must assess and clinically evaluate each employee on an individual basis and use your professional judgment to determine education and/or treatment, as well as a follow-up testing plan unique to the needs of the individual employee. For example, do not require the same and/or substantially similar education, treatment, and/or follow-up testing plan for most of the employees you assess.

  (f) You must provide a written report directly to the DER highlighting your specific recommendations for assistance (see § 40.311(c)).

  (g) For purposes of your role in the evaluation process, you must assume that a verified positive test result has conclusively established that the employee committed a DOT drug and alcohol regulation violation. You must not take into consideration in any way, as a factor in determining what your recommendation will be, any of the following:

    (1) A claim by the employee that the test was unjustified or inaccurate;

    (2) Statements by the employee that attempt to mitigate the seriousness of a violation of a DOT drug or alcohol regulation (*e.g.,* related to assertions of use of hemp oil, "medical marijuana" use, "contact positives," poppy seed ingestion, job stress); or

    (3) Personal opinions you may have about the justification or rationale for drug and alcohol testing.

(h)   In the course of gathering information for purposes of your evaluation in the case of a drug-related violation, you may consult with the MRO. As the MRO, you are required to cooperate with the SAP and provide available information the SAP requests. It is not necessary to obtain the consent of the employee to provide this information.

[65 FR 79526, Dec. 19, 2000, as amended at 88 FR 27650, May 2, 2023]

§ 40.295 May employees or employers seek a second SAP evaluation if they disagree with the first SAP's recommendations?

(a)   As an employee with a DOT drug and alcohol regulation violation, when you have been evaluated by a SAP, you must not seek a second SAP's evaluation in order to obtain another recommendation.

(b)   As an employer, you must not seek a second SAP's evaluation if the employee has already been evaluated by a qualified SAP. If the employee, contrary to paragraph (a) of this section, has obtained a second SAP evaluation, as an employer you may not rely on it for any purpose under this part.

§ 40.297 Does anyone have the authority to change a SAP's initial evaluation?

(a)   Except as provided in paragraph (b) of this section, no one (*e.g.*, an employer, employee, a managed-care provider, any service agent) may change in any way the SAP's evaluation or recommendations for assistance. For example, a third party is not permitted to make more or less stringent a SAP's recommendation by changing the SAP's evaluation or seeking another SAP's evaluation.

(b)   The SAP who made the initial evaluation may modify his or her initial evaluation and recommendations based on new or additional information (*e.g.*, from an education or treatment program).

(c)   The SAP, who is otherwise fully qualified under this subpart, must not perform evaluations outside the geographic jurisdiction for their credential(s). If the SAP who made the evaluation exceeds their geographic jurisdiction, the employee will not be required to seek the evaluation of a second SAP.

[65 FR 79526, Dec. 19, 2000, as amended at 88 FR 27650, May 2, 2023]

§ 40.299 What is the SAP's role and what are the limits on a SAP's discretion in referring employees for education and treatment?

(a)   As a SAP, upon your determination of the best recommendation for assistance, you will serve as a referral source to assist the employee's entry into an education and/or treatment program.

(b)   To prevent the appearance of a conflict of interest, you must not refer an employee requiring assistance to your private practice or to a person or organization from which you receive payment or to a person or organization in which you have a financial interest. You are precluded from making referrals to entities with which you are financially associated.

(c)   There are four exceptions to the prohibitions contained in paragraph (b) of this section. You may refer an employee to any of the following providers of assistance, regardless of your relationship with them:

   (1)   A public agency (*e.g.*, treatment facility) operated by a state, county, or municipality;

   (2)   The employer or a person or organization under contract to the employer to provide alcohol or drug treatment and/or education services (*e.g.*, the employer's contracted treatment provider);

(3) The sole source of therapeutically appropriate treatment under the employee's health insurance program (e.g., the single substance abuse in-patient treatment program made available by the employee's insurance coverage plan); or

(4) The sole source of therapeutically appropriate treatment reasonably available to the employee (e.g., the only treatment facility or education program reasonably located within the general commuting area).

§ 40.301 What is the SAP's function in the follow-up evaluation of an employee?

(a) As a SAP, after you have prescribed assistance under § 40.293, you must re-evaluate the employee to determine if the employee has successfully carried out your education and/or treatment recommendations.

(1) This is your way to gauge for the employer the employee's ability to demonstrate successful compliance with the education and/or treatment plan.

(2) Your evaluation may serve as one of the reasons the employer decides to return the employee to safety-sensitive duty.

(b) As the SAP making the follow-up evaluation determination, you must:

(1) Confer with or obtain appropriate documentation from the appropriate education and/or treatment program professionals where the employee was referred; and

(2) Conduct a clinical interview meeting the requirements of § 40.291(a)(1) with the employee to determine if the employee demonstrates successful compliance with your initial evaluation recommendations.

(c)

(1) If the employee has demonstrated successful compliance, you must provide a written report directly to the DER highlighting your clinical determination that the employee has done so with your initial evaluation recommendation (see § 40.311(d)).

(2) You may determine that an employee has successfully demonstrated compliance even though the employee has not yet completed the full regimen of education and/or treatment you recommended or needs additional assistance. For example, if the employee has successfully completed the 30-day in-patient program you prescribed, you may make a "successful compliance" determination even though you conclude that the employee has not yet completed the out-patient counseling you recommended or should continue in an aftercare program.

(d)

(1) As the SAP, if you believe, as a result of the follow-up evaluation, that the employee has not demonstrated successful compliance with your recommendations, you must provide written notice directly to the DER (see § 40.311(e)).

(2) As an employer who receives the SAP's written notice that the employee has not successfully complied with the SAP's recommendations, you must not return the employee to the performance of safety-sensitive duties.

(3) As the SAP, you may conduct additional follow-up evaluation(s) if the employer determines that doing so is consistent with the employee's progress as you have reported it and with the employer's policy and/or labor-management agreements.

(4)   As the employer, following a SAP report that the employee has not demonstrated successful compliance, you may take personnel action consistent with your policy and/or labor-management agreements.

[65 FR 79526, Dec. 19, 2000, as amended at 88 FR 27650, May 2, 2023]

§ 40.303 What happens if the SAP believes the employee needs additional treatment, aftercare, or support group services even after the employee returns to safety-sensitive duties?

(a)   As a SAP, if you believe that ongoing services (in addition to follow-up tests) are needed to assist an employee to maintain sobriety or abstinence from drug use after the employee resumes the performance of safety-sensitive duties, you must provide recommendations for these services in your follow-up evaluation report (see § 40.311(d)(10)).

(b)   As an employer receiving a recommendation for these services from a SAP, you may, as part of a return-to-duty agreement with the employee, require the employee to participate in the recommended services. You may monitor and document the employee's participation in the recommended services. You may also make use of SAP and employee assistance program (EAP) services in assisting and monitoring employees' compliance with SAP recommendations. Nothing in this section permits an employer to fail to carry out its obligations with respect to follow-up testing (see § 40.309).

(c)   As an employee, you are obligated to comply with the SAP's recommendations for these services. If you fail or refuse to do so, you may be subject to disciplinary action by your employer.

§ 40.305 How does the return-to-duty process conclude?

(a)   As the employer, if you decide that you want to permit the employee to return to the performance of safety-sensitive functions, you must ensure that the employee takes a return-to-duty test. This test cannot occur until after the SAP has determined that the employee has successfully complied with prescribed education and/or treatment. The employee must have a negative drug test result and/or an alcohol test with an alcohol concentration of less than 0.02 before resuming performance of safety-sensitive duties.

(b)   As an employer, you must not return an employee to safety-sensitive duties until the employee meets the conditions of paragraph (a) of this section. However, you are not required to return an employee to safety-sensitive duties because the employee has met these conditions. That is a personnel decision that you have the discretion to make, subject to collective bargaining agreements or other legal requirements.

(c)   As a SAP or MRO, you must not make a "fitness for duty" determination as part of this re-evaluation unless required to do so under an applicable DOT agency regulation. It is the employer, rather than you, who must decide whether to put the employee back to work in a safety-sensitive position.

(d)   As the employer, if a SAP who is otherwise fully qualified under this subpart performed a remote evaluation of the employee outside the geographic jurisdiction for their credential(s), the employee who they evaluated will not be required to seek the evaluation of a second SAP. If you decide that you want to permit the employee to return to the performance of safety-sensitive functions, you will proceed with the requirements of paragraph (a) of this section.

[65 FR 79526, Dec. 19, 2000, as amended at 88 FR 27650, May 2, 2023]

§ 40.307 What is the SAP's function in prescribing the employee's follow-up tests?

(a) As a SAP, for each employee who has committed a DOT drug or alcohol regulation violation, and who seeks to resume the performance of safety-sensitive functions, you must establish a written follow-up testing plan. You do not establish this plan until after you determine that the employee has successfully complied with your recommendations for education and/or treatment.

(b) You must present a copy of this plan directly to the DER (see § 40.311(d)(9)).

(c) You are the sole determiner of the number and frequency of follow-up tests and whether these tests will be for drugs, alcohol, or both, unless otherwise directed by the appropriate DOT agency regulation. For example, if the employee had a positive drug test, but your evaluation or the treatment program professionals determined that the employee had an alcohol problem as well, you should require that the employee have follow-up tests for both drugs and alcohol.

(d) However, you must, at a minimum, direct that the employee be subject to six unannounced follow-up tests in the first 12 months of safety-sensitive duty following the employee's return to safety-sensitive functions.

  (1) You may require a greater number of follow-up tests during the first 12-month period of safety-sensitive duty (*e.g.*, you may require one test a month during the 12-month period; you may require two tests per month during the first 6-month period and one test per month during the final 6-month period).

  (2) You may also require follow-up tests during the 48 months of safety-sensitive duty following this first 12-month period.

  (3) You are not to establish the actual dates for the follow-up tests you prescribe. The decision on specific dates to test is the employer's.

  (4) As the employer, you must not impose additional testing requirements (*e.g.*, under company authority) on the employee that go beyond the SAP's follow-up testing plan.

(e) The requirements of the SAP's follow-up testing plan "follow the employee" to subsequent employers or through breaks in service.

Example 1 to paragraph (e): The employee returns to duty with Employer A. Two months afterward, after completing the first two of six follow-up tests required by the SAP's plan, the employee quits his job with Employer A and begins to work in a similar position for Employer B. The employee remains obligated to complete the four additional tests during the next 10 months of safety-sensitive duty, and Employer B is responsible for ensuring that the employee does so. Employer B learns of this obligation through the inquiry it makes under § 40.25.

Example 2 to paragraph (e): The employee returns to duty with Employer A. Three months later, after the employee completes the first two of six follow-up tests required by the SAP's plan, Employer A lays the employee off for economic or seasonal employment reasons. Four months later, Employer A recalls the employee. Employer A must ensure that the employee completes the remaining four follow-up tests during the next nine months.

(f) As the SAP, you may modify the determinations you have made concerning follow-up tests. For example, even if you recommended follow-up testing beyond the first 12-months, you can terminate the testing requirement at any time after the first year of testing. You must not, however, modify the requirement that the employee take at least six follow-up tests within the first 12 months after returning to the performance of safety-sensitive functions.

(g) As the employer, SAP, or other service agent, you must not provide to the employee a copy of their drug and/or alcohol follow-up testing schedule prescribed by the SAP. No employer, SAP, or other service agent will indicate to the employee what the frequency or duration of the employee's follow-up testing schedule will be. The SAP can require follow-up testing for either or both drugs and alcohol for a drug-related or an alcohol-related violation.

[65 FR 79526, Dec. 19, 2000, as amended at 88 FR 27650, May 2, 2023]

§ 40.309 What are the employer's responsibilities with respect to the SAP's directions for follow-up tests?

(a) As the employer, you must carry out the SAP's follow-up testing requirements. You may not allow the employee to continue to perform safety-sensitive functions unless follow-up testing is conducted as directed by the SAP.

(b) You should schedule follow-up tests on dates of your own choosing, but you must ensure that the tests are unannounced with no discernable pattern as to their timing, and that the employee is given no advance notice.

(c) You cannot substitute any other tests (e.g., those carried out under the random testing program) conducted on the employee for this follow-up testing requirement.

(d) You cannot count a follow-up test that has been cancelled as a completed test. A cancelled follow-up test must be recollected.

§ 40.311 What are the requirements concerning SAP reports?

(a) As the SAP conducting the required evaluations, you must send the written reports required by this section in writing directly to the DER and not to a third party or entity for forwarding to the DER (except as provided in § 40.355(e)). You may, however, forward the document simultaneously to the DER and to a C/TPA.

(b) As an employer, you must ensure that you receive SAP written reports directly from the SAP performing the evaluation and that no third party or entity changed the SAP's report in any way.

(c) The SAP's written report, following an initial evaluation that determines what level of assistance is needed to address the employee's drug and/or alcohol problems, must be on the SAP's own letterhead (and not the letterhead of another service agent) signed and dated by the SAP, and must contain the following delineated items:

(1) Employee's name and SSN or employee ID No.;

(2) Employer's name and address;

(3) Reason for the assessment (specific violation of DOT regulations and violation date);

(4) Date(s) and format (i.e., face-to-face or remote) of the assessment;

    (5)   SAP's education and/or treatment recommendation; and

    (6)   SAP's telephone number.

(d)   The SAP's written report concerning a follow-up evaluation that determines the employee has demonstrated successful compliance must be on the SAP's own letterhead (and not the letterhead of another service agent), signed by the SAP and dated, and must contain the following items:

    (1)   Employee's name and SSN or employee ID No.;

    (2)   Employer's name and address;

    (3)   Reason for the initial assessment (specific violation of DOT regulations and violation date);

    (4)   Date(s) and format (*i.e.*, face-to-face or remote) of the initial assessment and synopsis of the treatment plan;

    (5)   Name of practice(s) or service(s) providing the recommended education and/or treatment;

    (6)   Inclusive dates of employee's program participation;

    (7)   Clinical characterization of employee's program participation;

    (8)   SAP's clinical determination as to whether the employee has demonstrated successful compliance;

    (9)   Follow-up testing plan;

    (10) Employee's continuing care needs with specific treatment, aftercare, and/or support group services recommendations; and

    (11) SAP's telephone number.

(e)   The SAP's written report concerning a follow-up evaluation that determines the employee has not demonstrated successful compliance must be on the SAP's own letterhead (and not the letterhead of another service agent), signed by the SAP and dated, and must contain the following items:

    (1)   Employee's name and SSN or employee ID No.;

    (2)   Employer's name and address;

    (3)   Reason for the initial assessment (specific DOT violation and date);

    (4)   Date(s) and format (*i.e.*, face-to-face or remote) of initial assessment and synopsis of treatment plan;

    (5)   Name of practice(s) or service(s) providing the recommended education and/or treatment;

    (6)   Inclusive dates of employee's program participation;

    (7)   Clinical characterization of employee's program participation;

    (8)   Date(s) of the first follow-up evaluation;

    (9)   Date(s) of any further follow-up evaluation the SAP has scheduled;

    (10) SAP's clinical reasons for determining that the employee has not demonstrated successful compliance; and

    (11) SAP's telephone number.

(f) As a SAP, you must also provide these written reports directly to the employee if the employee has no current employer and to the gaining DOT regulated employer in the event the employee obtains another transportation industry safety-sensitive position.

(g) As a SAP, you are to maintain copies of your reports to employers for 5 years, and your employee clinical records in accordance with Federal, state, and local laws regarding record maintenance, confidentiality, and release of information. You must make these records available, on request, to DOT agency representatives (*e.g.*, inspectors conducting an audit or safety investigation) and representatives of the NTSB in an accident investigation.

(h) As an employer, you must maintain your reports from SAPs for 5 years from the date you received them.

[65 FR 79526, Dec. 19, 2000, as amended at 88 FR 27650, May 2, 2023]

§ 40.313 Where is other information on SAP functions and the return-to-duty process found in this regulation?

You can find other information on the role and functions of SAPs in the following sections of this part:

§ 40.3—Definition.

§ 40.347—Service agent assistance with SAP-required follow-up testing.

§ 40.355—Transmission of SAP reports.

§ 40.329(c)—Making SAP reports available to employees on request.

Appendix E to Part 40—SAP Equivalency Requirements for Certification Organizations.

Subpart P—Confidentiality and Release of Information

§ 40.321 What is the general confidentiality rule for drug and alcohol test information?

Except as otherwise provided in this subpart, as a service agent or employer participating in the DOT drug or alcohol testing process, you are prohibited from releasing individual test results or medical information about an employee to third parties without the employee's specific written consent.

(a) A "third party" is any person or organization to whom other subparts of this regulation do not explicitly authorize or require the transmission of information in the course of the drug or alcohol testing process.

(b) "Specific written consent" means a statement signed by the employee that he or she agrees to the release of a particular piece of information to a particular, explicitly identified, person or organization at a particular time. "Blanket releases," in which an employee agrees to a release of a category of information (*e.g.*, all test results) or to release information to a category of parties (*e.g.*, other employers who are members of a C/TPA, companies to which the employee may apply for employment), are prohibited under this part.

§ 40.323 May program participants release drug or alcohol test information in connection with legal proceedings?

(a) As an employer, you may release information pertaining to an employee's drug or alcohol test without the employee's consent in certain legal proceedings.

    (1) These proceedings include a lawsuit (*e.g.*, a wrongful discharge action), grievance (*e.g.*, an arbitration concerning disciplinary action taken by the employer), or administrative proceeding (*e.g.*, an unemployment compensation hearing) brought by, or on behalf of, an employee and resulting from a positive DOT drug or alcohol test or a refusal to test (including, but not limited to, adulterated or substituted test results).

    (2) These proceedings also include a criminal or civil action resulting from an employee's performance of safety-sensitive duties, in which a court of competent jurisdiction determines that the drug or alcohol test information sought is relevant to the case and issues an order directing the employer to produce the information. For example, in personal injury litigation following a truck or bus collision, the court could determine that a post-accident drug test result of an employee is relevant to determining whether the driver or the driver's employer was negligent. The employer is authorized to respond to the court's order to produce the records.

(b) In such a proceeding, you may release the information to the decisionmaker in the proceeding (*e.g.*, the court in a lawsuit). You may release the information only with a binding stipulation that the decisionmaker to whom it is released will make it available only to parties to the proceeding.

(c) If you are a service agent, and the employer requests its employee's drug or alcohol testing information from you to use in a legal proceeding as authorized in paragraph (a) of this section (*e.g.*, the laboratory's data package), you must provide the requested information to the employer.

(d) As an employer or service agent, you must immediately notify the employee in writing of any information you release under this section.

§ 40.325 [Reserved]

§ 40.327 When must the MRO report medical information gathered in the verification process?

(a) As the MRO, you must, except as provided in paragraph (d) of this section, report drug test results and medical information you learned as part of the verification process to third parties without the employee's consent if you determine, in your reasonable medical judgment, that:

    (1) The information is likely to result in the employee being determined to be medically unqualified under an applicable DOT agency regulation; or

    (2) The information indicates that continued performance by the employee of his or her safety-sensitive function is likely to pose a significant safety risk.

(b) The third parties to whom you are authorized to provide information by this section include the employer, a physician or other health care provider responsible for determining the medical qualifications of the employee under an applicable DOT agency safety regulation, a SAP evaluating the employee as part of the return to duty process (see § 40.293(g)), a DOT agency, or the National Transportation Safety Board in the course of an accident investigation.

(c)   The MRO must not report such medical information using the CCF. Instead, the MRO must provide the information in a separate written communication (*e.g.,* letter, secure email). The information must state the specific nature of the MRO's safety concern (*e.g.,* the effects of a medication the employee is taking, the employee's underlying medical condition that the employee disclosed to the MRO).

(d)   If the law of a foreign country (*e.g.,* Canada) prohibits you from providing medical information to the employer, you may comply with that prohibition.

[65 FR 79526, Dec. 19, 2000, as amended at 88 FR 27650, May 2, 2023]

§ 40.329 What information must laboratories, MROs, and other service agents release to employees?

(a)   As an MRO or service agent you must provide, within 10 business days of receiving a written request from an employee, copies of any records pertaining to the employee's use of alcohol and/or drugs, including records of the employee's DOT-mandated drug and/or alcohol tests. You may charge no more than the cost of preparation and reproduction for copies of these records.

(b)   As a laboratory, you must provide, within 10 business days of receiving a written request from an employee, and made through the MRO, the records relating to the results of the employee's drug test (*i.e.,* laboratory report and data package). You may charge no more than the cost of preparation and reproduction for copies of these records.

(c)   As a SAP, you must make available to an employee, on request, a copy of all SAP reports (see § 40.311). However, you must redact follow-up testing information from the report before providing it to the employee.

[65 FR 79526, Dec. 19, 2000, as amended at 66 FR 41954, Aug. 9, 2001]

§ 40.331 To what additional parties must employers and service agents release information?

As an employer or service agent you must release information under the following circumstances:

(a)   If you receive a specific, written consent from an employee authorizing the release of information about that employee's drug or alcohol tests to an identified person, you must provide the information to the identified person. For example, as an employer, when you receive a written request from a former employee to provide information to a subsequent employer, you must do so. In providing the information, you must comply with the terms of the employee's consent.

(b)   If you are an employer, you must, upon request of DOT agency representatives, provide the following:

(1)   Access to your facilities used for this part and DOT agency drug and alcohol program functions.

(2)   All written, printed, and computer-based drug and alcohol program records and reports (including copies of name-specific records or reports), files, materials, data, documents/documentation, agreements, contracts, policies, and statements that are required by this part and DOT agency regulations. You must provide this information at your principal place of business in the time required by the DOT agency.

(3) All items in paragraph (b)(2) of this section must be easily accessible, legible, and provided in an organized manner. If electronic records do not meet these standards, they must be converted to printed documentation that meets these standards.

(c) If you are a service agent, you must, upon request of DOT agency representatives, provide the following:

(1) Access to your facilities used for this part and DOT agency drug and alcohol program functions.

(2) All written, printed, and computer-based drug and alcohol program records and reports (including copies of name-specific records or reports), files, materials, data, documents/documentation, agreements, contracts, policies, and statements that are required by this part and DOT agency regulations. You must provide this information at your principal place of business in the time required by the DOT agency.

(3) All items in paragraph (c)(2) of this section must be easily accessible, legible, and provided in an organized manner. If electronic records do not meet these standards, they must be converted to printed documentation that meets these standards.

(d) If requested by the National Transportation Safety Board as part of an accident investigation, you must provide information concerning post-accident tests administered after the accident.

(e) If requested by a Federal, state or local safety agency with regulatory authority over you or the employee, you must provide drug and alcohol test records concerning the employee.

(f) Except as otherwise provided in this part, as a laboratory you must not release or provide a specimen or a part of a specimen to a requesting party, without first obtaining written consent from ODAPC. DNA testing and other types of identity testing are not authorized and ODAPC will not give permission for such testing. If a party seeks a court order directing you to release a specimen or part of a specimen contrary to any provision of this part, you must take necessary legal steps to contest the issuance of the order (*e.g.,* seek to quash a subpoena, citing the requirements of § 40.13). This part does not require you to disobey a court order, however.

(g) Notwithstanding any other provision of this Part, as an employer of Commercial Motor Vehicle (CMV) drivers holding commercial driving licenses (CDLs) or as a third party administrator for owner-operator CMV drivers with CDLs, you are authorized to comply with State laws requiring you to provide to State CDL licensing authorities information about all violations of DOT drug and alcohol testing rules (including positive tests and refusals) by any CMV driver holding a CDL.

[65 FR 79526, Dec. 19, 2000, as amended at 66 FR 41955, Aug. 9, 2001; 73 FR 33737, June 13, 2008; 82 FR 52247, Nov. 13, 2017]

§ 40.333 What records must employers keep?

(a) As an employer, you must keep the following records for the following periods of time:

(1) You must keep the following records for five years:

(i) Records of alcohol test results indicating an alcohol concentration of 0.02 or greater;

(ii) Records of verified positive drug test results;

(iii) Documentation of refusals to take required alcohol and/or drug tests (including substituted or adulterated drug test results);

(iv) SAP reports; and

49 CFR Part 40 (up to date as of 3/05/2024)
Procedures for Transportation Workplace Drug and Alcohol Testing Programs
49 CFR 40.333(a)(1)(v)

    (v) All follow-up tests and schedules for follow-up tests.

  (2) You must keep records for three years of information obtained from previous employers under § 40.25 concerning drug and alcohol test results of employees.

  (3) You must keep records of the inspection, maintenance, and calibration of EBTs, for two years.

  (4) You must keep records of negative and cancelled drug test results and alcohol test results with a concentration of less than 0.02 for one year.

(b) You do not have to keep records related to a program requirement that does not apply to you (*e.g.,* a maritime employer who does not have a DOT-mandated random alcohol testing program need not maintain random alcohol testing records).

(c) You must maintain the records in a location with controlled access.

(d) A service agent may maintain these records for you. However, you must ensure that you can produce these records at your principal place of business in the time required by the DOT agency. For example, as a motor carrier, when an FMCSA inspector requests your records, you must ensure that you can provide them within two business days.

(e) If you store records electronically, where permitted by this part, you must ensure that the records are easily accessible, legible, and formatted and stored in an organized manner. If electronic records do not meet these criteria, you must convert them to printed documentation in a rapid and readily auditable manner, at the request of DOT agency personnel.

[65 FR 79526, Dec. 19, 2000, as amended at 66 FR 41955, Aug. 9, 2001]

Subpart Q—Roles and Responsibilities of Service Agents

§ 40.341 Must service agents comply with DOT drug and alcohol testing requirements?

(a) As a service agent, the services you provide to transportation employers must meet the requirements of this part and the DOT agency drug and alcohol testing regulations.

(b) If you do not comply, DOT may take action under the Public Interest Exclusions procedures of this part (see Subpart R of this part) or applicable provisions of other DOT agency regulations.

§ 40.343 What tasks may a service agent perform for an employer?

As a service agent, you may perform for employers the tasks needed to comply with DOT agency drug and alcohol testing regulations, subject to the requirements and limitations of this part.

§ 40.345 In what circumstances may a C/TPA act as an intermediary in the transmission of drug and alcohol testing information to employers?

(a) As a C/TPA or other service agent, you may act as an intermediary in the transmission of drug and alcohol testing information in the circumstances specified in this section only if the employer chooses to have you do so. Each employer makes the decision about whether to receive some or all of this information from you, acting as an intermediary, rather than directly from the service agent who originates the information (*e.g.,* an MRO or BAT).

(b)   The specific provisions of this part concerning which you may act as an intermediary are listed in appendix H to this part. These are the only situations in which you may act as an intermediary. You are prohibited from doing so in all other situations.

(c)   In every case, you must ensure that, in transmitting information to employers, you meet all requirements (*e.g.*, concerning confidentiality and timing) that would apply if the service agent originating the information (*e.g.*, an MRO or collector) sent the information directly to the employer. For example, if you transmit drug testing results from MROs to DERs, you must transmit each drug test result to the DER in compliance with the MRO requirements set forth in § 40.167.

[65 FR 79526, Dec. 19, 2000, as amended at 88 FR 27650, May 2, 2023]

§ 40.347 What functions may C/TPAs perform with respect to administering testing?

As a C/TPA, except as otherwise specified in this part, you may perform the following functions for employers concerning random selection and other selections for testing.

(a)   You may operate random testing programs for employers and may assist (*i.e.*, through contracting with laboratories or collection sites, conducting collections) employers with other types of testing (*e.g.*, pre-employment, post-accident, reasonable suspicion, return-to-duty, and follow-up).

(b)   You may combine employees from more than one employer or one transportation industry in a random pool if permitted by all the DOT agency drug and alcohol testing regulations involved.

   (1)   If you combine employees from more than one transportation industry, you must ensure that the random testing rate is at least equal to the highest rate required by each DOT agency.

   (2)   Employees not covered by DOT agency regulations may not be part of the same random pool with DOT covered employees.

(c)   You may assist employers in ensuring that follow-up testing is conducted in accordance with the plan established by the SAP. However, neither you nor the employer are permitted to randomly select employees from a "follow-up pool" for follow-up testing.

§ 40.349 What records may a service agent receive and maintain?

(a)   Except where otherwise specified in this part, as a service agent you may receive and maintain all records concerning DOT drug and alcohol testing programs, including positive, negative, and refusal to test individual test results. You do not need the employee's consent to receive and maintain these records.

(b)   You may maintain all information needed for operating a drug/alcohol program (*e.g.*, CCFs, ATFs, names of employees in random pools, random selection lists, copies of notices to employers of selected employees) on behalf of an employer.

(c)   If a service agent originating drug or alcohol testing information, such as an MRO or BAT, sends the information directly to the DER, he or she may also provide the information simultaneously to you, as a C/TPA or other service agent who maintains this information for the employer.

(d)   If you are serving as an intermediary in transmitting information that is required to be provided to the employer, you must ensure that it reaches the employer in the same time periods required elsewhere in this part.

(e) You must ensure that you can make available to the employer within two business days any information the employer is asked to produce by a DOT agency representative.

(f) On request of an employer, you must, at any time on the request of an employer, transfer immediately all records pertaining to the employer and its employees to the employer or to any other service agent the employer designates. You must carry out this transfer as soon as the employer requests it. You are not required to obtain employee consent for this transfer. You must not charge more than your reasonable administrative costs for conducting this transfer. You may not charge a fee for the release of these records.

(g) If you are planning to go out of business or your organization will be bought by or merged with another organization, you must immediately notify all employers and offer to transfer all records pertaining to the employer and its employees to the employer or to any other service agent the employer designates. You must carry out this transfer as soon as the employer requests it. You are not required to obtain employee consent for this transfer. You must not charge more than your reasonable administrative costs for conducting this transfer. You may not charge a fee for the release of these records.

[65 FR 79526, Dec. 19, 2000, as amended at 66 FR 41955, Aug. 9, 2001]

§ 40.351 What confidentiality requirements apply to service agents?

Except where otherwise specified in this part, as a service agent the following confidentiality requirements apply to you:

(a) When you receive or maintain confidential information about employees (e.g., individual test results), you must follow the same confidentiality regulations as the employer with respect to the use and release of this information.

(b) You must follow all confidentiality and records retention requirements applicable to employers.

(c) You may not provide individual test results or other confidential information to another employer without a specific, written consent from the employee. For example, suppose you are a C/TPA that has employers X and Y as clients. Employee Jones works for X, and you maintain Jones' drug and alcohol test for X. Jones wants to change jobs and work for Y. You may not inform Y of the result of a test conducted for X without having a specific, written consent from Jones. Likewise, you may not provide this information to employer Z, who is not a C/TPA member, without this consent.

(d) You must not use blanket consent forms authorizing the release of employee testing information.

(e) You must establish adequate confidentiality and security measures to ensure that confidential employee records are not available to unauthorized persons. This includes protecting the physical security of records, access controls, and computer security measures to safeguard confidential data in electronic data bases.

§ 40.353 What principles govern the interaction between MROs and other service agents?

As a service agent other than an MRO (e.g., a C/TPA), the following principles govern your interaction with MROs:

(a) You may provide MRO services to employers, directly or through contract, if you meet all applicable provisions of this part.

49 CFR Part 40 (up to date as of 3/05/2024)
Procedures for Transportation Workplace Drug and Alcohol Testing Programs

49 CFR 40.353(b)

(b) If you employ or contract for an MRO, the MRO must perform duties independently and confidentially. When you have a relationship with an MRO, you must structure the relationship to ensure that this independence and confidentiality are not compromised. Specific means (including both physical and operational measures, as appropriate) to separate MRO functions and other service agent functions are essential.

(c) Only your staff who are actually under the day-to-day supervision and control of an MRO with respect to MRO functions may perform these functions. This does not mean that those staff may not perform other functions at other times. However, the designation of your staff to perform MRO functions under MRO supervision must be limited and not used as a subterfuge to circumvent confidentiality and other requirements of this part and DOT agency regulations. You must ensure that MRO staff operate under controls sufficient to ensure that the independence and confidentiality of the MRO process are not compromised.

(d) Like other MROs, an MRO you employ or contract with must personally conduct verification interviews with employees and must personally make all verification decisions. Consequently, your staff cannot perform these functions.

§ 40.355 What limitations apply to the activities of service agents?

As a service agent, you are subject to the following limitations concerning your activities in the DOT drug and alcohol testing program.

(a) You must not require an employee to sign a consent, release, waiver of liability, or indemnification agreement with respect to any part of the drug or alcohol testing process covered by this part (including, but not limited to, collections, laboratory testing, MRO, and SAP services). No one may do so on behalf of a service agent.

(b) You must not act as an intermediary in the transmission of drug test results from the laboratory to the MRO. That is, the laboratory may not send results to you, with you in turn sending them to the MRO for verification. For example, a practice in which the laboratory transmits results to your computer system, and you then assign the results to a particular MRO, is not permitted.

(c) You must not transmit drug test results directly from the laboratory to the employer (by electronic or other means) or to a service agent who forwards them to the employer. All confirmed laboratory results must be processed by the MRO before they are released to any other party.

(d) You must not act as an intermediary in the transmission of alcohol test results of 0.02 or higher from the STT or BAT to the DER.

(e) Except as provided in paragraph (f) of this section, you must not act as an intermediary in the transmission of individual SAP reports to the actual employer. That is, the SAP may not send such reports to you, with you in turn sending them to the actual employer. However, you may maintain individual SAP summary reports and follow-up testing plans after they are sent to the DER, and the SAP may transmit such reports to you simultaneously with sending them to the DER.

(f) As an exception to paragraph (e) of this section, you may act as an intermediary in the transmission of SAP report from the SAP to an owner-operator or other self-employed individual.

(g) Except as provided in paragraph (h) of this section, you must not make decisions to test an employee based upon reasonable suspicion, post-accident, return-to-duty, and follow-up determination criteria. These are duties the actual employer cannot delegate to a C/TPA. You may, however, provide advice and information to employers regarding these testing issues and how the employer should schedule required testing.

(h) As an exception to paragraph (g) of this section, you may make decisions to test an employee based upon reasonable suspicion, post-accident, return-to-duty, and follow-up determination criteria with respect to an owner-operator or other self-employed individual.

(i) Except as provided in paragraph (j) of this section, you must not make a determination that an employee has refused a drug or alcohol test. This is a non-delegable duty of the actual employer. You may, however, provide advice and information to employers regarding refusal-to-test issues.

(j) As an exception to paragraph (i) of this section, you may make a determination that an employee has refused a drug or alcohol test, if:

(1) You schedule a required test for an owner-operator or other self-employed individual, and the individual fails to appear for the test without a legitimate reason; or

(2) As an MRO, you determine that an individual has refused to test on the basis of adulteration or substitution.

(k) You must not act as a DER. For example, while you may be responsible for transmitting information to the employer about test results, you must not act on behalf of the employer in actions to remove employees from safety-sensitive duties.

(l) In transmitting documents to laboratories, you must ensure that you send to the laboratory that conducts testing only Copy 1 of the CCF. You must not transmit other copies of the CCF or any ATFs to the laboratory.

(m) You must not impose conditions or requirements on employers that DOT regulations do not authorize. For example, as a C/TPA serving employers in the pipeline or motor carrier industry, you must not require employers to have provisions in their DOT plans that PHMSA or FMCSA regulations do not require.

(n) You must not intentionally delay the transmission of drug or alcohol testing-related documents concerning actions you have performed, because of a payment dispute or other reasons.

Example 1 to paragraph (n): A laboratory that has tested a specimen must not delay transmitting the documentation of the test result to an MRO because of a billing or payment dispute with the MRO or a C/TPA.

Example 2 to paragraph (n): An MRO or SAP who has interviewed an employee must not delay sending a verified test result or SAP report to the employer because of such a dispute with the employer or employee.

Example 3 to paragraph (n): A collector who has performed a specimen collection must not delay sending the drug specimen and CCF to the laboratory because of a payment or other dispute with the laboratory or a C/TPA.

Example 4 to paragraph (n):   A BAT who has conducted an alcohol test must not delay sending test result information to an employer or C/TPA because of a payment or other dispute with the employer or C/TPA.

(o)   While you must follow the DOT agency regulations, the actual employer remains accountable to DOT for compliance, and your failure to implement any aspect of the program as required in this part and other applicable DOT agency regulations makes the employer subject to enforcement action by the Department.

[65 FR 79526, Dec. 19, 2000, as amended at 66 FR 41955, Aug. 9, 2001; 71 FR 49384, Aug. 23, 2006; 75 FR 59108, Sept. 27, 2010; 88 FR 27650, May 2, 2023]

Subpart R—Public Interest Exclusions

§ 40.361 What is the purpose of a public interest exclusion (PIE)?

(a)   To protect the public interest, including protecting transportation employers and employees from serious noncompliance with DOT drug and alcohol testing rules, the Department's policy is to ensure that employers conduct business only with responsible service agents.

(b)   The Department therefore uses PIEs to exclude from participation in DOT's drug and alcohol testing program any service agent who, by serious noncompliance with this part or other DOT agency drug and alcohol testing regulations, has shown that it is not currently acting in a responsible manner.

(c)   A PIE is a serious action that the Department takes only to protect the public interest. We intend to use PIEs only to remedy situations of serious noncompliance. PIEs are not used for the purpose of punishment.

(d)   Nothing in this subpart precludes a DOT agency or the Inspector General from taking other action authorized by its regulations with respect to service agents or employers that violate its regulations.

§ 40.363 On what basis may the Department issue a PIE?

(a)   If you are a service agent, the Department may issue a PIE concerning you if we determine that you have failed or refused to provide drug or alcohol testing services consistent with the requirements of this part or a DOT agency drug and alcohol regulation.

(b)   The Department also may issue a PIE if you have failed to cooperate with DOT agency representatives concerning inspections, complaint investigations, compliance and enforcement reviews, or requests for documents and other information about compliance with this part or DOT agency drug and alcohol regulations.

§ 40.365 What is the Department's policy concerning starting a PIE proceeding?

(a)   It is the Department's policy to start a PIE proceeding only in cases of serious, uncorrected noncompliance with the provisions of this part, affecting such matters as safety, the outcomes of test results, privacy and confidentiality, due process and fairness for employees, the honesty and integrity of the testing program, and cooperation with or provision of information to DOT agency representatives.

(b) The following are examples of the kinds of serious noncompliance that, as a matter of policy, the Department views as appropriate grounds for starting a PIE proceeding. These examples are not intended to be an exhaustive or exclusive list of the grounds for starting a PIE proceeding. We intend them to illustrate the level of seriousness that the Department believes supports starting a PIE proceeding. The examples follow:

     (1) For an MRO, verifying tests positive without interviewing the employees as required by this part or providing MRO services without meeting the qualifications for an MRO required by this part;

     (2) For a laboratory, refusing to provide information to the Department, an employer, or an employee as required by this part; failing or refusing to conduct a validity testing program when required by this part; or a pattern or practice of testing errors that result in the cancellation of tests. (As a general matter of policy, the Department does not intend to initiate a PIE proceeding concerning a laboratory with respect to matters on which HHS initiates certification actions under its laboratory guidelines.);

     (3) For a collector, a pattern or practice of directly observing collections when doing so is unauthorized, or failing or refusing to directly observe collections when doing so is mandatory;

     (4) For collectors, BATs, or STTs, a pattern or practice of using forms, testing equipment, or collection kits that do not meet the standards in this part;

     (5) For a collector, BAT, or STT, a pattern or practice of "fatal flaws" or other significant uncorrected errors in the collection process;

     (6) For a laboratory, MRO or C/TPA, failing or refusing to report tests results as required by this part or DOT agency regulations;

     (7) For a laboratory, falsifying, concealing, or destroying documentation concerning any part of the drug testing process, including, but not limited to, documents in a "litigation package";

     (8) For SAPs, providing SAP services while not meeting SAP qualifications required by this part or performing evaluations without interviews meeting the requirements of § 40.291(a)(1);

     (9) For any service agent, maintaining a relationship with another party that constitutes a conflict of interest under this part (e.g., a laboratory that derives a financial benefit from having an employer use a specific MRO);

     (10) For any service agent, falsely representing that the service agent or its activities is approved or certified by the Department or a DOT agency (such representation includes, but is not limited to, the use of a Department or DOT agency logo, title, or emblem).

     (11) For any service agent, disclosing an employee's test result information to any party this part or a DOT agency regulation does not authorize, including by obtaining a "blanket" consent from employees or by creating a data base from which employers or others can retrieve an employee's DOT test results without the specific consent of the employee;

     (12) For any service agent, interfering or attempting to interfere with the ability of an MRO to communicate with the Department, or retaliating against an MRO for communicating with the Department;

     (13) For any service agent, directing or recommending that an employer fail or refuse to implement any provision of this part; or

(14) With respect to noncompliance with a DOT agency regulation, conduct that affects important provisions of Department-wide concern (*e.g.*, failure to properly conduct the selection process for random testing).

[65 FR 79526, Dec. 19, 2000, as amended at 82 FR 52247, Nov. 13, 2017; 88 FR 27650, May 2, 2023]

§ 40.367 Who initiates a PIE proceeding?

The following DOT officials may initiate a PIE proceeding:

(a) The drug and alcohol program manager of a DOT agency;

(b) An official of ODAPC, other than the Director; or

(c) The designee of any of these officials.

§ 40.369 What is the discretion of an initiating official in starting a PIE proceeding?

(a) Initiating officials have broad discretion in deciding whether to start a PIE proceeding.

(b) In exercising this discretion, the initiating official must consider the Department's policy regarding the seriousness of the service agent's conduct (see § 40.365) and all information he or she has obtained to this point concerning the facts of the case. The initiating official may also consider the availability of the resources needed to pursue a PIE proceeding.

(c) A decision not to initiate a PIE proceeding does not necessarily mean that the Department regards a service agent as being in compliance or that the Department may not use other applicable remedies in a situation of noncompliance.

§ 40.371 On what information does an initiating official rely in deciding whether to start a PIE proceeding?

(a) An initiating official may rely on credible information from any source as the basis for starting a PIE proceeding.

(b) Before sending a correction notice (see § 40.373), the initiating official informally contacts the service agent to determine if there is any information that may affect the initiating official's determination about whether it is necessary to send a correction notice. The initiating official may take any information resulting from this contact into account in determining whether to proceed under this subpart.

§ 40.373 Before starting a PIE proceeding, does the initiating official give the service agent an opportunity to correct problems?

(a) If you are a service agent, the initiating official must send you a correction notice before starting a PIE proceeding.

(b) The correction notice identifies the specific areas in which you must come into compliance in order to avoid being subject to a PIE proceeding.

(c) If you make and document changes needed to come into compliance in the areas listed in the correction notice to the satisfaction of the initiating official within 60 days of the date you receive the notice, the initiating official does not start a PIE proceeding. The initiating official may conduct appropriate fact finding to verify that you have made and maintained satisfactory corrections. When he or she is satisfied that you are in compliance, the initiating official sends you a notice that the matter is concluded.

§ 40.375 How does the initiating official start a PIE proceeding?

(a) As a service agent, if your compliance matter is not correctable (see § 40.373(a)), or if have not resolved compliance matters as provided in § 40.373(c), the initiating official starts a PIE proceeding by sending you a notice of proposed exclusion (NOPE). The NOPE contains the initiating official's recommendations concerning the issuance of a PIE, but it is not a decision by the Department to issue a PIE.

(b) The NOPE includes the following information:

(1) A statement that the initiating official is recommending that the Department issue a PIE concerning you;

(2) The factual basis for the initiating official's belief that you are not providing drug and/or alcohol testing services to DOT-regulated employers consistent with the requirements of this part or are in serious noncompliance with a DOT agency drug and alcohol regulation;

(3) The factual basis for the initiating official's belief that your noncompliance has not been or cannot be corrected;

(4) The initiating official's recommendation for the scope of the PIE;

(5) The initiating official's recommendation for the duration of the PIE; and

(6) A statement that you may contest the issuance of the proposed PIE, as provided in § 40.379.

(c) The initiating official sends a copy of the NOPE to the ODAPC Director at the same time he or she sends the NOPE to you.

§ 40.377 Who decides whether to issue a PIE?

(a) The ODAPC Director, or his or her designee, decides whether to issue a PIE. If a designee is acting as the decisionmaker, all references in this subpart to the Director refer to the designee.

(b) To ensure his or her impartiality, the Director plays no role in the initiating official's determination about whether to start a PIE proceeding.

(c) There is a "firewall" between the initiating official and the Director. This means that the initiating official and the Director are prohibited from having any discussion, contact, or exchange of information with one another about the matter, except for documents and discussions that are part of the record of the proceeding.

§ 40.379 How do you contest the issuance of a PIE?

(a) If you receive a NOPE, you may contest the issuance of the PIE.

(b) If you want to contest the proposed PIE, you must provide the Director information and argument in opposition to the proposed PIE in writing, in person, and/or through a representative. To contest the proposed PIE, you must take one or more of the steps listed in this paragraph (b) within 30 days after you receive the NOPE.

(1) You may request that the Director dismiss the proposed PIE without further proceedings, on the basis that it does not concern serious noncompliance with this part or DOT agency regulations, consistent with the Department's policy as stated in § 40.365.

(2) You may present written information and arguments, consistent with the provisions of § 40.381, contesting the proposed PIE.

(3) You may arrange with the Director for an informal meeting to present your information and arguments.

(c) If you do not take any of the actions listed in paragraph (b) of this section within 30 days after you receive the NOPE, the matter proceeds as an uncontested case. In this event, the Director makes his or her decision based on the record provided by the initiating official (*i.e.*, the NOPE and any supporting information or testimony) and any additional information the Director obtains.

§ 40.381 What information do you present to contest the proposed issuance of a PIE?

(a) As a service agent who wants to contest a proposed PIE, you must present at least the following information to the Director:

(1) Specific facts that contradict the statements contained in the NOPE (see § 40.375(b)(2) and (3)). A general denial is insufficient to raise a genuine dispute over facts material to the issuance of a PIE;

(2) Identification of any existing, proposed or prior PIE; and

(3) Identification of your affiliates, if any.

(b) You may provide any information and arguments you wish concerning the proposed issuance, scope and duration of the PIE (see § 40.375(b)(4) and (5)).

(c) You may provide any additional relevant information or arguments concerning any of the issues in the matter.

§ 40.383 What procedures apply if you contest the issuance of a PIE?

(a) DOT conducts PIE proceedings in a fair and informal manner. The Director may use flexible procedures to allow you to present matters in opposition. The Director is not required to follow formal rules of evidence or procedure in creating the record of the proceeding.

(b) The Director will consider any information or argument he or she determines to be relevant to the decision on the matter.

(c) You may submit any documentary evidence you want the Director to consider. In addition, if you have arranged an informal meeting with the Director, you may present witnesses and confront any person the initiating official presents as a witness against you.

(d) In cases where there are material factual issues in dispute, the Director or his or her designee may conduct additional fact-finding.

(e) If you have arranged a meeting with the Director, the Director will make a transcribed record of the meeting available to you on your request. You must pay the cost of transcribing and copying the meeting record.

§ 40.385 Who bears the burden of proof in a PIE proceeding?

(a) As the proponent of issuing a PIE, the initiating official bears the burden of proof.

(b) This burden is to demonstrate, by a preponderance of the evidence, that the service agent was in serious noncompliance with the requirements of this part for drug and/or alcohol testing-related services or with the requirements of another DOT agency drug and alcohol testing regulation.

§ 40.387 What matters does the Director decide concerning a proposed PIE?

(a) Following the service agent's response (see § 40.379(b)) or, if no response is received, after 30 days have passed from the date on which the service agent received the NOPE, the Director may take one of the following steps:

(1) In response to a request from the service agent (see § 40.379(b)(1)) or on his or her own motion, the Director may dismiss a PIE proceeding if he or she determines that it does not concern serious noncompliance with this part or DOT agency regulations, consistent with the Department's policy as stated in § 40.365.

(i) If the Director dismisses a proposed PIE under this paragraph (a), the action is closed with respect to the noncompliance alleged in the NOPE.

(ii) The Department may initiate a new PIE proceeding against you on the basis of different or subsequent conduct that is in noncompliance with this part or other DOT drug and alcohol testing rules.

(2) If the Director determines that the initiating official's submission does not have complete information needed for a decision, the Director may remand the matter to the initiating official. The initiating official may resubmit the matter to the Director when the needed information is complete. If the basis for the proposed PIE has changed, the initiating official must send an amended NOPE to the service agent.

(b) The Director makes determinations concerning the following matters in any PIE proceeding that he or she decides on the merits:

(1) Any material facts that are in dispute;

(2) Whether the facts support issuing a PIE;

(3) The scope of any PIE that is issued; and

(4) The duration of any PIE that is issued.

§ 40.389 What factors may the Director consider?

This section lists examples of the kind of mitigating and aggravating factors that the Director may consider in determining whether to issue a PIE concerning you, as well as the scope and duration of a PIE. This list is not exhaustive or exclusive. The Director may consider other factors if appropriate in the circumstances of a particular case. The list of examples follows:

(a) The actual or potential harm that results or may result from your noncompliance;

(b) The frequency of incidents and/or duration of the noncompliance;

(c) Whether there is a pattern or prior history of noncompliance;

(d) Whether the noncompliance was pervasive within your organization, including such factors as the following:

(1) Whether and to what extent your organization planned, initiated, or carried out the noncompliance;

(2) The positions held by individuals involved in the noncompliance, and whether your principals tolerated their noncompliance; and

(3) Whether you had effective standards of conduct and control systems (both with respect to your own organization and any contractors or affiliates) at the time the noncompliance occurred;

(e) Whether you have demonstrated an appropriate compliance disposition, including such factors as the following:

(1) Whether you have accepted responsibility for the noncompliance and recognize the seriousness of the conduct that led to the cause for issuance of the PIE;

(2) Whether you have cooperated fully with the Department during the investigation. The Director may consider when the cooperation began and whether you disclosed all pertinent information known to you;

(3) Whether you have fully investigated the circumstances of the noncompliance forming the basis for the PIE and, if so, have made the result of the investigation available to the Director;

(4) Whether you have taken appropriate disciplinary action against the individuals responsible for the activity that constitutes the grounds for issuance of the PIE; and

(5) Whether your organization has taken appropriate corrective actions or remedial measures, including implementing actions to prevent recurrence;

(f) With respect to noncompliance with a DOT agency regulation, the degree to which the noncompliance affects matters common to the DOT drug and alcohol testing program;

(g) Other factors appropriate to the circumstances of the case.

§ 40.391 What is the scope of a PIE?

(a) The scope of a PIE is the Department's determination about the divisions, organizational elements, types of services, affiliates, and/or individuals (including direct employees of a service agent and its contractors) to which a PIE applies.

(b) If, as a service agent, the Department issues a PIE concerning you, the PIE applies to all your divisions, organizational elements, and types of services that are involved with or affected by the noncompliance that forms the factual basis for issuing the PIE.

(c) In the NOPE (see § 40.375(b)(4)), the initiating official sets forth his or her recommendation for the scope of the PIE. The proposed scope of the PIE is one of the elements of the proceeding that the service agent may contest (see § 40.381(b)) and about which the Director makes a decision (see § 40.387(b)(3)).

(d) In recommending and deciding the scope of the PIE, the initiating official and Director, respectively, must take into account the provisions of paragraphs (e) through (j) of this section.

(e) The pervasiveness of the noncompliance within a service agent's organization (see § 40.389(d)) is an important consideration in determining the scope of a PIE. The appropriate scope of a PIE grows broader as the pervasiveness of the noncompliance increases.

(f) The application of a PIE is not limited to the specific location or employer at which the conduct that forms the factual basis for issuing the PIE was discovered.

(g) A PIE applies to your affiliates, if the affiliate is involved with or affected by the conduct that forms the factual basis for issuing the PIE.

(h) A PIE applies to individuals who are officers, employees, directors, shareholders, partners, or other individuals associated with your organization in the following circumstances:

   (1) Conduct forming any part of the factual basis of the PIE occurred in connection with the individual's performance of duties by or on behalf of your organization; or

   (2) The individual knew of, had reason to know of, approved, or acquiesced in such conduct. The individual's acceptance of benefits derived from such conduct is evidence of such knowledge, acquiescence, or approval.

(i) If a contractor to your organization is solely responsible for the conduct that forms the factual basis for a PIE, the PIE does not apply to the service agent itself unless the service agent knew or should have known about the conduct and did not take action to correct it.

(j) PIEs do not apply to drug and alcohol testing that DOT does not regulate.

(k) The following examples illustrate how the Department intends the provisions of this section to work:

Example 1 to § 40.391. Service Agent P provides a variety of drug testing services. P's SAP services are involved in a serious violation of this Part 40. However, P's other services fully comply with this part, and P's overall management did not plan or concur in the noncompliance, which in fact was contrary to P's articulated standards. Because the noncompliance was isolated in one area of the organization's activities, and did not pervade the entire organization, the scope of the PIE could be limited to SAP services.

Example 2 to § 40.391. Service Agent Q provides a similar variety of services. The conduct forming the factual basis for a PIE concerns collections for a transit authority. As in Example 1, the noncompliance is not pervasive throughout Q's organization. The PIE would apply to collections at all locations served by Q, not just the particular transit authority or not just in the state in which the transit authority is located.

Example 3 to § 40.391. Service Agent R provides a similar array of services. One or more of the following problems exists: R's activities in several areas—collections, MROs, SAPs, protecting the confidentiality of information—are involved in serious noncompliance; DOT determines that R's management knew or should have known about serious noncompliance in one or more areas, but management did not take timely corrective action; or, in response to an inquiry from DOT personnel, R's management refuses to provide information about its operations. In each of these three cases, the scope of the PIE would include all aspects of R's services.

Example 4 to § 40.391. Service Agent W provides only one kind of service (*e.g.,* laboratory or MRO services). The Department issues a PIE concerning these services. Because W only provides this one kind of service, the PIE necessarily applies to all its operations.

Example 5 to § 40.391. Service Agent X, by exercising reasonably prudent oversight of its collection contractor, should have known that the contractor was making numerous "fatal flaws" in tests.

Alternatively, X received a correction notice pointing out these problems in its contractor's collections. In neither case did X take action to correct the problem. X, as well as the contractor, would be subject to a PIE with respect to collections.

Example 6 to § 40.391. Service Agent Y could not reasonably have known that one of its MROs was regularly failing to interview employees before verifying tests positive. When it received a correction notice, Y immediately dismissed the erring MRO. In this case, the MRO would be subject to a PIE but Y would not.

Example 7 to § 40.391. The Department issues a PIE with respect to Service Agent Z. Z provides services for DOT-regulated transportation employers, a Federal agency under the HHS-regulated Federal employee testing program, and various private businesses and public agencies that DOT does not regulate. The PIE applies only to the DOT-regulated transportation employers with respect to their DOT-mandated testing, not to the Federal agency or the other public agencies and private businesses. The PIE does not prevent the non-DOT regulated entities from continuing to use Z's services.

§ 40.393 How long does a PIE stay in effect?

(a) In the NOPE (see § 40.375(b)(5)), the initiating official proposes the duration of the PIE. The duration of the PIE is one of the elements of the proceeding that the service agent may contest (see § 40.381(b)) and about which the Director makes a decision (see § 40.387(b)(4)).

(b) In deciding upon the duration of the PIE, the Director considers the seriousness of the conduct on which the PIE is based and the continued need to protect employers and employees from the service agent's noncompliance. The Director considers factors such as those listed in § 40.389 in making this decision.

(c) The duration of a PIE will be between one and five years, unless the Director reduces its duration under § 40.407.

§ 40.395 Can you settle a PIE proceeding?

At any time before the Director's decision, you and the initiating official can, with the Director's concurrence, settle a PIE proceeding.

§ 40.397 When does the Director make a PIE decision?

The Director makes his or her decision within 60 days of the date when the record of a PIE proceeding is complete (including any meeting with the Director and any additional fact-finding that is necessary). The Director may extend this period for good cause for additional periods of up to 30 days.

§ 40.399 How does the Department notify service agents of its decision?

If you are a service agent involved in a PIE proceeding, the Director provides you written notice as soon as he or she makes a PIE decision. The notice includes the following elements:

(a) If the decision is not to issue a PIE, a statement of the reasons for the decision, including findings of fact with respect to any material factual issues that were in dispute.

(b) If the decision is to issue a PIE—

49 CFR Part 40 (up to date as of 3/05/2024)
Procedures for Transportation Workplace Drug and Alcohol Testing Programs

49 CFR 40.399(b)(1)

(1) A reference to the NOPE;

(2) A statement of the reasons for the decision, including findings of fact with respect to any material factual issues that were in dispute;

(3) A statement of the scope of the PIE; and

(4) A statement of the duration of the PIE.

§ 40.401 How does the Department notify employers and the public about a PIE?

(a) The Department maintains a document called the "List of Excluded Drug and Alcohol Service Agents." This document may be found on the Department's web site (*http://www.transportation.gov/odapc*) . You may also request a copy of the document from ODAPC.

(b) When the Director issues a PIE, he or she adds to the List the name and address of the service agent, and any other persons or organizations, to whom the PIE applies and information about the scope and duration of the PIE.

(c) When a service agent ceases to be subject to a PIE, the Director removes this information from the List.

(d) The Department also publishes a FEDERAL REGISTER notice to inform the public on any occasion on which a service agent is added to or taken off the List.

[65 FR 79526, Dec. 19, 2000, as amended at 82 FR 52247, Nov. 13, 2017]

§ 40.403 Must a service agent notify its clients when the Department issues a PIE?

(a) As a service agent, if the Department issues a PIE concerning you, you must notify each of your DOT-regulated employer clients, in writing, about the issuance, scope, duration, and effect of the PIE. You may meet this requirement by sending a copy of the Director's PIE decision or by a separate notice. You must send this notice to each client within three business days of receiving from the Department the notice provided for in § 40.399(b).

(b) As part of the notice you send under paragraph (a) of this section, you must offer to transfer immediately all records pertaining to the employer and its employees to the employer or to any other service agent the employer designates. You must carry out this transfer as soon as the employer requests it.

[65 FR 79526, Dec. 19, 2000, as amended at 66 FR 41955, Aug. 9, 2001]

§ 40.405 May the Federal courts review PIE decisions?

The Director's decision is a final administrative action of the Department. Like all final administrative actions of Federal agencies, the Director's decision is subject to judicial review under the Administrative Procedure Act (5 U.S.C. 551 *et. seq*).

§ 40.407 May a service agent ask to have a PIE reduced or terminated?

(a) Yes, as a service agent concerning whom the Department has issued a PIE, you may request that the Director terminate a PIE or reduce its duration and/or scope. This process is limited to the issues of duration and scope. It is not an appeal or reconsideration of the decision to issue the PIE.

(b) Your request must be in writing and supported with documentation.

(c) You must wait at least nine months from the date on which the Director issued the PIE to make this request.

(d) The initiating official who was the proponent of the PIE may provide information and arguments concerning your request to the Director.

(e) If the Director verifies that the sources of your noncompliance have been eliminated and that all drug or alcohol testing-related services you would provide to DOT-regulated employers will be consistent with the requirements of this part, the Director may issue a notice terminating or reducing the PIE.

§ 40.409 What does the issuance of a PIE mean to transportation employers?

(a) As an employer, you are deemed to have notice of the issuance of a PIE when it appears on the List mentioned in § 40.401(a) or the notice of the PIE appears in the FEDERAL REGISTER as provided in § 40.401(d). You should check this List to ensure that any service agents you are using or planning to use are not subject to a PIE.

(b) As an employer who is using a service agent concerning whom a PIE is issued, you must stop using the services of the service agent no later than 90 days after the Department has published the decision in the FEDERAL REGISTER or posted it on its web site. You may apply to the ODAPC Director for an extension of 30 days if you demonstrate that you cannot find a substitute service agent within 90 days.

(c) Except during the period provided in paragraph (b) of this section, you must not, as an employer, use the services of a service agent that are covered by a PIE that the Director has issued under this subpart. If you do so, you are in violation of the Department's regulations and subject to applicable DOT agency sanctions (*e.g.*, civil penalties, withholding of Federal financial assistance).

(d) You also must not obtain drug or alcohol testing services through a contractor or affiliate of the service agent to whom the PIE applies.

Example to paragraph (d): Service Agent R was subject to a PIE with respect to SAP services. As an employer, not only must you not use R's own SAP services, but you also must not use SAP services you arrange through R, such as services provided by a subcontractor or affiliate of R or a person or organization that receives financial gain from its relationship with R.

(e) This section's prohibition on using the services of a service agent concerning which the Director has issued a PIE applies to employers in all industries subject to DOT drug and alcohol testing regulations.

Example to paragraph (e): The initiating official for a PIE was the FAA drug and alcohol program manager, and the conduct forming the basis of the PIE pertained to the aviation industry. As a motor carrier, transit authority, pipeline, railroad, or maritime employer, you are also prohibited from using the services of the service agent involved in connection with the DOT drug and alcohol testing program.

(f) The issuance of a PIE does not result in the cancellation of drug or alcohol tests conducted using the service agent involved before the issuance of the Director's decision or up to 90 days following its publication in the FEDERAL REGISTER or posting on the Department's web site, unless otherwise specified in the Director's PIE decision or the Director grants an extension as provided in paragraph (b) of this section.

Example to paragraph (f): The Department issues a PIE concerning Service Agent N on September 1. All tests conducted using N's services before September 1, and through November 30, are valid for all purposes under DOT drug and alcohol testing regulations, assuming they meet all other regulatory requirements.

§ 40.411 What is the role of the DOT Inspector General's office?

(a) Any person may bring concerns about waste, fraud, or abuse on the part of a service agent to the attention of the DOT Office of Inspector General.

(b) In appropriate cases, the Office of Inspector General may pursue criminal or civil remedies against a service agent.

(c) The Office of Inspector General may provide factual information to other DOT officials for use in a PIE proceeding.

§ 40.413 How are notices sent to service agents?

(a) If you are a service agent, DOT sends notices to you, including correction notices, notices of proposed exclusion, decision notices, and other notices, in any of the ways mentioned in paragraph (b) or (c) of this section.

(b) DOT may send a notice to you, your identified counsel, your agent for service of process, or any of your partners, officers, directors, owners, or joint venturers to the last known street address, fax number, or e-mail address. DOT deems the notice to have been received by you if sent to any of these persons.

(c) DOT considers notices to be received by you—

(1) When delivered, if DOT mails the notice to the last known street address, or five days after we send it if the letter is undeliverable;

(2) When sent, if DOT sends the notice by fax or five days after we send it if the fax is undeliverable; or

(3) When delivered, if DOT sends the notice by e-mail or five days after DOT sends it if the e-mail is undeliverable.

Appendix A to Part 40—DOT Standards for Urine Collection Kits

The Collection Kit Contents

1. *Collection Container*

   a. Single-use container, made of plastic, large enough to easily catch and hold at least 55 mL of urine voided from the body.

   b. Must have graduated volume markings clearly noting levels of 45 mL and above.

   c. Must have a temperature strip providing graduated temperature readings 32–38 °C/90–100 °F, that is affixed or can be affixed at a proper level on the outside of the collection container. Other methodologies (*e.g.,* temperature device built into the wall of the container) are acceptable provided the temperature measurement is accurate and such that there is no potential for contamination of the specimen.

49 CFR Part 40 (up to date as of 3/05/2024)
Procedures for Transportation Workplace Drug and Alcohol Testing Programs
49 CFR Appendix-A-to-Part-40 1.d.

d. Must be individually wrapped in a sealed plastic bag or shrink wrapping; or must have a peelable, sealed lid or other easily visible tamper-evident system.

e. May be made available separately at collection sites to address shy bladder situations when several voids may be required to complete the testing process.

2. *Plastic Specimen Bottles*

a. Each bottle must be large enough to hold at least 35 mL; or alternatively, they may be two distinct sizes of specimen bottles provided that the bottle designed to hold the primary specimen holds at least 35 mL of urine and the bottle designed to hold the split specimen holds at least 20 mL.

b. Must have screw-on or snap-on caps that prevent seepage of the urine from the bottles during shipment.

c. Must have markings clearly indicating the appropriate levels (30 mL for the primary specimen and 15 mL for the split) of urine that must be poured into the bottles.

d. Must be designed so that the required tamper-evident bottle seals made available on the CCF fit with no damage to the seal when the employee initials it nor with the chance that the seal overlap would conceal printed information.

e. Must be wrapped (with caps) together in a sealed plastic bag or shrink wrapping separate from the collection container; or must be wrapped (with cap) individually in sealed plastic bags or shrink wrapping; or must have peelable, sealed lid or other easily visible tamper-evident system.

f. Plastic material must be leach resistant.

3. *Leak-Resistant Plastic Bag*

a. Must have two sealable compartments or pouches which are leak-resistant; one large enough to hold two specimen bottles and the other large enough to hold the CCF paperwork.

b. The sealing methodology must be such that once the compartments are sealed, any tampering or attempts to open either compartment will be evident.

4. *Absorbent material*

Each kit must contain enough absorbent material to absorb the entire contents of both specimen bottles. Absorbent material must be designed to fit inside the leak-resistant plastic bag pouch into which the specimen bottles are placed.

5. *Shipping Container*

a. Must be designed to adequately protect the specimen bottles from shipment damage in the transport of specimens from the collection site to the laboratory (*e.g.,* standard courier box, small cardboard box, plastic container).

b. May be made available separately at collection sites rather than being part of an actual kit sent to collection sites.

c. A shipping container is not necessary if a laboratory courier hand-delivers the specimen bottles in the plastic leak-proof bags from the collection site to the laboratory.

Appendix B to Part 40—Oral Fluid Collection Kit Contents

1. Oral Fluid Collection Device

a. A single device, which can be subdivided in the employee's presence into an "A" specimen and a "B" split specimen bottle sufficient for laboratory testing, that is either of the following:

   (1) An oral fluid collection device made to collect a sufficient amount of oral fluid to permit an HHS-certified laboratory to analyze the specimen(s). For example, a device that directs the oral fluid into two separate collection bottles.

   (2) A device that uses buffering solution that collects a specimen using a single pad or dual pads joined for insertion together into the same region of the mouth, which can be subdivided into two separate collection bottles. Such a buffered device may use a diluent (or other component, process, or method that modifies the volume of the testable specimen). The volume specifications for the device must be consistent with those set by HHS.

b. Must have unit markings or other indicators that demonstrate the adequacy of the volume of oral fluid specimen collected.

c. Must be sufficiently transparent to permit a visual assessment of the contents without opening the specimen bottle.

d. Must be individually packaged in an easily visible tamper-evident system.

e. Must have the device's expiration date on the specimen bottles sent to the laboratory (*i.e.*, the shortest expiration date of any component).

f. Must not have components that substantially affect the composition of drugs and/or drug metabolites in the oral fluid specimen and/or interfere with an accurate analysis of the specimen.

g. Must maintain the integrity of the specimen during storage and transport so the specimen can be tested in an HHS-certified laboratory.

h. Must be designed so that the required tamper-evident bottle seals made available on the CCF fit without concealing the expiration date on the bottles, without damage to the seal when the collector dates and the employee initials it.

i. Must be approved by HHS for use by the specific HHS-certified laboratory that will test the specimen gathered by this device.

2. Instructions

Must include the manufacturer's instructions within the device's packaging. The instructions must provide sufficient detail to allow for an error-free collection when the instructions are followed.

3. Leak-Resistant Plastic Bag

a. Must have two sealable compartments or pouches that are leak-resistant; one large enough to hold two specimen bottles and the other large enough to hold the CCF paperwork, as applicable.

b. The sealing methodology must be such that once the compartments are sealed, any tampering or attempts to open either compartment will be evident.

4. Absorbent Material

Each kit must contain enough absorbent material to absorb the entire contents of both specimen bottles. Absorbent material must be designed to fit inside the leak-resistant plastic bag pouch into which the specimen bottles are placed.

5. Shipping Container

a. Must be designed to adequately protect the specimen bottles from damage during shipment of the specimens from the collection site to the laboratory (*e.g.*, standard courier box, small cardboard box, plastic container).

b. May be made available separately at collection sites rather than being part of an actual collection device sent to collection sites.

c. A shipping container is not necessary if a laboratory courier hand-delivers the specimen bottles in the leak-resistant plastic bags from the collection site to the laboratory.

[88 FR 27651, May 2, 2023]

Appendix C to Part 40 [Reserved]

Appendix D to Part 40—DOT Drug Testing Semi-Annual Laboratory Report to Employers

The following items are required on each laboratory report:

Reporting Period: (inclusive dates)

Laboratory Identification: (name and address)

Employer Identification: (name; may include Billing Code or ID code)

C/TPA Identification: (where applicable; name and address)

A. Urine Specimens

1. Urine Specimen Results Reported (Total Number) By Test Reason

(a) Pre-employment (number)

(b) Post-Accident (number)

(c) Random (number)

(d) Reasonable Suspicion/Cause (number)

(e) Return-to-Duty (number)

(f) Follow-up (number)

(g) Type of Test Not Noted on CCF (number)

2. Urine Specimens Reported

(a) Negative (number)

(b) Negative and Dilute (number)

3. Urine Specimens Reported as Rejected for Testing (Total Number) by Reason

    (a) Fatal flaw (number)

    (b) Uncorrected Flaw (number)

4. Urine Specimens Reported as Positive (Total Number) by Drug

    (a) Marijuana Metabolite (number)

    (b) Cocaine Metabolite (number)

    (c) Opioids (number)

        (1) Codeine (number)

        (2) Morphine (number)

        (3) 6–AM (number)

        (4) Hydrocodone (number)

        (5) Hydromorphone (number)

        (6) Oxycodone (number)

        (7) Oxymorphone (number)

    (d) Phencyclidine (number)

    (e) Amphetamines (number)

        (1) Amphetamine (number)

        (2) Methamphetamine (number)

        (3) MDMA (number)

        (4) MDA (number)

5. Urine Adulterated (Number)

6. Urine Substituted (Number)

7. Urine Invalid Result (Number)

B. Oral Fluid Specimens

1. Oral Fluid Specimen Results Reported (Total Number) by Test Reason

    (a) Pre-employment (number)

    (b) Post-Accident (number)

    (c) Random (number)

    (d) Reasonable Suspicion/Cause (number)

    (e) Return-to-Duty (number)

    (f) Follow-up (number)

    (g) Type of Test Not Noted on CCF (number)

2. Oral Fluid Specimens Reported

    (a) Negative (number)

    (b) Negative and Dilute (number)

3. Oral Fluid Specimens Reported as Rejected for Testing (Total Number) by Reason

    (a) Fatal flaw (number)

    (b) Uncorrected Flaw (number)

4. Oral Fluid Specimens Reported as Positive (Total Number) by Drug

    (a) Marijuana (number)

    (b) Cocaine and/or Cocaine Metabolite (number)

    (c) Opioids (number)

        (1) Codeine (number)

        (2) Morphine (number)

        (3) 6–AM (number)

        (4) Hydrocodone (number)

        (5) Hydromorphone (number)

        (6) Oxycodone (number)

        (7) Oxymorphone (number)

    (d) Phencyclidine (number)

    (e) Amphetamines (number)

        (1) Amphetamine (number)

        (2) Methamphetamine (number)

        (3) MDMA (number)

        (4) MDA (number)

5. Oral Fluid Adulterated (Number)

6. Oral Fluid Substituted (Number)

7. Oral Fluid Invalid Result (Number)

[88 FR 27651, May 2, 2023]

Appendix E to Part 40—Drug Testing Semi-Annual Laboratory Report to DOT

Mail, fax or email to: U.S. Department of Transportation, Office of Drug and Alcohol Policy and Compliance, 1200 New Jersey Avenue SE, Washington, DC 20590.

Fax: (202) 366–3897.

Email: ODAPCWebMail@dot.gov.

The following items are required on each report:

Reporting Period: (inclusive dates)

Laboratory Identification: (name and address)

1. Specimen Type:

   —oral fluid or urine

2. DOT agency

   —FMCSA, FAA, FRA, FTA, PHMSA, or USCG

3. Test Reason

   —Pre-Employment, Random, Reasonable Suspicion/Cause, Post-Accident, Return-to-Duty, Other, and Follow-up

   A. DOT Specimen Results Reported (total number)

   B. Negative Results Reported (total number)

      1. Negative (number)

      2. Negative-Dilute (number)

   C. Rejected for Testing Results Reported (total number) By Reason

      1. Fatal flaw (number)

      2. Uncorrected Flaw (number)

   D. Positive Results Reported (total number) By Drug

      1. Marijuana or Marijuana Metabolite (number)

      2. Cocaine and/or Cocaine Metabolite (number)

      3. Opioids (number)

         a. Codeine (number)

         b. Morphine (number)

         c. 6–AM (number)

         d. Hydrocodone (number)

         e. Hydromorphone (number)

         f. Oxycodone (number)

         g. Oxymorphone (number)

      4. Phencyclidine (number)

      5. Amphetamines (number)

      a.   Amphetamine (number)

      b.   Methamphetamine (number)

      c.   MDMA (number)

      d.   MDA (number)

   E.   Adulterated Results Reported (total number) By Reason (number)

   F.   Substituted Results Reported (total number)

   G.   Invalid Results Reported (total number) By Reason (number)

[88 FR 27652, May 2, 2023]

Appendix F to Part 40—Report Format: Split Specimen Failure To Reconfirm

Mail, fax, or submit electronically to: U.S. Department of Transportation, Office of Drug and Alcohol Policy and Compliance, 1200 New Jersey Avenue SE, Washington, DC 20590.

Fax: (202) 366–3897.

Submit Electronically: https://www.transportation.gov/odapc/mro-split-specimen-cancellation-notification.

The following items are required on each report:

1.   MRO name, address, phone number, and fax number.

2.   Collection site name, address, and phone number.

3.   Date of collection.

4.   Specimen I.D. number.

5.   Specimen type.

6.   Laboratory accession number.

7.   Primary specimen laboratory name, address, and phone number.

8.   Date result reported or certified by primary laboratory.

9.   Split specimen laboratory name, address, and phone number.

10.   Date split specimen result reported or certified by split specimen laboratory.

11.   Primary specimen results (*e.g.*, name of drug, adulterant) in the primary specimen.

12.   Reason for split specimen failure-to-reconfirm result (*e.g.*, drug or adulterant not present, specimen invalid, split not collected, insufficient volume).

13.   Actions taken by the MRO (*e.g.*, notified employer of failure to reconfirm and requirement for re-collection).

14.   Additional information explaining the reason for cancellation.

15.   Name of individual submitting the report (if not the MRO).

[88 FR 27652, May 2, 2023]

Appendix G to Part 40—SAP Equivalency Requirements for Certification Organizations

1. *Experience:* Minimum requirements are for three years of full-time supervised experience or 6,000 hours of supervised experience as an alcoholism and/or drug abuse counselor. The supervision must be provided by a licensed or certified practitioner. Supervised experience is important if the individual is to be considered a professional in the field of alcohol and drug abuse evaluation and counseling.

2. *Education:* There exists a requirement of 270 contact hours of education and training in alcoholism and/or drug abuse or related training. These hours can take the form of formal education, in-service training, and professional development courses. Part of any professional counselor's development is participation in formal and non-formal education opportunities within the field.

3. *Continuing Education:* The certified counselor must receive at least 40–60 hours of continuing education units (CEU) during each two year period. These CEUs are important to the counselor's keeping abreast of changes and improvements in the field.

4. *Testing:* A passing score on a national test is a requirement. The test must accurately measure the application of the knowledge, skills, and abilities possessed by the counselor. The test establishes a national standard that must be met to practice.

5. *Testing Validity:* The certification examination must be reviewed by an independent authority for validity (examination reliability and relationship to the knowledge, skills, and abilities required by the counseling field). The reliability of the exam is paramount if counselor attributes are to be accurately measured. The examination passing score point must be placed at an appropriate minimal level score as gauged by statistically reliable methodology.

6. *Measurable Knowledge Base:* The certification process must be based upon measurable knowledge possessed by the applicant and verified through collateral data and testing. That level of knowledge must be of sufficient quantity to ensure a high quality of SAP evaluation and referral services.

7. *Measurable Skills Base:* The certification process must be based upon measurable skills possessed by the applicant and verified through collateral data and testing. That level of skills must be of sufficient quality to ensure a high quality of SAP evaluation and referral services.

8. *Quality Assurance Plan:* The certification agency must ensure that a means exists to determine that applicant records are verified as being true by the certification staff. This is an important check to ensure that true information is being accepted by the certifying agency.

9. *Code of Ethics:* Certified counselors must pledge to adhere to an ethical standard for practice. It must be understood that code violations could result in de-certification. These standards are vital in maintaining the integrity of practitioners. High ethical standards are required to ensure quality of client care and confidentiality of client information as well as to guard against inappropriate referral practices.

10. *Re-certification Program:* Certification is not just a one-time event. It is a continuing privilege with continuing requirements. Among these are continuing education, continuing state certification, and concomitant adherence to the code of ethics. Re-certification serves as a protector of client interests by removing poor performers from the certified practice.

11. *Fifty State Coverage:* Certification must be available to qualified counselors in all 50 states and, therefore, the test must be available to qualified applicants in all 50 states. Because many companies are multi-state operators, consistency in SAP evaluation quality and opportunities is paramount. The test need not be given in all 50 states but should be accessible to candidates from all states.

12. *National Commission for Certifying Agencies (NCCA) Accreditation:* Having NCCA accreditation is a means of demonstrating to the Department of Transportation that your certification has been reviewed by a panel of impartial experts that have determined that your examination(s) has met stringent and appropriate testing standards.

[65 FR 79526, Dec. 19, 2000. Redesignated at 88 FR 27651, May 2, 2023]

Appendix H to Part 40—Drug and Alcohol Testing Information that C/TPAs May Transmit to Employers

1. If you are a C/TPA, you may, acting as an intermediary, transmit the information in the following sections of this part to the DER for an employer, if the employer chooses to have you do so. These are the only items that you are permitted to transmit to the employer as an intermediary. The use of C/TPA intermediaries is prohibited in all other cases, such as transmission of laboratory drug test results to MROs, the transmission of medical information from MROs to employers, the transmission of SAP reports to employers, the transmission of positive alcohol test results, and the transmission of medical information from MROs to employers.

2. In every case, you must ensure that, in transmitting the information, you meet all requirements (*e.g.*, concerning confidentiality and timing) that would apply if the party originating the information (*e.g.*, an MRO or collector) sent the information directly to the employer. For example, if you transmit MROs' drug testing results to DERs, you must transmit each drug test result to the DER in compliance with the requirements for MROs set forth in § 40.167.

Drug Testing Information

§ 40.25: Previous two years' test results

§ 40.35: Notice to collectors of contact information for DER

§ 40.61(a): Notification to DER that an employee is a "no show" for a drug test

§ 40.63(e): Notification to DER of a collection under direct observation

§ 40.65(b)(6) and (7) and (c)(2) and (3): Notification to DER of a refusal to provide a specimen or an insufficient specimen

§ 40.73(a)(9): Transmission of CCF copies to DER (However, MRO copy of CCF must be sent by collector directly to the MRO, not through the C/TPA.)

§ 40.111(a): Transmission of laboratory statistical report to employer

§ 40.127(f): Report of test results to DER

§§ 40.127(g), 40.129(d), 40.159(a)(4)(ii); 40.161(b): Reports to DER that test is cancelled

§ 40.129(e): Report of test results to DER

49 CFR Part 40 (up to date as of 3/05/2024)
Procedures for Transportation Workplace Drug and Alcohol Testing Programs

49 CFR Appendix-H-to-Part-40 2.

§ 40.129(g)(1): Report to DER of confirmed positive test in stand-down situation

§§ 40.149(b): Report to DER of changed test result

§ 40.155(a): Report to DER of dilute specimen

§ 40.167(b) and (c): Reports of test results to DER

§ 40.187(a)–(e) Reports to DER concerning the reconfirmation of tests

§ 40.191(d): Notice to DER concerning refusals to test

§ 40.193(b)(3): Notification to DER of refusal in shy bladder situation

§ 40.193(b)(4): Notification to DER of insufficient specimen

§ 40.193(b)(5): Transmission of CCF copies to DER (not to MRO)

§ 40.199: Report to DER of cancelled test and direction to DER for additional collection

§ 40.201: Report to DER of cancelled test

Alcohol Testing Information

§ 40.215: Notice to BATs and STTs of contact information for DER

§ 40.241(b)(1): Notification to DER that an employee is a "no show" for an alcohol test

§ 40.247(a)(2): Transmission of alcohol screening test results only when the test result is less than 0.02

§ 40.255(a)(4): Transmission of alcohol confirmation test results only when the test result is less than 0.02

§ 40.263(a)(3) and 263(b)(3): Notification of insufficient saliva and failure to provide sufficient amount of breath

[65 FR 79526, Dec. 19, 2000, as amended at 66 FR 41955, Aug. 9, 2001; 73 FR 35975, June 25, 2008. Redesignated and amended at 88 FR 27651, 27652, May 2, 2023]

Appendix I to Part 40—Alcohol Testing Form

The following form is the alcohol testing form required for use in the DOT alcohol testing program beginning January 1, 2011. Employers are authorized to use the form effective February 25, 2010.

U.S. Department of Transportation (DOT)
Alcohol Testing Form

(The instructions for completing this form are on the back of Copy 3)

Step 1: TO BE COMPLETED BY ALCOHOL TECHNICIAN

A: Employee Name _____

(Print)   (First, M.I., Last)

B: SSN or Employee ID No.

C: Employer Name _____
   Street
   City, Sate, Zip _____

   _____

   DER Name and
   Telephone No. _____

   DER Name   ( ) DER Phone Number

D: Reason for Test: Random   Reasonable Susp   Post-Accident   Return to Duty   Follow-up   Pre-employment

---

STEP 2: TO BE COMPLETED BY EMPLOYEE

I certify that I am about to submit to alcohol testing required by US Department of Transportation regulations and that the identifying information provided on the form is true and correct.

_____   ___/___/___
Signature of Employee   Date Month Day Year

STEP 3: TO BE COMPLETED BY ALCOHOL TECHNICIAN

(If the technician conducting the screening test is not the same technician who will be conducting the confirmation test, each technician must complete their own form.) I certify that I have conducted alcohol testing on the above named individual in accordance with the procedures established in the US Department of Transportation regulation, 49 CFR Part 40, that I am qualified to operate the testing device(s) identified, and that the results are as recorded.

TECHNICIAN: BAT   STT   DEVICE: SALIVA   BREATH*   15-Minute Wait: Yes   No

SCREENING TEST: (For BREATH DEVICE* write in the space below *only* if the testing device is *not* designed to *print.*)

Test #   Testing Device Name   Device Serial # *OR* Lot # & Exp Date   Activation Time   Reading Time   Result

CONFIRMATION TEST: Results *MUST* be affixed to each copy of this form or printed directly onto the form.

REMARKS: _____

_____

_____

_____

Alcohol Technician's Company   Company Street Address

(PRINT) Alcohol Technician's Name (First, M.I., Last)   Company City, State, Zip   ( ) Phone Number

_____   ___/___/___
Signature of Alcohol Technician   Date Month Day Year

STEP 4: TO BE COMPLETED BY EMPLOYEE IF TEST RESULT IS 0.02 OR HIGHER

I certify that I have submitted to the alcohol test, the results of which are accurately recorded on this form. I understand that I must not drive, perform safety-sensitive duties, or operate heavy equipment because the results are 0.02 or greater.

_____   ___/___/___
Signature of Employee   Date Month Day Year

Form DOT F 1380 (Rev. 5/2008)   OMB No. 2105-0529

COPY 1 – ORIGINAL – FORWARD TO THE EMPLOYER

Print Screening Results Here or Affix with Tamper Evident Tape

Print Confirmation Results Here or Affix with Tamper Evident Tape

Print Additional Results Here or Affix With Tamper Evident Tape

U.S. Department of Transportation (DOT)
Alcohol Testing Form
(The instructions for completing this form are on the back of Copy 3)

Print Screening Results Here or Affix with Tamper Evident Tape

Step 1: TO BE COMPLETED BY ALCOHOL TECHNICIAN

A: Employee Name _____
(Print)   (First, M.I., Last)

B: SSN or Employee ID No. _____

C: Employer Name _____
   Street _____
   City, State, Zip _____

DER Name and
Telephone No. _____
                DER Name   DER Phone Number

D: Reason for Test: ☐ Random   ☐ Reasonable Susp ☐ Post-Accident ☐ Return to Duty ☐ Follow-up ☐ Pre-employment

STEP 2: TO BE COMPLETED BY EMPLOYEE

I certify that I am about to submit to alcohol testing required by US Department of Transportation regulations and that the identifying information provided on the form is true and correct.

_____   ___/___/___
Signature of Employee   Date Month Day Year

Print Confirmation Results Here or Affix with Tamper Evident Tape

STEP 3: TO BE COMPLETED BY ALCOHOL TECHNICIAN

(If the technician conducting the screening test is not the same technician who will be conducting the confirmation test, each technician must complete their own form.) I certify that I have conducted alcohol testing on the above named individual in accordance with the procedures established in the US Department of Transportation regulation, 49 CFR Part 40, that I am qualified to operate the testing device(s) identified, and that the results are as recorded.

TECHNICIAN: ☐ BAT ☐ STT   DEVICE: ☐ SALIVA ☐ BREATH* 15-Minute Wait: ☐ Yes ☐ No

SCREENING TEST: *(For BREATH DEVICE* write in the space below only if the testing device is not designed to print.)*

Test #   Testing Device Name   Device Serial # OR Lot # & Exp Date   Activation Time   Reading Time   Result

CONFIRMATION TEST: Results *MUST* be affixed to each copy of this form or printed directly onto the form.

REMARKS: _____
_____
_____

Print Additional Results Here or Affix With Tamper Evident Tape

Alcohol Technician's Company _____   Company Street Address _____

(PRINT) Alcohol Technician's Name (First, M.I., Last)   Company City, State, Zip   Phone Number

Signature of Alcohol Technician _____   ___/___/___
                                                   Date Month Day Year

STEP 4: TO BE COMPLETED BY EMPLOYEE IF TEST RESULT IS 0.02 OR HIGHER

I certify that I have submitted to the alcohol test, the results of which are accurately recorded on this form. I understand that I must not drive, perform safety-sensitive duties, or operate heavy equipment because the results are 0.02 or greater.

_____   ___/___/___
Signature of Employee   Date Month Day Year

Form DOT F 1380 (Rev. 5/2008)   OMB No. 2105-0529

COPY 2 – EMPLOYEE RETAINS

49 CFR Part 40 (up to date as of 3/05/2024)
Procedures for Transportation Workplace Drug and Alcohol Testing Programs

49 CFR Appendix-H-to-Part-40 2.

U.S. Department of Transportation (DOT)
Alcohol Testing Form

(The instructions for completing this form are on the back of Copy 3)

Step 1: TO BE COMPLETED BY ALCOHOL TECHNICIAN

A: Employee Name _____

    (Print)   (First, M.I., Last)

B: SSN or Employee ID No. _____

C: Employer Name _____
    Street
    City, State, Zip _____

    DER Name and
    Telephone No. _____ ( ) _____
                DER Name   DER Phone Number

D: Reason for Test: ☐ Random ☐ Reasonable Susp ☐ Post-Accident ☐ Return to Duty ☐ Follow-up ☐ Pre-employment

---

STEP 2: TO BE COMPLETED BY EMPLOYEE

I certify that I am about to submit to alcohol testing required by US Department of Transportation regulations and that the identifying information provided on the form is true and correct.

_____   ___/___/___
Signature of Employee   Date Month Day Year

STEP 3: TO BE COMPLETED BY ALCOHOL TECHNICIAN

(If the technician conducting the screening test is not the same technician who will be conducting the confirmation test, each technician must complete their own form.) I certify that I have conducted alcohol testing on the above named individual in accordance with the procedures established in the US Department of Transportation regulation, 49 CFR Part 40, that I am qualified to operate the testing device(s) identified, and that the results are as recorded.

TECHNICIAN: ☐ BAT ☐ STT   DEVICE: ☐ SALIVA ☐ BREATH*   15-Minute Wait: ☐ Yes ☐ No

SCREENING TEST: *(For BREATH DEVICE* write in the space below only if the testing device is not designed to print.)*

_____ _____ _____ _____ _____ _____
Test #   Testing Device Name   Device Serial # *OR* Lot # & Exp Date   Activation Time   Reading Time   Result

CONFIRMATION TEST: *Results MUST be affixed to each copy of this form or printed directly onto the form.*

REMARKS: _____
_____
_____

_____   _____
Alcohol Technician's Company   Company Street Address

_____   _____ ( ) _____
(PRINT) Alcohol Technician's Name (First, M.I., Last)   Company City, State, Zip   Phone Number

_____   ___/___/___
Signature of Alcohol Technician   Date Month Day Year

STEP 4: TO BE COMPLETED BY EMPLOYEE IF TEST RESULT IS 0.02 OR HIGHER

I certify that I have submitted to the alcohol test, the results of which are accurately recorded on this form. I understand that I must not drive, perform safety-sensitive duties, or operate heavy equipment because the results are 0.02 or greater.

_____   ___/___/___
Signature of Employee   Date Month Day Year

Form DOT F 1380 (Rev. 5/2008)   OMB No. 2105-0529

Print Screening Results Here or Affix with Tamper Evident Tape

Print Confirmation Results Here or Affix with Tamper Evident Tape

Print Additional Results Here or Affix With Tamper Evident Tape

COPY 3 – ALCOHOL TECHNICIAN RETAINS

49 CFR Part 40 (up to date as of 3/05/2024)
Procedures for Transportation Workplace Drug and Alcohol Testing Programs

49 CFR Appendix-H-to-Part-40 2.

PAPERWORK REDUCTION ACT NOTICE (as required by 5 CFR 1320.21)

A federal agency may not conduct or sponsor, and a person is not required to respond to, nor shall a person be subject to a penalty for failure to comply with a collection of information subject to the requirements of the Paperwork Reduction Act unless that collection of information displays a current valid OMB Control Number. The OMB Control Number for this information collection is 2105-0529. Public reporting for this collection of information is estimated to be approximately 8 minutes per response, including the time for reviewing instructions, completing and reviewing the collection of information. All responses to this collection of information are mandatory. Send comments regarding this burden estimate or any other aspect of this collection of information, including suggestions for reducing this burden to: Information Collection Clearance Officer, U.S. Department of Transportation, Office of Drug and Alcohol Policy and Compliance, 1200 New Jersey Avenue, SE, Suite W62-300, Washington, D.C. 20590.

BACK OF PAGES 1 and 2

49 CFR Part 40 (up to date as of 3/05/2024)
Procedures for Transportation Workplace Drug and Alcohol Testing Programs

49 CFR Appendix-H-to-Part-40 2.

INSTRUCTIONS FOR COMPLETING THE U.S. DEPARTMENT OF TRANSPORTATION ALCOHOL TESTING FORM

NOTE: Use a ballpoint pen, press hard, and check all copies for legibility.

STEP 1   The Breath Alcohol Technician (BAT) or Screening Test Technician (STT) completes the information required in this step. Be sure to print the employee's name and check the box identifying the reason for the test.

NOTE: If the employee refuses to provide SSN or I.D. number, be sure to indicate this in the remarks section in STEP 3. Proceed with STEP 2.

STEP 2   Instruct the employee to read, sign, and date the employee certification statement in STEP 2.

NOTE: If the employee refuses to sign the certification statement, do not proceed with the alcohol test. Contact the designated employer representative.

STEP 3   The BAT or STT completes the information required in this step and checks the type of device (saliva or breath) being used. After conducting the alcohol screening test, do the following (as appropriate):

Enter the information for the screening test (test number, testing device name, testing device serial number or lot number and expiration date, time of test with any device-dependent activation times, and the results), on the front of the AFT. For a breath testing device capable of printing, the information may be part of the printed record.

NOTE: Be sure to enter the result of the test exactly as it is indicated on the breath testing device, e.g., 0.00, 0.02, 0.04, etc.

Affix the printed information to the front of the form in the space provided, or to the back of the form, in a tamper-evident manner (e.g., tape) such that it does not obscure the original printed information, or the device may print the results directly on the ATF. If the results of the screening test are less than 0.02, print, sign your name, and enter today's date in the space provided. The test process is complete.

If the results of the screening test are 0.02 or greater, a confirmation test must be administered in accordance with DOT regulations. An EVIDENTIAL BREATH TESTING device that is capable of printing confirmation test information must be used in conducting this test.

Ensure that a waiting period of at least 15 minutes occurs before the confirmation test begins. Check the box indicating that the waiting period lasted at least 15 minutes.

After conducting the alcohol confirmation test, affix the printed information to the front of the form in the space provided, or to the back of the form, in a tamper-evident manner (e.g., tape) such that it does not obscure the original information, or the device may print the results directly on the ATF. Print, sign your name, and enter the date in the space provided. Go to STEP 4.

STEP 4   If the employee has a breath alcohol confirmation test result of 0.02 or higher, instruct the employee to read, sign, and date the employee certification statement in STEP 4.

NOTE: If the employee refuses to sign the certification statement in STEP 4, be sure to indicate this in the remarks line in STEP 3.

Immediately notify the DER if the employee has a breath alcohol confirmation test result of 0.02 or higher.

Forward Copy 1 to the employer. Give Copy 2 to the employee. Retain Copy 3 for BAT/STT records.

BACK OF PAGE 3

49 CFR Part 40 (up to date as of 3/05/2024)
Procedures for Transportation Workplace Drug and Alcohol Testing Programs

49 CFR Appendix-H-to-Part-40 2.

[75 FR 8529, Feb. 25, 2010, as amended at 75 FR 13009, Mar. 18, 2010; 75 FR 38423, July 2, 2010. Redesignated at 88 FR 27651, May 2, 2023]

Appendix J to Part 40—DOT Drug and Alcohol Testing Management Information System (MIS) Data Collection Form

The following form is the MIS Data Collection form required for use to report calendar year MIS data. The instructions for this form are found at *https://www.transportation.gov/odapc*.

49 CFR Part 40 (up to date as of 3/05/2024)
Procedures for Transportation Workplace Drug and Alcohol Testing Programs

49 CFR Appendix-H-to-Part-40 2.

U.S. DEPARTMENT OF TRANSPORTATION DRUG AND ALCOHOL TESTING MIS DATA COLLECTION FORM

Calendar Year Covered by this Report: _____

OMB No. 2105-0529
Form DOT F 1385 (Rev. 4/2019)

I. Employer:
Company Name: _____

Doing Business As (DBA) Name (if applicable): _____

Address: _____ E-mail: _____

Name of Certifying Official: _____ Signature: _____

Telephone: (____) _____ Date Certified: _____
Prepared by (if different): _____ Telephone: (____) _____

C/TPA Name and Telephone (if applicable): _____ (____) _____

Check the DOT agency for which you are reporting MIS data; and complete the information on that same line as appropriate:

___ FMCSA – Motor Carrier: DOT #: _____ Owner-operator: (circle one) YES or NO   Exempt (Circle One) YES or NO
___ FAA – Aviation: Certificate # (if applicable): _____ Plan / Registration # (if applicable): _____
___ PHMSA – Pipeline: (Check) Gas Gathering___ Gas Transmission___ Gas Distribution___ Transport Hazardous Liquids___ Transport Carbon Dioxide___
___ FRA – Railroad: Total Number of observed/documented Part 219 "Rule G" Observations for covered employees: _____
___ USCG – Maritime: Vessel ID # (USCG- or State-Issued): _____ (If more than one vessel, list separately.)
___ FTA – Transit

II. Covered Employees (A) Enter Total Number Safety-Sensitive Employees In All Employee Categories: [_____]

(B) Enter Total Number of Employee Categories: [_____]

(C)

Employee Category	Total Number of Employees in this Category

If you have multiple employee categories, complete Sections I and II (A) & (B). Take that filled-in form and make one copy for each employee category and complete Sections II (C), III, and IV for each separate employee category.

III. Drug Testing Data

Type of Test	1 Total Number Of Test Results [Should equal the sum of Columns 2, 3, 9, 10, 11, and 12]	2 Verified Negative Results	3 Verified Positive Results – For One Or More Drugs	4 Positive For Marijuana	5 Positive For Cocaine	6 Positive For PCP	7 Positive For Opioids	8 Positive For Amphetamines	Refusal Results 9 Adulterated	10 Substituted	11 "Shy Bladder" – With No Medical Explanation	12 Other Refusals To Submit To Testing	13 Cancelled Results
Pre-Employment													
Random													
Post-Accident													
Reasonable Susp./Cause													
Return-to-Duty													
Follow-Up													
TOTAL													

IV. Alcohol Testing Data:

Type of Test	1 Total Number Of Screening Test Results [Should equal the sum of Columns 2, 3, 7, and 8]	2 Screening Tests With Results Below 0.02	3 Screening Tests With Results 0.02 Or Greater	4 Number Of Confirmation Tests Results	5 Confirmation Tests With Results 0.02 Through 0.039	6 Confirmation Tests With Results 0.04 Or Greater	Refusal Results 7 "Shy Lung" – With No Medical Explanation	8 Other Refusals To Submit To Testing	9 Cancelled Results
Pre-Employment									
Random									
Post-Accident									
Reasonable Susp./Cause									
Return-to-Duty									
Follow-Up									
TOTAL									

Made in the USA
Monee, IL
05 October 2024